New Testament Edition

The Word IN LIFE™ Study Bible

THOMAS NELSON PUBLISHERS
Nashville

The Word In Life Study Bible
New Testament Edition

Printed in the United States of America

3 4 5 6 7 8 9 10 11 12 — 98 97 96 95 94 93

Acknowledgments of sources of previously published material are
contained in a section beginning on page 934.

Introduction

This edition of the New Testament is part of *The Word In Life Study Bible,* the beginning of a new generation of study Bibles. Its purpose is to help you discover ways to relate the Word of God to you and the world you live in. This Bible makes it easy to bring the Word into your own world by taking you right into the world of the Bible.

The Word In Life Study Bible helps you get a clear understanding of God's Word by focusing on the surroundings of the biblical narrative. Stimulating articles get you thinking about how to relate the teachings of God's Word to life. The articles raise questions about what it means to live for God in today's world—about what a believer's role in the world is—and about how the Word in one life can touch the lives of others.

Features about the people, places, and customs of Jesus' world make the teachings of the Bible more vivid. You'll find friends in the Word of God. You'll feel at home where they lived. You'll discover that people aren't much different now than they were two thousand years ago. And you'll see that God's Word is more useful than you ever realized.

Explore the following pages and take a closer look at *The Word In Life Study Bible*—what it's meant to do, what it looks like, and how it works.

CONTENTS

BOOK ABBREVIATIONS IN BIBLICAL ORDER

OLD TESTAMENT:

Genesis	Gen.
Exodus	Ex.
Leviticus	Lev.
Numbers	Num.
Deuteronomy	Deut.
Joshua	Josh.
Judges	Judg.
Ruth	Ruth
1 Samuel	1 Sam.
2 Samuel	2 Sam.
1 Kings	1 Kin.
2 Kings	2 Kin.
1 Chronicles	1 Chr.
2 Chronicles	2 Chr.
Ezra	Ezra
Nehemiah	Neh.
Esther	Esth.
Job	Job
Psalms	Ps.
Proverbs	Prov.
Ecclesiastes	Eccl.
Song of Solomon	Song
Isaiah	Is.
Jeremiah	Jer.
Lamentations	Lam.
Ezekiel	Ezek.
Daniel	Dan.
Hosea	Hos.
Joel	Joel
Amos	Amos
Obadiah	Obad.
Jonah	Jon.
Micah	Mic.
Nahum	Nah.
Habakkuk	Hab.
Zephaniah	Zeph.
Haggai	Hag.
Zechariah	Zech.
Malachi	Mal.

NEW TESTAMENT:

Matthew	Matt.
Mark	Mark
Luke	Luke
John	John
Acts	Acts
Romans	Rom.
1 Corinthians	1 Cor.
2 Corinthians	2 Cor.
Galatians	Gal.
Ephesians	Eph.
Philippians	Phil.
Colossians	Col.
1 Thessalonians	1 Thess.
2 Thessalonians	2 Thess.
1 Timothy	1 Tim.
2 Timothy	2 Tim.
Titus	Titus
Philemon	Philem.
Hebrews	Heb.
James	James
1 Peter	1 Pet.
2 Peter	2 Pet.
1 John	1 John
2 John	2 John
3 John	3 John
Jude	Jude
Revelation	Rev.

ALPHABETICAL KEY TO BOOK ABBREVIATIONS

Acts	Acts
Amos	Amos
1, 2 Chr.	1, 2 Chronicles
Col.	Colossians
1, 2 Cor.	1, 2 Corinthians
Dan.	Daniel
Deut.	Deuteronomy
Eccl.	Ecclesiastes
Eph.	Ephesians
Esth.	Esther
Ex.	Exodus
Ezek.	Ezekiel
Ezra	Ezra
Gal.	Galatians
Gen.	Genesis
Hab.	Habakkuk
Hag.	Haggai
Heb.	Hebrews
Hos.	Hosea
Is.	Isaiah
James	James
Jer.	Jeremiah
Job	Job
Joel	Joel
John	John
1, 2, 3 John	1, 2, 3 John
Jon.	Jonah
Josh.	Joshua
Jude	Jude
Judg.	Judges
1, 2 Kin.	1, 2 Kings
Lam	Lamentations
Lev.	Leviticus
Luke	Luke
Mal.	Malachi
Mark	Mark
Matt.	Matthew
Mic.	Micah
Nah.	Nahum
Neh.	Nehemiah
Num.	Numbers
Obad.	Obadiah
1, 2 Pet.	1, 2 Peter
Phil.	Philippians
Philem.	Philemon
Prov.	Proverbs
Ps.	Psalms
Rev.	Revelation
Rom.	Romans
Ruth	Ruth
1, 2 Sam.	1, 2 Samuel
Song	Song of Solomon
1, 2 Thess.	1, 2 Thessalonians
1, 2 Tim.	1, 2 Timothy
Titus	Titus
Zech.	Zechariah
Zeph.	Zephaniah

WHY THIS KIND OF PUBLICATION?

Someone has well said that Scripture was not written merely to be studied, but to change our lives. Likewise, James exhorts us to be "doers of the word, and not hearers only" (James 1:22). And Jesus said, "By this My Father is glorified, that you bear much fruit; so you will be My disciples" (John 15:8). Clearly, the point of God's Word is not to make us "smarter sinners" but to help us become more like Jesus Christ by making the Word of God part of our lives.

However, applying biblical truth in this day and age is far from easy. In the first place, the fact that the Bible was written thousands of years ago in a different culture can sometimes make it difficult to understand. And even if we grasp what the writers were saying to their original readers, we still must make the connection to our own situation today. In the end, many people wonder: can Scripture really make any difference in our complex, modern world? Yes it can, and this publication helps to show the way. ◆

A "USER-FRIENDLY" STUDY BIBLE

THE WORD IN LIFE STUDY BIBLE HELPS YOU UNDERSTAND THE BIBLICAL TEXT.

Before you can apply Scripture, you must understand what Scripture means. That's why The Word In Life Study Bible *provides the kind of information you'll need to make sense of what the biblical text is talking about. The articles and other information (see below) provide the "who, what, when, where, how, and why" behind scores of passages, in an interesting, easy-to-understand way. Not only do they offer insight into the text, they also help you to understand the context of those passages, so that you can connect the words and events of biblical times with today.*

THE WORD IN LIFE STUDY BIBLE HELPS YOU APPLY SCRIPTURE TO EVERYDAY LIFE.

"Wow! This is the kind of Bible I need in my life," one reader said. "It just makes Scripture come alive. It's contemporary. It's relevant." As you read The Word In Life Study Bible, *you won't have to search and struggle for ways to apply God's Word; the articles suggest numerous possibilities for how Scripture makes a difference. That's especially helpful if you're one who is strapped for time or likes to quickly get to the point.*

THE WORD IN LIFE STUDY BIBLE CHALLENGES YOU TO DEVELOP YOUR OWN THINKING.

You won't find pat answers or a "packaged" theology in this study Bible. Instead, the articles are designed to provoke your thinking by relating the text of Scripture to the issues of today, providing information to guide your thinking. Sometimes the commentary will raise a question without answering it; sometimes it will suggest possible answers. Often it will point out things that you may not have considered before. The articles don't pretend to address every issue raised by the biblical text or to solve every theological problem. But they're guaranteed to make you think!

The Word In Life Study Bible introduces you to the people of Scripture.

For too many readers, the Bible can seem dull and lifeless, a book that only scholars and mystics might find interesting. But Scripture comes alive once we discover the people in the text. The Word In Life Study Bible *is designed to help you do that, to "make friends" with some of the fascinating characters that God chose to include in His Word. Almost fifty of them receive special attention through "Personality Profiles" that summarize what we know of them (see below). Even though these people lived long ago, you'll find that you have far more in common with them than you have differences. They experienced many of the same things you do. By learning what God did in their lives, you'll gain insight into what God is doing in yours.*

The Word In Life Study Bible makes the Bible easy to read.

"I know I should read the Bible more, but to be honest, I just don't have time!" Have you ever felt that way? If so, The Word In Life Study Bible *is for you. It was designed for busy people. In the first place, you'll enjoy how easy it is to read the New King James Version. A modern translation that preserves the stylistic beauty of the King James Version, the NKJV presents the eternal Word of God in everyday language that people can understand. You'll also find the material presented in bite-size units, with section headings to mark the text. The Scriptures are accompanied not by long, drawn-out treatises, but by straight-to-the-point articles and other information presented in simple, easily grasped terms.* ◆

Features to Look For

Introductory Articles

At the beginning of a book of the Bible you'll find information that explains why the book is important and what to pay attention to as you read it. You'll learn something of the background behind the book, including who the author and original readers were. You'll also get an idea of the issues the book addresses through a table of contents that describes some of the articles you'll find alongside the text.

Consider This

(symbols enlarged)

As mentioned above, God intended His Word to change people's lives. That's why occasionally you'll find a symbol that refers you to a nearby article relating in some way to the text indicated. These articles help to explain the Scriptural passages and highlight the significance of biblical truths for modern readers. In articles with this symbol, ways are offered for you to **consider** *how the passage applies to your life and the world around you.*

For Your Info

This symbol indicates articles that primarily offer **information** *about the text or its cultural context. Knowing the background of a biblical passage will help you understand it more accurately and make it more useful to you.*

Personality Profiles

One of the goals that the editors of The Word In Life Study Bible *had in developing their material was to introduce readers to the* **people** *of the Scriptures, including those who lived and worked in public places. One of the important ways that this study Bible does that is through personality profiles that highlight various individuals. These are not biographies, but summaries of what the Bible tells us about the person, what can be reasonably inferred from the text, and what other sources report about his or her life and legacy.*

You Are There

One of the most important windows on understanding the text of Scripture is knowing the **places** *where the events occurred. Unfortunately, ancient localities are unknown to most modern readers. The cities of Acts, for example, are little more than dots on a map for most of us. Yet when we examine the geography of the New Testament, we discover that the first-century Roman world was quite a bit like our own. The articles indicated by the "you are there" symbol will take you to places that you may never have "visited" before. Sometimes there's also information about what life was like for the people who lived there.*

A Closer Look

Sometimes the best way to understand a text of Scripture is to **compare** *the text to a related passage and/or its connected article. That's why you'll find symbols that "advertise" companion passages and articles that provide insight into the passage indicated.*

Quote Unquote

Occasionally you might be interested in knowing what someone else besides the writers of Scripture had to say about an idea raised in the biblical text, or about the text itself. That's not to suggest that these **quotations** *from various authors are on a par with Scripture. But one way to gain perspective on the implications of a passage is to read what someone has written, and then use that to reflect on what God has said.*

Themes to Consider

In designing The Word In Life Study Bible, *the editors wanted to create a resource that would help people deal with the issues of today, not yesterday. To that end, they identified a number of themes to highlight. Articles and other information provide a starting point for thought, study, and discussion of the following important areas:*

Work

For most of us, work is the most dominating area of life. It determines where we'll live, what kind of lifestyle we'll have, even who our friends will be. Yet how many of us are aware of how much the Bible says about work and workplace issues?

Economics

Who can doubt the importance of economic issues in a world increasingly tied together in a giant global marketplace? Of course, Scripture wasn't written to be an economics textbook. Nevertheless, it gives us principles relating to wealth, money, value, service, the environment, and other topics affecting both public policy and personal financial decisions.

Ethics

This is the issue of right and wrong, of integrity and character. In a day when truth and values have become relative, we need to return to God's unchanging Word as our absolute standard for ethical conduct and commitments.

Ethnicity

One has only to glance at a map of our modern world to recognize the impact of racial and ethnic differences. The landscape is strewn with wars, conflicts, and problems tied to long-standing ethnic tensions. How should Christians respond, especially living in an increasingly pluralistic society? As the early church discovered, the gospel has enormous implications for how we relate to others from different backgrounds.

The Church

Enormous opportunities and critical choices face the church today. A fresh look at the church's beginnings and its impact on the first-century world can offer valuable guidelines for the church's impact on the twenty-first-century world.

Laity

Elton Trueblood has pointed out that the first Reformation put the Word of God back into the hands of the people of God; now we face the prospect of a "second reformation" that can put the *work* of God back into the hands of the people of God. This means that "everyday" believers can participate in carrying out God's work and find meaning and value in their efforts.

The Family

Building marriages and families that honor God has perhaps never been harder than today. That's why *The Word In Life Study Bible* highlights passages, principles, and people that show us the fundamental truths—and the honest realities—of building healthy family relationships in a fallen world.

The City

Today for the first time in history, more people live in metropolitan than in rural areas. That has enormous implications for how Christians engage the world. Yet many believers have adopted a negative view of the city; some even see it as an evil. But when we read the Bible, we discover that the gospel "conquered" the Roman world by penetrating its major cities. The same thing can happen today.

Witness

One thing is certain about evangelism: both non-Christians and Christians feel uncomfortable with it. Yet Jesus has sent His followers into the world to communicate His message of salvation. Fortunately, the Bible gives us guidelines for carrying out the task in a way that is winsome, sensitive, and effective.

Women

One of the most significant developments in recent culture has been the growing awareness of and sensitivity to issues and concerns of women—their dignity, their needs, and their rights. *The Word In Life Study Bible* places a special emphasis on the many women of the Scriptures and their significant contribution to the ministry of Jesus and the growth of the church. It also highlights the condition of women in the ancient world and the biblical teaching that pertains to the lives of women both then and now.

The themes mentioned above are just some of the ones that are touched on. It wouldn't be possible to classify them all. But as you use The Word In Life Study Bible, *New Testament edition, it will stir up your thinking and show you other areas in which to apply God's Word to life.* ◆

How to Use the Symbol System

The section above concerning "Features to Look For" mentions four symbols that are used to designate various kinds of articles, tables, or related material in The Word In Life Study Bible.

From time to time as you read the biblical text, you will see one of those four symbols along the left side of the text, accompanied by a box containing information that will lead you to a feature that has to do with the biblical passage you are reading.

If the feature you are being sent to is on one of the two pages you are opened to (called a "spread"), then the box next to the symbol by the text will contain just chapter-and-verse information, designating one verse (for example, 1:10) or a range of verses (1:1–16). No page number is given. Just look on the spread you are opened to for a matching symbol accompanied by a box containing the name of the symbol (such as CONSIDER THIS) and matching chapter-and-verse information.

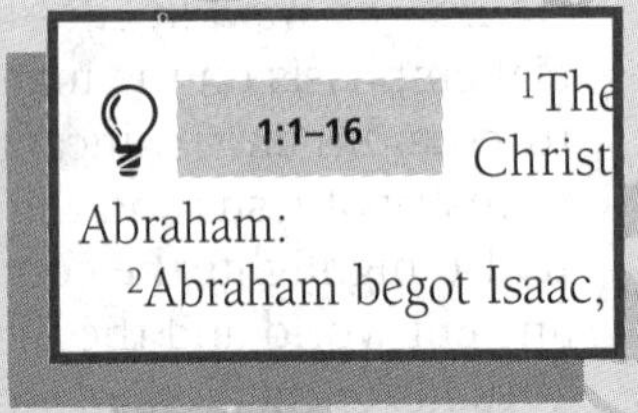

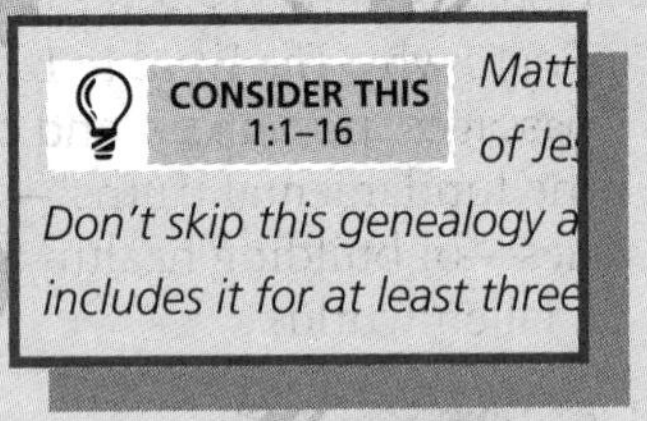

If the feature you are being sent to is someplace other than the spread you are opened to, then the box next to the symbol by the text will contain chapter-and-verse information and a page number. Just look on the designated page for a matching symbol accompanied by a box containing the name of the symbol and matching chapter-and-verse information.

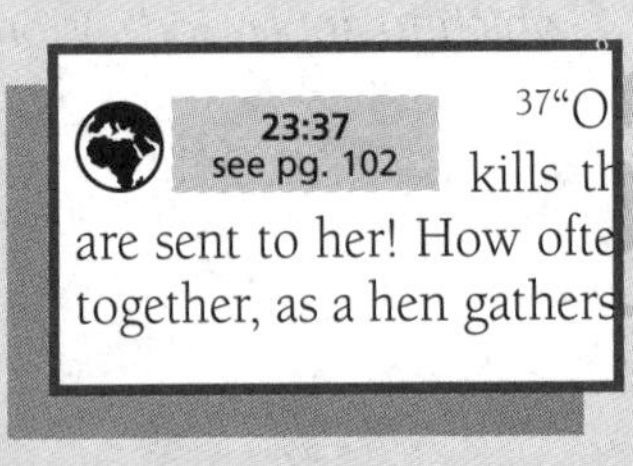

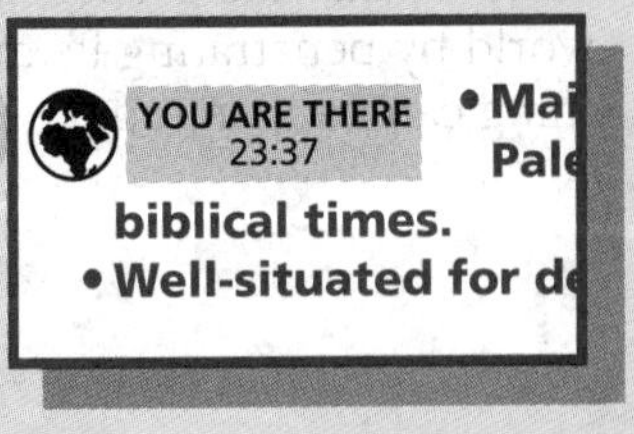

New King James Footnotes

your brethren[a] only, what do you do more *than* not even the tax collectors[b] do so? 48Therefore

As you read, you will often see a raised letter in the biblical text. Each raised letter designates a New King James footnote, to be found at the foot of the column of text. Each footnote is designated by the chapter and verse in which its raised letter is contained. Then you will see the raised letter, followed by the footnote. (The letter *a* is used for the first footnote connected to each verse. If a verse has more than one footnote connected to it, then the second footnote receives the letter *b*. The chapter and verse are not repeated in such cases.)

New King James footnotes contain helpful information about significant textual variations and alternate translations, as well as some explanations and references to other passages of Scripture.

Footnotes concerning textual variations make no evaluation of readings, but do clearly indicate the manuscript sources of readings. They objectively present the facts without such remarks as "the best manuscripts omit" or "the most reliable manuscripts read," which are value judgments that differ according to varying viewpoints on the text.

Where significant variations occur in the New Testament Greek manuscripts, textual notes are classified as followed:

1 NU-Text

These variations from the traditional text represent the text as published in the twenty-sixth edition of the Nestle-Aland Greek New Testament (N) and in the United Bible Societies' third edition (U), hence the abbreviation, "NU-Text."

Example:

As we forgive our debtors.

6:4 [a]NU-Text omits *openly.* *6:6* [a]NU-Text omits *openly.*

2 M-Text

These variations from the traditional text represent the Majority Text, which is based on the majority of surviving manuscripts. It should be noted that M stands for whatever reading is printed in the first edition of *The Greek New Testament According to the Majority Text,* whether supported by overwhelming, strong, or only a divided majority textual tradition.

Example:

be baptized by him. 14And John *tried to* prevent

3:11 [a]M-Text omits *and fire.*

The textual notes reflect the scholarship of the past 150 years and will assist the reader to observe the variations between the different manuscript traditions of the New Testament. Such information is generally not available in English translations of the New Testament.

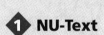

Other Features

Maps

Many maps appear throughout The Word In Life Study Bible. *They are designed to provide relevant geographical information in an accessible and easy-to-read format, on the same pages with the biblical text and related features.*

A number of locator maps *show you quickly where a certain place is with regard to its surrounding area.*

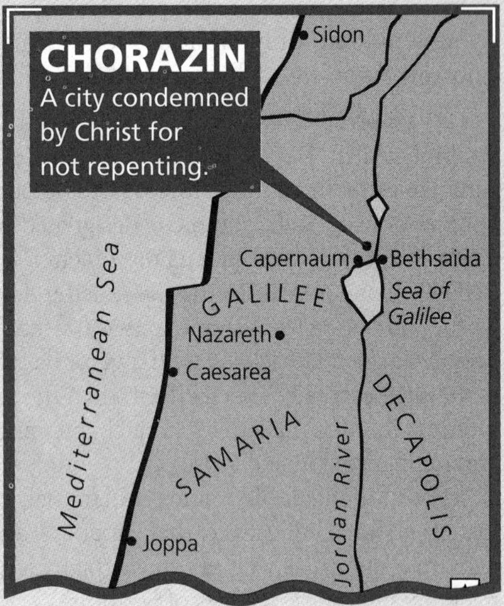

Tables

Information is often presented in the form of tables or lists, showing at a glance how various facts and ideas relate to each other.

THE TWELVE

Apostle	Description
Simon (Peter) (Mark 1:16)	Fisherman from Galilee, Andrew's brother
Andrew (John 1:40)	Fisherman from Galilee, Peter's brother
James	Son of Zebedee, brother to John; from Capernaum
John (Introduction to John)	Son of Zebedee, brother to James; from Capernaum
Philip	From Bethsaida
Bartholomew	[illegible]

In the back of *The Word In Life Study Bible*, New Testament edition, are four handy reference features:

Themes to Study (p. 938)

A list of *themes to study* includes information about articles and their related texts, arranged by subject. Using this feature, you can read in connected fashion the material that relates to certain themes or issues.

Index to Key Passages (p. 957)

This index directs you to passages in the New Testament that pertain to a variety of practical and spiritual topics. Passages are listed alphabetically within each topic by brief content summaries.

The Four Gospels Side by Side (p. 964)

This table shows the parallel passages in the four Gospels. By referring to it, you can find out what all four Gospels say about an event in the life of Jesus.

Jobs and Occupations Index (p. 971)

People in the Bible had to work for a living too. This feature describes the occupations mentioned in the Bible and offers a revealing glimpse into the daily lives of men and women in biblical times. You'll see many resemblances to the work world of today.

THE BOOKS OF THE NEW TESTAMENT

that your faith itself feels under siege, pay attention to 1 and 2 Peter! They were written for Christians in the crucible.

2 PETER—We Can Count on God 843
When we're being persecuted, sometimes it seems that just enduring it is all we can do. Coping may look like our only alternative to caving in. This letter offers great comfort to "coping Christians" by showing that we can rely on God, His Word, and the ultimate return of Jesus.

1 JOHN—Tough Love 849
John is often described as the "apostle of love" and 1, 2, and 3 John as the "love letters" of the New Testament. But these writings are not about sentimentalism. They're about "tough love," love that shoots straight, even if it hurts, because it cares for others and wishes them the best.

2 JOHN—The Test of Truth 863
Ideas and spiritual claims need to be given a simple but crucial litmus test: what do they say about Jesus? As believers today confront an onslaught of religious systems in a pluralistic society, this letter is particularly relevant.

3 JOHN—Imitate What Is Good 865
This letter confronts disloyalty in the church in a striking way. John sets descriptions of two leaders side by side and then encourages the reader to "imitate . . . what is good." Apparently John felt confident that a sensible person would know which man was worthy of imitation.

JUDE—The New Testament's Exposé of False Teachers 867
Using graphic word pictures and recalling a rogue's gallery of deceivers from years gone by, Jude documents a history of subversive forces that threatened to destroy the early church. In reading this letter, we are reminded that Christianity is no game.

REVELATION—Christ, the Lord of History 873
How will history end? That's the theme of this last book in the New Testament, which pulls the curtain back to reveal God's ultimate plan for the world. What we find is a dramatic tale told in highly symbolic language. Nevertheless, its point is easily grasped: Christ will be revealed as the Lord of history.

FAITH IMPACTS THE WORLD

Jesus not only affects one's private life, but one's public life as well. Christ's followers can recover that dimension of the gospel today. We can discover how to live out our faith in visible, public ways, as the "people of God" (1 Pet. 2:9–10), in order to powerfully impact our culture. But in doing so we need to consider: How does faith impact *the world?*

It helps to understand how our world operates. We can start by identifying three components of the "global village" in which we live and work:

(1) *The workplace,* made up of businesses, governments, and services.
(2) *Communities,* involving groupings of people such as cities, neighborhoods, and especially families.
(3) *Systems,* such as laws, traditions, and values, that support work and community life.

The world of (1) work and employment can be divided into three general sectors, as shown by the three towers in the accompanying diagram on page xx: business, government, and service. Each sector contains thousands of specific occupations and there is much overlap. Gatekeepers, power brokers, and other leaders exist for each sector.

The more general, and in many ways less formal, sectors of (2) community and family are represented by the larger horizontal disc that supports the workplace.

The undergirdings of society, (3) systems, are not as easily observed. They exist conceptually in our minds and hearts, quietly supporting and influencing the institutions, systems, and peoples of the world. Policies, traditions, values, laws, beliefs—like pilings sunk deep into the ground under tall buildings—are powerful supports that provide a foundation for society.

Some parts of the foundation are permanent in their value. But sometimes, as illustrated by the decaying columns, the nature of the foundation changes as unreliable supports crumble and the stronger foundations are relied upon even more and fortified if possible.

Behind it all is the sovereign God who sustains creation. Faith in Him enables truly meaningful social progress, as believers move back and forth between gathering for worship and scattering for engagement with the world.

How, Then, Does Christian Faith Impact the World?

Three ways that Christ's message impacts our world are:

(1) *Through followers of Christ.* These are individuals with an active faith who live out the gospel and proclaim it to the world through:

- sharing Christ by word and deed in their relationships and lifestyles;
- the proper handling of responsibilities and resources in their personal possession;

(continued)

(continued)

- informal networks of friendships, care groups, and guilds;
- active participation in the structures of society;
- recognized leaders who influence others in the society.

(2) *Through Christian institutions and structures.* In many cultures, believers have the privilege of owning or controlling organizations that present the gospel and its implications to the society. Some of these include:

- local churches, whose members and attenders can influence the larger community;
- service organizations that render human aid such as medical care, education, and help to the poor;
- media outlets, such as magazines, radio and television stations, and publishing houses.

(3) *Through lobbying and advocacy.* Here Christians attempt to influence the values of society and the people and institutions that determine them. This can mean either affirming support for beliefs with which Christians agree or restraining and resisting influences that seem opposed to Scripture. Christian advocacy might include:

- voting;
- running for office or supporting candidates and legislation;
- lobbying leaders and institutions to affect policies, procedures, and activities;
- pressing for business and community development that benefits people and their surroundings;
- demonstrating publicly for or against various activities;
- taking legal action.

We see that faith impacts more than just individuals. Jesus used images such as salt, light, leaven, and seeds to describe His kingdom's effect on the world. His gospel not only transforms persons but also institutions and the value structures that undergird society.

Evil and sin certainly pervade the world. In response, Jesus has sent us into the world to have influence for His sake (Mark 16:15). Through our work, our families, our prayers for the world and its leaders, our activity as good citizens, and our involvement in the structures of society, we can present Christ's message and have impact on a world that needs Him now more than ever. ◆

See diagram on next page.

. . . Christ came, who is over all,
the eternally blessed God. Amen.
—*Romans 9:5*

FAITH IMPACTS THE WORLD

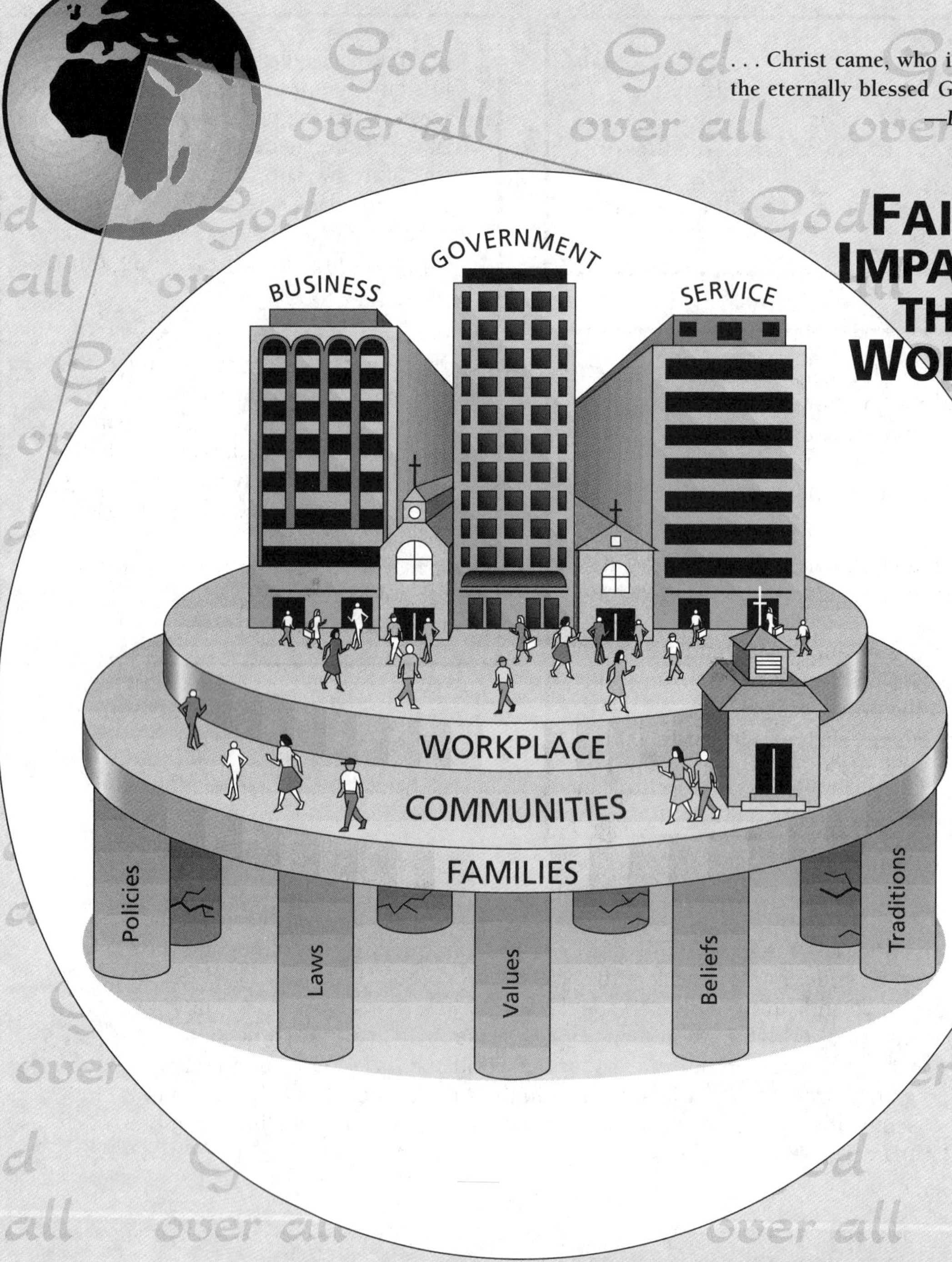

The workplace today includes many specific occupations, as it did in biblical times. See the Jobs and Occupations Index *on* *page 971* *for a detailed look at what work was like for the people of the Bible. You might see some parallels to your own situation.*

NEW TESTAMENT PANELISTS SPEAK OUT ON THE ISSUES

Imagine that we could observe a panel discussion including the major writers of the New Testament. We might ask them to explain how the gospel affects the issues of our day.

Naturally, we can't listen to such a discussion in person, but we can observe the writers' statements in Scripture, and try to estimate how they would respond.

That's what the table below does. It offers some scriptural comments by six New Testament writers as they relate to eight topics treated in The Word In Life Study Bible. *It also refers you to various annotations in which the passages and others are discussed.*

Use this table as a starting point for your own study of the issues. Examine the authors' statements in context and see what else they and the other New Testament writers have to say about applying biblical truth to everyday life.

MATTHEW	
Race and Ethnicity	•Matthew opens with a family tree of Jesus' ancestors. See "Jesus' Roots," Matt. 1:1–16. •The writer shows Jesus breaking through a wall of hatred and separation between Jews and Gentiles. See "Jews, Gentiles, and Jesus," Matt. 15:24.
The Church	•Christ's kingdom advances as His people live the gospel throughout the world. See "The King Declares His Kingdom," Matt. 4:17.
Laity	•Christ doesn't look for perfect people, but rather faithful people who will experience His forgiveness and grow. See "Would You Choose These for Leaders?" Matt. 26:35–74.
Witness	•It's easy to say that Jesus cares for the whole world. But sometimes it's easier to follow a pattern of religion that fits comfortably into our own culture. See "To All the Nations," Matt. 28:19.
Gender	•In certain remarks of Jesus we see an understanding of women and childbearing that varies from what was offered by the culture of His day. See "A New Respect for Women," Matt. 5:32.
Public Systems	•Matthew records a number of statements by Jesus that sound extreme to our ears (5:22, 30, 37, 39–42). How can we make sense out of them? See "The Morality of Christ," Matt. 5:17–48. •Believers today need to discover how to live out faith in visible, public ways, in order to have an impact in the world. See "The Public Side of Our Faith," Matt. 14:13–14.

Continued

Continued

MATTHEW	
Work	•One story that Jesus told offers an important lesson about success. See "True Success Means Faithfulness," Matt. 25:14–30.
The City	•Matthew called Jerusalem "the holy city," but it was also noisy, dirty, and smelly, not unlike cities today. How could such a city be considered "holy"? See "Can a Noisy, Dirty, Smelly City Also Be Holy?" Matt. 4:5. •Jesus used two symbols—salt and light—to remind us that following Him involves a person's public life, particularly through work and participation in the community. See "Sulfa Drugs and Street Lights," Matt. 5:13–16.

MARK	
Race and Ethnicity	•Jesus' Galilean roots demonstrated that His gospel was not just for the elite, but for everyone. See "Jesus the Galilean," Mark 1:14. •Jesus' encounter with a distraught woman gave His disciples a powerful lesson about dealing with foreigners. See "Jesus and Ethnicity," Mark 7:24–30.
The Church	•Jesus calls people to Him who are insignificant according to traditional ideas of importance. See "Significance for Little People," Mark 2:3–17.
Laity	•Is your significance tied too closely to achievements? God calls us to a far more stable basis for significance. See "A Kingdom Perspective on Significance," Mark 13:33.
Witness	•Mark shows that we must avoid the trap of evaluating our faith by how others respond to our communication of it. See "Is Your Witness Falling on Deaf Ears?" Mark 4:3–20.
Gender	•A question about divorce reveals that Jewish women in the first century were far more restricted than men in their grounds for divorce. See "Divorce," Mark 10:2–12.
Public System	•At times people have used a statement by Jesus to avoid caring for the poor. But is that what Jesus had in mind? See "Always the Poor," Mark 14:7.
Work	•Like His earthly father before Him, Jesus worked to make a living. See "Jesus the Carpenter," Mark 6:3. •Jesus modeled a principle that many of us today could stand to practice more—the principle of rest. See "Why Not Rest a While?" Mark 6:31.
The City	•No individual Christian can meet all of the desperate needs in today's cities. But does God really ask us to? See "People Priorities in the City," Mark 5:21–43.

LUKE	
Race and Ethnicity	•Luke shows that the Lord's salvation is for "all peoples," both Jews and Gentiles. See "An International Savior," Luke 2:29–31.
The Church	•The original leaders of the church were not exactly prize recruits for a new spiritual movement. See "Can Laity Get the Job Done?" Luke 9:1–62. •In the book of Acts, Luke goes on to demonstrate that God uses empowered laypeople like the Twelve—and like us today—to do His work. See "The Extraordinary Acts of Ordinary People," Introduction to Acts.
Laity	•Powerful results come from experienced believers mentoring younger believers in the faith. See "Discipleship—Or Mentoring?" Acts 9:26–30. •Dozens of churches sprang up in the first century, thanks to the Holy Spirit's coordinated use of three tentmakers, a fiery evangelist, and countless unnamed laity. See "The Ephesus Approach," Acts 19:8–41.
Witness	•What is the gospel, and why was it significant for Jesus—and us—to proclaim it? See "What Is the Gospel?" Luke 7:22. •God may have placed you in a strategic position to bring the gospel to someone. See "Where Has God Placed You?" Acts 8:26–39.
Gender	•If you're a man, are you growing in your appreciation of women as God's creation? Do you esteem the women God brings your way? See "Those Women Again!" Luke 24:11.
Public System	•Jesus' first sermon before His hometown crowd moves us to ask: Whom are we reaching out to with the good news about Christ? What issues does Jesus' gospel address in our times? See "Jesus' First Sermon Included Surprises," Luke 4:16–27.
Work	•Jesus saw His followers in the grip of a common way of thinking—competing to prove their significance. See "Competition versus Compassion," Luke 9:46–48. •Luke provides three examples to show that Christlike values don't always produce financial gain in the marketplace. See "People, Property, and Profitability," Acts 16:19.
The City	•When some people came to ask Jesus whether He was the Messiah, they found Him ministering among people who were just getting by on the margins of society. See "The Underclass," Luke 7:20–23. •Luke's account in Acts demonstrates that one reason Christianity prevailed in the Roman world was that it planted churches in dozens of the empire's major cities. See "Churches—Keys to the Cities," Acts 11:22.

JOHN	
Race and Ethnicity	•Jesus refused to play ethnic games when there was a matter of eternal life and death at stake. See "Ethnic Games With Religious Roots," John 4:19–23.
The Church	•To be effective, believers must remain "on line" with Jesus, drawing from His resources and obeying His commands. See "The Network," John 15:1–10. •John records a prayer of Jesus that shows that engagement with the world, not isolation, is His desire for His church. See "Called Into the World," John 17:18.
Laity	•Have you ever struggled with doubts or tough questions about Christ, the Christian faith, or the church? See "Skeptics Welcome," John 20:24–31.
Witness	•John presents back-to-back accounts that show two of the many different ways in which Jesus dealt with people. See "The Gospel in a Pluralistic Society," John 3:21. •One thing is certain about evangelism: both non-Christians and Christians feel uncomfortable with it. See "Whose Job Is Evangelism?" John 16:8.
Gender	•An attempt to humiliate a woman before Jesus results in His setting a new standard for judgment. See "A Double Standard," John 8:2–3. •Will there ever be an end to discrimination, elitism, and injustice? Will people ever regard each other as equals? See "Finally, Full Equality," Rev. 5:9–10.
Public System	•John's Gospel presents another man named John whose behavior seems to repudiate the common measures of success in our society. See "Success," John 3:30.
Work	•A statement by Jesus shows that God is a worker who continues to maintain the creation and provide for His creatures. See "God—The Original Worker," John 5:17. •John envisions "a new heaven and a new earth" in which work will be free of the painful toil and drudgery that now characterizes it. See "Fresh Fruit Salad!" Rev. 22:2.
The City	•Jesus tapped into one of the most powerful concepts of the Old Testament—the idea that a specific place on earth is made special because of God's presence there. See "Sacred Space," John 1:51. •In the book of Revelation, John presents Babylon as more than a city, but as an entire world system in rebellion against God. See "A Symbol of Evil," Rev. 14:8.

PETER	
Race and Ethnicity	•An officer of Rome's occupation troops in Palestine came to faith, and Peter realized that God wants Gentiles in the church. See "Ethnic Walls Break Down," Acts 10:44–45. •Peter paints a family portrait of God's people. See "God's Family Album," 1 Pet. 2:9–10.
The Church	•Peter's memorable declaration led to an important statement about the foundation on which the church is built. See "'You Are the Christ,'" Mark 8:27–33. •Peter urges clergy to maintain the utmost integrity when it comes to finances. See "Don't Fleece the Flock," 1 Pet. 5:2.
Laity	•Do you ever doubt God's willingness to forgive you over and over again? Peter might easily have felt that way. But Jesus reconnected with him and called him to genuine love and the continuation of His work. See "Forgiveness Abounds," John 21:15–23.
Witness	•At Pentecost, Peter proclaimed the message of Christ to a crowd of unbelievers in the best way he knew how, being faithful to the truth. The speech produced dramatic results. See "Carrots, Not Sticks," Acts 2:37–38.
Gender	•Peter recalls a heroine of the Old Testament as a model of good works and courageous faith. See "Sarah," 1 Pet. 3:6.
Public System	•Faced with a conflict between human authority and God's authority, Peter showed how believers can strike a balance between the two. See "'We Ought to Obey God Rather than Men,'" Acts 5:22–32.
Work	•Peter reminds us that the church is not a business, and when it imports marketplace practices, it needs to carefully evaluate them by the Scriptures. See "The Business of the Church," 1 Pet. 5:2–4.
The City	•Peter witnessed the birth of an international, multilingual church when he preached the gospel at Pentecost. See "Pluralism at Pentecost," Acts 2:5.

PAUL	
Race and Ethnicity	•It took Paul years to reevaluate his cultural perspectives and bring them in line with the heart of God. See "A Bigot Does an About-Face," Gal. 1:13–17. •Race is one of three major social distinctions that no longer matter in Christ. See "We Are Family!" Gal. 3:28.
The Church	•Suppose Paul were to visit your church—not the physical building, but the people. How would he evaluate your group? See "This Building Gets Landmark Status," Eph. 2:19–22.
Laity	•Paul didn't see himself as a super-saint. On the contrary, he grew in the faith with some difficulty. His view of himself changed over time. See "Hope for You—Watch Paul Grow," Gal. 1:11–24. •The vast majority of a church's faithful worshipers probably are available for ministries outside the church, out in the world among unbelievers. See "Is Your Church Upside-down or Right Side Up?" 1 Thess. 2:13–14.
Witness	•Rome was the greatest superpower of its day. Perhaps that's why Paul described the gospel to the believers there in terms of power—God's power to save. It's a gospel powerful enough to handle the empire, big enough to address issues on a global scale. See "The Super-Powerful Gospel," Introduction to Romans.
Gender	•The gospel requires a different understanding of sex and marriage than the one held by the surrounding culture. See "A New View of Sexuality," 1 Cor. 7:3–6. •Gender is one of three major social distinctions that no longer matter in Christ. See "We Are Family!" Gal. 3:28.
Public Systems	•Paul used his Roman citizenship to protect his rights, showing that there's no need to allow discrimination to hinder one's practice of the faith. See "Faith and Rights," Acts 22:25–29. •Paul offers some helpful perspectives on how to respond to the systems in which we live. See "Governmental Authority," Rom. 13:2.
Work	•Paul's statement recalling the curse that God leveled on creation reminds us of the commonly held idea that God imposed work as a curse to punish Adam and Eve's sin. But is that completely correct? See "Is Work a Curse?" Rom. 8:20. •What determines the spiritual value of a job? How does God assign significance? See "Are Some Jobs More Important Than Others?" 1 Cor. 12:28–31.
The City	•Paul intentionally went to cities. We see that the gospel has implications for the urban setting. See "Paul's Urban Strategy," Acts 16:4. •While there is a place for human responsibility, Paul tells us that people—including authorities—are not the ultimate enemy. See "Who Is the Enemy?" Eph. 6:10–13.

25 IMPORTANT FIGURES IN THE NEW TESTAMENT

One key to understanding the New Testament is to observe the people in the text, especially the way they relate to God and His work in the world. Obviously they lived in a somewhat different culture two thousand years ago. Yet, are the issues they faced, the questions they asked, the personalities they displayed, and the triumphs and failures they experienced really much different from our own?

Below, you are invited to examine twenty-five of the important figures in the New Testament. Some are models to follow; make them your friends and mentors. Others illustrate pitfalls to avoid; learn from their mistakes! Either way, study the fears and foibles, great deeds and misdeeds of these twenty-five, and allow the Scriptures to come alive through the personalities that God included in His Word.

(Italic titles and references indicate Personality Profiles.)

25 IMPORTANT FIGURES IN THE NEW TESTAMENT	
JESUS **Son of God**	•See: Matt. 16:16; 26:62–66; John 8:58. •Read: Ten Myths series, Myth #1: "Jesus Christ Was Only a Great Moral Teacher," Matt. 13:34–35.
Savior	•See: Matthew; Mark; Luke (especially 4:18–19); John. •Read: "An International Savior," Luke 2:29–32.
Lord	•See: Phil. 2:9–11. •Read: "Is Jesus Really Lord of All?" Luke 6:1–5; "Christ, the Lord of the World," Col. 1:15–18.
Messiah	•See: Matt. 16:16. •Read: "You Are the Christ," Mark 8:27–33.
Teacher of the Kingdom	•See: Matt. 5–7. •Read: "The King Declares His Kingdom," Matt. 4:17; "Work-World Stories Describe the Kingdom," Matt. 13:1.
Example for believers	•See: John 13:12–17; Phil. 2:5; 1 Pet. 2:21–23. •Read: "Being Like Jesus," Matt. 10:25.
PAUL **A leader of the church**	•See: Acts 13–28. •Read: *"Saul," Acts 13:2–3; "Paul," Acts 13:2–3.*

Continued

Continued

25 IMPORTANT FIGURES IN THE NEW TESTAMENT	
Mentor of numerous believers	•See: 1 Cor. 4:16; 11:1; 2 Tim. 2:2. •Read: "Discipleship—Or Mentoring?" Acts 9:26–30.
Apostle to the Gentiles	•See: Acts 9:15; Gal. 1:16; 2:9. •Read: "Paul Turns to the Gentiles," Acts 13:44–48; "Paul the Jew—Teacher of the Gentiles," 2 Tim. 1:3.
Business partner in tentmaking	•See: Acts 18:1–3. •Read: "Paul's 'Real' Job," Acts 18:1–3.
Author of more than a dozen New Testament letters	•See: Romans through Philemon, and (traditionally) Hebrews.
PETER **Disciple of Jesus**	•See: Matt. 10:2; John 1:40–42; 21:15–19. •Read: "The Twelve," Matt. 10:2; *"Simon Peter," Mark 1:16.*
A leader of the church	•See: Acts 1–15.
Evangelist	•See: Acts 2:14–42. •Read: "Off to a Good Start," Acts 2:1; "Ethnic Walls Break Down," Acts 10:44–45.
Author of two New Testament letters	•See: 1 and 2 Peter.
MARY, Jesus' Mother **Mother of Jesus**	•See: Matt. 1:18—2:23; Luke 1:26–56; 2:1–52. •Read: *"Mary the Mother of Jesus," Luke 1:26–56.*
International refugee	•See: Matt. 2:13–15, 19–23. •Read: "Asian-born Jesus Becomes a Refugee in Africa," Matt. 2:13–15.
PONTIUS PILATE **Roman procurator of Judea**	•See: John 18:28–40. •Read: "New Testament Political Rulers," Luke 3:1; "Roman Politics in the First Century A.D.," Luke 22:25.
Ruler who condemned Jesus to death	•See: John 19:1–16.
MARY of Magdala **Devoted follower of Jesus**	•See: Luke 8:1–3. •Read: *"Mary of Magdala," Luke 8:2.*
First person to see the resurrected Jesus	•See: Mark 16:9–10; John 20:14–18.

Continued

Continued

25 IMPORTANT FIGURES IN THE NEW TESTAMENT

JAMES **Brother of Jesus**	•See: Matt. 13:55; Gal. 1:19. •Read: *"James," Introduction to James.*
A leader of the church	•See: Acts 15:13–21; 21:18; Gal. 2:9.
Author of a New Testament letter	•See: James.
ELIZABETH **Mother of John the Baptist**	•See: Luke 1:5–25, 39–45, 57–66. •Read: "Elizabeth," Luke 1:24.
HEROD THE GREAT **King of Judea for Rome**	•See: Matt. 2:1–12. •Read: *"The Herods," Acts 12:1–2.*
Ruler who ordered the slaughter of babies in and near Bethlehem	•See: Matt. 2:16–18. •Read: "City Kids Die over Adult Matters," Matt. 2:16–18.
HERODIAS **Wife of Herod Antipas**	•See: Matt. 14:3. •Read: "Hateful Herodias," Matt. 14:3; *"The Herods," Acts 12:1–2.*
Schemer behind the execution of John the Baptist	•See: Matt. 14:1–12; Mark 6:17–28.
BARNABAS **Landowner in the early church**	•See: Acts 4:36–37. •Read: *"Barnabas," Acts 4:36–37.*
Mentor to Paul	•See: Acts 9:27; 11:22, 30; 12:25. •Read: "Barnabas—A Model for Mentoring," Acts 9:27.
Leader in the early church	•See: Acts 14:12–18.
TIMOTHY **Associate of Paul**	•See: Acts 16:3–7; 1 Thess. 1:1; 3:6. •Read: *"Timothy," Introduction to 2 Timothy.*
Project leader at Ephesus	•See: 1 Tim. 1:3; 4:6–16. •Read: "Discipleship—Or Mentoring?" Acts 9:26–30; "The Ephesus Approach," Acts 19:8–41.
Cross-cultural worker	•See: Acts 16:1–3.

Continued

Continued

25 Important Figures in the New Testament

PRISCILLA and AQUILA **Tent manufacturers**	•See: Acts 18:1–3. •Read: "Paul's 'Real' Job," Acts 18:1–3; *"Priscilla and Aquila," Rom. 16:3–5.*
Coworkers with Paul	•See: Acts 18:18–19; Rom. 16:3–5. •Read: "The Ephesus Approach," Acts 19:8–41.
Mentors to Apollos	•See: Acts 18:24–28. •Read: "Discipleship—Or Mentoring?" Acts 9:26–30; *"Apollos," Acts 18:24–28.*
LUKE **Gentile doctor**	•See: Col. 4:14. •Read: *"Luke," Introduction to Luke.*
Paul's associate	•See: Acts 16:10–17 ("we"); Philem. 24.
Author of Luke and Acts	•See: Luke 1:1–4; Acts 1:1. •Read: Introductions to Luke and Acts.
JUDAS ISCARIOT **Disciple of Jesus and treasurer of the Twelve**	•See: Matt. 10:4; John 12:6; 13:29. •Read: "The Twelve," Matt. 10:2; *"Judas Iscariot," Matt. 26:14.*
Betrayer of Jesus	•See: Luke 22:3–6, 47–53; John 13:21–30; 18:1–3. •Read: "Judas Iscariot, the Betrayer," Matt. 26:14–16.
ONESIMUS **Runaway slave of Philemon befriended by Paul and returned as a fellow believer**	•See: Philemon. •Read: Introduction to Philemon; *"Onesimus," "Philemon," both at Introduction to Philemon.*
LYDIA **Businesswoman of Philippi**	•See: Acts 16:14. •Read: "Lydia," Acts 16:14.
Host to the first church in Europe	•See: Acts 16:15, 40.
MATTHEW **Tax collector of Capernaum**	•See: Matt. 9:9. •Read: *"Matthew," Introduction to Matthew;* "Who Were Those Tax Collectors?" Matt. 9:10; "Taxes," Mark 12:14.
Disciple of Jesus	•See: Matt. 9:9–13; 10:3; Luke 5:27–32. •Read: "A Rich Man Enters the Kingdom," Matt. 9:9–13; "The Twelve," Matt. 10:2.
Author of Matthew	•Read: Introduction to Matthew.

Continued

25 Important Figures in the New Testament	
MARY of Bethany **Sister of Martha and Lazarus**	•See: Luke 10:38–42; John 11:1. •Read: *"Mary of Bethany," John 11:1–2.*
Devoted follower of Jesus	•See: Matt. 26:6–13; Mark 14:3–9; Luke 10:38–42; John 11:2; 12:1–8. •Read: "A Parting Gift," Mark 14:3–9.
MARTHA of Bethany **Sister of Mary and Lazarus**	•See: Luke 10:38–42; John 11:1. •Read: *"Martha of Bethany," Luke 10:38–42.*
A practical woman and follower of Jesus	•See: Luke 10:38–42; John 11:20–28.
ANANIAS and SAPPHIRA **Members of the early church who lied to the Holy Spirit**	•See: Acts 5:1–11. •Read: *"Ananias and Sapphira," Acts 5:1.*
PHILIP **Deacon (worker) in the early church**	•See: Acts 6:5. •Read: *"Philip the Evangelist," Acts 8:5–13.*
Communicator of the gospel	•See: Acts 8:4–13, 26–40. •Read: "The Conversion of Samaritans to the Gospel—And of Peter and John to Samaritans," Acts 8:4–25.
Father of daughters who prophesied	•See: Acts 21:8–9. •Read: "The Four Daughters of Philip," Acts 21:9.
APOLLOS **Eloquent speaker and itinerant lecturer**	•See: Acts 18:24—19:1. •Read: *"Apollos," Acts 18:24–28.*
Leader in the early church	•See: Acts 18:27–28; 1 Cor. 1:12; 4:1–6; 16:12. •Read: "Discipleship—Or Mentoring?" Acts 9:26–30; "The Ephesus Approach," Acts 19:8–41.

In addition to the ones mentioned above, the New Testament tells of numerous other prominent figures, including some from the Old Testament. See if you can identify the "biblical VIP'S" described in "Fathers and Prophets," Heb. 1:1, and "Who Are These People?" Heb. 11:2.

A Month-Long Journey with Jesus

Whatever else *The Word In Life Study Bible* accomplishes, the most important thing it could do for you is to help you know Jesus Christ. Nothing matters more than your relationship with Him. To help you get acquainted with Jesus, here are 31 readings (one for each day of the month) listed in the order of their appearance in the New Testament.

Day 1
Matt. 1:18—2:23
Jesus is born, then becomes a refugee as an evil king seeks to destroy Him. Finally His family returns home.

Day 2
Matt. 4:1–11
Jesus confronts very real temptations.

Day 3
Matt. 13:54–58
Jesus faces rejection based on His family, their work, and the small size of His hometown.

Day 4
Matt. 23:1–39
Jesus speaks out against deceit, pride, and hypocrisy.

Day 5
Matt. 25:31–46
Jesus judges according to mercy and compassion rather than outward displays of spirituality.

Day 6
Mark 4:1–41
Jesus begins to explain the kingdom of God, using stories and images from the workplace.

Day 7
Luke 2:1–52
Luke describes events connected with Jesus' birth—and tells of an incident during a boyhood trip to Jerusalem.

Day 8
Luke 4:14–37
Jesus goes public with His purpose, and immediately encounters opposition.

Day 9
Luke 6:17–49
Jesus teaches basic truths about attitudes, true charity, evaluating others, and making wise choices.

Day 10
Luke 9:18–36
Jesus talks with His followers about who He is.

Day 11
Luke 22:1—24:53
Jesus is betrayed, judged, executed, buried, resurrected, and reconnected with His followers.

Day 12
John 1:1–18
John, one of Jesus' followers, describes how God became a man through Christ—full of grace and truth.

Day 13
John 5:19–47
Jesus explains His relationship with His Father and the implications for us.

Day 14
John 6:35–51
Jesus teaches that He is the bread of life, and tells how people can find Him.

Day 15
John 8:12–30
Jesus announces that He is the light of the world.

Day 16
John 10:1–18
Jesus says that He is the good shepherd who seeks His Father's lost sheep.

Day 17
John 11:1—12:8
John describes Jesus' relationship with some of His friends, and their profound love and care for each other.

Day 18
John 14:1—15:8
Jesus explains that He is our source of spiritual life and productivity—the way to God.

Day 19
John 21:15–25
Jesus loved even the man who had denied Him and was jealous of another disciple.

Day 20
Acts 2:22–42
Peter explains Christ to a massive crowd in Jerusalem, and welcomes 3,000 people into the faith.

Day 21
Rom. 5:1–21
Paul explains how Christ sets people free from sin and makes them acceptable to God.

Day 22
1 Cor. 15:1–28
Paul teaches about Christ's resurrection and the destruction of our enemy, death.

Day 23
Eph. 1:3–14
Paul describes Christ's work for us from three vantage points: before creation, in the present, and in eternity.

Day 24
Phil. 2:5–16
Paul explains the choices Christ made in order to become a man, as well as the choices we should make in following Him.

Day 25
Col. 1:15–22
Paul states that Christ is Lord of all—yesterday, today, and tomorrow.

Day 26
1 Thess. 4:13—5:11
Paul explains that Jesus will return and bring history to its culmination.

Day 27
Heb. 1:1—2:18
The author of Hebrews describes Christ's complete and wonderful work on our behalf.

Day 28
Heb. 4:14—5:10
Christ has experienced every kind of test or trial we will ever face.

Day 29
Heb. 9:23—10:18
Jesus takes away sin, once and for all. Forgiveness is ours in Him.

Day 30
1 Pet. 1:1–12
Peter tells us that our salvation in Christ is a reality that even the angels and Old Testament prophets did not understand.

Day 31
Rev. 5:1–14; 22:1–21
Christ will rule heaven and earth and will welcome believers to an eternity with Him.

THE NEW TESTAMENT

Marching Orders!

No other person has ever touched the world in quite the way Jesus did. And no other book of the New Testament records Jesus' teaching in quite the way Matthew does. Built around five major addresses that Jesus gave to His followers, Matthew records the essence of Christ's message, the core commands that He not only wanted His people to live by, but to spread to "all the nations . . . teaching them to observe all things that I have commanded you" (Matt. 28:19–20).

Thus Matthew contains marching orders for Christ's followers today. He sends us into the world to have impact—not the impact of coercion or force, but the irresistible influence of lives that reflect His ways, His love, and His values.

How appropriate, then, that Matthew leads off the New Testament. All of the books that follow are God's Word, but Matthew sets the pace. It highlights the agenda of our Lord: "all things that I have commanded you."

Matthew

Christ sends us into the world to have impact.

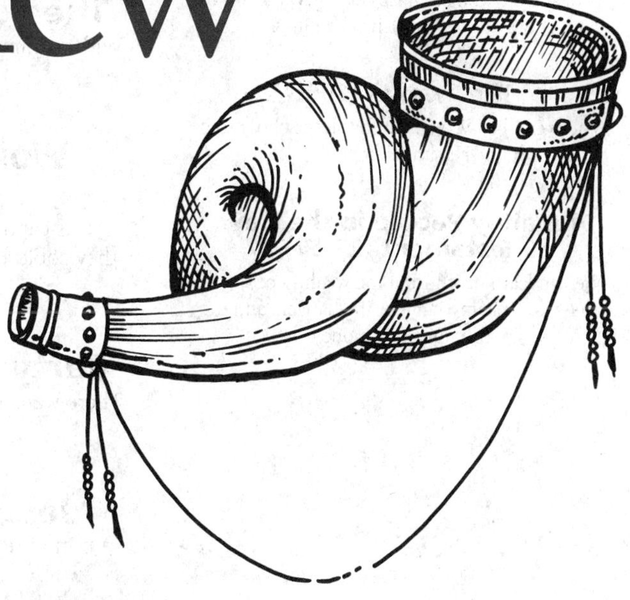

CONTENTS

Servant-Leaders (20:25–28)

Jesus revealed a unique style of authority—that whoever wishes to be great should become a "slave."

Whitewashed Tombs (23:27–28)

Jesus used a grim, arresting image to denounce His self-righteous enemies.

A Global Gospel with a Jewish Accent

For centuries, Jews had waited for a Messiah. They based their expectations on numerous Old Testament promises. For example, God told Abraham, the father of the nation, that through him "all the families of the earth [would] be blessed" (Gen. 12:3). To David, God's choice for Israel's king, God promised an enduring kingdom (2 Sam. 7:16). Through the prophets God renewed His pledge and provided details about the One who would fulfill it (Is. 7:14; 9:6–7; Dan. 2:44; 7:13–14).

Over the years, various figures came and went, some claiming to be the Messiah, others regarded by the people as likely candidates. But none proved convincing. None quite fulfilled the expectations of either the religious scholars who carefully studied the Scriptures, or the people who developed popular conceptions of what the Chosen One would accomplish.

What about the rabbi Jesus? He claimed to be God's Son. He performed extraordinary miracles that seemed to indicate divine power. He also taught with unprecedented authority and attracted a devoted band of followers. Yet hadn't He been rejected by the nation's leaders? Didn't He die a criminal's death? How, then, did He fulfill the promises of God? Was He really Israel's Messiah?

Matthew's Gospel answers with a resounding yes! He fills his account with Old Testament prophecies that point to Jesus as God's Chosen One (Matt. 1:23; 2:6, 15, 18, 23 to mention just a few). He wants his fellow Jews to study their Scriptures and find Jesus to be the Christ, the son of David, the son of Abraham, and the Son of God.

However, Matthew is not so much a Jewish Gospel as a global Gospel with a Jewish accent. In Jesus, all of us can find hope, no matter what our ethnic background. We don't have to be Jewish to be eligible for God's blessing and salvation. ◆

MATTHEW, THE SOCIAL OUTCAST

As a tax collector, Matthew was a member of a group that other Jews detested. Tax collectors were perceived not only as cheats, but mercenaries working for the Romans. Condemned by the religious leaders as unrighteous and ostracized by the general public as frauds and traitors, they found friends only among prostitutes, criminals, and other outcasts.

Yet Jesus selected Matthew to follow Him (Matt. 9:9). Scripture gives no indication why, but it does record the Lord's comment, "Go and learn what this means: 'I desire mercy and not sacrifice' [Hos. 6:6]. I did not come to call the righteous, but sinners to repentance" (v. 13). Apparently the call of Matthew was an act of pure mercy on the Lord's part—a choice that outraged self-satisfied religionists like the Pharisees.

They also criticized Jesus' willingness to attend a dinner that Matthew threw for Him (vv. 10–11). But Jesus knew whom He had come to help and where to find them. In Matthew, He had a direct entrée into the underworld of Jewish society, a class of people untouched by the religious legalists but deeply in need of a Savior. As the Great Physician (v. 12), Jesus was neither condoning nor glorifying lifestyles of sin, but merely reaching out to people who knew that they were sick and, as matters stood, completely lost. Matthew showed that Jesus can save anyone—that is, anyone who admits he needs saving. ◆

It's no wonder that Jews at the time of Jesus despised anyone associated with taxation: they were probably paying no less than 30 or 40 percent of their income on taxes and religious dues. See "Taxes," Mark 12:14.

Another tax collector who responded to Jesus was Zacchaeus of Jericho. See Luke 19:1–10.

PERSONALITY PROFILE: MATTHEW

Also known as: Levi. His given name, Matthew, meant "gift of Yahweh [the Hebrew term indicating God]."

Home: Capernaum (headquarters of Jesus' ministry); later Damascus, Syria.

Family: His father was Alphaeus.

Occupation: Tax collector; later an author, and pastor of a church in Damascus.

Special interests: Collecting Jesus' sermons and stories. He preserved them in a book that some call a new Torah because Jesus fulfilled so much Old Testament prophecy and restated much of the Mosaic Law.

Best known today as: The author of one of the Gospels.

HE SAW A MAN NAMED MATTHEW SITTING AT THE TAX OFFICE.
—Matthew 9:9

A Christian Torah

Tradition holds that after Jesus' departure, Matthew established a mostly Jewish church in or near Damascus of Syria and became its pastor. If so, his Gospel may have been a manual for Christian discipleship organized in a way that resembles the Pentateuch, the five books of Moses—Genesis, Exodus, Leviticus, Numbers, and Deuteronomy.

In Jesus' day, the Pentateuch was known as the Torah, which means "instruction" or "law." Moses warned the people to carefully observe all the words of the Law, the commandments of God (Deut. 32:46). The English word "law" does not convey all that Moses intended. Both the hearing and *the doing of the Law made the Torah. It was a manner of life, a way to live based on the covenant that God made with His people.*

In the same way, Matthew balances the teaching of Christ with the application of that truth in day-to-day life. He builds his material around five major speeches that Jesus gave, producing a sort of five-volume "Christian Torah":

5:1—7:27	*The Sermon on the Mount, given to a large crowd*
9:35—10:42	*Instructions to the Twelve, chosen by Christ*
13:1–52	*Parables of the kingdom, given on a crowded beach*
18:1–35	*Instructions on community, given to the disciples*
24:1—25:46	*The Olivet Discourse, also given to the disciples*

Before and after each of these teaching sections are action sections in which Jesus and His followers carry out God's Word. The book climaxes with what has been called the Great Commission, where Jesus instructs the Twelve to go throughout the world and make disciples, "teaching them to observe *all things that I have* commanded *you" (28:16–20, emphasis added). Discipleship involves not only truth believed, but truth applied.*

It's interesting how Matthew ties Jesus' earthly life to the history of Israel. For example, Jesus fled to Egypt as an infant (Matt. 2:13–15) just as Israel dwelt in Egypt beginning with Joseph (Gen. 39:1). Jesus was tempted by the devil in a wilderness (Matt. 4:1–11) just as Israel was tested in the wilderness (Ex. 15:22—32:35). The point is that Jesus was not some detached, heaven-sent Savior untouched by the pain that Israel experienced. On the contrary, Jesus was a full-fledged Hebrew who fulfilled the name Immanuel, "God with us" (Matt. 1:23).

Yet Matthew also shows Jesus reaching out to non-Jews and other "undesirables." In fact, Jesus' own ancestry was laced with "sinners" and "foreigners" (see "The Women in Jesus' Genealogy," Matt. 1:3–6). As a former tax collector, Matthew knew better than most that Jesus "did not come to call the righteous, but sinners to repentance" (9:13). The pastor/author wanted his congregation to understand that people don't have to be Jewish to be saved. ◆

THE LAND OF THE GOSPELS

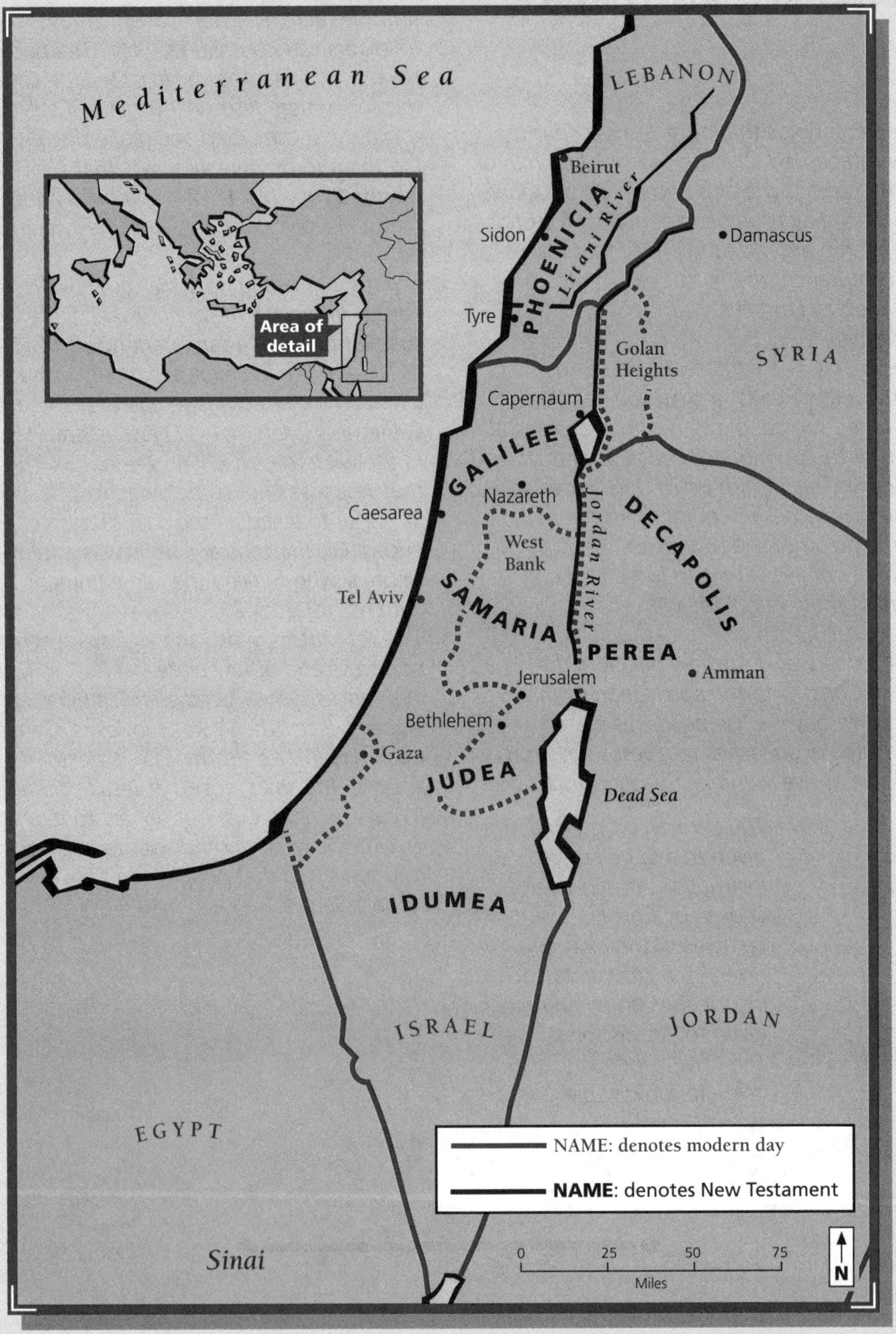

CHAPTER 1

The Background of Christ

1:1–16

[1]The book of the genealogy of Jesus
Christ, the Son of David, the Son of
Abraham:
[2]Abraham begot Isaac, Isaac begot Jacob, and Jacob begot

1:3–6 see pg. 8

Judah and his brothers. [3]Judah begot
Perez and Zerah by Tamar, Perez begot
Hezron, and Hezron begot Ram. [4]Ram begot Amminadab,
Amminadab begot Nahshon, and Nahshon begot Salmon.
[5]Salmon begot Boaz by Rahab, Boaz begot Obed by Ruth,
Obed begot Jesse, [6]and Jesse begot David the king.
David the king begot Solomon by her *who had been the wife*[a] of Uriah. [7]Solomon begot Rehoboam, Rehoboam begot
Abijah, and Abijah begot Asa.[a] [8]Asa begot Jehoshaphat, Je-
hoshaphat begot Joram, and Joram begot Uzziah. [9]Uzziah

(Bible text continued on page 9)

1:6 [a]Words in italic type have been added for clarity. They are not found in the original Greek. *1:7* [a]NU-Text reads *Asaph*.

JESUS' ROOTS

CONSIDER THIS 1:1–16 *Matthew opens with a family tree of Jesus' ancestors (vv. 1–16). Don't skip this genealogy and begin at v. 18! Matthew includes it for at least three important reasons:*

(1) To show that God's Son was also a real, flesh-and-blood human. This was a crucial concept for Matthew's first-century readers (see "Jesus, the Son of . . . ," Luke 3:23–38).

(2) To show that Jesus was the long-awaited Messiah of Israel. Notice the prominence of David and Abraham.

(3) To show that Jesus is also the international Christ, the Savior of the whole world. His genealogy reaches beyond Jews to include several ethnic groups that populated the Middle East during Israel's Old Testament history (see the accompanying article, "The Women In Jesus' Genealogy"). Jesus came to "make disciples of all the nations" (Matt. 28:19).

WHAT IT MEANS TO BE LIKE JESUS

CONSIDER THIS 1:1–17 *Jesus indicated that those who follow Him will become like Him (10:25). What does it mean to* **"be like Jesus"** *in today's complex world? Matthew paints eight portraits of what Christlikeness looks like, including:*

#1: To Be Like Jesus Means TO ACCEPT OUR ROOTS

Jesus' family tree hides nothing. His heritage was multiethnic and included several unattractive or embarrassing individuals. Indeed, the circumstances surrounding His own birth might have raised questions in the minds of some. But Jesus never denied His ancestry or allowed others to shame Him. If we want to be like Him, we need to understand and accept our roots in terms of culture, race, gender, and reputation. Moreover, like Jesus we want to avoid demeaning anyone else's heritage.

For a summary of all eight portraits of Christlikeness, see "What It Means to Be Like Jesus" at 10:25. The next item in the series can be found at 1:18—2:23.

CONSIDER THIS
1:3–6

THE WOMEN IN JESUS' GENEALOGY

Much has been made of the virgin Mary, but Matthew's genealogy (vv. 1–16) highlights four other women in Jesus' family. They were touched by scandal and remembered as "sinners" and "foreigners." Their inclusion can be an encouragement to us.

Tamar (v. 3; Gen. 38:1–30)

- Left a widow by Er, the firstborn son of Judah.
- Married Onan, Judah's second son, who refused to consummate the marriage and also died, leaving her childless—and therefore without means of support.
- Sent away to her home village by her father-in-law, Judah, who avoided responsibility to provide another husband.
- Eventually resorted to trickery, acting as a prostitute to cause Judah to father an heir and thereby provide economic security. The child also continued the line that eventually led to Jesus. Exposed as the father, irresponsible Judah acknowledged that Tamar was "more righteous than I" (Gen. 38:26).

Rahab (v. 5; Josh. 2:1–24; 6:22–25)

- A Canaanite harlot in Jericho.
- Protected two Hebrew spies in exchange for her own protection from the Israelites, who surrounded the city.
- Later married a Hebrew and gave birth to Boaz, David's great-grandfather.
- Praised in the New Testament as a person of faith (Heb. 11:31) and faithful action (James 2:25).

Ruth (v. 5; Ruth 1:1—4:22)

- A woman of Moab, a nation that began after the fall of Sodom when Lot committed incest with his daughters (Gen. 19:30–38). The Moabites became bitter enemies of Israel.
- Widowed when her Jewish husband died, and left without sons.
- Migrated to Israel with her mother-in-law, Naomi.
- Married Boaz (Rahab's son) and became the mother of Obed, making her David's great-grandmother. In effect, hostile Israel joined hated Moab to bring about God's will.

The Wife of Uriah (v. 6; 2 Sam. 11:1—12:25)

- Unnamed by Matthew, but known to be Bathsheba, wife of Uriah the Hittite.
- Attracted the eye of King David while bathing in ritual obedience on her roof, cleansing herself from her monthly flow.
- Summoned by the king, who committed adultery with her.
- Suffered the murder of her husband by David and the loss of the child that David had fathered.
- Married David, giving birth to a second child, Solomon, who became David's successor. (If Bathsheba was a Hittite like her first husband, then Solomon was half-Jew, half-Gentile. However, she was likely a Hebrew who married a Hittite sojourner.)

Jesus is the Messiah for women as well as men—even for women with (supposedly) checkered pasts and tainted bloodlines. He is the Messiah for all people, regardless of gender, race, or background. ◆

Matthew offers plenty of evidence to show Jesus' global connections. See Matt. 8:10.

begot Jotham, Jotham begot Ahaz, and Ahaz begot Hezekiah. 10Hezekiah begot Manasseh, Manasseh begot Amon,[a]
and Amon begot Josiah. 11Josiah begot Jeconiah and his
brothers about the time they were carried away to Babylon.
12And after they were brought to Babylon, Jeconiah begot
Shealtiel, and Shealtiel begot Zerubbabel. 13Zerubbabel begot Abiud, Abiud begot Eliakim, and Eliakim begot Azor.
14Azor begot Zadok, Zadok begot Achim, and Achim begot
Eliud. 15Eliud begot Eleazar, Eleazar begot Matthan, and
Matthan begot Jacob. 16And Jacob begot Joseph the husband of Mary, of whom was born Jesus who is called Christ.
1:1–17 see pg. 7
17So all the generations from Abraham
to David *are* fourteen generations, from
David until the captivity in Babylon *are* fourteen generations, and from the captivity in Babylon until the Christ *are*
fourteen generations.

The Birth of Christ

1:18—2:23 see pg. 10
18Now the birth of Jesus Christ was as
follows: After His mother Mary was be-
trothed to Joseph, before they came together, she was found
with child of the Holy Spirit. 19Then Joseph her husband,
being a just *man,* and not wanting to make her a public example, was minded to put her away secretly. 20But while he
thought about these things, behold, an angel of the Lord
appeared to him in a dream, saying, "Joseph, son of David,
do not be afraid to take to you Mary your wife, for that
which is conceived in her is of the Holy Spirit. 21And she
will bring forth a Son, and you shall call His name JESUS, for
He will save His people from their sins."
22So all this was done that it might be fulfilled which was
1:23
spoken by the Lord through the prophet,
saying: 23"Behold, the virgin shall be with
child, and bear a Son, and they shall call His name Immanuel,"[a] which is translated, "God with us."
24Then Joseph, being aroused from sleep, did as the angel
of the Lord commanded him and took to him his wife,
25and did not know her till she had brought forth her firstborn Son.[a] And he called His name JESUS.

CHAPTER 2

Wise Men Visit

1Now after Jesus was born in Bethlehem of Judea in the
days of Herod the king, behold, wise men from the East
came to Jerusalem, 2saying, "Where is He who has been
born King of the Jews? For we have seen His star in the East
and have come to worship Him."

1:10 [a]NU-Text reads *Amos.* *1:23* [a]Isaiah 7:14 *1:25* [a]NU-Text reads *a Son.*

WHAT'S IN A NAME?

CONSIDER THIS 1:23
Jesus was and is Immanuel, "God with us" (v. 23). God comes to us as people and lives in our world, rather than having us try the impossible of going to Him. Jesus does not take us out of the turmoil and pain of daily life, but rather walks *with us* as we live life.

It's a mistake to think of salvation as escape from the world instead of engagement with the world. God has a job for us to do right where we live and work. That's where Jesus is *with us;* that's where He gives us power (see Acts 1:8).

The name of Jesus played a powerful role in a five-act drama of which early Christians were a part. See "Jesus—The Name You Can Trust," Acts 3:1.

A POOR FAMILY COMES INTO WEALTH

CONSIDER THIS 2:11
What happened to the gifts presented to Jesus by the wise men (v. 11)? Scripture doesn't say. Clearly they reflected the Magi's worship of Christ at His birth. Yet we can speculate that they may have provided the means for His family's flight to Egypt (vv. 13–15).

The angel's warning and instructions to Joseph were sudden and unexpected. There was no time to save enough money for such a long journey—if saving was even an option. The family, after all, was poor (see "A Poor Family's Sacrifice," Luke 2:22–24). In fact, the costly gifts probably represented more wealth than either spouse had seen in a lifetime.

God promises to provide what is necessary for His children and to care for their needs (Matt. 6:19–34). In this instance, offerings of worship may have paid for a journey to Egypt and a new life in a strange land.

WHAT IT MEANS TO BE LIKE JESUS

CONSIDER THIS 1:18—2:23 *Jesus indicated that those who follow Him will become like Him (10:25). What does it mean to* **"be like Jesus"** *in today's complex world? Matthew paints eight portraits of what Christlikeness looks like, including:*

#2: To Be Like Jesus Means TO ENGAGE THE WORLD'S PAIN

Jesus' entry into human life was fraught with awkward tensions and human dilemmas: a miraculous but nevertheless embarrassing conception, an earthly father who was considering a quiet divorce, an outraged king resorting to infanticide, an early childhood in a strange culture, and a return to a homeland that remained hostile and dangerous. We, too, are all born into some troubles and circumstances. If we want to be like Jesus, we need to face up to the world and remain very much in it, despite all its troubles.

For a summary of all eight portraits of Christlikeness, see "What It Means to Be Like Jesus" at 10:25. The next item in the series can be found at 3:1–17.

2:3

3When Herod the king heard *this,* he
was troubled, and all Jerusalem with him.
4And when he had gathered all the chief priests and scribes
of the people together, he inquired of them where the
Christ was to be born.
5So they said to him, "In Bethlehem of Judea, for thus it is
written by the prophet:

6 'But you, Bethlehem, *in* the land of Judah,
Are not the least among the rulers of Judah;
For out of you shall come a Ruler
Who will shepherd My people Israel.' "[a]

7Then Herod, when he had secretly called the wise men,
determined from them what time the star appeared. 8And
he sent them to Bethlehem and said, "Go and search carefully for the young Child, and when you have found *Him,*
bring back word to me, that I may come and worship Him
also."
9When they heard the king, they departed; and behold,
the star which they had seen in the East went before them,
till it came and stood over where the young Child was.
10When they saw the star, they rejoiced with exceedingly

2:11 see pg. 9

great joy. 11And when they had come into
the house, they saw the young Child with
Mary His mother, and fell down and worshiped Him. And
when they had opened their treasures, they presented gifts
to Him: gold, frankincense, and myrrh.
12Then, being divinely warned in a dream that they
should not return to Herod, they departed for their own
country another way.

The Family Flees to Egypt

2:13–15

13Now when they had departed, behold, an angel of the Lord appeared to
Joseph in a dream, saying, "Arise, take the young Child and

2:6 [a]Micah 5:2

Herod the Great

A CLOSER LOOK 2:3 *Herod the Great (v. 3) was a highly ambitious leader who would stop at nothing to advance or protect his position. He routinely disposed of his enemies—even one of his wives and three of his sons. So it was no surprise that his immediate thought upon hearing the wise men's question—"Where is He who has been born King of the Jews?" (v. 2)—was to plan the infant's extermination. Read more about this ruler's infamy and the bloody family he came from in "The Herods," Acts 12:1–2.*

His mother, flee to Egypt, and stay there until I bring you word; for Herod will seek the young Child to destroy Him."

14When he arose, he took the young Child and His
mother by night and departed for Egypt, 15and was there
until the death of Herod, that it might be fulfilled which
was spoken by the Lord through the prophet, saying, "Out
of Egypt I called My Son."[a]

Herod Slaughters Infants

2:16–18 see pg. 12

16Then Herod, when he saw that he was deceived by the wise men, was exceedingly angry; and he sent forth and put to death all the male children who were in Bethlehem and in all its districts, from two years old and under, according to the time which
he had determined from the wise men. 17Then was fulfilled
what was spoken by Jeremiah the prophet, saying:

18 "A voice was heard in Ramah,
Lamentation, weeping, and great mourning,
Rachel weeping *for* her children,
Refusing to be comforted,
Because they are no more."[a]

The Family Returns to Nazareth

19Now when Herod was dead, behold, an angel of the
Lord appeared in a dream to Joseph in Egypt, 20saying,

2:15 [a]Hosea 11:1 *2:18* [a]Jeremiah 31:15

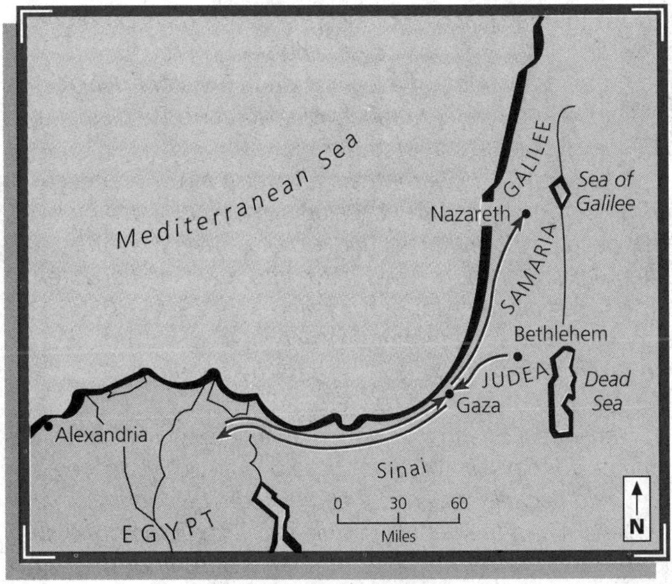

To Egypt and Back

"Out of Egypt I called My Son." —Matthew 2:15

Asian-born Jesus Becomes a Refugee in Africa

YOU ARE THERE 2:13–15 **Have you ever thought of Jesus as an intercontinental political refugee? He was, according to the Christmas story in vv. 13–15. Through His parents, the Asian-born Jesus sought political asylum in Africa, avoiding the infanticide ordered by King Herod, the ruthless ruler of Palestine.**

The text doesn't say where the family stayed. Perhaps they were absorbed into the one million Jews estimated to have lived in Alexandria at that time. Wherever they ended up, we know that Jesus, perhaps close to two years old at the start of the journey (2:16), spent at least some of His formative years in Egypt, displaced from His homeland. And when the family migrated back to Palestine (2:22–23), they did not settle in a privileged neighborhood, but in Nazareth in rural Galilee.

Jesus can identify with the many migrating peoples of the world today. He is an international Savior who knows the pain of forced migration. That is indeed good news for those who have been displaced by natural disasters, famine, or political unrest.

Herod shared a reputation for villainy with others in his family. See "The Herods," Acts 12:1–2.

"Arise, take the young Child and His mother, and go to the
land of Israel, for those who sought the young Child's life
are dead." 21Then he arose, took the young Child and His
mother, and came into the land of Israel.
22But when he heard that Archelaus was reigning over
Judea instead of his father Herod, he was afraid to go there.
And being warned by God in a dream, he turned aside into
the region of Galilee. 23And he came and dwelt in a city
called Nazareth, that it might be fulfilled which was spoken
by the prophets, "He shall be called a Nazarene."

CHAPTER 3

The Ministry of John the Baptist

3:1–17

1In those days John the Baptist came
preaching in the wilderness of Judea,
2and saying, "Repent, for the kingdom of heaven is at
hand!" 3For this is he who was spoken of by the prophet
Isaiah, saying:

> "The voice of one crying in the wilderness:
> 'Prepare the way of the LORD;
> Make His paths straight.' "[a]

3:4

4Now John himself was clothed in
camel's hair, with a leather belt around

3:3 [a]Isaiah 40:3

JOHN THE STREET PREACHER

CONSIDER THIS 3:4 **Would John the Baptist (v. 4) have been comfortable using today's media to proclaim his startling message? Probably not. Even for his own day he reflected none of the outward trappings of a successful ministry. He was not the head rabbi of a large city synagogue. He was not dressed in fine clothes. He did not sport a fine chariot. Nor did he enjoy sumptuous meals with leading citizens.**

Nevertheless, news about him spread far and wide, and people from throughout the region around Jerusalem and the Jordan came to hear him.

John illustrates the truth of Paul's words that "God has chosen the weak things of the world to put to shame the things which are mighty" (1 Cor. 1:27).

For the follower of Christ, how does success relate to wealth? See "Christians and Money," 1 Tim. 6:6–19.

CONSIDER THIS 2:16–18

CITY KIDS DIE OVER ADULT MATTERS

In the tragic account in vv. 16–18, we read of an entire village of baby boys being slaughtered, due to the insane rage of a jealous king. The story reminds us that growing numbers of children today die needlessly for the sins of adults.

Like Rachel (v. 18), mothers all over the world, particularly in urban ghettos and developing nations, weep over their dead children. Rachel had lots of experience with tears. Her father tricked her fiancé into marrying her sister and she remained childless for years (Gen. 29:1—30:24). Later, Jeremiah the prophet described her as wailing over the exiled tribes (Jer. 31:15, the passage quoted by Matthew).

The weeping and wailing in Bethlehem must have gone on for days. It could not have been quickly silenced, nor could Rachel's wailing be comforted. The babies of Bethlehem and the people in exile had a common bond: in both cases, innocent people suffered as a result of the proud, ungodly acts of powerful leaders.

his waist; and his food was locusts and wild honey. 5Then
Jerusalem, all Judea, and all the region around the Jordan
went out to him 6and were baptized by him in the Jordan,
confessing their sins.

7But when he saw many of the Pharisees and Sadducees
coming to his baptism, he said to them, "Brood of vipers!
Who warned you to flee from the wrath to come? 8There-
fore bear fruits worthy of repentance, 9and do not think to
say to yourselves, 'We have Abraham as *our* father.' For I say
to you that God is able to raise up children to Abraham
from these stones. 10And even now the ax is laid to the root
of the trees. Therefore every tree which does not bear good
fruit is cut down and thrown into the
fire. 11I indeed baptize you with water
unto repentance, but He who is coming after me is mightier
than I, whose sandals I am not worthy to carry. He will baptize you with the Holy Spirit and fire.[a] 12His winnowing fan
is in His hand, and He will thoroughly clean out His threshing floor, and gather His wheat into the barn; but He will
burn up the chaff with unquenchable fire."

3:11 see pg. 14

John Baptizes Jesus

13Then Jesus came from Galilee to John at the Jordan to
be baptized by him. 14And John *tried to* prevent Him, say-

3:11 [a]M-Text omits *and fire.*

Jesus can offer particular comfort to those who grieve the loss of a child. In effect, the babies of Bethlehem died for Him. He must have carried the pain of that throughout His life and onto the cross. It doubtless shaped His special concern for children (compare Matt. 18:6–7). And His concerned activity toward them beckons us to find ways to serve children today.

Matthew's retelling of this slaughter is a very significant part of the Christmas story. In a powerful way, it reminds city kids today that they need not die in vain: Jesus lived and died for them, too. ◆

What It Means To Be Like Jesus

CONSIDER THIS 3:1–17 *Jesus indicated that those who follow Him will become like Him (10:25). What does it mean to* **"be like Jesus"** *in today's complex world? Matthew paints eight portraits of what Christlikeness looks like, including:*

#3: To Be Like Jesus Means TO COMMIT OURSELVES TO OTHER BELIEVERS

John the Baptist was not your average individual. He was an unexpected child. He lived in the wilderness—the "other side of the tracks" for that day. He wore strange clothing and ate strange food. He was pugnacious, even offensive at times. Yet he helped launch Jesus' career. In return, Jesus had nothing but praise for him (11:7–15). If we want to be like Jesus, we must not pick and choose our brothers and sisters in God's family. We need to embrace other believers and demonstrate our unity in Christ, no matter how awkward or inconvenient.

For a summary of all eight portraits of Christlikeness, see "What It Means to Be Like Jesus" at 10:25. The next item in the series can be found at 4:1–11.

The Power of Humility

CONSIDER THIS 3:11 **How difficult is it for you to accept and admit that others are mightier than you? If you regard strength as the power to dominate, you'll always be intimidated by those who seem to have more than you—more expertise, more experience, more energy, more intelligence.**

John held a different understanding of strength (v. 11). He saw it as a gift from God to be used for divine purposes. That gave him tremendous power in his community (v. 5). His humility gave him the capacity to serve and to welcome others—in this case, Jesus—as valuable associates.

Like John, Paul challenged believers to cultivate humility. Not a groveling, abject demeanor, but rather an acknowledgment of what one is. See "Humility—The Scandalous Virtue," Phil. 2:3.

ing, "I need to be baptized by You, and are You coming to
me?"
15But Jesus answered and said to him, "Permit *it to be* so
now, for thus it is fitting for us to fulfill all righteousness."
Then he allowed Him.
16When He had been baptized, Jesus came up immediately from the water; and behold, the heavens were opened
to Him, and He[a] saw the Spirit of God descending like a
dove and alighting upon Him. 17And suddenly a voice *came*
from heaven, saying, "This is My beloved Son, in whom I
am well pleased."

CHAPTER 4

The Temptation of Jesus

4:1–11 see pg. 16

1Then Jesus was led up by the Spirit
into the wilderness to be tempted by the
devil. 2And when He had fasted forty days and forty nights,
afterward He was hungry. 3Now when the
tempter came to Him, he said, "If You are
the Son of God, command that these stones become
bread."
4But He answered and said, "It is written, 'Man shall not

4:3

3:16 [a]Or *he*

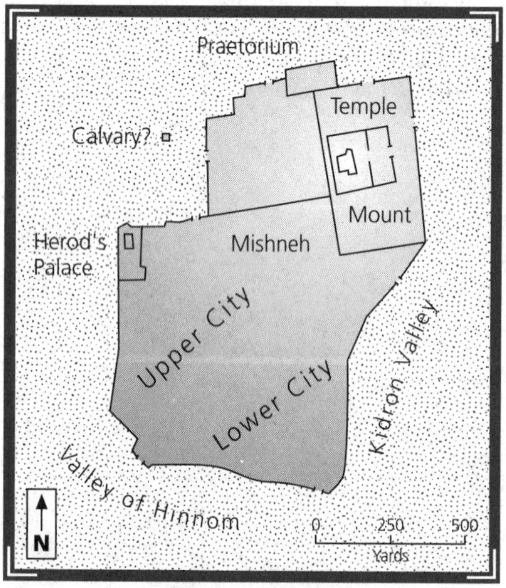

JERUSALEM

Can a Noisy, Dirty, Smelly City Also Be Holy?

YOU ARE THERE 4:5 *Matthew called Jerusalem "the holy city" (v. 5), but it was also noisy, dirty, and smelly. Gehenna, the town garbage dump and home to countless lepers, lay just outside the gates in a deep, narrow ravine, the Valley of Hinnom. Refuse, waste materials, and dead animals were burned there. Fires continually smouldered, and with the right wind, rank smells drifted north, blanketing the city and the temple mount with noxious odors.*

How could such a city be considered "holy"? Because God's presence was there, in the temple. That made it "sacred space" to the Hebrews (see John 1:51).

live by bread alone, but by every word that proceeds from
the mouth of God.' "[a]

4:5

5 Then the devil took Him up into the
holy city, set Him on the pinnacle of the
temple, 6 and said to Him, "If You are the Son of God, throw
Yourself down. For it is written:

'He shall give His angels charge over you,'

and,

'In *their* hands they shall bear you up,
Lest you dash your foot against a stone.' "[a]

7 Jesus said to him, "It is written again, 'You shall not
tempt the LORD your God.' "[a]

4:8–10 see pg. 16

8 Again, the devil took Him up on an
exceedingly high mountain, and showed
Him all the kingdoms of the world and their glory. 9 And he
said to Him, "All these things I will give You if You will fall
down and worship me."
10 Then Jesus said to him, "Away with you,[a] Satan! For it is
written, 'You shall worship the LORD your God, and Him
only you shall serve.' "[b]
11 Then the devil left Him, and behold, angels came and
ministered to Him.

Jesus Begins His Ministry

4:12–25 see pg. 17

12 Now when Jesus heard that John had
been put in prison, He departed to
Galilee. 13 And leaving Nazareth, He came and dwelt in Capernaum, which is by the sea, in the regions of Zebulun
and Naphtali, 14 that it might be fulfilled which was spoken
by Isaiah the prophet, saying:

15 "The land of Zebulun and the land of Naphtali,
By the way of the sea, beyond the Jordan,
Galilee of the Gentiles:
16 The people who sat in darkness have seen a great light,
And upon those who sat in the region and shadow of
death
Light has dawned."[a]

4:17 see pg. 18

17 From that time Jesus began to preach
and to say, "Repent, for the kingdom of
heaven is at hand."

(Bible text continued on page 17)

4:4 [a]Deuteronomy 8:3 *4:6* [a]Psalm 91:11, 12 *4:7* [a]Deuteronomy 6:16 *4:10* [a]M-Text reads *Get behind Me.* [b]Deuteronomy 6:13 *4:16* [a]Isaiah 9:1, 2

"YOU DON'T UNDERSTAND!"

CONSIDER THIS 4:3 **How often we hear someone dismiss the implications of faith for day-to-day life with the retort, "You don't understand! I live in the real world, where things are tough. They play by a different set of rules there. Christianity is all well and good, but isn't it a bit simplistic when it comes to real life?"**

The account of the temptation in vv. 1–11 offers a response to that sort of thinking. It shows that Jesus *does* understand real life. He faced real temptations—the same temptations that show up every day in the "real world."

Some people think that because He did not give in to what was offered, He must not have been "really" tempted; therefore, He can't "really" understand our situation. But that won't do. Scripture affirms that Satan's devices were real temptations that really tempted Him. And because He was able to resist them, He is able to help us do the same (Heb. 2:18). He completely understands our feelings—and how to do what is right in spite of them.

Temptation is not sin, but giving in is. See "Tired of Praying?" Luke 11:5–13.

Few teachings in Scripture have more practical, day-to-day implications than the truth that people are fallen, temptable, and subject to thinking and doing wrong. "Pay Attention to Temptation!" at 1 Cor. 10:12–13, explores the importance of that for Christians in today's workplace.

What It Means To Be Like Jesus

CONSIDER THIS 4:1–11 *Jesus indicated that those who follow Him will become like Him (10:25). What does it mean to* **"be like Jesus"** *in today's complex world? Matthew paints eight portraits of what Christlikeness looks like, including:*

#4: To Be Like Jesus Means TO ADMIT OUR VULNERABILITY TO TEMPTATION

Matthew's inclusion of the temptation is remarkable. It shows that the sinless Lord of the universe was tempted, just as we are (Heb. 4:15–16). If we want to be like Jesus, we must accept that temptation is real—as is the possibility of overcoming temptation. But we need to be open about our struggles. In doing so we honor God, recognize the power of sin, and encourage others to do likewise.

For a summary of all eight portraits of Christlikeness, see "What It Means to Be Like Jesus" at 10:25. The next item in the series can be found at 4:12–25.

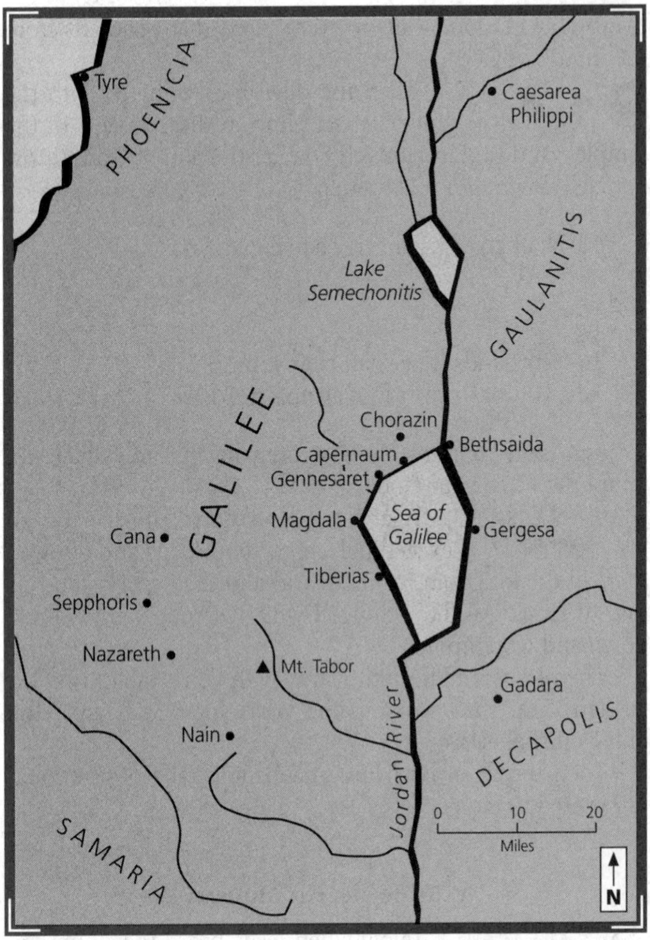

YOU ARE THERE 4:25 **JESUS' GALILEAN MINISTRY**

Wealth's Temptation

CONSIDER THIS 4:8–10 **For us who live in a materialistic culture, it's good to recognize that the desire for wealth and all that it symbolizes—prestige, power, luxury, authority—can be a powerful tool in Satan's hands. It was one of three strategies that the devil used to try to draw Christ away from His mission (vv. 8–10).**

Are you tempted by desires that are closely tied to wealth? If so, Christ's response in v. 10 challenges you to ask: Who or what are you going to worship and serve?

Opportunities for temptation sometimes seem endless. Yet Scripture offers several alternatives for dealing with temptation as we find it. See "Pay Attention to Temptation," 1 Cor. 10:12–13.

Most of Jesus' followers were not wealthy, but a few notable ones were. From them we can learn a great deal about the dangers and the disciplines of money. See the survey, "Wealthy People in the New Testament," Matt. 27:57.

Jesus Calls the Twelve

4:18–22

18 And Jesus, walking by the Sea of
Galilee, saw two brothers, Simon called
Peter, and Andrew his brother, casting a net into the sea; for
they were fishermen. 19 Then He said to them, "Follow Me,
and I will make you fishers of men." 20 They immediately
left *their* nets and followed Him.
21 Going on from there, He saw two other brothers, James
the son of Zebedee, and John his brother, in the boat with
Zebedee their father, mending their nets. He called them,
22 and immediately they left the boat and their father, and
followed Him.

Galilean Ministry

4:23

23 And Jesus went about all Galilee,
teaching in their synagogues, preaching
the gospel of the kingdom, and healing all kinds of sickness
and all kinds of disease among the people. 24 Then His fame
went throughout all Syria; and they brought to Him all sick
people who were afflicted with various diseases and torments, and those who were demon-possessed, epileptics,

4:25

and paralytics; and He healed them.
25 Great multitudes followed Him—from
Galilee, and *from* Decapolis, Jerusalem, Judea, and beyond
the Jordan.

CHAPTER 5

The Sermon on the Mount

5:1—7:27
see pg. 20

1 And seeing the multitudes, He went
up on a mountain, and when He was

(Bible text continued on page 20)

The Fishermen

A CLOSER LOOK 4:18–22

The fishermen Jesus called (vv. 18–22) eventually became members of an inner circle of Jesus' followers. See "The Twelve," Matt. 10:2.

Galilee

A CLOSER LOOK 4:23

Though Jesus launched His ministry in Galilee (v. 23) with great energy, there is little evidence that His message ever took firm root there after He left. See "Galilee," Mark 1:14.

WHAT IT MEANS TO BE LIKE JESUS

CONSIDER THIS 4:12–25

Jesus indicated that those who follow Him will become like Him (10:25). What does it mean to **"be like Jesus"** *in today's complex world? Matthew paints eight portraits of what Christlikeness looks like, including:*

#5: To Be Like Jesus Means TO PROCLAIM THE MESSAGE OF CHRIST

Jesus' life was *not* an open book, readable by all. To be sure, He lived a perfect, model life. But even that could not stand alone as an undeniable witness. His actions needed interpretation. So He supplemented His good *deeds* with good *news*. In the same way, we need to verbally declare our faith if we want to be like Christ. Certainly we need to back up our words with a Christlike lifestyle. But what we tell others gives meaning to our quiet walk and good deeds.

For a summary of all eight portraits of Christlikeness, see "What It Means to Be Like Jesus" at 10:25. The next item in the series can be found at 5:1—7:27.

"I WILL MAKE YOU FISHERS OF MEN."
—Matthew 4:19

CONSIDER THIS
4:17

The King Declares His Kingdom

Jesus initiated His public life with a simple but stiff challenge to repentance (v. 17). It was actually a familiar message—identical, in fact, to the message of John the Baptist, Jesus' forerunner (Matt. 3:2). Both urged their listeners to re-pent, to change their minds and hearts, not merely for the sake of change, but in light of what they called "the kingdom."

Jesus Is the King

The most important thing to notice is that a kingdom exists because Jesus is the King. He is the Messiah, the Savior promised by God in the Old Testament (1:22–23; 2:6; Is. 7:14; Mic. 5:2). He is not only Israel's King, but the international Christ for all the nations (see "Jesus' Roots," Matt. 1:1–16, and "Jesus' Global Connections," 8:10). At the beginning of His life, magi came to Herod, asking where they could find the King of the Jews (2:2). At the end of His life, Pilate asked Him, "Are you the King of the Jews?" He affirmed that He was (27:11–12), and Pilate sanctioned His crucifixion on that basis (27:37).

So in 4:17–25, the King was declaring His kingdom. Foretold by Scripture and announced by John, Jesus had come to establish His rule. However, He disappointed the expectations of many people—both then and now.

Where Is the Kingdom?

For a few brief decades, Israel had enjoyed a relatively prosperous, peaceful monarchy under David and his son, Solomon. Some Old Testament passages prophesied that the Messiah would reestablish that sort of kingdom. Was now the time? Would Jesus overthrow the iron rule of the Romans and set up a political state? He did not. In fact, He told the Roman governor Pilate that His kingdom was not of this world, that He did not have an army fighting on His behalf (John 18:36). And He told the Pharisees that the kingdom was not something tangible and observable, but was "within" them (Luke 17:20).

Then is Christ's kingdom simply a spiritual concept, a powerful but abstract ideal? No, because He made a definite promise to His disciples that they would rule the tribes of Israel in His kingdom (Matt. 19:23, 28). They apparently took Him literally (Acts 1:6).

When Is the Kingdom?

No less puzzling is the question of when the kingdom has or will come. As they began their ministries, John the Baptist and Jesus declared that the kingdom was "at hand." But a few years later, when Jesus' followers asked whether He was ready to restore Israel's kingdom, He put them off; that was something that only His Father could know, He told them (Acts 1:6–7). Sometimes the kingdom seemed to be a present reality (Matt. 12:28; 13:18–23; 21:43). At other times, it seemed to be a hope for the future (16:28; 20:20–23; 26:29).

Even today, theologians stridently debate over whether and in what form the kingdom has already been established, is currently in the process of being formed, is coming in the future, or is not coming at all. Like most questions that cannot be answered definitively to everyone's satisfaction, agreements are few and positions strongly defended.

What Is the Kingdom?

Is there any simple way to understand this puzzling doctrine of the kingdom? Probably not. Jesus' followers have not ceased to puzzle over His statements about it since the moment they were made. But most would generally agree that Christ's kingdom began in some way with His first coming. It continues to advance as His people live the gospel message throughout the world. However, it will not realize its ultimate completion until He returns.

What Difference Does It Make?

Whatever else we can say, the kingdom has to do with whatever Christ the King rules. That's why Jesus began His ministry with a call to repentance. Repentance means to change one's mind or purpose. In terms of the kingdom, it involves:

(1) A change in one's allegiance. If Christ is the King, He deserves our honor, loyalty, and obedience. We put ourselves under His authority and power. Whatever He says, we determine to do. That's the point of the oft-repeated lines in the Lord's Prayer, "Your kingdom come, Your will be done on earth as it is in heaven" (Matt. 6:10). Kingdom people submit their own will to the will of the King.

(2) A change in one's expectations. One of the difficulties people have with the idea of a kingdom is that it doesn't appear to be in place yet. The world seems to grow farther away from God by the day. As a result, it's easy to live for the here and now, as if this present life is all that matters. But the hope of the kingdom is that there is far more to life than what we see right now. Jesus made extraordinary promises in regard to a future kingdom, not only for Israel, but for all who follow Him as King. The kingdom may not yet be fulfilled completely, but it has been established and will last forever (6:13).

(3) A change in one's values. Our culture values achievement, success, independence, and image. Other cultures value other qualities. But the values of the kingdom reflect what matters to the King. Jesus described a number of His values in Matthew 5:3–10, a section of the Sermon on the Mount known as the Beatitudes (or, as some call them, the "beautiful attitudes"). Kingdom people adopt the King's values and make choices that reflect those values—in their jobs, families, and communities.

(4) A change in one's priorities. The real test of people's values is how they spend their time and money. Jesus spoke directly to that issue in terms of the kingdom (6:24–34). He did not demean the value of work or diminish the need for material goods. But He challenged His followers to bring kingdom values into their day-to-day lives. "Seeking first the kingdom" (6:33) puts a Christlike perspective on one's work and its outcomes.

(5) A change in one's lifelong mission. Some people are driven to accomplish great tasks with their lives. Others live aimlessly from day to day, lacking purpose or direction. Either way, Jesus affects the outlook of a person's life. He gives His followers purpose and a mission—to live as subjects of the kingdom and promote kingdom values in everyday life and work. Ultimately, He wants His followers to extend His message to the ends of the earth, so that all people have the opportunity to give their allegiance to Him as their Savior and King (28:18–20). ◆

What It Means To Be Like Jesus

CONSIDER THIS 5:1—7:27 *Jesus indicated that those who follow Him will become like Him (10:25). What does it mean to* **"be like Jesus"** *in today's complex world? Matthew paints eight portraits of what Christlikeness looks like, including:*

#6: To Be Like Jesus Means TO COMMIT TO CHANGED THINKING AND BEHAVIOR

In His Sermon on the Mount, Jesus explained the values of the kingdom. Money, prayer, relationships, possessions, information, and power were a few of the categories He redefined from God's perspective. He showed that following Him will involve radical change for most of us. It may mean undoing the way we've always done things and rethinking traditional sources of wisdom from our parents and culture. To become like Jesus involves a tough-minded review of our values and a thorough change in our behavior.

For a summary of all eight portraits of Christlikeness, see "What It Means to Be Like Jesus" at 10:25. The next item in the series can be found at 8:1—9:38.

5:2

seated His disciples came to Him. 2Then
He opened His mouth and taught them,
saying:

The Beatitudes

5:3 see pg. 22

3 "Blessed *are* the poor in spirit,
For theirs is the kingdom of heaven.
4 Blessed *are* those who mourn,
For they shall be comforted.

5:5

5 Blessed *are* the meek,
For they shall inherit the earth.
6 Blessed *are* those who hunger and thirst for righteousness,
For they shall be filled.
7 Blessed *are* the merciful,
For they shall obtain mercy.
8 Blessed *are* the pure in heart,
For they shall see God.
9 Blessed *are* the peacemakers,
For they shall be called sons of God.
10 Blessed are those who are persecuted for righteousness' sake,
For theirs is the kingdom of heaven.

11"Blessed are you when they revile and persecute you, and
say all kinds of evil against you falsely for My sake. 12Re-
joice and be exceedingly glad, for great *is* your reward in
heaven, for so they persecuted the prophets who were before you.

"You Are Salt and Light"

5:13–16 see pg. 24

13"You are the salt of the earth; but if
the salt loses its flavor, how shall it be
seasoned? It is then good for nothing but to be thrown out
and trampled underfoot by men.
14"You are the light of the world. A city that is set on a hill
cannot be hidden. 15Nor do they light a lamp and put it under a basket, but on a lampstand, and it gives light to all
who are in the house. 16Let your light so shine before men,

(Bible text continued on page 22)

The Meek

A CLOSER LOOK 5:5 *Nearly every society and every city in biblical times had a large* underclass, *people scraping by on the margins of society (v. 5). Jesus intentionally directed much of His life and ministry to that disadvantaged group. See Luke 7:22.*

A CLOSER LOOK
5:2

The Sermon on the Mount

"Repent, for the kingdom of heaven is at hand," Jesus warned as He began His public ministry in Galilee (Matt. 4:17). His message quickly spread and huge crowds came to hear Him from Galilee, from nearby Syria and the Decapolis, and from as far away as Jerusalem, Judea, and east of the Jordan River (vv. 24–25).

They came to hear about a kingdom. Instead, Jesus talked about a lifestyle—the lifestyle of those who intend to live in the kingdom. As perhaps thousands gathered on a hillside (or "mountain," 5:1; the exact location is unknown), Jesus began to fill out the implications of His appeal for repentance. It would mean far more than an outward show of piety. Indeed, Jesus urged His listeners to make such a complete change of heart and life that they would "be perfect, just as your Father in heaven is perfect" (v. 48).

Jesus may have spoken the contents of Matthew 5–7, known as the Sermon on the Mount, on more than one occasion. It is possible that the address lasted for some time as He described the new lifestyle of the kingdom, holding it up like a jewel with many facets, to be examined from many different angles. On the other hand, bits and pieces of the sermon can be found throughout the gospels. Like any good teacher, Jesus probably repeated much of His teaching at other times and places in order to drive home the message.

The Sermon on the Mount contains the core of Jesus' moral and ethical teaching:

The Beatitudes (5:3–12). True happiness comes from looking at life from God's perspective, which is often the reverse of the human point of view.

Salt and Light (5:13–16). Jesus wants His followers to influence the moral and spiritual climate of the world.

The Morality of the Kingdom (5:17–48). Jesus' listeners were familiar with the Old Testament Law and with the many traditions that generations of rabbis had added to it. But Jesus revealed a morality that went beyond the letter of the Law to its spirit.

Spiritual Disciplines (6:1–18). Practicing religion certainly involves behavior, but it goes beyond an outward show of spirituality to the hidden quality of one's character.

Treasures on Earth (6:19–34). Our relationship to money and material possessions reveals much about our relationship to God. Jesus does not denounce worldly goods, but He urges His listeners to place ultimate value on the treasures of heaven.

Judging Right and Wrong (7:1–6). Most of us are quick to point out the moral flaws of others. Jesus warns us to pay more attention to our own.

Asking and Receiving (7:7–12). When we approach God with a request, we can expect Him to deal with us as a loving father deals with his child. And just as God deals with us in love, He expects us to deal with others in love.

A Challenge to Obedience (7:13–29). Jesus wraps up His message with a challenge to change. The alternatives are clear: living a lifestyle that is worthy of the kingdom, resulting in life and joy; or ignoring the way of Christ, resulting in death and disaster.

In this manner, Jesus described the lifestyle of the kingdom. When He was finished, Matthew says that the people were "astonished" at His teaching (7:28; literally "overwhelmed" or "stunned"). They had come to hear a new teacher, but this one exceeded their expectations. His voice had an unusual but unmistakable ring of authority (v. 29). And no wonder: they were listening to the King Himself! ◆

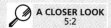

that they may see your good works and glorify your Father
in heaven.

The Morality of Christ

5:17–48 see pg. 24

17"Do not think that I came to destroy
the Law or the Prophets. I did not come
to destroy but to fulfill. 18For assuredly, I say to you, till
heaven and earth pass away, one jot or one tittle will by no
means pass from the law till all is ful-
filled. 19Whoever therefore breaks one of
the least of these commandments, and teaches men so, shall
be called least in the kingdom of heaven; but whoever does
and teaches *them*, he shall be called great in the kingdom of
heaven. 20For I say to you, that unless your righteousness
exceeds *the righteousness* of the scribes and Pharisees, you
will by no means enter the kingdom of heaven.

21"You have heard that it was said to those of old, 'You
shall not murder,[a] and whoever murders will be in danger
of the judgment.' 22But I say to you that whoever is angry
with his brother without a cause[a] shall be in danger of the
judgment. And whoever says to his brother, 'Raca!' shall be
in danger of the council. But whoever says, 'You fool!' shall

5:21 [a]Exodus 20:13; Deuteronomy 5:17 *5:22* [a]NU-Text omits *without a cause.*

CONSIDER THIS
5:3

THE WAY UP IS DOWN

Of all the virtues Christ commended in the Beatitudes, it is significant that the first is humility, being "poor in spirit" (v. 3). That underlies all the others:

- *You cannot mourn (v. 4) without appreciating how insufficient you are to handle life in your own strength. That is humility.*
- *You cannot be meek (v. 5) unless you have needed gentleness yourself. Knowing that need is humility.*
- *You cannot hunger and thirst for righteousness (v. 6) if you proudly think of yourself as already righteous. Longing to fill that spiritual appetite demands humility. In a parable that Luke recorded, a humble tax collector prayed, "God, be merciful to me a sinner!" He went away justified, unlike a proud Pharisee who boasted of his righteousness (Luke 18:13).*
- *You cannot be merciful (Matt. 5:7) without recognizing your own need for mercy. Jesus said that it's the person who is forgiven much that loves much (Luke 7:47). To*

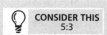

be in danger of hell fire. [23]Therefore if you bring your gift to
the altar, and there remember that your brother has something against you, [24]leave your gift there before the altar,
and go your way. First be reconciled to your brother, and
then come and offer your gift. [25]Agree with your adversary
quickly, while you are on the way with him, lest your adversary deliver you to the judge, the judge hand you over to
the officer, and you be thrown into prison. [26]Assuredly, I say
to you, you will by no means get out of there till you have
paid the last penny.

[27]"You have heard that it was said to those of old,[a] 'You
shall not commit adultery.'[b] [28]But I say to you that whoever
looks at a woman to lust for her has already committed adultery with her in his heart. [29]If your right eye causes
you to sin, pluck it out and cast *it* from you; for it is more
profitable for you that one of your members perish,
than for your whole body to be cast into hell. [30]And if
your right hand causes you to sin, cut it off and cast *it*
from you; for it is more profitable for you that one of your
members perish, than for your whole body to be cast into
hell.

(Bible text continued on page 26)

5:27 [a]NU-Text and M-Text omit *to those of old.* [b]Exodus 20:14; Deuteronomy 5:18

confess your sin and ask God and others for forgiveness takes humility.

- *You cannot be pure in heart (Matt. 5:8) if your heart is filled with pride. God promises to exalt the humble, not the proud (James 4:10).*
- *You cannot be a peacemaker (Matt. 5:9) if you believe that you are always right. To admit your own fallibility takes humility. Peace results when both warring parties move toward each other.*
- *Finally, identifying with Christ no matter what the reaction of others (vv. 10–12) demands a certain death to yourself and a renunciation of your own rights. Standing up under persecution demands Christlike humility.* ◆

Humility is the scandalous virtue! See Phil. 2:3.

What About the Old Testament Law?

CONSIDER THIS 5:19 **Jesus' critics claimed that His teaching encouraged people to violate the Mosaic Law, allowing them to get away with sin. Actually, He warned people to avoid the hypocrisies of the rabbis. While making an outward show of righteousness they took ethical shortcuts and carried out wicked schemes. In this portion of the the Sermon on the Mount (vv. 17–20), Jesus turned the tables on His opponents by appealing to the Law as the basis for His moral code—not the Law as they taught it, but as God intended it.**

Jesus' words are crucial for Christians today. While God does not require us to live by the specific regulations of the Old Testament Law, He still expects us to honor Old Testament morality. What might that look like in today's ethically complicated marketplace? See "Ten Commandments for Practical Living," James 2:8–13.

The Old Testament Law was part of the covenant that set Israel apart as God's people. It governed their worship, their relationship to God, and their social relationships with one another. See "The Law," Rom. 2:12.

CONSIDER THIS
5:13–16

Sulfa Drugs and Street Lights

Following Christ goes far beyond private spirituality. It also involves a believer's public life, particularly through work and participation in the community. Jesus used two metaphors to describe that dynamic: salt (v. 13) and light (vv. 14–16).

In Jesus' day, salt was used to preserve foods like fish from decay. In the same way, believers can help to preserve society from moral and spiritual decay. Of course, in our culture, salt has given way to chemical preservatives (many of which have come under attack in recent years for their alleged role in causing cancer). So Jesus might use a different metaphor were He speaking today.

Perhaps He would talk in terms of an infection-fighting drug, such as an antibiotic like penicillin, or the sulfa drugs developed in the '40s that have proved so valuable in fighting meningitis and pneumonia. Christians can help to ward off spiritual infections and diseases in the larger society. One of the most powerful arenas for influence is the workplace, particularly jobs that affect values, laws, and public opinion. That's why believers need to pursue careers in education, government, and journalism, among many others. They may not be able to transform the entire society, but they can use whatever influence they have to promote Christlike values and hinder evil.

CONSIDER THIS
5:17–48

The Morality of Christ

"Jesus was a great moral teacher. Mainly He taught that people should love each other." Have you ever heard someone summarize Christ's life and ministry that way?

It is true that Jesus was a great moral teacher. But of course, He was much more—He was also the Son of God (see "Ten Myths of Christianity, Myth #1: Jesus Christ Was Only a Great Moral Teacher," Matt. 13:34–35). Likewise, He certainly taught that people should love each other. But He taught a great deal more. In this section of the Sermon on the Mount (5:17–48), we discover much about Jesus' concept of morality.

Unfortunately, numerous misunderstandings have come from this passage. Jesus makes a number of statements that sound extreme to our ears (vv. 22, 30, 37, 39–42). How can we make sense out of them?

First, it's important to know that when Jesus referred to "the Law" and "the Prophets" (v. 17), He was referring to the express moral teaching of the Old Testament. His listeners were Jews, so their moral conduct and character were governed by those Scriptures. At least, they were supposed to be.

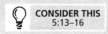

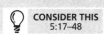

Jesus also called His followers "the light of the world" (v. 14), an image that fits perfectly into modern society. The Lord's first-century listeners would be astonished at the availability and importance of light in our culture. We use it not only to illuminate but also to communicate. Thus, Jesus wants us as His followers to shine, to be visible and attractive, not to bring attention to ourselves, but to bring people to God (v. 16). Again, our vocations are one of the primary means we have to reflect Christ to others.

Jesus' teaching here challenges us as His followers to ask: How are we engaging our society? What spiritual infections are we fighting to overcome? What positive changes are we trying to promote? What impact for God are we having through our work? Have we lost our saltiness (v. 13)? Are we standing like burned-out street lights, ineffective and waiting to be removed? Or are we shining brilliantly with the love and truth of Christ? ◆

Spreading Christ's message involves far more than just broadcasting a statement or a set of facts. See "Faith Impacts the World," Mark 16:15–16.

In reality, the people were taught a heavily doctored version of Old Testament truth by their rabbis. Sometimes these teachers stressed the letter of the Law, rather than its spirit, and sometimes they favored their own traditions over the actual teaching of God (12:9–12; 15:1–9). And sometimes they actually perverted the Law to suit their own ends (19:3–8). No wonder Jesus labeled them hypocrites and warned people not to follow their example (23:1–36).

That helps to explain the formula that Jesus uses here: "You have heard it said . . . but I say to you" (vv. 21–22, 27–28, 33–34, 38–39, 43–44). The people had heard the Law and the Prophets, but not in their purity. By contrast, Jesus spoke with integrity and authority to five areas of morality: murder (vv. 21–26), adultery (vv. 27–32), vows and oaths (vv. 33–37), vengeance (vv. 38–42), and love and hate (vv. 43–47).

Framing these remarks is an introduction in which the Lord appealed to His listeners to fulfill the Law (vv. 17–20) and a conclusion in which He challenged them to act as the Father would act (v. 48). ◆

"YOU HAVE HEARD THAT IT WAS SAID. . . . BUT I SAY TO YOU. . . ."
—Matthew 5:21–22

31“Furthermore it has been said, ‘Whoever divorces his
5:32 wife, let him give her a certificate of divorce.’ 32But I say to you that whoever divorces his wife for any reason except sexual immorality[a]
causes her to commit adultery; and whoever marries a
woman who is divorced commits adultery.
33“Again you have heard that it was said to those of old,
‘You shall not swear falsely, but shall perform your oaths to
the Lord.’ 34But I say to you, do not swear at all: neither by
heaven, for it is God’s throne; 35nor by the earth, for it is His
footstool; nor by Jerusalem, for it is the city of the great
King. 36Nor shall you swear by your head, because you cannot make one hair white or black. 37But let your ‘Yes’ be
‘Yes,’ and your ‘No,’ ‘No.’ For whatever is more than these is
from the evil one.
5:38–42 see pg. 28 38“You have heard that it was said, ‘An
eye for an eye and a tooth for a tooth.’[a]
39But I tell you not to resist an evil person. But whoever
slaps you on your right cheek, turn the other to him also.
40If anyone wants to sue you and take away your tunic, let
him have *your* cloak also. 41And whoever compels you to go
one mile, go with him two. 42Give to him who asks you, and
from him who wants to borrow from you do not turn away.
5:43–48 43“You have heard that it was said, ‘You
shall love your neighbor[a] and hate your
enemy.’ 44But I say to you, love your enemies, bless those
who curse you, do good to those who hate you, and pray
for those who spitefully use you and persecute you,[a] 45that
you may be sons of your Father in heaven; for He makes
His sun rise on the evil and on the good, and sends rain on
the just and on the unjust. 46For if you love those who love
you, what reward have you? Do not even the tax collectors
do the same? 47And if you greet your brethren[a] only, what
do you do more *than others*? Do not even the tax collectors[b]
do so? 48Therefore you shall be perfect, just as your Father
in heaven is perfect.

(Bible text continued on page 29)

5:32 [a]Or *fornication* *5:38* [a]Exodus 21:24; Leviticus 24:20; Deuteronomy 19:21
5:43 [a]Compare Leviticus 19:18 *5:44* [a]NU-Text omits three clauses from this verse, leaving, *“But I say to you, love your enemies and pray for those who persecute you.”*
5:47 [a]M-Text reads *friends.* [b]NU-Text reads *Gentiles.*

A New Respect for Women

CONSIDER THIS 5:32 *Greek, Roman, and Jewish laws of Jesus’ day afforded men many opportunities to divorce their wives. Perhaps the most painful for the women was infertility. But in vv. 31–32, Jesus insisted on a different understanding of women—and the relative importance of childbearing. Only the severing of the marriage bond through sexual immorality was to be grounds for divorce, not the lack of an heir.*

Living the Way God Wants Us To

A CLOSER LOOK 5:43–48 *Jesus’ moral standard seems high. But it’s not to be reached by just our own ability. When we are Christ’s, we are made into new creatures. The Holy Spirit lives through us as we become more like Jesus. See “New Creatures with New Character,” Gal. 5:22–23.*

There are two reasons not to feel frustrated by the expectations we see here: First, eternal life is not earned but is God’s gift. Second, godly principles enable us to live stable, joyful lives. See “Rules That Lead to Joy,” 1 John 2:3–6.

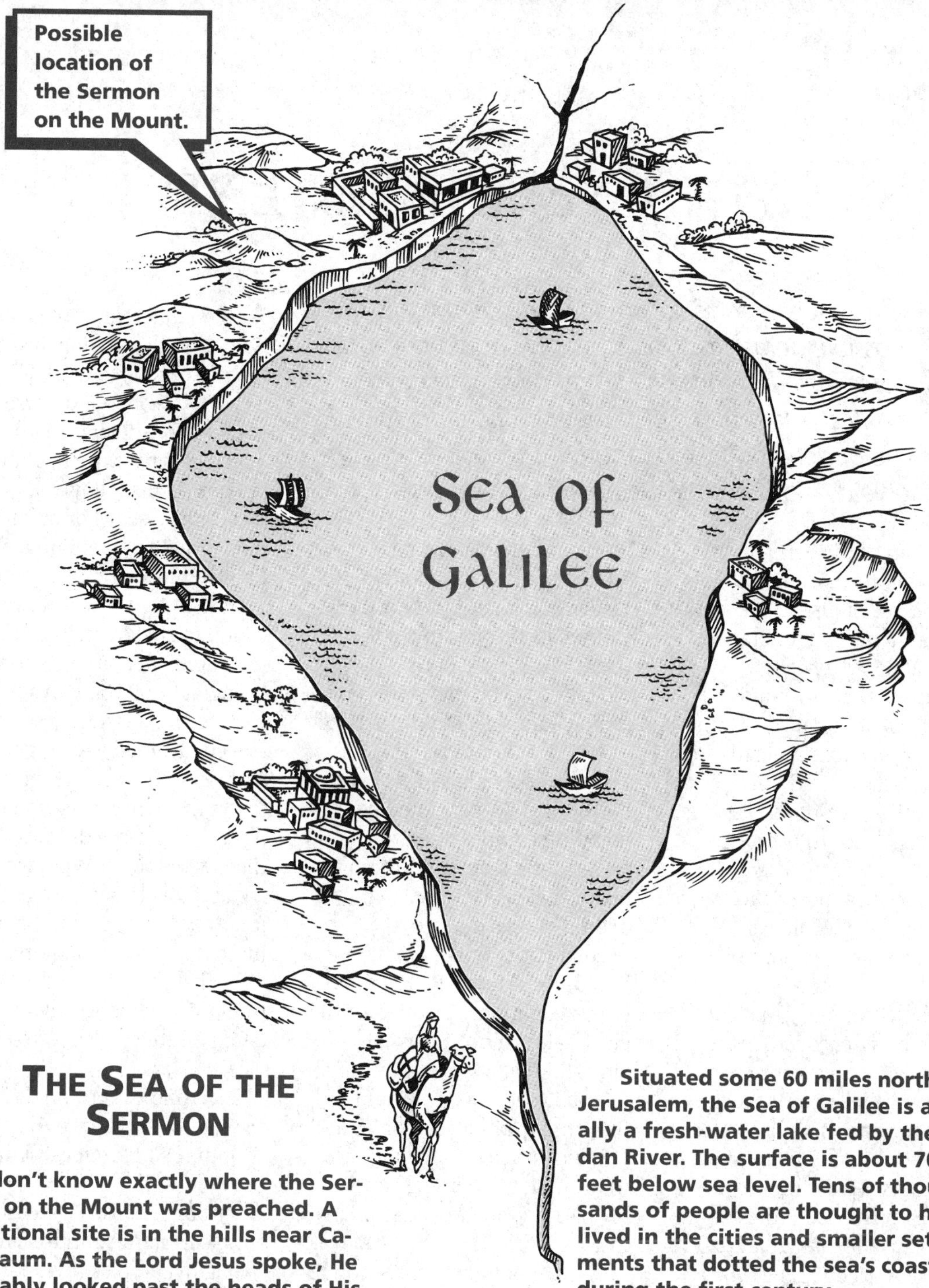

The Sea of the Sermon

We don't know exactly where the Sermon on the Mount was preached. A traditional site is in the hills near Capernaum. As the Lord Jesus spoke, He probably looked past the heads of His listeners from time to time, down toward the Sea of Galilee, which was closely connected with His earthly ministry. Much of the Lord's teaching and more than half of His recorded miracles occurred on or around this body of water.

Situated some 60 miles north of Jerusalem, the Sea of Galilee is actually a fresh-water lake fed by the Jordan River. The surface is about 700 feet below sea level. Tens of thousands of people are thought to have lived in the cities and smaller settlements that dotted the sea's coastline during the first century.

A fishing industry thrived on the Sea of Galilee. Peter, Andrew, James and John the sons of Zebedee, and probably many more of Jesus' followers derived their living from the sea. For more information see "The World of the Fishermen," Luke 5:1–11.

CONSIDER THIS
5:38–42

An Eye for an Eye

Jesus appears to make some stark, seemingly impossible demands: God's people should never use force in self-defense (v. 39); they should never contest a lawsuit (v. 40); they should comply with every type of demand (v. 41); and they should lend without reserve (v. 42). Could Jesus possibly be serious?

In this part of the Sermon on the Mount, the Lord is addressing the issue of justice. He was alluding to the Old Testament Law dealing with *public* vengeance. The Law limited damages in criminal cases to no more than the loss suffered—"an eye for an eye" (v. 38; Ex. 21:24–25). Nevertheless, as might be expected, people tended to justify *personal* vengeance by appealing to the same texts. We would call it "taking the law into your own hands."

But Jesus' morality challenged that. To be sure, some circumstances call for resistance and self-defense. The Law specifically sanctioned self-protection when there was no other apparent recourse (Ex. 22:2). Likewise, Jesus Himself protested when slapped (John 18:22–23).

But He warned against the needless use of force, particularly in revenge. In self-defense, the alternative to resistance may be injury or death. But in vengeance, one inflicts harm even though immediate danger is past. A slap on the cheek is little more than an insult. There's no place for violence in response to that. Furthermore, vengeance belongs to God (Deut. 32:35; see Rom. 12:19–21), who often uses governing authorities to carry it out (13:4).

In the case of lawsuits (Matt. 5:40), the Law permitted demanding a tunic (or shirt) in pledge for a loan, but prohibited taking a cloak (or coat) overnight, because it was needed for warmth (Ex. 22:26–27). However, Jesus' listeners commonly pressed for the cloak—for ruinous damages—almost literally "suing the pants off each other," as we would say. But Christ's point was that if lawsuits have to go to extremes, they ought to be in the extreme of charity. (Paul argued similarly in 1 Cor. 6:1–8.)

What about going the second mile (Matt. 5:41)? The word "compels" is a technical term meaning "to requisition or press into service." Ancient Persian law permitted postal carriers to *compel* private citizens to help carry their loads. The Romans were no different; for example, Roman soldiers compelled Simon of Cyrene to carry Jesus' cross (27:32). So Jesus was speaking of someone with legitimate authority who might compel one of His followers to go a "thousand paces," or one Roman mile, roughly nine-tenths of an English mile.

How should a believer respond to such requests? With resistance? Perhaps complying grudgingly, but only to a minimum degree? Again, Jesus challenged His followers to grace and integrity. Imagine the reputation that Christians would have if we always did twice what the law required! What would tax auditors think if we not only followed the rules, but paid more than the law required of us? What would our employers think if we consistently rendered double the expected service?

The same pattern holds in the case of lending (v. 42; see "Running to Extremes," Luke 6:29).

Throughout vv. 17–48, Jesus speaks in stark contrasts and strong hyperboles (overstatements for the sake of emphasis). The key to understanding this section is to keep in mind the major thrust of His teaching: good not evil, grace not vengeance, love not hatred. That is the morality of Christ. ◆

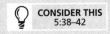

CHAPTER 6

Spiritual Disciplines

6:1–4

1“Take heed that you do not do your
charitable deeds before men, to be seen
by them. Otherwise you have no reward from your Father
in heaven. 2Therefore, when you do a charitable deed, do
not sound a trumpet before you as the hypocrites do in the
synagogues and in the streets, that they may have glory
from men. Assuredly, I say to you, they have their reward.
3But when you do a charitable deed, do not let your left
hand know what your right hand is doing, 4that your charitable deed may be in secret; and your Father who sees in secret will Himself reward you openly.[a]
5“And when you pray, you shall not be like the hypocrites. For they love to pray standing in the synagogues
and on the corners of the streets, that they may be seen by
men. Assuredly, I say to you, they have their reward. 6But
you, when you pray, go into your room, and when you have
shut your door, pray to your Father who *is* in the secret
place; and your Father who sees in secret will reward you
openly.[a] 7And when you pray, do not use vain repetitions as
the heathen *do.* For they think that they will be heard for
their many words.
8“Therefore do not be like them. For your Father knows
the things you have need of before you ask Him. 9In this
manner, therefore, pray:

Our Father in heaven,
Hallowed be Your name.
10 Your kingdom come.
Your will be done
On earth as *it is* in heaven.

6:11

11 Give us this day our daily bread.
12 And forgive us our debts,
As we forgive our debtors.

6:4 [a]NU-Text omits *openly.* *6:6* [a]NU-Text omits *openly.*

Our Daily Bread

A CLOSER LOOK 6:11

The request for daily bread (v. 11) acknowledges that God ultimately provides for our needs. He gives us skills and strength, jobs and income, and a world rich with resources to that end. For more on God's provision, see “God—The Original Worker,” John 5:17.

ANONYMOUS DONORS

CONSIDER THIS 6:1–4

Jesus' words in vv. 1–4 challenge a lot of what goes on today in fund-raising and charitable causes. As any fund-raiser knows, one of the biggest motivations for people who give large gifts is the prestige that results.

Jesus questioned that spirit of giving, however. He detested people who made a great show of presenting their gifts in the temple and elsewhere (Mark 12:41–44) as if they were generous and upright, but behind the scenes practiced the worst sorts of greed and immorality (Matt. 23:23–24). He was not attacking giving but hypocrisy.

How can we be sure that we are giving with the right motives? One way is to give anonymously (6:3–4). That way, our gifts will affect no one's opinion of us one way or the other. The matter will stay between us and God—and He can evaluate our motives.

“YOU SHALL NOT BE LIKE THE HYPOCRITES.”
—Matthew 6:5

6:13

13 And do not lead us into temptation,
But deliver us from the evil one.
For Yours is the kingdom and the power and the glory
forever. Amen.[a]

14"For if you forgive men their trespasses, your heavenly
Father will also forgive you. 15But if you do not forgive men
their trespasses, neither will your Father forgive your trespasses.
16"Moreover, when you fast, do not be like the hypocrites,
with a sad countenance. For they disfigure their faces that
they may appear to men to be fasting. Assuredly, I say to
you, they have their reward. 17But you, when you fast,
anoint your head and wash your face, 18so that you do not
appear to men to be fasting, but to your Father who *is* in

6:13 [a]NU-Text omits *For Yours* through *Amen.*

Do Not Lead Us into Temptation

A CLOSER LOOK 6:13

God has committed Himself to helping His children avoid, flee, confess, and resist temptation (v. 13). *See "Pay Attention to Temptation!" at 1 Cor. 10:12–13.*

CONSIDER THIS 6:19–34

Don't Worry!

Of the texts in Scripture that discuss money and work, vv. 19–34 are among the most frequently cited. Unfortunately, they are often used to imply that Jesus was against money and considered everyday work a distraction to things that "really" matter.

However, a careful reader will notice that Jesus condemned worry, *not work (vv. 25, 27–28, 31, 34). He never told us to stop working. Rather, He called us to correctly focus our faith on God, the ultimate supplier of our needs (v. 32).*

God provides for people in many ways. The most common is through everyday work. He expects us to work diligently with whatever resources He gives us (2 Thess. 3:6–12). Of course, sometimes that normal means of provision fails for a variety of reasons: ill health, divorce from or death of a provider, loss of a job, natural disaster, changing markets, and other circumstances beyond our control.

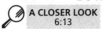

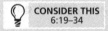

It is precisely the fear of those possibilities that tempts us to worry so much and forget about trusting God. Why rely on Him, we figure, if He can't keep us from troubles like that? Why not just rely on ourselves and trust to our

the secret *place;* and your Father who sees in secret will reward you openly.[a]

Treasures on Earth

6:19–34

[19]"Do not lay up for yourselves treasures on earth, where moth and rust destroy and where thieves break in and steal; [20]but lay up for yourselves treasures in heaven, where neither moth nor rust destroys and where thieves do not break in and steal. [21]For where your treasure is, there your heart will be also.

[22]"The lamp of the body is the eye. If therefore your eye is good, your whole body will be full of light. [23]But if your eye is bad, your whole body will be full of darkness. If therefore the light that is in you is darkness, how great *is* that darkness!

[24]"No one can serve two masters; for either he will hate the one and love the other, or else he will be loyal to the one and despise the other. You cannot serve God and mammon.

[25]"Therefore I say to you, do not worry about your life,

6:18 [a]NU-Text and M-Text omit *openly.*

own devices? All the while we forget that God never promised that we wouldn't face hard times, and that He has many ways to help us through them when we do: family members, church communities, neighbors, charities, inheritances, even public agencies and nonprofit groups.

Certainly we need to pay attention to our physical and material needs. But Jesus urged us to stop worrying about things so that they dominate our lives and values. We can't do that and serve God at the same time (v. 24). Instead, we need to redirect our focus onto God's kingdom and righteousness (v. 33). That means adopting the values of the King and bringing Him into our work and lives. Jesus said that's what "really" matters. ◆

God has given work as a gift to be used in service to others. See "People at Work," Heb. 2:7.

Contrary to what many people think, work is not a curse. See "Is Work a Curse?" Rom. 8:20–22.

Bringing Christ into our everyday work has a tangible effect on how we do our jobs. See "Your 'Workstyle,'" Titus 2:9–10.

"FOR WHERE YOUR TREASURE IS, THERE YOUR HEART WILL BE ALSO."
—Matthew 6:21

Judge Not!

CONSIDER THIS 7:1–5 **What was Jesus calling for when He ordered His followers to "judge not" (v. 1)? Did He want us to close our eyes to error and evil? Did He intend that managers forgo critical performance reviews of their employees? Or that news editors and art critics pull their punches? Or that juries refrain from judgment? Should we decline any assessment of others, since none of us is perfect?**

No, those would all be misapplications of Jesus' teaching. In the first place, He was not commanding blind acceptance, but grace toward others. Since all of us are sinners, we need to stop bothering with the failings of others and start attending to serious issues of our own (vv. 3–5). His words here extend His earlier exposé of hypocrisy (6:1–18). Don't blame or put down others while excusing or exalting yourself, Jesus was saying.

Is there room, then, to assess others, especially when we know we are not perfect? Yes, but only in Jesus' way: with empathy and fairness (7:12) and with a readiness to freely and fully forgive (Matt. 6:12, 14). When we are called upon to correct others, we should act like a good doctor whose purpose is to bring healing—not like an enemy who attacks.

Scripture gives clear guidelines to believers in cases where judgments need to be rendered. See Matt. 18:15–17; 1 Cor. 6:1–8; and Gal. 6:1–5.

what you will eat or what you will drink; nor about your
body, what you will put on. Is not life more than food and
the body more than clothing? 26Look at the birds of the air,
for they neither sow nor reap nor gather into barns; yet
your heavenly Father feeds them. Are you not of more value
than they? 27Which of you by worrying can add one cubit
to his stature?
28"So why do you worry about clothing? Consider the
lilies of the field, how they grow: they neither toil nor spin;
29and yet I say to you that even Solomon in all his glory was
not arrayed like one of these. 30Now if God so clothes the
grass of the field, which today is, and tomorrow is thrown
into the oven, *will He* not much more *clothe* you, O you of
little faith?
31"Therefore do not worry, saying, 'What shall we eat?' or
'What shall we drink?' or 'What shall we wear?' 32For after
all these things the Gentiles seek. For your heavenly Father
knows that you need all these things. 33But seek first the
kingdom of God and His righteousness, and all these things
shall be added to you. 34Therefore do not worry about tomorrow, for tomorrow will worry about its own things. Sufficient for the day *is* its own trouble.

CHAPTER 7

"Judge Not"

7:1–5
1"Judge not, that you be not judged.
2For with what judgment you judge, you
will be judged; and with the measure you use, it will be
measured back to you. 3And why do you look at the speck
in your brother's eye, but do not consider the plank in your
own eye? 4Or how can you say to your brother, 'Let me remove the speck from your eye'; and look, a plank *is* in your
own eye? 5Hypocrite! First remove the plank from your
own eye, and then you will see clearly to remove the speck
from your brother's eye.
6"Do not give what is holy to the dogs; nor cast your
pearls before swine, lest they trample them under their feet,
and turn and tear you in pieces.

Asking and Receiving

7"Ask, and it will be given to you; seek, and you will find;
knock, and it will be opened to you. 8For everyone who
asks receives, and he who seeks finds, and to him who
knocks it will be opened. 9Or what man is there among you
who, if his son asks for bread, will give him a stone? 10Or if
he asks for a fish, will he give him a serpent? 11If you then,

being evil, know how to give good gifts to your children,
how much more will your Father who is in heaven give
7:12
good things to those who ask Him!
[12]Therefore, whatever you want men to
do to you, do also to them, for this is the Law and the
Prophets.

A Challenge to Obedience

[13]"Enter by the narrow gate; for wide *is* the gate and
broad *is* the way that leads to destruction, and there are
many who go in by it. [14]Because[a] narrow *is* the gate and difficult *is* the way which leads to life, and there are few who
find it.
[15]"Beware of false prophets, who come to you in sheep's
clothing, but inwardly they are ravenous wolves. [16]You will
know them by their fruits. Do men gather grapes from
thornbushes or figs from thistles? [17]Even so, every good tree
bears good fruit, but a bad tree bears bad fruit. [18]A good
tree cannot bear bad fruit, nor *can* a bad tree bear good
fruit. [19]Every tree that does not bear good fruit is cut down
and thrown into the fire. [20]Therefore by their fruits you will
know them.
[21]"Not everyone who says to Me, 'Lord, Lord,' shall enter
the kingdom of heaven, but he who does the will of My
Father in heaven. [22]Many will say to Me in that day,
'Lord, Lord, have we not prophesied in Your name, cast
out demons in Your name, and done many wonders
in Your name?' [23]And then I will declare to them, 'I
never knew you; depart from Me, you who practice lawlessness!'
[24]"Therefore whoever hears these sayings of Mine, and
does them, I will liken him to a wise man who built his
house on the rock: [25]and the rain descended, the floods
came, and the winds blew and beat on that house; and it
did not fall, for it was founded on the rock.
[26]"But everyone who hears these sayings of Mine, and
does not do them, will be like a foolish man who built his
house on the sand: [27]and the rain descended, the floods
came, and the winds blew and beat on that house; and it
fell. And great was its fall."
7:29 see pg. 34
[28]And so it was, when Jesus had ended
these sayings, that the people were aston-
ished at His teaching, [29]for He taught them as one having
authority, and not as the scribes.

7:14 [a]NU-Text and M-Text read *How . . . !*

QUOTE UNQUOTE

CONSIDER THIS 7:12 *The "golden rule" (v. 12) is one of the best known teachings of Scripture. The great Reformer, Martin Luther, applied it specifically to the workplace:*

If you are a manual laborer, you find that the Bible has been put in your workshop, into your hand, into your heart. It teaches and preaches how you should treat your neighbor. Just look at your tools—at your needle or thimble, . . . your goods, your scales or yardstick or measure—and you will read this statement inscribed on them. Everywhere you look it stares at you. Nothing you handle every day is so tiny that it does not continually tell you this, if only you will listen. Indeed, there is no shortage of preaching. You have as many preachers as you have transactions, goods, tools, and other equipment in your house and home. All this is continually crying out to you: "Friend use me in your relations with your neighbor just as you would want your neighbor to use his property in his relations with you."

Martin Luther

Jesus had much more to say about the Law and the Prophets (v. 12). See "The Morality of Christ," Matt. 5:17–48.

CHAPTER 8

Jesus Heals a Leper

[1]When He had come down from the mountain,
great multitudes followed Him. [2]And
8:2
behold, a leper came and worshiped
Him, saying, "Lord, if You are willing, You can make me
clean."

[3]Then Jesus put out *His* hand and touched him, saying, "I
am willing; be cleansed." Immediately his leprosy was
cleansed.

[4]And Jesus said to him, "See that you tell no one; but go
your way, show yourself to the priest, and offer the gift that
Moses commanded, as a testimony to them."

Jesus' Authority

CONSIDER THIS 7:29

Scribes were members of a learned class in Israel who studied the Scriptures and tradition, and who served as copyists, editors, and teachers (see Luke 20:39). But while they held positions of authority, Jesus was a person of authority (v. 29). His authority was a function of who He was, not of what He had learned.

CONSIDER THIS 8:5–13

Under Authority

The centurion pointed out that, like Jesus, he was also "a man under authority" (v. 9). The encounter between the two suggests several lessons of authority and leadership:

(1) Effective leaders willingly admit when they need help (v. 5). The centurion faced a problem that went beyond his own considerable power. But he was willing to go outside his resources to enlist Jesus to deal with the situation.

(2) Effective leaders respond to matters of the heart and spirit (vv. 6, 8). The centurion was moved by compassion for his suffering servant, and perceived that Jesus had insight and power that went beyond a physician's skill.

(3) Effective leaders are able to approach others on their terms (vv. 5, 8). The centurion came in faith, pleading with Jesus to help his servant. As a Roman officer, he could have ordered Jesus, or offered Him money. But instead, he approached the Lord in a manner consistent with His nature.

(4) Effective leaders understand and accept the nature of authority (v. 9). The centurion understood what submission is all about. When he issued a command, his soldiers simply obeyed. He recognized that Jesus had the same authority over illness.

(5) Effective leaders invest trust in those under their authority (vv. 9–10). Great leaders display great faith in their people. The centurion trusted that Jesus could do what He said He would do.

Jesus Heals a Centurion's Servant

8:5–13

5 Now when Jesus had entered Capernaum, a centurion came to Him, plead-
ing with Him, 6 saying, "Lord, my servant is lying at home
paralyzed, dreadfully tormented."
7 And Jesus said to him, "I will come and heal him."
8 The centurion answered and said, "Lord, I am not worthy that You should come under my roof. But only speak a
word, and my servant will be healed. 9 For I also am a man
under authority, having soldiers under me. And I say to this
one, 'Go,' and he goes; and to another, 'Come,' and he
comes; and to my servant, 'Do this,' and he does *it*."

8:10 see pg. 36

10 When Jesus heard *it*, He marveled,
and said to those who followed, "As-
suredly, I say to you, I have not found such great faith, not

(Bible text continued on page 37)

(6) Effective leaders know who to trust (v. 10). *Trust is only as useful as the trustworthiness of the one in whom it is placed. The centurion's faith was marvelous because it was invested in the right person—Jesus. Leadership based on blind faith, either in others or in a system, is foolhardy.*

In light of these observations:

- *Do you rely too much on your own competence, or do you honestly assess both your strengths and your weaknesses?*
- *Do you respond to people only in terms of "the facts," or are you sensitive to the feelings and unexpressed needs of others (as well as your own)?*
- *Are you willing to meet and work with people on their terms, in their arena? Or must everyone come to you and play by your rules?*
- *Are you willing to be in charge, but unwilling to submit?*
- *In whom and in what do you place your faith?* ◆

Centurions played a powerful role in Rome's occupation of Palestine. See Mark 15:39.

In praising the centurion, Jesus tweaked the ethnic attitudes of the Jews. A Gentile with greater faith than any of them? Scandalous! See "A Soldier's Surprising Faith," Luke 7:1–10.

LEPROSY

FOR YOUR INFO 8:2

Lepers like the man mentioned in v. 2 were common in the ancient world. They suffered from a slowly progressing, ordinarily incurable skin disease that was believed to be highly contagious and therefore greatly feared. As a result, anyone who appeared to have leprosy, even if the symptoms were caused by some other condition, was banished from the community.

True leprosy is caused by a bacterium that spreads across the skin, creating sores, scabs, and white shining spots. The most serious problem, however, is a loss of sensation. Without the ability to feel, lepers injure their tissue, leading to further infection, deformity, muscle loss, and eventual paralysis. Fortunately, modern medicine has all but eliminated the disease.

Old Testament Law was quite detailed in its instructions regarding recognition and quarantine of leprous persons. Priests became the central figures for diagnosis, care of patients, and taking sanitary precautions to protect the rest of the community. The Law required that a leper be isolated from the rest of society (Lev. 13:45–46). Infected persons were required to wear mourning clothes, leave their hair in disorder, keep their beards covered, and cry "Unclean! Unclean!" so that others could avoid them. Any contact would defile the person who touched a leper.

Sometimes lepers were miraculously cured, as in the case of Moses (Ex. 4:7), Miriam, his sister (Num. 12:10), and Naaman (2 Kin. 5:1,10).

In the New Testament, Jesus intentionally healed lepers as a sign to vindicate His ministry. On one occasion He healed ten, but only one returned to thank Him (Luke 17:11–15).

CONSIDER THIS
8:10

Jesus' Global Connections

While Matthew's Gospel portrays Jesus in terms of His Jewish roots, it also shows that Jesus is an international Savior, a Messiah for the whole world. Notice some of Jesus' global connections:

Jesus' Roots (Matt. 1:1–16)

Jesus' genealogy includes at least two, and possibly three, Gentiles:

- David's great-great-grandmother, Rahab, a Canaanite prostitute of Jericho (Matt. 1:5; Josh. 2:1–24; 6:22–25).
- David's great-grandmother Ruth, a Moabite (Matt. 1:5; Ruth 1:1—4:22).
- Perhaps David's lover, Bathsheba, wife of Uriah the Hittite whom David murdered (Matt. 1:6; 2 Sam. 11:1—12:25). It is possible that Bathsheba was also a Hittite, though more likely she was a Hebrew who married a Hittite sojourner.

Wise Men from the East (Matt. 2:1–12)

In Matthew, the first worshipers of the baby Jesus were not Jews but Gentiles from the East. These wise men (*magi*) may have been astrologers from Persia (modern-day Iran). They came looking for the King of the Jews—their Messiah!

The Flight to Egypt (Matt. 2:13–14)

Egypt, a Gentile nation, provided a refuge for the infant Messiah from an outraged Herod the Great. In the same way, centuries before, Egypt had saved Jacob's family from starvation and had become a home where the family grew into a nation (Gen. 41:46—46:7).

Jesus' Childhood in Galilee (Matt. 2:22–23)

Jesus grew up in Nazareth, a small town of Galilee in the northern part of Palestine. The region was called Galilee of the Gentiles because of its mixed population (Matt. 4:15). Jesus began His ministry there, and many of His early followers were Gentiles from Syria and the Decapolis, a Gentile region (4:23–25).

"Undesirables" in Matthew

Jesus broke with many discriminatory traditions of His culture, reaching out to Samaritans, Gentiles, and other undesirables, as the following table of passages from Matthew shows:

A Variety of People and Responses

Text	People Involved	Jesus' Response
8:2–4	A leper, physically diseased and religiously unclean	Touched him when others would not
8:5–10	A Roman centurion	Healed his servant; praised his great faith
8:28–34	Two demon-possessed men from a Gentile region	Delivered them when the town rejected them
9:9–13	Matthew, a tax collector, and his disreputable friends	Called Matthew; dined with his friends
9:20–22	A hemorrhaging woman	Healed her; praised her faith
11:20–24	Tyre, Sidon, and Sodom (Gentile cities)	Said they will be better off than Jewish cities in the judgment, because of Jewish unbelief
12:39–42	Nineveh and the Queen of the South	Praised their repentance; said they would judge the generation of Jews that knew Jesus
14:34–36	People of Gennesaret, a Gentile region	Healed their sick
15:21–28	A Canaanite woman from the region of Tyre and Sidon	Healed her daughter; praised her great faith

◆

The roots of hostility between Jews and Gentiles stretched deep into Israel's history. See "Jews, Gentiles, and Jesus," Matt. 15:24.

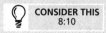

even in Israel! 11And I say to you that many will come from
east and west, and sit down with Abraham, Isaac, and Jacob
in the kingdom of heaven. 12But the sons of the kingdom
will be cast out into outer darkness. There will be weeping
and gnashing of teeth." 13Then Jesus said to the centurion,
"Go your way; and as you have believed, *so* let it be done
for you." And his servant was healed that same hour.

Peter's Mother-in-Law Healed

8:14–15

14Now when Jesus had come into Peter's house, He saw his wife's mother ly-
ing sick with a fever. 15So He touched her hand, and the
fever left her. And she arose and served them.[a]
16When evening had come, they brought to Him many
who were demon-possessed. And He cast out the spirits
with a word, and healed all who were sick, 17that it might
be fulfilled which was spoken by Isaiah the prophet, saying:

> "He Himself took our infirmities
> And bore *our* sicknesses."[a]

Following Jesus Has Its Costs

18And when Jesus saw great multitudes about Him, He
gave a command to depart to the other side. 19Then a certain scribe came and said to Him, "Teacher, I will follow
You wherever You go."

8:20 see pg. 38

20And Jesus said to him, "Foxes have
holes and birds of the air *have* nests, but
the Son of Man has nowhere to lay *His* head."
21Then another of His disciples said to Him, "Lord, let me
first go and bury my father."
22But Jesus said to him, "Follow Me, and let the dead
bury their own dead."

Jesus Calms a Storm

8:23–27

23Now when He got into a boat, His
disciples followed Him. 24And suddenly a
great tempest arose on the sea, so that the boat was covered
with the waves. But He was asleep. 25Then His disciples
came to *Him* and awoke Him, saying, "Lord, save us! We are
perishing!"
26But He said to them, "Why are you fearful, O you of

8:15 [a]NU-Text and M-Text read *Him.* *8:17* [a]Isaiah 53:4

A Surprise in Peter's Household

CONSIDER THIS 8:14–15

Households in Jesus' day tended to be much larger than those of today, with more children and more relatives from the extended family.

But Peter's home (v. 14) was somewhat unusual in that his mother-in-law lived with the family. Peter was not required by law or custom to provide her with a home. A widow usually moved back to her father's home, if he were still alive, or else joined a son's household.

It was fortunate for Peter's mother-in-law that Peter befriended Jesus. The Lord's compassion extended to widowed mothers-in-law even when He was a house guest! He healed her from her fever and she began to serve Him—a response that indicated a changed life and a deeply grateful attitude.

Does your faith cause you to respond to the needs of others like Jesus did?

The Storms of Galilee

A CLOSER LOOK 8:23–27

Galilee was and is the site of frequent violent storms such as the one described in vv. 23–27. For an explanation of this phenomenon, see the diagram, "What Kind of Storm Was This?" at Luke 8:22.

Jesus—A Homeless Man?

CONSIDER THIS 8:20 **Jesus was born poor and lived poor. His comment in v. 20 even suggests that He was homeless. He never celebrated poverty, but He did ask His followers to forsake the common belief that real security comes from having wealth (Matt. 6:19–34).**

Does that seem too difficult for those of us living in a society that craves financial security and independence? If so, consider that Christ is not asking us to do anything that He did not do Himself. He wants us to learn to hold what we have very lightly.

little faith?" Then He arose and rebuked the winds and the
sea, and there was a great calm. 27So the men marveled, saying, "Who can this be, that even the winds and the sea obey
Him?"

Two Demon-possessed Men Healed

28When He had come to the other side, to the country of
the Gergesenes,[a] there met Him two demon-possessed *men*,
coming out of the tombs, exceedingly fierce, so that no one
8:29 could pass that way. 29And suddenly they
cried out, saying, "What have we to do
with You, Jesus, You Son of God? Have You come here to
torment us before the time?"
30Now a good way off from them there was a herd of
many swine feeding. 31So the demons begged Him, saying,
"If You cast us out, permit us to go away[a] into the herd of
swine."
32And He said to them, "Go." So when they had come
out, they went into the herd of swine. And suddenly the

8:28 [a]NU-Text reads *Gadarenes.* *8:31* [a]NU-Text reads *send us.*

CONSIDER THIS 8:29

Spiritual Realities Beyond You

Jesus often encountered demons like those that possessed the men at Gadara (vv. 28–34). The mention of demons affirms the reality of powerful spiritual forces in the universe. Scripture has much to say about angels and demons.

***Angels** are members of an order of heavenly beings who are superior to humans in power and intelligence (Heb. 2:7; 2 Pet. 2:11). However, unlike God they are not all-powerful or all-knowing (Ps. 103:20; 2 Thess. 1:7). God often sends them to announce good news, such as the birth of Jesus (Luke 1:30–31), or to warn of coming dangers, such as the destruction of Sodom (Gen. 18:16—19:29).*

Angels played a particularly active role in the events surrounding Jesus' birth, resurrection, and ascension. They:

- *counseled Joseph to wed Mary (Matt. 1:20);*
- *warned Joseph to flee to Egypt with Mary and the Christ child (2:13);*
- *instructed Joseph to return the family to Palestine (2:19);*
- *foretold to Zacharias the birth of John the Baptist (Luke 1:11–38);*
- *announced to shepherds the birth of Christ (2:8–15);*
- *appeared to Jesus in the Garden of Gethsemane to strengthen Him (Luke 22:43);*

whole herd of swine ran violently down the steep place into the sea, and perished in the water.

33Then those who kept *them* fled; and they went away into the city and told everything, including what *had happened* to the demon-possessed *men.* 34And behold, the whole city came out to meet Jesus. And when they saw Him, they begged *Him* to depart from their region.

CHAPTER 9

Jesus Heals a Paralytic

1So He got into a boat, crossed over, and came to His own city.
2Then behold, they brought to Him a paralytic lying on a bed. When Jesus saw their faith, He said to the paralytic, "Son, be of good cheer; your sins are forgiven you."

3And at once some of the scribes said within themselves, "This Man blasphemes!"

9:4–8

4But Jesus, knowing their thoughts, said, "Why do you think evil in your hearts?
5For which is easier, to say, *'Your* sins are forgiven

(Bible text continued on page 41)

- *rolled back the stone from Jesus' empty tomb (Matt. 28:2);*
- *appeared to women at the empty tomb to announce Jesus' resurrection (Luke 24:4–7, 23; John 20:12);*
- *promised Jesus' return after His ascension (Acts 1:9–11).*

Since Pentecost, the frequency of angelic activity in human affairs appears to have diminished, perhaps because of the larger role played by the Holy Spirit in the lives of believers.

***Demons** are fallen angels that have been cast out of heaven. They seek to undermine the cause of righteousness in the world (1 Pet. 3:19–20; 2 Pet. 2:4; Jude 6). Scripture describes them with various names: "unclean spirits" (Mark 6:7), "wicked or evil spirits" (Luke 7:21; Acts 19:12–13), "spirit of divination" (Acts 16:16), "deceiving spirits" (1 Tim. 4:1), and "spirit of error" (1 John 4:6).* ◆

Scripture presents demons not as mythological creatures, but as real beings involved in historical events. See "Demons," Luke 11:14.

The Power of Forgiveness

CONSIDER THIS 9:4–8 **The crowd that watched Jesus heal the paralytic responded enthusiastically to His dramatic display of power (v. 8). But they overlooked His more significant ability to forgive sins—a power that deeply troubled the scribes (vv. 2–3).**

The power of forgiveness is immeasurable. Jesus challenged us as His followers to forgive others who have wronged or hurt us (6:14–15; 18:21–35). That may seem like a simple act, but anyone who has struggled with pain and anger knows that it takes enormous power to authentically forgive—to lay aside one's hurt and reach out to an offender with the embrace of a pardon. On the other side, forgiveness can release the wrongdoer from paralyzing guilt and even turn around the course of that person's life (James 5:19–20).

Forgiveness is as powerful and liberating as the healing of a paralytic. And it's a power that Jesus has delegated to His followers (John 20:23).

We are called to forgive others as Christ has forgiven us. See Col. 3:13.

CONSIDER THIS
9:9–13

A Rich Man Enters the Kingdom

Jesus said it would be hard for the rich to enter the kingdom of heaven (Matt. 19:23). The remark has led some to believe that rich people can't enter the kingdom, and others to feel that Jesus was opposed to wealth and the wealthy. But Matthew's response to Jesus' call (9:9–13) contradicts both of those assumptions.

The incident recorded here contrasts sharply with Jesus' encounter with the rich young ruler (Matt. 19:16–30; Mark 10:17–31; Luke 18:18–30). In many ways, the ruler seemed to make a more likely prospect than Matthew for membership in Jesus' burgeoning movement. (See table below.)

Yet despite the young ruler's apparent edge, it was Matthew who ended up following Jesus. The other "went away sorrowful" (19:22). What accounts for the difference? For one thing, the wealthy young man clearly perceived himself as already righteous (19:17–20). He felt that he was able to meet God's requirements on his own merits (19:16). But no one had to convince Matthew that he needed the Great Physician (9:11–12). As a tax collector, he was among the most despised members of Jewish society.

Yet there was a more fundamental difference between these two men, a difference that depended on Jesus' attitude more than on theirs. His words to the Pharisees explained the matter clearly: "I desire mercy and not sacrifice. For I did not come to call the righteous, but sinners, to repentance" (v. 13). In calling Matthew but turning away the rich young ruler, Jesus demonstrated in real-life parables precisely this point: that salvation depends on the mercy of God, not on the merits or sacrifice of people.

In the end, the crucial difference between the rich man who followed and the rich man who rejected was the merciful choice of God. Of course, none of us knows that choice beforehand. Therefore, we as believers need to be equally eager to present the gospel of Christ to everyone, rich or poor, wise or foolish, mighty or weak. ◆

Two Different Rich Men

Rich Young Ruler	Matthew
Probably enjoyed inherited wealth	Rich most likely because of his work as a tax collector
Had lived a good life	Like most tax collectors, was probably dishonest and ruthless
Came to Jesus	Sat at his tax table; Jesus approached him
Displayed interest in spiritual things	Was collecting money when Jesus found him
Indicated a willingness to make sacrifices to gain eternal life	Gave no such indication

Scripture has much to say to believers about their wealth. See "Christians and Money," 1 Tim. 6:6–19, and "Getting Yours," James 5:1–6.

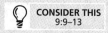

you,' or to say, 'Arise and walk'? 6But that you may know
that the Son of Man has power on earth to forgive sins"—
then He said to the paralytic, "Arise, take up your bed, and
go to your house." 7And he arose and departed to his house.
8Now when the multitudes saw *it,* they marveled[a] and
glorified God, who had given such power to men.

Matthew Follows Jesus

9As Jesus passed on from there, He saw a man named
Matthew sitting at the tax office. And He said to him, "Follow Me." So he arose and followed Him.

9:10

10Now it happened, as Jesus sat at the
table in the house, *that* behold, many tax
collectors and sinners came and sat down with Him and His
disciples. 11And when the Pharisees saw *it,* they said to His
disciples, "Why does your Teacher eat with tax collectors
and sinners?"

9:9–13

12When Jesus heard *that,* He said to
them, "Those who are well have no need
of a physician, but those who are sick. 13But go and learn
what *this* means: 'I desire mercy and not sacrifice.'[a] For I did
not come to call the righteous, but sinners, to repentance."[b]

The Old and the New

14Then the disciples of John came to Him, saying, "Why
do we and the Pharisees fast often,[a] but Your disciples do
not fast?"
15And Jesus said to them, "Can the friends of the bridegroom mourn as long as the bridegroom is with them? But
the days will come when the bridegroom will be taken away
from them, and then they will fast. 16No one puts a piece of
unshrunk cloth on an old garment; for the patch pulls away
from the garment, and the tear is made worse. 17Nor do
they put new wine into old wineskins, or else the wineskins
break, the wine is spilled, and the wineskins are ruined. But
they put new wine into new wineskins, and both are preserved."

Four Dramatic Healings

18While He spoke these things to them, behold, a ruler
came and worshiped Him, saying, "My daughter has just
died, but come and lay Your hand on her and she will live."
19So Jesus arose and followed him, and so *did* His disciples.

9:20–22 see pg. 43

20And suddenly, a woman who had a
flow of blood for twelve years came from
behind and touched the hem of His garment. 21For she said

(Bible text continued on page 43)

9:8 [a]NU-Text reads *were afraid.* *9:13* [a]Hosea 6:6 [b]NU-Text omits *to repentance.*
9:14 [a]NU-Text brackets *often* as disputed.

Who Were Those Tax Collectors?

CONSIDER THIS 9:10

Tax collectors (v. 10) were agents or contract workers who collected taxes for the government during Bible times. Some translations incorrectly call them "publicans," but publicans were wealthy men, usually non-Jewish, who contracted with the Roman government to be responsible for the taxes of a particular district. They were often backed by military force. By contrast, tax collectors were employed by publicans to do the actual collecting of monies. They were Jews, usually not very wealthy.

Tax collectors gathered several different types of taxes. Depending on the kind of rule in a given Jewish province, Rome levied a land tax, a poll tax, even a tax for the operation of the temple (Matt. 17:24–27). Some provinces, like Galilee, were not under an imperial governor, so their taxes remained in the province rather than going to the imperial treasury at Rome. Perhaps these inequities prompted the Pharisees in Judea (an imperial province) to ask Jesus, "Is it lawful to pay taxes to Caesar, or not?" (Matt. 22:17).

As a class, tax collectors were despised by their fellow Jews, and were generally associated with "sinners" (Matt. 9:10–11; Mark 2:15). They often gathered more than the government required and pocketed the excess amount—a practice that John the Baptist specifically preached against (Luke 3:12–13). But tax collectors were also hated because their fellow citizens viewed them as mercenaries working for the Roman oppressors.

In Jesus' day, Jews were probably paying no less than 30 or 40 percent of their income on taxes and religious dues. See "Taxes," Mark 12:14.

Zacchaeus was called the chief tax collector in Jericho, which may mean he was a publican. Nevertheless, he responded to Jesus' call. See Luke 19:1–10.

YOU ARE THERE
9:35

JESUS—A CITY PREACHER

Popular opinion frequently regards the Bible in general and the ministry of Jesus in particular in rural terms. Perhaps it's the Christmas story, with its quaint references to a donkey, a manger, and shepherds. Perhaps it's the memorable parables, such as the sower and the seed, the wheat and the weeds, and the prodigal son. Perhaps it's Jesus' origins in a small town. Whatever the cause, the popular image of Jesus and His world seems fixed on a rural environment. But that is somewhat misleading.

Palestine in Jesus' day was undergoing rapid urban development. Its population of around 2.5 to 3 million people lived in numerous preindustrial cities and towns that revolved around Jerusalem, the hub of the region. The Holy City had a population conservatively estimated by modern scholars at between 55,000 and 90,000. (Josephus, a first-century Jewish historian, placed the number at 3 million; the Talmud gives an incredible 12 million.)

So as Jesus carried out His ministry, He focused on the urban centers of Palestine (v. 35; 11:1; Luke 4:43; 13:22) and visited Jerusalem at least three times. This brought Him into contact with a greater number and wider variety of people than He would have encountered in a purely rural campaign—women, soldiers, religious leaders, the rich, merchants, tax collectors, Gentiles, prostitutes, beggars, and the poor. These He attracted in large crowds as He visited each city.

Jesus' urban strategy established a model for His disciples and the early church. When He sent the disciples on preaching tours, He directed them toward cities (Matt. 10:5, 11–14; Luke 10:1, 8–16). And later, the movement spread throughout the Roman empire by using an urban strategy that planted communities of believers in no less than 40 cities by the end of the first century (see "Churches—Keys to the Cities," Acts 11:22).

In light of the vital role that cities played in the ministry of Jesus, we who follow Him today need to ask: What are we doing to relate the message of Christ to our increasingly urban, multicultural, and pluralistic world? Our Lord's example in urban Palestine has much to teach us. ◆

Jerusalem dominated life in first-century Palestine. To find out why, see Matt. 23:37.

Don't miss the explosive start of the worldwide church! See "A Surprising First Fulfillment of Acts 1:8," Acts 2:8–11.

An urban strategy for ministry can be explosive—and unpredictable. See "The Ephesus Approach: How the Gospel Penetrates a City," Acts 19:8–41.

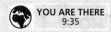

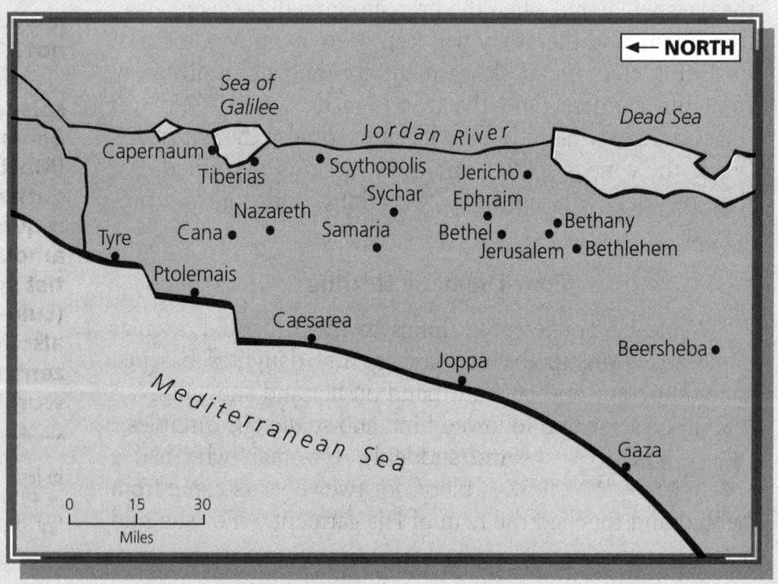

CITIES OF PALESTINE IN CHRIST'S TIME

to herself, "If only I may touch His garment, I shall be made
well." 22But Jesus turned around, and when He saw her He
said, "Be of good cheer, daughter; your faith has made you
well." And the woman was made well from that hour.

9:23

23When Jesus came into the ruler's
house, and saw the flute players and the
noisy crowd wailing, 24He said to them, "Make room, for
the girl is not dead, but sleeping." And they ridiculed Him.
25But when the crowd was put outside, He went in and
took her by the hand, and the girl arose. 26And the report of
this went out into all that land.

27When Jesus departed from there, two blind men followed Him, crying out and saying, "Son of David, have
mercy on us!"

28And when He had come into the house, the blind men
came to Him. And Jesus said to them, "Do you believe that I
am able to do this?"

They said to Him, "Yes, Lord."

29Then He touched their eyes, saying, "According to your
faith let it be to you." 30And their eyes were opened. And Jesus sternly warned them, saying, "See *that* no one knows *it.*"
31But when they had departed, they spread the news about
Him in all that country.

32As they went out, behold, they brought to Him a man,
mute and demon-possessed. 33And when the demon was

The Mourners

CONSIDER THIS 9:23 *In the ancient world, paid professional mourners (v. 23), most often women, aided families in their public expression of grief upon the death of a loved one. They composed poems or dirges praising the deceased, which they chanted to the accompaniment of a flute or other musical instrument in an attempt to stir the audience emotionally. They usually wore sackcloth and scattered dust in the air and on their heads. Weeping, wailing, and beating their breasts, they created an unmistakable tone of grief. There was no denial of death or distancing themselves from loss.*

Perhaps Jesus was making use of the image of professional mourners when He spoke of those who mourn in the Sermon on the Mount (Matt. 5:2).

The Hemorrhaging Woman

CONSIDER THIS 9:20–22 **For twelve years the woman in vv. 20–22 had sought a cure for her condition. Perhaps worse than the drain on her physical strength and finances was the stigma of uncleanness. Jews considered women ritually unclean during menstruation, and whoever touched a menstruating woman was made unclean until evening. If a woman experienced bleeding other than at her normal menses, she was considered unclean until the bleeding stopped (Lev. 15:19–27). That meant exclusion from participating in the life and worship of the community.**

Scripture is silent on the source of this woman's livelihood. Perhaps she lived off an inheritance, or perhaps she was divorced and her dowry had been returned to her. Whatever her means of support, it was gone. Jesus was her last hope.

So she approached Him, breaking a rule that made it an unclean person's responsibility to keep away from others. In desperation, she reached out and touched Jesus.

Perceiving that power had gone out from Him, Jesus sought her out. Perhaps as she explained her disease the crowd backed away, not wanting to contaminate themselves. But Jesus didn't withdraw. Rather He drew her to Him with the affectionate term "daughter" and sent her away in peace, healed at last.

Who are the "untouchables" in your world? Who is desperately trying to reach out for help? How can you respond to their needs with Christlikeness?

WHAT IT MEANS TO BE LIKE JESUS

CONSIDER THIS 8:1—9:38 *Jesus indicated that those who follow Him will become like Him (10:25). What does it mean to* **"be like Jesus"** *in today's complex world? Matthew paints eight portraits of what Christlikeness looks like, including:*

#7: To Be Like Jesus Means TO SERVE OTHERS

The Sermon on the Mount (Matt. 5–7) was immediately followed by "deeds in the valley" (Matt. 8–9). Christlike values lead to servant actions—and it was obedient action that Jesus cared about, not just sermonizing (7:21–29). Jesus modeled how to *do* the will of God by actively serving more than 25 different people (chs. 8–9). These included such undesirables as lepers, an officer of the Roman occupation troops, the sick, the demon-possessed, cave dwellers, tax collectors, and a diseased, outcast woman. If we want to be like Jesus, we need to befriend those who are weak, under oppression, or without Christ. Like Him, we need to become "a friend of sinners" (11:19). He offered much more than religious information—He served them.

For a summary of all eight portraits of Christlikeness, see "What It Means to Be Like Jesus" at 10:25. The next item in the series can be found at 10:1–42.

cast out, the mute spoke. And the multitudes marveled,
saying, "It was never seen like this in Israel!"
34But the Pharisees said, "He casts out demons by the
ruler of the demons."

Jesus Feels Compassion for the Crowds

9:35 see pg. 42

35Then Jesus went about all the cities
and villages, teaching in their syna-
gogues, preaching the gospel of the kingdom, and healing
every sickness and every disease among the people.[a] 36But
when He saw the multitudes, He was moved with compassion for them, because they were weary[a] and scattered, like
sheep having no shepherd. 37Then He said to His disciples,
"The harvest truly *is* plentiful, but the laborers *are* few.

8:1—9:38

38Therefore pray the Lord of the harvest
to send out laborers into His harvest."

CHAPTER 10

The Twelve

10:1–42

1And when He had called His twelve
disciples to *Him,* He gave them power
over unclean spirits, to cast them out, and to heal all kinds

10:2

of sickness and all kinds of disease. 2Now
the names of the twelve apostles are
these: first, Simon, who is called Peter, and Andrew his
brother; James the *son* of Zebedee, and John his brother;
3Philip and Bartholomew; Thomas and Matthew the tax collector; James the *son* of Alphaeus, and Lebbaeus, whose surname was[a] Thaddaeus; 4Simon the Cananite,[a] and Judas Iscariot, who also betrayed Him.

Jesus Sends and Warns the Twelve

5These twelve Jesus sent out and commanded them, saying: "Do not go into the way of the Gentiles, and do not enter a city of the Samaritans. 6But go rather to the lost sheep

10:7–10 see pg. 46

of the house of Israel. 7And as you go,
preach, saying, 'The kingdom of heaven
is at hand.' 8Heal the sick, cleanse the lepers, raise the
dead,[a] cast out demons. Freely you have received, freely
give. 9Provide neither gold nor silver nor copper in your
money belts, 10nor bag for *your* journey, nor two tunics, nor
sandals, nor staffs; for a worker is worthy of his food.
11"Now whatever city or town you enter, inquire who in it
is worthy, and stay there till you go out. 12And when you go
into a household, greet it. 13If the household is worthy, let
your peace come upon it. But if it is not worthy, let your

9:35 [a]NU-Text omits *among the people.* *9:36* [a]NU-Text and M-Text read *harassed.*
10:3 [a]NU-Text omits *Lebbaeus, whose surname was.* *10:4* [a]NU-Text reads *Cananaean.*
10:8 [a]NU-Text reads *raise the dead, cleanse the lepers;* M-Text omits *raise the dead.*

peace return to you. 14And whoever will not receive you
nor hear your words, when you depart from that house or
city, shake off the dust from your feet. 15Assuredly, I say to
you, it will be more tolerable for the land of Sodom and
Gomorrah in the day of judgment than for that city!
16"Behold, I send you out as sheep in the midst of wolves.
Therefore be wise as serpents and harmless as doves. 17But
beware of men, for they will deliver you up to councils and
scourge you in their synagogues. 18You will be brought before governors and kings for My sake, as a testimony to
them and to the Gentiles. 19But when they deliver you up,
do not worry about how or what you should speak. For it
will be given to you in that hour what you should speak;
20for it is not you who speak, but the Spirit of your Father
who speaks in you.

(Bible text continued on page 47)

FOR YOUR INFO
10:2

THE TWELVE

Apostle	Description
Simon (Peter) (Mark 1:16)	Fisherman from Galilee, Andrew's brother
Andrew (John 1:40)	Fisherman from Galilee, Peter's brother
James	Son of Zebedee, brother to John; from Capernaum
John (Introduction to John)	Son of Zebedee, brother to James; from Capernaum
Philip	From Bethsaida
Bartholomew (Nathanael)	From Cana in Galilee
Thomas (Didymus)	Possibly also a fisherman
Matthew (Levi) (Matt. 9:9)	Tax collector in Capernaum; son of Alphaeus, possibly James' brother
James	Son of Alphaeus, possibly Matthew's brother
Lebbaeus Thaddeus (Judas)	May have taken the name Thaddeus ("warm-hearted") because of the infamy that came to be attached to the name Judas
Simon (the Cananite)	From Cana; one of the Zealots, Jewish revolutionaries who opposed Rome
Judas Iscariot (Matt. 26:14)	From Kerioth, and possibly the only Judean among the Twelve

(Biblical references are to Personality Profiles.)

Matthew called these twelve "apostles." What did that term mean? See 2 Cor. 11:5.

WHAT IT MEANS TO BE LIKE JESUS

CONSIDER THIS
10:1–42

*Jesus indicated that those who follow Him will become like Him (10:25). What does it mean to **"be like Jesus"** in today's complex world? Matthew paints eight portraits of what Christlikeness looks like, including:*

#8: To Be Like Jesus Means TO AFFIRM OTHER LEADERS

Jesus invested Himself in the development of other people, particularly the Twelve. He gave them responsibility and authority, resisting the temptation to get the job done "right" by doing it Himself. In doing so, He accepted the risk that they might fail. Of course, He gave them adequate preparation before sending them out, and on their return He affirmed them on their successful completion of the mission. Jesus calls us to help others grow. If we want to be like Him, we will share the joys and risks of working together with our brothers and sisters.

For a summary of all eight portraits of Christlikeness, see "What It Means to Be Like Jesus" at 10:25. This is the last item in the series.

CONSIDER THIS
10:7–10

A Prayer of the Laity

He was born into a noble family in Assisi, Italy in 1182. Although christened Giovanni Bernadone, he went by the nickname Francis —a reminder that his merchant father had been away in France when he was born. The privileges of his childhood fostered a pursuit of wealth, education, and fun, and when he came of age he joined the army as the simplest avenue to achieving those goals.

But young Francis' life took a dramatic turn when serious illness interrupted his plans. While convalescing, he took a new and profound interest in religion. Once on his feet, he made a pilgrimage to Rome, a common discipline for the spiritually devoted.

But he was shocked at what he found there. Lepers and beggars languished in cathedrals fallen into disrepair. Moved to compassion and inspired by his newfound faith, he exercised one of the few options available to concerned laity at the time: he sold his horse and some of his father's cloth supplies and gave the money to a local priest, assuming that the cleric would restore the buildings. But to his surprise, the priest rejected the gift when he learned that it had come from the Bernadone family's commercial ventures. To make matters worse, Francis' father disowned him upon learning of his actions.

Penniless, he managed to find refuge with a bishop. But he continued his mission to the poor, begging enough money over a two-year span to repair four church buildings. It was during that period that he heard a sermon on Matthew 10:7–10. The text galvanized his thinking, and he made a decision to live the rest of his life as a beggar, serving the poor through preaching and healing.

His example motivated others to follow. A wealthy woman from Assisi began a sister movement, as well as one for married laity. Those who joined were reacting against widespread corruption in the church and a general confusion about the meaning and practice of spirituality for laypeople. Not all of the newcomers were sincere. Some tried to introduce changes away from a singleminded focus on the poor and unbelievers. And, as the movement became fashionable, Francis had to constantly resist the clergy's attempts to bring the work under their auspices and "upgrade" the status of the lay workers to agents of the church.

The spirit of Francis' vision was captured in a prayer that he penned, "Make me an instrument of Thy peace." Today, it has become quite well known. Perhaps its popularity springs from its simple yet eloquent statement of the aspirations of a very concerned and committed layperson who determined to make a difference for God in the world as he found it. ◆

The Prayer of St. Francis

Lord,
Make me an instrument of Thy peace;
Where there is hatred, let me sow love;
Where there is injury, pardon;
Where there is doubt, faith;
Where there is despair, hope;
Where there is darkness, light; and
Where there is sadness, joy.
Divine Master,
Grant that I may not so much
seek to be consoled as to console;
To be understood as to understand;
To be loved as to love;
For it is in giving that we receive;
It is in pardoning that we are pardoned;
And it is in dying
that we are born to eternal life.

[21]"Now brother will deliver up brother to death, and a father *his* child; and children will rise up against parents and
cause them to be put to death. [22]And you will be hated by
all for My name's sake. But he who endures to the end will
be saved. [23]When they persecute you in this city, flee to
another. For assuredly, I say to you, you will not have
gone through the cities of Israel before the Son of Man
comes.

[24]"A disciple is not above *his* teacher, nor a servant above
10:25 his master. [25]It is enough for a disciple
that he be like his teacher, and a servant
like his master. If they have called the master of the house
Beelzebub,[a] how much more *will they call* those of his
household! [26]Therefore do not fear them. For there is nothing covered that will not be revealed, and hidden that will
not be known.

[27]"Whatever I tell you in the dark, speak in the light; and
what you hear in the ear, preach on the housetops. [28]And
do not fear those who kill the body but cannot kill the soul.
But rather fear Him who is able to destroy both soul and
body in hell. [29]Are not two sparrows sold for a copper coin?
And not one of them falls to the ground apart from your Father's will. [30]But the very hairs of your head are all numbered. [31]Do not fear therefore; you are of more value than
many sparrows.

[32]"Therefore whoever confesses Me before men, him I will
also confess before My Father who is in heaven. [33]But whoever denies Me before men, him I will also deny before My
Father who is in heaven.

[34]"Do not think that I came to bring peace on earth. I did
not come to bring peace but a sword. [35]For I have come to
'set a man against his father, a daughter against her mother,
and a daughter-in-law against her mother-in-law'; [36]and 'a
man's enemies will be those of his *own* household.'[a] [37]He
who loves father or mother more than Me is not worthy of
Me. And he who loves son or daughter more than Me is not
worthy of Me. [38]And he who does not take his cross and
follow after Me is not worthy of Me. [39]He who finds his
life will lose it, and he who loses his life for My sake will
find it.

[40]"He who receives you receives Me, and he who receives
Me receives Him who sent Me. [41]He who receives a prophet
in the name of a prophet shall receive a prophet's reward.
And he who receives a righteous man in the name of a
righteous man shall receive a righteous man's reward. [42]And
whoever gives one of these little ones only a cup of cold *water* in the name of a disciple, assuredly, I say to you, he shall
by no means lose his reward."

10:25 [a]NU-Text and M-Text read *Beelzebul.* *10:36* [a]Micah 7:6

WHAT IT MEANS TO BE LIKE JESUS

CONSIDER THIS 10:25 **Jesus' statement in v. 25 implies that His disciples will be like Him. To His first-century followers, that included the prospect of persecution and martyrdom. But what else does it mean to "be like Jesus," especially for Christians in today's marketplace? Eight portraits in Matthew's eye-witness account give us some clues:**

#1: To be like Jesus means to accept our roots (1:1–17).

#2: To be like Jesus means to engage the world's pain and struggle (1:18—2:23).

#3: To be like Jesus means to commit ourselves to other believers, no matter how "weird" they appear to be (3:1–17).

#4: To be like Jesus means to admit our vulnerability to temptation (4:1–11).

#5: To be like Jesus means to openly proclaim the message of Christ (4:12–25).

#6: To be like Jesus means to commit ourselves to changed thinking and behavior (5:1—7:27).

#7: To be like Jesus means to serve others, especially those who are oppressed or without Christ (8:1—9:38).

#8: To be like Jesus means to affirm others in leadership (10:1–42).

For more on each of these points, see the articles at the texts indicated.

Some Surprising Evidence

CONSIDER THIS 11:2–6 **John the Baptist wanted reassurance about who Jesus was and what He was doing (vv. 2–3). Jesus replied with a list of things He had done that revealed God's presence, power, and love (vv. 4–5). The most telling evidence was His work among the poor, the downtrodden, and the needy.**

Our culture today wants to know whether Christ is still alive among His people. Like John, observers are asking whether those of us who claim to be Christ's followers are truly of God, or whether they should look elsewhere. They especially pay attention to our posture toward the poor. So it's worth asking: Are we as involved and concerned with the material needs of our neighbors as we are with their spiritual needs? Do we respond to physical needs as intentionally as Christ did, even if we have only material help to offer rather than miracles of healing? Is there unmistakable evidence of Christ working within us?

Scripture has a great deal to say about Christians' responsibilities to the poor and needy. See "I Have Not Coveted," Acts 20:33–38; "Giving It All Away," 1 Cor. 13:3; "Christ Became Poor," 2 Cor. 8:9; and "Take a Cardiogram," 1 John 3:16–21.

CHAPTER 11

Jesus Speaks about John the Baptist

1 Now it came to pass, when Jesus finished commanding
His twelve disciples, that He departed from there to teach
and to preach in their cities.

11:2–6 2 And when John had heard in prison
about the works of Christ, he sent two of[a]
his disciples 3 and said to Him, "Are You the Coming One,
or do we look for another?"

4 Jesus answered and said to them, "Go and tell John the
things which you hear and see: 5 *The* blind see and *the* lame
walk; *the* lepers are cleansed and *the* deaf hear; *the* dead are
raised up and *the* poor have the gospel preached to them.
6 And blessed is he who is not offended because of Me."

7 As they departed, Jesus began to say to the multitudes
concerning John: "What did you go out into the wilderness
to see? A reed shaken by the wind? 8 But what did you go
out to see? A man clothed in soft garments? Indeed, those
who wear soft *clothing* are in kings' houses. 9 But what did
you go out to see? A prophet? Yes, I say to you, and more
than a prophet. 10 For this is *he* of whom it is written:

'Behold, I send My messenger before Your face,
Who will prepare Your way before You.'[a]

11 "Assuredly, I say to you, among those born of women
there has not risen one greater than John the Baptist; but he
who is least in the kingdom of heaven is greater than he.
12 And from the days of John the Baptist until now the kingdom of heaven suffers violence, and the violent take it by
force. 13 For all the prophets and the law prophesied until
John. 14 And if you are willing to receive *it,* he is Elijah who
is to come. 15 He who has ears to hear, let him hear!

16 "But to what shall I liken this generation? It is like children sitting in the marketplaces and calling to their companions, 17 and saying:

'We played the flute for you,
　　And you did not dance;
We mourned to you,
　　And you did not lament.'

18 For John came neither eating nor drinking, and they say,
'He has a demon.' 19 The Son of Man came eating and drinking, and they say, 'Look, a glutton and a winebibber, a
friend of tax collectors and sinners!' But wisdom is justified
by her children."[a]

11:2 [a]NU-Text reads *by* for *two of.* *11:10* [a]Malachi 3:1 *11:19* [a]NU-Text reads *works.*

Unbelieving Cities Condemned

[20]Then He began to rebuke the cities in which most of
His mighty works had been done, because they did not re-
11:21 pent: [21]"Woe to you, Chorazin! Woe to
you, Bethsaida! For if the mighty works
which were done in you had been done in Tyre and Sidon,
they would have repented long ago in sackcloth and ashes.
[22]But I say to you, it will be more tolerable for Tyre and
Sidon in the day of judgment than for you. [23]And you, Capernaum, who are exalted to heaven, will be[a] brought down
to Hades; for if the mighty works which were done in you
had been done in Sodom, it would have remained until this
day. [24]But I say to you that it shall be more tolerable for the
land of Sodom in the day of judgment than for you."

An Invitation

[25]At that time Jesus answered and said, "I thank You,
Father, Lord of heaven and earth, that You have hidden
these things from *the* wise and prudent and have revealed
them to babes. [26]Even so, Father, for so it seemed good in
Your sight. [27]All things have been delivered to Me by My
Father, and no one knows the Son except the Father. Nor
does anyone know the Father except the Son, and *the one* to
whom the Son wills to reveal *Him.* [28]Come to Me, all *you*
who labor and are heavy laden, and I will give you rest.
[29]Take My yoke upon you and learn from Me, for I am gentle and lowly in heart, and you will find rest for your souls.
[30]For My yoke *is* easy and My burden is light."

CHAPTER 12

Sabbath Controversies

12:1–13 [1]At that time Jesus went through the
grainfields on the Sabbath. And His disci-
ples were hungry, and began to pluck heads of grain and to
eat. [2]And when the Pharisees saw *it,* they said to Him,
"Look, Your disciples are doing what is not lawful to do on
the Sabbath!"
[3]But He said to them, "Have you not read what David did
when he was hungry, he and those who were with him:

11:23 [a]NU-Text reads *will you be exalted to heaven? No, you will be.*

Why This Anger?

A CLOSER LOOK 12:1–13 *What was it that so enraged the Pharisees when they saw the disciples picking grain and Jesus healing a man's withered hand? And why did Jesus refuse to allow their grumbling to go unchallenged? See "Jesus Confronts the Legalists," Luke 6:1–11.*

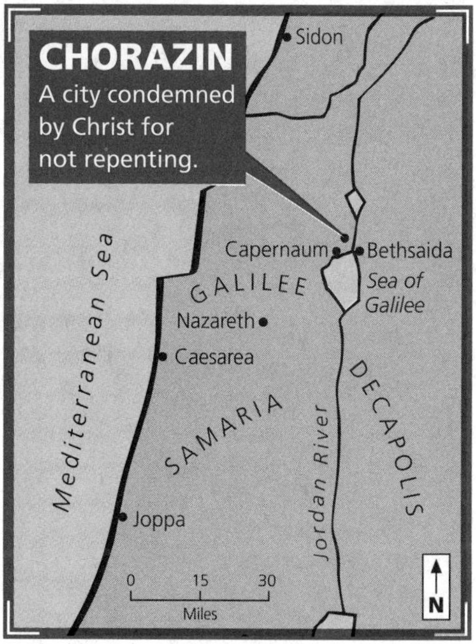

Chorazin

YOU ARE THERE 11:21

- **A town north of the Sea of Galilee, built on the basalt hills two and one-half miles north of Capernaum.**
- **Name means "secret."**
- **Mentioned in the Talmud as a distribution point for wheat.**
- **Known for the black, volcanic rock ruins of its synagogue. The famed *cathedra Mosis,* a carved judgment seat of Moses (compare Matt. 23:2), has been found there (in modern-day Khirbet Kerazeh).**

4how he entered the house of God and ate the showbread
which was not lawful for him to eat, nor for those who were
with him, but only for the priests? 5Or have you not read in
the law that on the Sabbath the priests in the temple profane the Sabbath, and are blameless? 6Yet I say to you that
in this place there is *One* greater than the temple. 7But if
you had known what *this* means, 'I desire mercy and not
sacrifice,'[a] you would not have condemned the guiltless.
8For the Son of Man is Lord even[a] of the Sabbath."

9Now when He had departed from there, He went into
their synagogue. 10And behold, there was a man who had a
withered hand. And they asked Him, saying, "Is it lawful to
heal on the Sabbath?"—that they might accuse Him.

11Then He said to them, "What man is there among you
who has one sheep, and if it falls into a pit on the Sabbath,
will not lay hold of it and lift *it* out? 12Of how much more
value then is a man than a sheep? Therefore it is lawful to
do good on the Sabbath." 13Then He said to the man,
"Stretch out your hand." And he stretched *it* out, and it was

12:7 [a]Hosea 6:6 *12:8* [a]NU-Text and M-Text omit *even*.

CONSIDER THIS
12:31–32

No Forgiveness!

People speak of committing the "unpardonable sin," but in His severe comments to the Pharisees (vv. 31–32), Jesus indicated that it is more than just a figure of speech—it is a matter with eternal consequences!

Can people ever sin so badly that God cannot forgive them? The answer is yes and no. It's important to realize that the blood of Jesus Christ on the cross paid for all of the sin of the world (John 1:29; Rom. 5:12–21; 8:3). There is no sin that God has not overcome through Christ. That means that no one ever has to fear going beyond the scope of God's grace or power. Sometimes people despair because they have committed certain sins that to them seem unforgivable. But no matter what their failure has been, God can and will forgive their sin if they come to Him in repentance (Acts 2:38; 1 John 1:9).

At the same time, it is possible to willfully place oneself beyond the grace of God—to persist in rebellion and sin and resist His call to repentance. This, essentially, is what the Pharisees and other Jewish leaders did (compare Acts 7:51–52). Jesus had healed a demon-possessed man by the power of the Holy Spirit (v. 28). His enemies claimed that He cast them out by the power of Satan ("Beelze-

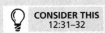

12:14

restored as whole as the other. [14]Then the
Pharisees went out and plotted against
Him, how they might destroy Him.

Jesus Seeks a Low Profile

[15]But when Jesus knew *it,* He withdrew from there. And
great multitudes[a] followed Him, and He healed them all.
[16]Yet He warned them not to make Him known, [17]that it
might be fulfilled which was spoken by Isaiah the prophet,
saying:

18 "Behold! My Servant whom I have chosen,
My Beloved in whom My soul is well pleased!

12:15 [a]NU-Text brackets *multitudes* as disputed.

Political Intrigue

A CLOSER LOOK 12:14

The Pharisees feared Jesus as much as they hated Him. They were concerned that His popularity might have political repercussions, drawing Roman troops to the area and causing the loss of what little independence the nation had. So they plotted to destroy Him. The mastermind behind their plans was Caiaphas the high priest, a Sadducee rather than a Pharisee, but equally opposed to Jesus. Find out more about this man at Matt. 26:3.

bub," v. 24). The accusation was evidence that they had rejected Him.

It also slandered the Holy Spirit, revealing their spiritual blindness, a warping and perversion of their moral nature that put them beyond hope of repentance and faith—and therefore beyond forgiveness.

Is there an "unpardonable sin?" Not for those who cry out like the tax collector in a parable of Jesus, "God, be merciful to me a sinner!" (Luke 18:13). But those who, like the Pharisee in the same parable (as well the Pharisees in this incident), trust to their own self-righteousness, reject Christ, and slander His Holy Spirit—they reveal a spiritual cancer so advanced that they are beyond any hope of healing and forgiveness. ◆

Our culture tends to dismiss demon possession as a quaint, archaic way of trying to explain physical and psychological conditions. But the Bible presents demons and demon possession not as myth, but as reality. See "Demons," Luke 11:14.

"OF HOW MUCH MORE VALUE THEN IS A MAN THAN A SHEEP?"
—Matthew 12:12

I will put My Spirit upon Him,
And He will declare justice to the Gentiles.
19 He will not quarrel nor cry out,
Nor will anyone hear His voice in the streets.
20 A bruised reed He will not break,
And smoking flax He will not quench,
Till He sends forth justice to victory;
21 And in His name Gentiles will trust."[a]

Allegations of Satanism

22Then one was brought to Him who was demon-possessed, blind and mute; and He healed him, so that the blind and[a] mute man both spoke and saw. 23And all the multitudes were amazed and said, "Could this be the Son of David?"

24Now when the Pharisees heard *it* they said, "This *fellow* does not cast out demons except by Beelzebub,[a] the ruler of the demons."

12:21 [a]Isaiah 42:1–4 *12:22* [a]NU-Text omits *blind and.* *12:24* [a]NU-Text and M-Text read *Beelzebul.*

CONSIDER THIS
12:43–45

Turning Back Is Awful

Do you intend to overcome evil? If so, make sure to replace it with good or else, as Jesus warns, the evil may return with its friends, producing more evil than ever (vv. 43–45).

This teaching warns us to persevere in the journey of faith. That can be hard to do when everything in us wants to quit, the way an exhausted long-distance runner wants to drop out of a marathon. Besides (we reason), look how far we've already come!

Yes, but God's goal is not just to make us nicer people or better people, but to make us Christlike people. That won't happen completely until we're with Him. For now, He wants us to keep growing in that direction. Stopping short can bring disaster. In a warning similar to Jesus' words here, the writer of Hebrews urges us to "go on to perfection" and describes in sobering words the fate of those who "fall away" (Heb. 6:1–12).

Fortunately, God lends us help to prevent us from falling back. As Hebrews also says, He disciplines us for our good. His stern efforts can feel harsh, but they are the loving protection of a caring Father (12:3–11). ◆

It is dangerous to compare ourselves with others when evaluating our worth. God has a better way of self-assessment. See "Do You Suffer from 'Comparisonitis'?" Rom. 12:3.

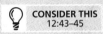

[25]But Jesus knew their thoughts, and said to them: "Every
kingdom divided against itself is brought to desolation, and
every city or house divided against itself will not stand. [26]If
Satan casts out Satan, he is divided against himself. How
then will his kingdom stand? [27]And if I cast out demons by
Beelzebub, by whom do your sons cast *them* out? Therefore
they shall be your judges. [28]But if I cast out demons by the
Spirit of God, surely the kingdom of God has come upon
you. [29]Or how can one enter a strong man's house and
plunder his goods, unless he first binds the strong man?
And then he will plunder his house. [30]He who is not with
Me is against Me, and he who does not gather with Me scatters abroad.

12:31–32 see pg. 50

[31]"Therefore I say to you, every sin and
blasphemy will be forgiven men, but the
blasphemy *against* the Spirit will not be forgiven men.
[32]Anyone who speaks a word against the Son of Man, it will
be forgiven him; but whoever speaks against the Holy
Spirit, it will not be forgiven him, either in this age or in the
age to come.
[33]"Either make the tree good and its fruit good, or else
make the tree bad and its fruit bad; for a tree is known by
its fruit. [34]Brood of vipers! How can you, being evil, speak
good things? For out of the abundance of the heart the
mouth speaks. [35]A good man out of the good treasure of his
heart[a] brings forth good things, and an evil man out of the
evil treasure brings forth evil things. [36]But I say to you that
for every idle word men may speak, they will give account
of it in the day of judgment. [37]For by your words you will
be justified, and by your words you will be condemned."
[38]Then some of the scribes and Pharisees answered, saying, "Teacher, we want to see a sign from You."
[39]But He answered and said to them, "An evil and adulterous generation seeks after a sign, and no sign will be
given to it except the sign of the prophet Jonah. [40]For as
Jonah was three days and three nights in the belly of the
great fish, so will the Son of Man be three days and three
nights in the heart of the earth. [41]The men of Nineveh will
rise up in the judgment with this generation and condemn
it, because they repented at the preaching of Jonah; and indeed a greater than Jonah *is* here. [42]The queen of the South
will rise up in the judgment with this generation and condemn it, for she came from the ends of the earth to hear the
wisdom of Solomon; and indeed a greater than Solomon *is*
here.

12:43–45

[43]"When an unclean spirit goes out of a
man, he goes through dry places, seeking

(Bible text continued on page 55)

12:35 [a]NU-Text and M-Text omit *of his heart.*

Family Loyalty

CONSIDER THIS 12:46–50 *Ancient society placed great emphasis on faithfulness to blood relatives. So Jesus' words in vv. 48–50 must have sounded quite foreign to the crowd. He seemed to be breaking with tradition and disowning His family. But notice: Jesus didn't deny that the woman and the men at the door were His family. He merely pushed beyond the normal understanding of family to a larger reality—the claims of spiritual kinship. This new "family" included anyone who does the will of the Father in heaven.*

In no way was Jesus denying the value or benefits of solid family relationships. See "The Family: A Call to Long-Term Work," Eph. 5:21.

CONSIDER THIS
13:1

WORK-WORLD STORIES DESCRIBE THE KINGDOM

Jesus captivated His listeners by presenting truth in terms that they could understand. Here in chapter 13 we find no less than eight different images from the work world. Clearly, Jesus knew how to relate to the world in which everyday people lived and worked.

No wonder: Jesus probably spent most of His life working in His family's carpentry business. We know almost nothing of His youth from adolescence until He began His public ministry at about age 30. But we know that His father was a carpenter (Matt. 13:55) and that Jesus also practiced the trade (Mark 6:3). Carpenters worked with wood, metal, and stone to produce furniture and farm implements, and constructed houses and public buildings.

Jesus may have continued His occupation even after He began to teach and travel. Rabbis (or teachers) of the day commonly spent anywhere from one-third to one-half of their time working (most likely with their hands) to provide for themselves. And while Jesus' opponents, many of them rabbis, attacked Him on numerous grounds, they never accused Him of laziness or freeloading. Indeed, He was known to them as a carpenter.

That reputation passed on to the early church. One writer described Jesus as "working as a carpenter when among men, making ploughs and yokes, by which He taught the symbols of righteousness and an active life."

Little wonder, then, that Jesus' teaching was filled with workplace images and analogies such as those recorded here. Using parables—brief tales illustrating moral principles—He frequently spoke about the nature of His kingdom. Matthew 13 collects eight of these as listed below (with possible interpretations):

(1) *The parable of the soils (vv. 1–23)* addresses the receptivity of those who hear about the kingdom.

(2) *The parable of the wheat and the weeds (vv. 24–30)* warns that people who pretend to be part of the kingdom may be able to fool others, but they can't fool God.

(3) *The parable of the mustard seed (vv. 31–32)* is a promise that the kingdom would become a force to be reckoned with. Do not despise small beginnings!

(4) *The parable of the leaven (v. 33)* describes the influence of the kingdom: it quietly but effectively spreads among people and accomplishes significant results.

(5) *The parable of the hidden treasure (v. 44)* puts a value on the kingdom: it's the most important thing one can possess.

(6) *The parable of the pearl of great price (vv. 45–46)* also describes the kingdom's value: it's worth sacrificing everything in order to possess it.

(continued on next page)

rest, and finds none. 44Then he says, 'I will return to my
house from which I came.' And when he comes, he finds *it*
empty, swept, and put in order. 45Then he goes and takes
with him seven other spirits more wicked than himself, and
they enter and dwell there; and the last *state* of that man is
worse than the first. So shall it also be with this wicked generation."

Family Loyalty

12:46–50 see pg. 53

46While He was still talking to the multitudes, behold, His mother and brothers
stood outside, seeking to speak with Him. 47Then one said
to Him, "Look, Your mother and Your brothers are standing
outside, seeking to speak with You."
48But He answered and said to the one who told Him,
"Who is My mother and who are My brothers?" 49And He
stretched out His hand toward His disciples and said, "Here
are My mother and My brothers! 50For whoever does the
will of My Father in heaven is My brother and sister and
mother."

CHAPTER 13

Parables by the Sea

13:1

1On the same day Jesus went out of the
house and sat by the sea. 2And great mul-
titudes were gathered together to Him, so that He got into a
boat and sat; and the whole multitude stood on the shore.

Soils

3Then He spoke many things to them in parables, saying:
"Behold, a sower went out to sow. 4And as he sowed, some
seed fell by the wayside; and the birds came and devoured
them. 5Some fell on stony places, where they did not have
much earth; and they immediately sprang up because they
had no depth of earth. 6But when the sun was up they were
scorched, and because they had no root they withered away.
7And some fell among thorns, and the thorns sprang up
and choked them. 8But others fell on good ground and
yielded a crop: some a hundredfold, some sixty, some thirty.
9He who has ears to hear, let him hear!"
10And the disciples came and said to Him, "Why do You
speak to them in parables?"
11He answered and said to them, "Because it has been giv-
en to you to know the mysteries of the kingdom of heav-
en, but to them it has not been given. 12For whoever has,
to him more will be given, and he will have abundance;
but whoever does not have, even what he has will be taken
away from him. 13Therefore I speak to them in parables,

(continued from previous page)

(7) *The parable of the dragnet* (vv. 47–50) warns that a day of reckoning is coming, when those who accept the kingdom will be separated from those who reject it.

(8) *The parable of the householder* (vv. 51–52) places a responsibility on those who understand about the kingdom to share their insight with others.

Jesus' stories connected with the real world of agriculture (sowing, harvesting, growing), the food industry (baking, fishing), real estate (land purchasing, home ownership), and retailing (the sale of pearls). His images and language helped bring His message alive to common people. It showed clearly that God takes an interest in the workplace, and desires people to serve Him in the "secular" arena.

Work is one of the most important means that believers today have to accomplish God's purposes. See "Faith Impacts the World," Mark 16:15–16.

Like Jesus, Paul was able to support himself through a "secular" occupation. See "Paul's 'Real' Job," Acts 18:1–3.

If Jesus might have supported Himself while carrying out His ministry, is there any reason why modern Christian leaders shouldn't at least consider that as an option today? See "Paying Vocational Christian Workers," 1 Cor. 9:1–23.

because seeing they do not see, and hearing they
do not hear, nor do they understand. [14]And in
them the prophecy of Isaiah is fulfilled, which
says:

> 'Hearing you will hear and shall not
> understand,
> And seeing you will see and not perceive;
> 15 For the hearts of this people have grown dull.
> *Their* ears are hard of hearing,
> And their eyes they have closed,
> Lest they should see with *their* eyes and hear
> with *their* ears,
> Lest they should understand with *their* hearts
> and turn,
> So that I should[a] heal them.'[b]

[16]But blessed *are* your eyes for they see, and your
ears for they hear; [17]for assuredly, I say to you that
many prophets and righteous *men* desired to see
what you see, and did not see *it,* and to hear what
you hear, and did not hear *it.*

[18]"Therefore hear the parable of the sower:
[19]When anyone hears the word of the kingdom,
and does not understand *it,* then the wicked *one*
comes and snatches away what was sown in his
heart. This is he who received seed by the wayside.
[20]But he who received the seed on stony places,
this is he who hears the word and immediately receives it with joy; [21]yet he has no root in himself,
but endures only for a while. For when tribulation or persecution arises because of the word, immediately he stumbles. [22]Now he who received
seed among the thorns is he who hears the word,
and the cares of this world and the deceitfulness of riches choke the word, and he becomes unfruitful. [23]But he who received seed on
the good ground is he who hears the word and understands *it,* who indeed bears fruit and produces: some a hundredfold, some sixty, some
thirty."

Wheat and Tares

[24]Another parable He put forth to them, saying:
"The kingdom of heaven is like a man who sowed
good seed in his field; [25]but while men slept, his
enemy came and sowed tares among the wheat and
went his way. [26]But when the grain had sprouted
and produced a crop, then the tares also appeared.
[27]So the servants of the owner came and said to
him, 'Sir, did you not sow good seed in your field?
How then does it have tares?' [28]He said to them,
'An enemy has done this.' The servants said to him,
'Do you want us then to go and gather them up?'
[29]But he said, 'No, lest while you gather up the
tares you also uproot the wheat with them. [30]Let
both grow together until the harvest, and at the
time of harvest I will say to the reapers, "First
gather together the tares and bind them in bundles to burn them, but gather the wheat into my
barn." ' "

A Mustard Seed

[31]Another parable He put forth to them, saying:
"The kingdom of heaven is like a mustard seed,
which a man took and sowed in his field, [32]which
indeed is the least of all the seeds; but when it is
grown it is greater than the herbs and becomes a
tree, so that the birds of the air come and nest in its
branches."

Leaven

13:33 see pg. 58

[33]Another parable He spoke to
them: "The kingdom of heaven
is like leaven, which a woman took and hid in
three measures[a] of meal till it was all leavened."

The Use of Parables

13:34–35

[34]All these things Jesus spoke
to the multitude in parables; and
without a parable He did not speak to them, [35]that
it might be fulfilled which was spoken by the
prophet, saying:

> "I will open My mouth in parables;
> I will utter things kept secret from the
> foundation of the world."[a]

Wheat and Tares Explained

[36]Then Jesus sent the multitude away and went
into the house. And His disciples came to Him,
saying, "Explain to us the parable of the tares of the
field."

(Bible text continued on page 58)

13:15 [a]NU-Text and M-Text read *would.* [b]Isaiah 6:9, 10 *13:33* [a]Greek *sata,* approximately two pecks in all *13:35* [a]Psalm 78:2

CONSIDER THIS
13:34–35

MYTH #1

10 MYTHS ABOUT CHRISTIANITY

MYTH: JESUS CHRIST WAS ONLY A GREAT MORAL TEACHER

Many people today accept a number of myths about Christianity, with the result that they never respond to Jesus as He really is. This is one of ten articles that speak to some of those misconceptions. For a list of all ten, see 1 Tim. 1:3–4.

People marveled at the teaching of Jesus. Whether He spoke in interesting parables (v. 34) or gave more straightforward, extended discourses (for instance, Matt. 5–7), people followed Him everywhere, hanging on His every word (Matt. 7:28). "No man ever spoke like this Man!" His listeners remarked (John 7:46). And they were right. Jesus was a master teacher and communicator.

Moreover, beyond simply teaching the highest moral and spiritual principles ever known, Jesus actually *lived* them. He told people to love their enemies; He forgave those who crucified Him. He told people to lay down their lives for others; He laid down His own life for the world. He told people not to worry about material possessions; He owned no more than the clothes on His back. Jesus' example makes Him the most remarkable of all teachers.

And yet that legacy almost makes it too easy for people to dismiss Him, ignoring both His message and His person: "Jesus? Yes, He was a great moral teacher." What they really mean is that, for them, Jesus was *only* a teacher—a great teacher, perhaps the greatest the world has ever seen, but a teacher and nothing more.

Neither He nor His followers would allow for that. Jesus was either very much more than a great teacher or else very much less than one. For in addition to His great moral precepts, He made astonishing claims that no other sane person has ever made, and behaved in ways that no other decent human has. For instance:

- He claimed to forgive people's sins (Matt. 9:2; Luke 7:47–48).
- He accepted people's worship (Matt. 8:2–3; 9:18–19; 14:33).
- He said that He alone was the way to God, the truth of God, and the life of God (John 5:40; 6:44; 7:16–17; 14:6).
- He said that He had come to seek and to save the lost (Luke 19:10).
- He promised that He would rise from the dead (Matt. 20:19; 27:63).
- He claimed that humanity would ultimately be accountable to Him (Matt. 7:21–23; 25:31–46).
- He claimed to be God and allowed others to call Him God (Matt. 16:15–16; 26:63–64; John 8:58).

These are astonishing claims. Any teacher who would make them had better be telling the truth or else He would be the worst of all liars and neither great nor moral.

The evidence suggests that Jesus was telling the truth. For in addition to His explicit claims are the implicit claims of fulfilled Old Testament prophecies and the performance of supernatural miracles. And there is also the fact that countless others who have examined His words and actions have come away convinced that He was not merely a great moral teacher, but the very Son of God. Among them have been determined and supposedly unshakable skeptics like Thomas and adamant opponents like the brilliant Saul of Tarsus who ended up becoming His most ardent follower.

(continued on next page)

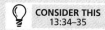

[37]He answered and said to them: "He who sows the good
seed is the Son of Man. [38]The field is the world, the good
seeds are the sons of the kingdom, but the tares are the sons
of the wicked *one.* [39]The enemy who sowed them is the
devil, the harvest is the end of the age, and the reapers are
the angels. [40]Therefore as the tares are gathered and burned
in the fire, so it will be at the end of this age. [41]The Son of
Man will send out His angels, and they will gather out of
His kingdom all things that offend, and those who practice
lawlessness, [42]and will cast them into the furnace of fire.
There will be wailing and gnashing of teeth. [43]Then the
righteous will shine forth as the sun in the kingdom of their
Father. He who has ears to hear, let him hear!

◆ ◆ ◆ ◆ ◆ ◆ ◆ ◆ ◆ ◆ ◆ ◆ ◆ ◆

MYTH #1
10 MYTHS ABOUT CHRISTIANITY

(continued from previous page)

To believe that Jesus was simply a great moral teacher is untenable. As C. S. Lewis put it,

> *A man who was merely a man and said the sort of things Jesus said would not be a great moral teacher. He would either be a lunatic—on a level with the man who says he is a poached egg—or else He would be the Devil of Hell. You must make your choice. Either this man was, and is, the Son of God: or else a madman or something worse. You can shut Him up for a fool, you can spit at Him and kill Him as a demon; or you can fall at His feet and call Him Lord and God. But let us not come with any patronizing nonsense about His being a great human teacher. He has not left that open to us. He did not intend to.*

(C. S. Lewis, *Mere Christianity,* p. 56) ◆

FIFTY POUNDS OF FLOUR

CONSIDER THIS
13:33

Perhaps when Jesus told the parable of the leaven (v. 33), laughter rippled through the crowd from the women who were listening. "Doesn't He know anything about baking?" they might have chuckled—or maybe Jesus was humoring them with an inside joke.

Jewish women did not use fresh yeast each day to leaven their barley or wheat bread, but a small piece of fermented dough from the previous day's batch. However, three measures was an enormous amount of flour—close to fifty pounds! How could that much flour be leavened by the usual amount of previously leavened dough?

Jesus' parable—and its point—must have come to mind every day afterwards as the women kneaded their dough. Fifty pounds of flour leavened by such a small amount of dough . . . the kingdom of God brought about by way of such a small number of faithful people.

Two other images that Jesus used to describe the influence His followers can have on society were salt and light. See "Sulfa Drugs and Street Lights," Matt. 5:13–16.

On another occasion, Jesus talked about leaven in a much more negative connection. See "Danger Ahead," Mark 8:14–21.

Hidden Treasure

13:44–46

44"Again, the kingdom of heaven is like
treasure hidden in a field, which a man
found and hid; and for joy over it he goes and sells all that
he has and buys that field.

A Pearl of Great Price

45"Again, the kingdom of heaven is like a merchant seeking beautiful pearls, 46who, when he had found one pearl of
great price, went and sold all that he had and bought it.

A Dragnet

47"Again, the kingdom of heaven is like a dragnet that was
cast into the sea and gathered some of every kind, 48which,
when it was full, they drew to shore; and they sat down and
gathered the good into vessels, but threw the bad away. 49So
it will be at the end of the age. The angels will come forth,
separate the wicked from among the just, 50and cast them
into the furnace of fire. There will be wailing and gnashing
of teeth."

A Householder

51Jesus said to them,[a] "Have you understood all these
things?"

They said to Him, "Yes, Lord."[b]

13:52 see pg. 60

52Then He said to them, "Therefore
every scribe instructed concerning[a] the
kingdom of heaven is like a householder who brings out of
his treasure *things* new and old."

Jesus Dishonored in His Own Country

53Now it came to pass, when Jesus had finished these
parables, that He departed from there. 54When He had
come to His own country, He taught them in their synagogue, so that they were astonished and said, "Where did
this *Man* get this wisdom and *these* mighty works? 55Is this
not the carpenter's son? Is not His mother called Mary? And
His brothers James, Joses,[a] Simon, and Judas? 56And His sisters, are they not all with us? Where then did this *Man* get
all these things?" 57So they were offended at Him.

But Jesus said to them, "A prophet is not without honor
except in his own country and in his own house." 58Now
He did not do many mighty works there because of their
unbelief.

(Bible text continued on page 61)

13:51 [a]NU-Text omits *Jesus said to them.* [b]NU-Text omits *Lord.* *13:52* [a]Or *for*
13:55 [a]NU-Text reads *Joseph.*

The Incomparable Value of the Kingdom

CONSIDER THIS 13:44–46 **The two parables in vv. 44–46 describe the incomparable value of the kingdom. Nothing was worth more, Jesus told His followers. Nothing is too great to sacrifice for it—certainly not material wealth (Matt. 6:33; 19:16–30).**

In light of Jesus' words here, maybe it's worth pausing to reflect on your own life and choices. What has your commitment to Christ cost you? Or has it cost you anything? Has it made any difference in decisions about your career, lifestyle, investments, or purchases? What would you sell in order to gain the King and His kingdom (v. 46)?

CONSIDER THIS
13:52

Treasures New and Old

One of the most exciting aspects of Christian truth is that it is inexhaustible. One can never come to the end of it. No matter how long we may have been in the faith, no matter how much theology we may master, we can never come to the end of what God has revealed in Christ and in the Bible. Jesus spoke to this fact in His parable of the householder (v. 52).

The key to understanding this parable is the question Jesus asked His followers: "Have you understood all these things?" (v. 51). "These things" refers to the series of parables on the kingdom that He had just told (vv. 1–50). Amazingly, the disciples answered yes. Apparently they thought they had absorbed everything Jesus had to say.

But how could they? They could not possibly perceive the vast implications of these stories for day-to-day life, let alone the theological issues involved in a doctrine as complex as the kingdom. Theologians still debate these matters (see "The King Declares His Kingdom," Matt. 4:17).

Jesus recognized that the disciples were claiming more insight than they actually possessed. So He gave them the parable of the householder to characterize the situation.

Householders were what we would call heads of households, persons with authority over what went on in a given home.

If one were to visit the home, the master of the house might bring out some of the treasures of the home to delight and impress his guest. He might bring out something old—perhaps one of the family heirlooms—or something new—maybe a recent purchase.

Jesus likened His disciples to heads of the family in possession of His truth. Over the years they would tell people about the "old treasures"—the basics of the gospel—and about "new treasures"—the way in which His teaching applied to new situations.

In effect, they would be like "scribe[s] instructed concerning the kingdom of heaven" (v. 52). Scribes were a learned class of scholars who studied the Scriptures and served as copyists, editors, and teachers. They occupied a prestigious position, as only ordained teachers could transmit and create religious tradition. Just as the Jewish scribes studied the Law, recalling old truths recognized for centuries as well as "new" truths that applied Scripture to the demands of new situations, so the disciples were storing up Jesus' teaching and—someday—would repeat it to others, write it down, and teach from it, passing on "things new and old."

Today we possess the written record of these treasures. But like Jesus' first disciples, we can find both old and new. As we confront situations, we can look back to the "old" truths, the fundamental things that never change, and we can also discern how to apply biblical truth to new issues in ways that are fresh and alive. ◆

To become a scribe required constant study, often beginning at age 14 and continuing to the age of 40. Learn more about these elite scholars of Jewish society at Luke 20:39.

CHAPTER 14

Herod Executes John the Baptist

14:1
1 At that time Herod the tetrarch heard
the report about Jesus 2 and said to his
servants, "This is John the Baptist; he is risen from the dead,
14:3
and therefore these powers are at work in
him." 3 For Herod had laid hold of John
and bound him, and put *him* in prison for the sake of Herodias, his brother Philip's wife. 4 Because John had said to
him, "It is not lawful for you to have her." 5 And although he
wanted to put him to death, he feared the multitude, because they counted him as a prophet.
14:6–10
6 But when Herod's birthday was celebrated, the daughter of Herodias danced
before them and pleased Herod. 7 Therefore he promised
with an oath to give her whatever she might ask.
8 So she, having been prompted by her mother, said, "Give
me John the Baptist's head here on a platter."
9 And the king was sorry; nevertheless, because of the
oaths and because of those who sat with him, he commanded *it* to be given to *her.* 10 So he sent and had John beheaded in prison. 11 And his head was brought on a platter
and given to the girl, and she brought *it* to her mother.
12 Then his disciples came and took away the body and
buried it, and went and told Jesus.

Jesus Feeds 5,000

14:13–14
see pg. 62
13 When Jesus heard *it,* He departed
from there by boat to a deserted place by
Himself. But when the multitudes heard it, they followed
Him on foot from the cities. 14 And when Jesus went out He
saw a great multitude; and He was moved with compassion
for them, and healed their sick. 15 When it was evening, His
disciples came to Him, saying, "This is a deserted place, and
the hour is already late. Send the multitudes away, that they
may go into the villages and buy themselves food."

Herod the Tetrarch

A CLOSER LOOK 14:1

The son of King Herod, Herod Antipas inherited the title of "tetrarch" (ruler of a fourth part; see Luke 9:7). Read about his infamous family in "The Herods," Acts 12:1–2.

Herod's Rash Promise

A CLOSER LOOK 14:6–10

Charmed by his stepdaughter and no doubt intoxicated, Herod rashly made a promise that cost John the Baptist his life (vv. 6–10). "A Reckless Choice" at Mark 6:23, discusses how decisions with far-reaching consequences are often made in haste, in a flush of wild excitement.

HATEFUL HERODIAS

CONSIDER THIS 14:3

Herodias (v. 3) was a powerful woman. The wife of Palestine's appointed ruler, she enjoyed privilege and position. But one thing she had no control over was the outspoken tongue of John the Baptist.

John had publicly condemned Herodias' marriage to Herod Antipas. A granddaughter of Herod the Great, Herodias had first married her father's brother, Herod Philip I. But she left Philip to marry his half-brother, Herod Antipas, who divorced his wife to marry Herodias.

John denounced their immorality, and Herodias was determined to silence the troublesome prophet. So she persuaded Herod to have John arrested and imprisoned. However, she could not convince her husband to execute the man.

Eventually, however, an opportunity presented itself when Herod's lust led him to foolishly promise Herodias' daughter Salome anything (v. 7). The extent of Herodias' evil and cunning is evident from her daughter's unusual request. Imagine the control she must have had over the girl's mind!

The Bible records terrible stories truthfully. This woman's choice, to use her daughter to work her vengeance on an innocent man, ranks among the worst.

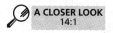

16But Jesus said to them, "They do not need to go away.
You give them something to eat."
17And they said to Him, "We have here only five loaves
and two fish."
18He said, "Bring them here to Me." 19Then He commanded the multitudes to sit down on the grass. And He
took the five loaves and the two fish, and looking up to
heaven, He blessed and broke and gave the loaves to the
disciples; and the disciples gave to the multitudes. 20So they
all ate and were filled, and they took up twelve baskets full
of the fragments that remained. 21Now those who had eaten
were about five thousand men, besides women and children.

CONSIDER THIS
14:13–14

The Public Side of Our Faith

Much of the Christianity that has come down to us today dwells on private spirituality—prayers, private devotions and Bible reading, self-examination and confession, personal holiness, individual acts of charity, and so on. This is all to the good, inasmuch as Christ is a Person who seeks a relationship with individuals.

But what about the public *side of our faith? For example:*

- *How do we as believers live as Christians in the public arenas—work, community, relationships, civic responsibilities, and so on?*
- *What about our communities of faith, such as our churches? How vibrant and strategic is our collective witness as God's people to a watching world?*

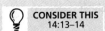

Jesus Walks on Water

22Immediately Jesus made His disciples get into the boat
and go before Him to the other side, while He sent the multitudes away. 23And when He had sent the multitudes away,
He went up on the mountain by Himself to pray. Now
when evening came, He was alone there. 24But the boat was
now in the middle of the sea,[a] tossed by the waves, for the
wind was contrary.

14:25 see pg. 64

25Now in the fourth watch of the night
Jesus went to them, walking on the sea.
26And when the disciples saw Him walking on the sea, they

14:24 [a]NU-Text reads *many furlongs away from the land.*

- *In what ways do we as believers influence our society as a whole—its institutions, its needs, and its values?*

These are broad, complex questions that have no easy answers. But we cannot afford to ignore them—not when we consider the public side of Jesus' ministry. Unlike others of His day who withdrew from society to practice and perfect their own, private spirituality (such as the Essenes, Matt. 16:1), Jesus actively engaged His culture. He participated in its rituals. He focused His work on its cities (see "Jesus—A City Preacher," Matt. 9:35). He interacted with its leaders. He welcomed its crowds (as seen here in vv. 13–14). He particularly reached out to its poor—not only the financially poor but the "poor in spirit," those left behind, those left without hope.

In short, Jesus not only affects our private lives, but our public lives as well. We need to recover that dimension of the gospel today. As believers we are no longer simply individuals, but have been made part of a "royal priesthood" and a "holy nation." Out of those who were once "no people," we are now "the people of God" (1 Pet. 2:9–10). We need to discover how to live out our faith in visible, public ways, as the collective people of God, in order to powerfully impact our world. ◆

Jesus used two metaphors to describe a believer's public life, particularly work and participation in the community. See "Sulfa Drugs and Street Lights," Matt. 5:13–16.

HE SAW A GREAT MULTITUDE; AND HE WAS MOVED WITH COMPASSION FOR THEM. . . .
—Matthew 14:14

were troubled, saying, "It is a ghost!" And they cried out for fear.

27But immediately Jesus spoke to them, saying, "Be of good cheer! It is I; do not be afraid."

28And Peter answered Him and said, "Lord, if it is You, command me to come to You on the water."

29So He said, "Come." And when Peter had come down
out of the boat, he walked on the water to go to Jesus. 30But
when he saw that the wind *was* boisterous,[a] he was afraid;
and beginning to sink he cried out, saying, "Lord, save me!"

31And immediately Jesus stretched out *His* hand and
caught him, and said to him, "O you of little faith, why did
you doubt?" 32And when they got into the boat, the wind
ceased.

33Then those who were in the boat came and[a] worshiped Him, saying, "Truly You are the Son of God."

14:30 [a]NU-Text brackets *that* and *boisterous* as disputed. *14:33* [a]NU-Text omits *came and.*

FOR YOUR INFO
14:25

Telling Time

Matthew records that Jesus came walking on the sea "in the fourth watch of the night" (v. 25). That would make it near sunrise, indicating that the disciples had spent virtually the entire night struggling with the stormy conditions!

In those days, time was not reckoned as precisely as it is today. In cultures that lacked electricity and were far more agriculturally based than our own, time was an approximation. Thus when the men of Jabesh Gilead came to Saul for help, he promised them, "Tomorrow, by the time the sun is hot, you shall have help" (1 Sam. 11:9), indicating that reinforcements would arrive sometime in midmorning. Likewise, God is said to have walked in the garden of Eden "in the cool of the day" (Gen. 3:8), suggesting evening.

However, the Hebrews did divide the period of daylight (yom) *into 12 hours, as follows:*

Sunrise	*6:00 a.m.*
1st hour	*7:00 a.m.*
2nd hour	*8:00 a.m.*
3rd hour	*9:00 a.m.*
4th hour	*10:00 a.m.*
5th hour	*11:00 a.m.*
6th hour	*12:00 noon*
7th hour	*1:00 p.m.*

Many Healed in Gennesaret

[34]When they had crossed over, they came to the land of[a] Gennesaret. [35]And when the men of that place recognized Him, they sent out into all that surrounding region, brought to Him all who were sick, [36]and begged Him that they might only touch the hem of His garment. And as many as touched *it* were made perfectly well.

CHAPTER 15

Debates over Tradition

15:1–3

[1]Then the scribes and Pharisees who were from Jerusalem came to Jesus, saying, [2]"Why do Your disciples transgress the tradition of the elders? For they do not wash their hands when they eat bread."

14:34 [a]NU-Text reads *came to land at.*

◆ ◆ ◆ ◆ ◆ ◆ ◆ ◆ ◆ ◆ ◆ ◆ ◆ ◆ ◆

8th hour	*2:00 p.m.*
9th hour	*3:00 p.m.*
10th hour	*4:00 p.m.*
11th hour	*5:00 p.m.*
12th hour	*6:00 p.m.*

Obviously these times could vary substantially, depending on the season. To complicate matters, the Romans reckoned the day (as we do) in two twelve-hour periods beginning at midnight and noon.

Nighttime was divided into "watches," so called because of the changing shifts of watchmen who stood guard on city walls and at the gates. In the New Testament, the influence of the Romans created four watches estimated as follows (again depending on the season):

	Beginning around . . .
1st watch	*6:00 p.m.*
2nd watch	*9:00 p.m.*
3rd watch	*midnight*
4th watch	*3:00 a.m.* ◆

TRADITION

CONSIDER THIS 15:1–3 **Tradition. Is it the bedrock of intelligent change or the stumbling block to any change? Should leaders embrace and personify traditional values, or should they be mavericks, breaking with tradition and striking out in new directions?**

Jesus rebuked the scribes and Pharisees for allowing their rabbinic traditions to actually supersede the express commands of God (v. 3). The specific issue here was a tradition about ritual washings connected with the preparation and serving of food. Not only must one's hands be washed, but also the bowls, cups, pitchers, and other utensils.

In modern American culture we do not follow the rigid pronouncements of a priestly class. Yet there are numerous traditions and expectations—most of which are unspoken—that govern our behavior in powerful ways. This creates tension for believers in the workplace, particularly managers. They are called upon to be both sustainers and breakers of tradition. There are no simple formulas to help one decide how to respond to tradition, but it might help to reflect on questions such as:

- **What values and principles does the tradition seek to embody? How do those square with the values of Christ?**
- **Why does the tradition exist? Why is it maintained? Are there any major objections to it?**
- **In maintaining a tradition, who benefits and who suffers? If it changes, who might be helped or hurt? How would the organization be affected?**

Tradition is an important area in which faith impacts the world. See Mark 16:15–16.

3He answered and said to them, "Why do you also transgress the commandment of God because of your tradition?
4For God commanded, saying, 'Honor your father and your
mother';[a] and, 'He who curses father or mother, let him be
put to death.'[b] 5But you say, 'Whoever says to his father or
mother, "Whatever profit you might have received from me
is a gift to God"— 6then he need not honor his father or
mother.'[a] Thus you have made the commandment[b] of God
of no effect by your tradition. 7Hypocrites! Well did Isaiah
prophesy about you, saying:

8 'These people draw near to Me with their mouth,
And[a] honor Me with *their* lips,
But their heart is far from Me.
9 And in vain they worship Me,
Teaching *as* doctrines the commandments of men.' "[a]

Jesus Denounces the Pharisees

10When He had called the multitude to *Himself*, He said
to them, "Hear and understand: 11Not what goes into the
mouth defiles a man; but what comes out of the mouth, this
defiles a man."
12Then His disciples came and said to Him, "Do You
know that the Pharisees were offended when they heard
this saying?"
13But He answered and said, "Every plant which My heavenly Father has not planted will be uprooted. 14Let them
alone. They are blind leaders of the blind. And if the blind
leads the blind, both will fall into a ditch."
15Then Peter answered and said to Him, "Explain this
parable to us."
16So Jesus said, "Are you also still without understanding?
17Do you not yet understand that whatever enters the
mouth goes into the stomach and is eliminated? 18But those
things which proceed out of the mouth come from the
heart, and they defile a man. 19For out of the heart proceed
evil thoughts, murders, adulteries, fornications, thefts, false
witness, blasphemies. 20These are *the things* which defile a
man, but to eat with unwashed hands does not defile a
man."

A Canaanite Woman's Plea

15:21–28

21Then Jesus went out from there and
departed to the region of Tyre and Sidon.
22And behold, a woman of Canaan came from that region

(Bible text continued on page 68)

PERSISTENCE PAYS OFF

CONSIDER THIS 15:21–28 **Jesus took His disciples to the seacoast towns of Tyre and Sidon (v. 21), probably to rest (Mark 7:24). As far as we can tell, He had no intention of preaching or healing in that area.**

But as so often happens when one has no intention of being available, someone interrupted His vacation. Today, phone calls prove to be the major source of interruptions. But in ancient times it was worse: interruptions arrived at one's doorstep and stayed until someone answered.

In this instance, a woman who supposedly had no claim on Jesus' attention begged Him to deliver her daughter from demons. She had probably already tried to heal the girl and failed. In ancient societies, women usually tended the sick and nursed the dying.

Jesus hardly encouraged this woman. As He pointed out, she had no ethnic or religious claim on Him. But somehow she recognized that He was capable of doing what she could not—heal her daughter. In the end, her courage, faith, and sheer persistence won out.

How persistent are you in crying out to God for people who matter a lot to you? Like the woman, will you keep coming back to God in faith?

Jesus' treatment of the woman seems a contradiction to His image. She came in utter sincerity and with great respect, yet He put her off with severe words. Why would He do that? See "Jesus and Ethnicity," Mark 7:24–30.

On another occasion, Jesus told His followers an interesting story about the need for persistence in prayer. See Luke 18:1–8.

15:4 [a]Exodus 20:12; Deuteronomy 5:16 [b]Exodus 21:17 *15:6* [a]NU-Text omits *or mother.* [b]NU-Text reads *word.* *15:8* [a]NU-Text omits *draw near to Me with their mouth, And.* *15:9* [a]Isaiah 29:13

CONSIDER THIS
15:24

JEWS, GENTILES, AND JESUS

At the time Jesus was born, Hebrews saw the world divided into two types of people—Jews and everyone else. Jews regarded foreigners (known as Gentiles, or "nations") as morally unclean and spiritually lost. Jews were God's people; Gentiles were not. The attitude was well expressed by Peter upon meeting Cornelius, a Roman centurion: "You know how unlawful it is for a Jewish man to keep company with or go to one of another nation" (Acts 10:28).

The roots of this separation stretched deep into Israel's history. One important development occurred in about 450 B.C. when a remnant of Jews returned from captivity in Babylon to rebuild Jerusalem. Their leader, Ezra the priest, called for purification from all pagan influences, such as foreign-born wives (Ezra 10:2–4).

Later, after centuries of domination by the Greeks and Romans, Jews developed a hatred for all Gentiles and tried to avoid contact with foreigners. According to Tacitus, a Roman historian, "they regard the rest of mankind with all the hatred of enemies" (*Histories,* v. 5).

In Matthew's Gospel we see a recognition of the tension between the two groups. He presents Jesus as the long-awaited Christ of the Jews (Matt. 15:24). Jesus fulfilled numerous Old Testament messianic prophecies (for example, Matt. 1:23; 2:6, 14, 18, 23). But Matthew also shows Jesus breaking through the Jew/Gentile wall of hatred and separation. Jesus dealt with Jews and Gentiles alike, shattering the caste system of His day—and shocking His Jewish brothers.

What ethnic or racial walls would Jesus tear down in the modern era? Perhaps He would have joined black slaves in the United States and lived among them as an equal. Perhaps He would have violated the customs of segregation and eaten with blacks in white restaurants earlier in this century. Perhaps He would open His door to Haitians in Miami, Chinese in Vancouver, or Vietnamese in Houston. Perhaps He would make friends with Palestinians in Israel, or reach out to Moslems in Iraq and Iran. Perhaps He would heal both Roman Catholics and Protestants in Northern Ireland.

Racism and ethnic hatred have never been God's desire. They come from the sin of men and women. Jesus repudiated such sin wherever He found it. As Matthew shows, His heart is for all the nations. ◆

While Matthew's Gospel portrays Jesus in terms of His Jewish roots, it also shows that Jesus is an international Savior, a Messiah for the whole world. See "Jesus' Global Connections," Matt. 8:10.

Part-Jew, part-Gentile, Samaritans were treated with unusual scorn by their Hebrew cousins. See John 4:4.

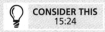

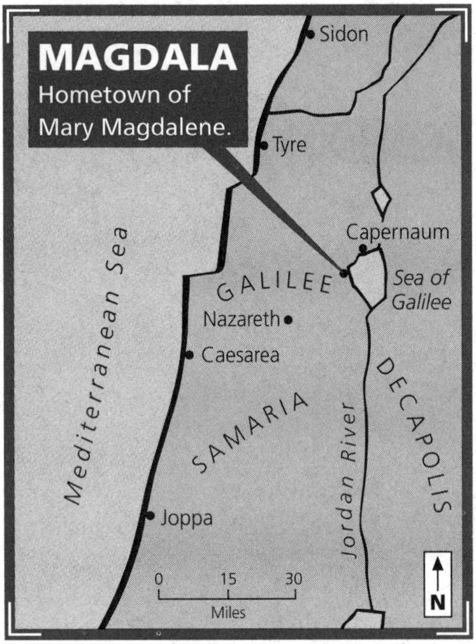

MAGDALA

YOU AREA THERE 15:39

- A city on the west shore of the Sea of Galilee, a short distance from Tiberias.
- Also known as Taricheae and called *Migdal* ("tower"), suggesting its significance militarily.
- A flourishing center of the region's fishing industry, shipping salted and pickled fish to Jerusalem, Damascus, and even as far away as Spain.
- Also known for agriculture, shipbuilding, and trade.
- Mostly Gentile in population and very wealthy.
- Boasted a hippodrome (stadium for chariot racing).
- Modern-day Mejdel the likely site of the ancient city.

and cried out to Him, saying, "Have mercy on me, O Lord,
Son of David! My daughter is severely demon-possessed."
23But He answered her not a word.
And His disciples came and urged Him, saying, "Send her
away, for she cries out after us."

15:24 see pg. 67

24But He answered and said, "I was not
sent except to the lost sheep of the house
of Israel."
25Then she came and worshiped Him, saying, "Lord, help
me!"
26But He answered and said, "It is not good to take the
children's bread and throw *it* to the little dogs."
27And she said, "Yes, Lord, yet even the little dogs eat the
crumbs which fall from their masters' table."
28Then Jesus answered and said to her, "O woman, great
is your faith! Let it be to you as you desire." And her daughter was healed from that very hour.

Jesus Heals on a Mountain

29Jesus departed from there, skirted the Sea of Galilee,
and went up on the mountain and sat down there. 30Then
great multitudes came to Him, having with them *the* lame,
blind, mute, maimed, and many others; and they laid them
down at Jesus' feet, and He healed them. 31So the multitude
marveled when they saw *the* mute speaking, *the* maimed
made whole, *the* lame walking, and *the* blind seeing; and
they glorified the God of Israel.

Jesus Feeds 4,000

32Now Jesus called His disciples to *Himself* and said, "I
have compassion on the multitude, because they have now
continued with Me three days and have nothing to eat. And
I do not want to send them away hungry, lest they faint on
the way."
33Then His disciples said to Him, "Where could we get
enough bread in the wilderness to fill such a great multitude?"
34Jesus said to them, "How many loaves do you have?"
And they said, "Seven, and a few little fish."
35So He commanded the multitude to sit down on the
ground. 36And He took the seven loaves and the fish and
gave thanks, broke *them* and gave *them* to His disciples;
and the disciples *gave* to the multitude. 37So they all ate and
were filled, and they took up seven large baskets full of the
fragments that were left. 38Now those who ate were four

15:39

thousand men, besides women and children. 39And He sent away the multitude,
got into the boat, and came to the region of Magdala.[a]

15:39 [a]NU-Text reads *Magadan.*

CHAPTER 16

Leaders Ask for a Sign

16:1 see pg. 70

1Then the Pharisees and Sadducees
came, and testing Him asked that He
would show them a sign from heaven. 2He answered and
said to them, "When it is evening you say, '*It will be* fair
weather, for the sky is red'; 3and in the morning, '*It will be*
foul weather today, for the sky is red and threatening.' Hypocrites![a] You know how to discern the face of the sky, but
you cannot *discern* the signs of the times. 4A wicked and
adulterous generation seeks after a sign, and no sign shall
be given to it except the sign of the prophet[a] Jonah." And
He left them and departed.

"Beware of the Leaven of the Pharisees"

5Now when His disciples had come to the other side, they
had forgotten to take bread. 6Then Jesus said to them, "Take
heed and beware of the leaven of the Pharisees and the Sadducees."

7And they reasoned among themselves, saying, "*It is* because we have taken no bread."

8But Jesus, being aware of *it,* said to them, "O you of little
faith, why do you reason among yourselves because you
have brought no bread?[a] 9Do you not yet understand, or remember the five loaves of the five thousand and how many
baskets you took up? 10Nor the seven loaves of the four
thousand and how many large baskets you took up? 11How
is it you do not understand that I did not speak to you concerning bread?—*but* to beware of the leaven of the Pharisees
and Sadducees." 12Then they understood that He did not
tell *them* to beware of the leaven of bread, but of the doctrine of the Pharisees and Sadducees.

"You Are the Christ"

16:13–20

13When Jesus came into the region of
Caesarea Philippi, He asked His disciples,
saying, "Who do men say that I, the Son of Man, am?"

(Bible text continued on page 72)

16:3 [a]NU-Text omits *Hypocrites.* *16:4* [a]NU-Text omits *the prophet.* *16:8* [a]NU-Text reads *you have no bread.*

"YOU CANNOT DISCERN THE SIGNS OF THE TIMES."
—Matthew 16:3

Standing at the Gates of Hell

A CLOSER LOOK 16:13–20

When Jesus queried His disciples as to His identity (vv. 13, 15), they were standing in the shadow of a city named in honor of Rome's emperor. See "You Are the Christ," Mark 8:27–33, and "Caesarea," Acts 10:24.

FOR YOUR INFO 16:1

PARTY POLITICS OF JESUS' DAY

What were the politics of Jesus? We may speculate on what His preferences might be today. But what political ideals did He favor during His earthly life? What leaders did He endorse, if any? What causes did He support? For that matter, was political choice even an issue for Him? Did politics even matter?

In the end, it would be difficult if not impossible to determine any satisfactory answers. Jesus seemed acutely aware of the power brokers in His society. He also showed remarkable skill at political gamesmanship. But He never addressed or practiced politics in any formal sense. And He lived in a system completely different from our own.

However, even if we cannot know precisely what Jesus' affiliations were, we can at least understand some of the political dynamics at work in Palestine in the first half of the first century. For example, we know that there were at least five major political parties among the Hebrews of that day.

The Herodians—Loyal Defenders of the Status Quo

- Took their name from Herod the Great (37–4 B.C.) and his supporters. (See "The Herods," Acts 12:1–2.)
- Supported the adoption of Graeco-Roman culture and policies in Palestine.
- Like the Pharisees, favored local political autonomy. Fearing military intervention by Rome, they stridently resisted challengers to the status quo, such as the Zealots, John the Baptist, Jesus, and the apostles.
- Joined forces with other parties in the plot to eliminate Jesus (Matt. 22:16; Mark 3:6; 12:13).

The Pharisees—Religious Legalists

- Probably derived from a group of the faithful called the *Hasidim*.
- Name means "to separate."
- Shared similar views with the Essenes, but chose to stay within the

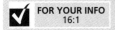

larger society. Nevertheless, many chose to study the Law on their own, having lost respect for the priesthood as a result of its corruption.

- Many served on the council (see Acts 6:12).
- Considered the doctors of the Law; scribes were considered laymen.
- Collected and preserved the Talmud and the Mishnah, voluminous products of oral tradition and Old Testament commentary.
- By reputation, legalistic and fanatically devoted to rabbinic tradition. Some even refused to eat with non-Pharisees for fear of being contaminated by food not rendered ritually clean.
- Like the Herodians, favored local political autonomy.
- Differed with the Sadducees over the doctrine of the resurrection.
- Understood the coming kingdom as a literal fulfillment of the promise to David for a King to reign over Israel forever.
- Maintained an elaborate theology of angels, believing them to intervene in human affairs.

The Sadducees—The Urban Elite

- May have derived from Zadok, high priest under King David.
- Tended to represent the aristocrats, priests, merchants, and urban elite in Jerusalem and other cities in Judea.
- Hostile to Jesus and His followers.
- Many served on the council. Most of the high priests in the days of Jesus and the apostles were Sadducees.
- Denied the resurrection or life after death, along with the doctrines of everlasting punishment and a literal kingdom.
- Denied that God controls history, insisting on free will and the responsibility of humans to make wise choices according to the Law.
- Held only to the Law of Moses (the first five books of the Old Testament) as supremely authoritative.
- Denied the existence of angels.

The Zealots—Firebrands of Revolution

- Ardent nationalists who awaited an opportunity to revolt against Rome.
- Resisted paying taxes to Rome or to the temple.
- One particular tax revolt against Rome, led by Judas the Galilean (6 B.C.), secured Galilee's reputation as a seedbed of revolutionaries.
- Blamed by some for the collapse of Judea to Rome in the war of A.D. 66–70. Josephus, a Jewish historian, claimed that they degenerated into mere assassins or *sicarii* ("dagger-men").
- Sided with the Pharisees in supporting Jewish Law.
- Opposed the Herodians and Sadducees, who tried to maintain the political status quo.
- Intolerant of the Essenes and later the Christians for their tendencies toward nonviolence.
- Two recruited by Jesus were Judas Iscariot and Simon the Cananite.

The Essenes—Detached Purists

- A sect of ascetics that thrived between the middle of the second century B.C. until the Jewish-Roman war in A.D. 66–70.
- Once members of the *Hasidim,* but unlike the Pharisees separated from society, withdrawing into monastic communities like Qumran where the Dead Sea scrolls were found.
- Known today mostly through secondary sources.
- Lived in societies that held property in common.
- Believed in the immortality of the soul, angels, and an elaborate scheme of end-times prophecies. Some were looking for as many as three different Messiahs.
- Known for celibacy, pacifism, opposition to slavery, caring for their own sick and elderly, trading only within their own sect, simplicity in meals and dress, and the rejection of all ostentatious display.
- Paid more attention to ceremonial purity than did even the Pharisees, and carefully guarded the Sabbath.
- Practiced ritual baptism and a communal dinner called the messianic banquet.
- May have influenced some early Christian practices and rituals. ◆

In addition to the regional and local politics of Palestine, Jesus and His followers lived under the enormous influence of Rome. See *"Roman Politics in the First Century A.D.," Luke 22:25.*

14So they said, "Some *say* John the Baptist, some Elijah,
and others Jeremiah or one of the prophets."
15He said to them, "But who do you say that I am?"
16Simon Peter answered and said, "You are the Christ, the
Son of the living God."
17Jesus answered and said to him, "Blessed are you, Simon Bar-Jonah, for flesh and blood has not revealed *this* to

16:18

you, but My Father who is in heaven.
18And I also say to you that you are Peter,
and on this rock I will build My church, and the gates of
Hades shall not prevail against it. 19And I will give you the
keys of the kingdom of heaven, and whatever you bind on
earth will be bound in heaven, and whatever you loose on
earth will be loosed[a] in heaven."
20Then He commanded His disciples that they should tell
no one that He was Jesus the Christ.

Following Christ Means Sacrifice

21From that time Jesus began to show to His disciples that
He must go to Jerusalem, and suffer many things from the
elders and chief priests and scribes, and be killed, and be
raised the third day.

16:22–23
see pg. 74

22Then Peter took Him aside and began
to rebuke Him, saying, "Far be it from
You, Lord; this shall not happen to You!"
23But He turned and said to Peter, "Get behind Me, Satan!
You are an offense to Me, for you are not mindful of the
things of God, but the things of men."
24Then Jesus said to His disciples, "If anyone desires to
come after Me, let him deny himself, and take up his cross,
and follow Me. 25For whoever desires to save his life will
lose it, but whoever loses his life for My sake will find it.
26For what profit is it to a man if he gains the whole world,
and loses his own soul? Or what will a man give in exchange for his soul? 27For the Son of Man will come in the
glory of His Father with His angels, and then He will reward each according to his works. 28Assuredly, I say to you,
there are some standing here who shall not taste death till
they see the Son of Man coming in His kingdom."

"FOR WHAT PROFIT IS IT TO A MAN IF HE GAINS THE WHOLE WORLD, AND LOSES HIS OWN SOUL?"
—Matthew 16:26

CHAPTER 17

The Transfiguration

1Now after six days Jesus took Peter, James, and John his
brother, led them up on a high mountain by themselves;
2and He was transfigured before them. His face shone like

(Bible text continued on page 74)

16:19 [a]*Or will have been bound . . . will have been loosed*

CONSIDER THIS
16:18

"The Gates of Hell"

Jesus referred to "the gates of Hades" (hell) in His bold statement to Peter (v. 18). For Matthew's original readers, the word "gates" held special significance.

Ancient cities erected walls to protect themselves from invaders. Here and there along the walls they inserted massive gates to allow traffic in and out. In times of trouble, they could close the gates against attacking armies or bandits.

City gates, then, tended to be thoroughfares through which communications and commerce passed with frequency. Not surprisingly, bazaars and forums tended to congregate around a city's gates, so that they became an important arena in a town's public life. Goods were traded there and decision-makers gathered to hear news and deliberate on events of the day. Such gates exist to this day in some cities of the world.

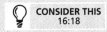

Given this phenomenon, "gates" became a metaphor signifying the economic and political life of a walled city. The influential and powerful did their business "in the gates." For example, the husband of the virtuous women of Proverbs 31 is "known in the gates, when he sits among the elders of the land" (Prov. 31:23). Boaz, the intended husband of Ruth, went to the gate to buy a marriage license (Ruth 4:1–12; also Deut. 25:7). War plans were devised and military treaties signed in the gates (Judg. 5:8, 11). Kings sat in the gates to address their people (2 Sam. 19:8). Even conspirators against kings hatched their plots and were exposed in the gates (Esth. 2:19–23).

So when Jesus spoke of the gates of Hades, He was drawing on a powerful image. Matthew's original readers would have seen it as a political metaphor, the way we use the terms *City Hall, the White House,* or *the Capitol* today. For them, the gates of Hades were not just a spiritual abstraction but actual forces of evil at work among human systems—the Roman government, for instance. While not evil in and of itself, first-century government was quickly becoming corrupted and also anti-Christian.

Jesus was alluding to a spiritual warfare of cosmic proportions. His followers are pitted against the powers of hell itself, which not only attack individual believers but seek to corrupt institutions, enlisting them in their campaign against Christ. Satan's guises can take many forms, as a look at any day's news will attest. (See "Spiritual Realities Beyond You," Matt. 8:29.)

Fortunately, Jesus also promised that in the end the gates of Hades would not succeed. That offers great hope to believers who live in difficult places and contend for good against powerful entities that, in ways known and unknown, are backed by spiritual forces of wickedness. In the midst of the fight Jesus has declared: "I will build My church!" ◆

the sun, and His clothes became as white as the light. 3And
behold, Moses and Elijah appeared to them, talking with
Him. 4Then Peter answered and said to Jesus, "Lord, it is
good for us to be here; if You wish, let us[a] make here three
tabernacles: one for You, one for Moses, and one for Elijah."

17:5 see pg. 76

5While he was still speaking, behold, a
bright cloud overshadowed them; and
suddenly a voice came out of the cloud, saying, "This is My
beloved Son, in whom I am well pleased. Hear Him!" 6And
when the disciples heard *it,* they fell on their faces and were
greatly afraid. 7But Jesus came and touched them and said,
"Arise, and do not be afraid." 8When they had lifted up
their eyes, they saw no one but Jesus only.

9Now as they came down from the mountain, Jesus commanded them, saying, "Tell the vision to no one until the Son of Man is risen from the dead."

10And His disciples asked Him, saying, "Why then do the scribes say that Elijah must come first?"

11Jesus answered and said to them, "Indeed, Elijah is
coming first[a] and will restore all things. 12But I say to you
that Elijah has come already, and they did not know him
but did to him whatever they wished. Likewise the Son of
Man is also about to suffer at their hands." 13Then the disciples understood that He spoke to them of John the Baptist.

17:4 [a]NU-Text reads *I will.* *17:11* [a]NU-Text omits *first.*

CONSIDER THIS
16:22–23

Living Within Your Limits

Are you impulsive? Are you quick to step forward with a plan of action? As the exchange between Peter and the Lord in vv. 22–23 shows there were times when Peter liked to take charge quickly and set the agenda for himself and others. But just as often he found himself in over his head:

- *When Jesus came walking on water to a storm-tossed boat that held His terrified disciples, Peter demanded that He show that it was He by bidding Peter also to walk on water. After a few steps, Peter noticed the wind and the waves and promptly sank, requiring Jesus to rescue him again (Matt. 14:22–32).*
- *He overstated his commitment to Christ, claiming that "even if I have to die with You, I will not deny You!" (26:35). Yet only a few hours later he denied having any association with the Lord (26:69–75).*
- *He took charge of defending Jesus against Roman soldiers when they came to arrest Him—even though he*

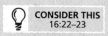

Jesus Heals an Epileptic Boy

14And when they had come to the multitude, a man came
to Him, kneeling down to Him and saying, 15"Lord, have
mercy on my son, for he is an epileptic[a] and suffers severely; for he often falls into the fire and often into the water. 16So I brought him to Your disciples, but they could not
cure him."
17Then Jesus answered and said, "O faithless and perverse
generation, how long shall I be with you? How long shall I
bear with you? Bring him here to Me." 18And Jesus rebuked
the demon, and it came out of him; and the child was cured
from that very hour.
19Then the disciples came to Jesus privately and said,
"Why could we not cast it out?"
20So Jesus said to them, "Because of your unbelief;[a] for assuredly, I say to you, if you have faith as a mustard seed,
you will say to this mountain, 'Move from here to there,'
and it will move; and nothing will be impossible for you.
21However, this kind does not go out except by prayer and
fasting."[a]

Jesus Predicts His Betrayal

22Now while they were staying[a] in Galilee, Jesus said to
them, "The Son of Man is about to be betrayed into the

(Bible text continued on page 77)

17:15 [a]Literally *moonstruck* *17:20* [a]NU-Text reads *little faith.* *17:21* [a]NU-Text omits this verse. *17:22* [a]NU-Text reads *gathering together.*

had failed to "watch and pray" with Christ as had been requested (26:36–46; John 18:1–11).

- *He refused to allow Jesus to wash his feet at the Last Supper, then called on Him to wash his hands and his head as well (John 13:5–11).*

Eventually Peter's leadership skills were captured in a more controlled spirit and he became a significant figure in the early church. Despite many false starts as a result of Peter's impetuous nature, Jesus enlisted this impulsive but loyal follower to "feed My sheep" (John 21:17).

Have your personality and skills become more mature and thoughtful? Or are you still in the raw stage, ready to jump at the first idea that occurs to you? ◆

Peter was not the only man who made an unlikely candidate for Jesus' "leadership training program." See "Would You Choose These for Leaders?" Matt. 26:35–74.

"O FAITHLESS AND PERVERSE GENERATION, HOW LONG SHALL I BE WITH YOU?"
—Matthew 17:17

FOR YOUR INFO
17:5

THE NAMES OF JESUS

The voice that the disciples heard during the Transfiguration said that Jesus was "My beloved Son" (v. 5). This term indicates a unique relationship that Jesus has with God the Father. Elsewhere Scripture calls Jesus by other names and titles to indicate other aspects of His nature, character, and roles:

Name or Title	Description
Adam (1 Cor. 15:45)	The first Adam brought death through sin; Jesus, "the last Adam," brought life through His righteousness.
The Alpha and the Omega (Rev. 21:6)	Jesus is eternal, "the Beginning and the End." Alpha is the first letter in the Greek alphabet, omega is the last.
Apostle (Heb. 3:1)	"Messenger." Jesus came to bring the good news of salvation to humanity.
The bread of life (John 6:35, 48)	Jesus is the heavenly manna, the spiritual food, given by the Father to those who ask for it.
The chief cornerstone (Eph. 2:20)	Jesus is the foundation of the church.
The Chief Shepherd (1 Pet. 5:4)	The title that Peter called Jesus, indicating His oversight of His "flock," the church.
The Christ (Matt. 1:1, 17; 16:16; Luke 2:11; John 1:40)	From the Greek word *Christos,* "Messiah" or "Anointed One." Jesus fulfills the Old Testament promise of a Messiah.
The Consolation of Israel (Luke 2:25)	Jesus came to bring comfort to the nation (Is. 40:1–2).
The firstborn from the dead (Col. 1:18)	Jesus overcame death in order to give life to believers.
The firstborn over all creation (Col. 1:15)	As God's Son, Jesus rules over everything that exists.
The good shepherd (John 10:11, 14; compare Heb. 13:20)	An image that Jesus used to describe His relationship to His people.
The head of the body, the church (Eph. 1:22–23; 4:15–16; Col. 1:18)	Jesus is the leader of His people and the source of their life.
High Priest (Heb. 3:1)	Like the Old Testament high priest, Jesus stands between God and people to offer an acceptable sacrifice for sin.
The Holy One of God (Mark 1:24; John 6:69)	Jesus is the sinless Messiah promised by God.
I AM (John 8:58)	A name by which God made Himself known to Moses (Ex. 3:14), related to the verb "to be."
The image of the invisible God (Col. 1:15)	Jesus expresses God in bodily form.
Immanuel (Matt. 1:23)	"God with us" (Is. 7:14).
Jesus (Matt. 1:21; Luke 1:30; Acts 9:5)	The name that God instructed Joseph and Mary to call their Son.
King of Kings and Lord of Lords (Rev. 19:16)	The formal title that Jesus has received, indicating His supremacy as the one to whom "every knee should bow" (Phil. 2:9–11).
King of the Jews (Matt. 2:2; 27:11–12; John 19:19)	As Messiah, Jesus is Israel's king, fulfilling God's promises to David (2 Sam. 7:12–16).
The Lamb of God (John 1:29, 35)	Jesus became the atoning sacrifice for sin.
The light of the world (John 9:5)	Jesus brings truth and hope to light in the midst of spiritual darkness.
Lord (Luke 2:11; 1 Cor. 2:8; Phil. 2:11)	A title indicating ultimate sovereignty.
Mediator between God and men (1 Tim. 2:5)	Jesus reestablishes the relationship between God and people.

Continued

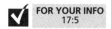

hands of men, 23and they will kill Him, and the third day
He will be raised up." And they were exceedingly sorrowful.

Jesus and Taxation

17:24–27 see pg. 78

24When they had come to Capernaum,[a]
those who received the *temple* tax came
to Peter and said, "Does your Teacher not pay the *temple*
tax?"
25He said, "Yes."
And when he had come into the house, Jesus anticipated
him, saying, "What do you think, Simon? From whom do
the kings of the earth take customs or taxes, from their sons
or from strangers?"
26Peter said to Him, "From strangers."
Jesus said to him, "Then the sons are free. 27Nevertheless,
lest we offend them, go to the sea, cast in a hook, and take
the fish that comes up first. And when you have opened its
mouth, you will find a piece of money;[a] take that and give it
to them for Me and you."

CHAPTER 18

"Who Is Greatest in the Kingdom?"

1At that time the disciples came to Jesus, saying, "Who
then is greatest in the kingdom of heaven?"
2Then Jesus called a little child to Him, set him in the

17:24 [a]NU-Text reads *Capharnaum* (here and elsewhere). *17:27* [a]Greek *stater,* the exact amount to pay the temple tax (didrachma) for two

Continued

Name or Title	Description
The only Begotten of the Father (John 1:14)	Jesus is God's only Son.
The Prophet (Mark 6:15; John 7:40; Acts 3:22)	Jesus is the leader that God promised to "raise up" like Moses (Deut. 18:15, 18–19).
Rabbi (John 1:38; 3:2)	Friends and enemies alike recognized Jesus as Teacher.
Savior (Luke 1:47; 2:11)	Jesus came to save people from their sins.
Seed (of Abraham; Gal. 3:16)	God made promises to Abraham and his "Seed," whom Paul identified as Christ (Gen. 13:15; 17:8).
The Son of Abraham (Matt. 1:1)	Jesus descended from Abraham and fulfills the promises of God to Abraham (Gen. 22:18).
The Son of David (Matt. 1:1)	Jesus descended from David and fulfills the promises of God to David (2 Sam. 7:12–16).
The Son of God (John 1:24; 9:35–37)	Jesus is one of three Persons of the Trinity (Father, Son, and Holy Spirit).
The Son of Man (Matt. 18:11; John 1:51)	Though fully God, Jesus took on a human body (compare Phil. 2:5–8).
The Word (John 1:1; Rev. 19:13)	Jesus is fully God and therefore is the full expression of God.

midst of them, 3and said, "Assuredly, I say to you, unless
you are converted and become as little children, you will by
no means enter the kingdom of heaven. 4Therefore whoever
humbles himself as this little child is the greatest in the
kingdom of heaven. 5Whoever receives one little child like
this in My name receives Me.

6"But whoever causes one of these little ones who believe
in Me to sin, it would be better for him if a millstone were
hung around his neck, and he were drowned in the depth
of the sea. 7Woe to the world because of offenses! For offenses must come, but woe to that man by whom the offense comes!

18:8–9

8"If your hand or foot causes you to sin,
cut it off and cast *it* from you. It is better
for you to enter into life lame or maimed, rather than having two hands or two feet, to be cast into the everlasting

CONSIDER THIS
17:24–27

JESUS AND TAXATION

The odd episode in vv. 24–27 turns out to be a subtle and winsome reminder that Jesus claimed to be God. It's also a lesson in the proper exercise of moral liberty.

The temple tax of half a shekel was assessed annually on all Jews 20 years old and above. It paid for the support of the temple system (Ex. 30:13–15). Apparently Jesus and Peter had not yet paid their taxes, though Peter's response to the tax collectors indicated that they soon would (Matt. 17:24–25).

The irony, however, is that the temple tax collectors were demanding taxes from the Messiah Himself! How ludicrous—as Jesus pointed out in His question to Peter about who is taxed by a ruler (v. 25). As God's Son, Jesus was the Lord of the temple; technically, He was exempt from taxation.

God put His stamp of approval on Jesus' reasoning with the miracle of the coin (v. 27). Peter found "a piece of

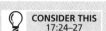

fire. 9And if your eye causes you to sin, pluck it out and cast
it from you. It is better for you to enter into life with one
eye, rather than having two eyes, to be cast into hell fire.
10"Take heed that you do not despise one of these little
ones, for I say to you that in heaven their angels always see
the face of My Father who is in heaven. 11For the Son of
Man has come to save that which was lost.[a]
12"What do you think? If a man has a hundred sheep, and
one of them goes astray, does he not leave the ninety-nine
and go to the mountains to seek the one that is straying?
13And if he should find it, assuredly, I say to you, he rejoices
more over that *sheep* than over the ninety-nine that did not
go astray. 14Even so it is not the will of your Father who is
in heaven that one of these little ones should perish.
15"Moreover if your brother sins against you, go and tell

18:11 [a]NU-Text omits this verse.

money" (a stater, a four-drachma coin) in the fish's mouth—the exact amount needed for the two of them. The collectors were satisfied, and the transaction cost Peter and Jesus nothing.

But consider: Jesus voluntarily paid the tax to avoid offending the religious leaders that the collectors represented (v. 27). In doing so, He demonstrated something about how His followers should live.

We as Christians are properly free in many areas because of our relationship with God. We are not bound by legalistic rules about eating, drinking, or special observances. Nonetheless, we must be careful not to use our liberty in a manner that offends other people. If the Son of God paid a voluntary tax in order to avoid offending those who did not understand who He was, how much more should we, as God's children, bend over backwards at times to avoid offending those who do not understand our liberty? ◆

Scripture offers help for believers in handling the "gray" areas of life in which God has prescribed no specific behavior. See "Matters of Conscience," Rom. 14:1–23; and "Gray Areas," 1 Cor. 8:1–13.

There were so many taxes during Jesus' time that the Jews were probably paying between 30 and 40 percent of their income on taxes and religious dues. See "Taxes," Mark 12:14.

EXAGGERATING TO MAKE A POINT

CONSIDER THIS 18:8–9 **Was Jesus speaking literally when He told His followers to cut off their hand or foot if it caused them to sin (v. 8)? Did He intend for them actually to rip out their eye if it caused them to sin (v. 9)? No, Jesus was using a customary teaching method called *hyperbole*—exaggerating to make a point. He frequently spoke in that manner, perhaps to hold His listeners' attention, to touch their imagination, or to show a bit of humor.**

After all, it's a bit silly to imagine what would happen if people actually followed these instructions literally. It's hard to sin without using a hand, a foot, or an eye, so it wouldn't be long before we all would be paralyzed and blind. Without our faculties, we simply couldn't function. And that's precisely Jesus' point. Sin makes it difficult if not impossible to function spiritually in the way God created us. Moreover, sin can do what no amputation can—keep us from God. That's why, to catch Jesus' serious point, it *would* be better to do without an arm or a leg than to live forever apart from God.

SEVENTY TIMES SEVEN—STILL NOT ENOUGH!

CONSIDER THIS 18:21–35 **If Peter gasped when Jesus told him to forgive his brother up to seventy times seven times (v. 22), he must have gagged when he heard the parable that followed.**

The first servant owed 10,000 talents to the king (v. 24). The second servant owed 100 denarii to the first servant (v. 28). This was an extraordinary difference in indebtedness. A talent was a lot of money, perhaps $1,000 in today's currency. But in that culture, it probably represented far more. A talent equalled 6,000 denarii, and one denarius was what a common laborer could earn in one day, about 16¢ to 18¢.

So the first servant owed at least $10 million, but from the standpoint of common wages, *he would have had to work 60 million days to pay off his debt!* By contrast, the second servant owed $16 to $18, which he could earn in 100 days. In other words, the first servant owed the king more than the second servant owed the first servant by a ratio of at least 600,000-to-1!

Somehow, after Jesus finished that parable, seventy times seven probably didn't look so bad to Peter!

The power of forgiveness is immeasurable. It is a power that Jesus used often and even delegated to His followers. See "The Power of Forgiveness," Matt. 9:4–8.

The talent was one of several units of money in the ancient world. See the table, "Money in the New Testament," Rev. 16:21.

him his fault between you and him alone. If he hears you,
you have gained your brother. 16But if he will not hear, take
with you one or two more, that 'by the mouth of two or
three witnesses every word may be established.'[a] 17And if he
refuses to hear them, tell *it* to the church. But if he refuses
even to hear the church, let him be to you like a heathen
and a tax collector.

18"Assuredly, I say to you, whatever you bind on earth
will be bound in heaven, and whatever you loose on earth
will be loosed in heaven.

19"Again I say[a] to you that if two of you agree on earth
concerning anything that they ask, it will be done for them
by My Father in heaven. 20For where two or three are gathered together in My name, I am there in the midst of them."

About Forgiveness

18:21–35 21Then Peter came to Him and said,
"Lord, how often shall my brother sin
against me, and I forgive him? Up to seven times?"

22Jesus said to him, "I do not say to you, up to seven
times, but up to seventy times seven. 23Therefore the kingdom of heaven is like a certain king who wanted to settle
accounts with his servants. 24And when he had begun to
settle accounts, one was brought to him who owed him ten
thousand talents. 25But as he was not able to pay, his master
commanded that he be sold, with his wife and children and
all that he had, and that payment be made. 26The servant
therefore fell down before him, saying, 'Master, have patience with me, and I will pay you all.' 27Then the master of
that servant was moved with compassion, released him, and
forgave him the debt.

28"But that servant went out and found one of his fellow
servants who owed him a hundred denarii; and he laid
hands on him and took *him* by the throat, saying, 'Pay me
what you owe!' 29So his fellow servant fell down at his feet[a]
and begged him, saying, 'Have patience with me, and I will
pay you all.'[b] 30And he would not, but went and threw him
into prison till he should pay the debt. 31So when his fellow
servants saw what had been done, they were very grieved,
and came and told their master all that had been done.
32Then his master, after he had called him, said to him, 'You
wicked servant! I forgave you all that debt because you
begged me. 33Should you not also have had compassion on
your fellow servant, just as I had pity on you?' 34And his
master was angry, and delivered him to the torturers until
he should pay all that was due to him.

35"So My heavenly Father also will do to you if each of

18:16 [a]Deuteronomy 19:15 *18:19* [a]NU-Text and M-Text read *Again, assuredly, I say.*
18:29 [a]NU-Text omits *at his feet.* [b]NU-Text and M-Text omit *all.*

you, from his heart, does not forgive his brother his trespasses."[a]

CHAPTER 19

Marriage and Divorce

19:1–15
see pg. 82

1Now it came to pass, when Jesus had
finished these sayings, *that* He departed
from Galilee and came to the region of Judea beyond the
Jordan. 2And great multitudes followed Him, and He healed
them there.
3The Pharisees also came to Him, testing Him, and saying
to Him, "Is it lawful for a man to divorce his wife for *just*
any reason?"
4And He answered and said to them, "Have you not read
that He who made[a] *them* at the beginning 'made them male
and female,'[b] 5and said, 'For this reason a man shall leave
his father and mother and be joined to his wife, and the two
shall become one flesh' ?[a] 6So then, they are no longer two
but one flesh. Therefore what God has joined together, let
not man separate."
7They said to Him, "Why then did Moses command to
give a certificate of divorce, and to put her away?"
8He said to them, "Moses, because of the hardness of your
hearts, permitted you to divorce your wives, but from the
beginning it was not so. 9And I say to you, whoever divorces his wife, except for sexual immorality,[a] and marries
another, commits adultery; and whoever marries her who is
divorced commits adultery."
10His disciples said to Him, "If such is the case of the man
with *his* wife, it is better not to marry."
11But He said to them, "All cannot accept this saying, but
only *those* to whom it has been given: 12For there are eunuchs who were born thus from *their* mother's womb, and
there are eunuchs who were made eunuchs by men, and
there are eunuchs who have made themselves eunuchs for
the kingdom of heaven's sake. He who is able to accept *it*,
let him accept *it*."

Jesus Blesses Children

19:13–15

13Then little children were brought to
Him that He might put *His* hands on

(Bible text continued on page 84)

18:35 [a]NU-Text omits *his trespasses.* *19:4* [a]NU-Text reads *created.* [b]Genesis 1:27; 5:2
19:5 [a]Genesis 2:24 *19:9* [a]Or *fornication*

"WHAT GOD HAS JOINED TOGETHER, LET NOT MAN SEPARATE."
—Matthew 19:6

Please Bless Our Children

A CLOSER LOOK
19:13–15

In Jesus' day it was customary to ask famous rabbis to bless one's children. See "The Friend of Children" at Mark 10:13–16.

CONSIDER THIS
19:1–15

The Challenge of Commitment

Commitment is in jeopardy these days. Some even call it the "C" word, as if to shame it as something we won't even acknowledge. After all, the demands and costs are too great. Today, convenience usually wins out over the sacrifice involved in being committed to someone or something.

The situation was no less confused in Jesus' day. As He began to unveil a new way of life for His followers, critics appeared and challenged Him on the difficulties of keeping the marriage commitment (vv. 3, 7). Even His disciples quivered as they perceived the costs of maintaining one's marriage vows (v. 10). Later, they wanted to send away some bothersome children in order to deal with more "important" things (v. 13). It seems that Jesus was surrounded by men who were a little unsure about domestic matters.

The discussion of divorce followed appropriately on the heels of Jesus' remarks about the merits of boundless forgiveness (18:21–35). What better way to lead into the topic of commitment? Jesus didn't ignore the problems and failures of human relationships. Those very shortcomings are what make forgiveness—and commitment—crucial.

YOU ARE THERE
19:14

Children and Childcare

When Jesus welcomed the little children (v. 14), He was making a major statement to everyone standing by about the value and significance of children.

Perhaps the disciples, who rebuked the mothers who brought their babies to Jesus (v. 13), had adopted the prevailing Graeco-Roman view of childhood as an insignificant phase of life. To be sure, children were necessary for a family's survival, but they were not valued for their own sake.

Indeed, unwanted infants in pagan cultures were routinely abandoned on roadsides and at garbage dumps. Tragically, gender and economics often determined an infant's fate: more girls than boys were exposed since girls represented a future financial burden while boys could eventually contribute to the family's income.

Most exposed infants died but a few were rescued and raised to become slaves, gladiators, or prostitutes. Children were held in such low esteem in Jesus' time that some professional beggars collected exposed children, mutilated them, and then used their misery to gain sympathy and thus increase profits from their begging.

However, among the Jews children were traditionally

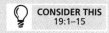

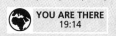

Those lessons were reinforced in Jesus' next encounter, with a rich man who wanted to ensure his possession of eternal life (19:16–30). The man proposed rule-keeping as the standard by which he should be judged, but Jesus countered with an appeal for service (v. 21). True wealth involved a higher commitment—serving the Lord and others rather than the idol of material gain (vv. 23, 29).

Followers of Christ need to be known for their commitment—to marriage, to family, to community, to work, above all to Christ. Such loyalty often means messy obedience, but it is the way of Christ. How desperately that is needed in a day when people make vows of convenience rather than commitment. ◆

Commitment makes all the difference when it comes to family relationships. See "Family: A Call to Long-term Work," Eph. 5:21—6:4.

Commitment is one of the hallmarks of a godly "workstyle." See Titus 2:9–10.

Peter echoed Jesus' words on marital faithfulness in his instructions to husbands, 1 Pet. 2:11–17.

considered a blessing from God, and childlessness a curse. In fact, children were so desired that barrenness was grounds for divorce.

Jewish fathers had ultimate authority over all aspects of their children's lives, but both fathers and mothers were instructed by the Law to nurture and care for their children. Fathers were particularly obligated to teach their children God's commands and to raise them as members of God's chosen people (Deut. 6:6–8). In return, children were obliged to honor both mother and father (5:16).

Mothers usually took care of infants who typically nursed until the age of two or three. In some wealthy Greek and Roman homes, women employed wet nurses and, as the children grew, slaves who were assigned to their total care. Poor women, however, worked while their babies hung from slings on their backs. But as soon as the children were old enough, they were taught to help.

First-century women did not have to confront the childcare dilemma faced by many women today. Their work and their homes were tightly linked, so they did not have to surmount the challenges of specialization and separation. ◆

"LET THE LITTLE CHILDREN COME TO ME. . . ."
—Matthew 19:14

19:14
see pg. 82

them and pray, but the disciples rebuked
them. 14But Jesus said, "Let the little children come to Me, and do not forbid them; for of such is the
kingdom of heaven." 15And He laid *His* hands on them and
departed from there.

A Rich Young Man's Question

19:16–26

16Now behold, one came and said to
Him, "Good[a] Teacher, what good thing
shall I do that I may have eternal life?"
17So He said to him, "Why do you call Me good?[a] No one
is good but One, *that is,* God.[b] But if you want to enter into
life, keep the commandments."
18He said to Him, "Which ones?"
Jesus said, "'You shall not murder,' 'You shall not commit
adultery,' 'You shall not steal,' 'You shall not bear false witness,' 19'Honor your father and *your* mother,'[a] and, 'You
shall love your neighbor as yourself.' "[b]
20The young man said to Him, "All these things I have
kept from my youth.[a] What do I still lack?"
21Jesus said to him, "If you want to be perfect, go, sell
what you have and give to the poor, and you will have treasure in heaven; and come, follow Me."
22But when the young man heard that saying, he went
away sorrowful, for he had great possessions.
23Then Jesus said to His disciples, "Assuredly, I say to you
that it is hard for a rich man to enter the kingdom of
heaven. 24And again I say to you, it is easier for a camel to
go through the eye of a needle than for a rich man to enter
the kingdom of God."
25When His disciples heard *it,* they were greatly astonished, saying, "Who then can be saved?"
26But Jesus looked at *them* and said to them, "With men
this is impossible, but with God all things are possible."

**"It is easier for a camel to go through the eye of a needle than for a rich man to enter the kingdom of God."
—Matthew 19:24**

Rewards for the Twelve

27Then Peter answered and said to Him, "See, we have left
all and followed You. Therefore what shall we have?"

19:16 [a]NU-Text omits *Good.* *19:17* [a]NU-Text reads *Why do you ask Me about what is good?* [b]NU-Text reads *There is One who is good.* *19:19* [a]Exodus 20:12–16; Deuteronomy 5:16–20 [b]Leviticus 19:18 *19:20* [a]NU-Text omits *from my youth.*

"What Do I Still Lack?"

A CLOSER LOOK
19:16–26

The rich young ruler asked the classic question of many who appear to have it all: "What do I still lack?" (v. 20). "The Man Who Had It All—Almost" (Mark 10:17–27) discusses the Lord's mysterious response and challenging perspective on wealth. In a similar situation (Luke 10:25–37), Jesus urged people to put feet on their good intentions.

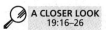

28So Jesus said to them, "Assuredly I say to you, that in
the regeneration, when the Son of Man sits on the throne of
His glory, you who have followed Me will also sit on twelve
19:29
thrones, judging the twelve tribes of Israel. 29And everyone who has left houses
or brothers or sisters or father or mother or wife[a] or children or lands, for My name's sake, shall receive a hundredfold, and inherit eternal life. 30But many *who are* first will be
last, and the last first.

CHAPTER 20

A Parable about Wages

20:1–16
see pg. 86
1"For the kingdom of heaven is like a
landowner who went out early in the
morning to hire laborers for his vineyard. 2Now when he
had agreed with the laborers for a denarius a day, he sent
them into his vineyard. 3And he went out about the third
hour and saw others standing idle in the marketplace, 4and
said to them, 'You also go into the vineyard, and whatever is
right I will give you.' So they went. 5Again he went out
about the sixth and the ninth hour, and did likewise. 6And
about the eleventh hour he went out and found others
standing idle,[a] and said to them, 'Why have you been
standing here idle all day?' 7They said to him, 'Because no
one hired us.' He said to them, 'You also go into the vineyard, and whatever is right you will receive.'[a]
8"So when evening had come, the owner of the vineyard
said to his steward, 'Call the laborers and give them *their*
wages, beginning with the last to the first.' 9And when those
came who *were hired* about the eleventh hour, they each received a denarius. 10But when the first came, they supposed
that they would receive more; and they likewise received
each a denarius. 11And when they had received *it,* they
complained against the landowner, 12saying, 'These last *men*
have worked *only* one hour, and you made them equal to us
who have borne the burden and the heat of the day.' 13But
he answered one of them and said, 'Friend, I am doing you
no wrong. Did you not agree with me for a denarius? 14Take
what is yours and go your way. I wish to give to this last
man *the same* as to you. 15Is it not lawful for me to do what

19:29 [a]NU-Text omits *or wife.* *20:6* [a]NU-Text omits *idle.* *20:7* [a]NU-Text omits the last clause of this verse.

A Pushy Mother

CONSIDER THIS
20:20–23
Overzealous mothers are not exclusive to the twentieth century, as the incident in vv. 20–23 makes clear. The woman's name remains unknown; she is remembered only as the mother of Zebedee's sons (James and John). Perhaps she was so caught up in managing her sons' lives that she had no other life, and therefore required no other designation than "mother." Naturally, she would have claimed that she only wanted what was best for her sons.

But when Jesus found out what she was seeking, He gave her and her sons a warning. He knew that suffering had to come before glory. Could James and John endure that suffering? The two men were quick to promise that they would. (Perhaps their mother prompted them to say so by giving them a stern look.) Jesus assured them that they would have the chance to back up their words.

Perhaps later James and John regretted making such bold promises. But how often are we like them—eager to promise whatever we have to in order to get what we want? Perhaps worse, how often do we push our children into things based on our own needs for pride and significance?

An Eternal Inheritance

A CLOSER LOOK
19:29
To have Christ is to have everything *(v. 29). "What's in It for Me?" (Eph. 1:11) describes the inheritance we will enjoy as God's children.*

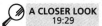

I wish with my own things? Or is your eye evil because I am good?' [16]So the last will be first, and the first last. For many are called, but few chosen."[a]

Jesus Predicts His Death

[17]Now Jesus, going up to Jerusalem, took the twelve disciples aside on the road and said to them, [18]"Behold, we are going up to Jerusalem, and the Son of Man will be betrayed to the chief priests and to the scribes; and they will condemn Him to death, [19]and deliver Him to the Gentiles to mock and to scourge and to crucify. And the third day He will rise again."

20:16 [a]NU-Text omits the last sentence of this verse.

CONSIDER THIS
20:1–16

Jesus and Unjust Pay

Anyone who feels that they are not paid what they are worth can appreciate the reaction of the workers in the parable Jesus told (vv. 1–16). He spoke of an employer who hired workers for a full day, others for two-thirds of a day, others for half a day, and others for even less. Yet he paid them all the same (v. 9–11)! Naturally those who had worked longer demanded, "What's going on here?" (vv. 11–12). Good question!

The first thing to notice is that none of the workers was employed before the landowner hired them (vv. 3, 6, 7). The fact that they got a job was due to the employer's goodwill, not to anything they brought to the situation. Furthermore, the landowner promised the first group fair wages of a day's pay (a denarius, *v. 2; see "Money in the New Testament," Rev. 16:21) and the rest an undetermined amount ("whatever is right"). As it turned out, he paid everyone an entire day's wage.*

Jesus was trying to help His followers grasp something important about grace in the kingdom of God. They had been asking about the kingdom's makeup and benefits earlier (Matt. 19:16, 25, 27). Jesus was not encouraging unjust pay scales and discrimination. He was merely illustrating the nature of God's grace in terms that His followers could understand.

In the kingdom of God, grace is given because of the nature of the Giver, not the worthiness of the recipient. Receiving God's grace is a privilege for sinners—who, after all, really deserve nothing but condemnation. ◆

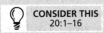

A Mother's Big Request

20:20–23 see pg. 85
20 Then the mother of Zebedee's sons
came to Him with her sons, kneeling
down and asking something from Him.
21 And He said to her, "What do you wish?"
She said to Him, "Grant that these two sons of mine may
sit, one on Your right hand and the other on the left, in
Your kingdom."
22 But Jesus answered and said, "You do not know what
you ask. Are you able to drink the cup that I am about to
drink, and be baptized with the baptism that I am baptized
with?"[a]
They said to Him, "We are able."
23 So He said to them, "You will indeed drink My cup, and
be baptized with the baptism that I am baptized with;[a] but
to sit on My right hand and on My left is not Mine to give,
but *it is for those* for whom it is prepared by My Father."
24 And when the ten heard *it,* they were greatly displeased
20:25–28
with the two brothers. 25 But Jesus called
them to *Himself* and said, "You know that
the rulers of the Gentiles lord it over them, and those who
are great exercise authority over them. 26 Yet it shall not be
so among you; but whoever desires to become great among
you, let him be your servant. 27 And whoever desires to be
20:28 see pg. 88
first among you, let him be your slave—
28 just as the Son of Man did not come to
be served, but to serve, and to give His life a ransom for
many."

Two Blind Men Healed at Jericho

20:29
29 Now as they went out of Jericho, a
great multitude followed Him. 30 And be-
hold, two blind men sitting by the road, when they heard
that Jesus was passing by, cried out, saying, "Have mercy on
us, O Lord, Son of David!"
31 Then the multitude warned them that they should be
quiet; but they cried out all the more, saying, "Have mercy
on us, O Lord, Son of David!"
32 So Jesus stood still and called them, and said, "What do
you want Me to do for you?"

20:22 [a]NU-Text omits *and be baptized with the baptism that I am baptized with.*
20:23 [a]NU-Text omits *and be baptized with the baptism that I am baptized with.*

The Dangerous Road to Jericho

A CLOSER LOOK 20:29 *Jericho was notorious for the beggars and thieves who camped nearby, plundering travelers along the narrow, winding mountain road up to Jerusalem. See Luke 10:30.*

SERVANT-LEADERS

CONSIDER THIS 20:25–28 **Responding to a controversy among the disciples (vv. 25–28), Jesus revealed a unique style of authority—servant leadership. What does it mean to be a "slave" in order to become great (v. 27)? What does it mean to define leadership in terms of servanthood? Jesus suggested that both involve seeking the highest good for others—good as evaluated from God's perspective.**

In light of Jesus' own example—particularly in giving up His own life as a "ransom for many" (v. 28)—we can observe that servant leadership means:

- **seeing ourselves as called by God to serve/lead others.**
- **knowing intimately the people we serve/lead.**
- **caring deeply about the people we serve/lead.**
- **being willing to sacrifice our own convenience to meet the needs of the people we serve/lead.**

33They said to Him, "Lord, that our eyes may be opened."
34So Jesus had compassion and touched their eyes. And immediately their eyes received sight, and they followed Him.

CHAPTER 21

Jesus Enters Jerusalem

21:1

1Now when they drew near Jerusalem,
and came to Bethphage,[a] at the Mount of
Olives, then Jesus sent two disciples, 2saying to them, "Go
into the village opposite you, and immediately you will find
a donkey tied, and a colt with her. Loose *them* and bring
them to Me. 3And if anyone says anything to you, you shall
say, 'The Lord has need of them,' and immediately he will
send them."
4All[a] this was done that it might be fulfilled which was
spoken by the prophet, saying:

5 "Tell the daughter of Zion,
'Behold, your King is coming to you,
Lowly, and sitting on a donkey,
A colt, the foal of a donkey.' "[a]

6So the disciples went and did as Jesus commanded them.
7They brought the donkey and the colt, laid their clothes on

21:1 [a]M-Text reads *Bethsphage.* *21:4* [a]NU-Text omits *All.* *21:5* [a]Zechariah 9:9

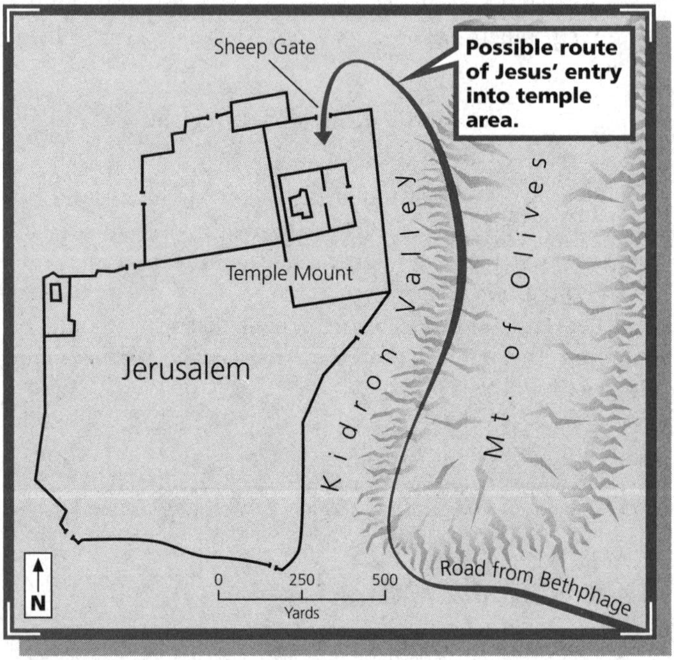

YOU ARE THERE 21:1 **JESUS' ENTRY**

QUOTE UNQUOTE

CONSIDER THIS 20:28 *Just as Jesus came to serve, He calls His followers to a life of service:*

That Christianity should be equated in the public mind, inside as well as outside the Church, with "organized religion" merely shows how far we have departed from the New Testament. For the last thing the Church exists to be is an organization for the religious. Its charter is to be the servant of the world.

John A.T. Robinson, *Honest To God*

Jesus used a powerful image when He compared true leadership to slavery. See "Slaves," Rom. 6:16.

21:8–11
see pg. 90

them, and set *Him*[a] on them. 8And a very
great multitude spread their clothes on
the road; others cut down branches from the trees and
spread *them* on the road. 9Then the multitudes who went
before and those who followed cried out, saying:

"Hosanna to the Son of David!
'Blessed *is* He who comes in the name of the Lord!'[a]
Hosanna in the highest!"

10And when He had come into Jerusalem, all the city was
moved, saying, "Who is this?"
11So the multitudes said, "This is Jesus, the prophet from
Nazareth of Galilee."

Jesus Purges the Temple

12Then Jesus went into the temple of God[a] and drove out
all those who bought and sold in the temple, and overturned the tables of the money changers and the seats of
those who sold doves. 13And He said to them, "It is written,
'My house shall be called a house of prayer,'[a] but you have
made it a 'den of thieves.' "[b]
14Then *the* blind and *the* lame came to Him in the temple,
and He healed them. 15But when the chief priests and
scribes saw the wonderful things that He did, and the children crying out in the temple and saying, "Hosanna to the
Son of David!" they were indignant 16and said to Him, "Do
You hear what these are saying?"
And Jesus said to them, "Yes. Have you never read,

'Out of the mouth of babes and nursing infants
You have perfected praise'? "[a]

17Then He left them and went out of the city to Bethany,
and He lodged there.

Jesus Curses a Fig Tree

18Now in the morning, as He returned to the city, He was
hungry. 19And seeing a fig tree by the road, He came to it
and found nothing on it but leaves, and said to it, "Let no
fruit grow on you ever again." Immediately the fig tree withered away.
20And when the disciples saw *it,* they marveled, saying,
"How did the fig tree wither away so soon?"
21So Jesus answered and said to them, "Assuredly, I say to
you, if you have faith and do not doubt, you will not only
do what was done to the fig tree, but also if you say to this

(*Bible text continued on page 92*)

21:7 [a]NU-Text reads *and He sat.* *21:9* [a]Psalm 118:26 *21:12* [a]NU-Text omits *of God.*
21:13 [a]Isaiah 56:7 [b]Jeremiah 7:11 *21:16* [a]Psalm 8:2

" 'MY HOUSE SHALL BE CALLED A HOUSE OF PRAYER,' BUT YOU HAVE MADE IT A 'DEN OF THIEVES.' "
—Matthew 21:13

CONSIDER THIS
21:8–11

A New Style of Fame

If you've ever encountered a famous person, you may have felt somewhat intimidated, especially if that person seemed arrogant. People of status and image can easily make us feel inferior, as if we have nothing to offer by comparison. No wonder we long for the traits of compassion and humility in society's leaders.

Jesus became famous among His own people. But as He entered Jerusalem, the capital of Palestine, He modeled a new style for handling acclaim from the crowd. The city was wild with excitement during its peak season of tourists and celebration. What a moment for Jesus to bring His campaign to a climax! He even had the prophecies of Zechariah 9:9 and Isaiah 62:11 to bolster His confidence.

But instead of a parade of chariots and trumpets and a well-orchestrated ceremony, Jesus chose to ride into town on a donkey, a common beast of burden; no prancing warhorse for Him! And instead of walking arm-in-arm with powerful city officials and other celebrities, He was accompanied only by a small band of common fishermen, rural Galileans, and even a former tax collector. For once, the common folks had a parade (Matt. 21:8, 10).

Once arrived at the end of the parade route, Jesus did

CONSIDER THIS
21:23–27

A Challenge to Authority

Sooner or later, almost all leaders have their authority questioned. Sometimes they are challenged directly, but more often indirectly by rumor and innuendo.

Jesus faced a direct challenge to His authority from the chief priests and elders, the top leadership in Israel (vv. 23–27). In this instance He didn't argue with them, but simply tossed the ball back into their court. He showed that one very effective way of responding to threatening questions is to ask questions in return.

But observe two aspects of the interaction between Jesus and the Jewish leaders:

(1) The motives of the challengers. *The scribes and Pharisees had no interest in an honest understanding of the nature or source of Jesus' authority. They were only concerned with protecting their own interests and power. In light of their behavior, you might ask yourself whether you ever question or resist people in authority over you because you are afraid or jealous of them.*

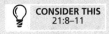

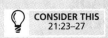

not go to the halls of the powerful. Instead He marched into the place of worship, a national center for the Jews. There He overthrew the tables of unjust businesses that manipulated the poor and made the temple a place of moneymaking (vv. 12–13). He focused on the blind, the lame, and children (vv. 14–16). And when He completed the day's tasks, He spent the night not in the fashionable home of a city leader but in a humble house in a nearby suburb, Bethany (v. 17).

Jesus' final activities before His death focused on those most ready to hear of His love, forgiveness, and hope—the little people in (or even outside) the system of privilege and power (Luke 4:18).

Do you know people who need to be invited to join the humble King's procession? Are there coworkers, neighbors, or family members who need to receive good news through you? How are you dealing with the temptation to rub shoulders only with the powerful and elite? ◆

Jesus liked to surround Himself with relatively average people of little social standing or influence. See "The Little People at Jesus' Death," Matt. 27:32.

" 'Blessed is He who comes in the name of the Lord!' "
—Matthew 21:9

(2) The security of Jesus. *Jesus was neither upset nor caught off guard by His attackers. For one thing, He had endured their criticism before, and no doubt expected it to increase. But He also knew with absolute certainty about the very thing that His challengers were attacking: He knew who He was and whose authority He wielded (28:18). His response is a reminder that intimidation is something we allow to occur. People may threaten and confront us, but only we allow ourselves to feel fear. The real question is, are we certain who we are as followers of the King?* ◆

To understand more about Jesus' sense of identity, see "Being Like Jesus," Matt. 10:25.

mountain, 'Be removed and be cast into the sea,' it will be
done. 22And whatever things you ask in prayer, believing,
you will receive."

Pharisees Challenge Jesus' Authority

21:23–27
see pg. 90

23Now when He came into the temple,
the chief priests and the elders of the
people confronted Him as He was teaching, and said, "By
what authority are You doing these things? And who gave
You this authority?"

21:24–27

24But Jesus answered and said to them,
"I also will ask you one thing, which if
you tell Me, I likewise will tell you by what authority I do
these things: 25The baptism of John—where was it from?
From heaven or from men?"
And they reasoned among themselves, saying, "If we say,

CONSIDER THIS
21:24–27

IS EVASION ETHICAL?

As you deal with people at work and in your family, you no doubt encounter situations where it might seem better not to reveal the whole truth. What should you do? Is anything less than the actual, complete truth ever ethical or biblical? Can believers practice cunning when Scripture calls us to be honest (for example, Eph. 4:15, 25, 29)?

Christ faced this dilemma when certain leaders challenged His authority (Matt. 21:23). He replied by asking them a question that was almost impossible for them to answer (vv. 24–27). Was He being fair?

Observe the context. Jesus' inquisitors were powerful religious leaders who felt threatened by His assault on their hypocrisies and His impact on the people. He had just challenged one of their sources of revenue by throwing the money changers out of the temple (vv. 12–17). Now they were launching a counterassault by challenging His authority.

Rather than being unethically evasive, Jesus was merely diverting an evil plot in a discrete manner by posing a difficult question. A simple yes or no answer would have played right into their hands. It probably would have touched off a confrontation prematurely. Jesus was more interested in accomplishing His long-range purposes than in exposing these hateful leaders on the spot.

Have you developed the ability to discern the gray areas of conflict and competition? Do you take a long-term view when you face confrontation? ◆

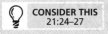

'From heaven,' He will say to us, 'Why then did you not believe him?' [26]But if we say, 'From men,' we fear the multitude, for all count John as a prophet." [27]So they answered
Jesus and said, "We do not know."
And He said to them, "Neither will I tell you by what authority I do these things.

A Parable about Two Sons

[28]"But what do you think? A man had two sons, and he
came to the first and said, 'Son, go, work today in my vineyard.' [29]He answered and said, 'I will not,' but afterward he
regretted it and went. [30]Then he came to the second and
said likewise. And he answered and said, 'I *go,* sir,' but he
did not go. [31]Which of the two did the
will of *his* father?"

21:31–32 see pg. 94

They said to Him, "The first."
Jesus said to them, "Assuredly, I say to you that tax collectors and harlots enter the kingdom of God before you.
[32]For John came to you in the way of righteousness, and
you did not believe him; but tax collectors and harlots believed him; and when you saw *it,* you did not afterward relent and believe him.

A Parable about a Vineyard Owner

[33]"Hear another parable: There was a certain landowner
who planted a vineyard and set a hedge around it, dug a
winepress in it and built a tower. And he leased it to vinedressers and went into a far country. [34]Now when vintage-
time drew near, he sent his servants to the vinedressers, that
they might receive its fruit. [35]And the vinedressers took his
servants, beat one, killed one, and stoned another. [36]Again
he sent other servants, more than the first, and they did
likewise to them. [37]Then last of all he sent his son to them,
saying, 'They will respect my son.' [38]But when the vinedressers saw the son, they said among themselves, 'This is
the heir. Come, let us kill him and seize his inheritance.'
[39]So they took him and cast *him* out of the vineyard and
killed *him.*
[40]"Therefore, when the owner of the vineyard comes,
what will he do to those vinedressers?"
[41]They said to Him, "He will destroy those wicked men
miserably, and lease *his* vineyard to other vinedressers who
will render to him the fruits in their seasons."
[42]Jesus said to them, "Have you never read in the Scriptures:

'The stone which the builders rejected
Has become the chief cornerstone.

" 'THE STONE WHICH THE BUILDERS REJECTED HAS BECOME THE CHIEF CORNERSTONE.' "
—Matthew 21:42

This was the LORD's doing,
And it is marvelous in our eyes' ?[a]

43"Therefore I say to you, the kingdom of God will be
taken from you and given to a nation bearing the fruits of it.
44And whoever falls on this stone will be broken; but on
whomever it falls, it will grind him to powder."
45Now when the chief priests and Pharisees heard His
parables, they perceived that He was speaking of them.
46But when they sought to lay hands on Him, they feared
the multitudes, because they took Him for a prophet.

CHAPTER 22

A Parable about a Rejected Invitation

1And Jesus answered and spoke to them again by parables
22:2–14 and said: 2"The kingdom of heaven is like
a certain king who arranged a marriage
for his son, 3and sent out his servants to call those who
were invited to the wedding; and they were not willing to
come. 4Again, he sent out other servants, saying, 'Tell those

21:42 [a]Psalm 118:22, 23

CONSIDER THIS
21:31–32

"HARLOTS ENTER THE KINGDOM"

Jesus' startling statement about prostitutes (vv. 31–32) was not an endorsement of that lifestyle but a condemnation of the self-righteousness and especially the unbelief of Israel's religious leaders. Faith was the key to the kingdom; yet even prostitutes were showing more faith in Christ than those who were viewed as "righteous."

Prostitution has been a part of religious rites since at least 3,000 B.C. In Babylon, Syria, Canaan, Arabia, and Phoenicia intercourse with a temple prostitute was believed to induce fertility among humans, animals, and crops. The historian Herodotus tells of a Babylonian custom that required every woman to sit in the temple of the goddess Ishtar until chosen by a stranger for sexual relations. A desirous man would toss a coin in a woman's lap. If she accepted the coin and his sexual advances, she would have paid her obligation to the goddess and be free to return to her normal life.

In Israel, however, ritual prostitution was forbidden (Deut. 23:17). Laws existed to prevent priests from marrying prostitutes (Lev. 21:7), and income from prostitution could not be used to pay vows in the temple (Deut. 23:18).

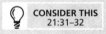

who are invited, "See, I have prepared my dinner; my oxen
and fatted cattle *are* killed, and all things *are* ready. Come to
the wedding." ' 5But they made light of it and went their
ways, one to his own farm, another to his business. 6And
the rest seized his servants, treated *them* spitefully, and
killed *them*. 7But when the king heard *about it*, he was furious. And he sent out his armies, destroyed those murderers,
and burned up their city. 8Then he said to his servants, 'The
wedding is ready, but those who were invited were not worthy. 9Therefore go into the highways, and as many as you
find, invite to the wedding.' 10So those servants went out
into the highways and gathered together all whom they
found, both bad and good. And the wedding *hall* was filled
with guests.
11"But when the king came in to see the guests, he saw a
man there who did not have on a wedding garment. 12So he
said to him, 'Friend, how did you come in here without a
wedding garment?' And he was speechless. 13Then the king
said to the servants, 'Bind him hand and foot, take him
away, and[a] cast *him* into outer darkness; there will be weeping and gnashing of teeth.'
14"For many are called, but few *are* chosen."

22:13 [a]NU-Text omits *take him away, and.*

Nevertheless, commercial prostitutes practiced their trade rather freely in Hebrew society. They were easily recognizable by their hairstyle, head ornaments, or perhaps a special mark on their foreheads. Their clothing and jewelry signaled their availability, and like streetwalkers everywhere, they frequented particular locales well known as meeting spots. Payments were accepted in money, grain, wine, or livestock. It was even common to accept a pledge until the payment could be fulfilled.

In Jesus' day, prostitutes endured the particular condemnation of the religious elite, especially the Pharisees, who avoided all outward contact with such people. By contrast, Jesus became known as a friend of sinners who welcomed those in need of forgiveness (Matt. 11:19; Luke 7:36–50). His words on this occasion showed that people don't have to become religiously "proper" before they can believe. God responds to faith no matter how troubled one's personal life may be. What an encouragement to start now to put trust in Jesus and be among the first in the kingdom! ◆

WORSE THAN RUDE

CONSIDER THIS 22:2–14 **Jesus' parable of the king's wedding feast for his son (vv. 2–14) turns on an important detail of Jewish marriage custom. Wedding hosts sent out two invitations for a wedding. The first was sent far in advance to let people know that a wedding was being prepared and they were invited. This was necessary because weddings were major events that could last as long as a week. Furthermore, it took time for the replies to come back.**

When all the preparations were complete, messengers were sent out with a second invitation telling the guests that the feast was ready and it was time for the celebration to begin. To turn down that second invitation—which was the one the guests in the parable refused (v. 3)—was not merely bad manners. It was considered a rejection of the host family's hospitality and a complete insult to their dignity.

God had sent Israel an early "invitation" to His Son's wedding through the Old Testament Law and prophets. Now that Jesus had arrived, proclaiming the second invitation, the nation was rejecting Him—a perilous choice.

TRICK QUESTIONS FOILED

CONSIDER THIS 22:23–33 **Have you ever seen someone try to manipulate someone else by asking for one thing in order to get another? Perhaps you've tried to outwit or embarrass someone with a less-than-direct approach.**

The Sadducees did precisely that when they tried to trap Jesus in front of a crowd (vv. 23–33). Using the subject of serial marriage relationships, they attempted to paint Him into a corner on His teaching about the resurrection, a belief that they rejected (v. 23).

Jesus confronted them on their thinly veiled pretext and at the same time affirmed the resurrection. He even used the very Scriptures they loved to quote: v. 32 is from Exodus 3:6. Jesus refused to let them get away with using subtle inferences to twist things to their own advantage. He cut to the heart of the matter.

There's nothing wrong with being discreet, using inference, or stating things subtly and diplomatically. Some situations call for planting seed ideas in someone else's thinking, then allowing time for the idea to take shape. Here, however, Jesus was challenging selfish manipulation and trickery which had no benefit for others.

Are you known as a speaker of truth among your peers? Are there ways you could be more forthright and helpful in your communications?

Speaking truth in love is one of the main characteristics of Christlike character. See Eph. 4:15.

Jesus Confounds His Challengers

[15]Then the Pharisees went and plotted how they might
entangle Him in *His* talk. [16]And they sent to Him their disciples with the Herodians, saying, "Teacher, we know that
You are true, and teach the way of God in truth; nor do You
care about anyone, for You do not regard the person of
men. [17]Tell us, therefore, what do You think? Is it lawful to
pay taxes to Caesar, or not?"
[18]But Jesus perceived their wickedness, and said, "Why
do you test Me, *you* hypocrites? [19]Show Me the tax money."
So they brought Him a denarius.
[20]And He said to them, "Whose image and inscription *is*
this?"
[21]They said to Him, "Caesar's."
And He said to them, "Render therefore to Caesar the
things that are Caesar's, and to God the things that are
God's." [22]When they had heard *these words,* they marveled,
and left Him and went their way.

22:23–33 [23]The same day the Sadducees, who
say there is no resurrection, came to Him
and asked Him, [24]saying: "Teacher, Moses said that if a man
dies, having no children, his brother shall marry his wife
and raise up offspring for his brother. [25]Now there were
with us seven brothers. The first died after he had married,
and having no offspring, left his wife to his brother. [26]Like-
wise the second also, and the third, even to the seventh.
[27]Last of all the woman died also. [28]Therefore, in the resurrection, whose wife of the seven will she be? For they all
had her."
[29]Jesus answered and said to them, "You are mistaken,
not knowing the Scriptures nor the power of God. [30]For in
the resurrection they neither marry nor are given in marriage, but are like angels of God[a] in heaven. [31]But concerning the resurrection of the dead, have you not read what
was spoken to you by God, saying, [32]'I am the God of Abraham, the God of Isaac, and the God of Jacob'?[a] God is
not the God of the dead, but of the living." [33]And when
the multitudes heard *this,* they were astonished at His teaching.

The Greatest of the Commandments

22:34–40 see pg. 98 [34]But when the Pharisees heard that He
had silenced the Sadducees, they gath-
ered together. [35]Then one of them, a lawyer, asked *Him a
question,* testing Him, and saying, [36]"Teacher, which *is* the
great commandment in the law?"
[37]Jesus said to him, " 'You shall love the LORD your God

22:30 [a]NU-Text omits *of God.* *22:32* [a]Exodus 3:6, 15

with all your heart, with all your soul, and with all your
mind.'[a] 38This is *the* first and great commandment. 39And
the second *is* like it: 'You shall love your neighbor as yourself.'[a] 40On these two commandments hang all the Law and
the Prophets."

Jesus Silences the Pharisees

41While the Pharisees were gathered together, Jesus asked
them, 42saying, "What do you think about the Christ?
Whose Son is He?"
They said to Him, "*The Son* of David."
43He said to them, "How then does David in the Spirit call
Him 'Lord,' saying:

44 'The LORD said to my Lord,
"Sit at My right hand,
Till I make Your enemies Your footstool" ' ?[a]

45If David then calls Him 'Lord,' how is He his Son?" 46And
no one was able to answer Him a word, nor from that day
on did anyone dare question Him anymore.

CHAPTER 23

Jesus Denounces the Scribes and Pharisees

23:1–30

1Then Jesus spoke to the multitudes
and to His disciples, 2saying: "The scribes
and the Pharisees sit in Moses' seat. 3Therefore whatever
they tell you to observe,[a] *that* observe and do, but do not do
according to their works; for they say, and do not do. 4For
they bind heavy burdens, hard to bear, and lay *them* on
men's shoulders; but they *themselves* will not move them
with one of their fingers. 5But all their works they do to be
seen by men. They make their phylacteries broad and en-
large the borders of their garments. 6They love the best
places at feasts, the best seats in the synagogues, 7greetings
in the marketplaces, and to be called by men, 'Rabbi,
Rabbi.' 8But you, do not be called 'Rabbi'; for One is your
Teacher, the Christ,[a] and you are all brethren. 9Do not call
anyone on earth your father; for One is your Father, He
who is in heaven. 10And do not be called teachers; for
One is your Teacher, the Christ. 11But he who is greatest
among you shall be your servant. 12And whoever exalts
himself will be humbled, and he who humbles himself will
be exalted.

22:37 [a]Deuteronomy 6:5 *22:39* [a]Leviticus 19:18 *22:44* [a]Psalm 110:1 *23:3* [a]NU-Text omits *to observe.* *23:8* [a]NU-Text omits *the Christ.*

QUOTE UNQUOTE

CONSIDER THIS
23:1–30

Jesus denounced the Pharisees for their abuse of spiritual authority. Perhaps their daily contact with religion made them callous to it:

Someone has said, "None are so unholy as those whose hands are cauterized with holy things"; sacred things may become profane by becoming matters of the job.

C.S. Lewis, Letter to Sheldon Vanauken, Jan. 5, 1951

Woe to the Scribes and Pharisees

13"But woe to you, scribes and Pharisees, hypocrites! For
you shut up the kingdom of heaven against men; for you
neither go in *yourselves*, nor do you allow those who are entering to go in. 14Woe to you, scribes and
Pharisees, hypocrites! For you devour
widows' houses, and for a pretense make long prayers.
Therefore you will receive greater condemnation.[a]

23:14

15"Woe to you, scribes and Pharisees, hypocrites! For you
travel land and sea to win one proselyte, and when he is
won, you make him twice as much a son of hell as yourselves.

16"Woe to you, blind guides, who say, 'Whoever swears by
the temple, it is nothing; but whoever swears by the gold of
the temple, he is obliged *to perform it.*' 17Fools and blind!
For which is greater, the gold or the temple that sanctifies[a]
the gold? 18And, 'Whoever swears by the altar, it is nothing;
but whoever swears by the gift that is on it, he is obliged *to*

23:14 [a]NU-Text omits this verse. *23:17* [a]NU-Text reads *sanctified.*

CONSIDER THIS
22:34–40

WHAT KIND OF LOVE IS THIS?

"Love" is a very confusing concept these days. People use the word "love" to describe very different relationships: people "love" their dog . . . a certain type of car . . . a brand of pizza . . . a sexually intimate partner . . . another person for whom they have deep feelings. What can "love" possibly mean if it applies equally well to dogs, machines, food, sex, or close companions?

The Bible is not confused or vague about the powerful concept it calls love. Greek, the international language of Jesus' day and the language in which the New Testament was written, had four distinct words for love, each with its own shade of meaning:

(1) Erōs *denoted the relationship between male and female, including physical desire, craving, and longing. That word for love is not used in the New Testament.*

(2) Stergos *described affection and was applied especially to the mutual love between family members. It is not used in the New Testament either.*

(3) Philos *reflected the care and concern that friends have for each other, what we would call brotherly love. Peter spoke of this kind of love when he and Jesus discussed his future task of serving others (John 21:15–17).*

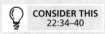

perform it.' 19Fools and blind! For which is greater, the gift
or the altar that sanctifies the gift? 20Therefore he who
swears by the altar, swears by it and by all things on it. 21He
who swears by the temple, swears by it and by Him who
dwells[a] in it. 22And he who swears by heaven, swears by the
throne of God and by Him who sits on it.

23:23–24 see pg. 100

23"Woe to you, scribes and Pharisees,
hypocrites! For you pay tithe of mint and
anise and cummin, and have neglected the weightier *matters* of the law: justice and mercy and faith. These you
ought to have done, without leaving the others undone.
24Blind guides, who strain out a gnat and swallow a camel!

25"Woe to you, scribes and Pharisees, hypocrites! For you
cleanse the outside of the cup and dish, but inside they are
full of extortion and self-indulgence.[a] 26Blind Pharisee, first
cleanse the inside of the cup and dish, that the outside of
them may be clean also.

(Bible text continued on page 101)

23:21 [a]M-Text reads *dwelt*. *23:25* [a]M-Text reads *unrighteousness*.

(4) Agapē *described a unique type of supreme love involving a conscious and deliberate choice to do good for another, a commitment based on the willful choice of the lover, not the qualities of the person receiving the love.* Agapē *love is perhaps best seen in God's love for the world (John 3:16) and in the love that God calls believers to display (1 Cor. 13:1–13).*

When Jesus recalled the greatest of the commandments, both of which had to do with love (Matt. 22:34–40), He was calling for agapē *love, a sustained and conscious choice to graciously serve God, neighbor, and self, expecting nothing in return. Followers of Christ learn this kind of love as God loves them first. He then commands us to live in the same way toward others (1 John 3:11–24). God's love empowers us to love by choice rather than just emotion or senses, and to sustain our love even in the face of hostility or rejection.*

God wants to deliver a new kind of love—agapē love—to families, workplaces, and communities through His people. Who around you needs that kind of intentional touch of compassion and grace? ◆

GROWING FAT AT THE POOR'S EXPENSE

CONSIDER THIS 23:14 **Jesus chastised the Pharisees for growing fat at the expense of widows (v. 14). Unfortunately, not much has changed from that day to this. We still see people with lots of power but few scruples grow rich by dislodging widows and other less powerful folks from what little they own.**

Sadly, there are loan sharks and other flimflam artists who con the poor. But there are also more respectable businesspeople whose activities can hurt the powerless. For example, occasionally some "urban renewal projects" have driven the poor from one slum to another in a frantic search for housing that costs more than before.

Then there are those who buy, sell, close down, and bankrupt companies with little regard for the impact on workers or communities, whose only motive appears to be personal financial gain.

Jesus never condemned business or investment. But His stiff rebuke of the Pharisees challenges any of us involved in finance and deal-making to carefully weigh the ethics of our choices. Woe to us if we devour the resources of the disadvantaged.

Scripture has much more to say about our use and abuse of wealth. See "Christians and Money," 1 Tim. 1:6–19; and "Getting Yours," James 5:1–6.

CONSIDER THIS
23:23–24

TITHING

Jesus' words to the Pharisees (v. 23) raise the issue of tithing. Should Christians today pay tithes? Or are we free from that practice?

For that matter, what is a *tithe*? The word means "a tenth part." In the Old Testament, God commanded the Israelites to give tithes—one-tenth of their produce or income—for one of three reasons:

(1) To support the Levites, who were responsible for the tabernacle and worship (Num. 18:20–24).

(2) To support various feasts and sacrifices (Deut. 14:22–27), some of which lasted more than one or two days and were times of joyous celebration and thanksgiving.

(3) To establish a pool of resources to help the poor, orphans and widows, and strangers in the land (Deut. 14:28–29).

In the New Testament, neither Christ nor the apostles gave any explicit instructions about tithing. However, Jesus clearly endorsed it, as He did all the Law (v. 23; Matt. 5:17–20). He denounced the hypocritical way that the Pharisees ignored the "weightier matters" of the Law—justice, mercy, and faith. But those "heavy duty" issues by no means negated such "lightweight matters" as tithing.

So what is the place of tithing for believers today? Several principles might be considered:

(1) As Christians, our allegiance is not to the Old Testament Law, which was primarily given to Israel, but to Christ.

(2) Our giving needs to spring from a love of Christ, not a slavish obedience to a percentage standard. When Abraham gave the first tithe recorded in the Bible (Gen. 14:17–20), he did it as an expression of gratitude for God's deliverance of him in battle. Throughout Scripture, loving God and worshiping Him are at the heart of tithing.

(3) All of what we have ultimately comes from and belongs to God—not just what we give away, but also what we keep. So He has total claim on 100 percent of our income, not just 10 percent.

(4) Ten percent makes a great starting point for giving. However, studies indicate that as a group, Christians in the United States give nowhere near that much of their income away—to ministries or charities of any kind. In fact, while per capita income has increased, church members have actually *decreased* their contributions to churches.

(5) The New Testament is clear that vocational Christian workers have a right to financial support from those to whom they minister (1 Cor. 9:13–14; Gal. 6:6). Likewise, many churches and other ministries assist the poor, orphans and widows, and strangers. So it seems legitimate to expect believers to donate money to those causes.

(6) No matter how much we give or to whom, Matt. 23:23 indicates that our first priority should be to ensure that justice is carried out around us, that we show mercy to our "neighbors," and that we practice our faith and not just talk about it. In the end, it is through our obedience that Jesus increases our faith. ◆

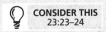

23:27–28

27“Woe to you, scribes and Pharisees,
hypocrites! For you are like whitewashed
tombs which indeed appear beautiful outwardly, but inside
are full of dead *men's* bones and all uncleanness. 28Even so
you also outwardly appear righteous to men, but inside you
are full of hypocrisy and lawlessness.
29“Woe to you, scribes and Pharisees, hypocrites! Because
you build the tombs of the prophets and adorn the monuments of the righteous, 30and say, ‘If we had lived in the
days of our fathers, we would not have been partakers with
them in the blood of the prophets.’
31“Therefore you are witnesses against yourselves that you
are sons of those who murdered the prophets. 32Fill up,
then, the measure of your fathers' *guilt.* 33Serpents, brood of
vipers! How can you escape the condemnation of hell?
34Therefore, indeed, I send you prophets, wise men, and
scribes: *some* of them you will kill and crucify, and *some* of
them you will scourge in your synagogues and persecute
from city to city, 35that on you may come all the righteous
blood shed on the earth, from the blood of righteous Abel
to the blood of Zechariah, son of Berechiah, whom you
murdered between the temple and the altar. 36Assuredly, I
say to you, all these things will come upon this generation.

Jerusalem's Refusal

23:37
see pg. 102

37“O Jerusalem, Jerusalem, the one who
kills the prophets and stones those who
are sent to her! How often I wanted to gather your children
together, as a hen gathers her chicks under *her* wings, but
you were not willing! 38See! Your house is left to you desolate; 39for I say to you, you shall see Me
no more till you say, ‘Blessed *is* He who
comes in the name of the LORD!’ ”[a]

23:37–39

CHAPTER 24

Jesus Predicts the Temple's Destruction

1Then Jesus went out and departed from the temple, and
His disciples came up to show Him the buildings of the
temple. 2And Jesus said to them, “Do you not see all these
things? Assuredly, I say to you, not *one* stone shall be left
here upon another, that shall not be thrown down.”

23:39 [a]Psalm 118:26

Jesus Weeps for the Children

A CLOSER LOOK 23:37–39 *Jesus wanted to gather together the lost children of Jerusalem (v. 37). Was He speaking only in spiritual terms? See “Good Men Cry,” Luke 13:34.*

WHITEWASHED TOMBS

CONSIDER THIS 23:27–28 *Jesus drew upon a grim, arresting image in His denunciation of the self-righteous Pharisees (vv. 27–28). At the end of a Jewish funeral procession, which everyone was obliged to join, the body was placed on a rock shelf in a tomb. Once the flesh had decomposed, the bones would be collected and removed, allowing the shelf to be reused. Since Jews were made ritually unclean by touching graves (Num. 19:16), rocks used to seal tombs were whitewashed as a warning to stay away. The glaze gave the tombs a clean image on the outside—even though there were decomposing corpses on the inside.*

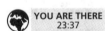

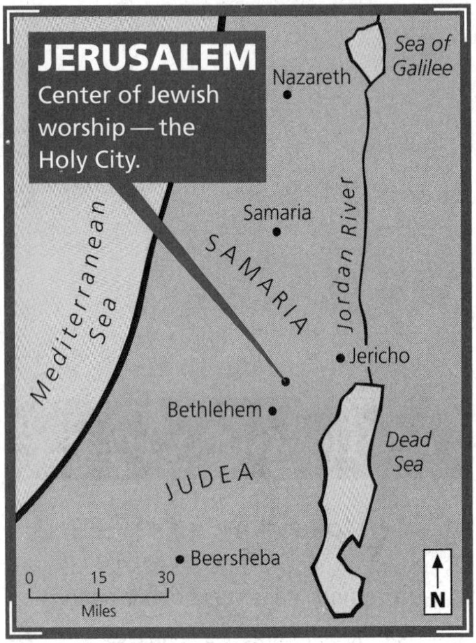

JERUSALEM

YOU ARE THERE 23:37

- **Main city of Palestine in biblical times.**
- **Well-situated for defense on two triangular ridges that converged to the south, bordered by the Kidron Valley on the east and the Valley of Hinnom on the west.**
- **Appears in the Bible as early as Abraham (Gen. 14:18), though the site had probably been inhabited for centuries before.**
- **Captured by David and made the capital of Israel.**
- **Site of Solomon's temple and, in the first century, Herod's temple.**
- **Estimated population in Jesus' day probably 60,000 to 70,000, though estimates range from 40,000 to 12 million.**
- **Besieged and destroyed by Rome in A.D. 70.**
- **Relatively small geographically, but a sizable metropolitan area with numerous suburban towns.**

(continued on next page)

3Now as He sat on the Mount of Olives, the disciples
came to Him privately, saying, "Tell us, when will these
things be? And what *will be* the sign of Your coming, and of
the end of the age?"
4And Jesus answered and said to them: "Take heed that
no one deceives you. 5For many will come in My name,
saying, 'I am the Christ,' and will deceive many. 6And you
will hear of wars and rumors of wars. See that you are not
troubled; for all[a] *these things* must come to pass, but the end
is not yet. 7For nation will rise against nation, and kingdom
against kingdom. And there will be famines, pestilences,[a]
and earthquakes in various places. 8All these *are* the beginning of sorrows.

Terrible Times to Come

9"Then they will deliver you up to tribulation and kill
you, and you will be hated by all nations for My name's
sake. 10And then many will be offended, will betray one another, and will hate one another. 11Then many false
prophets will rise up and deceive many. 12And because lawlessness will abound, the love of many will grow cold. 13But
he who endures to the end shall be saved. 14And this gospel
of the kingdom will be preached in all the world as a witness to all the nations, and then the end will come.
15"Therefore when you see the 'abomination of desolation,'[a] spoken of by Daniel the prophet, standing in the holy
place" (whoever reads, let him understand), 16"then let
those who are in Judea flee to the mountains. 17Let him
who is on the housetop not go down to take anything out
of his house. 18And let him who is in the field not go back
to get his clothes. 19But woe to those who are pregnant and
to those who are nursing babies in those days! 20And pray
that your flight may not be in winter or on the Sabbath.
21For then there will be great tribulation, such as has not
been since the beginning of the world until this time, no,
nor ever shall be. 22And unless those days were shortened,
no flesh would be saved; but for the elect's sake those days
will be shortened.
23"Then if anyone says to you, 'Look, here *is* the Christ!'
or 'There!' do not believe *it*. 24For false christs and false
prophets will rise and show great signs and wonders to deceive, if possible, even the elect. 25See, I have told you beforehand.
26"Therefore if they say to you, 'Look, He is in the desert!'
do not go out; *or* 'Look, *He is* in the inner rooms!' do not
believe *it*. 27For as the lightning comes from the east and
flashes to the west, so also will the coming of the Son of

24:6 [a]NU-Text omits *all*. *24:7* [a]NU-Text omits *pestilences*. *24:15* [a]Daniel 11:31; 12:11

Man be. 28For wherever the carcass is, there the eagles will
be gathered together.
29"Immediately after the tribulation of those days the sun
will be darkened, and the moon will not give its light; the
stars will fall from heaven, and the powers of the heavens
will be shaken. 30Then the sign of the Son of Man will appear in heaven, and then all the tribes of the earth will
mourn, and they will see the Son of Man coming on the
clouds of heaven with power and great glory. 31And He will
send His angels with a great sound of a trumpet, and they
will gather together His elect from the four winds, from one
end of heaven to the other.
32"Now learn this parable from the fig tree: When its
branch has already become tender and puts forth leaves,
you know that summer *is* near. 33So you also, when you see
all these things, know that it[a] is near—at the doors! 34As-
suredly, I say to you, this generation will by no means pass
away till all these things take place. 35Heaven and earth will
pass away, but My words will by no means pass away.

Faithful and Foolish Living

36"But of that day and hour no one knows, not even the
angels of heaven,[a] but My Father only. 37But as the days of
Noah *were,* so also will the coming of the Son of Man be.
38For as in the days before the flood, they were eating and
drinking, marrying and giving in marriage, until the day
that Noah entered the ark, 39and did not know until the
flood came and took them all away, so also will the coming
of the Son of Man be. 40Then two *men* will be in the field:
24:41 one will be taken and the other left.
41Two *women will be* grinding at the mill:
one will be taken and the other left. 42Watch therefore, for
you do not know what hour[a] your Lord is coming. 43But
know this, that if the master of the house had known what
hour the thief would come, he would have watched and not
allowed his house to be broken into. 44Therefore you also
be ready, for the Son of Man is coming at an hour you do
not expect.
45"Who then is a faithful and wise servant, whom his
master made ruler over his household, to give them food in
due season? 46Blessed *is* that servant whom his master,

24:33 [a]Or *He* *24:36* [a]NU-Text adds *nor the Son.* *24:42* [a]NU-Text reads *day.*

(continued from previous page)

THE HOLY CITY

For centuries before and after Christ, Jerusalem has been viewed as more than just a city. It stands as a great symbol of the Bible and the Near East. As the center of Judaism and Hebrew culture, it bore the brunt of Jesus' dramatic cry of anguish over its rejection of Him (Matt. 23:37–38). He knew all too well that in a matter of years Jerusalem would indeed be left desolate by a myriad of Roman siege troops.

Jesus visited Jerusalem several times. Yet its population as a whole never did respond to the Son of God. Nor did it accept Christ's followers later when they tried to penetrate it with His message. Known as the Holy City (Matt. 4:5), Jerusalem nevertheless rejected the Holy One of Israel, the Messiah.

An Everyday Task

A CLOSER LOOK 24:41

Jesus promised that His return would burst into common, everyday life, as pictured in two women grinding grain (v. 41). See Luke 17:35.

The first headquarters of the early church was at Jerusalem, but the city's supremacy was short-lived. See "Jerusalem—Merely the Beginning," Acts 1:12–26.

when he comes, will find so doing. 47Assuredly, I say to you
that he will make him ruler over all his goods. 48But if that
evil servant says in his heart, 'My master is delaying his
coming,' [a] 49and begins to beat *his* fellow servants, and to
eat and drink with the drunkards, 50the master of that servant will come on a day when he is not looking for *him* and
at an hour that he is not aware of, 51and will cut him in two
and appoint *him* his portion with the hypocrites. There
shall be weeping and gnashing of teeth.

CHAPTER 25

A Parable about Ten Virgins

1"Then the kingdom of heaven shall be likened to ten virgins who took their lamps and went out to meet the bridegroom. 2Now five of them were wise, and five *were* foolish.
3Those who *were* foolish took their lamps and took no oil
with them, 4but the wise took oil in their vessels with their
lamps. 5But while the bridegroom was delayed, they all
slumbered and slept.

6"And at midnight a cry was *heard:* 'Behold, the bridegroom is coming;[a] go out to meet him!' 7Then all those virgins arose and trimmed their lamps. 8And the foolish said
to the wise, 'Give us *some* of your oil, for our lamps are going out.' 9But the wise answered, saying, '*No,* lest there
should not be enough for us and you; but go rather to those
who sell, and buy for yourselves.' 10And while they went to
buy, the bridegroom came, and those who were ready went
in with him to the wedding; and the door was shut.
11"Afterward the other virgins came also, saying, 'Lord,
Lord, open to us!' 12But he answered and said, 'Assuredly, I
say to you, I do not know you.'
13"Watch therefore, for you know neither the day nor the
hour[a] in which the Son of Man is coming.

A Parable about Investment

25:14–30

14"For *the kingdom of heaven is* like a
man traveling to a far country, *who* called
his own servants and delivered his goods to them. 15And to
one he gave five talents, to another two, and to another one,
to each according to his own ability; and immediately he
went on a journey. 16Then he who had received the five talents went and traded with them, and made another five talents. 17And likewise he who *had received* two gained two
more also. 18But he who had received one went and dug in
the ground, and hid his lord's money. 19After a long time the

24:48 [a]NU-Text omits *his coming.* *25:6* [a]NU-Text omits *is coming.* *25:13* [a]NU-Text omits the rest of this verse.

lord of those servants came and settled accounts with them.
[20]"So he who had received five talents came and brought five other talents, saying, 'Lord, you delivered to me five talents; look, I have gained five more talents besides them.'
[21]His lord said to him, 'Well *done,* good and faithful servant; you were faithful over a few things, I will make you ruler over many things. Enter into the joy of your lord.' [22]He also
who had received two talents came and said, 'Lord, you delivered to me two talents; look, I have gained two more talents besides them.' [23]His lord said to him, 'Well *done,* good and faithful servant; you have been faithful over a few things, I will make you ruler over many things. Enter into the joy of your lord.'
[24]"Then he who had received the one talent came and said, 'Lord, I knew you to be a hard man, reaping where you have not sown, and gathering where you have not scattered seed. [25]And I was afraid, and went and hid your talent
in the ground. Look, *there* you have *what is* yours.'
[26]"But his lord answered and said to him, 'You wicked and lazy servant, you knew that I reap where I have not sown, and gather where I have not scattered seed. [27]So you
ought to have deposited my money with the bankers, and at my coming I would have received back my own with interest. [28]Therefore take the talent from him, and give *it* to
him who has ten talents.
[29]'For to everyone who has, more will be given, and he will have abundance; but from him who does not have, even what he has will be taken away. [30]And cast the unprofitable servant into the outer darkness. There will be weeping and gnashing of teeth.'

Judgment of the Nations

25:31–46 see pg. 106

[31]"When the Son of Man comes in His glory, and all the holy[a] angels with Him, then He will sit on the throne of His glory. [32]All the nations
will be gathered before Him, and He will separate them one from another, as a shepherd divides *his* sheep from the goats. [33]And He will set the sheep on His right hand, but
25:34
the goats on the left. [34]Then the King will
say to those on His right hand, 'Come, you blessed of My Father, inherit the kingdom prepared for you from the foundation of the world: [35]for I was hungry

25:31 [a]NU-Text omits *holy.*

TRUE SUCCESS MEANS FAITHFULNESS

CONSIDER THIS 25:14–30 **The story of the talents (vv. 14–30) is about the kingdom of heaven (v. 14), but it offers an important lesson about success. God measures our success not by what we have, but by what we do with what we have—for all that we have is a gift from Him. We are really only managers to whom He has entrusted resources and responsibilities.**

The key thing He looks for is *faithfulness* (vv. 21, 23), doing what we can to obey and honor Him with whatever He has given us. We may or may not be "successful" as our culture measures success, in terms of wealth, prestige, power, or fame. In the long run that hardly matters. What counts is whether we have faithfully served God with what He has entrusted to us. By all means we must avoid wasting our lives, the way the third servant wasted his talents, by failing to carry out our Master's business.

A talent was worth a lot of money. See "Seventy Times Seven—Still Not Enough," Matt. 18:21–35.

Jesus told a different version of this parable in Luke 19:15–27.

Prepared for You

A CLOSER LOOK 25:34 *God's children will enjoy an inheritance that is beyond comprehension. See "What's In It for Me?" at Eph. 1:11.*

THE FINAL EXAM

CONSIDER THIS 25:31–46 **Have you ever wondered whether God is going to give you a "final exam" when you stand before Him? If you pass you go to heaven, but if you fail . . . ? Fortunately, Jesus has already taken that exam for us—and passed (Eph. 2:4–10). Nevertheless, Matt. 25:31–46 reveals a final exam for the nations at Christ's return with one six-part question:**

EXAM FOR THE NATIONS

Were you a friend of Jesus when He was *hungry*?	yes	no
Were you a friend of Jesus when He was *thirsty*?	yes	no
Were you a friend of Jesus when He was *a stranger*?	yes	no
Were you a friend of Jesus when He was *naked*?	yes	no
Were you a friend of Jesus when He was *sick*?	yes	no
Were you a friend of Jesus when He was *in prison*?	yes	no

The point is that those being examined at that time will have made certain choices: whether or not to feed the hungry, to give drink to the thirsty, to befriend the strangers, to clothe the naked, to heal the sick, to befriend the prisoners. Who ever said that life was a series of meaningless choices? And who can say that the evidence Christ will look for at His return is not the same evidence He wants to see in believers today? To love Jesus is to love all who need our care.

Who are those in need nearest you? See "Who Was the Neighbor?" Luke 10:37.

and you gave Me food; I was thirsty and you gave Me drink;
I was a stranger and you took Me in; 36I *was* naked and you
clothed Me; I was sick and you visited Me; I was in prison
and you came to Me.'
37"Then the righteous will answer Him, saying, 'Lord,
when did we see You hungry and feed *You,* or thirsty and
give *You* drink? 38When did we see You a stranger and take
You in, or naked and clothe *You?* 39Or when did we see You
sick, or in prison, and come to You?' 40And the King will
answer and say to them, 'Assuredly, I say to you, inasmuch
as you did *it* to one of the least of these My brethren, you
did *it* to Me.'
41"Then He will also say to those on the left hand, 'Depart
from Me, you cursed, into the everlasting fire prepared for
the devil and his angels: 42for I was hungry and you gave
Me no food; I was thirsty and you gave Me no drink; 43I was
a stranger and you did not take Me in, naked and you did
not clothe Me, sick and in prison and you did not visit Me.'
44"Then they also will answer Him,[a] saying, 'Lord, when
did we see You hungry or thirsty or a stranger or naked or
sick or in prison, and did not minister to You?' 45Then He
will answer them, saying, 'Assuredly, I say to you, inasmuch
as you did not do *it* to one of the least of these, you did not
do *it* to Me.' 46And these will go away into everlasting punishment, but the righteous into eternal life."

25:44 [a]NU-Text and M-Text omit *Him.*

PERSONALITY PROFILE: CAIAPHAS

FOR YOUR INFO 26:3 **Also known as:** Joseph. His given name, Caiaphas, meant "a searcher."

Home: Jerusalem.

Occupation: High priest of Israel from A.D. 18 to 36.

Family: His father-in-law was Annas, also a high priest. Both father and son were Sadducees (see "Party Politics of Jesus' Day," Matt. 16:1) from aristocratic families in Israel.

Special interests: Maintaining the political and religious status quo.

Best known today as: The judge at the trial leading to Jesus' crucifixion.

CHAPTER 26

Leaders Plot to Kill Jesus

1Now it came to pass, when Jesus had finished all these sayings, *that* He said to His disciples, 2"You know that after two days is the Passover, and the Son of Man will be delivered up to be crucified."

26:3

26:3–5

3Then the chief priests, the scribes,[a] and the elders of the people assembled at the palace of the high priest, who was
called Caiaphas, 4and plotted to take Jesus by trickery and kill *Him.* 5But they said, "Not during the feast, lest there be an uproar among the people."

26:3 [a]NU-Text omits *the scribes.*

FOR YOUR INFO
26:3–5

CAIAPHAS, THE RELIGIOUS POWER BROKER

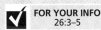

As the high priest, Caiaphas was the most influential member of the Sanhedrin, or council, the highest ruling body and supreme court of the Jews (see "Stephen's Trial and Murder," Acts 6:12). However, while the position afforded him vast authority, it provided little job security. High priests served at the whim of Rome, and between 37 B.C. and A.D. 67, the empire appointed no fewer than 28 men to the position. The fact that Caiaphas held onto the job for 18 years is a tribute to his political savvy and, some felt, was evidence that he was in league with Rome.

There may be some truth to that, but if so, his concern was not to protect Rome's interests as much as Israel's. He feared lest the slightest civil disorder would mobilize Roman troops and lead to the nation's downfall. So when Jesus came, drawing the attention of vast numbers of the people and performing astounding miracles, especially the raising of Lazarus, Caiaphas determined that He would have to be destroyed (John 11:45–50).

This led to a well conceived plot in which Jesus was arrested, an illegal trial was held, and false evidence was brought against Him (Matt. 26:3–4, 57–68). By playing Pilate the Roman governor and Herod the Jewish king against each other, and by whipping up the people into a mob (Luke 22:66—23:25), Caiaphas triumphantly orchestrated Jesus' conviction leading to execution.

To Caiaphas' amazement, however, the sparks that he thought he had doused flamed up again with renewed power. The apostles began preaching the gospel in Jerusalem (and beyond) with great effect. And, like Jesus, they began performing miracles that not only drew the people's attention, but their response to the message about Christ (Acts 3:1—4:13). ◆

A Woman Anoints Jesus for Burial

26:6–13

6And when Jesus was in Bethany at the
house of Simon the leper, 7a woman
came to Him having an alabaster flask of very costly fragrant oil, and she poured *it* on His head as He sat *at the*
26:8–9
table. 8But when His disciples saw *it,* they
were indignant, saying, "Why this waste?
9For this fragrant oil might have been sold for much and
given to *the* poor."
10But when Jesus was aware of *it,* He said to them, "Why
do you trouble the woman? For she has done a good work
for Me. 11For you have the poor with you always, but Me
you do not have always. 12For in pouring this fragrant oil
on My body, she did *it* for My burial. 13Assuredly, I say to
you, wherever this gospel is preached in the whole world,
what this woman has done will also be told as a memorial
to her."

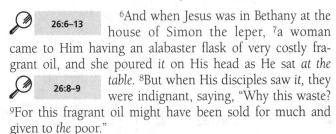

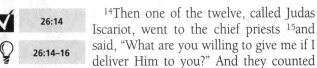

Judas Sells Out

26:14

14Then one of the twelve, called Judas
Iscariot, went to the chief priests 15and
26:14–16
said, "What are you willing to give me if I
deliver Him to you?" And they counted
out to him thirty pieces of silver. 16So from that time he
sought opportunity to betray Him.

A Final Passover Meal

17Now on the first *day of the Feast* of Unleavened Bread
the disciples came to Jesus, saying to Him, "Where do You
want us to prepare for You to eat the Passover?"
18And He said, "Go into the city to a certain man, and say
to him, 'The Teacher says, "My time is at hand; I will keep
the Passover at your house with My disciples." ' "
19So the disciples did as Jesus had directed them; and
they prepared the Passover.
20When evening had come, He sat down with the twelve.

(Bible text continued on page 110)

Preparing Jesus for His Death

A CLOSER LOOK 26:6–13

The woman who anointed Jesus turns out to have been Mary, Lazarus' sister. See "Funeral Preparations," John 12:1–8.

Squandering Wealth on Worship

A CLOSER LOOK 26:8–9

What the disciples saw as waste (vv. 8–9) the Lord saw as worship. The tension still exists. Is it right for a community of believers to spend millions on new church facilities when there are so many poor and homeless on the streets? Moreover, don't they, too, deserve the benefits of art and beauty? "A Parting Gift" (Mark 14:3–9) says more about this incident at Simon's home.

Personality Profile: Judas Iscariot

FOR YOUR INFO 26:14

Name meant: "Praise of the Lord."

Home: Probably Kerioth in southern Judah.

Family: His father was Simon Iscariot.

Occupation: Unknown, although he may have had some background in finance or accounting; he kept track of the money box for Jesus and the other disciples; John calls him a thief (John 12:6).

Best known then and now as: The disciple who betrayed Jesus to His enemies.

CONSIDER THIS 26:14–16

Judas Iscariot, the Betrayer

The New Testament never mentions Judas Iscariot without reminding the reader that he was the man who betrayed Jesus (for example, Matt. 10:4; Mark 3:19; John 12:4). Consequently, to this day the name Judas is a symbol of betrayal.

Why did he do it? His portrayal in the Gospels suggests that he had a keen interest in money. But the amount that the priests paid him—30 pieces of silver—was relatively small. Besides, he had access to the disciples' money box and apparently was known for helping himself to its contents (John 12:6).

Some have suggested that Judas thought that his betrayal would force Jesus into asserting His true power and overthrowing the Romans. Others have suggested that Judas became convinced that Jesus was a false Messiah and that the true Messiah was yet to come. Or perhaps he was upset over Jesus' seemingly casual attitude toward the Law in regard to associating with sinners and violating the Sabbath.

In the end, no one knows what Judas' exact motives were for turning against Jesus. He remains a shadowy figure in the Gospel accounts, unknown by his companions, unfaithful to his Lord, and unmourned in his death. ◆

Judas took his own life. Ironically, his death was memorialized in the purchase of a plot of ground for a cemetery. See "Field of Blood," Acts 1:19.

The New Testament mentions several other Judases. One was a brother of Jesus and probably the author of the book of Jude (Matt. 13:55). See the introduction to Jude.

21Now as they were eating, He said, "Assuredly, I say to you,
one of you will betray Me."
22And they were exceedingly sorrowful, and each of them
began to say to Him, "Lord, is it I?"
23He answered and said, "He who dipped *his* hand with
Me in the dish will betray Me. 24The Son of Man indeed
goes just as it is written of Him, but woe to that man by
whom the Son of Man is betrayed! It would have been good
for that man if he had not been born."
25Then Judas, who was betraying Him, answered and
said, "Rabbi, is it I?"

He said to him, "You have said it."

26And as they were eating, Jesus took bread, blessed[a] and
broke *it*, and gave *it* to the disciples and said, "Take, eat;
this is My body."
27Then He took the cup, and gave thanks, and gave *it* to
them, saying, "Drink from it, all of you. 28For this is My
blood of the new[a] covenant, which is shed for many for the
remission of sins. 29But I say to you, I will not drink of this
fruit of the vine from now on until that day when I drink it
new with you in My Father's kingdom."

26:26 [a]M-Text reads *gave thanks for.* *26:28* [a]NU-Text omits *new.*

CONSIDER THIS
26:35–74

WOULD YOU CHOOSE THESE FOR LEADERS?

Jesus was close to the end of His earthly ministry. His life was about to come to an agonizing end at the hands of bitter opponents. Shortly thereafter, those He had trained would be assuming the reins of His new movement.

That transition period would prove to be rather awkward. It didn't help that it was forced on the group by hostile outsiders. But the most troubling aspect was what happened to Jesus' associates, the ones who would have to carry His banner into the future. During those final days and hours, they began to fall apart:

- *Bravado caused them to overstate their commitment (v. 35). When the moment of truth came, they deserted the Lord (v. 56).*
- *Even though the Lord asked them to keep watch with Him during His final hours of freedom, they fell asleep twice (vv. 40, 43).*
- *At the very moment when Jesus was standing trial and enduring mockery and beatings, Peter, who had led the others in declaring their loyalty (v. 35), denied any association with Him (vv. 69–75).*

In short, the disciples hardly seem to have had the "right stuff" for continuing the important work that Jesus

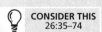

30And when they had sung a hymn, they went out to the Mount of Olives.

31Then Jesus said to them, "All of you will be made to stumble because of Me this night, for it is written:

'I will strike the Shepherd,
And the sheep of the flock will be scattered.'[a]

32But after I have been raised, I will go before you to Galilee."

33Peter answered and said to Him, "Even if all are made to stumble because of You, I will never be made to stumble."

34Jesus said to him, "Assuredly, I say to you that this night, before the rooster crows, you will deny Me three times."

26:35–74

35Peter said to Him, "Even if I have to die with You, I will not deny You!"

And so said all the disciples.

Jesus Prays in the Garden of Gethsemane

36Then Jesus came with them to a place called Geth-

26:36

semane, and said to the disciples, "Sit here while I go and pray over there."

26:31 [a]Zechariah 13:7

◆ ◆ ◆ ◆ ◆ ◆ ◆ ◆ ◆ ◆ ◆ ◆ ◆ ◆ ◆

began. Yet, even after all that He went through, Jesus returned to that very group of followers after His resurrection and declared that they were still His chosen representatives, the ones appointed to continue His work. He even affirmed His commitment to stick with them to the end (28:19–20).

Jesus' treatment of the disciples shows that failure is not the unforgivable act. In fact, it seems to be the crucible out of which character is formed. It is certainly not a sifting-out process to eliminate weak or useless people. Christ does not look for perfect people, but rather faithful *people who can experience His forgiveness and grow.*

Do you stick with people even though they stumble? Do you allow the shortcomings of your spouse, children, boss, coworkers, and neighbors to open up bright futures? Do you give yourself freedom to fail? ◆

The Twelve were all men. But women also played an important role in Jesus' life and ministry. *See "The Women Who Followed Jesus," Luke 8:1–3.*

God has always valued faithfulness over perfection when it comes to handing out acclaim. *See "The Hall of Faithfulness," Heb. 11:1–40.*

Praying in a Workplace

CONSIDER THIS 26:36

Jesus chose a familiar place of work in which to pray one of His final prayers (v. 36). The area around Jerusalem was rich with olive groves, and many people were employed at the commercial oil presses, or gethsemanes, to produce the city's only export product.

The particular garden mentioned here was a place to which Jesus often went alone or with His disciples for prayer or relaxation. As a result, Judas had no trouble finding Him when he led the party to arrest Him (John 18:1–2). The exact site of the garden is unknown, but it may have been located on the Mount of Olives, just east of Jerusalem across the Kidron Valley, opposite the temple (Mark 13:3; John 18:1).

37And He took with Him Peter and the two sons of
Zebedee, and He began to be sorrowful and deeply distressed. 38Then He said to them, "My soul is exceedingly
sorrowful, even to death. Stay here and watch with Me."
39He went a little farther and fell on His face, and prayed,
saying, "O My Father, if it is possible, let this cup pass from
Me; nevertheless, not as I will, but as You *will*."
40Then He came to the disciples and found them sleeping, and said to Peter, "What! Could you not watch with Me
26:41 one hour? 41Watch and pray, lest you enter into temptation. The spirit indeed *is*
willing, but the flesh *is* weak."
42Again, a second time, He went away and prayed, saying,
"O My Father, if this cup cannot pass away from Me unless[a]
I drink it, Your will be done." 43And He came and found
them asleep again, for their eyes were heavy.
44So He left them, went away again, and prayed the third
time, saying the same words. 45Then He came to His disciples and said to them, "Are *you* still sleeping and resting?
Behold, the hour is at hand, and the Son of Man is being
betrayed into the hands of sinners. 46Rise, let us be going.
See, My betrayer is at hand."

"PUT YOUR SWORD IN ITS PLACE, FOR ALL WHO TAKE THE SWORD WILL PERISH BY THE SWORD."
—Matthew 26:52

Jesus Betrayed

47And while He was still speaking, behold, Judas, one of
the twelve, with a great multitude with swords and clubs,
came from the chief priests and elders of the people.
48Now His betrayer had given them a sign, saying,
"Whomever I kiss, He is the One; seize Him." 49Immedi-
ately he went up to Jesus and said, "Greetings, Rabbi!" and
kissed Him.
50But Jesus said to him, "Friend, why have you come?"
Then they came and laid hands on Jesus and took Him.
51And suddenly, one of those *who were* with Jesus stretched
out *his* hand and drew his sword, struck the servant of the
high priest, and cut off his ear.
52But Jesus said to him, "Put your sword in its place, for
all who take the sword will perish[a] by the sword. 53Or do
you think that I cannot now pray to My Father, and He will

26:42 [a]NU-Text reads *if this may not pass away unless.* *26:52* [a]M-Text reads *die.*

Lest You Enter into Temptation

A CLOSER LOOK 26:41 *Prayer is one of the most important strategies believers can use to avoid temptation (v. 41). Only by God's help can we resist. See "Pay Attention to Temptation!" at 1 Cor. 10:12–13.*

provide Me with more than twelve legions of angels? 54How
then could the Scriptures be fulfilled, that it must happen
thus?"
55In that hour Jesus said to the multitudes, "Have you
come out, as against a robber, with swords and clubs to take
Me? I sat daily with you, teaching in the temple, and you
did not seize Me. 56But all this was done that the Scriptures
of the prophets might be fulfilled."
Then all the disciples forsook Him and fled.

Jesus Is Brought Before the High Priest

57And those who had laid hold of Jesus led *Him* away to
Caiaphas the high priest, where the scribes and the elders
were assembled. 58But Peter followed Him at a distance to
the high priest's courtyard. And he went in and sat with the
servants to see the end.

26:59–68

59Now the chief priests, the elders,[a]
and all the council sought false testimony
against Jesus to put Him to death, 60but found none. Even
though many false witnesses came forward, they found
none.[a] But at last two false witnesses[b] came forward 61and
said, "This *fellow* said, 'I am able to destroy the temple of
God and to build it in three days.' "
62And the high priest arose and said to Him, "Do You answer nothing? What *is it* these men testify against You?"
63But Jesus kept silent. And the high priest answered and
said to Him, "I put You under oath by the living God: Tell
us if You are the Christ, the Son of God!"
64Jesus said to him, "*It is as* you said. Nevertheless, I say
to you, hereafter you will see the Son of Man sitting at the
right hand of the Power, and coming on the clouds of
heaven."
65Then the high priest tore his clothes, saying, "He has
spoken blasphemy! What further need do we have of witnesses? Look, now you have heard His blasphemy! 66What
do you think?"
They answered and said, "He is deserving of death."
67Then they spat in His face and beat Him; and others
struck *Him* with the palms of their hands, 68saying, "Prophesy to us, Christ! Who is the one who struck You?"

Peter Denies Knowing Jesus

69Now Peter sat outside in the courtyard. And a servant
girl came to him, saying, "You also were with Jesus of
Galilee."
70But he denied it before *them* all, saying, "I do not know
what you are saying."

26:59 [a]NU-Text omits *the elders.* *26:60* [a]NU-Text puts a comma after *but found none,* does not capitalize *Even,* and omits *they found none.* [b]NU-Text omits *false witnesses.*

No Right Answers

CONSIDER THIS 26:59–68 **Have you ever been trapped in a situation where there is no good alternative? Jesus faced that as He stood trial before Caiaphas and the Jewish elders (v. 59). They were determined to do away with Him by any means, even resorting to false witnesses (vv. 59–62). The situation was so distorted and malicious that there was no good response. So Jesus remained silent (v. 63).**

As their anger intensified, the high priest placed Jesus "under oath by the living God" (v. 63). This meant that Jesus was bound by Law to answer and answer truthfully. In effect, Caiaphas was coercing a response. Jesus rewarded him by giving the very response he expected and wanted—a claim to be "the Christ, the Son of God." This sent His accusers into a frenzy as it allowed them to impose their prearranged verdict (vv. 65–68).

Some situations cannot be salvaged. There is no way out and the worst happens. Like Jesus, however, believers can take hope that even in those moments, God remains in control. Ultimately, He will see that justice is done (Rom. 12:19).

TAINTED MONEY

CONSIDER THIS 27:3–10 **The chief priests knew that the coins tossed back at them by Judas were unacceptable to God (v. 6). It was blood money, money they had paid to apprehend their enemy, Jesus (26:14–16). Yet they turned around and used it to buy a cemetery for the poor—a good deed, yet hypocritical all the same.**

Do you ever present "tainted" money to the Lord—money not necessarily obtained through outright crime, but perhaps through deception, shady deal-making, or dirty politics? When we donate money to churches, missions, schools, ministries to the poor, and the like, we hide nothing from God. He knows all of our motives. He knows whether our gifts are from the first and best of what we've accumulated, or whether we're giving "leftovers." He knows whether our gifts cost us little or nothing (2 Sam. 24:21–24). And He certainly knows—and hates—whatever we have come by unjustly (Mal. 1:6–14). We deceive no one but ourselves if we pretend to honor God while giving Him the fruit of unrighteousness.

The early church found out just how much God disapproves of tainted money. See "Real Estate Deal Deadly," Acts 5:2–10.

71 And when he had gone out to the gateway, another *girl*
saw him and said to those *who were* there, "This *fellow* also
was with Jesus of Nazareth."

72 But again he denied with an oath, "I do not know the
Man!"

73 And a little later those who stood by came up and said
to Peter, "Surely you also are *one* of them, for your speech
betrays you."

74 Then he began to curse and swear, *saying,* "I do not
know the Man!"

Immediately a rooster crowed. 75 And Peter remembered
the word of Jesus who had said to him, "Before the rooster
crows, you will deny Me three times." So he went out and
wept bitterly.

CHAPTER 27

Jesus Is Taken to Pilate

1 When morning came, all the chief priests and elders of
the people plotted against Jesus to put Him to death. 2 And
when they had bound Him, they led Him away and delivered Him to Pontius[a] Pilate the governor.

Judas Hangs Himself

27:3–10 3 Then Judas, His betrayer, seeing that
He had been condemned, was remorseful
and brought back the thirty pieces of silver to the chief
priests and elders, 4 saying, "I have sinned by betraying innocent blood."

And they said, "What *is that* to us? You see *to it!*"

5 Then he threw down the pieces of silver in the temple
and departed, and went and hanged himself.

6 But the chief priests took the silver pieces and said, "It is
not lawful to put them into the treasury, because they are
the price of blood." 7 And they consulted together and
bought with them the potter's field, to bury strangers in.
8 Therefore that field has been called the Field of Blood to
this day.

9 Then was fulfilled what was spoken by Jeremiah the
prophet, saying, "And they took the thirty pieces of silver,
the value of Him who was priced, whom they of the children of Israel priced, 10 and gave them for the potter's field,
as the LORD directed me."[a]

Jesus Before Pilate

11 Now Jesus stood before the governor. And the governor
asked Him, saying, "Are You the King of the Jews?"

27:2 [a]NU-Text omits *Pontius.* *27:10* [a]Jeremiah 32:6–9

Jesus said to him, "*It is as* you say." 12And while He was
being accused by the chief priests and elders, He answered
nothing.

13Then Pilate said to Him, "Do You not hear how many
things they testify against You?" 14But He answered him not
one word, so that the governor marveled greatly.

15Now at the feast the governor was accustomed to releas-

27:16

ing to the multitude one prisoner whom
they wished. 16And at that time they had
a notorious prisoner called Barabbas.[a] 17Therefore, when
they had gathered together, Pilate said to them, "Whom do
you want me to release to you? Barabbas, or Jesus who is
called Christ?" 18For he knew that they had handed Him
over because of envy.

19While he was sitting on the judgment seat, his wife sent
to him, saying, "Have nothing to do with that just Man, for
I have suffered many things today in a dream because of
Him."

20But the chief priests and elders persuaded the multitudes that they should ask for Barabbas and destroy Jesus.
21The governor answered and said to them, "Which of the
two do you want me to release to you?"

They said, "Barabbas!"

22Pilate said to them, "What then shall I do with Jesus
who is called Christ?"

They all said to him, "Let Him be crucified!"

23Then the governor said, "Why, what evil has He done?"

But they cried out all the more, saying, "Let Him be crucified!"

24When Pilate saw that he could not prevail at all, but
rather *that* a tumult was rising, he took water and washed
his hands before the multitude, saying, "I am innocent of
the blood of this just Person.[a] You see *to it*."

25And all the people answered and said, "His blood *be* on
us and on our children."

26Then he released Barabbas to them; and when he had
scourged Jesus, he delivered *Him* to be crucified.

(Bible text continued on page 117)

27:16 [a]NU-Text reads *Jesus Barabbas.* *27:24* [a]NU-Text omits *just.*

BUT HE ANSWERED HIM NOT ONE WORD, SO THAT THE GOVERNOR MARVELED GREATLY.
—Matthew 27:14

The Prisoner Barabbas

A CLOSER LOOK 27:16

But for a remarkable set of circumstances, the "notorious prisoner called Barabbas" (v. 16) probably would have remained unknown to history. See "'Not This Man But Barabbas!'" Mark 15:7.

FOR YOUR INFO
27:32

THE LITTLE PEOPLE AT JESUS' DEATH

Have you ever noticed that Jesus tended to surround Himself with or be surrounded by relatively average people of little social standing or influence?

At Jesus' birth, various kinds of "little people" were involved: a minor priest and his barren wife, a small town girl and a poor carpenter, shepherds, an elderly woman, and others. A similar cast appeared during Jesus' final days and hours, including Simon, who was compelled to carry His cross (v. 32). Many of these people showed curiosity about Christ, demonstrated understanding and loyalty, or provided needed services and acts of compassion. (See table below.)

Unlike many who rise to positions of prominence and leadership, Jesus never lost touch with the little people of society. He did not insulate Himself from difficulties by surrounding Himself with the powerful, the wealthy, and the privileged. His birth, life, and death involved countless ordinary folks who could perceive His message about true values and needs.

Are you in touch with the unnamed and unnoticed? How can you serve them? What can you learn from them? ◆

ORDINARY PEOPLE WHO SAW JESUS TO THE CROSS

Simon the leper, who had been an untouchable outcast	Hosts Jesus as his house guest (Matt. 26:6)
An unnamed woman (probably Mary of Bethany; see John 11:2; compare 12:1–8)	Uses expensive ointment to anoint Jesus' head (26:7)
An unnamed homeowner in Jerusalem	Opens his home to Jesus and the Twelve for their last meal together (26:18)
The disciples, Jesus' chosen successors from rural Galilee	Overstate their faith (26:35); join Jesus in a garden during the final hours before His arrest (26:40, 43, 56)
An unnamed servant girl	Asks Peter about his association with Jesus (26:69)
Another girl in the crowd	Also asks Peter about his association with Jesus (26:71)
Unnamed crowd members	Also enquire about Peter's association with Jesus (26:71)
Judas	Betrays Christ; later breaks down with guilt and commits suicide (27:3–5)
Barabbas, a convicted criminal	Is freed instead of Jesus due to a mob's demands (27:16, 26)
Simon of Cyrene, a man in the watching crowd	Is conscripted to carry Jesus' cross (27:32)
Two dying robbers	Are executed with Jesus (27:38, 44)
An unnamed crowd member	Offers Jesus a drink as He is in His death throes (27:48)
An unnamed Roman centurion	Observes that Jesus must be the Son of God (27:54)
Some loyal women from Galilee	Look on from afar (27:55–56)

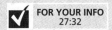

Soldiers Mock Jesus

27Then the soldiers of the governor took Jesus into the
Praetorium and gathered the whole garrison around Him.
28And they stripped Him and put a scarlet robe on Him.
29When they had twisted a crown of thorns, they put *it* on
His head, and a reed in His right hand. And they bowed the
knee before Him and mocked Him, saying, "Hail, King of
the Jews!" 30Then they spat on Him, and took the reed and
struck Him on the head. 31And when they had mocked
Him, they took the robe off Him, put His *own* clothes on
Him, and led Him away to be crucified.

The Crucifixion

27:32

32Now as they came out, they found a
man of Cyrene, Simon by name. Him
they compelled to bear His cross. 33And when they had
come to a place called Golgotha, that is to say, Place of a
Skull, 34they gave Him sour[a] wine mingled with gall to
drink. But when He had tasted *it,* He would not drink.
35Then they crucified Him, and divided His garments,
casting lots,[a] that it might be fulfilled which was spoken by
the prophet:

> "They divided My garments among them,
> And for My clothing they cast lots."[b]

36Sitting down, they kept watch over Him there. 37And they
put up over His head the accusation written against Him:

THIS IS JESUS THE KING OF THE JEWS.

38Then two robbers were crucified with Him, one on the
right and another on the left.
39And those who passed by blasphemed Him, wagging
their heads 40and saying, "You who destroy the temple and
build *it* in three days, save Yourself! If You are the Son of
God, come down from the cross."
41Likewise the chief priests also, mocking with the scribes
and elders,[a] said, 42"He saved others; Himself He cannot
save. If He is the King of Israel,[a] let Him now come down
from the cross, and we will believe Him.[b] 43He trusted in
God; let Him deliver Him now if He will have Him; for He
said, 'I am the Son of God.' "
44Even the robbers who were crucified with Him reviled
Him with the same thing.

(Bible text continued on page 119)

27:34 [a]NU-Text omits *sour.* *27:35* [a]NU-Text and M-Text omit the rest of this verse. [b]Psalm 22:18 *27:41* [a]M-Text reads *with the scribes, the Pharisees, and the elders.* *27:42* [a]NU-Text reads *He is the King of Israel!* [b]NU-Text and M-Text read *we will believe in Him.*

AND THEY BOWED THE KNEE BEFORE HIM AND MOCKED HIM. —Matthew 27:29

FOR YOUR INFO
27:57

WEALTHY PEOPLE IN THE NEW TESTAMENT

Most of Jesus' followers were not wealthy, but a few notable ones, like Joseph of Arimathea (v. 57), were. We can learn a great deal from the wealthy people recorded in the New Testament, about the dangers and the disciplines of money.

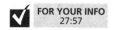

Persons	What They Did With Their Wealth	Lessons To Be Learned
Zacchaeus the tax collector (Luke 19:1–10)	• Before faith, cheated citizens and abused the poor. • After faith, repented and made restitution.	(1) Ill-gotten gain must be repaid. (2) God saves and changes us—all the way down to our pocketbooks.
Joseph of Arimathea (Matt. 27:57–61; Mark 15:42–46; Luke 23:50–53)	• Pre-paid his own funeral. • Donated his tomb for the burial of Jesus.	(3) Forsaking treasures on earth for the kingdom will be rewarded.
Women supporters of Christ (Luke 8:3*; Luke 23:55–24:10; Mark 15:40; 16:1)	• Supported Jesus' work. • Assisted in His burial (probably donated expensive perfume).	(4) Generosity characterizes those who follow Jesus.
Roman centurion who believed (Matt. 8:5–13; Luke 7:5)	• Showed kindness toward the Jews. • Paid for the building of a synagogue. • Showed compassion for his ill servant.	(5) When we love people it shows in the things we do and the projects we support.
Rich young ruler (Matt. 19:16–30; Mark 10:17–31; Luke 18:18–30)	• Unwilling to part with his wealth when tested by Jesus.	(6) Those who cling to wealth have difficulty getting into the kingdom. (7) Righteousness cannot be earned, but must be received as a gift. (8) "Many who are first will be last, and the last first."
Philemon (Philem. 1*)	• Owned slaves and other property. • Forgave a runaway slave, both morally and financially.	(9) People are more valuable than property.
Joseph, called Barnabas (Acts 4:36–37*)	• Sold land and gave the proceeds to believers.	(10) Partnership in the gospel may mean putting your money where believers hurt.
Ananias and Sapphira (Acts 5:1–11*)	• Sold land and tried to deceive the church about the proceeds to gain a reputation.	(11) God is not fooled by gracious appearances but sees the heart and acts accordingly.
Rich Christians written about by James (James 2:1–7)	• Exploited the tendency of some to cater to them because of their wealth. • Dragged other believers into court and slandered Jesus' name.	(12) God favors those who are rich in faith; they will inherit the kingdom.
Lydia (Acts 16:13–15*, 40)	• Hosted the first church in Europe in her home.	(13) We should use our resources and homes to accomplish God's purposes.
Cornelius the centurion (Acts 10:1–48*)	• Generous to the poor. • Sought out Peter concerning the faith.	(14) Fear of God should prompt us to admit our own need for a Savior.
The Ethiopian treasurer (Acts 8:26–40)	• Nurtured his belief in God by traveling to Jerusalem. • Invited Philip to explain more about the faith.	(15) Stewardship of money and study of Scripture go hand in hand—as do business trips and worship services.
Simon the Sorcerer (Acts 8:9–25)	• Longed for spiritual power and thought it could be bottled and sold.	(16) The gifts of God cannot be bought.

Your checkbook is a diary of your values. God calls believers to be compassionate, merciful, and just to all. Does your checkbook reflect such values? Does it show a pattern of godly concern for people?

***See profiles of these people at the texts indicated.**

Wealth is a major topic in the New Testament. Jesus often warned about its dangers. See Matt. 6:24; Mark 10:17–31; and Luke 12:13–21. Likewise, Paul challenged believers to use their resources in a Christlike way. See "Christians and Money," 1 Tim. 6:6–19.

45Now from the sixth hour until the ninth hour
there was darkness over all the land. 46And about
the ninth hour Jesus cried out with a loud voice,
saying, "Eli, Eli, lama sabachthani?" that is, "My
God, My God, why have You forsaken Me?"[a]
47Some of those who stood there, when they
heard *that,* said, "This Man is calling for Elijah!"
48Immediately one of them ran and took a sponge,
filled *it* with sour wine and put *it* on a reed, and offered it to Him to drink.
49The rest said, "Let Him alone; let us see if Elijah
will come to save Him."
50And Jesus cried out again with a loud voice,
and yielded up His spirit.
51Then, behold, the veil of the temple was torn in
two from top to bottom; and the earth quaked, and
the rocks were split, 52and the graves were opened;
and many bodies of the saints who had fallen
asleep were raised; 53and coming out of the graves
after His resurrection, they went into the holy city
and appeared to many.
54So when the centurion and those with
him, who were guarding Jesus, saw the earthquake and the things that had happened, they
feared greatly, saying, "Truly this was the Son of
God!"
55And many women who followed Jesus from
Galilee, ministering to Him, were there looking on

27:56

from afar, 56among whom were
Mary Magdalene, Mary the
mother of James and Joses,[a] and the mother of
Zebedee's sons.

Jesus Is Buried in a Borrowed Tomb

27:57

57Now when evening had
come, there came a rich man
from Arimathea, named Joseph, who himself had

27:58–61

also become a disciple of Jesus.
58This man went to Pilate and
asked for the body of Jesus. Then Pilate com-

27:59–60

manded the body to be given to
him. 59When Joseph had taken
the body, he wrapped it in a clean linen cloth,
60and laid it in his new tomb which he had hewn
out of the rock; and he rolled a large stone against
the door of the tomb, and departed. 61And Mary
Magdalene was there, and the other Mary, sitting
opposite the tomb.
62On the next day, which followed the Day of
Preparation, the chief priests and Pharisees gathered together to Pilate, 63saying, "Sir, we remember,
while He was still alive, how that deceiver said, 'After three days I will rise.' 64Therefore command
that the tomb be made secure until the third day,
lest His disciples come by night[a] and steal Him
away, and say to the people, 'He has risen from the
dead.' So the last deception will be worse than the
first."
65Pilate said to them, "You have a guard; go your
way, make *it* as secure as you know how." 66So they
went and made the tomb secure, sealing the stone
and setting the guard.

CHAPTER 28

The Resurrection

28:1–10
see pg. 120

1Now after the Sabbath, as the
first *day* of the week began to
dawn, Mary Magdalene and the other Mary came

(Bible text continued on page 121)

27:46 [a]Psalm 22:1 *27:56* [a]NU-Text reads *Joseph.* *27:64* [a]NU-Text omits *by night.*

Mary—A Common Name for Some Uncommon Women

A CLOSER LOOK
27:56

At least six Marys are mentioned in the New Testament. Why was the name so common? See "Why So Many Marys?" Mark 15:40.

For a listing of other women who followed Jesus, see Luke 8:1.

A Borrowed Tomb

A CLOSER LOOK
27:58–61

Just as God provided for Jesus' needs at His birth (see "A Poor Family Comes into Wealth," Matt. 2:11), He provided for His needs in death (27:57–61). "A Burial Fit for a King" at Mark 15:42—16:1 talks about the gift of a borrowed tomb.

Expensive Funerals

A CLOSER LOOK
27:59–60

It is common for people to spend a great deal on funerals, sometimes more than they should. See "A Burial Fit for a King," Mark 15:42—16:1, for more on honoring the dead without breaking the bank.

CONSIDER THIS
28:1–10

MYTH #2

10 MYTHS ABOUT CHRISTIANITY

MYTH: There Is No Evidence That Jesus Rose from the Dead

Many people today accept a number of myths about Christianity, with the result that they never respond to Jesus as He really is. This is one of ten articles that speak to some of those misconceptions. For a list of all ten, see 1 Tim. 1:3–4.

All four Gospels give an account of Jesus' resurrection (vv. 1–10; Mark 16:1–18; Luke 24:1–12; John 20:1–29). Moreover, the rest of the New Testament speaks with a tremendous sense of confidence about an empty tomb and the triumph of Christ over death.

And no wonder. If true, the resurrection is the most amazing news the world has ever heard. It means there is a God after all. It means that Jesus really is God's Son. It means that Christ is alive—today—and we can know Him and be touched by His life and power. It means that we need not fear death the way we once did; we are not destined to oblivion but to spend eternity with God. It also means that knowing God is of the utmost importance right now, while we can.

These are important implications, so the question of whether Jesus actually rose from the dead is crucial. At least four lines of evidence indicate that He did:

(1) *Jesus really was dead.* Every source we have indicates that Jesus was publicly executed before large crowds. He was certified as dead by both a centurion in charge of the execution—a professional whose job it was to determine that death had taken place—and by the regional governor, Pilate, who sent to have the matter checked. This is an important point because some skeptics claim that Jesus was not really dead, that He was only near death but revived in the cool of the tomb.

(2) *The tomb was found empty.* Jesus was buried in a new tomb, one that had never before been used (John 19:41). That means it was in perfect condition and would have been easy to locate. But when Jesus' friends arrived on the second morning after His death, His body was gone. All the accounts agree on this.

The empty tomb was no less astonishing to Jesus' enemies than it was to His friends. His enemies had been working for years to see Him dead and buried. Having accomplished their goal, they took pains to post a guard and seal the tomb with an enormous boulder. Nevertheless, on Easter morning the tomb was found empty.

Who emptied it? Either men or God. If men, which ones? Jesus' enemies would have been the least likely to have stolen the body. Even if they had, they would certainly have produced it later to refute the claims of the disciples that Jesus was alive. What about Jesus' friends? Unlikely, since the accounts show them to have been very demoralized after the crucifixion. Nor would they have willingly suffered persecution and death for what they knew to be a lie.

(3) *Jesus appeared after His death to many witnesses.* In a garden, on a road, in an upstairs room, by a lake—each of the Gospels recounts Jesus' post-resurrection appearances to His fearful, doubting followers over a period of forty days. Were these hallucinations? That seems implausible, since they happened to too many people, among them hardheaded fishermen, steadfast women, civil servants, and the ultimate skeptic, Thomas.

(4) *Countless people have encountered the living Jesus and been changed by Him.* The resurrection is not simply a matter of intellectual curiosity or theological argument, but of personal experience. From the first century to today there have been innumer-

(continued on next page)

to see the tomb. [2]And behold, there was a great earthquake;
for an angel of the Lord descended from heaven, and came
and rolled back the stone from the door,[a] and sat on it. [3]His
countenance was like lightning, and his clothing as white as
snow. [4]And the guards shook for fear of him, and became
like dead *men.*

[5]But the angel answered and said to the women, "Do not
be afraid, for I know that you seek Jesus who was crucified.
28:6 [6]He is not here; for He is risen, as He
said. Come, see the place where the Lord
lay. [7]And go quickly and tell His disciples that He is risen
from the dead, and indeed He is going before you into
Galilee; there you will see Him. Behold, I have told you."

[8]So they went out quickly from the tomb with fear and
great joy, and ran to bring His disciples word.

(Bible text continued on page 123)

28:2 [a]NU-Text omits *from the door.*

MYTH #2 10 MYTHS ABOUT CHRISTIANITY

(continued from previous page)

able people who have turned from being totally opposed or indifferent to Christianity to being utterly convinced that it is true. What changed them? They met the living Jesus. He has invited them to respond to Him in faith and challenged them to live according to His way. Jesus is as alive now as He was that first Easter morning. He still invites people to know Him today. ◆

CONSIDER THIS
28:6

Don't Miss God's Help

Do you feel uneasy when it comes to religion and spirituality? Do issues of faith and morality create fear? The women who went to the tomb on the first Easter Sunday were terribly frightened by what they found—or rather, by what they didn't *find, for the tomb was empty (v. 6)!*

Fortunately, God understands when spiritual matters invade the safety of our world. He offers help to overcome our fears and deal with whatever has come our way. For Mary and Mary Magdalene, He sent an angel to comfort and enlighten them about the reality of Christ's resurrection. He also sent an angel to Joseph, the earthly father of Jesus, when he was troubled by his fiancée's miraculous pregnancy (1:18–25).

So it was for many others in Scripture, who were no less troubled by spiritual events and truths than many of us are today. In addition to angels, God's help has included other people, dramatic and even miraculous demonstrations of His power, direct promises, and the enormous comfort of His Word. These helps show that God appreciates the impact of spiritual light suddenly shining in a dark world. He helps us overcome the shock not only of what *He has spoken, but* that *He has spoken.*

The question remains, will we respond to His message? No matter how awkward we may feel about matters of faith, we dare not avoid them. God opens up these scary places in our lives only because He wants to restore us to Himself. ◆

YOU ARE THERE
28:19

To All the Nations

Jesus sent His followers to make disciples of all the nations (ethnē, *"peoples"; v. 19*)*. That mandate may seem obvious to us today. After all, we live at the end of 2,000 years of Christian outreach based on this and similar passages. Christianity now is an overwhelmingly Gentile religion subscribed to by roughly one-third of the world's population. And with modern technology, it appears to be a relatively simple task to expand that outreach even further.*

Yet in many ways we are just like Jesus' original disciples. They wanted a local hero, a Messiah just for Israel, one who would follow their customs and confirm their prejudices. So they were no doubt stunned by the scope and far-reaching implications of the global, cross-cultural vision that Jesus now presented. He was turning out to be more than the King of the Jews; He was the international Christ, the Savior of the entire world.

Actually, Jesus had been showing them this since the beginning of His ministry. Matthew recorded again and again His work among the Gentiles (Matt. 8:10; 15:24). The writer even cited Isaiah 42:1–4, that Jesus would "declare justice to the Gentiles [nations] . . . and in His name Gentiles will trust" (12:14–21). Yet the disciples had a hard time believing it. Could their Lord really be interested in "all the nations"? They certainly weren't.

(continued on next page)

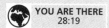

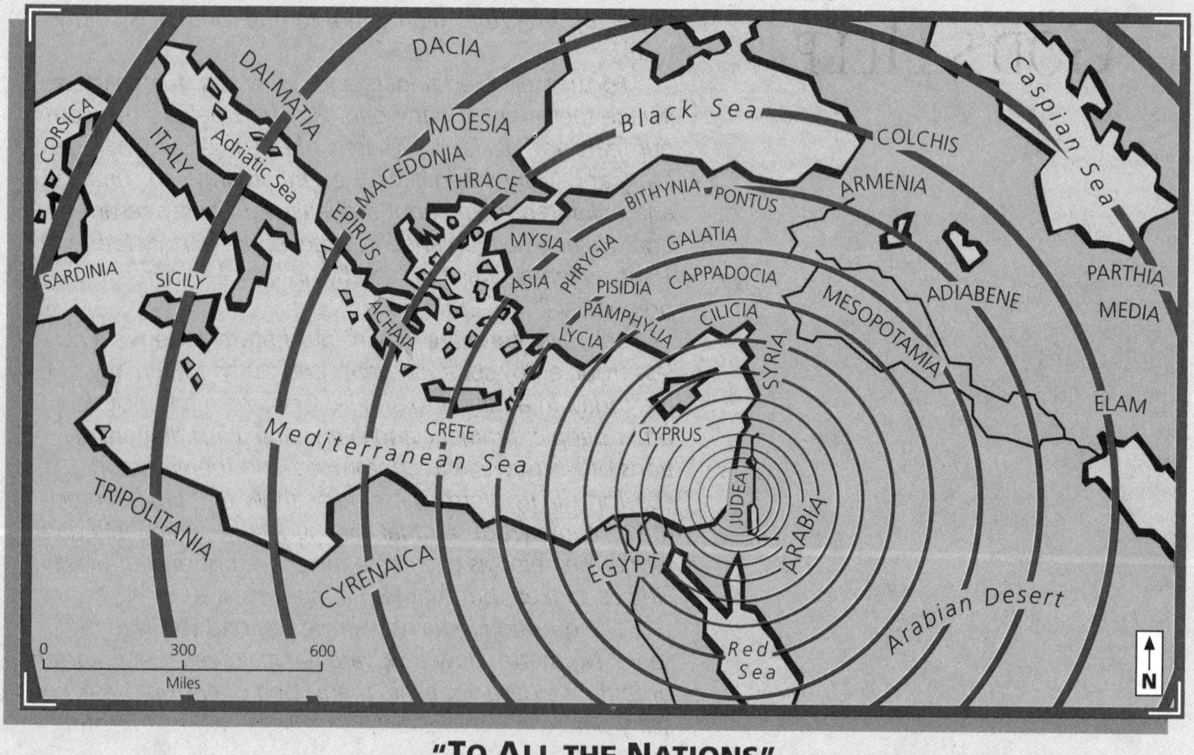

"To All the Nations"

9And as they went to tell His disciples,[a] behold, Jesus met
them, saying, "Rejoice!" So they came and held Him by the
feet and worshiped Him. 10Then Jesus said to them, "Do not
be afraid. Go *and* tell My brethren to go to Galilee, and
there they will see Me."

The Guards Are Bribed

11Now while they were going, behold, some of the guard
came into the city and reported to the chief priests all the
things that had happened. 12When they had assembled with
the elders and consulted together, they gave a large sum of
money to the soldiers, 13saying, "Tell them, 'His disciples
came at night and stole Him *away* while we slept.' 14And if
this comes to the governor's ears, we will appease him and
make you secure." 15So they took the money and did as
they were instructed; and this saying is commonly reported
among the Jews until this day.

Jesus Sends His Followers into the World

16Then the eleven disciples went away into Galilee, to the
mountain which Jesus had appointed for them. 17When
they saw Him, they worshiped Him; but some doubted.

28:18

28:19

18And Jesus came and spoke to them,
saying, "All authority has been given to
Me in heaven and on earth. 19Go therefore[a] and make disciples of all the na-
tions, baptizing them in the name of the Father and of the
Son and of the Holy Spirit, 20teaching them to observe all
things that I have commanded you; and lo, I am with you
always, *even* to the end of the age." Amen.[a]

28:19 [a]M-Text omits *therefore.* *28:20* [a]NU-Text omits *Amen.*

Jesus' Power

A CLOSER LOOK 28:18

The power that gave Jesus authority and that He promised to His followers (vv. 18–19) was not the power of force or political authority. It was an ability to accomplish a very specific task. See "Power," Acts 1:8.

(continued from previous page)

Are we? It's easy to pay lip service to the idea that Jesus cares for the whole world. But isn't it easier to follow a Christ that fits comfortably into our own culture?

Culture, after all, is the key. Jesus told His Galilean followers to "make disciples," and they did—*Jewish* disciples. But they experienced profound culture-shock when the Holy Spirit brought new groups into the fellowship, including Hellenist disciples (Acts 6:1–7), Samaritan disciples (8:4–25), and eventually even Gentile disciples of all kinds (10:1—11:18; 15:1–21).

Today the bulk of new disciples are non-white and non-Western. Not surprisingly, they bring very different cultural perspectives into the church. So one of the greatest challenges believers will face in the coming years is the same one that the original disciples faced at the inauguration of the movement: to not only believe but to *accept* that Jesus really is for all the nations. ◆

One of the key people responsible for helping communicate the message about Christ throughout the Roman world was "Luke, the Gentile Author." Find out more about him at the introduction to Luke.

The spread of the gospel to "all the nations" began in an explosive way just a few days after Jesus' words in Matthew 28. See "A Surprising First Fulfillment of Acts 1:8," Acts 2:8–11.

As the gospel spread to people of different cultures, there was always the danger of believers going their separate ways. That's why Paul challenged Christians to pursue unity in the body of Christ and charity among the peoples of the world. See "Are We One People?" Rom. 11:13–24.

The Action-oriented Christ

There are four Gospels. Which one should you read first? Probably the Gospel of Mark. Even though it is placed second among the four, it's an ideal book for "entry-level" readers. Like a television drama, Mark's Gospel portrays the life of Jesus in simple, straightforward, action-packed vignettes. In fact, *action* is the hallmark of the book: Jesus reveals Himself here more by what He does than by what He says.

If you like stories, you'll love reading Mark. The author opens with a view of crowds streaming into the wilderness to be baptized by John the Baptist (1:4–5). A close-up shows John predicting the coming of the Messiah (1:6–8). Then Jesus appears, and John baptizes Him (1:9–11). Dissolve to another wilderness setting, where Jesus endures a lonely vigil as Satan tests Him, wild beasts haunt Him, and angels attend Him (1:12–13). Time passes, and arid wilderness gives way to seaside Galilee, where Jesus launches His ministry with an appeal for repentance (1:14–15).

And so it goes, as Mark heaps up scenes of an action-oriented Christ, going places and doing things. The overall message is that Jesus is the Son of God (1:1, 11; 9:7; 14:61–62; 15:39) who came "[not] to be served, but to serve, and to give His life a ransom for many" (10:45).

Mark

Jesus is the Son of God who came to serve.

C O N T E N T S

Mark's Vivid Portrayal of People

A R T I C L E S

Life—The Big Picture (12:28–34)

Unfortunately, many Christians have developed some dangerous attitudes that push God to the fringes of their lives. Some popular myths need to be explored—and exploded.

A Parting Gift (14:3–9)

Sensing that her days with Jesus were drawing to a close, a woman poured out a costly gift of oil worth about a year's wages.

Why So Many Marys? (15:40)

Mary was a popular name in first-century Palestine. It honored one of Israel's most famous women.

Faith Impacts the World (16:15–16)

Jesus had global impact in mind for His followers. But spreading Christ's message and having an impact requires that we understand how our world operates.

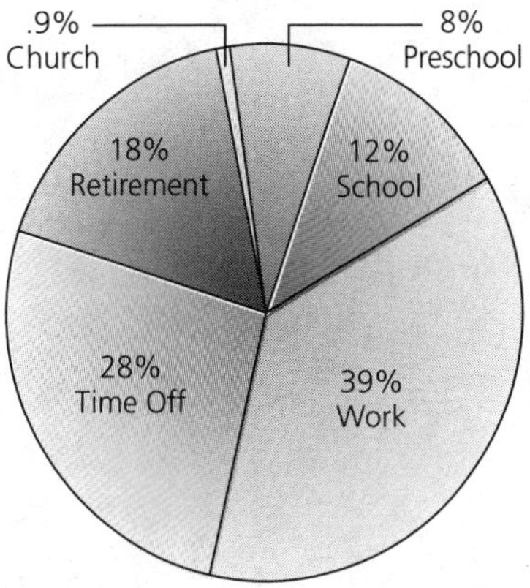

HOW THE TYPICAL 75-YEAR-OLD AMERICAN WILL HAVE SPENT LIFE

Tales of the Fisherman

The vivid, direct style of Mark's Gospel and its attention to detail provide a sense of authenticity and immediacy that could come only from an eyewitness to the events recorded. But was Mark himself a participant in the story? Probably not.

The book never mentions the name of its author. However, in about A.D. 125, Papias, bishop of Hierapolis in Asia Minor, claimed that Mark created this Gospel by writing down Peter's recollections of Jesus' life. Subsequent tradition agrees with Papias in ascribing the book to Mark.

So possibly what we have here are the memoirs of Peter. Ministering to Christians in Rome, he may have recalled his memories of Jesus in order to create a Gospel for Christians under persecution by Nero. If so, it's no wonder that the narrative reads so easily: as a fisherman, Peter was probably quite skilled in holding an audience with a good story.

Fortunately, Mark wrote it all down. Mark had not followed Jesus during His lifetime—though he may have been present at the arrest of Jesus, leaving an "anonymous signature" in the story of a young man who fled naked (Mark 14:51–52). Mark was a native of Jerusalem, and the church often met for prayer at his mother's house (Acts 12:12). Thanks to his cousin Barnabas (Col. 4:10), he was mentored in the faith (Acts 15:37–39) and became a valued associate of Paul (2 Tim. 4:11) and Peter (1 Pet. 5:13). Mark probably traveled with Peter to Rome, where tradition holds that he composed his Gospel in the early 60s. ◆

John Mark

Church tradition holds that John Mark was known to have stumpy fingers. Evidently that did not impede him from writing the first Gospel. Turn to Acts 15:37 to learn more about the man Peter described as "my son" (1 Pet. 5:13).

CHAPTER 1

John the Baptist Prepares the Way

1The beginning of the gospel of Jesus Christ, the Son of
God. 2As it is written in the Prophets:[a]

"Behold, I send My messenger before Your face,
Who will prepare Your way before You." [b]
3"The voice of one crying in the wilderness:
'Prepare the way of the LORD;
Make His paths straight.' "[a]

4John came baptizing in the wilderness and preaching a
1:5 baptism of repentance for the remission
of sins. 5Then all the land of Judea, and
those from Jerusalem, went out to him and were all baptized by him in the Jordan River, confessing their sins.
1:6 6Now John was clothed with camel's
hair and with a leather belt around his
waist, and he ate locusts and wild honey. 7And he preached,
saying, "There comes One after me who is mightier than I,
whose sandal strap I am not worthy to stoop down and

(Bible text continued on page 130)

1:2 [a]NU-Text reads *Isaiah the prophet.* [b]Malachi 3:1 *1:3* [a]Isaiah 40:3

JOHN, A VOICE CRYING IN THE WILDERNESS

All four Gospels present John as a preacher in the wilderness (Matt. 3:1; Mark 1:4; Luke 3:2; John 1:23). Even in his own day he must have seemed odd. He lived in the wild. He ate locusts and honey. He seemed given to extremes of humility—for example, declaring that "[Jesus] must increase, but I must decrease" (John 3:30), and that he was not worthy even to loose Jesus' sandal strap (1:27).

But the main thing that impressed people about John was that he fearlessly preached a message of repentance to any who would listen—and many did. Crowds flocked to hear him from throughout Judea, including the main city of Jerusalem. In addition to everyday folk, he attracted great sinners like the tax gatherers, respectable socialites like the religious leaders, and even Gentiles like the Roman soldiers. What was his winsome message? "Brood of vipers! Who warned you to flee from the wrath to come?" (Luke 3:7).

As one might have expected, he eventually offended the wrong person—Herodias, wife of the King Herod (see "Hateful Herodias," Matt. 14:3). John condemned the

PERSONALITY PROFILE: JOHN THE BAPTIST

FOR YOUR INFO 1:6 **In his day, often confused with:** The Old Testament prophet, Elijah; one of the other prophets; the Messiah.

Home: Born and raised in a town of Judah, but lived most of his adult life in the Judean wilderness, near the Jordan River.

Family: Son of Zacharias and Elizabeth.

Occupation: Preacher and prophet.

Best known today for: Preparing the way for Jesus the Messiah.

royal couple for their illicit marriage. Outraged, Herodias had her husband arrest the prophet and badgered him to execute him. But the king refused, fearing to kill a man he knew to be holy and just. However, Herodias knew ways to accomplish her evil ends, and eventually had her way (Mark 6:14–29).

John's influence continued to live on after his death. Several of his disciples became followers of Jesus (for example, Andrew, John 1:35–40). And nearly 30 years later, when Paul arrived at Ephesus to preach the gospel, he encountered a group of John's disciples (Acts 19:1–7).

The last of the Old Testament prophets, John was declared by Jesus to be the greatest of men (Matt. 11:11–14). He fulfilled the purpose for which he was sent—to pave the way for Jesus. ◆

Even evaluated by the standards of his own day, John the Baptist reflected none of the outward trappings of a successful ministry. See "John the Street Preacher," Matt. 3:4, to learn about the "wealth" of John.

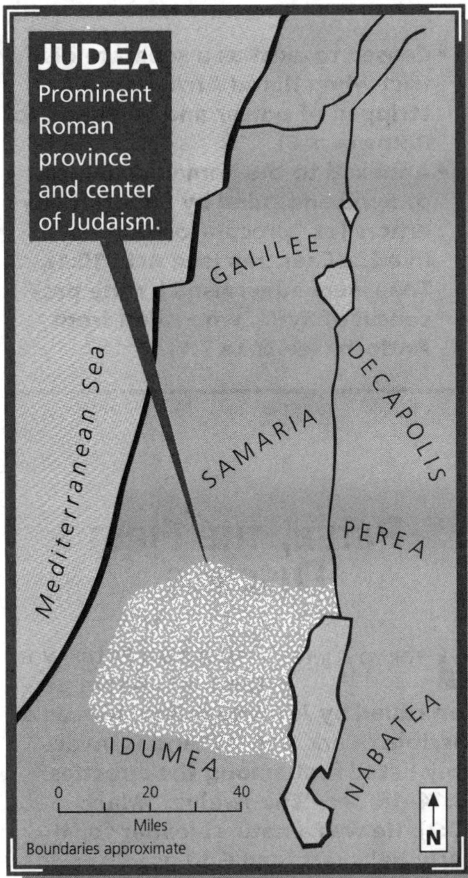

JUDEA

YOU ARE THERE 1:5 **• The most prominent Roman province of Palestine in the first century.**

• Contained four distinctive types of land: coastal plains near the Mediterranean Sea, lowlands in the south, hill country, and desert.

• Named by the Greeks and Romans from a term used of the Hebrew captives who had returned to the promised land after the Babylonian exile, most of whom were of the tribe of Judah.

• Under the Persians, a district administered by a governor, usually a Jew (Ezra 5:8; Hag. 1:14; 2:2).

(continued on next page)

(continued from previous page)

- **Ceased to exist as a separate district when Herod Archelaus was stripped of power and banished to Rome (A.D. 6).**
- **Annexed to the Roman province of Syria and ruled by imperial governors (or "procurators") who lived at Caesarea (see Acts 10:1). They were supervised by the proconsul of Syria, who ruled from Antioch (see Luke 3:1).**

PETER, THE FIRST DISCIPLE

FOR YOUR INFO 1:16 **Fisherman Peter was the first known person called by Jesus to follow Him as a disciple (Mark 1:16–18) and is invariably listed first among the apostles (3:14–16; see "The Twelve," Matt. 10:2). He was a natural leader for the early believers, and God used him to break new ground for the movement that Jesus initiated. Among Peter's "firsts":**

- **First apostle to recognize Jesus as the Christ (Matt. 16:13–17).**
- **First ordinary person to walk on water (Matt. 14:28–30).**
- **First apostle to see the risen Lord (Luke 24:34; 1 Cor. 15:5).**
- **Preached the first sermon after the coming of the Holy Spirit (Acts 2:14–40).**
- **First apostle to break the barrier between Jews and Gentiles (Acts 10:1—11:18).**
- **First apostle to be associated with the writing of a Gospel. Early church tradition says that Peter died in Rome. Papias (A.D. 125) claimed that Peter's preaching led his interpreter, Mark, to write the first Gospel.**

---

loose. 8I indeed baptized you with water, but He will baptize you with the Holy Spirit."

John Baptizes Jesus

9It came to pass in those days *that* Jesus came from
Nazareth of Galilee, and was baptized by John in the Jordan. 10And immediately, coming up from[a] the water, He saw
the heavens parting and the Spirit descending upon Him
like a dove. 11Then a voice came from heaven, "You are My
beloved Son, in whom I am well pleased."

Jesus Faces Temptation in the Wilderness

1:12–13 12Immediately the Spirit drove Him
into the wilderness. 13And He was there
in the wilderness forty days, tempted by Satan, and was
with the wild beasts; and the angels ministered to Him.

(Bible text continued on page 132)

1:10 [a]NU-Text reads *out of.*

The "Real" World

A CLOSER LOOK 1:12–13 *Jesus understands real life. He faced real temptations—the same temptations that show up every day in the "real" world. See "You Don't Understand!" at Matt. 4:3.*

PERSONALITY PROFILE: SIMON PETER

Also known as: Simon (his given name); renamed Cephas (Aramaic), or Peter (Greek), or "The Rock" or "Rocky" (English) by Christ.

Home: Bethsaida and Capernaum on the north shore of the Sea of Galilee.

Family: His father's name was Jonah; his younger brother was Andrew; he was married and his wife traveled with him as he spread the message about Jesus.

Occupation: Commercial fisherman; later one of Jesus' first representatives.

Best known today for: His declaration that Jesus was the Christ, and his denial of Christ.

YOU ARE THERE
1:21

The Synagogue

In Jesus' day, synagogues (v. 21) were common throughout Palestine. Synagogues (from the Greek sunagōgē, *meaning "a leading or bringing together") were local congregations of Jews that met for the reading and explanation of Scripture and for prayer. The original emphasis was not on preaching but instruction in the law of Moses.*

Synagogues began during the Babylonian captivity experience. Lacking a temple but longing for communion with God, Jewish captives in Babylon met in local groups for worship and Torah reading. Some of the captives eventually returned to their land, where Zerubbabel rebuilt the temple and Ezra the scribe promoted the reading of the Law and prayer (Neh. 8). But many Jews remained in Persia and spread elsewhere, notably to Alexandria, Egypt. Both in and outside of Palestine, Jews continued to meet in synagogues, which became centers of community life.

Some synagogues functioned as local courts of justice which could sentence offenders as well as inflict the punishment of scourging (Matt. 10:17; 23:34). They also became grammar schools teaching children to read. And much of Jewish social life revolved around synagogue activities.

By Jesus' time, synagogues were well-established and had customary officials, including:

Elders, a board made up of devout and respected men who regulated the policies of the synagogue. Custom seated the elders in the chief seats at the front of the synagogue (see Matt. 23:6).

A ruler of the synagogue, appointed by the elders, whose duty was to attend to matters concerning the building and the planning of the services. There could be more than one ruler. On one occasion, a ruler named Jairus approached Jesus about healing his daughter (Mark 5:21–43).

The minister (chazzan), who had charge of the sacred scrolls kept in the ark, attended to the lamps, and kept the building clean. If an offender was found guilty by the council of elders, this official was the one who administered the number of lashes prescribed for the scourging. During the week he taught children how to read.

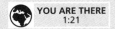

The delegate of the congregation. This was not a permanent office. Before each service the ruler chose a capable person to read the Scripture lesson, lead in prayer, and preach or comment on the Scripture. Jesus was selected for this office in the synagogue in Nazareth (Luke 4:16–20).

The interpreter. The Scriptures were written in Hebrew, but by Jesus' day most Jews in Palestine spoke Aramaic, a language related to Hebrew but different enough to call for an interpreter.

Almoners, two or three persons who received money or other necessities for the poor.

A synagogue could not be formed unless there were at least ten Jewish men in the community—apparently a condition met in a great many towns throughout the Roman world, as Paul found synagogues at Damascus (Acts 9:2), Salamis (13:5), Antioch in Pisidia (13:14), Iconium (14:1), Thessalonica (17:1), Berea (17:10), Athens (17:16–17), and Ephesus (19:1, 8). Indeed, whenever Paul entered a city to preach the gospel, he invariably spoke first in the synagogue before reaching out to the larger community.

Not surprisingly, synagogue worship had a profound influence on Christian worship. The Jewish service began with a recitation of the *shema* by the

(continued on next page)

(continued from previous page)

people. *Shema* ("Hear") is the first Hebrew word in the passage, "Hear, O Israel: The Lord our God, the Lord is one!" (Deut. 6:4–9). The speaker for the day then led the congregation in prayer as they stood facing Jerusalem with hands extended. At the close of the prayer the people said "Amen."

The chosen speaker stood and read the Law while the interpreter translated it into Aramaic. Then a passage from the Prophets was read and translated. For the commentary or sermon, the speaker usually sat down. After the sermon, a priest, if one was present, pronounced a benediction and the people said "Amen." Since the earliest Christians were Jews, they tended to follow this synagogue pattern in their own assemblies. ◆

Jesus Launches His Ministry

1:14

[14]Now after John was put in prison, Jesus came to Galilee, preaching the gospel
of the kingdom[a] of God, [15]and saying, "The time is fulfilled,
and the kingdom of God is at hand. Repent, and believe in
the gospel."

Jesus Calls Fishermen to Follow Him

1:16 see pg. 130

[16]And as He walked by the Sea of
Galilee, He saw Simon and Andrew his
brother casting a net into the sea; for they were fishermen.
[17]Then Jesus said to them, "Follow Me, and I will make you
become fishers of men." [18]They immediately left their nets
and followed Him.
[19]When He had gone a little farther from there, He saw
James the *son* of Zebedee, and John his brother, who also
were in the boat mending their nets. [20]And immediately He
called them, and they left their father Zebedee in the boat
with the hired servants, and went after Him.

Demons Are Cast Out at Capernaum

1:21 see pg. 131

[21]Then they went into Capernaum, and
immediately on the Sabbath He entered
the synagogue and taught. [22]And they were astonished at

1:14 [a]NU-Text omits *of the kingdom.*

Jesus the Galilean

In New Testament times there were two Galilees, upper and lower. Jesus of Nazareth grew up in densely populated lower Galilee. Among its urban centers He carried out most of His ministry (Mark 1:14). In fact, as many as eleven of His twelve disciples may have come from that region, the exception being Judas Iscariot (see "The Twelve," Matt. 10:2).

Galilee represented the periphery of traditional Jewish life, a cultural frontier between the Hebraic and Graeco-Roman worlds. As a result, Galileans were scorned by their neighbors in Judea. Judeans used the term "Galilean" as a synonym for fool, heathen, sinner, or worse. Most significantly for Jesus, they were certain that no prophet could come from Galilee (John 7:52).

Yet, a prophet did come from Galilee. It was there that Jesus announced the character of His message (Luke 4:14–19) and demonstrated its power. He performed at least 33 known miracles there, and of 32 recorded parables, 19 were spoken in Galilee.

His teaching, for He taught them as one having authority,
and not as the scribes.
23Now there was a man in their synagogue with an unclean spirit. And he cried out, 24saying, "Let *us* alone! What
have we to do with You, Jesus of Nazareth? Did You come
to destroy us? I know who You are—the Holy One of
God!"
25But Jesus rebuked him, saying, "Be quiet, and come out
of him!" 26And when the unclean spirit had convulsed him
and cried out with a loud voice, he came out of him. 27Then
they were all amazed, so that they questioned among themselves, saying, "What is this? What new doctrine *is* this? For
with authority[a] He commands even the unclean spirits, and
they obey Him." 28And immediately His fame spread
throughout all the region around Galilee.

Jesus Heals Simon's Mother-in-Law

1:29–31 see pg. 134
29Now as soon as they had come out of
the synagogue, they entered the house of
Simon and Andrew, with James and John. 30But Simon's
wife's mother lay sick with a fever, and they told Him about
her at once. 31So He came and took her by the hand and
lifted her up, and immediately the fever left her. And she
served them.

1:27 [a]NU-Text reads *What is this? A new doctrine with authority.*

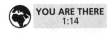

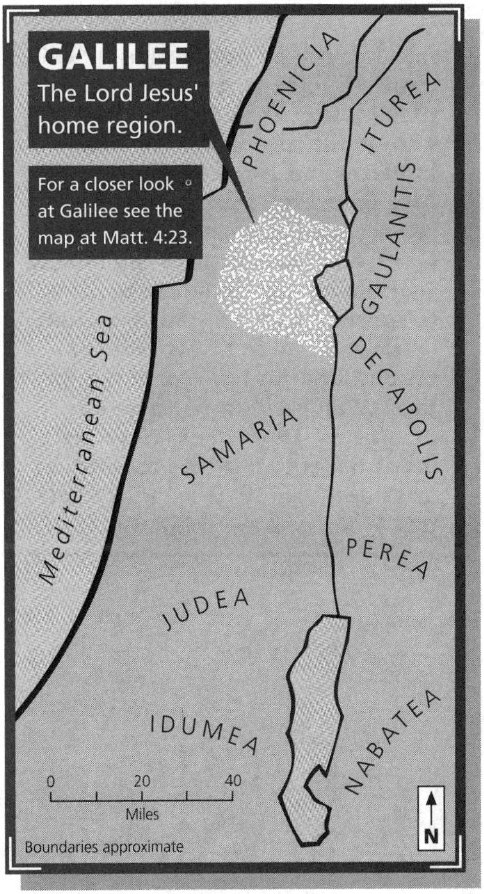

In short, the Galilee district was also the arena for Jesus' public ministry. He demonstrated that His gospel was not just for the elite, but for all. It was for those living at the margins of traditional, acceptable society. It did not start at the top and move down, but at the bottom and moved up, from the periphery to the center.

And yet, there is little evidence that His message ever took firm root in Galilee after He left. His predictions about Capernaum, Chorazin, and other Galilean cities came true (Matt. 11:20–24). In their unbelief they rejected Him—their one and only Prophet and King. ◆

"Can any good thing come out of Galilee?" Jesus' enemies cried. To find out, see John 7:52.

The Sea of Galilee was no place to be caught in a storm. Sudden outbursts of violent weather occur there to this day. See "What Kind of Storm Was This?" Luke 8:22–25.

GALILEE

YOU ARE THERE 1:14

- **The Roman province of northern Palestine extending from Mount Hermon in the north to Mount Carmel in the south, between the Mediterranean Sea and the Jordan River.**
- **Unlike Judea, remained under the rule of the Herods (see Acts 12:1–2) during the first half of the first century.**
- **Herod the Great depopulated Judea by resettling Jews in new or rebuilt cities in Samaria and Galilee.**
- **Galilee, meaning "circuit," "district," or "cylinder," was surrounded and heavily influenced by Gentiles. Jews to the south de-**

(continued on next page)

(continued from previous page)

rided its mixed population by calling it "Galilee [circle] of the Gentiles [nations]" (Is. 9:1; Matt. 4:15).

- **Known for its prosperous fishing industry and fertile lands.**
- **Also benefited from trade as a crossroads between Egypt to the south and Damascus to the north.**
- **Economic independence, political toleration, and religious freedom made the region a seedbed for revolutionaries against Rome. In fact, "Galilean" came to be used in a derogatory way in New Testament times to indicate revolutionaries and bandits (see "Party Politics of Jesus' Day," Matt. 16:1).**

Many Healed in Galilee

1:32–34

32At evening, when the sun had set,
they brought to Him all who were sick
and those who were demon-possessed. 33And the whole city
was gathered together at the door. 34Then He healed many
who were sick with various diseases, and cast out many
demons; and He did not allow the demons to speak, because they knew Him.
35Now in the morning, having risen a long while before

The Great Physician

A CLOSER LOOK 1:32–34

Throughout His ministry, Jesus healed many people whose diseases made them outcasts of society. On the other hand, He also healed several well-connected folks whose maladies were of prime concern to their families, friends, and employers. See " 'Who Sinned?': Health and Disease in the Bible," John 9:2–3.

YOU ARE THERE 1:29–31

JEWISH HOMEMAKING

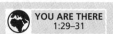

Mark recounts Jesus' visit to the home of two of His new followers, Simon and Andrew. There He healed Simon's mother-in-law, after which, the text says, "she served them." Her service likely involved far more than cooking a meal.

In Jewish homes of the day, work began at sunrise. After a simple breakfast of curds and bread, the women went to the nearest well or stream to fill their jars with fresh water for the day's needs.

Some of the water was used to make the daily bread. The women ground kernels of wheat or barley by hand on the family millstone (see "Grinding the Grain," Luke 17:35), then added water and some of the previous day's dough that had yeast in it. Kneaded and left to rise, the dough was shaped into several large, flat disks and baked in the household oven. The oven was fueled by grasses and brush gathered by the women and their children.

Other chores included spinning wool, weaving, making clothes and linens, mending, washing, producing pottery and other utensils for cooking, and preparing food. Far more than hobbies, these tasks were absolutely necessary to the family's survival. In that pre-industrial society, each household had to rely on its own labor and skills. Women acquired these from their mothers and in turn passed them on to their children.

Perhaps for that reason, first-century Jewish women enjoyed a "seamlessness" in their lives between work and home: the two were not separate categories of life, but

daylight, He went out and departed to a solitary place; and
there He prayed. 36And Simon and those *who were* with
Him searched for Him. 37When they found Him, they said
to Him, "Everyone is looking for You."
38But He said to them, "Let us go into the next towns, that I may preach there also, because for this purpose I have come forth."
39And He was preaching in their synagogues throughout all Galilee, and casting out demons.
40Now a leper came to Him, imploring Him, kneeling down to Him and saying to Him, "If You are willing, You can make me clean."
41Then Jesus, moved with compassion, stretched out *His*
hand and touched him, and said to him, "I am willing; be
cleansed." 42As soon as He had spoken, immediately the
leprosy left him, and he was cleansed. 43And He strictly

parts of an integrated whole. Caring for children and providing for essentials such as food and clothing were highly valued in Hebrew culture.

Nor was a woman's work confined to material needs. The wife provided essential leadership in the home, shaping the cultural and religious values of her children. Formal schooling was rare, so she tutored them in craft skills and literacy. She was also expected to help them follow the customs and faith of Israel. It was through her that her children's Jewish heritage was determined.

The woman was responsible for preparing the home for the Sabbath. She filled the lamps with olive oil, prepared Sabbath food and special treats, and collected an extra day's water. No wonder that on each Sabbath, as part of the evening ceremony, her husband would recite to her Proverbs 31:10–31, an acknowledgement of her vital and varied work. ◆

Women were the primary caregivers to infants and children. See "Children and Childcare," Matt. 19:14.

Not all first-century women centered their lives around domestic responsibilities totally. Lydia was a successful businesswoman in the purple trade (see profile at Acts 16:14) and Priscilla manufactured tents with her husband (see profile at Rom. 16:3–5).

Evidence from the first century reveals that women worked as wool workers, midwives, hairdressers, nurses, vendors, entertainers, political leaders, and even construction workers. See "Women and Work in the Ancient World," 1 Cor. 7:32–35.

"LET US GO INTO THE NEXT TOWNS. . . ."
—Mark 1:38

44warned him and sent him away at once, and said to him, "See that you say nothing to anyone; but go your way, show yourself to the priest, and offer for your cleansing those things which Moses commanded, as a testimony to them."

45However, he went out and began to proclaim *it* freely, and to spread the matter, so that Jesus could no longer openly enter the city, but was outside in deserted places; and they came to Him from every direction.

CHAPTER 2

Persistence Brings Healing and Forgiveness

1And again He entered Capernaum after *some* days, and it was heard that He was in the house. 2Immediately[a] many gathered together, so that there was no longer room to receive *them,* not even near the door. And He preached the word to them. 3Then they came to Him, bringing a paralytic who was carried by four *men.* 4And when they could not come near Him because of the crowd, they uncovered the roof where He was. So when they had broken through, they let down the bed on which the paralytic was lying.

2:3–17

ALL THE MULTITUDE CAME TO HIM, AND HE TAUGHT THEM. —Mark 2:13

5When Jesus saw their faith, He said to the paralytic, "Son, your sins are forgiven you."

6And some of the scribes were sitting there and reasoning in their hearts, 7"Why does this *Man* speak blasphemies like this? Who can forgive sins but God alone?"

8But immediately, when Jesus perceived in His spirit that they reasoned thus within themselves, He said to them, "Why do you reason about these things in your hearts? 9Which is easier, to say to the paralytic, '*Your* sins are forgiven you,' or to say, 'Arise, take up your bed and walk'? 10But that you may know that the Son of Man has power on earth to forgive sins"—He said to the paralytic, 11"I say to you, arise, take up your bed, and go to your house." 12Immediately he arose, took up the bed, and went out in the presence of them all, so that all were amazed and glorified God, saying, "We never saw *anything* like this!"

Levi (Matthew) Called

13Then He went out again by the sea; and all the multitude came to Him, and He taught them. 14As He passed by, He saw Levi the *son* of Alphaeus sitting at the tax office. And He said to him, "Follow Me." So he arose and followed Him.

(Bible text continued on page 138)

2:2 [a]NU-Text omits *Immediately.*

CONSIDER THIS
2:3–17

SIGNIFICANCE FOR LITTLE PEOPLE

Who really counts in life? Do those without position, power, health, or wealth really matter? Or is their only hope in somehow climbing to the top of the heap?

Each of the four Gospel writers helps the reader meet the significant people in Jesus' life. Most were distinctly insignificant when evaluated by the traditional criteria for importance. The paralytic let down from the roof (v. 3), for example, blended into the background until touched by Jesus. Likewise, the rest were generally not wealthy or famous, nor were they social, business, or government leaders. They were little people of the world with problems and needs similar to ours.

Note the cluster of people in each of the writers' first few chapters:

Matthew

- Four women touched by scandal (1:3, 5–6)
- A young couple dealing with a complicated engagement (1:18–21)
- Three advisors from a foreign government (2:1–12)
- Countless baby boys who are slaughtered (2:16–18)
- A wilderness man who becomes Jesus' forerunner (3:1–17)

Mark

- Four fishermen (1:16–20)
- A man oppressed by a demon (1:23–27)
- A feverish mother-in-law (1:29–31)
- Many sick and oppressed (1:32–34)
- An outcast leper (1:40–42)
- A paralytic (2:1–12)
- A despised tax-collector (2:13–17)

Luke

- A barren elderly couple (1:5–25)
- An expectant couple (1:26–38)
- A baby born amid confusion (1:57–80)
- Startled shepherds (2:8–20)
- An aged, saintly man (2:25–35)
- An elderly widow with a gift of prophecy (2:36–38)

John

- A puzzling religious pioneer (1:19–35)
- Two fishermen (1:35–42)
- The fishermen's friend (1:43–44)
- A skeptical critic (1:45–51)
- An enquirer who prefers a low profile (3:1–21)
- A minority woman touched by scandal (4:1–42)
- A nobleman's ill son (4:46–54)

As Scripture introduces the Savior, it shows us lots of little people, and for good reason: the people ready for God's help are not the ones insulated from trouble by possessions, health, or status, but those who know their needs. Brokenness makes one ready to turn to God for help. In Him is the forgiveness and hope that can overcome human limitation.

Are you trapped in the world's system of climbing over others to gain significance? Or have you allowed God to help you break that bondage? If so, are you following Jesus among the "little people," wherever they are struggling and groping for help? ◆

QUOTE UNQUOTE

CONSIDER THIS 2:17 *One modern-day writer intentionally seeks to broaden her appeal, in the spirit of Jesus' words about who it was He came to help:*

I do not write my books for either Christians or women. If I understand the Gospel, it tells us that we are to spread the Good News to all four corners of the world, not limiting the giving of light to people who already have seen the light. If my stories are incomprehensible to Jews or Muslims or Taoists, then I have failed as a Christian writer. We do not draw people to Christ by loudly discrediting what they believe, by telling them how wrong they are and how right we are, but by showing them a light that is so lovely that they want with all their hearts to know the source of it.

Madeleine L'Engle, *Walking On Water,* p. 122

Jesus Dines with Levi and His Friends

15Now it happened, as He was dining in *Levi's* house, that
many tax collectors and sinners also sat together with Jesus
and His disciples; for there were many, and they followed
Him. 16And when the scribes and[a] Pharisees saw Him eating
with the tax collectors and sinners, they said to His disciples, "How *is it* that He eats and drinks with tax collectors
and sinners?"

2:17 17When Jesus heard *it,* He said to them,
"Those who are well have no need of a
physician, but those who are sick. I did not come to call *the*
righteous, but sinners, to repentance."[a]

Cloth and Wineskins

18The disciples of John and of the Pharisees were fasting.
Then they came and said to Him, "Why do the disciples of
John and of the Pharisees fast, but Your disciples do not
fast?"

19And Jesus said to them, "Can the friends of the bridegroom fast while the bridegroom is with them? As long as
they have the bridegroom with them they cannot fast. 20But
the days will come when the bridegroom will be taken away
from them, and then they will fast in those days. 21No one
sews a piece of unshrunk cloth on an old garment; or else
the new piece pulls away from the old, and the tear is made
worse. 22And no one puts new wine into old wineskins; or
else the new wine bursts the wineskins, the wine is spilled,
and the wineskins are ruined. But new wine must be put
into new wineskins."

Sabbath Controversies

2:23—3:6 23Now it happened that He went
through the grainfields on the Sabbath;
and as they went His disciples began to pluck the heads of
grain. 24And the Pharisees said to Him, "Look, why do they
do what is not lawful on the Sabbath?"

25But He said to them, "Have you never read what David
did when he was in need and hungry, he and those with
him: 26how he went into the house of God *in the days* of
Abiathar the high priest, and ate the showbread, which is

2:16 [a]NU-Text reads *of the.* *2:17* [a]NU-Text omits *to repentance.*

No Tolerance for Intolerance

A CLOSER LOOK 2:23—3:6 *The Pharisees were like some intolerant religionists of our own day, and Jesus refused to put up with them. See "Jesus Confronts the Legalists," Luke 6:1–11, for a discussion of the Sabbath controversies.*

not lawful to eat except for the priests, and also gave some
to those who were with him?"
27And He said to them, "The Sabbath was made for man,
and not man for the Sabbath. 28Therefore the Son of Man is
also Lord of the Sabbath."

CHAPTER 3

1And He entered the synagogue again, and a man was
there who had a withered hand. 2So they watched Him
closely, whether He would heal him on the Sabbath, so that
they might accuse Him. 3And He said to the man who had
the withered hand, "Step forward." 4Then He said to them,
"Is it lawful on the Sabbath to do good or to do evil, to save
life or to kill?" But they kept silent. 5And when He had
looked around at them with anger, being grieved by the
hardness of their hearts, He said to the man, "Stretch out
your hand." And he stretched *it* out, and his hand was restored as whole as the other.[a] 6Then the Pharisees went out
and immediately plotted with the Herodians against Him,
how they might destroy Him.

Massive Crowds Follow Jesus

7But Jesus withdrew with His disciples to the sea. And a
great multitude from Galilee followed Him, and from Judea
8and Jerusalem and Idumea and beyond the Jordan; and
those from Tyre and Sidon, a great multitude, when they
heard how many things He was doing, came to Him. 9So He
told His disciples that a small boat should be kept ready for
Him because of the multitude, lest they should crush Him.
10For He healed many, so that as many as had afflictions
pressed about Him to touch Him. 11And the unclean spirits,
whenever they saw Him, fell down before Him and cried
out, saying, "You are the Son of God." 12But He sternly
warned them that they should not make Him known.

Jesus Calls the Twelve

3:13–19

13And He went up on the mountain
and called to *Him* those He Himself
wanted. And they came to Him. 14Then He appointed
twelve,[a] that they might be with Him and that He might
send them out to preach, 15and to have power to heal sick-

3:5 [a]NU-Text omits *as whole as the other.* *3:14* [a]NU-Text adds *whom He also named apostles.*

"THE SABBATH WAS MADE FOR MAN, AND NOT MAN FOR THE SABBATH."
—Mark 2:27

A Diverse Group

A CLOSER LOOK 3:13–19

The twelve that Jesus appointed to be His followers came from an interesting variety of backgrounds. See Matt. 10:2.

nesses and[a] to cast out demons: 16Simon,[a] to whom He gave
the name Peter; 17James the *son* of Zebedee and John the
brother of James, to whom He gave the name Boanerges,
that is, "Sons of Thunder"; 18Andrew, Philip, Bartholomew,
Matthew, Thomas, James the *son* of Alphaeus, Thaddaeus,
Simon the Cananite; 19and Judas Iscariot, who also betrayed
Him. And they went into a house.

"**WHO IS MY MOTHER, OR MY BROTHERS?"**
—Mark 3:33

Jesus' Family Tries to Slow Him Down

20Then the multitude came together again, so that they
could not so much as eat bread. 21But when His own people
heard *about this,* they went out to lay hold of Him, for they
said, "He is out of His mind."

Scribes Call Jesus Satanic

3:22

22And the scribes who came down
from Jerusalem said, "He has Beelzebub,"
and, "By the ruler of the demons He casts out demons."
23So He called them to *Himself* and said to them in parables: "How can Satan cast out Satan? 24If a kingdom is divided against itself, that kingdom cannot stand. 25And if a
house is divided against itself, that house cannot stand.
26And if Satan has risen up against himself, and is divided,
he cannot stand, but has an end. 27No one can enter a
strong man's house and plunder his goods, unless he first
binds the strong man. And then he will plunder his house.
28"Assuredly, I say to you, all sins will be forgiven the sons
of men, and whatever blasphemies they may utter; 29but he
who blasphemes against the Holy Spirit never has forgiveness, but is subject to eternal condemnation"— 30because
they said, "He has an unclean spirit."

3:15 [a]NU-Text omits *to heal sicknesses and.* *3:16* [a]NU-Text reads *and He appointed the twelve: Simon . . . .*

FOR YOUR INFO
3:22

PAGAN GODS IN THE NEW TESTAMENT

Name	Description	Reference
BEELZEBUB	A heathen god considered by the Jews to be the supreme evil spirit	Mark 3:22
DIANA	In Roman mythology, the goddess of the moon, hunting, wild animals, and virginity	Acts 19:24, 27–28
HERMES	The Greek god of commerce, science, invention, cunning, eloquence, and theft	Acts 14:12
MAMMON	The Aramaic word for *riches*, personified by Jesus as a false god	Luke 16:9, 11
MOLOCH	National god of the Ammonites whose worship involved child sacrifice	Acts 7:43
REMPHAN	An idol worshiped by Israel in the wilderness	Acts 7:43
TWIN BROTHERS	In Greek mythology, the twin sons of Zeus	Acts 28:11
ZEUS	The supreme god of the ancient Greeks	Acts 14:12–13

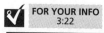

"Who Are My Mother and Brothers?"

3:31–35

31Then His brothers and His mother
came, and standing outside they sent to
Him, calling Him. 32And a multitude was sitting around
Him; and they said to Him, "Look, Your mother and Your
brothers[a] are outside seeking You."
33But He answered them, saying, "Who is My mother, or
My brothers?" 34And He looked around in a circle at those
who sat about Him, and said, "Here are My mother and My
brothers! 35For whoever does the will of God is My brother
and My sister and mother."

CHAPTER 4

Jesus Teaches by the Sea

1And again He began to teach by the sea. And a great
multitude was gathered to Him, so that He got into a boat
and sat *in it* on the sea; and the whole multitude was on the

4:2 see pg. 144

land facing the sea. 2Then He taught
them many things by parables, and said
to them in His teaching:

A Parable about Soils

4:3–20 see pg. 142

3"Listen! Behold, a sower went out to
sow. 4And it happened, as he sowed, *that*
some *seed* fell by the wayside; and the birds of the air[a] came
and devoured it. 5Some fell on stony ground, where it did
not have much earth; and immediately it sprang up because
it had no depth of earth. 6But when the sun was up it was
scorched, and because it had no root it withered away. 7And
some *seed* fell among thorns; and the thorns grew up and
choked it, and it yielded no crop. 8But other *seed* fell on
good ground and yielded a crop that sprang up, increased
and produced: some thirtyfold, some sixty, and some a hundred."
9And He said to them,[a] "He who has ears to hear, let him
hear!"
10But when He was alone, those around Him with the
twelve asked Him about the parable. 11And He said to
them, "To you it has been given to know the mystery of the
kingdom of God; but to those who are outside, all things
come in parables, 12so that

'Seeing they may see and not perceive,
And hearing they may hear and not understand;
Lest they should turn,
And *their* sins be forgiven them.' "[a]

3:32 [a]NU-Text and M-Text add *and Your sisters.* *4:4* [a]NU-Text and M-Text omit *of the air.*
4:9 [a]NU-Text and M-Text omit *to them.* *4:12* [a]Isaiah 6:9, 10

For or Against Family?

CONSIDER THIS 3:31–35

Conflict seems inevitable within families. Family members can always find something to disagree about—personal values, current events, politics, possessions, sex, money, feelings. Why do some of the most bitter fights occur between people who married for love? How can people who are so familiar with each other sometimes find themselves so far apart?

One reason is that families are unions of sinners, and sinners will be themselves no matter how intense their love and commitment for each other (1 John 1:8, 10). This has been so from the beginning: the first eight families in Scripture displayed many kinds of dysfunction, revealing their condition as sinful human beings. Perhaps God recorded their stories to let us know that even though He instituted the family unit, families are made up of sinners who will inevitably hurt each other.

Was Jesus "too good" to associate with His family of origin? His words in Mark 3:33–35 might seem to imply that. But He was merely distinguishing between human expectations about how families should relate and what the values of the kingdom had to say about family relations. He was not against His own parents and siblings; He just wanted to stress obedience to God.

"His own people" had already shown that they understood very little about Jesus or the values of His kingdom (vv. 20–21). They were limited by their own sinfulness, and needed God's help like everyone else.

Scripture has much to say about healthy ways families can interrelate. See "The Family: A Call to Long-term Work," Eph. 5:21.

13And He said to them, "Do you not understand this parable? How then will you understand all the parables? 14The
sower sows the word. 15And these are the ones by the wayside where the word is sown. When they hear, Satan comes
immediately and takes away the word that was sown in
their hearts. 16These likewise are the ones sown on stony
ground who, when they hear the word, immediately receive
it with gladness; 17and they have no root in themselves, and
so endure only for a time. Afterward, when tribulation or
persecution arises for the word's sake, immediately they
stumble. 18Now these are the ones sown among thorns; *they
are* the ones who hear the word, 19and the cares of this
world, the deceitfulness of riches, and the desires for other
things entering in choke the word, and it becomes unfruitful. 20But these are the ones sown on good ground, those
who hear the word, accept *it,* and bear fruit: some thirtyfold, some sixty, and some a hundred."

Warnings

21Also He said to them, "Is a lamp brought to be put under a basket or under a bed? Is it not to be set on a lampstand? 22For there is nothing hidden which will not be revealed, nor has anything been kept secret but that it should
come to light. 23If anyone has ears to hear, let him hear."

CONSIDER THIS
4:3–20

Is Your Witness Falling on Deaf Ears?

Do you find some of your coworkers or neighbors totally uninterested in the Christian faith? Are some even openly hostile? Have you become a target for their venom?

Jesus called us to be His witnesses (Acts 1:6–8), but that is not a call to convert others. Conversion is the responsibility of the Holy Spirit (John 16:8–11). That means that we need not measure our success in witnessing by the number who respond. If that were the case, Jesus would have often been considered a failure: many who heard Him—and even some who followed Him—turned out to be uninterested (John 6:60–66).

The fact is that people are in various conditions when it comes to spiritual matters, as Jesus' story of the four kinds of soils illustrates (Mark 4:3–20). One thing we as "farmers" can't do is change the soil. But we can offer good seed and do the best we can to nurture whatever faith sprouts up (1 Cor. 3:7–9). One way to do that is by continually working out our faith in day-to-day life (Phil. 2:12–13; James 2:14–26), making it available for others to consider rather than hiding it (Mark 4:21–23). How others react is between them and God.

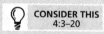

24Then He said to them, "Take heed what you hear. With
the same measure you use, it will be measured to you; and
to you who hear, more will be given. 25For whoever has, to
him more will be given; but whoever does not have, even
what he has will be taken away from him."

A Growing Seed

26And He said, "The kingdom of God is as if a man
should scatter seed on the ground, 27and should sleep by
night and rise by day, and the seed should sprout and grow,
he himself does not know how. 28For the earth yields crops
by itself: first the blade, then the head, after that the full
grain in the head. 29But when the grain ripens, immediately
he puts in the sickle, because the harvest has come."

A Mustard Seed

30Then He said, "To what shall we liken the kingdom of
God? Or with what parable shall we picture it? 31*It is* like a
mustard seed which, when it is sown on the ground, is
smaller than all the seeds on earth; 32but when it is sown, it
grows up and becomes greater than all herbs, and shoots
out large branches, so that the birds of the air may nest under its shade."

(Bible text continued on page 145)

That's not to suggest that we should be detached or uncaring about others and their responses. Scripture challenges us to love others as we have been loved. One way is to make available to them our experience of faith—and make ourselves available to God to be used with anybody, anywhere, anytime.

We ought to avoid the trap of evaluating our faith by how others respond to us. The Spirit of God converts people—we don't. If we do, our converts are on shaky ground. The story is told of an evangelist traveling on an airplane who sat across the aisle from a noisy drunk. After watching the fellow carry on for a while, the minister's seatmate turned and sarcastically remarked, "I understand he's one of your converts!"

The evangelist replied, "Must be. If he were God's, he wouldn't act that way." ◆

The Holy Spirit is the great evangelist, but Scripture also urges us to work with the Spirit in influencing others with the gospel. To understand our role in this joint venture, see "Whose Job Is Evangelism?" John 16:8.

One of the most important ways that we can give evidence of our faith in Christ is through the way we do our work. See "Your 'Workstyle,'" Titus 2:9–10.

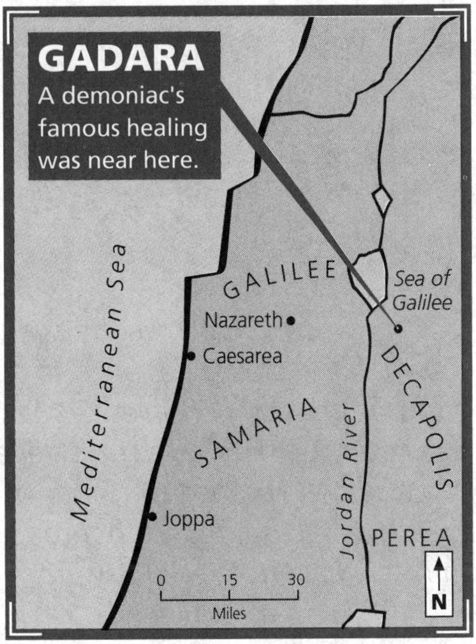

GADARA

YOU ARE THERE 5:1

- **A town located six miles southeast of the Sea of Galilee, east of the Jordan on the edge of the Arabian desert.**
- **Surrounding region known as the country of the Gadarenes (Mark 5:1; Luke 8:26) or Gergesenes (Matt. 8:28), but see the textual footnotes for variants.**

FOR YOUR INFO
4:2

PARABLES

Jesus frequently taught using parables (v. 2), short, simple stories designed to communicate spiritual truths and principles. Sometimes these were extended tales with character and plot development; sometimes they were little more than figures of speech that illustrated truth through comparisons or examples drawn from everyday life.

Jesus was a master of the parabolic form, but He was not the first to use parables. Several appear in the Old Testament. For example: Nathan's parable of a rich man who took a small ewe lamb belonging to a poor man (2 Sam. 12:1–4); the wise woman of Tekoa's parable of a widow whose two sons fought until one was killed (2 Sam. 14:5–7); and Solomon's parable of the sluggard (Prov. 24:30–34).

The advantage of stories like these is that they impress the listener with a vivid, imaginative picture of the truth. That doesn't mean, however, that they are always easy to understand. Even Jesus' disciples were sometimes confused as to the meaning of His parables (Matt. 13:24–30, 36–43). Furthermore, Jesus sometimes spoke in parables to reveal truth to His followers but to conceal it from those who had rejected Him (Matt. 13:10–17; Mark 4:10–12; Luke 8:9–10). Thus He fulfilled the prophecy of Isaiah 6:9–10. Like a double-edged sword, His words cut two ways—enlightening those who sought the truth but blinding the disobedient.

Interpreting Parables

Most of Jesus' parables have one central point, and there is no need for fanciful, speculative interpretation. To find that central meaning, it helps if we as modern-day readers can understand what the parable meant in the time of Jesus and relate the story to His proclamation of the kingdom and to His miracles. After all, the parables were more than simple folk stories; they were expressions of Christ's view of God, humanity, salvation, and the new epoch which began with His ministry.

A good example of this approach are the parables dealing with the four "lost" things in Luke 15:3–32: the lost sheep, the lost coin, and the two lost sons. The context shows that Jesus told these stories while eating with tax collectors and sinners (vv. 1–2). The Pharisees and scribes, the religious elite of the day, were criticizing Him because, in their view, He was transgressing the Law.

In response, Jesus told the three parables. God rejoices more, He said, over the repentance of one sinner (such as those sitting with Him at the table) than over "ninety-nine just persons who need no repentance" (v. 7; such as the religious professionals who congratulated themselves on their own self-achieved "goodness"). Likewise, the prodigal son (vv. 11–24) illustrated the tax collectors and sinners, while the older son (vv. 25–32) illustrated the scribes and Pharisees.

Parables are one of the most engaging forms of teaching in Scripture. If you or someone you know has struggled with understanding and applying God's truth, you might consider reading the parables. In a powerful way, they stimulate the imagination and bring eternal truth to everyday life. ◆

Jesus probably spent most of His life working in His family's carpentry business. No wonder He knew how to present truth in terms that normal people could understand. See "Work-World Stories Describe the Kingdom," Matt. 13:1.

The Use of Parables

4:33–34

33And with many such parables He
spoke the word to them as they were able
to hear *it.* 34But without a parable He did not speak to
them. And when they were alone, He explained all things to
His disciples.

Jesus Stills a Great Storm

35On the same day, when evening had come, He said to
them, "Let us cross over to the other side." 36Now when
they had left the multitude, they took Him along in the boat
as He was. And other little boats were also with Him. 37And
a great windstorm arose, and the waves beat into the boat,
so that it was already filling. 38But He was in the stern,
asleep on a pillow. And they awoke Him and said to Him,
"Teacher, do You not care that we are perishing?"
39Then He arose and rebuked the wind, and said to the
sea, "Peace, be still!" And the wind ceased and there was a
great calm. 40But He said to them, "Why are you so fearful?
How *is it* that you have no faith?"[a] 41And they feared exceedingly, and said to one another, "Who can this be, that
even the wind and the sea obey Him!"

CHAPTER 5

A Demon-possessed Man Finds Help

5:1
see pg. 143

1Then they came to the other side of
the sea, to the country of the Gadarenes.[a]
2And when He had come out of the boat, immediately there
met Him out of the tombs a man with an unclean spirit,
3who had *his* dwelling among the tombs; and no one could
bind him,[a] not even with chains, 4because he had often
been bound with shackles and chains. And the chains had
been pulled apart by him, and the shackles broken in
pieces; neither could anyone tame him. 5And always, night
and day, he was in the mountains and in the tombs, crying
out and cutting himself with stones.
6When he saw Jesus from afar, he ran and worshiped
Him. 7And he cried out with a loud voice and said, "What
have I to do with You, Jesus, Son of the Most High God? I
implore You by God that You do not torment me."
8For He said to him, "Come out of the man, unclean
spirit!" 9Then He asked him, "What *is* your name?"
And he answered, saying, "My name *is* Legion; for we are
many." 10Also he begged Him earnestly that He would not
send them out of the country.

4:40 [a]NU-Text reads *Have you still no faith?* *5:1* [a]NU-Text reads *Gerasenes.* *5:3* [a]NU-Text adds *anymore.*

FAITH UNFOLDS SLOWLY

CONSIDER THIS 4:33–34 **How much do you understand about the faith? Do you wish you knew more? Perhaps others intimidate you with their knowledge and familiarity with Scripture.**

If so, Jesus' work with His disciples (vv. 33–34) can lend some helpful perspective. Just as our biological lives unfold slowly, so do our spiritual lives. God offers us what we can understand as soon as we can handle it, but not before. Most parents would consider explicit lessons on sexuality to be premature for preschoolers. Likewise, driving lessons for first graders would be inappropriate. And some athletic activities can cause great damage if children engage in them too early in their development. In the same way, God holds back certain lessons until we're mature enough to handle them.

Jesus called the disciples to follow Him one day at a time (Luke 9:23). But He also promised them that the Spirit would come later and lead them into truths that they could not handle then (John 16:12–16). Like those first disciples, we as Jesus' modern-day followers are not to know the end from the beginning, but to learn something from Him every day, applying it to our lives. Faith is not a badge to be worn or knowledge to be flaunted, but a little seed to be nurtured (vv. 26–32).

Jesus told a parable to illustrate the way in which His followers would slowly understand spiritual truth. See "Treasures New and Old," Matt. 13:52.

11 Now a large herd of swine was feeding there near the
mountains. 12 So all the demons begged Him, saying, "Send
us to the swine, that we may enter them." 13 And at once Jesus[a] gave them permission. Then the unclean spirits went
out and entered the swine (there were about two thousand);
and the herd ran violently down the steep place into the
sea, and drowned in the sea.

14 So those who fed the swine fled, and they told *it* in the
city and in the country. And they went out to see what it
was that had happened. 15 Then they came to Jesus, and saw
the one *who had been* demon-possessed and had the legion,
sitting and clothed and in his right mind. And they were
afraid. 16 And those who saw it told them how it happened
to him *who had been* demon-possessed, and about the
swine. 17 Then they began to plead with Him to depart from
their region.

18 And when He got into the boat, he who had been
demon-possessed begged Him that he might be with Him.
19 However, Jesus did not permit him, but said to him, "Go
home to your friends, and tell them what great things the
Lord has done for you, and how He has had compassion on
you." 20 And he departed and began to
proclaim in Decapolis all that Jesus had
done for him; and all marveled.

5:20

(Bible text continued on page 148)

5:13 [a]NU-Text reads *And He gave.*

The City of the Dead

Gadara was either the site of or near the site of Jesus' dramatic healing of a man possessed by demons calling themselves Legion (Mark 5:1–20; Matt. 8:28–34; Luke 8:26–39). Matthew records that Jesus healed two demon-possessed men; Mark and Luke refer to only one. Perhaps that particular man was the more violent of the two.

At any rate, the incident took place at a "necropolis," or city of the dead (Mark 5:2–3, 5). Then as now, certain people lived among the dead. The Gospels say that the demon-possessed man had been driven away from normal society. In modern Cairo, nearly one million people live in cemeteries, with houses literally built on tombs. The arrangement continues a long-standing practice in the Middle East.

But not only does this dramatic story take place at a necropolis, it follows an equally riveting incident—the stilling of the storm (4:35–41). Mark shows that Jesus was the master of both the storm at sea and the storm inside the head of the poor cemetery dweller.

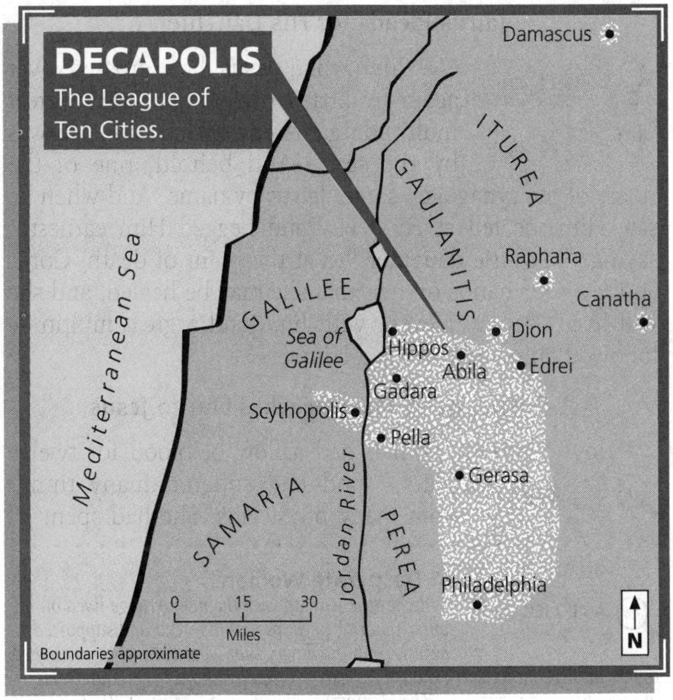

The man, or rather the demons, identified themselves as Legion (5:9). Roman legions of between 5,000 and 6,000 soldiers marched along the King's Highway that ran from the Gulf of Aqaba north to Syria, through the Decapolis—right beside the lakeside cemetery where the man lived. In a similar way, thousands of demonic spirits marched through the man's body, tormenting him day and night.

Jesus cast them out, and they entered a herd of pigs which they drowned in the lake (vv. 11–13). Some have used this incident to accuse Jesus of being both environmentally and economically insensitive. But to Jesus, one demented person was worth more than a herd of pigs or the economic impact of losing them. He didn't cause their loss—the demons did—or approve of it, but He permitted it in order to save the man. Here as elsewhere, He showed that people matter more than products or profits. ◆

Decapolis

YOU ARE THERE 5:20

- **The region also known as the Transjordan east of Galilee and Samaria.**
- **Name means "League of Ten Cities." Alphabetically, these included:**
  - **Canatha**
  - **Damascus, the chief city (see Acts 9:2)**
  - **Dion**
  - **Gadara**
  - **Gerasa (modern Jerash, Jordan)**
  - **Hippos**
  - **Pella, an ancient settlement not mentioned in the Bible, but a sanctuary for Christians during the Jewish-Roman War of A.D. 67–70**
  - **Philadelphia (Old Testament Rabbah or Rabbath Ammon, chief city of the Ammonites, perpetual enemies of the Israelites since at least the thirteenth century B.C.; present-day Amman)**
  - **Raphana**
  - **Scythopolis**
  - **and later, Abila and Edrei.**
- **Accessed in Roman times by the King's Highway and three other major roads, making it a major trade route in the empire.**
- **Region tended to favor Greek culture more than Hebrew.**
- **Visited by Jesus, who drew large crowds mostly of Gentiles (Matt. 4:25; Mark 5:20; 7:31). Word no doubt spread quickly through the transportation links afforded by the league.**

Jairus Pleads for His Daughter

5:21–43

5:22–23

21Now when Jesus had crossed over
again by boat to the other side, a great
multitude gathered to Him; and He was
by the sea. 22And behold, one of the
rulers of the synagogue came, Jairus by name. And when he
saw Him, he fell at His feet 23and begged Him earnestly,
saying, "My little daughter lies at the point of death. Come
and lay Your hands on her, that she may be healed, and she
will live." 24So *Jesus* went with him, and a great multitude
followed Him and thronged Him.

A Desperate Woman Reaches Out to Jesus

25Now a certain woman had a flow of blood for twelve
years, 26and had suffered many things
from many physicians. She had spent all

5:26

A CLOSER LOOK 5:26

A Desperate Woman

Whether the woman with the hemorrhage lived off an inheritance or perhaps was divorced and supported herself from the dowry that would have been returned to her, her livelihood was exhausted. Jesus was her last hope. Fortunately, He did not disappoint her. *See "The Hemorrhaging Woman," Matt. 9:20–22.*

CONSIDER THIS 5:21–43

People Priorities in the City

Believers today can feel overwhelmed as they look at the many needs in the world around them. Where should they start? How can they make any difference? Who needs help the most?

Jesus modeled several lessons in dealing with the needs of people when He disembarked from His sail across the Sea of Galilee (v. 21). He found Himself confronted by two individuals with critical needs: a well-off, well-connected, and well-respected synagogue ruler whose twelve-year-old daughter was terminally ill (vv. 22–24); and an obscure elderly woman who had spent her livelihood on an ineffectual medical system, yet still suffered from chronic bleeding (vv. 25–28).

The man, with all his connections, got to Jesus first. But as Jesus was on His way across town, the woman—unnamed, unannounced, and, from the crowd's point of view, unwanted—grabbed Him. It was the desperate act of someone who knew she was going to die unless a miracle of some sort took place.

A little girl who had been living for twelve years (v. 42) and an old lady who had been dying for twelve years (v. 25). What would Jesus do?

To complicate matters, the woman's touch rendered

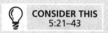

that she had and was no better, but rather grew worse.
27When she heard about Jesus, she came behind *Him* in the
crowd and touched His garment. 28For she said, "If only I
may touch His clothes, I shall be made well."
29Immediately the fountain of her blood was dried up,
and she felt in *her* body that she was healed of the affliction.
30And Jesus, immediately knowing in Himself that power
had gone out of Him, turned around in the crowd and said,
"Who touched My clothes?"
31But His disciples said to Him, "You see the multitude
thronging You, and You say, 'Who touched Me?' "
32And He looked around to see her who had done this
thing. 33But the woman, fearing and trembling, knowing
what had happened to her, came and fell down before Him
and told Him the whole truth. 34And He said to her,
"Daughter, your faith has made you well. Go in peace, and
be healed of your affliction."

Jesus Heals Jairus' Daughter

35While He was still speaking, *some* came from the ruler
of the synagogue's *house* who said, "Your daughter is dead.
Why trouble the Teacher any further?"

Jesus ritually unclean (Lev. 15:25–27). Technically, He was now prohibited from helping the little girl until the next day. But neither the woman nor Jesus cared about that in the least: she was more amazed at her immediate healing, and Jesus was aware that His power had been activated (vv. 29–30). He was able to distinguish the incidental touch of the crowd from the person who reached out in faith.

Jesus called her "daughter" (v. 34). Perhaps He was referring to her Jewish ancestry. He called a woman in a similar situation a daughter of Abraham (Luke 13:16). But the term also put her on an equal footing with the daughter of the ruler—and put Jesus in sympathy with Jairus as a parent in pain. Perhaps that's why Jairus continued to trust Jesus even as his crisis worsened (vv. 35–36).

No individual Christian can meet all the desperate needs in today's urban arena. But does God really ask us to? If Jesus' example in Mark 5 is any indication, we need to do what we can to respond to the individuals He sends our way. We also need to remember that chronically ill old ladies mean just as much to God as bright, privileged schoolgirls. ◆

A Respected Leader Takes a Risk

CONSIDER THIS 5:22–23 **Personal crises can cause us to break with our peers and cultural traditions in order to seek help. Jairus (v. 22) risked his job as the ruler of the synagogue by turning to Jesus. This leader was well-known in his town, and his actions were carefully watched by people. But he was desperate to save his daughter's life, so he went to Jesus as a last resort.**

Jesus was a controversial rabbi. Some Jews followed Him, but many others took great offense at His teaching (3:6). So when Jairus fell at Jesus' feet, he must have known that some in his synagogue would sharply criticize him.

When Jesus arrived at Jairus' home, He took the daughter by the hand. In doing so, He risked a violation of Jewish custom. By touching her dead body, Jesus was making Himself ritually unclean. Moreover, by touching a woman, He was doing something that Jewish men, and particularly rabbis, were told not to do.

Jairus risked his secure, prestigious job because he loved his daughter more than his career. Jesus risked His reputation as a teacher in order to bring the daughter back to life.

Whom do you love enough to risk your career for?

Jesus the Carpenter

CONSIDER THIS 6:3 **Like His earthly father before Him, Jesus worked as a carpenter (v. 3). Possibly He continued to practice His trade while traveling about to teach and heal.**

He certainly derived no income from His ministry. Only officials of the temple and religious courts drew salaries. The rest of the religious teachers and leaders were either independently wealthy or supported themselves through a trade or profession.

Jesus did receive support from several wealthy women (see "The Women Who Followed Jesus," Luke 8:1–3). And He was welcomed as a guest into many homes. But of all the complaints that His enemies lodged against Him—that He failed to keep the Sabbath, that He ate and drank with sinners, that He made Himself out to be God—they never accused Him of being lazy. Indeed, Jesus' own townsfolk were amazed at His teaching because He was "just a carpenter."

One Pharisee who joined the Christian movement supported himself by manufacturing tents. See "Paul's 'Real' Job," Acts 18:1–3.

If Jesus may have supported Himself through "secular" employment while carrying out His ministry, is there any reason why modern Christian leaders shouldn't at least consider that as an option today? See "Paying Vocational Christian Workers," 1 Cor. 9:1–23.

36As soon as Jesus heard the word that was spoken, He
said to the ruler of the synagogue, "Do not be afraid; only
believe." 37And He permitted no one to follow Him except
Peter, James, and John the brother of James. 38Then He
came to the house of the ruler of the synagogue, and saw a
tumult and those who wept and wailed loudly. 39When He
came in, He said to them, "Why make this commotion and
weep? The child is not dead, but sleeping."
40And they ridiculed Him. But when He had put them all
outside, He took the father and the mother of the child, and
those *who were* with Him, and entered where the child was
lying. 41Then He took the child by the hand, and said to
her, "Talitha, cumi," which is translated, "Little girl, I say to
you, arise." 42Immediately the girl arose and walked, for she
was twelve years *of age.* And they were overcome with great
amazement. 43But He commanded them strictly that no one
should know it, and said that *something* should be given her
to eat.

CHAPTER 6

Unbelief in Jesus' Own Country

1Then He went out from there and came to His own
country, and His disciples followed Him. 2And when the
Sabbath had come, He began to teach in the synagogue.
And many hearing *Him* were astonished, saying, "Where *did*
this Man *get* these things? And what wisdom *is* this which is
given to Him, that such mighty works are performed by His
hands! 3Is this not the carpenter, the Son
of Mary, and brother of James, Joses, Ju-
das, and Simon? And are not His sisters here with us?" So
they were offended at Him.

6:3

4But Jesus said to them, "A prophet is not without honor
except in his own country, among his own relatives, and in
his own house." 5Now He could do no mighty work there,
except that He laid His hands on a few sick people and
healed *them.* 6And He marveled because of their unbelief.
Then He went about the villages in a circuit, teaching.

The Twelve Are Sent Out

7And He called the twelve to *Himself,* and began to send
them out two *by* two, and gave them power over unclean
spirits. 8He commanded them to take nothing for the journey except a staff—no bag, no bread, no copper in *their*
money belts— 9but to wear sandals, and not to put on two
tunics.
10Also He said to them, "In whatever place you enter a
house, stay there till you depart from that place. 11And
whoever[a] will not receive you nor hear you, when you de-

6:11 [a]NU-Text reads *whatever place.*

part from there, shake off the dust under your feet as a testimony against them.[b] Assuredly, I say to you, it will be more
tolerable for Sodom and Gomorrah in the day of judgment
than for that city!"
12So they went out and preached that *people* should repent. 13And they cast out many demons, and anointed with
oil many who were sick, and healed *them.*

Herod Hears and Fears

6:14

14Now King Herod heard *of Him,* for
His name had become well known. And
he said, "John the Baptist is risen from the dead, and therefore these powers are at work in him."

6:14–16

15Others said, "It is Elijah."
And others said, "It is the Prophet, or[a]
like one of the prophets."
16But when Herod heard, he said, "This is John, whom I
beheaded; he has been raised from the dead!" 17For Herod
himself had sent and laid hold of John, and bound him in
prison for the sake of Herodias, his brother Philip's wife; for
he had married her. 18Because John had said to Herod, "It is
not lawful for you to have your brother's wife."
19Therefore Herodias held it against him and wanted to
kill him, but she could not; 20for Herod feared John, knowing that he *was* a just and holy man, and he protected him.
And when he heard him, he did many things, and heard
him gladly.

The Murder of John the Baptist

21Then an opportune day came when Herod on his birthday gave a feast for his nobles, the high officers, and the
chief *men* of Galilee. 22And when Herodias' daughter herself
came in and danced, and pleased Herod and those who sat
with him, the king said to the girl, "Ask me whatever you

6:23

want, and I will give *it* to you." 23He also
swore to her, "Whatever you ask me, I
will give you, up to half my kingdom."
24So she went out and said to her mother, "What shall I
ask?"
And she said, "The head of John the Baptist!"

6:11 [b]NU-Text omits the rest of this verse. *6:15* [a]NU-Text and M-Text omit *or.*

Herod the Tetrarch

A CLOSER LOOK 6:14

Called King Herod in v. 14, this man was also known as Herod Antipas or, with his formal title, Herod the tetrarch (ruler of a fourth part; *see Luke 9:7*). *The son of Herod the Great, he came from a long line of brilliant but immoral royalty. Don't miss "The Herods," Acts 12:1–2.*

"You Remind Me of . . ."

CONSIDER THIS 6:14–16

Jesus' reputation traveled far and wide, even to the king (v. 14). But who was this Man with such extraordinary power and authority? Herod and his counselors compared Jesus to some very special people—John the Baptist, Elijah, the Old Testament prophets.

Their exercise in trying to identify Jesus raises an interesting question: When others observe you and the way you use power and authority, to whom do they compare you? How might someone complete the sentence, "When I think of [*YOUR NAME*], I'm most reminded of . . ." whom?

A Reckless Choice

CONSIDER THIS 6:23

Someone has well said that there are good decisions and there are quick decisions, but there are few good quick decisions. Herod made a very bad decision on the spur of the moment when he rewarded his stepdaughter with a blank check (v. 23).

It's easy to condemn Herod for his foolishness. Yet how often we act in a similar manner, making decisions that have the most far-reaching consequences in haste, in a flush of wild excitement. Carried away by our passions, we choose impulsively, to our misfortune.

Herod's mistake is easily understood. He was drunk, he was distracted, he was impulsive by nature. Believers ought never to make their decisions in such a manner. As Paul challenges us, we need to live as wise people, not as fools (Eph. 5:14–17).

WHY NOT REST A WHILE?

CONSIDER THIS 6:31 When the Twelve returned from their preaching tour (vv. 7, 12, 30), Jesus took them aside for a bit of rest and relaxation (v. 31). In doing so, He modeled a principle that many of us today could stand to practice more—the principle of rest.

Rest may seem to be the last thing we need, given industry's obsession with productivity and our culture's reputation as a "leisure society." But God wants us to adopt His values, not the values of our culture. One thing He values is leisure. He values work as well (see "God—The Original Worker," John 5:17 and "People at Work," Heb. 2:7). But rest is something God Himself does (Gen. 2:2), which means that rest is good in and of itself. In fact, God actually commanded His people Israel to rest (Ex. 20:8–11).

Have you determined how much time you actually need to spend at work? Have you carefully considered how to balance your time and energy between workplace commitments and your family? Are you perhaps working too much, not because the job demands it, but because you won't trust God to supply your needs through a reasonable amount of work? Perhaps you need to take Jesus' advice: "Come aside . . . and rest a while."

25Immediately she came in with haste to the king and
asked, saying, "I want you to give me at once the head of
John the Baptist on a platter."
26And the king was exceedingly sorry; *yet,* because of the
oaths and because of those who sat with him, he did not
want to refuse her. 27Immediately the king sent an executioner and commanded his head to be brought. And he
went and beheaded him in prison, 28brought his head on a
platter, and gave it to the girl; and the girl gave it to her
mother. 29When his disciples heard *of it,* they came and
took away his corpse and laid it in a tomb.

Jesus Feeds 5,000

30Then the apostles gathered to Jesus and told Him all
things, both what they had done and what they had taught.
6:31 31And He said to them, "Come aside by
yourselves to a deserted place and rest a
while." For there were many coming and going, and they
did not even have time to eat. 32So they departed to a deserted place in the boat by themselves.
33But the multitudes[a] saw them departing, and many
knew Him and ran there on foot from all the cities. They arrived before them and came together to Him. 34And Jesus,
when He came out, saw a great multitude and was moved
with compassion for them, because they were like sheep
not having a shepherd. So He began to teach them many
things. 35When the day was now far spent, His disciples
came to Him and said, "This is a deserted place, and already
the hour *is* late. 36Send them away, that they may go into
the surrounding country and villages and buy themselves
bread;[a] for they have nothing to eat."
37But He answered and said to them, "You give them
something to eat."
And they said to Him, "Shall we go and buy two hundred
denarii worth of bread and give them *something* to eat?"
38But He said to them, "How many loaves do you have?
Go and see."
And when they found out they said, "Five, and two fish."
39Then He commanded them to make them all sit down
in groups on the green grass. 40So they sat down in ranks,
in hundreds and in fifties. 41And when He had taken the
five loaves and the two fish, He looked up to heaven,
blessed and broke the loaves, and gave *them* to His disciples
to set before them; and the two fish He divided among *them*
all. 42So they all ate and were filled. 43And they took up
twelve baskets full of fragments and of the fish. 44Now those
who had eaten the loaves were about[a] five thousand men.

6:33 [a]NU-Text and M-Text read *they.* *6:36* [a]NU-Text reads *something to eat* and omits the rest of this verse. *6:44* [a]NU-Text and M-Text omit *about.*

Jesus Walks on Water

6:45

45Immediately He made His disciples
get into the boat and go before Him to
the other side, to Bethsaida, while He sent the multitude
away. 46And when He had sent them away, He departed to
the mountain to pray. 47Now when evening came, the boat
was in the middle of the sea; and He *was* alone on the land.
48Then He saw them straining at rowing, for the wind was
against them. Now about the fourth watch of the night He
came to them, walking on the sea, and would have passed
them by. 49And when they saw Him walking on the sea,
they supposed it was a ghost, and cried out; 50for they all
saw Him and were troubled. But immediately He talked
with them and said to them, "Be of good cheer! It is I; do
not be afraid." 51Then He went up into the boat to them,
and the wind ceased. And they were greatly amazed in
themselves beyond measure, and marveled. 52For they had
not understood about the loaves, because their heart was
hardened.

Many Healed in Gennesaret

6:53 see pg. 154

53When they had crossed over, they
came to the land of Gennesaret and an-
chored there. 54And when they came out of the boat, immediately the people recognized Him, 55ran through that
whole surrounding region, and began to carry about on
beds those who were sick to wherever they heard He was.
56Wherever He entered, into villages, cities, or the country,
they laid the sick in the marketplaces, and begged Him that
they might just touch the hem of His garment. And as many
as touched Him were made well.

CHAPTER 7

Jesus Answers the Pharisees

1Then the Pharisees and some of the scribes came together to Him, having come from Jerusalem. 2Now when[a]
they saw some of His disciples eat bread with defiled, that
is, with unwashed hands, they found fault. 3For the Pharisees and all the Jews do not eat unless they wash *their*
hands in a special way, holding the tradition of the elders.
4*When they come* from the marketplace, they do not eat unless they wash. And there are many other things which they
have received and hold, *like* the washing of cups, pitchers,
copper vessels, and couches.

7:2 [a]NU-Text omits *when* and *they found fault.*

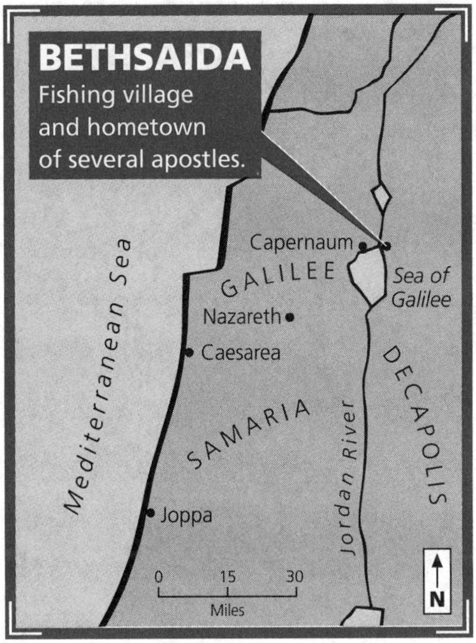

BETHSAIDA

YOU ARE THERE 6:45

- A town (or possibly two) located on the north shore of the Sea of Galilee (modern-day Golan Heights).
- Name in Aramaic meant "fish town" (not the same as *Bethesda,* having to do with wells and healing).
- Located near the Decapolis (Mark 5:20), total population for the surrounding seaside area was greater in the first century than today.
- In New Testament times, the entire city was employed in the fishing industry.
- Situated near the heavily used King's Highway running alongside the Sea of Galilee.
- Home town to several of the apostles: brothers James and John, Simon and Andrew, and Philip.
- Inhabitants denounced by Jesus for their lack of faith (Matt. 11:21; Luke 10:13).
- Possible home of the early Christian sign of the fish.

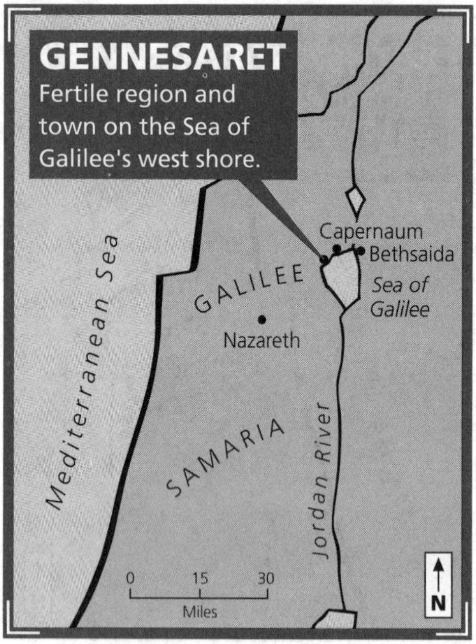

GENNESARET

YOU ARE THERE 6:53

- **A plain extending a mile from the Sea of Galilee along a five-mile section of the north shore.**
- **Name means "garden of riches"; the district's rich, loamy soil caused figs, olives, palms, and other trees to grow well there.**
- **Also the name of a town on the west shore, the fortified city of Naphtali (Josh. 19:35), often called by its Hebrew name, *Chinnereth*.**

[5]Then the Pharisees and scribes asked Him, "Why do
Your disciples not walk according to the tradition of the elders, but eat bread with unwashed hands?"
[6]He answered and said to them, "Well did Isaiah prophesy of you hypocrites, as it is written:

'This people honors Me with *their* lips,
But their heart is far from Me.
[7] And in vain they worship Me,
Teaching *as* doctrines the commandments of
men.'[a]

[8]For laying aside the commandment of God, you hold the
tradition of men[a]—the washing of pitchers and cups, and
many other such things you do."

7:9–13

[9]He said to them, "*All too* well you reject the commandment of God, that you
may keep your tradition. [10]For Moses said, 'Honor your father and your mother';[a] and, 'He who curses father or
mother, let him be put to death.'[b] [11]But you say, 'If a man
says to his father or mother, "Whatever profit you might
have received from me *is* Corban"—' (that is, a gift *to God*),
[12]then you no longer let him do anything for his father or
his mother, [13]making the word of God of no effect through
your tradition which you have handed down. And many
such things you do."
[14]When He had called all the multitude to *Himself*, He
said to them, "Hear Me, everyone, and understand: [15]There
is nothing that enters a man from outside which can defile
him; but the things which come out of him, those are the
things that defile a man. [16]If anyone has ears to hear, let
him hear!"[a]
[17]When He had entered a house away from the crowd,
His disciples asked Him concerning the parable. [18]So
He said to them, "Are you thus without understanding
also? Do you not perceive that whatever enters a man
from outside cannot defile him, [19]because it does not
enter his heart but his stomach, and is eliminated, *thus*
purifying all foods?"[a] [20]And He said, "What comes out
of a man, that defiles a man. [21]For from within, out of
the heart of men, proceed evil thoughts, adulteries, fornications, murders, [22]thefts, covetousness, wickedness,
deceit, lewdness, an evil eye, blasphemy, pride, foolishness. [23]All these evil things come from within and defile a
man."

7:7 [a]Isaiah 29:13 *7:8* [a]NU-Text omits the rest of this verse. *7:10* [a]Exodus 20:12; Deuteronomy 5:16 [b]Exodus 21:17 *7:16* [a]NU-Text omits this verse. *7:19* [a]NU-Text ends quotation with *eliminated,* setting off the final clause as Mark's comment that Jesus has declared all foods clean.

Jesus Heals a Gentile Woman

7:24

24From there He arose and went to the
region of Tyre and Sidon.[a] And He en-
tered a house and wanted no one to know *it,* but He could
not be hidden. 25For a woman whose young daughter had
an unclean spirit heard about Him, and she came and fell at
His feet. 26The woman was a Greek, a Syro-Phoenician by
birth, and she kept asking Him to cast the demon out of her

7:24–30 see pg. 156

daughter. 27But Jesus said to her, "Let the
children be filled first, for it is not good
to take the children's bread and throw *it* to the little dogs."
28And she answered and said to Him, "Yes, Lord, yet even
the little dogs under the table eat from the children's
crumbs."
29Then He said to her, "For this saying go your way; the
demon has gone out of your daughter."
30And when she had come to her house, she found the
demon gone out, and her daughter lying on the bed.

A Deaf and Mute Man Healed

31Again, departing from the region of Tyre and Sidon, He
came through the midst of the region of Decapolis to the
Sea of Galilee. 32Then they brought to Him one who was
deaf and had an impediment in his speech, and they begged
Him to put His hand on him. 33And He took him aside
from the multitude, and put His fingers in his ears, and He
spat and touched his tongue. 34Then, looking up to heaven,
He sighed, and said to him, "Ephphatha," that is, "Be
opened."
35Immediately his ears were opened, and the impediment
of his tongue was loosed, and he spoke plainly. 36Then He
commanded them that they should tell no one; but the
more He commanded them, the more widely they proclaimed *it.* 37And they were astonished beyond measure,
saying, "He has done all things well. He makes both the
deaf to hear and the mute to speak."

CHAPTER 8

Jesus Feeds 4,000

1In those days, the multitude being very great and having
nothing to eat, Jesus called His disciples *to Him* and said to

(Bible text continued on page 157)

7:24 [a]NU-Text omits *and Sidon.*

HONOR YOUR PARENTS

CONSIDER THIS 7:9–13 *Giving equal honor to both father and mother (v. 10) was a requirement of the Law (Ex. 20:12). Indeed, the Law decreed stiff punishment for those who cursed their parents (Lev. 20:9). According to Jewish wisdom literature, only a fool would disobey his mother or mock his father (Prov. 30:17).*

Nevertheless, the scribes and the Pharisees of Jesus' day had found a way around these commands, at least in part (Mark 7:11–12). Their man-made tradition was more important than keeping the Law. No wonder Jesus called them hypocrites (v. 6).

A Beautiful Vacation Spot

A CLOSER LOOK 7:24 *Apparently Jesus' trip to Tyre and Sidon was meant to be a pleasant rest at the seashore (v. 24). He picked a beautiful spot for a spiritual retreat. See "Tyre and Sidon" at Luke 6:17.*

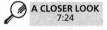

CONSIDER THIS
7:24–30

Jesus and Ethnicity

Jesus' encounter with the Syro-Phoenician woman (vv. 24–30; Matt. 15:21–28) could raise some troubling questions about racial and ethnic attitudes. His treatment of the woman seems to be a contradiction of His image as the international Christ, the Savior of the whole world. Notice:

The Conversation of Jesus and the Syro-Phoenician Woman

The Gentile Woman...	But Jesus...
•Sought Jesus out (v. 25).	•Tried to hide from her (v. 24).
•Begged mercy for her demon-possessed daughter (vv. 25–26; Matt. 15:22).	•Ignored her cries (Matt. 15:23). •Seemed to agree with His disciples that she should be sent away (Matt. 15:23–24).
•Called Him "Lord" (v. 28; Matt. 15:25) and "Son of David" (Matt. 15:22). •Worshiped Him (v. 25; Matt. 15:25).	•Said He only came for the Jews (Matt. 15:24).
•Did not object to being called a dog (v. 28; Matt. 15:27).	•Implied that she was a dog (Jews frequently referred to Gentiles as "dogs"; v. 27; Matt. 15:26). •Implied that because she was not a Jew, she was not a child of God and could not be helped (Matt. 15:24, 26).
•Asked only for the "crumbs" left over from Jesus' work with the Jews (v. 28; Matt. 15:27).	

Finally, because of the woman's persistent faith, Jesus praised her and healed her daughter (v. 29; Matt. 15:28).

But what are we to make of His treatment of her? The woman came in utter sincerity and with great respect, yet Jesus rebuffed her with hard words. Why would He do that? Does God want us to relate to people from other races and ethnic groups like that?

Perhaps the key is to consider that Jesus' words were intended less for the woman's ears than for His disciples'. Maybe it was to them, not the woman, that He said, "I was not sent except to the lost sheep of the house of Israel" (Matt. 15:24). They wanted Him to heal her daughter and send her away, but He refused—by appealing to their own national pride and exclusivism.

In other words, Jesus may have turned this incident into a living parable to show His disciples how hardened they were in their attitudes against Gentiles. Tyre, the setting for this story, was only 50 miles from the Galilee region where most of the Twelve had grown up. But it was an entirely different culture, dominated by Greek influences and populated almost exclusively by Gentiles. Many of them had already come south to learn more about Jesus (Mark 3:8). Now Jesus was taking His followers north on a crash course in cross-cultural awareness.

So upon encountering the woman, it could be that Jesus treated her the way His disciples would have treated her. Perhaps He wanted to illustrate in a way they would never forget that despite rejection, Gentiles like the woman deeply hungered for God's grace and power. In the end, Jesus' high praise for the woman's faith and the healing of her daughter repudiated the notion that God was concerned only with Israel.

How would Jesus have to treat someone today to illustrate prejudice among His followers? ◆

Racism and ethnic hatred have never been God's desire, and Jesus repudiated such sin wherever He found it. See "Jews, Gentiles, and Jesus," Matt. 15:24.

them, 2“I have compassion on the multitude, because they
have now continued with Me three days and have nothing
to eat. 3And if I send them away hungry to their own
houses, they will faint on the way; for some of them have
come from afar.”
4Then His disciples answered Him, “How can one satisfy
these people with bread here in the wilderness?”
5He asked them, “How many loaves do you have?”
And they said, “Seven.”
6So He commanded the multitude to sit down on the
ground. And He took the seven loaves and gave thanks,
broke *them* and gave *them* to His disciples to set before
them; and they set *them* before the multitude. 7They also
had a few small fish; and having blessed them, He said
to set them also before *them.* 8So they ate and were filled,
and they took up seven large baskets of leftover fragments. 9Now those who had eaten were about four thousand. And He sent them away, 10immediately got into the
boat with His disciples, and came to the region of Dal-
manutha.

The Pharisees Demand a Sign

8:11–12 see pg. 158

11Then the Pharisees came out and began to dispute with Him, seeking from
Him a sign from heaven, testing Him. 12But He sighed
deeply in His spirit, and said, “Why does this generation
seek a sign? Assuredly, I say to you, no sign shall be given to
this generation.”

Jesus Warns His Disciples

13And He left them, and getting into the boat again, departed to the other side. 14Now the disciples[a] had forgotten to take bread, and
they did not have more than one loaf with them in the boat.
15Then He charged them, saying, “Take heed, beware of the
leaven of the Pharisees and the leaven of Herod.”
16And they reasoned among themselves, saying, “*It is* because we have no bread.”
17But Jesus, being aware of *it,* said to them, “Why do you
reason because you have no bread? Do you not yet perceive
nor understand? Is your heart still[a] hardened? 18Having
eyes, do you not see? And having ears, do you not hear?
And do you not remember? 19When I broke the five loaves
for the five thousand, how many baskets full of fragments
did you take up?”

8:14–21 see pg. 160

(Bible text continued on page 159)

8:14 [a]NU-Text and M-Text read *they.* *8:17* [a]NU-Text omits *still.*

“How MANY LOAVES DO YOU HAVE?” —Mark 8:5

FOR YOUR INFO
8:11–12

THE MIRACLES OF JESUS

"No sign [miracle] shall be given to this generation!" Jesus declared to the Pharisees (v. 12). Jesus wanted to avoid giving in to his opponents' demand for a miracle, but He had performed plenty of miracles already and would perform many more, as the following table shows:

Miracle	Matthew	Mark	Luke	John
Healed a leper	8:2–4	1:40–45	5:12–16	
Healed a centurion's servant	8:5–13		7:1–10	
Healed Peter's mother-in-law	8:14–15	1:29–31	4:38–39	
Healed the sick in the evening	8:16–17	1:32–34	4:40–41	
Stilled the storm	8:23–27	4:35–41	8:22–25	
Cast out demons and sent them into swine	8:28–34	5:1–20	8:26–39	
Healed a paralytic	9:1–8	2:1–12	5:18–26	
Raised Jairus' daughter	9:18–19, 23–26	5:22–24, 35–43	8:40–42, 49–56	
Healed a woman with a hemorrhaging	9:20–22	5:25–34	8:43–48	
Healed two blind men	9:27–31			
Healed a demon-possessed, mute man	9:32–33			
Healed a man with a withered hand	12:9–14	3:1–6	6:6–11	
Healed a demon-possessed, blind, and mute man	12:22		11:14	
Fed more than 5,000 people	14:13–21	6:30–44	9:10–17	6:1–14
Walked on the Sea of Galilee	14:22–27	6:45–52		6:16–21
Enabled Peter to walk on the Sea of Galilee	14:28–33			
Healed the Syro-Phoenician woman's daughter	15:21–28	7:24–30		
Fed more than 4,000 people	15:32–39	8:1–10		
Healed an epileptic boy	17:14–18	9:17	9:38–42	
Sent Peter to find a coin in a fish's mouth	17:24–27			
Healed two blind men near Jericho	20:29–34			
Caused a fig tree to wither	21:18–19	11:12–14, 20–21		
Returned from the dead	28:1–10	16:1–14	24:1–43	20:1–29
Cast out an unclean spirit		1:23–28	4:33–37	
Healed a deaf mute		7:31–37		
Healed the blind man at Bethsaida		8:22–26		
Healed blind Bartimaeus		10:46–52	18:35–43	
Escaped from a hostile crowd			4:28–30	
Caused a great catch of fish			5:1–11	
Raised a widow's son at Nain			7:11–17	
Healed an infirm, bent woman			13:11–13	

Continued

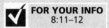

They said to Him, "Twelve."
20"Also, when I broke the seven for the four thousand,
how many large baskets full of fragments did you take up?"
And they said, "Seven."
21So He said to them, "How *is it* you do not understand?"

A Blind Man Healed at Bethsaida

22Then He came to Bethsaida; and they brought a blind
man to Him, and begged Him to touch him. 23So He took
the blind man by the hand and led him out of the town.
And when He had spit on his eyes and put His hands on
him, He asked him if he saw anything.
24And he looked up and said, "I see men like trees, walking."
25Then He put *His* hands on his eyes again and made him
look up. And he was restored and saw everyone clearly.
26Then He sent him away to his house, saying, "Neither go
into the town, nor tell anyone in the town."[a]

8:26 [a]NU-Text reads *"Do not even go into the town."*

"How is it you do not understand?" —Mark 8:21

Continued

Miracle	Matthew	Mark	Luke	John
Healed a man with dropsy			14:1–4	
Healed ten lepers			17:11–19	
Healed Malchus' ear			22:47–51	18:10
Turned water into wine				2:1–11
Healed a nobleman's son				4:46–54
Healed an infirm man at Bethsaida				5:1–15
Healed a man born blind				9:1–41
Raised Lazarus				11:1–44
Caused a second great catch of fish				21:1–14

Even though Jesus performed astonishing miracles, most of His Jewish brothers and sisters rejected Him as their Messiah. Today many people reject Christianity on similar grounds, claiming that Christianity and science conflict. *See "Ten Myths about Christianity, Myth #3: Science Is in Conflict with Christian Faith," John 4:48.*

Peter Calls Jesus "the Christ"

8:27

27Now Jesus and His disciples went out
to the towns of Caesarea Philippi; and on
the road He asked His disciples, saying to them, "Who do
men say that I am?"
28So they answered, "John the Baptist; but some *say,* Elijah; and others, one of the prophets."

8:27–33
see pg. 162

29He said to them, "But who do you say
that I am?"
Peter answered and said to Him, "You are the Christ."
30Then He strictly warned them that they should tell no
one about Him.

Jesus Rebukes Peter

31And He began to teach them that the Son of Man must
suffer many things, and be rejected by the elders and chief
priests and scribes, and be killed, and after three days rise
again. 32He spoke this word openly. Then Peter took Him

CONSIDER THIS
8:14–21

DANGER AHEAD

Yeast, or leaven, is a powerful fungus that can cause a lump of dough to rise into bread, ferment liquids into alcohol, or cause painful infections. When Jesus spoke of yeast in His comments about the Pharisees and Herod (v. 15), His disciples were quite confused. What could He mean? What was the leaven of the Pharisees and Herod?

Jesus reminded His followers of His miracles of feeding the five thousand and the four thousand (vv. 19–21; 6:35–44; 8:1–9). What was the response of the Pharisees? They disputed with Him and tried to test Him by appealing for a miracle (v. 11). In short, they refused to believe—despite the miraculous provision of meals for more than nine thousand people! Furthermore, they were already in league with Herod and his supporters to destroy Jesus (3:6; 12:13), just as Herod had done away with John the Baptist (6:14–29).

Clearly, Jesus was warning His followers against the insidious infection of unbelief. Like yeast in dough, a lack of faith can permeate one's life until it breaks out in open rebellion against God. No wonder the Lord was so dis-

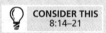

aside and began to rebuke Him. 33But when He had turned
around and looked at His disciples, He rebuked Peter, saying, "Get behind Me, Satan! For you are not mindful of the
things of God, but the things of men."

Discipleship Is Costly

34When He had called the people to *Himself,* with His disciples also, He said to them, "Whoever desires to come after
Me, let him deny himself, and take up his cross, and follow
Me. 35For whoever desires to save his life will lose it, but
whoever loses his life for My sake and the gospel's will save
it. 36For what will it profit a man if he gains the whole
world, and loses his own soul? 37Or what will a man give in
exchange for his soul? 38For whoever is ashamed of Me and
My words in this adulterous and sinful generation, of him
the Son of Man also will be ashamed when He comes in the
glory of His Father with the holy angels."

pleased with the disciples' lack of perception (8:17–18). Perhaps the yeast of unbelief was already at work among them. After all, they had apparently failed to understand the significance of a feeding miracle the first time around (6:52); now they were missing it a second time!

Jesus had grave concern about the condition of His followers' faith. He knew that there was danger ahead. Powerful enemies would lay hold of Him, and the disciples would be sorely tested. No wonder He took measures to keep a low profile (vv. 26, 30). He wanted to avoid exposing these men to the full force of His opponents before their faith was ready to handle such a trial.

None of us knows what dangers lie ahead for our faith. We may be headed for trials and challenges that we never imagined. Is our faith ready to meet whatever challenges come our way? Or have we let the yeast of unbelief gain a foothold, breaking down our trust in God and spreading resistance to Him throughout our life? ◆

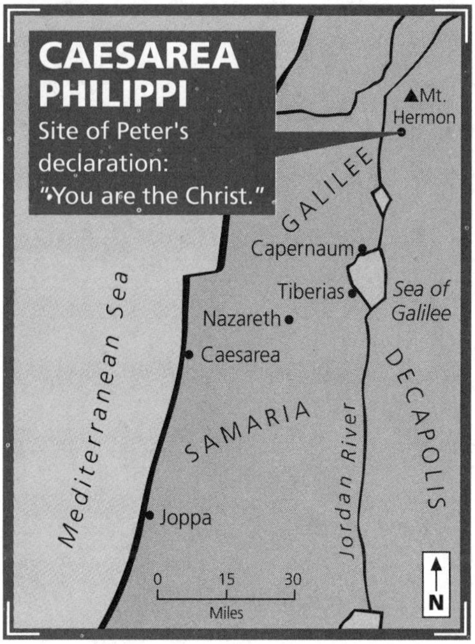

Caesarea Philippi

YOU ARE THERE 8:27

- **City on the southwestern slope of Mount Hebron in northern Palestine.**
- **Known as Paneas (or Panias) in New Testament times, but renamed by Philip the tetrarch in honor of Caesar Augustus.**
- **Not to be confused with Caesarea, Herod's seaport jewel on the Mediterranean (see Acts 8:40; 10:1).**
- **Perhaps the northernmost extent of Jesus' ministry.**
- **High cliffs nearby housed a cave dedicated to the Greek god Pan. Other rock cuts held statues dedicated to the mythical nymphs.**

CHAPTER 9

Jesus Is Transfigured

9:1–13

[1]And He said to them, "Assuredly, I say
to you that there are some standing here
who will not taste death till they see the kingdom of God
present with power."
[2]Now after six days Jesus took Peter, James, and John,
and led them up on a high mountain apart by themselves;
and He was transfigured before them. [3]His clothes became
shining, exceedingly white, like snow, such as no launderer
on earth can whiten them. [4]And Elijah appeared to them
with Moses, and they were talking with Jesus. [5]Then Peter
answered and said to Jesus, "Rabbi, it is good for us to be
here; and let us make three tabernacles: one for You, one for

The "A" Team?

A CLOSER LOOK 9:1–13 *The actions of Peter, James, and John during the Transfiguration (vv. 1–13) raise questions as to their fitness for leadership. But Jesus not only kept them and the rest of the Twelve on His team, He kept all of them as His first team! He showed that undeveloped rookies can be developed into servant-leaders—over time.* *See "Can Laity Get the Job Done?" Luke 9:1–62.*

YOU ARE THERE 8:27–33

"You Are the Christ"

Peter's memorable declaration, "You are the Christ" (v. 29) was made near Caesarea Philippi (v. 27), a town named in honor of Caesar Augustus.

In Old Testament times, the city was a center of the Canaanites' Baal worship. Later the Greeks substituted their god Pan for Baal, and later the Romans used it to develop worship of their emperors.

Significantly, Jesus took His followers outside of Palestine to a center of pagan, Gentile deities, where He asked them two vital questions:

- *"Who do men say that I am?" (v. 27).*
- *"Who do you say that I am?" (v. 29).*

The answer to the first question was easy enough. People believed that He was more or less a powerful religious leader such as John the Baptist, Elijah, or one of the Old Testament prophets. Even King Herod's counselors saw Him that way (6:14–16).

But Peter had finally settled in His own mind who Jesus was, so he immediately stepped forward to answer the

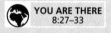

Moses, and one for Elijah"— 6because he did not know
what to say, for they were greatly afraid.
7And a cloud came and overshadowed them; and a voice
came out of the cloud, saying, "This is My beloved Son.
Hear Him!" 8Suddenly, when they had looked around, they
saw no one anymore, but only Jesus with themselves.
9Now as they came down from the mountain, He commanded them that they should tell no one the things they
had seen, till the Son of Man had risen from the dead. 10So
they kept this word to themselves, questioning what the rising from the dead meant.
11And they asked Him, saying, "Why do the scribes say
that Elijah must come first?"
12Then He answered and told them, "Indeed, Elijah is
coming first and restores all things. And how is it written
concerning the Son of Man, that He must suffer many
things and be treated with contempt? 13But I say to you that
Elijah has also come, and they did to him whatever they
wished, as it is written of him."

A Young Demon-possessed Man Healed

14And when He came to the disciples, He saw a great
multitude around them, and scribes disputing with them.
15Immediately, when they saw Him, all the people were

second question: "You are the Christ, the son of the living God" (8:29; Matt. 16:16).

It may be that Jesus looked at the great rock cliffs standing nearby as He replied, "Blessed are you, Simon Bar-Jonah [that is, Simon, son of Jonah] . . . . And I also say to you that you are Peter ["Rock"], and on this rock I will build My church" (Matt. 16:17–18).

Some have understood "rock" to mean the bedrock of faith, like the faith Peter was demonstrating here. Others believe that Peter himself (and for some, the other disciples as well) was the rock, the key figure on whom the church was to stand, and that his successors have continued that foundational role. Another view, based on the language Jesus used, is that Jesus made a word play on Peter's name to indicate Himself as the Rock on which His church is built.

The key point of the incident, however, is that Jesus is the Christ. Standing in the shadow of a city named in honor of Rome's emperor, Jesus was declared to be the the very Son of God. He was more than just the Messiah of the Jews; He was the Savior of the whole world. ◆

"THIS IS MY BELOVED SON. HEAR HIM!"
—Mark 9:7

Are You Confused about Greatness, Too?

CONSIDER THIS 9:33–37 **Significance is a tricky achievement. Too often it is built upon fame, money, marketing, power, position, or possessions.**

The disciples were caught up in a value system based on these things, which caused them to compete with each other (v. 34). In fact, the dispute over greatness resurfaced later (10:35–45). The quest for significance through power was an insidious problem.

Jesus noticed His followers' thinking and challenged it (9:35). He pointed out that true greatness is in serving others rather than outdoing them. Later He suggested the same thing to a rich ruler (10:21).

To drive His point home, Jesus gathered a child in His arms and said that to welcome a child is to welcome both Christ and His Father (vv. 36–37). No wonder the apostle Paul, in writing to believers in Galatia, identified many childlike characteristics as highly valued works of the Spirit (Gal. 5:22–25). He contrasted those traits with some ugly ones that often accompany competition (Gal. 5:16–21).

Do you need to rework your value system? Are you addicted to fame and fortune? A good test is to ask yourself, *Where do children and the poor stand among my priorities?*

One of the most debilitating diseases of the modern world is "comparisonitis"—the tendency to measure one's worth by comparing oneself to other people. Do you suffer from it? Find out at Rom. 12:3.

greatly amazed, and running to *Him,* greeted Him. 16And
He asked the scribes, "What are you discussing with them?"
17Then one of the crowd answered and said, "Teacher, I
brought You my son, who has a mute spirit. 18And wherever it seizes him, it throws him down; he foams at the
mouth, gnashes his teeth, and becomes rigid. So I spoke to
Your disciples, that they should cast it out, but they could
not."
19He answered him and said, "O faithless generation, how
long shall I be with you? How long shall I bear with you?
Bring him to Me." 20Then they brought him to Him. And
when he saw Him, immediately the spirit convulsed him,
and he fell on the ground and wallowed, foaming at the
mouth.
21So He asked his father, "How long has this been happening to him?"
And he said, "From childhood. 22And often he has
thrown him both into the fire and into the water to destroy
him. But if You can do anything, have compassion on us
and help us."
23Jesus said to him, "If you can believe,[a] all things *are*
possible to him who believes."
24Immediately the father of the child cried out and said
with tears, "Lord, I believe; help my unbelief!"
25When Jesus saw that the people came running together,
He rebuked the unclean spirit, saying to it, "Deaf and dumb
spirit, I command you, come out of him and enter him no
more!" 26Then *the spirit* cried out, convulsed him greatly,
and came out of him. And he became as one dead, so that
many said, "He is dead." 27But Jesus took him by the hand
and lifted him up, and he arose.
28And when He had come into the house, His disciples
asked Him privately, "Why could we not cast it out?"
29So He said to them, "This kind can come out by nothing but prayer and fasting."[a]

Jesus Predicts His Death

30Then they departed from there and passed through
Galilee, and He did not want anyone to know *it.* 31For He
taught His disciples and said to them, "The Son of Man is
being betrayed into the hands of men, and they will kill
Him. And after He is killed, He will rise the third day." 32But
they did not understand this saying, and were afraid to ask
Him.

A Discussion about Rank

9:33–37 33Then He came to Capernaum. And
when He was in the house He asked

9:23 [a]NU-Text reads "*'If You can!' All things . . . .*" 9:29 [a]NU-Text omits *and fasting.*

them, "What was it you disputed among yourselves on the
road?" 34 But they kept silent, for on the road they had disputed among themselves who *would be the* greatest. 35 And
He sat down, called the twelve, and said to them, "If anyone
desires to be first, he shall be last of all and servant of all."
36 Then He took a little child and set him in the midst of
them. And when He had taken him in His arms, He said to
them, 37 "Whoever receives one of these little children in My
name receives Me; and whoever receives Me, receives not
Me but Him who sent Me."

Taking Sides

38 Now John answered Him, saying, "Teacher, we saw
someone who does not follow us casting out demons in
Your name, and we forbade him because he does not follow
us."

39 But Jesus said, "Do not forbid him, for no one who
works a miracle in My name can soon afterward speak evil
of Me. 40 For he who is not against us is on our[a] side. 41 For
whoever gives you a cup of water to drink in My name, because you belong to Christ, assuredly, I say to you, he will
by no means lose his reward.

42 "But whoever causes one of these little ones who believe
in Me to stumble, it would be better for him if a millstone
were hung around his neck, and he were thrown into the
sea. 43 If your hand causes you to sin, cut it off. It is better
for you to enter into life maimed, rather than having two
hands, to go to hell, into the fire that shall never be
quenched— 44 where

'Their worm does not die,
And the fire is not quenched.'[a]

45 And if your foot causes you to sin, cut it off. It is better for
you to enter life lame, rather than having two feet, to be
cast into hell, into the fire that shall never be quenched—
46 where

'Their worm does not die,
And the fire is not quenched.'[a]

47 And if your eye causes you to sin, pluck it out. It is better
for you to enter the kingdom of God with one eye, rather
than having two eyes, to be cast into hell fire— 48 where

'Their worm does not die,
And the fire is not quenched.'[a]

49 "For everyone will be seasoned with fire,[a] and every sacrifice will be seasoned with salt. 50 Salt *is* good, but if the salt

9:40 [a]M-Text reads *against you is on your side.* *9:44* [a]NU-Text omits this verse.
9:46 [a]NU-Text omits the last clause of verse 45 and all of verse 46. *9:48* [a]Isaiah 66:24
9:49 [a]NU-Text omits the rest of this verse.

"IF ANYONE DESIRES TO BE FIRST, HE SHALL BE LAST OF ALL. . . ."
—Mark 9:35

loses its flavor, how will you season it? Have salt in yourselves, and have peace with one another."

CHAPTER 10

Jesus Teaches about Divorce

1 Then He arose from there and came to the region of
Judea by the other side of the Jordan. And multitudes gathered to Him again, and as He was accustomed, He taught
them again.

10:2–12

2 The Pharisees came and asked Him,
"Is it lawful for a man to divorce *his*
wife?" testing Him.
3 And He answered and said to them, "What did Moses
command you?"
4 They said, "Moses permitted *a man* to write a certificate
of divorce, and to dismiss *her.*"
5 And Jesus answered and said to them, "Because of the
hardness of your heart he wrote you this precept. 6 But from
the beginning of the creation, God 'made them male and female.'[a] 7 'For this reason a man shall leave his father and
mother and be joined to his wife, 8 and the two shall become one flesh';[a] so then they are no longer two, but one
flesh. 9 Therefore what God has joined together, let not man
separate."
10 In the house His disciples also asked Him again about
the same *matter.* 11 So He said to them, "Whoever divorces
his wife and marries another commits adultery against her.
12 And if a woman divorces her husband and marries another, she commits adultery."

Jesus Lets Children Come to Him

10:13–16

13 Then they brought little children to
Him, that He might touch them; but the
disciples rebuked those who brought *them.* 14 But when Jesus saw *it,* He was greatly displeased and said to them, "Let
the little children come to Me, and do not forbid them; for
of such is the kingdom of God. 15 Assuredly, I say to you,
whoever does not receive the kingdom of God as a little
child will by no means enter it." 16 And He took them up in
His arms, laid *His* hands on them, and blessed them.

A Rich Man Asks about Eternal Life

10:17–27
see pg. 168

17 Now as He was going out on the
road, one came running, knelt before
Him, and asked Him, "Good Teacher, what shall I do that I
may inherit eternal life?"

10:6 [a]Genesis 1:27; 5:2 *10:8* [a]Genesis 2:24

DIVORCE

CONSIDER THIS 10:2–12 *In the first century, Jewish men were allowed to divorce their wives for many different reasons (v. 2). Depending on which interpretation of the Torah one followed, a man could even send his wife away if she burned a meal.*

By contrast, women were far more restricted in their grounds for divorce. One of the few had to do with her husband's occupation. If he were a copper smelter, tanner, or dung collector, she could get a divorce, even if she knew before she married what his trade was, on the grounds that she couldn't have known how awful the smell would be.

18So Jesus said to him, "Why do you call Me good? No
one *is* good but One, *that is,* God. 19You know the commandments: 'Do not commit adultery,' 'Do not murder,' 'Do
not steal,' 'Do not bear false witness,' 'Do not defraud,'
'Honor your father and your mother.' "[a]
20And he answered and said to Him, "Teacher, all these
things I have kept from my youth."
21Then Jesus, looking at him, loved him, and said to him,
"One thing you lack: Go your way, sell whatever you have
and give to the poor, and you will have treasure in heaven;
and come, take up the cross, and follow Me."
22But he was sad at this word, and went away sorrowful,
for he had great possessions.

Jesus Speaks about Riches

23Then Jesus looked around and said to His disciples,
"How hard it is for those who have riches to enter the kingdom of God!" 24And the disciples were astonished at His
words. But Jesus answered again and said to them, "Children, how hard it is for those who trust in riches[a] to enter
the kingdom of God! 25It is easier for a camel to go through
the eye of a needle than for a rich man to enter the kingdom of God."
26And they were greatly astonished, saying among themselves, "Who then can be saved?"
27But Jesus looked at them and said, "With men *it is* impossible, but not with God; for with God all things are possible."

Rewards for the Twelve

28Then Peter began to say to Him, "See, we have left all
and followed You."
29So Jesus answered and said, "Assuredly, I say to you,
there is no one who has left house or brothers or sisters or
father or mother or wife[a] or children or lands, for My sake
and the gospel's, 30who shall not receive a hundredfold now
in this time—houses and brothers and sisters and mothers
and children and lands, with persecutions—and in the age
to come, eternal life. 31But many *who are* first will be last,
and the last first."

Jesus Again Predicts His Death

10:32–37 see pg. 169

32Now they were on the road, going up
to Jerusalem, and Jesus was going before
them; and they were amazed. And as they followed they
were afraid. Then He took the twelve aside again and began

10:19 [a]Exodus 20:12–16; Deuteronomy 5:16–20 *10:24* [a]NU-Text omits *for those who trust in riches.* *10:29* [a]NU-Text omits *or wife.*

The Friend of Children

CONSIDER THIS 10:13–16 *In Jesus' day it was common for mothers to ask famous rabbis to bless their children. With Jesus, however, they sought more than a blessing; they wanted the touch of this Rabbi (v. 13). No doubt the power of His touch had become well known.*

Mark did not explain why the disciples tried to keep the children away. Perhaps they viewed the little ones as ritually unclean, or, like most of society, unworthy of an important man's attention.

But Jesus rebuked the disciples and invited the children into His arms (v. 16). The way that He spoke to them and embraced them must have shocked those who stood by. Such tenderness and respect were rarely given children in that society.

Perhaps the disciples had adopted the prevailing Graeco-Roman view of childhood as an insignificant phase of life. Children were not valued for their own sake. See "Children and Childcare," Matt. 19:14.

to tell them the things that would happen to Him: 33"Behold, we are going up to Jerusalem, and the Son of Man will
be betrayed to the chief priests and to the scribes; and they
will condemn Him to death and deliver Him to the Gentiles; 34and they will mock Him, and scourge Him, and spit
on Him, and kill Him. And the third day He will rise again."

James and John's Request

35Then James and John, the sons of Zebedee, came to
Him, saying, "Teacher, we want You to do for us whatever
we ask."
36And He said to them, "What do you want Me to do for
you?"
37They said to Him, "Grant us that we may sit, one on
Your right hand and the other on Your left, in Your glory."
38But Jesus said to them, "You do not know what you ask.
Are you able to drink the cup that I drink, and be baptized
with the baptism that I am baptized with?"
39They said to Him, "We are able."
So Jesus said to them, "You will indeed drink the cup that
I drink, and with the baptism I am baptized with you will
be baptized; 40but to sit on My right hand and on My left is
not Mine to give, but *it is for those* for whom it is prepared."
41And when the ten heard *it,* they began to be greatly dis-

CONSIDER THIS
10:17–27

THE MAN WHO HAD IT ALL—ALMOST

He was young, well-mannered, well-educated, and well-off. He was sincere, honest, and above reproach. Maybe he also had an engaging personality and a winsome smile. Certainly Jesus found him likable; He even tried to recruit him (v. 21). He was the man who had everything—except eternal life. And he could have had that, too. All he had to do was get rid of his money and follow Jesus.

But it wasn't to be. Elsewhere Jesus had said that no one can serve both God and money (Matt. 6:24). Here was living proof of that principle. In coming to Jesus, the rich young ruler came to a fork in the road. He had to choose which one he would serve—money or Jesus. Apparently he chose money.

Jesus never condemned people for being rich. Nor does Scripture condemn the possession or the accumulation of money. But Jesus warned people about what He called "the deceitfulness of riches" (Mark 4:19). He understood the powerful but ultimately fatal attraction of money as a substitute for God.

Jesus perceived that tendency in the rich young ruler.

pleased with James and John. 42But Jesus called them to *Himself* and said to them, "You know that those who are considered rulers over the Gentiles lord it over them, and their great ones exercise authority over them. 43Yet it shall not be so among you; but whoever desires to become great among you shall be your servant. 44And whoever of you desires to be first shall be slave of all. 45For even the Son of Man did not come to be served, but to serve, and to give His life a ransom for many."

Blind Bartimaeus Sees

10:46

46Now they came to Jericho. As He went out of Jericho with His disciples and a great multitude, blind Bartimaeus, the son of Timaeus, sat by the road begging. 47And when he heard that it was Jesus of Nazareth, he began to cry out and say, "Jesus, Son of David, have mercy on me!"

48Then many warned him to be quiet; but he cried out all the more, "Son of David, have mercy on me!"

Jericho

A CLOSER LOOK 10:46 *Blind Bartimaeus (v. 46) was but one of countless beggars who lined the road to Jericho in Jesus' day.* *See "Jericho" at Luke 10:30.*

The man was placing far too much value on his wealth. So Jesus told him to give it away, to free himself from its entanglements. It's worth noting that Jesus did not give that same advice to every other rich person He encountered. But it was a requirement for this young ruler.

There are many rich young rulers today, people who have or are well on their way to having relatively sizable assets. Some are Christians and some are not. But sooner or later they all must answer the question that this man asked Jesus: "What do I need to do to inherit eternal life?" (10:17).

Jesus' response is still the same: there's nothing you can do, only God can give eternal life (v. 27). But He gives it freely and graciously to those who follow Him (vv. 29–30). However, that's especially hard for the rich (v. 23). They have a competing offer, and it's very attractive. ◆

Scripture offers an alternative to greed. See "Christians and Money," 1 Tim. 6:6–19.

No Better than Gentiles

CONSIDER THIS 10:32–37 *On the final trip to Jerusalem, something of a power struggle began to emerge among Jesus' disciples. James and John were the first to try to obtain positions of power in the coming kingdom (vv. 35–37).*

Jesus rebuked them in an interesting way. He compared them to the leaders of the Gentiles that they so despised (v. 42)—people like Pilate and Augustus and all their governors, tax collectors, soldiers, and centurions. The disciples detested those people as living only for themselves. Yet Jesus implied that this was the way His disciples were acting when they jockeyed for positions of power. The comparison must have challenged them to the core. Jesus was telling them, "You are no different than Gentiles!"

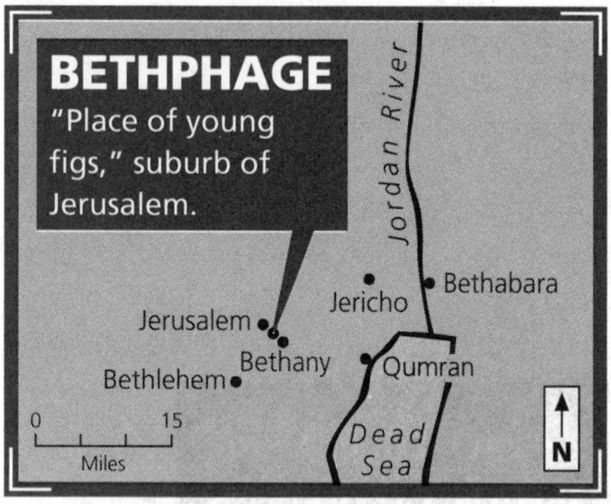

Bethphage

YOU ARE THERE 11:1

- **A village near Bethany, along the road from Jerusalem to Jericho (possibly modern Moslem town of Abu Dis); or perhaps somewhere between Bethany and the Mount of Olives.**
- **A "suburb" of Jerusalem.**
- **Name in Aramaic meant "place of young figs," a species that never appeared ripe, even when edible—perhaps giving rise to Jesus' parable of the unripe figs (Mark 11:12–14, 20–26; see "Bethany," John 11:1).**
- **First stop in Jesus' triumphal entry into Jerusalem (Mark 11:1; Matt. 21:1; Luke 19:29).**
- **Modern-day Bethphage hosts a Franciscan monastery (see "A Prayer of the Laity," Matt. 10:7–10).**

49So Jesus stood still and commanded him to be called.
Then they called the blind man, saying to him, "Be of good cheer. Rise, He is calling you."
50And throwing aside his garment, he rose and came to Jesus.
51So Jesus answered and said to him, "What do you want Me to do for you?"
The blind man said to Him, "Rabboni, that I may receive my sight."
52Then Jesus said to him, "Go your way; your faith has made you well." And immediately he received his sight and followed Jesus on the road.

CHAPTER 11

The Triumphal Entry into Jerusalem

11:1

1Now when they drew near Jerusalem,
to Bethphage[a] and Bethany, at the Mount
of Olives, He sent two of His disciples; 2and He said to
them, "Go into the village opposite you; and as soon as you
have entered it you will find a colt tied, on which no one
has sat. Loose it and bring *it.* 3And if anyone says to you,
'Why are you doing this?' say, 'The Lord has need of it,' and
immediately he will send it here."
4So they went their way, and found the[a] colt tied by the
door outside on the street, and they loosed it. 5But some of
those who stood there said to them, "What are you doing,
loosing the colt?"
6And they spoke to them just as Jesus had commanded.
So they let them go. 7Then they brought the colt to Jesus

11:1–11

and threw their clothes on it, and He sat
on it. 8And many spread their clothes on
the road, and others cut down leafy branches from the trees
and spread *them* on the road. 9Then those who went before
and those who followed cried out, saying:

"Hosanna!
'Blessed *is* He who comes in the name of the LORD!'[a]
10 Blessed *is* the kingdom of our father David
That comes in the name of the Lord![a]
Hosanna in the highest!"

11:1 [a]M-Text reads *Bethsphage.* *11:4* [a]NU-Text and M-Text read *a.* *11:9* [a]Psalm 118:26
11:10 [a]NU-Text omits *in the name of the Lord.*

A Parade for the Common People

A CLOSER LOOK 11:1–11 *For once, the common folks in Jerusalem had a parade (vv. 8–9). But the Man they celebrated traveled into town in a manner unlike any other celebrity they had seen. See "A New Style of Fame," Matt. 21:8–11.*

11And Jesus went into Jerusalem and into the temple. So
when He had looked around at all things, as the hour was
already late, He went out to Bethany with the twelve.

Jesus Curses a Fig Tree

11:12–26

12Now the next day, when they had
come out from Bethany, He was hungry.
13And seeing from afar a fig tree having leaves, He went to
see if perhaps He would find something on it. When He
came to it, He found nothing but leaves, for it was not the
season for figs. 14In response Jesus said to it, "Let no one eat
fruit from you ever again."
And His disciples heard *it.*

Jesus Drives Merchants from the Temple

15So they came to Jerusalem. Then Jesus went into the
temple and began to drive out those who bought and sold
in the temple, and overturned the tables of the money
changers and the seats of those who sold doves. 16And He
would not allow anyone to carry wares through the temple.
17Then He taught, saying to them, "Is it not written, 'My
house shall be called a house of prayer for all nations' ?[a] But
you have made it a 'den of thieves.' "[b]
18And the scribes and chief priests heard it and sought
how they might destroy Him; for they feared Him, because
all the people were astonished at His teaching. 19When
evening had come, He went out of the city.

Lessons from the Cursed Fig Tree

20Now in the morning, as they passed by, they saw the fig
tree dried up from the roots. 21And Peter, remembering,
said to Him, "Rabbi, look! The fig tree which You cursed
has withered away."
22So Jesus answered and said to them, "Have faith in God.
23For assuredly, I say to you, whoever says to this mountain,
'Be removed and be cast into the sea,' and does not doubt in
his heart, but believes that those things he says will be
done, he will have whatever he says. 24Therefore I say to
you, whatever things you ask when you pray, believe that
you receive *them,* and you will have *them.*
25"And whenever you stand praying, if you have anything
against anyone, forgive him, that your Father in heaven may
also forgive you your trespasses. 26But if you do not forgive,
neither will your Father in heaven forgive your trespasses."[a]

Leaders Question Jesus' Authority

27Then they came again to Jerusalem. And as He was
walking in the temple, the chief priests, the scribes, and the

11:17 [a]Isaiah 56:7 [b]Jeremiah 7:11 *11:26* [a]NU-Text omits this verse.

Jesus and the Fig Tree

CONSIDER THIS 11:12–26

Why did Jesus destroy an innocent fig tree and then promise mountain-moving powers (vv. 12–14, 20–24)? The context of these events and statements is important. Jesus and His disciples were entering Jerusalem, where He was about to be killed (Mark 15). When He came upon the fig tree, He used it as an illustration and a warning of what ultimately awaits those who oppose the kingdom of God—like the Jewish leaders of that day. Rather than bearing useful fruit, the nation was misusing its privileges as God's people (11:12–18).

Cursing the fig tree was not a wanton act of environmental destruction but a teaching method for Jesus' disciples. They would soon be very confused and frightened by events. Perhaps the memory of that graphic illustration would help.

As for moving mountains into the sea by prayer, Jesus was talking about the power of forgiveness (v. 25). He was not holding out false hopes of the free use of power to one's personal advantage. Instead, He was showing the significance of moving heaven and earth with another power—forgiving one's enemies.

Jesus frequently used contrasts to highlight spiritual truths. In Matt. 6:5–15, for example, He spoke of attention-getting prayers on the one hand (v. 5) and unseen prayers of forgiveness on the other (vv. 6, 14–15).

The power of forgiveness is immeasurable. It's a power that Jesus has delegated to us as His followers. *See "The Power of Forgiveness," Matt. 9:4–8.*

elders came to Him. 28And they said to Him, "By what authority are You doing these things? And who gave You this
authority to do these things?"
29But Jesus answered and said to them, "I also will ask
you one question; then answer Me, and I will tell you by
what authority I do these things: 30The baptism of John—
was it from heaven or from men? Answer Me."
31And they reasoned among themselves, saying, "If we
say, 'From heaven,' He will say, 'Why then did you not believe him?' 32But if we say, 'From men' "—they feared the
people, for all counted John to have been a prophet indeed.
33So they answered and said to Jesus, "We do not know."
And Jesus answered and said to them, "Neither will I tell
you by what authority I do these things."

CHAPTER 12

A Parable about a Vineyard Owner

12:1–12

1Then He began to speak to them in
parables: "A man planted a vineyard and
set a hedge around *it,* dug *a place for* the wine vat and built
a tower. And he leased it to vinedressers and went into a far
country. 2Now at vintage-time he sent a servant to the vinedressers, that he might receive some of the fruit of the vineyard from the vinedressers. 3And they took *him* and beat
him and sent *him* away empty-handed. 4Again he sent them
another servant, and at him they threw stones,[a] wounded
him in the head, and sent *him* away shamefully treated.
5And again he sent another, and him they killed; and many
others, beating some and killing some. 6Therefore still having one son, his beloved, he also sent him to them last, saying, 'They will respect my son.' 7But those vinedressers said
among themselves, 'This is the heir. Come, let us kill him,
and the inheritance will be ours.' 8So they took him and
killed *him* and cast *him* out of the vineyard.
9"Therefore what will the owner of the vineyard do? He
will come and destroy the vinedressers, and give the vineyard to others. 10Have you not even read this Scripture:

'The stone which the builders rejected
Has become the chief cornerstone.

(Bible text continued on page 174)

12:4 [a]NU-Text omits *and at him they threw stones.*

"SO THEY TOOK HIM AND KILLED HIM AND CAST HIM OUT OF THE VINEYARD."
—Mark 12:8

Who Owns What?

A CLOSER LOOK
12:1–12

The parable of the vineyard owner (vv. 1–12) challenges the idea that our significance is determined by how much we own and how much what we own is worth. See "Owners or Tenants?" Luke 20:9–19.

FOR YOUR INFO
12:14

TAXES

When the Pharisees and Herodians tested Jesus with a question about taxes (v. 14), they were raising a highly explosive issue. Feelings of resentment over taxes ran extremely deep among the Jews, who had endured a history of heavy taxation for millennia.

Taxes may have originated with the custom of giving presents for protection from harm (Gen. 32:13–21; 33:10; 43:11).

In Egypt, Joseph warned of seven years of famine after seven years of abundance. Pharaoh then put him in charge of raising revenues. He collected a 20 percent tax to store up food and buy land for Pharaoh—during the famine as well as the time of plenty (Gen. 47:20–26).

During the Exodus, Moses asked for voluntary contributions to construct the tabernacle (Ex. 25:2; 35:5, 21). The Law prescribed that every male over the age of 20 was to give half a shekel for the service of the tabernacle (Ex. 30:11–16).

When Israel asked Samuel for a king, he warned the people that heavy taxes would result—10 percent of nearly everything the people produced, as well as confiscation of land and servants. "You will cry out in that day because of your king whom you have chosen for yourselves," he predicted (1 Sam. 8:14–18). His words came true almost right away.

Under David and Solomon, several taxes were established: a 10 percent tax on the produce of land and livestock (1 Sam. 8:15, 17); compulsory military service for one month each year (1 Chr. 27:1); import duties (1 Kin. 10:15); and tribute paid by subject peoples (2 Sam. 8:6; 2 Kin. 3:4). The taxes became so oppressive under Solomon that they contributed to the split in the kingdom after his death (1 Kin. 12:4).

When the Persians came, they set up a new system. Instead of paying tribute, each province in the Persian Empire was required to collect its own taxes. Persian rulers called *satraps* collected taxes for their own provinces, from which they paid a fixed amount into the royal treasury. Revenues were derived from tribute, custom, and toll (Ezra 4:13). Priests and religious servants were exempt (Ezra 7:24). A tax was also collected for maintenance of the governor's household. Again, the taxes were crushing. Many people were forced to mortgage their fields and vineyards, and some even sold their own children into slavery (Neh. 5:1–5).

During the period between the Old and the New Testament, the Jews were first under the Egyptian Ptolemaic rule (301–198 B.C.) and later under the Syrian Seleucid rule (198–63 B.C.). Under the Ptolemies, taxing privileges were farmed out to the highest bidders. People came to Alexandria from the various provinces to bid for the privilege of collecting taxes from their own people. Contractors would tax their people up to double the amount required by law in order to make a handsome profit. These tax collectors were even given military assistance to enforce their demands.

The same type of system probably continued under the Syrians. A poll tax, a salt tax, and a crown tax were enforced during this time. The Syrians taxed as much as one-third of the grain, one-half of the fruit, and a portion of the tithes which the Jews paid to support the temple.

When the Romans captured Jerusalem in 63 B.C., a tax of 10,000 talents was temporarily imposed on the Jews. Julius

(continued on next page)

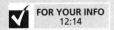

(continued from previous page)

Caesar later reformed the system by reducing taxes and levying no tax during the sabbatic years. But soon the Herods came to power.

The Herods instituted a poll tax and a tax on fishing rights. Customs were collected on trade routes by men like Levi in Capernaum (Matt. 9:9; Mark 2:14; Luke 5:27). The city may have also been a place for port duties and fishing tolls. Some items sold for 1,000 per cent above their original prices because of all the taxes. There may have been a sales tax on slaves, oil, clothes, hides, and furs.

Over and above these taxes were religious dues, generally between 10 and 20 percent of a person's income before government tax. As a result, during Jesus' time, the Jews were probably paying between 30 and 40 percent of their income on taxes and religious dues.

No wonder the Pharisees asked, "Is it lawful to pay taxes to Caesar, or not?" ◆

Jesus' example in paying taxes proves instructive. See "Jesus and Taxation," Matt. 17:24–27.

11 This was the LORD's doing,
And it is marvelous in our eyes'? "[a]

12 And they sought to lay hands on Him, but feared the multitude, for they knew He had spoken the parable against them. So they left Him and went away.

A Test Regarding Taxes

13 Then they sent to Him some of the Pharisees and the

12:14
see pg. 173

Herodians, to catch Him in *His* words.
14 When they had come, they said to Him,
"Teacher, we know that You are true, and care about no
one; for You do not regard the person of men, but teach the
way of God in truth. Is it lawful to pay taxes to Caesar, or
not? 15 Shall we pay, or shall we not pay?"
But He, knowing their hypocrisy, said to them, "Why do
you test Me? Bring Me a denarius that I may see *it*." 16 So
they brought *it*.
And He said to them, "Whose image and inscription *is*
this?" They said to Him, "Caesar's."
17 And Jesus answered and said to them, "Render to Caesar the things that are Caesar's, and to God the things that are God's."
And they marveled at Him.

Jesus Confounds the Sadducees

12:18–27

18 Then *some* Sadducees, who say there
is no resurrection, came to Him; and they
asked Him, saying: 19 "Teacher, Moses wrote to us that if a
man's brother dies, and leaves *his* wife behind, and leaves
no children, his brother should take his wife and raise up
offspring for his brother. 20 Now there were seven brothers.
The first took a wife; and dying, he left no offspring. 21 And
the second took her, and he died; nor did he leave any offspring. And the third likewise. 22 So the seven had her and
left no offspring. Last of all the woman died also. 23 Therefore, in the resurrection, when they rise, whose wife will
she be? For all seven had her as wife."
24 Jesus answered and said to them, "Are you not therefore
mistaken, because you do not know the Scriptures nor the

(Bible text continued on page 176)

12:11 [a]Psalm 118:22, 23

How Would You Respond?

A CLOSER LOOK 12:18–27

As the Sadducees saw Jesus gaining popularity and influence, they schemed to undo Him with trick questions (vv. 18–27). If you had been in His shoes, would you have known how to respond to their trickery? See "Retaliation Foiled," Luke 20:20–26.

CONSIDER THIS
12:28–34

Life—The Big Picture

*When Jesus recited the greatest of the commandments (vv. 29–30), He repeated the word "all" four times. What aspects of life was He including? Later, Paul emphasized that "*all *things were created" through and for Christ (Col. 1:15–18, italics added). How much of "all" is* all?

Here's how a typical American who lives to be 75 years old will have spent life:

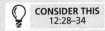

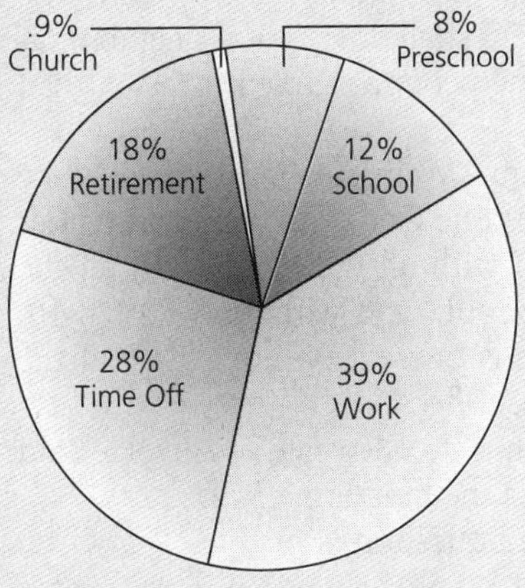

In light of this use of time, when does a person "love the Lord God" as Jesus commanded? Is that limited to what one does for an hour or so on Sunday morning? If so, then worship takes up a mere 3,900 hours, or 0.9 percent, of one's waking life—assuming that one goes to church *every* Sunday for 75 years!

Is that what Jesus or Paul had in mind? No, Christ is Lord of *all* of life—not just Sunday mornings, but weekdays, too, including time at work. Furthermore, He is Lord not only of our time, but of our money and possessions as well. Unfortunately, many Christians in the West have developed some dangerous attitudes in these areas that push God to the fringes of life. For example:

Myth: One-seventh of our time belongs to God. Some Christians speak of Sunday as "the Lord's day," a day for religion. And so it might be if Christians worshiped from sunup to sundown. But for most people Sunday worship means an hour-long service before an afternoon of televised sporting events. Thus the "day of worship" is effectively reduced to less than one-twentieth of the week.

That was never what God intended. Originally, the seventh day or Sabbath rest was viewed as the completion of the week, not a break or separation from the work week. It was a time for review, celebration, and restoration.

Yet already by Jesus' day there were major distortions regarding the Sabbath. It had become a day of legalistic ritual. Jesus sought to restore it as a day of compassion and worship (Luke 6:1–11; John 5:1–18).

Dedicating *all* of our time to God does not mean apportioning so much to family, so much to a job, so much for ourselves, and a little left over for God. No, all 168 hours of the week, all 52 weeks of the year, and all of the years of a lifetime belong to God and are on loan to us to manage for Him.

Myth: Ten percent of our money belongs to God. Some Christians believe that God expects them to give a flat 10 percent of their income to church and other ministries. The reality is that on the average, American believers give only 2.3 percent of their income to religious or charitable causes of any kind.

The underlying principle that needs to be considered is that God has given us the ability to earn money, so actually all 100 percent of our earnings belong to Him. We are called to manage our money—not just what we give away, but what we keep, too—according to His values. Tithing was intended as a discipline to remind God's people that all of what they have or earn belongs to Him. Originally a voluntary activity (Gen. 14:13–24; 28:20–22), it was intended for the care of others and as a representation of the worship of God (Deut. 26:1–19).

(continued on next page)

(continued from previous page)

Tithing was never intended to replace obedience to *all* of God's commands (Matt. 23:23–24).

Myth: Only some real estate belongs to God. Too many Christians have fallen into a dangerous pattern of identifying a few buildings as the Lord's property—religious institutions like churches, schools, and church-owned hospitals. By implication, other real estate is ours to do with as we please.

However, Scripture opposes that view. Paul says that "all things were created through Him and for Him" (Col. 1:16). Even our bodies are "temples of God" (1 Cor. 6:19). God calls us to serve Him in *all* that we do (Col. 3:17). Therein lies the path to true blessing, peace, and truth. Christ has come to break our bondage to anything less. Equipped by His Spirit within us and instructed by His written Word, we can live *wholly* for the kingdom. ◆

power of God? 25For when they rise from the dead, they
neither marry nor are given in marriage, but are like angels
in heaven. 26But concerning the dead, that they rise, have
you not read in the book of Moses, in the *burning* bush *pas-*
sage, how God spoke to him, saying, 'I *am* the God of Abraham, the God of Isaac, and the God of Jacob' ?[a] 27He is not
the God of the dead, but the God of the living. You are
therefore greatly mistaken."

The Greatest of the Commandments

12:28–34 see pg. 175

28Then one of the scribes came, and
having heard them reasoning together,
perceiving[a] that He had answered them well, asked Him,
"Which is the first commandment of all?"
29Jesus answered him, "The first of all the commandments
is: 'Hear, O Israel, the LORD our God, the LORD is one. 30And
you shall love the LORD your God with all your heart, with
all your soul, with all your mind, and with all your
strength.'[a] This *is* the first commandment.[b] 31And the
second, like *it, is* this: 'You shall love your neighbor as
yourself.'[a] There is no other commandment greater than
these."
32So the scribe said to Him, "Well *said,* Teacher. You have
spoken the truth, for there is one God, and there is no other
but He. 33And to love Him with all the heart, with all the
understanding, with all the soul,[a] and with all the strength,
and to love one's neighbor as oneself, is more than all the
whole burnt offerings and sacrifices."
34Now when Jesus saw that he answered wisely, He said
to him, "You are not far from the kingdom of God."
But after that no one dared question Him.

Jesus Turns the Tables on the Pharisees

35Then Jesus answered and said, while He taught in the
temple, "How *is it* that the scribes say that the Christ is the
Son of David? 36For David himself said by the Holy Spirit:

'The LORD said to my Lord,
"Sit at My right hand,
Till I make Your enemies Your footstool." '[a]

37Therefore David himself calls Him 'Lord'; how is He *then*
his Son?"
And the common people heard Him gladly.
38Then He said to them in His teaching, "Beware of the
scribes, who desire to go around in long robes, *love* greet-

12:26 [a]Exodus 3:6, 15 *12:28* [a]NU-Text reads *seeing.* *12:30* [a]Deuteronomy 6:4, 5 [b]NU-Text omits this sentence. *12:31* [a]Leviticus 19:18 *12:33* [a]NU-Text omits *with all the soul.* *12:36* [a]Psalm 110:1

ings in the marketplaces, [39]the best seats in the synagogues,
and the best places at feasts, [40]who devour widows' houses,
and for a pretense make long prayers. These will receive
greater condemnation."

A Poor Widow's Contribution

12:41–44

[41]Now Jesus sat opposite the treasury
and saw how the people put money into
the treasury. And many *who were* rich put in much. [42]Then
one poor widow came and threw in two mites,[a] which
make a quadrans. [43]So He called His disciples to *Himself* and said to them, "Assuredly, I say to you that this poor widow has put in more
than all those who have given to the treasury; [44]for they all
put in out of their abundance, but she out of her poverty
put in all that she had, her whole livelihood."

12:43–44

CHAPTER 13

Jesus Predicts the Temple's Destruction

[1]Then as He went out of the temple, one of His disciples
said to Him, "Teacher, see what manner
of stones and what buildings *are here!*"

13:1–37 see pg. 178

[2]And Jesus answered and said to him, "Do you see these
great buildings? Not *one* stone shall be left upon another,
that shall not be thrown down."

Signs of the End

[3]Now as He sat on the Mount of Olives opposite the temple, Peter, James, John, and Andrew asked Him privately,
[4]"Tell us, when will these things be? And what *will be* the
sign when all these things will be fulfilled?"
[5]And Jesus, answering them, began to say: "Take heed
that no one deceives you. [6]For many will come in My name,
saying, 'I am *He*,' and will deceive many. [7]But when you
hear of wars and rumors of wars, do not be troubled; for
such things must happen, but the end *is* not yet. [8]For nation
will rise against nation, and kingdom against kingdom. And
there will be earthquakes in various places, and there will

12:42 [a]Greek *lepta,* very small copper coins worth a fraction of a penny

Down to Her Last Penny

A CLOSER LOOK 12:41–44

The poor widow in v. 42 was so destitute that she was literally in danger of death. For more on this incident, see "How Poor Was the Widow?" Luke 21:1–4.

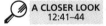

IT'S ALL RELATIVE

CONSIDER THIS 12:43–44

What did Jesus mean when He said that the widow had put more money into the treasury than anyone else (v. 43)? Clearly, He was indicating that economic value is relative. The widow's contribution would have been nothing but spare change to the rich who preceded her. But to her, two mites represented enormous value. It was "*all* that she had, her *whole* livelihood" (v. 44, italics added). Replacing it would be difficult, if not impossible; as a poor widow, she was probably unemployable. Giving it to God meant that she could not use it to buy her next crust of bread.

But Jesus indicated that God placed moral rather than economic value on her tiny offering. Her gift showed that she was giving herself entirely to God and trusting in Him to meet her needs. Her use of money disclosed the moral and spiritual condition of her heart.

be famines and troubles.[a] These *are* the beginnings of sorrows.

9"But watch out for yourselves, for they will deliver you up to councils, and you will be beaten in the synagogues. You will be brought[a] before rulers and kings for My sake, for a testimony to them.
10And the gospel must first be preached to all the nations.
11But when they arrest *you* and deliver you up, do not worry beforehand, or premeditate[a] what you will speak. But whatever is given you in that hour, speak that; for it is not you who speak, but the Holy Spirit.
12Now brother will betray brother to death, and a father *his* child; and children will rise up against parents and cause them to be put to death.
13And you will be hated by all for My name's sake. But he who endures to the end shall be saved.

14"So when you see the 'abomination of desolation,'[a] spoken of by Daniel the prophet,[b] standing where it ought not" (let the reader understand), "then let those who are in Judea flee to the mountains.
15Let him who is on the housetop not go down into the house, nor enter to take anything out of

13:8 [a]NU-Text omits *and troubles.* *13:9* [a]NU-Text and M-Text read *will stand.* *13:11* [a]NU-Text omits *or premeditate.* *13:14* [a]Daniel 11:31; 12:11 [b]NU-Text omits *spoken of by Daniel the prophet.*

CONSIDER THIS
13:1–37

ISSUES FOR DOOMSDAY

As you look at events in the world today, you may feel anxious about how history is going to turn out. Perhaps you're confused and troubled about end times. The buildup of weapons, the warnings of religious prophets of doom, shaky economies, and the turmoil of nations may feel very unsettling.

Jesus' words in Mark 13 (and Matt. 24:1–51 and Luke 21:5–36) speak to these issues. They left an indelible impression on His followers. What touched off the discussion was the disciples' comments on the solidity and significance of a downtown building (Mark 13:1). Jesus replied by noting how temporary such structures actually are (v. 2). Later, in a quiet setting (v. 3), He went into far more detail about the end of history as we know it and the stresses believers would undergo (vv. 4–37). Rather than avoid the topic, He spoke of:

- *deception, wars, earthquakes, and famines as the beginning of sorrows (vv. 5–8).*
- *how His followers would experience testing as His witnesses before councils, governors, and kings (vv. 9–11).*
- *how family members would turn against each other (vv. 12–13).*

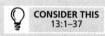

his house. 16And let him who is in the field not go back to get his clothes. 17But woe to those who are pregnant and to those who are nursing babies in those days! 18And pray that your flight may not be in winter. 19For *in* those days there will be tribulation, such as has not been since the beginning of the creation which God created until this time, nor ever shall be. 20And unless the Lord had shortened those days, no flesh would be saved; but for the elect's sake, whom He chose, He shortened the days.

21"Then if anyone says to you, 'Look, here *is* the Christ!' or, 'Look, *He is* there!' do not believe it. 22For false christs and false prophets will rise and show signs and wonders to deceive, if possible, even the elect. 23But take heed; see, I have told you all things beforehand.

24"But in those days, after that tribulation, the sun will be darkened, and the moon will not give its light; 25the stars of heaven will fall, and the powers in the heavens will be shaken. 26Then they will see the Son of Man coming in the clouds with great power and glory. 27And then He will send His angels, and gather together His elect from the four winds, from the farthest part of earth to the farthest part of heaven.

(Bible text continued on page 181)

- *how distress and deception would eventually reign, but such times would be limited by God (vv. 14–25).*
- *His eventual return for His own (vv. 15–31).*
- *the fact that no one knows precisely when He will return—and thus the need for His followers to be watchful and dutiful in serving God (vv. 32–37).*

Jesus contrasted the strength and beauty of a downtown building with the faithful loyalty and service of His followers (vv. 2, 9, 13, 33–37). Human structures will inevitably crumble and fall, but the righteous works of God will last forever. Therefore, believers ought to stand firm, serving God faithfully—not just building monuments to their own accomplishments, and certainly not falling prey to the seductive dangers of the times. ◆

Paul emphasized exactly the same things as Jesus when he wrote his second letter to the Thessalonians and addressed the issue of troubled times (2 Thess. 2:1–17).

"FOR IN THOSE DAYS THERE WILL BE TRIBULATION. . . ."
—Mark 13:19

CONSIDER THIS
13:33

A KINGDOM PERSPECTIVE ON SIGNIFICANCE

Jesus wants His followers to evaluate turbulent times of change (v. 33) not just from the perspective of history but even more from the perspective of His kingdom. As believers, we are citizens of eternity. Therefore, our confidence needs to be rooted in something far more important than our positions and achievements here and now. It's not that the here and now has no importance. But as we live our lives, God wants us to be loyal workers for His kingdom, serving the people He sends our way.

Is your significance tied too closely to achievements—building buildings, reaching business goals, acquiring material possessions, climbing career ladders? There's nothing inherently wrong with these. But if you lost them, would your confidence completely crumble? If your sense of worth depends on them, what happens when you reach the top of the ladder, only to discover that the ladder is leaning against the wrong wall?

The problem is that our world has a system of values that is upside down from the way God determines value. It lacks any sense of what Scripture describes as "calling," or what Christians later termed "vocation"—a perspective that God has called and equipped people to serve Him through their work in the world. Instead, our cul- [illegible] encourages us to climb a [illegible] ladder that is ultimately self-serving, and often self-destructive.

Climbing that ladder can be very misleading. The higher one goes, the more one's identity, value, and security tend to depend on the nature of one's work. But what happens if we lose our position, titles, or high-level compensation? Perhaps this explains why severe emotional problems—drug and alcohol abuse, abuse of spouse and children, divorce, even suicide—often accompany job loss. If our significance relies on our job, then it dies with our job.

God calls us to a far more stable basis for significance. He wants us to establish our identity in the fact that we are His children, created by Him to carry out good works as responsible people in His kingdom (Eph. 2:10). This is our calling or vocation from God. According to Scripture, our calling:

- is irrevocable (Rom. 11:29).
- is from God; He wants to let us share in Christ's glory (2 Thess. 2:14).
- is a function of how God has designed us (Eph. 2:10).
- is an assurance that God will give us everything we need to serve Him, including the strength to remain faithful to Him (1 Cor. 1:7–9).
- is what we should be proclaiming as our true identity (1 Pet. 2:5, 9).
- carries us through suffering (1 Pet. 2:19–21).
- is rooted in peace, no matter what the circumstances in which we find ourselves (1 Cor. 7:15–24).
- is focused on eternal achievements, not merely temporal ones (Phil. 3:13—4:1).

Above all else, believers are called to character development, service to others, and loyalty to God. These can be accomplished wherever we live or work, whatever our occupational status or position in society. If we pursue these, we can enjoy great satisfaction and significance. No matter what happens on the job, we can join Paul in saying, "We know that all things work together for good to those who love God, to those who are called according to His purpose" (Rom. 8:28). ◆

28“Now learn this parable from the fig tree: When its
branch has already become tender, and puts forth leaves,
you know that summer is near. 29So you also, when you see
these things happening, know that it[a] is near—at the
doors! 30Assuredly, I say to you, this generation will by no
means pass away till all these things take place. 31Heaven
and earth will pass away, but My words will by no means
pass away.
32“But of that day and hour no one knows, not even the

13:33

angels in heaven, nor the Son, but only
the Father. 33Take heed, watch and pray;
for you do not know when the time is. 34*It is* like a man going to a far country, who left his house and gave authority
to his servants, and to each his work, and commanded the
doorkeeper to watch. 35Watch therefore, for you do not
know when the master of the house is coming—in the
evening, at midnight, at the crowing of the rooster, or in the
morning— 36lest, coming suddenly, he find you sleeping.
37And what I say to you, I say to all: Watch!”

CHAPTER 14

Leaders Plot to Do Away with Jesus

1After two days it was the Passover and *the Feast* of Unleavened Bread. And the chief priests and the scribes
sought how they might take Him by trickery and put *Him*
to death. 2But they said, “Not during the feast, lest there be
an uproar of the people.”

A Woman Anoints Jesus with Costly Oil

14:3–9

3And being in Bethany at the house of
Simon the leper, as He sat at the table, a
woman came having an alabaster flask of very costly oil of
spikenard. Then she broke the flask and poured *it* on His
head. 4But there were some who were indignant among
themselves, and said, “Why was this fragrant oil wasted?
5For it might have been sold for more than three hundred
denarii and given to the poor.” And they criticized her
sharply.
6But Jesus said, “Let her alone. Why do you trouble her?

13:29 [a]Or *He*

Important Preparations

A CLOSER LOOK 14:3–9 *It's difficult for us today to appreciate the significance that burial rituals had for ancient peoples (v. 8). Nearly every ancient religion gave explicit and sometimes elaborate instructions for preparing and burying the dead. See “Funeral Preparations,” John 12:1–8.*

A Parting Gift

CONSIDER THIS 14:3–9 **What the disciples saw as waste (vv. 4–9) the Lord saw as worship. The woman's gift of costly oil was worth about one year's average wages, yet she poured it out, apparently sensing that her days with Jesus were drawing to a close.**

This incident raises the issue of how one's material wealth enters into worship. While Jesus was still physically present and available to her, the woman did “what she could” (v. 8). She took one of her most valuable possessions and gave it to Jesus in an unusual act of devotion. A waste? Not to the One she honored by it.

Today Jesus is not physically among us. Yet while we are alive, we control a certain measure of the world's resources. So we might ask: What act of worship might we give while we have opportunity? How might we honor the Lord materially?

There are no easy answers. But did Jesus give us a clue when He told His disciples that just as the woman had done Him “a good work,” so they could do good to the poor at any time (v. 6)?

The woman's act was the first step in preparing Jesus' body for the grave. See “A Burial Fit for a King,” Mark 15:42—16:1.

14:7

14:3–9
see pg. 181

She has done a good work for Me. 7For
you have the poor with you always, and
whenever you wish you may do them good; but Me you do
not have always. 8She has done what she
could. She has come beforehand to
anoint My body for burial. 9Assuredly, I say to you, wherever this gospel is preached in the whole world, what this
woman has done will also be told as a memorial to her."

Judas Betrays Jesus

10Then Judas Iscariot, one of the twelve, went to the chief
priests to betray Him to them. 11And when they heard *it,*
they were glad, and promised to give him money. So he
sought how he might conveniently betray Him.

The Upper Room

12Now on the first day of Unleavened Bread, when they
killed the Passover *lamb,* His disciples said to Him, "Where
do You want us to go and prepare, that You may eat the
Passover?"
13And He sent out two of His disciples and said to them,
"Go into the city, and a man will meet you carrying a
pitcher of water; follow him. 14Wherever he goes in, say to
the master of the house, 'The Teacher says, "Where is the
guest room in which I may eat the Passover with My disciples?" ' 15Then he will show you a large upper room, furnished *and* prepared; there make ready for us."
16So His disciples went out, and came into the city, and
found it just as He had said to them; and they prepared the
Passover.
17In the evening He came with the twelve. 18Now as they
sat and ate, Jesus said, "Assuredly, I say to you, one of you
who eats with Me will betray Me."
19And they began to be sorrowful, and to say to Him one
by one, "*Is* it I?" And another *said,* "*Is* it I?"[a]
20He answered and said to them, "*It is* one of the twelve,
who dips with Me in the dish. 21The Son of Man indeed
goes just as it is written of Him, but woe to that man by
whom the Son of Man is betrayed! It would have been good
for that man if he had never been born."
22And as they were eating, Jesus took bread, blessed and
broke *it,* and gave *it* to them and said, "Take, eat;[a] this is My
body."
23Then He took the cup, and when He had given thanks
He gave *it* to them, and they all drank from it. 24And He
said to them, "This is My blood of the new[a] covenant,

14:19 [a]NU-Text omits this sentence. *14:22* [a]NU-Text omits *eat.* *14:24* [a]NU-Text omits *new.*

Always the Poor

CONSIDER THIS 14:7 *Unfortunately, some people use Jesus' statement in v. 7 as an escape hatch to avoid caring for the poor. "Jesus Himself said there will always be poor people," the logic goes, "so what good does it do to offer aid? The problem won't go away." But Jesus had nothing of the sort in mind. On the contrary, He was mandating that we should always care for those who have need.*

which is shed for many. 25Assuredly, I say to you, I will no
longer drink of the fruit of the vine until that day when I
drink it new in the kingdom of God."
26And when they had sung a hymn, they went out to the
Mount of Olives.
27Then Jesus said to them, "All of you will be made to
stumble because of Me this night,[a] for it is written:

'I will strike the Shepherd,
And the sheep will be scattered.'[b]

28"But after I have been raised, I will go before you to
Galilee."
29Peter said to Him, "Even if all are made to stumble, yet I
will not *be*."
30Jesus said to him, "Assuredly, I say to you that today,
even this night, before the rooster crows twice, you will
deny Me three times."
31But he spoke more vehemently, "If I have to die with
You, I will not deny You!"
And they all said likewise.

Jesus Prays in the Garden of Gethsemane

14:32 32Then they came to a place which was
named Gethsemane; and He said to His
disciples, "Sit here while I pray." 33And He took Peter,
James, and John with Him, and He began to be troubled
and deeply distressed. 34Then He said to them, "My soul is
exceedingly sorrowful, *even* to death. Stay here and watch."
35He went a little farther, and fell on the ground, and
prayed that if it were possible, the hour might pass from
Him. 36And He said, "Abba, Father, all things *are* possible
for You. Take this cup away from Me; nevertheless, not
what I will, but what You *will*."
37Then He came and found them sleeping, and said to Peter, "Simon, are you sleeping? Could you not watch one
14:38 hour? 38Watch and pray, lest you enter
into temptation. The spirit indeed *is* willing, but the flesh *is* weak."

14:27 [a]NU-Text omits *because of Me this night.* [b]Zechariah 13:7

"THE SPIRIT INDEED IS WILLING, BUT THE FLESH IS WEAK." —Mark 14:38

Gethsemane

A CLOSER LOOK 14:32 *Jesus chose a familiar place of work in which to pray (v. 32). See, "Praying in a Workplace," Matt. 26:36.*

Watch and Pray!

A CLOSER LOOK 14:38 *Jesus told His disciples to pray to avoid succumbing to temptation (v. 38). He knew that only God could help them avoid, flee, confess, and resist it. See "Pay Attention to Temptation!" at 1 Cor. 10:12–13.*

39Again He went away and prayed, and spoke the same words. 40And when He returned, He found them asleep again, for their eyes were heavy; and they did not know what to answer Him.
41Then He came the third time and said to them, "Are you still sleeping and resting? It is enough! The hour has come; behold, the Son of Man is being betrayed into the hands of sinners. 42Rise, let us be going. See, My betrayer is at hand."

Judas Brings About Jesus' Arrest

43And immediately, while He was still speaking, Judas, one of the twelve, with a great multitude with swords and clubs, came from the chief priests and the scribes and the elders. 44Now His betrayer had given them a signal, saying, "Whomever I kiss, He is the One; seize Him and lead *Him* away safely."
45As soon as he had come, immediately he went up to Him and said to Him, "Rabbi, Rabbi!" and kissed Him.
46Then they laid their hands on Him and took Him. 47And one of those who stood by drew his sword and struck the servant of the high priest, and cut off his ear.
48Then Jesus answered and said to them, "Have you come out, as against a robber, with swords and clubs to take Me?

CONSIDER THIS
14:53–64

IS THERE ENOUGH EVIDENCE TO CONVICT YOU?

Are you a "closet" Christian, an undercover follower of Christ, keeping your faith a secret? Would your friends or coworkers describe you as a loyal believer? Is there any evidence that could be used to convict you of practicing the faith?

The religious and political leaders of Israel wanted to rid themselves of Jesus. They tried every means possible to convict Him of a crime. They paid an informant from among Jesus' own followers—but he returned their money and declared the Lord to be innocent (vv. 43–46; Matt. 27:3–5). They orchestrated an armed mob to intimidate Him—but He kept His cool and restrained His followers (Matt. 26:51–54). The leaders even presented witnesses to testify against Him in court—but the witnesses either perjured themselves or contradicted each other (Mark 14:55–56).

People tried to convict Jesus of a crime—something bad—for which they lacked even a shred of evidence. Suppose you were on trial instead of Jesus. What would be some of the best evidence against you, that you were "guilty" of following Christ—something good, and something for which there should be evidence? Would

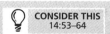

49I was daily with you in the temple teaching, and you did
not seize Me. But the Scriptures must be fulfilled."
50Then they all forsook Him and fled.
51Now a certain young man followed Him, having a linen
cloth thrown around *his* naked *body.* And the young men
laid hold of him, 52and he left the linen cloth and fled from
them naked.

Jesus Taken to the High Priest

14:53–64

53And they led Jesus away to the high
priest; and with him were assembled all
the chief priests, the elders, and the scribes. 54But Peter followed Him at a distance, right into the courtyard of the
high priest. And he sat with the servants and warmed himself at the fire.
55Now the chief priests and all the council sought testimony against Jesus to put Him to death, but found none.
56For many bore false witness against Him, but their testi-
monies did not agree.
57Then some rose up and bore false witness against Him,
saying, 58"We heard Him say, 'I will destroy this temple
made with hands, and within three days I will build an-

there be anything conclusive? Here is a checklist to consider:

EVIDENCE OF FOLLOWING JESUS

- ____ Displays the "beautiful attitudes" described by Jesus in His Sermon on the Mount (Matt. 5:3–16).
- ____ Thinks with a transformed mind, expresses a spirit of genuine love, and shows respect for authority (Rom. 12:1–2; 13:1–7).
- ____ Reflects the "lifestyle of love" (1 Cor. 13).
- ____ Displays the fruits of the Spirit described by Paul (Gal. 5:22–26).
- ____ Looks out for the interests of others in the humility of Christ (Phil. 2:1–4).
- ____ Rejoices always, prays without ceasing, and in everything gives thanks (1 Thess. 5:16–18).
- ____ Carries out works of faith and compassion (James 2:14–17), controls the tongue (3:1–11), and is known for wisdom (3:13).
- ____ Holds to the truth about Jesus (2 John 4, 3 John 3–4) and defends it (Jude 3).

Is there enough evidence to convict you of faith in Christ? ◆

"THEN THEY ALL FORSOOK HIM AND FLED."
—Mark 14:50

other made without hands.' " [59]But not even then did their
testimony agree.
[60]And the high priest stood up in the midst and asked Jesus, saying, "Do You answer nothing? What *is it* these men
testify against You?" [61]But He kept silent and answered
nothing.
Again the high priest asked Him, saying to Him, "Are You
the Christ, the Son of the Blessed?"
[62]Jesus said, "I am. And you will see the Son of Man sitting at the right hand of the Power, and coming with the
clouds of heaven."
[63]Then the high priest tore his clothes and said, "What
further need do we have of witnesses? [64]You have heard the
blasphemy! What do you think?"
And they all condemned Him to be deserving of death.
[65]Then some began to spit on Him, and to blindfold Him,
and to beat Him, and to say to Him, "Prophesy!" And the
officers struck Him with the palms of their hands.[a]

Peter Denies His Lord

[66]Now as Peter was below in the courtyard, one of the
servant girls of the high priest came. [67]And when she saw
Peter warming himself, she looked at him and said, "You
also were with Jesus of Nazareth."
[68]But he denied it, saying, "I neither know nor understand what you are saying." And he went out on the porch,
and a rooster crowed.
[69]And the servant girl saw him again, and began to say to

14:65 [a]NU-Text reads *received Him with slaps.*

"AND THEY ALL CONDEMNED HIM TO BE DESERVING OF DEATH." —Mark 14:64

PERSONALITY PROFILE: BARABBAS

FOR YOUR INFO 15:7

Name meant: "Son of Abbas."

Home: Unknown, but because he was a revolutionary, he might have been from Galilee, known as a seedbed for resistors against Rome (see "Galilee," Mark 1:14).

Occupation: Unknown, but he may have worked as a member of the Zealots, ardent nationalists who wanted to throw off Roman occupation of Palestine.

Best known today for: Being released instead of Jesus by Pilate (v. 15).

those who stood by, "This is one of them." 70But he denied
it again.
And a little later those who stood by said to Peter again,
"Surely you are *one* of them; for you are a Galilean, and
your speech shows *it*."[a]
71Then he began to curse and swear, "I do not know this
Man of whom you speak!"
72A second time *the* rooster crowed. Then Peter called to
mind the word that Jesus had said to him, "Before the
rooster crows twice, you will deny Me three times." And
when he thought about it, he wept.

14:70 [a]NU-Text omits *and your speech shows it.*

"Not This Man but Barabbas!"

But for a remarkable set of circumstances, Barabbas probably would have remained unknown to history. He was just another one of the sicarii ("dagger-men") who assassinated Roman officials in the vain hope of driving them out of Palestine. Occasionally, when political conditions were right, such men managed to gain a small following and create serious trouble. For example, in 6 B.C. Judas the Galilean led a tax revolt. But the Romans quickly executed him and scattered his followers.

In a similar way, the authorities had arrested Barabbas and others on charges of insurrection and murder (Mark 15:7; Luke 23:19). The prisoners knew well what fate awaited them—crucifixion, a grisly form of execution that the Romans reserved for political criminals. The public spectacle of nailing rebels to an upraised cross was a potent deterrent to political opposition.

But Barabbas was not to die in that manner. The arrest of Jesus, the political maneuverings of Caiaphas the high priest (see "Caiaphas, the Religious Power Broker," Matt. 26:3) and of Herod and Pilate (23:6–12), and the custom of releasing a prisoner during the feast of the Passover (Mark 15:6) combined to open a way for Barabbas to go free.

What finally secured his liberty were the cries of the mob to have him released (John 18:40). Pilate found it hard to believe that they actually preferred Barabbas, and when they kept demanding that Jesus be crucified, Pilate asked, "Shall I crucify your king?" (19:15). At that point the chief priests claimed, "We have no king but Caesar!" and the governor released Barabbas. What a peculiar irony that a revolutionary against Rome should be released by the cry, "We have no king but Caesar!" ◆

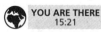

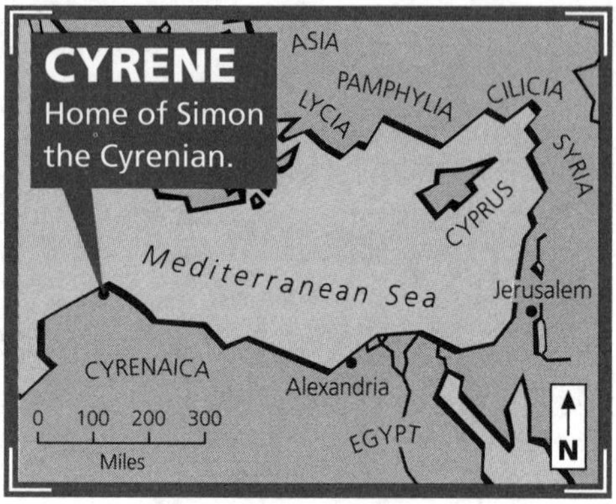

CYRENE

YOU ARE THERE 15:21

- **A city on the north coast of Africa, midway between Carthage and Alexandria.**
- **Under the Romans, capital of the province of Cyrenaica (ancient and modern Libya).**
- **Built on beautiful tableland 2,000 feet above sea level but only 16 miles from the sea.**
- **A major crossroads for trade, commerce, and tourism.**
- **Renowned as an intellectual center.**
- **In New Testament times, home to a large Jewish population.**
- **Site of a Jewish revolt in A.D. 115–116 in which 200,000 people were killed.**
- **Stricken by a disastrous earthquake in A.D. 365.**
- **Invaded by the Arabs in A.D. 642.**
- **Uninhabited today.**

CHAPTER 15

Jesus Brought Before Pilate

1Immediately, in the morning, the chief priests held a consultation with the elders and scribes and the whole council; and they bound Jesus, led *Him* away, and delivered *Him* to Pilate. 2Then Pilate asked Him, "Are You the King of the Jews?"

He answered and said to him, "*It is as* you say."

3And the chief priests accused Him of many things, but He answered nothing. 4Then Pilate asked Him again, saying, "Do You answer nothing? See how many things they testify against You!"[a] 5But Jesus still answered nothing, so that Pilate marveled.

6Now at the feast he was accustomed to releasing one prisoner to them, whomever they requested. 7And there was one named Barabbas, *who was* chained with his fellow rebels; they had committed murder in the rebellion. 8Then the multitude, crying aloud,[a] began to ask *him to do* just as he had always done for them. 9But Pilate answered them, saying, "Do you want me to release to you the King of the Jews?" 10For he knew that the chief priests had handed Him over because of envy.

15:7 see pg. 186

11But the chief priests stirred up the crowd, so that he should rather release Barabbas to them. 12Pilate answered and said to them again, "What then do you want me to do *with Him* whom you call the King of the Jews?"

13So they cried out again, "Crucify Him!"

14Then Pilate said to them, "Why, what evil has He done?"

But they cried out all the more, "Crucify Him!"

15So Pilate, wanting to gratify the crowd, released Barabbas to them; and he delivered Jesus, after he had scourged *Him,* to be crucified.

Soldiers Mock Jesus

16Then the soldiers led Him away into the hall called Praetorium, and they called together the whole garrison. 17And they clothed Him with purple; and they twisted a crown of thorns, put it on

15:17–20

15:4 [a]NU-Text reads *of which they accuse You.* 15:8 [a]NU-Text reads *going up.*

Mocked by Wealth

A CLOSER LOOK 15:17–20

The outrageous incident in vv. 17–20 is a reminder that the symbols of wealth can be used to send many kinds of messages—including mockery and disrespect, as happened here. See "Discrimination on the Basis of Wealth," John 19:1–6.

His *head,* 18and began to salute Him, "Hail, King of the
Jews!" 19Then they struck Him on the head with a reed and
spat on Him; and bowing the knee, they worshiped Him.
20And when they had mocked Him, they took the purple off
Him, put His own clothes on Him, and led Him out to crucify Him.

The Crucifixion

15:21

21Then they compelled a certain man,
Simon a Cyrenian, the father of Alexan-
der and Rufus, as he was coming out of the country and
passing by, to bear His cross. 22And they brought Him to
the place Golgotha, which is translated, Place of a Skull.
23Then they gave Him wine mingled with myrrh to drink,
but He did not take *it.* 24And when they
crucified Him, they divided His gar-
ments, casting lots for them to determine what every man
should take.

15:24

25Now it was the third hour, and they crucified Him.
26And the inscription of His accusation was written above:

THE KING OF THE JEWS.

27With Him they also crucified two robbers, one on His
right and the other on His left. 28So the Scripture was fulfilled[a] which says, "And He was numbered with the transgressors."[b]
29And those who passed by blasphemed Him, wagging
their heads and saying, "Aha! *You* who destroy the temple
and build *it* in three days, 30save Yourself, and come down
from the cross!"
31Likewise the chief priests also, mocking among themselves with the scribes, said, "He saved others; Himself He
cannot save. 32Let the Christ, the King of Israel, descend
now from the cross, that we may see and believe."[a]
Even those who were crucified with Him reviled Him.
33Now when the sixth hour had come, there was darkness
over the whole land until the ninth hour. 34And at the ninth
hour Jesus cried out with a loud voice, saying, "Eloi, Eloi,

15:28 [a]Isaiah 53:12 [b]NU-Text omits this verse.

SIMON OF CYRENE

As Jesus staggered under the weight of His cross, Roman soldiers pressed into service a man known as Simon the Cyrenean to help Him (Mark 15:21). Little is known of this man who came to the Lord's aid, but he had probably made the pilgrimage from his home in Africa to Jerusalem for the Passover. Perhaps after the dramatic events in which he played a small part he stayed, like many Hellenistic Jews, until Pentecost. We know that men from Cyrene were among the crowd that witnessed the birth of the church (Acts 2:10).

We suspect that Simon became a believer, because Mark recorded his sons' names, Alexander and Rufus. (Alexander was probably a popular name among the Cyreneans; Alexander the Great had captured the city in 331 B.C.) Paul mentioned Rufus, along with his mother, in his greetings to the Romans (Rom. 16:13). Thus the family was well known to the early church.

Jesus Died Poor

A CLOSER LOOK 15:24

Jesus not only was born poor and lived poor, He died poor. The soldiers tore the clothes off his back and divided them among themselves (v. 24), leaving Him with not a single material possession to pass on to His family or friends. "Jesus—A Homeless Man?" (Matt. 8:20) addresses His lack of earthly wealth and what that means for us today.

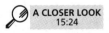

lama sabachthani?" which is translated, "My God, My God,
why have You forsaken Me?"[a]
35Some of those who stood by, when they heard *that,* said,
"Look, He is calling for Elijah!" 36Then someone ran and
filled a sponge full of sour wine, put *it* on a reed, and offered *it* to Him to drink, saying, "Let Him alone; let us see if
Elijah will come to take Him down."
37And Jesus cried out with a loud voice, and breathed His
last.
38Then the veil of the temple was torn in two from top to
15:39
bottom. 39So when the centurion, who
stood opposite Him, saw that He cried
out like this and breathed His last,[a] he said, "Truly this Man
was the Son of God!"
15:40 see pg. 192
40There were also women looking on
from afar, among whom were Mary Mag-
dalene, Mary the mother of James the Less and of Joses, and

15:34 [a]Psalm 22:1 *15:39* [a]NU-Text reads *that He thus breathed His last.*

FOR YOUR INFO
15:39

CENTURIONS

Roman centurions (v. 39) were non-commissioned officers who commanded battle groups called "centuries," each comprising at least 100 men. Akin to sergeants in a modern army, centurions often led Rome's local police forces in occupied territories.

Centurions were responsible for keeping track of individuals who posed a threat to Rome's security. Because Jesus drew thousands of people to hear Him, He was perhaps kept under surveillance. That may account for the accurate knowledge that one officer seemed to have of Him (Luke 7:1–10).

The Roman Army

1 Contubernum	*= 8 soldiers*		
1 Century	*= 10 Contubernums*	*= 80 to 100 men*	
1 Cohort	*= 6 Centuries*	*= 500 to 600 men*	
1 Legion	*= 10 Cohorts*	*= 6,000 men*	

At the time of Jesus, Rome had an estimated 500,000 troops in its army.

Legions were placed in two major Roman cities of Palestine, Sebaste in Samaria and Caesarea on the Mediterranean. A military force was also kept in Jerusalem at the Antonia fortress, guarding Herod's temple palace.

Salome, [41]who also followed Him and ministered to Him
when He was in Galilee, and many other women who came
up with Him to Jerusalem.

Jesus Is Buried

15:42—16:1 [42]Now when evening had come, because it was the Preparation Day, that is,
the day before the Sabbath, [43]Joseph of Arimathea, a prominent council member, who was himself waiting for the
kingdom of God, coming and taking courage, went in to Pilate and asked for the body of Jesus. [44]Pilate marveled that
He was already dead; and summoning the centurion, he
asked him if He had been dead for some time. [45]So when he
found out from the centurion, he granted the body to
Joseph. [46]Then he bought fine linen, took Him down, and
wrapped Him in the linen. And he laid Him in a tomb
which had been hewn out of the rock, and rolled a stone
against the door of the tomb. [47]And Mary Magdalene and
Mary *the mother* of Joses observed where He was laid.

During Jewish feasts, Rome moved additional troops into the city to ensure order.

It was to a Gentile Roman centurion and his troops that fell the gruesome task of crucifying Jesus and the two men with Him. The officer had likely observed Jesus' trial, final march to the execution, crucifixion, and response to the crowd that mocked Him. He had seen the sky turn black at midday, felt the earth quake, and heard Jesus' last, exhausted death cry. A Gentile who probably had little regard for Hebrew religion, he was left with no doubt that the man he had seen die was not only "a righteous man" (Luke 23:47), but was in fact the very Son of God (Mark 15:39; Matt. 27:54). ◆

Another centurion who responded to the message about Christ was Cornelius. Read about him at Acts 10:1.

A Burial Fit for a King

CONSIDER THIS 15:42—16:1 **How much should you spend on a funeral? A fortune, or only enough to pay for the barest essentials?**

The four Gospel writers recorded that Jesus' body was treated as a rich man's corpse might be—which is not surprising since rich people buried Him:

- ***Joseph of Arimathea* bought fine linen to wrap the body in before laying it in his own very expensive tomb (v. 43–46; Matt. 27:60).**
- ***Nicodemus* helped with the arrangements and brought 100 pounds of myrrh and aloes, costly substances used to perfume and wrap the body (John 19:39).**
- ***Women who had supported Jesus* in His ministry, including Mary Magdalene, Mary the mother of James, and Salome, prepared spices and fragrant oils to place on the body as soon as the Sabbath was over (Mark 16:1; Luke 23:56).**

Those who took charge of Jesus' burial did so out of love, not guilt. And under the circumstances, they obviously were not trying to make a prideful show of their wealth. Rather they honestly expressed their grief, devotion, respect, adoration, and desire to protect the Lord's body from His enemies. They did what they could according to their desires and financial resources, and in keeping with the laws, customs, and traditions of their day.

The first step in preparing Jesus' body for the grave was actually a woman's curious act of devotion. See "A Parting Gift," Mark 14:3–9.

It is difficult for us today to appreciate the significance that burial rituals had for ancient peoples. See "Funeral Preparations," John 12:1–8.

CHAPTER 16

An Angel Announces the Resurrection

16:1–8 see pg. 194

1Now when the Sabbath was past,
Mary Magdalene, Mary *the mother* of
James, and Salome bought spices, that they might come and
anoint Him. 2Very early in the morning, on the first *day* of
the week, they came to the tomb when the sun had risen.
3And they said among themselves, "Who will roll away the
stone from the door of the tomb for us?" 4But when they
looked up, they saw that the stone had been rolled away—
for it was very large. 5And entering the tomb, they saw a
young man clothed in a long white robe sitting on the right
side; and they were alarmed.
6But he said to them, "Do not be alarmed. You seek Jesus
of Nazareth, who was crucified. He is risen! He is not here.
See the place where they laid Him. 7But go, tell His disciples—and Peter—that He is going before you into Galilee;
there you will see Him, as He said to you."
8So they went out quickly[a] and fled from the tomb, for

16:8 [a]NU-Text and M-Text omit *quickly.*

QUOTE UNQUOTE

CONSIDER THIS 16:15 *Some Christians today feel that the church is not fulfilling the bold mandate prescribed by Christ in v. 15:*

The modern religious crisis . . . is its fearful retreat into the comfortable womb of community, where there is no outward mission, and where the retreating community inevitably begins to die—as if a fetus from within chooses its own abortion.

National Catholic Reporter, October 27, 1989, p. 1

FOR YOUR INFO 15:40

WHY SO MANY MARYS?

In reading the New Testament, one discovers that Mary was a popular name in first-century Palestine. For example, we find:

- *Mary of Nazareth, the mother of Jesus (Luke 1:26—2:52).*
- *Mary of Bethany, the sister of Martha and Lazarus (Luke 10:38–42; John 11). She anointed Jesus with perfume before His death (John 12:3).*
- *Mary of Magdala, a financial supporter of Jesus (Luke 8:2–3). The Lord had cast seven demons out of her. She watched Jesus' crucifixion and was the first witness of His resurrection (Mark 15:40; 16:9).*
- *Mary the mother of James and Joses. She was present at Jesus' crucifixion and was probably the same woman described as the "other" Mary (Matt. 27:61; 28:1) and Mary the wife of Clopas (John 19:25).*
- *Mary the mother of Mark, making her a relative of Barnabas (Acts 12:12; Col. 4:10).*
- *Mary of Rome, known simply as a woman who worked hard for Paul and his companions (Rom. 16:6).*

Why were so many Jewish women named Mary? The name is the Greek form of the Hebrew Miriam, *which was the name of one of Israel's most famous women:*

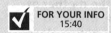

they trembled and were amazed. And they said nothing to
anyone, for they were afraid.

Jesus Appears to Many Witnesses

9 Now when *He* rose early on the first *day* of the week, He
appeared first to Mary Magdalene, out of whom He had cast
seven demons. 10 She went and told those who had been
with Him, as they mourned and wept. 11 And when they
heard that He was alive and had been seen by her, they did
not believe.

12 After that, He appeared in another form to two of them
as they walked and went into the country. 13 And they went
and told *it* to the rest, *but* they did not believe them either.

Final Instructions

14 Later He appeared to the eleven as they sat at the table;
and He rebuked their unbelief and hardness of heart, because they did not believe those who had seen Him after He
had risen. 15 And He said to them, "Go
into all the world and preach the gospel
to every creature. 16 He who believes and
is baptized will be saved; but he who

16:15

16:15–16

(Bible text continued on page 195)

- *Miriam was the sister of Moses (Num. 26:59) and one of the nation's first prophets (Ex. 15:20).*
- *She, her brother, and Aaron were the leadership team that God appointed to lead Israel out of Egypt and through the wilderness toward the Promised Land (Mic. 6:4).*
- *Miriam displayed courage early in life when she saved her baby brother from death (Ex. 2:4–7).*
- *Later, after Israel escaped across the Red Sea from the Egyptian army, she helped lead the people in songs of celebration and praise (Ex. 15:20–21).*
- *However, on one occasion she spoke against Moses. As a consequence she experienced God's judgment by contracting leprosy. For seven days she was shut out of the camp, the time required before a person healed of leprosy could rejoin the community (Num. 12:1–15).*
- *While she was on "forced sick leave," the people remained in one place until she returned to her work of leading the people (Num. 12:15).* ◆

Faith Impacts the World

CONSIDER THIS 16:15–16 **Jesus sent His followers into "all the world" (v. 15). Clearly He had global impact in mind. But spreading Christ's message involves more than just broadcasting a statement or set of facts. How does faith *impact* the world?**

One way is through followers of Christ who live out the gospel and proclaim it to the world. That's why the lifestyles and relationships of believers are so important. People are watching to see how we as Christians handle our responsibilities and resources. Is there any evidence that Christ really makes a difference in our lives?

Another way is through Christian institutions, such as local churches, parachurch organizations, and the Christian media. If you work or volunteer for one of these kinds of organizations, you have an important opportunity to touch the needs of the world with Christ's love and power.

A third sphere of influence is through lobbying and advocacy. Here Christians attempt to influence the institutions and people that control society. This might mean something as simple as voting, or something as complex as running for office or working to enact a particular piece of legislation. In our culture, Christians have the right to participate actively in public policy decisions, and we should use that right in ways that we believe honor the Lord.

As we attempt to take Christ's message to "all the world," it helps to understand how our world operates. See the diagram located at pages xviii–xx, "Faith Impacts the World," to find out more about how we can be salt and light in a world that needs Jesus.

Evidence for the Resurrection—Jesus' Appearances

Dead people don't ordinarily rise again. History stands on the fact that death is inevitable, and no human can avoid it. But Jesus broke that cycle. He conquered death by rising from the grave (vv. 1–8), and verified His resurrection by appearing to many of His followers:

Resurrection Appearances

Who Sees Him	Where	When	Reference
Mary Magdalene, **Mary** the mother of James, and **Salome**	At the tomb	Early Sunday morning	Matt. 28:1–10; Mark 16:1–8; Luke 24:1–12; John 20:1–9
Mary Magdalene	At the tomb	Early Sunday morning	Mark 16:9–11; John 20:11–18
Peter	Jerusalem	Sunday	Luke 24:34; 1 Cor. 15:5
Two travelers	Road to Emmaus	Midday Sunday	Luke 24:13–32
Ten disciples	Upper room	Sunday evening	Mark 16:14; Luke 24:36–43; John 20:19–25
Eleven disciples	Upper room	One week later	John 20:26–29; 1 Cor. 15:5
Seven disciples	Fishing in Galilee	Dawn	John 21:1–23
Eleven disciples	Galilee	Much later	Matt. 28:16–20; Mark 16:15–18
500 followers	Probably Galilee	Later	1 Cor. 15:6
James the apostle	Unknown	Later	1 Cor. 15:7
Disciples, leading women, Jesus' brothers, and others	Mount of Olives	40 days after the resurrection	Luke 24:46–53; Acts 1:3–14
Saul of Tarsus	Road to Damascus	Midday, years later	Acts 9:1–9; 1 Cor. 15:8

As Christians we can have hope in life after death because Jesus broke the bondage of death (1 Cor. 15:12–24, 35–58). ◆

The resurrection is the most amazing news the world has ever heard. For more on this most incredible event of history, see "Ten Myths About Christianity, Myth #2: There Is No Evidence that Jesus Rose from the Dead," Matt. 28:1–10.

does not believe will be condemned. 17And these signs will
follow those who believe: In My name they will cast out
demons; they will speak with new tongues; 18they[a] will take
up serpents; and if they drink anything deadly, it will by no
means hurt them; they will lay hands on the sick, and they
will recover."

The Ascension and Its Effect

19So then, after the Lord had spoken to them, He was received up into heaven, and sat down at the right hand of
God. 20And they went out and preached everywhere, the
Lord working with *them* and confirming the word through
the accompanying signs. Amen.[a]

16:18 [a]NU-Text reads *and in their hands they will.* *16:20* [a]Verses 9–20 are bracketed in NU-Text as not original. They are lacking in Codex Sinaiticus and Codex Vaticanus, although nearly all other manuscripts of Mark contain them.

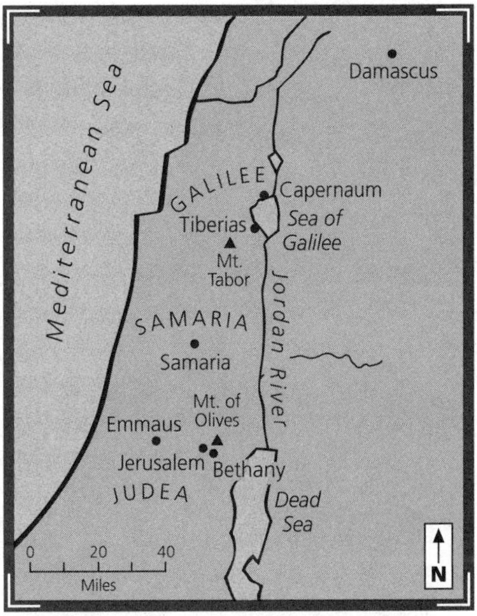

RESURRECTION APPEARANCES

The Global Gospel

Who was Jesus of Nazareth and what difference does it make? That's the question Luke answers in this carefully researched account that reads like a newspaper serial of the life of Christ.

Luke tells a story that has universal appeal. The Jesus that he portrays reaches out to people of every class and background—Jews, Samaritans, Gentiles, Roman soldiers, the poor, women, children, the powerful, the powerless, the sick, the fearful, the devout, the irreligious. He has something to offer everyone. Perhaps that's why some of today's most popular selections of Scripture come from this book—the Christmas story, the Good Samaritan, the Prodigal Son.

Jesus of Nazareth was a carpenter from an obscure town in an insignificant Roman province. Nevertheless, Luke will help you discover Him to be the international Christ whose words and works have global implications.

Luke

The Jesus that he portrays reaches out to people of every class and background.

C O N T E N T S

Whom Did Jesus Touch?

Elizabeth (1:24)
A childless woman finds hope and a heritage in the coming of God's Son.

Mary (1:27)
A young girl receives a visit from a heavenly messenger whose news turns her world upside down.

A Tax Official's Party-going Friends (5:28–29)
Levi throws a feast to introduce Jesus to his friends, who happen to be among the power brokers of society.

The Underclass (7:22)
In the cities Jesus found those on the margins of society—and intentionally directed much of His life and ministry to their plight.

A Self-Righteous Leader and a Humble Sinner (7:36–50)
A disreputable woman crashes Simon's party to find the One who could give her forgiveness and hope.

Mary of Magdala (8:2)
Jesus rescues a woman from demonic bondage and gains her lifelong loyalty.

Nine Ingrates—and One Thankful Leper (17:11–19)
Ten men walk away after Jesus heals them from leprosy. Only one returns to say thanks.

Two Confused Followers (24:13–32)
After His resurrection, Jesus walks for hours with two of His followers, but they recognize Him only when He leaves.

A R T I C L E S

Jesus Is for Gentiles, Too (1:1–4)
Luke shows that the gospel is not just for a select nation. Jesus offers forgiveness and salvation freely to all people.

New Testament Political Rulers (3:1)
We can tell closely when Jesus began His public ministry, thanks to Luke's listing of Roman officials. Other major political leaders of the Roman Empire and Palestine in the first century are shown in this table.

The Underclass (7:20–22)
Nearly every society and every city in biblical times had a large *underclass*—people scraping by on the margins of society. Jesus reached out to them, setting an example for His followers.

What Is the Gospel? (7:22)
Jesus came preaching the *gospel*, literally "the good news." What is the gospel, and why was it significant for Jesus to preach it?

The Women Who Followed Jesus (8:1–3)
The Gospel writers show that many women, frequently overlooked, were among the followers of Jesus.

Can Laity Get the Job Done? (9:1–62)
Jesus sent out His followers to preach and heal. They had no training or credentials other than their association with Christ Himself. Can people like that be effective today?

Who Was the Neighbor? (10:37)

One of Jesus' most popular parables reduces an abstract theological question to a simple, practical challenge: "Go and do likewise!"

Watch Out for Greed! (12:15)

Jesus warned us to guard against *covetousness*—longing for what we don't have. He was not telling us to watch for it in others, but in ourselves.

Set for Life—But What about Eternity? (16:19–31)

It can be a dangerous thing to have it made in this life. With wealth, status, and power, who needs God?

LUKE, THE GENTILE AUTHOR

To the best of our knowledge, the entire Bible, Old Testament and New, was composed by Hebrew writers, with the exception of one man—the "beloved physician," Luke. A Greek from Antioch of Syria (according to one tradition), he was well educated and thoroughly acquainted with the Roman world. His writings, the Gospel of Luke and Acts, show a far more cultured form of Greek than the rest of the New Testament.

How did Luke come to write nearly one-fourth of the New Testament? He probably began by traveling with Paul on parts of his second, third, and final journeys. At three places in Acts, the narrative changes to the first person ("we," Acts 16:10–17; 20:5—21:18; 27:1—28:16). That probably indicates that Luke was personally present during those episodes.

While Paul was imprisoned at Caesarea for two years (Acts 24:24–27), Luke may have used the time to visit Galilee and Judea, gathering firsthand accounts of Jesus' life. He may have interviewed Mary, Jesus' mother, as his account describes details of her pregnancy and motherhood that the other three gospel writers leave out: for example, her song of praise (Luke 1:46–55) and her habit of reflection on the events of which she was a part (2:19, 51). Who better to pay attention to the virgin birth from Mary's point of view than a physician?

Luke 1:1 implies that the doctor may also have visited Matthew, Mark, or John, the other Gospel writers, or perhaps others from the Twelve who remained in Palestine. Whoever his sources were, Luke's detailed descriptions indicate that they were actual participants. There was no need to resort to legends and hearsay. Instead, writing as a disciplined, careful historian and inspired by the Holy Spirit, Luke compiled the material into a skillfully crafted document, a certifiable record of Jesus' life.

If, as is probable, Luke was a Gentile, then it's no surprise that his Gospel seems to highlight Gentiles and their response to Jesus. For example, Matthew traces Jesus' genealogy back to Abraham, the father of the Jews (Matt. 1:2), but Luke traces it back to Adam, the father of the human race (Luke 3:38). Furthermore, Luke's narrative continues into Acts, where He shows the gospel moving beyond its Jewish origins to include peoples of every race.

One early source states that Luke had no wife or children, which would have made it easy for him to travel with Paul. Elsewhere Paul refers to him affectionately as a "fellow laborer" (Philem. 24), a term of high esteem. ◆

The Gospel of Luke is only volume one of a two-volume set. Volume two begins at Acts 1:1.

The First of Two Volumes

By the time Nero ascended to the title of Caesar over an increasingly troubled realm, the Christian movement had spread to most of the Roman empire's major cities. Yet the authorities did not at first view the new religion as a significant threat. Indeed, they still regarded it as a minor sect of Judaism. Nevertheless, the Christians' insistence on the divinity of Christ and their refusal to pay homage to the emperors eventually brought state-supported persecution.

Against this backdrop Luke wrote his Gospel and the book of Acts. The two-part narrative could have been intended as a legal document for the apostle Paul, who awaited trial at Rome (Acts 22:11; 25:11; 28:30–31). In his Gospel, Luke presents "all that Jesus began both to do and teach" (Acts 1:1). In Acts, he goes on to describe how Jesus' followers continued their Lord's work.

The key link between these two accounts is the Holy Spirit. While John's Gospel has much to say about the person of the Spirit, Luke-Acts emphasizes the activity of the Spirit in the ministry of Jesus and the early church. In the Gospel, John the Baptist and his parents are filled with the Spirit (Luke 1:15, 41, 67), as is Simeon (2:25–35). Jesus begins his ministry "in the power of the Spirit" (4:14; also 4:1, 18; 10:21), and He promises the Spirit to His disciples in their hour of need (12:12). Jesus is not alone; the Spirit is always with Him, within Him, empowering Him to accomplish God's purpose. ◆

Personality Profile: Luke

Also known as: The "beloved physician" (Col. 4:14).

Home: Antioch of Syria; later Philippi and other cities where Christian communities were started.

Background: Born into a cultured, educated Gentile family.

Profession: Primarily a physician, though he became a historian and author, and even did some evangelism.

Best known today for: Writing about one-fourth of the New Testament (Luke and Acts). His works emphasize the impact of the gospel on people considered "second-class" in Jewish culture at the time—Gentiles, women, the poor—as well as the topics of prayer and the work of the Holy Spirit.

LUKE THE BELOVED PHYSICIAN. . . .
—Colossians 4:14

CHAPTER 1

Luke's Preface

1:1–4 1 Inasmuch as many have taken in hand
to set in order a narrative of those things
which have been fulfilled[a] among us, 2 just as those who
from the beginning were eyewitnesses and ministers of the
word delivered them to us, 3 it seemed good to me also, having had perfect understanding of all things from the very
first, to write to you an orderly account, most excellent
Theophilus, 4 that you may know the certainty of those
things in which you were instructed.

An Angel Promises Zacharias a Son

1:5 5 There was in the days of Herod, the
king of Judea, a certain priest named
Zacharias, of the division of Abijah. His wife *was* of the
daughters of Aaron, and her name *was* Elizabeth. 6 And they
were both righteous before God, walking in all the commandments and ordinances of the Lord blameless. 7 But they
had no child, because Elizabeth was barren, and they were
both well advanced in years.
8 So it was, that while he was serving as priest before God
in the order of his division, 9 according to the custom of the
priesthood, his lot fell to burn incense when he went into
the temple of the Lord. 10 And the whole multitude of the
people was praying outside at the hour of incense. 11 Then
an angel of the Lord appeared to him, standing on the right
side of the altar of incense. 12 And when Zacharias saw *him*,
he was troubled, and fear fell upon him.
1:5–25 see pg. 202 13 But the angel said to him, "Do not be
afraid, Zacharias, for your prayer is
heard; and your wife Elizabeth will bear you a son, and you
shall call his name John. 14 And you will have joy and gladness, and many will rejoice at his birth. 15 For he will be
great in the sight of the Lord, and shall drink neither wine
nor strong drink. He will also be filled with the Holy Spirit,
even from his mother's womb. 16 And he will turn many of
the children of Israel to the Lord their God. 17 He will also
go before Him in the spirit and power of Elijah, 'to turn the
hearts of the fathers to the children,'[a] and the disobedient to
•

(Bible text continued on page 203)

1:1 [a]*Or are most surely believed* *1:17* [a]Malachi 4:5, 6

King Herod

A CLOSER LOOK 1:5 *King Herod, also known as Herod the Great, was highly intelligent, charming, and a brilliant politician. Yet his memory lives in infamy for the violence, incest, and intrigue that marked his family. Read about it in "The Herods," Acts 12:1–2.*

JESUS IS FOR GENTILES, TOO

CONSIDER THIS 1:1–4 **Luke's Gospel (as well as Acts) is addressed to someone named Theophilus. Little is known about this person, though speculation abounds. Was this an individual or a group of believers? Was Theophilus, which means "lover of God," his given name or a name taken after conversion (a common practice)? The title "most excellent" (Luke 1:3) indicates prominence and a high rank in Roman society. However, the title is dropped in Acts 1:1. Did Theophilus lose his position in the intervening years?**

One thing seems apparent: Luke was writing to and for a Gentile reader. In fact, a major emphasis of the account is that the gospel is not just for a select nation. Jesus offers forgiveness and salvation freely to all humanity, regardless of race, gender, or social merit. Luke shows that the good news is for:

- **Samaritans (Luke 9:52–56; 10:30–37; 17:11–19)**
- **Gentiles (2:32; 3:6, 8; 4:25–27; 7:9; 10:1; 24:47)**
- **Jews (1:32–33, 54)**
- **Women (1:26–56; 7:36–50; 8:1–3; 10:38–42)**
- **Outcasts such as tax collectors, widows, lepers, and the disabled (3:12; 4:27; 5:27–32; 7:11–15, 22–23, 37–50; 14:1–6; 15:1; 17:12; 19:2–10)**
- **The poor (1:53; 2:7; 6:20; 7:22)**
- **The rich (19:2; 23:50)**

Personality Profile: Zacharias

FOR YOUR INFO 1:5–25

Often confused with: Zechariah, the name of dozens of other men in the Bible, or Zacharias the priest who was murdered in the temple, also called Zechariah (Matt. 23:35; Luke 11:51).

Home: The Judean hill country.

Family: Descended from Abijah, who was a priest in David's day and a descendent of Aaron. His wife was Elizabeth, also from a family of priestly descent. John the Baptist was their son.

Occupation: Priest and therefore a local leader in his town's religious community.

Best known today for: Faltering in his faith when God was answering his prayer.

CONSIDER THIS 1:18–19

Can You Be Trusted?

Told by the angel Gabriel that he and his wife would have a son, Zacharias expressed doubt (v. 18) based on their advanced age. But implicit in his comments was a lack of trust in Gabriel himself. The angel responded with the simple statement, "I am Gabriel, who stands in the presence of God." No appeal to evidence; no attempt at persuasion. Just a simple declaration of his position before God. That alone was enough to ensure that the messenger was absolutely trustworthy.

Were Gabriel a liar, God would have banished him long before. But his continued presence before God indicated that he must have been truthful, as none but the truthful can stand in God's presence.

Consider the implications of that for the character of believers today. If we know God, we are to be like Him (2 Pet. 1:3–4; 1 John 3:2). As He is faithful and true (Rev. 3:14; 19:11; 22:6), we must be faithful and true. Wouldn't it be something if the claim "I am a Christian" were enough to establish one's integrity!

Yet that is far from the case today. For example, how

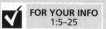

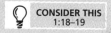

the wisdom of the just, to make ready a people prepared for
the Lord."

1:18–19

18And Zacharias said to the angel,
"How shall I know this? For I am an old
man, and my wife is well advanced in years."
19And the angel answered and said to him, "I am Gabriel,
who stands in the presence of God, and was sent to speak
to you and bring you these glad tidings. 20But behold, you
will be mute and not able to speak until the day these
things take place, because you did not believe my words
which will be fulfilled in their own time."

Personality Profile: Elizabeth

FOR YOUR INFO 1:24

Home: Hill country of Judea.

Family: Descended from a priestly family; wife of Zacharias, a priest; mother of John the Baptist; a relative of Mary of Nazareth.

Occupation: Homemaker.

Best known today as: The mother of John the Baptist.

many "Christian businesspeople" bring disrepute to the name of Christ by failing to pay their bills, abusing contracts, performing sloppy work, or making excuses rather than fulfilling commitments? Even some churches and Christian ministries cheat vendors, short-change visiting speakers and musicians, misrepresent their finances, or pay employees far below a fair wage for their work.

What a tragedy! If Gabriel's confident statement is any indication of the integrity that should mark God's workers, then it ought to be that one need only be identified as a Christian to erase all doubt. Of all people, Christ's followers should pursue an unimpeachable reputation for integrity. ◆

"I won't hire Christians!" says one business owner, himself a believer. See 1 Tim. 6:1–2.

How you do your job can make the gospel attractive to coworkers and customers. What impression are you making? See "Your 'Workstyle,'" Titus 2:9–10.

"... To make ready a people prepared for the Lord."
—Luke 1:17

21And the people waited for Zacharias, and marveled that
he lingered so long in the temple. 22But when he came out,
he could not speak to them; and they perceived that he had
seen a vision in the temple, for he beckoned to them and
remained speechless.
23So it was, as soon as the days of his service were completed, that he departed to his own
house. 24Now after those days his wife
Elizabeth conceived; and she hid herself five months, saying, 25"Thus the Lord has dealt with me, in the days when
He looked on *me,* to take away my reproach among people."

1:24 see pg. 203

Mary Learns that She Will Bear the Messiah

26Now in the sixth month the angel Gabriel was sent by
God to a city of Galilee named Nazareth,
27to a virgin betrothed to a man whose
name was Joseph, of the house of David. The virgin's name

1:27

CONSIDER THIS 1:38

The Maidservant of the Lord

When Gabriel appeared to Mary of Nazareth (Luke 1:26–38), she was perhaps no more than 15 years old. His startling announcement—that she would soon bear the very Son of the Highest—meant the end of a normal life. Mary's name would forever be on the lips of gossips and rumor-mongers. Joseph, her husband-to-be, could decide to end their betrothal through a public, humiliating divorce. Even if he "put her away secretly" (Matt. 1:19), she would still have to return in shame to her father's home or else survive on her own by whatever means she could.

Faced with these ruinous prospects that she had neither caused nor sought, Mary would have had plenty of reason to balk at Gabriel's message. Instead she accepted her assignment: "Let it be to me according to your word" (Luke 1:38). Her response was submissive obedience to the clearly revealed will of God. It was her duty as one of God's people.

Preparations and Follow Through

After Gabriel's departure, Mary took practical action by visiting her relative, Elizabeth, during the third trimester before John's birth (Luke 1:39–56). She might well have helped Elizabeth prepare items for the coming baby, even as she herself produced or acquired what she would need in her new home with Joseph. We can imagine that Mary

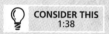

1:26–56
see pg. 206

was Mary. 28And having come in, the angel said to her, "Rejoice, highly favored
one, the Lord *is* with you; blessed *are* you among women!"[a]
29But when she saw *him,*[a] she was troubled at his saying,
and considered what manner of greeting this was. 30Then
the angel said to her, "Do not be afraid, Mary, for you have
found favor with God. 31And behold, you will conceive in
your womb and bring forth a Son, and shall call His name
JESUS. 32He will be great, and will be called the Son of the
Highest; and the Lord God will give Him the throne of His
father David. 33And He will reign over the house of Jacob
forever, and of His kingdom there will be no end."
34Then Mary said to the angel, "How can this be, since I
do not know a man?"
35And the angel answered and said to her, "*The* Holy
Spirit will come upon you, and the power of the Highest
will overshadow you; therefore, also, that Holy One who is
to be born will be called the Son of God. 36Now indeed,

1:28 [a]NU-Text omits *blessed are you among women.* *1:29* [a]NU-Text omits *when she saw him.*

learned much from this older, righteous woman as she listened to her and observed her marriage to Zacharias.

Once Jesus was born and the family set up housekeeping in Nazareth (2:39–40), Mary apparently settled into a fairly routine life as a homemaker. (The tasks involved are described in "Jewish Homemaking," Mark 1:29–31.) As she carried out responsibilities such as drawing water, baking bread, and spinning wool, she would have tied her Baby on her back or carried Him in a sling over her shoulder.

Luke was careful to record the family's obedience to Jewish law in having Jesus circumcised (2:21), in regard to Mary's purification (2:22), and in the presentation of Jesus and a sacrifice at the temple (2:22–24). Assuming that such observance carried over into the home, Mary probably provided Jesus' earliest instruction in the ways and values of the Hebrews.

Empty Nest

The New Testament mentions little of Mary's life after Jesus' birth. She is not listed among the earliest followers; indeed, Jesus seemed to treat her with some remoteness (8:19–21; 11:27–28). Nevertheless, she stood at the cross (John 19:25–27) and was among the first believers in Acts who awaited the Holy Spirit (Acts 1:14). ◆

BETROTHAL

FOR YOUR INFO 1:27

Betrothal (v. 27) was a mutual promise or contract for a future marriage (Deut. 20:7; Jer. 2:2). Not to be entirely equated with the modern concept of engagement, betrothal followed the selection of the bride by the prospective husband. The contract was negotiated by a friend or agent representing the bridegroom and by the parents representing the bride. It was confirmed by oaths and was accompanied with presents to the bride and often to the bride's parents.

Betrothal was celebrated by a feast. In some instances, it was customary for the bridegroom to place a ring on the bride's finger as a token of love and fidelity. In Hebrew custom, betrothal was actually part of the marriage process. A change of intention by one of the partners after he or she was betrothed was a serious matter, subject in some instances to a fine.

Betrothal was much more closely linked with marriage than our modern engagement. But the actual marriage took place only when the bridegroom took the bride to his home and the marriage was consummated in the sexual union.

What Kind of "Hill Country" Was This?

YOU ARE THERE 1:39

Mary's journey into the Judean hill country was no leisurely stroll along a country road. Given the difficulties and dangers that the landscape posed, her support network—Elizabeth and family—must have been especially valuable to her.

The mountainous terrain that she traversed did have a certain rugged beauty: desert yellows, a glimpse of the Dead Sea, violet-red mountains, and perhaps a few groves of fruit trees grown on terraced slopes. One main north-south road linked the region's principal cities—Jerusalem to the north, Bethlehem, Beth-zur, and Hebron to the south.

Beyond that, the hill country was rather bleak. The eastern slopes were mostly impassable desert, stretching 10 to 15 miles from their highest point, 3000 feet near Hebron, down to the Dead Sea, the lowest point on earth at 1,300 feet below sea level. The vast wasteland was broken only by imposing cliffs and canyons and a few forts and oases, such as En Gedi. It was an area fit for fugitives, rebels, and hermits—but certainly not for a pregnant woman.

Elizabeth your relative has also conceived a son in her old
age; and this is now the sixth month for her who was called
barren. 37For with God nothing will be impossible."

1:38 see pg. 204

38Then Mary said, "Behold the maidservant of the Lord! Let it be to me according to your word." And the angel departed from her.

Elizabeth and Mary Praise God

1:39

39Now Mary arose in those days and
went into the hill country with haste, to a
city of Judah, 40and entered the house of Zacharias and
greeted Elizabeth. 41And it happened, when Elizabeth heard
the greeting of Mary, that the babe leaped in her womb; and
Elizabeth was filled with the Holy Spirit. 42Then she spoke
out with a loud voice and said, "Blessed *are* you among
women, and blessed *is* the fruit of your womb! 43But why *is*
this *granted* to me, that the mother of my Lord should come
to me? 44For indeed, as soon as the voice of your greeting
sounded in my ears, the babe leaped in my womb for joy.
45Blessed *is* she who believed, for there will be a fulfillment
of those things which were told her from the Lord."

1:46–55

46And Mary said:

"My soul magnifies the Lord,
47 And my spirit has rejoiced in God my Savior.

Personality Profile: Mary, the Mother of Jesus

FOR YOUR INFO 1:26–56

Also known as: Miryam (of Nazareth); the Virgin.

Sometimes confused with: Mary of Bethany, the sister of Martha and Lazarus (John 11:1; 12:1–8); Mary, the mother of James and Joses (Matt. 27:55–61); and Mary, the mother of John Mark (Acts 12:12).

Home: Nazareth.

Family: Married to Joseph; they had four other sons—James, Joses, Judas, and Simon—as well as daughters; she was a relative of Elizabeth, John the Baptist's mother.

Occupation: Homemaker.

Best known today as: The mother of Jesus.

48 For He has regarded the lowly state of His maidservant;
For behold, henceforth all generations will call me
blessed.
49 For He who is mighty has done great things for me,
And holy *is* His name.
50 And His mercy *is* on those who fear Him
From generation to generation.
51 He has shown strength with His arm;
He has scattered *the* proud in the imagination of their
hearts.
52 He has put down the mighty from *their* thrones,
And exalted *the* lowly.
53 He has filled *the* hungry with good things,
And *the* rich He has sent away empty.
54 He has helped His servant Israel,
In remembrance of *His* mercy,
55 As He spoke to our fathers,
To Abraham and to his seed forever."

56And Mary remained with her about three months, and
returned to her house.

John the Baptist Is Born

57Now Elizabeth's full time came for her to be delivered,
and she brought forth a son. 58When her neighbors and relatives heard how the Lord had shown great mercy to her,
they rejoiced with her.
59So it was, on the eighth day, that they came to circumcise the child; and they would have called him by the name
of his father, Zacharias. 60His mother answered and said,
"No; he shall be called John."
61But they said to her, "There is no one among your relatives who is called by this name." 62So they made signs to
his father—what he would have him called.
63And he asked for a writing tablet, and wrote, saying,
"His name is John." So they all marveled. 64Immediately his
mouth was opened and his tongue *loosed,* and he spoke,
praising God. 65Then fear came on all who dwelt around
them; and all these sayings were discussed throughout all
the hill country of Judea. 66And all those who heard *them*
kept *them* in their hearts, saying, "What kind of child will
this be?" And the hand of the Lord was with him.
67Now his father Zacharias was filled with the Holy Spirit,
and prophesied, saying:

68 "Blessed *is* the Lord God of Israel,
For He has visited and redeemed His people,
69 And has raised up a horn of salvation for us
In the house of His servant David,

A Public Statement

CONSIDER THIS 1:46–55 *Mary's song (vv. 46–55) crackles with implications for society. Known as the Magnificat (from magnificare, the first word in the Latin version), it praises the Lord for the great things He has done (v. 49). But notice who it is He helps: the "lowly," including Mary (vv. 48–49, 52); those who fear Him (v. 50); the hungry (v. 53); and Israel (v. 54). By contrast, He scatters the proud (v. 51); puts down the mighty (v. 52); and sends away the rich empty-handed (v. 53).*

Jesus' birth is good news for the poor. In fact, He Himself was born into poverty (see 2:24). So here, as elsewhere in Luke's account, the poor are valued. They can identify with Jesus, right from His birth. They identify with the hope that "His mercy is on those who fear Him from generation to generation" (v. 50).

What does it mean to "fear" the Lord? See Luke 12:4–7.

For more on the poverty of Jesus and his family, see "A Poor Family Comes into Wealth," Matt. 2:11, and "Jesus—A Homeless Man?" Matt. 8:20.

Wealth was an important topic for Jesus. See "Don't Worry!" Matt. 6:19–34. Later, James warned those who live lavish lifestyles while ignoring their hurting neighbors that they are storing up judgment for themselves. See "Getting Yours," James 5:1–6.

THE CENSUS

FOR YOUR INFO 2:1–3 **Just as the United States numbers its population every ten years, so governments in biblical times kept track of their citizens. Four major censuses are mentioned in Scripture: under Moses (Num. 1:1–3), under David (1 Chr. 21:1–2), upon the Hebrews' return from captivity under Ezra and Nehemiah (Ezra 2:1–67; Neh. 7:4–72), and the one mentioned here in vv. 1–3, when Quirinius was imperial legate in the Roman province of Syria.**

Censuses were important for taxation, administration, military planning and conscription, recruitment of (sometimes forced) labor for public works projects, and for tithes and offerings to maintain religious institutions. Caesar Augustus used censuses to inventory the resources and needs of his empire, to raise money, and to determine where to allocate his troops. The Romans are believed to have held an empire-wide census every 14 years, and Luke could have been referring to one of those.

In biblical times, as today, censuses had major political implications. They certainly aided the strategic delivery of services. But registration was experienced by many as a tool of exploitation and oppression, especially where government was maintained without the choice of the governed and with little concern for their welfare. Such was the case in Israel under the Romans.

Nevertheless, God used a census to bring Joseph and Mary to Bethlehem, where Jesus was born, in fulfillment of His plan.

70 As He spoke by the mouth of His holy prophets,
Who *have been* since the world began,
71 That we should be saved from our enemies
And from the hand of all who hate us,
72 To perform the mercy *promised* to our fathers
And to remember His holy covenant,
73 The oath which He swore to our father Abraham:
74 To grant us that we,
Being delivered from the hand of our enemies,
Might serve Him without fear,
75 In holiness and righteousness before Him all the days of our life.

76 "And you, child, will be called the prophet of the Highest;
For you will go before the face of the Lord to prepare His ways,
77 To give knowledge of salvation to His people
By the remission of their sins,
78 Through the tender mercy of our God,
With which the Dayspring from on high has visited[a] us;
79 To give light to those who sit in darkness and the shadow of death,
To guide our feet into the way of peace."

80So the child grew and became strong in spirit, and was in the deserts till the day of his manifestation to Israel.

CHAPTER 2

The Birth of Jesus

2:1

1And it came to pass in those days *that*
a decree went out from Caesar Augustus
that all the world should be registered. 2This census first

2:1–3

took place while Quirinius was governing
Syria. 3So all went to be registered, everyone to his own city.
4Joseph also went up from Galilee, out of the city of Nazareth, into Judea, to the city of David, which is called Bethlehem, because he was of the house and lineage of
David, 5to be registered with Mary, his betrothed wife,[a] who
was with child. 6So it was, that while they were there, the
days were completed for her to be delivered. 7And she
brought forth her firstborn Son, and wrapped Him in swaddling cloths, and laid Him in a manger, because there was no room for them in the inn.

1:78 [a]NU-Text reads *shall visit.* 2:5 [a]NU-Text omits *wife.*

8Now there were in the same country shepherds living
out in the fields, keeping watch over their flock by night.
9And behold,[a] an angel of the Lord stood before them, and
the glory of the Lord shone around them, and they were
greatly afraid. 10Then the angel said to them, "Do not be
afraid, for behold, I bring you good tidings of great joy
2:11 which will be to all people. 11For there is
born to you this day in the city of David
a Savior, who is Christ the Lord. 12And this *will be* the sign
to you: You will find a Babe wrapped in swaddling cloths,
lying in a manger."

2:9 [a]NU-Text omits *behold.*

PERSONALITY PROFILE: AUGUSTUS

FOR YOUR INFO 2:1 **Also known as:** Gaius Octavius, his given name (born 63 B.C.); renamed Octavian; given the title Augustus in 27 B.C when he became emperor of Rome.

Home: A small town in Italy, but eventually Rome as the seat of power.

Family: Julius Caesar was his great-uncle by marriage. When Caesar was murdered in 44 B.C., Octavius was named his adopted son and heir, and even called the "son of a god." His first wife was Scribonia, whom he married for political reasons and hated. His second wife, Livia Drusilla, he loved although he cheated on her. His daughter Julia he exiled for moral offenses. His adopted son, Tiberius, was his aide and eventual heir.

Profession: Emperor of Rome and leader of its many institutions.

Best known today for: Bringing decades of civil war to an end and establishing Rome as a unified world power. Patient, shrewd, and a master of propaganda, he was a genius in administration and overhauled every aspect of Roman life—even the roads. During his 44-year reign, he established the *Pax Romana* ("Peace of Rome"), a state of control in which Roman culture flourished worldwide.

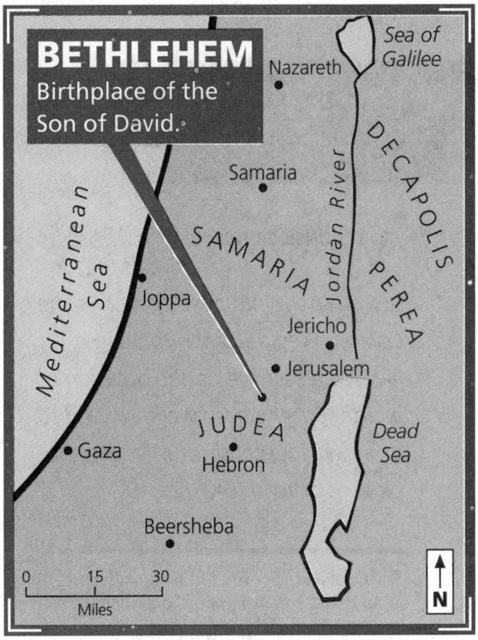

BETHLEHEM

YOU ARE THERE 2:11

- **The name of two towns mentioned in Scripture, the most famous of which was the birthplace of Jesus, five miles south of Jerusalem.**
- **Name means "House of Bread." The district was known for its agriculture.**
- **Called the City of David because of its association with Israel's second king (1 Sam. 17:12). The prophet Samuel anointed David king there, and David never lost his affection for the city.**
- **Predicted to be the birthplace of the Messiah (Mic. 5:2).**
- **The site of Jesus' birth was likely a cave near the town (sometimes stables were built into caves). Helena, mother of Constantine, erected the Church of the Nativity at the reputed birthplace in A.D. 330. Today a successor church, built by Emperor Justinian (A.D. 527–565), still stands.**

A Poor Family's Sacrifice

CONSIDER THIS 2:22–24 *Luke's Gospel reveals that Jesus was born into poverty (v. 24). The Law required a woman to bring a lamb as a sacrifice on the occasion of a birth. But the poor were allowed to offer two inexpensive turtledoves or pigeons instead (Lev. 12:6–8).*

For more on the poverty of Jesus and his family, see "A Poor Family Comes into Wealth," Matt. 2:11, and "Jesus—A Homeless Man?" Matt. 8:20.

An International Savior

CONSIDER THIS 2:29–31 *Simeon declared the international significance of the baby Jesus. The Lord's salvation is for "all peoples," both Jews and Gentiles. The old man's blessing was not his own invention, but came from the Holy Spirit (mentioned three times in vv. 25–27).*

13 And suddenly there was with the angel a multitude of
the heavenly host praising God and saying:

14 "Glory to God in the highest,
And on earth peace, goodwill toward men!"[a]

15 So it was, when the angels had gone away from them
into heaven, that the shepherds said to one another, "Let us
now go to Bethlehem and see this thing that has come to
pass, which the Lord has made known to us." 16 And they
came with haste and found Mary and Joseph, and the Babe
lying in a manger. 17 Now when they had seen *Him,* they
made widely[a] known the saying which was told them concerning this Child. 18 And all those who heard *it* marveled at
those things which were told them by the shepherds. 19 But
Mary kept all these things and pondered *them* in her heart.
20 Then the shepherds returned, glorifying and praising God
for all the things that they had heard and seen, as it was
told them.

Jesus Is Presented in the Temple

21 And when eight days were completed for the circumcision of the Child,[a] His name was called JESUS, the name
given by the angel before He was conceived in the womb.
22 Now when the days of her purification according to the
2:22–24 law of Moses were completed, they
brought Him to Jerusalem to present *Him*
to the Lord 23 (as it is written in the law of the Lord, "Every
male who opens the womb shall be called holy to the
LORD"),[a] 24 and to offer a sacrifice according to what is said
in the law of the Lord, "A pair of turtledoves or two
young pigeons."[a]
2:25–35 25 And behold, there was a man in
Jerusalem whose name was Simeon, and
this man was just and devout, waiting for the Consolation
of Israel, and the Holy Spirit was upon him. 26 And it had
been revealed to him by the Holy Spirit that he would not
see death before he had seen the Lord's Christ. 27 So he came
by the Spirit into the temple. And when the parents
brought in the Child Jesus, to do for Him according to the
custom of the law, 28 he took Him up in his arms and
blessed God and said:

2:29–31
29 "Lord, now You are letting Your
servant depart in peace,
According to Your word;
30 For my eyes have seen Your salvation
31 Which You have prepared before the face of all peoples,

2:14 [a]NU-Text reads *toward men of goodwill.* *2:17* [a]NU-Text omits *widely.*
2:21 [a]NU-Text reads *for His circumcision.* *2:23* [a]Exodus 13:2, 12, 15 *2:24* [a]Leviticus 12:8

32 A light to *bring* revelation to the Gentiles,
And the glory of Your people Israel."

33And Joseph and His mother[a] marveled at those things
which were spoken of Him. 34Then Simeon blessed them,
and said to Mary His mother, "Behold, this *Child* is destined
for the fall and rising of many in Israel, and for a sign which
will be spoken against 35(yes, a sword will pierce through
your own soul also), that the thoughts of many hearts may
be revealed."

2:36–38 see pg. 213

36Now there was one, Anna, a prophetess, the daughter of Phanuel, of the tribe
of Asher. She was of a great age, and had lived with a husband seven years from her virginity; 37and this woman *was*
a widow of about eighty-four years,[a] who did not depart
from the temple, but served *God* with fastings and prayers
night and day. 38And coming in that instant she gave thanks
to the Lord,[a] and spoke of Him to all those who looked for
redemption in Jerusalem.

Young Jesus Visits the Teachers

39So when they had performed all things according to the
law of the Lord, they returned to Galilee, to their *own* city,
Nazareth. 40And the Child grew and became strong in
spirit,[a] filled with wisdom; and the grace of God was upon
Him.
41His parents went to Jerusalem every year at the Feast of

2:42 see pg. 213

the Passover. 42And when He was twelve
years old, they went up to Jerusalem according to the custom of the feast. 43When they had finished the days, as they returned, the Boy Jesus lingered behind in Jerusalem. And Joseph and His mother[a] did not
know *it;* 44but supposing Him to have been in the company,
they went a day's journey, and sought Him among *their* relatives and acquaintances. 45So when they did not find Him,

2:46–47 see pg. 212

they returned to Jerusalem, seeking Him.
46Now so it was *that* after three days they
found Him in the temple, sitting in the midst of the teachers, both listening to them and asking them questions.
47And all who heard Him were astonished at His understanding and answers. 48So when they saw Him, they were
amazed; and His mother said to Him, "Son, why have You
done this to us? Look, Your father and I have sought You
anxiously."
49And He said to them, "Why did you seek Me? Did you
not know that I must be about My Father's business?" 50But

2:33 [a]NU-Text reads *And His father and mother.* *2:37* [a]NU-Text reads *a widow until she was eighty-four.* *2:38* [a]NU-Text reads *to God.* *2:40* [a]NU-Text omits *in spirit.* *2:43* [a]NU-Text reads *And His parents.*

SIMEON

CONSIDER THIS 2:25–35

There was nothing special about Simeon that qualified him to take up the Christ child in his arms and bless Him (v. 28). To our knowledge he was not an ordained religious leader, he had no credentials or special authority. He was simply a "just and devout" man who had a close walk with the Holy Spirit (vv. 25–27).

Thus, Simeon, whose name means "God hears," is an example of how God honors those who engage in lifetimes of quiet prayer and constant watchfulness. Simeon was a man of patient faith, yet his wait for the Messiah must have seemed interminable. He likely had many opportunities for doubt, as numerous would-be Messiahs sounded false alarms in the land.

Yet somehow he knew that the Redeemer would first come not as a great, heavenly champion wrapped in banners of nationalism, nor with a political agenda of violence, but as a Baby carried in the arms of His parents. His kingdom would prove to be a stumbling block to some and the Rock of salvation to others, both Jew and Gentile. Simeon also knew that the young couple standing before him would be hurt by the controversy that would eventually surround their Son (vv. 34–35).

they did not understand the statement which He spoke to them.

51 Then He went down with them and came to Nazareth, and was subject to them, but His mother kept all these things in her heart. 52 And Jesus increased in wisdom and stature, and in favor with God and men.

CONSIDER THIS
2:46–47

Jesus the Student

What kind of student was Jesus? Did He come into the world already knowing everything He needed to know? Was He able to acquire knowledge without even studying? The snapshot of Jesus in the temple (vv. 46–47) suggests otherwise. Though He apparently held His seniors spellbound with questions and responses, He nevertheless went through a lifelong process of education, learning and growing through "on-the-job training" from expert teachers.

Luke paints a picture of Jesus as a model student. The rabbis He encountered at Jerusalem were the preeminent experts in Judaism who researched, developed, and applied the body of Old Testament Law and rabbinical tradition to issues of the day. Some were members of the council, the governing tribunal of Judea. These teachers were fond of waxing eloquent on religious and legal questions in the temple courtyard for the benefit of any who would listen (Matt. 6:5; 7:28–29; 23:1–7).

Nevertheless, Jesus made strategic use of these authorities during His visit to the big city for Passover. Now age 12, He was considered a man. So He went to the temple to learn all He could about the Law of God. He proved to be an avid student, listening carefully and asking questions about His "Father's business" (Luke 2:49). Rather than embarrass His parents and offend His teachers by spouting off what He knew, He humbly subjected Himself to the discipline of education (v. 51). His turn to teach would come later. For now, He accepted the role of a learner.

It's a good example for all of us who must go through school and learn on the job. Like Jesus, we need to learn all we can from the best teachers we can find, showing ourselves to be teachable, with an attitude of humility. ◆

Jesus' teachers were probably among an elite class of scholars called scribes, who spent their entire lives studying the Law and tradition. See Luke 20:39.

The council, which included many of the temple rabbis, was the highest ruling body and supreme court of the Jews. See Acts 6:12.

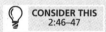

CHAPTER 3

John the Baptist Begins His Ministry

3:1
see pg. 214

1Now in the fifteenth year of the reign
of Tiberius Caesar, Pontius Pilate being
governor of Judea, Herod being tetrarch of Galilee, his
brother Philip tetrarch of Iturea and the region of Trachonitis, and Lysanias tetrarch of Abilene, 2while Annas and Caiaphas were high priests,[a] the word of God came to John the
son of Zacharias in the wilderness. 3And he went into all the
region around the Jordan, preaching a baptism of repentance for the remission of sins, 4as it is written in the book
of the words of Isaiah the prophet, saying:

"The voice of one crying in the wilderness:
'Prepare the way of the LORD;
Make His paths straight.
5 Every valley shall be filled
And every mountain and hill brought low;
The crooked places shall be made straight
And the rough ways smooth;
6 And all flesh shall see the salvation of God.' "[a]

7Then he said to the multitudes that came out to be baptized by him, "Brood of vipers! Who warned you to flee

(Bible text continued on page 215)

3:2 [a]NU-Text and M-Text read *in the high priesthood of Annas and Caiaphas.*
3:6 [a]Isaiah 40:3–5

ANNA

FOR YOUR INFO
2:36–38

Prophets such as Anna (vv. 36–38) were known for their spiritual wisdom and the proclamation of God's word to the people. Anna spent her time in the temple, serving God through fasting and prayers. When Joseph and Mary brought Jesus to the temple for presentation, Anna recognized Him as the One who would bring redemption to Israel.

No doubt many of Anna's prayers over the years had expressed a longing for God's Anointed. Her many years in the temple had probably given her a keen knowledge of the Scriptures, which were read there regularly.

Along with Simeon, Anna helped to testify to Jesus as God's Redeemer. Her testimony as a woman would have counted for little in Jewish courts of the day. But Luke includes her in his Gospel, perhaps to highlight one of the changes that Jesus the

(continued on page 215)

FOR YOUR INFO
2:42

JEWISH FEASTS

Feast of	Month on Jewish Calendar	Day	Corresponding Month	References
Passover	Nisan	14	Mar.–Apr.	Ex. 12:1–14; Matt. 26:17–20
*Unleavened Bread	Nisan	15–21	Mar.–Apr.	Ex. 12:15–20
Firstfruits	Nisan or Sivan	16 6	Mar.–Apr. May–June	Lev. 23:9–14; Num. 28:26
*Pentecost (Harvest or Weeks)	Sivan	6 (50 days after barley harvest)	May–June	Deut. 16:9–12; Acts 2:1
Trumpets, *Rosh Hashanah*	Tishri	1, 2	Sept.–Oct.	Num. 29:1–6
Day of Atonement, *Yom Kippur*	Tishri	10	Sept.–Oct.	Lev. 23:26–32; Heb. 9:7
*Tabernacles (Booths or Ingathering)	Tishri	15–22	Sept.–Oct.	Neh. 8:13–18; John 7:2
Dedication (Lights), *Hanukkah*	Chislev	25 (8 days)	Nov.–Dec.	John 10:22
Purim (Lots)	Adar	14, 15	Feb.–Mar.	Esth. 9:18–32

*The three major feasts for which all males of Israel were required to travel to the temple in Jerusalem (Ex. 23:14–19)

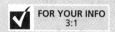

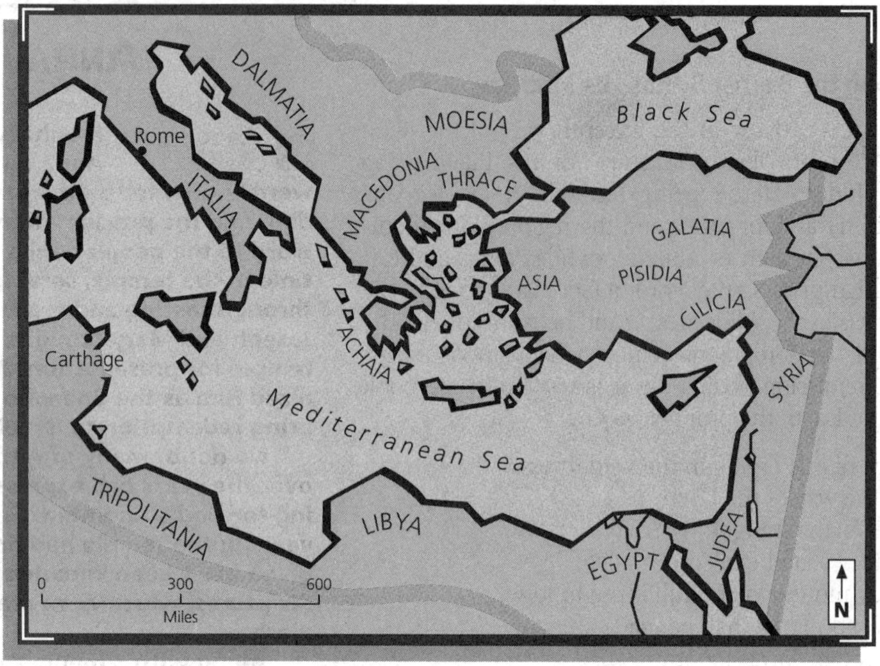

ROMAN POWER IN BIBLE LANDS

FOR YOUR INFO
3:1

NEW TESTAMENT POLITICAL RULERS

We can almost name the day on which Jesus began His public ministry, thanks to Luke's list of Roman officials (v. 1). The accompanying table shows some of the other major political leaders of the Roman Empire and Palestine in the first century.

The Roman empire was far less centralized than most. For all its size and age, its bureaucracy and army were relatively small. For nearly a thousand years the system worked. But much depended on the good will of client kingdoms. Those that complied with Rome's wishes were treated leniently. By granting them a degree of autonomy, Rome could concentrate its limited armed forces on trouble spots. Rebellions were brutally crushed, creating a strong deterrent to revolt and an incentive to remain loyal to the Caesar and his empire. ◆

What powers did Rome's government hold over Jesus and His fellow citizens in Judea? See "Roman Politics in the First Century A.D.," Luke 22:25.

from the wrath to come? 8Therefore bear fruits worthy of repentance, and do not begin to say to yourselves, 'We have
Abraham as *our* father.' For I say to you that God is able to
raise up children to Abraham from these stones. 9And even
now the ax is laid to the root of the trees. Therefore every
tree which does not bear good fruit is cut down and thrown
into the fire."
10So the people asked him, saying, "What shall we do
then?"

(continued from page 213)

Redeemer wanted to bring about among His followers. No longer should they regard women as untrustworthy witnesses, but as full members of a new community of faith in Christ.

Another woman became an important witness after Jesus' resurrection. See "Mary the Reliable Witness," Luke 8:2.

NEW TESTAMENT POLITICAL RULERS

Roman Emperor	Rulers of Palestine		
	Herod the Great (37–4 B.C.)		
	Judea	Galilee and Perea	Other Provinces
Augustus Caesar (31 B.C.–A.D. 14)	Archelaus (4 B.C.–A.D. 6)	Herod Antipas (4 B.C.–A.D. 39)	Herod Philip II (4 B.C.–A.D. 34) (Iturea and Trachonitis)
	Coponius (A.D. 6–8)		Lysanias (Dates uncertain) (Abilene)
	Ambivius (A.D. 9–12)		
	Annius Rufus (A.D. 12–15)		
Tiberius Caesar (A.D. 14–37)	Valerius Gratus (A.D. 15–26)		
	Pontius Pilate (A.D. 26–36)		
Caligula (A.D. 37–41)	Marcellus (A.D. 37)		
	Herod Agrippa I (A.D. 37–44)		
Claudius (A.D. 41–54)	Cuspius Fadus (A.D. 44–46)		
	Tiberius Alexander (A.D. 46–48)	Herod Agrippa II (Began to rule in A.D. 34 in other provinces and in A.D. 39 in Galilee and Perea.)	
	Ventidius Cumanus (A.D. 48–52)		
	M. Antonius Felix (A.D. 52–60)		
Nero (A.D. 54–68)	Porcius Festus (A.D. 60–62)		
	Clodius Albinus (A.D. 62–64)		
	Gessius Florus (A.D. 64–66)		
Galba, Otho, Vitellius (A.D. 68–69)	Jewish Revolt (A.D. 66–70)		
Vespasian (A.D. 69–79)			
Titus (A.D. 79–81)			
Domitian (A.D. 81–96)			

THREE DANGERS OF POWER

CONSIDER THIS 3:14

Like fire, power can be used to accomplish good. But always lurking in its shadow is the temptation of abuse—to use power for self-centered gains that harm others, and to avoid accountability for that harm. Responding to the Roman soldiers who policed Jerusalem (v. 14), John raised three issues in regard to the abuse of power:

(1) Intimidation. **We can use our power to push others around, especially those who are too weak or afraid to push back. Using power in that way is ungodly and harmful. Ultimately such power users destroy themselves, for their subordinates serve them without loyalty and with increasing resentment.**

(2) False accusations. **We can use our power to make snap decisions and judgments. But power used in that way keeps us in the dark, since others will be too afraid to tell us when we're wrong. When things go awry, it's all too easy to start blaming people under us and around us.**

(3) Discontent. **If we use our power in self-centered, hurtful ways, we'll tend to increase our appetite for power and seek more, perhaps by pressuring superiors or by cheating and stealing.**

The power of the gospel is a complete contrast to the power of intimidation, blame, and discontent. See "Power," Acts 1:8.

11He answered and said to them, "He who has two tunics,
let him give to him who has none; and he who has food, let
him do likewise."
12Then tax collectors also came to be baptized, and said
to him, "Teacher, what shall we do?"
13And he said to them, "Collect no more than what is appointed for you."

3:14

14Likewise the soldiers asked him, saying, "And what shall we do?"
So he said to them, "Do not intimidate anyone or accuse
falsely, and be content with your wages."
15Now as the people were in expectation, and all reasoned
in their hearts about John, whether he was the Christ *or*
not, 16John answered, saying to all, "I indeed baptize you
with water; but One mightier than I is coming, whose sandal strap I am not worthy to loose. He will baptize you with
the Holy Spirit and fire. 17His winnowing fan *is* in His hand,
and He will thoroughly clean out His threshing floor, and
gather the wheat into His barn; but the chaff He will burn
with unquenchable fire."
18And with many other exhortations he preached to the
people. 19But Herod the tetrarch, being rebuked by him
concerning Herodias, his brother Philip's wife,[a] and for all
the evils which Herod had done, 20also added this, above
all, that he shut John up in prison.

Jesus Is Baptized

21When all the people were baptized, it came to pass that
Jesus also was baptized; and while He prayed, the heaven
was opened. 22And the Holy Spirit descended in bodily
form like a dove upon Him, and a voice came from heaven
which said, "You are My beloved Son; in You I am well
pleased."

The Genealogy of Christ

3:23–38

23Now Jesus Himself began *His ministry at* about thirty years of age, being (as was
supposed) *the* son of Joseph, *the son* of Heli, 24*the son* of
Matthat,[a] *the son* of Levi, *the son* of Melchi, *the son* of Janna,
the son of Joseph, 25*the son* of Mattathiah, *the son* of Amos,
the son of Nahum, *the son* of Esli, *the son* of Naggai, 26*the son*
of Maath, *the son* of Mattathiah, *the son* of Semei, *the son* of
Joseph, *the son* of Judah, 27*the son* of Joannas, *the son* of
Rhesa, *the son* of Zerubbabel, *the son* of Shealtiel, *the son*
of Neri, 28*the son* of Melchi, *the son* of Addi, *the son* of
Cosam, *the son* of Elmodam, *the son* of Er, 29*the son* of Jose,

3:19 [a]NU-Text reads *his brother's wife.* *3:24* [a]This and several other names in the genealogy are spelled somewhat differently in the NU-Text. Since the New King James Version uses the Old Testament spelling for persons mentioned in the New Testament, these variations, which come from the Greek, have not been footnoted.

the son of Eliezer, *the son* of Jorim, *the son* of Matthat, *the son*
of Levi, 30*the son* of Simeon, *the son* of Judah, *the son* of
Joseph, *the son* of Jonan, *the son* of Eliakim, 31*the son* of Me-
lea, *the son* of Menan, *the son* of Mattathah, *the son* of
Nathan, *the son* of David, 32*the son* of Jesse, *the son* of Obed,
the son of Boaz, *the son* of Salmon, *the son* of Nahshon, 33*the
son* of Amminadab, *the son* of Ram, *the son* of Hezron, *the
son* of Perez, *the son* of Judah, 34*the son* of Jacob, *the son* of
Isaac, *the son* of Abraham, *the son* of Terah, *the son* of Nahor,
35*the son* of Serug, *the son* of Reu, *the son* of Peleg, *the son*
of Eber, *the son* of Shelah, 36*the son* of
Cainan, *the son* of Arphaxad, *the son* of
Shem, *the son* of Noah, *the son* of Lamech, 37*the son*

3:36–38
see pg. 219

CONSIDER THIS
3:23–38

JESUS, THE SON OF . . .

Have you ever been tempted to skip over vv. 23–38 as just another boring genealogy? Why, you may ask, did God fill up pages of Scripture with passages like this one, or its counterpart in Matt. 1:1–16? Why not just get right to the story?

One answer is that these verses were a major piece of the story. For one thing, they demonstrated Jesus' descent from King David, establishing His credentials as Messiah. Also, they showed that Jesus was fully human. Nowadays skeptics question the divinity of Christ. By contrast, some in the first century doubted whether Jesus was really human. Perhaps He was just an immaterial Spirit being, they said, a "heavenly Jesus" who only appeared to be human.

To answer that challenge, Luke and other church leaders stressed Christ's biological and personal roots. The first few chapters of Luke and Matthew, for example, describe Jesus' infancy to show that He was born just like any other flesh-and-blood human being (even though His conception was miraculous). Luke especially highlights Jesus' mother, Mary, and His earthly father, Joseph. He also grounds the story in a precise moment of Roman and Jewish history (Luke 3:1–2).

Today, many of us are eager to trace our genealogy and discover our roots, the stock of people from which we've come. Luke does us a favor by cataloging Jesus' roots. He shows us that not only was Jesus the Son of God, He was also the Son of Man. He is one of us! ◆

Be sure to compare Luke's list of Jesus' forebears with "Jesus' Roots," Matt. 1:1–16.

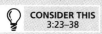

of Methuselah, *the son* of Enoch, *the son* of Jared, *the son* of Mahalalel, *the son* of Cainan, 38*the son* of Enosh, *the son* of Seth, *the son* of Adam, *the son* of God.

CHAPTER 4

Jesus Faces 40 Days of Temptation

4:1–13

4:1–13

1Then Jesus, being filled with the Holy Spirit, returned from the Jordan and was
led by the Spirit into[a] the wilderness, 2be-
ing tempted for forty days by the devil. And in those days He ate nothing, and afterward, when they had ended, He was hungry.
3And the devil said to Him, "If You are the Son of God, command this stone to become bread."
4But Jesus answered him, saying,[a] "It is written, 'Man shall not live by bread alone, but by every word of God.' "[b]

4:5–8 see pg. 220

5Then the devil, taking Him up on a high mountain, showed Him[a] all the

4:1 [a]NU-Text reads *in.* *4:4* [a]Deuteronomy 8:3 [b]NU-Text omits *but by every word of God.* *4:5* [a]NU-Text reads *And taking Him up, he showed Him.*

Real Temptation?

A CLOSER LOOK 4:1–13

Was Jesus really tempted, the same way that people are tempted today in the "real" world? To find out, see "You Don't Understand!" Matt. 4:3.

CONSIDER THIS 4:1–13

UNDER THE CIRCUMSTANCES

In addition to the substance of what was happening when Satan tempted Jesus, we see an environmental aspect in this passage as well. Jesus was tempted in three very different settings:

(1) In a barren desert (vv. 1–4). *In the ancient world, deserts were believed to be inhabited by spirits that engaged in never-ending warfare. In fact, some of the early church fathers went into desert caves as a way to engage in spiritual warfare and develop spiritual disciplines. Unfortunately, they sometimes lost contact with the everyday world in which life has to be lived.*

Centuries earlier, Israel had run into major problems in the desert, rebelling against God and wandering for forty years before entering the promised land (Num. 14:29–35).

(2) On a mountain (vv. 5–8). *A mountain setting may seem an unlikely environment for temptation. But in the ancient world, many religious shrines were carved or carried into mountains, where they became sources of idolatry and superstition. Today, mountain retreats, even those*

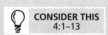

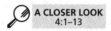

kingdoms of the world in a moment of time. 6And the devil
said to Him, "All this authority I will give You, and their
glory; for *this* has been delivered to me, and I give it to
whomever I wish. 7Therefore, if You will worship before
me, all will be Yours."
8And Jesus answered and said to him, "Get behind Me,
Satan![a] For[b] it is written, 'You shall worship the LORD your
God, and Him only you shall serve.' "[c]
9Then he brought Him to Jerusalem, set Him on the pinnacle of the temple, and said to Him, "If You are the Son of
God, throw Yourself down from here. 10For it is written:

'He shall give His angels charge over you,
To keep you,'

11and,

'In *their* hands they shall bear you up,
Lest you dash your foot against a stone.' "[a]

12And Jesus answered and said to him, "It has been said,
'You shall not tempt the LORD your God.' "[a]
13Now when the devil had ended every temptation, he
departed from Him until an opportune time.

4:8 [a]NU-Text omits *Get behind Me, Satan.* [b]NU-Text and M-Text omit *For.* [c]Deuteronomy 6:13 *4:11* [a]Psalm 91:11, 12 *4:12* [a]Deuteronomy 6:16

owned and operated by religious organizations, can become like shrines that tempt people to run away from problems. It's easy to prefer an exciting, memorable "mountain-top experience" to the grinding reality of day-to-day life in the "valley." Retreats and vacations can be valuable, but they can also become a vain religion if they are used to avoid reality.

(3) In Jerusalem, a city (vv. 9–13). *Like us, Jesus was tempted to take command of a city. Any city—especially "the holy city"—can sorely tempt a person with power. Power itself is morally neutral, but like fire it has grave potential to destroy people when mishandled. One has only to review the political history of cities like New York, Chicago, Hong Kong, or Beirut to appreciate that grim reality.*

Jesus' temptation touched the environment in three different ways. What environments pose temptations—and opportunities—for you? ◆

JESUS' FAMILY EXPERIENCED PAIN, TOO

CONSIDER THIS 3:36–38 **Luke's review of Jesus' forebears shows His direct association with broken people—a fact that offers hope to anyone struggling with inherited pain. Very early in the record we find family members with deep problems:**

- ***Adam* (v. 37) was cast out of an ideal situation because he disobeyed in the garden of Eden (Gen. 3:23, 24).**
- ***Seth* (v. 38) was a baby conceived out of the grief caused by one brother's murder and another's alienation. Seth was named as a substitute child by his grieving mother (Gen. 4:25).**
- ***Lamech* (v. 36) was a descendant of Cain who lived under his ancestor's curse of vengeance. Lamech acted out those haunting fears by killing yet another (Gen. 4:19–24).**
- ***Noah* (v. 36) brings us to the Bible's first case of alcohol abuse. He caused embarrassment to his sons during a drunken stupor in which he lay naked (Gen. 9:20–23).**

The people listed in Luke's genealogy are more than just names on a list. Each was a person who needed God's rescue from sin and unhealth.

Like Luke, Matthew begins his account of Jesus' life with a family tree checkered by scandal. See "Jesus' Roots," Matt. 1:1–16, and "The Women in Jesus' Genealogy," Matt. 1:3–6.

"ALL WILL BE YOURS"

CONSIDER THIS 4:5–8 **Satan promised to give Jesus authority over all the kingdoms of the world. "The father of lies" spoke the truth when he boldly declared, "This has been delivered to me, and I give it to whomever I wish" (v. 6). He neglected, of course, to mention *who* had delivered the world powers to him—God the Son Himself, who possessed authority over the entire created universe (Col. 1:15–17)!**

No wonder Jesus turned him down, one might say. But notice: Jesus did not respond by laying claim to His rightful authority. No, rather than focusing on the substance of the offer, He responded to its cost. To accept it would have required idolatry—a violation of His Father's unique position as the Lord God who *alone* deserves worship.

Jesus' response compels us to ask: When we receive an enticing offer that, in effect, promises "all will be yours" (v. 7), what do we focus on—the benefits or the costs? The benefits may be extremely attractive. But what are the costs? Does it involve "selling out" our Lord by compromising His commands, His values, or His honor? If so, then the cost is simply too high, and we need to respond as He did: "Get behind me, Satan!"

Matthew and Mark also record Jesus' temptation (Matt. 4:1–11; Mark 1:12–13). It was a major event in His life and preparation for ministry. Moses, too, confronted the "passing pleasures of sin," but like Jesus he resisted (Heb. 11:24–26).

Jesus Starts His Work and Meets Rejection

14Then Jesus returned in the power of the Spirit to
Galilee, and news of Him went out through all the surrounding
region. 15And He taught in their synagogues, being
glorified by all.

4:16–27

16So He came to Nazareth, where He
had been brought up. And as His custom
was, He went into the synagogue on the Sabbath day, and

4:17 see pg. 222

4:17–21 see pg. 222

stood up to read. 17And He was handed
the book of the prophet Isaiah. And
when He had opened the book, He found
the place where it was written:

4:18 see pg. 223

18 "The Spirit of the LORD *is* upon Me,
Because He has anointed Me
To preach the gospel to *the* poor;
He has sent Me to heal the brokenhearted,[a]
To proclaim liberty to *the* captives
And recovery of sight to *the* blind,
To set at liberty those who are oppressed;
19 To proclaim the acceptable year of the LORD."[a]

20Then He closed the book, and gave *it* back to the attendant
and sat down. And the eyes of all who were in the synagogue
were fixed on Him. 21And He began to say to them,
"Today this Scripture is fulfilled in your hearing." 22So all
bore witness to Him, and marveled at the gracious words
which proceeded out of His mouth. And they said, "Is this
not Joseph's son?"

23He said to them, "You will surely say this proverb to Me,
'Physician, heal yourself! Whatever we have heard done in
Capernaum,[a] do also here in Your country.' " 24Then He
said, "Assuredly, I say to you, no prophet is accepted in his
own country. 25But I tell you truly, many widows were in Israel
in the days of Elijah, when the heaven was shut up
three years and six months, and there was a great famine
throughout all the land; 26but to none of them was Elijah
sent except to Zarephath,[a] *in the region* of Sidon, to a
woman *who was* a widow. 27And many lepers were in Israel
in the time of Elisha the prophet, and none of them was
cleansed except Naaman the Syrian."

28So all those in the synagogue, when they heard these
things, were filled with wrath, 29and rose up and thrust
Him out of the city; and they led Him to the brow of the
hill on which their city was built, that they might throw
Him down over the cliff. 30Then passing through the midst
of them, He went His way.

(Bible text continued on page 222)

4:18 [a]NU-Text omits *to heal the brokenhearted.* *4:19* [a]Isaiah 61:1, 2 *4:23* [a]Here and elsewhere the NU-Text spelling is *Capharnaum.* *4:26* [a]Greek *Sarepta*

CONSIDER THIS
4:16–27

Jesus' First Sermon Included Surprises

Jesus launched His public ministry with a dramatic first sermon in the synagogue at Nazareth. Using Isaiah 61:1–2 as His text, He announced that He *was the One anointed by the Spirit to preach the gospel (v. 18), the good news.*

Jesus also said that the "acceptable year of the Lord" had come (v. 19), a reference to the Old Testament concept of the Jubilee Year (Lev. 25:8–19). Every fifty years, the Israelites were to set their slaves free, cancel each other's debts, and restore lands to their original owners. Apparently Jesus intended to make a dramatic difference in the lives of people, not only spiritually, but sociologically and economically as well.

Jesus' claims startled the hometown crowd for at least two reasons. First, He reminded His listeners of whom the good news was for: the poor, the brokenhearted, the captives (or prisoners), the blind, and the oppressed. At first, the people welcomed these words (v. 22). Perhaps they understood Jesus figuratively to mean them.

But soon they began to question His right to make such claims. "We know this fellow, don't we?" they asked in effect (v. 22). "Isn't He Joseph's boy? Isn't He one of us? Can He really be the One to fulfill Isaiah's prophecy?" They doubted His credentials.

Jesus rose to the occasion by throwing them another curve ball: "I'm especially impressed with the poor widow of Sidon," one might paraphrase His words (vv. 25–26). "She reminds Me that God often works outside of Israel; He even works in the lives of women. I'm also impressed with Naaman [v. 27]. He reminds me that God works in the lives of Syrian generals. Both cases indicate that prophets like Elijah and Elisha frequently had to go to the nations outside Israel to find people who would respond to God."

Such a radical message disturbed that small-town community. They loved the way that young Jesus read the Bible. But they were likely also concerned with preserving Jewish orthodoxy and reversing the region's reputation as a seedbed of radicals and "sinners" who were ignorant and/or disrespectful of the Law. Jesus' words might well have represented a threat to the image they wanted to project to the watching world. Once Jesus' neighbors realized what He was really saying—that His heroes and models were not always the usual Jewish models—they determined to reject Him. In fact, in their rage they almost killed Him (vv. 28–29).

The reaction of Jesus' hometown crowd moves us to ask: Whom are we reaching out to with the good news about Christ? What issues does Jesus' gospel address in our times? Are we like the Nazareth listeners, so committed to preserving the status quo that God has to go around us to accomplish His work? Nothing could be more tragic than that Jesus would pass through our midst and go on His way (v. 30). ◆

Jesus had a great deal to say about how we as His people should respond to those in need around us. See "Some Surprising Evidence," Matt. 11:2–6.

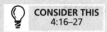

"Here Am I! Send Me!"

FOR YOUR INFO 4:17–21 **It was a time of greatness for Judah. King Uzziah had ruled for 52 years—longer than any previous king of Judah or Israel. Wise, pious, and powerful, the ruler had extended the nation's territory and brought about great prosperity. Most importantly, he had sought the Lord, influenced by a prophet named Zechariah who encouraged him to honor and obey God (2 Chr. 26:5).**

Yet upon Uzziah's death, the Lord appeared to Isaiah in a vision and warned that the nation was about to undergo His judgment. "Whom shall I send [to give this message to the people]?" He asked. "Who will go for Us?" Isaiah replied, "Here am I! Send me" (Is. 6:8).

So God sent Isaiah to Judah, knowing that most of the people would reject his message (v. 10). Jesus found in the record of Isaiah's call a prediction of His own rejection by the people of His day (Matt. 13:14–15). Yet at the same time, no other Old Testament prophet made as many references to the coming Messiah as did Isaiah.

According to a popular Jewish tradition, Isaiah met his death by being sawed in half during the reign of the evil king Manasseh of Judah. The writer to the Hebrews may have had that in mind as he listed some of the heroes of the faith (Heb. 11:37–38).

One of Isaiah's major emphases was the Messiah as a suffering servant, a role that Jesus fulfilled. See Luke 24:27.

A Demon Is Cast Out at Capernaum

4:31 see pg. 225

31Then He went down to Capernaum, a
city of Galilee, and was teaching them on
the Sabbaths. 32And they were astonished at His teaching,
for His word was with authority. 33Now in the synagogue
there was a man who had a spirit of an unclean demon.
And he cried out with a loud voice, 34saying, "Let *us* alone!
What have we to do with You, Jesus of Nazareth? Did You
come to destroy us? I know who You are—the Holy One of
God!"
35But Jesus rebuked him, saying, "Be quiet, and come out
of him!" And when the demon had thrown him in *their*
midst, it came out of him and did not hurt him. 36Then
they were all amazed and spoke among themselves, saying,
"What a word this *is!* For with authority and power He
commands the unclean spirits, and they come out." 37And
the report about Him went out into every place in the surrounding region.

Jesus Heals Simon's Mother-in-Law

38Now He arose from the synagogue and entered Simon's
house. But Simon's wife's mother was sick with a high fever,
and they made request of Him concerning her. 39So He
stood over her and rebuked the fever, and it left her. And
immediately she arose and served them.

Personality Profile: Isaiah

FOR YOUR INFO 4:17 **Name means:** "Jehovah has saved."

Home: Probably Jerusalem.

Family: May have been related to the royal house of Judah; married to a woman he called "the prophetess" (Is. 8:3); two sons, Shear-Jashub ("A Remnant Shall Return") and Maher-Shalal-Hash-Baz ("Speed the Spoil, Hasten the Booty").

Occupation: Early years spent as an official of King Uzziah of Judah; later called to be a prophet.

Best known today as: The Old Testament prophet who so vividly predicted the coming of the Messiah.

Jesus Travels and Heals

4:40 see pg. 224

40When the sun was setting, all those
who had any that were sick with various
diseases brought them to Him; and He laid His hands on
every one of them and healed them. 41And demons also
came out of many, crying out and saying, "You are the
Christ,[a] the Son of God!"
And He, rebuking *them,* did not allow them to speak, for
they knew that He was the Christ.
42Now when it was day, He departed and went into a deserted place. And the crowd sought Him and came to Him,
and tried to keep Him from leaving them; 43but He said to
them, "I must preach the kingdom of God to the other cities
also, because for this purpose I have been sent." 44And He
was preaching in the synagogues of Galilee.[a]

CHAPTER 5

Fish Caught and Fishermen Called

5:1–11 see pg. 228

1So it was, as the multitude pressed
about Him to hear the word of God, that
He stood by the Lake of Gennesaret, 2and saw two boats
standing by the lake; but the fishermen had gone from
them and were washing *their* nets. 3Then He got into one of
the boats, which was Simon's, and asked him to put out a
little from the land. And He sat down and taught the multitudes from the boat.
4When He had stopped speaking, He said to Simon,
"Launch out into the deep and let down your nets for a
catch."
5But Simon answered and said to Him, "Master, we have
toiled all night and caught nothing; nevertheless at Your
word I will let down the net." 6And when they had done
this, they caught a great number of fish, and their net was
breaking. 7So they signaled to *their* partners in the other
boat to come and help them. And they came and filled both
the boats, so that they began to sink. 8When Simon Peter
saw *it,* he fell down at Jesus' knees, saying, "Depart from
me, for I am a sinful man, O Lord!"
9For he and all who were with him were astonished at the
catch of fish which they had taken; 10and so also *were* James
and John, the sons of Zebedee, who were partners with Simon. And Jesus said to Simon, "Do not be afraid. From now
on you will catch men." 11So when they had brought their
boats to land, they forsook all and followed Him.

4:41 [a]NU-Text omits *the Christ.* *4:44* [a]NU-Text reads *Judea.*

THE SPIRIT OF THE LORD IS UPON . . . YOU!

CONSIDER THIS 4:18

If you've ever assumed that God's work in the world is accomplished primarily by ordained clergy, then you need to look carefully at Jesus' words to the hometown crowd of Nazareth. "The Spirit of the Lord is upon Me," He declared, applying an Old Testament prophecy to Himself (vv. 18–19; Is. 61:1–2). "Today this Scripture is fulfilled in your hearing" (v. 21).

The promise fulfilled was that the Messiah had come and would do all of the things foretold in the ancient text. But the text went on to make more promises about what would happen *after* the Messiah's initial work: "You shall be named the priests of the LORD, they shall call you the servants of our God" (Is. 61:6).

This would be a profound change. The tasks of "ministry" would no longer be done just by priests, rabbis, or clergy, but by all of God's people. Just as the Spirit of the Lord had come upon Christ, enabling Him to accomplish God's work, so the Spirit would enable Christ's followers to accomplish God's work, too.

If you are a believer in Christ, God has empowered you with His Spirit. Are you carrying out His assignments for you?

Paul affirmed the idea of everyday believers carrying out the work of God in Eph. 4:12–13. Likewise, Peter calls us "a holy priesthood" in 1 Pet. 2:9–10.

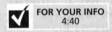

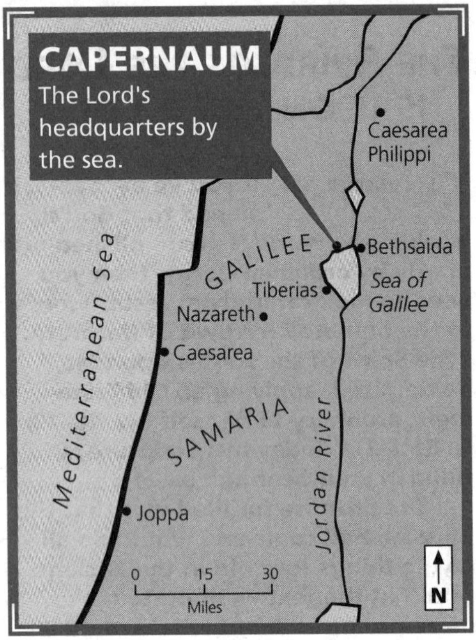

Jesus Heals a Leper

5:12–15 see pg. 229

12And it happened when He was in a
certain city, that behold, a man who was
full of leprosy saw Jesus; and he fell on *his* face and implored Him, saying, "Lord, if You are willing, You can make
me clean."
13Then He put out *His* hand and touched him, saying,
"I am willing; be cleansed." Immediately the leprosy left
him. 14And He charged him to tell no one, "But go and
show yourself to the priest, and make an offering for your
cleansing, as a testimony to them, just as Moses commanded."
15However, the report went around concerning Him all
the more; and great multitudes came together to hear, and
to be healed by Him of their infirmities. 16So He Himself *of-*
ten withdrew into the wilderness and prayed.

FOR YOUR INFO
4:40

HE HEALED THEM ALL

Jesus backed up His claim of being the Messiah by healing the sick (v. 40). Later, His followers used similar miracles to verify their message. Not only did healing demonstrate Christ's divine power over disease and infirmity, it revealed God's heart of compassion. The Great Physician and the apostles treated people with:

Disabilities or Conditions from Birth

- *paralytics (Matt. 9:1–8; Acts 9:32–35)*
- *the blind (Matt. 9:27–31; Mark 8:22–25; 10:46–52; Luke 7:21; 18:35–43; John 9:1–12)*
- *the mute (Matt. 9:32–34)*
- *a deaf and mute man (Mark 7:31–37)*
- *the lame (John 5:1–15; Acts 3:1–11; 14:8–10)*
- *a man with a deformed hand (Matt. 12:9–13)*
- *crowds of lame, blind, mute, and maimed (Matt. 15:30)*

Diseases of a Permanent or Semi-permanent Nature

- *a woman with a flow of blood (Matt. 9:20–22)*
- *a leper (Matt. 8:1–4; Luke 5:12–14; 17:11–17)*
- *a woman bent over with an 18-year infirmity (Luke 13:11–16)*
- *a man with dropsy, or swelling (Luke 14:1–6)*

A Paralyzed Man Brought to Jesus

5:17–26
see pg. 227

17Now it happened on a certain day, as
He was teaching, that there were Phari-
sees and teachers of the law sitting by, who had come out of
every town of Galilee, Judea, and Jerusalem. And the power
of the Lord was *present* to heal them.[a] 18Then behold, men
brought on a bed a man who was paralyzed, whom they
sought to bring in and lay before Him. 19And when they
could not find how they might bring him in, because of the
crowd, they went up on the housetop and let him down
with *his* bed through the tiling into the midst before Jesus.
20When He saw their faith, He said to him, "Man, your
sins are forgiven you."
21And the scribes and the Pharisees began to reason, say-

5:17 [a]NU-Text reads *present with Him to heal.*

Spiritual and Psychological Conditions

- *the demon-possessed (Matt. 8:28–34; Mark 5:1–20; 9:14–29; Luke 4:33–37; 7:21; Acts 5:12–16; 16:16–18; 19:11–12)*
- *a demon-possessed, blind, and mute man (Matt. 12:22)*
- *an epileptic (Matt. 17:14–21)*

Sickness

- *those with unspecified sickness (Matt. 14:34–36; Mark 1:32–34; Luke 4:40; 7:21; Acts 5:12–16; 19:11–12)*
- *people afflicted with a fever (Mark 1:29–31; John 4:46–54)*
- *a man suffering from dysentery (Acts 28:7–8)*

Death

- *Jairus' daughter (Mark 5:22–24, 35–43)*
- *the widow of Nain's son (Luke 7:11–17)*
- *Lazarus (John 11:38–44)*
- *Tabitha of Joppa (Acts 9:36–43)*
- *Eutychus (Acts 20:9–12)* ◆

The Bible mentions more than 40 specific diseases or disabilities and alludes frequently to sickness and health issues generally. It seems to accept that concerns over physical health are universal, inescapable, and problematic. See " 'Who Sinned?' Health and Disease in the Bible," John 9:2–3.

CAPERNAUM

YOU ARE THERE
4:31

- **The most important, prosperous city on the northwestern shore of the Sea of Galilee.**
- **Name means "village of Nahum" (not the Old Testament prophet).**
- **Economic and political hub of the Galilee region in the first century A.D. Situated on a road from Jerusalem to Damascus, it was a crossroads of international trade and commerce and was near the border between the tetrarchies of Philip and Herod Antipas.**
- **Blessed with fertile land and a mild climate. The area grew date palms, walnut trees, olives, figs, wheat, and wildflowers, and today even grows bananas.**
- **Offered many options for employment: agriculture, trade, fishing, even tax collection, a lucrative but not well-respected enterprise (Matt. 9:9–17).**
- **Center of Jesus' Galilean ministry, and called by Matthew Jesus' "own city" (Matt. 9:1–2). Two of Jesus' disciples are known to have had a home there, Simon Peter and Andrew (Mark 1:29–31; Luke 4:38).**
- **Archaeological excavations have uncovered ruins of a synagogue built on the site of the city's synagogue of Jesus' time. One block away is the foundation of an early church that excavators are convinced was built on the site of Peter's house (Mark 1:9; 8:14; Luke 4:38), the place where Jesus often stayed while in Capernaum.**

The densely populated Galilee region figured prominently in Jesus' life. He carried out most of His ministry there, and as many as eleven of His twelve disciples may have come from the region. See "Galilee," Mark 1:14.

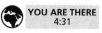

ing, "Who is this who speaks blasphemies? Who can forgive
sins but God alone?"
22But when Jesus perceived their thoughts, He answered
and said to them, "Why are you reasoning in your hearts?
23Which is easier, to say, 'Your sins are forgiven you,' or to
say, 'Rise up and walk'? 24But that you may know that the
Son of Man has power on earth to forgive sins"—He said to
the man who was paralyzed, "I say to you, arise, take up
your bed, and go to your house."
25Immediately he rose up before them, took up what he
had been lying on, and departed to his own house, glorifying God. 26And they were all amazed, and they glorified
God and were filled with fear, saying, "We have seen strange
things today!"

Levi Follows Jesus and Hosts a Dinner

27After these things He went out and saw a tax collector
named Levi, sitting at the tax office. And He said to him,
5:28–29 see pg. 230
"Follow Me." 28So he left all, rose up, and
followed Him.
29Then Levi gave Him a great feast in his own house. And
there were a great number of tax collectors and others who
sat down with them. 30And their scribes and the Pharisees[a]
complained against His disciples, saying, "Why do You eat
and drink with tax collectors and sinners?"
31Jesus answered and said to them, "Those who are well
have no need of a physician, but those who are sick. 32I
have not come to call *the* righteous, but sinners, to repentance."

New Wine and Old Wineskins

33Then they said to Him, "Why do[a] the disciples of John
fast often and make prayers, and likewise those of the Pharisees, but Yours eat and drink?"
34And He said to them, "Can you make the friends of the
bridegroom fast while the bridegroom is with them? 35But
the days will come when the bridegroom will be taken away
from them; then they will fast in those days."
5:36–39 see pg. 231
36Then He spoke a parable to them:
"No one puts a piece from a new garment
on an old one;[a] otherwise the new makes a tear, and also
the piece that was *taken* out of the new does not match the
old. 37And no one puts new wine into old wineskins; or else
the new wine will burst the wineskins and be spilled, and
the wineskins will be ruined. 38But new wine must be put
into new wineskins, and both are preserved.[a] 39And no one,

"NEW WINE MUST BE PUT INTO NEW WINESKINS. . . ." —Luke 5:38

5:30 [a]NU-Text reads *But the Pharisees and their scribes.* *5:33* [a]NU-Text omits *Why do,* making the verse a statement. *5:36* [a]NU-Text reads *No one tears a piece from a new garment and puts it on an old one.* *5:38* [a]NU-Text omits *and both are preserved.*

having drunk old *wine,* immediately[a] desires new; for he
says, 'The old is better.' "[b]

CHAPTER 6

Plucking Grain on the Sabbath

6:1–11
see pg. 230

[1]Now it happened on the second Sabbath after the first[a] that He went through
the grainfields. And His disciples plucked the heads of grain
and ate *them,* rubbing *them* in *their* hands. [2]And some of the
Pharisees said to them, "Why are you doing what is not
lawful to do on the Sabbath?"
[3]But Jesus answering them said, "Have you not even read
this, what David did when he was hungry, he and those
who were with him: [4]how he went into the house of God,
took and ate the showbread, and also gave some to those
with him, which is not lawful for any but the priests to eat?"

6:1–5
see pg. 232

[5]And He said to them, "The Son of Man
is also Lord of the Sabbath."

Doing Good on the Sabbath

[6]Now it happened on another Sabbath, also, that He entered the synagogue and taught. And a man was there
whose right hand was withered. [7]So the scribes and Pharisees watched Him closely, whether He would heal on the
Sabbath, that they might find an accusation against Him.
[8]But He knew their thoughts, and said to the man who had
the withered hand, "Arise and stand here." And he arose
and stood. [9]Then Jesus said to them, "I will ask you one
thing: Is it lawful on the Sabbath to do good or to do evil,
to save life or to destroy?"[a] [10]And when He had looked
around at them all, He said to the man,[a] "Stretch out your
hand." And he did so, and his hand was restored as whole
as the other.[b] [11]But they were filled with rage, and discussed
with one another what they might do to Jesus.

Twelve Named as Apostles

6:12–16

[12]Now it came to pass in those days
that He went out to the mountain to pray,

5:39 [a]NU-Text omits *immediately.* [b]NU-Text reads *good.* *6:1* [a]NU-Text reads *on a Sabbath.* *6:9* [a]M-Text reads *to kill.* *6:10* [a]NU-Text and M-Text read *to him.* [b]NU-Text omits *as whole as the other.*

The Twelve: Similar or Diverse?

A CLOSER LOOK 6:12–16

On the one hand, the twelve disciples were a rather similar group: all men, all Jews, and all but one (Judas Iscariot) apparently from Galilee. On closer inspection, however, they turn out to be fairly different in their backgrounds and outlook. See "The Twelve" at Matt. 10:2 to find out more about Jesus' diverse followers.

ARE YOU A FRIEND OF SOMEONE IN NEED?

CONSIDER THIS 5:17–26

The news was out: help was available for the sick! But a certain paralytic had no way to get to it. Physically disabled people like him were not only immobile, but usually poor. Useless to society and lacking help from the government, they invariably lived as social outcasts.

But some men knew of this man's dilemma and came to his need. They helped him get to a house where Jesus was teaching. Yet enormous crowds made access impossible. Fortunately, the men were determined and resourceful: they literally tore the roof off in order to connect their friend with the Helper (v. 19).

Jesus noticed "*their* faith" (v. 20, italics added) and healed the paralyzed man.

Is there someone near you who is cut off from needed services—health care, transportation, access to community resources, financial assistance, or advocacy in the workplace? Can you band together with others to provide what is needed in the tradition of the unnamed but faithful helpers described in Luke 5?

and continued all night in prayer to God. 13And when it
was day, He called His disciples to *Himself*; and from them
He chose twelve whom He also named apostles: 14Simon,
whom He also named Peter, and Andrew his brother; James
and John; Philip and Bartholomew; 15Matthew and Thomas;
James the *son* of Alphaeus, and Simon called the Zealot;
16Judas *the son* of James, and Judas Iscariot who also became
a traitor.

Crowds Come from Near and Far

6:17
see pg. 233
17And He came down with them and
stood on a level place with a crowd of
His disciples and a great multitude of people from all Judea

(Bible text continued on page 230)

YOU ARE THERE
5:1–11

THE WORLD OF THE FISHERMEN

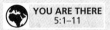

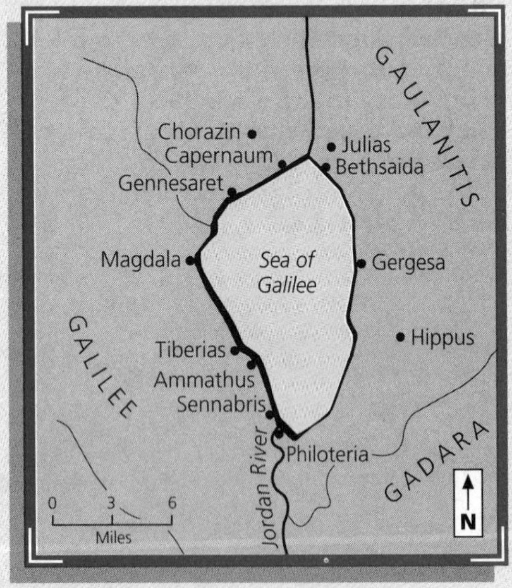

THE SEA OF GALILEE

Even though several of Jesus' disciples came from "Fish Town," He denounced it for its lack of faith. See "Bethsaida," Mark 6:45.

Fishing on the Sea of Galilee was big business. This now-famous body of water, 8 miles wide and 13 miles long, lay beside a fertile plain renowned for its agriculture. In Jesus' day, nine cities crowded its shorelines, each with no less than 15,000 citizens, possibly making the region's total population greater than Jerusalem's.

The names of the Galilean towns reflect the importance of fishing to the life and economy of the area. For example, at Tarichaea, "the place of salt fish," workers packed fish for shipment to Jerusalem and export to Rome. Bethsaida—from which at least four fishermen left their nets to follow Jesus (Matt. 4:18–22; John 1:44)—means "fish town"; most of the town was employed in the fishing industry.

Shoals just offshore were a fisherman's paradise. In Jesus' day, hundreds of fishing boats trawled the lake. Galileans ate little meat besides fish. It came highly salted, as there was no other way of preserving the "catch of the day."

Two kinds of nets were used—the sagēnē *and the* amphiblēstron. *The* sagēnē *(Matt. 13:47) was larger. Fitted with both weighted and buoyant material, it was used for trawling. In water, it stood almost upright and bagged fish as it was dragged behind a boat. The smaller* amphiblēstron *was shaped like an umbrella and was used for casting off the side of a boat (see Mark 1:16).*

The fisherman's day did not end with a return to shore. Mending and washing nets, preserving fish, maintaining boats and supplies, training and supervising crews, and negotiating with merchants and others in the shipping industry made for long, tiring hours. ◆

CONSIDER THIS
5:12–15

WHAT DOES LEPROSY HAVE TO DO WITH AIDS?

In Jesus' day, leprosy was a slowly progressing, chronic, highly infectious, incurable skin disease with large social implications. Today, leprosy is rare thanks to sulfone drugs and better hygiene. Now known as Hansen's Disease, the once-dreaded malady has been virtually eliminated. Much of that medical work has been done by Christians who followed Jesus' example in reaching out to a class of people that society had rejected (vv. 12–15; compare 17:11–15).

Now the world struggles with acquired immune deficiency syndrome (AIDS), a scourge that bears some remarkable similarities to leprosy. Biologically the diseases are quite different. But like the lepers of the ancient world, many AIDS sufferers are socially ostracized out of fear that they will contaminate others.

The situation is complicated by the fact that many AIDS cases have resulted from sex outside of monogamous, heterosexual marriage or from intravenous drug abuse—behaviors that oppose biblical precepts and principles. That introduces a moral dimension to the problem. But if there are moral issues involved in the spread of AIDS, there is also a moral issue involved in determining a Christlike response to AIDS.

In biblical times, leprosy was thought to be very contagious and hereditary. It was also believed to be a divine punishment for sin, even though the actual instances of that, such as Miriam (Num. 12:9–10) and Uzziah (2 Chr. 26:16–23), were exceptional. The Law was very specific about the diagnosis and treatment of leprosy (see Lev. 13). If a priest detected suspicious symptoms—pimples, scabs, sores, nodules, or white spots on the skin "like snow"—he ordered a quarantine of the infected person for seven days to protect the rest of the society. If the symptoms did not fade away within a week, another week of quarantine was prescribed.

Weeks could drag into months and months into years. Quarantined persons became social outcasts, living outside the Israelite camp. They fended for themselves as best they could. Some perhaps received occasional supplies from relatives, but most were reduced to begging.

Those who actually had the dreaded disease slowly wasted away. As the disease took away sensation, they easily injured themselves without feeling pain, leading to deformity and "half-eaten flesh" (Num. 12:12) and, eventually, death.

Quarantines never cured a leper. Only divine intervention could. God healed Moses (Ex. 4:6–7), Miriam (Num. 12:11–15), and Naaman (2 Kin. 5:1–15) in order to reveal His power and call people to follow Him. So when Jesus healed lepers, it demonstrated His divine nature and caused people to turn to Him.

What would Jesus do today? Surely His compassionate treatment of lepers is instructive for those of us living in a day of AIDS. We may debate the extent to which AIDS could be a divine punishment for sinful behavior. But we can and should continue to seek for a cure, just as leprosy was eventually cured through modern medicine. In the meantime, believers need to consider what a Christlike response would be to those with AIDS. Jesus reached out to lepers with love and healing. What compassionate, redemptive responses can we show toward our own, modern-day "lepers"? ◆

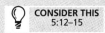

and Jerusalem, and from the seacoast of Tyre and Sidon,
who came to hear Him and be healed of their diseases,
18 as well as those who were tormented with unclean spirits. And they were healed.
19 And the whole multitude sought to touch Him, for power went out from Him and healed *them* all.

Jesus Pronounces Blessings

6:20–26

20 Then He lifted up His eyes toward His disciples, and said:

"Blessed *are you* poor,
For yours is the kingdom of God.
21 Blessed *are you* who hunger now,
For you shall be filled.
Blessed *are you* who weep now,
For you shall laugh.
22 Blessed are you when men hate you,
And when they exclude you,

Levi's Feast—A Career Transition Party

CONSIDER THIS 5:28–29 *As Levi was about to leave his professional life to follow the Lord, he came up with an interesting idea: a feast where some of the power brokers of the society—who happened to be his friends—could meet his new friend, Jesus. Maybe it could be compared to an office good-bye party—but with a surprise guest! Can your coworkers detect any of your loyalty to Christ?*

The Blessing—and Woes—of Wealth

A CLOSER LOOK 6:20–26 *The blessings of vv. 20–23, contrasted with the woes of vv. 24–26, should warn us to reflect carefully on God's perspective on wealth and poverty. See "Don't Worry!" at Matt. 6:19–34 for more on this issue.*

CONSIDER THIS 6:1–11

Jesus Confronts the Legalists

A pleasant day's hike through the grainfields turned sour when Jesus and His disciples ran into some Pharisees (vv. 1–2). Ever on the lookout for infractions of their traditions especially by Jesus and His followers, these legalists objected to the disciples "harvesting" grain in violation of the Sabbath. Never mind the group's hunger. For that matter, never mind that they were obviously snacking: after all, how could a handful of tiny heads of wheat or barley make a satisfying meal?

But the Pharisees would take Scripture out of context or add to it in order to condemn people for normal, God-given behavior. They ignored God's love and the freeness of His grace.

The Pharisees had lost sight of the intent of the Law and had taken upon themselves the impossible task of earning God's favor through moral perfectionism. The more they labored to "keep the Law," the more they wrapped themselves in an ever-expanding cloak of man-made rules and regulations. Worse, they judged everyone around them by their impossible standards.

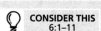

And revile *you*, and cast out your name as evil,
For the Son of Man's sake.
23 Rejoice in that day and leap for joy
For indeed your reward *is* great in heaven,
For in like manner their fathers did to the prophets.

Jesus Pronounces Woes

24 "But woe to you who are rich,
For you have received your consolation.
25 Woe to you who are full,
For you shall hunger.
Woe to you who laugh now,
For you shall mourn and weep.
26 Woe to you[a] when all[b] men speak well of you,
For so did their fathers to the false prophets.

"Love Your Enemies"

6:27–31 see pg. 234

27"But I say to you who hear: Love your
enemies, do good to those who hate you,
28bless those who curse you, and pray for those who spitefully use you. 29To him who strikes you
on the *one* cheek, offer the other also.

6:29 see pg. 234

6:26 [a]NU-Text and M-Text omit *to you.* [b]M-Text omits *all.*

Jesus challenged them by using the very Scriptures they claimed to honor (vv. 3–4). Furthermore, according to Matthew's account of this incident, Jesus questioned their basic attitudes, which seemed to have more to do with ritual than with the mercy that God values (Matt. 12:7).

Yet the critics only seemed to harden in their legalism, continuing to dog Jesus' steps on another Sabbath, when He visited one of their synagogues (vv. 6–7).

Legalists may be the hardest people to reach with the message of God's love. Jesus never won the Pharisees over as a group. But neither did He allow their abuse of Scripture or people to go unchallenged. ◆

The Sabbath controversies raise legitimate questions: How should Christians observe a day of rest? Is it okay to work on Sundays? See "Are Sundays Special?" Rom. 14:5–13, and "The Sabbath," Heb. 4:1–13.

Does Change Threaten You?

CONSIDER THIS 5:36–39 **A stubborn allegiance to old habits and traditions can sometimes seriously hinder maturing faith. Every believer should pay attention to that, because new life in Christ inevitably leads to innovation and timely change. Fear of change is understandable, but too much fear may be a sign of sinful resistance or of clinging to the past only because it feels safe and familiar.**

Jesus understood our human tendency toward predictability and the natural resistance to new things. He also knew that not all changes are good, and He never advocated change for the sake of change. But He warned against making tradition, particularly religious tradition, the standard by which all things should be tested (vv. 36–39). His parable of the wineskins pleads for at least the openness to consider something new. It affirms timely change in matters of growth and new life.

Are you resistant to the dynamics of change in your life, work, family, or church? If so, could you be resisting the very work of God or the ongoing dynamic of life itself? Pay attention to Jesus' image of the wineskins!

And from him who takes away your cloak, do not withhold
your tunic either. [30]Give to everyone who asks of you. And
from him who takes away your goods do not ask *them* back.
[31]And just as you want men to do to you, you also do to
them likewise.
[32]"But if you love those who love you, what credit is that
to you? For even sinners love those who love them. [33]And if
you do good to those who do good to you, what credit is
that to you? For even sinners do the same. [34]And if you
lend *to those* from whom you hope to receive back, what
credit is that to you? For even sinners lend to sinners to receive as much back. [35]But love your enemies, do good, and
lend, hoping for nothing in return; and your reward will be
great, and you will be sons of the Most High. For He is kind
to the unthankful and evil. [36]Therefore be merciful, just as
your Father also is merciful.

"Judge Not"

[37]"Judge not, and you shall not be judged. Condemn not,
and you shall not be condemned. Forgive, and you will be
forgiven. [38]Give, and it will be given to you: good measure,
pressed down, shaken together, and running over will be
put into your bosom. For with the same measure that you
use, it will be measured back to you."
[39]And He spoke a parable to them: "Can the blind lead
the blind? Will they not both fall into the ditch? [40]A disciple
is not above his teacher, but everyone who is perfectly
trained will be like his teacher. [41]And why do you look at
the speck in your brother's eye, but do not perceive the
plank in your own eye? [42]Or how can you say to your
brother, 'Brother, let me remove the speck that *is* in your
eye,' when you yourself do not see the plank that *is* in
your own eye? Hypocrite! First remove the plank from your
own eye, and then you will see clearly to remove the speck
that is in your brother's eye.

A Tree Is Known by Its Fruit

[43]"For a good tree does not bear bad fruit, nor does a bad
tree bear good fruit. [44]For every tree is known by its own
fruit. For *men* do not gather figs from thorns, nor do they
gather grapes from a bramble bush. [45]A good man out
of the good treasure of his heart brings forth good; and an
evil man out of the evil treasure of his heart[a] brings forth
evil. For out of the abundance of the heart his mouth
speaks.

6:45 [a]NU-Text omits *treasure of his heart.*

Is Jesus Really Lord of All?

CONSIDER THIS 6:1–5 **Is Jesus Lord of only the things we dedicate to Him, or is He Lord of everything and everyone? Are some things more "sacred" than others?**

To the Pharisees, the Sabbath day was so sacred that they could not accept Jesus and His friends gathering a handful of grain and eating it on that day (v. 1). Jesus was violating their extreme view of the separation between rest and work. He added to their consternation by reminding them of King David who entered the temple and ate the ceremonial showbread (vv. 3–4; 1 Sam. 21:1–6).

Jesus was not only challenging the Pharisees' view of holiness, He was establishing Himself as the Lord of the Sabbath, and in fact of all creation (v. 5; Col. 1:15–18). As Lord, He was free to determine what was permissible on the Sabbath day of rest. More importantly, as Lord He will not be boxed in by people's categories of "sacred" and "secular." He is Lord of *all.*

In what areas of life do we try to keep Jesus from being Lord? How do we try to limit His authority in order to preserve our own views and further our own interests?

When we say that Jesus is Lord of all, how much of "all" is all? See "Life—The Big Picture," Mark 12:28–34.

The Foundation of a House

46“But why do you call Me ‘Lord, Lord,’ and not do the
things which I say? 47Whoever comes to Me, and hears My
sayings and does them, I will show you whom he is like:
48He is like a man building a house, who dug deep and laid
the foundation on the rock. And when the flood arose, the
stream beat vehemently against that house, and could not
shake it, for it was founded on the rock.[a] 49But he who
heard and did nothing is like a man who built a house on
the earth without a foundation, against which the stream
beat vehemently; and immediately it fell.[a] And the ruin of
that house was great.”

CHAPTER 7

A Centurion’s Great Faith

1Now when He concluded all His sayings in the hearing
of the people, He entered Capernaum. 2And a certain centurion’s servant, who was dear to him, was sick and ready to
die. 3So when he heard about Jesus, he sent elders of the
Jews to Him, pleading with Him to come and heal his servant. 4And when they came to Jesus, they begged Him
earnestly, saying that the one for whom He should do this
was deserving, 5“for he loves our nation, and has built us a
synagogue.”
6Then Jesus went with them. And when He was already
not far from the house, the centurion sent friends to Him,
saying to Him, “Lord, do not trouble Yourself, for I am not
worthy that You should enter under my roof. 7Therefore I
did not even think myself worthy to come to You. But say
the word, and my servant will be healed. 8For I also am a
man placed under authority, having soldiers under me. And
I say to one, ‘Go,’ and he goes; and to another, ‘Come,’ and
he comes; and to my servant, ‘Do this,’ and he does *it*.”

7:1–10 see pg. 235

9When Jesus heard these things, He
marveled at him, and turned around and
said to the crowd that followed Him, “I say to you, I have
not found such great faith, not even in Israel!” 10And those
who were sent, returning to the house, found the servant
well who had been sick.[a]

A Dead Man Raised at Nain

7:11 see pg. 237

11Now it happened, the day after, *that*
He went into a city called Nain; and
many of His disciples went with Him, and a large crowd.

(Bible text continued on page 236)

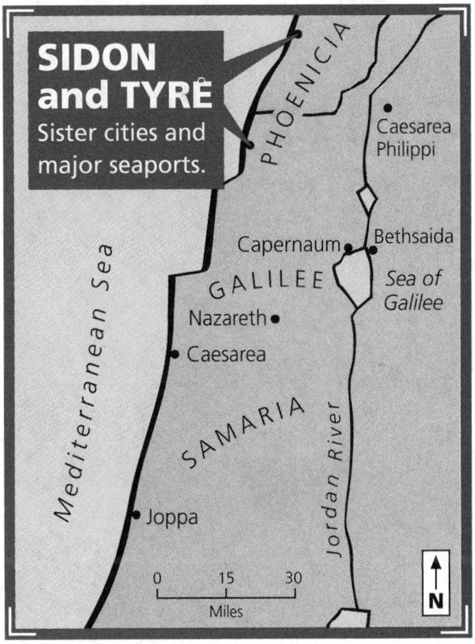

TYRE AND SIDON

YOU ARE THERE 6:17

- **Sister cities and major seaports about 20 miles apart on the Mediterranean coast, in Phoenicia (modern Lebanon) north of Galilee.**
- **Tyre (*rock*) was a rocky, coastal city on the mainland and a small island city just offshore; Sidon (*fishery*), built on a hill, stretched across several small islands connected by bridges.**
- **Introduced pagan practices to Israel and resisted conquest.**
- **Frequently denounced by Hebrew prophets.**
- **Renowned for shipping and shipbuilding, fishing, purple (an expensive dye; see “Lydia,” Acts 16:14), masonry, carpentry, pottery, and glassware.**
- **Used by Jesus to warn His Hebrew listeners: had Tyre and Sidon received the attention that cities like Chorazin and Capernaum did, their pagan citizens would have been converted (Luke 10:13–16).**

6:48 [a]NU-Text reads *for it was well built.* *6:49* [a]NU-Text reads *collapsed.* *7:10* [a]NU-Text omits *who had been sick.*

CONSIDER THIS
6:27–31

Love My Enemies?

The Law commanded Hebrews to love their neighbors (Lev. 19:18), but Jesus challenged His followers to love even their enemies (v. 27). Later He would be asked, "Who is my neighbor?" (Luke 10:29). Here we might ask, "Who are our enemies?"

Many believers today might think of our enemies as those we find unpleasant, people we just don't like. But that's not strong enough. By "enemies" Jesus meant those we actually hate, *and those who* hate us, *for whatever reason.*

Jesus' listeners didn't need to look far to understand who it was He was talking about. Verse 17 notes that a huge crowd had gathered around Him, including Gentiles from the seacoast cities of Tyre and Sidon. These centers of Baal worship had troubled the Hebrews for generations by introducing pagan ideas and practices. Elsewhere, Roman occupation troops held sway over the region, exploiting the Jews through oppressive taxation and political manipulation.

CONSIDER THIS
6:29

Running to Extremes

Did Christ intend for us to take what He said in vv. 27–36 literally? *It sounds noble to love our enemies, bless those who curse us, and pray for those who spite us. But what about physical abuse, robbery, or endless appeals for help (vv. 29–30)? Surely He didn't mean those words the way they sound. Or does Christianity encourage people to run to dangerous extremes?*

It's legitimate to notice that Jesus often used hyperbole and stark contrasts in His comments here (see "The Sermon on the Mount," Matt. 5:2). So when we read Jesus' words today, it's easy to set up all kinds of exceptions and qualifications to soften them. But in the process, do we miss His point? Do we distort His message?

Jesus was not calling here for unhealthy responses, nor setting forth a political or social agenda, nor offering a statement of public policy, nor constructing a model for business and finance. Instead, He posed a tough challenge to His followers—to those "who hear" (v. 27): What difference does our faith make in the way we respond to people in need? That's the key—our response to human need. That shows the true condition of our hearts. Do we respond to people as God Himself does, with mercy (v. 36)?

The test comes when we are faced with extremes. As

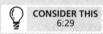

So it was immediately clear to the crowd who their enemies were—who was likely to curse and shame them (v. 28), who was likely to strike and rob them (v. 29), and who was likely to exploit them (v. 30). "Love your enemies," Jesus told them. Love those you hate, and who hate you.

Those of us who follow Jesus in today's world also have "enemies." Basically we are no different from those first believers. If we look carefully, we will recognize people we hate, *and who* hate us. *The bitterness may spring from racial, ethnic, political, economic, moral, gender, religious, or ideological conflicts. But they go beyond mere likes and dislikes. So Jesus' challenge to us is the same: "Love your enemies. Love those you hate, and who hate you."* ◆

On another occasion Jesus came back to the issue of loving one's neighbor. See Luke 10:27.

◆ ◆ ◆ ◆ ◆ ◆ ◆ ◆ ◆ ◆ ◆ ◆ ◆ ◆

Jesus pointed out, it's easy to love those who love us (v. 32). It's easy to give when we know we'll get back (v. 34). But God loves people who do not love Him, and gives to those who will never even thank Him, let alone give back to Him (v. 35).

Even God's enemies have needs that only He can meet. In His mercy, He meets those needs. Do we? When faced with people in genuine need, do we look only at their character, and base our response on that alone? Or do we look at their needs and do what we can to meet them?

We may question how far Jesus wants us to go in the various situations described in vv. 29–30. But we need never question how far God is willing to go to show mercy. That's what we need to take literally and imitate practically. ◆

Many misunderstandings have arisen from Jesus' statements in vv. 27–36. His words sound extreme to our ears. How can we make sense of them? See "The Morality of Christ," Matt. 5:17–48.

A Soldier's Surprising Faith

CONSIDER THIS
7:1–10

Jesus stepped on the toes of His Jewish listeners by praising a Roman centurion's faith (v. 9). He was impressed that the centurion—a soldier who knew all about power and authority—recognized Jesus' power and authority over disease. He marveled at the officer's faith—just as He later marveled at the lack of faith among the citizens of Capernaum (10:13–16).

But in praising the centurion, Jesus also tweaked the ethnic attitudes of the Jews. A Gentile with greater faith than any of them? Scandalous! His words must have enraged them, just as His sermon in Nazareth proved explosive (4:16–30).

[12]And when He came near the gate of the city, behold, a
dead man was being carried out, the only son of his
mother; and she was a widow. And a large crowd from the
city was with her. [13]When the Lord saw her, He had compassion on her and said to her, "Do not weep." [14]Then He
came and touched the open coffin, and those who carried
him stood still. And He said, "Young man, I say to you,
arise." [15]So he who was dead sat up and began to speak.
And He presented him to his mother.
[16]Then fear came upon all, and they glorified God, saying,
"A great prophet has risen up among us"; and, "God has visited His people." [17]And this report about Him went
throughout all Judea and all the surrounding region.

"He Who Is Least in the Kingdom"

[18]Then the disciples of John reported to him concerning
all these things. [19]And John, calling two of his disciples to
him, sent *them* to Jesus,[a] saying, "Are You the Coming One,
or do we look for another?"
7:20–23
[20]When the men had come to Him,
they said, "John the Baptist has sent us to
You, saying, 'Are You the Coming One, or do we look for
another?' " [21]And that very hour He cured many of infirmities, afflictions, and evil spirits; and to many blind He gave
sight.

7:19 [a]NU-Text reads *the Lord.*

CONSIDER THIS
7:20–23

THE UNDERCLASS

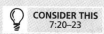

Nearly every society and every city in biblical times had a large underclass*—people scraping by on the margins of society. Tending to congregate in the cities, the underclass included the poor, the sick, the disabled, the lepers, the blind, the insane, the demon-possessed, widows, orphans, runaways, castaways, and refugees. Lacking resources to provide for even their basic needs, many turned to begging, stealing, menial labor, slavery, and prostitution. Few cultures made provision for these desperate, destitute wanderers, and so they remained largely powerless to change their condition.*

Yet it was to the underclass that Jesus intentionally directed much of His life and ministry. They were among the "blessed" in His opening remarks in the Sermon on the Mount (Matt. 5:3–10). And He declared that He had come to bring them good news in his inaugural sermon at Nazareth (Luke 4:17–18). So it was no surprise that when John's questioning disciples came to ask whether He was

7:22 see pg. 238
[22]Jesus answered and said to them, "Go
and tell John the things you have seen
and heard: that *the* blind see, *the* lame walk, *the* lepers are
cleansed, *the* deaf hear, *the* dead are raised, *the* poor have
the gospel preached to them. [23]And blessed is *he* who is not
offended because of Me."
[24]When the messengers of John had departed, He began
to speak to the multitudes concerning John: "What did you
go out into the wilderness to see? A reed shaken by the
7:25
wind? [25]But what did you go out to see?
A man clothed in soft garments? Indeed
those who are gorgeously appareled and live in luxury are
in kings' courts. [26]But what did you go out to see? A
prophet? Yes, I say to you, and more than a prophet. [27]This
is *he* of whom it is written:

> 'Behold, I send My messenger before Your face,
> Who will prepare Your way before You.'[a]

[28]For I say to you, among those born of women there is not
a greater prophet than John the Baptist;[a] but he who is least
in the kingdom of God is greater than he."

(Bible text continued on page 240)

7:27 [a]Malachi 3:1 *7:28* [a]NU-Text reads *there is none greater than John.*

John Who?

A CLOSER LOOK 7:25 *Even for his own day, John's ministry had none of the outward trappings of success. See "John the Street Preacher," Matt. 3:4.*

indeed the Messiah, they found Him ministering among the underclass (7:20–21).

Nor was it any surprise that the early church continued this outreach. They used their resources to meet material needs among their own members (Acts 2:44–45; 4:32, 34–35). They attracted the sick and afflicted (5:12–16). They appointed leaders to manage social programs for widows (6:1–6). They sent famine relief (11:27–30). They urged new leaders to remember the poor (Gal. 2:10). They even evaluated their success in part by how much they collected in charitable contributions (Rom. 15:26–27).

To what extent will Christians today follow in the footsteps of Jesus and the first believers? Our cities, like theirs, are filling up with an underclass. How can we offer "good news" to them? Can we touch their bodies as well as their souls? Do we take them as seriously as our Savior did? ◆

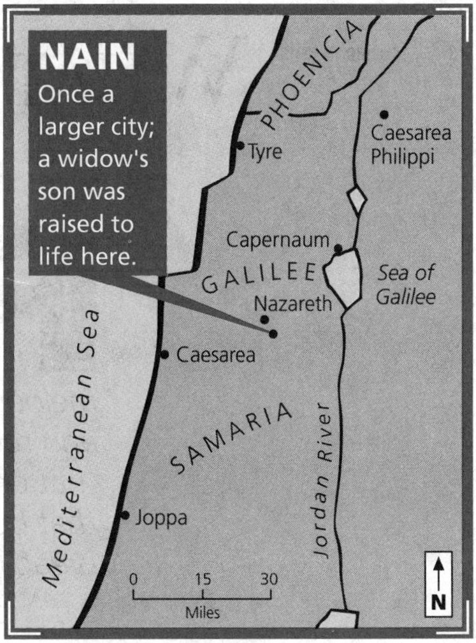

NAIN

YOU ARE THERE 7:11

- **Town in southwest Galilee, overlooking the Plain of Esdraelon.**
- **Name means *pleasant* or *delightful.* The view was certainly pleasant, and a spring contributed to groves of olives and figs.**
- **A small village now, though probably much larger at the time of Christ's visit (7:11).**
- **Located near numerous caves and tombs.**

CONSIDER THIS
7:22

What Is the Gospel?

Fewer and fewer people today understand the meaning and significance of the term "gospel." To many it is little more than a category of the music industry—songs with simple melodies and harmonies that honor traditional themes and religious devotion. Yet Jesus told John's followers that one way they could tell He was the Messiah was that because of His coming, "the poor have the gospel *preached to them" (v. 22, emphasis added).*

What is the gospel, and why was it significant for Jesus to preach it? The Greek word translated *gospel* can mean either "a reward for bringing good news" or simply "good news." From the standpoint of the New Testament, the ultimate good news is that Jesus Christ has come as the Messiah, the Savior of the world. He has come to save people from sin and restore them to God.

The Good News

That is indeed good news because it speaks to the very bad news that apart from God's intervention, all the world would be lost and without hope. As Paul declared in Romans, his monumental work explaining the gospel, "All have sinned and fall short of the glory of God" (Rom. 3:23). The good news is that "while we were still sinners, Christ died for us" (5:8). Indeed, Christ's death, which dealt with sin, and His resurrection from the dead form the core of the gospel message and ground that message in historical events (1 Cor. 15:1–4).

Obviously, though, Jesus had not yet gone to the cross at the time John's followers came, asking whether He was the Christ. Nevertheless, His message of the kingdom was good news because it revealed that God was finally bringing about the salvation promised in the Old Testament. Jesus' coming was like a fireman arriving on the scene of a fire or an emergency medical team arriving at an accident. The situation was not yet remedied, but the remedy was at hand. That was good news!

The Gospel for the Poor

But Jesus said it was especially good news for the poor (Luke 7:22). He had told the hometown crowd at Nazareth the same thing, that He had come "to preach the gospel to the poor" (4:18). Likewise, in the Sermon on the Mount He taught, "Blessed are you poor, for yours is the kingdom of God" (Luke 6:20). In what sense was

Jesus' message of the kingdom particularly for the poor?

You might say Jesus was announcing an "up-side-down kingdom." Whereas the kingdoms of the world are set up by and for the powerful and the advantaged, His kingdom was offered to the destitute, the wretched, the broken, and the hopeless, to those stripped of their dignity and self-respect. The "poor in spirit" were not merely the humble, but the humiliated, those who have had their spirits crushed and are knocked down by circumstances.

The poor were easy to spot in Jesus' day. They included widows and orphans, slaves and prisoners, the sick and demon-possessed, the homeless and the hungry. In our own day we could add people grieving the loss of a loved one or the end of a marriage, those who have lost jobs, or those who have been victimized by crime or injustice.

To these Jesus preached good news. He invited them to become part of a new family, a new community, the church. The rich are invited as well, but as in the parable of the slighted invitation, most reject the offer, feeling sufficient in themselves to take care of their needs (see "Worse than Rude," Matt. 22:2–14).

But those who accept Jesus' invitation do so by believing in His work on the cross on their behalf. That involves more than mere intellectual agreement to a theoretical truth. It means admitting their sinful condition and placing trust in Jesus to deal with their sin. It means entering into a vital relationship with the living Christ Himself.

The Purpose of the Gospel

When people believe, Christ begins to fashion them into a community of faith, the body of Christ (Eph. 2:1—3:11; 1 Pet. 2:9–10). His ultimate purpose in the gospel is to create a new people who live out the message, relationships, and values of His kingdom, a kingdom in which justice replaces injustice, community replaces rugged individualism, and compassion reigns over competition and neglect of others.

Thus the gospel is not merely a private relationship with God, but a public expression of godliness as well. The good news about Jesus certainly affects one's personal life, transforming individual attitudes and habits. But it challenges us to look beyond our own self-interests to the interests of others, both those in our network of relationships and in the world in general (Rom. 12:3–8; Eph. 4:1–16; Phil. 2:1–11). To embrace the gospel is to live no longer for oneself, but to live for Christ.

Spreading the Gospel

Moreover, Christ has commissioned His followers to spread the good news about Him throughout the world. This involves both the verbal proclamation of gospel truth and the demonstration of gospel reality in the lives of believers. Both can happen in a variety of ways: through preaching and teaching, through Christian worship and daily disciplines of spiritual life, through works of mercy and programs of compassion that meet basic human needs, or through believers taking moral stands (see "Faith Impacts the World," Mark 16:15).

The Four Gospels

During the second century, the term "gospel" came to mean the authoritative message about Jesus that the apostles had left and especially the four written accounts of His life and teaching, Matthew, Mark, Luke, and John. Mark was probably the first to be written, but all were created to be more than mere biographies about an historical figure. Each portrays the Lord in a particular way to show His saving significance for all people and to call them to respond in faith to His good news. ◆

THE GOOD NEWS
WHILE WE WERE STILL SINNERS CHRIST DIED FOR US....

29And when all the people heard *Him,* even the tax collectors justified God, having been baptized with the baptism of
John. 30But the Pharisees and lawyers rejected the will of
God for themselves, not having been baptized by him.
31And the Lord said,[a] "To what then shall I liken the men
of this generation, and what are they like? 32They are like
children sitting in the marketplace and calling to one another, saying:

'We played the flute for you,
  And you did not dance;
We mourned to you,
  And you did not weep.'

33For John the Baptist came neither eating bread nor drinking wine, and you say, 'He has a demon.' 34The Son of Man
has come eating and drinking, and you say, 'Look, a glutton
and a winebibber, a friend of tax collectors and sinners!'
35But wisdom is justified by all her children."

A Sinner at Simon's Dinner

7:36–50 36Then one of the Pharisees asked Him
to eat with him. And He went to the
Pharisee's house, and sat down to eat. 37And behold, a
woman in the city who was a sinner, when she knew that
Jesus sat at the table in the Pharisee's house, brought an alabaster flask of fragrant oil, 38and stood at His feet behind
Him weeping; and she began to wash His feet with her
tears, and wiped *them* with the hair of her head; and she
kissed His feet and anointed *them* with the fragrant oil.
39Now when the Pharisee who had invited Him saw *this,* he
spoke to himself, saying, "This Man, if He were a prophet,
would know who and what manner of woman *this is* who is
touching Him, for she is a sinner."
40And Jesus answered and said to him, "Simon, I have
something to say to you."
So he said, "Teacher, say it."
41"There was a certain creditor who had two debtors. One
owed five hundred denarii, and the other fifty. 42And when
they had nothing with which to repay, he freely forgave
them both. Tell Me, therefore, which of them will love him
more?"
43Simon answered and said, "I suppose the *one* whom he
forgave more."
And He said to him, "You have rightly judged." 44Then
He turned to the woman and said to Simon, "Do you see
this woman? I entered your house; you gave Me no water
for My feet, but she has washed My feet with her tears and

7:31 [a]NU-Text and M-Text omit *And the Lord said.*

SIMON'S SPOILED PARTY

CONSIDER THIS 7:36–50 *The incident in vv. 36–50 contrasts a respectable Pharisee, Simon, against a disreputable, unnamed woman. Luke describes her as a "sinner" (v. 37), a general term describing both those who failed to keep the ritual laws as well as those who flaunted the moral laws. How she gained entrance to Simon's feast is unclear.*

The religious leader was probably restricted from even talking to the woman. Extensive Jewish religious laws had developed in the first century to ensure moral purity. Many men suspected women of being sexually aggressive and eager to trap unsuspecting men. So Jewish men in general and teachers of the Law in particular—such as Simon and Jesus—were to have as little to do with women as possible.

Jesus knew what kind of life the woman lived, possibly by her hairstyle and the clothes she wore. Yet He accepted her anyway, violating taboos against speaking with her or allowing her to touch Him. In return, she gave to Jesus what Simon, the host, should have given—a kiss of welcome, a washing of the feet, and oil for the skin. These comforts were not merely symbolic but practical expressions of hospitality.

wiped *them* with the hair of her head. 45 You gave Me no kiss, but this woman has not ceased to kiss My feet since the time I came in. 46 You did not anoint My head with oil, but this woman has anointed My feet with fragrant oil. 47 Therefore I say to you, her sins, *which are* many, are forgiven, for she loved much. But to whom little is forgiven, *the same* loves little."

48 Then He said to her, "Your sins are forgiven."

49 And those who sat at the table with Him began to say to themselves, "Who is this who even forgives sins?"

50 Then He said to the woman, "Your faith has saved you. Go in peace."

CHAPTER 8

Many Women Provide for Jesus

8:1–3 see pg. 242

1 Now it came to pass, afterward, that He went through every city and village, preaching and bringing the glad tidings of the kingdom of God. And the twelve *were* with Him,

8:2 see pg. 243

2 and certain women who had been healed of evil spirits and infirmities—Mary called Magdalene, out of whom had come seven demons, 3 and Joanna the wife of Chuza, Herod's steward, and Susanna, and many others who provided for Him[a] from their substance.

A Parable about a Sower

8:4 see pg. 244

4 And when a great multitude had gathered, and they had come to Him from every city, He spoke by a parable: 5 "A sower went out to sow his seed. And as he sowed, some fell by the wayside; and it was trampled down, and the birds of the air devoured it. 6 Some fell on rock; and as soon as it sprang up, it withered away because it lacked moisture. 7 And some fell among thorns, and the thorns sprang up with it and choked it. 8 But others fell on good ground, sprang up, and yielded a crop a hundredfold." When He had said these things He cried, "He who has ears to hear, let him hear!"

The Purpose of Parables

9 Then His disciples asked Him, saying, "What does this parable mean?"

10 And He said, "To you it has been given to know the mysteries of the kingdom of God, but to the rest *it is given* in parables, that

'Seeing they may not see,
And hearing they may not understand.'[a]

(Bible text continued on page 243)

"YOUR FAITH HAS SAVED YOU. GO IN PEACE."
—Luke 7:50

8:3 [a]NU-Text and M-Text read *them*. *8:10* [a]Isaiah 6:9

THE WOMEN WHO FOLLOWED JESUS

FOR YOUR INFO 8:1–3 **The Gospel writers show us that many women, frequently overlooked, were among the followers of Jesus. Several appear by name:**

Mary, called Magdalene (Matt. 27:56; Mark 15:40; Luke 8:2; 24:10). Invariably mentioned first, perhaps because of her dramatic healing or because she was the most prominent.

Joanna, the wife of Chuza (Luke 8:3; 24:10). Chuza managed the king's household, so Joanna had access to Herod's court — infamous for its extravagant parties and sexual immorality (see "The Herods," Acts 12:1-2).

Susanna (Luke 8:3).

Mary, the mother of James and Joses (Matt. 27:56; Mark 15:40; Luke 24:10).

Salome (Mark 15:40).

The mother of the sons of Zebedee (James and John; Matt. 27:56). Remembered for her request that Christ allow her sons to sit in favored positions in His kingdom (Matt 20:20-24).

In addition to the above, the writers state clearly that "many" other women followed Jesus (for example, see Matt. 27:55; Mark 15:41; Luke 8:3; 24:1). Luke indicates that women provided materially for Jesus and the disciples—a curious statement in that Jewish women of the time generally did not have much control over their families' resources. Nor did women commonly travel with a rabbi (see "Jesus—A Rabbi for Women, Too," 23:49). Indeed, strict codes tended to distance Jewish leaders from women, so much so that by Jesus' time a rabbi was not even to speak to his wife in public.

But Jesus apparently thought little of such taboos. There is no indication that He discouraged women from being His followers. They listened to His teaching, accompanied Him in His travels, stood by Him at His crucifixion, gave witness to His resurrection, and eventually helped spread His message throughout the Roman world. ◆

Just as women assisted Jesus in His life and ministry, so they played a major role in the early church. See "Women and the Growth of Christianity," Phil. 4:3.

The Parable of the Sower Explained

11"Now the parable is this: The seed is the word of God.
12Those by the wayside are the ones who hear; then the
devil comes and takes away the word out of their hearts,
lest they should believe and be saved. 13But the ones on the
rock *are those* who, when they hear, receive the word with
joy; and these have no root, who believe for a while and in
time of temptation fall away. 14Now the ones *that* fell among
thorns are those who, when they have heard, go out and are
choked with cares, riches, and pleasures of life, and bring
no fruit to maturity. 15But the ones *that* fell on the good
ground are those who, having heard the word with a noble
and good heart, keep *it* and bear fruit with patience.

A Lamp on a Lampstand

16"No one, when he has lit a lamp, covers it with a vessel
or puts *it* under a bed, but sets *it* on a lampstand, that those
who enter may see the light. 17For nothing is secret that will
not be revealed, nor *anything* hidden that will not be known
and come to light. 18Therefore take heed how you hear. For
whoever has, to him *more* will be given; and whoever does
not have, even what he seems to have will be taken from
him."

Jesus' Mother and Brothers Come to Him

8:19–21

19Then His mother and brothers came
to Him, and could not approach Him be-

Who Is My Family?

A CLOSER LOOK 8:19–21

Was Jesus disowning his family (v. 21)? Was He ashamed of His disbelieving relatives? See "Family Loyalty" at Matt. 12:46–50.

Personality Profile: Mary of Magdala

FOR YOUR INFO 8:2

Also known as: Mary Magdalene.

Home: Raised in Magdala, a large city on the Sea of Galilee.

Best known today for: Being freed from seven demons by Jesus and becoming one of His most devoted followers.

Mary the Reliable Witness

The Gospels mention Mary of Magdala by name more than any other female disciple. One reason may be the dramatic turnaround in her life that the Lord brought about by casting out seven demons. She responded by supporting His ministry and joining with several other women who traveled with Him (Luke 8:1–3).

Mary's loyalty proved unwavering right to the end. While the Twelve fled after Jesus' arrest, Mary stood by at His crucifixion (Matt. 27:56; Mark 15:40; John 19:25). She also helped prepare His body for burial (Matt. 27:61; Mark 15:47; Luke 23:55). Perhaps it was to reward her undying devotion that the Lord allowed her to be the first person to meet Him after His resurrection (Mark 16:9–10; John 20:14–18).

Curiously, however, the disciples refused to believe Mary's report of the risen Lord. In fact, they dismissed it as an "idle tale" (Mark 16:11; Luke 24:11). Perhaps their skepticism betrayed long-held doubts about Mary's credibility: after all, hadn't she been possessed by seven demons? Moreover, Jewish culture raised its men to consider the testimony of women as inferior.

Nevertheless, Jesus chose Mary to report the good news of His resurrection to His other followers. Later, He rebuked them for their unwillingness to believe her (Mark 16:14). Thanks to Him, she was a changed person. Moreover, she was a reliable witness, having proven her trustworthiness through her perseverance and steadfastness in the face of danger and doubt.

cause of the crowd. 20And it was told Him *by some,* who
said, "Your mother and Your brothers are standing outside,
desiring to see You."
21But He answered and said to them, "My mother and My
brothers are these who hear the word of God and do it."

". . . HEAR THE WORD OF GOD AND DO IT." —Luke 8:21

A Great Storm Obeys Jesus

8:22–25 see pg. 246

22Now it happened, on a certain day,
that He got into a boat with His disciples.
And He said to them, "Let us cross over to the other side of
the lake." And they launched out. 23But as they sailed He
fell asleep. And a windstorm came down on the lake, and
they were filling *with water,* and were in jeopardy. 24And
they came to Him and awoke Him, saying, "Master, Master,
we are perishing!"
Then He arose and rebuked the wind and the raging of
the water. And they ceased, and there was a calm. 25But He
said to them, "Where is your faith?"
And they were afraid, and marveled, saying to one another, "Who can this be? For He commands even the winds
and water, and they obey Him!"

FOR YOUR INFO 8:4

THE PARABLES OF JESUS CHRIST	Matthew	Mark	Luke
Lamp Under a Basket	5:14–16	4:21, 22	8:16, 17 11:33–36
A Wise Man Builds on Rock and a Foolish Man Builds on Sand	7:24–27		6:47–49
Unshrunk (New) Cloth on an Old Garment	9:16	2:21	5:36
New Wine in Old Wineskins	9:17	2:22	5:37, 38
The Sower	13:3–23	4:2–20	8:4–15
The Tares (Weeds)	13:24–30		
The Mustard Seed	13:31, 32	4:30–32	13:18, 19
The Leaven	13:33		13:20, 21
The Hidden Treasure	13:44		
The Pearl of Great Price	13:45, 46		
The Dragnet	13:47–50		
The Lost Sheep	18:12–14		15:3–7
The Unforgiving Servant	18:23–35		
The Laborers in the Vineyard	20:1–16		
The Two Sons	21:28–32		
The Wicked Vinedressers	21:33–45	12:1–12	20:9–19
The Wedding Feast	22:2–14		
The Fig Tree	24:32–44	13:28–32	21:29–33
The Wise and Foolish Virgins	25:1–13		

A Demon-possessed Man Healed

26Then they sailed to the country of the Gadarenes,[a]
which is opposite Galilee. 27And when He stepped out on
the land, there met Him a certain man from the city who
had demons for a long time. And he wore no clothes,[a] nor
did he live in a house but in the tombs. 28When he saw
Jesus, he cried out, fell down before Him, and with a loud
voice said, "What have I to do with You, Jesus, Son of the
Most High God? I beg You, do not torment me!" 29For He
had commanded the unclean spirit to come out of the man.
For it had often seized him, and he was kept under guard,
bound with chains and shackles; and he broke the bonds
and was driven by the demon into the wilderness.

30Jesus asked him, saying, "What is your name?"

And he said, "Legion," because many demons had entered him. 31And they begged Him that He would not command them to go out into the abyss.

32Now a herd of many swine was feeding there on the

8:26 [a]NU-Text reads *Gerasenes.* *8:27* [a]NU-Text reads *who had demons and for a long time wore no clothes.*

THE PARABLES OF JESUS CHRIST (cont.)	Matthew	Mark	Luke
The Talents	25:14–30		
The Growing Seed		4:26–29	
The Absent Householder		13:33–37	
The Creditor and Two Debtors			7:41–43
The Good Samaritan			10:30–37
A Friend in Need			11:5–13
The Rich Fool			12:16–21
The Watchful Servants			12:35–40
The Faithful Servant and the Evil Servant			12:42–48
The Barren Fig Tree			13:6–9
The Great Supper			14:16–24
Building a Tower and a King Making War			14:25–35
The Lost Coin			15:8–10
The Lost Son			15:11–32
The Unjust Steward			16:1–13
The Rich Man and Lazarus			16:19–31
Unprofitable Servants			17:7–10
The Persistent Widow			18:1–8
The Pharisee and the Tax Collector			18:9–14
The Minas			19:11–27

mountain. So they begged Him that He would permit them
to enter them. And He permitted them. 33Then the demons
went out of the man and entered the swine, and the herd
ran violently down the steep place into the lake and
drowned.
34When those who fed *them* saw what had happened,
they fled and told *it* in the city and in the country. 35Then
they went out to see what had happened, and came to
Jesus, and found the man from whom the demons had departed, sitting at the feet of Jesus, clothed and in his right
mind. And they were afraid. 36They also who had seen *it*
told them by what means he who had been demon-possessed was healed. 37Then the whole multitude of the
surrounding region of the Gadarenes[a] asked Him to depart
from them, for they were seized with great fear. And He got
into the boat and returned.
38Now the man from whom the demons had departed
begged Him that he might be with Him. But Jesus sent him

8:37 [a]NU-Text reads *Gerasenes.*

YOU ARE THERE
8:22–25

What Kind of Storm Was This?

The Sea of Galilee was no place to be caught in a storm. The kind of weather that caught Jesus and His disciples occurs there to this day. As one traveler described it:

> The sun had scarcely set when the wind began to rush down towards the lake, and it continued all night long, with increasing violence, so that when we reached the shore the next morning the face of the lake was like a huge, boiling caldron . . . .
>
> We had to double-pin all the tent-ropes, and frequently were obliged to hang on with our whole weight upon them to keep the quivering tabernacle from being carried up bodily into the air.

The reason for such gale-force winds is the surrounding landscape. The lake is 700 feet below sea level, and is fed by rivers that have cut deep ravines surrounded by flat plains that are in turn hedged in by mountains. The ravines act like wind siphons or tunnels, gathering cooler air from the mountains as it crosses the plains. When the air mass runs into the hot lake shore, violent storms are whipped up with no warning.

Several of the disciples were experienced fishermen, well acquainted with such storms. However, they had never seen winds like those that attacked their boat (v. 23), for they turned to the Lord in utter terror, certain that all

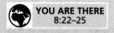

8:38–39 away, saying, 39"Return to your own house, and tell what great things God has done for you." And he went his way and proclaimed throughout the whole city what great things Jesus had done for him.

A Girl Restored to Life and a Woman Healed

40So it was, when Jesus returned, that the multitude welcomed Him, for they were all waiting for Him. 41And be-
hold, there came a man named Jairus, and he was a ruler of the synagogue. And he fell down at Jesus' feet and begged Him to come to his house, 42for he had an only daughter
about twelve years of age, and she was dying.

The First Gentile Evangelist?

A CLOSER LOOK 8:38–39 *The restored man was most likely a Gentile from the city of Gadara (vv. 38–39). Jesus sent him back home to tell his family and friends of God's power and grace—possibly making him the first known Gentile evangelist. See "Gadara," Mark 5:1.*

was lost. Yet their fear of the wind and the waves gave way to wonder and awe when Jesus turned and calmed the sea. ◆

Jesus drew most of His followers from the Galilee region, and carried out most of His ministry there. See "Galilee," Mark 1:14.

Why it Storms Over Galilee

Storms rapidly form over the Sea of Galilee when air masses from the surrounding higher plains and mountains are funneled through deep river ravines to meet the warm shore air rising off the lake.

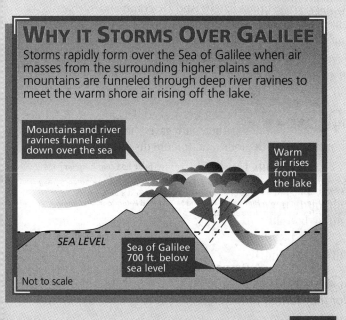

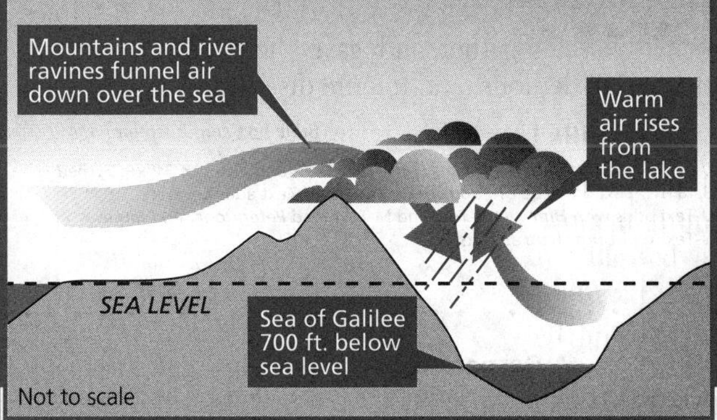

"Tell what great things God has done for you."
—Luke 8:39

8:43–44
But as He went, the multitudes
thronged Him. 43 Now a woman, having a
flow of blood for twelve years, who had spent all her livelihood on physicians and could not be healed by any, 44 came
from behind and touched the border of His garment. And
immediately her flow of blood stopped.
45 And Jesus said, "Who touched Me?"
When all denied it, Peter and those with him[a] said, "Master, the multitudes throng and press You, and You say, 'Who
touched Me?' "[b]
46 But Jesus said, "Somebody touched Me, for I perceived
power going out from Me." 47 Now when the woman saw
that she was not hidden, she came trembling; and falling
down before Him, she declared to Him in the presence of
all the people the reason she had touched Him and how she
was healed immediately.
48 And He said to her, "Daughter, be of good cheer;[a] your
faith has made you well. Go in peace."
49 While He was still speaking, someone came from the
ruler of the synagogue's *house,* saying to him, "Your daughter is dead. Do not trouble the Teacher."[a]
50 But when Jesus heard *it,* He answered him, saying, "Do
not be afraid; only believe, and she will be made well."
51 When He came into the house, He permitted no one to go
in[a] except Peter, James, and John,[b] and the father and
mother of the girl. 52 Now all wept and mourned for her;
but He said, "Do not weep; she is not dead, but sleeping."
53 And they ridiculed Him, knowing that she was dead.
54 But He put them all outside,[a] took her by the hand and
called, saying, "Little girl, arise." 55 Then her spirit returned,
and she arose immediately. And He commanded that she be
given *something* to eat. 56 And her parents were astonished,
but He charged them to tell no one what had happened.

"YOUR FAITH HAS MADE YOU WELL. GO IN PEACE." —Luke 8:48

CHAPTER 9

Jesus Sends Out the Twelve

9:1–62
1 Then He called His twelve disciples
together and gave them power and au-
thority over all demons, and to cure diseases. 2 He sent them

(Bible text continued on page 250)

8:45 [a]NU-Text omits *and those with him.* [b]NU-Text omits *and You say, 'Who touched Me?'* *8:48* [a]NU-Text omits *be of good cheer.* *8:49* [a]NU-Text adds *anymore.* *8:51* [a]NU-Text adds *with Him.* [b]NU-Text and M-Text read *Peter, John, and James.* *8:54* [a]NU-Text omits *put them all outside.*

A Desperate Grasp for Help

A CLOSER LOOK 8:43–44
For more on this woman's attempt to find relief, see "A Desperate Woman," Mark 5:26.

CONSIDER THIS
9:1–62

CAN LAITY GET THE JOB DONE?

Are you surprised by Jesus' choice of His leadership team? A close reading of Luke 9 suggests that the Twelve were not exactly prize recruits for a new spiritual movement. They showed some frightening patterns and embarrassing traits that might cause a manager to wonder, "Who hired these people? How in the world can they possibly get the job done?"

Jesus recruited them, and He delegated real power and authority to them to get the job done (v. 1), not just token responsibilities, as often happens when leaders "delegate" tasks to subordinates (vv. 2–6). When they reported back from their first assignment (v. 10), He took them aside for a "performance review" at a private place near Bethsaida, a small fishing village on the north of Galilee and hometown to several team members. From that point, the Twelve made eight identifiable mistakes that we might assume would disqualify them from leadership:

(1) *They acted from a short-sighted vision.* When their retreat was interrupted by a crowd eager to meet Jesus, all they could see was their limited resources in a desert place (vv. 12–13).

(2) *Some of them fell asleep at a moment of great opportunity.* When Jesus met with Moses and Elijah, two of the greatest leaders in Israel's history, Peter, James, and John were caught napping (vv. 28–32).

(3) *They tried to preserve the status quo.* Peter wanted to hang on to a good experience and build monuments to it (vv. 33–36).

(4) *They gave way to fear of the unknown.* Jesus healed an epileptic boy, but fear caused the Twelve not to ask questions when they were confused (vv. 43–45).

(5) *They competed to see who would be top dog.* The disciples argued over greatness and privilege rather than concern themselves with serving others. Contrast that with Jesus' treatment of seekers, especially "children" and "the least" (vv. 46–48).

(6) *They dallied in partisan politics.* Encountering a rival teacher, the disciples tried to claim exclusive rights to God's activity. By contrast, Jesus included any and all who were sincerely interested in serving God in His name (vv. 49–50).

(7) *They plotted a dirty tricks campaign.* When their ethnic enemies proved inhospitable, the Twelve turned vicious. Jesus replied by issuing one of His strongest rebukes (vv. 51–56).

(8) *They bit off more than they could chew.* As they traveled along, Jesus' followers overstated their commitment; in the end they failed to deliver what they promised (vv. 57–62).

Despite these shortcomings, Jesus not only kept the Twelve on His team, He kept them as His first team! He showed that undeveloped rookies can be developed into servant-leaders—over time. Even though they were weak, competitive, self-centered, unrealistic about themselves, and insensitive to others, He kept working with them. The Lord's hopes were rewarded, but only after His death and resurrection. Luke 9 is merely the beginning of the story. The outcome can be found in Acts, where Luke goes on to show that God uses empowered laypeople like the Twelve—and like us today—to do His work.

Can we as laity do the work of God? Absolutely! But as we do, we need to take a serious look at ourselves and ask God to help us purge out those mistaken attitudes that we share with Jesus' early leaders. ◆

Who were the twelve men that Jesus chose to spread His message in Luke 9? See "The Twelve," Matt. 10:2.

Herod's Curiosity

CONSIDER THIS 9:7 **Herod's interest in Jesus (vv. 7–9) is a reminder that pragmatic politicians often seem at a loss when it comes to the subtle doctrines of religion. Just as his father Herod the Great was "troubled" at the birth of the Christ child (Matt. 2:3), so Herod Antipas was "perplexed" by Jesus.**

The ruler wanted to find out exactly who it was he was dealing with. No sooner had he done away with John the Baptist than this new figure, Jesus, had appeared. The speculations of his advisors must have exasperated him, for while they put a religious "spin" on events, they explained nothing.

The tragedy is that even when Herod eventually got his wish and met Jesus face to face, Jesus remained an enigma to him (Luke 23:7–9). No doubt the Lord recognized that Herod's curiosity was not born of faith. Politicians, whose job it is to wield power, have often perceived the extraordinary power in religion, and many have sought to either eliminate it or make it their ally. Such was likely the case with Herod. His interest in Jesus surely had more to do with political expediency than any religious sincerity.

So it was with most of the other authorities that encountered Jesus, His followers, and the gospel. None of them recognized who it was they were dealing with; if they had, Paul later wrote, "they would not have crucified the Lord of glory" (1 Cor. 2:8).

Herod Antipas was given Galilee and Perea to rule, inheriting the title of "tetrarch" (ruler of a fourth part). *Rome liked to divide conquered territories into four parts under separate rulers. For more on the infamous family of Herod, see the article at Acts 12:1–2.*

to preach the kingdom of God and to heal the sick. 3And
He said to them, "Take nothing for the journey, neither
staffs nor bag nor bread nor money; and do not have two
tunics apiece.
4"Whatever house you enter, stay there, and from there
depart. 5And whoever will not receive you, when you go
out of that city, shake off the very dust from your feet as a
testimony against them."
6So they departed and went through the towns, preaching
the gospel and healing everywhere.

Herod Seeks to See Jesus

9:7 7Now Herod the tetrarch heard of all
that was done by Him; and he was per-
plexed, because it was said by some that John had risen
from the dead, 8and by some that Elijah had appeared, and
by others that one of the old prophets had risen again.
9Herod said, "John I have beheaded, but who is this of
whom I hear such things?" So he sought to see Him.

Jesus Feeds 5,000

10And the apostles, when they had returned, told Him all
that they had done. Then He took them and went aside privately into a deserted place belonging to the city called
Bethsaida. 11But when the multitudes knew *it,* they followed
Him; and He received them and spoke to them about the
kingdom of God, and healed those who had need of healing. 12When the day began to wear away, the twelve came
and said to Him, "Send the multitude away, that they may
go into the surrounding towns and country, and lodge and
get provisions; for we are in a deserted place here."
13But He said to them, "You give them something to eat."
And they said, "We have no more than five loaves and
two fish, unless we go and buy food for all these people."
14For there were about five thousand men.
Then He said to His disciples, "Make them sit down in
groups of fifty." 15And they did so, and made them all sit
down.
16Then He took the five loaves and the two fish, and
looking up to heaven, He blessed and broke *them,* and gave
them to the disciples to set before the multitude. 17So they
all ate and were filled, and twelve baskets of the leftover
fragments were taken up by them.

Peter Recognizes Jesus as the Christ

18And it happened, as He was alone praying, *that* His disciples joined Him, and He asked them, saying, "Who do the
crowds say that I am?"
19So they answered and said, "John the Baptist, but some

say Elijah; and others *say* that one of the old prophets has risen again."

20He said to them, "But who do you say that I am?"

Peter answered and said, "The Christ of God."

Jesus Predicts His Death

21And He strictly warned and commanded them to tell this to no one, 22saying, "The Son of Man must suffer many things, and be rejected by the elders and chief priests and scribes, and be killed, and be raised the third day."

23Then He said to *them* all, "If anyone desires to come after Me, let him deny himself, and take up his cross daily,[a] and follow Me. 24For whoever desires to save his life will lose it, but whoever loses his life for My sake will save it.

9:25

25For what profit is it to a man if he gains the whole world, and is himself destroyed or lost? 26For whoever is ashamed of Me and My words, of him the Son of Man will be ashamed when He comes in His *own* glory, and *in His* Father's, and of the holy angels. 27But I tell you truly, there are some standing here who shall not taste death till they see the kingdom of God."

The Transfiguration

28Now it came to pass, about eight days after these sayings, that He took Peter, John, and James and went up on the mountain to pray. 29As He prayed, the appearance of His face was altered, and His robe *became* white *and* glistening. 30And behold, two men talked with Him, who were Moses and Elijah, 31who appeared in glory and spoke of His decease which He was about to accomplish at Jerusalem. 32But Peter and those with him were heavy with sleep; and when they were fully awake, they saw His glory and the two men who stood with Him. 33Then it happened, as they were parting from Him, *that* Peter said to Jesus, "Master, it is good for us to be here; and let us make three tabernacles: one for You, one for Moses, and one for Elijah"—not knowing what he said.

34While he was saying this, a cloud came and overshadowed them; and they were fearful as they entered the cloud. 35And a voice came out of the cloud, saying, "This is My beloved Son.[a] Hear Him!" 36When the voice had ceased, Jesus was found alone. But they kept quiet, and told no one in those days any of the things they had seen.

A Man's Demon-possessed Son Healed

37Now it happened on the next day, when they had come down from the mountain, that a great multitude met Him.

9:23 [a]M-Text omits *daily*. **9:35** [a]NU-Text reads *This is My Son, the Chosen One.*

The Real Bottom Line

CONSIDER THIS 9:25 **Businesspeople commonly talk about the "bottom line," usually meaning the *financial* bottom line. In v. 25 Christ challenges us to look at another bottom line—the final accounting each of us will give to God for how we have spent our lives.**

Clearly one can be very successful from a human point of view and yet be finally lost. Moreover, a careless Christian's works will be judged adversely. That can happen both actively and passively. Actively, we can sell out to the world's values by lying to a customer, cheating on a deal, or running over others to advance our position. Passively, we can drift away from God by leaving Him out of our work and lives, or perhaps by sacrificing our families in order to pursue wealth and status. Either way, the "bottom line" is clear: we will bring ourselves to ultimate loss.

Jesus had more to say about what really matters to God in the story of the talents. See "True Success Means Faithfulness," Matt. 25:14–30.

9:38–42

38Suddenly a man from the multitude cried out, saying, "Teacher, I implore You, look on my son, for he is my only child. 39And behold, a spirit seizes him, and he suddenly cries out; it convulses him so that he foams *at the mouth;* and it departs from him with great difficulty, bruising him. 40So I implored Your disciples to cast it out, but they could not."

41Then Jesus answered and said, "O faithless and perverse generation, how long shall I be with you and bear with you? Bring your son here." 42And as he was still coming, the demon threw him down and convulsed *him.* Then Jesus rebuked the unclean spirit, healed the child, and gave him back to his father.

Jesus Again Predicts His Death

43And they were all amazed at the majesty of God.

But while everyone marveled at all the things which Jesus did, He said to His disciples, 44"Let these words sink down into your ears, for the Son of Man is about to be betrayed

CONSIDER THIS
9:38–42

WHATEVER BECAME OF "DEMON POSSESSION"?

For all the good they've contributed to the healing professions and pastoral care, some theories of psychology have done a great disservice by casting doubt on the objective reality of evil and the devil. That presents a problem for those who read the Bible's accounts of demon possession (for example, vv. 38–42) and believe that demonic powers can play a hand in physical illnesses.

Some schools of psychology reduce religious experience to nothing but unconscious drives projected onto the external world. Satan, they say, is no more than a personification of one's deepest, darkest emotions. Likewise, God is reduced to the embodiment of a fully authenticated self, parental ideals, social mores, or universal symbols of goodness.

Without question, a genuine encounter with God or with Satan may involve intense emotional and psychological experiences. But that does not make either one any less real. The existence of Satan and demons is affirmed in scores of scriptural texts. (A demon is a fallen angel or spirit that has joined with Satan in his futile rebellion against God.) At war with Jesus and His followers, these evil powers have played a major role in such events as the fall, the flood, and Jesus' crucifixion, and will figure in the tribulations that will someday wrack the earth and in the final judgment.

The Gospels record several dozen encounters between

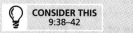

into the hands of men." [45]But they did not understand this saying, and it was hidden from them so that they did not perceive it; and they were afraid to ask Him about this saying.

Teaching about Rank

9:46–48

[46]Then a dispute arose among them as to which of them would be greatest.
[47]And Jesus, perceiving the thought of their heart, took a little child and set him by Him, [48]and said to them, "Whoever
receives this little child in My name receives Me; and whoever receives Me receives Him who sent Me. For he who is
least among you all will be great."
[49]Now John answered and said, "Master, we saw someone
casting out demons in Your name, and we forbade him because he does not follow with us."
[50]But Jesus said to him, "Do not forbid *him,* for he who is
not against us[a] is on our[b] side."

9:50 [a]NU-Text reads *you.* [b]NU-Text reads *your.*

Jesus and the powers of evil. In many of those instances, demon possession had produced any number of physical maladies and manifestations:

- *deafness (Mark 9:25)*
- *muteness (Matt. 12:22; Mark 9:17–25)*
- *bodily deformity (Luke 13:10–17)*
- *blindness (Matt. 12:22)*
- *epileptic seizure (Luke 9:39)*

Ailments like these did not automatically imply demon possession. In fact, distinctions were made between possession and physical illness unrelated to evil spirits (Matt. 4:24; 10:8; Mark 1:32; Luke 6:17–18).

By casting out demons and restoring people both physically and spiritually, Jesus showed that the kingdom of God was as real as, and more powerful than, the forces of Satan (Matt. 10:7–8; 12:28). Today, that same work has been delegated to the church (Luke 10:17; Acts 16:18). Psychology is often helpful in the task, but it is no match for the kingdom of darkness. Only the "whole armor of God" can help believers prevail (Eph. 6:10–18). ◆

One of Jesus' primary purposes was to overcome the power of Satan, which is why He regularly challenged the demonic realm. See "Demons," Luke 11:14.

Competition versus Compassion

CONSIDER THIS 9:46–48

Do you compete to prove your significance? Do you crave greatness? Do you measure your self-worth not only by whether you win, but by how much?

Jesus saw that His followers were in the grip of this common way of thinking (v. 46). So He placed a child in front of them and affirmed that childlikeness is more desirable to God than competition. He went so far as to state that welcoming the child in His name would be like welcoming Him. While the disciples aspired to positions of power and prestige, their Lord exalted the humble act of serving a child as more important.

Jesus calls us to follow a very different value system than our world's. Position, success, and beating the competition fade in comparison to caring for those around us who are weak and forgotten. He beckons us as His followers to replace competition with compassion.

Who near you needs affirmation and help?

Samaritans Reject Jesus

9:51–56

51 Now it came to pass, when the time
had come for Him to be received up, that
He steadfastly set His face to go to Jerusalem, 52 and sent
messengers before His face. And as they went, they entered
a village of the Samaritans, to prepare for Him. 53 But they
did not receive Him, because His face was *set* for the journey to Jerusalem. 54 And when His disciples James and John
saw *this,* they said, "Lord, do You want us to command fire
to come down from heaven and consume them, just as Elijah did?"[a]
55 But He turned and rebuked them,[a] and said, "You do
not know what manner of spirit you are of. 56 For the Son of
Man did not come to destroy men's lives but to save *them.*"[a]
And they went to another village.

9:54 [a]NU-Text omits *just as Elijah did.* *9:55* [a]NU-Text omits the rest of this verse.
9:56 [a]NU-Text omits the first sentence of this verse.

CONSIDER THIS
9:51–56

Condemnation or Compassion?

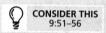

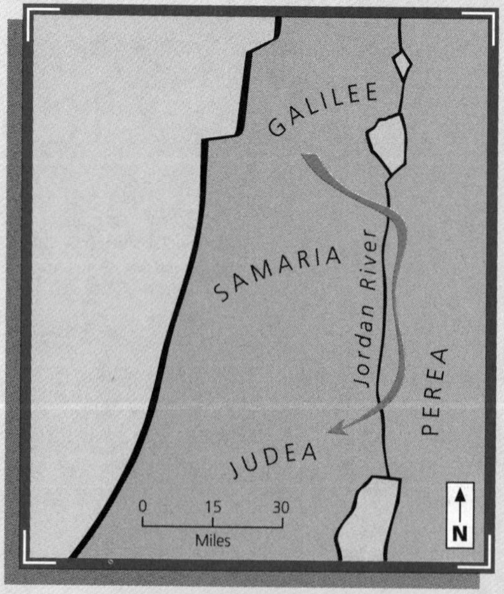

BYPASSING SAMARIA

Heading south from Galilee to Jerusalem (v. 51), Jesus traveled with His disciples through Samaria (v. 52). Prejudiced against the Samaritans (John 4:9), Jews commonly bypassed this region by journeying down the east bank of the Jordan River. But Jesus deliberately chose the more direct route, as if to seek out conflict rather than avoid it.

Confrontation erupted at the first village. The Samaritans did not want Jesus or His followers there, nor did the disciples want to be there. Neither group could see past the other's ethnic identity. But the disciples turned exceptionally ugly. Insulted by the villagers' rejection of their Lord, they were itching to call down fire from heaven—with the justification (according to most manuscripts), "just as Elijah did."

Their response shows how terribly destructive centuries of hatred and bitterness can be. In their case, it actually distorted their interpretation of Scripture. For Elijah had called down fire to consume a sacrifice, not people. In fact, he prayed for the demonstration of God's power in order to turn people back to the Lord, not to punish them (1 Kin. 18:36–39).

No wonder Jesus utterly rebuked this response. He realized that His followers were blinded by their presumption of religious and ethnic superiority. In rebuke, He reminded them of His mission: to save lives—even Samaritan lives—not to destroy them.

The Costs of Discipleship

57Now it happened as they journeyed on the road, *that* someone said to Him, "Lord, I will follow You wherever You go."

9:58

58And Jesus said to him, "Foxes have holes and birds of the air *have* nests, but the Son of Man has nowhere to lay *His* head."

59Then He said to another, "Follow Me."

But he said, "Lord, let me first go and bury my father."

60Jesus said to him, "Let the dead bury their own dead, but you go and preach the kingdom of God."

Nowhere to Lay His Head

A CLOSER LOOK 9:58

Like John the Baptist before Him, Jesus lived without a home (v. 58). He was born into relative poverty and never left it (2:24). For more on Jesus' lifestyle, see "A Poor Family Comes into Wealth," Matt. 2:11, and "Jesus—A Homeless Man?" Matt. 8:20.

We as Jesus' followers today need to consider this incident carefully. Who do we regard with condemnation rather than compassion? Is it someone of another race or a different ideology? Our differences may arise from legitimate concerns. But if we would just as soon see someone eliminated in order to reinforce our feelings of ethnic, racial, moral, theological, or spiritual superiority, then we need the rebuke of Jesus' words: "You do not know what manner of spirit you are of" (v. 55).

As we read in John 3:17, "God did not send His Son into the world to condemn the world, but that the world through Him might be saved." ◆

This incident was only one in a series of courses that Jesus taught on relating to Samaritans. His next lesson proved to be one of the most memorable. See "Who Was the Neighbor?" Luke 10:37.

The disciples had grown up in a culture deeply divided along ethnic lines. To find out more about the Samaritan minority, see "'Jews Have No Dealings with Samaritans,'" John 4:9.

"THE SON OF MAN HAS NOWHERE TO LAY HIS HEAD."
—Luke 9:58

61And another also said, "Lord, I will follow You, but let
me first go *and* bid them farewell who are at my house."
62But Jesus said to him, "No one, having put his hand to
the plow, and looking back, is fit for the kingdom of God."

CHAPTER 10

Jesus Sends Out Seventy Workers

10:1

1After these things the Lord appointed
seventy others also,[a] and sent them two
by two before His face into every city and place where He
Himself was about to go. 2Then He said to them, "The harvest truly *is* great, but the laborers *are* few; therefore pray
the Lord of the harvest to send out laborers into His harvest. 3Go your way; behold, I send you out as lambs among

10:1 [a]NU-Text reads *seventy-two others.*

CONSIDER THIS
10:1

DELEGATION AND AFFIRMATION

Is delegation hard for you? When faced with a choice between letting others do a task or doing it yourself, do you tend to sigh, "It's easier to do it myself"? Do you give others, such as coworkers, relatives, or friends, not only the responsibility but the needed authority to get the job done—even if it means seeing it done their way instead of yours?

Certainly Jesus had more reason than any of us to avoid delegating His work to others. When it came to proclaiming His kingdom, He had every right to lack confidence in His band of followers. He had experienced their failings firsthand (Luke 9:10–50). Yet He sent out seventy workers with full appointment to preach and heal on His behalf (10:1, 16).

In doing so, Jesus affirmed the often heard but less often practiced concept of people and their development as the most important task of a manager. Certainly He gave the seventy workers detailed instructions before sending them off (vv. 2–12). But a study of His discipleship methods shows that He was just as concerned with their growth as He was that the task be accomplished or done in a certain way.

Jesus accomplished the work He came to do. He hardly needed seventy neophytes to help Him! But He was clear that people matter, and that His disciples would grow only if they held real responsibility and authority. No wonder the seventy returned "with joy," excited by their experiences (v. 17). They would never be the same again.

Whom do you need to give more responsibility to and affirm with greater encouragement? ◆

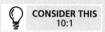

wolves. 4Carry neither money bag, knapsack, nor sandals;
and greet no one along the road. 5But whatever house you
enter, first say, 'Peace to this house.' 6And if a son of peace is
there, your peace will rest on it; if not, it will return to you.
7And remain in the same house, eating and drinking such
things as they give, for the laborer is worthy of his wages.
Do not go from house to house. 8Whatever city you enter,
and they receive you, eat such things as are set before you.
9And heal the sick there, and say to them, 'The kingdom of
God has come near to you.' 10But whatever city you enter,
and they do not receive you, go out into its streets and say,
11'The very dust of your city which clings to us[a] we wipe off
against you. Nevertheless know this, that the kingdom of
God has come near you.' 12But[a] I say to you that it will be
more tolerable in that Day for Sodom than for that city.
13"Woe to you, Chorazin! Woe to you, Bethsaida! For if
the mighty works which were done in you had been done
in Tyre and Sidon, they would have repented long ago, sitting in sackcloth and ashes. 14But it will be more tolerable
10:15 for Tyre and Sidon at the judgment than
for you. 15And you, Capernaum, who are
exalted to heaven, will be brought down to Hades.[a] 16He
who hears you hears Me, he who rejects you rejects Me, and
he who rejects Me rejects Him who sent Me."

The Joy of Jesus

17Then the seventy[a] returned with joy, saying, "Lord, even
the demons are subject to us in Your name."
18And He said to them, "I saw Satan fall like lightning
from heaven. 19Behold, I give you the authority to trample
on serpents and scorpions, and over all the power of the enemy, and nothing shall by any means hurt you. 20Neverthe-
less do not rejoice in this, that the spirits are subject to you,
but rather[a] rejoice because your names are written in
heaven."
21In that hour Jesus rejoiced in the Spirit and said, "I
thank You, Father, Lord of heaven and earth, that You have
hidden these things from *the* wise and prudent and revealed
them to babes. Even so, Father, for so it seemed good in
Your sight. 22All[a] things have been delivered to Me by My
Father, and no one knows who the Son is except the Father,
and who the Father is except the Son, and *the one* to whom
the Son wills to reveal *Him*."
23Then He turned to *His* disciples and said privately,
"Blessed *are* the eyes which see the things you see; 24for I

10:11 [a]NU-Text reads *our feet.* *10:12* [a]NU-Text and M-Text omit *But.* *10:15* [a]NU-Text reads *will you be exalted to heaven? You will be thrust down to Hades!* *10:17* [a]NU-Text reads *seventy-two.* *10:20* [a]NU-Text and M-Text omit *rather.* *10:22* [a]M-Text reads *And turning to the disciples He said, "All . . . .*

Capernaum, City of Unfulfilled Potential

YOU ARE THERE 10:15 **Jesus visited Capernaum after performing His first miracle at nearby Cana (John 2:1–12). His ministry in Capernaum was a fulfillment of Old Testament prophecy concerning the Messiah (Is. 9:1; Matt. 4:13–15). Jesus wanted the people of Capernaum to embrace His message with wholehearted faith. In addition to their bondage to the Romans, to their economic systems, to their petty political factions and kingdoms, and to their religious traditions, they were also in bondage to sin. He wanted them to turn to Him for salvation and deliverance and to reflect His light to the surrounding peoples, strategically located as they were.**

But the majority of Galileans were not responsive to His warnings to repent (Matt. 4:17), despite the many miracles He performed there. In the end, Jesus denounced Capernaum, along with her neighbors, Chorazin and Bethsaida (Matt. 11:23–24), prophesying that they would all come to ruin (Luke 10:13–15). His words were fulfilled when the prosperous city was destroyed during the Jewish-Roman war of A.D. 66–70. Rebuilt later as a center of Judaism, Capernaum was destroyed for good by the Arabs in the seventh century.

Love Your Neighbor

CONSIDER THIS 10:27–28 **How easy it is to excuse ourselves when we see someone in need by thinking, "There's no reason why I should get involved. Those people are strangers, and I have no obligation to them."**

But Scripture doesn't let us off that easily. Obviously we can't help every needy person we come across. Or can we? We can at least pray! At any rate, the lawyer's restatement of Leviticus 19:18 (v. 27) and Christ's response (v. 28) show that in fact we do have an obligation to strangers—even though we've made no commitments to them.

As Jesus goes on to show in the parable of the good Samaritan (vv. 29–37), we who intend to follow Him have a responsibility to everyone in the human race, because everyone is our neighbor. We are to demonstrate "mercy" to all (v. 37). Or, as Paul later wrote, "do good to all" (Gal. 6:10).

It is not enough to love just one's neighbor, however. Jesus challenges His followers to love even their enemies, Luke 6:27–31.

tell you that many prophets and kings have desired to see what you see, and have not seen *it,* and to hear what you hear, and have not heard *it.*"

A Parable about a Good Samaritan

25And behold, a certain lawyer stood up and tested Him,
saying, "Teacher, what shall I do to inherit eternal life?"
26He said to him, "What is written in the law? What is
your reading *of it?*"
10:27–28
27So he answered and said, " 'You shall
love the LORD your God with all your
heart, with all your soul, with all your strength, and with all
your mind,'[a] and 'your neighbor as yourself.' "[b]
28And He said to him, "You have answered rightly; do this
and you will live."
29But he, wanting to justify himself, said to Jesus, "And
who is my neighbor?"
10:30
30Then Jesus answered and said: "A
certain *man* went down from Jerusalem
to Jericho, and fell among thieves, who stripped him of his
clothing, wounded *him,* and departed, leaving *him* half
10:30–37
dead. 31Now by chance a certain priest
came down that road. And when he saw
him, he passed by on the other side. 32Likewise a Levite,
when he arrived at the place, came and looked, and passed
by on the other side. 33But a certain Samaritan, as he journeyed, came where he was. And when he saw him, he had
compassion. 34So he went to *him* and bandaged his wounds,
pouring on oil and wine; and he set him on his own animal,
10:35
brought him to an inn, and took care of
him. 35On the next day, when he de-
parted,[a] he took out two denarii, gave *them* to the inn-
keeper, and said to him, 'Take care of him; and whatever
more you spend, when I come again, I will repay you.' 36So
which of these three do you think was neighbor to him who
fell among the thieves?"
10:37 see pg. 261
37And he said, "He who showed mercy
on him."
Then Jesus said to him, "Go and do likewise."

10:27 [a]Deuteronomy 6:5 [b]Leviticus 19:18 *10:35* [a]NU-Text omits *when he departed.*

Heartstrings and Purse Strings

A CLOSER LOOK 10:35 *Heartstrings and purse strings are often tied together. The Samaritan was praised for mercy, but one way he showed it was through generosity (v. 35). For more on the ties between the heart and wealth, see "Don't Worry!" Matt. 6:19–34; "Christians and Money," 1 Tim. 6:6–19; and "Getting Yours," James 5:1–6.*

Jesus at Martha and Mary's House

10:38
[38]Now it happened as they went that
He entered a certain village; and a certain
woman named Martha welcomed Him into her house.
[39]And she had a sister called Mary, who also sat at Jesus'[a]
feet and heard His word. [40]But Martha was distracted with
much serving, and she approached Him and said, "Lord, do
You not care that my sister has left me to serve alone?
Therefore tell her to help me."
[41]And Jesus[a] answered and said to her, "Martha, Martha,
10:38–42 see pg. 260
you are worried and troubled about
many things. [42]But one thing is needed,
and Mary has chosen that good part, which will not be
taken away from her."

10:39 [a]NU-Text reads *the Lord's.* *10:41* [a]NU-Text reads *the Lord.*

The Village of Bethany

A CLOSER LOOK 10:38 *The "certain village" that Jesus visited (v. 38) was Bethany, a suburb of Jerusalem and a favorite stopover for Jesus on His trips to and from the city. Find out more about Bethany at John 11:18.*

THE GOOD NEIGHBOR

CONSIDER THIS 10:30–37 *The parable in vv. 30–37 takes place along the road from Jerusalem to Jericho. Descending through rugged, mountainous terrain, the route was ideal for ambush. There were many hiding places for bandits and little likelihood of help for the unfortunate victim.*

But even though the story takes place in a rural setting, it speaks to a number of important urban issues: racial and ethnic divisions, violent crime, even the struggle of small businesses to collect on their debts. The Samaritan—the good neighbor—addresses each of these needs. He does not eliminate the problems, but he acts as an agent of mercy to overcome them in small but effective ways.

His example challenges us as modern Christians, especially those of us living in cities among countless victims like the hapless man in the parable, to consider how we can be neighbors. How can we "go and do likewise"?

JERICHO

YOU ARE THERE 10:30

- **Ancient city located northeast of Jerusalem on the west bank of the Jordan River.**
- **Name means "city of palms" (Deut. 34:3).**
- **Made famous by the Old Testament report of its dramatic defeat by Joshua and the Israelites (Josh. 6:1–21).**
- **Site of Herod the Great's winter palace.**
- **Notorious for the beggars and thieves who camped nearby, plundering travelers along the narrow, winding mountain road up to Jerusalem.**

Herod was fond of building projects, but is remembered more for political corruption. See "The Herods," Acts 12:1–2.

CHAPTER 11

Instructions on Prayer

1Now it came to pass, as He was praying in a certain
place, when He ceased, *that* one of His disciples said to
Him, "Lord, teach us to pray, as John also taught his disciples."

"YOUR WILL BE DONE ON EARTH. . . ." —Luke 11:2

PERSONALITY PROFILE: MARTHA OF BETHANY

CONSIDER THIS 10:38–42

Home: Bethany, near Jerusalem.

Family: Sister of Mary and Lazarus (John 11:1).

Occupation: Homemaker.

Known today for: Being "distracted" in her preparations when Jesus and His disciples came to visit.

MARTHA, THE "PRACTICAL" ONE

Jesus' visit to Martha's home (Luke 10:38–42) has given rise to a caricature of Martha as obsessively "practical," as opposed to Mary, her "spiritual" sister. In fact, some would use this incident to reinforce a hierarchy of "spiritual" concerns over "secular" ones: it is more important to "sit at Jesus' feet"—that is, to engage in religious pursuits such as prayer or attending church—than to be "distracted" with everyday tasks such as work or household chores.

But it would be unfair to read Jesus' words to Martha as a rebuke for her preparations. After all, He had come as a guest to her home with His disciples. Someone was obligated to prepare a meal—a large meal. Assuming Jesus and the twelve, plus Mary, Martha, and Lazarus, there were at least 17 hungry people. No wonder Martha was "distracted [literally, drawn away*] with much serving" (v. 40). She could not sit and chat with her guests if she was to prepare the food.*

So what was Jesus getting at in vv. 41–42? Only this: that in addition to her marvelous preparations, Martha needed to add spiritual sensitivity. He was in no way set-

[2]So He said to them, "When you pray, say:

Our Father in heaven,[a]
Hallowed be Your name.
Your kingdom come.[b]
Your will be done
On earth as *it is* in heaven.
3 Give us day by day our daily bread.
4 And forgive us our sins,
For we also forgive everyone who is indebted to us.
And do not lead us into temptation,
But deliver us from the evil one."[a]

11:5–13 see pg. 264

[5]And He said to them, "Which of you shall have a friend, and go to him at midnight and say to him, 'Friend, lend me three loaves; [6]for a friend of mine has come to me on his journey, and I have nothing to set before him'; [7]and he will answer from within and say, 'Do not trouble me; the door is now shut, and my children are with me in bed; I cannot rise and give to you'? [8]I say to you, though he will not rise and give to him because he is his friend, yet because of his persistence he will rise and give him as many as he needs.

(Bible text continued on page 263)

11:2 [a]NU-Text omits *Our* and *in heaven.* [b]NU-Text omits the rest of this verse.
11:4 [a]NU-Text omits *But deliver us from the evil one.*

ting up a dichotomy between the sacred and the secular, but merely emphasizing that in the midst of her busyness, Martha should not lose sight of who He was and why He had come. Without question, Mary had that insight, and Jesus was keen to preserve it.

Apparently Martha profited from Jesus' exhortation, for when her brother Lazarus died, she recognized His ability as the Christ to raise him from the dead (John 11:27).

Like Martha, we today are called on to strike a balance between faithful, diligent service in our day-to-day responsibilities and a constant attitude of dependence on the Lord. ◆

What was involved in Martha's preparations for her guests? See "Jewish Homemaking," Mark 1:29–31.

Are you quiet, withdrawn, or shy? If so, Martha's sister, Mary, may be a model for you. She demonstrates that preaching sermons or leading movements are not the only ways to follow Jesus. See John 11:1.

WHO WAS THE NEIGHBOR?

CONSIDER THIS 10:37 **The parable of the good Samaritan (vv. 30–37) is one of Jesus' most popular. It reduces an abstract theological question, "What shall I do to inherit eternal life" (v. 25), to a simpler, more practical challenge: "Go and do likewise [i.e., show mercy]" (v. 37).**

The story begins with the lawyer's self-justifying question, "Who is my neighbor?" But Jesus turned the question around: "Which of these three do you think was neighbor to him who fell among the thieves?" What matters, Jesus implied, is not identifying needs, but meeting them. The question is not *Who is my neighbor?*, but rather *Am I a neighbor to others?*

What makes the story so poignant, however, is the contrast between the Jewish priest and Levite who avoid the half-dead victim, and the Samaritan who shows him compassion. Jesus was playing on the deep-seated animosity that existed between the two groups (see "Samaria," John 4:4). He knew His listeners would find it hard enough to show mercy, but unthinkable that a Samaritan would illustrate how. Prejudiced people find it almost impossible to think that their ethnic enemies might be compassionate human beings.

Jesus' challenge to "go and do likewise" is a test for us as we consider the many racial and ethnic divisions in the world today. God is interested in mercy, not maintaining prejudice.

Jesus' own disciples were blinded by ethnic pride. They thought Samaritans ought to be destroyed. See "Condemnation or Compassion?" Luke 9:51–56.

On another occasion, a Samaritan's faith put Jews to shame. See "Where Are the Others?" Luke 17:11–19.

FOR YOUR INFO
11:14

DEMONS

Popular culture tends to dismiss demons as nothing but an imaginative fantasy similar to the "daemons" of Greek mythology, supposedly supernatural beings that mediated between the gods and humans. But Scripture presents demons not as mythological creatures, but as real beings involved in historical events. Jesus, for example, frequently encountered demons during His ministry, as in the case of the demon-possessed mute (v. 14).

DEMONS in the NEW TESTAMENT

- unclean spirits (Matt. 10:1; Mark 6:7)
- Legion, probably a collective name for a group of demons rather than the name of a single demon (Mark 5:9; Luke 8:30)
- wicked or evil spirits (Luke 7:21; Acts 19:12–13)
- a spirit of divination (Acts 16:16)
- deceiving spirits (1 Tim. 4:1)
- the spirit of error (1 John 4:6)
- spirits of demons (Rev. 16:14)

Demons are fallen angels who joined with Satan in rebellion against God. The Bible does not explicitly discuss their origin, but the New Testament does speak of the fall and later imprisonment of a group of angels (2 Pet. 2:4; Jude 6). Their rebellion apparently occurred before God's creation of the world. Afterward, Satan and his followers roamed the new creation, eventually contaminating the human race with wickedness (Gen. 3; Matt. 25:41; Rev. 12:9). To this day they continue to oppose God's purposes and undermine the cause of righteousness.

Demon Possession

One of Jesus' primary purposes was to overcome the power of Satan, which is why He regularly challenged the demonic realm (Matt. 12:25–29; Luke 11:17–22; John 12:31; 1 John 3:8). One of His most compassionate activities was to release persons possessed by demons.

Again, our culture tends to dismiss demon possession as a quaint, archaic way of trying to explain physical and psychological conditions. But the Bible never suggests that all ailments are the result of demonic activity, only that demons can afflict people with physical symptoms such as muteness (Matt. 12:22; Mark 9:17, 25), deafness (Mark 9:25), blindness (Matt. 12:22), and bodily deformity (Luke 13:10–17). The Gospels actually distinguish between sickness and demon possession (Matt. 4:24; Mark 1:32; Luke 6:17–18).

Demons can also cause mental and emotional problems (Matt. 8:28; Acts 19:13–16). The demon-possessed might rant and rave (Mark 1:23–24; John 10:20), have uncontrolled fits (Luke 9:37–42; Mark 1:26), and behave in an antisocial manner (Luke 8:27, 35).

In casting out demons, Jesus and His disciples used methods that differed radically from the mystical rites so often employed in that time. Through His simple command Jesus expelled them (Mark 1:25; 5:8; 9:25). His disciples did the same, adding only the authority of Jesus' name to their command (Luke 10:17; Acts 16:18). Even some who were not His followers invoked the Lord's power (Luke 9:49; Acts 19:13).

Despite these straightforward means, Jesus' enemies accused

(continued on next page)

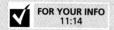

9"So I say to you, ask, and it will be given to you; seek,
and you will find; knock, and it will be opened to you.
10For everyone who asks receives, and he who seeks finds,
and to him who knocks it will be opened. 11If a son asks for
bread[a] from any father among you, will he give him a stone?
Or if *he asks* for a fish, will he give him a serpent instead of
a fish? 12Or if he asks for an egg, will he offer him a scorpion? 13If you then, being evil, know how to give good gifts
to your children, how much more will *your* heavenly Father
give the Holy Spirit to those who ask Him!"

Jesus' Power Called Satanic

11:14

14And He was casting out a demon,
and it was mute. So it was, when the de-
mon had gone out, that the mute spoke; and the multitudes
marveled. 15But some of them said, "He casts out demons
by Beelzebub,[a] the ruler of the demons."
16Others, testing *Him,* sought from Him a sign from
heaven. 17But He, knowing their thoughts, said to them:
"Every kingdom divided against itself is brought to desolation, and a house *divided* against a house falls. 18If Satan also
is divided against himself, how will his kingdom stand? Because you say I cast out demons by Beelzebub. 19And if I
cast out demons by Beelzebub, by whom do your sons cast
them out? Therefore they will be your judges. 20But if I cast
out demons with the finger of God, surely the kingdom of
God has come upon you. 21When a strong man, fully
armed, guards his own palace, his goods are in peace. 22But
when a stronger than he comes upon him and overcomes
him, he takes from him all his armor in which he trusted,
and divides his spoils. 23He who is not with Me is against
Me, and he who does not gather with Me scatters.
24"When an unclean spirit goes out of a man, he goes
through dry places, seeking rest; and finding none, he says,
'I will return to my house from which I came.' 25And when
he comes, he finds *it* swept and put in order. 26Then he
goes and takes with *him* seven other spirits more wicked
than himself, and they enter and dwell there; and the last
state of that man is worse than the first."

Obedience More Important than Family Ties

11:27–28
see pg. 265

27And it happened, as He spoke these
things, that a certain woman from the
crowd raised her voice and said to Him, "Blessed *is* the
womb that bore You, and *the* breasts which nursed You!"
28But He said, "More than that, blessed *are* those who
hear the word of God and keep it!"

11:11 [a]NU-Text omits the words from *bread* through *for* in the next sentence.
11:15 [a]NU-Text and M-Text read *Beelzebul.*

(continued from previous page)

Him of being in alliance with Satan's kingdom (Mark 3:22; Luke 11:15; John 8:48). The same accusation was made against Jesus' forerunner, John the Baptist (Matt. 11:18; Luke 7:33). But Jesus' works of goodness and righteousness showed that these claims could not be true (Matt. 12:25–29; Luke 11:17–22).

The Final Victory

Following the resurrection of Jesus and His return to heaven, demons have continued their warfare against Him and His followers (Rom. 8:38–39; Eph. 6:12). Yet Satan and his allies will ultimately be overthrown by God. After Christ returns, the devil and his angels will be defeated and thrown into the lake of fire and brimstone (Matt. 25:41; Rev. 20:10)—a doom with which the demons are quite familiar (Matt. 8:29). God will achieve the final victory in a conflict that has been going on since the beginning of time. ◆

Some theories of psychology have tried to cast doubt on the objective reality of evil and the devil. That presents a problem for some who read the Bible's accounts of demon possession. See "Whatever Became of 'Demon Possession'?" Luke 9:38–42.

TIRED OF PRAYING?

CONSIDER THIS 11:5–13 **Do you ever feel impatient with God? Does He seem late in answering your requests or meeting your needs?**

Jesus spoke to the issues of how to pray, how long to pray, and how long God might take to respond. One day His disciples asked Him to teach them to pray (v. 1). He told a story about someone with a need who was

(continued on next page)

Jesus Warns the Crowds

29And while the crowds were thickly gathered together,
He began to say, "This is an evil generation. It seeks a sign,
and no sign will be given to it except the sign of Jonah the
prophet.[a] 30For as Jonah became a sign to the Ninevites, so
11:31 also the Son of Man will be to this generation. 31The queen of the South will rise
up in the judgment with the men of this generation and
condemn them, for she came from the ends of the earth to
hear the wisdom of Solomon; and indeed a greater than
Solomon *is* here. 32The men of Nineveh will rise up in the
judgment with this generation and condemn it, for they re-

11:29 [a]NU-Text omits *the prophet.*

FOR YOUR INFO 11:31

WHO WAS THE QUEEN OF SHEBA?

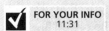

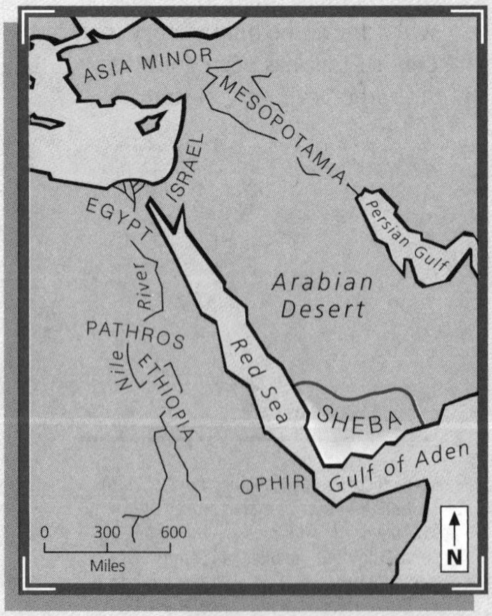

SHEBA

The Queen of Sheba, known in the New Testament as the Queen of the South (v. 31), visited Solomon to examine his wisdom (1 Kin. 10:1–13). She ruled a country that was most likely in southwest Arabia, a mighty commercial power specializing in the trade of perfume and incense. During her visit, she probably negotiated a trade agreement as well as provisions for safe passage of her merchants' caravans through Israel's territory.

Having heard astonishing reports of Solomon's wisdom and splendor, she found him exceeding his reputation. In response, she worshiped the God of Israel (1 Kin. 10:9) and presented Solomon with an abundance of gold, jewels, and more spices than the kingdom had ever received before. In exchange, Solomon was equally generous, giving her "all she desired, whatever she asked, besides what [he] had given her according to the royal generosity" (1 Kin. 10:13).

Commenting on her story, Jesus warned His listeners that this queen would rise up in judgment on their generation. When she came to Solomon and saw his greatness, her response was not jealousy or denial, but awe and thanksgiving. She acknowledged Solomon's greatness and honored his God. By contrast, Jesus' generation had met one greater than Solomon—the Messiah Himself—and its response had been unbelief (v. 29; compare Matt. 12:38). So He predicted that a woman who ruled a powerful country would someday put them to shame because she, like Solomon, was wise. ◆

Women played a major role in Jesus' life and work. See "The Women Around Jesus," John 19:25.

pented at the preaching of Jonah; and indeed a greater than
Jonah *is* here.
33"No one, when he has lit a lamp, puts *it* in a secret place
or under a basket, but on a lampstand, that those who
come in may see the light. 34The lamp of the body is the
eye. Therefore, when your eye is good, your whole body
also is full of light. But when *your eye* is bad, your body also
is full of darkness. 35Therefore take heed that the light
which is in you is not darkness. 36If then your whole body
is full of light, having no part dark, *the* whole *body* will be
full of light, as when the bright shining of a lamp gives you
light."

Pharisees and Lawyers Rebuked

37And as He spoke, a certain Pharisee asked Him to dine
with him. So He went in and sat down to eat. 38When the
Pharisee saw *it*, he marveled that He had not first washed
before dinner.
39Then the Lord said to him, "Now you Pharisees make
the outside of the cup and dish clean, but your inward part
is full of greed and wickedness. 40Foolish ones! Did not He
who made the outside make the inside also? 41But rather
give alms of such things as you have; then indeed all things
are clean to you.
11:42 42"But woe to you Pharisees! For you
tithe mint and rue and all manner of
herbs, and pass by justice and the love of God. These you
ought to have done, without leaving the others undone.
43Woe to you Pharisees! For you love the best seats in the
synagogues and greetings in the marketplaces. 44Woe to
you, scribes and Pharisees, hypocrites![a] For you are like
graves which are not seen, and the men who walk over *them*
are not aware *of them.*"
45Then one of the lawyers answered and said to Him,
"Teacher, by saying these things You reproach us also."
46And He said, "Woe to you also, lawyers! For you load
men with burdens hard to bear, and you yourselves do not
touch the burdens with one of your fingers. 47Woe to you!
For you build the tombs of the prophets, and your fathers
killed them. 48In fact, you bear witness that you approve the
deeds of your fathers; for they indeed killed them, and you
build their tombs. 49Therefore the wisdom of God also said,
'I will send them prophets and apostles, and *some* of them

11:44 [a]NU-Text omits *scribes and Pharisees, hypocrites.*

The Tithe

A CLOSER LOOK 11:42 *"Tithing" (Matt. 23:23–24) explains the tithe that Jesus was talking about in v. 42.*

(continued from previous page)

very persistent in asking a neighbor for help (vv. 5–8).

The story makes it clear that our ability to ask does not equal God's response or its timing. God is not a celestial bellhop waiting at our beck and call. Neither does He rely on us to define our needs, outline solutions, or say when or how He should act. No, God does those for us—which is just as well since He is all-wise.

God delights in His children developing the habit and freedom of asking Him for help (vv. 9–10). But He won't leave us trapped in our limited perception of the situation (vv. 11–13). Sooner or later He will answer our prayers, but in His own time. He asks us to trust Him to know what is needed and when.

Our calling, then, is to ask—even persistently—and to grow in the process. One of the surprising benefits of praying is how much *we* change. Sometimes, that in itself is the answer to our prayers.

Who Is Blessed?

CONSIDER THIS 11:27–28 *Notice how Jesus responded to the praise of His mother (vv. 27–28). He didn't deny that she was blessed, but focused attention on the real source of blessing—hearing and doing the Word of God. Mary was an outstanding model of that at the time of His conception, since she both heard and responded to God's words to her (see "The Maidservant of the Lord," Luke 1:26–56).*

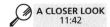

The Right Kind of Fear

CONSIDER THIS 12:4–7 **Every culture seems to be afraid of someone. The Hebrews feared and hated the Romans because of the ruthless might of their occupation troops. Eventually those fears were realized as Rome viciously destroyed Jerusalem in A.D. 70 (see "Jerusalem Surrounded," Luke 21:20). In recent years, the West feared destruction from Soviet nuclear missiles. Today there is growing alarm and outrage over drug- and gang-related violence in cities.**

But in Luke 12:4–7 we see that Jesus redefines fear by rearranging our view so we look at things from God's perspective. He draws upon the Old Testament concept of the "fear of the Lord" (Prov. 1:7). This is not a fawning, cringing dread that keeps us wallowing in anxiety, but a respect for who God is—the One who holds ultimate power. When we have a balanced view of God, it puts our thinking in a proper framework. We view everybody and everything in relation to God's holiness, righteousness, and love. We can't ignore physical threats and violence, but we dare not ignore the One who holds sway over our eternal destiny.

Will You Get What's Coming to You?

CONSIDER THIS 12:13–15 **The man we read of in v. 13 appealed to Jesus for justice. He wanted to make sure that he was going to get his inheritance. But Jesus turned the issue**

(continued on next page)

they will kill and persecute,' 50that the blood of all the
prophets which was shed from the foundation of the world
may be required of this generation, 51from the blood of Abel
to the blood of Zechariah who perished between the altar
and the temple. Yes, I say to you, it shall be required of this
generation.
52"Woe to you lawyers! For you have taken away the key
of knowledge. You did not enter in yourselves, and those
who were entering in you hindered."
53And as He said these things to them,[a] the scribes and
the Pharisees began to assail *Him* vehemently, and to cross-
examine Him about many things, 54lying in wait for Him,
and seeking to catch Him in something He might say, that
they might accuse Him.[a]

CHAPTER 12

Hypocritical Leaders Warned Against

1In the meantime, when an innumerable multitude of
people had gathered together, so that they trampled one another, He began to say to His disciples first *of all,* "Beware of
the leaven of the Pharisees, which is hypocrisy. 2For there is
nothing covered that will not be revealed, nor hidden that
will not be known. 3Therefore whatever you have spoken in
the dark will be heard in the light, and what you have spoken in the ear in inner rooms will be proclaimed on the
housetops.

12:4–7

4"And I say to you, My friends, do not
be afraid of those who kill the body, and
after that have no more that they can do. 5But I will show
you whom you should fear: Fear Him who, after He has
killed, has power to cast into hell; yes, I say to you, fear
Him!

12:6–7 see pg. 268

6"Are not five sparrows sold for two
copper coins?[a] And not one of them is
forgotten before God. 7But the very hairs of your head are
all numbered. Do not fear therefore; you are of more value
than many sparrows.
8"Also I say to you, whoever confesses Me before men,
him the Son of Man also will confess before the angels of
God. 9But he who denies Me before men will be denied before the angels of God.
10"And anyone who speaks a word against the Son of
Man, it will be forgiven him; but to him who blasphemes
against the Holy Spirit, it will not be forgiven.
11"Now when they bring you to the synagogues and mag-

11:53 [a]NU-Text reads *And when He left there.* *11:54* [a]NU-Text omits *and seeking* and *that they might accuse Him.* *12:6* [a]Greek *assarion,* a coin of very small value

istrates and authorities, do not worry about how or what
you should answer, or what you should say. 12For the Holy
Spirit will teach you in that very hour what you ought to
say."

A Parable about a Rich Fool

12:13–15

13Then one from the crowd said to
Him, "Teacher, tell my brother to divide
the inheritance with me."
14But He said to him, "Man, who made Me a judge or an
arbitrator over you?" 15And He said to
them, "Take heed and beware of cov-
etousness,[a] for one's life does not consist in the abundance
of the things he possesses."
16Then He spoke a parable to them, saying: "The ground
of a certain rich man yielded plentifully. 17And he thought
within himself, saying, 'What shall I do, since I have no
room to store my crops?' 18So he said, 'I will do this: I will
pull down my barns and build greater, and there I will store
all my crops and my goods. 19And I will say to my soul,
"Soul, you have many goods laid up for many years; take
your ease; eat, drink, *and* be merry." ' 20But God said to
him, 'Fool! This night your soul will be required of you;
then whose will those things be which you have provided?'
21"So *is* he who lays up treasure for himself, and is not
rich toward God."

12:15 see pg. 269

Priorities and Comforts of the Kingdom

12:22–34

22Then He said to His disciples, "Therefore I say to you, do not worry about
your life, what you will eat; nor about the body, what you
will put on. 23Life is more than food, and the body *is more*
than clothing. 24Consider the ravens, for they neither sow
nor reap, which have neither storehouse nor barn; and God
feeds them. Of how much more value are you than the
birds? 25And which of you by worrying can add one cubit
to his stature? 26If you then are not able to do *the* least, why
are you anxious for the rest? 27Consider the lilies, how they
grow: they neither toil nor spin; and yet I say to you, even
Solomon in all his glory was not arrayed like one of these.
28If then God so clothes the grass, which today is in the
field and tomorrow is thrown into the oven, how much
more *will He clothe* you, O *you* of little faith?

12:15 [a]NU-Text reads *all covetousness.*

Don't Worry!

A CLOSER LOOK 12:22–34

This passage raises important questions about the impact of wealth on our lives. See "Don't Worry!" Matt. 6:19–34.

(continued from previous page)

from the material to the spiritual. He was far more concerned about the man's covetous spirit than his family's estate.

The Old Testament, which governed Hebrew life, had a great deal to say about family estates and the succession of land and property. Sometimes Christians have understood such teaching as merely foreshadowing the spiritual inheritance of New Testament believers. But our earthly, material estates are not to be treated as insignificant. An inheritance is a responsibility that God wants both parents and children to view and manage properly.

Here, Jesus showed grave concern that the man did not view his physical inheritance properly, but rather with a greedy attitude—a major problem because it threatened his spiritual inheritance, his eternal destiny.

The Lord's response and the parable following it (vv. 16–21) challenge us to ask: What is our perspective on the inheritance coming to us in this world? Will it be a blessing and a resource to be managed responsibly before God? Or, like this man and the man in the parable, are we trying to fashion a life out of the abundance of our possessions? If so, we need to pay attention to vv. 20–21.

There are three kinds of inheritance in Scripture: the earthly inheritance, such as the kind mentioned in this passage; the believer's inheritance "in Christ" (see "What's In It for Me?" Eph. 1:11); and Christ's inheritance of the redeemed children of God (see Eph. 1:18).

Jesus told another story about an inheritance: A son squandered his portion of the estate—but it turned out to be the best thing that could happen. See Luke 15:11–32.

Jesus frequently changed the subject from material concerns to spiritual ones. See, for example, Luke 4:5–8; 8:19–21; 10:38–42; 11:27–28.

29"And do not seek what you should eat or what you
should drink, nor have an anxious mind. 30For all these
things the nations of the world seek after, and your Father
knows that you need these things. 31But seek the kingdom
of God, and all these things[a] shall be added to you.
32"Do not fear, little flock, for it is your Father's good
pleasure to give you the kingdom. 33Sell what you have and
give alms; provide yourselves money bags which do not
grow old, a treasure in the heavens that does not fail, where
no thief approaches nor moth destroys. 34For where your
treasure is, there your heart will be also.

12:35–48
see pg. 270

35"Let your waist be girded and *your*
lamps burning; 36and you yourselves be
like men who wait for their master, when he will return
from the wedding, that when he comes and knocks they
may open to him immediately. 37Blessed *are* those servants
whom the master, when he comes, will find watching. Assuredly, I say to you that he will gird himself and have them
sit down *to eat,* and will come and serve them. 38And if he
should come in the second watch, or come in the third
watch, and find *them* so, blessed are those servants. 39But
know this, that if the master of the house had known what
hour the thief would come, he would have watched and[a]
not allowed his house to be broken into. 40Therefore you

12:31 [a]NU-Text reads *His kingdom, and these things.* *12:39* [a]NU-Text reads *he would not have allowed.*

CONSIDER THIS
12:6–7

GOD AND THE ENVIRONMENT

In the middle of warning people against hypocrisy, Jesus made an interesting comparison. He said that God values people more than He values sparrows (vv. 6–7). The point is that people matter to God. But so do the rest of God's creatures. Indeed, "not one of them is forgotten."

Scripture clearly shows God's intense concern for every aspect of the creation, particularly its conservation. For example:

- *In the beginning, God commanded Adam and Eve to cultivate and keep the garden. That kind of stewardship ruled out wanton destruction (Gen. 2:15).*
- *Later, God was sorry that He had created humanity because of their total wickedness (Gen. 6:5–6). So He determined to destroy everyone through a flood. However, He saved not only Noah and his family, but the other creatures as well (Gen. 6:13–14, 19–22).*
- *After the flood, God made a covenant with both people and animals that "all flesh shall never again be cut off by the water of the flood" (Gen. 9:8–11).*

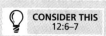

also be ready, for the Son of Man is coming at an hour you
do not expect."

A Parable about a Faithful Manager

[41]Then Peter said to Him, "Lord, do You speak this parable *only* to us, or to all *people?*"
[42]And the Lord said, "Who then is that faithful and wise
steward, whom *his* master will make ruler over his household, to give *them their* portion of food in due season?
[43]Blessed *is* that servant whom his master will find so doing
when he comes. [44]Truly, I say to you that he will make him
ruler over all that he has. [45]But if that servant says in his
heart, 'My master is delaying his coming,' and begins to
beat the male and female servants, and to eat and drink and
be drunk, [46]the master of that servant will come on a day
when he is not looking for *him,* and at an hour when he is
not aware, and will cut him in two and appoint *him* his portion with the unbelievers. [47]And that servant who knew his
master's will, and did not prepare *himself* or do according to
his will, shall be beaten with many *stripes.* [48]But he who did
not know, yet committed things deserving of stripes, shall
be beaten with few. For everyone to whom much is given,
from him much will be required; and to whom much has
been committed, of him they will ask the more.
[49]"I came to send fire on the earth, and how I wish it were
already kindled! [50]But I have a baptism to be baptized with,

- *Later, God instructed the Hebrews to allow their cropland to be rested (left fallow) every seventh year in order to rejuvenate it and preserve it (Ex. 23:10–11; Lev. 25:2–7; 26:34–35).*
- *The Law also forbade the unnecessary destruction of fruit and nut trees and the killing of mother birds, even for food (Deut. 20:19–20; 22:6–7).*

Without question, God cares about what He has created. And He has charged us to wisely manage those resources (Gen. 1:26), for our good and for His glory. As we face increasingly complex environmental issues, we need to view the earth as a sacred trust from God's hands, for which He will hold us accountable. If He cares about every single bird on the planet, shouldn't we? ◆

Watch Out for Greed!

CONSIDER THIS 12:15 **Jesus gave a direct, unequivocal command to guard against *covetousness* (v. 15)—longing for something we don't have, especially for what belongs to someone else. He was not telling us to watch for it in others, but in ourselves.**

According to this verse and the following parable, covetousness, or greed, is based on the foolish belief that what matters in life is how much one has. It may be money (as is the case here), or status, power, intelligence, beauty, even spiritual blessings; it is possible to covet anything that can be acquired. The idea is that having that thing will make us content. But biblically, only God can—and will—satisfy our real needs, as Jesus goes on to show (12:22–31).

To covet is to be discontented with what God brings our way. Yet our consumer-oriented culture excels at stoking the fires of discontent. In subtle yet powerful ways, we come to believe that whatever we have, it's not enough. We need more, we need bigger, we need better.

So more than ever, we need to pay attention to Jesus' warning: *Watch out for greed!*

Sometimes people attempt to enlist God in their selfish pursuit of material things. See "The Dangers of Prosperity Theology," 1 Tim. 6:3–6.

If we're supposed to avoid covetousness, what does a lifestyle of contentment look like? See Phil. 4:10–13.

What's wrong with wanting more? Paul warns us to watch out—we could be worshipping idols! See "Do-It-Yourself Idolatry," Col. 3:5.

AUTHORITY AND RESPONSIBILITY

CONSIDER THIS 12:35–48 **All of us must deal with authority and responsibility. The parables Jesus told (vv. 35–48) talk about the believer's faithfulness to God. But they also remind us of faithful conduct on the job.**

To be sure, our work relationships are more complicated—and civilized—than those between slaves and masters. But in light of the principles raised in this passage, we might ask: Are we as productive when our supervisors are gone as when they are looking over us? Do we try to anticipate their needs and desires, or do we wait until told what to do? Do we pray for our bosses and the work we do under them?

Jesus has a high regard for faithfulness. In this passage He challenges us to carry out our spiritual responsibilities in a faithful, diligent way. But clearly we need to fulfill our everyday work responsibilities with the same reliable, faithful spirit.

Paul explicitly challenges workers to diligence, whether or not the boss is around (Eph. 6:5–8). Moreover, faithfulness is a mark of a Christlike "workstyle." See Titus 2:9–10.

and how distressed I am till it is accomplished! ⁵¹Do *you* suppose that I came to give peace on earth? I tell you, not at all, but rather division. ⁵²For from now on five in one house will be divided: three against two, and two against three. ⁵³Father will be divided against son and son against father, mother against daughter and daughter against mother, mother-in-law against her daughter-in-law and daughter-in-law against her mother-in-law."

The Signs of the Times

12:54–56 ⁵⁴Then He also said to the multitudes, "Whenever *you see* a cloud rising out of the west, immediately you say, 'A shower is coming'; and so it is. ⁵⁵And when you see the south wind blow, you say, 'There will be hot weather'; and there is. ⁵⁶Hypocrites! You can discern the face of the sky and of the earth, but how *is it* you do not discern this time?

⁵⁷"Yes, and why, even of yourselves, do you not judge what is right? ⁵⁸When you go with your adversary to the magistrate, make every effort along the way to settle with him, lest he drag you to the judge, the judge deliver you to the officer, and the officer throw you into prison. ⁵⁹I tell you, you shall not depart from there till you have paid the very last mite."

CHAPTER 13

The Need for Repentance

¹There were present at that season some who told Him about the Galileans whose blood Pilate had mingled with their sacrifices. ²And Jesus answered and said to them, "Do you suppose that these Galileans were worse sinners than all *other* Galileans, because they suffered such things? ³I tell you, no; but unless you repent you will all likewise perish. ⁴Or those eighteen on whom the tower in Siloam fell and killed them, do you think that they were worse sinners than all *other* men who dwelt in Jerusalem? ⁵I tell you, no; but unless you repent you will all likewise perish."

⁶He also spoke this parable: "A certain *man* had a fig tree planted in his vineyard, and he came seeking fruit on it and found none. ⁷Then he said to the keeper of his vineyard, 'Look, for three years I have come seeking fruit on this fig tree and find none. Cut it down; why does it use up the ground?' ⁸But he answered and said to him, 'Sir, let it alone this year also, until I dig around it and fertilize *it*. ⁹And if it bears fruit, *well*. But if not, after that*ᵃ* you can cut it down.' "

13:9 ᵃNU-Text reads *And if it bears fruit after that, well. But if not, you can cut it down.*

A Crippled Woman Finds Help

[10]Now He was teaching in one of the synagogues on the
13:10–17 see pg. 272 Sabbath. [11]And behold, there was a
woman who had a spirit of infirmity
eighteen years, and was bent over and could in no way raise
herself up. [12]But when Jesus saw her, He called *her* to *Him*
and said to her, "Woman, you are loosed from your infirmity." [13]And He laid *His* hands on her, and immediately she
was made straight, and glorified God.
[14]But the ruler of the synagogue answered with indignation, because Jesus had healed on the Sabbath; and he said
to the crowd, "There are six days on which men ought to
work; therefore come and be healed on them, and not on
the Sabbath day."
[15]The Lord then answered him and said, "Hypocrite![a]
Does not each one of you on the Sabbath loose his ox or
donkey from the stall, and lead *it* away to water it? [16]So
ought not this woman, being a daughter of Abraham,
whom Satan has bound—think of it—for eighteen years, be
loosed from this bond on the Sabbath?" [17]And when He
said these things, all His adversaries were put to shame; and
all the multitude rejoiced for all the glorious things that
were done by Him.

A Parable about a Mustard Seed

13:18–21 see pg. 272 [18]Then He said, "What is the kingdom
of God like? And to what shall I compare
it? [19]It is like a mustard seed, which a man took and put in
his garden; and it grew and became a large[a] tree, and the
birds of the air nested in its branches."

A Parable about Hidden Leaven

[20]And again He said, "To what shall I liken the kingdom
of God? [21]It is like leaven, which a woman took and hid in
three measures[a] of meal till it was all leavened."

The Exclusivity of the Kingdom

13:22–23 see pg. 273 [22]And He went through the cities and
villages, teaching, and journeying toward
Jerusalem. [23]Then one said to Him, "Lord, are there few
who are saved?"
And He said to them, [24]"Strive to enter through the narrow gate, for many, I say to you, will seek to enter and will
not be able. [25]When once the Master of the house has risen
up and shut the door, and you begin to stand outside and
knock at the door, saying, 'Lord, Lord, open for us,' and He

13:15 [a]NU-Text and M-Text read *Hypocrites.* *13:19* [a]NU-Text omits *large.* *13:21* [a]Greek *sata,* approximately two pecks in all

CURRENT AFFAIRS

CONSIDER THIS 12:54–56 **In vv. 54–56, Jesus rebuked the people of Israel for their failure to recognize the real issues and forces at work among them. Many were farmers and fishermen who were quite skilled at discerning when the weather was about to change. But they failed to detect the momentous message and change that Christ was now bringing to the earth.**

What about you? Are you up on current affairs, yet unaware of God's global work and purposes? Are you quick to read the winds of change at your job, in the economy, in politics, and in public opinion, while you fail to observe God's Word regarding your work, your relationships, and your family? Are you up on all the latest gossip about celebrities, yet ignorant of what the Lord of the universe is up to?

The Value of a Disabled Woman

CONSIDER THIS 13:10–17 **The incident in vv. 10–17 put the ruler of the synagogue and his fellow rabbis to shame. Jesus rebuked them for showing more concern for their animals than for a disabled woman. They grumbled about profaning the Sabbath, but Jesus pointed out that *any* time is appropriate to meet a genuine need; *any* day—even the Sabbath—is a proper day for acts of mercy.**

Actually, of all the days on which the woman could have been given rest from her affliction, the Sabbath—a day of rest—was perhaps the most appropriate.

(continued on next page)

will answer and say to you, 'I do not know you, where you
are from,' 26then you will begin to say, 'We ate and drank in
Your presence, and You taught in our streets.' 27But He will
say, 'I tell you I do not know you, where you are from. Depart from Me, all you workers of iniquity.' 28There will be
weeping and gnashing of teeth, when you see Abraham
and Isaac and Jacob and all the prophets in the kingdom
of God, and yourselves thrust out. 29They will come from
the east and the west, from the north and the south,
and sit down in the kingdom of God. 30And indeed there
are last who will be first, and there are first who will be
last."

Jesus Mourns over Jerusalem

31On that very day[a] some Pharisees came, saying to Him,
"Get out and depart from here, for Herod wants to kill
You."
32And He said to them, "Go, tell that fox, 'Behold, I cast
out demons and perform cures today and tomorrow, and
the third *day* I shall be perfected.' 33Nevertheless I must

13:31 [a]NU-Text reads *In that very hour.*

CONSIDER THIS 13:18–21

Little Things Mean a Lot

Do you tend to be impressed by bigness? Do you measure something's significance by whether it's bigger than anything else? Have you noticed the impact of little things, like the usefulness of a pinhead or the danger of a little bit of electricity in the wrong place?

Jesus described the kingdom and faith as starting out small, but ultimately having a big effect (vv. 18–21; 17:6; Matt. 13:31; 17:20; Mark 4:31). He likened the kingdom to a small seed that grows into a tree-like plant, just as today we speak of the acorn becoming an oak tree. He also borrowed an image from the baking industry, likening the kingdom to leaven, a piece of fermented dough that was added to a new batch, causing it to rise.

In our own culture, where people tend to equate significance with magnitude, these parables remind us of the power of small but potent faith and of simple but solid kingdom values. Paul listed these lasting things: love, joy, peace, patience, kindness, goodness, faithfulness, gentleness, and self-control (Gal. 5:22–23).

God's challenge to us as His people is not to be impressed by power, success, or super-achievement, but to give ourselves to the so-called little things, the things of His kingdom. Therein lies ultimate significance. ◆

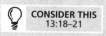

journey today, tomorrow, and the *day* following; for it cannot be that a prophet should perish outside of Jerusalem.

13:34

34"O Jerusalem, Jerusalem, the one who
kills the prophets and stones those who
are sent to her! How often I wanted to gather your children together, as a hen *gathers* her brood under *her* wings, but
you were not willing! 35See! Your house is left to you deso-
late; and assuredly,[a] I say to you, you shall not see Me until *the time* comes when you say, 'Blessed is He who comes in the name of the LORD!' "[b]

CHAPTER 14

Jesus Heals on the Sabbath

1Now it happened, as He went into the house of one of the rulers of the Pharisees to eat bread on the Sabbath, that
they watched Him closely. 2And behold, there was a certain

14:1–6 see pg. 274

man before Him who had dropsy. 3And
Jesus, answering, spoke to the lawyers and Pharisees, saying, "Is it lawful to heal on the Sabbath?"[a]

4But they kept silent. And He took *him* and healed him,
and let him go. 5Then He answered them, saying, "Which of you, having a donkey[a] or an ox that has fallen into a pit, will not immediately pull him out on the Sabbath day?"

13:35 [a]NU-Text and M-Text omit *assuredly.* [b]Psalm 118:26 *14:3* [a]NU-Text adds *or not.* *14:5* [a]NU-Text and M-Text read *son.*

Good Men Cry

CONSIDER THIS 13:34

Jesus cried out as He came upon Jerusalem, mourning the lost children of Israel (v. 34). Clearly He was speaking of "children" in spiritual terms. But spiritual desolation is often reflected in outward ways. The fastest growing category of street people today are the children of the homeless in our cities. What would be Jesus' cry upon seeing them? What is our own response?

This was not the last time that Jesus would weep over Jerusalem. See Luke 19:41.

(continued from previous page)

Jesus put a name on the legalists' attitude and behavior: hypocrisy. He wanted everyone to see that the outward appearance of righteousness often masks inner unrighteousness.

Jesus faced a similar situation somewhat earlier. He was no less direct in His condemnation of legalism. See "Jesus Confronts the Legalists," Luke 6:1–11.

Sorting Out Membership

CONSIDER THIS 13:22–23

Do you try to sort out who is saved and who is not? Do you find yourself making judgments about people's faith and its quality?

One of Jesus' followers asked Him how many others were being saved (v. 23). The Lord's response turned the questioner's attention away from others and toward his own quality of faith and the implications of that (vv. 24–30). Jesus even said that outward association with Him is not enough to ensure salvation (vv. 26–27). And He warned that those who seem to be the least likely candidates for the kingdom will enter ahead of others (v. 30).

Are you spending more energy trying to nail down who is and isn't going to heaven than on developing a walk with Christ that encourages others to pursue Him as Savior?

The Letter and the Spirit

CONSIDER THIS 14:1–6 **The Sabbath-day controversy (vv. 1–6) shows a tension between the letter of the Law and its spirit. The Old Testament was clear about keeping the Sabbath holy by resting from work (Ex. 20:8–11). But Jesus was known for doing the "work" of healing on the Sabbath (Luke 13:10–17). Was He breaking the Law or not? The lawyers and Pharisees couldn't say (v. 6).**

Jesus let them stew over the issue, but clearly He was convinced that He was acting well within the Law. If He appeared to break it, it was only because His enemies paid more attention to superficial, external ways of "keeping" the Law than to its underlying moral spirit. Furthermore, over the centuries their predecessors had heaped up countless traditions on top of the Law, creating a mammoth set of expectations that no one could fulfill.

In our own day, even believers sometimes try to live by a rigid set of dos and don'ts that go beyond the clear teaching of Scripture. Like the Pharisees, we are tempted to be more concerned about the externals of the faith than the larger principles of "justice and the love of God" (Luke 11:42). Given His treatment of the self-righteous Pharisees, what would Jesus say to us?

What does it mean to keep the Sabbath holy? See "Are Sundays Special?" Rom. 14:5–13, and "The Sabbath," Heb. 4:1–13.

14:1–6 [6]And they could not answer Him regarding these things.

A Parable about Seating at a Dinner

[7]So He told a parable to those who were invited, when He
noted how they chose the best places, saying to them:
[8]"When you are invited by anyone to a wedding feast, do
not sit down in the best place, lest one more honorable than
you be invited by him; [9]and he who invited you and him
come and say to you, 'Give place to this man,' and then you
begin with shame to take the lowest place. [10]But when you
are invited, go and sit down in the lowest place, so that
when he who invited you comes he may say to you, 'Friend,
go up higher.' Then you will have glory in the presence of
those who sit at the table with you. [11]For whoever exalts
himself will be humbled, and he who humbles himself will
be exalted."

14:12–14 [12]Then He also said to him who invited
Him, "When you give a dinner or a sup-
per, do not ask your friends, your brothers, your relatives,
nor rich neighbors, lest they also invite you back, and you
be repaid. [13]But when you give a feast, invite *the* poor, *the*
maimed, *the* lame, *the* blind. [14]And you will be blessed, because they cannot repay you; for you shall be repaid at the
resurrection of the just."

A Parable about a Slighted Invitation

[15]Now when one of those who sat at the table with Him
heard these things, he said to Him, "Blessed *is* he who shall
eat bread[a] in the kingdom of God!"

14:15 [a]M-Text reads *dinner.*

"Do You Mind If I Heal?"

A CLOSER LOOK 14:1–6 *Jesus sparked plenty of controversy by healing on the Sabbath. His question in v. 3 appears ironic, as if asking "permission" to perform a miracle of mercy. Maybe His recent encounter with a synagogue ruler was still fresh in His mind (13:10–17).*

Jesus never won many legalists to His cause. But neither did He allow their abuse of Scripture or people to go unchallenged. See "Jesus Confronts the Legalists," Luke 6:1–11.

Care for the Poor

A CLOSER LOOK 14:12–14 *"Some Surprising Evidence" at Matt. 11:2–6 explores our responsibility toward the poor.*

14:16–24 16Then He said to him, "A certain man
gave a great supper and invited many,
17and sent his servant at supper time to say to those who
were invited, 'Come, for all things are now ready.' 18But they
all with one *accord* began to make excuses. The first said to
him, 'I have bought a piece of ground, and I must go and
see it. I ask you to have me excused.' 19And another said, 'I
have bought five yoke of oxen, and I am going to test them.
I ask you to have me excused.' 20Still another said, 'I have
married a wife, and therefore I cannot come.' 21So that servant came and reported these things to his master. Then the
master of the house, being angry, said to his servant, 'Go
out quickly into the streets and lanes of the city, and bring
in here *the* poor and *the* maimed and *the* lame and *the*
blind.' 22And the servant said, 'Master, it is done as you
commanded, and still there is room.' 23Then the master said
to the servant, 'Go out into the highways and hedges, and
compel *them* to come in, that my house may be filled. 24For
I say to you that none of those men who were invited shall
taste my supper.' "

More about the Costs of Discipleship

14:25–32 25Now great multitudes went with
Him. And He turned and said to them,
26"If anyone comes to Me and does not hate his father and
mother, wife and children, brothers and sisters, yes, and his
own life also, he cannot be My disciple. 27And whoever
does not bear his cross and come after Me cannot be My
disciple. 28For which of you, intending to build a tower,
does not sit down first and count the cost, whether he has
enough to finish *it*— 29lest, after he has laid the foundation,
and is not able to finish, all who see *it* begin to mock him,
30saying, 'This man began to build and was not able to finish.' 31Or what king, going to make war against another
king, does not sit down first and consider whether he is
able with ten thousand to meet him who comes against him
with twenty thousand? 32Or else, while the other is still a
great way off, he sends a delegation and asks conditions of
peace. 33So likewise, whoever of you does not forsake all
that he has cannot be My disciple.
34"Salt *is* good; but if the salt has lost its flavor, how shall
it be seasoned? 35It is neither fit for the land nor for the

Excuse Me!

A CLOSER LOOK 14:16–24 *The guests in Jesus' parable asked to be excused from the feast (v. 18). Jesus' listeners undoubtedly recognized that this was a gross impropriety. See "Worse than Rude," Matt. 22:2–14.*

THE COST OF FOLLOWING JESUS

CONSIDER THIS 14:25–32 **Following Jesus has its privileges—but also its costs, as vv. 25–32 reveal:**

- **The cost of *service* (v. 26). Jesus' followers must serve Him before all others.**
- **The cost of *sacrifice* (v. 27). Jesus' followers must subordinate their own interests to the interests of Christ.**
- **The cost of *self-assessment* (vv. 28–30). Jesus' followers must be fully in touch with who they are and how Christ has equipped and empowered them to do what He asks.**
- **The cost of *strategy* (vv. 31–33). Jesus' followers must think through the issues and have the courage to act in the face of uncertainty.**

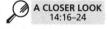

Confused Value?

CONSIDER THIS 15:1–31 *In Luke 15, Jesus tells three parables about a lost sheep (vv. 4–7), a lost coin (vv. 8–10), and a lost son (vv. 11–32). Each story reflects God's concern for lost people, the tremendous value He places on every individual, and the great joy He feels "over one sinner who repents" (v. 10).*

In the first two stories, Jesus points out the natural value that humans place on their possessions. A shepherd loses one sheep out of a hundred (only 1 percent of his flock), yet he goes out and scours the countryside until he finds it and returns it to the fold. Likewise, a woman loses one coin out of ten (only 10 percent of her collection), yet she searches high and low until she finds it.

But in the third story, the loss is a worthless son—not unlike the tax collectors and sinners listening to Jesus (v. 1). We can imagine that Jesus' critics, the Pharisees, found it easy to write off such unrighteous people. Surely they were hopelessly lost in sin and shame.

But Jesus' parable shows that God views every sinner with compassion, not as merely a possession, but as a person—indeed, as a lost but loved son. He longs for each one to return to Him.

dunghill, *but* men throw it out. He who has ears to hear, let
him hear!"

CHAPTER 15

A Parable about a Lost Sheep

15:1–31 1Then all the tax collectors and the sinners drew near to Him to hear Him. 2And
the Pharisees and scribes complained, saying, "This Man receives sinners and eats with them." 3So He spoke this parable to them, saying:
4"What man of you, having a hundred sheep, if he loses
one of them, does not leave the ninety-nine in the wilderness, and go after the one which is lost until he finds it?
5And when he has found *it,* he lays *it* on his shoulders, rejoicing. 6And when he comes home, he calls together *his*
friends and neighbors, saying to them, 'Rejoice with me, for
I have found my sheep which was lost!' 7I say to you that
likewise there will be more joy in heaven over one sinner
who repents than over ninety-nine just persons who need
no repentance.

A Parable about a Lost Coin

15:8–10 8"Or what woman, having ten silver
coins,[a] if she loses one coin, does not
light a lamp, sweep the house, and search carefully until she
finds *it?* 9And when she has found *it,* she calls *her* friends
and neighbors together, saying, 'Rejoice with me, for I have
found the piece which I lost!' 10Likewise, I say to you, there
is joy in the presence of the angels of God over one sinner
who repents."

A Parable about a Lost Son

11Then He said: "A certain man had two sons. 12And the
younger of them said to *his* father, 'Father, give me the portion of goods that falls *to me.*' So he divided to them *his*
livelihood. 13And not many days after, the younger son
gathered all together, journeyed to a far country, and there
wasted his possessions with prodigal living. 14But when he
had spent all, there arose a severe famine in that land, and
he began to be in want. 15Then he went and joined himself
to a citizen of that country, and he sent him into his fields
to feed swine. 16And he would gladly have filled his stomach with the pods that the swine ate, and no one gave him
anything.
17"But when he came to himself, he said, 'How many of

15:8 [a]Greek *drachma,* a valuable coin often worn in a ten-piece garland by married women

my father's hired servants have bread enough and to spare,
and I perish with hunger! 18I will arise and go to my father,
and will say to him, "Father, I have sinned against heaven
and before you, 19and I am no longer worthy to be called
your son. Make me like one of your hired servants." '
20"And he arose and came to his father. But when he was
still a great way off, his father saw him and had compassion,
and ran and fell on his neck and kissed him. 21And the son
said to him, 'Father, I have sinned against heaven and in
your sight, and am no longer worthy to be called your son.'
22"But the father said to his servants, 'Bring[a] out the best
robe and put *it* on him, and put a ring on his hand and sandals on *his* feet. 23And bring the fatted calf here and kill *it,*
and let us eat and be merry; 24for this my son was dead and
is alive again; he was lost and is found.' And they began to
be merry.

15:25–30
see pg. 278

25"Now his older son was in the field.
And as he came and drew near to the
house, he heard music and dancing. 26So he called one of
the servants and asked what these things meant. 27And he
said to him, 'Your brother has come, and because he has received him safe and sound, your father has killed the fatted
calf.'
28"But he was angry and would not go in. Therefore his
father came out and pleaded with him. 29So he answered
and said to *his* father, 'Lo, these many years I have been
serving you; I never transgressed your commandment at
any time; and yet you never gave me a young goat, that I
might make merry with my friends. 30But as soon as this
son of yours came, who has devoured your livelihood with
harlots, you killed the fatted calf for him.'
31"And he said to him, 'Son, you are always with me, and
all that I have is yours. 32It was right that we should make
merry and be glad, for your brother was dead and is alive
again, and was lost and is found.' "

CHAPTER 16

A Parable about an Unjust Steward

16:1–13
see pg. 278

1He also said to His disciples: "There
was a certain rich man who had a stew-
ard, and an accusation was brought to him that this man
was wasting his goods. 2So he called him and said to him,
'What is this I hear about you? Give an account of your
stewardship, for you can no longer be steward.'
3"Then the steward said within himself, 'What shall I do?

15:22 [a]NU-Text reads *Quickly bring.*

THE WOMAN WHO SEARCHED AS GOD SEARCHES

YOU ARE THERE 15:8–10

The impact of the parable in vv. 8–10 is easily lost on us as modern readers, who think nothing of tossing a penny in a fountain or losing a quarter in a pay phone. We need to understand that the lost coin was probably a drachma, *a Greek coin worth a day's wage. How many of us would not search high and low to find a missing paycheck? That's what the woman in the parable was doing.*

Actually, her coin was probably part of a set of ten silver coins. The women of Jesus' day commonly wore such collections as jewelry. So not only had she lost a valuable coin, she had a flawed piece of jewelry. What bride today does not get down on her hands and knees to search the carpet or the yard to find her missing diamond? That's what this woman was doing.

Jesus likens her search for the precious coin to God's search for each one of us.

A Shrewd Manager

CONSIDER THIS 16:1–13 **What is the point of the parable in vv. 1–13? Was Christ commending the manager (or steward) for cheating his boss (v. 8)? No, He was merely observing that people go to great lengths to secure favorable treatment when they are in legal or financial trouble. They may cheat others or pervert the law to do it, but in a way their conduct reveals a certain wisdom, a prudent concern for oneself. If only they took similar pains with their eternal destiny (vv. 9–12)!**

Verse 9 speaks of "unrighteous mammon." Jesus was not implying that money (mammon) is inherently evil, only that material wealth is temporal in nature and will not go with us into eternal life. It will "fail." Therefore, we should use our wealth wisely in this life. In fact, we should "make friends" with it—that is, use it

(continued on next page)

For my master is taking the stewardship away from me. I
cannot dig; I am ashamed to beg. 4I have resolved what to
do, that when I am put out of the stewardship, they may receive me into their houses.'
5"So he called every one of his master's debtors to *him,*
and said to the first, 'How much do you owe my master?'
6And he said, 'A hundred measures[a] of oil.' So he said to
him, 'Take your bill, and sit down quickly and write fifty.'
7Then he said to another, 'And how much do you owe?' So
he said, 'A hundred measures[a] of wheat.' And he said to
him, 'Take your bill, and write eighty.' 8So the master commended the unjust steward because he had dealt shrewdly.
For the sons of this world are more shrewd in their generation than the sons of light.
9"And I say to you, make friends for yourselves by unrighteous mammon, that when you fail,[a] they may receive
you into an everlasting home. 10He who *is* faithful in *what is*
least is faithful also in much; and he who is unjust in *what*
is least is unjust also in much. 11Therefore if you have not
been faithful in the unrighteous mammon, who will commit to your trust the true *riches?* 12And if you have not been
faithful in what is another man's, who will give you what is
your own?
13"No servant can serve two masters; for either he will

16:6 [a]Greek *batos,* eight or nine gallons each (Old Testament *bath*) *16:7* [a]Greek *koros,* ten or twelve bushels each (Old Testament *kor*) *16:9* [a]NU-Text reads *it fails.*

CONSIDER THIS 15:25–30

Are You the Older Brother?

If you grew up in the church or have been a believer for many years, it's worth looking carefully at the prodigal son's older brother (v. 25). He's one of the most intriguing characters in all of Jesus' parables—a case study in what can happen to people who have been around religion for a long time.

In contrast to the father, who shows nothing but mercy to his long lost son who has finally come home, the older brother sneers at the joy and celebration heaped on his brother. He is not merely jealous, but outraged at what he perceives as injustice. How could the father kill the fatted calf just because his wayward, ne'er-do-well son had come back, while seeming to neglect the faithful, diligent loyalty of his other son (vv. 29–30)?

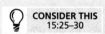

That was the attitude of the Pharisees who were among those listening to this story (vv. 2–3). And in a larger sense, it would become the attitude of Jews in general as the gospel spread to the Gentiles (for example, Acts 11:1–3). How could Jesus be so friendly toward known

hate the one and love the other, or else he will be loyal to the one and despise the other. You cannot serve God and mammon."

Jesus Denounces the Pharisees

14Now the Pharisees, who were lovers of money, also
heard all these things, and they derided Him. 15And He said
to them, "You are those who justify yourselves before men,
but God knows your hearts. For what is highly esteemed
among men is an abomination in the sight of God.
16"The law and the prophets *were* until John. Since that
time the kingdom of God has been preached, and everyone
is pressing into it. 17And it is easier for heaven and earth to
pass away than for one tittle of the law to fail.
18"Whoever divorces his wife and marries another commits adultery; and whoever marries her who is divorced
from *her* husband commits adultery.

The Rich Man and Lazarus

16:19–31 see pg. 280

19"There was a certain rich man who
was clothed in purple and fine linen and
fared sumptuously every day. 20But there was a certain beggar named Lazarus, full of sores, who was laid at his gate,
21desiring to be fed with the crumbs which fell[a] from the

(Bible text continued on page 281)

16:21 [a]NU-Text reads *with what fell.*

sinners, such as the tax gatherers, and so distant from people like the Pharisees who carefully practiced the finer points of the Law? How could God be compassionate toward Gentiles, while the Jews, who had been His people for generations, were passed by?

Have you ever felt that way when someone came into the faith? Have you ever felt that more attention is paid to new converts than to those who have followed biblical teaching all their lives? If so, Jesus' parable contains a comfort and a challenge. The comfort is that God never forgets who His children are and has great treasures stored up for them (v. 31). The challenge is to maintain a proper perspective—the perspective of compassion and mercy that is at the heart of the Father (v. 32). ◆

(continued from previous page)

in a way that brings others into the kingdom of Christ (vv. 8–9).

Jesus' words in vv. 10–11 make it plain that He is not denouncing money. On the contrary, our level of responsibility in His kingdom will depend on how we manage the resources that God gives us in this life. In fact, we might ask: What condition are our finances in? Are we overseeing our material resources prudently and faithfully?

The "bottom line" of this passage is found in vv. 12–13. All our earthly goods ultimately come from God and belong to Him. They are not really ours; we only manage them on His behalf. Any other outlook leads to a divided mind. We can't serve God if we're convinced that our money and property belong to us. We'll inevitably end up serving them.

We can't serve God and mammon. See "Don't Worry!" Matt. 6:19–34.

Jesus encountered a man who had a "divided mind" about money—and it cost the fellow everything. See "The Man Who Had It All—Almost," Mark 10:17–27.

CONSIDER THIS
16:19–31

SET FOR LIFE—BUT WHAT ABOUT ETERNITY?

The parable in vv. 19–31 draws a stark contrast between the rich man and the poor beggar Lazarus. The key to understanding it is to notice who Jesus told it to—the Pharisees, whom Luke describes as "lovers of money" (v. 14). Like the rich man, they were set for life—but not for eternity. They displayed an image of righteousness but were actually hypocrites (v. 15). Careful to preserve the letter of a greatly expanded Mosaic tradition, they violated the spirit of the Mosaic Law. Worst of all, they rejected Jesus as the Christ (v. 31).

So Jesus told the parable to rebuke them. He was not saying that all the poor will go to heaven and all the rich will go to hell. He was warning those who live as though this life were all that matters: they are playing with fire!

Clearly, it is a dangerous thing to have it made in this life. The insensitive rich man received his "good things" during his lifetime (v. 25). He was like the men described in Psalm 17:14 who "have their portion in this life," but have no portion in the life to come. Likewise, Psalm 73 talks about the wicked who appear to have it all: They live above the everyday problems that everyone else faces. They wear their pride like jewelry. They have more wealth than they can possibly use. Yet they belittle those who live hand-to-mouth. With all of their status and power they strut through life, giving not a care for God. Who needs Him?

But in eternity, the tables turn, as the rich man discovers to his horror (v. 23). The parable concludes on an ominous note. Jesus describes the hardness of people who are determined to reject God. Despite plenty of evidence to warn them that they are headed for ruin, they persist in their ways—just as the Pharisees did.

This grim parable moves one to ask: "What portion do I value most in life? Which am I more interested in—being set for life or set for eternity?" The writer of Psalm 73 made his commitment clear (vv. 25–26):

> Whom have I in heaven but You?
> And there is none upon earth
> that I desire besides You.
> My flesh and my heart fail;
> But God is the strength of
> my heart and my portion
> forever. ◆

Modern believers do well to carefully study what Paul wrote about money, given the emphasis on material things in our culture. *See "Christians and Money," 1 Tim. 6:6–19.*

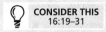

rich man's table. Moreover the dogs came and licked his
sores. 22So it was that the beggar died, and was carried by
the angels to Abraham's bosom. The rich man also died and
was buried. 23And being in torments in Hades, he lifted up
his eyes and saw Abraham afar off, and Lazarus in his bosom.
24"Then he cried and said, 'Father Abraham, have mercy
on me, and send Lazarus that he may dip the tip of his finger in water and cool my tongue; for I am tormented in this
flame.' 25But Abraham said, 'Son, remember that in your
lifetime you received your good things, and likewise
Lazarus evil things; but now he is comforted and you are
tormented. 26And besides all this, between us and you there
is a great gulf fixed, so that those who want to pass from
here to you cannot, nor can those from there pass to us.'
27"Then he said, 'I beg you therefore, father, that you
would send him to my father's house, 28for I have five
brothers, that he may testify to them, lest they also come to
this place of torment.' 29Abraham said to him, 'They have
Moses and the prophets; let them hear them.' 30And he said,
'No, father Abraham; but if one goes to them from the dead,
they will repent.' 31But he said to him, 'If they do not hear
Moses and the prophets, neither will they be persuaded
though one rise from the dead.' "

CHAPTER 17

Forgiveness

1Then He said to the disciples, "It is impossible that no
offenses should come, but woe *to him* through whom they
do come! 2It would be better for him if a millstone were
hung around his neck, and he were thrown into the sea,
than that he should offend one of these little ones. 3Take
heed to yourselves. If your brother sins against you,[a] rebuke
him; and if he repents, forgive him. 4And if he sins against
you seven times in a day, and seven times in a day returns
to you,[a] saying, 'I repent,' you shall forgive him."

About Faith and Faithfulness

17:5–10

5And the apostles said to the Lord, "Increase our faith."
6So the Lord said, "If you have faith as a mustard seed,
you can say to this mulberry tree, 'Be pulled up by the roots
and be planted in the sea,' and it would obey you. 7And
which of you, having a servant plowing or tending sheep,
will say to him when he has come in from the field, 'Come

17:3 [a]NU-Text omits *against you.* *17:4* [a]M-Text omits *to you.*

DOING YOUR DUTY

CONSIDER THIS 17:5–10 **Jesus' words in vv. 6–10 raise many puzzling questions. Did He intend that we should never thank people for doing what is expected of them? Should workers never expect praise for doing their jobs? Why are the workers "unprofitable" if in fact they did what was their duty? Should we always do more than expected? Was this a sermon on initiative and creativity? Who was Jesus addressing, bosses or employees?**

Actually, He was responding to the disciples' request for more faith (v. 5). That's a key to understanding this passage. Jesus had just challenged His followers to forgive others freely and repeatedly (17:1–4). But they replied, "Give us more faith," as if it took great faith to forgive.

But it does not. Forgiveness is not some supernatural ability that only God can give. It is not the product of great faith, but rather of simple obedience. That's what the servant in the parable must do—obey his master. It doesn't take great trust on the part of the servant to get a meal prepared; it just takes doing it. In the same way, forgiveness is *expected* of us as Christ's followers, since Christ has forgiven us. We are *obligated* to forgive others, so there's no reward attached to it.

The disciples expected a payoff for following Jesus (9:46–48; Matt. 20:20–28). But Jesus wanted them to see that following Him *was* a reward in itself!

WHERE ARE THE OTHERS?

CONSIDER THIS 17:11–19 **Once again Jesus chose a route that made it likely that He would encounter Samaritans (v. 11; see map at Luke 9:51–56). And once again Luke's account has to do with the tension between Jews and Samaritans.**

It's easy to see why Jesus would ask, "Where are the nine?" (v. 17). He was amazed at their lack of gratitude. But why did He call the one man who did return a "foreigner"? Luke singles out the fact that he was a Samaritan. That meant that he and Jesus were divided by a cultural wall that was virtually impenetrable. In fact, it was said to be unlawful for a Jew even to associate with a "foreigner" (compare Acts 10:28). Yet Jesus openly violated that taboo as He marveled at the Samaritan's thankful heart.

What of the other nine? Were they not Samaritans as well? Possibly, since this incident was taking place in or near Samaria. But is it not equally possible, given Luke's comment and Jesus' remark, that the other nine were not Samaritans, but Jews who had been driven away from the Jewish community to the Samaritans because of their leprous condition?

If so, their ingratitude was inexcusable. There was no racial wall separating them from Jesus. The only barrier had been their leprosy—and Jesus had removed that. They had every reason to turn in faith toward the Lord; but instead they turned away.

By contrast, a man who had every reason to stay away from Jesus returned and gave glory to God. As a

(continued on next page)

at once and sit down to eat'? 8But will he not rather say to
him, 'Prepare something for my supper, and gird yourself
and serve me till I have eaten and drunk, and afterward you
will eat and drink'? 9Does he thank that servant because he
did the things that were commanded him? I think not.[a] 10So
likewise you, when you have done all those things which
you are commanded, say, 'We are unprofitable servants. We
have done what was our duty to do.' "

Ten Lepers Healed in Samaria

17:11–19 11Now it happened as He went to
Jerusalem that He passed through the
midst of Samaria and Galilee. 12Then as He entered a certain
village, there met Him ten men who were lepers, who stood
afar off. 13And they lifted up *their* voices and said, "Jesus,
Master, have mercy on us!"
14So when He saw *them,* He said to them, "Go, show
yourselves to the priests." And so it was that as they went,
they were cleansed.
15And one of them, when he saw that he was healed, returned, and with a loud voice glorified God, 16and fell
down on *his* face at His feet, giving Him thanks. And he was
a Samaritan.
17So Jesus answered and said, "Were there not ten
cleansed? But where *are* the nine? 18Were there not any
found who returned to give glory to God except this foreigner?" 19And He said to him, "Arise, go your way. Your
faith has made you well."

The Kingdom of God and the Day of the Lord

20Now when He was asked by the Pharisees when the
kingdom of God would come, He answered them and said,
"The kingdom of God does not come with observation;
21nor will they say, 'See here!' or 'See there!'[a] For indeed, the
kingdom of God is within you."
22Then He said to the disciples, "The days will come
when you will desire to see one of the days of the Son of
Man, and you will not see *it.* 23And they will say to you,
'Look here!' or 'Look there!'[a] Do not go after *them* or follow
them. 24For as the lightning that flashes out of one *part* under heaven shines to the other *part* under heaven, so also
the Son of Man will be in His day. 25But first He must suffer
many things and be rejected by this generation. 26And as it
was in the days of Noah, so it will be also in the days of the
Son of Man: 27They ate, they drank, they married wives,
they were given in marriage, until the day that Noah en-

17:9 [a]NU-Text ends verse with *commanded;* M-Text omits *him.* *17:21* [a]NU-Text reverses *here* and *there.* *17:23* [a]NU-Text reverses *here* and *there.*

tered the ark, and the flood came and destroyed them all.
28Likewise as it was also in the days of Lot: They ate, they
drank, they bought, they sold, they planted, they built;
29but on the day that Lot went out of Sodom it rained fire
and brimstone from heaven and destroyed *them* all. 30Even
so will it be in the day when the Son of Man is revealed.
31"In that day, he who is on the housetop, and his goods
are in the house, let him not come down to take them away.
And likewise the one who is in the field, let him not turn
back. 32Remember Lot's wife. 33Whoever
seeks to save his life will lose it, and who-
ever loses his life will preserve it. 34I tell you, in that night
there will be two *men* in one bed: the one will be taken and
the other will be left. 35Two *women* will
be grinding together: the one will be
taken and the other left. 36Two *men* will be in the field: the
one will be taken and the other left."[a]
37And they answered and said to Him, "Where, Lord?"
So He said to them, "Wherever the body is, there the
eagles will be gathered together."

17:32

17:35 see pg. 284

CHAPTER 18

A Parable about an Unjust Judge

1Then He spoke a parable to them, that men always
ought to pray and not lose heart, 2saying: "There was in a
certain city a judge who did not fear God nor regard man.
3Now there was a widow in that city; and she came to him,
saying, 'Get justice for me from my adversary.' 4And he
would not for a while; but afterward he said within himself,
'Though I do not fear God nor regard man, 5yet because this
widow troubles me I will avenge her, lest by her continual
coming she weary me.' "
6Then the Lord said, "Hear what the unjust judge said.
7And shall God not avenge His own elect who cry out day
and night to Him, though He bears long with them? 8I tell
you that He will avenge them speedily. Nevertheless, when
the Son of Man comes, will He really find faith on the
earth?"

A Pharisee and a Tax Collector

18:9–14 see pg. 285

9Also He spoke this parable to some
who trusted in themselves that they were
righteous, and despised others: 10"Two men went up to the
temple to pray, one a Pharisee and the other a tax collector.
11The Pharisee stood and prayed thus with himself, 'God, I
thank You that I am not like other men—extortioners, un-

17:36 [a]NU-Text and M-Text omit verse 36.

(continued from previous page)

result, he received what the other nine—and most of the rest of Israel—did not: spiritual healing, and not just physical.

At times Jesus chose to take His disciples through Samaria and challenged their prejudices—sometimes with explosive results. See "Condemnation or Compassion?" Luke 9:51–56.

Lepers were common in the ancient world. They suffered from a slowly progressing, ordinarily incurable skin disease that was believed to be highly contagious and therefore greatly feared. Anyone who appeared to have leprosy, even if the symptoms were caused by some other condition, was banished from the community. See Matt. 8:2.

The Infamous Mrs. Lot

CONSIDER THIS 17:32 *Jesus warned His followers to remember Lot's wife (v. 32). By including this instruction in his Gospel, Luke made sure we would do that!*

Mrs. Lot was forced to leave her prosperous home in Sodom, taking only what she could carry. Angels had come to warn her and her husband of God's impending judgment on the city. They told her not to look back—not to linger, not to long for her old way of life. But she did and as a result, judgment fell on her as well: she was turned into a pillar of salt (Gen. 19:15–26).

The example of Lot's wife reminds us that the return of Christ will be just as sudden as the judgment on Sodom—and the consequences of longing for an old way of life just as severe.

just, adulterers, or even as this tax collector. 12I fast twice a
week; I give tithes of all that I possess.' 13And the tax collector, standing afar off, would not so much as raise *his* eyes to
heaven, but beat his breast, saying, 'God, be merciful to me
a sinner!' 14I tell you, this man went down to his house justified *rather* than the other; for everyone who exalts himself
will be humbled, and he who humbles himself will be exalted."

"He who humbles himself will be exalted." —Luke 18:14

"Let Children Come to Me"

18:15–17

15Then they also brought infants to
Him that He might touch them; but
when the disciples saw *it,* they rebuked them. 16But Jesus
called them to *Him* and said, "Let the little children come to
Me, and do not forbid them; for of such is the kingdom of
God. 17Assuredly, I say to you, whoever does not receive the
kingdom of God as a little child will by no means enter it."

Jesus Encounters a Rich Young Ruler

18:18–30 see pg. 286

18Now a certain ruler asked Him, saying, "Good Teacher, what shall I do to inherit eternal life?"
19So Jesus said to him, "Why do you call Me good? No
one *is* good but One, *that is,* God. 20You know the commandments: 'Do not commit adultery,' 'Do not murder,' 'Do

Please Bless Our Children

A CLOSER LOOK 18:15–17

In Jesus' day it was customary to ask famous rabbis to bless one's children. See "The Friend of Children" at Mark 10:13–16.

Grinding the Grain

YOU ARE THERE 17:35

Jesus' allusion to two women grinding grain (v. 35) speaks to the suddenness of His return in the middle of ordinary, everyday life. Grinding grain was a daily task, as meal was not stored in large quantities. It was a job reserved for women in Jewish culture. Most households owned their own hand-mill, a round, medium-sized stone that rotated around a wooden post inserted through a hole in the center. It could be worked by one woman but was easiest with two (v. 35). One woman fed in the grain while the other worked the stone to crush the hulls. The task required little mental effort but a lot of muscle.

not steal,' 'Do not bear false witness,' 'Honor your father
and your mother.' "[a]
21And he said, "All these things I have kept from my
youth."
22So when Jesus heard these things, He said to him, "You
still lack one thing. Sell all that you have and distribute to
the poor, and you will have treasure in heaven; and come,
follow Me."
23But when he heard this, he became very sorrowful, for
he was very rich.
24And when Jesus saw that he became very sorrowful, He
said, "How hard it is for those who have riches to enter the
kingdom of God! 25For it is easier for a camel to go through
the eye of a needle than for a rich man to enter the kingdom of God."
26And those who heard it said, "Who then can be saved?"
27But He said, "The things which are impossible with men
are possible with God."

Rewards for Self-Sacrifice

28Then Peter said, "See, we have left all[a] and followed
You."
29So He said to them, "Assuredly, I say to you, there is no
one who has left house or parents or brothers or wife or
children, for the sake of the kingdom of God, 30who shall
not receive many times more in this present time, and in
the age to come eternal life."

Jesus Predicts His Death

31Then He took the twelve aside and said to them, "Behold, we are going up to Jerusalem, and all things that are
written by the prophets concerning the Son of Man will be
accomplished. 32For He will be delivered to the Gentiles
and will be mocked and insulted and spit upon. 33They will
scourge *Him* and kill Him. And the third day He will rise
again."
34But they understood none of these things; this saying
was hidden from them, and they did not know the things
which were spoken.

A Blind Man Healed Near Jericho

18:35–43
see pg. 287

35Then it happened, as He was coming
near Jericho, that a certain blind man sat
by the road begging. 36And hearing a multitude passing by,
he asked what it meant. 37So they told him that Jesus of
Nazareth was passing by. 38And he cried out, saying, "Jesus,
Son of David, have mercy on me!"

18:20 [a]Exodus 20:12–16; Deuteronomy 5:16–20 *18:28* [a]NU-Text reads *our own.*

COMPARISONITIS WILL KILL YOU

CONSIDER THIS 18:9–14 **How do you establish your identity? Are you always comparing yourself to others? If so, you suffer from "comparisonitis," a malady that can kill you! Consider the Pharisee in Jesus' parable (vv. 9–14). He was so proud of himself that he started off his prayer with a comparison: "God, I thank you that I am not like other men."**

Do you do that? Do you try to build up your self-esteem by looking down on others less fortunate or gifted than you? If so, you are standing on shaky ground because your identity becomes uncertain. You can never be sure about yourself on those terms. Sooner or later, someone is bound to come along who is better than you in some way. You also risk loneliness, because no one cultivates friends by always finding fault with others in order to feel better about oneself.

In contrast to the Pharisee, the second man in Jesus' parable looked to God in order to see himself properly. Doing so exposed his sin but it also brought about God's forgiveness and restoration. This man shows us the path to true identity. It is based on honesty about ourselves and becoming like Christ.

Paul was aware of how deadly "comparisonitis" can be. That's why he offers an antidote for it. See "Do You Suffer from 'Comparisonitis'?" Rom. 12:3.

Holding Wealth or Serving Others?

CONSIDER THIS
18:18–30

Do you feel that your life would be better if only you were wealthy? Would your friends describe you as generous? These two issues were at stake in the encounter between Jesus and the rich young ruler (vv. 18–30). The young man was wealthy enough for this life, but he wanted to know about eternal life. He was confident that he was living a clean life, but he was fearful of his destiny and came seeking security for his future.

Jesus did not challenge the young ruler's claims about his life, but rather focused on what was most important to him—his wealth. *Was it available for others?* was the probing question. Jesus made service to others the indication of fitness for eternal life. Real wealth involves following Jesus, living not to be served but to serve others and to gives one's life for others (Matt. 20:28).

This episode poses a challenge: Where is your attention focused, on accumulation or servanthood?

Jesus perceived that the rich young ruler placed far too much value on his wealth and told him to give it away. Jesus did not give that same advice to every other rich person He encountered. But it was a requirement for this young man. See "The Man Who Had It All—Almost," Mark 10:17–27.

39 Then those who went before warned him that he should
be quiet; but he cried out all the more, "Son of David, have
mercy on me!"
40 So Jesus stood still and commanded him to be brought
to Him. And when he had come near, He asked him, 41 saying, "What do you want Me to do for you?"
He said, "Lord, that I may receive my sight."
42 Then Jesus said to him, "Receive your sight; your faith
has made you well." 43 And immediately he received his
sight, and followed Him, glorifying God. And all the people, when they saw *it,* gave praise to God.

CHAPTER 19

Zacchaeus Believes

19:1–10
see pg. 288

1 Then *Jesus* entered and passed
through Jericho. 2 Now behold, *there was*
a man named Zacchaeus who was a chief tax collector, and
he was rich. 3 And he sought to see who Jesus was, but
could not because of the crowd, for he was of short stature.
4 So he ran ahead and climbed up into a sycamore tree to
see Him, for He was going to pass that *way.* 5 And when
Jesus came to the place, He looked up and saw him,[a] and
said to him, "Zacchaeus, make haste and come down, for
today I must stay at your house." 6 So he made haste and
came down, and received Him joyfully. 7 But when they saw
it, they all complained, saying, "He has gone to be a guest
with a man who is a sinner."
8 Then Zacchaeus stood and said to the Lord, "Look, Lord,
I give half of my goods to the poor; and if I have taken anything from anyone by false accusation, I restore fourfold."
9 And Jesus said to him, "Today salvation has come to this
house, because he also is a son of Abraham; 10 for the Son of
Man has come to seek and to save that which was lost."

A Parable about an Unfaithful Steward

19:11–27
see pg. 289

11 Now as they heard these things, He
spoke another parable, because He was
near Jerusalem and because they thought the kingdom of
God would appear immediately. 12 Therefore He said: "A certain nobleman went into a far country to receive for himself
a kingdom and to return. 13 So he called ten of his servants,
delivered to them ten minas,[a] and said to them, 'Do business till I come.' 14 But his citizens hated him, and sent a
delegation after him, saying, 'We will not have this *man* to
reign over us.'

19:5 [a]NU-Text omits *and saw him.* *19:13* [a]The *mina* (Greek *mna,* Hebrew *minah*) was worth about three months' salary.

15"And so it was that when he returned, having received
the kingdom, he then commanded these servants, to whom
he had given the money, to be called to him, that he might
know how much every man had gained by trading. 16Then
came the first, saying, 'Master, your mina has earned ten
minas.' 17And he said to him, 'Well *done*, good servant; because you were faithful in a very little, have authority over
ten cities.' 18And the second came, saying, 'Master, your
mina has earned five minas.' 19Likewise he said to him, 'You
also be over five cities.'
20"Then another came, saying, 'Master, here is your mina,
which I have kept put away in a handkerchief. 21For I
feared you, because you are an austere man. You collect
what you did not deposit, and reap what you did not sow.'
22And he said to him, 'Out of your own mouth I will judge
you, *you* wicked servant. You knew that I was an austere
man, collecting what I did not deposit and reaping what I
did not sow. 23Why then did you not put
my money in the bank, that at my coming I might have collected it with interest?'

19:23

Banking

FOR YOUR INFO 19:23

When Jesus incorporated a bank into his parable of the talents (v. 23), He was referring to a relatively recent development in Jewish society. Institutional banking was not known in ancient Israel until the time of the Babylonian captivity (586 B.C.) because money as such did not exist at that time. Lending money at interest (a traditional function of banks) was forbidden in the Law (Ex. 22:25; Deut. 23:19–20). People protected their valuables by burying them or depositing them in temples or palaces.

During the captivity the Israelites became familiar with Babylonian banking practices. Some Jews joined the industry and became prominent bank officers. By New Testament times banking had become an established institution.

Although Jesus' parable shows that bankers received money for safekeeping and also paid interest, the most common New Testament reference to banking is to moneychanging (Matt. 21:12).

Holy Interruptions

CONSIDER THIS 18:35–43

How full is your schedule? Is it booked so tightly that only an act of God seems able to force an adjustment?

Jesus certainly had a demanding task with lots of responsibility. God sent Him to earth to gain salvation for all and to launch the church—and gave Him little more than three years to do it! Yet somehow Jesus' value system allowed for what we would call interruptions. People barged into His presence, even when His associates tried to prevent them.

Such was the case for a blind beggar by a roadside near Jericho (vv. 35–38). The man called out to Jesus as He and his leadership team were on their way to major events in Jerusalem. Then as now, well-traveled roads were cluttered with such inconveniences. Some tried to ignore the beggar, or at least keep him away. But amazingly, Jesus stopped and met the man's needs.

It's interesting that Jesus' very next encounter, with a known government crook, was also an interruption (Luke 19:1–10). Yet again, Jesus set aside His travel plans and turned aside to Zacchaeus' home to talk with him and meet his family and friends.

Do you have room for others in your life, especially the "little people" such as your children, an entry-level employee, a visitor to your church, or someone poor? When Jesus took time to serve a forgotten castaway, it caused everyone nearby to give praise to God (v. 43). Watch out for God's holy interruptions!

A Remedy for Tax Fraud

CONSIDER THIS 19:1–10 **Luke describes Zacchaeus as a tax collector (v. 2). His first-century readers would have understood that to mean that Zacchaeus was a cheating, corrupt lackey of the Roman government. In fact, he was a *chief* tax collector, which probably meant that he was "public enemy number one" to the Jews in Jericho, even worse than the notorious bandits on the city's main highway.**

But Jesus reached out to the curious Zacchaeus, prompting him to change his ways. In fact, Zacchaeus came up with his own formula for making restitution on the tax fraud he had practiced: a 400 percent rebate to those he had knowingly cheated, plus half of his net worth to go to the poor (v. 8). By paying restitution, he showed a new respect for the Old Testament Law (Ex. 22:1). Giving away his possessions was not a requirement of the Law, but it revealed his change of heart.

Imagine a corrupt public official or shady corporate financier today following that formula. Imagine a pastor challenging a businessperson in his congregation to repay four times what was made on a crooked deal. It sounds simplistic. But Zacchaeus was truly repentant. He was like the tax collector Jesus had recently mentioned in a parable who cried out, "God, be merciful to me a sinner!" (18:13).

Zacchaeus may have been a higher-ranking "publican" rather than an ordinary tax collector. Either way, he would have been despised by the citizens of Jericho. See "Who Were Those Tax Collectors," Matt. 9:10, and "Taxes," Mark 12:14.

24"And he said to those who stood by, 'Take the mina
from him, and give *it* to him who has ten minas.' 25(But
they said to him, 'Master, he has ten minas.') 26'For I say to
you, that to everyone who has will be given; and from him
who does not have, even what he has will be taken away
from him. 27But bring here those enemies of mine, who
did not want me to reign over them, and slay *them* before
me.' "

Jesus' Triumphal Entry into Jerusalem

28When He had said this, He went on ahead, going up to
Jerusalem. 29And it came to pass, when He drew near to
Bethphage[a] and Bethany, at the mountain called Olivet, *that*
He sent two of His disciples, 30saying, "Go into the village
opposite *you*, where as you enter you will find a colt tied,
on which no one has ever sat. Loose it and bring *it here.*
31And if anyone asks you, 'Why are you loosing *it?*' thus you
shall say to him, 'Because the Lord has need of it.' "
32So those who were sent went their way and found *it* just
as He had said to them. 33But as they were loosing the colt,
the owners of it said to them, "Why are you loosing the
colt?"
34And they said, "The Lord has need of him." 35Then they
brought him to Jesus. And they threw their own clothes on
the colt, and they set Jesus on him. 36And as He went, *many*
spread their clothes on the road.
37Then, as He was now drawing near the descent of the
Mount of Olives, the whole multitude of the disciples began
to rejoice and praise God with a loud voice for all the
mighty works they had seen, 38saying:

" 'Blessed *is* the King who comes in the name of the
LORD!'[a]
Peace in heaven and glory in the highest!"

39And some of the Pharisees called to Him from the
crowd, "Teacher, rebuke Your disciples."
40But He answered and said to them, "I tell you that if
these should keep silent, the stones would immediately cry
out."

Jesus Weeps over Jerusalem

19:41–46 see pg. 290
41Now as He drew near, He saw the city
and wept over it, 42saying, "If you had
known, even you, especially in this your day, the things *that
make* for your peace! But now they are hidden from your
eyes. 43For days will come upon you when your enemies
will build an embankment around you, surround you and

19:29 [a]M-Text reads *Bethsphage.* *19:38* [a]Psalm 118:26

close you in on every side, 44 and level you, and your children within you, to the ground; and they will not leave in
you one stone upon another, because you did not know the
time of your visitation."

Jesus Purges the Temple

45 Then He went into the temple and began to drive out
those who bought and sold in it,[a] 46 saying to them, "It is
written, 'My house is[a] a house of prayer,'[b] but you have
made it a 'den of thieves.' "[c]
47 And He was teaching daily in the temple. But the chief
priests, the scribes, and the leaders of the people sought to
destroy Him, 48 and were unable to do anything; for all the
people were very attentive to hear Him.

CHAPTER 20

Jesus' Authority Questioned

1 Now it happened on one of those days, as He taught the
people in the temple and preached the gospel, *that* the chief
priests and the scribes, together with the elders, confronted
Him 2 and spoke to Him, saying, "Tell us, by what authority
are You doing these things? Or who is he who gave You this
authority?"
3 But He answered and said to them, "I also will ask you
one thing, and answer Me: 4 The baptism of John—was it
from heaven or from men?"
5 And they reasoned among themselves, saying, "If we say,
'From heaven,' He will say, 'Why then[a] did you not believe
him?' 6 But if we say, 'From men,' all the people will stone
us, for they are persuaded that John was a prophet." 7 So
they answered that they did not know where *it was* from.
8 And Jesus said to them, "Neither will I tell you by what
authority I do these things."

A Parable about Wicked Vinedressers

20:9–19 see pg. 290

9 Then He began to tell the people this
parable: "A certain man planted a vine-
yard, leased it to vinedressers, and went into a far country
for a long time. 10 Now at vintage-time he sent a servant to
the vinedressers, that they might give him some of the fruit
of the vineyard. But the vinedressers beat him and sent *him*
away empty-handed. 11 Again he sent another servant; and
they beat him also, treated *him* shamefully, and sent *him*
away empty-handed. 12 And again he sent a third; and they
wounded him also and cast *him* out.

19:45 [a]NU-Text reads *those who were selling.* *19:46* [a]NU-Text reads *shall be.* [b]Isaiah 56:7 [c]Jeremiah 7:11 *20:5* [a]NU-Text and M-Text omit *then.*

A JOB TO DO

CONSIDER THIS 19:11–27

The parable recorded in vv. 12–27 describes a case of absentee ownership and on-site management. Actually, it reflected the government in Palestine, in which Rome "owned" the region but left it in the hands of local governors, such as the infamous Herods (see Acts 12:1–2).

The reason that Jesus told this story is given in v. 11: the kingdom of God would be delayed, and He wanted His followers to know some of the implications of that delay. Chief among them is that we as believers have a job to do. We've been given resources to manage until the Lord returns (v. 13). These include our skills, jobs, time, wealth, mental capacities, physical bodies, and so on. Eventually we will give a full accounting for how we have used these (v. 15).

Jesus delivered this lesson in the form of a parable and was obviously talking about more than the management of money. Yet it's clear that He expects His followers to live out their everyday, temporal lives with an eye toward His return. He will ask us what we have done with our lives, and reward us accordingly.

This story is very similar to the parable of the talents, Matt. 25:14–30, probably a story that Jesus told frequently.

Rom. 14:12 and 1 Pet. 4:5 also speak of the accounting believers will make to God for what He has entrusted to us.

COMPASSION AND ANGER IN ONE PERSON?

CONSIDER THIS 19:41–46 **It isn't easy to show both compassion and anger in appropriate ways. With most people it seems like it's one or the other, often in extremes—sugar-coated sentimentality or vicious, destructive rage, neither of which helps anyone.**

In vv. 41–46, we see that Jesus acted out of both compassion and anger. As He drew near Jerusalem and saw the plight of its people, He was moved to grief, and His eyes filled with tears (v. 41). But before long He saw one source of the city's problem—the unjust moneychangers in

(continued on next page)

13"Then the owner of the vineyard said, 'What shall I do?
I will send my beloved son. Probably they will respect *him*
when they see him.' 14But when the vinedressers saw him,
they reasoned among themselves, saying, 'This is the heir.
Come, let us kill him, that the inheritance may be ours.'
15So they cast him out of the vineyard and killed *him*.
Therefore what will the owner of the vineyard do to them?
16He will come and destroy those vinedressers and give the
vineyard to others."

And when they heard *it* they said, "Certainly not!"
17Then He looked at them and said, "What then is this
that is written:

> 'The stone which the builders rejected
> Has become the chief cornerstone' ?[a]

18Whoever falls on that stone will be broken; but on
whomever it falls, it will grind him to powder."
19And the chief priests and the scribes that very hour
sought to lay hands on Him, but they feared the people[a]—for they knew He had spoken this parable against
them.

20:17 [a]Psalm 118:22 *20:19* [a]M-Text reads *but they were afraid.*

CONSIDER THIS 20:9–19

OWNERS OR TENANTS?

Are we the owners of possessions like money, houses, land, cars, clothing, TV sets, and so forth? Our culture tells us that we are. In fact, many messages tell us that significance is determined by how much we own and how much what we own is worth.

But the parable of the vineyard owner (vv. 9–19) challenges that way of looking at things. Jesus tells of tenants or workers who scheme to steal a vineyard from its owner rather than return its produce to him. They value the land, the trees, and the fruit more than people—they beat the owner's representatives (vv. 10–12)—and even more than life itself—they kill the owner's own son (vv. 14–15).

In the same way, the community leaders among Jesus' listeners harbored the same desire to kill Him (v. 19). At that point, however, they were prevented from acting by the rest of the people. But eventually they would have their way. Just as their forebears had rejected the prophets that God had sent, so they would now reject God's own Son in a futile effort to keep the nation under their control. But they would only succeed in bringing down God's judgment.

Jesus Tested about Tax Payment

20:20–26 [20]So they watched *Him,* and sent spies
who pretended to be righteous, that they
might seize on His words, in order to deliver Him to the power and the authority of the governor.
[21]Then they asked Him, saying, "Teacher, we know that You say and teach rightly, and You do not show personal favoritism, but teach the way of God in truth: [22]Is it lawful for us to pay taxes to Caesar or not?"
[23]But He perceived their craftiness, and said to them, "Why do you test Me?[a] [24]Show Me a denarius. Whose image and inscription does it have?"

They answered and said, "Caesar's."

[25]And He said to them, "Render therefore to Caesar the things that are Caesar's, and to God the things that are God's."

[26]But they could not catch Him in His words in the presence of the people. And they marveled at His answer and kept silent.

20:23 [a]NU-Text omits *Why do you test Me?*

◆ ◆ ◆ ◆ ◆ ◆ ◆ ◆ ◆ ◆ ◆ ◆ ◆ ◆ ◆

This parable challenges us to consider what God has entrusted to our care, and what He expects from us. No matter what He has given us, we are like tenants; the true Owner of all things is the Creator God. He has loaned us our lives, our families, our skills, and all our resources. He calls us to manage those gifts in a way that honors Him.

That means that we must resist getting so tied to our possessions and the accumulation of more possessions that we are tempted to resort to evil or even violence to keep them. We must hold things with the attitude of tenants, keeping in mind who really owns them—God who loaned them to us for His glory and the service of others. ◆

One of the most important resources that God has entrusted to us is our work. Whatever we do for a living, God wants us to do it as though we were working for Him. See "Who's the Boss?" Col. 3:22–24, and "People at Work," Heb. 2:7.

The Bible has much to offer believers today about how they handle their wealth. See "Christians and Money," 1 Tim. 6:6–19.

(continued from previous page)

the temple. With stern but controlled anger, He drove them out, taking care to put a name on their offense: "robbery" (vv. 45–46).

As you consider Jesus' responses in these two situations, it's worth asking: What moves you to tears? What injustices make you indignant? What productive or corrective action do you take in light of how you feel? Do you even allow yourself to react emotionally to the pain around you, or do you choose detached, dispassionate analysis or just plain apathy?

RETALIATION FOILED

CONSIDER THIS 20:20–26 **When highly competitive people are overshadowed or intimidated they often resort to ugly tactics to try to regain their superiority. An unhealthy need for importance, success, and power can bring out the worst in anyone. Have you noticed this pattern among coworkers, family members, or yourself?**

As community leaders saw Jesus once again gaining popularity and influence, they schemed to ensnare Him (vv. 9–19). They even enlisted agents for their plot (v. 20). Unfortunately, there always seems to be a ready supply of help for evil designs.

But Jesus refused to stoop to their methods (vv. 23–25). As they tried to undo Him, He foiled their plans with grace and truth.

Do you know how to respond to trickery or evil when it is intended for you?

Scripture challenges us that rather than being overcome by evil, we should overcome evil with good. See "Do Not Avenge Yourself," Rom. 12:19–21.

Jesus Tested about Resurrection

27Then some of the Sadducees, who deny that there is a
resurrection, came to *Him* and asked Him, 28saying:
"Teacher, Moses wrote to us *that* if a man's brother dies,
having a wife, and he dies without children, his brother
should take his wife and raise up offspring for his brother.
29Now there were seven brothers. And the first took a wife,
and died without children. 30And the second[a] took her as
wife, and he died childless. 31Then the third took her, and
in like manner the seven also; and they left no children,[a]
and died. 32Last of all the woman died also. 33Therefore, in
the resurrection, whose wife does she become? For all seven
had her as wife."

20:34

34Jesus answered and said to them,
"The sons of this age marry and are given
in marriage. 35But those who are counted worthy to attain

(Bible text continued on page 294)

20:30 [a]NU-Text ends verse 30 here. *20:31* [a]NU-Text and M-Text read *the seven also left no children.*

"THE SONS OF THIS AGE MARRY AND ARE GIVEN IN MARRIAGE." —Luke 20:34

CONSIDER THIS
20:34

FAMILIES OF THE GOSPELS

As Jesus affirmed in His reply to the scheming Sadducees, marriages and families are fundamental institutions of life (v. 34). The Gospels support that view by portraying many different kinds of families, some large, some quite small. As the accompanying chart shows, some faced severe difficulties and "dysfunctions" not unlike those that families face today. The New Testament openly addresses these conditions and offers honest hope.

Judging by Acts and the New Testament letters, acceptance of the faith seemed often to be a decision of an entire family or clan during the early days of the church. See "Families of the Early Church," Acts 16:31–34.

FAMILIES OF THE GOSPELS

Gospel Appearances: Matthew Mark Luke John

Family Name	Description
•Zacharias •His wife Elizabeth •Son John the Baptist	The father is a temple priest on a rotating basis. He and his wife face a surprise pregnancy late in life that poses unique problems, especially for him. Later, their son John announces the arrival of the long-awaited Messiah.
•Joseph •His wife Mary •Jesus •Other sons and daughters	The father is a carpenter in the Galilean village of Nazareth. He and his fiancée face the delicate challenge of a supernatural pregnancy during their engagement. Their Child is delivered in a common stable and they become political refugees because of the new Baby. They struggle to understand their growing Son.
•Peter •His brother Andrew •Peter's mother-in-law	The family runs a fishing business on Lake Galilee. The two sons leave the business to follow Jesus. Later Peter's mother-in-law becomes sick as Jesus visits Peter's home.
•Zebedee •His wife, the mother of James and John •James •John	The family has a fishing business along with Peter's family on Lake Galilee. The mother approaches Jesus about positions of power for her sons in His kingdom. Both sons eventually hold significant leadership positions in the growing movement.
•The Herods	Powerful provincial rulers of Roman Palestine; the family name is remembered for violence, incest, and political intrigue. Herod the Great responds viciously to rumors of a new king born in the realm. Herod Antipas becomes a lover of his niece Herodias, who had been married to his brother Philip before leaving him for Antipas. The couple murders John the Baptist for criticizing their relationship.
•A Canaanite woman •Her demonized daughter	A despised minority woman displays relentless faith, winning Christ's approval and help for her daughter.
•A man •His epileptic son	Jesus heals the afflicted boy after His disciples could not.
•Jairus •His wife •His 12-year-old daughter	The father is a synagogue ruler who turns to Jesus when his daughter is on the verge of dying. When Jesus arrives the child is dead, but Jesus restores her to life.
•Anna	An 84-year-old widow and prophetess who serves in the temple rejoices to see the Christ child.
•A Roman centurion of Capernaum	Jesus heals his highly valued servant.
•A widow of Nain •Her only son	Jesus shows compassion on the woman by restoring her dead son to life.
•Joanna •Chuza, her husband	The wife of Herod's steward provides money for Jesus and joins several other women as His followers.
•Mary •Her sister Martha •Their brother Lazarus	Mary treats Jesus as a valued spiritual director. Sister Martha serves Him as a diligent worker. Brother Lazarus becomes a close friend. When he dies, Jesus restores him to life.
•A woman of Samaria •Her five previous husbands •Her lover	She meets Jesus at a well in Samaria and discovers Him to be the Living Water.
•A royal official of Cana •His son	After Jesus restores the boy to health, the entire household believes in Him.
•A woman caught in adultery	Jesus protects her from vindictive religious leaders.
•A man born blind •His parents	After Jesus restores his sight, the man is ostracized by the religious leaders for remaining loyal to Jesus.

that age, and the resurrection from the dead, neither marry
nor are given in marriage; 36nor can they die anymore, for
they are equal to the angels and are sons of God, being sons
of the resurrection. 37But even Moses showed in the *burning*
bush *passage* that the dead are raised, when he called the
Lord 'the God of Abraham, the God of Isaac, and the God of
Jacob.'[a] 38For He is not the God of the dead but of the living, for all live to Him."

The Scribes Confounded

20:39

39Then some of the scribes answered
and said, "Teacher, You have spoken

20:37 [a]Exodus 3:6, 15

FOR YOUR INFO
20:39

SCRIBES

The scribes who challenged Jesus (v. 39) were members of a learned class in Israel who studied the Scriptures and served as copyists, editors, and teachers.

The era of the scribes began after the Jews returned from captivity in Babylon. Ezra the scribe directed that the Law be read before the entire nation (Neh. 8–10), signaling a return to exact observance of all the laws and rites that had been given. At first the priests were responsible for the scientific study and professional communication of this legal code. But that job eventually passed to the scribes. Unfortunately, their official interpretation of the meaning of the Law soon became more important than the Law itself.

From their position of strength, scribes began to enforce their rules and practices with binding authority. By the time of Jesus, they had become a new upper class. Large numbers of priests in Jerusalem joined the profession, including the Jewish historian, Josephus. Others came from the ordinary classes, including merchants, carpenters, tent makers, and even day laborers, like Hillel, who became a famous Jewish teacher. Most probably kept their former occupations, since scribes were not paid for their services and had to earn a living in other ways.

Prospective scribes went through a set course of study for several years, centered at Jerusalem. Students were in continual contact with the teacher, listening to his instruction. The disciple-scribe first had to master all the traditional material and a unique method of interpretation. The aim was to give the apprentice competence in making decisions on questions of religious legislation and justice.

well." 40But after that they dared not question Him anymore.
41And He said to them, "How can they say that the Christ
is the Son of David? 42Now David himself said in the Book
of Psalms:

'The LORD said to my Lord,
"Sit at My right hand,
43 Till I make Your enemies Your footstool." '[a]

44Therefore David calls Him 'Lord'; how is He then his
Son?"
45Then, in the hearing of all the people, He said to His

20:43 [a]Psalm 110:1

Within this course of study, according to tradition, there were "secrets" of interpretation to be learned, forbidden degrees of knowledge, which were not to be expounded before three or more persons. Some chapters in the Bible were to be explained only to sages, and certain teaching was hidden from the masses because they could not be trusted to understand and apply the Law.

Ordination required constant study, often beginning at age 14 and continuing to the age of 40. Once qualified, scribes could act as judges, be called rabbis, and occupy positions in law, government, and education. They joined the chief priests and aristocratic families who made up the Jewish council. They were held in great esteem by the people, as only ordained teachers could transmit and create the tradition.

Sometimes the Gospels refer to scribes as lawyers, a title identifying them as experts in the Mosaic Law (Matt. 22:35; Luke 7:30). In Jesus' day, they were usually associated with the Pharisees (Matt. 12:38; Mark 7:5; Luke 6:7). The two groups developed attitudes of pride based on their professional privileges. Jesus strongly warned against that posture and boldly attacked the religious hypocrisy of these religious leaders (Matt. 23). ◆

Luke records that the legal masters at Jerusalem were astonished at one boy's grasp of their material. See "Jesus the Student," Luke 2:46–47.

Jesus drew upon the image of a scribe in a parable He taught to show that we can never come to the end of what God has revealed. See "Treasures New and Old," Matt. 13:52.

"HE IS NOT THE GOD OF THE DEAD BUT OF THE LIVING." —Luke 20:38

disciples, 46"Beware of the scribes, who desire to go around in long robes, love greetings in the marketplaces, the best seats in the synagogues, and the best places at feasts, 47who devour widows' houses, and for a pretense make long prayers. These will receive greater condemnation."

CHAPTER 21

A Poor Widow's Contribution

21:1–4

1And He looked up and saw the rich
putting their gifts into the treasury, 2and
He saw also a certain poor widow putting in two mites. 3So
He said, "Truly I say to you that this poor widow has put in

FOR YOUR INFO 21:20

JERUSALEM SURROUNDED

Those living in Jerusalem at the time of Christ had reason to believe His prediction that the city would eventually fall to an invading army (v. 20; see also 19:41–44). Political tensions were at a breaking point.

The Jews bitterly resented Rome's occupation of their homeland, which brought the corrupting influence of Greek culture, crushing taxes, and cruel government. Some, like the Zealots, fanned the flames of revolution by leading tax revolts and launching terrorist strikes against Roman troops and officials (see "Party Politics of Jesus' Day," Matt. 16:1).

The final chapter in the drama began in A.D. 66 when a skirmish broke out between Jews and Gentiles over the desecration of the synagogue at Caesarea. Unable to prevail politically, the Jews retaliated religiously by banning all sacrifices on behalf of foreigners, even for the emperor himself. Furthermore, access to the temple grounds at Jerusalem would be strictly limited to Jewish countrymen.

Meanwhile, the Roman procurator ordered an enormous payment from the temple treasury. The Jews balked and assumed that the ruler would back down. Instead, he unleashed troops on the city who raped and pillaged at will, even resorting to flogging and crucifixion. The slaughter claimed about 3,600 Jewish lives, including children.

The city went into riot. Arsonists torched official buildings along with the home of the high priest, long suspected of collusion with the empire. Elsewhere, Jews overran Roman fortresses and ambushed a legion of reinforcements, capturing arms for the revolt at Jerusalem. In the end, the Romans retreated, temporarily leaving the Holy City in the hands of the rebels.

more than all; [4]for all these out of their abundance have put in offerings for God,[a] but she out of her poverty put in all the livelihood that she had."

Jesus Teaches about the End Times

[5]Then, as some spoke of the temple, how it was adorned with beautiful stones and donations, He said, [6]"These things which you see—the days will come in which not *one* stone shall be left upon another that shall not be thrown down."

[7]So they asked Him, saying, "Teacher, but when will these things be? And what sign *will there be* when these things are about to take place?"

21:4 [a]NU-Text omits *for God*.

◆ ◆ ◆ ◆ ◆ ◆ ◆ ◆ ◆ ◆ ◆ ◆ ◆ ◆ ◆ ◆ ◆

Yet no matter how brave or committed the Jewish revolutionaries may have been, they were no match for the professional armies of Rome. Emperor Nero dispatched Vespasian, his top general, to the region. Beginning in Galilee and working his way south, he systematically cut off Jerusalem's lines of supply—and escape—from Babylonia, the Mediterranean, and Egypt. By A.D. 70, he was poised to launch the final assault on Jerusalem.

However, Vespasian returned to Rome to succeed Nero as emperor, leaving his son Titus to complete the campaign. Advancing on the city from the north, the east, and the west, his legions erected siege walls and finally took the city, fulfilling Jesus' prophecy. Herod's temple was destroyed only three years after its completion (compare Luke 21:5–6), the priesthood and the council were abolished, and all Jews were expelled from the remains of the city.

Jesus wept to think of such carnage (Matt. 23:37–39). Yet it was one of the prices His generation paid for rejecting Him as its Messiah. Today, as we read about Jesus' grim prediction and its tragic fulfillment in A.D. 70, we are challenged to ask a sobering question: If the destruction of Jerusalem came about just as Jesus said, what other prophecies did He make that might have to do with us, that we ought to take literally and seriously? ◆

Jerusalem fell despite the fact that it was walled and well-situated for defense on two triangular ridges. See Matt. 23:37.

HOW POOR WAS THE WIDOW?

☑ FOR YOUR INFO 21:1–4 **Jesus called the widow in vv. 1–4 "poor." The word He used referred to a person so destitute that she was literally in danger of death.**

It is hard to reckon what the two mites that she threw into the treasury would be worth in today's currency. But even in her day they were not much. Each mite was worth about one-thirty-second of a denarius, the daily wage of a soldier, which would be less than fifty cents today.

The important thing to note is that the two coins were "all the livelihood that she had" (v. 21). She was truly destitute—the sort of widow who would later be eligible for support from the church (1 Tim. 5:5). Nevertheless, she gave generously to the temple. Jesus praised her for her faithfulness, even though it meant sacrifice.

In doing so, the Lord showed that God's accounting differs from ours. He pays attention to our attitudes in giving more than the absolute dollar amount of our gifts.

Widows were common in the ancient world, and usually poor, as their gender was a disadvantage in the ancient economies. However, Luke tells about one instance when the church stepped in to help struggling widows. See "A Growing Movement Confronts Ethnic Prejudice," Acts 6:2–6. See also "Widows," 1 Tim. 5:3.

8And He said: "Take heed that you not be deceived. For
many will come in My name, saying, 'I am *He*,' and, 'The
time has drawn near.' Therefore[a] do not go after them. 9But
when you hear of wars and commotions, do not be terrified; for these things must come to pass first, but the end
will not come immediately."

10Then He said to them, "Nation will rise against nation,
and kingdom against kingdom. 11And there will be great
earthquakes in various places, and famines and pestilences;
and there will be fearful sights and great signs from heaven.
12But before all these things, they will lay their hands on
you and persecute *you*, delivering *you* up to the synagogues
and prisons. You will be brought before kings and rulers for
My name's sake. 13But it will turn out for you as an occasion
for testimony. 14Therefore settle *it* in your hearts not to
meditate beforehand on what you will answer; 15for I will
give you a mouth and wisdom which all your adversaries
will not be able to contradict or resist. 16You will be
betrayed even by parents and brothers, relatives and
friends; and they will put *some* of you to death. 17And you
will be hated by all for My name's sake. 18But not a hair of
your head shall be lost. 19By your patience possess your
souls.

"I WILL GIVE YOU A MOUTH AND WISDOM. . . ."
—Luke 21:15

21:20 see pg. 296

20"But when you see Jerusalem surrounded by armies, then know that its
desolation is near. 21Then let those who are in Judea flee to
the mountains, let those who are in the midst of her depart,
and let not those who are in the country enter her. 22For
these are the days of vengeance, that all things which are
written may be fulfilled. 23But woe to those who are pregnant and to those who are nursing babies in those days! For
there will be great distress in the land and wrath upon this
people. 24And they will fall by the edge of the sword, and be
led away captive into all nations. And Jerusalem will be
trampled by Gentiles until the times of the Gentiles are fulfilled.

25"And there will be signs in the sun, in the moon, and in
the stars; and on the earth distress of nations, with perplex-
ity, the sea and the waves roaring; 26men's hearts failing
them from fear and the expectation of those things which
are coming on the earth, for the powers of the heavens will
be shaken. 27Then they will see the Son of Man coming in a
cloud with power and great glory. 28Now when these things
begin to happen, look up and lift up your heads, because
your redemption draws near."

29Then He spoke to them a parable: "Look at the fig tree,
and all the trees. 30When they are already budding, you see
and know for yourselves that summer is now near. 31So you

21:8 [a]NU-Text omits *Therefore*.

also, when you see these things happening, know that the
kingdom of God is near. 32Assuredly, I say to you, this generation will by no means pass away till all things take place.
33Heaven and earth will pass away, but My words will by no
means pass away.

21:34–36

34“But take heed to yourselves, lest
your hearts be weighed down with
carousing, drunkenness, and cares of this life, and that Day
come on you unexpectedly. 35For it will come as a snare on
all those who dwell on the face of the whole earth. 36Watch
therefore, and pray always that you may be counted
worthy[a] to escape all these things that will come to pass,
and to stand before the Son of Man.”
37And in the daytime He was teaching in the temple, but
at night He went out and stayed on the mountain called
Olivet. 38Then early in the morning all the people came to
Him in the temple to hear Him.

CHAPTER 22

Judas Conspires to Betray Jesus

1Now the Feast of Unleavened Bread drew near, which is
called Passover. 2And the chief priests and the scribes
sought how they might kill Him, for they feared the people.
3Then Satan entered Judas, surnamed Iscariot, who was
numbered among the twelve. 4So he went his way and conferred with the chief priests and captains, how he might betray Him to them. 5And they were glad, and agreed to give
him money. 6So he promised and sought opportunity to betray Him to them in the absence of the multitude.

Jesus and the Twelve Eat the Passover

7Then came the Day of Unleavened Bread, when the

22:7

Passover must be killed. 8And He sent
Peter and John, saying, “Go and prepare
the Passover for us, that we may eat.”
9So they said to Him, “Where do You want us to prepare?”
10And He said to them, “Behold, when you have entered
the city, a man will meet you carrying a pitcher of water;

21:36 [a]NU-Text reads *may have strength.*

Passover

FOR YOUR INFO 22:7 **The Passover and Feast of Unleavened Bread (v. 7) was the first of three great festivals of the Hebrews.**

The name Passover recalls the deliverance of Israel from slavery in Egypt (Ex. 12:1—13:16). God sent His angel to kill all the firstborn sons of the Egyptians in order to persuade Pharaoh to let His people go. Hebrew families were instructed to sacrifice a lamb and smear its blood on the doorpost of their house as a signal to God that His angel should “pass over” them during the judgment.

Passover was observed on the fourteenth day of the first month, Abib (March-April), with the service beginning in the evening (Lev. 23:6). It was on the evening of this day that Israel left Egypt in haste. Unleavened bread was used in the celebration as a reminder that the people had no time to leaven their bread before they ate their final meal as slaves in Egypt.

In New Testament times, Passover became a pilgrim festival. Large numbers gathered in Jerusalem to observe the annual celebration. Thus an unusually large crowd was on hand to take part in the events surrounding Jesus’ entry into the city (Luke 19:37–39) and His arrest, trial, and crucifixion (23:18, 27, 35, 48). Apparently many stayed on until the Feast of Pentecost, when they heard Peter’s persuasive sermon (Acts 2:1–41).

Like the blood of the lambs which saved the Hebrews from destruction in Egypt, the blood of Jesus, the ultimate Passover Lamb, saves us from the power of sin and death.

The Cares of This Life

A CLOSER LOOK 21:34–36 *Jesus warned us about becoming weighed down with the “cares of this life” (v. 34). He was not suggesting that everyday affairs are unimportant. But isn’t it all too easy to get so wrapped up in the pressures and pace of life that we ignore our Lord? For more on this critical issue, see “Don’t Worry!” Matt. 6:19–34.*

In celebrating His final Passover meal, Jesus ate food that was highly symbolic. See Matt. 26:19.

Passover was one of three major feasts celebrated by the Jews. To find out about the others, see the table, “Jewish Feasts,” Luke 2:42.

LEADERSHIP EQUALS HUMILITY?

CONSIDER THIS 22:24–27 **Are you in a position of leadership in your job, in government, in your family, or in your church? In vv. 24–27, Jesus shows that biblical leadership starts with humility, by *serving* others.**

The autocratic, authoritarian leadership style has fallen out of favor among many today. Yet a subtle, far more powerful approach has appeared, characterized by manipulation and selfish ambition. Masking their true intentions, many new-style "leaders" pretend to offer a "win-win" arrangement; but they have no real concern for others, except insofar as others can help them achieve their objectives.

Both styles are out of the question if we want to lead with Christlikeness. He asks us to take the posture of a *servant*—to genuinely concern ourselves with the rights, the needs, and the welfare of those we lead. Christ Himself has provided the example of true servant-leadership: not to be served, but to serve and to give (Matt. 20:28).

Paul encouraged believers to develop the same attitude that Christ had. See "Humility—The Scandalous Virtue," Phil. 2:3.

follow him into the house which he enters. 11 Then you shall
say to the master of the house, 'The Teacher says to you,
"Where is the guest room where I may eat the Passover with
My disciples?" ' 12 Then he will show you a large, furnished
upper room; there make ready."
13 So they went and found it just as He had said to them,
and they prepared the Passover.
14 When the hour had come, He sat down, and the twelve[a]
apostles with Him. 15 Then He said to them, "With *fervent*
desire I have desired to eat this Passover with you before I
suffer; 16 for I say to you, I will no longer eat of it until it is
fulfilled in the kingdom of God."
17 Then He took the cup, and gave thanks, and said, "Take
this and divide *it* among yourselves; 18 for I say to you,[a] I
will not drink of the fruit of the vine until the kingdom of
God comes."
19 And He took bread, gave thanks and broke *it*, and gave
it to them, saying, "This is My body which is given for you;
do this in remembrance of Me."
20 Likewise He also *took* the cup after supper, saying, "This
cup *is* the new covenant in My blood, which is shed
for you. 21 But behold, the hand of My betrayer *is* with
Me on the table. 22 And truly the Son of Man goes as it has
been determined, but woe to that man by whom He is betrayed!"
23 Then they began to question among themselves, which
of them it was who would do this thing.

22:24–27

22:25 see pg. 302

22:24–30

24 Now there was also a dispute among
them, as to which of them should be
considered the greatest. 25 And He said to
them, "The kings of the Gentiles exercise
lordship over them, and those who exercise authority over
them are called 'benefactors.' 26 But not so
among you; on the contrary, he who is
greatest among you, let him be as the younger, and he who
governs as he who serves. 27 For who *is* greater, he who sits
at the table, or he who serves? *Is* it not he who sits at the
table? Yet I am among you as the One who serves.
28 "But you are those who have continued with Me in My
trials. 29 And I bestow upon you a kingdom, just as My Father bestowed *one* upon Me, 30 that you may eat and drink
at My table in My kingdom, and sit on thrones judging the
twelve tribes of Israel."
31 And the Lord said,[a] "Simon, Simon! Indeed, Satan has
asked for you, that he may sift *you* as wheat. 32 But I have
prayed for you, that your faith should not fail; and when
you have returned to *Me*, strengthen your brethren."

22:14 [a]NU-Text omits *twelve.* *22:18* [a]NU-Text adds *from now on.* *22:31* [a]NU-Text omits *And the Lord said.*

33But he said to Him, "Lord, I am ready to go with You,
both to prison and to death."
34Then He said, "I tell you, Peter, the rooster shall not
crow this day before you will deny three times that you
know Me."
35And He said to them, "When I sent you without money
bag, knapsack, and sandals, did you lack anything?"
So they said, "Nothing."
36Then He said to them, "But now, he who has a money
bag, let him take *it,* and likewise a knapsack; and he who
has no sword, let him sell his garment and buy one. 37For I
say to you that this which is written must still be accomplished in Me: 'And He was numbered with the transgressors.'[a] For the things concerning Me have an end."
38So they said, "Lord, look, here *are* two swords."
And He said to them, "It is enough."

Jesus Prays in Gethsemane

22:39–46 see pg. 305

39Coming out, He went to the Mount
of Olives, as He was accustomed, and His
disciples also followed Him. 40When He came to the place,
He said to them, "Pray that you may not enter into temptation."
41And He was withdrawn from them about a stone's
throw, and He knelt down and prayed, 42saying, "Father, if
it is Your will, take this cup away from Me; nevertheless not
My will, but Yours, be done." 43Then an angel appeared to
Him from heaven, strengthening Him. 44And being in
agony, He prayed more earnestly. Then His sweat became
like great drops of blood falling down to the ground.[a]
45When He rose up from prayer, and had come to His
disciples, He found them sleeping from sorrow. 46Then He
said to them, "Why do you sleep? Rise and pray, lest you
enter into temptation."

The Arrest of Jesus

47And while He was still speaking, behold, a multitude;
and he who was called Judas, one of the twelve, went before
them and drew near to Jesus to kiss Him. 48But Jesus said to
him, "Judas, are you betraying the Son of Man with a kiss?"
49When those around Him saw what was going to happen, they said to Him, "Lord, shall we strike with the
sword?" 50And one of them struck the
servant of the high priest and cut off his
right ear.

22:50 see pg. 304

51But Jesus answered and said, "Permit even this." And
He touched his ear and healed him.

(Bible text continued on page 306)

22:37 [a]Isaiah 53:12 *22:44* [a]NU-Text brackets verses 43 and 44 as not in the original text.

The Quest for Greatness

CONSIDER THIS 22:24–30 **Is it wrong to desire greatness—to be a great salesperson, a great athlete, a great scholar, or a great performer? Shouldn't we all seek excellence in what we do? Does God not want us to experience great achievements?**

Jesus' words to the disciples in vv. 24–30 touch on this complex issue. As He did so often, the Lord challenged the motives of His followers rather than their desires. He realized that they wanted greatness for its own sake, in order to lord it over others. They sought position and power as means to personal gain, not service to others.

Jesus defined leadership for His disciples in a unique way. See "Servant-Leaders," Matt. 20:25–28.

FOR YOUR INFO
22:25

ROMAN POLITICS IN THE FIRST CENTURY A.D.

Jesus and His followers were well acquainted with the "kings of the Gentiles" and their authority (v. 25). Rome exercised a small but effective government over Judea and the other territories in its empire. The hierarchy of officials included:

ROMAN LEADERSHIP POSITIONS

Position or title	Name and/or New Testament example	Description of position	Historical significance
Emperor or Caesar	Augustus Caesar, 31 B.C.–A.D. 14 (Luke 2:1); Tiberius, A.D. 14–37 (Luke 3:1); Gaius Caligula, A.D. 37–41; Claudius, A.D. 41–54 (Acts 18:2); Nero, A.D. 54–68; Galba, A.D. 68–69; Otho, A.D. 69; Vitellius, A.D. 69; Vespasian, A.D. 69–79; Titus, A.D. 79–81; Domitian, A.D. 81–96; Nerva, A.D. 96–98; Trajan, A.D. 98–117	•Sovereign ruler of the Roman Empire. •Augustus (Octavian) ruled with as much practicality and goodwill as possible. •A standing army was needed to preserve law and order only in those outlying provinces still struggling with conflict. Wherever possible, provincial rule was delegated to local authorities or to Roman senators, called proconsuls.	•The title *Caesar* was taken from the family name of Julius Caesar, father of the Roman Empire.
Proconsul or Senator	Junius Gallio in Achaia (Acts 18:12); Sergius Paulus in Cyprus (Acts 13:7–12)	•Rulers of the *senatorial* provinces. •The Senate met twice each month for legislative, administrative, and judicial purposes. •Senators were chosen by lot to rule in the provinces. •In the time of Augustus, the Senate comprised 600 members of the Roman aristocracy. •Proconsuls were appointed for one–year terms and tended to act expediently, enriching themselves before returning to Rome, where they remained politically active.	•Senatorial provinces were usually older, more stable, and nearer to Rome. Those named in the New Testament include Achaea, Asia, Bithynia, Crete, Cyrene, Cyprus, Macedonia, and Pontus. •Roman Law was approved by the Senate and implemented locally by procurators, proconsuls, and, when necessary, the Roman army. •When the silversmiths of Ephesus complained against Paul (Acts 19:38), proconsuls were mentioned as the appropriate officials to settle the dispute.
Procurator	Pilate (Luke 3:1); Felix (Acts 23:24); Festus (Acts 24:27)	•Relatively low-ranking rulers of the *imperial* provinces. •A procurator could gain political freedoms for the region he governed by demonstrating the area's loyalty to Rome and reverence for the emperor.	•Imperial provinces, such as Judea, tended to lie on the frontiers of the empire, in areas of conflict. •They required large standing armies to maintain order under the command of appointed governors.

(continued)

Procurator *(continued)*		•Privileges might include self–government, freedom from taxation, and freedom of religion. •The procurator had to maintain law and order in his jurisdiction, putting down any threat to the social order, and, if necessary, calling in the Roman army.	•Provinces mentioned in the New Testament include Judea, Syria, Galatia, Cappadocia and Egypt.
Legate (also called governor)	Quirinius, in Syria (Luke 2:2)	•A subordinate ruler under a proconsul who commanded troops, handled administrative tasks and, in the larger provinces, collected revenue.	•At the time of Augustus, there were 11 senatorial provinces (under senatorial supervision) and 21 imperial provinces (directly under the emperor or his agents).
Prefect (also called governor)		•Commanded non–Roman auxiliary troops and governed the smaller provinces, mostly as chief financial officers.	•Senators, procurators, legates, and prefects all preferred that local leaders handle most legal problems; theirs was the court of last resort.
King	Herod the Great (Matt. 2:1); Herod Agrippa (Acts 25:24)	•Under Rome, little more than puppet governors appointed by the emperor.	•Even Egypt was ruled by a viceroy representing Rome as a successor to the Pharaohs and the Ptolemaic dynasty (323–30 B.C.). They ruled in the wake of Alexander the Great.
Tetrarch	Herod Antipas (Matt. 14:1; Acts 13:1); Lysanias; Herod Philip (Luke 3:1)	•Literally "ruler of a fourth part." •The sons of Herod the Great disputed their father's will in 4 B.C. Archelaus received half of his father's territory, making him an ethnarch; Antipas and Philip both received one–fourth and became tetrarchs.	•*Tetrarch* came to designate any petty prince or local magistrate in the Middle East.
Praetorian Guard	Paul was "kept in Herod's Praetorium" (Acts 23:35)	•Official guard of the Roman emperor and the elite corps of the empire. •Their salaries and privileges exceeded those of other Roman soldiers.	•Originally stationed in Rome, the Praetorian Guard was later dispersed throughout the provinces. •The Guard was disbanded in the third century A.D., due to their threat to the emperor himself.
Centurion	The man who showed greater faith than any in Israel (Luke 7:2–10); the man who believed Jesus to be the Son of God after His death on the cross (Matt. 27:54; Mark 15:39; Luke 23:47)	•A non–commissioned officer commanding at least 100 soldiers. •Most served for life, much longer than the required 20 years. •Sixty centuries made up a *legion*, a force of 6,000 troops.	
Sergeant		•A local law enforcement officer.	

In addition to the kinds of officials listed, local leadership for each region might include priests, landlords, and merchant guilds. In Judea, rival factions attempted to gain influence with Rome, creating a dangerous instability. The conflicts came to a head after Jesus' departure, and Rome finally sent troops that laid siege to Jerusalem and destroyed it in A.D. 70. ◆

Luke mentions by name some of the Roman officials of the empire and Palestine in the first century. See "New Testament Political Rulers," Luke 3:1.

In addition to the Roman authorities listed here, there were at least five major political parties among the Jews in the first century A.D. See "Party Politics of Jesus' Day," Matt. 16:1.

FOR YOUR INFO
22:50

Peter's Poor Aim

Total confusion reigned in the Garden of Gethsemane as Judas led a band to arrest Jesus. The chaos boiled over when Peter drew a sword and swept the air with a stroke that lopped off the ear of Malchus, one of the arresting party (v. 50; John 18:10).

Peter's impulsive act could have spelled disaster. Jesus and the Twelve were completely outnumbered and ill equipped to defend themselves against a mob that included soldiers from the Roman cohort. The arresting party might even have been looking for a pretext to use violence against this supposedly dangerous rabbi. Fortunately, Jesus acted swiftly to regain control of the situation by healing Malchus' ear and addressing the crowd (vv. 51–53).

Another stroke of fortune was probably Peter's bad aim. It's interesting that the account details an injury to Malchus' right ear. Modern readers might assume that Pe-

CONSIDER THIS
22:56–57

The Servant Girl

Fear of the truth and its consequences can lead even the strongest among us to hide behind lies and half-truths. So it was for Peter, the stouthearted fisherman and leader among the apostles. No doubt fearing for his life as he sat in the courtyard of the high priest's house, Peter denied to a servant girl that he had any connection with Jesus (vv. 56–57).

Normally Peter would have paid little attention to the young woman, who was merely a doorkeeper in Caiaphas' household (John 18:15–17; see "Caiaphas," Matt. 26:3). But having watched his Master's arrest and perhaps having learned from John, who gained him access to the courtyard, about the events taking place inside, Peter told an outright lie. Apparently he feared what the girl might say or do if he admitted to being one of Jesus' followers.

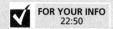

It's interesting to contrast this situation with Peter's later encounter with another doorkeeper, the servant girl Rhoda (Acts 12:1–17). On that occasion, it was not Peter who was afraid of the servant girl, but the servant girl who was astonished and overjoyed at seeing Peter, who had been miraculously delivered from jail. By that point, of

ter would have swung his sword laterally, with the blade parallel to the ground. But a first-century swordsman was more likely to sweep out his sword and come down on the head of an opponent with a vertical, chopping stroke. In battle, the idea was to place a well-aimed blow on the seam of an enemy's helmet, splitting it open and wounding the head.

Perhaps this was Peter's intention, but he aimed wide to the left. Perhaps, too, Malchus saw the blow coming and ducked to his left, exposing his right ear.

In any event, Peter caused no mortal injury. But he certainly drew attention to himself. Malchus happened to be a servant of Caiaphas, the high priest (see Matt. 26:3). Later, one of Malchus' relatives recognized Peter warming himself by a fire outside Pilate's court. "Did I not see you in the garden?" he asked suspiciously, a claim that Peter denied (John 18:26). ◆

◆ ◆ ◆ ◆ ◆ ◆ ◆ ◆ ◆ ◆ ◆ ◆ ◆ ◆

course, Peter had repented of denying Jesus and had received the Holy Spirit, who filled him with power and boldness to stand before not only the high priest (4:5–6, 18–21), but King Herod as well.

What place in your life is so vulnerable that you would tell an outright lie—even to someone that you would normally regard as inconsequential—rather than reveal the truth? Like Peter, are you afraid of the consequences of being identified with Jesus? If so, you need a dose of the Spirit's power to give you the courage to be honest (see Acts 1:8). ◆

The servant girl was among the many domestics of the ancient world who helped women attend to the chores of their households and provided care for children. Find out more about this large class of servants in "Slaves," Rom. 6:16.

Runaway slaves faced severe punishment, even death, if caught and returned to their masters. However, the gospel produced a different outcome for one slave and his owner. See the introduction to Philemon.

Prayerlessness Comes Before a Fall

CONSIDER THIS 22:39–46

Temptation is tough. It's a test. It's an enticement to do wrong. It may involve great pleasure, a chance to escape risk, or illegitimate gain. Whatever the offering, it's usually attractive.

But Scripture calls giving in to tempting opportunities sin. It even warns us that repeatedly giving way to temptation can result in falling away permanently with a total loss of interest in returning to God (Heb. 6:6–8, according to one interpretation). Clearly we need God's strength, and wisdom to flee (1 Cor. 6:18; 1 Tim. 6:11).

As Jesus and His closest companions faced great danger, they were afraid and tired (vv. 42–45). Jesus knew how vulnerable and confused that condition can make a person. He urged His followers to join Him in prayer so that they would not fall into temptation (v. 40). They could not face the trials to come without new strength from God.

Earlier Jesus had taught His followers to ask the Father not to lead them into temptation (Matt. 6:13). There is no sin in being tempted. In fact, temptation is a sign that our spiritual lives are strong enough to recognize values that conflict with godliness. But giving in is sin. That's why it's crucial to take time to declare to God our weakness, weariness, and need for help in the midst of testing.

It may also help to have others pray with us, just as Jesus did in His hour of need. Do you have others you can turn to for prayer in times of difficulty? Are you available when others have that need?

One of the best ways that we as believers can support each other is to be available for encouraging prayer. See "Are You a Friend of Someone in Need?" Luke 5:17–26.

[52]Then Jesus said to the chief priests, captains of the
temple, and the elders who had come to Him, "Have you
come out, as against a robber, with swords and clubs?
[53]When I was with you daily in the temple, you did not
try to seize Me. But this is your hour, and the power of
darkness."

Peter Denies Knowing the Lord

[54]Having arrested Him, they led *Him* and brought Him
into the high priest's house. But Peter followed at a distance.
[55]Now when they had kindled a fire in the midst of the
courtyard and sat down together, Peter sat among them.
22:56–57 see pg. 304
[56]And a certain servant girl, seeing him as
he sat by the fire, looked intently at him
and said, "This man was also with Him."
[57]But he denied Him,[a] saying, "Woman, I do not know
Him."
[58]And after a little while another saw him and said, "You
also are of them."
But Peter said, "Man, I am not!"
[59]Then after about an hour had passed, another confi-
dently affirmed, saying, "Surely this *fellow* also was with
Him, for he is a Galilean."
[60]But Peter said, "Man, I do not know what you are saying!"
Immediately, while he was still speaking, the rooster[a]
crowed. [61]And the Lord turned and looked at Peter. Then
Peter remembered the word of the Lord, how He had said
to him, "Before the rooster crows,[a] you will deny Me three
times." [62]So Peter went out and wept bitterly.

"THIS IS YOUR HOUR, AND THE POWER OF DARKNESS."
—Luke 22:53

Jesus Is Beaten

[63]Now the men who held Jesus mocked Him and beat
Him. [64]And having blindfolded Him, they struck Him on
the face and asked Him,[a] saying, "Prophesy! Who is the one
who struck You?" [65]And many other things they blasphe-
mously spoke against Him.

Jesus Is Condemned by the Council

[66]As soon as it was day, the elders of the people, both
chief priests and scribes, came together and led Him into
their council, saying, [67]"If You are the Christ, tell us."
But He said to them, "If I tell you, you will by no means
believe. [68]And if I also ask *you*, you will by no means an-

22:57 [a]NU-Text reads *denied it.* *22:60* [a]NU-Text and M-Text read *a rooster.* *22:61* [a]NU-Text adds *today.* *22:64* [a]NU-Text reads *And having blindfolded Him, they asked Him.*

swer Me or let *Me* go.[a] 69Hereafter the Son of Man will sit
on the right hand of the power of God."
70Then they all said, "Are You then the Son of God?"
So He said to them, "You *rightly* say that I am."
71And they said, "What further testimony do we need?
For we have heard it ourselves from His own mouth."

CHAPTER 23

Jesus Is Brought to Pilate and Herod

23:1–25

1Then the whole multitude of them
arose and led Him to Pilate. 2And they
began to accuse Him, saying, "We found this *fellow* perverting the[a] nation, and forbidding to pay taxes to Caesar, saying that He Himself is Christ, a King."
3Then Pilate asked Him, saying, "Are You the King of the
Jews?"
He answered him and said, "*It is as* you say."
4So Pilate said to the chief priests and the crowd, "I find
no fault in this Man."
5But they were the more fierce, saying, "He stirs up the
people, teaching throughout all Judea, beginning from
Galilee to this place."
6When Pilate heard of Galilee,[a] he asked if the Man were
a Galilean. 7And as soon as he knew that He belonged to
Herod's jurisdiction, he sent Him to Herod, who was also

23:8

in Jerusalem at that time. 8Now when
Herod saw Jesus, he was exceedingly
glad; for he had desired for a long *time* to see Him, because
he had heard many things about Him, and he hoped to see
some miracle done by Him. 9Then he questioned Him with
many words, but He answered him nothing. 10And the chief
priests and scribes stood and vehemently accused Him.
11Then Herod, with his men of war, treated Him with contempt and mocked *Him,* arrayed Him in a gorgeous robe,
and sent Him back to Pilate. 12That very day Pilate and
Herod became friends with each other, for previously they
had been at enmity with each other.

(Bible text continued on page 309)

22:68 [a]NU-Text omits *also* and *Me or let Me go.* *23:2* [a]NU-Text reads *our.* *23:6* [a]NU-Text omits *of Galilee.*

Herod Finally Meets Jesus

A CLOSER LOOK 23:8

In v. 8, Herod Antipas finally meets an old nemesis. Having allowed himself to be manipulated into executing John the Baptist (Matt. 14:1–12; Mark 6:17–28), he was frightened by the coming of Jesus, wondering whether John had come back to life (Luke 9:7–9). Jesus' enemies tried to make use of that fear, but to no avail (13:31–33). For more on Herod and his infamous family, see "The Herods," Acts 12:1–2.

Convenience Makes for Odd Choices

CONSIDER THIS 23:1–25

Faced with difficulty, most of us tend to choose convenience and expediency over sacrifice and integrity, particularly when the personal costs are likely to be high. Our desire to avoid negative outcomes can stir up odd reactions in us.

Jesus triggered some odd choices of convenience and expediency in the political system of Jerusalem. For example:

- **Two leaders who had been longtime enemies suddenly became allies and friends (v. 12).**
- **Pilate chose to free Barabbas, an insurrectionist and murderer (v. 19), and allow the execution of Jesus, the innocent man (v. 22), in order to maintain order and appease an angry mob (vv. 23–25).**
- **The rulers chose popularity with the people, and the people chose fawning subservience to the rulers, over justice for the accused (vv. 23–24; Matt. 27:20, 25; John 19:15).**

These kinds of sinful tendencies are part of the reason Christ came to die. He wants to save us from opportunistic, self-serving ways of life, because ultimately they lead to death. Evil alliances, political manipulation, rigged votes, and injustice are a stench in the nostrils of God (Is. 2:5—3:26).

As believers, we may have to make odd choices, too. But ours should be rooted in Christlike values of love, truth, and humility, rather than expedience, popularity, and selfishness.

Crucifixion

The Romans used one of the most painful methods of torture ever devised to put Jesus to death (v. 33). Crucifixion was used by many nations of the ancient world, including Assyria, Media, and Persia. The idea may have originated from the practice of hanging up the bodies of executed persons on stakes for public display. This discouraged civil disobedience and mocked defeated military foes (Gen. 40:19; 1 Sam. 31:8–13).

Ancient writers do not tell us much about when or how execution on a stake or cross came about, or how it was carried out. But we know that the Assyrians executed captured enemies by forcing their living bodies down onto pointed stakes. This barbaric cruelty was not actually crucifixion but impalement.

No one knows when the crossbeam was added. But Ezra 6:11 provides clear evidence that the Persians continued to use impalement as a method of execution. Likewise, the references to "hanging" in Esther 2:23 and 5:14 probably refer to either impalement or crucifixion. Rope hangings were not used in Persia during the biblical period. The word translated "gallows" refers not to a scaffold but to a pole or stake.

Crucifixion on a stake or cross was practiced by the Greeks, notably Alexander the Great, who hung 2,000 people on crosses when the city of Tyre was destroyed. During the period between Greek and Roman control of Palestine, the Jewish ruler Alexander Jannaeus crucified 800 Pharisees who opposed him. But such executions were condemned as detestable and abnormal even in that day as well as by the later Jewish historian, Josephus.

From the early days of the Roman Republic, death on the cross was used for rebellious slaves and bandits, although Roman citizens were rarely subjected to it. The practice continued well beyond the New Testament period as one of the supreme punishments for military and political crimes such as desertion, spying, revealing secrets, rebellion, and sedition. However, following the conversion of Constantine, the cross became a sacred symbol and its use as a means of execution was abolished.

Crucifixion involved attaching the victim with nails through the wrists or with leather thongs to a crossbeam attached to a vertical stake. Sometimes blocks or pins were put on the stake to give the victim support as he hung suspended from the crossbeam. At times the feet were also nailed to the vertical stake. As the victim hung dangling by the arms, blood could no longer circulate to his vital organs. Only by supporting himself on the seat or pin could he gain some relief.

But gradually exhaustion set in, and death followed, although usually not for several days. If the victim had been severely beaten, he would not live that long. To hasten death, the executioners sometimes broke the victim's legs with a club. Then he could no longer support his body to keep blood circulating, and death by suffocation quickly followed. Usually bodies were left to rot or to be eaten by scavengers.

To the Jewish people, crucifixion represented the most disgusting form of death: "He who is hanged is accursed of God" (Deut. 21:23). Yet the Jewish council sought and obtained Roman authorization to have Jesus crucified (Mark 15:13–15).

The apostle Paul summed up the crucial importance of His manner of death when he wrote, "We preach Christ crucified, to the Jews a stumbling block and to the Greeks foolishness, but to those who are called, both Jews and Greeks, Christ the power of God and the wisdom of God" (1 Cor. 1:23–24). Out of the ugliness and agony of crucifixion, God accomplished the greatest good of all—the redemption of sinners. ◆

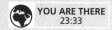

Pilate Sentences Jesus to Death

13Then Pilate, when he had called together the chief
priests, the rulers, and the people, 14said to them, "You have
brought this Man to me, as one who misleads the people.
And indeed, having examined *Him* in your presence, I have
found no fault in this Man concerning those things of
which you accuse Him; 15no, neither did Herod, for I sent
you back to him;[a] and indeed nothing deserving of death
has been done by Him. 16I will therefore chastise Him and
release *Him*" 17(for it was necessary for him to release one to
them at the feast).[a]

18And they all cried out at once, saying, "Away with this
Man, and release to us Barabbas"— 19who had been thrown
into prison for a certain rebellion made in the city, and for
murder.

20Pilate, therefore, wishing to release Jesus, again called
out to them. 21But they shouted, saying, "Crucify *Him,* crucify Him!"

22Then he said to them the third time, "Why, what evil
has He done? I have found no reason for death in Him. I
will therefore chastise Him and let *Him* go."

23But they were insistent, demanding with loud voices
that He be crucified. And the voices of these men and of the
chief priests prevailed.[a] 24So Pilate gave sentence that it
should be as they requested. 25And he released to them[a] the
one they requested, who for rebellion and murder had been
thrown into prison; but he delivered Jesus to their will.

The Crucifixion

26Now as they led Him away, they laid hold of a certain
man, Simon a Cyrenian, who was coming from the country,
and on him they laid the cross that he might bear *it* after
Jesus.

27And a great multitude of the people followed Him, and
women who also mourned and lamented Him. 28But Jesus,
turning to them, said, "Daughters of Jerusalem, do not
weep for Me, but weep for yourselves and for your children.
29For indeed the days are coming in which they will say,
'Blessed *are* the barren, wombs that never bore, and breasts
which never nursed!' 30Then they will begin 'to say to the
mountains, "Fall on us!" and to the hills, "Cover us!" '[a] 31For
if they do these things in the green wood, what will be done
in the dry?"

32There were also two others, criminals, led with Him to
be put to death. 33And when they had
come to the place called Calvary, there

23:33

"NOTHING DESERVING OF DEATH HAS BEEN DONE BY HIM."
—Luke 23:15

23:15 [a]NU-Text reads *for he sent Him back to us.* *23:17* [a]NU-Text omits verse 17.
23:23 [a]NU-Text omits *and of the chief priests.* *23:25* [a]NU-Text and M-Text omit *to them.*
23:30 [a]Hosea 10:8

they crucified Him, and the criminals, one on the right
hand and the other on the left. 34Then Jesus said, "Father,
forgive them, for they do not know what they do."[a]
And they divided His garments and cast lots. 35And the
people stood looking on. But even the rulers with them
sneered, saying, "He saved others; let Him save Himself if
He is the Christ, the chosen of God."
36The soldiers also mocked Him, coming and offering
Him sour wine, 37and saying, "If You are the King of the
Jews, save Yourself."
38And an inscription also was written over Him in letters
of Greek, Latin, and Hebrew:[a]

THIS IS THE KING OF THE JEWS.

39Then one of the criminals who were hanged blasphemed Him, saying, "If You are the Christ,[a] save Yourself
and us."
40But the other, answering, rebuked him, saying, "Do you
not even fear God, seeing you are under the same condem-

23:34 [a]NU-Text brackets the first sentence as a later addition. *23:38* [a]NU-Text omits *written* and *in letters of Greek, Latin, and Hebrew.* *23:39* [a]NU-Text reads *Are You not the Christ?*

CONSIDER THIS
23:49

Jesus—A Rabbi for Women, Too

Luke mentions that Jesus had a following among the women of His day (v. 49; see "The Women Who Followed Jesus," 8:1–3). From what we know about Jewish culture in the first century, their presence and loyalty probably offended many Jews.

Jewish tradition frowned upon women studying with rabbis. Some rabbis actually considered it sinful to teach women the Law. Women were permitted in the synagogues, but custom required them to sit apart from the men. Menstruation made them unclean each month according to the Law (Lev. 15:19). Women were often viewed as the cause of men's sexual sins. To prevent any temptation, Jewish men were instructed not to speak to a woman in public—even to one's wife. And they were never to touch a woman in public.

But not only did Jesus speak to women in public (John 4:27), he dared to take them by the hand (Mark 5:41). He encouraged a woman who desired to follow Him, even when it conflicted with her household duties (Luke 10:42). And as He tried to help people understand the kingdom of

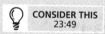

nation? [41]And we indeed justly, for we receive the due reward of our deeds; but this Man has done nothing wrong."
[42]Then he said to Jesus, "Lord,[a] remember me when You
come into Your kingdom."
[43]And Jesus said to him, "Assuredly, I say to you, today
you will be with Me in Paradise."
[44]Now it was[a] about the sixth hour, and there was darkness over all the earth until the ninth hour. [45]Then the sun
was darkened,[a] and the veil of the temple was torn in two.
[46]And when Jesus had cried out with a loud voice, He said,
"Father, 'into Your hands I commit My spirit.' "[a] Having said
this, He breathed His last.
[47]So when the centurion saw what had happened, he
glorified God, saying, "Certainly this was a righteous
Man!"
[48]And the whole crowd who came together to that sight,
seeing what had been done, beat their breasts and returned.
23:49 [49]But all His acquaintances, and the
women who followed Him from Galilee,
stood at a distance, watching these things.

23:42 [a]NU-Text reads *And he said, "Jesus, remember me.* *23:44* [a]NU-Text adds *already.*
23:45 [a]NU-Text reads *obscured.* *23:46* [a]Psalm 31:5

God, He used illustrations that women as well as men could relate to.

Though excluded from the inner courts of the temple, Jewish women were welcome among Jesus' followers. He showed that rules of "clean" and "unclean" no longer determined who could approach God. He had come to open a new way, and everyone was welcome to participate. In doing so, He turned the world upside down.

What about your world? Do you see people—whether women or men—the way Jesus does? What one change would you need to make to treat someone more like the Savior did? ◆

Find out more about the significant part women played in Jesus' life and work in "The Women around Jesus," John 19:25. Women helped communicate the gospel throughout the Roman world. See "Women and the Spread of Christianity," Phil. 4:3, and "Paul's Female Coworkers," Rom. 16:12.

"FATHER, 'INTO YOUR HANDS I COMMIT MY SPIRIT.' "
—Luke 23:46

Friends Bury Jesus in a Borrowed Tomb

23:50–56 50Now behold, *there was* a man named
Joseph, a council member, a good and
just man. 51He had not consented to their decision and
deed. *He was* from Arimathea, a city of the Jews, who himself was also waiting[a] for the kingdom of God. 52This man
went to Pilate and asked for the body of Jesus. 53Then he
took it down, wrapped it in linen, and laid it in a tomb *that*
was hewn out of the rock, where no one had ever lain before. 54That day was the Preparation, and the Sabbath drew
near.

55And the women who had come with Him from Galilee
followed after, and they observed the tomb and how His
body was laid. 56Then they returned and prepared spices
and fragrant oils. And they rested on the Sabbath according
to the commandment.

23:51 [a]NU-Text reads *who was waiting.*

CONSIDER THIS
23:50–56

A REMARKABLE COALITION

We live in a world where groups of people tend to exclude others rather than include them. Seldom do people from vastly different backgrounds band together, unless it's to fight a common enemy. Distinctions such as race, money, position, language, and gender often keep people from cooperating with each other.

But for those who followed Jesus, divisive walls began to break down. As a result of His influence, people who were far apart socially began to come together for the benefit of others.

Such was the case at Jesus' burial. His death brought about a surprising coalition: two men who were prominent Jewish leaders, and two women, one who had been delivered from demon possession and the other an obscure mother (vv. 50–56). Who were these people?

Joseph of Arimathea *was a wealthy community leader and a member of the Jewish council. He had access to Pilate and gained permission to take away Jesus' body. He helped prepare the body for burial and deliver it to his own tomb (vv. 50–53; Matt. 27:57–60; Mark 15:42–46).*

Nicodemus *was also a member of the council (John 3:1–2). He challenged some of the accusations against*

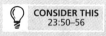

CHAPTER 24

The Resurrection

1Now on the first *day* of the week, very early in the morning, they, and certain *other women* with them,[a] came to the
tomb bringing the spices which they had prepared. 2But
they found the stone rolled away from the tomb. 3Then they
went in and did not find the body of the Lord Jesus. 4And it
happened, as they were greatly[a] perplexed about this, that
behold, two men stood by them in shining garments.
5Then, as they were afraid and bowed *their* faces to the
earth, they said to them, "Why do you seek the living
among the dead? 6He is not here, but is risen! Remember
how He spoke to you when He was still in Galilee, 7saying,
'The Son of Man must be delivered into the hands of sinful
men, and be crucified, and the third day rise again.' "

24:1 [a]NU-Text omits *and certain other women with them.* *24:4* [a]NU-Text omits *greatly.*

Jesus (7:50–51). After the Lord's death, he brought nearly 100 pounds of embalming supplies (19:39–42).

Mary Magdalene *came from Galilee. She had been demon-possessed before following Jesus (Luke 8:2). Along with other women she observed the tragic ordeal of the crucifixion (23:49). After Joseph retrieved the body, she helped with the embalming (v. 56). Later, after Jesus' resurrection, she helped spread the amazing news that He was alive (24:10).*

Mary of Galilee *was the mother of James and Joses (Mark 15:40). Little else is known about her, but she played enough of a part in the burial coalition to have her participation recorded in Scripture.*

Does your faith connect you with people different from yourself? Believers often have more in common with other believers than they do with family, friends, or coworkers. That fact can sometimes be just the bit of evidence needed to make the faith attractive to its worst critics. ◆

Mary Magdalene and Mary of Galilee were only two of a number of Jesus' female followers. *See "The Women Who Followed Jesus," Luke 8:1–3.*

AND THEY REMEMBERED HIS WORDS. THEN THEY RETURNED. . . .
—Luke 24:8–9

THOSE WOMEN AGAIN!

CONSIDER THIS 24:11 **The discounting of women by men is a pattern that has persisted throughout history. Jesus' male disciples found it easy to dismiss Mary Magdalene, Joanna, Mary, and the other women when they reported the empty tomb and a conversation with the risen Lord (v. 11).**

The news should have been encouraging, given the confusion that dominated the group after their Master's cruel death. But the men rejected the words of these women. It didn't seem to matter that the women had followed Jesus just as closely and in fact had stood by Him through His ordeal rather than betray Him (as Judas had), or deny Him (as Peter had), or run away in fear (as all the men had).

Male skepticism of women's testimony raises questions about the masculine mind. Why are some men so insecure that they must exalt themselves over the other sex to feel significant? Can true companionship survive that kind of distrust? Sooner or later, men can expect to pay for that kind of abuse, especially since both male and female are created in God's image and vested with authority and responsibility together (Gen. 1:26–31; 2:18–25).

If you're a man, are you growing in your appreciation of woman as God's creation? Do you esteem the women God brings your way? Are you learning to listen to them, partner with them, and even follow their lead toward godliness?

8And they remembered His words. 9Then they returned
from the tomb and told all these things to the eleven and to
24:10 all the rest. 10It was Mary Magdalene,
Joanna, Mary *the mother* of James, and
the other *women* with them, who told these things to the
24:11 apostles. 11And their words seemed to
them like idle tales, and they did not believe them. 12But Peter arose and ran to the tomb; and
stooping down, he saw the linen cloths lying[a] by themselves; and he departed, marveling to himself at what had
happened.

Jesus Appears on the Road to Emmaus

13Now behold, two of them were traveling that same day
to a village called Emmaus, which was seven miles[a] from
Jerusalem. 14And they talked together of all these things
which had happened. 15So it was, while they conversed and
reasoned, that Jesus Himself drew near and went with
them. 16But their eyes were restrained, so that they did not
know Him.
17And He said to them, "What kind of conversation *is* this
that you have with one another as you walk and are sad?"[a]
18Then the one whose name was Cleopas answered and
said to Him, "Are You the only stranger in Jerusalem, and
have You not known the things which happened there in
these days?"
19And He said to them, "What things?"
So they said to Him, "The things concerning Jesus of
Nazareth, who was a Prophet mighty in deed and word before God and all the people, 20and how the chief priests and
our rulers delivered Him to be condemned to death, and
crucified Him. 21But we were hoping that it was He who
was going to redeem Israel. Indeed, besides all this, today is
the third day since these things happened. 22Yes, and certain women of our company, who arrived at the tomb early,
astonished us. 23When they did not find His body, they
came saying that they had also seen a vision of angels who
said He was alive. 24And certain of those *who were* with us
went to the tomb and found *it* just as the women had said;
but Him they did not see."
25Then He said to them, "O foolish ones, and slow of

24:12 [a]NU-Text omits *lying.* *24:13* [a]Literally *sixty stadia* *24:17* [a]NU-Text reads *as you walk? And they stood still, looking sad.*

Mary—An Important Name

A CLOSER LOOK 24:10 *In naming their daughters Mary, Hebrew parents honored one of Israel's most famous women. See "Why So Many Marys?" Mark 15:40.*

heart to believe in all that the prophets have spoken!
26Ought not the Christ to have suffered these things and to

24:27
see pg. 316

enter into His glory?" 27And beginning
at Moses and all the Prophets, He ex-
pounded to them in all the Scriptures the things concerning
Himself.

28Then they drew near to the village where they were going, and He indicated that He would have gone farther.
29But they constrained Him, saying, "Abide with us, for it is
toward evening, and the day is far spent." And He went in
to stay with them.

30Now it came to pass, as He sat at the table with them,
that He took bread, blessed and broke *it,* and gave it to
them. 31Then their eyes were opened and they knew Him;
and He vanished from their sight.

32And they said to one another, "Did not our heart burn
within us while He talked with us on the road, and while
He opened the Scriptures to us?" 33So they rose up that very
hour and returned to Jerusalem, and found the eleven and
those *who were* with them gathered together, 34saying, "The
Lord is risen indeed, and has appeared to Simon!" 35And
they told about the things *that had happened* on the
road, and how He was known to them in the breaking of
bread.

Jesus Appears to His Apostles

36Now as they said these things, Jesus Himself stood in
the midst of them, and said to them, "Peace to you." 37But
they were terrified and frightened, and supposed they had
seen a spirit. 38And He said to them, "Why are you troubled? And why do doubts arise in your hearts? 39Behold My
hands and My feet, that it is I Myself. Handle Me and see,
for a spirit does not have flesh and bones as you see I have."

40When He had said this, He showed them His hands and
His feet.[a] 41But while they still did not believe for joy, and
marveled, He said to them, "Have you any food here?" 42So
they gave Him a piece of a broiled fish and some honeycomb.[a] 43And He took *it* and ate in their presence.

Final Instructions

44Then He said to them, "These *are* the words which I
spoke to you while I was still with you, that all things must
be fulfilled which were written in the Law of Moses and *the*

24:45–49

Prophets and *the* Psalms concerning Me."
45And He opened their understanding,
that they might comprehend the Scriptures.

24:40 [a]Some printed New Testaments omit this verse. It is found in nearly all Greek manuscripts. *24:42* [a]NU-Text omits *and some honeycomb.*

His Last Words

CONSIDER THIS 24:45–49 **What would you like to be your last words to your closest family and friends? Whatever they might be, imagine the impact if you returned from the grave to speak them!**

Jesus did. He came back from the dead to give His followers a final word. As a result, His instructions carry unusual weight and have come to be known as the "Great Commission," because Jesus charged His followers with a mighty task. All four writers of His life provide a version of this mandate (vv. 45–49; Matt. 28:18–20; Mark 16:15–16; John 20:21–23; Acts 1:6–8). Jesus gives us the privilege and responsibility of telling the good news about His provision of forgiveness and eternal life to all who will listen.

Do your friends know what Christ has done for them? Do they know what He has done and is doing in your life? Can you afford to deprive them of having that good news so they can consider it for themselves?

46Then He said to them, "Thus it is written, and thus it
was necessary for the Christ to suffer and to rise[a] from the
dead the third day, 47and that repentance and remission of
sins should be preached in His name to all nations, beginning at Jerusalem. 48And you are wit-
nesses of these things. 49Behold, I send
the Promise of My Father upon you; but
tarry in the city of Jerusalem[a] until you
are endued with power from on high."

24:48 see pg. 318

24:49

24:46 [a]NU-Text reads *written, that the Christ should suffer and rise.* *24:49* [a]NU-Text omits *of Jerusalem.*

Wait for the Power!

A CLOSER LOOK 24:49

Jesus told His followers to wait in Jerusalem for power (v. 49). He had a job for them to do, but they were not to attempt it through their own ability, but to wait for empowerment from God. See Acts 1:8 for a description of the power that Jesus promised.

FOR YOUR INFO 24:27

The Suffering Christ

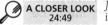

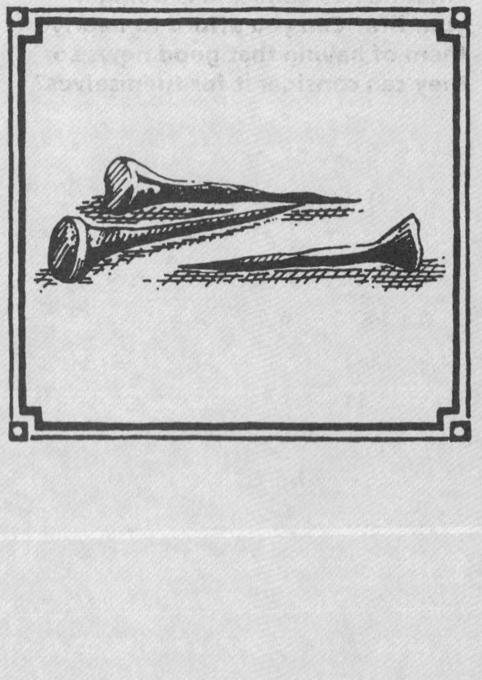

Would you be able to explain to someone where the Scriptures speak about Jesus, "beginning at Moses and all the Prophets" (v. 27)? That's what the Lord did with two of His disciples on the road to Emmaus. He explained how the Old Testament—the only inspired Scriptures in existence at that time—foretold His coming as the Messiah.

An entire list of the Old Testament texts to which Jesus probably referred would be too lengthy to publish here. But one book that He undoubtedly spent a lot of time on was Isaiah. No other Old Testament prophet made as many references to the coming Messiah as did Isaiah. Notice his emphasis on the Messiah as a suffering servant, a role that Jesus fulfilled:

Isaiah's Prophecy Fulfilled in Christ

The Suffering Servant	Jesus
Would be widely rejected (53:1, 3)	Jesus "came to His own, and His own did not receive Him" (John 1:11; compare 12:37–38).
Would be disfigured by suffering (52:14; 53:2)	Pilate had Jesus scourged (beaten); Roman soldiers placed a crown of thorns on His head, struck Him on the head with a stick, and spat on Him (Mark 15:15, 17, 19).
Would voluntarily accept the pain, suffering, and death that sinners deserve (53:7–8)	As the Good Shepherd, Jesus laid down His life for His "sheep" (John 10:11; compare 19:30).
Would make atonement for sin through His blood (52:15)	Believers are redeemed and saved through the blood of Christ (1 Pet. 1:18–19).

Continued

The Ascension

50And He led them out as far as Bethany, and He lifted up
His hands and blessed them. 51Now it came to pass, while
He blessed them, that He was parted from them and carried
up into heaven. 52And they worshiped Him, and returned
to Jerusalem with great joy, 53and were continually in the
temple praising and[a] blessing God. Amen.[b]

24:53 [a]NU-Text omits *praising and.* [b]NU-Text omits *Amen.*

Continued	
Would take upon Himself the grief of human sin and sorrow (53:4–5)	Jesus was "delivered up because of our offenses" (Rom. 4:25); He "bore our sins in His own body on the tree" and by His stripes we were healed (1 Pet. 2:24–25).
Would die on behalf of "the iniquity [sin] of us all" (53:6, 8)	God made Jesus "who knew no sin to be sin for us" (2 Cor. 5:21).
Would die in order to make "intercession for the transgressors" (53:12)	Jesus was crucified between two robbers, one on His right and the other on His left (Mark 15:27–28; compare Luke 22:37). More generally, He is the one "Mediator between God and men" (1 Tim. 2:5).
Would be buried in a rich man's tomb (53:9)	Joseph of Arimathea placed the body of Jesus in his own new tomb (John 19:38–42).
Would bring salvation to those who believed in Him (53:10–11)	Jesus promised that whoever believes in Him would not perish but have everlasting life (John 3:16). The early church proclaimed that same message (Acts 16:31).
Would be "exalted and extolled and be very high" (52:13)	God has "highly exalted [Jesus] and given Him the name" of Lord, to whom "every knee should bow" (Phil. 2:9–11).

According to Jewish tradition, Isaiah underwent suffering of his own: he met his death by being sawed in half during the reign of the evil king Manasseh of Judah. Find out more about this major Old Testament prophet at Luke 4:17.

"BEHOLD, I SEND THE PROMISE OF MY FATHER UPON YOU."
—Luke 24:49

CONSIDER THIS
24:48

WITNESSING—JESUS' STYLE

Does evangelism make you nervous? If so, it will help to study carefully how Jesus interacted with people. Whom did He meet? How did He connect with them? Where did the encounters take place? Who initiated contact? What happened in the conversation?

Like Jesus' original followers, believers today are sent into the world to be His witnesses (v. 48; compare Matt. 28:18–20; Acts 1:8). We can learn much about how to handle that assignment by asking questions of the four narratives of Jesus' life—Matthew, Mark, Luke, and John. They include more than 40 meetings between Jesus and various individuals.

Who started the conversation?

In nine cases, Jesus initiated the conversations.

Examples:

- a Samaritan woman (John 4:7–42)
- a crippled beggar (John 5:1–15)

In 25 instances, it was the other party who started the discussion. Jesus responded to other people's inquiries.

Examples:

- a rich young ruler (Matt. 19:16–30)
- a demoniac (Mark 5:1–20)
- Jairus, a synagogue ruler (Mark 5:21–43)
- a hemorrhaging woman (Mark 5:24–34)

Other conversations were triggered by third parties.

Examples:

- tax collectors and other "sinners," invited to a party by Matthew (Matt. 9:9–13)
- Herod, introduced by Pilate (Luke 23:6–16)
- Nathaniel, invited by Philip (John 1:45–51)
- an adulterous woman brought by the scribes (John 8:1–11)

Where did the conversation take place?

The majority of Jesus' interactions occurred in the workplace.

Examples:

- with James and John (Matt. 4:21–22)
- with a Samaritan woman (John 4:7–42)
- with a lame man (John 5:1–15)

Many took place in homes.

Examples:

- at Peter's house with his mother-in-law (Mark 1:29–31)
- with a Syro-Phoenician woman (Mark 7:24–30)
- at Zacchaeus' house (Luke 19:1–10)

Few were in religious settings. Instead, Jesus talked with people about spiritual issues where they were most familiar. He did not need a special environment or control over the circumstances to discuss things of eternal significance.

What was discussed?

Jesus asked questions in more than half of the conversations He had. This is similar to God's first response to the first sinners in history, when He asked four questions of Adam and Eve (Gen. 3:9, 11, 13).

Examples:

- an adulterous woman (John 8:1–11)
- the scribes (Luke 5:17–26)
- His mother and brothers (Matt. 12:46–50)
- the Pharisees (Luke 6:6–11)

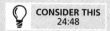

He connected with people's thoughts and feelings. He understood that new ideas need to be connected with existing frames of reference if they are to last. He seldom pressed for "closure" or a decision. Instead, He understood that time is required for ideas to simmer and for people to own them before they act on them.

What can we learn from Jesus' example?

- Jesus knew how to take initiative.
- Jesus responded to the initiatives of others.
- Jesus left room in his schedule for interruptions by friends and others enlisting his help.
- Jesus usually met people on their own turf.
- Jesus was interested in establishing common ground with others.

Witnessing is a science, an art, and a mystery. It involves connecting your faith with people's experience in a way that they can understand it, in their own time and manner. It means cooperating with whatever God's Spirit may be doing with them and leaving the results to Him. ◆

Both non-Christians and Christians seem to feel uncomfortable with evangelism. That's one reason why many believers remain silent when it comes to spiritual matters. *See "Whose Job Is Evangelism?" John 16:8.*

A Gospel for the Thinking Person

The first-century world was a swirl of ideas, values, and symbols, not unlike our own. John's is a Gospel that is especially good for the thinking person. Unlike Matthew, Mark, and Luke, which present comprehensive and similar ("synoptic") overviews of the Lord's life, John is a highly stylized arrangement of carefully selected events and words, all directed toward one major purpose: that readers might find life by believing in Jesus as the Christ. John's goal is not belief for its own sake, but belief in order to have *life* (John 20:30–31).

For that reason, this book is vitally important for modern-day Christians. We tend to apply our faith only to certain private and "religious" settings, but leave it behind when we go into the public arena. The message of John cuts through that way of thinking and living. Jesus is our bridge between that which is eternal, spiritual, and supernatural, and the everyday, human, natural world. He is the divine Word of God, yet He became human and lived our experience (1:1, 14).

How can our faith become relevant to the day-to-day circumstances we face? In the Gospel of John, Jesus shows us. He lived the message that He preached. And as we come to know Him and follow Him, we can experience the *life* that He gives.

John

Christ is the divine Word of God, yet He became human.

C O N T E N T S

Individuals Encounter Christ

A R T I C L E S

Under Authority (12:49)

Jesus modeled for us two principles of leading and following.

The Cost of Following Jesus (15:18–25)

Sooner or later, following Christ has a cost, and those who think they can get by without paying it are misguided. In fact, if there's no cost, is there really any genuine commitment?

Whose Job Is Evangelism? (16:8)

John shows that bringing people to faith is a cooperative effort between Christians and the Holy Spirit.

The Women around Jesus (19:25)

Women played a major part in Jesus' life and work. This listing summarizes their participation.

THE SEVEN SIGNS OF JOHN'S GOSPEL

A famous author once said that the key to good writing is not in knowing what to put into a story, but what to leave out. Imagine, then, the problem of writing down the story of Jesus, especially if you had been an eyewitness and even a participant in the events. Of all that Jesus said and did, what would you include? What would you leave out?

John solved the problem by determining what he wanted his Gospel to accomplish: he wanted his readers to know that "Jesus is the Christ, the Son of God, and that believing [they might] have life in His name" (John 20:31). To that end, he organized his account around seven miracles that Jesus performed, seven "signs" pointing to His divine nature:

THE SIGNS AND THEIR MEANINGS

Turns water into wine (2:1–12)	Jesus is the source of life.
Heals a nobleman's son (4:46–54)	Jesus is master over distance.
Heals a lame man at the pool of Bethesda (5:1–17)	Jesus is master over time.
Feeds 5,000 (6:1–14)	Jesus is the bread of life.
Walks on water, stills a storm (6:15–21)	Jesus is master over nature.
Heals a man blind from birth (9:1–41)	Jesus is the light of the world.
Raises Lazarus from the dead (11:17–45)	Jesus has power over death.

The fact that there are seven sign miracles is significant. In the Jewish view of life, the number seven signified perfection or completion. John's Gospel presents the seven miracles like a diamond refracting seven bands of color. Upon closer inspection, each one turns out to be rooted in Old Testament understanding of the Messiah. John's point is that Jesus is perfect and complete. His miracles show His true colors—that He is the Messiah that Israel has been looking for, and that He alone offers eternal life.

This way of presenting things may seem strange to some modern readers. But the Gospel of John, though probably the last Gospel to be written, was Christianity's first statement of the message of Jesus in a way that would relate to the thought-forms of its day. It is more meticulously and artistically composed than any prize-winning narrative or award-winning film. ◆

JOHN—THE APOSTLE OF LOVE

John and his brother James came from the prosperous family of Zebedee, a successful fisherman who owned his own boat and had hired servants (Mark 1:19–20). Together with Simon and Andrew, with whom they were in partnership (Luke 5:10), the brothers became loyal followers of Jesus. Their mother Salome also joined the fellowship and supported Jesus' ministry (Mark 15:4–41; Luke 8:3).

Modern Christians regard John as the "apostle of love" because of the frequent appearance of that theme in his writings and because the Gospel of John refers to him as the disciple whom Jesus loved (John 13:23). But he certainly didn't start out as a model of charity.

Apparently headstrong and opinionated, Jesus dubbed John and his brother the Sons of Thunder (Mark 3:17). On one occasion they created a storm of protest and indignation from the other disciples by asking if they could sit on Jesus' right and left hands in glory (Mark 10:35–45). On another occasion they suggested calling down fire from heaven on an unreceptive Samaritan village; Jesus rebuked them (Luke 9:51–56).

Somehow John's exposure to Jesus worked an amazing change in his life. After the Lord's departure, he became a leader of the Christian movement, as might be expected. But now his perspective was different. When word came that the gospel had spread to the Samaritans, John was sent with Peter to investigate. Whereas before he had wanted to destroy Samaritans, now he helped bring them the Holy Spirit (Acts 8:14–25). The son of thunder had become a son of love!

Church tradition holds that after the execution of his brother James, John eventually migrated to Ephesus, from which he wrote or oversaw the writing of five New Testament documents. From there he was banished to the island of Patmos, but later returned to Ephesus where he died sometime after A.D. 98. ◆

PERSONALITY PROFILE: JOHN

Name means: "Yahweh is gracious."

Home: Probably raised in Capernaum on the north shore of the Sea of Galilee; later lived at Ephesus; banished to the island of Patmos in old age.

Family: Father was Zebedee; mother was probably Salome; younger brother of James. Salome and Mary may have been sisters (Matt. 27:56; John 19:25); if so, James and John would have been cousins to Jesus.

Occupation: Commercial fisherman; later, one of Jesus' disciples and a member of His inner circle; also an author of a Gospel, three New Testament letters, and Revelation.

Best known today for: His close relationship to Jesus, and his New Testament writings.

CHAPTER 1

The Word

1 In the beginning was the Word, and the Word was with
God, and the Word was God. 2 He was in the beginning
1:3 with God. 3 All things were made through
Him, and without Him nothing was
made that was made. 4 In Him was life, and the life was the
light of men. 5 And the light shines in the darkness, and the
darkness did not comprehend[a] it.
6 There was a man sent from God, whose name *was* John.
7 This man came for a witness, to bear witness of the Light,
that all through him might believe. 8 He was not that Light,
but *was sent* to bear witness of that Light. 9 That was the true
Light which gives light to every man coming into the
world.[a]
10 He was in the world, and the world was made through
Him, and the world did not know Him. 11 He came to His
own,[a] and His own[b] did not receive Him. 12 But as many as
received Him, to them He gave the right to become children
of God, to those who believe in His name: 13 who were
born, not of blood, nor of the will of the flesh, nor of the
will of man, but of God.
1:14 see pg. 326 14 And the Word became flesh and
dwelt among us, and we beheld His
glory, the glory as of the only begotten of the Father, full of
grace and truth.
15 John bore witness of Him and cried out, saying, "This
was He of whom I said, 'He who comes after me is preferred before me, for He was before me.' "
16 And[a] of His fullness we have all received, and grace for
grace. 17 For the law was given through Moses, *but* grace and
truth came through Jesus Christ. 18 No one has seen God at
any time. The only begotten Son,[a] who is in the bosom of
the Father, He has declared *Him*.

The Testimony of John the Baptist

19 Now this is the testimony of John, when the Jews sent
priests and Levites from Jerusalem to ask him, "Who are
you?"
20 He confessed, and did not deny, but confessed, "I am
not the Christ."
21 And they asked him, "What then? Are you Elijah?"
He said, "I am not."
"Are you the Prophet?"
And he answered, "No."

1:5 [a]Or *overcome* *1:9* [a]Or *That was the true Light which, coming into the world, gives light to every man.* *1:11* [a]That is, His own things or domain [b]That is, His own people *1:16* [a]NU-Text reads *For.* *1:18* [a]NU-Text reads *only begotten God.*

THE DIVINE PARTNERSHIP

CONSIDER THIS 1:3 **Christ was fully involved in the work of creation (v. 3). In fact, all three persons of the Trinity worked together to bring the world into existence—Father (Gen. 1:1; John 5:17), Son (John 1:10; Col. 1:16), and Holy Spirit (Gen. 1:2; Job 33:4).**

Many people tend to think of God's divine partnership only in terms of the work of salvation. But the three members of the Godhead are just as involved in the ongoing work of providing and caring for all creatures and maintaining the created order. In fact, their creative work continues even now in the heavens, as God prepares eternal dwelling places for believers (John 14:2–3; Rev. 21:1–2, 5).

Remarkably, this working, Triune God invites people to work with Him as junior members in the partnership, to accomplish His work in the world. In our day-to-day jobs, God asks us to do only what He has been doing from the beginning.

Perhaps you've never thought of God as a worker, but that's how He first appears in Scripture. See "God—The Original Worker," John 5:17.

Your own work is an extension of God's work in the world. See "People at Work," Heb. 2:7.

[22]Then they said to him, "Who are you, that we may give
an answer to those who sent us? What do you say about
yourself?"
[23]He said: "I *am*

'The voice of one crying in the wilderness:
"Make straight the way of the LORD," '[a]

as the prophet Isaiah said."

1:23 [a]Isaiah 40:3

God Among Us

CONSIDER THIS 1:14 *The first fourteen verses of John 1 were probably a hymn for the early church. They remind us that Jesus is God's* Word *(v. 1), "word" being a Greek term that means a* thought *expressed. Jesus is the human expression of God. He is light and flesh, to use John's metaphors (vv. 4–5, 14). To see Jesus is to see God, and to know Jesus is to experience God's grace and truth.*

It is no accident, then, that believers are called to practice community and witness publicly. The gospel is both what we say and how we live. Just as Christ became flesh and "dwelt among us," so we are to "flesh out" the good news about Christ in our everyday world.

Personality Profile: Andrew

FOR YOUR INFO 1:40 **Name means:** "Manly."

Home: Bethsaida and Capernaum, on the northwest coast of the Sea of Galilee.

Family: Father's name was Jonah; brother was Simon Peter (see Mark 1:16).

Occupation: Fisherman; later one of Jesus' followers and, according to tradition, an apostle to Scythia (now Russia).

Known today as: The person who introduced Simon to the Lord.

Andrew the Networker

In addition to working in his family's commercial fishing enterprise, Andrew followed the teaching of John the Baptist and was considered one of his disciples (John 1:35–40). Thus he heard John declare that Jesus was the Lamb of God—a clear reference to Him as the Messiah. Eager to know more about this new Teacher, Andrew pursued Jesus, prompting an invitation to spend an evening with Him. The meeting convinced Andrew that he had indeed met the long-awaited Christ.

The text is quite clear that the first thing Andrew did after coming to this conclusion was to find his brother, Simon, and tell him the extraordinary news: "We have found the Messiah!" He then brought his brother to meet Jesus (vv. 41–42).

Later, after Jesus called both of the brothers to follow Him as His disciples, Andrew and the others found themselves on one occasion confronted by thousands of people. Jesus asked His disciples where they could buy food for the crowd to eat, a proposition that staggered them.

24Now those who were sent were from the Pharisees.
25And they asked him, saying, "Why then do you baptize if
you are not the Christ, nor Elijah, nor the Prophet?"
26John answered them, saying, "I baptize with water, but
there stands One among you whom you do not know. 27It is
He who, coming after me, is preferred before me, whose
sandal strap I am not worthy to loose."

1:28

28These things were done in Bethabara[a]
beyond the Jordan, where John was baptizing.
29The next day John saw Jesus coming toward him, and
said, "Behold! The Lamb of God who takes away the sin of
the world! 30This is He of whom I said, 'After me comes a
Man who is preferred before me, for He was before me.' 31I
did not know Him; but that He should be revealed to Israel,
therefore I came baptizing with water."
32And John bore witness, saying, "I saw the Spirit descending from heaven like a dove, and He remained upon
Him. 33I did not know Him, but He who sent me to baptize
with water said to me, 'Upon whom you see the Spirit descending, and remaining on Him, this is He who baptizes
with the Holy Spirit.' 34And I have seen and testified that
this is the Son of God."

1:28 [a]NU-Text and M-Text read *Bethany*.

But Andrew had made the acquaintance of a boy with a handful of barley loaves and a couple of fish. He brought this meager supply to the attention of the Lord, who then multiplied it to feed the entire crowd of about 5,000 (6:4–14).

Shortly before Jesus' arrest, certain Greeks desired to meet Him. Once again, Andrew acted as a go-between, carrying their request to his Teacher (12:20–22). All of these incidents suggest that Andrew was a networker, a man who liked to put people together—and especially to put them together with Jesus. He serves as a model for believers today in bringing others to Christ.

Tradition holds that Andrew devoted the later years of his life to spreading the news about Jesus to Scythia, the region north of the Black Sea. Some say that he was martyred at Patrae in Achaia by crucifixion on an X-shaped cross. ◆

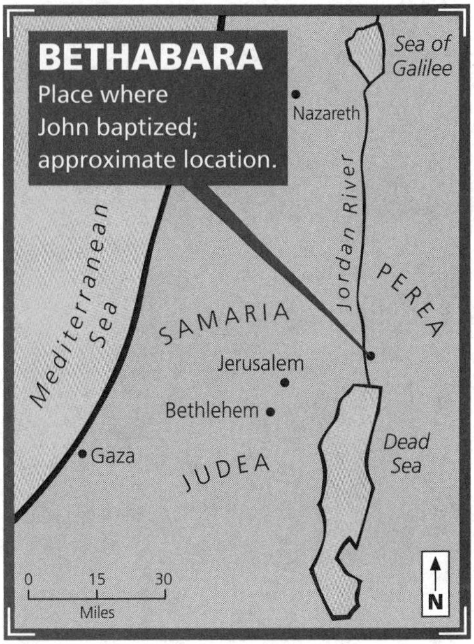

BETHABARA

YOU ARE THERE 1:28

- **A ford or crossing on the Jordan River at which John the Baptist carried out his work. The exact location is unknown.**
- **Name means "house of the ford," though it may also be another name for Bethany.**

Jesus Recruits His First Followers

35Again, the next day, John stood with two of his disciples. 36And looking at Jesus as He walked, he said, "Behold
the Lamb of God!"
37The two disciples heard him speak, and they followed
Jesus. 38Then Jesus turned, and seeing them following, said
to them, "What do you seek?"
They said to Him, "Rabbi" (which is to say, when translated, Teacher), "where are You staying?"
39He said to them, "Come and see." They came and saw
where He was staying, and remained with Him that day
(now it was about the tenth hour).

1:40 see pg. 326

40One of the two who heard John
speak, and followed Him, was Andrew,
Simon Peter's brother. 41He first found his own brother Simon, and said to him, "We have found the Messiah" (which
is translated, the Christ). 42And he brought him to Jesus.
Now when Jesus looked at him, He said, "You are Simon
the son of Jonah.[a] You shall be called Cephas" (which is
translated, A Stone).
43The following day Jesus wanted to go to Galilee, and He
found Philip and said to him, "Follow Me." 44Now Philip

1:45

was from Bethsaida, the city of Andrew
and Peter. 45Philip found Nathanael and
said to him, "We have found Him of whom Moses in the

1:42 [a]NU-Text reads *John.*

CONSIDER THIS
1:46

NAZARETH—THE OTHER SIDE OF THE TRACKS

Nazareth was a community on "the other side of the tracks." Located less than five miles from Sepphoris, the splendid capital city of Galilee, it knew quite well the impact on Palestine of Greek culture and Roman wealth and power. Yet Nazareth shared in none of those benefits. Its situation on a steep promontory ensured that its citizens would remain outsiders in the city below.

Someone has said that "God made the garden, evil men made the city, but the devil made the small town." Little towns can be vicious with rumors, gossip, and memories that refuse to die. They can also prove remarkably resistant to change. Nazareth in Jesus' day was possibly that kind of town.

Nevertheless, God chose Nazareth as the place where Jesus would grow up and invest most of His life. That fact demonstrates that while God cares deeply about cities, He also invests in small communities and various kinds of neighborhoods. Nazareth is a gift to anyone who comes from an unfashionable place, such as a dying inner city or

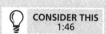

law, and also the prophets, wrote—Jesus of Nazareth, the
son of Joseph."
1:46
46And Nathanael said to him, "Can
anything good come out of Nazareth?"
Philip said to him, "Come and see."
47Jesus saw Nathanael coming toward Him, and said of
him, "Behold, an Israelite indeed, in whom is no deceit!"
48Nathanael said to Him, "How do You know me?"
Jesus answered and said to him, "Before Philip called
you, when you were under the fig tree, I saw you."
49Nathanael answered and said to Him, "Rabbi, You are
the Son of God! You are the King of Israel!"
50Jesus answered and said to him, "Because I said to you,
'I saw you under the fig tree,' do you believe? You will see
1:51 see pg. 330
greater things than these." 51And He said
to him, "Most assuredly, I say to you,
hereafter[a] you shall see heaven open, and the angels of God
ascending and descending upon the Son of Man."

CHAPTER 2

A Marriage Feast at Cana

2:1 see pg. 331
1On the third day there was a wedding
in Cana of Galilee, and the mother of
Jesus was there. 2Now both Jesus and His disciples were

(Bible text continued on page 331)

1:51 [a]NU-Text omits *hereafter.*

a declining rural town. Nazareth says that such a person, too, can receive God's love and serve the world.

If they want to, that is. Nazareth chose to reject its home-grown leader in dramatic fashion (Luke 4:16–30). Jesus left and as far as we know, never went back. However, His mother and brothers remained. They had to endure the scorn of their neighbors, who may have circulated rumors about Jesus' birth and His mental condition. The family might have suspected that Jesus' career would end in a martyr's death. For a while, even His brothers doubted His claims (John 7:5).

Can anything good come out of a Nazareth? Or out of a seedy neighborhood? Or out of an abandoned, forgotten piece of real estate? In Jesus, we see the answer is yes! ◆

Galilee, the province in which Nazareth was located, was a seedbed for revolutionaries against Rome. See "Galilee," Mark 1:14.

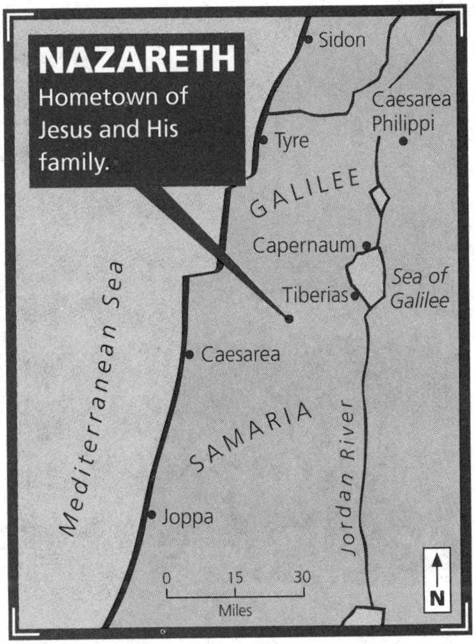

NAZARETH

YOU ARE THERE 1:45

- **Name meant "watchtower"; also "shoot" or "sprout."**
- **Close enough to the main trade routes to maintain contact with the outside world, but its remote location contributed to a certain aloofness and independence. Its people, for example, spoke a crude dialect of Aramaic.**
- **Not highly regarded, as reflected in Nathanael's remark, "Can anything good come out of Nazareth?" (John 1:46).**
- **Hometown of Joseph and Mary and boyhood home of Jesus.**
- **Today, Nazareth is a mostly Arab village of about 65,000 to 70,000 residents. Tours frequent the Church of the Carpenter and a house in which Jesus allegedly grew up.**
- **Recent archaeological digs have uncovered sites for numerous Roman garrisons and cities within five miles of Nazareth.**

CONSIDER THIS
1:51

SACRED SPACE

In His conversation with Nathanael, Jesus alluded to the Old Testament incident we call Jacob's ladder (v. 51; Gen. 28:12). Jacob had a dream in which angels passed to and from heaven, where God stood and repeated promises He had made to Jacob's father and grandfather. Waking up, Jacob exclaimed, "Surely, the Lord is in this place."

By reminding Nathanael of that story, Jesus tapped into one of the most powerful concepts of Old Testament theology—the idea that a specific place on earth is made special because of God's presence there. To the Hebrews, wherever God or His representatives touched the ground, that spot became "Bethel," or sacred space (literally, "House of God"). They built altars in those places to commemorate God's visitation.

Jesus told Nathanael that someday angels would ascend and descend upon *Him.* That put a radically new twist on things: now there was not only sacred space, but a sacred *Person.* Eventually, that truth came to have enormous implications, such as:

(1) *Those who have Christ become temples of God.* We as believers become sacred space, or better yet, sacred people because of God's presence within us. Paul described us as "temple[s] of the Holy Spirit" (1 Cor. 6:19).

(2) *Every place that we take Jesus becomes a special place.* God is in Christ and Christ is in us, so wherever we are—in the city, in the marketplace, at home—that place becomes sacred space because Christ is there, *in us.* As a result . . .

(3) *We can view our workplaces, neighborhoods, and communities from a new perspective.* We don't have to write them off as "secular" territory. And no longer are cathedrals and churches the only hallowed buildings in town. An office with Christians in it who expect God to work there becomes as special a place as any religious shrine. Even a fig tree can become the place where God carries out His purposes, as Nathanael discovered (John 1:50). Furthermore . . .

(4) *We need no longer view the inner city as throw-away real estate or a God-forsaken ghetto.* Any neighborhood, no matter how scarred and broken, can become a Bethel. If Christ's people are there, Christ is there. That sort of vision can transform a community and lend its

(continued on next page)

2:3
see pg. 332
invited to the wedding. 3And when they
ran out of wine, the mother of Jesus said
to Him, "They have no wine."
4Jesus said to her, "Woman, what does your concern have
to do with Me? My hour has not yet come."
5His mother said to the servants, "Whatever He says to
you, do *it*."
6Now there were set there six waterpots of stone, according to the manner of purification of the Jews, containing
twenty or thirty gallons apiece. 7Jesus said to them, "Fill the
waterpots with water." And they filled them up to the brim.
8And He said to them, "Draw *some* out now, and take *it* to
the master of the feast." And they took *it*. 9When the master
of the feast had tasted the water that was made wine, and

The Seven Signs of John's Gospel

Water into Wine

CONSIDER THIS 2:1–12 *Jesus' miracle of turning water into wine (vv. 1–12) was loaded with symbolism. Its placement at the beginning of John's Gospel is significant.*

For Jews, wine represented life and abundance. No proper wedding would be without it. Wine symbolized the life of the party and the expectation of a good life to come for the newlyweds. But at Cana, just as the young couple prepared to launch a new life, the unthinkable happened—they ran out of wine. That may have been a common problem in that day, given that wedding festivities often lasted as long as a week. Nevertheless, it was discouraging and probably quite an embarrassment to the host. The party immediately began to wind down.

But Jesus seized the moment to reveal to His followers something of who He was. By producing wine from water, He astounded His disciples and encouraged their faith (v. 11).

However, the product was not merely wine, but the best wine (v. 10) In the same way, Jesus was the new wine bringing abundant life to Judaism, which, like the wedding, had run out of life and become spiritually empty.

(continued from previous page)

people significance and hope.

Jesus demonstrated the power of that new vision by going to the most sacred spot in Israel, the temple, and restoring it to its purpose of worship (2:13–22). Later He went to Samaria, to Mount Gerazim, the sacred place of the Samaritans (4:19–24), where He defined true worship. Then He went to a sacred pool in Jerusalem, Bethesda, where He healed a lame man (5:1–4). And so it goes throughout John's Gospel.

Sacred space is a vital concept for us who need a God as big as the city and as powerful as today's workplace. We carry with us the very Lord of the universe. He can make every place that we enter a place of grace and truth for us and for others. ◆

Cana

YOU ARE THERE 2:1

- **A town near Nazareth, exact location unknown, though possibly at modern Kirf Kenna, four miles north of Nazareth, or perhaps the ruined city of Khirbet Kana, nine miles north of Nazareth.**
- **Name meant "place of reeds"; at Kirf Kenna, water springs and shady fig trees are still found.**
- **Mentioned in Scripture only by John, as the site of Jesus' first recorded miracle (John 2:1–11; 4:46) and the home of Nathanael (21:2).**

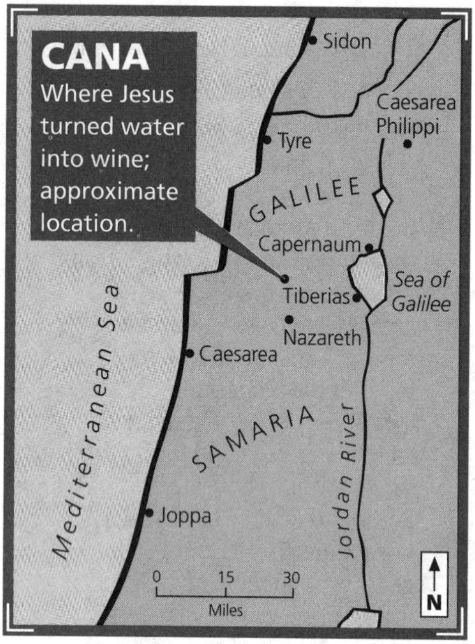

did not know where it came from (but the servants who
had drawn the water knew), the master of the feast called
the bridegroom. 10And he said to him, "Every man at the
beginning sets out the good wine, and when the *guests* have
well drunk, then the inferior. You have kept the good wine
until now!"

2:1–12 see pg. 331

11This beginning of signs Jesus did in
Cana of Galilee, and manifested His
glory; and His disciples believed in Him.

2:12

12After this He went down to Capernaum, He, His mother, His brothers, and
His disciples; and they did not stay there many days.

Merchants Evicted from the Temple

13Now the Passover of the Jews was at hand, and Jesus
went up to Jerusalem. 14And He found in the temple those
who sold oxen and sheep and doves, and the money chang-

2:13–25

ers doing business. 15When He had made
a whip of cords, He drove them all out of
the temple, with the sheep and the oxen, and poured out
the changers' money and overturned the tables. 16And He
said to those who sold doves, "Take these things away! Do
not make My Father's house a house of merchandise!"

Good and Angry

A CLOSER LOOK 2:13–25

What injustices cause your blood to boil? Jesus showed how to be both compassionate and angry in appropriate ways (vv. 13–25). See "Compassion and Anger in One Person?" Luke 19:41–46.

WINEMAKING

YOU ARE THERE 2:3

Wine was a common beverage throughout biblical times. Galilee in particular was known for its cultivation of grapes and knowledge of the winemaking process.

Galilean women and children pressed grapes in a winepress dug out of limestone. Often an artificial cave constructed near the work area served as a wine cellar.

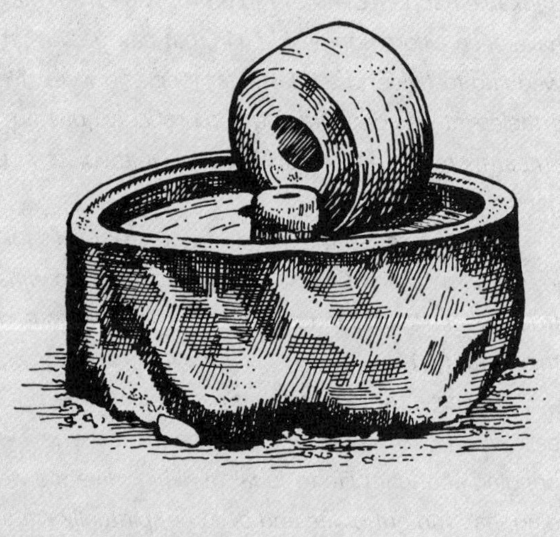

[17]Then His disciples remembered that it was written, "Zeal
for Your house has eaten[a] Me up."[b]
[18]So the Jews answered and said to Him, "What sign do
You show to us, since You do these things?"
2:19–20 [19]Jesus answered and said to them,
"Destroy this temple, and in three days I
will raise it up."
[20]Then the Jews said, "It has taken forty-six years to build
this temple, and will You raise it up in three days?"
[21]But He was speaking of the temple of His body. [22]There-
fore, when He had risen from the dead, His disciples remembered that He had said this to them;[a] and they believed
the Scripture and the word which Jesus had said.
[23]Now when He was in Jerusalem at the Passover, during
the feast, many believed in His name when they saw the
signs which He did. [24]But Jesus did not commit Himself to
them, because He knew all *men*, [25]and had no need that
anyone should testify of man, for He knew what was in
man.

CHAPTER 3

Nicodemus Visits Jesus by Night

[1]There was a man of the Pharisees named Nicodemus, a
ruler of the Jews. [2]This man came to Jesus by night and said
to Him, "Rabbi, we know that You are a teacher come from
God; for no one can do these signs that You do unless God
is with him."
[3]Jesus answered and said to him, "Most assuredly, I say to
you, unless one is born again, he cannot see the kingdom of
God."
[4]Nicodemus said to Him, "How can a man be born when
he is old? Can he enter a second time into his mother's
womb and be born?"
[5]Jesus answered, "Most assuredly, I say to you, unless one
is born of water and the Spirit, he cannot enter the kingdom of God. [6]That which is born of the flesh is flesh, and
that which is born of the Spirit is spirit. [7]Do not marvel that
I said to you, 'You must be born again.' [8]The wind blows
where it wishes, and you hear the sound of it, but cannot
tell where it comes from and where it goes. So is everyone
who is born of the Spirit."
[9]Nicodemus answered and said to Him, "How can these
things be?"
[10]Jesus answered and said to him, "Are you the teacher of
Israel, and do not know these things? [11]Most assuredly, I say

(Bible text continued on page 335)

2:17 [a]NU-Text and M-Text read *will eat.* [b]Psalm 69:9 2:22 [a]NU-Text and M-Text omit *to them.*

WHAT HAPPENED TO MARY?

CONSIDER THIS 2:12 **Jesus' mother, brothers, and disciples accompanied Him during His early travels to Capernaum (v. 12). But after this scene, Jesus' mother disappears from John's account until Jesus' crucifixion (19:25–27). Was Mary a follower of her Son? Perhaps not in the sense of one who traveled with Him. It could be that over time she came to understand better her Son's divine nature and call. After His departure, she was found among those in the upper room who prayed and waited for the promise of the Holy Spirit (Acts 1:14).**

BUILDING THE TEMPLE

YOU ARE THERE 2:19–20 **During Jesus' time, the temple at Jerusalem was undergoing extensive reconstruction and renovation. Desiring favor among the Jews, King Herod pledged to build a magnificent temple that would perhaps recall some of the glory of Solomon's temple (1 Kin. 6:1). Work began in 19 B.C. and was carried on until A.D. 64.**

At first the priests opposed Herod, suspicious that his real intent was to either do away with the temple altogether or erect something profane in its place. But Herod proved he was serious, hiring 10,000 laborers and ordering 1,000 wagons for hauling cream-colored stone. When finished, the structure shone so brightly in the Mediterranean sun that it was difficult to look at directly.

Still the priests feared that this most sacred place would be profaned.

(continued on next page)

(continued from previous page)

So Herod had 1,000 of them trained as carpenters and masons so that only priestly hands would construct the Most Holy Place. Unfortunately, the priests themselves turned out to be their own worst enemies: poor craftsmen, they did work that sometimes collapsed and had to be replaced.

But it was an exercise in futility. In A.D. 70, Roman armies surrounded Jerusalem, captured it, and completely destroyed Herod's temple (see "Jerusalem Surrounded," Luke 21:20).

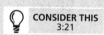

The temple was but one of many splendid edifices that the family of the Herods built while they governed Palestine. Unfortunately, they are remembered more for their infamous family history than their brilliant architectural achievements. See "The Herods," Acts 12:1–2.

CONSIDER THIS
3:21

THE GOSPEL IN A PLURALISTIC SOCIETY

Jesus' nighttime meeting with Nicodemus (vv. 1–21) and His midday encounter with the Samaritan woman (4:5–42) show two of the many different ways in which He dealt with people. Whether it had to do with a respected urban leader like Nicodemus or a hardened, street-wise loner like the woman of Samaria, Jesus approached people on their own terms, as individuals with unique concerns. He modeled for us what it means to live, work, and communicate the gospel message in a pluralistic society.

Nicodemus was an upper-class Jew, a Pharisee from one of the prominent families of Jerusalem. He approached Jesus, alone, at night. The Lord confronted him with his need to be "born again," then let him go away to think things over. The next time we see him, he is defending Jesus on a procedural matter (7:45–52). But Nicodemus apparently didn't openly identify with Jesus until after the crucifixion, when he helped prepare His body for burial (19:39).

The Samaritan woman, on the other hand, had lived a scandalous lifestyle with a succession of husbands and then with a live-in companion. As a result, her community despised her. She also probably came from mixed ancestry,

to you, We speak what We know and testify what We have
seen, and you do not receive Our witness. 12If I have told
you earthly things and you do not believe, how will you believe if I tell you heavenly things? 13No one has ascended to
heaven but He who came down from heaven, *that is,* the
Son of Man who is in heaven.[a] 14And as Moses lifted up the
serpent in the wilderness, even so must the Son of Man be
lifted up, 15that whoever believes in Him should not perish
but[a] have eternal life. 16For God so loved the world that He
gave His only begotten Son, that whoever believes in Him
should not perish but have everlasting life. 17For God did
not send His Son into the world to condemn the world, but
that the world through Him might be saved.
18"He who believes in Him is not condemned; but he who
does not believe is condemned already, because he has not
believed in the name of the only begotten Son of God.
19And this is the condemnation, that the light has come into
the world, and men loved darkness rather than light, because their deeds were evil. 20For everyone practicing evil
hates the light and does not come to the light, lest his deeds
should be exposed. 21But he who does
the truth comes to the light, that his

3:21

3:13 [a]NU-Text omits *who is in heaven.* *3:15* [a]NU-Text omits *not perish but.*

for which the Jews despised her. She was spoken to by Jesus in broad daylight, in public, first by herself but later in the company of others. He told her of "living water" and the need to worship in spirit and truth. She responded much more quickly than Nicodemus. Furthermore, hers may have been not so much an individual choice as a clan decision (4:39–41).

John went on to record many other ways Jesus dealt with people, and many ways they responded to Him. Some became believers after they were fed (6:4–14), others after they were healed (9:1–38), and others after they had seen the resurrected Christ (20:24–29). Some responded to the Lord's miracles, others to His teaching. There was no one kind of response to Jesus.

We as believers today must present the gospel in an increasingly pluralistic world. Like Jesus, we need to use many different approaches. What are some of the creative means you can use to influence friends and coworkers for Christ? ◆

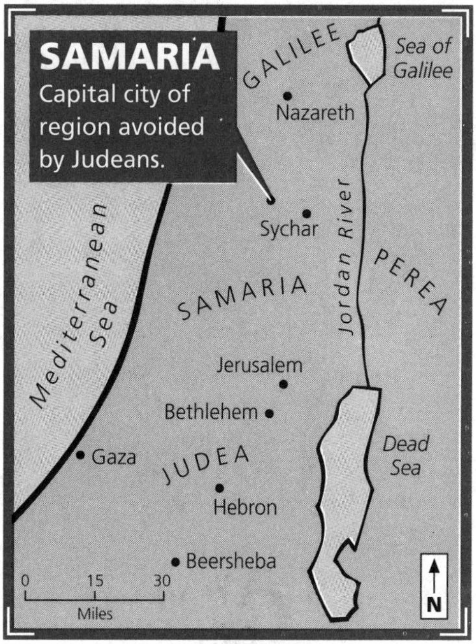

SAMARIA

YOU ARE THERE 4:4

- **The central province of Palestine under the Romans. Its key city, also called Samaria, had been the capital of the northern kingdom of Israel before its fall to Assyria (722 B.C.).**
- **Noted for rich, fertile farmlands that produced valuable grain crops, olives, and grapes.**
- **Served by five major roads, which encouraged trade with Phoenicia, Syria, and Egypt.**
- **Historically, a prime target of invaders due to its reputation for prosperity.**

Jesus taught His followers a series of courses on relating to Samaritans. For two of the more memorable, see "Condemnation or Compassion?" Luke 9:51–56, and "Who Was the Neighbor?" Luke 10:37.

In going from Jerusalem to the end of the earth, the gospel had to go through Samaria. See "Opportunities Look Like Barriers," Acts 1:4.

deeds may be clearly seen, that they have been done in God."

John the Baptist Teaches about Jesus

22 After these things Jesus and His disciples came into the land of Judea, and there He remained with them and baptized. 23 Now John also was baptizing in Aenon near Salim, because there was much water there. And they came and were baptized. 24 For John had not yet been thrown into prison.

25 Then there arose a dispute between *some* of John's disciples and the Jews about purification. 26 And they came to John and said to him, "Rabbi, He who was with you beyond the Jordan, to whom you have testified—behold, He is baptizing, and all are coming to Him!"

27 John answered and said, "A man can receive nothing unless it has been given to him from heaven. 28 You yourselves bear me witness, that I said, 'I am not the Christ,' but, 'I have been sent before Him.' 29 He who has the bride is the bridegroom; but the friend of the bridegroom, who stands and hears him, rejoices greatly because of the bridegroom's voice. Therefore this joy of mine is fulfilled. 30 He must increase, but I *must* decrease. 31 He who comes from above is above all; he who is of the earth is earthly and speaks of the earth. He who comes from heaven is above all. 32 And what He has seen and heard, that He testifies; and no one receives His testimony. 33 He who has received His testimony has certified that God is true. 34 For He whom God has sent speaks the words of God, for God does not give the Spirit by measure. 35 The Father loves the Son, and has given all things into His hand. 36 He who believes in the Son has everlasting life; and he who does not believe the Son shall not see life, but the wrath of God abides on him."

3:30

"A MAN CAN RECEIVE NOTHING UNLESS IT HAS BEEN GIVEN TO HIM FROM HEAVEN."
—John 3:27

CHAPTER 4

Jesus Encounters a Samaritan Woman

1 Therefore, when the Lord knew that the Pharisees had heard that Jesus made and baptized more disciples than John 2 (though Jesus Himself did not baptize, but His disciples), 3 He left Judea and departed again to Galilee. 4 But He needed to go through Samaria.

4:4 see pg. 335

5 So He came to a city of Samaria which is called Sychar, near the plot of ground that Jacob gave to his son Joseph. 6 Now Jacob's well was

4:5 see pg. 339

(Bible text continued on page 338)

CONSIDER THIS
3:30

SUCCESS

To what extent should Christ's followers today pursue success? John's declaration that "He must increase, but I must decrease" (v. 30) seems to repudiate the idea of personal achievement, recognition, or material gain—common measures of success in our society. Indeed, John himself showed none of the outward trappings of a successful ministry (see "John the Street Preacher," Matt. 3:4).

So should believers avoid success as the world defines it? Can people be successful in their careers as well as in their spiritual lives, or are the two mutually exclusive? Some Christians say that success on the job creates credibility for them to talk about Christ with coworkers. Others, however, claim that they have no interest in being successful. But is that a genuine conviction, or are they merely avoiding the rough-and-tumble of a competitive marketplace? Would God prefer that His people be *failures* on the job, in society, or in life?

Questions like these barely scratch the surface of the complex, emotional issue of success. The people of Jesus' day were no less interested in prospering than we are, even if they defined success in slightly different terms. So it's not surprising that Scripture speaks to human ambition and achievement. It seems to affirm at least three important principles, as illustrated by John the Baptist:

(1) *Success is always measured by a set of standards established by some person or group.* Many people of John's day felt that they were assured of the blessing of God simply because they were descendants of Abraham. Their religious leaders aggressively promoted and reinforced that idea (Matt. 3:7–9; Luke 3:8; John 8:39). John challenged them to reconsider that way of thinking. What mattered, he said, was faith in Jesus. That was the ultimate criterion by which God would measure people's lives. Thus, unbelief would result in the ultimate failure—eternal death (3:36).

(2) *Why and how we pursue success is just as important as whether or not we achieve it.* John's listeners were ordinary people caught up in the everyday scramble to get ahead. But in their pursuit of gain they tended to ignore the needs of others and to take ethical shortcuts. John challenged them to make internal changes (that is, to repent) and to demonstrate those changes in their day-to-day responsibilities through charity, honesty, and justice (Luke 3:8, 10–14).

John himself was able to carry out his ministry because he had the right perspective on the assignment that God had given him. He recognized that he was merely a forerunner to the Christ, not the Christ Himself (John 3:28–29). He knew that Jesus' ministry was going to grow and expand, slowly eliminating the need for John—hence his statement that "He must increase, but I must decrease."

(3) *Obtaining success always carries a cost.* John warned the people of God's judgment using a simple, well-known image: "Even now the ax is laid to the root of the trees. Therefore, every tree which does not bear fruit is cut down and thrown into the fire" (Luke 3:9). Just as a lumberjack would lay his ax at the foot of a tree while he decided which trees in a forest to cut, so God had sent John and Jesus as His final messengers before letting His judgment fall.

The people could choose what they wanted to do—whether to continue in their self-satisfied ways of unbelief, or whether to turn toward God in repentance and obedience. Either way, there would be a cost involved. Unfortunately, most of them chose to reject John's message and later Jesus' message, with tragic results (see "Jerusalem Surrounded," Luke 21:20).

For John, the cost of faithfully proclaiming his message was imprisonment and, eventu-

(continued on next page)

(continued from previous page)

ally, execution (Matt. 14:1–12). Yet he gained a treasure all out of proportion to the price of martyrdom—-the praise of Christ (11:7–11).

So should believers pursue success? Judging from the experience of John the Baptist and the people who followed him, the issue seems to be not so much *whether* we should pursue it, but *how.* In light of John's message, it's worth considering three crucial questions:

- Who sets the standards by which I measure success?
- What are my motives and behavior in pursuing success?
- What price am I willing to pay to achieve success? ◆

Jesus told a parable in which He showed that "True Success Means Faithfulness." See Matt. 25:14–30.

Like John, Paul challenged the idea of people looking out chiefly for Number One. See "Humility—The Scandalous Virtue," Phil. 2:3.

there. Jesus therefore, being wearied from *His* journey, sat
thus by the well. It was about the sixth hour.
[7]A woman of Samaria came to draw water. Jesus said to
her, "Give Me a drink." [8]For His disciples had gone away
into the city to buy food.

4:9
see pg. 340

[9]Then the woman of Samaria said to
Him, "How is it that You, being a Jew, ask
a drink from me, a Samaritan woman?" For Jews have no
dealings with Samaritans.
[10]Jesus answered and said to her, "If you knew the gift of
God, and who it is who says to you, 'Give Me a drink,' you
would have asked Him, and He would have given you living water."
[11]The woman said to Him, "Sir, You have nothing to draw
with, and the well is deep. Where then do You get that living water? [12]Are You greater than our father Jacob, who
gave us the well, and drank from it himself, as well as his
sons and his livestock?"
[13]Jesus answered and said to her, "Whoever drinks of this
water will thirst again, [14]but whoever drinks of the water
that I shall give him will never thirst. But the water that I
shall give him will become in him a fountain of water
springing up into everlasting life."
[15]The woman said to Him, "Sir, give me this water, that I
may not thirst, nor come here to draw."
[16]Jesus said to her, "Go, call your husband, and come
here."
[17]The woman answered and said, "I have no husband."
Jesus said to her, "You have well said, 'I have no husband,' [18]for you have had five husbands, and the one
whom you now have is not your husband; in that you
spoke truly."

4:19–23
see pg. 341

[19]The woman said to Him, "Sir, I perceive that You are a prophet. [20]Our
fathers worshiped on this mountain, and you *Jews* say that
in Jerusalem is the place where one ought to worship."
[21]Jesus said to her, "Woman, believe Me, the hour is coming when you will neither on this mountain, nor in
Jerusalem, worship the Father. [22]You worship what you do
not know; we know what we worship, for salvation is of the
Jews. [23]But the hour is coming, and now is, when the true
worshipers will worship the Father in spirit and truth; for
the Father is seeking such to worship Him. [24]God *is* Spirit,
and those who worship Him must worship in spirit and
truth."
[25]The woman said to Him, "I know that Messiah is coming" (who is called Christ). "When He comes, He will tell us
all things."
[26]Jesus said to her, "I who speak to you am *He.*"

4:27 see pg. 342
27And at this *point* His disciples came,
and they marveled that He talked with a
woman; yet no one said, "What do You seek?" or, "Why are
You talking with her?"

4:4–42 see pg. 342
28The woman then left her waterpot,
went her way into the city, and said to
the men, 29"Come, see a Man who told me all things that I
ever did. Could this be the Christ?" 30Then they went out of
the city and came to Him.
31In the meantime His disciples urged Him, saying,
"Rabbi, eat."
32But He said to them, "I have food to eat of which you
do not know."
33Therefore the disciples said to one another, "Has anyone
brought Him *anything* to eat?"
34Jesus said to them, "My food is to do the will of Him
who sent Me, and to finish His work. 35Do you not say,
'There are still four months and *then* comes the harvest'? Behold, I say to you, lift up your eyes and look at the fields,
for they are already white for harvest! 36And he who reaps
receives wages, and gathers fruit for eternal life, that both
he who sows and he who reaps may rejoice together. 37For
in this the saying is true: 'One sows and another reaps.' 38I
sent you to reap that for which you have not labored; others
have labored, and you have entered into their labors."
39And many of the Samaritans of that city believed in Him
because of the word of the woman who testified, "He told
me all that I *ever* did." 40So when the Samaritans had come
to Him, they urged Him to stay with them; and He stayed
there two days. 41And many more believed because of His
own word.
42Then they said to the woman, "Now we believe, not because of what you said, for we ourselves have heard *Him*
and we know that this is indeed the Christ,[a] the Savior of
the world."

Jesus Heals a Nobleman's Son

43Now after the two days He departed from there and
went to Galilee. 44For Jesus Himself testified that a prophet
has no honor in his own country. 45So when He came to
Galilee, the Galileans received Him, having seen all the
things He did in Jerusalem at the feast; for they also had
gone to the feast.

4:46–54 see pg. 343
46So Jesus came again to Cana of
Galilee where He had made the water
wine. And there was a certain nobleman whose son was
sick at Capernaum. 47When he heard that Jesus had come
out of Judea into Galilee, he went to Him and implored

4:42 [a]NU-Text omits *the Christ.*

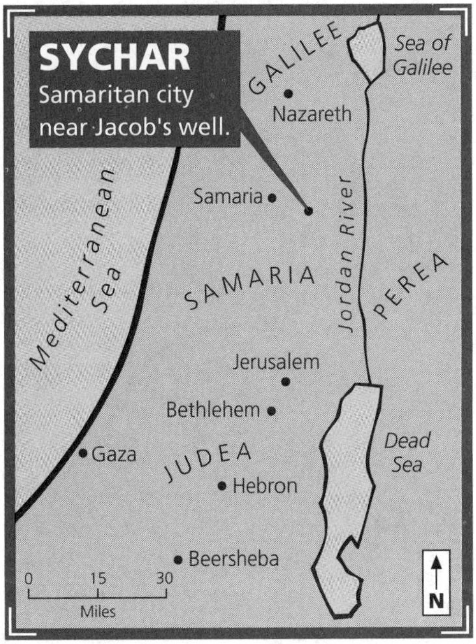

SYCHAR

YOU ARE THERE 4:5

- **A Samaritan city mentioned only once in the Bible (John 4:5).**
- **Exact location unknown, though it could be the same as ancient Askar, one mile north of Jacob's well, or possibly Shechem, a city of great historical significance (Gen. 33:18).**
- **Today some 300 Samaritan descendants live in Nablus, site of ancient Shechem.**

Him to come down and heal his son, for he was at the point

4:48
see pg. 344

of death. [48]Then Jesus said to him, "Unless you *people* see signs and wonders, you will by no means believe."

[49]The nobleman said to Him, "Sir, come down before my child dies!"

4:50

[50]Jesus said to him, "Go your way; your son lives." So the man believed the word that Jesus spoke to him, and he went his way. [51]And as he

A Wealthy Man Believes

A CLOSER LOOK
4:50

The nobleman who sought Jesus' help (v. 46) became a true child of God because he believed the words of Christ (v. 50). His status with God was based on his faith, not his wealth. Anyone whose greatest aspiration is status and wealth, rather than faith, has embarked on a course that can only end in eternal poverty. See "Christians and Money," 1 Tim. 6:7–19, and "Getting Yours," James 5:1–6. To find out about some of the other wealthy people in the New Testament, see Matt. 27:57.

CONSIDER THIS
4:9

"Jews Have No Dealings with Samaritans"

Hatred between Jews and Samaritans was fierce and long-standing. In some ways, it dated all the way back to the days of the patriarchs. Jacob (or Israel) had twelve sons, whose descendants became twelve tribes. Joseph, his favorite, was despised by the other brothers (Gen. 37:3–4), and they attempted to do away with him.

But God intervened and not only preserved Joseph's life, but used him to preserve the lives of the entire clan. Before his death, Jacob gave Joseph a blessing in which he called him a "fruitful bough by a well" (Gen. 49:22). The blessing was fulfilled, as the territory allotted to the tribes of Joseph's two sons, Ephraim ("doubly fruitful") and Manasseh, was the fertile land that eventually became Samaria.

Later, Israel divided into two kingdoms. The northern kingdom, called Israel, established its capital first at Shechem, a revered site in Jewish history, and later at the hilltop city of Samaria.

In 722 B.C. Assyria conquered Israel and took most of its people into captivity. The invaders then brought in Gentile colonists "from Babylon, Cuthah, Ava, Hamath, and from Sepharvaim" (2 Kin. 17:24) to resettle the land. The foreigners brought with them their pagan idols, which the remaining Jews began to worship alongside the God of Israel (2 Kin. 17:29–41). Intermarriages also took place (Ezra 9:1—10:44; Neh. 13:23–28).

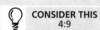

was now going down, his servants met him and told *him*,
saying, "Your son lives!"
52Then he inquired of them the hour when he got better.
And they said to him, "Yesterday at the seventh hour the
fever left him." 53So the father knew that *it was* at the same
hour in which Jesus said to him, "Your son lives." And he
himself believed, and his whole household.
54This again *is* the second sign Jesus did when He had
come out of Judea into Galilee.

CHAPTER 5

Jesus Heals a Paralyzed Man

5:1–17 see pg. 343

1After this there was a feast of the Jews,
and Jesus went up to Jerusalem. 2Now
there is in Jerusalem by the Sheep *Gate* a pool, which is

(Bible text continued on page 345)

Meanwhile, the southern kingdom of Judah fell to Babylon in 600 B.C. Its people, too, were carried off into captivity. But 70 years later, a remnant of 43,000 was permitted to return and rebuild Jerusalem. The people who now inhabited the former northern kingdom—the Samaritans—vigorously opposed the repatriation and tried to undermine the attempt to reestablish the nation. For their part, the full-blooded, monotheistic Jews detested the mixed marriages and worship of their northern cousins. So walls of bitterness were erected on both sides and did nothing but harden for the next 550 years.

There are countless modern parallels to the Jewish-Samaritan enmity—indeed, wherever peoples are divided by racial and ethnic barriers. Perhaps that's why the Gospels and Acts provide so many instances of Samaritans coming into contact with the message of Jesus. It is not the person from the radically different culture on the other side of the world that is hardest to love, but the nearby neighbor whose skin color, language, rituals, values, ancestry, history, and customs are different from one's own.

Jews had no dealings with the Samaritans. With whom do you have no dealings? ◆

ETHNIC GAMES WITH RELIGIOUS ROOTS

CONSIDER THIS 4:19–23

Jesus must have made the woman at the well very uncomfortable when He spoke with such detailed, personal knowledge of her past (v. 17). Perhaps that's why she began to play ethnic games with Him, falling back on her religious roots (vv. 19–20).

Samaritans were good at that. Nearby was Mount Ebal, where Joshua had renewed Israel's covenant with God (Josh. 8:30–35). According to the Jewish Torah (Deut. 27:4–6), Mount Ebal was also where Moses built an altar to celebrate the Israelites entering the Promised Land. But the Samaritans held that Mount Gerizim, also nearby, was the only true place of worship. The Samaritans built an altar there in 400 B.C., but the Jews destroyed it in 128 B.C. That only added to the historic enmity between the two groups—and provided ammunition for the woman to challenge Jesus.

Today, many people still play ethnic games with their religious roots. In Mexico City, for example, some churches are located on top of Aztec or Mayan shrines. Some Mexicans, seeking to recover their Indian roots and throw off their Spanishness, literally dig deep into their past to promote paganism and reject Christianity. Similar behavior can be found among other groups exploring and recovering their roots. Like the Samaritans in Jesus' day, they want to affirm who they are as a people.

Jesus understood this woman's need for ethnic identity and security. But He challenged her and her neighbors with a deeper issue—their need to turn to God and become true worshipers of Him. He refused to play ethnic games when there was a matter of eternal life and death at stake.

JESUS SPEAKS TO A WOMAN

CONSIDER THIS
4:27

The disciples marveled that their rabbi was speaking to a woman (v. 27). In their day it was considered disreputable and beneath his dignity for a rabbi to speak to a woman in public. But Jesus chose a more inclusive posture than His religious peers.

Women were not the only group that Jesus reached out to in contrast to other rabbis. See "Please Bless Our Children," Matt. 19:13–15.

CONSIDER THIS
4:4–42

THE ROAD LESS TRAVELED

For Jews in Jesus' day, the main road to Jerusalem went around *Samaria. But He intentionally went* through *Samaria (v. 4), where He taught His disciples a lesson in cross-cultural communication.*

Finding a woman at Jacob's well in Sychar (vv. 5–7), Jesus struck up a conversation which quickly turned personal. Before long, the woman was on the verge of conversion. But Jesus understood that in her culture women lacked authority to make substantive decisions on their own. Those were made by men, often tribally, within clans. In fact, it was unusual for a man, particularly a rabbi, to hold serious conversation with a woman in public, as Jesus was doing. Perhaps that's one reason why the woman left as soon as the disciples showed up (vv. 27–28).

However, another reason was so that she could go and tell her "significant others," her network of family and friends, about Jesus (vv. 28–30). The woman left her waterpot at the well, maybe because she was in a hurry, though she may have left it there to avoid having to carry it around; after all, she clearly intended to return. At any rate, v. 28 specifically points out that she approached "the men" in the community first—perhaps a clue that they were indeed the decision makers.

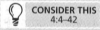

The Seven Signs of John's Gospel

THE NOBLEMAN'S SON

CONSIDER THIS 4:46–54

The key to understanding the significance of Jesus' second sign miracle (vv. 46–54) is geography. The nobleman and his dying son lived in Capernaum, the main city of the Galilee region (see Luke 4:31). But Jesus was 20 miles away at Cana (where, significantly, His first sign miracle had taken place, John 2:1–12). That means that the nobleman walked a 40-mile round trip—a two-day trek by foot—to implore Jesus to heal his son. But Jesus merely spoke a word (v. 50), producing results 20 miles away, in a world that knew nothing of phones, faxes, or modems. No wonder the incident produced faith (v. 53). Jesus was the master of distance.

But it was also true that she had been married to or had lived with or been intimate with a number of the men in that clan (vv. 17–18). In that respect, she was like many public aid mothers today living in common-law marriages. Those connections might have made her a unique "gatekeeper" or social organizer in the community. She could unlock the village for Jesus. Once she did, He stayed there for two days (v. 43).

What does Jesus' example say about communicating the gospel message today? Northern European and American cultures tend to value individual choice. But elsewhere, many cultures are more clannish. Inter- and intra-family relationships have a powerful bearing on how the message will be received. Western believers need to respect that and use it to advantage as they cross over into cultures different from their own.

Jesus followed the less-traveled road directly into Samaria to bring not just an individual woman, but an entire community to faith. Have you chosen the road less traveled to walk with Jesus into cultures different than your own? ◆

The Seven Signs of John's Gospel

THE MAN AT BETHESDA

CONSIDER THIS 5:1–17

Jesus' third sign miracle revolves around the issue of time. The man at the pool of Bethesda had lain there for 38 years—an entire lifetime as a helpless cripple. Indeed, he had probably started lying there before Jesus was even born. Imagine the disappointment he must have experienced time after time when the angel stirred up the pool, but always he had arrived too late to experience healing. Yet Jesus healed him and immediately he was able to walk. Jesus showed Himself to be the master of time. However, was Israel ready for Him (v. 16)?

CONSIDER THIS
4:48

MYTH #3

10 MYTHS ABOUT CHRISTIANITY

MYTH: SCIENCE IS IN CONFLICT WITH CHRISTIAN FAITH

Many people today accept a number of myths about Christianity, with the result that they never respond to Jesus as He really is. This is one of ten articles that speak to some of those misconceptions. For a list of all ten, see 1 Tim. 1:3–4.

The people of Jesus' day demanded miraculous signs as a condition for belief (v. 48). Yet even though Jesus performed astonishing miracles, His Jewish brothers and sisters by and large rejected Him as their Messiah (1:11). Today many people reject Christianity on similar grounds. We live in a natural world, they say, a world that can be explained by science. Since Christianity relies on faith, it no longer applies in our modern, scientific world. In fact, Christianity and science conflict.

The interesting thing is that while many top scientists do not make this claim, many untrained people do. They have bought into a number of myths, including:

Science can be proved; Christianity cannot. The truth is that both science and Christianity deal with *evidence.* Science examines evidence about our world from things that we can see, touch, measure, and calculate. Christianity is based on evidence about our world from the life, teaching, death, and resurrection of Jesus. Both deal with matters that are very much open to examination.

Of course, it is a misconception that science can be "proved." The heart of the scientific method is to allow the evidence to lead one where it will. But in that case, one cannot "prove" a scientific hypothesis, but only support it with evidence. In fact, one of the fundamental tenets of science is that it takes only one contrary instance to bring down an entire hypothesis. For centuries Newton's theories of gravity seemed irrefutably "proven." Then along came Einstein. Today his thinking is giving way to new discoveries.

Science is progressive; Christianity resists progress. There is some truth to this—but only some. At certain times in history, Christianity has opposed ideas that seemed to challenge its worldview. Yet at other times Christianity—that is to say, Christians—have been (and still are) on the vanguard of scientific progress. Indeed, modern science is largely the product of inquiring believers.

Science is logical; Christianity involves a leap of faith. Without question there is a logic and an order in scientific inquiry. But the same is true for the philosophical, historical, ethical, and theological disciplines of Christianity. Our faith is not opposed to reason. At points it may go beyond reason. But it is a reasonable faith. It hangs together logically.

At the same time, science demands an element of faith. Faith is not, as one schoolboy defined it, believing what you know is not true; faith involves self-commitment on the basis of evidence. In science, one must commit oneself to the belief that the world we see and touch is real, that nature is uniform, and that it operates according to the principle of cause-and-effect. Without these prior "leaps of faith," reasonable though they are, one cannot undertake science.

Science deals with the laws of nature; Christianity thrives on miracles. If science involves a closed, physical universe with fixed, unalterable laws, then the concept of miracles, which in-

(continued on next page)

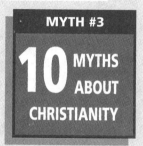

called in Hebrew, Bethesda,[a] having five porches. 3 In these
lay a great multitude of sick people, blind, lame, paralyzed,
waiting for the moving of the water. 4 For an angel went
down at a certain time into the pool and stirred up the water; then whoever stepped in first, after the stirring of the
water, was made well of whatever disease he had.[a] 5 Now a
certain man was there who had an infirmity thirty-eight
years. 6 When Jesus saw him lying there, and knew that he
already had been *in that condition* a long time, He said to
him, "Do you want to be made well?"

7 The sick man answered Him, "Sir, I have no man to put
me into the pool when the water is stirred up; but while I
am coming, another steps down before me."

5:8–18

8 Jesus said to him, "Rise, take up your
bed and walk." 9 And immediately the
man was made well, took up his bed, and walked.

And that day was the Sabbath. 10 The Jews therefore said
to him who was cured, "It is the Sabbath; it is not lawful for
you to carry your bed."

11 He answered them, "He who made me well said to me,
'Take up your bed and walk.' "

12 Then they asked him, "Who is the Man who said to
you, 'Take up your bed and walk'?" 13 But the one who was
healed did not know who it was, for Jesus had withdrawn,
a multitude being in *that* place. 14 Afterward Jesus found
him in the temple, and said to him, "See, you have been
made well. Sin no more, lest a worse thing come upon
you."

15 The man departed and told the Jews that it was Jesus
who had made him well.

Jesus Responds to His Critics

5:16–17
see pg. 346

5:17
see pg. 347

16 For this reason the Jews persecuted
Jesus, and sought to kill Him,[a] because
He had done these things on the Sabbath.
17 But Jesus answered them, "My Father
has been working until now, and I have been working."

5:2 [a]NU-Text reads *Bethzatha.* *5:4* [a]NU-Text omits *waiting for the moving of the water* at the end of verse 3, and all of verse 4. *5:16* [a]NU-Text omits *and sought to kill Him.*

MYTH #3 10 MYTHS ABOUT CHRISTIANITY

(continued from previous page)

volve the local, temporary suspension of natural laws, will prove intolerable. But that is a nineteenth-century view of science. Few scientists of stature today support such a view.

Moreover, the so-called "laws of nature" are not prescriptive but *descriptive*. They do not determine what may happen; they describe what normally does happen. Therefore, science can legitimately say that miracles do not usually occur in nature. But it would be illegitimate to claim that miracles are impossible. Such a claim speaks outside the limits of science. If God has really come into this world in Christ, is it so surprising that He would perform miracles, as the Gospels report?

Science is not in conflict with Christianity. To be sure, some scientists are. But other scientists are passionately committed Christians, just like people in other walks of life. There are reasons why people choose for or against Christ, but those reasons are found elsewhere than in science. ◆

"You Can't Get Healed on the Sabbath!"

A CLOSER LOOK 5:8–18

Ever on the lookout for infractions of their traditions and especially eager to catch Jesus and His followers in sin, the Pharisees quibbled over a formerly lame man carrying his bed on the Sabbath (v. 10). Jesus' Sabbath-day miracles sparked no end of controversy with these legalists. But He refused to let their objections go unchallenged. See "Jesus Confronts the Legalists," Luke 6:1–11.

[18]Therefore the Jews sought all the more to kill Him, because He not only broke the Sabbath, but also said that God
was His Father, making Himself equal with God. [19]Then Jesus answered and said to them, "Most assuredly, I say to
you, the Son can do nothing of Himself, but what He sees
the Father do; for whatever He does, the Son also does in
like manner. [20]For the Father loves the Son, and shows Him
all things that He Himself does; and He will show Him
greater works than these, that you may marvel. [21]For as the
Father raises the dead and gives life to *them,* even so the
Son gives life to whom He will. [22]For the Father judges no
one, but has committed all judgment to the Son, [23]that all
should honor the Son just as they honor the Father. He who
does not honor the Son does not honor the Father who sent
Him.

[24]"Most assuredly, I say to you, he who hears My word
and believes in Him who sent Me has everlasting life, and
shall not come into judgment, but has passed from death
into life. [25]Most assuredly, I say to you, the hour is coming,
and now is, when the dead will hear the voice of the Son of
God; and those who hear will live. [26]For as the Father has
life in Himself, so He has granted the Son to have life in
Himself, [27]and has given Him authority to execute judgment also, because He is the Son of Man. [28]Do not marvel at
this; for the hour is coming in which all who are in the
graves will hear His voice [29]and come forth—those who
have done good, to the resurrection of life, and those who
have done evil, to the resurrection of condemnation. [30]I can
of Myself do nothing. As I hear, I judge; and My judgment
is righteous, because I do not seek My own will but the will
of the Father who sent Me.

[31]"If I bear witness of Myself, My witness is not true.
[32]There is another who bears witness of Me, and I know
that the witness which He witnesses of Me is true. [33]You
have sent to John, and he has borne witness to the truth.
[34]Yet I do not receive testimony from man, but I say these
things that you may be saved. [35]He was the burning and
shining lamp, and you were willing for a time to rejoice in
his light. [36]But I have a greater witness than John's; for the
works which the Father has given Me to finish—the very
works that I do—bear witness of Me, that the Father has
sent Me. [37]And the Father Himself, who sent Me, has testified of Me. You have neither heard His voice at any time,
nor seen His form. [38]But you do not have His word abiding
in you, because whom He sent, Him you do not believe.
[39]You search the Scriptures, for in them you think you have
eternal life; and these are they which testify of Me. [40]But
you are not willing to come to Me that you may have life.

(Bible text continued on page 348)

Does God Work on Sundays?

CONSIDER THIS 5:16–17 **Jesus offered an odd retort to His critics in the controversy over observance of the Sabbath (vv. 16–17). Genesis 2:2–3 said that God "rested" from His work on the seventh day of creation and "sanctified" it, or set it apart as something special. Later, the third of the Ten Commandments made the seventh day a holy day, a Sabbath or day of rest in Israel (Ex. 20:8–11). Many Christians continue this practice today (on Sundays).**

According to rabbinical legal tradition, the healed man was violating the Sabbath rest by carrying his bed (v. 10), as was Jesus by healing him on that day (v. 16). But Jesus said that even God "breaks" His own Sabbath by continuing to work (v. 17). Even though He has completed the Creation, He continues to maintain it and provide for His creatures—even on Sundays.

The point was that it's never the wrong day to do good.

CONSIDER THIS
5:17

GOD—THE ORIGINAL WORKER

God is a worker! Perhaps you've never thought of Him that way. But that's how He first appears in Scripture. In the creation account (Gen. 1–2) He wears no end of occupational hats: strategic planner, designer, civil engineer, real estate developer, project manager, artist, and many more. Using these skills, He created something that was "very good" (1:31). How good? As good as God! No wonder the creation is said to "glorify," or praise God. His work is worth honoring, and it honors Him. (See Is. 43:7; 60:21.)

Furthermore, God continues to work (John 5:17), maintaining the creation and providing for His creatures. He also carries out the work of salvation. And He uses people to help Him accomplish these tasks. Think what that means:

(1) *Work itself is inherently good.* God didn't mind "getting His hands dirty," so to speak, in creating the universe. Genesis says He "worked" to bring it into existence (2:2). But that means work must be good in and of itself, since by definition, God can only do what is good. It also means work reflects the activity of God. The engineer who designs a bridge, the zoologist who studies animals, and the farmer who raises crops all carry out jobs that God did at the beginning of the world.

(2) *Your work is important; it matters.* The work that God gives you has dignity to it. In fact, God created you "in His image" (Gen. 1:26–27). Just as He works, so He has created you to work. Genesis even says that God has placed human beings in authority over the creation as His managers. As you use the abilities He's given you, you can be a partner, a coworker with Him to carry out His work.

For example, God can use: the nurse to meet the health needs of patients; the grocer to distribute food to customers; the researcher to provide accurate information; the lawyer to promote justice for clients; the career homemaker to nurture growing children. God values these kinds of jobs because they help to carry out His purposes in the world. These things matter to Him.

(3) *There's no such thing as "secular" or "sacred" work.* God certainly uses ministers and missionaries to meet spiritual and personal needs around the world. But they are not the only people doing "God's work." God is just as interested in the physical, emotional, intellectual, and other needs that people have. He also cares about the management of the earth itself. It takes all kinds of skills, and all kinds of people, to do what God wants done in the world.

(4) *You should do your work in a way that honors God.* Your work has dignity; you're created in God's image as a worker; you're a coworker with God; you have God-given abilities to carry out important tasks that He wants done. All of this says that what you do for work and how you do it should bring glory to God. He should be pleased with it—and with you as you do it. ◆

Our work isn't exactly the same as God's work, is it? See "Creation: 'Very Good,' But Not Sacred!" Heb. 11:3.

Doesn't Genesis say that God "rested" from His work? See "Does God Work on Sundays?" John 5:16–17.

Many people assume that work is a part of the curse. Is it? See Rom. 8:20–22.

The Seven Signs of John's Gospel

FEEDING THE 5,000

CONSIDER THIS 6:1–14 *John writes that the crowd that followed Jesus did so in response to His miracles (v. 2), a link to the healing of the lame man in John 5:1–17. This leads to a fourth sign miracle, the feeding of the 5,000.*

What Jesus did was remarkable in every way. Consider, for example, that even today very few facilities in the United States can accommodate 5,000 people for a sit-down meal. Yet Jesus miraculously provided for at least that many—with leftovers! John mentions that they filled twelve *baskets—perhaps one for each disciple, or perhaps one for each of the twelve tribes of Israel. The overall result was faith: Jesus must be the Messiah, the crowd concluded (v. 14).*

Yet doubt and rejection were soon to follow. Detractors pointed out that Jesus' lunch may have been impressive, but it was only one meal. By contrast, Moses had fed Israel in the wilderness for 40 years (vv. 30–31). Incredibly, they had missed the point of the sign: Jesus was not merely a deliveryman, He was the bread of life itself (vv. 32–58).

41"I do not receive honor from men. 42But I know you,
that you do not have the love of God in you. 43I have come
in My Father's name, and you do not receive Me; if another
comes in his own name, him you will receive. 44How can
you believe, who receive honor from one another, and do
not seek the honor that *comes* from the only God? 45Do not
think that I shall accuse you to the Father; there is *one* who
accuses you—Moses, in whom you trust. 46For if you believed Moses, you would believe Me; for he wrote about
Me. 47But if you do not believe his writings, how will you
believe My words?"

CHAPTER 6

Jesus Feeds 5,000

6:1–14

1After these things Jesus went over
the Sea of Galilee, which is *the Sea* of
Tiberias. 2Then a great multitude followed Him, because
they saw His signs which He performed on those who were
diseased. 3And Jesus went up on the mountain, and there
He sat with His disciples.
4Now the Passover, a feast of the Jews, was near. 5Then Jesus lifted up *His* eyes, and seeing a great multitude coming
toward Him, He said to Philip, "Where shall we buy bread,
that these may eat?" 6But this He said to test him, for He
Himself knew what He would do.
7Philip answered Him, "Two hundred denarii worth of
bread is not sufficient for them, that every one of them may
have a little."
8One of His disciples, Andrew, Simon Peter's brother, said
to Him, 9"There is a lad here who has five barley loaves and
two small fish, but what are they among so many?"
10Then Jesus said, "Make the people sit down." Now there
was much grass in the place. So the men sat down, in number about five thousand. 11And Jesus took the loaves, and
when He had given thanks He distributed *them* to the disciples, and the disciples[a] to those sitting down; and likewise
of the fish, as much as they wanted. 12So when they were
filled, He said to His disciples, "Gather up the fragments
that remain, so that nothing is lost." 13Therefore they gathered *them* up, and filled twelve baskets with the fragments
of the five barley loaves which were left over by those who
had eaten. 14Then those men, when they
had seen the sign that Jesus did, said,
"This is truly the Prophet who is to come into the world."

6:14–15

Jesus Walks on Water

6:15–21

15Therefore when Jesus perceived that
they were about to come and take Him

6:11 [a]NU-Text omits *to the disciples, and the disciples.*

by force to make Him king, He departed again to the
mountain by Himself alone.
[16]Now when evening came, His disciples went down to
the sea, [17]got into the boat, and went over the sea toward
Capernaum. And it was already dark, and Jesus had not
come to them. [18]Then the sea arose because a great wind
was blowing. [19]So when they had rowed about three or four
miles,[a] they saw Jesus walking on the sea and drawing near
the boat; and they were afraid. [20]But He said to them, "It is
I; do not be afraid." [21]Then they willingly received Him into
the boat, and immediately the boat was at the land where
they were going.

"I Am the Bread of Life"

[22]On the following day, when the people who were standing on the other side of the sea saw that there was no other
boat there, except that one which His disciples had
entered,[a] and that Jesus had not entered the boat with His
disciples, but His disciples had gone away alone— [23]how-
ever, other boats came from Tiberias, near the place where
they ate bread after the Lord had given thanks— [24]when the
people therefore saw that Jesus was not there, nor His disciples, they also got into boats and came to Capernaum, seeking Jesus. [25]And when they found Him on the other side of
the sea, they said to Him, "Rabbi, when did You come
here?"
[26]Jesus answered them and said, "Most assuredly, I say to
you, you seek Me, not because you saw the signs, but because you ate of the loaves and were filled. [27]Do not labor
for the food which perishes, but for the food which endures
to everlasting life, which the Son of Man will give you, because God the Father has set His seal on Him."
[28]Then they said to Him, "What shall we do, that we may
work the works of God?"
[29]Jesus answered and said to them, "This is the work of
God, that you believe in Him whom He sent."
[30]Therefore they said to Him, "What sign will You perform then, that we may see it and believe You? What work
will You do? [31]Our fathers ate the manna in the desert; as it
is written, 'He gave them bread from heaven to eat.' "[a]
[32]Then Jesus said to them, "Most assuredly, I say to you,
Moses did not give you the bread from heaven, but My
Father gives you the true bread from heaven. [33]For the
bread of God is He who comes down from heaven and gives
life to the world."
[34]Then they said to Him, "Lord, give us this bread always."

6:19 [a]Literally *twenty-five or thirty stadia* *6:22* [a]NU-Text omits *that* and *which His disciples had entered.* *6:31* [a]Exodus 16:4; Nehemiah 9:15; Psalm 78:24

Preventing Kingdom Confusion

CONSIDER THIS 6:14–15 **Throughout history people have longed for leaders to whom they can attach themselves. They often tie their own aspirations to the charisma and vision of a famous person, using that person to achieve their own ends, which are sometimes quite incompatible.**

Jesus knew the pattern well. He came to accomplish the work that His Father had given Him. But others quickly attached their own agendas and values to His plans (v. 15). Jesus resisted the mixed intentions of some of His followers and admirers because His kingdom differed fundamentally from their expectations.

What exactly was Jesus' concept of the kingdom, and what difference does it make for people today? See "The King Declares His Kingdom," Matt. 4:17.

The Seven Signs of John's Gospel

Miracles at Sea

CONSIDER THIS 6:15–21 *The fifth sign miracle that John included in his Gospel was a private affair for the disciples alone (vv. 15–21). What happened on the troubled Sea of Galilee revealed Jesus as master of the elements. John makes no explanatory comment on this incident, but its impact on the disciples is evident in Peter's words: "We have come to believe and know that You are the Christ, the Son of the living God" (v. 69, emphasis added).*

6:35

[35]And Jesus said to them, "I am the
bread of life. He who comes to Me shall
never hunger, and he who believes in Me shall never thirst.
[36]But I said to you that you have seen Me and yet do not believe. [37]All that the Father gives Me will come to Me, and
the one who comes to Me I will by no means cast out. [38]For
I have come down from heaven, not to do My own will, but
the will of Him who sent Me. [39]This is the will of the Father
who sent Me, that of all He has given Me I should lose
nothing, but should raise it up at the last day. [40]And this is
the will of Him who sent Me, that everyone who sees the
Son and believes in Him may have everlasting life; and I
will raise him up at the last day."

Jesus' Listeners Are Confounded

[41]The Jews then complained about Him, because He said,
"I am the bread which came down from heaven." [42]And
they said, "Is not this Jesus, the son of Joseph, whose father
and mother we know? How is it then that He says, 'I have
come down from heaven'?"
[43]Jesus therefore answered and said to them, "Do not

FOR YOUR INFO
6:35

THE BREAD OF LIFE

When Jesus called Himself the "bread of life" (v. 35; also vv. 32–33, 41, 48), He was using as an image more than a staple of the diet, He was drawing on a rich symbol of Jewish life.

Bread played an important role in Israel's worship. During the celebration of Pentecost, two loaves of leavened bread were offered as sacrifices (Lev. 23:17). In the tabernacle, and later in the temple, the Levites placed twelve loaves of unleavened bread, or bread without yeast, before the Lord each week to symbolize God's presence with the twelve tribes (Ex. 25:30).

Throughout the Exodus, God miraculously sustained His people by sending manna from heaven each morning (Ex. 16). The bread-like manna was a "small round substance as fine as frost" (v. 14). It looked "like white coriander seed" and tasted like "wafers made with honey" (v. 31) or "pastry prepared with oil" (Num. 11:8).

It was this manna that Jesus was recalling when He called Himself "the true bread from heaven" (John 6:32), "the bread which came down from heaven" (6:41), and the "bread of life" (vv. 48–51, 58). Symbolically, Jesus is the heavenly manna, the spiritual or supernatural food given by the Father to those who ask, seek, and knock (v. 45; Matt. 7:7–8).

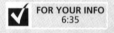

6:44 murmur among yourselves. 44No one can
come to Me unless the Father who sent
Me draws him; and I will raise him up at the last day. 45It is
written in the prophets, 'And they shall all be taught by
God.'[a] Therefore everyone who has heard and learned[b] from
the Father comes to Me. 46Not that anyone has seen the
Father, except He who is from God; He has seen the Father.
47Most assuredly, I say to you, he who believes in Me[a] has
everlasting life. 48I am the bread of life. 49Your fathers ate
the manna in the wilderness, and are dead. 50This is the
bread which comes down from heaven, that one may eat of
it and not die. 51I am the living bread which came down
from heaven. If anyone eats of this bread, he will live forever; and the bread that I shall give is My flesh, which I
shall give for the life of the world."

52The Jews therefore quarreled among themselves, saying,
"How can this Man give us *His* flesh to eat?"

53Then Jesus said to them, "Most assuredly, I say to you,
unless you eat the flesh of the Son of Man and drink His

6:45 [a]Isaiah 54:13 [b]M-Text reads *hears and has learned.* *6:47* [a]NU-Text omits *in Me.*

However, it's also interesting that Jesus' "bread of life discourse" (as John 6:26–58 is called) was given during Passover, also known as the Feast of Unleavened Bread (vv. 4, 22; see "Passover," Luke 22:7). Passover celebrated the deliverance of Israel from slavery in Egypt. On the night before leaving Egypt, the Israelites made unleavened bread, as they had no time to let their bread rise before taking flight (Ex. 12:8; 13:6–7).

In this context, Jesus had just fed at least 5,000 people (John 6:1–14), an event that led directly to the bread of life discourse (vv. 22–27). Clearly, He was indicating that He was God's provision for the people's deepest spiritual needs. Just as God had provided for His people as they came out of Egypt, so Jesus had provided physical food for the 5,000 and was ready to provide spiritual nourishment and life to all of them as well.

Tragically, the people balked at His teaching (vv. 30–31, 41–42, 52, 60). Their hearts were hardened in unbelief. Soon, many began to turn away (v. 66). But to those who believed, like Peter who declared, "You are the Christ, the Son of the Living God" (v. 69), Jesus gave abundant and eternal life. ◆

YOU ALONE CAN'T BRING THEM TO JESUS

CONSIDER THIS 6:44

Do you stagger under a heavy load of expectation that you alone (or that you primarily) are responsible for bringing your friends and coworkers to faith? Do you feel guilty because you can't get them converted? If so, you may be surprised to discover that not even Jesus felt that kind of load for the lost!

While explaining how people enter the kingdom, Jesus clearly declared that it is God the Father who draws them (v. 44). That means that people's response to the gospel does not depend primarily on you or on Jesus. Elsewhere, Jesus taught that:

- **"All that the Father gives Me will come to Me" (v. 37).**
- **"No one can come to Me unless it has been granted to him by My Father" (v. 65).**

Clearly, the responsibility for conversion ultimately belongs to the Father. Then is there anything we can do as Christ's followers to motivate others toward the Savior? Yes, we can give evidence of how God works in our lives as we grow. We can offer clear, truthful information about the gospel as we have opportunity. And we can invite and even urge others to believe.

But the ultimate responsibility for salvation is God's, not ours. So relax! Live the faith, talk about it, and offer it to others. But let the dynamic of conversion be from God alone.

Unfortunately, some believers run to the other extreme: they fold their hands and shut their mouths when it comes to evangelism. After all, it's up to God to bring people to faith. Is that what Jesus intended? See "Whose Job Is Evangelism?" John 16:8.

blood, you have no life in you. 54Whoever eats My flesh and
drinks My blood has eternal life, and I will raise him up at
the last day. 55For My flesh is food indeed,[a] and My blood is
drink indeed. 56He who eats My flesh and drinks My blood
abides in Me, and I in him. 57As the living Father sent Me,
and I live because of the Father, so he who feeds on Me will
live because of Me. 58This is the bread which came down
from heaven—not as your fathers ate the manna, and are
dead. He who eats this bread will live forever."

59These things He said in the synagogue as He taught in
Capernaum.

Many Followers Abandon Jesus

6:60–67

60Therefore many of His disciples,
when they heard *this,* said, "This is a hard
saying; who can understand it?"

61When Jesus knew in Himself that His disciples complained about this, He said to them, "Does this offend you?
62*What* then if you should see the Son of Man ascend where
He was before? 63It is the Spirit who gives life; the flesh
profits nothing. The words that I speak to you are spirit,
and *they* are life. 64But there are some of you who do not
believe." For Jesus knew from the beginning who they were
who did not believe, and who would betray Him. 65And He
said, "Therefore I have said to you that no one can come to
Me unless it has been granted to him by My Father."

66From that *time* many of His disciples went back and
walked with Him no more. 67Then Jesus said to the twelve,
"Do you also want to go away?"

"HE WHO FEEDS ON ME WILL LIVE BECAUSE OF ME." —John 6:57

Peter Declares that Jesus Is the Christ

68But Simon Peter answered Him, "Lord, to whom shall
we go? You have the words of eternal life. 69Also we have
come to believe and know that You are the Christ, the Son
of the living God."[a]

70Jesus answered them, "Did I not choose you, the twelve,
and one of you is a devil?" 71He spoke of Judas Iscariot, *the
son* of Simon, for it was he who would betray Him, being
one of the twelve.

6:55 [a]NU-Text reads *true food* and *true drink.* *6:69* [a]NU-Text reads *You are the Holy One of God.*

The Desertion of the Disciples

A CLOSER LOOK 6:60–67

Jesus attracted large crowds, and from them quite a number of disciples *or "learners." However, when His teaching became costly and hard to accept (v. 60), many deserted Him—but not all. To find out more about these dedicated followers, see "The Twelve," Matt. 10:2, and "The Women Who Followed Jesus," Luke 8:1–3.*

CHAPTER 7

Jesus' Brothers Doubt Him

1After these things Jesus walked in Galilee; for He did not
want to walk in Judea, because the Jews[a] sought to kill
7:2 Him. 2Now the Jews' Feast of Tabernacles
was at hand. 3His brothers therefore said
to Him, "Depart from here and go into Judea, that Your disciples also may see the works that You are doing. 4For no
one does anything in secret while he himself seeks to be
7:5 known openly. If You do these things,
show Yourself to the world." 5For even
His brothers did not believe in Him.
6Then Jesus said to them, "My time has not yet come, but
your time is always ready. 7The world cannot hate you, but
it hates Me because I testify of it that its works are evil. 8You
go up to this feast. I am not yet[a] going up to this feast, for
My time has not yet fully come." 9When He had said these
things to them, He remained in Galilee.

Jesus Attends the Feast of Tabernacles

10But when His brothers had gone up, then He also went
up to the feast, not openly, but as it were in secret. 11Then
the Jews sought Him at the feast, and said, "Where is He?"
12And there was much complaining among the people concerning Him. Some said, "He is good"; others said, "No, on
the contrary, He deceives the people." 13However, no one
spoke openly of Him for fear of the Jews.
14Now about the middle of the feast Jesus went up into
the temple and taught. 15And the Jews marveled, saying,
"How does this Man know letters, having never studied?"
16Jesus[a] answered them and said, "My doctrine is not
Mine, but His who sent Me. 17If anyone wills to do His will,
he shall know concerning the doctrine, whether it is from
God or *whether* I speak on My own *authority.* 18He who
speaks from himself seeks his own glory; but He who seeks
the glory of the One who sent Him is true, and no unrighteousness is in Him. 19Did not Moses give you the law, yet
none of you keeps the law? Why do you seek to kill Me?"

7:1 [a]That is, the ruling authorities *7:8* [a]NU-Text omits *yet.* *7:16* [a]NU-Text and M-Text read *So Jesus.*

The Feast of Tabernacles

A CLOSER LOOK 7:2 *The Feast of Tabernacles (v. 2) was one of three great feast days in the life of the Hebrews. It offered Jesus an ideal moment of opportunity in which to declare Himself publicly. See "Jewish Feasts," Luke 2:42, and "'We Interrupt This Program . . . ,'" John 7:37.*

DOES ANYONE BELIEVE YOU?

CONSIDER THIS 7:5 **If you ever feel discouraged because family, friends, or coworkers refuse to accept the gospel, you may take some comfort from the fact that even Jesus' own brothers did not believe that He was the Christ (v. 5). Even though they had seen His miracles and listened to His teaching, they still balked at the idea of placing faith in Jesus as the Son of God.**

This is important to notice, because it shows that the person who hears the gospel bears responsibility for responding in faith, while the person who shares the gospel bears responsibility for communicating with faithfulness. If we as believers ever start holding ourselves responsible for whether unbelievers accept or reject the message of Christ, we are headed for trouble!

That's not to suggest that we can be careless in our witness or ignore our credibility. Notice that Jesus' brothers rejected Him *in spite of* His works and words. Is that true of us? Or do people dismiss our faith because our lives show little evidence that what we say we believe is true or that it makes any difference to us?

Eventually, at least some of Jesus' brothers did believe in Him. James, probably the oldest, became a leader in the church (Acts 15:13–21) and wrote the New Testament letter that bears his name. Likewise, the author of Jude may have been the half-brother of Jesus. Ultimately, both urged Christians to practice and defend their *faith* (James 2:2–26; Jude 3).

Maybe you have decided that since it's up to God to bring people to faith, you can relax and keep quiet about the gospel. Is that a realistic attitude? See "Whose Job Is Evangelism?" John 16:8.

[20]The people answered and said, "You have a demon.
Who is seeking to kill You?"

7:21–24

[21]Jesus answered and said to them,
"I did one work, and you all marvel.
[22]Moses therefore gave you circumcision (not that it is from
Moses, but from the fathers), and you circumcise a man on
the Sabbath. [23]If a man receives circumcision on the Sabbath, so that the law of Moses should not be broken, are
you angry with Me because I made a man completely well
on the Sabbath? [24]Do not judge according to appearance,
but judge with righteous judgment."

[25]Now some of them from Jerusalem said, "Is this not He
whom they seek to kill? [26]But look! He speaks boldly, and
they say nothing to Him. Do the rulers know indeed that
this is truly[a] the Christ? [27]However, we know where this
Man is from; but when the Christ comes, no one knows
where He is from."

[28]Then Jesus cried out, as He taught in the temple, saying, "You both know Me, and you know where I am from;
and I have not come of Myself, but He who sent Me is true,
whom you do not know. [29]But[a] I know Him, for I am from
Him, and He sent Me."

[30]Therefore they sought to take Him; but no one laid a
hand on Him, because His hour had not yet come. [31]And
many of the people believed in Him, and said, "When the
Christ comes, will He do more signs than these which this
Man has done?"

[32]The Pharisees heard the crowd murmuring these things
concerning Him, and the Pharisees and the chief priests
sent officers to take Him. [33]Then Jesus said to them,[a] "I
shall be with you a little while longer, and *then* I go to Him
who sent Me. [34]You will seek Me and not find *Me,* and
where I am you cannot come."

[35]Then the Jews said among themselves, "Where does He
intend to go that we shall not find Him? Does He intend to
go to the Dispersion among the Greeks and teach the
Greeks? [36]What is this thing that He said, 'You will seek Me
and not find Me, and where I am you cannot come'?"

7:26 [a]NU-Text omits *truly.* *7:29* [a]NU-Text and M-Text omit *But.* *7:33* [a]NU-Text and M-Text omit *to them.*

"DO NOT JUDGE ACCORDING TO APPEARANCE BUT JUDGE WITH RIGHTEOUS JUDGMENT."
—John 7:24

Blind Guides

A CLOSER LOOK 7:21–24

The Pharisees had grown so out of touch with the intent of the Law that they could no longer distinguish between appearance and reality. Jesus challenged them by appealing to the very Scriptures they held so dear (vv. 22–23). Here as elsewhere, He refused to let them abuse Him or others with their hypocrisy. See "Jesus Confronts the Legalists," Luke. 6:1–11.

Jesus Provides Living Water

7:37
see pg. 356

37On the last day, that great *day* of the
feast, Jesus stood and cried out, saying,
"If anyone thirsts, let him come to Me and drink. 38He who
believes in Me, as the Scripture has said, out of his heart
will flow rivers of living water." 39But this He spoke concerning the Spirit, whom those believing[a] in Him would receive; for the Holy[b] Spirit was not yet *given,* because Jesus
was not yet glorified.
40Therefore many[a] from the crowd, when they heard this
saying, said, "Truly this is the Prophet." 41Others said, "This
is the Christ."
But some said, "Will the Christ come out of Galilee?
42Has not the Scripture said that the Christ comes from the
seed of David and from the town of Bethlehem, where
David was?" 43So there was a division among the people because of Him. 44Now some of them wanted to take Him,
but no one laid hands on Him.
45Then the officers came to the chief priests and Pharisees, who said to them, "Why have you not brought Him?"
46The officers answered, "No man ever spoke like this
Man!"
47Then the Pharisees answered them, "Are you also deceived? 48Have any of the rulers or the Pharisees believed in
Him? 49But this crowd that does not know the law is accursed."
50Nicodemus (he who came to Jesus by night,[a] being one
of them) said to them, 51"Does our law judge a man before
it hears him and knows what he is doing?"

7:52

52They answered and said to him, "Are
you also from Galilee? Search and look,
for no prophet has arisen[a] out of Galilee."
53And everyone went to his *own* house.[a]

CHAPTER 8

1But Jesus went to the Mount of Olives.

A Woman Caught in Adultery

8:2–3

2Now early[a] in the morning He came
again into the temple, and all the people

7:39 [a]NU-Text reads *who believed.* [b]NU-Text omits *Holy.* *7:40* [a]NU-Text reads *some.* *7:50* [a]NU-Text reads *before.* *7:52* [a]NU-Text reads *is to rise.* *7:53* [a]The words *And everyone* through *sin no more* (8:11) are bracketed by NU-Text as not original. They are present in over 900 manuscripts. *8:2* [a]M-Text reads *very early.*

No Prophet from Galilee

A CLOSER LOOK 7:52

Pharisees and other citizens of Judea looked upon their brothers from Galilee with scorn. To them, a "Galilean" was a fool, heathen, sinner, or worse. See "Jesus the Galilean," Mark 1:14.

A Double Standard?

CONSIDER THIS 8:2–3

The woman presented to Jesus (v. 3) must have been utterly humiliated at being dragged into the temple by self-righteous men who were only using her to try to trick the Teacher they hated. According to the Law, adultery required capital punishment of *both* parties (Lev. 20:10). Did the accusers forget to bring the man? Or had they allowed a double standard to creep in?

If so, Jesus refrained from challenging their hypocrisy, but He did set a new standard for judgment: Let someone perfect decide the case (v. 7; compare Matt. 5:48). Ironically, He was the only one who fit that qualification, and He did decide the case—declining to condemn the woman, but admonishing her to "go and sin no more."

Are there double standards in your moral judgments? Are you eager to point out the speck in someone else's eye, while ignoring the plank in your own (Matt. 7:4–5)? Or, perhaps, like the woman, you've experienced the forgiveness of God for grave offenses against His holiness. If so, live in His grace—and sin no more.

came to Him; and He sat down and taught them. [3]Then the
scribes and Pharisees brought to Him a woman caught in
adultery. And when they had set her in the midst, [4]they said
to Him, "Teacher, this woman was caught[a] in adultery, in
the very act. [5]Now Moses, in the law, commanded[a] us that
such should be stoned.[b] But what do You say?"[c] [6]This they
said, testing Him, that they might have *something* of which
to accuse Him. But Jesus stooped down and wrote on the
ground with *His* finger, as though He did not hear.[a]

[7]So when they continued asking Him, He raised Himself
up[a] and said to them, "He who is without sin among you,
let him throw a stone at her first." [8]And again He stooped
down and wrote on the ground. [9]Then those who heard *it*,
being convicted by *their* conscience,[a] went out one by one,

8:4 [a]M-Text reads *we found this woman.* *8:5* [a]M-Text reads *in our law Moses commanded.* [b]NU-Text and M-Text read *to stone such.* [c]M-Text adds *about her.* *8:6* [a]NU-Text and M-Text omit *as though He did not hear.* *8:7* [a]M-Text reads *He looked up.* *8:9* [a]NU-Text and M-Text omit *being convicted by their conscience.*

CONSIDER THIS
7:37

"We Interrupt This Program . . ."

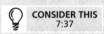

Jesus' cry in v. 37 was far more dramatic than most modern readers realize. He chose a time when Jerusalem was packed with holiday visitors and a crucial moment in the festivities when He could attract the most attention. It would be as if someone broke into the broadcast of a presidential state-of-the-union address or the kickoff of a Super Bowl to announce, "We interrupt this program to bring you a special report."

The annual Feast of Tabernacles (or Booths, or Tents, 7:2) swelled Jerusalem with an overflow of festive crowds. Every Jewish family within 20 miles of the city was required to move out of its home and live in a booth or tent in remembrance of Israel's wanderings in the wilderness. Many chose to move into the city for the week. Reunions and parties alternated with solemn processions from the temple down to the Pool of Siloam, a reservoir (9:7). Pushing its way through the crowded streets, the throng sang Psalms 113 to 118 in anticipation of God's righteous reign over Jerusalem.

Jesus chose to keep a low profile at this year's festival (7:2–10). He taught in the temple (v. 14), but waited for the right moment to declare Himself publicly. It came on the last day of the feast (v. 37), probably at the climax of the daily processional.

As on the previous six days, the high priest filled a goblet of water from Siloam and carried it back to the

beginning with the oldest *even* to the last. And Jesus was left
alone, and the woman standing in the midst. 10When Jesus
had raised Himself up and saw no one but the woman, He
said to her,[a] "Woman, where are those accusers of yours?[b]
Has no one condemned you?"
11She said, "No one, Lord."
And Jesus said to her, "Neither do I condemn you; go
and[a] sin no more."

"I Am the Light of the World"

12Then Jesus spoke to them again, saying, "I am the light
of the world. He who follows Me shall not walk in darkness, but have the light of life."
13The Pharisees therefore said to Him, "You bear witness
of Yourself; Your witness is not true."

8:10 [a]NU-Text omits *and saw no one but the woman;* M-Text reads *He saw her and said.* [b]NU-Text and M-Text omit *of yours.* *8:11* [a]NU-Text and M-Text add *from now on.*

temple, where he poured it out for all the people to see. Each day at that point the crowds chanted, "Oh, give thanks to the LORD" (Ps. 118:1), and "Save now, I pray, O LORD; O LORD, I pray, send now prosperity" (118:25), and again, "Oh, give thanks to the LORD." Then they shook myrtle, willow, and palm branches toward the altar, as if to remind God of His promises. Then, after a pause, sacrifices were offered.

On the last day, however, just after the crowds had not only waved their branches but, as was the custom, literally shook them to pieces in a frenzy of enthusiasm, a voice suddenly cried out: "If anyone thirsts, let him come to Me and drink" (John 7:37, emphasis added). Jesus' timing couldn't have been more perfect or His claim more explicit: He was declaring Himself to be none other than the long-awaited Christ who would pour out the Holy Spirit, as many in the crowd immediately recognized (vv. 39–43).

In many ways v. 37 acts as the pivot for John's account. From that point on, the hostility of Jesus' enemies mounted until they finally arrested Him (18:12) in vain hopes of shutting off the "living water." ◆

The Feast of Tabernacles was one of three major festivals for the Hebrews of Jesus' day. See "Jewish Feasts," Luke 2:42.

"HE WHO FOLLOWS ME SHALL NOT WALK IN DARKNESS, BUT HAVE THE LIGHT OF LIFE."
—John 8:12

[14]Jesus answered and said to them, "Even if I bear witness
of Myself, My witness is true, for I know where I came from
and where I am going; but you do not know where I come
from and where I am going. [15]You judge according to the
flesh; I judge no one. [16]And yet if I do judge, My judgment
is true; for I am not alone, but I *am* with the Father who
sent Me. [17]It is also written in your law that the testimony
of two men is true. [18]I am One who bears witness of Myself,
and the Father who sent Me bears witness of Me."
[19]Then they said to Him, "Where is Your Father?"
Jesus answered, "You know neither Me nor My Father. If
you had known Me, you would have known My Father
also."
[20]These words Jesus spoke in the treasury, as He taught in
the temple; and no one laid hands on Him, for His hour
had not yet come.
[21]Then Jesus said to them again, "I am going away, and

CONSIDER THIS
8:48

Jesus Is Called a Samaritan Demoniac

John 8 records a heated, even bitter, confrontation between Jesus and the Jews, led by the Pharisees. The Lord became particularly blunt with the religious leaders because they refused to accept His claims, imperiling not only their own spiritual standing but that of Israel.

Exchange between Jesus and the Pharisees

Jesus told the Pharisees...	The Pharisees responded...
I know where I came from and where I'm going (8:14–18).	You were born illegitimately (8:19).
You do not know God (8:19).	No response.
You will die in your sin (8:21, 24).	Who are You? (8:25).
[My] truth will make you free (8:31–32).	We've never needed freedom (8:33).
You are the slaves of sin (8:34–38).	We are children of Abraham (8:39).
You are murderers and liars, doing the deeds of your father (8:39–41).	We are not illegitimate [like You]; besides, God is our Father (8:41).
Your father is the devil, a murderer and liar (8:42–47).	You're nothing but a Samaritan and have a demon! (8:48).
I have power even over death (8:49–51).	Who do You think You are? (8:52–54).
My Father honors Me [as His Son]; but you are liars (8:54–56).	You're just a young upstart, yet You claim to have seen Abraham! (8:57).
I AM (8:58; compare Gen. 17:1; Ex. 3:14).	They picked up stones to throw at Him (8:59).

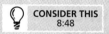

you will seek Me, and will die in your sin. Where I go you
cannot come."
22So the Jews said, "Will He kill Himself, because He says,
'Where I go you cannot come'?"
23And He said to them, "You are from beneath; I am from
above. You are of this world; I am not of this world.
24Therefore I said to you that you will die in your sins; for if
you do not believe that I am *He,* you will die in your sins."
25Then they said to Him, "Who are You?"
And Jesus said to them, "Just what I have been saying to
you from the beginning. 26I have many things to say and to
judge concerning you, but He who sent Me is true; and I
speak to the world those things which I heard from Him."
27They did not understand that He spoke to them of the
Father.
28Then Jesus said to them, "When you lift up the Son of

(Bible text continued on page 361)

Calling Jesus a demon-crazed Samaritan was about the most insulting thing His opponents could think to say. "Samaritan" and "demoniac" were virtual synonyms in their minds. The names expressed all of the bitterness, rage, and contempt they felt toward Jesus.

By the way, what names would people call you as you stand for God's truth at your job or in your community? What hate words would you cringe to hear? ◆

Jews and Samaritans were deeply divided by ethnic barriers. In fact, they had almost no dealings with each other—not unlike many societies today. See John 4:4.

"IF YOU DO NOT BELIEVE THAT I AM HE, YOU WILL DIE IN YOUR SINS."
—John 8:24

CONSIDER THIS
8:52–59

Many Men Would Be Gods, But Only One God Would Be Man

History is crowded with men who claimed to be gods. Christianity is unique in that it reveals that the one God became man, in the person of Jesus Christ. That is the dramatic import of Jesus' words, "Before Abraham was, I AM" (v. 58). I AM was an expression by which God was known to the Hebrews (Ex. 3:14). In using such words, Jesus was declaring that God Himself was standing before the crowd.

By contrast, consider others in history who wanted their followers to regard them as gods, or who were given such adulation after they died:

King Tutankhamen

The boy king of Egypt, who reigned during the fourteenth century B.C., was regarded as a god. We know a lot about him since the discovery in 1922 of his tomb of gold. He died at 18.

Siddhartha Gautama

The first "Enlightened One," or *Buddha,* was born into royalty (c. 563–483 B.C.). However, he renounced all luxury and became a wandering ascetic searching for and later teaching a "middle way" to transcend the human condition. After his death, the Buddha was deified by his followers, who spread his teachings from India to southern and eastern Asia.

Alexander the Great

When the great military general of Macedonia overthrew the Persian Empire (c. 334–323 B.C.), he became a legend bigger than life. He attempted to fuse the Macedonians and the Persians into one master race of which he would be the supreme being. He demanded the same divine recognition from his subject people that they gave to the Greek gods, Heracles and Dionysus. Nevertheless, an illness claimed his life at age 33.

Julius Caesar

A Roman general and statesman, Caesar changed the course of the Graeco-Roman world by conquering Gaul (58–50 B.C.) and winning the Roman Civil War (49–45 B.C.). Crowned emperor, he had military and literary genius that was matched only by his carnal appetite. After his murder in 44 B.C. he was granted status as a god.

King Herod Agrippa I

The grandson of Herod the Great (see "The Herods," Acts 12:1–2) executed James the apostle and tried to do the same with Peter. Later, Agrippa's subjects in Tyre and Sidon, weary of his anger, attempted to make peace with him. Listening to one of his orations, they humored him by shouting, "The voice of a god and not of a man!" Apparently pleased with this sudden elevation in his status, he failed to correct their theology. God struck him for his arrogance so that he was eaten by worms and died (12:20–23).

Napoleon Bonaparte

The renowned French general and emperor made numerous reforms in government, education, and the military. The Napoleonic Code became a basis for civil law throughout the West. A military genius, he waged war and consolidated power throughout Europe (1800–1810). But he died in exile at age 51.

Vladimir Lenin

A militant Marxist, Lenin led the Bolshevik Revolution (1917)

(continued on next page)

Man, then you will know that I am *He,* and *that* I do nothing of Myself; but as My Father taught Me, I speak these
things. [29]And He who sent Me is with Me. The Father has
not left Me alone, for I always do those things that please
Him." [30]As He spoke these words, many believed in Him.
[31]Then Jesus said to those Jews who believed Him, "If you
abide in My word, you are My disciples indeed. [32]And you
shall know the truth, and the truth shall make you free."
[33]They answered Him, "We are Abraham's descendants,
and have never been in bondage to anyone. How *can* You
say, 'You will be made free'?"
[34]Jesus answered them, "Most assuredly, I say to you,
whoever commits sin is a slave of sin. [35]And a slave does
not abide in the house forever, *but* a son abides forever.
[36]Therefore if the Son makes you free, you shall be free indeed.
[37]"I know that you are Abraham's descendants, but you
seek to kill Me, because My word has no place in you. [38]I
speak what I have seen with My Father, and you do what
you have seen with[a] your father."
[39]They answered and said to Him, "Abraham is our
father."
Jesus said to them, "If you were Abraham's children, you
would do the works of Abraham. [40]But now you seek to kill
Me, a Man who has told you the truth which I heard from
God. Abraham did not do this. [41]You do the deeds of your
father."
Then they said to Him, "We were not born of fornication;
we have one Father—God."
[42]Jesus said to them, "If God were your Father, you would
love Me, for I proceeded forth and came from God; nor
have I come of Myself, but He sent Me. [43]Why do you not
understand My speech? Because you are not able to listen to
My word. [44]You are of *your* father the devil, and the desires
of your father you want to do. He was a murderer from the
beginning, and does not stand in the truth, because there is
no truth in him. When he speaks a lie, he speaks from his
own *resources,* for he is a liar and the father of it. [45]But because I tell the truth, you do not believe Me. [46]Which of
you convicts Me of sin? And if I tell the truth, why do you
not believe Me? [47]He who is of God hears God's words;
therefore you do not hear, because you are not of God."
8:48 see pg. 358
[48]Then the Jews answered and said to
Him, "Do we not say rightly that You are
a Samaritan and have a demon?"
[49]Jesus answered, "I do not have a demon; but I honor
My Father, and you dishonor Me. [50]And I do not seek My
own glory; there is One who seeks and judges. [51]Most as-

8:38 [a]NU-Text reads *heard from.*

(continued from previous page)

and became the first head of the former Soviet Union. His writings vastly expanded and promoted the Communist worldview, and he hoped they would stimulate other proletarian revolutions. He died at the age of 54 after a long, paralyzing illness. He was the closest thing to a "god" that the Soviets would allow. His body was put on view in Moscow.

Adolf Hitler

The mad dictator of Nazi Germany (1932–45) was unequaled in his ability to wield hypnotic power over masses of people. He knew how to manipulate events and people to his own ends, but his attempts to build a master race resulted only in a holocaust of evil. He died by his own hand in 1945.

Only Jesus Backed Up His Claim

Many more pretenders could be listed. But only Jesus demonstrated that He was God by His words and actions. He healed the sick, raised the dead, forgave sins, and lived by the moral precepts that He taught. In fact, He fulfilled every code of righteousness without ever sinning. Most importantly, He backed up His claim of being God by conquering death. No one else in history has ever done that. Others have been regarded as divine, but all have fallen short of God's glory—except Jesus. ◆

suredly, I say to you, if anyone keeps My word he shall
never see death."

8:52–59
see pg. 360

52Then the Jews said to Him, "Now we
know that You have a demon! Abraham
is dead, and the prophets; and You say, 'If anyone keeps My
word he shall never taste death.' 53Are You greater than our
father Abraham, who is dead? And the prophets are dead.
Who do You make Yourself out to be?"
54Jesus answered, "If I honor Myself, My honor is nothing. It is My Father who honors Me, of whom you say that
He is your[a] God. 55Yet you have not known Him, but I
know Him. And if I say, 'I do not know Him,' I shall be a
liar like you; but I do know Him and keep His word. 56Your
father Abraham rejoiced to see My day, and he saw *it* and
was glad."
57Then the Jews said to Him, "You are not yet fifty years
old, and have You seen Abraham?"
58Jesus said to them, "Most assuredly, I say to you, before
Abraham was, I AM."
59Then they took up stones to throw at Him; but Jesus
hid Himself and went out of the temple,[a] going through the
midst of them, and so passed by.

CHAPTER 9

Jesus Heals a Man Born Blind

9:1–41

9:2–3

1Now as *Jesus* passed by, He saw a man
who was blind from birth. 2And His disciples asked Him, saying, "Rabbi, who
sinned, this man or his parents, that he
was born blind?"
3Jesus answered, "Neither this man nor his parents
sinned, but that the works of God should be revealed in
him. 4I[a] must work the works of Him who sent Me while it
is day; *the* night is coming when no one can work. 5As long
as I am in the world, I am the light of the world."
6When He had said these things, He spat on the ground
and made clay with the saliva; and He anointed the eyes of
the blind man with the clay. 7And He said to him, "Go,
wash in the pool of Siloam" (which is translated, Sent). So
he went and washed, and came back seeing.
8Therefore the neighbors and those who previously had
seen that he was blind[a] said, "Is not this he who sat and
begged?"
9Some said, "This is he." Others *said*, "He is like him."[a]

(Bible text continued on page 364)

8:54 [a]NU-Text and M-Text read *our.* *8:59* [a]NU-Text omits the rest of this verse.
9:4 [a]NU-Text reads *We.* *9:8* [a]NU-Text reads *a beggar.* *9:9* [a]NU-Text reads *"No, but he is like him."*

The Seven Signs of John's Gospel

Jesus Heals the Blind Man

CONSIDER THIS
9:1–41

The sixth sign miracle featured in John's Gospel reveals Jesus as the light of the world (v. 5). He was also unique among the prophets in that none of them had cured blindness (vv. 30–33).

The healing of the blind man speaks to the problem of human suffering. Then as now, sickness was often assumed to be divine punishment for someone's sin. Like Job's counselors (Job 4:7–9; 8:2–8; 11:4–20), Jesus' disciples asked, "Whose sin caused this man's blindness?" (v. 2). But Jesus replied with a radically new truth: God can use human suffering to reveal His glory (v. 3). Jesus immediately showed what He was talking about by healing the man's blindness, thereby revealing Himself to be the Son of God.

CONSIDER THIS
9:2–3

"Who Sinned?" Health and Disease in the Bible

When Jesus' disciples asked Him whose sin had caused a man's blindness (v. 2), they were reflecting a common perception about health and disease in the ancient world. In their minds, physical maladies and suffering were the result of sin and/or God's judgment.

Viewed from our perspective 2,000 years later, their question seems quaint and simplistic. Yet was it really? Even with all of our culture's medical technology, we still wrestle the same issue: what is the ultimate cause of sickness and death? We may understand the scientific explanations and even know how to prevent or cure countless ills. But we still look for a larger meaning behind physical health and disease.

The Bible mentions more than 40 specific diseases or disabilities and alludes frequently to sickness and health issues generally. It seems to accept that concerns about physical health are universal, inescapable, and problematic.

The Great Physician

Jesus devoted considerable time and teaching to health issues, provoking many questions in the process. The most challenging aspect of His work was the miracles of physical healing that He performed. They confounded those who saw them first-hand no less than they trouble us today.

The Gospel writers make it clear that Jesus' first-century witnesses had no problem believing that He actually healed the sick and even raised the dead. They never accused Him of charlatanism. Apparently they accepted the miracles as miracles. But what they struggled with profoundly was the source of His power to perform them and the resulting implications. The curious wondered whether He might not be the Messiah (John 7:31); His enemies accused Him of being in league with the devil (8:48; 10:19–21; Matt. 9:34).

What most troubled people was that the miracles signaled the arrival of the kingdom of God. It was not the healings themselves that they anguished over, but what they were going to do with the One who claimed to be the Christ on the basis of those healings. Was He or wasn't He? And were they ready to receive Him or not?

Modern Skepticism

Today our culture challenges the credibility of the miraculous itself. Capable of accomplishing many physical feats once thought to be "impossible" (flying, curing leprosy, seeing inside the body noninvasively), and lacking many (some would say any) current examples of miracles, skeptics look for some "rational" explanation. "Perhaps Jesus knew more about the body than the average first-century Jew and cleverly manipulated physical forces in a way that people assumed the miraculous," some say. "Perhaps He only appeared to heal, duping the simple like so many modern-day pretenders. Perhaps the miracles never really occurred; they were simply imagined by later believers eager to embellish the myth of a God-man."

Other explanations have been put forth in the last two centuries. They all reflect the skepticism of our age. Yet in the end, one comes out at the same place as those who originally challenged the authority of the miracles: "If I cast out demons by the

(continued on next page)

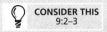

(continued from previous page)

Spirit of God, surely the kingdom of God has come upon you" (Matt. 12:28). In other words, is it really the possibility of miracles that troubles moderns? Or is it the staggering probability that the One who performed them is in fact God Himself? ◆

JESUS AND THE PHYSICAL

- **Most of the healings that Jesus performed were intended to reveal His divine power and authority (John 9:2–3).**
- **He healed people from all walks of life, both the untouchables and the well-off and well-connected.**
- **He did not heal everyone (Matt. 13:58).**
- **He recognized and dealt with the emotional side of illness—feelings of sadness, anger, disorientation, anxiety, conflict, fear, and aggression.**
- **He exhibited patience, compassion, and courage when confronting the sick.**
- **He never used spells, charms, incantations, drugs, incense, or herbs to ward off evil spirits or to heal people of their diseases. His power came directly from His person.**
- **He drew a parallel between physical sickness and spiritual need (Mark 2:15–17).**
- **He often linked the healing of disease with faith and the forgiveness of sins.**
- **He refused to see all sickness as a sign of God's judgment.**
- **He refused to allow religious traditions and taboos to prevent Him from relieving pain and suffering.**

(continued on next page)

He said, "I am *he.*"
10Therefore they said to him, "How were your eyes
opened?"
11He answered and said, "A Man called Jesus made clay
and anointed my eyes and said to me, 'Go to the pool of[a]
Siloam and wash.' So I went and washed, and I received
sight."
12Then they said to him, "Where is He?"
He said, "I do not know."
13They brought him who formerly was blind to the Pharisees.
14Now it was a Sabbath when Jesus made the clay and
opened his eyes. 15Then the Pharisees also asked him again
how he had received his sight. He said to them, "He put
clay on my eyes, and I washed, and I see."
16Therefore some of the Pharisees said, "This Man is not
from God, because He does not keep the Sabbath."
Others said, "How can a man who is a sinner do such
signs?" And there was a division among them.
17They said to the blind man again, "What do you say
about Him because He opened your eyes?"
He said, "He is a prophet."
18But the Jews did not believe concerning him, that he
had been blind and received his sight, until they called the
parents of him who had received his sight. 19And they
asked them, saying, "Is this your son, who you say was
born blind? How then does he now see?"
20His parents answered them and said, "We know that
this is our son, and that he was born blind; 21but by what
means he now sees we do not know, or who opened his
eyes we do not know. He is of age; ask him. He will speak
for himself." 22His parents said these *things* because they
feared the Jews, for the Jews had agreed already that if anyone
confessed *that* He *was* Christ, he would be put out of
the synagogue. 23Therefore his parents said, "He is of age;
ask him."
24So they again called the man who was blind, and said to
him, "Give God the glory! We know that this Man is a sinner."
25He answered and said, "Whether He is a sinner *or not* I
do not know. One thing I know: that though I was blind,
now I see."
26Then they said to him again, "What did He do to you?
How did He open your eyes?"
27He answered them, "I told you already, and you did not
listen. Why do you want to hear *it* again? Do you also want
to become His disciples?"
28Then they reviled him and said, "You are His disciple,
but we are Moses' disciples. 29We know that God spoke to

9:11 [a]NU-Text omits *the pool of.*

Moses; *as for* this *fellow,* we do not know where He is from."
30The man answered and said to them, "Why, this is a
marvelous thing, that you do not know where He is from;
yet He has opened my eyes! 31Now we know that God does
not hear sinners; but if anyone is a worshiper of God and
does His will, He hears him. 32Since the world began it has
been unheard of that anyone opened the eyes of one who
was born blind. 33If this Man were not from God, He could
do nothing."
34They answered and said to him, "You were completely
born in sins, and are you teaching us?" And they cast him
out.
35Jesus heard that they had cast him out; and when He
had found him, He said to him, "Do you believe in the Son
of God?"[a]
36He answered and said, "Who is He, Lord, that I may believe in Him?"
37And Jesus said to him, "You have both seen Him and it
is He who is talking with you."
38Then he said, "Lord, I believe!" And he worshiped Him.
39And Jesus said, "For judgment I have come into this
world, that those who do not see may see, and that those
who see may be made blind."
40Then *some* of the Pharisees who were with Him heard
these words, and said to Him, "Are we blind also?"
41Jesus said to them, "If you were blind, you would have
no sin; but now you say, 'We see.' Therefore your sin remains.

CHAPTER 10

"I Am the Good Shepherd"

1"Most assuredly, I say to you, he who does not enter the
sheepfold by the door, but climbs up some other way, the
same is a thief and a robber. 2But he who enters by the door
is the shepherd of the sheep. 3To him the doorkeeper
opens, and the sheep hear his voice; and he calls his own
sheep by name and leads them out. 4And when he brings
out his own sheep, he goes before them; and the sheep follow him, for they know his voice. 5Yet they will by no
means follow a stranger, but will flee from him, for they do
not know the voice of strangers." 6Jesus used this illustration, but they did not understand the things which He
spoke to them.
7Then Jesus said to them again, "Most assuredly, I say to
you, I am the door of the sheep. 8All who *ever* came before
Me[a] are thieves and robbers, but the sheep did not hear

9:35 [a]NU-Text reads *Son of Man.* 10:8 [a]M-Text omits *before Me.*

(continued from previous page)

- **His power to heal threatened the established authorities.**
- **His immediate followers experienced the same power over physical maladies, a sign that their message was from God.**
- **Sometimes illness and death showed God's judgment (Acts 5:1–11; 12:19–23).**
- **His followers were not spared from physical afflictions. God used their sufferings to form character.**
- **We can look forward to a time when suffering, sorrow, pain, and disease will come to an end (Rom. 8:18; Rev. 21:4).**

Not only did healing demonstrate Christ's divine power over disease and infirmity, it revealed God's heart of compassion. "He Healed Them All" (Luke 4:40) lists some of the diseases and disabilities that Jesus and His followers treated.

THE POWER OF SELF-SACRIFICE

CONSIDER THIS 10:17–18 **What does power look like in the lives of people you know? Does it mean aggressively making things happen? Does it mean political or financial muscle? Jesus described His power as the right and ability to lay down His life for others (vv. 17–18).**

For whom or what would you lay down your life? Is there a cause so noble or people so dear that you would willingly let go of life itself? The world may not view that kind of self-sacrifice as power. But we who follow Christ can know the profound power of love—looking out not only for our own interests, but also for the interests of others (Phil. 2:4).

Jesus' first followers experienced a dynamic power that changed the world. See "Power," Acts 1:8.

The Feast of Dedication

FOR YOUR INFO 10:22 **The Feast of Dedication (v. 22) was a minor feast held in the Jewish month of Chislev (November-December). We know it today as Hanukkah, or the Feast of Lights. It was not a feast prescribed by Old Testament Law. Rather it originated as a celebration of the cleansing of the temple after its desecration by Antiochus Epiphanes, one of the cruelest rulers of all time.**

A member of the Seleucid dynasty of Syria, Antiochus IV (175–164 B.C.) was surnamed Epiphanes, meaning "God manifest." His enemies, however, called him Epimanes, or "madman." Enterprising and ambitious, he desired to unify his empire by spreading Greek civilization and culture. This brought him into direct conflict with the Jews.

In a show of utter contempt for their religion, Antiochus erected an altar to the Greek god Zeus over the altar in the temple at Jerusalem. He also forced Jews to participate in heathen festivities and ordered them put to death if caught with the Law in their possession.

In 165 B.C., a man named Judas Maccabeus led a successful revolt that overthrew Seleucid domination of Palestine. The temple was cleansed on the 25th of Chislev, around December 25th by our calendar. Antiochus retreated to Persia, where, true to his nickname, he died a madman.

them. 9I am the door. If anyone enters by Me, he will be
saved, and will go in and out and find pasture. 10The thief
does not come except to steal, and to kill, and to destroy. I
have come that they may have life, and that they may have
it more abundantly.
11"I am the good shepherd. The good shepherd gives His
life for the sheep. 12But a hireling, *he who is* not the shepherd, one who does not own the sheep, sees the wolf coming and leaves the sheep and flees; and the wolf catches the
sheep and scatters them. 13The hireling flees because he is a
hireling and does not care about the sheep. 14I am the good
shepherd; and I know My *sheep,* and am known by My
own. 15As the Father knows Me, even so I know the Father;
and I lay down My life for the sheep. 16And other sheep I
have which are not of this fold; them also I must bring, and
they will hear My voice; and there will be one flock *and* one
shepherd.

10:17–18 see pg. 365

17"Therefore My Father loves Me, because I lay down My life that I may take
it again. 18No one takes it from Me, but I lay it down of Myself. I have power to lay it down, and I have power to take
it again. This command I have received from My Father."
19Therefore there was a division again among the Jews because of these sayings. 20And many of them said, "He has a
demon and is mad. Why do you listen to Him?"
21Others said, "These are not the words of one who has a
demon. Can a demon open the eyes of the blind?"

Jesus Attends the Feast of Dedication

10:22

22Now it was the Feast of Dedication in
Jerusalem, and it was winter. 23And Jesus
walked in the temple, in Solomon's porch. 24Then the Jews
surrounded Him and said to Him, "How long do You keep
us in doubt? If You are the Christ, tell us plainly."
25Jesus answered them, "I told you, and you do not believe. The works that I do in My Father's name, they bear
witness of Me. 26But you do not believe, because you are
not of My sheep, as I said to you.[a] 27My sheep hear My
voice, and I know them, and they follow Me. 28And I give
them eternal life, and they shall never perish; neither shall
anyone snatch them out of My hand. 29My Father, who has
given *them* to Me, is greater than all; and no one is able to
snatch *them* out of My Father's hand. 30I and *My* Father are
one."

10:31

31Then the Jews took up stones again
to stone Him. 32Jesus answered them,
"Many good works I have shown you from My Father. For
which of those works do you stone Me?"

10:26 [a]NU-Text omits *as I said to you.*

33The Jews answered Him, saying, "For a good work we
do not stone You, but for blasphemy, and because You, being a Man, make Yourself God."
34Jesus answered them, "Is it not written in your law, 'I
said, "You are gods" '?[a] 35If He called them gods, to whom
the word of God came (and the Scripture cannot be broken), 36do you say of Him whom the Father sanctified and
sent into the world, 'You are blaspheming,' because I said, 'I
am the Son of God'? 37If I do not do the works of My
Father, do not believe Me; 38but if I do, though you do not
believe Me, believe the works, that you may know and believe[a] that the Father *is* in Me, and I in Him." 39Therefore
they sought again to seize Him, but He escaped out of their
hand.

Jesus Returns to the River Jordan

10:40–42 see pg. 369

40And He went away again beyond the
Jordan to the place where John was bap-
tizing at first, and there He stayed. 41Then many came to
Him and said, "John performed no sign, but all the things
that John spoke about this Man were true." 42And many believed in Him there.

CHAPTER 11

Lazarus Raised from the Dead

11:1–2 see pg. 369

11:2 see pg. 370

1Now a certain *man* was sick, Lazarus
of Bethany, the town of Mary and her sister Martha. 2It was *that* Mary who
anointed the Lord with fragrant oil and
wiped His feet with her hair, whose brother Lazarus was
sick. 3Therefore the sisters sent to Him, saying, "Lord, behold, he whom You love is sick."
4When Jesus heard *that,* He said, "This sickness is not
unto death, but for the glory of God, that the Son of God
may be glorified through it."
5Now Jesus loved Martha and her sister and Lazarus. 6So,
when He heard that he was sick, He stayed two more days
in the place where He was. 7Then after this He said to *the*
disciples, "Let us go to Judea again."
8*The* disciples said to Him, "Rabbi, lately the Jews sought
to stone You, and are You going there again?"
9Jesus answered, "Are there not twelve hours in the day?
If anyone walks in the day, he does not stumble, because he
sees the light of this world. 10But if one walks in the night,
he stumbles, because the light is not in him." 11These things

10:34 [a]Psalm 82:6 *10:38* [a]NU-Text reads *understand.*

STONING

FOR YOUR INFO 10:31 *The intensity of the Jews' hostility against Jesus can be seen in their readiness to stone Him (v. 31; 8:59). Stoning was an ancient method of capital punishment reserved for the most serious crimes against the Mosaic Law, including:*

- *child sacrifice (Lev. 20:2).*
- *consultation with mediums and occultists (Lev. 20:27).*
- *blasphemy (Lev. 24:16).*
- *Sabbath-breaking (Num. 15:32–36).*
- *the worship of false gods (Deut. 13:10).*
- *rebellion against parents (Deut. 21:21).*
- *adultery (Ezek. 16:40).*
- *certain cases of direct disobedience against God's express command (Josh. 7:25).*

Stoning was usually carried out by the men of the community (Deut. 21:21) upon the testimony of at least two witnesses, who were to cast the first stones (17:5–7). The execution usually took place outside the camp or city (Lev. 24:14, 23; 1 Kin. 21:10, 13).

Jesus must have known He was headed for trouble when His enemies "surrounded" Him (literally, "closed in on Him,") as He walked in Solomon's porch (vv. 23–24). In the same way, a victim of stoning would be surrounded as the executioners cut all means of escape from their fury.

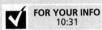

He said, and after that He said to them, "Our friend Lazarus
sleeps, but I go that I may wake him up."
12Then His disciples said, "Lord, if he sleeps he will get
well." 13However, Jesus spoke of his death, but they thought
that He was speaking about taking rest in sleep.
14Then Jesus said to them plainly, "Lazarus is dead. 15And

(Bible text continued on page 370)

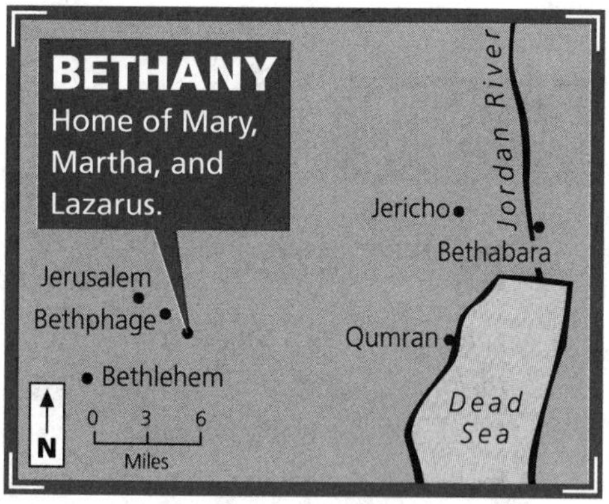

BETHANY

YOU ARE THERE 11:18

- **A village about two miles east of Jerusalem on the southeast slope of the Mount of Olives, on the road to Jericho.**
- **Name meant "house of an unripe fig," though its modern Arab**

(continued on next page)

PERSONALITY PROFILE: LAZARUS

FOR YOUR INFO 11:1–45

Not to be confused with: The man named Lazarus in one of Jesus' parables (Luke 16:19–31).

Home: Bethany, near Jerusalem.

Family: Brother of Mary and Martha.

Occupation: Unknown.

Known today as: A man whom Jesus raised from the dead.

CONSIDER THIS 11:25

"I AM THE RESURRECTION AND THE LIFE"

It was after the raising of Lazarus from the dead that the chief priests, Pharisees, and other religious leaders finally determined to put Jesus to death (John 11:53). Until now, the conflict between them and the upstart rabbi had been little more than a war of words. But the raising of Lazarus was an incredible miracle, witnessed by many. Jesus had raised at least two others, but those events had taken place in faraway Galilee (Mark 5:22–24, 35–43; Luke 7:11–17). By contrast, Lazarus' resurrection occurred in Bethany, a suburb of Jerusalem (John 11:18).

Not surprisingly, the miracle caused many to believe in Jesus (v. 45). It provided undeniable proof that Jesus' bold claim must be true: "I am the resurrection and the life . . . and whoever lives and believes in Me shall never die" (v. 25). Indeed, Lazarus became something of a curiosity, drawing numerous onlookers who wanted to see for themselves the man whom Jesus had brought back to life (12:9).

It was this kind of publicity that the leaders especially feared. Disputes over religious matters were one thing; a rapidly growing movement led by a popular Messiah-

Personality Profile: Mary of Bethany

FOR YOUR INFO 11:1–2

Not to be confused with: Mary, the mother of Jesus (Luke 1:26–56); Mary of Magdala (8:2); Mary, the mother of James and Joses (Matt. 27:55–61); Mary, the mother of John Mark (Acts 12:12).

Home: Bethany, a suburb of Jerusalem on the road to Jericho.

Family: Sister of Martha and Lazarus.

Best known today for: Sitting at Jesus' feet to worship and learn while her sister, Martha, served Him and His hungry disciples (Luke 10:38–42).

figure was something else. It was bound to have political repercussions, as the Romans were ever on the lookout for signs of rebellion (see "Jerusalem Surrounded," Luke 21:20).

It was Caiaphas the high priest (see Matt. 26:3) who saw the usefulness of that fact. Why sacrifice the entire nation for the sake of Jesus, when Jesus could be sacrificed for the sake of the nation (John 11:49–52)? Thus the religious leaders began to scheme how they might bring Jesus before the Romans and, hopefully, have Him put away on a charge of rebellion. And even though Lazarus had just been brought back from the dead, they plotted to do away with him as well, as he was living evidence of Jesus' power (12:10–11).

The plan succeeded brilliantly except for one detail that Caiaphas and his fellow leaders either overlooked or refused to believe: in arranging His death, they handed Him an opportunity to prove once and for all that He had spoken the truth when He said, "I am the resurrection and the life." ◆

(continued from previous page)

name is el-'Azariyeh, "home of Lazarus."

- **A favorite stopover for Jesus on His trips to and from Jerusalem. He stayed with His close friends Mary, Martha, and Lazarus.**
- **Modern Bethany offers a tomb site that some claim to be the authentic tomb of Lazarus, whom Jesus raised from the dead (John 11:1–44).**

A nearby village, Bethphage ("place of young figs") along with Bethany may have given rise to Jesus' parable of the unripe figs (Luke 13:6–9). See "Bethphage," Mark 11:1.

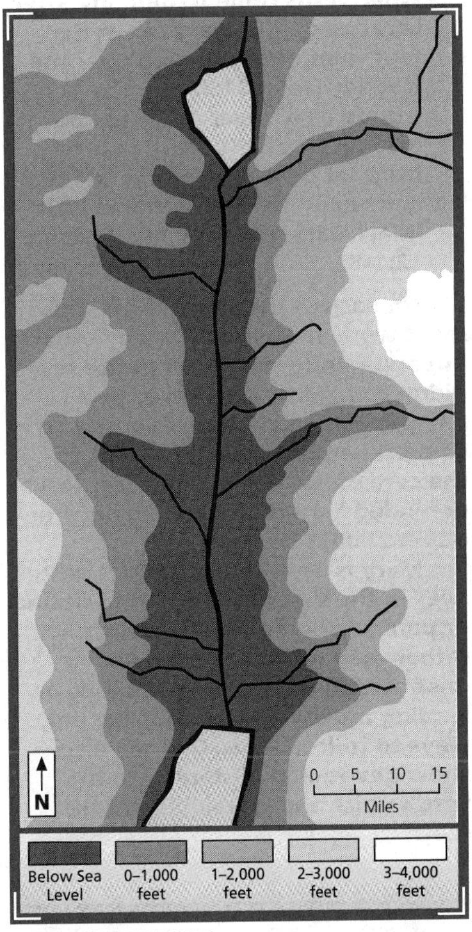

YOU ARE THERE 10:40–42

The Jordan River Valley

I am glad for your sakes that I was not there, that you may
believe. Nevertheless let us go to him."
16 Then Thomas, who is called the Twin, said to his fellow
disciples, "Let us also go, that we may die with Him."
17 So when Jesus came, He found that he had already been
11:18 see pg. 368
in the tomb four days. 18 Now Bethany
was near Jerusalem, about two miles[a]
away. 19 And many of the Jews had joined the women
around Martha and Mary, to comfort them concerning their
brother.
20 Now Martha, as soon as she heard that Jesus was coming, went and met Him, but Mary was sitting in the house.
21 Now Martha said to Jesus, "Lord, if You had been here,
my brother would not have died. 22 But even now I know
that whatever You ask of God, God will give You."
23 Jesus said to her, "Your brother will rise again."
24 Martha said to Him, "I know that he will rise again in
the resurrection at the last day."
11:25 see pg. 368
25 Jesus said to her, "I am the resurrection and the life. He who believes in Me,
though he may die, he shall live. 26 And whoever lives and
believes in Me shall never die. Do you believe this?"
27 She said to Him, "Yes, Lord, I believe that You are the
Christ, the Son of God, who is to come into the world."
28 And when she had said these things, she went her way
and secretly called Mary her sister, saying, "The Teacher has
come and is calling for you." 29 As soon as she heard *that,*
she arose quickly and came to Him. 30 Now Jesus had not
yet come into the town, but was[a] in the place where Martha
met Him. 31 Then the Jews who were with her in the house,
and comforting her, when they saw that Mary rose up
quickly and went out, followed her, saying, "She is going to
the tomb to weep there."[a]
32 Then, when Mary came where Jesus was, and saw Him,
she fell down at His feet, saying to Him, "Lord, if You had
been here, my brother would not have died."
33 Therefore, when Jesus saw her weeping, and the Jews
who came with her weeping, He groaned in the spirit
and was troubled. 34 And He said, "Where have you laid
him?"
They said to Him, "Lord, come and see."
35 Jesus wept. 36 Then the Jews said, "See how He loved
him!"
37 And some of them said, "Could not this Man, who
opened the eyes of the blind, also have kept this man from
dying?"
38 Then Jesus, again groaning in Himself, came to the

11:18 [a]Literally *fifteen stadia* *11:30* [a]NU-Text adds *still.* *11:31* [a]NU-Text reads *supposing that she was going to the tomb to weep there.*

The Devoted Mary

CONSIDER THIS 11:2 **Scripture records only one sentence spoken by Mary of Bethany (John 11:32), and even that wasn't original: her sister Martha had already said the same thing (v. 21)! But what Mary may have lacked in outspokenness, she more than made up for in devotion to Jesus. All three portraits of her in the Gospels show her at the Lord's feet:**

- **During one of Jesus' visits to her home, Mary sat at His feet, listening (Luke 10:38–42).**
- **When Jesus came to Bethany after Lazarus' death, Mary fell at His feet, completely broken over the tragedy (John 11:32).**
- **During a Passover meal just before Jesus' death, Mary poured fragrant oil on His head and feet, and wiped His feet with her hair (Matt. 26:6–13; Mark 14:3–9; John 12:1–8).**

On each of these occasions, this quiet woman was criticized by others. But apparently she didn't notice or didn't care. Mary seemed to be a woman who made choices based on a commitment to Jesus that went to the core of her being. In return, Jesus defended her actions, giving her freedom to be His disciple.

Mary is a model for anyone who lives in the shadow of a strong sibling or parent, or who prefers to listen rather than to speak. She demonstrates that preaching sermons or leading movements are not the only ways to follow Jesus. One can also show devotion by listening to the Lord's voice and worshiping at His feet.

Mary's sister, Martha, was an industrious, practical woman who never hesitated to speak her mind. Learn more about her at Luke 10:38–42.

tomb. It was a cave, and a stone lay against it. [39]Jesus said,
"Take away the stone."
Martha, the sister of him who was dead, said to Him,
"Lord, by this time there is a stench, for he has been *dead*
four days."
[40]Jesus said to her, "Did I not say to you that if you would
11:17–45 see pg. 372
believe you would see the glory of God?"
[41]Then they took away the stone *from the*
place where the dead man was lying.[a] And Jesus lifted up
His eyes and said, "Father, I thank You that You have heard
Me. [42]And I know that You always hear Me, but because of
the people who are standing by I said *this*, that they may be-
11:1–45 see pg. 368
lieve that You sent Me." [43]Now when He
had said these things, He cried with a
loud voice, "Lazarus, come forth!" [44]And he who had died
came out bound hand and foot with graveclothes, and his
face was wrapped with a cloth. Jesus said to them, "Loose
him, and let him go."

Leaders Plot to Destroy Jesus

[45]Then many of the Jews who had come to Mary, and had
seen the things Jesus did, believed in Him. [46]But some of
them went away to the Pharisees and told them the things
Jesus did. [47]Then the chief priests and the Pharisees gathered a council and said, "What shall we do? For this Man
works many signs. [48]If we let Him alone like this, everyone
will believe in Him, and the Romans will come and take
away both our place and nation."
11:49
[49]And one of them, Caiaphas, being
high priest that year, said to them, "You
know nothing at all, [50]nor do you consider that it is expedient for us[a] that one man should die for the people, and not
that the whole nation should perish." [51]Now this he did not
say on his own *authority;* but being high priest that year he
prophesied that Jesus would die for the nation, [52]and not
for that nation only, but also that He would gather together
in one the children of God who were scattered abroad.
[53]Then, from that day on, they plotted to put Him to
11:54
death. [54]Therefore Jesus no longer
walked openly among the Jews, but went
from there into the country near the wilderness, to a city
called Ephraim, and there remained with His disciples.

11:41 [a]NU-Text omits *from the place where the dead man was lying.* *11:50* [a]NU-Text reads *you.*

Caiaphas

A CLOSER LOOK 11:49

Troubled by the confusion created by the raising of Lazarus, Caiaphas, the high priest, scorned his fellow leaders as know-nothings (v. 49). But what do we know about the man Caiaphas? See Matt. 26:3.

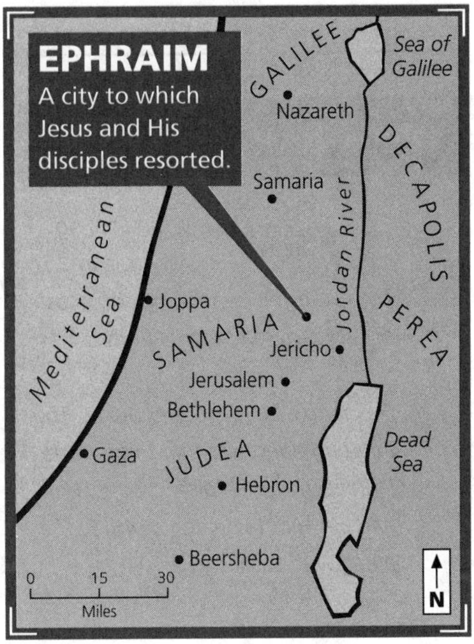

EPHRAIM

YOU ARE THERE 11:54

- **A city surrounded by mountains, four miles east of Bethel and fourteen miles northeast of Jerusalem.**
- **Also known as Ephron and Ephrain. Ephraim was of one of the twelve tribes of Israel.**
- **Name meant "doubly fruitful" or "double grain land."**
- **Identified with the Old Testament city of Ophrah (Josh. 18:23; 1 Sam. 13:17), at site of modern et-Taiyibeh.**

The Seven Signs of John's Gospel

JESUS RAISES LAZARUS

CONSIDER THIS 11:17–45 *The final sign miracle in John's Gospel is the climax of Jesus' signs: He raised Lazarus from the dead (vv. 41–44), proving to all that He was master even over death. The amazing thing was that this miracle led directly to the plot to arrest Him and put Him to death (vv. 46–53), along with Lazarus (12:10–11)!*

55 And the Passover of the Jews was near, and many went
from the country up to Jerusalem before the Passover, to
purify themselves. 56 Then they sought Jesus, and spoke
among themselves as they stood in the temple, "What do
you think—that He will not come to the feast?" 57 Now both
the chief priests and the Pharisees had given a command,
that if anyone knew where He was, he should report *it*, that
they might seize Him.

CHAPTER 12

Mary Anoints Jesus with Costly Oil

12:1–8

1 Then, six days before the Passover, Jesus came to Bethany, where Lazarus was
who had been dead,[a] whom He had raised from the dead.
2 There they made Him a supper; and Martha served, but
Lazarus was one of those who sat at the table with Him.
3 Then Mary took a pound of very costly oil of spikenard,
anointed the feet of Jesus, and wiped His feet with her hair.
And the house was filled with the fragrance of the oil.

12:1 [a]NU-Text omits *who had been dead.*

YOU ARE THERE 12:1–8

FUNERAL PREPARATIONS

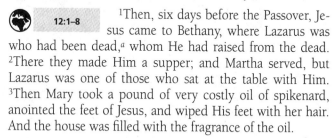

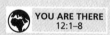

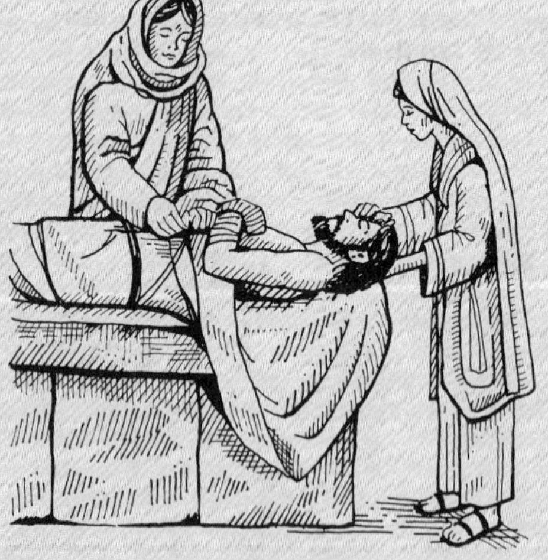

Jesus told the dinner crowd that Mary was preparing Him for His burial (v. 7). It's difficult for us today to appreciate the significance that burial rituals had for ancient peoples. Nearly every ancient religion gave explicit and sometimes elaborate instructions for preparing and burying the dead.

For Hebrews at the time of Christ, women and men participated in the mourning ritual, but women likely prepared the corpse for interment. First they washed the body, then scented it with fragrant oil, an act of devotion that might be repeated at the tomb.

The oil that Mary used on Jesus (v. 3) was probably nard, a perfume used by women. Imported from India, it was extremely costly and was known for its strong fragrance. It was the same perfume used by the woman that Solomon praised in his Song of Solomon (1:12; 4:13).

Washed and scented, the body was dressed in the person's own clothes or else wrapped in specially prepared sheets. Then, as soon as possible, it was carried upon a bier to the tomb. Relatives, friends, and professional mourners (see Matt. 9:23) formed a procession, and anyone meeting it was obliged to show honor to the

12:4–7

[4]But one of His disciples, Judas Iscariot, Simon's *son,* who would betray Him,
said, [5]"Why was this fragrant oil not sold for three hundred
denarii[a] and given to the poor?" [6]This he said, not that he
cared for the poor, but because he was a thief, and had the
money box; and he used to take what was put in it.
[7]But Jesus said, "Let her alone; she has kept[a] this for the
day of My burial. [8]For the poor you have with you always,
but Me you do not have always."

The Curious Gather

[9]Now a great many of the Jews knew that He was there;
and they came, not for Jesus' sake only, but that they might
also see Lazarus, whom He had raised from the dead. [10]But
the chief priests plotted to put Lazarus to death also, [11]be-
cause on account of him many of the Jews went away and
believed in Jesus.

12:5 [a]About one year's wages for a worker *12:7* [a]NU-Text reads *that she may keep.*

Why Not Give to the Poor?

A CLOSER LOOK 12:4–7

Judas Iscariot's greedy heart was clearly revealed in this incident (vv. 4–6). But Jesus responded with a puzzling statement (vv. 7–8). For an explanation, see "A Parting Gift," Mark 14:3–9.

deceased and the relatives by joining. A eulogy was often delivered at the grave site.

The body was placed on a shelf in the tomb, which was then sealed by a heavy, tight-fitting slab. Jews were expected to visit the tomb often, partly as a precaution against burying someone who only seemed dead. ◆

For further details see "Burial" at 1 Cor. 15:42.

"FOR THE POOR YOU HAVE WITH YOU ALWAYS, BUT ME YOU DO NOT HAVE ALWAYS."
—John 12:8

A Parade Welcomes Jesus to Jerusalem

[12]The next day a great multitude that had come to the
feast, when they heard that Jesus was coming to Jerusalem,
[13]took branches of palm trees and went out to meet Him,
and cried out:

"Hosanna!
'Blessed *is* He who comes in the name of the LORD!'[a]
The King of Israel!"

[14]Then Jesus, when He had found a young donkey, sat on
it; as it is written:

15 "Fear not, daughter of Zion;
Behold, your King is coming,
Sitting on a donkey's colt."[a]

[16]His disciples did not understand these things at first;
but when Jesus was glorified, then they remembered that
these things were written about Him and *that* they had
done these things to Him.
[17]Therefore the people, who were with Him when He
called Lazarus out of his tomb and raised him from the
dead, bore witness. [18]For this reason the people also met
Him, because they heard that He had done this sign. [19]The
Pharisees therefore said among themselves, "You see that
you are accomplishing nothing. Look, the world has gone
after Him!"

Jesus Sums Up His Teaching

12:20–36 [20]Now there were certain Greeks
among those who came up to worship at
the feast. [21]Then they came to Philip, who was from Bethsaida of Galilee, and asked him, saying, "Sir, we wish to see
Jesus."
[22]Philip came and told Andrew, and in turn Andrew and
Philip told Jesus.
[23]But Jesus answered them, saying, "The hour has come
that the Son of Man should be glorified. [24]Most assuredly, I
say to you, unless a grain of wheat falls into the ground and
dies, it remains alone; but if it dies, it produces much grain.
[25]He who loves his life will lose it, and he who hates his
life in this world will keep it for eternal life. [26]If anyone
serves Me, let him follow Me; and where I am, there My servant will be also. If anyone serves Me, him *My* Father will
honor.
[27]"Now My soul is troubled, and what shall I say? 'Father,
save Me from this hour'? But for this purpose I came to this
hour. [28]Father, glorify Your name."

12:13 [a]Psalm 118:26 *12:15* [a]Zechariah 9:9

Jesus Excludes Only the Faithless

CONSIDER THIS 12:20–36 *Jesus was at an annual Jewish festival called Passover (12:1). It was a major feast, lasting several days and attended by people from all over the Roman Empire (see Luke 22:7).*

When Gentiles at the Passover requested a meeting with Jesus, He responded by telling His Jewish followers that He was going to draw all peoples to Himself (v. 32). Later He affirmed that nothing can save someone from judgment but faith in Him and His saving work on the cross (vv. 46, 48). Nothing else helps, nor does the lack of any other qualification prohibit anyone from coming to Jesus for salvation.

Then a voice came from heaven, *saying,* "I have both glorified *it* and will glorify *it* again."
29Therefore the people who stood by and heard *it* said
that it had thundered. Others said, "An angel has spoken to
Him."
30Jesus answered and said, "This voice did not come because of Me, but for your sake. 31Now is the judgment of
this world; now the ruler of this world will be cast out.
32And I, if I am lifted up from the earth, will draw all *peoples*
to Myself." 33This He said, signifying by what death He
would die.
34The people answered Him, "We have heard from the
law that the Christ remains forever; and how *can* You say,
'The Son of Man must be lifted up'? Who is this Son of
Man?"
35Then Jesus said to them, "A little while longer the light
is with you. Walk while you have the light, lest darkness
overtake you; he who walks in darkness does not know
where he is going. 36While you have the light, believe in the
light, that you may become sons of light." These things Jesus spoke, and departed, and was hidden from them.

Unbelief Persists

37But although He had done so many signs before them,
they did not believe in Him, 38that the word of Isaiah the
prophet might be fulfilled, which he spoke:

"Lord, who has believed our report?
And to whom has the arm of the LORD been revealed?"[a]

39Therefore they could not believe, because Isaiah said
again:

40 "He has blinded their eyes and hardened their hearts,
Lest they should see with *their* eyes,
Lest they should understand with *their* hearts and turn,
So that I should heal them." [a]

41These things Isaiah said when[a] he saw His glory and
spoke of Him.

12:42–43

42Nevertheless even among the rulers
many believed in Him, but because of the
Pharisees they did not confess *Him,* lest they should be put
out of the synagogue; 43for they loved the praise of men
more than the praise of God.

Jesus Makes His Final Claims

44Then Jesus cried out and said, "He who believes in Me,
believes not in Me but in Him who sent Me. 45And he who

12:38 [a]Isaiah 53:1 *12:40* [a]Isaiah 6:10 *12:41* [a]NU-Text reads *because.*

THE FEAR OF REJECTION

CONSIDER THIS 12:42–43 **As John points out in vv. 42–43, the Pharisees held a powerful grip on Jewish society in Jesus' day, stifling dissent through fear. Apparently Jesus had some support even at the highest levels of society. But it did Him no good, as fear of rejection overcame the impulse for justice and truth.**

Have you ever been embarrassed or afraid to identify publicly with Christ because of possible rejection by others, especially superiors? Scripture is clear that one price of authentic discipleship will almost certainly be some rejection and persecution (15:18–25; 2 Tim. 3:12). To believe that you can avoid any tough choices between acceptance by the world and loyalty to God is both naive and dangerous. If God does not hold your highest allegiance, how real can He be to you in any meaningful way?

The Pharisees were one of a number of major political parties among the Hebrews in the first century. See "Party Politics of Jesus' Day," Matt. 16:1.

sees Me sees Him who sent Me. [46]I have come *as* a light into
the world, that whoever believes in Me should not abide in
darkness. [47]And if anyone hears My words and does not believe,[a] I do not judge him; for I did not come to judge the
world but to save the world. [48]He who rejects Me, and does
not receive My words, has that which judges him—the
12:49 word that I have spoken will judge him
in the last day. [49]For I have not spoken
on My own *authority;* but the Father who sent Me gave Me a
command, what I should say and what I should speak.
[50]And I know that His command is everlasting life. Therefore, whatever I speak, just as the Father has told Me, so I
speak."

CHAPTER 13

Jesus Washes the Disciples' Feet

13:1–20 [1]Now before the Feast of the Passover,
when Jesus knew that His hour had come
that He should depart from this world to the Father, having
loved His own who were in the world, He loved them to
the end.

13:2–17 [2]And supper being ended,[a] the devil
having already put it into the heart of Ju-
das Iscariot, Simon's *son,* to betray Him, [3]Jesus, knowing

12:47 [a]NU-Text reads *keep them.* 13:2 [a]NU-Text reads *And during supper.*

THE ORDER OF THE TOWEL

CONSIDER THIS 13:1–20

Leadership is a fascinating topic. Business books offer models of leadership as diverse as Attila the Hun, Oriental warlords, and Abraham Lincoln. But Jesus painted a different picture of leadership.

As He wrapped up His work, Jesus held a dinner for His closest associates. Instead of delivering a state-of-the-union address or naming a successor, He chose to leave His seat at the head of the table and pick up some household servant's equipment—a basin of water and a towel. He then washed the feet of every person at the table—even Judas, His betrayer (vv. 1–20). Foot-washing was usually performed by household servants as an act of hospitality to weary, dusty guests (compare Luke 7:44). Leaders and hosts did not stoop to such a menial task. But Jesus did.

(continued on next page)

CONSIDER THIS 12:49

UNDER AUTHORITY

Jesus faithfully represented His Father to the world (v. 49). Consider two implications of that for Christians today:

(1) As believers, we are to live under Christ's authority, and therefore we are responsible for faithfully representing Christ in our places of work. To do so we must be intimately familiar with Jesus—what He said, what His commands are, and what His purposes are. That means serious and continuous exploration of the Scriptures.

(2) As employees under human authorities, we are responsible for faithfully representing our organizations in general and our superiors in particular to other people. To do so we must be intimately familiar with the values, goals, policies, and procedures of our employers.

Neither of these is an easy assignment. It's all too common to misrepresent the statements of the Lord or our superiors to suit our own purposes. It's also easy to hear from them only what we want to hear.

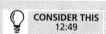

that the Father had given all things into His hands, and that
He had come from God and was going to God, 4rose from
supper and laid aside His garments, took a towel and girded
Himself. 5After that, He poured water into a basin and began to wash the disciples' feet, and to wipe *them* with the
towel with which He was girded. 6Then He came to Simon
Peter. And *Peter* said to Him, "Lord, are You washing my
feet?"

7Jesus answered and said to him, "What I am doing you
do not understand now, but you will know after this."

8Peter said to Him, "You shall never wash my feet!"

Jesus answered him, "If I do not wash you, you have no
part with Me."

9Simon Peter said to Him, "Lord, not my feet only, but
also *my* hands and *my* head!"

10Jesus said to him, "He who is bathed needs only to
wash *his* feet, but is completely clean; and you are clean,
but not all of you." 11For He knew who would betray Him;
therefore He said, "You are not all clean."

12So when He had washed their feet, taken His garments,
and sat down again, He said to them, "Do you know what I
have done to you? 13You call Me Teacher and Lord, and you
say well, for *so* I am. 14If I then, *your* Lord and Teacher, have
washed your feet, you also ought to wash one another's feet.
15For I have given you an example, that you should do as I
have done to you. 16Most assuredly, I say to you, a servant is
not greater than his master; nor is he who is sent greater

Are there any checks and balances to guard against those temptations? Jesus modeled two principles for us. First, He asked questions and listened to answers: for example, with Nicodemus (3:1–21) and with the woman at the well (4:1–26). Furthermore, He was clear about His mission and secure in His position. As a result, He never felt compelled to prove or promote Himself. In this He differed from many of the leaders of His day, who "loved the praise of men more than the praise of God" (12:43). ◆

Scripture has much more to say about our relationship to our employers. See "Who's the Boss?" Col. 3:22–24.

(continued from previous page)

Seated once again at the table, the Lord asked whether His followers understood what He had done (John 13:12). He then exhorted them to adopt the same posture of serving others, thereby following His example. He assured them that they would be blessed if they did (vv. 15–17).

Jesus still calls believers today to become members of the "Order of the Towel." As Christ's followers, we need to lead others by serving them.

In a related incident, Jesus spelled out what servant-leadership means. See "Servant-Leaders," Matt. 20:25–28.

A Model of Servant-Leadership

CONSIDER THIS 13:2–17

When Jesus washed His disciples' feet (vv. 3–5), He demonstrated a fundamental principle that He regularly stressed to His followers: To lead others, one must serve others. This is as true in public life and the business world as it is in the church. No number of corporate memos or rah-rah speeches exhorting workers to commit themselves to an organization or its clients will have as powerful an impact as a person of authority modeling consistently and clearly the attitude of a servant: placing others' needs before one's own, committing oneself to doing concrete things to meet those needs, and looking for neither favors nor reciprocity from the people one serves.

THE HALLMARK OF LOVE

CONSIDER THIS 13:31–35 **A key test of our commitment to Christ is our love for other believers (vv. 31–35). It is not just our words that express our love, but our attitudes and actions as well. Jesus did not say that others would know we are His disciples by what we say, or how we dress, or what we know, or the label of our denomination. He said, "as I have loved you" (v. 34). Shortly afterward, He laid down His life for those first believers.**

"... HAVE LOVE FOR ONE ANOTHER." —John 13:35

than he who sent him. 17If you know these things, blessed
are you if you do them.

18"I do not speak concerning all of you. I know whom I
have chosen; but that the Scripture may be fulfilled, 'He
who eats bread with Me[a] has lifted up his heel against Me.'[b]
19Now I tell you before it comes, that when it does come to
pass, you may believe that I am *He.* 20Most assuredly, I say
to you, he who receives whomever I send receives Me; and
he who receives Me receives Him who sent Me."

Judas Leaves to Betray Jesus

21When Jesus had said these things, He was troubled in
spirit, and testified and said, "Most assuredly, I say to you,
one of you will betray Me." 22Then the disciples looked at
one another, perplexed about whom He spoke.

23Now there was leaning on Jesus' bosom one of His disciples, whom Jesus loved. 24Simon Peter therefore motioned
to him to ask who it was of whom He spoke.

25Then, leaning back[a] on Jesus' breast, he said to Him,
"Lord, who is it?"

26Jesus answered, "It is he to whom I shall give a piece of
bread when I have dipped *it.*" And having dipped the
bread, He gave *it* to Judas Iscariot, *the son* of Simon. 27Now
after the piece of bread, Satan entered him. Then Jesus said
to him, "What you do, do quickly." 28But no one at the table
knew for what reason He said this to him. 29For some
thought, because Judas had the money box, that Jesus had
said to him, "Buy *those things* we need for the feast," or that
he should give something to the poor.

30Having received the piece of bread, he then went out
immediately. And it was night.

A New Commandment

13:31–35

31So, when he had gone out, Jesus said,
"Now the Son of Man is glorified, and
God is glorified in Him. 32If God is glorified in Him, God
will also glorify Him in Himself, and glorify Him immediately. 33Little children, I shall be with you a little while
longer. You will seek Me; and as I said to the Jews, 'Where I
am going, you cannot come,' so now I say to you. 34A new
commandment I give to you, that you love one another; as I
have loved you, that you also love one another. 35By this all
will know that you are My disciples, if you have love for
one another."

Jesus Predicts Peter's Denial

36Simon Peter said to Him, "Lord, where are You going?"
Jesus answered him, "Where I am going you cannot

13:18 [a]NU-Text reads *My bread.* [b]Psalm 41:9 *13:25* [a]NU-Text and M-Text add *thus.*

follow Me now, but you shall follow Me afterward."
37 Peter said to Him, "Lord, why can I not follow You
now? I will lay down my life for Your sake."
38 Jesus answered him, "Will you lay down your life for
My sake? Most assuredly, I say to you, the rooster shall not
crow till you have denied Me three times.

CHAPTER 14

"I Am the Way, the Truth, and the Life"

1 "Let not your heart be troubled; you believe in God, believe also in Me. 2 In My Father's house are many mansions;[a]
if *it were* not *so,* I would have told you. I go to prepare a
place for you.[b] 3 And if I go and prepare a place for you, I
will come again and receive you to Myself; that where I am,
there you may be also. 4 And where I go you know, and the
way you know."
5 Thomas said to Him, "Lord, we do not know where You
are going, and how can we know the way?"
6 Jesus said to him, "I am the way, the truth, and the life.
No one comes to the Father except through Me.
7 "If you had known Me, you would have known My
Father also; and from now on you know Him and have seen
Him."
8 Philip said to Him, "Lord, show us the Father, and it is
sufficient for us."
9 Jesus said to him, "Have I been with you so long, and yet
you have not known Me, Philip? He who has seen Me has
seen the Father; so how can you say, 'Show us the Father'?
10 Do you not believe that I am in the Father, and the Father
in Me? The words that I speak to you I do not speak on My
own *authority;* but the Father who dwells in Me does the
works. 11 Believe Me that I *am* in the Father and the Father
in Me, or else believe Me for the sake of the works themselves.

14:12–13

12 "Most assuredly, I say to you, he who
believes in Me, the works that I do he
will do also; and greater *works* than these he will do, because I go to My Father. 13 And whatever you ask in My
name, that I will do, that the Father may be glorified in the
Son. 14 If you ask[a] anything in My name, I will do *it.*

The Holy Spirit Is Promised

14:16–18

15 "If you love Me, keep[a] My commandments. 16 And I will pray the Father, and
He will give you another Helper, that He may abide with

14:2 [a]Literally *dwellings* [b]NU-Text adds a word which would cause the text to read either *if it were not so, would I have told you that I go to prepare a place for you?* or *if it were not so I would have told you; for I go to prepare a place for you.* *14:14* [a]NU-Text adds *Me.* *14:15* [a]NU-Text reads *you will keep.*

EMPOWERING LEADERSHIP

CONSIDER THIS 14:12–13 *Jesus' promise in vv. 12–13 shows that noble leadership seeks to empower others to achieve results even greater than the leader has achieved. The true leader seeks to achieve great goals more than great personal gain. Rather than being intimidated by his followers' potential, he rejoices in their growth, development, and achievements.*

Jesus used a unique style of authority to lead His disciples. To find out more about it, see "Servant-Leaders," Matt. 20:25–28.

WITH US

CONSIDER THIS 14:16–18 *Jesus calls the Holy Spirit the Helper (vv. 16–17). The Greek word,* paraclete, *means "one called alongside to help." In giving us the Holy Spirit, Jesus shows that leadership is not so much the ability to walk ahead of someone as the willingness to walk* beside *someone. Followers need support as well as direction, a hand that helps as well as a finger that points.*

Peace in the Chaos

CONSIDER THIS 14:25–28 **We live in a turbulent world. Change is rapid and frequently dramatic. Jesus said that He alone can provide the help and peace we need to live and work with integrity and wholeness (vv. 25–28). Certainly our work cannot be depended on for that. No job is engaging enough, no position powerful enough, and no material rewards substantial enough to give us the kind of inner peace and confidence we long for. Only Christ will never leave us nor forsake us.**

you forever— 17the Spirit of truth, whom the world cannot
receive, because it neither sees Him nor knows Him; but
you know Him, for He dwells with you and will be in you.
18I will not leave you orphans; I will come to you.
19"A little while longer and the world will see Me no
more, but you will see Me. Because I live, you will live also.
20At that day you will know that I *am* in My Father, and you
in Me, and I in you. 21He who has My commandments and
keeps them, it is he who loves Me. And he who loves Me
will be loved by My Father, and I will love him and manifest Myself to him."
22Judas (not Iscariot) said to Him, "Lord, how is it that
You will manifest Yourself to us, and not to the world?"
23Jesus answered and said to him, "If anyone loves Me, he
will keep My word; and My Father will love him, and We
will come to him and make Our home with him. 24He who
does not love Me does not keep My words; and the word
which you hear is not Mine but the Father's who sent Me.

14:25–28
25"These things I have spoken to you
while being present with you. 26But the
Helper, the Holy Spirit, whom the Father will send in My
name, He will teach you all things, and bring to your remembrance all things that I said to you. 27Peace I leave with

CONSIDER THIS 15:1–10

The Network

Computer networks have become important systems in today's competitive marketplace. They enable teams of workers in different offices, at regional sites, and even from around the world to join together on tasks that would otherwise be difficult if not impossible.

One way of setting up a network is to use a central computer to handle the main programming, storage, and communication functions, with remote workstations for individual input and retrieval. This is similar to the situation that Jesus described in His image of the vine and the branches (vv. 1–10):

(1) Jesus is the key (v. 1). *Like the central processing unit of a computer system, Jesus provides the life, the direction, and the commands for His followers, those of us "on-line."*

(2) To be effective, believers must maintain their relationship with Jesus (v. 4). *In order to use the features of a network, a user must remain attached to the network. If one "signs off," there is no more access to the central computer or to others in the network. Likewise, if we allow sin to disrupt our walk with Christ, we lose fellowship with Him and with other believers (1 John 1:6–7).*

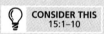

you, My peace I give to you; not as the world gives do I give
to you. Let not your heart be troubled, neither let it be
afraid. 28You have heard Me say to you, 'I am going away
and coming *back* to you.' If you loved Me, you would rejoice because I said,[a] 'I am going to the Father,' for My
Father is greater than I.
29"And now I have told you before it comes, that when it
does come to pass, you may believe. 30I will no longer talk
much with you, for the ruler of this world is coming, and
he has nothing in Me. 31But that the world may know that I
love the Father, and as the Father gave Me commandment,
so I do. Arise, let us go from here.

CHAPTER 15

"I Am the Vine"

15:1–10

1"I am the true vine, and My Father is
the vinedresser. 2Every branch in Me that
does not bear fruit He takes away;[a] and every *branch* that
bears fruit He prunes, that it may bear more fruit. 3You are
already clean because of the word which I have spoken to

14:28 [a]NU-Text omits *I said.* *15:2* [a]Or *lifts up*

(3) Jesus wants His followers to be productive (vv. 5–8). *Companies install computer networks so that their employees can get their work done. The systems cost too much to be treated as toys or to be underutilized. Correspondingly, the relationship that believers have with God was purchased through Christ's blood, so we need to take it seriously. Christ wants us to enjoy walking with Him, but He also wants us to accomplish His purposes.*

(4) To love Jesus is to follow His commands (vv. 9–10). *Occasionally network users receive an "error message" indicating that they have not followed the instructions of the program correctly. By the same token, Jesus has given us commands to follow, and the only way to experience His life and power is to obey those commands. To do so is not only practical, but an expression of our love for the Lord.*

Are you "on-line" with Jesus, drawing on His resources and obeying His commands? Is your life productive, accomplishing the tasks and responsibilities that He has assigned to you? ◆

"EVERY BRANCH THAT BEARS FRUIT HE PRUNES, THAT IT MAY BEAR MORE FRUIT."
—John 15:2

you. [4]Abide in Me, and I in you. As the branch cannot bear
fruit of itself, unless it abides in the vine, neither can you,
unless you abide in Me.
[5]"I am the vine, you *are* the branches. He who abides in
Me, and I in him, bears much fruit; for without Me you can
do nothing. [6]If anyone does not abide in Me, he is cast out
as a branch and is withered; and they gather them and
throw *them* into the fire, and they are burned. [7]If you abide
in Me, and My words abide in you, you will[a] ask what you
desire, and it shall be done for you. [8]By this My Father is
glorified, that you bear much fruit; so you will be My disciples.
[9]"As the Father loved Me, I also have loved you; abide in
My love. [10]If you keep My commandments, you will abide
in My love, just as I have kept My Father's commandments
and abide in His love.

"Love One Another"

[11]"These things I have spoken to you, that My joy may remain in you, and *that* your joy may be full. [12]This is My
commandment, that you love one another as I have loved
you. [13]Greater love has no one than this, than to lay down
one's life for his friends. [14]You are My friends if you do
whatever I command you. [15]No longer do I call you servants, for a servant does not know what his master is doing;
but I have called you friends, for all things that I heard from
My Father I have made known to you. [16]You did not choose
Me, but I chose you and appointed you that you should go
and bear fruit, and *that* your fruit should remain, that whatever you ask the Father in My name He may give you.
[17]These things I command you, that you love one another.

15:18–20

15:18–25

[18]"If the world hates you, you know
that it hated Me before *it hated* you. [19]If
you were of the world, the world would
love its own. Yet because you are not of
the world, but I chose you out of the world, therefore the
world hates you. [20]Remember the word that I said to you,
'A servant is not greater than his master.' If they persecuted
Me, they will also persecute you. If they kept My word, they
will keep yours also. [21]But all these things they will do to
you for My name's sake, because they do not know Him
who sent Me. [22]If I had not come and spoken to them, they
would have no sin, but now they have no excuse for their
sin. [23]He who hates Me hates My Father also. [24]If I had not
done among them the works which no one else did, they
would have no sin; but now they have seen and also hated
both Me and My Father. [25]But *this happened* that the word

15:7 [a]NU-Text omits *you will.*

QUOTE UNQUOTE

CONSIDER THIS 15:18–20 *Just as the world rejected Jesus, it will reject His followers (vv. 18–20). One writer offers a few reasons why:*

A real Christian is an odd number anyway. He feels supreme love for One whom he has never seen; talks familiarly every day to Someone he cannot see; expects to go to heaven on the virtue of Another; empties himself in order to be full; admits he is wrong so he can be declared right; goes down in order to get up; is strongest when he is weakest; richest when he is poorest; and happiest when he feels the worst. He dies so he can live; forsakes in order to have; gives away so he can keep; sees the invisible; hears the inaudible; and knows that which passeth knowledge.

A. W. Tozer

might be fulfilled which is written in their law, 'They hated
Me without a cause.'[a]
26"But when the Helper comes, whom I shall send to
you from the Father, the Spirit of truth who proceeds from
the Father, He will testify of Me. 27And you also will bear
witness, because you have been with Me from the beginning.

CHAPTER 16

The Work of the Spirit

1"These things I have spoken to you, that you should not
be made to stumble. 2They will put you out of the synagogues;
yes, the time is coming that whoever kills you will
think that he offers God service. 3And these things they will
do to you[a] because they have not known the Father nor Me.
4But these things I have told you, that when the[a] time
comes, you may remember that I told you of them.
"And these things I did not say to you at the beginning,
because I was with you.
5"But now I go away to Him who sent Me, and none of
you asks Me, 'Where are You going?' 6But because I have
said these things to you, sorrow has filled your heart. 7Nevertheless
I tell you the truth. It is to your advantage that I
go away; for if I do not go away, the Helper will not come to
16:8 see pg. 384
you; but if I depart, I will send Him to
you. 8And when He has come, He will
convict the world of sin, and of righteousness, and of judgment:
9of sin, because they do not believe in Me; 10of righteousness,
because I go to My Father and you see Me no
more; 11of judgment, because the ruler of this world is
judged.
12"I still have many things to say to you, but you cannot
bear *them* now. 13However, when He, the Spirit of truth, has
come, He will guide you into all truth; for He will not speak
on His own *authority,* but whatever He hears He will speak;
and He will tell you things to come. 14He will glorify Me,
for He will take of what is Mine and declare *it* to you. 15All
things that the Father has are Mine. Therefore I said that He
will take of Mine and declare *it* to you.[a]

Temporary Sorrow, Then Permanent Joy

16"A little while, and you will not see Me; and again a little
while, and you will see Me, because I go to the Father."

(Bible text continued on page 386)

15:25 [a]Psalm 69:4 *16:3* [a]NU-Text and M-Text omit *to you.* *16:4* [a]NU-Text reads *their.*
16:15 [a]NU-Text and M-Text read *He takes of Mine and will declare it to you.*

THE COST OF FOLLOWING JESUS

CONSIDER THIS 15:18–25

Are you prepared to be *hated* because of your commitment to Jesus Christ? Perhaps you expect to be misunderstood occasionally or even chided by associates for "going overboard" on religion. But Jesus used strong words in vv. 18–25: "hate" and "persecute." He indicated that our true commitments will be made clear when they start to cost us something.

What has your faith cost you? A promotion or some other career opportunity? Criticism or even ostracism by coworkers or family? Legal action? Or nothing at all? Sooner or later, following Christ has a cost, and those who think they can get by without paying it are misguided. In fact, if there's no cost, is there really any genuine commitment? Jesus' words suggest not.

However, it's also possible for our actions or words to cause offense because they are inappropriate. In that case, the hostility we may receive is not persecution. Like Jesus (1:14), we are called to be people of grace and truth, not obnoxious and rude. True persecution involves unmerited hostility for doing good works in the pattern of Christ (1 Pet. 2:12–21).

Fear of rejection is one of the main reasons believers hesitate to declare their true colors. See John 12:42–43.

CONSIDER THIS 16:8

WHOSE JOB IS EVANGELISM?

One thing is certain about evangelism: both non-Christians and Christians feel uncomfortable with it. Bring up the topic of religion (let alone the gospel) with your unbelieving workmates, and the atmosphere suddenly tenses up. It's as if spiritual matters are out of place in a professional setting.

Consequently, many Christians fold their hands and shut their mouths when it comes to evangelism. They've decided it's up to God to bring people to faith. But they're not going to participate in the process.

Of course, in a way it is up to God to bring about salvation, as v. 8 shows. The Holy Spirit is *the* great evangelist. Yet other passages urge us as believers to work *with* the Spirit in influencing others with the gospel. To understand our role in this joint venture, we need to rediscover the evangelistic work of the Spirit. This involves:

Common grace. No matter how bad things get in the world—plagued as it is with war, poverty, famine, disease, crime, family chaos, and so on—things would be far worse if it weren't for God's Spirit. The Spirit moves throughout the world, restraining the full onslaught of evil and promoting whatever is good. The Spirit does this for believers and unbelievers alike; hence the name, "common grace."

Because of this gracious work, the unbeliever is in a position to accept God's offer of salvation, and therefore benefits from divine grace whether salvation occurs or not (Ps. 104:24–30).

Spiritual awakening. Unaware that God restrains evil and promotes good, an unbeliever can be glib about life and unapproachable concerning spiritual issues. So the Spirit's job is to awaken the unbeliever to his or her true spiritual condition. The Spirit may use a disturbing conscience, a declining hope, or a gripping fear. Other instruments include the law, government, and human kindness (Is. 57:20–21; Joel 2:28–32; Rom. 2:1–6, 15–16).

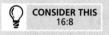

Conviction of sin. When the Spirit pricks an unbeliever's conscience, there may be feelings of acute guilt and fear of God's judgment (John 16:8; Acts 5:1–11). Such a person can become quite hostile, and even attack nearby believers. This is important to know; rejection of the gospel does not necessarily reflect failure on our part as Christ's representatives (though anger is justifiable if we're insensitive in our approach).

Regeneration. This part of evangelism is one that Christians too often take credit for, even though it is the work of the Spirit. Regeneration involves the giving of new life to a lost sinner (John 3:5–8). Only the Spirit can do that. As believers, we can do nothing but help this birthing process along.

Sealing and equipping. Finally, the Spirit "seals" the new believer in Christ; that is, the Spirit confirms and guarantees the believer's place in God's family and provides assurance of salvation (2 Cor. 5:5; Eph. 1:13). Moreover, the Spirit equips the new Christian to live and act as Christ's follower by providing spiritual power and gifts, and bonding believers together. New appetites develop—a love for Scripture, a hatred of evil, and a desire to share the faith.

In light of these evangelistic efforts of God's Spirit, how can believers cooperate with God in evangelism? Here are four ways:

Identify with Christ. We can start by publicly (yet sensitively) acknowledging our life in Christ, declaring our spiritual commitments and convictions. We can also act with Christ-like love toward others and demonstrate integrity in our work and lifestyle. And we can identify with the people of God. That doesn't mean we have to endorse everything that other Christians do. But we accept and affirm that we are part of God's family (John 13:14–15; 17:14–19; Phil. 3:17).

Proclaim the gospel. Jesus preached repentance and the forgiveness of sins. Similarly, He asks us to verbally communicate the gospel message to our relatives, friends, and coworkers. Naturally, we must avoid preaching more than we practice. However, evangelism demands more than a "silent witness." As important as it is, our lives alone are not enough to guide people toward Christ's work for them. We must also provide information that presents Christ's message clearly and persuasively (Matt. 4:17; Col. 1:26–29).

Appeal for a decision. God gives people a choice to accept or reject His salvation offer. Therefore, as the Spirit gives us opportunity, we should present the gospel and then ask the person to decide what to do with Jesus (2 Cor. 5:18–20). For instance: "Is there any reason why you can't give yourself to Jesus Christ and accept the work that He has done for you?" We can act as Christ's ambassadors, appealing to others to accept His gift of new life.

In a way we're like midwives, carefully assisting in a new birth. Obviously, timing is crucial. To try to force premature delivery by high-pressure tactics and insistence on a decision only produces hostility, sometimes even rejection. It can create lasting wounds that close people's minds to the gospel.

Nurture and train new believers. We can continue to work with the Spirit to help new Christians get established in their faith. As a mother nurtures her newborn child, so we can nurture a baby believer (1 Thess. 2:7–8; 2 Tim. 2:2). We can assist the person in resisting temptation, developing new values, building relationships with other Christians, and gaining insight into the Bible. We can invite the "newborn" to pray with us, discuss God's Word, and worship the Lord.

Evangelism, then, is a cooperative effort between the Holy Spirit and those of us who follow Christ. As we interact with our associates, we should consider: How is the Spirit working in this person, and how can I contribute to the process? We can act like farmers, sometimes sowing new seeds, other times watering what someone else has planted. Occasionally we must root out an offensive weed left by someone else. But always our objective should be to reap a harvest to the glory of God (see John 4:34–38; 1 Cor. 3:5–7). ◆

What is the gospel we are called to proclaim? See Luke 7:22.

How you do your job affects your coworkers' attitude toward your witness. See "Your 'Workstyle,'" Titus 2:9–10.

A Woman in Labor

CONSIDER THIS 16:21–22 **An alternative translation to *sorrow* (v. 21) is "pain." There were few options available to first-century women for pain relief during labor. Since births took place at home, all of the disciples had probably heard a woman scream out in pain while giving birth.**

As in most undeveloped countries today, childbearing in biblical times was often fatal for the child, the mother, or both. Many pagan women sought help from their gods, along with special charms, to protect them during pregnancy and delivery.

So Jesus was using a graphic metaphor by comparing the coming "sorrow" of His followers with that of a woman in labor. He was indicating that their pain could not be avoided. But He did give them a hope: He promised that they would see Him again, and when they did their joy would be as great as a woman whose baby has finally been delivered safely.

Do you live with the hope of seeing Jesus, even as you confront the pain of this world?

17Then *some* of His disciples said among themselves,
"What is this that He says to us, 'A little while, and you will
not see Me; and again a little while, and you will see Me';
and, 'because I go to the Father'?" 18They said therefore,
"What is this that He says, 'A little while'? We do not know
what He is saying."

19Now Jesus knew that they desired to ask Him, and He
said to them, "Are you inquiring among yourselves about
what I said, 'A little while, and you will not see Me; and
again a little while, and you will see Me'? 20Most assuredly, I
say to you that you will weep and lament, but the world
will rejoice; and you will be sorrowful, but your sorrow
16:21–22 will be turned into joy. 21A woman, when
she is in labor, has sorrow because her
hour has come; but as soon as she has given birth to the
child, she no longer remembers the anguish, for joy that
a human being has been born into the world. 22There-
fore you now have sorrow; but I will see you again and
your heart will rejoice, and your joy no one will take from
you.

23"And in that day you will ask Me nothing. Most assuredly, I say to you, whatever you ask the Father in My
name He will give you. 24Until now you have asked nothing
in My name. Ask, and you will receive, that your joy may
be full.

25"These things I have spoken to you in figurative language; but the time is coming when I will no longer
speak to you in figurative language, but I will tell you
plainly about the Father. 26In that day you will ask in
My name, and I do not say to you that I shall pray the
Father for you; 27for the Father Himself loves you, because you have loved Me, and have believed that I came
forth from God. 28I came forth from the Father and have
come into the world. Again, I leave the world and go to the
Father."

29His disciples said to Him, "See, now You are speaking
plainly, and using no figure of speech! 30Now we are sure
that You know all things, and have no need that anyone
should question You. By this we believe that You came forth
from God."

31Jesus answered them, "Do you now believe? 32Indeed
the hour is coming, yes, has now come, that you will be
scattered, each to his own, and will leave Me alone. And yet
I am not alone, because the Father is with Me. 33These
things I have spoken to you, that in Me you may have
peace. In the world you will[a] have tribulation; but be of
good cheer, I have overcome the world."

16:33 [a]NU-Text and M-Text omit *will.*

CHAPTER 17

Jesus Prays for His Followers Then

17:1 1Jesus spoke these words, lifted up His
eyes to heaven, and said: "Father, the
hour has come. Glorify Your Son, that Your Son also may
glorify You, 2as You have given Him authority over all flesh,
that He should[a] give eternal life to as many as You have
given Him. 3And this is eternal life, that they may know
You, the only true God, and Jesus Christ whom You have
sent. 4I have glorified You on the earth. I have finished the
work which You have given Me to do. 5And now, O Father,
glorify Me together with Yourself, with the glory which I
had with You before the world was.

6"I have manifested Your name to the men whom You
have given Me out of the world. They were Yours, You gave
them to Me, and they have kept Your word. 7Now they have
known that all things which You have given Me are from
You. 8For I have given to them the words which You have
given Me; and they have received *them,* and have known
surely that I came forth from You; and they have believed
that You sent Me.

9"I pray for them. I do not pray for the world but for
those whom You have given Me, for they are Yours. 10And
all Mine are Yours, and Yours are Mine, and I am glorified
in them. 11Now I am no longer in the world, but these are
in the world, and I come to You. Holy Father, keep through
Your name those whom You have given Me,[a] that they may
be one as We *are.* 12While I was with them in the world,[a] I
kept them in Your name. Those whom You gave Me I have
kept;[b] and none of them is lost except the son of perdition,
that the Scripture might be fulfilled. 13But now I come to
You, and these things I speak in the world, that they may
have My joy fulfilled in themselves. 14I have given them
Your word; and the world has hated them because they are
not of the world, just as I am not of the world. 15I do not
pray that You should take them out of the world, but that
You should keep them from the evil one. 16They are not of
the world, just as I am not of the world. 17Sanctify them by

(Bible text continued on page 389)

17:2 [a]M-Text reads *shall.* *17:11* [a]NU-Text and M-Text read *keep them through Your name which You have given Me.* *17:12* [a]NU-Text omits *in the world.* [b]NU-Text reads *in Your name which You gave Me. And I guarded them;* (or *it;*).

"I DO NOT PRAY THAT YOU SHOULD TAKE THEM OUT OF THE WORLD. . . ." —John 17:15

A CLOSER LOOK 17:1

Gethsemane

Jesus' high priestly prayer recorded in this chapter was probably said in a familiar place of work. See "Praying in a Workplace," Matt. 26:36.

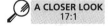

CONSIDER THIS
17:18

CALLED INTO THE WORLD

Should followers of Christ withdraw from the world to set up their own exclusive communities or retreat from society into "Christian ghettos"? Not if they are to fulfill Christ's prayer in v. 18. Engagement, not isolation, is His desire.

Some early Christians sought refuge in the catacombs of Rome. But that practice was only temporary, and they were forced there only by the most extreme persecutions. Normally, they could be found actively participating in the society.

Actually, Scripture recognizes a tension between separation and involvement. Passages like Romans 12:2 and 1 Peter 1:14–16 urge us to pursue a distinctive, holy lifestyle. Our commitments, character, and conduct should contrast vividly with those of people who do not know or follow God. On the other hand, Jesus calls us to live and work side by side with those very same people. He sends us *into the world* to make an impact (see Matt. 5:13–16, and "Faith Impacts the World," Mark 16:15).

Naturally, that can lead to conflict. If our loyalty is given to Christ, we can expect tension with others who follow a different course. Whether we undergo mild teasing and insults or open hostility and even violence, "normal" Christianity involves conflict with the world to which we are called (see 2 Tim. 3:12; 1 Pet. 4:12–14). Fortunately, the New Testament gives us plenty of examples to follow:

Jesus. The Lord Himself came into the world to offer a new relationship with God. He didn't have to. He could have remained in His heavenly position. Yet He voluntarily left it all to die for us, and to deliver to a rebellious humanity God's offer of forgiveness, love, and acceptance (Phil. 2:5–8).

When Christ came into the world, His listeners showed initial interest. Yet gradually most of them turned against Him. Knowing full well the fate that awaited Him, He entered Jerusalem, ready to face persecution, arrest, and even death. His followers tried to divert Him (Mark 8:31–33), but He was determined to follow God's call into the world. Isolation and safety were not options.

Paul. The church's greatest messenger started out hating anyone who followed Jesus. Yet Christ Himself stopped him in his vengeful tracks and redirected his life to become a globe-trotting messenger of faith and forgiveness.

However, Paul's first days as a Christian were spent in an isolated "retreat" in Arabia. But this withdrawal lasted only for a time, and only so that Saul could emerge as Paul, *the apostle.* He crisscrossed the empire, bringing the gospel to dozens of cities and towns. These encounters led to numerous misunderstandings, deportations, arrests, physical abuse, and attempts on his life. Probably Paul sometimes longed for the safer, quieter days of his Arabian retreat. But once he responded to God's call to engage the world, there was no turning back. He also challenged others to live, work, and witness among the lost (1 Cor. 4:16–20).

Peter. Peter struggled throughout his life to break out of the separatist mentality he had grown up with. He didn't like the prospect of suffering and rejection, and at times took steps to forestall it (see Mark 8:31–38; Luke 22:54–62; John 18:10–11). He liked even less the idea of sharing God's good news of salvation with Samaritans and Gentiles.

But Christ kept calling Peter back to re-engage the world (for example, see Acts 10). In the end, he learned the necessity and the value of suffering (1 Pet. 4:1–2) and called others to do likewise (2:11–12).

Barnabas. A respected landowner, Barnabas enjoyed a relatively "safe" calling as a

(continued on next page)

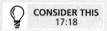

17:18
Your truth. Your word is truth. 18As You
sent Me into the world, I also have sent
them into the world. 19And for their sakes I sanctify Myself,
that they also may be sanctified by the truth.

Jesus Prays for His Followers Now

20"I do not pray for these alone, but also for those who
will[a] believe in Me through their word; 21that they all may
be one, as You, Father, *are* in Me, and I in You; that they
also may be one in Us, that the world may believe that You
sent Me. 22And the glory which You gave Me I have given
them, that they may be one just as We are one: 23I in them,
and You in Me; that they may be made perfect in one, and
that the world may know that You have sent Me, and have
loved them as You have loved Me.
24"Father, I desire that they also whom You gave Me may
be with Me where I am, that they may behold My glory
which You have given Me; for You loved Me before the
foundation of the world. 25O righteous Father! The world
has not known You, but I have known You; and these have
known that You sent Me. 26And I have declared to them
Your name, and will declare *it,* that the love with which You
loved Me may be in them, and I in them."

CHAPTER 18

Jesus Is Arrested

18:1–11
1When Jesus had spoken these words,
He went out with His disciples over the
Brook Kidron, where there was a garden, which He and His
disciples entered. 2And Judas, who betrayed Him, also
knew the place; for Jesus often met there with His disciples.
3Then Judas, having received a detachment *of troops,* and officers from the chief priests and Pharisees, came there with
lanterns, torches, and weapons. 4Jesus therefore, knowing
all things that would come upon Him, went forward and
said to them, "Whom are you seeking?"
5They answered Him, "Jesus of Nazareth."
Jesus said to them, "I am *He.*" And Judas, who betrayed
Him, also stood with them. 6Now when He said to them, "I
am *He,*" they drew back and fell to the ground.
7Then He asked them again, "Whom are you seeking?"
And they said, "Jesus of Nazareth."
8Jesus answered, "I have told you that I am *He.* Therefore,
if you seek Me, let these go their way," 9that the saying
might be fulfilled which He spoke, "Of those whom You
gave Me I have lost none."

17:20 [a]NU-Text and M-Text omit *will.*

(continued from previous page)

leader of the infant church in Jerusalem. But he accepted an assignment to visit Antioch and investigate rumors of Gentile converts to the predominantly Jewish movement. Sure enough, he found that God was bringing all nations into the fellowship. So he sought out Paul, an unknown, to help him establish the new converts in the faith (Acts 11:19–26). Later, they traveled to Jerusalem to defend and extend this new "worldly" thrust in the growing work of God (Acts 15). ◆

THE BLESSING OF A CLEAN CONSCIENCE

CONSIDER THIS 18:1–11 **Would you feel free to welcome others to attempt to assassinate your character? Would you even help them? Jesus did. He had such a clean conscience and a secure trust in God that justice would ultimately prevail, and that His enemies could do no lasting harm, that He actually aided His accusers. He welcomed them (v. 4), identified Himself for them (vv. 5, 8), and even protected them from retaliation by His own loyalists (v. 11). Jesus demonstrated grace in the face of hostility.**

Jesus' innocence did not protect Him from suffering, pain, or death. But it gave Him a confidence rooted in a larger reality than life on earth. Because He answered to God's judgment (John 12:23–33; 14:1–4), He was free to suffer, even unjustly. He left justice up to God and did not resort to retaliation.

10Then Simon Peter, having a sword, drew it and struck
the high priest's servant, and cut off his right ear. The servant's name was Malchus.
11So Jesus said to Peter, "Put your sword into the sheath.
Shall I not drink the cup which My Father has given Me?"
12Then the detachment *of troops* and the captain and the
officers of the Jews arrested Jesus and bound Him. 13And
they led Him away to Annas first, for he was the father-in-
law of Caiaphas who was high priest that year. 14Now it was
Caiaphas who advised the Jews that it was expedient that
one man should die for the people.

Peter Denies Knowing Jesus

15And Simon Peter followed Jesus, and so *did* another[a]
disciple. Now that disciple was known to the high priest,
and went with Jesus into the courtyard of the high priest.
16But Peter stood at the door outside. Then the other disciple, who was known to the high priest, went out and spoke
to her who kept the door, and brought Peter in. 17Then the
servant girl who kept the door said to Peter, "You are not
also *one* of this Man's disciples, are you?"
He said, "I am not."
18Now the servants and officers who had made a fire of
coals stood there, for it was cold, and they warmed themselves. And Peter stood with them and warmed himself.
19The high priest then asked Jesus about His disciples and
His doctrine.
20Jesus answered him, "I spoke openly to the world. I always taught in synagogues and in the temple, where the
Jews always meet,[a] and in secret I have said nothing. 21Why
do you ask Me? Ask those who have heard Me what I said
to them. Indeed they know what I said."
22And when He had said these things, one of the officers
who stood by struck Jesus with the palm of his hand, saying, "Do You answer the high priest like that?"
23Jesus answered him, "If I have spoken evil, bear witness
of the evil; but if well, why do you strike Me?"
24Then Annas sent Him bound to Caiaphas the high
priest.
25Now Simon Peter stood and warmed himself. Therefore
they said to him, "You are not also *one* of His disciples, are
you?"
He denied *it* and said, "I am not!"
26One of the servants of the high priest, a relative *of him*
whose ear Peter cut off, said, "Did I not see you in the garden with Him?" 27Peter then denied again; and immediately
a rooster crowed.

"I SPOKE OPENLY TO THE WORLD. . . . AND IN SECRET I HAVE SAID NOTHING." —John 18:20

18:15 [a]M-Text reads *the other.* *18:20* [a]NU-Text reads *where all the Jews meet.*

Jesus Is Taken to Pilate

28 Then they led Jesus from Caiaphas to the Praetorium,
and it was early morning. But they themselves did not go
into the Praetorium, lest they should be defiled, but that
they might eat the Passover. 29 Pilate then went out to them
and said, "What accusation do you bring against this Man?"
30 They answered and said to him, "If He were not an evildoer, we would not have delivered Him up to you."
31 Then Pilate said to them, "You take Him and judge Him
according to your law."
Therefore the Jews said to him, "It is not lawful for us to
put anyone to death," 32 that the saying of Jesus might be
fulfilled which He spoke, signifying by what death He
would die.
33 Then Pilate entered the Praetorium again, called Jesus,
and said to Him, "Are You the King of the Jews?"
34 Jesus answered him, "Are you speaking for yourself
about this, or did others tell you this concerning Me?"
35 Pilate answered, "Am I a Jew? Your own nation and the
chief priests have delivered You to me. What have You
done?"
36 Jesus answered, "My kingdom is not of this world. If My
kingdom were of this world, My servants would fight, so
that I should not be delivered to the Jews; but now My
kingdom is not from here."
18:37–38
37 Pilate therefore said to Him, "Are You
a king then?"
Jesus answered, "You say *rightly* that I am a king. For this
cause I was born, and for this cause I have come into the
world, that I should bear witness to the truth. Everyone
who is of the truth hears My voice."
38 Pilate said to Him, "What is truth?" And when he had
said this, he went out again to the Jews, and said to them, "I
find no fault in Him at all.
39 "But you have a custom that I should release someone
to you at the Passover. Do you therefore want me to release
to you the King of the Jews?"
18:40
40 Then they all cried again, saying,
"Not this Man, but Barabbas!" Now
Barabbas was a robber.

A Political Terrorist Goes Free

A CLOSER LOOK 18:40 *Barabbas was not only a robber (v. 40), he was a political terrorist, one of the* sicarii *("dagger-men") who assassinated Roman officials in the vain hope of driving them out of Palestine. Find out more at Mark 15:7 about how this revolutionary escaped the usual punishment of crucifixion.*

QUOTE UNQUOTE

CONSIDER THIS 18:37–38 *Pilate tossed the question to Jesus, "What is truth?" (v. 38). As an unbeliever, Pilate had no basis for measuring ultimate truth.*

To the non-believer, the person who sees no cosmos in chaos, we are all the victims of the darkness which surrounds our choices; we have lost our way; we do not know what is right and what is wrong; we cannot tell our left hand from our right. There is no meaning.

Madeleine L'Engle, *Walking On Water*, p. 27

Discrimination on the Basis of Wealth

CONSIDER THIS 19:1–6 **The soldiers seemed to enjoy mocking Christ (vv. 2–3). But they were also mocking wealth and authority, perhaps having lived and worked too long under Rome's iron fist. The crown of thorns was a grisly caricature of the ultimate symbol of royalty. But the purple robe was the genuine item: the purple dye used to make it was very costly and only the very rich could afford it.**

This incident reminds us that wealth and its symbols can be used to send many kinds of messages. Frequently wealth is the starting point for deciding who should be respected, accepted, included, and honored, and who should not. Scripture explicitly states that sin lies at the root of such judgments (James 2:1–9).

Do you judge people, in your heart of hearts, by their possessions and financial achievements? Do you work hard at getting close to people of position and wealth? Do your friends come from many different levels on the social and economic ladder?

In Jesus' day, purple cloth was ranked in value with gold and was important not only for adorning emperors and temples but for tribute and international trade. *See "The Trade in Purple," Acts 16:14.*

There is a marked contrast between how our culture measures success and how God evaluates true success and wealth. *See "Success," John 3:30, and "Christians and Money," 1 Tim. 6:7–19.*

CHAPTER 19

Pilate Sends Jesus to Be Crucified

19:1–6
1So then Pilate took Jesus and scourged
Him. 2And the soldiers twisted a crown of
thorns and put *it* on His head, and they put on Him a purple robe. 3Then they said,[a] "Hail, King of the Jews!" And
they struck Him with their hands.
4Pilate then went out again, and said to them, "Behold, I
am bringing Him out to you, that you may know that I find
no fault in Him."
5Then Jesus came out, wearing the crown of thorns and
the purple robe. And *Pilate* said to them, "Behold the Man!"
6Therefore, when the chief priests and officers saw Him,
they cried out, saying, "Crucify *Him,* crucify *Him!*"
Pilate said to them, "You take Him and crucify *Him,* for I
find no fault in Him."
7The Jews answered him, "We have a law, and according
to our[a] law He ought to die, because He made Himself the
Son of God."
8Therefore, when Pilate heard that saying, he was the
more afraid, 9and went again into the Praetorium, and said
to Jesus, "Where are You from?" But Jesus gave him no answer.

19:10–11
10Then Pilate said to Him, "Are You not
speaking to me? Do You not know that I
have power to crucify You, and power to release You?"
11Jesus answered, "You could have no power at all against
Me unless it had been given you from above. Therefore the
one who delivered Me to you has the greater sin."
12From then on Pilate sought to release Him, but the Jews
cried out, saying, "If you let this Man go, you are not Caesar's friend. Whoever makes himself a king speaks against
Caesar."
13When Pilate therefore heard that saying, he brought Jesus out and sat down in the judgment seat in a place that is
called *The* Pavement, but in Hebrew, Gabbatha. 14Now it
was the Preparation Day of the Passover, and about the
sixth hour. And he said to the Jews, "Behold your King!"
15But they cried out, "Away with *Him,* away with *Him!*
Crucify Him!"
Pilate said to them, "Shall I crucify your King?"
The chief priests answered, "We have no king but Caesar!"
16Then he delivered Him to them to be crucified. Then
they took Jesus and led *Him* away.[a]

19:3 [a]NU-Text reads *And they came up to Him and said.* *19:7* [a]NU-Text reads *the law.* *19:16* [a]NU-Text omits *and led Him away.*

The Crucifixion

17And He, bearing His cross, went out to a place called
the Place of a Skull, which is called in Hebrew, Golgotha, 18where they crucified Him, and two others with
Him, one on either side, and Jesus in the center. 19Now Pilate wrote a title and put *it* on the cross. And the writing
was:

JESUS OF NAZARETH, THE KING OF THE JEWS.

20Then many of the Jews read this title, for the place where
Jesus was crucified was near the city; and it was written in
Hebrew, Greek, *and* Latin.
21Therefore the chief priests of the Jews said to Pilate, "Do
not write, 'The King of the Jews,' but, 'He said, "I am the
King of the Jews." ' "
22Pilate answered, "What I have written, I have written."

19:23–24

23Then the soldiers, when they had
crucified Jesus, took His garments and
made four parts, to each soldier a part, and also the tunic.
Now the tunic was without seam, woven from the top in
one piece. 24They said therefore among themselves, "Let us
not tear it, but cast lots for it, whose it shall be," that the
Scripture might be fulfilled which says:

"They divided My garments among them,
And for My clothing they cast lots."[a]

Therefore the soldiers did these things.

19:25
see pg. 394

25Now there stood by the cross of Jesus His mother, and His mother's sister,
Mary the *wife* of Clopas, and Mary Magdalene. 26When
Jesus therefore saw His mother, and the disciple whom He
loved standing by, He said to His mother, "Woman, behold your son!" 27Then He said to the disciple, "Behold
your mother!" And from that hour that disciple took her to
his own *home*.

19:24 [a]Psalm 22:18

SEEING BEHIND POWER

CONSIDER THIS 19:10–11 **Pilate assumed that he had more power than Jesus because he had authority to condemn Him to death (v. 10). But Jesus knew that all power ultimately comes from God, even the power of the state (v. 11; Rom. 13:1). Indeed, one of the reasons Jesus could submit to the injustices of His trial was that He was submitting to God's will (18:11). Pilate and those under him were merely exercising limited authority. Meanwhile, God's purposes were being fulfilled.**

What sort of power do you have—in your work, at home, in your community? Do you recognize that your authority ultimately comes from God, and that you are ultimately accountable to Him for the use of that power?

Submission to authority is never easy. Yet Scripture challenges believers to subject themselves to whatever governments they live under. See "Governmental Authority," Rom. 13:2.

Success or Failure?

A CLOSER LOOK 19:23–24 *Would you consider your life a success if, at its conclusion, you had only the clothes on your back? That was the sum total of Jesus' wealth—and the soldiers took those away, leaving Him nothing (v. 24). For many of us, that kind of poverty would mark us as failures. "Jesus—A Homeless Man?" (Matt. 8:20) addresses the Lord's lack of earthly possessions and what that means for us today. As for the question* What is success? *see "Christians and Money," 1 Tim. 6:7–19.*

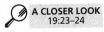

28After this, Jesus, knowing[a] that all things were now accomplished, that the Scripture might be fulfilled, said, "I
thirst!" 29Now a vessel full of sour wine was sitting there;
and they filled a sponge with sour wine, put *it* on hyssop,
and put *it* to His mouth. 30So when Jesus had received the
sour wine, He said, "It is finished!" And bowing His head,
He gave up His spirit.

31Therefore, because it was the Preparation *Day,* that the
bodies should not remain on the cross on the Sabbath (for
that Sabbath was a high day), the Jews asked Pilate that
their legs might be broken, and *that* they might be taken
away. 32Then the soldiers came and broke the legs of the
first and of the other who was crucified with Him. 33But
when they came to Jesus and saw that He was already dead,
they did not break His legs. 34But one of the soldiers
pierced His side with a spear, and immediately blood and
water came out. 35And he who has seen has testified, and
his testimony is true; and he knows that he is telling the
truth, so that you may believe. 36For these things were done
that the Scripture should be fulfilled, "Not *one* of His bones
shall be broken."[a] 37And again another Scripture says, "They
shall look on Him whom they pierced."[a]

19:28 [a]M-Text reads *seeing.* *19:36* [a]Exodus 12:46; Numbers 9:12; Psalm 34:20
19:37 [a]Zechariah 12:10

FOR YOUR INFO
19:25

THE WOMEN AROUND JESUS

Jesus went to His death attended by a loyal following of women who had stood by Him throughout His ministry (v. 25). Women played a major part in Jesus' life and work. It was a woman or women who . . .

- *Nurtured Him as He grew up (Luke 2:51)*
- *Traveled with Him and helped finance His ministry (Luke 8:1–3)*
- *Listened to Him teach (Luke 10:39)*
- *Were featured in His parables (Matt. 13:33; 24:41)*
- *Shared the good news that He was the Messiah (John 4:28–30)*
- *Offered hospitality to Him and His companions (Mark 1:29–31)*
- *Were treated by Him with respect and compassion (John 4:5–27; 11:32–33)*
- *Were healed by Him (Matt. 9:20–22; Luke 13:10–17)*

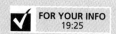

Jesus' Body Laid in Joseph's Tomb

19:38–42

38After this, Joseph of Arimathea, being
a disciple of Jesus, but secretly, for fear of
the Jews, asked Pilate that he might take away the body of
Jesus; and Pilate gave *him* permission. So he came and took
the body of Jesus. 39And Nicodemus, who at first came to
Jesus by night, also came, bringing a mixture of myrrh and
aloes, about a hundred pounds. 40Then they took the body
of Jesus, and bound it in strips of linen with the spices, as
the custom of the Jews is to bury. 41Now in the place where
He was crucified there was a garden, and in the garden a
new tomb in which no one had yet been laid. 42So there
they laid Jesus, because of the Jews' Preparation *Day,* for the
tomb was nearby.

Jesus' Funeral

A CLOSER LOOK 19:38–42

Jesus' body was treated as a rich man's corpse might be—which could be due to the fact that rich people buried Him. See "A Burial Fit for a King," Mark 15:42—16:1.

- *Were praised by Him for their faith (Mark 7:24–30)*
- *Were commended by Him for their generosity (Mark 12:41–44)*
- *Worshiped Him and prepared His body for burial before His crucifixion (Matt. 26:6–13)*
- *Stood by Him at the cross (Matt. 27:55; John 19:25)*
- *Assisted in His burial (Mark 16:1; Luke 23:55—24:1)*
- *First saw Him resurrected (John 20:16)*
- *Went to tell the rest of His followers that He was risen from the dead (John 20:18)* ◆

Meet some of the individual women who followed Jesus at Luke 8:1–3.

How were first-century women involved in the spread of the gospel? See "Women and the Growth of Christianity," Phil. 4:3.

HE WHO HAS SEEN . . . KNOWS THAT HE IS TELLING THE TRUTH, SO THAT YOU MAY BELIEVE. —John 19:35

Skeptics Welcome

CONSIDER THIS 20:24–31 **Have you ever struggled with doubts or troubling questions about Christ, the Christian faith, or the church? Do you sometimes feel that tough questions are not welcome or acceptable among believers?**

Thomas (v. 24) was a classic skeptic. Even though he had traveled with Jesus and learned from His teaching for at least three years, he needed time, evidence, and personal convincing before he would accept the resurrection (vv. 25–26). But Jesus responded to his doubt by inviting him to check it all out. He presented Himself for Thomas' inspection (vv. 26–27) and did not chide him for wanting to be certain.

Jesus seeks to honor the mind and heart of every seeker or doubter. He knows that easily developed loyalties often lack staying power. By contrast, many tenacious people who probe the corners of their doubts and fears finally reach the truth—and faith in the *truth* is what Christ desires. He even promised that the Spirit would aid those who seek it (16:12–16).

The encounter with Thomas welcomes every skeptic to bring his or her doubts to God. He delights in hearing our arguments and questions.

If you're a skeptic when it comes to issues of faith and God, you may find some friends in the Old Testament books of Habakkuk, Job, and Psalms.

CHAPTER 20

The Resurrection

20:1–31 1Now the first *day* of the week Mary
Magdalene went to the tomb early, while
it was still dark, and saw *that* the stone had been taken
away from the tomb. 2Then she ran and came to Simon Peter, and to the other disciple, whom Jesus loved, and said to
them, "They have taken away the Lord out of the tomb, and
we do not know where they have laid Him."
3Peter therefore went out, and the other disciple, and
were going to the tomb. 4So they both ran together, and the
other disciple outran Peter and came to the tomb first. 5And
he, stooping down and looking in, saw the linen cloths lying *there;* yet he did not go in. 6Then Simon Peter came, following him, and went into the tomb; and he saw the linen
cloths lying *there,* 7and the handkerchief that had been
around His head, not lying with the linen cloths, but folded
together in a place by itself. 8Then the other disciple, who
came to the tomb first, went in also; and he saw and believed. 9For as yet they did not know the Scripture, that He
must rise again from the dead. 10Then the disciples went
away again to their own homes.

Jesus Appears to Mary and the Disciples

11But Mary stood outside by the tomb weeping, and as
she wept she stooped down *and looked* into the tomb. 12And
she saw two angels in white sitting, one at the head and the
other at the feet, where the body of Jesus had lain. 13Then
they said to her, "Woman, why are you weeping?"
She said to them, "Because they have taken away my
Lord, and I do not know where they have laid Him."
14Now when she had said this, she turned around and
saw Jesus standing *there,* and did not know that it was Jesus. 15Jesus said to her, "Woman, why are you weeping?
Whom are you seeking?"
She, supposing Him to be the gardener, said to Him, "Sir,
if You have carried Him away, tell me where You have laid
Him, and I will take Him away."
16Jesus said to her, "Mary!"

The First Easter

A CLOSER LOOK 20:1–31 *John's account of that first Easter Sunday (vv. 1–31) is part of an important body of evidence pointing to the resurrection as a historical fact. See "Evidence for the Resurrection—Jesus' Appearances," Mark 16:1–8.*

She turned and said to Him,[a] "Rabboni!" (which is to say,
Teacher).
17Jesus said to her, "Do not cling to Me, for I have not yet
ascended to My Father; but go to My brethren and say to
them, 'I am ascending to My Father and your Father, and *to*
My God and your God.' "
18Mary Magdalene came and told the disciples that she
had seen the Lord,[a] and *that* He had spoken these things to
her.
19Then, the same day at evening, being the first *day* of the
week, when the doors were shut where the disciples were
assembled,[a] for fear of the Jews, Jesus came and stood in the
midst, and said to them, "Peace *be* with you." 20When He
had said this, He showed them *His* hands and His side.
Then the disciples were glad when they saw the Lord.
21So Jesus said to them again, "Peace to you! As the
Father has sent Me, I also send you." 22And when He had
said this, He breathed on *them,* and said to them, "Receive
the Holy Spirit. 23If you forgive the sins of any, they are
forgiven them; if you retain the *sins* of any, they are re-
tained."

20:24–31

24Now Thomas, called the Twin, one of
the twelve, was not with them when Je-
sus came. 25The other disciples therefore said to him, "We
have seen the Lord."
So he said to them, "Unless I see in His hands the print of
the nails, and put my finger into the print of the nails, and
put my hand into His side, I will not believe."
26And after eight days His disciples were again inside, and
Thomas with them. Jesus came, the doors being shut, and
stood in the midst, and said, "Peace to you!" 27Then He said
to Thomas, "Reach your finger here, and look at My hands;
and reach your hand *here,* and put *it* into My side. Do not
be unbelieving, but believing."
28And Thomas answered and said to Him, "My Lord and
my God!"
29Jesus said to him, "Thomas,[a] because you have seen Me,
you have believed. Blessed *are* those who have not seen and
yet have believed."

The Purpose of John's Gospel

20:30–31

30And truly Jesus did many other signs
in the presence of His disciples, which
are not written in this book; 31but these are written that you
may believe that Jesus is the Christ, the Son of God, and
that believing you may have life in His name.

20:16 [a]NU-Text adds *in Hebrew.* *20:18* [a]NU-Text reads *disciples, "I have seen the Lord," . . .* *20:19* [a]NU-Text omits *assembled.* *20:29* [a]NU-Text and M-Text omit *Thomas.*

The Purpose of John's Gospel

A CLOSER LOOK 20:30–31

Whereas Luke tells his reader in the opening verses of Luke (1:1–4) and Acts (1:1–3) what those books are about and why he wrote them, John hangs the key to his Gospel at the back door of his narrative (John 20:30–31). That was a common practice in ancient writings. What we would call a preface was often placed at the end of a book, where it summarized the writer's purpose.

John's "preface" tells us that he wanted his readers to find faith and life from his narrative. That's why he included seven sign miracles that show Jesus as the authentic, life-giving Son of God. See "The Seven Signs of John's Gospel" in the introduction to the book.

Forgiveness Abounds

CONSIDER THIS 21:15–23 **Do you ever feel hopeless regarding your faith? Do you doubt God's willingness to forgive you over and over again?**

Peter (v. 15) might easily have felt that way. He had risen to a position of leadership among Jesus' followers. He had even been given the "keys of the kingdom" (Matt. 16:19). And he had positioned himself as the defender of Christ when Roman soldiers came to arrest Him (John 18:10). But when he felt the heat of a national trial, conviction, and death, Peter denied three times that he even knew Christ (18:15–18, 25–27) and afterward disappeared. What Jesus had predicted about him came true (John 13:31–38).

So when Jesus engaged Peter in a conversation on the shore (21:15–23), Peter might easily have felt that he was already disqualified from further service for the Lord. After all, as we would say, three strikes and you're out. But Jesus reconnected with Peter and called him to genuine love and the continuation of His work.

Second and third chances are not often available in families, communities, or workplaces. All you have to do is fail once too often, and you're gone. But Christ offers tangible love and boundless forgiveness—to those who own up to their failures and repent (Luke 7:47). Can we offer anything less to our coworkers, families, and friends?

Abundant forgiveness is something that Scripture stresses over and over for followers of Christ. See Matt. 18:21–22; Luke 17:3; Gal. 6:1.

CHAPTER 21

A Great Catch of Fish

1After these things Jesus showed Himself again to the disciples at the Sea of Tiberias, and in this way He showed
Himself: 2Simon Peter, Thomas called the Twin, Nathanael of
Cana in Galilee, the *sons* of Zebedee, and two others of His
disciples were together. 3Simon Peter said to them, "I am
going fishing."

They said to him, "We are going with you also." They
went out and immediately[a] got into the boat, and that night
they caught nothing. 4But when the morning had now
come, Jesus stood on the shore; yet the disciples did not
know that it was Jesus. 5Then Jesus said to them, "Children,
have you any food?"

They answered Him, "No."

6And He said to them, "Cast the net on the right side of
the boat, and you will find *some.*" So they cast, and now
they were not able to draw it in because of the multitude of
fish.

7Therefore that disciple whom Jesus loved said to Peter,
"It is the Lord!" Now when Simon Peter heard that it was
the Lord, he put on *his* outer garment (for he had removed
it), and plunged into the sea. 8But the other disciples came
in the little boat (for they were not far from land, but about
two hundred cubits), dragging the net with fish. 9Then, as
soon as they had come to land, they saw a fire of coals
there, and fish laid on it, and bread. 10Jesus said to them,
"Bring some of the fish which you have just caught."

11Simon Peter went up and dragged the net to land, full
of large fish, one hundred and fifty-three; and although
there were so many, the net was not broken. 12Jesus said to
them, "Come *and* eat breakfast." Yet none of the disciples
dared ask Him, "Who are You?"—knowing that it was the
Lord. 13Jesus then came and took the bread and gave it to
them, and likewise the fish.

14This *is* now the third time Jesus showed Himself to His
disciples after He was raised from the dead.

Jesus Commissions Peter

21:15–23 15So when they had eaten breakfast, Jesus said to Simon Peter, "Simon, *son* of
Jonah,[a] do you love Me more than these?"

He said to Him, "Yes, Lord; You know that I love You."

He said to him, "Feed My lambs."

16He said to him again a second time, "Simon, *son* of
Jonah,[a] do you love Me?"

21:3 [a]NU-Text omits *immediately.* *21:15* [a]NU-Text reads *John.* *21:16* [a]NU-Text reads *John.*

He said to Him, "Yes, Lord; You know that I love You."
He said to him, "Tend My sheep."
17 He said to him the third time, "Simon, *son* of Jonah,[a] do
you love Me?" Peter was grieved because He said to him the
third time, "Do you love Me?"

21:15–17

And he said to Him, "Lord, You know
all things; You know that I love You."
Jesus said to him, "Feed My sheep. 18 Most assuredly, I say
to you, when you were younger, you girded yourself and
walked where you wished; but when you are old, you will
stretch out your hands, and another will gird you and carry
you where you do not wish." 19 This He spoke, signifying by
what death he would glorify God. And when He had spoken this, He said to him, "Follow Me."
20 Then Peter, turning around, saw the disciple whom Jesus loved following, who also had leaned on His breast at
the supper, and said, "Lord, who is the one who betrays
You?" 21 Peter, seeing him, said to Jesus, "But Lord, what
about this man?"
22 Jesus said to him, "If I will that he remain till I come,
what *is that* to you? You follow Me."
23 Then this saying went out among the brethren that this
disciple would not die. Yet Jesus did not say to him that he
would not die, but, "If I will that he remain till I come,
what *is that* to you?"
24 This is the disciple who testifies of these things, and
wrote these things; and we know that his testimony is true.
25 And there are also many other things that Jesus did,
which if they were written one by one, I suppose that even
the world itself could not contain the books that would be
written. Amen.

21:17 [a]NU-Text reads *John.*

"DO YOU LOVE ME? . . . FEED MY SHEEP."
—John 21:17

A CLOSER LOOK 21:15–17

The Meaning of Love

For a discussion of love and its actions see "Loving God Is More than Enthusiasm," 1 John 5:1–3.

Trade in Ancient Israel

While the strip of land that Israel inhabited had little in the way of proven natural resources, its location geographically made it a strategic corridor through which much of the military and economic traffic between Europe, Asia, and Africa had to pass. As a result, Israel became a major factor in international trade and commerce and a much-prized possession of ancient empires.

The major route through Palestine was the "**Way of the Sea**" (Is. 9:1), an ancient and important highway that ran along the coast to Joppa before turning inland in the north (see "Travel," Acts 13:4). Despite their proximity to the Mediterranean, the Hebrews never liked the sea and never had a navy. Solomon built a **merchant fleet** to sail from Ezion Geber, a port and refinery on the Red Sea, but many of the crews were Phoenician (1 Kin. 9:27), and the ships often sailed with King Hiram's Phoenician fleet (1 Kin. 10:22).

What the Israelites gave up on the water, however, they more than made up for on the land. **Grain**, especially **wheat and barley**, grew abundantly in the shallow valleys along the foothills of Judea and Samaria and became major export crops. **Figs, grapes, and olives** were plentiful in the hill country of Judea.

Hebron produced magnificent **grapes** which it turned into large quantities of **raisins and wine** for domestic consumption and export. **Olives** were used as food or crushed for **cooking oil**. **Olive oil** was also used in lamps or as a body rub, making it a major product of the region.

Palestine also boasted large herds of **sheep and goats** from which **wool and cloth** were produced. **Fish** were taken along the Mediterranean coast and especially at the Sea of Galilee. Along the northern section of the Mediterranean coast could be found the **murex shell**, used to make a very valuable dye called **purple** (see "The Trade in Purple," Acts 16:14). Extensive **textile industries**, using both wool and the **linen** made from **flax** grown on the coastal plain, produced the distinctive Tyrian **purple cloth** that was in great demand throughout the Mediterranean world.

The southern end of the Jordan Valley was the source of a large and profitable **salt-mining industry**. **Asphalt or bitumen** was easily obtained from the **tar pits** in the Dead Sea area. This substance was used as **caulk** in boats and rafts, as **mortar** in building, and for making **monuments and jewelry**. Israel exported few metals except during the reign of Solomon when **copper mines** in Sinai and the **iron mines** in Syria were worked commercially. However, **timber** from the Lebanon mountains was a major trade item.

Little **pottery** was exported, except for simple containers for wine and oil. This may have been because Israelite pottery was more practical and less artistic than Philistine and Greek pottery. However, a major industry was the manufacture of **millstones** from the high-quality **basalt stone** found in the volcanic hills of northern Gilead. These were shipped as far away as Spain, Italy, and North Africa.

Ezekiel 27:1–24 lists numerous products that were traded through the city of Tyre (see "Tyre and Sidon," Luke 6:17): **fir, cedar, oak, ivory, ebony, fine embroidered linen, blue and purple cloth and clothes, white wool, finished garments and multicolored apparel, saddlecloths for riding, caulk, silver, gold, iron, tin, lead, vessels of bronze, emeralds, corals, rubies, precious stones, wheat, millet, honey, the herb cassia, spices, cane, oil, balm, horses, mules, lambs, rams, goats, wine, luxury goods, and slaves.** ◆

The Extraordinary Acts of Ordinary People

Tradition has assigned this book the title, "The Acts of the Apostles," as if Peter, Paul, and a handful of other spiritual giants alone carried out the significant work of the early church. But actually the account shows that the Holy Spirit *and a whole lot of ordinary people* took the message of Christ "to the end of the earth."

This is one of the most timely books, because it illustrates what happens when everyday people, filled with God's power, apply their faith to everyday life and society.

Acts

Everyday people, filled with God's power, apply their faith.

C O N T E N T S

People Just Like You

A R T I C L E S

Christ Collides with Culture

Acts shows the gospel's impact on a variety of cultures and societies as it builds into a movement. It internationalizes across gender, ethnic, lingual, geographic, occupational, and economic boundaries in places as diverse as . . .

Jerusalem (1:12–26; 7:1–53; 8:1). **The Holy City witnesses the dramatic birth of the church but then gets left behind as the gospel spreads out across the Roman Empire.**

Samaria (8:5). **Samaritans experience ethnic separation until a minority preacher invites them to join the community of faith.**

Damascus (9:2). **A "political football" in the ancient world becomes an amplifier for the Christian message.**

Tarsus (11:25). **The empire's second most important center of learning and the headquarters of the tent manufacturing industry produces one of Christianity's most influential messengers.**

Antioch (13:1). **A multiethnic church in the third-largest city of the Roman Empire becomes headquarters for New Testament Christianity.**

Cyprus (13:4). **This Mediterranean island was a frequent port of call for early Christian travelers.**

Philippi (16:12). **A retirement community becomes the gateway to Christianity's march to the West.**

Athens (17:15). **Curious philosophers lend an ear to the new message about Christ—but prefer debate to commitment.**

Alexandria (18:24). **This center of education and scholarship is the source of the world's first popular translation of the Bible.**

Ephesus (19:10). **A shrine of first-century paganism goes haywire when the gospel upsets its economy.** ◆

The Second of Two Volumes

Acts is the second volume of a two-part account. Luke's Gospel narrates "all that Jesus began *both to do and teach" (Acts 1:1, emphasis added). In Acts, Luke continues the account of what happened after Christ returned to heaven and His followers spread out across the Roman Empire.*

However, the book ends abruptly, leading some scholars to suggest that Luke was working on or at least had planned a third installment. The message of Acts could have served two important purposes. First, it would have shown believers that rebellion and retaliation against Rome were not the way of Jesus. Instead, faithfulness to the message and lifestyle of the gospel was called for.

In addition, Luke may have written Acts (along with the Gospel of Luke) as a legal document for use in Paul's trial in Rome (see 22:11; 25:11; 28:30–31). His presentation of the Christian movement would have been evidence to show that believers posed no threat to the government. ◆

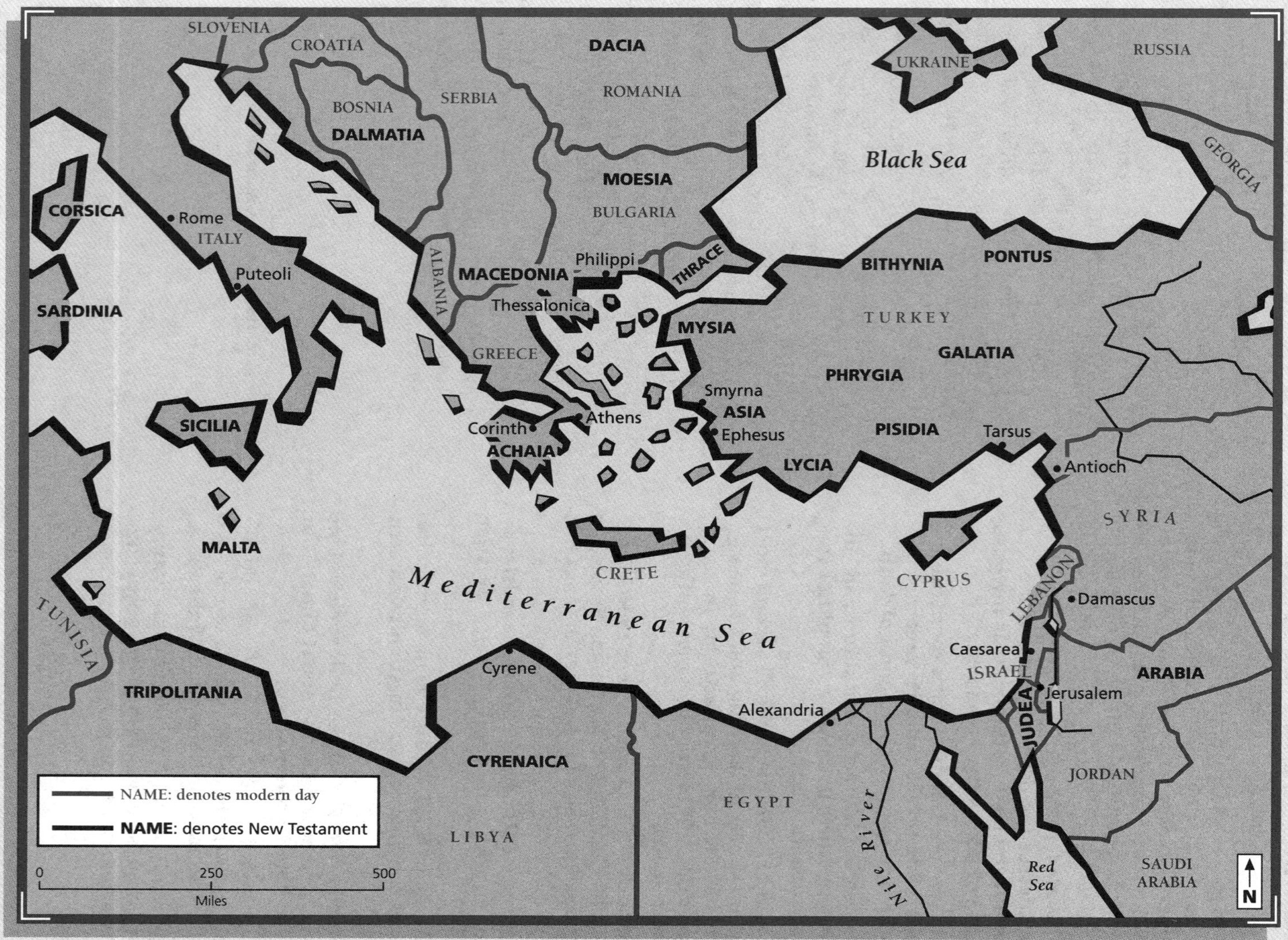

THE WORLD OF THE EARLY CHURCH

CHAPTER 1

The Second of Two Volumes

1 The former account I made, O Theophilus, of all that Jesus began both to do and teach, 2 until the day in which He
was taken up, after He through the Holy Spirit had given
commandments to the apostles whom He had chosen, 3 to
whom He also presented Himself alive after His suffering by
many infallible proofs, being seen by them during forty
days and speaking of the things pertaining to the kingdom
of God.

Jesus Ascends to Heaven

1:4 see pg. 406

4 And being assembled together with
them, He commanded them not to depart
from Jerusalem, but to wait for the Promise of the Father,
"which," *He said,* "you have heard from Me; 5 for John truly
baptized with water, but you shall be baptized with the
Holy Spirit not many days from now." 6 Therefore, when
they had come together, they asked Him, saying, "Lord, will
You at this time restore the kingdom to Israel?" 7 And He
said to them, "It is not for you to know times or seasons

1:8

which the Father has put in His own authority. 8 But you shall receive power
when the Holy Spirit has come upon you; and you shall be
witnesses to Me[a] in Jerusalem, and in all Judea and Samaria,
and to the end of the earth."

9 Now when He had spoken these things, while they
watched, He was taken up, and a cloud received Him out of
their sight. 10 And while they looked steadfastly toward
heaven as He went up, behold, two men stood by them in
white apparel, 11 who also said, "Men of Galilee, why do you
stand gazing up into heaven? This *same* Jesus, who was
taken up from you into heaven, will so come in like manner
as you saw Him go into heaven."

Waiting—and Choosing a New Apostle

1:12–26 see pg. 408

1:13

12 Then they returned to Jerusalem from
the mount called Olivet, which is near
Jerusalem, a Sabbath day's journey. 13 And
when they had entered, they went up
into the upper room where they were staying: Peter, James,
John, and Andrew; Philip and Thomas; Bartholomew and

(Bible text continued on page 407)

1:8 [a]NU-Text reads *My witnesses.*

The Apostles

A CLOSER LOOK 1:13

Who were these men who met with others in the upper room, waiting for the promise of the Spirit? See "The Twelve," Matt. 10:2.

POWER

CONSIDER THIS 1:8 **At the beginning of Acts, Jesus' followers appear confused and fearful. But by the end of the book they are well on their way to transforming the Roman world with the gospel. What accounts for this dramatic change? Verse 8 provides the answer: "You shall receive *power.*" But notice:**

(1) The power promised was not force or political authority. **Israel had enjoyed superiority under David and Solomon, but those days were a distant memory. Jesus was not indicating a revival of Jewish dominance. Instead, the word "power" means *ability* or *capacity.* Jesus promised that once the Holy Spirit came upon them, His followers would have a new ability.**

(2) The ability had more to do with being than doing. **The believers would "be witnesses," not just "do witnessing." Evangelism is a process, not just an event. It involves a total lifestyle, not just occasional efforts.**

(3) The power came from without, not from within. **The believers were not to manufacture their own ways of proclaiming the gospel, but to look for supernatural ability from the Spirit to make them effective in gospel presentation. The power came when the Holy Spirit arrived, not before.**

(4) The believers were to be witnesses to Christ, not to themselves. **They were to make disciples not to themselves but to the risen Lord (Matt. 28:18–20).**

CONSIDER THIS
1:4

Opportunities Look Like Barriers

A Grand Strategy

Speaking on the Mount of Olives at Bethany (vv. 4, 12), Jesus outlined a vision that would affect the whole world (v. 8). He began by pointing to the starting point of gospel penetration—Jerusalem, two miles to the west. From there the message would spread to the the surrounding region, Judea, and its estranged cousin to the north, Samaria. Eventually it would reach the entire world (though the crowd in Acts 1 probably understood "the end of the earth" as meaning the extent of the Roman Empire).

While Jesus' mandate sounds admirable today, it probably met with less than enthusiasm then. All of the places mentioned represented trouble and danger, both real and imagined. Jews—which almost all of Jesus' listeners were—were a small minority in the Roman Empire.

In fact, most of the apostles came from the Galilee region, north of Samaria. Galileans endured the scorn of their Jewish brothers from Judea, especially those from Jerusalem, who considered themselves more pure and orthodox, less contaminated by foreign influences. The lake region was derided as "Galilee of the Gentiles." Even the Galilean accent was chided.

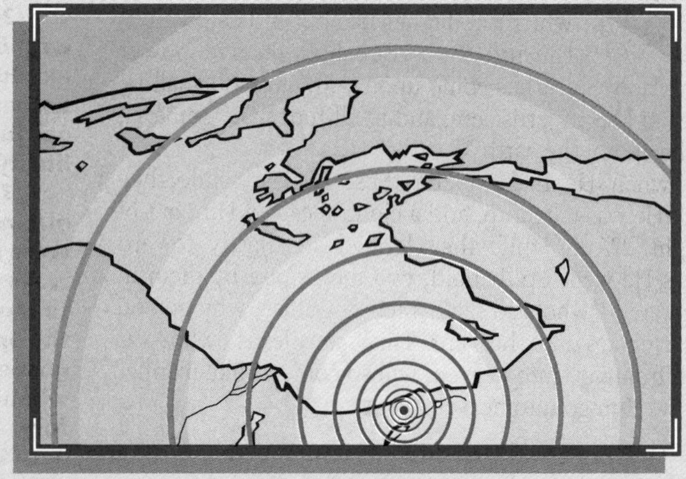

THE SPREAD OF THE GOSPEL

Jerusalem

Jerusalem was not the apostles' home, but it was Judea's key city, center of its religious, political, economic, and cultural life. Jesus' crucifixion had recently taken place there. Leaders still plotted to stamp out what was left of His movement.

Yet Christ told His followers to start their witness there, in the place of greatest hostility and intimidation. They must have wondered: Could He protect them from the inevitable opposition they would encounter? Would they suffer the same terrible end that He had?

Judea and Samaria

The relationship of Jerusalem to Judea was that of urban center to province, or of city to state. By penetrating the city, the gospel would also permeate the city's surroundings.

However, Jesus was careful to link Judea to Samaria, its cousin to the north. The two regions endured a bitter rivalry dating to the seventh century B.C., when the Assyrians colonized Samaria with non-Jews who intermarried with Israelites and thereby "corrupted" the race. Judea, which means "Jewish," considered itself the home of pure Judaism

(continued on next page)

Matthew; James *the son* of Alphaeus and Simon the Zealot;
1:14
and Judas *the son* of James. [14]These all
continued with one accord in prayer and
supplication,[a] with the women and Mary the mother of Jesus, and with His brothers.
[15]And in those days Peter stood up in the midst of the
disciples[a] (altogether the number of names was about a
hundred and twenty), and said, [16]"Men *and* brethren, this
Scripture had to be fulfilled, which the Holy Spirit spoke
before by the mouth of David concerning Judas, who became a guide to those who arrested Jesus; [17]for he was
numbered with us and obtained a part in this ministry."
[18](Now this man purchased a field with the wages of iniquity; and falling headlong, he burst open in the middle and
1:19 see pg. 409
all his entrails gushed out. [19]And it became known to all those dwelling in
Jerusalem; so that field is called in their own language, Akel
Dama, that is, Field of Blood.)
[20]"For it is written in the Book of Psalms:

'Let his dwelling place be desolate,
And let no one live in it';[a]

and,

'Let[b] another take his office.'[c]

[21]"Therefore, of these men who have accompanied us all
the time that the Lord Jesus went in and out among us,
[22]beginning from the baptism of John to that day when He

1:14 [a]NU-Text omits *and supplication.* *1:15* [a]NU-Text reads *brethren.* *1:20* [a]Psalm 69:25 [b]Psalm 109:8 [c]Greek *episkopen,* position of overseer

AN INCLUSIVE PRAYER MEETING

CONSIDER THIS 1:14 *The first prayer meeting of the new movement was notable for its inclusiveness, particularly of women (v. 14). Jewish religious gatherings separated men and women and assigned them different roles. By contrast, the apostles were joined by women who had followed Christ, including His mother. Together they formed a unified group of dedicated followers. God intended all of them to be His witnesses.*

(continued from previous page)

and viewed Samaria with contempt. As John points out in his account of the woman at the well at Sychar, "Jews have no dealings with Samaritans" (John 4:9).

In reaching Judea with the gospel, the Galilean apostles would have to surmount barriers of regional pride and cultural arrogance. But in moving into Samaria, they would have to overcome long-held ethnic prejudices.

The End of the Earth

Talk of the gospel spreading to "the end of the earth" signaled the eventual inclusion of Gentiles—the ultimate shock to the apostles. In their mind, the world was divided into Jews and non-Jews (Gentiles or "foreigners"). Extremely orthodox Jews would have nothing to do with Gentiles. Even Jews like the apostles, who had grown up alongside of Gentiles, avoided contact as much as possible.

For the gospel to spread to the Gentiles, then, Jesus' followers would have to overcome centuries of racial, religious, and cultural prejudice and break down well-established walls of separation. Eventually they did—but not without great conflict and tension (see "Ethnic Walls Break Down," Acts 10:44–45; and "'Sure You're Saved . . . Sort of,'" Acts 15:1–21). ◆

How strong was the antagonism between Jews and Samaritans? See "'Jews Have No Dealings with Samaritans,'" John 4:9.

was taken up from us, one of these must become a witness
with us of His resurrection."
23And they proposed two: Joseph called Barsabas, who
was surnamed Justus, and Matthias. 24And they prayed and
said, "You, O Lord, who know the hearts of all, show which
of these two You have chosen 25to take part in this ministry
and apostleship from which Judas by transgression fell, that
he might go to his own place." 26And they cast their lots,
and the lot fell on Matthias. And he was numbered with the
eleven apostles.

CHAPTER 2

The Day of Pentecost

2:1 see pg. 410

1When the Day of Pentecost had fully
come, they were all with one accord[a] in
one place. 2And suddenly there came a sound from heaven,
as of a rushing mighty wind, and it filled the whole house
where they were sitting. 3Then there appeared to them divided tongues, as of fire, and *one* sat upon each of them.
4And they were all filled with the Holy Spirit and began to

2:1 [a]NU-Text reads *together.*

CONSIDER THIS
1:12–26

JERUSALEM—MERELY THE BEGINNING

The first headquarters of the church was Jerusalem, but the city's supremacy was short-lived. By the time Paul returned there on his way to Rome (Acts 21:15—23:31), only a shadow remained of the Pentecostal euphoria that characterized the first believers. Three factors could account for this:

1. Jerusalem was not the leaders' home. *Home for most of Jesus' followers was the Galilee region to the north (see "Opportunities Look Like Barriers," 1:4; and "The Twelve," Matt. 10:2). While they set up headquarters in Jerusalem, they probably never viewed it with the same loyalty as their hometowns of Cana, Bethsaida, or Capernaum. In fact, the city and its leaders never ceased to oppose their efforts, beginning with the arrest of Peter and John (Acts 4:1–3) and climaxing with the arrest of Paul (21:30).*

2. Christianity in Jerusalem excluded rather than included. *Following Pentecost, the new believers enjoyed an unusual sense of community, sharing, and fellowship. But as Samaritans and Gentiles responded to the gospel, the Jewish believers struggled to accept them (10:1–48; 15:1–31).*

Jerusalem remained the center of a Judaistic Christianity that assumed Gentiles had to become like Jews to be

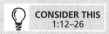

speak with other tongues, as the Spirit gave them utterance.
2:5 see pg. 410
5And there were dwelling in Jerusalem
Jews, devout men, from every nation un-
der heaven. 6And when this sound occurred, the multitude
came together, and were confused, because everyone heard
them speak in his own language. 7Then they were all
amazed and marveled, saying to one another, "Look, are not
2:8–11 see pg. 412
all these who speak Galileans? 8And how
is it that we hear, each in our own language in which we were born? 9Parthians and Medes and
Elamites, those dwelling in Mesopotamia, Judea and Cappadocia, Pontus and Asia, 10Phrygia and Pamphylia, Egypt
and the parts of Libya adjoining Cyrene, visitors from
Rome, both Jews and proselytes, 11Cretans and Arabs—we
hear them speaking in our own tongues the wonderful
works of God." 12So they were all amazed and perplexed,
saying to one another, "Whatever could this mean?"
13Others mocking said, "They are full of new wine."

Peter Speaks and Many Respond

14But Peter, standing up with the eleven, raised his voice
and said to them, "Men of Judea and all who dwell in

◆ ◆ ◆ ◆ ◆ ◆ ◆ ◆ ◆ ◆ ◆ ◆ ◆ ◆ ◆

completely acceptable to God. As a result, the influence of the Jerusalem church waned as more and more Gentiles came to faith. Eventually Antioch eclipsed Jerusalem as the capital of New Testament Christianity (see "Antioch," 13:1).

3. The gospel was meant to be spread. *As Jesus' words predicted (1:8), the gospel would reach the ends of the earth. The spark that ignited in Galilee (Luke 4:14–22) would eventually explode in Jerusalem, home of Israel's religion and politics. Jerusalem would act as a springboard to launch the good news throughout the Mediterranean and eventually to Rome and beyond. Then the church would survive long after Jerusalem's destruction by the Romans in* A.D. *70 (see "Jerusalem Surrounded," Luke 21:20).* ◆

For an introduction to the Holy City, see "Jerusalem," Matt. 23:37. Even though it waned as a center of Christian activity, Jerusalem figured prominently in the events of Acts. See "Stephen's New View of History," Acts 7:1–53, and "Rome or Bust," Acts 19:21.

FIELD OF BLOOD

FOR YOUR INFO 1:19

The tragic end of Judas Iscariot, who betrayed Jesus (see Matt. 26:14), was memorialized in the purchase of a plot of ground for a cemetery, appropriately named the Field of Blood (Acts 1:19).

Matthew informs us that the field was purchased by the chief priests with the 30 pieces of silver which they had paid Judas for betraying Jesus. Remorseful at having betrayed innocent blood, Judas flung the money onto the floor of the temple and went out and hanged himself. The priests would not put the coins in the temple treasury because they were tainted with "the price of blood." So they used them instead to buy the potter's field in which to bury foreigners and strangers (Matt. 27:3–10).

As Luke words it in Acts 1:18, Judas "purchased a field with the wages of iniquity." Matthew's account shows that Judas did not personally buy the field; he "bought" it only in the sense that his own money was used by the chief priests to purchase the land.

Tradition holds that this plot of ground is on the Hill of Evil Counsel, a level spot overlooking the Valley of Hinnom south of Jerusalem.

Jerusalem, let this be known to you, and heed my words.
15For these are not drunk, as you suppose, since it is *only*
the third hour of the day. 16But this is what was spoken by
the prophet Joel:

17 'And it shall come to pass in the last days, says God,
That I will pour out of My Spirit on all flesh;
Your sons and your daughters shall prophesy,
Your young men shall see visions,
Your old men shall dream dreams.
18 And on My menservants and on My maidservants
I will pour out My Spirit in those days;
And they shall prophesy.
19 I will show wonders in heaven above
And signs in the earth beneath:
Blood and fire and vapor of smoke.
20 The sun shall be turned into darkness,
And the moon into blood,
Before the coming of the great and awesome day of the
LORD.
21 And it shall come to pass
That whoever calls on the name of the LORD
Shall be saved.'[a]

22"Men of Israel, hear these words: Jesus of Nazareth, a
Man attested by God to you by miracles, wonders, and

2:21 [a]Joel 2:28–32

OFF TO A GOOD START

FOR YOUR INFO 2:1 **The Spirit's timing for the launch of the church could not have been better. The drama that unfolds in Acts 2–3 coincides perfectly with the meaning and significance of the Feast of Weeks (or Pentecost) then underway in Jerusalem. The diverse crowds that packed the city to celebrate the festival became a ready audience for the events that took place.**

There were three great annual feasts in Jewish life (see "Jewish Feasts," Luke 2:42): the Feast of Unleavened Bread (or Passover), the Feast of Weeks (or Harvest, or Pentecost), and the Feast of Tabernacles (or Booths; see "'We Interrupt This Program . . . ,'" John 7:37). On all three occasions, thousands of Jews made pilgrimages to the temple at Jerusalem.

The Feast of Weeks, or Pentecost, took its name from the fact that it occurred seven weeks, or fifty days, after Passover. Each family offered thanks to God for the just-completed grain harvest by giving the firstfruits of its produce to the temple priests. Pentecost was a day of celebration; no work was carried out. Everyone was expected to participate—husbands and wives, parents and children, servants, priests, widows, orphans, even visitors and foreigners. The days of slavery in Egypt were recalled, and the people were reminded to observe God's Law.

On this day, then, God's Spirit chose to descend on the 120 believers gathered in the upper room. The event followed by fifty days the death of Jesus on the cross and turned into a spiritual harvest: 3,000 people responded to Peter's proclamation of the gospel (Acts 3:41), becoming the firstfruits of the church.

PLURALISM AT PENTECOST

CONSIDER THIS 2:5 *What happened at Pentecost began to reverse what happened at ancient Babel (Gen. 11:1–9). At Babel God confused the languages of the peoples and dispersed the nations abroad in order to stop their evil from multiplying. At Pentecost He brought Jews from many nations together in Jerusalem. Once again there was confusion (v. 6), but this time it came from the fact that everyone heard ordinary men and women, filled with the Holy Spirit, speaking in the various languages of the ancient world. Then an international, multilingual church was born when the onlookers heard the gospel preached and believed it.*

signs which God did through Him in your midst, as you
yourselves also know— 23Him, being delivered by the determined purpose and foreknowledge of God, you have
taken[a] by lawless hands, have crucified, and put to death;
24whom God raised up, having loosed the pains of death,
because it was not possible that He should be held by it.
25For David says concerning Him:

'I foresaw the LORD always before my face,
For He is at my right hand, that I may not be shaken.
26 Therefore my heart rejoiced, and my tongue was glad;
Moreover my flesh also will rest in hope.
27 For You will not leave my soul in Hades,
Nor will You allow Your Holy One to see corruption.
28 You have made known to me the ways of life;
You will make me full of joy in Your presence.'[a]

29"Men *and* brethren, let *me* speak freely to you of the patriarch David, that he is both dead and buried, and his
tomb is with us to this day. 30Therefore, being a prophet,
and knowing that God had sworn with an oath to him that
of the fruit of his body, according to the flesh, He would
raise up the Christ to sit on his throne,[a] 31he, foreseeing
this, spoke concerning the resurrection of the Christ, that
His soul was not left in Hades, nor did His flesh see corruption. 32This Jesus God has raised up, of which we are all
witnesses. 33Therefore being exalted to the right hand of
God, and having received from the Father the promise of
the Holy Spirit, He poured out this which you now see and
hear.
34"For David did not ascend into the heavens, but he says
himself:

'The LORD said to my Lord,
"Sit at My right hand,
35 Till I make Your enemies Your footstool." '[a]

36"Therefore let all the house of Israel know assuredly that
God has made this Jesus, whom you crucified, both Lord
and Christ."

2:37–38

37Now when they heard *this,* they were
cut to the heart, and said to Peter and the
rest of the apostles, "Men *and* brethren, what shall we do?"
38Then Peter said to them, "Repent, and let every one of
you be baptized in the name of Jesus Christ for the remission of sins; and you shall receive the gift of the Holy Spirit.

(Bible text continued on page 413)

2:23 [a]NU-Text omits *have taken.* *2:28* [a]Psalm 16:8–11 *2:30* [a]NU-Text omits *according to the flesh, He would raise up the Christ* and completes the verse with *He would seat one on his throne.* *2:35* [a]Psalm 110:1

CARROTS, NOT STICKS

CONSIDER THIS
2:37–38

As believers, we are called to proclaim the message of Christ to unbelievers in the best way we know how, being faithful to the truth. That's really all that Peter did at Pentecost (vv. 14–36), but his speech produced dramatic results: the small band of Christ's followers added 3,000 believers that day (v. 41).

In the same way, each of us needs to speak up as best we can when the opportunity presents itself. What we say will reflect our understanding of the faith at the time. We may not sound as impressive as Peter or a minister or some other believer. But at least our message will be authentic.

Notice that Peter did not call for an immediate response. Only after God's Spirit had "cut to the heart" those in the audience and they asked for help (v. 37) did he explain what they ought to do (v. 38).

In the same way we need to offer the "carrot" of truth to others—the facts of the gospel and our experience of it—and let the Holy Spirit wield the "stick" of conviction. We should strive for impact and understanding before pressing for a decision. That might take weeks or years, or just moments. But we need the sensitive timing of a midwife as we assist in the spiritual birthing process.

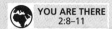

A SURPRISING FIRST FULFILLMENT OF ACTS 1:8

The harvest feast of Pentecost brought together thousands of Jews (including converts to Judaism) from all over the Roman Empire. This made it possible to bring about at least a partial fulfillment of the promise of Acts 1:8—that the gospel would spread "to the end of the earth"—much sooner than the apostles expected.

The 3,000 who converted following Peter's Pentecost speech (2:14–41) stayed for a while in Jerusalem but eventually returned to their homelands, taking their newfound faith with them.

NATIONS OF PENTECOST

Parthia: Included parts of modern-day Iran, Iraq, and Turkey. Part of the Persian Empire conquered by the Greeks in 330 B.C., it broke away in 250 B.C. and built an empire of its own. Even the Romans could not conquer it, and it became the other first-century superpower.

Media: A mountainous region southwest of Parthia. It aligned either with Assyria or Babylon to suit its interests. Like the Parthians, Medes were Indo-European peoples whose religion was the dualistic Zoroastrianism.

Elam: Home to an ancient people who struggled with the Babylonians, Assyrians, and Persians for control of Mesopotamia. After defeating the Northern Kingdom of Israel in 722 B.C., the Assyrians deported some Elamites to Samaria, and some Samaritan Jews to Elam.

Mesopotamia: The land between the Tigris and Euphrates Rivers in modern-day Iraq, homeland of the Jewish patriarch Abram (Abraham) and later of the feared Babylonians.

Judea: The Graeco-Roman name for the homeland of the Jews.

Cappadocia: A large Roman province in eastern Asia Minor, now Turkey.

Pontus: A Roman province in northern Asia Minor on the Black Sea coast. A mountainous region, it produced olives, grain, and timber.

Asia: A strategic Roman province that included the cities of Ephesus, Smyrna, and Pergamos, which vied for domination of the region. Its wealth and culture were legendary, and positions in its government were among the most prized in all the Roman Empire.

(continued on next page)

39For the promise is to you and to your children, and to all who are afar off, as many as the Lord our God will call."

Early Organization

40And with many other words he testified and exhorted them, saying, "Be saved from this perverse generation." 41Then those who gladly[a] received his word were baptized; and that day about three thousand souls were added *to them.* 42And they continued steadfastly in the apostles' doctrine and fellowship, in the breaking of bread, and in prayers. 43Then fear came upon every soul, and many wonders and signs were done through the apostles. 44Now all who believed were together, and had all things in common, 45and sold their possessions and goods, and divided them among all, as anyone had need.

2:42–47 see pg. 415

46So continuing daily with one accord in the temple, and breaking bread from house to house, they ate their food with gladness and simplicity of heart, 47praising God and having favor with all the people. And the Lord added to the church[a] daily those who were being saved.

2:46–47 see pg. 414

CHAPTER 3

Peter Heals a Lame Man

3:1 see pg. 416

1Now Peter and John went up together to the temple at the hour of prayer, the ninth *hour.* 2And a certain man lame from his mother's womb was carried, whom they laid daily at the gate of the temple which is called Beautiful, to ask alms from those who entered the temple; 3who, seeing Peter and John about to go into the temple, asked for alms. 4And fixing his eyes on him, with John, Peter said, "Look at us." 5So he gave them his attention, expecting to receive something from them. 6Then Peter said, "Silver and gold I do not have, but what I do have I give you: In the name of Jesus Christ of Nazareth, rise up and walk." 7And he took him by the right hand and lifted *him* up, and immediately his feet and ankle bones received strength. 8So he, leaping up, stood and walked and entered the temple with them—walking, leaping, and praising God. 9And all the people saw him walking and praising God. 10Then they knew that it was he who sat begging alms at the Beautiful Gate of the temple; and they were filled with wonder and amazement at what had happened to him.

2:41 [a]NU-Text omits *gladly.* *2:47* [a]NU-Text omits *to the church.*

(continued from previous page)

Phrygia: A large, mountainous, inland region divided by the Romans between Galatia in the east and Asia in the west.

Pamphylia: The southern coast of Asia Minor. Its name means "a region of every tribe."

Egypt: Homeland of the ancient north African empire. By the time of Christ an estimated one million Jews lived in Alexandria (Hebrews dispersed from Palestine after the fall of Israel to the Assyrians in 722 B.C. and of Judah to the Babylonians in 597–581 B.C.).

Libya and Cyrene: The same region as modern-day Libya on the northern coast of Africa. Founded by the Greeks, Cyrene was established by the Romans as the provincial capital of Libya. In New Testament times it was an intellectual center with a large Jewish population.

Rome: Capital of the empire, and therefore the symbolic center of Luke's world. ◆

Peter Speaks Again

11Now as the lame man who was healed held on to Peter
and John, all the people ran together to them in the porch
3:12 see pg. 417
which is called Solomon's, greatly
amazed. 12So when Peter saw *it,* he responded to the people: "Men of Israel, why do you marvel
at this? Or why look so intently at us, as though by our own
power or godliness we had made this man walk? 13The God
of Abraham, Isaac, and Jacob, the God of our fathers, glorified His Servant Jesus, whom you delivered up and denied
in the presence of Pilate, when he was determined to let

CONSIDER THIS
2:46–47

Reconnecting Sunday and Monday

*Does the faith you celebrate on Sunday sometimes feel disconnected from the "real world" you face on Monday? The newly formed group of believers (vv. 46–47) closed that gap by practicing a rhythm of two kinds of experiences—*gathering *for growth and worship balanced by* scattering *into the world for work and to communicate the gospel to non-Christian friends and coworkers.*

Notice this rhythm of gathering for refinement and scattering for engagement as we see it progressing in Acts 4–9:

Believers Gathered for Refinement	Believers Scattered for Engagement
Donate money from asset sales to care for their poor (4:36–37).	
Discipline those who practice deceit in giving to the poor (5:1–11).	
	Meet in public to care for the sick; many are converted (5:12–21).
	Are arrested and tried on charges of civil disobedience (5:22–42).
	Go to the Samaritans with the gospel; challenge Simon, a leading sorcerer (8:3–13).
Meet to discuss and confirm Samaritan work (8:14–17).	
Discipline a new believer for misuse of Holy Spirit (8:18–24).	
	Take the gospel to an Ethiopian government official on a highway (8:26–40).
Confirm and nurture the new faith of Saul (9:10–22).	
Accept Saul into the fellowship, even though he had persecuted them (9:26–28).	

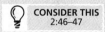

Him go. 14But you denied the Holy One and the Just, and
asked for a murderer to be granted to you, 15and killed the
Prince of life, whom God raised from the dead, of which we
are witnesses. 16And His name, through faith in His name,
has made this man strong, whom you see and know. Yes,
the faith which *comes* through Him has given him this perfect soundness in the presence of you all.

17"Yet now, brethren, I know that you did *it* in ignorance,
as *did* also your rulers. 18But those things which God foretold by the mouth of all His prophets, that the Christ would
suffer, He has thus fulfilled. 19Repent therefore and be con-

◆ ◆ ◆ ◆ ◆ ◆ ◆ ◆ ◆ ◆ ◆ ◆ ◆ ◆ ◆

This pattern continues throughout Acts as the narrative moves back and forth between internal meetings of the church and external encounters with the surrounding culture. The account includes more than twenty refinement narratives and more than fifty engagement narratives. We clearly see a connection between the development of faith and its delivery.

Believers today could help to reconnect Sundays and Mondays by moving through this same cycle. The gathering process might include worship services, praise gatherings, prayer meetings, fellowship over meals, and teaching for growth. Such encounters prepare us for Monday's world of work and responsibility, filled as it often is with pressures, conflicts, and opportunities to engage unbelievers as they inspect or perhaps even oppose our faith.

Rather than being disconnected, these two worlds need to be vitally connected. The refinement of our faith as we gather for growth supplies much-needed strength as we engage the world Monday through Saturday. On the other hand, the realities of life outside the fellowship can alert us to areas where we need to grow in faith.

Are you reconnecting Sunday and Monday by practicing this rhythm? Is there a link between the resources of your faith community and the demands of your world? Are there ways to improve the connections? ◆

NEW LIFE MEANS NEW LIFESTYLES

CONSIDER THIS 2:42–47 *The converts from Peter's sermon remained in Jerusalem for a while, perhaps as guests of the handful of local believers. They celebrated their new life in Christ in five important ways (vv. 42–47):*

(1) they listened to the apostles' teaching;
(2) they practiced community by sharing meals;
(3) they worshiped God with praise;
(4) they demonstrated lifestyle changes by sharing their possessions with each other; and
(5) they cared for each others' needs.

These essential behaviors of the first believers form a challenging summary of behaviors that should characterize believers today.

verted, that your sins may be blotted out, so that times of
refreshing may come from the presence of the Lord, [20]and
that He may send Jesus Christ, who was preached to you
before,[a] [21]whom heaven must receive until the times of
restoration of all things, which God has spoken by the
mouth of all His holy prophets since the world began. [22]For
Moses truly said to the fathers, 'The LORD your God will
raise up for you a Prophet like me from your brethren. Him
you shall hear in all things, whatever He says to you. [23]And
it shall be *that* every soul who will not hear that Prophet
shall be utterly destroyed from among the people.'[a] [24]Yes,
and all the prophets, from Samuel and those who follow, as

3:20 [a]NU-Text and M-Text read *Christ Jesus, who was ordained for you before.*
3:23 [a]Deuteronomy 18:15, 18, 19

CONSIDER THIS
3:1

JESUS—THE NAME YOU CAN TRUST

Using none of the sophisticated marketing strategies of today's corporate giants, a small-town carpenter's name managed to become a byword in the first-century world. Why? Because there was power *in His name.*

Jesus means "Jehovah [God] is salvation" or "Jehovah delivers." Early Christians discovered just how true to His name Jesus was. In Acts 3–4, Luke records a sequence of events resembling a five-act drama, in which the name of Jesus features prominently.

THE FIVE-ACT DRAMA OF ACTS 3–4

Act One, 3:1–10	The lame man healed at the gate.	The name of Jesus healed him (3:6).
Act Two, 3:11–26	Peter's sermon identifies Jesus with the "I Am" of Israel's history. Jesus is Lord!	Faith in the name of Jesus brings salvation (3:16, 26).
Act Three, 4:1–12	Peter and John imprisoned and tried.	No other name but Jesus can be called on to bring salvation to all the earth (4:12).
Act Four, 4:13–22	Peter and John warned and released.	Though opposed, the name of Jesus rings true—"God delivers" (4:18, 21).
Act Five, 4:23–37	The church responds by worshiping Jesus, caring for each other, and witnessing about Christ.	Signs and wonders continue to be done through the name of Jesus (4:30).

How is the name "Jesus" used in today's workplace? Probably not in the same way as recorded here! Why might that be? Is it possible that Christians today have lost confidence in the power behind Jesus' name? ◆

A related name, "Christian," was used to malign early believers. See "The First 'Christians,'" Acts 11:26.

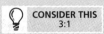

many as have spoken, have also foretold[a] these days. 25You
are sons of the prophets, and of the covenant which God
made with our fathers, saying to Abraham, 'And in your
seed all the families of the earth shall be blessed.'[a] 26To you
first, God, having raised up His Servant Jesus, sent Him to
bless you, in turning away every one *of you* from your iniquities."

CHAPTER 4

Peter and John Arrested; More Respond

1Now as they spoke to the people, the priests, the captain
of the temple, and the Sadducees came upon them, 2being
greatly disturbed that they taught the people and preached
in Jesus the resurrection from the dead. 3And they laid
hands on them, and put *them* in custody until the next day,
for it was already evening. 4However, many of those who
heard the word believed; and the number of the men came
to be about five thousand.

Peter and John Face the Council

4:5

5And it came to pass, on the next day,
that their rulers, elders, and scribes, 6as
well as Annas the high priest, Caiaphas, John, and Alexander, and as many as were of the family of the high priest,
were gathered together at Jerusalem. 7And when they had
set them in the midst, they asked, "By what power or by
what name have you done this?"
8Then Peter, filled with the Holy Spirit, said to them,
"Rulers of the people and elders of Israel: 9If we this day are
judged for a good deed *done* to a helpless man, by what
means he has been made well, 10let it be known to you all,
and to all the people of Israel, that by the name of Jesus
Christ of Nazareth, whom you crucified, whom God raised
from the dead, by Him this man stands here before you
whole. 11This is the 'stone which was rejected by you
builders, which has become the chief
cornerstone.'[a] 12Nor is there salvation in
any other, for there is no other name under heaven given
among men by which we must be saved."

4:12
see pg. 418

(Bible text continued on page 419)

3:24 [a]NU-Text and M-Text read *proclaimed.* *3:25* [a]Genesis 22:18; 26:4; 28:14
4:11 [a]Psalm 118:22

Caiaphas

A CLOSER LOOK 4:5 *This same Caiaphas had once himself been the high priest of Israel, making him the most influential member of the Jewish council. He figured prominently in the trial of Jesus. See Matt. 26:3.*

Seizing the Opportunity

CONSIDER THIS 3:12 **When God is at work, people will marvel. The people in Jerusalem marveled at the healing of a lame man (v. 11). People today may be just as surprised by social or personal changes that God brings about. Often that makes them ready and even eager to hear believers as we explain the message of Christ. Curiosity opens an opportunity for us to speak up. We can help "open the eyes" of others to see God's hand behind what they have observed, the way Peter did (3:12–26).**

Of course, like Peter and John we may also trigger a hostile reaction from some (4:1–4). Our explanation might confront the anger or confusion that often accompanies conviction—the realization that one has offended God. But belonging to God means that we speak the truth anyway, no matter what the outcome.

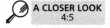

CONSIDER THIS
4:12

MYTH #4

10 MYTHS ABOUT CHRISTIANITY

MYTH: IT DOESN'T MATTER WHAT YOU BELIEVE, ALL RELIGIONS ARE BASICALLY THE SAME

Many people today accept a number of myths about Christianity, with the result that they never respond to Jesus as He really is. This is one of ten articles that speak to some of those misconceptions. For a list of all ten, see 1 Tim. 1:3–4.

Peter describes the exclusiveness of Christianity by claiming that "there is no other name" that can save (v. 12). That doesn't play well in our pluralistic society where tolerance is a chief virtue. Indeed, many people feel that an exclusive commitment to any one religious system is pointless, since they assume that all religions are basically the same.

Most of us would never apply such reasoning to any other realm of life. Imagine a student saying, "It doesn't matter what answer I give in algebra, Latin, history, or geography. They all come to the same thing in the end."

So why do so many people apply the same shaky reasoning to religion? Perhaps one motivation is the strong desire to see everyone getting along in our global village. Christianity, Islam, Hinduism, Buddhism—all kinds of faiths drive the peoples of the world. If one system claims exclusivity, it's bound to create hostility among the others. But the fact is, religion is already one of the greatest sources there is of national and international conflicts—which seems incredibly odd if "all religions are basically the same." Obviously they are not.

Another reason why people accept this myth is because they think that faith itself is what really matters. One can believe in anything, they reason, as long as one believes in something. But they misunderstand faith. Faith is only as good as the object in which it is placed. Like a rope, it matters enormously what one attaches it to. One can believe in anything—but not just anything will reward one's commitment. Only what is true.

A third reason why people adopt the all-religions-are-the-same line of thinking is that it helps them avoid a decision. If all religions are the same, they don't have to choose any one. In other words, they can avoid religion altogether. How convenient!

But they are committing themselves to a deception. The assumption that we are all looking for God and will find Him in the end is false both to the nature of people and to the nature of God. In the first place, we are not all looking for God. Many people today have absolutely no interest in God or religion. They are not atheists, just committed secularists. Moreover, there are far more motives behind the practice of religion than a search or desire for God. Political power, tradition, standing in the community, a desire for increased fertility or wealth, even sexual gratification are among the forces driving countless people back to their centers of worship. Looking for God? Hardly.

Nor is there any guarantee that people will find Him in the end. If there is a God at all, He obviously lives in realms beyond us. Otherwise all of us would already know Him from birth. But the religions of the world, including today's New Age systems, recognize that people do not naturally and instinctively know God, which is why they promise their followers access to Him. The problem is, they offer competing and often conflicting versions of who God is and how we can know Him.

Christianity is unique in that it claims that instead of people gaining access to God, God has made Himself known to people. His ultimate self-disclosure was in Jesus Christ. No longer is He the unknown God. Although

(continued on next page)

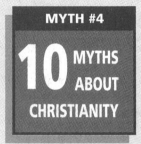

4:13
[13]Now when they saw the boldness of
Peter and John, and perceived that they
were uneducated and untrained men, they marveled. And
they realized that they had been with Jesus. [14]And seeing
the man who had been healed standing with them, they
4:15
could say nothing against it. [15]But when
they had commanded them to go aside
out of the council, they conferred among themselves, [16]say-
ing, "What shall we do to these men? For, indeed, that a
notable miracle has been done through them *is* evident to
all who dwell in Jerusalem, and we cannot deny *it.* [17]But so
that it spreads no further among the people, let us severely
threaten them, that from now on they speak to no man in
this name."

[18]So they called them and commanded them not to speak
at all nor teach in the name of Jesus. [19]But Peter and John
answered and said to them, "Whether it is right in the sight
of God to listen to you more than to God, you judge. [20]For
we cannot but speak the things which we have seen and
heard." [21]So when they had further threatened them, they
let them go, finding no way of punishing them, because of
the people, since they all glorified God for what had been
done. [22]For the man was over forty years old on whom this
miracle of healing had been performed.

Peter and John Released

[23]And being let go, they went to their own *companions*
and reported all that the chief priests and elders had said to
them. [24]So when they heard that, they raised their voice to
God with one accord and said: "Lord, You *are* God, who
made heaven and earth and the sea, and all that is in them,
[25]who by the mouth of Your servant David[a] have said:

'Why did the nations rage,
And the people plot vain things?
26 The kings of the earth took their stand,
And the rulers were gathered together
Against the LORD and against His Christ.'[a]

[27]"For truly against Your holy Servant Jesus, whom You
anointed, both Herod and Pontius Pilate, with the Gentiles
and the people of Israel, were gathered together [28]to do

4:25 [a]NU-Text reads *who through the Holy Spirit, by the mouth of our father, Your servant David.* *4:26* [a]Psalm 2:1, 2

The Council

A CLOSER LOOK 4:15 *In arguing their case before the council (v. 15), Peter and John were standing before the supreme court of the Jews. See "Stephen's Trial and Murder," Acts 6:12.*

MYTH #4 10 MYTHS ABOUT CHRISTIANITY

(continued from previous page)

"no one has seen God at any time," Jesus "has declared Him" (John 1:18).

So does Christianity claim that all other religions are totally wrong? Of course not. Most have some measure of truth in them. Islam and Judaism in particular have a great deal of truth in them. They are like candles that bring a bit of light into a very dark world. Nevertheless, all religions pale into insignificance at the dawn that has come with Christ. He fulfills the hopes, the aspirations, the virtues, and the insights of whatever is true and good in all faiths. ◆

QUOTE UNQUOTE

CONSIDER THIS 4:13 *The council marveled that untrained "laymen" like Peter and John could speak with such boldness and authority (v. 13). Yet the same thing happens today:*

Most words of a clergyman are minimized [by non-clergy] simply because he is supposed to say them . . . . The contrast in effect is often enormous when a layman's remarks are taken seriously, even though he says practically the same words. His words are given full weight, not because he is a more able exponent, but because he is wholly free from any stigma of professionalism.

Elton Trueblood, *Your Other Vocation,* pp. 40–41

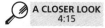

Being Renewed and Renewed

CONSIDER THIS 4:31 **A person of faith among non-believing coworkers can face misunderstanding, challenges to his or her values, or outright opposition. One's lifestyles, convictions, and even "workstyle" can trigger such responses. It can be very draining, like swimming against the tide.**

The new believers in Acts felt stress, too. They encountered the arrest of their leaders (4:1–3), rage and plots against them (4:25), and threats (4:21, 29). In response, they prayed together and were filled with the Holy Spirit yet again (v. 31). The previous filling (2:4) needed to be renewed.

As modern-day believers we, too, face the drain of unfriendly encounters in our lives and work. Like the Christians in Acts, we need to gather regularly for spiritual refueling. Worship services and small groups can provide that essential element, supplying the power we need to follow Christ in this world.

Do you have such a place? If not, consider gathering a small group of believers at your job or in your neighborhood to pray together and talk about life in Christ.

One church has a long history of linking prayer for its people with the work they carry out. See "Coventry," Heb. 10:19–25.

What is your "workstyle"? See Titus 2:9–10.

Sharing Things in Common

CONSIDER THIS 4:32–35 **The first Christians were extraordinarily generous. In fact, "they had all things in common" (vv. 32–35), an ideal that**

(continued on next page)

whatever Your hand and Your purpose determined before to
be done. [29]Now, Lord, look on their threats, and grant to
Your servants that with all boldness they may speak Your
word, [30]by stretching out Your hand to heal, and that signs
and wonders may be done through the name of Your holy
Servant Jesus."

4:31

[31]And when they had prayed, the place
where they were assembled together was
shaken; and they were all filled with the Holy Spirit, and
they spoke the word of God with boldness.

More Organizational Development

4:32–35

[32]Now the multitude of those who believed were of one heart and one soul;
neither did anyone say that any of the things he possessed
was his own, but they had all things in common. [33]And
with great power the apostles gave witness to the resurrection of the Lord Jesus. And great grace was upon them all.
[34]Nor was there anyone among them who lacked; for all
who were possessors of lands or houses sold them, and
brought the proceeds of the things that were sold, [35]and laid
them at the apostles' feet; and they distributed to each as
anyone had need.

4:36–37 see pg. 422
4:36–37 see pg. 422
4:37—5:11 see pg. 422

[36]And Joses,[a] who was also named
Barnabas by the apostles (which is translated Son of Encouragement), a Levite of
the country of Cyprus, [37]having land,
sold *it,* and brought the money and laid *it*
at the apostles' feet.

CHAPTER 5

5:1 see pg. 423
5:2–10

[1]But a certain man named Ananias,
with Sapphira his wife, sold a possession.
[2]And he kept back *part* of the proceeds,
his wife also being aware *of it,* and
brought a certain part and laid *it* at the apostles' feet. [3]But
Peter said, "Ananias, why has Satan filled your heart to lie
to the Holy Spirit and keep back *part* of the price of the
land for yourself? [4]While it remained, was it not your own?
And after it was sold, was it not in your own control? Why
have you conceived this thing in your heart? You have not
lied to men but to God."
[5]Then Ananias, hearing these words, fell down and
breathed his last. So great fear came upon all those who

4:36 [a]NU-Text reads *Joseph.*

heard these things. 6And the young men arose and wrapped
him up, carried *him* out, and buried *him*.
7Now it was about three hours later when his wife came
in, not knowing what had happened. 8And Peter answered
her, "Tell me whether you sold the land for so much?"
She said, "Yes, for so much."
9Then Peter said to her, "How is it that you have agreed
together to test the Spirit of the Lord? Look, the feet of
those who have buried your husband *are* at the door, and
they will carry you out." 10Then immediately she fell down
at his feet and breathed her last. And the young men came
in and found her dead, and carrying *her* out, buried *her* by
5:1–11 see pg. 423
her husband. 11So great fear came upon
all the church and upon all who heard
these things.

Growing Respect among the People

5:12–16 see pg. 424
12And through the hands of the apostles many signs and wonders were done
among the people. And they were all with one accord in
Solomon's Porch. 13Yet none of the rest dared join them, but
the people esteemed them highly. 14And believers were increasingly added to the Lord, multitudes of both men and
women, 15so that they brought the sick out into the streets
and laid *them* on beds and couches, that at least the shadow
of Peter passing by might fall on some of them. 16Also a
multitude gathered from the surrounding cities to
Jerusalem, bringing sick people and those who were tormented by unclean spirits, and they were all healed.

Real Estate Deal Deadly

CONSIDER THIS 5:2–10 *If Sapphira's consent was required to sell the property (vv. 2, 9), it would have been unusual since first-century women's legal powers were limited compared to those of modern women. In any case, she knew about the sale and, unfortunately, the deceit. She chose to participate in it rather than oppose her husband and hold to the truth.*

As a spouse, do you choose to "keep the peace" even when you know you are denying what is right?

(continued from previous page)

pure communism advocated but never achieved. So were these first believers in some sense communists?

No. In the first place, they were not setting up an economic system here, but simply responding to each other with gracious, Christlike compassion. Such behavior was one powerful result of the outpouring of the Spirit (Acts 2:1–4). Unfortunately, not all New Testament believers demonstrated that kind of concern (5:1–11; 1 Cor. 6:8; James 4:1–2).

Furthermore, Scripture never mandates an equal distribution of goods, nor does it call for the elimination of property or ownership. This passage (along with 2:44–45) is a historical account, not a doctrinal treatise. It documents the work of God in building the early church.

In that day, as in ours, there were both rich and poor Christians (2 Cor. 8:2; 1 Tim. 6:17–19). And when the New Testament does address issues such as wealth, care for the poor, work, equality, widows, slaves, and public justice, it inevitably calls believers to compassion and generosity; but not to asceticism, the idea that one can become more godly through self-denial and renouncing worldly wealth. In fact, Paul warns against that (Col. 2:18–23). The Bible condemns the love of wealth, not its possession, as a root of all kinds of evil (1 Tim. 6:9–10).

Reading about these early Christians, modern believers are challenged to consider: Do we, with our much higher standard of living, show the same commitment to generosity as these believers? If we, too, are filled with the Spirit of Christ, then we ought to respond to the needs of people with the love of Christ.

WEALTH—HOLD IT LIGHTLY

CONSIDER THIS 4:37—5:11 **Whether we own land, buildings, things, or cash, wealth is tricky to handle. How we hold these assets speaks volumes about our values. If we hold them too tightly, the results will likely be possessiveness, stinginess, manipulation, and elitism.**

Barnabas converted some land that he owned into a cash gift for needy believers (4:36–37). Notice how he *let go* of the money, laying it at the apostles' feet to be administered by them. By contrast, Ananias and Sapphira practiced a similar transaction for the same need, but lied about it (5:1–2). Apparently they wanted to look good among the believers, but they also wanted to secretly hold onto some of their money from the sale.

God calls us as believers to hold our resourses lightly. After all, everything that we have comes from Him. He gives it to us as a trust to be managed—not a treasure to be hoarded.

Perhaps it was to avoid situations like the one mentioned in this passage that Jesus warned His followers that when doing a charitable deed, "Do not let your left hand know what your right hand is doing." See "Anonymous Donors," Matt. 6:1–4.

BARNABAS—"JOE ENCOURAGEMENT"

CONSIDER THIS 4:36–37 **The apostles chose the perfect Christian name for Joses of Cyprus when they called him Barnabas—Son of Encouragement. Every appearance of Barnabas in Scripture finds him encouraging others in the faith. In fact, he serves as the supreme model for how**

(continued on next page)

Religious Leaders Try to Stop the Apostles

17Then the high priest rose up, and all those who *were*
with him (which is the sect of the Sadducees), and they
were filled with indignation, 18and laid their hands on the
apostles and put them in the common prison. 19But at night
an angel of the Lord opened the prison doors and brought
them out, and said, 20"Go, stand in the temple and speak to
the people all the words of this life."
21And when they heard *that,* they entered the temple early
in the morning and taught. But the high priest and those
with him came and called the council together, with all the
elders of the children of Israel, and sent to the prison to
have them brought.

5:22–32 see pg. 425

22But when the officers came and did
not find them in the prison, they re-
turned and reported, 23saying, "Indeed we found the prison
shut securely, and the guards standing outside[a] before the
doors; but when we opened them, we found no one inside!"
24Now when the high priest,[a] the captain of the temple, and
the chief priests heard these things, they wondered what the
outcome would be. 25So one came and told them, saying,[a]
"Look, the men whom you put in prison are standing in the
temple and teaching the people!"
26Then the captain went with the officers and brought

5:23 [a]NU-Text and M-Text omit *outside.* *5:24* [a]NU-Text omits *the high priest.*
5:25 [a]NU-Text and M-Text omit *saying.*

PERSONALITY PROFILE: BARNABAS

FOR YOUR INFO 4:36–37

Given name: Joses (Joseph).

Renamed (by the apostles): Barnabas, which means "Son of Encouragement."

Home: Cyprus.

Family: A Levite by background.

A primary responsibility: Landowner.

Best known today for: Recruiting and mentoring promising young leaders such as Saul and John Mark.

them without violence, for they feared the people, lest they
should be stoned. 27And when they had brought them, they
set *them* before the council. And the high priest asked them,
28saying, "Did we not strictly command you not to teach in
this name? And look, you have filled Jerusalem with your
doctrine, and intend to bring this Man's blood on us!"
29But Peter and the *other* apostles answered and said: "We
ought to obey God rather than men. 30The God of our
fathers raised up Jesus whom you murdered by hanging on
a tree. 31Him God has exalted to His right hand *to be* Prince
and Savior, to give repentance to Israel and forgiveness of
sins. 32And we are His witnesses to these things, and *so* also
is the Holy Spirit whom God has given to those who obey
Him."
33When they heard *this,* they were furious and plotted to
kill them. 34Then one in the council stood up, a Pharisee
named Gamaliel, a teacher of the law held in respect by all
the people, and commanded them to put the apostles outside for a little while. 35And he said to them: "Men of Israel,
take heed to yourselves what you intend to do regarding
these men. 36For some time ago Theudas rose up, claiming
to be somebody. A number of men, about four hundred,
joined him. He was slain, and all who obeyed him were
scattered and came to nothing. 37After this man, Judas of
Galilee rose up in the days of the census, and drew away
many people after him. He also perished, and all who
obeyed him were dispersed. 38And now I say to you, keep
away from these men and let them alone; for if this plan or
this work is of men, it will come to nothing; 39but if it is of

Personality Profile: Ananias and Sapphira

FOR YOUR INFO 5:1 **Names mean:** "God is gracious" (Ananias) and "beautiful" (Sapphira).

Not to be confused with: Ananias, the disciple in Damascus, who was the first believer to visit Saul after his dramatic conversion (Acts 9:10); Ananias the high priest (23:2).

Remembered today for: Lying to Peter about donating money to the church and being struck dead by the Holy Spirit for their deception.

(continued from previous page)

to mentor young believers. Numerous churches can trace their beginnings back to the efforts of "Joe Encouragement" (see "Discipleship—Or Mentoring?" and "Kingdom-Style Mentoring," Acts 9:26–30).

An interesting sidelight: Though Levites traditionally lived off the temple system, Barnabas had real estate. But on coming into the faith he sold it and donated the proceeds for the care of the poor (4:36–37). Later, he joined with Paul in refusing to make a living from the gospel (1 Cor. 9:6).

Ananias and Sapphira—Playing Games with God

CONSIDER THIS 5:1–11 **The dramatic account of Ananias and Sapphira (Acts 5:1–11) immediately after the mention of Barnabas (4:36–37) draws a stark contrast between two kinds of people. On the one hand, Barnabas serves as a positive model of sincere faith, as evidenced by his open-handed generosity. On the other hand, Ananias and Sapphira serve as negative models.**

Externally, they appeared the same. Like Barnabas, they sold land and brought money to the church, where they "laid it at the apostles' feet" (4:37; 5:2). But internally, they had a radically different commitment.

The sins that Peter named—lying to the Holy Spirit (v. 3) and testing the Spirit (v. 9)—indicate that they were playing games with God. Peter noted that the source of their deception was Satan. As the ultimate liar (John 8:44), Satan had filled their hearts with lies, in contrast to the Holy Spirit, who fills the heart with truth (14:16–17; Eph. 5:6–21). And like Israel, they were testing the Spirit (1 Cor. 10:1–13), testing the limits of

(continued on next page)

(continued from previous page)

what He would permit, trying to see how much they could get away with.

God dealt severely with this couple by making an example of them. As a result, fear came upon the church (Acts 5:5, 11)—not a cringing fear of dread, but a heightened respect for God's holiness, His moral purity. The incident still stands as a bold warning to believers today about relating to God. No one is perfect, and God forgives. But when given a chance to confess the truth, it's important to confess the truth, not lie as they did.

God, you cannot overthrow it—lest you even be found to
fight against God."
40And they agreed with him, and when they had called
for the apostles and beaten *them,* they commanded that they
should not speak in the name of Jesus, and let them go.
41So they departed from the presence of the council, rejoicing that they were counted worthy to suffer shame for His[a]
name. 42And daily in the temple, and in every house, they
did not cease teaching and preaching Jesus *as* the Christ.

CHAPTER 6

Ethnic Tensions

6:1 see pg. 426

1Now in those days, when *the number*
of the disciples was multiplying, there

5:41 [a]NU-Text reads *the name;* M-Text reads *the name of Jesus.*

A Confusing Reputation

CONSIDER THIS 5:12–16 **Seeing loyalty to God's kingdom often triggers peculiar responses from unbelievers. Many will keep a safe distance, as happened to the early church (v. 13), while others enthusiastically join up (v. 14).**

What will bring the hesitant watchers across the line? Time, reasonable evidence, and the work of the Holy Spirit will. That's why we as believers need to give others space to sort things out. Many times quick transitions don't have lasting power.

We must not measure our evangelistic effectiveness by responses, but by whether we have been faithful in our witness. The commands of God must be our yardstick—not the reactions of others.

Believers are called to present the message of Christ in the best way they know how when the opportunity presents itself. See "Carrots, Not Sticks," Acts 2:37–38.

Leaders Start as Servants

CONSIDER THIS 6:5–6 *Two factors probably led to the neglect of the Hellenist (Greek-speaking) widows (v. 1): dramatic numerical growth and cultural prejudice by native-born Jews against their foreign-born brothers and sisters. Something had to be done, because first-century widows had almost no means of support. Sometimes a widow was left with no options but begging or prostitution to survive. Those in the church relied on the daily distribution of food.*

Church leaders appointed seven men, probably from among the Hellenists, to manage the program (vv. 5–6). Note that their first assignment in ministry involved what we might call "social work." In fact, it involved a task that their culture defined as women's or slaves' work—serving meals. We don't know what struggles that must have created, but perhaps the requirements of good character, Spirit filling, and wisdom had something to do with what these men would need to break out of traditional cultural ways.

Having served well, at least some of these workers extended their service into cross-cultural evangelism (v. 8; 8:5–40).

arose a complaint against the Hebrews by the Hellenists,[a]
because their widows were neglected in the daily distribu-
6:2–6 see pg. 426
tion. 2Then the twelve summoned the
multitude of the disciples and said, "It is
not desirable that we should leave the word of God and
serve tables. 3Therefore, brethren, seek out from among you
seven men of *good* reputation, full of the Holy Spirit and
wisdom, whom we may appoint over this business; 4but we
will give ourselves continually to prayer and to the ministry
of the word."

6:5–6
5And the saying pleased the whole
multitude. And they chose Stephen, a
man full of faith and the Holy Spirit, and Philip, Prochorus,
Nicanor, Timon, Parmenas, and Nicolas, a proselyte from
Antioch, 6whom they set before the apostles; and when they
had prayed, they laid hands on them.

7Then the word of God spread, and the number of the
disciples multiplied greatly in Jerusalem, and a great many
of the priests were obedient to the faith.

Stephen Arrested

8And Stephen, full of faith[a] and power, did great wonders
6:9 see pg. 428
and signs among the people. 9Then there
arose some from what is called the Syna-
gogue of the Freedmen (Cyrenians, Alexandrians, and those
from Cilicia and Asia), disputing with Stephen. 10And they
were not able to resist the wisdom and the Spirit by which
he spoke. 11Then they secretly induced men to say, "We
have heard him speak blasphemous words against Moses
6:12 see pg. 428
and God." 12And they stirred up the people, the elders, and the scribes; and they
came upon *him*, seized him, and brought *him* to the council.
13They also set up false witnesses who said, "This man does
not cease to speak blasphemous[a] words against this holy
place and the law; 14for we have heard him say that this
Jesus of Nazareth will destroy this place and change the
customs which Moses delivered to us." 15And all who sat in
the council, looking steadfastly at him, saw his face as the
face of an angel.

CHAPTER 7

Stephen Faces the Council

7:1–53 see pg. 430
1Then the high priest said, "Are these
things so?"

2And he said, "Brethren and fathers, listen: The God of
glory appeared to our father Abraham when he was in

6:1 [a]That is, Greek-speaking Jews *6:8* [a]NU-Text reads *grace.* *6:13* [a]NU-Text omits *blasphemous.*

"We Ought to Obey God Rather than Men"

CONSIDER THIS 5:22–32 **What should Christians do when faced with a conflict between human authority and God's authority? Notice what Peter and the other apostles did (vv. 22–32):**

(1) Their aim was to serve and glorify God. They were not motivated by ego or out to protect their own power.

(2) Their point of disobedience was specific and particular. They did not resist the authority of the Jewish council in total.

(3) They approached the situation with a spirit of submissiveness toward both the council and God. They did not harbor rebellious anger toward authority in general.

(4) They delivered a positive, factual message about God's plan and power in loving truth. They did not slander or show disrespect to their superiors.

(5) They accepted the cost of being loyal to the truth without rancor or bitterness.

Society's Divisions Affect Believers

CONSIDER THIS 6:1 **Oftentimes the values that a society holds are reflected in and embraced by the church whether they are biblical or not. Coming to faith in Christ does not automatically change one's view of the world and its people. We may reproduce and even defend sinful attitudes and actions that are normal for our surrounding culture.**

The early church faced that problem (v. 1). Hellenist widows, traditionally neglected by the Jews, were now being neglected by Hebrew Christians who had brought that attitude with them into the church.

Likewise, later church history shows that Christians were among those who advocated and even promoted such evils as slavery, segregation, apartheid, and the holocaust. To be sure, Christians were also among those objecting to and overthrowing those practices. But many chose to accept cultural norms that were opposed to Christ's message.

This reality forces us to ask some troubling questions: What values in modern society do we uncritically accept? How are divisions in our culture revealed in our churches, at work, and in our neighborhoods? How does the gospel of Jesus challenge those attitudes? What changes do we need to make?

A Growing Movement Confronts Ethnic Prejudice

CONSIDER THIS 6:2–6 **Success never means the end of problems; it just means a new set of problems. The community of believers in**

(continued on next page)

7:3–44 see pg. 429

Mesopotamia, before he dwelt in Haran,
3and said to him, 'Get out of your coun-
try and from your relatives, and come to a land that I will
show you.'[a] 4Then he came out of the land of the Chaldeans
and dwelt in Haran. And from there, when his father was
dead, He moved him to this land in which you now dwell.
5And *God* gave him no inheritance in it, not even *enough* to
set his foot on. But even when *Abraham* had no child, He
promised to give it to him for a possession, and to his descendants after him. 6But God spoke in this way: that his
descendants would dwell in a foreign land, and that they
would bring them into bondage and oppress *them* four hundred years. 7'And the nation to whom they will be in
bondage I will judge,'[a] said God, 'and after that they shall
come out and serve Me in this place.'[b] 8Then He gave him
the covenant of circumcision; and so *Abraham* begot Isaac
and circumcised him on the eighth day; and Isaac *begot* Jacob, and Jacob *begot* the twelve patriarchs.

9"And the patriarchs, becoming envious, sold Joseph into
Egypt. But God was with him 10and delivered him out of all
his troubles, and gave him favor and wisdom in the presence of Pharaoh, king of Egypt; and he made him governor
over Egypt and all his house. 11Now a famine and great
trouble came over all the land of Egypt and Canaan, and
our fathers found no sustenance. 12But when Jacob heard
that there was grain in Egypt, he sent out our fathers first.
13And the second *time* Joseph was made known to his
brothers, and Joseph's family became known to the
Pharaoh. 14Then Joseph sent and called his father Jacob and
all his relatives to *him*, seventy-five[a] people. 15So Jacob went
down to Egypt; and he died, he and our fathers. 16And they
were carried back to Shechem and laid in the tomb that
Abraham bought for a sum of money from the sons of
Hamor, *the father* of Shechem.

17"But when the time of the promise drew near which
God had sworn to Abraham, the people grew and multiplied in Egypt 18till another king arose who did not know
Joseph. 19This man dealt treacherously with our people, and
oppressed our forefathers, making them expose their babies, so that they might not live. 20At this time Moses was
born, and was well pleasing to God; and he was brought up
in his father's house for three months. 21But when he was
set out, Pharaoh's daughter took him away and brought him

7:22 see pg. 429

up as her own son. 22And Moses was
learned in all the wisdom of the Egyptians, and was mighty in words and deeds.

7:3 [a]Genesis 12:1 *7:7* [a]Genesis 15:14 [b]Exodus 3:12 *7:14* [a]Or *seventy* (compare Exodus 1:5)

23"Now when he was forty years old, it came into his
heart to visit his brethren, the children of Israel. 24And seeing one of *them* suffer wrong, he defended and avenged him
who was oppressed, and struck down the Egyptian. 25For
he supposed that his brethren would have understood that
God would deliver them by his hand, but they did not understand. 26And the next day he appeared to two of them as
they were fighting, and *tried to* reconcile them, saying,
'Men, you are brethren; why do you wrong one another?'
27But he who did his neighbor wrong pushed him away,
saying, 'Who made you a ruler and a judge over us? 28Do
you want to kill me as you did the Egyptian yesterday?'[a]
29Then, at this saying, Moses fled and became a dweller in
the land of Midian, where he had two sons.

30"And when forty years had passed, an Angel of the
Lord[a] appeared to him in a flame of fire in a bush, in the
wilderness of Mount Sinai. 31When Moses saw *it,* he marveled at the sight; and as he drew near to observe, the voice
of the Lord came to him, 32*saying,* 'I *am* the God of your
fathers—the God of Abraham, the God of Isaac, and the
God of Jacob.'[a] And Moses trembled and dared not look.
33'Then the LORD said to him, "Take your sandals off your
feet, for the place where you stand is holy ground. 34I have
surely seen the oppression of My people who are in Egypt; I
have heard their groaning and have come down to deliver
them. And now come, I will send you to Egypt." '[a]

35"This Moses whom they rejected, saying, 'Who made
you a ruler and a judge?'[a] is the one God sent *to be* a ruler
and a deliverer by the hand of the Angel who appeared to
him in the bush. 36He brought them out, after he had
shown wonders and signs in the land of Egypt, and in the
Red Sea, and in the wilderness forty years.

37"This is that Moses who said to the children of Israel,[a]
'The LORD your God will raise up for you a Prophet like me
from your brethren. Him you shall hear.'[b]

38"This is he who was in the congregation in the wilderness with the Angel who spoke to him on Mount Sinai, and
with our fathers, the one who received the living oracles to
give to us, 39whom our fathers would not obey, but rejected.
And in their hearts they turned back to Egypt, 40saying to
Aaron, 'Make us gods to go before us; *as for* this Moses who
brought us out of the land of Egypt, we do not know what
has become of him.'[a] 41And they made a calf in those days,
offered sacrifices to the idol, and rejoiced in the works of
their own hands. 42Then God turned and gave them up to

(Bible text continued on page 429)

7:28 [a]Exodus 2:14 *7:30* [a]NU-Text omits *of the Lord.* *7:32* [a]Exodus 3:6, 15
7:34 [a]Exodus 3:5, 7, 8, 10 *7:35* [a]Exodus 2:14 *7:37* [a]Deuteronomy 18:15 [b]NU-Text and M-Text omit *Him you shall hear.* *7:40* [a]Exodus 32:1, 23

(continued from previous page)

Jerusalem discovered that as they experienced significant development in their life together. Their group was constantly growing and changing (Acts 1:15; 2:41, 47; 4:4, 32; 5:14). There was amazing agreement among them (2:46; 4:32; 5:12). And their material needs were being met through sacrificial generosity (2:45; 4:34, 36).

Nevertheless, a situation developed that threatened to fracture this successful movement (6:1). The immediate problem had to do with the daily distribution to widows, but the underlying issue was ethnic tension between the *Hebrews,* Jews born in Judea and Galilee, and the *Hellenists,* Greek-speaking Jews born outside of Palestine. The clash could have destroyed the church or divided it into two Christian ethnic communities. Notice how the apostles responded (vv. 2–6):

(1) They met face-to-face with the Hellenists (the powerful with the powerless).

(2) They listened to the complaints and acknowledged their legitimacy.

(3) Together with the Hellenists, they devised guidelines for godly leaders and chose seven with names that suggest they were from among the Hellenist minority.

(4) They approved and commissioned the new leaders through the laying on of hands and committed themselves to work with them.

(5) They gave the new leaders authority over the distribution.

(6) They shared power and resources and affirmed the dignity of the newly chosen leaders.

Result? "The word of God spread, and multiplied greatly in Jerusalem" (v. 7).

What problems do you or your church confront as a result of success? What steps are you taking to manage those problems in a way that serves people and honors God?

THE HELLENISTS

FOR YOUR INFO 6:9

Stephen's opponents came from the Synagogue of the Freedmen (Acts 6:9), a center of religious life in Jerusalem for a minority known as the Hellenists.

- **Two groups of Hebrews in the Roman Empire:**
  - ***Jews,* natives of Palestine who spoke Aramaic.**
  - **Others born elsewhere, known as *Hellenists* because they spoke Greek, the common trade language.**
- **Hellenists were despised by the Jews, who viewed them as "contaminated" by Gentiles.**
- **But Hellenists responded in large numbers to the gospel.**

PERSONALITY PROFILE: STEPHEN

Name means: "Crown" or "crown-bearer."

Background: A Hellenist (Greek-speaking) Jew.

Occupation: Unknown, but he became a manager of the church's food distribution program in response to an ethnic problem (Acts 6:1–7); later became an evangelist.

Known for: Faith, spiritual power, and wisdom. He turned the tables on the council, in effect putting them on trial for rejecting Jesus. As a result of his death, widespread persecution of the church broke out, scattering believers far and wide.

Best known today as: The first Christian martyr.

CONSIDER THIS 6:12

STEPHEN'S TRIAL AND MURDER

Ethnic tension played a decisive role in the trial and death of Stephen, the church's first martyr. Other members of the early church faced the council (v. 12; 4:1–23), but it was Stephen, probably a Hellenist, who first died for his faith.

Hellenists, Jews born outside of Palestine, were among those first attracted by the gospel. Treated as second-class citizens by native-born Jews, many found acceptance in the early church. But it could be that as the new faith threatened to further alienate Hellenistic Jews from the full-blooded majority, some Hellenists (6:9) had a motive to try to discredit the Christian movement.

Their opposition focused on Stephen, a dynamic, emerging leader who enjoyed in the church a prominence that would have been denied him in the Hebrew community. His trial and murder (Acts 7) show that the Hellenists were willing to sacrifice one of their own as a demonstration of loyalty to the ruling system.

The strategy worked. Stephen's death precipitated a great persecution of believers, sanctioned by the council and led by a new young leader, Saul of Tarsus (8:1–3; 9:1–2).

The Council

The council, or Sanhedrin, was the highest ruling body and supreme court of the Jews.

worship the host of heaven, as it is written in the book of the Prophets:

'Did you offer Me slaughtered animals and sacrifices
during forty years in the wilderness,
O house of Israel?
43 You also took up the tabernacle of Moloch,
And the star of your god Remphan,
Images which you made to worship;
And I will carry you away beyond Babylon.'[a]

44"Our fathers had the tabernacle of witness in the wilderness, as He appointed, instructing Moses to make it according to the pattern that he had seen, 45which our fathers,
having received it in turn, also brought with Joshua into the
land possessed by the Gentiles, whom God drove out before
the face of our fathers until the days of David, 46who found
favor before God and asked to find a dwelling for the God
of Jacob. 47But Solomon built Him a house.

7:43 [a]Amos 5:25–27

- *Led by the high priest, the most powerful Jewish official in the city.*
- *71 members, including priests, leading men (elders), and experts in Mosaic law (scribes).*
- *In the first century, dominated by two major parties, Pharisees and Sadducees (see "Party Politics of Jesus' Day," Matt. 16:1).*
- *Allowed by Rome to oversee religious, civil, and criminal issues in the province of Judea.*
- *Politically: could appoint kings and high priests, make war, gerrymander the city, and expand the temple.*
- *Judicially: could judge traitorous priests, false prophets, rebel leaders, and rebellious tribes.*
- *Religiously: could ordain certain services, such as the Day of Atonement.*
- *Had its own police force.*
- *Prevented by Rome from exercising capital punishment.*
- *Prominent members mentioned in the Bible:*
  - *Joseph of Arimathea (Mark 15:43)*
  - *Annas and Caiaphas, high priests (Luke 3:2)*
  - *Nicodemus (John 3:1; 7:50)*
  - *Gamaliel (Acts 5:34)*
  - *Ananias (23:2)*
  - *Possibly Tertullus, an orator (24:1–2)*
  - *Possibly Saul, a student of Gamaliel (22:3)* ◆

Little Is Much with God

CONSIDER THIS 7:3–44 **God delights in working through people who are disadvantaged. Stephen mentioned three from the Old Testament as he explained the faith (vv. 3–44):**

- ***Abraham and Sarah.* God chose a childless immigrant couple to found the Israelite nation as a witness to all the nations (vv. 3–8).**
- ***Joseph.* From a favored child sold by jealous brothers into the international slave trade, God shaped a national leader who rescued his family and his adopted country from famine and death (vv. 9–14).**
- ***Moses.* God developed a liberator and nation-builder from a minority child marked for slaughter, who later murdered an opponent and fled, fearing his people's rejection (vv. 20–44).**

The Value of Learning

CONSIDER THIS 7:22 **"It doesn't matter whether you have an education," some people say, "God can use you anyway." True, God can use anyone, with or without formal education. But Moses' learning "in all the wisdom of the Egyptians" (v. 22) proved to be a valuable asset when the Lord called Him to lead Israel out of captivity.**

Moses spent the first third of his life—40 years—in Egypt. Raised among royalty, he was exposed to the impressive culture of the pharaohs. The curriculum likely included political science, public administration, religion, history, literature, geometry, and perhaps even engineering and hydraulics.

(continued on next page)

(continued from previous page)

But that was not the end of Moses' education. He spent another 40 years in "graduate school" in the desert, studying animal husbandry while interning as a shepherd. He also learned about public health and primitive communities. Altogether, the first two-thirds of Moses' life prepared him for his most challenging job—leading Israel through the wilderness.

Intelligence and education alone don't make someone fit to serve God. Indeed, an educated person can hide behind his or her learning in order to avoid dealing with God. Young Saul fell into that trap (Acts 22:3–5), as did his fellow Pharisees. So did the philosophers at Athens (17:16–34). But as Stephen pointed out, the problem is not with the intellect but with the will; the danger comes not from embracing knowledge but from resisting God (7:51).

48"However, the Most High does not dwell in temples
made with hands, as the prophet says:

49 'Heaven *is* My throne,
And earth *is* My footstool.
What house will you build for Me? says the LORD,
Or what *is* the place of My rest?
50 Has My hand not made all these things?'[a]

51"*You* stiff-necked and uncircumcised in heart and ears!
You always resist the Holy Spirit; as your fathers *did*, so *do*
you. 52Which of the prophets did your fathers not persecute? And they killed those who foretold the coming of the
Just One, of whom you now have become the betrayers and
murderers, 53who have received the law by the direction of
angels and have not kept *it*."

Stephen Stoned to Death

54When they heard these things they were cut to the
heart, and they gnashed at him with *their* teeth. 55But he,
being full of the Holy Spirit, gazed into heaven and saw the
glory of God, and Jesus standing at the right hand of God,
56and said, "Look! I see the heavens opened and the Son of
Man standing at the right hand of God!"

7:50 [a]Isaiah 66:1, 2

CONSIDER THIS
7:1–53

STEPHEN'S NEW VIEW OF HISTORY

Political change can often lead to changed perspectives on history. The destruction of Jerusalem and its temple by the Romans in A.D. 70 forced the Hebrews to radically rethink the significance of Jerusalem and its institutions. Early Christians, however, began changing their view well before the city's fall, as Stephen's speech before the council shows (vv. 1–53).

Stephen and his fellow Christians departed from the earlier view that the world revolved around Israel, and Israel in turn revolved around Jerusalem's temple and the Law. They still saw Jerusalem as more than just a city, but they made it into a new symbol of a higher ideal (see "The Holy City," Matt. 23:37). Stephen's eloquent history lesson makes four points in this regard:

(1) The founding of the Hebrew nation occurred in Mesopotamia, not Jerusalem (vv. 2–5).
(2) God's liberation of His people occurred at locations outside of Palestine—in Egypt, at the Red Sea, and in the Sinai wilderness—not in Jerusalem (vv. 9–36).

7:57–60

57Then they cried out with a loud
voice, stopped their ears, and ran at him
with one accord; 58and they cast *him* out of the city and
stoned *him*. And the witnesses laid down their clothes at the
feet of a young man named Saul. 59And they stoned
Stephen as he was calling on *God* and saying, "Lord Jesus,
receive my spirit." 60Then he knelt down and cried out with
a loud voice, "Lord, do not charge them with this sin." And
when he had said this, he fell asleep.

CHAPTER 8

8:1

1Now Saul was consenting to his death.

Persecution by Saul Scatters Believers

8:1

At that time a great persecution arose
against the church which was at Jerusa-
lem; and they were all scattered throughout the regions of
Judea and Samaria, except the apostles. 2And devout men

Saul

A CLOSER LOOK 8:1

Saul enjoyed advantages that allowed him to rise quickly as a leading opponent of the church. See "Saul," Acts 13:2–3.

(3) The Law was given in the desert, not Jerusalem (v. 38).

(4) God doesn't live only in a temple or any other physical building; He never did and He never will (vv. 39–50).

Needless to say, Stephen's view of history brought the conflict between the new movement and the city fathers to a boil. Outraged, the council stoned Stephen to death and allowed Saul to start persecuting believers openly (7:54—8:3). Yet by God's design, that only helped to expand the church (8:4). God had always intended for believers to move beyond Jerusalem, but it took persecution to get them moving.

Stephen's perspective on Jerusalem challenges us as modern Christians to reflect on our loyalty to beloved institutions. Our highest allegiance must be to Christ. ◆

Stephen was the first Christian to die for the faith. Find out more about him at Acts 6:12.

Resistance—Unpopular Obedience

CONSIDER THIS 7:57–60

Whistle-blowers and other workplace gadflies who go against prevailing values and popular opinion usually face rough treatment. They put themselves, their relationships, and sometimes even their jobs at risk. Stephen's determination to stand up for tough truth went even further: it cost him his life (vv. 57–60).

Before you engage in potentially costly causes, make sure you are sacrificing for the right thing. Are you attacking people, with a spirit of hostility and judgment? That kind of negative motivation is not what God wants. He gives us a far more positive, noble vision to honor, as Stephen illustrates. He stood for the truth of the gospel. His focus was not on attacking his opponents, but on affirming the message of Christ. While his accusers turned on him, he turned the other cheek, following the example of His Lord.

The Message Leaves Jerusalem

CONSIDER THIS 8:1

Was Jerusalem supposed to be the center of the early church? Verse 1 might give that impression, since all the believers were scattered *except the apostles.* But Antioch, not Jerusalem, was destined to be the headquarters of the burgeoning international movement (see "Antioch," 13:1).

Jerusalem served chiefly as a launching pad for the gospel—quite a

(continued on next page)

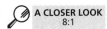

(continued from previous page)

contrast from its role as the center of gravity for the worship of God in the Old Testament. But as Stephen made plain in his trial (7:1–53), many great acts of God happened *outside* of Palestine.

Jerusalem had once served as the religious center for God's people. But God changed that. The gospel started in Jerusalem, then moved into Judea and Samaria, just as the Lord had said it would (see "Opportunities Look Like Barriers," Acts 1:4).

For a more complete profile of Jerusalem, see Matt. 23:37.

From Jerusalem, the gospel continued to spread throughout the Roman empire. See "The Movement Expands Beyond Palestine," Acts 11:19–26.

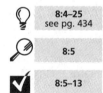

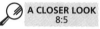

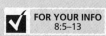

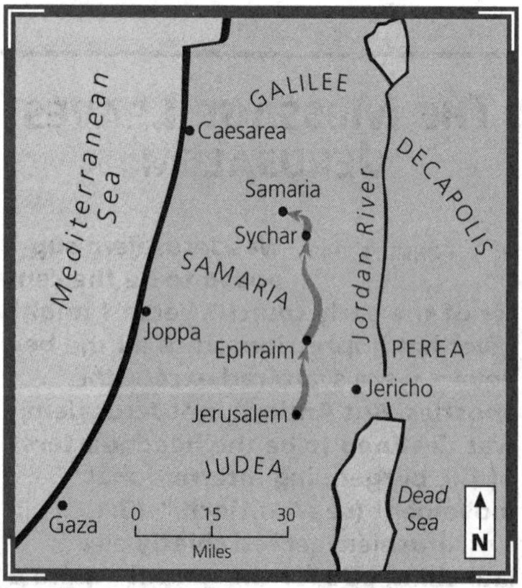

PHILIP'S JOURNEY TO SAMARIA

carried Stephen *to his burial,* and made great lamentation
over him.
3As for Saul, he made havoc of the church, entering every
house, and dragging off men and women, committing *them*
to prison.

The Message Spreads to Samaria

8:4–25 see pg. 434
8:5
8:5–13

4Therefore those who were scattered
went everywhere preaching the word.
5Then Philip went down to the[a] city of
Samaria and preached Christ to them.
6And the multitudes with one accord
heeded the things spoken by Philip, hear-
ing and seeing the miracles which he did. 7For unclean
spirits, crying with a loud voice, came out of many who
were possessed; and many who were paralyzed and lame
were healed. 8And there was great joy in that city.

8:5 [a]Or a

Samaria

A CLOSER LOOK 8:5

Philip's journey to Samaria (v. 5) was not the first occasion on which the gospel had been preached to Samaritans. See "Samaria," John 4:4.

PERSONALITY PROFILE: PHILIP THE EVANGELIST

FOR YOUR INFO 8:5–13

Name means: "Lover of horses."

Not to be confused with: Philip the apostle, one of the Twelve (see Matt. 10:2).

Home: The Mediterranean seaport of Caesarea (see Acts 10:1).

Family: Included four gifted daughters (21:8–9).

Occupation: Vocation unknown, but helped oversee the daily distribution of food to Hellenist widows (6:1–7). Later he crossed cultural barriers to take the message of Christ to Samaria.

Best known today for: His encounter with the Ethiopian treasurer (8:26–40).

8:9
9But there was a certain man called Simon, who previously practiced sorcery in
the city and astonished the people of Samaria, claiming that
he was someone great, 10to whom they all gave heed, from
the least to the greatest, saying, "This man is the great
8:9–24
power of God." 11And they heeded him
because he had astonished them with his
sorceries for a long time. 12But when they believed Philip as
he preached the things concerning the kingdom of God and
the name of Jesus Christ, both men and women were bap-
8:5–13
tized. 13Then Simon himself also believed; and when he was baptized he
continued with Philip, and was amazed, seeing the miracles
and signs which were done.
14Now when the apostles who were at Jerusalem heard
that Samaria had received the word of God, they sent Peter
and John to them, 15who, when they had come down,
prayed for them that they might receive the Holy Spirit.
16For as yet He had fallen upon none of them. They had
only been baptized in the name of the Lord Jesus. 17Then
they laid hands on them, and they received the Holy Spirit.
8:18–19 see pg. 434
18And when Simon saw that through
the laying on of the apostles' hands the
Holy Spirit was given, he offered them money, 19saying,
"Give me this power also, that anyone on whom I lay hands
may receive the Holy Spirit."
20But Peter said to him, "Your money perish with you, because you thought that the gift of God could be purchased
with money! 21You have neither part nor portion in this
matter, for your heart is not right in the sight of God. 22Re-
pent therefore of this your wickedness, and pray God if per-

Personality Profile: Simon the Magician

FOR YOUR INFO 8:9

Referred to as: "The great power of God."

Home: Samaria.

Occupation: Sorcerer, meaning that he was involved in occult practices (see Rev. 18:23).

Remembered today for: Trying to buy the power of the Holy Spirit with money.

Four Glimpses of Philip

CONSIDER THIS 8:5–13

The book of Acts sketches four scenes of Philip. Notice how they touch on many issues confronting the church today:

1. **He helped manage a *social service* for widows in Jerusalem (Acts 6:1–7).**
2. **He worked *cross-culturally* in Samaria in an *urban* environment (8:5–13).**
3. **He transcended *racial, cultural, and other barriers* as he explained the gospel to a black Ethiopian treasurer who had been made a eunuch by his government. Note that Philip was not afraid to touch the man or baptize him (8:26–40).**
4. **He welcomed Paul into his home and presented four *daughters who prophesied* (21:8–9).**

Simon—Infatuated with Power

CONSIDER THIS 8:9–24

Simon illustrates a common habit of new believers—trying to use their newfound faith to justify old, sinful habits, or, in their zeal, "help God out." In his case, preoccupation with power, especially spiritual power, motivated him to try to buy the Holy Spirit's power (Acts 8:19). It took a sharp rebuke from Peter to help him realize that following Christ involves fundamental changes in one's motives and attitudes. Old values must give way to new (2 Cor. 5:17).

In the end, Simon may have changed his ways, as his plea for mercy suggests (Acts 8:24). Nevertheless, his name lives in infamy in the term "simony," which means the buying or selling of a church office.

"GIVE ME POWER!"

CONSIDER THIS 8:18–19 **Simon's request (vv. 18–19) was motivated by the same illusion of power that drives so many in today's business, political, and entertainment arenas. Popular culture invests actors, sports figures, and other celebrities with the appearance of unusual significance. Even among Christians there exists a strong tendency to create power figures out of preachers, singers, writers, and parachurch leaders. But God's power has little or nothing to do with outward appearances or worldly acclaim.**

Simon had adopted the world's

(continued on next page)

haps the thought of your heart may be forgiven you. 23For I
see that you are poisoned by bitterness and bound by iniquity."
24Then Simon answered and said, "Pray to the Lord for
me, that none of the things which you have spoken may
come upon me."
25So when they had testified and preached the word of
the Lord, they returned to Jerusalem, preaching the gospel
in many villages of the Samaritans.

An Ethiopian Official Receives the Gospel

8:26–39 see pg. 440

8:27

8:27–39

26Now an angel of the Lord spoke to
Philip, saying, "Arise and go toward the
south along the road which goes down from Jerusalem to
Gaza." This is desert. 27So he arose and
went. And behold, a man of Ethiopia, a
eunuch of great authority under Candace the queen of the
Ethiopians, who had charge of all her treasury, and had
come to Jerusalem to worship, 28was returning.
And sitting in his chariot, he was

(Bible text continued on page 436)

CONSIDER THIS 8:4–25

THE CONVERSION OF SAMARITANS TO THE GOSPEL—AND OF PETER AND JOHN TO SAMARITANS

Jesus said that His disciples were to be His witnesses not only in Jerusalem, but also to Judea, Samaria, and the ends of the earth (Acts 1:8). As chapter 8 opens, several years had probably gone by, but the church had not yet left Jerusalem. In fact, it took persecution to move the Lord's people to obedience.

Why was that? Jerusalem was not the apostles' home. The church had no buildings there. The authorities certainly had not welcomed it. Why, then, the reluctance to leave?

One probable factor was that the apostles had grown up in a culture deeply divided along ethnic lines. For them to preach the gospel to Jews at Jerusalem was a challenge, but a manageable one. But to preach to Samaritans was hard. (To appreciate how hard, see " 'Jews Have No Dealings with Samaritans,' " John 4:9.) Perhaps that's why the apostles chose to stay in Jerusalem despite Saul's persecution (Acts 8:1).

But a man who was probably a Hellenistic (Greek-speaking) Jew, Philip, crossed the Jewish-Samaritan barrier (see accompanying profile). A veteran of cross-cultural work (6:1–7), Philip knew by personal experience what it meant to be a second-class citizen. When he preached Jesus in the city of Samaria, multitudes responded. The gospel breached the wall of separation.

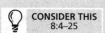

Personality Profile: The Treasurer of Ethiopia

FOR YOUR INFO 8:27–39

Home: Ethiopia.

Background: A black, unmarried male officer of the royal household; made a eunuch as a precautionary measure, a common practice performed on servants who served a woman or worked among the wives of a king.

Occupation: Treasurer of Ethiopia under Queen Candace.

News of the revival reached the apostles in Jerusalem, and they dispatched Peter and John to investigate. The two Galileans must have been stunned and no doubt humbled by what they found. John, who once had asked to call down fire from heaven on unbelieving Samaritans (Luke 9:52–54), now joined Peter in praying for the Holy Spirit to come upon the new believers.

Ironically, Peter condemned Simon the magician for trying to purchase the Spirit's power with money. "I see that you are poisoned by bitterness and bound by iniquity," he told him (Acts 8:23). But the poison of bitterness and the bondage of iniquity also were behind those who allowed ethnic differences to prevent Samaritans and others from entering the kingdom.

As they returned to Jerusalem, Peter and John were changed men. Notice that they finally began to preach in the Samaritan villages (v. 25). The wall of ethnic hatred was breaking down. Samaritans were now embracing the gospel—and at least two of the apostles were beginning to embrace Samaritans. ◆

Coming to faith in Christ does not automatically change one's view of the world and its people. See "Society's Divisions Affect Believers," Acts 6:1.

(continued from previous page)

perspective on power. Showered with uncritical adulation (vv. 9–10), he became obsessed with himself and his supposed importance. Tragically, he viewed others through the same distorted lens.

What about you? Have you succumbed to the illusion of power? Consider:

(1) How much time and energy do you devote to fantasizing about how great you could become?

(2) Do you pay attention only to those who stroke your ego? Or do you listen to those who aren't impressed with your status and will level with you about weaknesses?

(3) How much do status and position define who you are? Suppose you were to lose it all—what then?

God's power is vastly different from the world's. See "Power," Acts 1:8.

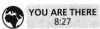

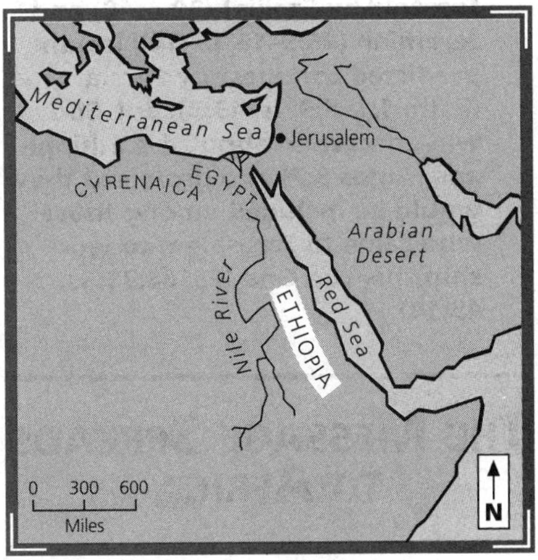

Ethiopia

YOU ARE THERE 8:27

• An ancient African nation south of Egypt, including the Egyptian territory south of Aswan (Syene; Ezek. 29:10).

(continued on next page)

(continued from previous page)

- **Name means "burnt face."**
- **Sometimes called Nubia or Cush.**
- **Known for its rivers, the Blue Nile and the White Nile (Is. 18:1), its papyrus boats (18:2), and its precious topaz gems (Job 28:19).**
- **Controlled by Egypt until after the time of David (1000 B.C.).**
- **Peopled by descendants of Ham, the father of Cush (Ethiopia; Gen. 10:6; 1 Chr. 1:8–10) as well as of Mizraim (Egypt). Ethiopia and Egypt were closely connected throughout their histories (Is. 20:3–5; Ezek. 30:4–5).**
- **Ethiopians known for their size and smooth, black skin (Is. 18:2; Jer. 13:23) and their military prowess (2 Sam. 18:21–32; 2 Chr. 12:3; 14:9–13; Jer. 46:9).**
- **Attained its greatest strength during the time of Hezekiah (700 B.C.), possibly because of internal disunity within Egypt.**
- **Conquest of Ethiopia by Babylon foretold by Ezekiel (30:4–10) and Jeremiah (46:9–10,13–14); Isaiah predicted conquest by Persia (Esth. 1:1; 8:9; Is. 43:3). But God was concerned about the Ethiopians (Amos 9:7) and promised they would be included among those who came to Jerusalem to worship the true God (Ps. 68:31; Is. 45:14).**

The Message Spreads to Africa

CONSIDER THIS 8:27–39 **The Ethiopian treasurer was probably a convert to Judaism. He had a great yearning to know the God of Israel, as demonstrated by his reading of Isaiah 53 (Acts 8:28–33) and by the fact that he had to travel at least 750 miles one way to worship in Jerusalem. The trip would have taken him and his ser-**

(continued on next page)

reading Isaiah the prophet. 29Then the Spirit said to Philip,
"Go near and overtake this chariot."
30So Philip ran to him, and heard him reading the
prophet Isaiah, and said, "Do you understand what you are
reading?"
31And he said, "How can I, unless someone guides me?"
And he asked Philip to come up and sit with him. 32The
place in the Scripture which he read was this:

"He was led as a sheep to the slaughter;
And as a lamb before its shearer is silent,
So He opened not His mouth.
33 In His humiliation His justice was taken away,
And who will declare His generation?
For His life is taken from the earth."[a]

34So the eunuch answered Philip and said, "I ask you, of
whom does the prophet say this, of himself or of some
other man?" 35Then Philip opened his mouth, and beginning at this Scripture, preached Jesus to him. 36Now as they
went down the road, they came to some water. And the eunuch said, "See, *here is* water. What hinders me from being
baptized?"
37Then Philip said, "If you believe with all your heart, you
may."
And he answered and said, "I believe that Jesus Christ is
the Son of God."[a]
38So he commanded the chariot to stand still. And both
Philip and the eunuch went down into the water, and he
8:27–39
baptized him. 39Now when they came up
out of the water, the Spirit of the Lord
caught Philip away, so that the eunuch saw him no more;
and he went on his way rejoicing. 40But Philip was found at
Azotus. And passing through, he preached in all the cities
till he came to Caesarea.

CHAPTER 9

Jesus Stops Saul Near Damascus

1Then Saul, still breathing threats and murder against the
9:2 see pg. 438
disciples of the Lord, went to the high
priest 2and asked letters from him to the
synagogues of Damascus, so that if he found any who were
of the Way, whether men or women, he might bring them
bound to Jerusalem.

8:33 [a]Isaiah 53:7, 8 *8:37* [a]NU-Text and M-Text omit this verse. It is found in Western texts, including the Latin tradition.

[3]As he journeyed he came near Damascus, and suddenly
a light shone around him from heaven. [4]Then he fell to the
ground, and heard a voice saying to him, "Saul, Saul, why
are you persecuting Me?"
[5]And he said, "Who are You, Lord?"
Then the Lord said, "I am Jesus, whom you are persecuting.[a] It *is* hard for you to kick against the goads."
[6]So he, trembling and astonished, said, "Lord, what do
You want me to do?"
Then the Lord *said* to him, "Arise and go into the city,
and you will be told what you must do."
[7]And the men who journeyed with him stood speechless,
hearing a voice but seeing no one. [8]Then Saul arose from
the ground, and when his eyes were opened he saw no one.
But they led him by the hand and brought *him* into Damascus. [9]And he was three days without sight, and neither ate
nor drank.

Ananias Reaches Out Cautiously

9:10
see pg. 440
[10]Now there was a certain disciple at
Damascus named Ananias; and to him
the Lord said in a vision, "Ananias."
And he said, "Here I am, Lord."
[11]So the Lord *said* to him, "Arise and go to the street
called Straight, and inquire at the house of Judas for *one*
called Saul of Tarsus, for behold, he is praying. [12]And in
a vision he has seen a man named Ananias coming in
and putting *his* hand on him, so that he might receive his
sight."
[13]Then Ananias answered, "Lord, I have heard from many
about this man, how much harm he has done to Your saints
in Jerusalem. [14]And here he has authority from the chief
priests to bind all who call on Your name."
9:15
see pg. 438
[15]But the Lord said to him, "Go, for he
is a chosen vessel of Mine to bear My
name before Gentiles, kings, and the children of Israel.
[16]For I will show him how many things he must suffer for
My name's sake."
9:10–18
see pg. 438
[17]And Ananias went his way and entered the house; and laying his hands on
him he said, "Brother Saul, the Lord Jesus,[a] who appeared
to you on the road as you came, has sent me that you may
receive your sight and be filled with the Holy Spirit." [18]Im-
mediately there fell from his eyes *something* like scales, and
he received his sight at once; and he arose and was baptized.

(Bible text continued on page 440)

9:5 [a]NU-Text and M-Text omit the last sentence of verse 5 and begin verse 6 with *But arise and go.* *9:17* [a]M-Text omits *Jesus.*

(continued from previous page)

vants at least thirty days by chariot. How long would he have stayed? A month? Then he faced a return trip. So he spent at least a quarter of a year to travel to Jerusalem to worship God.

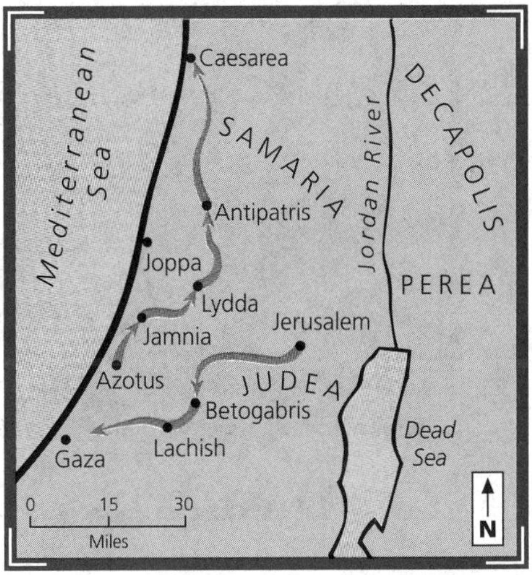

PHILIP AND THE ETHIOPIAN TREASURER

What he heard in the city about the followers of Jesus and their persecution is not recorded. But he responded warmly to Philip and the message about Christ, and became the first known witness—black or white—to Africa. For the second time in Acts 8, the gospel moved outside of the narrow confines of Jerusalem and Judea.

Once again God used Philip, the Greek-speaking Hellenist table-server, to accomplish the task rather than Peter, John, or the other apostles, who were just beginning to realize that the gospel reaches out to all peoples—Hellenists, Samaritans, even Gentiles of all colors and races.

Who was the curious man that the treasurer met on the road to Gaza? See "Philip the Evangelist," Acts 8:5–13.

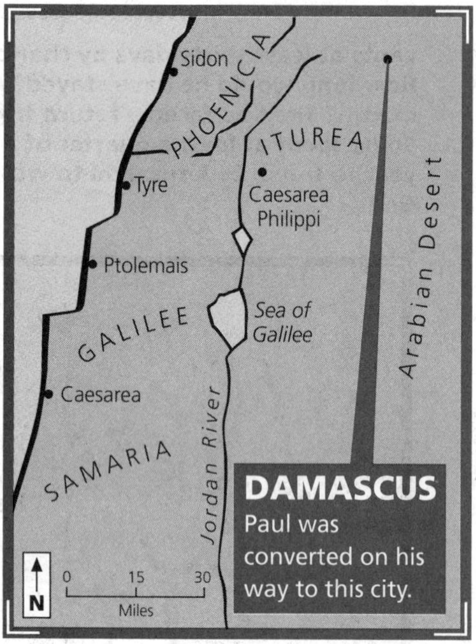

DAMASCUS

YOU ARE THERE 9:2 • Major city of the "Decapolis," ten cities located east of the Jordan River.

- A transportation and commercial hub for Palestine and Egypt to the south, the Tigris and Euphrates River valleys to the east, and Antioch and Asia Minor to the north. It sat at the intersection of the two main international highways of the ancient Near East, the Way of the Sea and the King's Highway (see "Travel in the Ancient World," Acts 13:3–4).
- Flat, surrounded by hills, it was never easy to defend.
- Heavily populated by Jews, later by Christians.
- Under Rome, governed itself as a free city, minting its own coinage, which added to its commercial prospects.
- Walled and laid out in a rectangle, with two parallel streets running its length. One was (and is) "the street called Straight."

ANANIAS—SCARED BUT OBEDIENT

CONSIDER THIS 9:10–18 Saul's reputation as a ruthless persecutor of Christians preceded him to Damascus (Acts 9:1, 10). Perhaps hearing that Saul was headed that way, Ananias mentally prepared himself to be hunted down, arrested, imprisoned, and ultimately martyred for following the new movement called the Way. In any case, he was no doubt stunned by the Lord's command to go and meet this dangerous enemy face-to-face! His words of protest indicate great fear.

But twice God commanded, "Go" (vv. 11, 15), and to his credit, Ananias—scared as he may have been—went obediently to lay hands on Saul that he might receive the Holy Spirit, and to baptize him. As a result, he witnessed the spiritual birth of early Christianity's greatest spokesperson. He also saw a dramatic demonstration of the truth that God's grace can overcome anyone's background.

Ananias' story challenges believers today to consider: Who might God want us to approach with the message of His grace? Who that we know is the least likely to respond to Christ—yet just might if only someone would reach out in faith and obedience?

The man whom Ananias went to visit had been raised in a way that made him the perfect choice to lead the opposition against the growing Christian movement—but later to lead the movement itself. See "Saul" and "Paul," Acts 13:2–3.

A RADICALLY CHANGED PERCEPTION

CONSIDER THIS 9:15 Have you ever avoided someone who seems dangerous? Ananias felt that way about Saul. He knew very well that Saul was a determined persecutor of believers, a government hit man assigned to purge the land of Christ's followers (9:1–2, 13–14). Saul terrified Ananias, and the frightened believer told God so.

But God assured him that the "impossible" can happen (v. 15). An enemy can become a partner. In fact, this particular enemy had changed and needed Ananias' help (vv. 17–18).

Do you harbor deep doubts about certain people, convinced that they will never change, never enter the faith? In light of Ananias' experience, perhaps it's time to review your perspective.

Another case in which an early believer needed to radically change his perception was Philemon, the owner of a runaway slave named Onesimus. See the Introduction to Philemon.

Barnabas—A Model for Mentoring

CONSIDER THIS 9:27

Barnabas' example serves as a textbook case in kingdom-style mentoring. This model mentor . . .

- Befriended Saul (Paul) as a new believer (9:26–27).
- Recruited a forgotten Saul from his home in Tarsus to help him stabilize a new group of multiethnic believers at Antioch, a year-long project (11:25–26).
- Helped organize an international team of leaders in prayer, fasting, and decision-making. Result: he launched out with Paul to bring the gospel to peoples in the western empire (13:1–3).
- Moved Paul to the forefront of leadership. "Barnabas and Saul" (13:7) became "Paul and his party" (13:13).
- Contended with ethnic hostility, personal attacks, and idol worship (13:46—14:20).
- Resisted well-meaning but misguided attempts at Lystra to make him and Paul into gods of Greek culture (14:8–18).
- Took the lead with Paul in defending Gentile believers before the Jerusalem church council (15:1–4, 12).
- Stood up to Paul over a negative assessment of young John Mark (15:36–38). Notice: Encouragers like Barnabas need not avoid conflict.
- Gave John Mark a second chance, taking him with him to Cyprus (15:39). He was vindicated several years later when Paul described John Mark as "useful to me for ministry" (2 Tim. 4:11).

The apostles chose the perfect Christian name for Joses of Cyprus when they called him Barnabas. Find out more about "Joe Encouragement" at Acts 4:36–37.

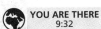

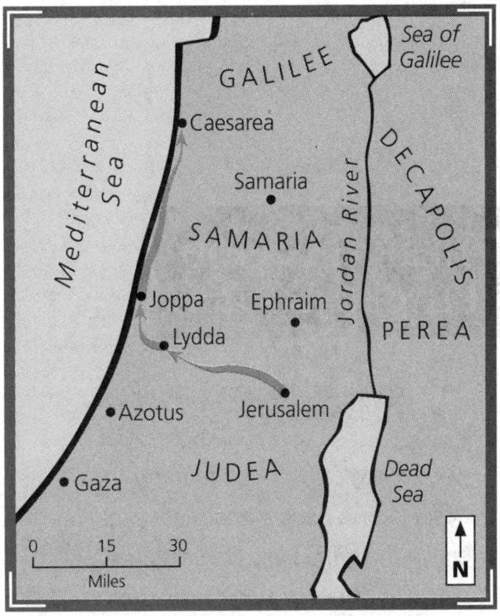

Peter's Journey to the Sea

Lydda

YOU ARE THERE 9:32

- Known as Lod in Old Testament times (1 Chr. 8:12) and today.
- Variously occupied by Jews, Greeks, Romans, Arabs, and Crusaders.
- In Peter's day, renowned for its legacy of Jewish scholarship and commerce.
- Burned in A.D. 70 by the Romans.
- Became a center of Christianity in the fourth century.
- Captured from the Arabs by Israel in 1948 and settled by Jewish immigrants.
- Famous today for its defense industry, paper products, food preserves, and electrical appliances.

19So when he had received food, he was strengthened.
Then Saul spent some days with the disciples at Damascus.

Believers Doubt Saul's Conversion

20Immediately he preached the Christ[a] in the synagogues,
that He is the Son of God.
21Then all who heard were amazed, and said, "Is this not
he who destroyed those who called on this name in
Jerusalem, and has come here for that purpose, so that he
might bring them bound to the chief priests?"

9:2–25 see pg. 442

22But Saul increased all the more in
strength, and confounded the Jews who
dwelt in Damascus, proving that this *Jesus* is the Christ.
23Now after many days were past, the Jews plotted to kill
him. 24But their plot became known to Saul. And they
watched the gates day and night, to kill him. 25Then the
disciples took him by night and let *him* down through the
wall in a large basket.

9:26–30 see pg. 444

26And when Saul had come to Jerusalem, he tried to join the disciples; but
they were all afraid of him, and did not believe that he was

9:27 see pg. 439

a disciple. 27But Barnabas took him and
brought *him* to the apostles. And he declared to them how he had seen the Lord on the road, and
that He had spoken to him, and how he had preached
boldly at Damascus in the name of Jesus. 28So he was with
them at Jerusalem, coming in and going out. 29And he
spoke boldly in the name of the Lord Jesus and disputed
against the Hellenists, but they attempted to kill him.

9:20 [a]NU-Text reads *Jesus.*

Where Has God Placed You?

CONSIDER THIS 8:26–39 *The Ethiopian treasurer (v. 27) was strategically placed to bring the gospel to his people and their leaders. In the same way, God may have placed you in a strategic position to bring the gospel to someone.*

Are you taking advantage of that opportunity?

Personality Profile: Ananias the Disciple

FOR YOUR INFO 9:10 **Not to be confused with:** Ananias, the deceptive property owner (Acts 5:1); Ananias, the notorious high priest (23:2).

Home: Damascus in Syria.

Best known today as: The believer sent by God to bring into the faith Saul of Tarsus, the zealous government agent who persecuted Christians.

30 When the brethren found out, they brought him down to
Caesarea and sent him out to Tarsus.
31 Then the churches[a] throughout all Judea, Galilee, and
Samaria had peace and were edified. And walking in the
fear of the Lord and in the comfort of the Holy Spirit, they
were multiplied.

Peter Heals Aeneas and Raises Tabitha

9:32 see pg. 439

32 Now it came to pass, as Peter went
through all *parts of the country,* that he
also came down to the saints who dwelt in Lydda. 33 There
he found a certain man named Aeneas, who had been
bedridden eight years and was paralyzed. 34 And Peter said
to him, "Aeneas, Jesus the Christ heals you. Arise and make
your bed." Then he arose immediately. 35 So all who dwelt at
Lydda and Sharon saw him and turned to the Lord.

9:36

36 At Joppa there was a certain disciple
named Tabitha, which is translated Dor-
cas. This woman was full of good works and charitable
deeds which she did. 37 But it happened in those days that
she became sick and died. When they had washed her, they
laid *her* in an upper room. 38 And since Lydda was near
Joppa, and the disciples had heard that Peter was there,
they sent two men to him, imploring *him* not to delay in
coming to them. 39 Then Peter arose and went with them.
When he had come, they brought *him* to the upper room.
And all the widows stood by him weeping, showing the tunics and garments which Dorcas had made while she was

9:31 [a]NU-Text reads *church . . . was edified.*

"JESUS THE CHRIST HEALS YOU. ARISE AND MAKE YOUR BED."
—Acts 9:34

PERSONALITY PROFILE: TABITHA

FOR YOUR INFO 9:36

Also known as: Dorcas, which means "gazelle."

Home: Joppa, the Mediterranean seaport (see accompanying map).

Special skills: Deft at sewing; she made clothing for destitute widows (Acts 9:36, 39).

Best known today for: Being raised from the dead by Peter, a miracle that demonstrated the gospel's truth and power (compare Mark 16:15–18; John 14:12–14).

with them. 40But Peter put them all out, and knelt down
and prayed. And turning to the body he said, "Tabitha,
arise." And she opened her eyes, and when she saw Peter
she sat up. 41Then he gave her *his* hand and lifted her up;
and when he had called the saints and widows, he presented her alive. 42And it became known
throughout all Joppa, and many believed
on the Lord. 43So it was that he stayed many days in Joppa
with Simon, a tanner.

9:42

YOU ARE THERE
9:2–25

An Amplifier for the Gospel

Damascus was a political football in the ancient world, not unlike places today that are torn by rival claims of ownership.

Damascus turned out to be an important city in the life of the church. Christians fled there from the persecution that followed Stephen's death (Acts 8:1, 4). Their faith attracted the attention of the council in Jerusalem, and Saul, the zealous Pharisee in charge of the anti-Christian campaign, was dispatched to investigate and make arrests (9:1–2).

Saul's (that is, Paul's) dramatic conversion on the Damascus road has been celebrated throughout Christian history. Less well known is that Damascus became a strategic center for Paul and the gospel. Certainly the church there must have been powerfully encouraged by the incredible turn of events that Paul's conversion entailed. During his lengthy stay (three years, according to Gal. 1:17–18), he became a champion of the gospel and probably helped win many Damascenes to the faith—so much so that he was forced to flee the city, just as earlier he had forced others to run (9:23–25).

Nevertheless, Damascus continued to be an amplifier for the gospel, as travelers through the Decapolis heard the good news there and spread it throughout the ancient world. Tradition holds that the apostle Matthew became a Syrian pastor and established a church in or near the city. The gospel that he wrote reflects his concern for Syrian believers (see the Introduction to Matthew).

A Christian church can still be found in Damascus—on a street called Straight. The Antiochian Orthodox Church and the Syrian Orthodox Church are both headquartered there. ◆

Cities in general can be enormously strategic in amplifying the message of Christ. See "Ghetto Blaster," Acts 19:10.

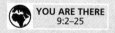

CHAPTER 10

An Ethnic Wall Comes Down

10:1

1There was a certain man in Caesarea
called Cornelius, a centurion of what was
called the Italian Regiment, 2a devout *man* and one who
feared God with all his household, who gave alms generously to the people, and prayed to God always. 3About the
ninth hour of the day he saw clearly in a vision an angel of
God coming in and saying to him, "Cornelius!"
4And when he observed him, he was afraid, and said,
"What is it, lord?"
So he said to him, "Your prayers and your alms have
come up for a memorial before God. 5Now send men to
Joppa, and send for Simon whose surname is Peter. 6He is
lodging with Simon, a tanner, whose house is by the sea.[a]
He will tell you what you must do." 7And when the angel
who spoke to him had departed, Cornelius called two of his
household servants and a devout soldier from among those
who waited on him continually. 8So when he had explained
all *these* things to them, he sent them to Joppa.

(Bible text continued on page 445)

10:6 [a]NU-Text and M-Text omit the last sentence of this verse.

PERSONALITY PROFILE: CORNELIUS

FOR YOUR INFO 10:1

Home: Stationed in Caesarea, Rome's administrative center in Palestine.

Occupation: Centurion. A Roman officer was designated a centurion if he oversaw at least 100 soldiers. As head of the Italian Regiment, he probably had about 600 men under his command.

Known to be: God-fearing, prayerful, and generous. He was drawn to Jewish monotheism as opposed to the pagan idolatry and immorality common among Romans of that day.

Best known today as: The second recorded Gentile convert to Christianity (an Ethiopian treasurer was first, Acts 8:26–40). He sent men to fetch Simon Peter, 36 miles away, in response to a vision from God.

JOPPA

YOU ARE THERE 9:42

- **A Mediterranean seaport, the only natural harbor between Egypt and the Bay of Acco (Haifa).**
- **Named Joppa, or "beautiful," because of the way sunlight reflected off its buildings and city walls.**
- **Known today as Jaffa or Yafo, a southern suburb of Tel Aviv.**
- **Although ideally situated for Israel's maritime use, Joppa was rarely under Israel's control. As a result, the nation never developed much of a navy during Old Testament times, which prevented it from dominating the Mediterranean.**

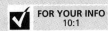

CONSIDER THIS
9:26–30

DISCIPLESHIP—OR MENTORING?

In the Great Commission (as it is frequently labeled; Matt. 28:19), Jesus commanded His disciples to "Go . . . and make disciples." The objective was not that they attract their own disciples, but that they win new followers of Jesus. Acts tells the story of how the Spirit-filled apostles obeyed that command.

But closely related to the making of disciples is the *mentoring* of leaders. Here in Acts 9 Saul's conversion starts one dynamic chain of mentoring that extends through the rest of the New Testament (see the accompanying diagram, "Kingdom-Style Mentoring").

"Mentoring" has become a buzzword among Western business and professional people. But the concept is as old as Homer's *Odyssey* (c. 900–810 B.C.), in which Odysseus entrusts to his friend, Mentor, the education of Telemachus, his son. A mentor, then, is a trusted counselor or guide—typically an older, more experienced person who imparts valuable wisdom to someone younger. Countless figures throughout history have recalled the powerful influence of mentors on their development.

The Old Testament is filled with mentoring relationships: Jethro, a wealthy livestock owner, helped his overworked son-in-law, Moses, learn to delegate authority (Ex. 18:1–27); Deborah, judge over Israel, summoned Barak to military leadership and helped him triumph over Jabin, a Canaanite king, bringing forty years of peace to the land (Judg. 4:4–24); Eli, a priest of the Lord (but a failure as a father) raised young Samuel to succeed him (1 Sam. 1:1—3:21); the prophet Elijah, who oversaw the evil end of Ahab and Jezebel, passed his office on to young Elisha, who received a double portion of his spirit (2 Kin. 2:1–15).

Barnabas, a wealthy landowner in the early church, became an advocate and guide for Saul, the former enemy and persecutor of the movement (Acts 9:26–30). Over time, with Barnabas' coaching and encouragement, Saul (later called Paul) became the central figure in the early spread of the gospel.

Close observation reveals four key functions of a kingdom-style mentor:

(1) Mentors *care* about those who follow them. Their primary interest is not what they can gain from the relationship, but with what they can give to it. They also realize how much they have to learn from their protégés. Ultimately, they fulfill Paul's admonition to look out not only for their own interests, but also for the interests of others (Phil. 2:4).

(2) Mentors *convey* wisdom and skill. Through modeling and coaching, and eventually by turning over responsibility to their followers, kingdom-style mentors seek to make their disciples more capable than the mentors have been (Matt. 10:25).

(3) Mentors *correct* their followers when they are wrong. An excellent example is Barnabas' challenge to Paul over taking John Mark along on the second missionary journey (Acts 15:36–39). Later Paul changed his perspective, and asked Timothy to bring John Mark to him (2 Tim. 4:11). Kingdom-style mentors do not avoid confrontation.

(4) Mentors *connect* their followers to significant others. As Acts 9 shows, Saul's entrée into the early church was Barnabas. Kingdom-style mentors introduce their protégés to relationships and resources that will further their development and increase their opportunities. ◆

Barnabas was so well regarded in the early church for his encouragement of others that his name was changed from Joses to Barnabas, which means "Son of Encouragement." Learn more about this model of kingdom-style mentoring at Acts 4:36–37.

9The next day, as they went on their journey and drew
near the city, Peter went up on the housetop to pray, about
the sixth hour. 10Then he became very hungry and wanted
to eat; but while they made ready, he fell into a trance 11and
saw heaven opened and an object like a great sheet bound
at the four corners, descending to him and let down to the
earth. 12In it were all kinds of four-footed animals of the
earth, wild beasts, creeping things, and birds of the air.
13And a voice came to him, "Rise, Peter; kill and eat."
14But Peter said, "Not so, Lord! For I have never eaten
anything common or unclean."
15And a voice *spoke* to him again the second time, "What
God has cleansed you must not call common." 16This was
done three times. And the object was taken up into heaven
again.
17Now while Peter wondered within himself what this vision which he had seen meant, behold, the men who had
been sent from Cornelius had made inquiry for Simon's
house, and stood before the gate. 18And they called and
asked whether Simon, whose surname was Peter, was lodging there.

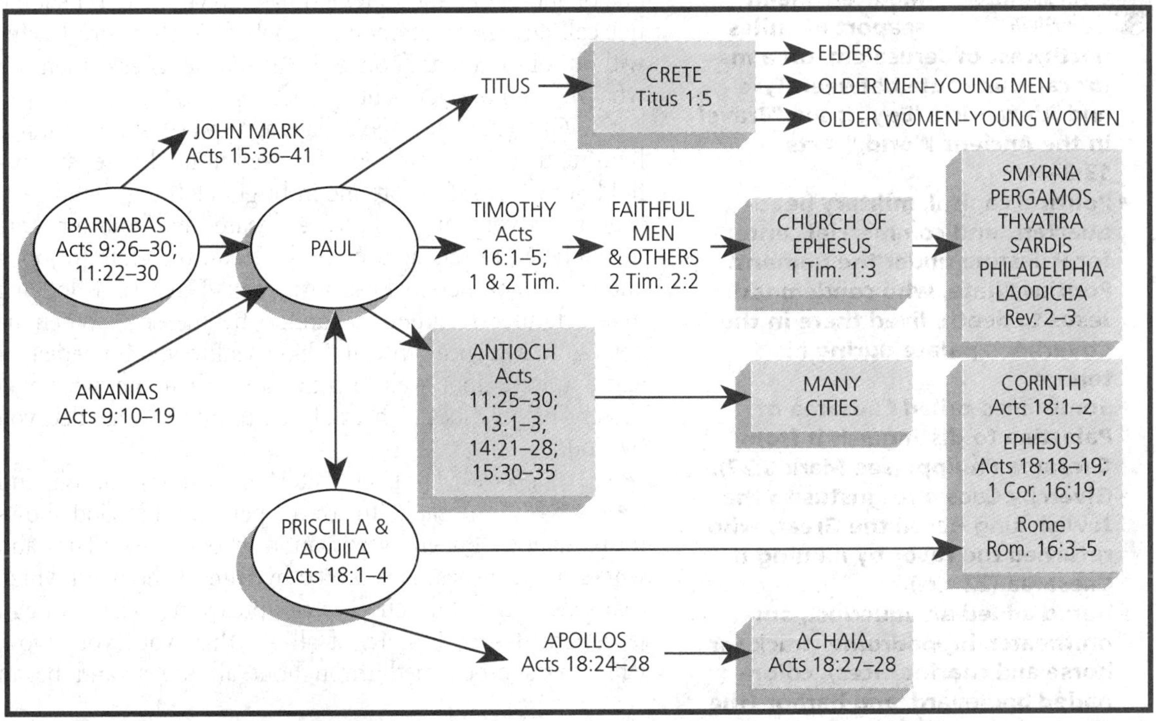

KINGDOM–STYLE MENTORING

Powerful results stem from experienced believers mentoring younger believers in the faith. Not only individuals, but entire communities benefit as the gospel transforms lives.

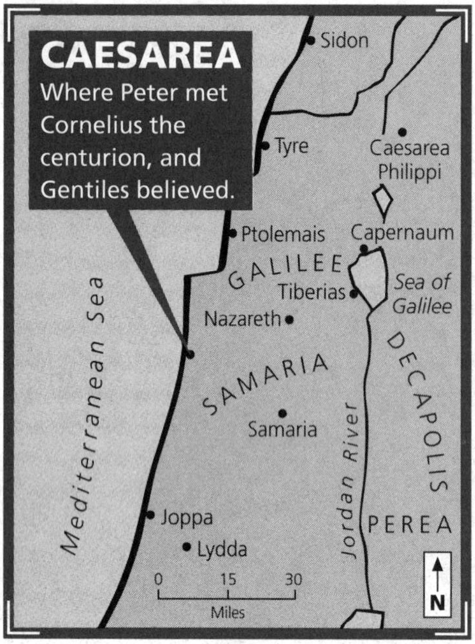

CAESAREA

YOU ARE THERE 10:24

- **Mediterranean seaport 60 miles northwest of Jerusalem, on a major caravan route between Tyre and Alexandria (Egypt; see "Travel in the Ancient World," Acts 13:3–4).**
- **Political capital, military headquarters, and commercial center for Palestine under the Romans. Pontius Pilate, who condemned Jesus to death, lived there in the governor's palace during his tenure.**
- **Sometimes called Caesarea of Palestine to distinguish it from Caesarea Philippi (see Mark 8:27).**
- **Given by Caesar Augustus to the Jewish king Herod the Great, who returned the favor by naming it Caesarea (22 B.C.).**
- **Herod added an aqueduct, amphitheater, hippodrome (track for horse and chariot races), colonnaded boulevard, and harbor (the city had no natural harbor).**
- **Herod also built a Roman temple**

(continued on next page)

19While Peter thought about the vision, the Spirit said to
him, "Behold, three men are seeking you. 20Arise therefore,
go down and go with them, doubting nothing; for I have
sent them."
21Then Peter went down to the men who had been sent to
him from Cornelius,[a] and said, "Yes, I am he whom you
seek. For what reason have you come?"
22And they said, "Cornelius *the* centurion, a just man, one
who fears God and has a good reputation among all the nation of the Jews, was divinely instructed by a holy angel to
summon you to his house, and to hear words from you."
23Then he invited them in and lodged *them*.
On the next day Peter went away with them, and some
brethren from Joppa accompanied him.

10:24

24And the following day they entered
Caesarea. Now Cornelius was waiting for
them, and had called together his relatives and close
friends. 25As Peter was coming in, Cornelius met him and
fell down at his feet and worshiped *him*. 26But Peter lifted
him up, saying, "Stand up; I myself am also a man." 27And
as he talked with him, he went in and found many who had
come together. 28Then he said to them, "You know how unlawful it is for a Jewish man to keep company with or go to
one of another nation. But God has shown me that I should
not call any man common or unclean. 29Therefore I came
without objection as soon as I was sent for. I ask, then, for
what reason have you sent for me?"
30So Cornelius said, "Four days ago I was fasting until this
hour; and at the ninth hour[a] I prayed in my house, and behold, a man stood before me in bright clothing, 31and said,
'Cornelius, your prayer has been heard, and your alms are
remembered in the sight of God. 32Send therefore to Joppa
and call Simon here, whose surname is Peter. He is lodging
in the house of Simon, a tanner, by the sea.[a] When he
comes, he will speak to you.' 33So I sent to you immediately,
and you have done well to come. Now therefore, we are all
present before God, to hear all the things commanded you
by God."

10:34 see pg. 450

34Then Peter opened *his* mouth and
said: "In truth I perceive that God shows
no partiality. 35But in every nation whoever fears Him and
works righteousness is accepted by Him. 36The word which
God sent to the children of Israel, preaching peace through
Jesus Christ—He is Lord of all— 37that word you know,
which was proclaimed throughout all Judea, and began

10:21 [a]NU-Text and M-Text omit *who had been sent to him from Cornelius.*
10:30 [a]NU-Text reads *Four days ago to this hour, at the ninth hour.* *10:32* [a]NU-Text omits the last sentence of this verse.

from Galilee after the baptism which John preached: 38how
God anointed Jesus of Nazareth with the Holy Spirit and
with power, who went about doing good and healing all
who were oppressed by the devil, for God was with Him.
39And we are witnesses of all things which He did both in
the land of the Jews and in Jerusalem, whom they[a] killed by
hanging on a tree. 40Him God raised up on the third day,
and showed Him openly, 41not to all the people, but to witnesses chosen before by God, *even* to us who ate and drank
with Him after He arose from the dead. 42And He commanded us to preach to the people, and to testify that it is
He who was ordained by God *to be* Judge of the living and
the dead. 43To Him all the prophets witness that, through
His name, whoever believes in Him will receive remission
of sins."

10:44–45
see pg. 448

44While Peter was still speaking these
words, the Holy Spirit fell upon all those
who heard the word. 45And those of the circumcision who
believed were astonished, as many as came with Peter, because the gift of the Holy Spirit had been poured out on the
Gentiles also. 46For they heard them speak with tongues
and magnify God.

Then Peter answered, 47"Can anyone forbid water, that
these should not be baptized who have received the Holy
Spirit just as we *have?*" 48And he commanded them to be
baptized in the name of the Lord. Then they asked him to
stay a few days.

CHAPTER 11

Peter Defends His Visit to Gentiles

1Now the apostles and brethren who were in Judea heard

11:2–18
see pg. 451

that the Gentiles had also received the
word of God. 2And when Peter came up
to Jerusalem, those of the circumcision contended with
him, 3saying, "You went in to uncircumcised men and ate
with them!"

4But Peter explained *it* to them in order from the beginning, saying: 5"I was in the city of Joppa praying; and in a
trance I saw a vision, an object descending like a great
sheet, let down from heaven by four corners; and it came to
me. 6When I observed it intently and considered, I saw
four-footed animals of the earth, wild beasts, creeping
things, and birds of the air. 7And I heard a voice saying to

(Bible text continued on page 450)

10:39 [a]NU-Text and M-Text add *also.*

(continued from previous page)

honoring Augustus. Filled with statues of the emperor, it offended the Jewish population, one of the prominent minority groups in the city.

- **Home to Philip the evangelist (see Acts 8:5).**
- **Paul kept there for two years in Herod's Praetorium, which housed an elite corps of Roman soldiers (23:23–35; 24:27), perhaps including Cornelius the centurion (see related article at 10:44–45).**
- **In the later Roman Empire, a major headquarters for the church and a center of learning.**

Herod the Great was politically astute but ruthless. He routinely exterminated his enemies, including one of his wives and three of his sons. See "The Herods," Acts 12:1–2.

CONSIDER THIS
10:44–45

Ethnic Walls Break Down

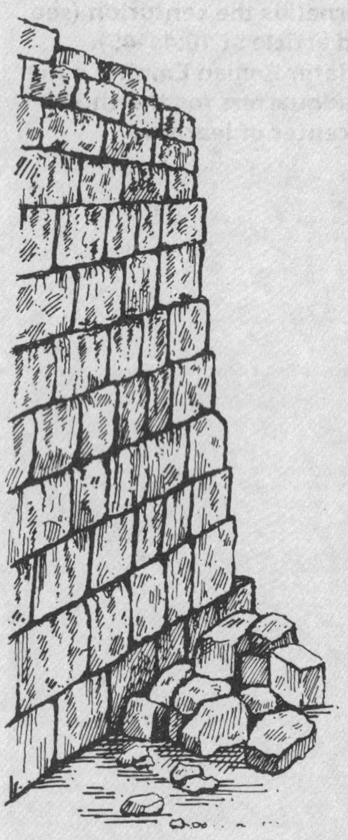

A major breakthrough in race relations is described in Acts 10. For years a virtual wall between Jews and Gentiles had hampered the apostles in sharing Jesus with the Gentile world. But when Peter met Cornelius—an officer of Rome's occupation troops in Palestine—two conversions took place: Cornelius, his family, and his friends came to faith; and Peter came to realize that God wants Gentiles in the church.

God easily could have used Philip the evangelist (see 8:5) to bring the gospel to Cornelius. After all, he lived in Caesarea and had already shown his willingness to share the gospel across ethnic lines. But no, God called Peter to bring His message to the Roman centurion. Apparently He wanted to break down barriers against Gentiles in Peter's heart.

How Peter Saw Cornelius

- *Living in Caesarea,* Roman military capital of Palestine (10:1).
- *A centurion,* commander of 100 occupying Roman troops (10:1).
- *Of the Italian Regiment,* all men from Italy (10:1).
- *Gentile* (10:1).
- *Unclean,* like the unclean animals of the Old Testament dietary laws (10:11–16).
- *Unlawful for a Jew to visit,* as he was from another nation (10:28).
- *Uncircumcised,* therefore not right to eat with (11:3).

In Peter's mind, these factors disqualified Cornelius from serving him dinner, let alone coming to faith. But Peter was following a "Jewish gospel."

God's intention had been that Hebrews would treat their Gentile neighbors cordially (Num. 35:15; Deut. 10:19; Ezek. 47:2). Of course, He also charged His people to exclude heathen practices, particularly idolatry (Lev. 18:24—19:4; Deut. 12:29–31). Intermarriage was condemned, though sometimes allowed (compare Ex. 34:16; Deut. 7:3; Ezra 9:12; 10:2–44; Neh. 10:30). But the main concern was moral purity.

Through rabbinic tradition strict separation became the rule. By Peter's day, four hundred years of Greek and Roman oppression had only hardened Jewish resolve to avoid as much contact as possible with foreigners.

Peter and the other Jewish believers brought these attitudes with them into the church, which made it almost impossible for them to reach out to Gentiles.

How God Saw Cornelius

- *Devout* (10:2).
- *A God-fearer,* along with his household (10:2).
- *Generous to the poor* (10:2).
- *A man of prayer* whose prayers and alms were received by God (10:2, 4).
- *Obedient to God's angel* (10:7–8).
- *Cleansed by God,* so not unclean (10:15).
- *Crucial for Peter to visit* (10:5, 19–20).

God's view of Cornelius was a contrast to Peter's. Because of Christ, God was ready to throw the doors of faith wide open to Gentiles: "What God has cleansed you must not call common," He sternly declared to Peter (vv. 9–16). Because of Christ, the centurion could be "cleansed" from sin and be acceptable to God.

But Peter was confused. Should he break with his culture and visit this Gentile, violating traditional codes handed down as if carrying the force of God's law? He had at least two days to sort out his thoughts as he walked to Caesarea to meet Cornelius. His emotional struggle can be seen in his first words to the assembled group: "You know how unlawful it is for a Jewish man to keep company with or go to one of another nation" (v. 28).

But God broke down the wall in Peter's heart by pouring out the Holy Spirit on these Gentile believers (vv. 44–45).

Peter's New Perspective

- "In truth I perceive that *God shows no partiality*" (10:34, italics added).
- "But *in every nation* whoever fears Him . . . is accepted by Him" (10:35, italics added).
- "Jesus Christ . . . is Lord of *all*" (10:36, italics added).
- "*Whoever believes* in Him will receive remission of sins" (10:43, italics added).
- "Can *anyone* forbid water, that *these* should not be baptized who have received the Holy Spirit *just as we have?*" (10:47, italics added).
- "God gave *them* the *same gift* as He gave us when we believed" (11:17, italics added).
- "*Who was I* that I could withstand God?" (11:17, italics added).

Breaking Down Barriers Today

Attitudes of prejudice and legalism trouble the church today just as they did the early church. Believers sometimes mingle cultural biases with biblical mandates, creating wrenching controversies over numerous sensitive issues. Certainly issues need to be addressed, particularly when essentials of the faith are at stake. But one of those biblical essentials is that believers eagerly seek out *all* people, look at them from God's perspective, love them for the gospel's sake, and rejoice over those that respond in faith. Can the church ever afford to wall itself off through fear or prejudice? Doing so would be to turn away from God's compassionate heart. ◆

The incident at Caesarea was not the first time that the early church had to deal with ethnic issues. See "A Growing Movement Confronts Ethnic Prejudice," Acts 6:2–6, and "Society's Divisions Affect Believers," Acts 6:1.

Peter's visit with Cornelius recalls an earlier meeting he had with Samaritans. See "The Conversion of Samaritans to the Gospel—and of Peter and John to Samaritans," Acts 8:4–25.

CONSIDER THIS
10:34

COME ONE, COME ALL!

God never shows partiality (v. 34), but people often do. Luke peppers his Acts account with incidents of ethnic tension and prejudice, and also their resolution in Christ. He shows that the door of faith is open to the whole world, Jews and Gentiles alike.

1:8 / Jesus sends His followers out "to the end of the earth."	
2:5–12, 37–41 / 3,000 **Hellenist Jews** from throughout the Roman world come to faith at Pentecost.	
6:1–7 / Reconciliation occurs between **Hellenist and native-born Jews.** Stephen, Philip, and other Hellenist leadership emerge.	
8:1, 4 / Persecuted believers scatter from Jerusalem throughout **Samaria**, telling their story.	
8:5–8 / Philip preaches the gospel to the **Samaritans**, who respond in multitudes.	
8:14–17, 25 / Peter and John visit the new **Samaritan believers**, pray that they would receive the Spirit, and begin preaching in **Samaritan cities.**	
8:26–40 / Philip meets a black official from **Ethiopia** and leads him to faith.	
10:1–48 / Peter baptizes Cornelius, a **Roman centurion of Caesarea**, and his relatives and close friends after seeing the Spirit come upon them.	
11:19–26 / The gospel spreads to **Antioch** and a multiethnic church is born.	
13:1—14:26 / Barnabas and Saul (Paul) take the gospel to **Asia Minor**, preaching first in synagogues but then turning to the Gentiles.	
15:1–33 / A meeting is held at Jerusalem to resolve controversy over the inclusion of **Gentiles** in the church.	
16:1–4 / Paul recruits **Timothy**, a young believer from a mixed background.	
17:16–34 / Paul preaches to the **intellectuals in Athens**, and some respond in faith.	
18:5–11 / Paul turns to the **Gentiles in Corinth**, establishing a multiethnic church.	
21:17–36 / Paul explains his **Gentile ministry** to the believers in Jerusalem, and takes Greeks into the temple, creating a riot.	

me, 'Rise, Peter; kill and eat.' 8But I said, 'Not so, Lord! For
nothing common or unclean has at any time entered my
mouth.' 9But the voice answered me again from heaven,
'What God has cleansed you must not call common.' 10Now
this was done three times, and all were drawn up again into
heaven. 11At that very moment, three men stood before the
house where I was, having been sent to me from Caesarea.
12Then the Spirit told me to go with them, doubting nothing. Moreover these six brethren accompanied me, and we
entered the man's house. 13And he told us how he had seen
an angel standing in his house, who said to him, 'Send men
to Joppa, and call for Simon whose surname is Peter, 14who
will tell you words by which you and all your household
will be saved.' 15And as I began to speak, the Holy Spirit fell
upon them, as upon us at the beginning. 16Then I remembered the word of the Lord, how He said, 'John indeed baptized with water, but you shall be baptized with the Holy
Spirit.' 17If therefore God gave them the same gift as *He gave*
us when we believed on the Lord Jesus Christ, who was I
that I could withstand God?"

18When they heard these things they became silent; and
they glorified God, saying, "Then God has also granted to
the Gentiles repentance to life."

The Message Spreads to Antioch

11:19–26
see pg. 453

19Now those who were scattered after
the persecution that arose over Stephen
traveled as far as Phoenicia, Cyprus, and Antioch, preaching the word to no one but the Jews only. 20But some of
them were men from Cyprus and Cyrene, who, when
they had come to Antioch, spoke to the Hellenists, preaching the Lord Jesus. 21And the hand of the Lord was
with them, and a great number believed and turned to the
Lord.

11:22
see pg. 452

22Then news of these things came to
the ears of the church in Jerusalem, and
they sent out Barnabas to go as far as Antioch. 23When he
came and had seen the grace of God, he was glad, and encouraged them all that with purpose of heart they should
continue with the Lord. 24For he was a good man, full of
the Holy Spirit and of faith. And a great many people were
added to the Lord.

11:25
see pg. 454

11:26
see pg. 455

25Then Barnabas departed for Tarsus to
seek Saul. 26And when he had found
him, he brought him to Antioch. So it
was that for a whole year they assembled
with the church and taught a great many people. And the
disciples were first called Christians in Antioch.

Famine Relief for Judea

27And in these days prophets came from Jerusalem to An-
11:28
tioch. 28Then one of them, named Agabus, stood up and showed by the Spirit that there was going to be a great famine throughout all the world, which also happened in the days of Claudius

◆ ◆ ◆ ◆ ◆ ◆ ◆ ◆ ◆ ◆ ◆ ◆ ◆ ◆ ◆

PERSONALITY PROFILE: CLAUDIUS

FOR YOUR INFO 11:28

Also known as: Tiberius Claudius Nero Germanicus (his full given name).

Home: Rome.

Family: Married and divorced three wives in succession, by whom he had five children. His fourth wife, Agrippina, fed him poison after forcing him to adopt her son, Nero, and proclaim him heir.

Profession: Fourth emperor of Rome (A.D. 41–54), crowned after the Praetorian Guard found him trembling in a corner following the murder of his predecessor, Caligula. Having been a sickly child and rather ugly and ill-mannered, he was considered unfit for public life.

Accomplishments: Planted Roman colonies throughout the empire; wrote some 30 books having to do with Roman history.

Regarded as: A fool. Seneca even wrote a satire entitled, *The Pumpkinification of the Divine Claudius.*

Best known today for: Putting down a riot "instigated by one Chrestus," which led to the expulsion of Jews and some Christians from Rome, including Aquila and Priscilla (Acts 18:1–2; see Rom. 16:3–5). A worldwide famine is also reported to have occurred during his reign (Acts 11:28).

For more on the powerful emperors and others who ruled the Roman Empire and Palestine in the first century, see "New Testament Political Rulers," Luke 3:1.

CONFLICT RESOLUTION

CONSIDER THIS 11:2–18

It seems that no matter what one does, conflicts are bound to happen. Peter's report of his visit to Cornelius aroused hostility and opposition among some of the believers at Jerusalem (vv. 2–3). His behavior in Joppa, socializing with the hated and feared Gentiles, was unacceptable—even scandalous.

But Peter responded with a clear, honest description of what happened (vv. 4–17). He filled in the gaps in their understanding and gently interpreted his activities. As a result, he not only achieved understanding, but created acceptance and approval for the new converts (v. 18).

Is there a need for advocacy, interpretation, or gentle persuasion in your world? Can you be a source of grace and truth between adversaries?

Peter's encounter with the believers at Jerusalem was not the end of the controversy over Gentiles in the church. See "Sure You're Saved . . . Sort Of," Acts 15:1–21.

Caesar. 29Then the disciples, each according to his ability,
determined to send relief to the brethren dwelling in Judea.
30This they also did, and sent it to the elders by the hands
of Barnabas and Saul.

CHAPTER 12

Herod Executes James and Has Peter Arrested

12:1–2
see pg. 458

1Now about that time Herod the king
stretched out *his* hand to harass some
from the church. 2Then he killed James the brother of John
with the sword. 3And because he saw that it pleased the
Jews, he proceeded further to seize Peter also. Now it was
during the Days of Unleavened Bread. 4So when he had arrested him, he put *him* in prison, and delivered *him* to four
squads of soldiers to keep him, intending to bring him before the people after Passover.

CONSIDER THIS
11:22

CHURCHES—KEYS TO THE CITIES

Christianity eventually prevailed as the dominant worldview and social force in the Roman world. One reason: it planted churches in dozens of the empire's major cities by the end of the first century. Christians spread the gospel "to the end of the earth" (Acts 1:8) by establishing strategic, visible communities in urban areas such as Antioch (11:22, 26; see 13:1). These groups of believers stood apart from the culture in their beliefs and values, yet engaged the culture in their daily lives and work.

The New Testament word for "church," ekklēsia, *means assembly or congregation. In the Greek world, the* ekklēsia *was a public assembly called together by a herald to discuss legal issues and make community decisions. For example, Paul faced such a gathering at Ephesus, a town meeting that turned into a riot (19:32–41). But* ekklēsia *always referred to people—originally to the citizens of a city, and later to a gathering of believers. There is no evidence that it meant a church building until the fourth century* A.D.

Interestingly, eight times out of ten the New Testament uses the word ekklēsia *to refer to all of the believers in a specific city, such as "the church that was at Antioch" (13:1) or "the church of God which is at Corinth" (1 Cor. 1:2). Elsewhere it implies all Christian believers, regardless of geographic location or time in history—what is often called the universal (or catholic) church (Eph. 1:22; 3:10, 21; 5:23–32).*

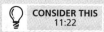

Peter Is Miraculously Released

5Peter was therefore kept in prison, but constant[a] prayer
was offered to God for him by the church. 6And when
Herod was about to bring him out, that night Peter was
sleeping, bound with two chains between two soldiers; and
the guards before the door were keeping the prison. 7Now
behold, an angel of the Lord stood by *him*, and a light shone
in the prison; and he struck Peter on the side and raised
him up, saying, "Arise quickly!" And his chains fell off *his*
hands. 8Then the angel said to him, "Gird yourself and tie
on your sandals"; and so he did. And he said to him, "Put
on your garment and follow me." 9So he went out and followed him, and did not know that what was done by the
angel was real, but thought he was seeing a vision. 10When
they were past the first and the second guard posts, they

12:5 [a]NU-Text reads *constantly* (or *earnestly*).

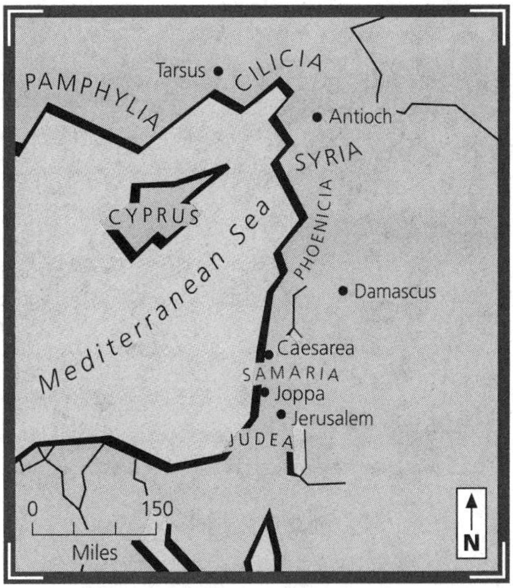

EARLY CHURCH EXPANSION

In forming churches, the early Christians did not drop out of society, nor did they form congregations that competed with each other for members (though sometimes members competed with each other, 1 Cor. 1:10–12). Instead, they lived and worked as members of the larger community. Meanwhile, they related to the other believers in their cities as members of a common family in Christ. This proved to be a radical concept—so powerful, in fact, that by the end of the second century, one author was able to write:

> *Christians are not distinguished from the rest of mankind by either country, speech, customs; the fact is, they nowhere settle in cities of their own; they use no peculiar language; they cultivate no eccentric mode of life . . . .*
>
> *Yet while they dwell in both Greek and non-Greek cities, as each one's lot was cast, and conform to the customs of the country in dress, food, and mode of life in general, the whole tenor of their way of living stamps it as worthy of admiration and admittedly extraordinary.*

This remarkable reputation of the early Christians compels modern believers to ask: What will the church today be remembered for? ◆

THE MOVEMENT EXPANDS BEYOND PALESTINE

YOU ARE THERE 11:19–26 **Though the apostles remained in Jerusalem, the majority of believers there scattered (v. 19) in the face of deadly attacks by Saul and others following Stephen's death (Acts 8:1–3; 9:1; 22:4–5; 26:10–11). As the Christians searched for places to rebuild their lives, some related the gospel to Jews only. But others who spoke Greek (like those from Cyprus and Cyrene, modern-day Libya) crossed ethnic barriers, particularly at Antioch.**

Jerusalem was never intended to be the headquarters of Christianity. See "Jerusalem—Merely the Beginning," Acts 1:12–26, and "The Message Leaves Jerusalem," Acts 8:1.

TARSUS

YOU ARE THERE 11:25

- **One of the world's oldest cities, with a continuous history dating back several thousand years.**
- **Capital of the province of Cilicia under the Romans, on the southeast coast of Asia Minor, with a culture heavily influenced by the Greeks.**
- **City where Cleopatra first met Mark Antony.**
- **A free city under Caesar Augustus, meaning it enjoyed self-government and tax-exempt status.**
- **Noted as a center of learning, with schools rivaling those of Alexandria.**
- **Center for the garment and tent-making industries. A goat hair fabric called cilicium was used to make tents. Paul may have picked up this trade as a boy.**
- **Population in Roman times may have been 500,000.**
- **A sizable Jewish population and synagogue by the first century.**

Tarsus' greatest claim to fame proved to be the apostle Paul. To learn more about this dynamic leader, see the profile at Acts 13:2–3.

came to the iron gate that leads to the city, which opened to
them of its own accord; and they went out and went down
one street, and immediately the angel departed from him.
11And when Peter had come to himself, he said, "Now I
know for certain that the Lord has sent His angel, and has
delivered me from the hand of Herod and *from* all the expectation of the Jewish people."

12:12–17

12So, when he had considered *this*, he
came to the house of Mary, the mother of
John whose surname was Mark, where many were gathered
together praying. 13And as Peter knocked at the door of the
gate, a girl named Rhoda came to answer. 14When she recognized Peter's voice, because of *her* gladness she did not
open the gate, but ran in and announced that Peter stood
before the gate. 15But they said to her, "You are beside yourself!" Yet she kept insisting that it was so. So they said, "It is
his angel."
16Now Peter continued knocking; and when they opened
the door and saw him, they were astonished. 17But motioning to them with his hand to keep silent, he declared to
them how the Lord had brought him out of the prison. And
he said, "Go, tell these things to James and to the brethren."
And he departed and went to another place.
18Then, as soon as it was day, there was no small stir
among the soldiers about what had become of Peter. 19But
when Herod had searched for him and not found him, he
examined the guards and commanded that *they* should be
put to death.

MARY'S HOUSE

CONSIDER THIS 12:12–17 *Mary, John Mark's mother (v. 12), contributed immeasurably to the growth of the early church by opening her home as a meeting place for believers at Jerusalem. As homeowner and host she probably had a prominent role in the gatherings.*

Like her nephew, Barnabas (see 4:36–37; Col. 4:10), Mary apparently enjoyed some wealth, as demonstrated by her employment of the maid Rhoda. Released from prison, Peter went immediately to this center of Christian activity.

And he went down from Judea to Caesarea, and stayed *there.*

An Angel of God Strikes Down Herod

20Now Herod had been very angry with the people of Tyre
and Sidon; but they came to him with one accord, and having made Blastus the king's personal aide their friend, they
asked for peace, because their country was supplied with
food by the king's *country.*
21So on a set day Herod, arrayed in royal apparel, sat on
his throne and gave an oration to them. 22And the people
kept shouting, "The voice of a god and not of a man!"
23Then immediately an angel of the Lord struck him, because he did not give glory to God. And he was eaten by
worms and died.
24But the word of God grew and multiplied.

Barnabas and Saul Are Sent Out

25And Barnabas and Saul returned from[a] Jerusalem when
they had fulfilled *their* ministry, and they also took with
them John whose surname was Mark.

CHAPTER 13

13:1 see pg. 461
13:1–3 see pg. 460
13:2–3 see pg. 456

1Now in the church that was at Antioch
there were certain prophets and teachers:
Barnabas, Simeon who was called Niger,
Lucius of Cyrene, Manaen who had been
brought up with Herod the tetrarch, and
Saul. 2As they ministered to the Lord and
fasted, the Holy Spirit said, "Now separate to Me Barnabas
and Saul for the work to which I have called them." 3Then,
having fasted and prayed, and laid hands on them, they
sent *them* away.

A Governor Believes

13:3–4 see pg. 462
13:5 see pg. 466

4So, being sent out by the Holy Spirit,
they went down to Seleucia, and from
there they sailed to Cyprus. 5And when
they arrived in Salamis, they preached
the word of God in the synagogues of the Jews. They also
had John as *their* assistant.

13:6 see pg. 466

6Now when they had gone through the
island[a] to Paphos, they found a certain
sorcerer, a false prophet, a Jew whose name *was* Bar-Jesus,
7who was with the proconsul, Sergius Paulus, an intelligent
man. This man called for Barnabas and Saul and sought to
hear the word of God. 8But Elymas the sorcerer (for so his

(Bible text continued on page 458)

12:25 [a]NU-Text and M-Text read *to.* *13:6* [a]NU-Text reads *the whole island.*

A New Reality Gets a New Name

CONSIDER THIS 11:26 **As Jesus' band of followers grew into a movement, they were called the Way (Acts 9:2), probably a reference to Christ's statement, "I am the Way" (John 14:6). For the most part, members of the Way had been Jewish believers.**

But in Antioch there was an infusion of other ethnic groups, and observers were perplexed as to what to call the multicultural body. The new reality required a new name. Standard ethnic designations—Jews, Greeks, Romans, Gentiles—no longer fit. So the Antiochians seized on the one factor that united the diverse community—Christ. Actually, the term "Christians," or Christ-followers, was a sarcastic put-down (Acts 11:26). But the term stuck and even became a name of honor.

Are there perceptions of the faith where you live and work that are inadequate? Can you change some of those with a display of what following Christ actually involves? Are there ways in which coworkers, friends, or relatives can be touched by the faith, ways that will cause a breakthrough in understanding?

The name of Jesus held extraordinary power for the first believers. See "Jesus—The Name You Can Trust," Acts 3:1.

Saul of Tarsus

FOR YOUR INFO 13:2–3 **Few backgrounds could have better prepared Saul to be the chief persecutor of the early church. He was born at Tarsus—"no mean city," as he liked to describe it (21:39)—a major Roman city on the coast of southeast Asia Minor. Tarsus was a center for the tentmaking industry, and perhaps that influenced Saul to choose that craft as an occupation. Teachers of the Law, which Saul eventually became, were not paid for their services and had to earn a living in other ways (see "Scribes," Luke 20:39).**

However, Saul said that he was "brought up" in Jerusalem "at the feet of Gamaliel," the most illustrious rabbi of the day (Acts 22:3) and a highly respected member of the Jewish council (5:34; see "The Council," Acts 6:12). In making that statement, Saul was describing a process of technical training in the Law that prepared him to become one of the Pharisees, the religious elite of Judaism. For many Jewish youth, the rigorous course of study began at age 14 and continued to the age of 40.

Apparently Saul was an apt pupil. He claimed to have outstripped his peers in enthusiasm for ancestral traditions and in his zeal for the Law (Phil. 3:4–6). Probably through Gamaliel, he had opportunity to observe the council and come to know many of its principals and some of its inner workings.

So it was that he chanced to be present when the conflict between the council and the early church came to a head in the stoning of Stephen (7:57—8:1). He had likely watched earlier encounters between the council and members of the Way, such as those with Peter and John (4:5–18; 5:17–40). But apparently the incident with Stephen galvanized his commitment to traditional Judaism and set him off on a mission to seek out and destroy as many believers as he could (8:1–3).

Personality Profile: Saul

Also known as: Paul, perhaps his Roman name; but as far as we know, he was always called Saul prior to his conversion (see the accompanying profile on post-conversion Paul).

Home: Born at Tarsus (see Acts 11:25); brought up in Jerusalem (see Matt. 23:37).

Family: Saul was a Jew but was born a Roman citizen (Acts 22:28), which means his father, who was a Pharisee (23:6), must have been a Roman citizen before him.

Profession: Tentmaker by trade (see 18:1–3); trained as a Pharisee under Rabbi Gamaliel, he became the Jewish council's chief agent of anti-Christian activity.

Life-changing experience: Before his conversion—probably witnessing Stephen's defense before the council and subsequent execution by stoning (7:1—8:1)

Best known today for: His ardent persecution of Christians.

He made havoc of the church.
—Acts 8:3

PAUL, THE APOSTLE TO THE GENTILES

Ironically, Paul's background not only prepared him to be the early church's chief opponent, but also to become its leading spokesperson. Devout, energetic, outspoken, stubborn, and exacting, Paul became far more troublesome to the Jews than he had ever been to the Christians, not in terms of violence, but ideology. Indeed, he lived with a price on his head as his former colleagues among the Jews sought to destroy him (Acts 9:23–25, 29; 23:12–15; 2 Cor. 11:26, 32–33).

Perhaps the chief irony of Paul's life was his calling to be the "apostle to the Gentiles" (Acts 9:15; Gal. 1:16; 2:7–9). Paul had been a Pharisee, the very title meaning "to separate." Some Pharisees even refused to eat with non-Pharisees for fear of being contaminated by food not rendered ritually clean. They also separated from women, from lepers, from Samaritans, and especially from Gentiles (or "foreigners").

So for Paul to take the gospel to the Gentiles was a reversal of his life and a thorough repudiation of his background as a Pharisee. Perhaps three people proved invaluable in helping him make this dramatic change: Barnabas, who like Paul was a Hellenistic Jew and came from a Levite background—he embraced Paul and mentored him in the faith when no one else would come near him (see Acts 4:36–37); and Priscilla and Aquila, fellow tentmakers—they joined Paul in business in Corinth and probably discussed the faith and its implications with Paul much as they did with Apollos (18:1–3; 24–28; see Rom. 16:3–5).

Paul eventually became Christianity's leading evangelist and theologian. But even as his status in the church rose, his perspective on himself changed. At first he saw himself as an important Christian leader, but then as "the least of the apostles" (1 Cor. 15:9). Later he realized that he was capable of "nothing good" (Rom. 7:18) and was "less than the the least of all the saints" (Eph. 3:8). Finally he described himself as the "chief" of sinners (1 Tim. 1:15)—and threw himself on God's mercy and grace.

The fearsome Pharisee of Pharisees became the fearless apostle to the Gentiles whose credo was, "To live is Christ, and to die is gain" (Phil. 1:21).

PERSONALITY PROFILE: PAUL

Also known as: Saul, his Jewish name, perhaps given in memory of Israel's first king, a member of the tribe of Benjamin, to which Paul's family belonged; but following his conversion he was known as Paul.

Home: Settled in Antioch of Syria (see Acts 13:1), but traveled throughout the Roman empire, with extended stays in Corinth (see Introduction to 2 Corinthians) and Ephesus (see Introduction to Ephesians).

Family: Luke mentions a sister and her son (Acts 23:16).

Profession: Tentmaker by trade (see 18:1–3); he became not only a leader in the church, but its most well-known and widely traveled spokesperson, and a major New Testament writer.

Life-changing experience: A vision of Christ on the Damascus road, which led to his conversion and call as an apostle (9:1–31; Gal. 1:1–24).

Best known today as: The apostle to the Gentiles.

Paul's transformation into the "apostle to the Gentiles" did not take place overnight. It took him at least ten years to reevaluate his cultural perspectives and bring them in line with the heart of God for the world. See "A Bigot Does an About-Face," Gal. 1:13–17.

name is translated) withstood them, seeking to turn the
proconsul away from the faith. 9Then Saul, who also *is*
called Paul, filled with the Holy Spirit, looked intently at
him 10and said, "O full of all deceit and all fraud, *you* son of
the devil, *you* enemy of all righteousness, will you not cease
perverting the straight ways of the Lord? 11And now, in-

FOR YOUR INFO
12:1–2

THE HERODS

Backed by Roman authority, the family of the Herods exerted ruthless control over Palestine during the time of Christ and the founding of the church. Although they built many splendid edifices and strengthened Judea militarily, they are remembered infamously for a family history full of violence, incest, and political intrigue.

Antipater

- *Cunning, wealthy, ambitious.*
- *Leveraged Jewish civil unrest with Roman muscle to take control (47 B.C.).*
- *Installed his son Herod ("the Great") as governor of Judea.*
- *Died of poisoning.*

Herod the Great

- *Intelligent, charming in manners, a master of statecraft, and like his father, highly ambitious.*
- *Survived Jewish challenges to his rule through skillful politicking with Roman authorities, hard fighting, and extermination of his enemies, including one of his wives and three of his sons.*
- *Proclaimed king of the Jews by the Romans, a position he held at the birth of Christ (Matt. 2:1).*
- *Married a total of ten women who bore him at least 15 children.*
- *Rebuilt the temple to regain the Jews' favor. But he also built temples to pagan gods.*
- *Deteriorated mentally and physically in later years, but before dying divided his kingdom among three sons.*

Herod Archelaus

- *Oldest of Herod's sons, with the worst reputation.*
- *Given Judea by his father (Matt. 2:22).*
- *Angered the Jews by marrying his half-brother's widow.*
- *Deposed and banished in A.D. 6, leaving Judea a Roman province.*

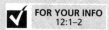

deed, the hand of the Lord *is* upon you, and you shall be
blind, not seeing the sun for a time."
And immediately a dark mist fell on him, and he went
around seeking someone to lead him by
the hand. 12Then the proconsul believed,
when he saw what had been done, being
astonished at the teaching of the Lord.

13:4–12 see pg. 464

13:4–12 see pg. 465

Herod Antipas

- *Depicted in Scripture as wholly immoral.*
- *Given Galilee and Perea by his father, Herod the Great, inheriting the title of tetrarch (ruler of a fourth part).*
- *Childhood companion of Manaen, who was a leader in the church at Antioch (Acts 13:1).*
- *Divorced his first wife to marry Herodias, wife of his half-brother and also his niece.*
- *Maneuvered by Herodias into executing John the Baptist (Matt. 14:1–12; Mark 6:17–28).*
- *Exiled by Caligula after Herodias' brother Agrippa accused him of plotting against Rome.*

Herod Philip II

- *The one bright spot in the family—dignified, modest, and just.*
- *Given the northeastern territories of Iturea and the region of Trachonitis by his father Herod the Great (Luke 3:1).*

Herod Agrippa I

- *Grandson of Herod the Great.*
- *Installed by Caligula, he eventually ruled all of Jewish Palestine.*
- *Executed the apostle James and persecuted the early church (Acts 12:1–2).*
- *Struck down by God for his arrogance (12:21–23).*

Herod Agrippa II

- *Son of Agrippa I.*
- *Had an incestuous relationship with his sister, Bernice.*
- *Heard Paul's defense of his ministry (Acts 25:13—26:32).*
- *Fled Palestine for Rome during the Jewish revolts, where he died in A.D. 100.* ◆

Find out about the other major political leaders of the Roman Empire and Palestine in the first century in the table, "New Testament Political Rulers," Luke 3:1.

"WILL YOU NOT CEASE PERVERTING THE STRAIGHT WAYS OF THE LORD?"
—Acts 13:10

Barnabas and Paul Turn to the Gentiles

13:13 see pg. 468
13Now when Paul and his party set sail
from Paphos, they came to Perga in Pamphylia; and John, departing from them, returned to
13:13–14 see pg. 466
Jerusalem. 14But when they departed
from Perga, they came to Antioch in Pi-
sidia, and went into the synagogue on the Sabbath day and
13:14–52 see pg. 466
sat down. 15And after the reading of the
Law and the Prophets, the rulers of the
synagogue sent to them, saying, "Men *and* brethren, if you
have any word of exhortation for the people, say on."
16Then Paul stood up, and motioning with *his* hand said,
"Men of Israel, and you who fear God, listen: 17The God of

YOU ARE THERE 13:1–3

ANTIOCH: A MODEL FOR THE MODERN CHURCH?

Even though first-century Christians made regular pilgrimages to Jerusalem and met annually in the upper room, the city of Antioch—not Jerusalem—was the center of early Christianity. In fact, modern churches might consider Antioch as a model for what God's people ought to be and do.

Like most cities today, Antioch was racially diverse and culturally pluralistic. As a result, when the scattered believers arrived there (Acts 11:19–20), they had to wrestle with how to make the gospel meaningful for a diversity of groups. Four factors help to account for their success.

(1) They saw ethnic division as a barrier to overcome rather than a status quo to be maintained. *Antioch walled off the four dominant ethnic groups of its population, Greek, Syrian, African, and Jewish. But the gospel breaks down walls of separation and hostility (Eph. 2:14–22) and brings diverse peoples together in Christ. We know that the Antioch believers broke through the ethnic barriers because . . .*

(2) They soon had multiethnic leadership. *The church employed and deployed pastors, teachers, and evangelists who reflected the composition of the community. Notice the cross-section of the city represented by the leadership team in Acts 13:1:*

- *Barnabas, a Hellenist from Cyprus raised in a priestly family. Appropriately, he was the first major leader of the new group (see 4:36; 11:22–23).*
- *Simeon (Niger), an African.*
- *Lucius of Cyrene, also of African descent.*
- *Manaen, a childhood companion of Herod Antipas (the ruler who killed John the Baptist, Mark 6:17–28), per-*

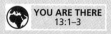

this people Israel[a] chose our fathers, and exalted the people
when they dwelt as strangers in the land of Egypt, and with
an uplifted arm He brought them out of it. 18Now for a time
of about forty years He put up with their ways in the
wilderness. 19And when He had destroyed seven nations in
the land of Canaan, He distributed their land to them by al-
lotment.
20"After that He gave *them* judges for about four hundred
and fifty years, until Samuel the prophet. 21And afterward
they asked for a king; so God gave them Saul the son of
Kish, a man of the tribe of Benjamin, for forty years. 22And

(Bible text continued on page 464)

13:17 [a]M-Text omits *Israel.*

haps even a relative, and surely a privileged member of society.

- *Saul, a Hellenistic Jew from Tarsus with rabbinical training who had Roman citizenship. Note how Barnabas intentionally recruited this young, untried leader for the work (Acts 11:25–26).*

(3) They sent out ministry teams. *Just as the church at Antioch had been established by believers fleeing from Jerusalem, it, too, sent out ministry teams to tell the story of Jesus. Paul used Antioch as his base of operation for three successive tours (13:1–3; 15:36–41; and 18:22–23). Moreover, Antioch served as a crossroads for travelers from the Tigris and Euphrates River valleys to the east, Asia Minor to the north, and Egypt to the south. So the church was able to maintain an international outreach in its own hometown.*

(4) They joined together to accomplish projects of compassion. *A famine in Judea became an opportunity for the multiethnic Christians at Antioch to serve their predominantly Jewish brothers in Judea (11:27–30). Paul recognized how powerful the "politics of compassion" could be at uniting otherwise disconnected churches. "Remember the poor" became his rallying cry to bring together believers in Ephesus, Corinth, Thessalonica, Galatia, and Rome with those at Jerusalem (for example, 20:17–18, 35; 2 Cor. 8:1—9:15; Gal. 2:10).*

Overall, Antioch became the model for how the church ought to function when surrounded by diversity and cultural pluralism. ◆

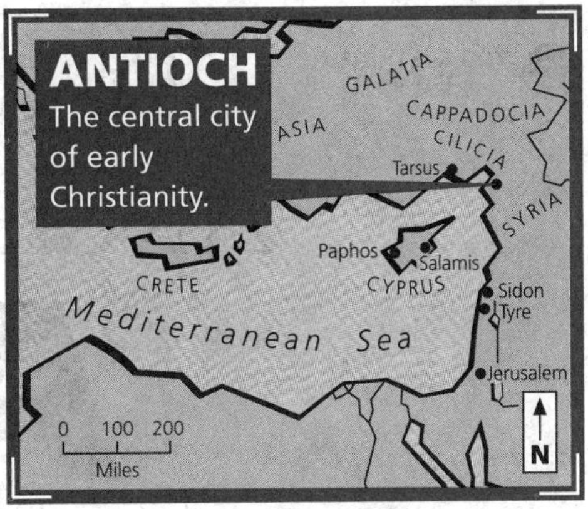

ANTIOCH

YOU ARE THERE 13:1

- **One of 16 cities named Antioch, sometimes called "Antioch of Syria" to distinguish it.**
- **Third largest city of the Roman empire, with 500,000 to 800,000 residents.**
- **Noted for its political power, bustling trade and commerce, a vibrant intellectual life, and religious tolerance.**
- **Divided by walls into four quadrants—Greek, Syrian, African, and Jewish.**
- **City where followers of the Way were first called "Christians" (Acts 11:26) and main headquarters of the early church.**
- **Known today as Antakiya in Turkey, a town of 35,000.**

YOU ARE THERE
13:3–4

Travel in the Ancient World

As they set off on their travels for "the work" to which God had called them, Barnabas and Saul traveled through Seleucia (vv. 3–4), the seaport for Antioch. The city was important to the Romans because it provided access to one of the major east-west land trade routes of the Mediterranean region, the Way of the Sea.

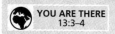

The Way of the Sea

The Way of the Sea (Is. 9:1), also called "the way of the land of the Philistines" (Ex. 13:17) and, later, the Via Maris, was the most important international highway throughout the biblical period. Originating in Egypt, it ran north along the coast to a pass over the Carmel ridge, through the Valley of Jezreel to Hazor, and eventually to Damascus. From there one could either head north through Syria toward Asia Minor, or east toward Mesopotamia, eventually linking up with the Euphrates River, which the highway followed to the Persian Gulf.

Many of the most important political and commercial centers of the ancient world were located along this road and its branches. Citizens thrived on supplying the needs and security of the many caravans traveling east and west.

However, it was the strategic military value of this roadway that ancient empires prized the most. By controlling a key city like Damascus or the passes at Megiddo and Hazor, an army could effectively shut down the Way of the Sea—or keep it open for its own troops or merchants. As a result, Palestine became a major factor in international politics and trade.

The King's Highway

A second major highway in the region was the King's Highway (Num. 20:17; 21:22). The northern portion was also called "the way to Bashan" (Num. 21:33) or "the road to Bashan" (Deut. 3:1). The King's Highway ran north and south along the length of the Transjordanian Highlands, near the desert to the east of the Sea of Galilee, Jordan River, and the Dead Sea, and linked Damascus (and the Way of the Sea) with Elath on the Gulf of Aqaba.

This route provided a secondary road to Egypt and access to the spice routes of Arabia. It was often controlled by semi-nomadic people who prevented the founding of settlements along its length. In certain periods, however, the route was guarded by a network of fortresses.

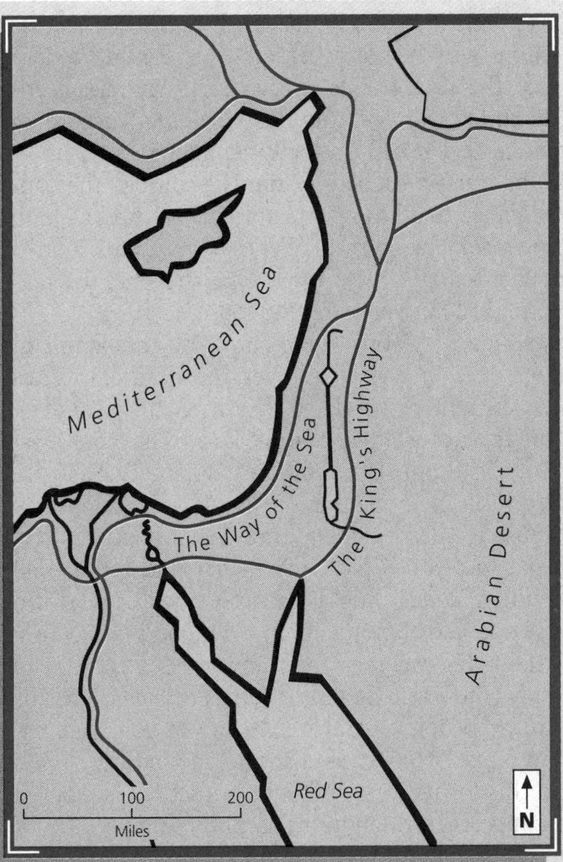

MAJOR LAND ROUTES

Secondary Road Systems

Within the region of Palestine, an internal system of roads provided communication between the many regions of the country. One north-south route, called the Way of the Wilderness of Edom and the Way of the Wilderness of Moab was located to the east of the King's Highway, along the fringe of the desert. It avoided the dry streambeds whose deep canyons divided the Transjordanian Highlands into its main geographical regions.

Other regional roads mentioned in the Bible include: "the way to the mountains of the Amorites" in the south (Deut. 1:19); "the road to Beth Shemesh" linking that city with Jerusalem (1 Sam. 6:9); "the road to Beth Horon," north of and parallel to the road to Beth Shemesh (1 Sam. 13:18); and "the way of the wilderness" west of Jericho to Ai (Josh. 8:15).

For people of means or position, such as the Ethiopian treasurer (Acts 8:26–28), travel along these roads might be by chariot or by portable chairs (Song 3:6–10). Horses were used mostly for military purposes (Acts 23:23–24).

For most people, however, the only way to get about was on foot or donkeyback. Foot travelers could average about 16 miles a day. Thus under normal circumstances, the trip that Joseph and Mary took from Nazareth to Bethlehem (Luke 2:1–7) probably took at least five days.

Sea Journeys

For long distances, ship travel was common (Jon. 1; Acts 13:4; 27:1–44). In addition to Seleucia, some other major ports were beautiful Cyrene in northern Africa (see Mark 15:21); Caesarea of Palestine (see Acts 10:1); Tarsus, the hometown of Saul (see Acts 11:25); Corinth, perhaps the most celebrated city of the Roman Empire (see Introduction to 2 Corinthians); Syracuse, once home port of the world's best navy (see Acts 28:12); and Puteoli, gateway to Rome (see 28:13).

The islands of Crete (see Introduction to Titus) and especially Cyprus (see Acts 13:4) also served as major crossroads for shipping across the Mediterranean.

None of these locations, however, could top Alexandria for its reputation as a center of shipbuilding (see 18:24). Cargo ships usually had little room for passengers, though occasionally they carried voyagers on the open deck or in the hold with the cargo (Jon. 1:5). Paul sailed on such a vessel on the last leg of his trip to Rome (Acts 28:11).

Despite his earlier shipwreck (27:13–44) and his allusion to the various "perils" of travel (2 Cor. 11:26), travel in Paul's day was relatively simple and considerably safer than in the earlier times. The establishment of Roman control over the Mediterranean put an effective end to piracy and highway robbery in the region. Furthermore, the well-maintained Roman road system linked every corner of the empire and made travel much easier. ◆

Thanks to Israel's location on the Way of the Sea, it became a major exporter of agricultural goods. See "Trade in Ancient Israel" at the conclusion of John.

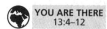

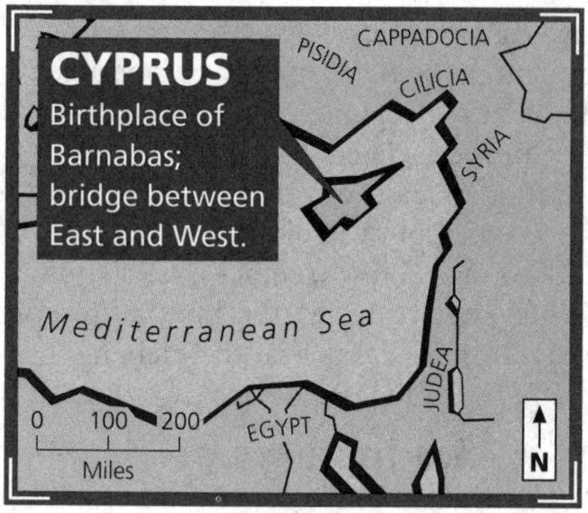

CYPRUS

YOU ARE THERE 13:4–12

- **First called Cyprus by the Greek poet, Homer; also known as "Copper Country."**
- **Its mostly Greek population was seldom independent of a stronger nation; accountable to Rome at the time of Christianity's rise.**
- **Dramatically variable climate—from warm water at sea level to snow in the mountains.**
- **Home to Barnabas (see Acts 4:36) and Mnason (21:16); a frequent port of call for early Christian travelers (11:19–20; 13:4–12). It was also where Barnabas took John Mark after separating from Paul (15:36–39).**
- **The modern Greek Orthodox Church honors Barnabas there as the patron saint of the Cyprus church.**

when He had removed him, He raised up for them David as
king, to whom also He gave testimony and said, 'I have
found David[a] the *son* of Jesse, a man after My *own* heart,
who will do all My will.'[b] 23 From this man's seed, according
to *the* promise, God raised up for Israel a Savior—Jesus—[a]
24 after John had first preached, before His coming, the baptism of repentance to all the people of Israel. 25 And as John
was finishing his course, he said, 'Who do you think I am? I
am not *He*. But behold, there comes One after me, the sandals of whose feet I am not worthy to loose.'

26 "Men *and* brethren, sons of the family of Abraham, and
those among you who fear God, to you the word of this salvation has been sent. 27 For those who dwell in Jerusalem,
and their rulers, because they did not know Him, nor even
the voices of the Prophets which are read every Sabbath,
have fulfilled *them* in condemning *Him*. 28 And though they
found no cause for death *in Him*, they asked Pilate that He
should be put to death. 29 Now when they had fulfilled all
that was written concerning Him, they took *Him* down
from the tree and laid *Him* in a tomb. 30 But God raised Him
from the dead. 31 He was seen for many days by those who
came up with Him from Galilee to Jerusalem, who are His
witnesses to the people. 32 And we declare to you glad tidings—that promise which was made to the fathers. 33 God
has fulfilled this for us their children, in that He has raised
up Jesus. As it is also written in the second Psalm:

> 'You are My Son,
> Today I have begotten You.'[a]

34 And that He raised Him from the dead, no more to return
to corruption, He has spoken thus:

> 'I will give you the sure mercies of David.'[a]

35 Therefore He also says in another *Psalm*:

> 'You will not allow Your Holy One to see corruption.'[a]

36 "For David, after he had served his own generation by
the will of God, fell asleep, was buried with his fathers, and
saw corruption; 37 but He whom God raised up saw no corruption. 38 Therefore let it be known to you, brethren, that
through this Man is preached to you the forgiveness of sins;
39 and by Him everyone who believes is justified from all
things from which you could not be justified by the law of
Moses. 40 Beware therefore, lest what has been spoken in the
prophets come upon you:

13:22 [a]Psalm 89:20 [b]1 Samuel 13:14 *13:23* [a]M-Text reads *for Israel salvation.*
13:33 [a]Psalm 2:7 *13:34* [a]Isaiah 55:3 *13:35* [a]Psalm 16:10

41 'Behold, you despisers,
Marvel and perish
For I work a work in your days,
A work which you will by no means believe,
Though one were to declare it to you.' "[a]

42So when the Jews went out of the synagogue,[a] the Gentiles begged that these words might be preached to them
the next Sabbath. 43Now when the congregation had broken
up, many of the Jews and devout proselytes followed Paul
and Barnabas, who, speaking to them, persuaded them to
continue in the grace of God.

13:44–48 44On the next Sabbath almost the
whole city came together to hear the
word of God. 45But when the Jews saw the multitudes, they
were filled with envy; and contradicting and blaspheming,
they opposed the things spoken by Paul. 46Then Paul and

(Bible text continued on page 468)

13:41 [a]Habakkuk 1:5 13:42 [a]Or *And when they went out of the synagogue of the Jews;* NU-Text reads *And when they went out of the synagogue, they begged.*

Some Prominent Women Oppose the Gospel

CONSIDER THIS 13:50 *The devout and prominent women who opposed Paul (v. 50) may have been Jews, but more likely they were Roman citizens.*

The first century saw tremendous changes in women's roles. Though Roman law technically kept a woman under a guardian, in practice it was easy for her to do as she pleased. In Asia Minor, women ran businesses, held municipal offices, and participated in public life. Women were gaining increasing wealth and, with it, influence. Those who had civic and social ambitions were heavily pressured to donate money for building projects, athletic contests, and religious cults.

The tragedy of the women of Pisidian Antioch was that once they gained access to the political and social power structures of their community, they used them to reject the gospel and protect their own interests.

Cyprus, a Geographic Hyphen

CONSIDER THIS 13:4–12 **In the first century—as well as today—Cyprus functioned much like a Heathrow, the international airport in England, hosting travelers who criss-crossed the ancient Mediterranean. These included Christians like Paul and Barnabas who sailed to Asia Minor, Greece, and Italy with the message of Christ.**

Cyprus was thus a "hyphen," a bridge between East and West. As such, its coastal cities were frequently exposed to new ideas and influences, which they tended to adopt, much like coastal cities today.

Modern Cyprus has become the offshore headquarters for many corporations, governmental agencies, nonprofit organizations, and ministries that used to be located in Beirut. In this way it still acts as a hyphen, contributing strategically to the flow of ideas and people between East and West.

Paul Turns to the Gentiles

CONSIDER THIS 13:44–48 *Paul's decision to turn to the Gentiles (v. 46) was a crossroads in the Christian movement. From then on, Paul extended the gospel as freely to Gentiles as to Jews.*

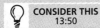

Salamis

YOU ARE THERE 13:5

- Principal city of ancient Cyprus, not to be confused with the modern town and island of Salamis off the coast of Greece.
- Boasted a deep water harbor which made the town a commercial success; now silted over.
- Traded in copper, flax, wine, fruit, and honey.
- Included an influential Jewish colony when Paul and Barnabas arrived on the first leg of their first journey.
- Traditional site of Barnabas' martyrdom at the hands of a Jewish mob.

Paphos

YOU ARE THERE 13:6

- Roman capital of Cyprus.
- Less significant than neighboring Salamis which had a better harbor.
- Site of a famous temple to the Syrian goddess Astarte (Greek Aphrodite, the goddess of beauty, love, and fertility).

Perga

YOU ARE THERE 13:13–14

- Capital city of Pamphylia, a Roman province on the southwest coast of Asia Minor.
- Situated inland to defend against pirates who roamed the coast.
- Boasted many structures typical of Graeco-Roman cities, including an acropolis, a walled lower city, colonnaded streets, an *agora,* or marketplace, public baths, a stadium seating 12,000, a theater,

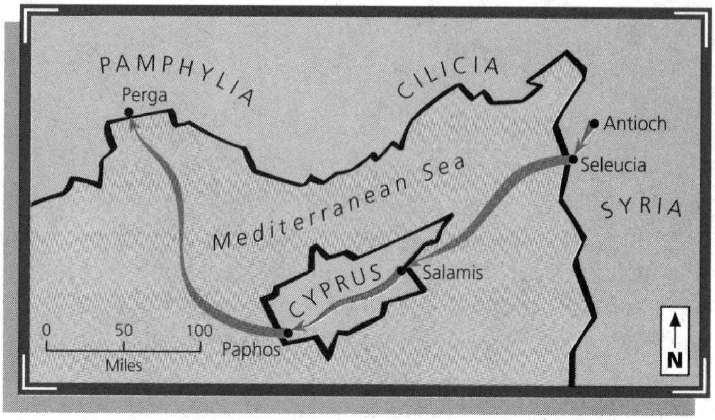

Paul's First Journey, Part One

and a temple to the goddess Artemis (Roman Diana).

- The nearby port city of Attalia, founded by Rome in the second century B.C., eventually overshadowed Perga's waterway and prosperity. Perga fell into decay—its ruins are still visible—while Attalia (modern Adalia) remains to this day.
- Visited twice by Paul (Acts 13:13–14; 14:25). This was the first instance of Paul preaching in a predominantly pagan environment. There is no evidence that he had much success.

Antioch in Pisidia

YOU ARE THERE 13:14–52

- One of 16 Antiochs in the ancient world.
- A commercial and administrative center on the east-west highway from Ephesus to Syria.
- Noted for its worship of pagan deities and a temple to Caesar Augustus.
- The city had a rare mix of native Phrygians, Greeks, Jews, and Roman colonists, making it one of the most ethnically diverse cities in the empire.
- Antioch's relative openness to the gospel, in contrast to the indifference of Perga, motivated Paul to begin a strategy that he frequently used elsewhere: speaking first to leading Jews and Gentile God-fearers at the synagogue, then mixing with the pagan Greeks and Roman colonists.

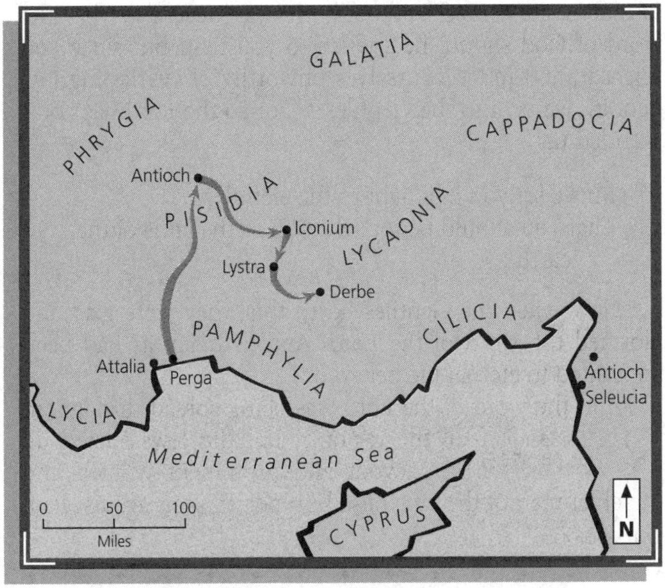

PAUL'S FIRST JOURNEY, PART TWO

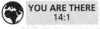

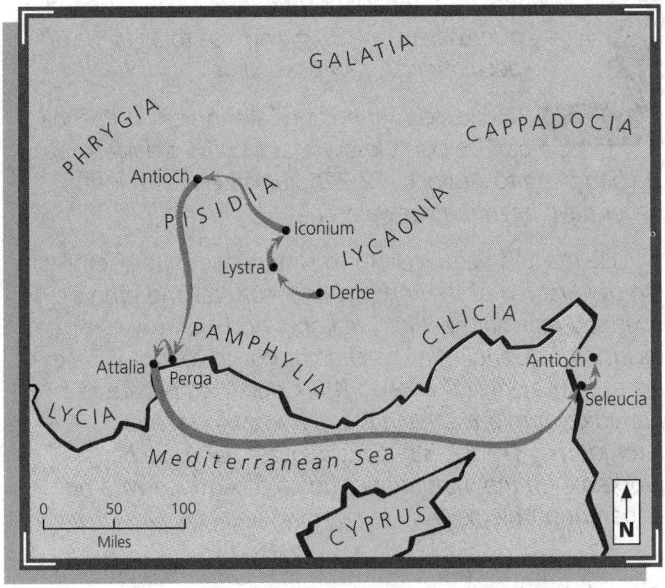

PAUL'S FIRST JOURNEY, PART THREE

ICONIUM

YOU ARE THERE 14:1

- Capital of the Roman province of Lycaonia in central Asia Minor.
- Largely Greek, the city was at one time named Claudiconium, reflecting privileges conferred by the Roman emperor Claudius.
- Several major routes—west to Antioch and Ephesus, south to Lystra and Derbe—led to and from this important crossroads.
- Bordering a huge plateau, Iconium was well watered and fertile, prospering from wheat fields and apricot and plum orchards.
- The Iconium church may have been the first to read Paul's letter to the Galatians, as well as the first letter of Peter.
- Known today as Konya, in Turkey.

LYSTRA

YOU ARE THERE 14:8

- An obscure town on the plains of Lycaonia in central Asia Minor, about 45 miles from the Mediterranean.
- Only 25 miles from Iconium but closer to Derbe in its politics and Roman culture.
- A Roman road system, the Via Sebaste, connected Lystra, Iconium, Derbe, and the other cities in the region.

DERBE

YOU ARE THERE 14:20

- A city in the southeastern part of the Roman province of Lycaonia.
- Now believed to be the unexcavated site of Kerti Huyuk in south central Asia Minor.
- Politically and culturally aligned with Lystra in the Roman province of Galatia.
- Home to Gaius, a traveling companion of Paul (Acts 20:4).
- Surviving inscriptions suggest a succession of bishops in Derbe. One of them, Daphnus, was present at the Council of Constantinople in A.D. 381. So apparently Paul's efforts in this little town were not in vain.

Barnabas grew bold and said, "It was necessary that the
word of God should be spoken to you first; but since you
reject it, and judge yourselves unworthy of everlasting life,
behold, we turn to the Gentiles. 47For so the Lord has commanded us:

'I have set you *as* a light to the Gentiles,
That you should be for salvation to the ends of the
earth.' "[a]

48Now when the Gentiles heard this, they were glad and
glorified the word of the Lord. And as many as had been
appointed to eternal life believed.
49And the word of the Lord was being spread throughout
all the region. 50But the Jews stirred up
the devout and prominent women and
the chief men of the city, raised up persecution against Paul

13:50 see pg. 465

13:47 [a]Isaiah 49:6

CONSIDER THIS 13:13

WHY DID JOHN MARK GO HOME?

Luke does not tell us why John Mark returned to Jerusalem (v. 13), giving rise to all kinds of speculation. A few possibilities:

He was young and felt homesick. *Possibly, but we don't know exactly how old Mark was. He had been to Antioch (12:25), but otherwise might never have been outside Palestine.*

He reacted negatively to the interaction with Gentiles. *On the first leg of the trip (Cyprus), cultural and ethnic overload may have set in. We know how controversial the inclusion of Gentiles in the church proved to be for believers at Jerusalem (15:1-29). If Mark departed because of prejudice, it might explain Paul's refusal to take him on a later journey (15:37–38). On the other hand, he had worked with the multiethnic church at Antioch with no apparent problems (12:25).*

He didn't want to work with Paul. *We know that Paul was a hard charger and that his standards were quite high. Perhaps Mark didn't measure up, or perhaps the relational chemistry didn't work, and so Mark decided to go home rather than endure a lengthy trip with a demanding person. But later Paul was eager to have him on board (2 Tim. 4:11) and included him among his fellow laborers (Philem. 24).*

He got seasick. *No evidence for that except that Mark left as soon as the party hit the mainland at Perga in Pamphylia. But why return home over seasickness?*

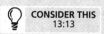

and Barnabas, and expelled them from their region. 51But
they shook off the dust from their feet against them, and
came to Iconium. 52And the disciples were filled with joy
and with the Holy Spirit.

CHAPTER 14

Conflict at Iconium

14:1 see pg. 467

1Now it happened in Iconium that they
went together to the synagogue of the
Jews, and so spoke that a great multitude both of the Jews
and of the Greeks believed. 2But the unbelieving Jews
stirred up the Gentiles and poisoned their minds against the
brethren. 3Therefore they stayed there a long time, speaking
boldly in the Lord, who was bearing witness to the word of
His grace, granting signs and wonders to be done by their
hands.
4But the multitude of the city was divided: part sided

He was afraid. *In Antioch, Mark met a diverse community of believers who showed extraordinary concern and compassion for each other (see "Antioch: A Model for the Modern Church?" Acts 13:1). But on Cyprus he encountered characters like Elymas the sorcerer (13:6–12) and discovered that in gospel outreach, opponents use live ammunition. So he might have left out of fear.*

The pace was too hard. *Luke calls Mark an "assistant" (13:5), which probably involved making arrangements for travel, food, and lodging, and possibly some teaching. Again, Paul's pace may have outstripped the young man's capacities, and once they arrived at Perga he decided to throw in the towel. But this is pure speculation.*

Scripture doesn't tell us why John Mark made the decision to go home. But the encouraging thing is that his return didn't disqualify him from the faith or diminish his spirituality, no matter how strongly Paul felt about it later (15:38–39). With time and the encouragement of Barnabas, Mark developed into one of the key leaders of the early church who had a lasting impact on the faith. ◆

The man who "deserted" Paul and Barnabas turned out to be a key figure in the Christian movement—thanks to Barnabas. See "John Mark," Acts 15:37.

Confusing Responses

CONSIDER THIS 14:11–19

The gospel can trigger intense responses, both positive and negative. At Lystra, Barnabas and Paul were initially hailed as Greek gods after healing a crippled man (vv. 11–12). But at Iconium, their message offended the Jews (14:1–2), who viewed the apostles not as gods, but devils.

The good news can either raise a person's hopes or strike fear at levels that are hard to perceive. That's why believers today need to be ready for extreme reactions when they present the gospel.

Attalia

YOU ARE THERE 14:25

- **Key seaport on the coast of Pamphylia in south central Asia Minor, serving Perga, the regional capital, eight miles inland.**
- **Archaeologists have found evidence of a double wall, an ancient aqueduct, and a triple gateway constructed under the reign of Hadrian, who visited in A.D. 130.**
- **Alternately conquered by Turks and Europeans during the Crusades.**
- **Known today as Adalia (Antalya), this major seaport on Turkey's Gulf of Adalia is the "Turkish Riviera," with tourism the major industry.**

with the Jews, and part with the apostles. 5And when a violent attempt was made by both the Gentiles and Jews, with
their rulers, to abuse and stone them, 6they became aware
of it and fled to Lystra and Derbe, cities of Lycaonia, and to
the surrounding region. 7And they were preaching the
gospel there.

Enthusiasm Turns to Violence

14:8 see pg. 467

8And in Lystra a certain man without
strength in his feet was sitting, a cripple
from his mother's womb, who had never walked. 9*This* man
heard Paul speaking. Paul, observing him intently and seeing that he had faith to be healed, 10said with a loud voice,
"Stand up straight on your feet!" And he leaped and

14:11–19 see pg. 469

walked. 11Now when the people saw
what Paul had done, they raised their
voices, saying in the Lycaonian *language,* "The gods have
come down to us in the likeness of men!" 12And Barnabas
they called Zeus, and Paul, Hermes, because he was the
chief speaker. 13Then the priest of Zeus, whose temple was
in front of their city, brought oxen and garlands to the gates,
intending to sacrifice with the multitudes.

14But when the apostles Barnabas and Paul heard this,
they tore their clothes and ran in among the multitude, crying out 15and saying, "Men, why are you doing these things?
We also are men with the same nature as you, and preach to
you that you should turn from these useless things to the
living God, who made the heaven, the earth, the sea, and all
things that are in them, 16who in bygone generations allowed all nations to walk in their own ways. 17Nevertheless
He did not leave Himself without witness, in that He did
good, gave us rain from heaven and fruitful seasons, filling
our hearts with food and gladness." 18And with these sayings they could scarcely restrain the multitudes from sacrificing to them.

19Then Jews from Antioch and Iconium came there; and
having persuaded the multitudes, they stoned Paul *and*
dragged *him* out of the city, supposing him to be dead.

14:20 see pg. 467

20However, when the disciples gathered
around him, he rose up and went into
the city. And the next day he departed with Barnabas to
Derbe.

"WE MUST THROUGH MANY TRIBULATIONS ENTER THE KINGDOM OF GOD."
—Acts 14:22

Paul and Barnabas Retrace Their Steps

21And when they had preached the gospel to that city and
made many disciples, they returned to Lystra, Iconium, and
Antioch, 22strengthening the souls of the disciples, exhorting *them* to continue in the faith, and *saying,* "We must
through many tribulations enter the kingdom of God." 23So

when they had appointed elders in every church, and prayed with fasting, they commended them to the Lord in whom they had believed. [24]And after they had passed

14:25 see pg. 469

through Pisidia, they came to Pamphylia.
[25]Now when they had preached the word in Perga, they went down to Attalia. [26]From there they sailed to Antioch, where they had been commended to the grace of God for the work which they had completed.

[27]Now when they had come and gathered the church together, they reported all that God had done with them, and that He had opened the door of faith to the Gentiles. [28]So they stayed there a long time with the disciples.

CHAPTER 15

A Controversy over Doctrine Boils Over

15:1–21 see pg. 472

[1]And certain *men* came down from Judea and taught the brethren, "Unless you are circumcised according to the custom of Moses, you

15:2

cannot be saved." [2]Therefore, when Paul and Barnabas had no small dissension and dispute with them, they determined that Paul and Barnabas and certain others of them should go up to Jerusalem, to the apostles and elders, about this question.

[3]So, being sent on their way by the church, they passed through Phoenicia and Samaria, describing the conversion of the Gentiles; and they caused great joy to all the brethren. [4]And when they had come to Jerusalem, they were received by the church and the apostles and the elders; and they reported all things that God had done with them. [5]But some of the sect of the Pharisees who believed rose up, saying, "It is necessary to circumcise them, and to command *them* to keep the law of Moses."

15:6 see pg. 473

[6]Now the apostles and elders came together to consider this matter. [7]And when there had been much dispute, Peter rose up and said to them: "Men and brethren, you know that a good while ago God chose among us, that by my mouth the Gentiles should hear the word of the gospel and believe. [8]So God, who knows the heart, acknowledged them by giving them the Holy Spirit, just as *He did* to us, [9]and made no distinction between us and them, purifying their hearts by faith. [10]Now therefore, why do you test God by putting a yoke on the neck of the disciples which neither our fathers nor we were able to bear? [11]But we believe that through the grace of the Lord Jesus Christ[a] we shall be saved in the same manner as they."

15:11 [a]NU-Text and M-Text omit *Christ*.

Growth Leads to New Understanding

CONSIDER THIS 15:2 *An encounter with a different culture can sometimes force believers to evaluate what they believe and why. In Antioch the church ran into a pluralistic society made up of several different groups, prompting the question, "What about circumcision and the Law?" The council at Jerusalem came together to address that issue and formulate a biblical response (vv. 2, 6). In this sense Antioch could be called the mother not only of Christian missions and church government, but of biblical theology as well.*

"Antioch—A Model for the Modern Church?" tells this story in more detail, Acts 13:1.

Who Was the Leader?

CONSIDER THIS 15:12 *Note the order in which Luke mentions the two leaders in v. 12—Barnabas before Paul. Apparently Barnabas took the lead before the council, rather than Paul, as compared to other settings (for instance, 13:13, 43, 46, 50; 15:2, 35).*

15:12
see pg. 471

[12]Then all the multitude kept silent and
listened to Barnabas and Paul declaring
how many miracles and wonders God had worked through
them among the Gentiles. [13]And after they had become
silent, James answered, saying, "Men *and* brethren, listen to
me: [14]Simon has declared how God at the first visited the
Gentiles to take out of them a people for His name. [15]And
with this the words of the prophets agree, just as it is written:

16 'After this I will return
And will rebuild the tabernacle of David, which has fallen down;
I will rebuild its ruins,
And I will set it up;
17 So that the rest of mankind may seek the LORD,
Even all the Gentiles who are called by My name,
Says the LORD who does all these things.'[a]

[18]"Known to God from eternity are all His works.[a]
[19]Therefore I judge that we should not trouble those from

15:17 [a]Amos 9:11, 12 *15:18* [a]NU-Text (combining with verse 17) reads *Says the Lord, who makes these things known from eternity (of old).*

CONSIDER THIS
15:1–21

"Sure You're Saved . . . Sort Of"

In Acts 15 we see a simmering controversy that finally boiled over. The year was about A.D. 48. Paul and Barnabas had just returned to Antioch from their first preaching tour and reported the exciting news that God had opened the door of faith to the Gentiles (14:26–27). Now men who claimed to speak for the church in Judea came with a disturbing message: to be saved, Gentiles must become Jews. They must reject their ethnic backgrounds and instead accept the tenets of Hebrew religion and culture.

If true, that would mean that perhaps half the church at Antioch was not saved, along with the majority of new believers in the new churches established by Paul and Barnabas in Pisidia and Galatia. No wonder the debate that ensued created great tension and bitterness (15:2, 6–7, 24)!

Nor was it easily resolved. Paul reported that Peter went along with the error when the false teachers arrived. Even Barnabas was swayed (Gal. 2:11–16). The crisis was so great that Paul, Barnabas, and others journeyed to Jerusalem for a full-scale debate with the apostles and elders there.

The discussion turned on three important presentations:

among the Gentiles who are turning to God, [20]but that we write to them to abstain from things polluted by idols, *from* sexual immorality,[a] *from* things strangled, and *from* blood.
[21]For Moses has had throughout many generations those who preach him in every city, being read in the synagogues every Sabbath."

A Letter of Reconciliation Is Sent

15:22–35 see pg. 474
[22]Then it pleased the apostles and elders, with the whole church, to send chosen men of their own company to Antioch with Paul and Barnabas, *namely,* Judas who was also named Barsabas,[a] and Silas, leading men among the brethren.
[23]They wrote this *letter* by them:

The apostles, the elders, and the brethren,

To the brethren who are of the Gentiles in Antioch, Syria, and Cilicia:

(*Bible text continued on page 475*)

15:20 [a]Or *fornication* *15:22* [a]NU-Text and M-Text read *Barsabbas.*

(1) Peter's reminder of his meeting with Cornelius (Acts 10:1–48), in which God gave the Holy Spirit to Gentiles.
(2) Barnabas and Paul's account of their recent travels through Asia Minor, in which God worked miraculously among the Gentiles.
(3) James' conclusion that these events correlated with the prophetic words of Amos 9:11–12.

The conclusion, as described in the letter to the Galatians, was, "There is neither Jew nor Greek . . . slave nor free . . . male nor female; for you are all one in Christ Jesus" (Gal. 3:28).

However, the issues of Acts 15 have continued to trouble the church in one form or another to this day. It is difficult to separate one's culture and worldview from one's understanding the gospel. Even in the church we often find our security in sameness and sometimes exclude those who differ. Diversity feels uncomfortable. But in light of Acts 15, we might consider what it would take to address our concerns honestly and biblically. ◆

Issues of Faith and Culture

CONSIDER THIS 15:6 **As the gospel expanded "to the end of the earth" (Acts 1:8), the first Christians encountered new cultures that challenged accepted beliefs and practices. Then as now, the frontiers of mission required the church to meet as an international body to sort out issues of faith and culture (15:6).**

Some controversies involve "truth issues," others "love issues," and others both truth and love issues. Truth issues call for clarity of doctrine and understanding of Scripture. Love issues call for open-mindedness and toleration. The situation in Acts 15 required the early church to deal with both.

What issues in today's church are truth-related? What issues are love issues demanding tolerance for legitimate differences of opinion and practice? What issues demand the perspective of both truth and love?

CONSIDER THIS
15:22–35

A Church That Defies Market Research

As the twentieth century closes and the twenty-first century begins, the population of the United States is becoming increasingly diverse. Can the church prosper in a pluralistic society? Yes, judging by Acts. In fact, the response of the council at Jerusalem to an influx of Gentile believers (vv. 22–35) suggests that Christians must allow for cultural differences if they want their churches to thrive.

The collections of people who responded to the gospel and banded together in the first century defy much of modern market research and ideas about church growth. Modern thinking holds that groups of people with similar sociological backgrounds ("homogeneous" groups) grow more quickly than ones with different backgrounds ("heterogeneous") because like attracts like. Therefore, churches should target people of the same race, demographic profile, socioeconomic status, and so forth.

But the untidy collection of Acts believers seems to contradict that model. Churches sprouted up spontaneously in response to God's grace more than through social marketing.

Heterogeneous Backgrounds

- They came from *all classes* of society, from the wealthy and privileged to destitute beggars, slaves, and even criminals.
- They represented the *many cultures* of that day—Roman, Greek, Hebrew, African, Arab.
- They varied widely in their *political allegiances and power,* from government, military, and civic leaders to reactionaries, revolutionaries, and displaced refugees.
- Their *leadership* was male and female, old and young.
- They came from all manner of *religious traditions*—pagan sorcery and mystery cults, Greek and Roman mythology, idol worship, and Judaism.

A Diversity of Abilities and Callings

- *Landholders* such as Barnabas (4:34–37), Ananias and Sapphira (5:1–11), Mnason (21:16) and Publius (28:7–10).
- *Health care workers and therapists* including Dr. Luke (Acts 1:1; see also Col. 4:14; 2 Tim. 4:11).
- *Lecturers and teachers* such as Stephen (6:8–10), Philip (8:4–5), Priscilla and Aquila (18:26), Apollos (18:24–28), and of course Peter, Paul, and the other apostles.
- *Government officials and civic leaders,* including the Ethiopian treasurer (8:26–40), Saul before his conversion (8:3; 9:1–2; 26:9–11), the proconsul Sergius Paulus (13:6–12), a Philippian jailer (16:22–34), Dionysius (17:34), and Crispus (18:8).

Individual converts came from many other, equally diverse industries:

- Dorcas, who possibly worked in the *tailoring and garment industry* (9:36–42).
- Simon, employed in *leather tanning* (9:43).
- Cornelius, a centurion from the Italian Regiment of the *Roman military* (10:1–48).
- Rhoda, a *domestic* (12:12–17).
- Lydia, who *manufactured, imported, and exported clothing* for the rich (16:13–15, 40).
- *Tentmakers* Priscilla and Aquila (18:1–3).

Innovative Programs

- Advocacy by Barnabas on behalf of Saul (9:26–27); by Paul and Barnabas on behalf of a slave girl, freeing her from oppressive masters (16:16–21); and by Ephesian believers on behalf of Apollos (18:27–28).

(continued on next page)

Greetings.

24 Since we have heard that some who went out from us
have troubled you with words, unsettling your souls,
saying, "*You must* be circumcised and keep the law"[a]—
to whom we gave no *such* commandment— 25it seemed
good to us, being assembled with one accord, to send
chosen men to you with our beloved Barnabas and
Paul, 26men who have risked their lives for the name of
our Lord Jesus Christ. 27We have therefore sent Judas
and Silas, who will also report the same things by word
of mouth. 28For it seemed good to the Holy Spirit, and
to us, to lay upon you no greater burden than these
necessary things: 29that you abstain from things offered
to idols, from blood, from things strangled, and from
sexual immorality.[a] If you keep yourselves from these,
you will do well.

Farewell.

30So when they were sent off, they came to Antioch; and
when they had gathered the multitude together, they delivered the letter. 31When they had read it, they rejoiced over
its encouragement. 32Now Judas and Silas, themselves being
prophets also, exhorted and strengthened the brethren with
many words. 33And after they had stayed *there* for a time,
they were sent back with greetings from the brethren to the
apostles.[a]

15:24 [a]NU-Text omits *saying, "You must be circumcised and keep the law".* *15:29* [a]Or *fornication* *15:33* [a]NU-Text reads *to those who had sent them.*

◆ ◆ ◆ ◆ ◆ ◆ ◆ ◆ ◆ ◆ ◆ ◆ ◆ ◆ ◆

PERSONALITY PROFILE: SILAS

FOR YOUR INFO 15:34

Also known as: Silvanus, meaning "person of the woods."

First gained notice as: One of four church leaders from Jerusalem named to write and deliver to Antioch a pivotal decision on the status of Gentile converts (Acts 15:22).

Best known today as: Paul's traveling companion on his second journey after the apostle had rejected John Mark (15:36–41). Silas' Roman citizenship and ties to the Jerusalem church proved useful to their work as messengers of Christ. He also became Paul's literary assistant.

(continued from previous page)

- *Charity and hospitality,* often anonymously and on a large scale, to meet both social and spiritual needs (2:45; 4:32; 11:29–30; 28:13–15).
- *Ethnic reconciliation* as deacons acted on behalf of neglected widows (6:1–6); as Philip carried the gospel across ethnic barriers (8:4–17, 26–40); as Peter met with the Gentile, Cornelius, and defended his actions to the Jewish leaders at Jerusalem (10:1—11:30); as Paul and Barnabas brought together Gentiles and Jews at Antioch in Pisidia (13:46–52); as the council at Jerusalem accepted Gentiles into the faith, sending Judas and Silas as emissaries to welcome them (15:1–35); as Paul recruited Timothy into gospel work (16:1–5).

The early church was a diverse, grass-roots, from-the-ground-up movement that drew people together in surprising ways. It turned them inside out, toward one another in service and love. Its example challenges believers today to ask: How are we allowing for cultural differences in our pluralistic society? ◆

15:34
see pg. 475

34However, it seemed good to Silas to
remain there.[a] 35Paul and Barnabas also
remained in Antioch, teaching and preaching the word of
the Lord, with many others also.

Paul and Barnabas Part

36Then after some days Paul said to Barnabas, "Let us now
go back and visit our brethren in every city where we have
preached the word of the Lord, *and see* how they are doing."

15:34 [a]NU-Text and M-Text omit this verse.

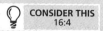

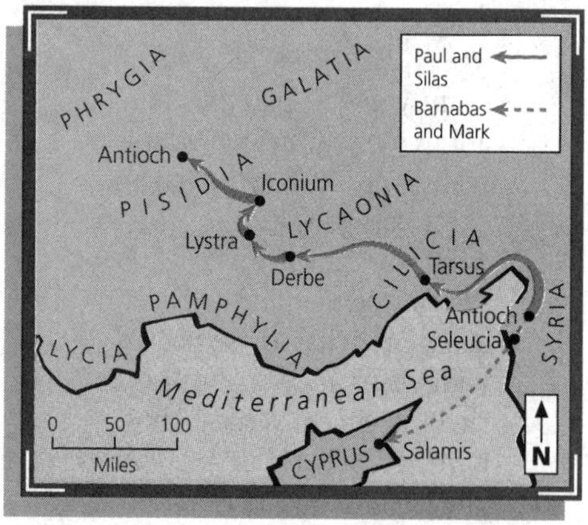

PAUL'S SECOND JOURNEY, PART ONE

CONSIDER THIS
16:4

PAUL'S URBAN STRATEGY

Iconium. Lystra. Derbe. Philippi. Ephesus. Corinth. Antioch. Athens. For most people today, names like these indicate merely dots on a map. But they were major cities in the Roman world, centers of influence that attracted Christian messengers such as Paul (v. 4). The message of Christ was a message for the city—for its marketplace, arts, academies, councils, courts, prisons, temples, and synagogues.

Paul was from the beautiful coastal seaport of Tarsus, "no mean city" as he described it (Acts 21:39; see 11:25), with an estimated half-million residents. He was brought up in Jerusalem, one of the largest cities in the empire. Thus he was no stranger to city life. In fact, as a spokesperson for the Christian movement, he preferred working in urban centers. This strategy offered several advantages:

(1) He could use a common language, Greek. *Older ethnic languages prevailed among rural peoples, but multicultural city dwellers spoke to each other in* koinē *("common") Greek.*

(2) He could anticipate greater receptivity. *Urban peoples were perhaps more likely to entertain new ideas and consider change.*

(3) He could influence networks. *As crossroads of communication and commerce, cities tended to amplify the Christian message to their surrounding areas (see "Ghetto Blaster," 19:10).*

(4) He could affect multiple ethnic groups. *The gospel is inclusive and multiethnic, uniting people of every background. Cities brought into close proximity Jews and Gentiles, men and women, rich and poor. The message of Christ brought them together.*

15:37
see pg. 478

15:37–39

15:39
see pg. 478

37Now Barnabas was determined to take
with them John called Mark. 38But Paul
insisted that they should not take with
them the one who had departed from
them in Pamphylia, and had not gone with them to the
work. 39Then the contention became so
sharp that they parted from one another.
And so Barnabas took Mark and sailed to Cyprus; 40but
Paul chose Silas and departed, being commended by the
brethren to the grace of God. 41And he went through Syria
and Cilicia, strengthening the churches.

◆ ◆ ◆ ◆ ◆ ◆ ◆ ◆ ◆ ◆ ◆ ◆ ◆ ◆ ◆

(5) He could reach the workplace. *As a tentmaker, Paul identified with the great numbers of artisans who populated Roman cities. In fact, urban areas were often divided into districts according to crafts, and workers formed guilds to enhance their trades. Paul used these coalitions to advantage in spreading the message.*

(6) He could make use of the Roman legal system. *Paul believed that his message had relevance for the political, economic, and religious institutions of his day. As a Roman citizen, he expected—and even demanded—justice. He also used the courts to attract a larger audience for the gospel.*

Paul intentionally went to the cities. The gospel he proclaimed had implications for an urban setting. To him, the message of Christ spoke not only to the private individual, but to public society as well. Given the increasingly urban nature of the modern world, he would likely urge Christians today to pay attention to cities. Those who want to have influence will benefit from a careful study of Paul's urban strategy. ◆

From the very beginning, the church was known for its inclusiveness (see Acts 1:13). One of the best models could be found at Antioch (see Acts 13:1).

Christianity conquered Rome by invading its cities. It penetrated the cities by establishing dozens of urban churches by the end of the first century. See "Churches—Keys to Cities," Acts 11:22.

To see how explosive—and unpredictable—Paul's urban strategy could be, read "The Ephesus Approach: How the Gospel Penetrates a City," Acts 19:8–41.

JOHN MARK—"USEFUL FOR MINISTRY"

CONSIDER THIS
15:37–39

John Mark is a case study in second chances. Spurned by Paul because he had gone home to Jerusalem instead of continuing on a journey to Asia Minor (Acts 13:13; 15:38), John Mark was fortunate in that his cousin was the mentoring model, Barnabas (see 4:36–37). Just as he had done with Paul when no one else would come near him, Barnabas took John Mark home with him to Cyprus where he nurtured him personally and spiritually.

Thanks to Barnabas, John Mark turned out to be a special gift to the early church. He became a valued associate of Peter and probably traveled with him to Rome, where tradition holds that he composed his Gospel by writing down Peter's memories of Jesus' life and teaching (see "Tales of the Fisherman," Introduction to Mark).

Paul also finally recognized the value of John Mark. Late in life, he wrote to Timothy, urging him to "get Mark and bring him with you, for he is useful to me for ministry" (2 Tim. 4:11). Indeed he was. Early church tradition says that he was the first evangelist to Alexandria, Egypt, and the first bishop of that city. He won a great number of sincerely committed converts there.

Luke does not tell us why John Mark returned to Jerusalem, giving rise to all kinds of speculation. See "Why Did John Mark Go Home?" Acts 13:13.

The Tension between Truth and Love

CONSIDER THIS 15:39 *The account states that the split between Paul and Barnabas was contentious (v. 39), and the outcome was ugly. Paul was known to emphasize issues of truth, arguing for high doctrinal standards (see "Issues of Faith and Culture," Acts 15:6). Barnabas felt the same commitment to doctrinal purity, but when it came to people, it seems that the "Son of Encouragement" tended to emphasize issues of love. He was a risk-taker who held onto those who fell through the cracks. So it's not surprising that he embraced John Mark (15:39), just as he had embraced Paul when none of the other believers would touch him because of his past (11:25).*

To Paul's credit, he later reconciled with John Mark and Barnabas (Col. 4:10–11; 2 Tim. 4:11).

Where do you tend to place your emphasis in the tension between truth and love? Are there times when your commitment to doctrinal truth causes you to forget that no matter how right or wrong others may be, they are people who need to be loved?

CHAPTER 16

Timothy Is Recruited for the Work

16:1–3

1Then he came to Derbe and Lystra.
And behold, a certain disciple was there,
named Timothy, *the* son of a certain Jewish woman who believed, but his father *was* Greek. 2He was well spoken of by
the brethren who were at Lystra and Iconium. 3Paul wanted
to have him go on with him. And he took *him* and circumcised him because of the Jews who were in that region, for
they all knew that his father was Greek.

16:4 see pg. 476

4And as they went through the cities,
they delivered to them the decrees to keep, which were determined by the apostles and elders at Jerusalem. 5So the
churches were strengthened in the faith, and increased in
number daily.

Timothy

A CLOSER LOOK 16:1–3 *It's interesting that Paul recruited Timothy (vv. 1–3) for the same trip from which he had just rejected John Mark (15:37–41). What did he see in the young man from Lystra? See the profile at the Introduction to 2 Timothy. Eventually Timothy took on a major assignment—a multiethnic church at Ephesus. See "Discipleship—Or Mentoring?" Acts 9:26–30.*

Personality Profile: John Mark

FOR YOUR INFO 15:37 **Not to be confused with:** John, one of the Twelve and a close friend of Jesus.

Family: Son of Mary, who owned a house in Jerusalem where the church often prayed (Acts 12:12–17); cousin to Barnabas (see 4:36–37; Col. 4:10). Peter referred to Mark as his "son" (1 Pet. 5:13).

Background: His family was wealthy enough to own a large home with at least one servant. It frequently hosted gatherings of believers.

Best known today for: Leaving Paul and Barnabas on their first gospel tour after visiting Cyprus (Acts 13:13); later writing the Gospel that bears his name, Mark.

The Spirit Directs the Team Westward

6 Now when they had gone through Phrygia and the region of Galatia, they were forbidden by the Holy Spirit to
preach the word in Asia. 7 After they had
come to Mysia, they tried to go into
Bithynia, but the Spirit[a] did not permit
them. 8 So passing by Mysia, they came
down to Troas. 9 And a vision appeared to Paul in the night.
A man of Macedonia stood and pleaded with him, saying,
"Come over to Macedonia and help us." 10 Now after he had
seen the vision, immediately we sought to go to Macedonia,
concluding that the Lord had called us to preach the gospel
to them.

16:7 see pg. 480

16:8 see pg. 480

A Clothier Turns to Christ

11 Therefore, sailing from Troas, we ran a straight course to
Samothrace, and the next *day* came to
Neapolis, 12 and from there to Philippi,
which is the foremost city of that part of Macedonia, a
colony. And we were staying in that city for some days.

16:12 see pg. 481

16:7 [a]NU-Text adds *of Jesus.*

Personality Profile: Lydia

FOR YOUR INFO 16:14–15

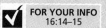

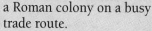

Home: Originally Thyatira (see Rev. 2:18), a large industrial city and leading exporter of purple dye; relocated to Philippi (see accompanying article), a Roman colony on a busy trade route.

Family: Unknown, though the text mentions her "household" (Acts 16:15).

Occupation: Owner of a business that traded in an exotic dye known as purple, along with cloth dyed in it.

Best known today for: Becoming the first known convert to Christianity in the West and hosting the first church in Europe in her home.

The Trade in Purple

FOR YOUR INFO 16:14

Lydia's hometown, Thyatira, was a thriving manufacturing and commercial center. Its trade in purple was renowned in the Roman world. The most expensive of dyes and a mark of wealth or royalty, purple came from the murex, a shellfish found only along the northeastern section of the Mediterranean coast. Purple cloth was ranked in value with gold and was important not only for adorning emperors and temples but for tribute and international trade.

We don't know when or why Lydia relocated to Philippi, but it was a smart business move. A Latin inscription found there mentions the dying trade and its economic importance to the city. Philippi was the leading Roman colony of the region, located on the major east-west highway connecting Europe to the Middle East. Its people were known for trying to outdo Rome in dress and manners.

Lydia probably belonged to a local dyer's guild, a professional association. Guilds sometimes involved such pagan customs and practices as worship of the trade's patron god, feasts using food sacrificed to idols, and loose sexual morality.

Lydia's conversion didn't change her occupation, but it dramatically changed her loyalty. Her business contacts likely introduced Paul to the "movers and shakers" of the Macedonian area.

To get better acquainted with Lydia and the church that met in her house, read Paul's letter to the Philippians.

MYSIA

YOU ARE THERE 16:7

- A Roman province, the westernmost portion of Asia Minor (present-day Turkey).
- Never granted independent status, so its precise boundaries are unknown.
- Passively allied with the Trojans during the legendary Trojan War.
- Apparently of little interest to Paul, who hastily "passed by Mysia" on his way to Troas (Acts 16:8). No evidence of other Christian outreach here.

TROAS

YOU ARE THERE 16:8

- A major city on the coast of Mysia in northwest Asia Minor (modern Turkey).
- Name means "the region around Troy"; the city was located on the rugged Troad Plain 10 miles south of legendary Troy.
- In Paul's day, called Alexandria Troas in honor of Alexander the Great.
- A key Roman seaport, offering the shortest route from Asia to Greece.
- Visited by Paul at least three times: en route to Macedonia (Acts 16:11); after his journey in Ephesus (20:6; 2 Cor. 2:12); and once when he left his cloak and books at the house of Carpus (2 Tim. 4:13).

A TURNING POINT IN WESTERN CIVILIZATION

Paul's vision and subsequent trip from Troas to Neapolis (Acts 16:9–11) proved to be a major fork in the road for Western civilization. One small step for Paul became one giant leap

(continued on next page)

16:13

13And on the Sabbath day we went out of
the city to the riverside, where prayer
was customarily made; and we sat down and spoke to the

16:14 see pg. 479

women who met *there.* 14Now a certain
woman named Lydia heard *us.* She was a
seller of purple from the city of Thyatira, who worshiped
God. The Lord opened her heart to heed the things spoken

16:14–15 see pg. 479

by Paul. 15And when she and her household were baptized, she begged *us,* say-
ing, "If you have judged me to be faithful to the Lord, come
to my house and stay." So she persuaded us.

A DIFFERENT APPROACH

CONSIDER THIS 16:13

Paul began his ministry in Philippi among women he met by the river (v. 13). His normal approach was through the synagogues. But apparently Philippi lacked even ten male Jews, which was the required number to form a synagogue. Yet there were spiritually hungry women meeting for prayer. Perhaps they met outside the city because their monotheism was considered strange by the dominant pagan culture. At any rate, God answered their prayers by bringing the gospel to their community.

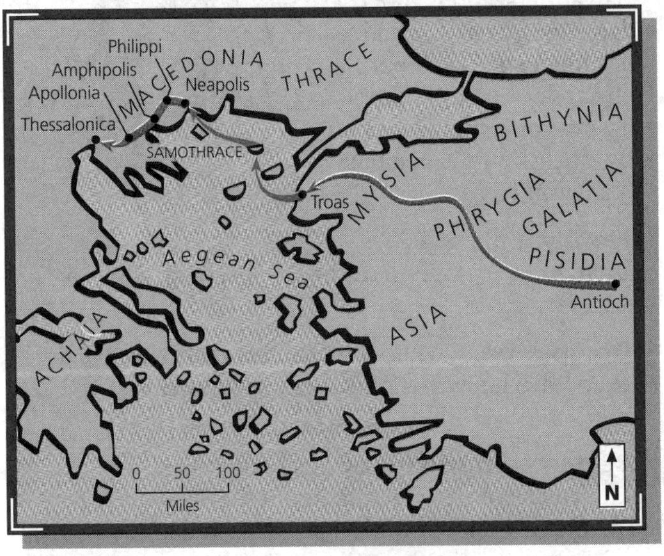

PAUL'S SECOND JOURNEY, PART TWO

A Slave Girl Finds Faith and Freedom

16:16–24 see pg. 482

16Now it happened, as we went to
prayer, that a certain slave girl possessed
with a spirit of divination met us, who brought her masters
much profit by fortune-telling. 17This girl followed Paul and
us, and cried out, saying, "These men are the servants of the
Most High God, who proclaim to us the way of salvation."
18And this she did for many days.
But Paul, greatly annoyed, turned and said to the spirit,
"I command you in the name of Jesus Christ to come out of
her." And he came out that very hour.
19But when her masters saw that their
hope of profit was gone, they seized Paul and Silas and
dragged *them* into the marketplace to the authorities.

16:19 see pg. 482

20And they brought them to the magistrates, and said,
"These men, being Jews, exceedingly trouble our city; 21and
they teach customs which are not lawful for us, being Romans, to receive or observe." 22Then the multitude rose up
together against them; and the magistrates tore off their
clothes and commanded *them* to be beaten with rods. 23And
when they had laid many stripes on them, they threw *them*
into prison, commanding the jailer to keep them securely.
24Having received such a charge, he put them into the inner
prison and fastened their feet in the stocks.

A Jailer and His Family Believe

25But at midnight Paul and Silas were praying and singing
hymns to God, and the prisoners were listening to them.
26Suddenly there was a great earthquake, so that the foundations of the prison were shaken; and immediately all the
doors were opened and everyone's chains were loosed.
27And the keeper of the prison, awaking from sleep and seeing the prison doors open, supposing the prisoners had
fled, drew his sword and was about to kill himself. 28But
Paul called with a loud voice, saying, "Do yourself no harm,
for we are all here."
29Then he called for a light, ran in, and fell down trembling before Paul and Silas. 30And he brought them out and
said, "Sirs, what must I do to be saved?"

16:31–34 see pg. 484

31So they said, "Believe on the Lord Jesus Christ, and you will be saved, you
and your household." 32Then they spoke the word of the
Lord to him and to all who were in his house. 33And he
took them the same hour of the night and washed *their*
stripes. And immediately he and all his family were baptized. 34Now when he had brought them into his house, he
set food before them; and he rejoiced, having believed in
God with all his household.

(continued from previous page)

for Christianity as it spread west, gaining a foothold at Philippi in Macedonia, moving on into Europe, and eventually pervading the entire western hemisphere.

PHILIPPI

YOU ARE THERE 16:12

- **A city in eastern Macedonia (modern Greece) 10 miles inland from the Aegean Sea.**
- **Name means "city of Philip."**
- **Founded in 356 B.C. by the great Macedonian king, Philip, father of Alexander the Great.**
- **Honored by Caesar Augustus with the placement of a Roman military colony with the pretentious name *Colonia Augusta Julia Philippensis.* Parcels of land were used to reward retired soldiers.**
- **A "gateway city" on the Egnatian Way, the highway connecting the Empire from east to west.**
- **At one time boasted vast gold and silver mines.**

PHILIPPI—GATEWAY FOR THE GOSPEL

Just as all roads led to Rome, so much of the traffic to Rome from the east funneled through Philippi, which served as a gateway to Greece and Italy. Thus the city served as a gateway for the gospel once a church was established there. However, Paul had not planned to visit Philippi until a timely vision persuaded him to change direction (Acts 16:9–10).

Pride, self-importance, and affluence marked the people he found there, as they basked in the city's rich political and military history.

To find out more about the church that Paul founded in Philippi, see his letter to the Philippians.

Be Willing to Pay the Price

CONSIDER THIS 16:16–24 **The gospel frequently challenges systems of privilege, oppression, and injustice. Such was the case in Paul's encounter with the slave girl at Philippi (vv. 16–24). She was imprisoned in a pathetic situation that afforded her no options. But when Paul**

(continued on next page)

Paul and Silas Are Released

35And when it was day, the magistrates sent the officers,
saying, "Let those men go."
36So the keeper of the prison reported these words to
Paul, saying, "The magistrates have sent to let you go. Now
therefore depart, and go in peace."
37But Paul said to them, "They have beaten us openly, uncondemned Romans, *and* have thrown *us* into prison. And
now do they put us out secretly? No indeed! Let them come
themselves and get us out."
38And the officers told these words to the magistrates, and
they were afraid when they heard that they were Romans.
39Then they came and pleaded with them and brought *them*

CONSIDER THIS 16:19

People, Property, and Profitability

The gospel can produce radical changes as it affects people, property, and profitability. Consider three instructive examples from Acts:

Simon "the Great" (Acts 8:9–13, 18–24)

- *A sorcerer with a large following.*
- *The gospel threatened his profitable business by demonstrating a greater power.*
- *Hoping to expand his repertoire, he offered to buy the apostles' power.*
- *Rebuked by the apostles, who called him to true repentance.*

The Slave Girl at Philippi (Acts 16:16–40)

- *Paul's gospel freed a fortune-teller from her occult bondage.*
- *Owned by a syndicate of investors, she had powers that earned them good money.*
- *Realizing their loss, they seized Paul and Silas and hauled them before the authorities.*
- *Punishment: beatings and jail.*
- *But lockup only led to further conversions.*
- *Morning brought embarrassment to the city as officials learned of the travelers' Roman citizenship.*

The Silversmiths at Ephesus (Acts 19:1–41)

- *Paul lectured daily in the school of Tyrannus, resulting in many conversions.*
- *Sales of silver statues of Diana (the Greek goddess of fertility) fell off, triggering an emergency "Chamber of Commerce" meeting.*
- *Artisans complained that Paul's gospel had reduced*

out, and asked *them* to depart from the city. 40So they went
out of the prison and entered *the house of* Lydia; and when
they had seen the brethren, they encouraged them and departed.

CHAPTER 17

Converts and Conflict in Thessalonica

17:1 1Now when they had passed through
Amphipolis and Apollonia, they came to
Thessalonica, where there was a synagogue of the Jews.
2Then Paul, as his custom was, went in to them, and for
three Sabbaths reasoned with them from the Scriptures,

(Bible text continued on page 486)

* *trade, ruined their reputations, and impugned their goddess.*
* *A riot was incited and Paul's associates were dragged before a lynch mob.*
* *The city clerk eventually restored peace and Paul quietly went on his way.*

Good Ethics—Not Always Good Business

Christlike values do not necessarily produce financial gain in the marketplace. Sometimes they produce just the opposite. Scripture has no argument with making a profit except when it compromises people or the truth. At that point the gospel raises questions that any responsible believer must face. For example, a contract goes unsigned because a Christian refuses to offer money under the table. A sale is lost because a Christian refuses to lie to a customer. A promotion slips by because a Christian sets limits on the intrusion of work into his or her family and personal life.

Make no mistake, many people are receptive toward Christian principles at home and church, and even on the job—as long as such principles cost nothing. But the test of Christian commitment often lies in what one is willing to sacrifice.

What have your Christian convictions cost you? If nothing, are you making tradeoffs that you can't afford to make? Do you sometimes value possessions or power more than people? ◆

How you apply your faith to your work is one of the most important ways you have of communicating Christ to others. See "Your 'Workstyle,'" Titus 2:9–10.

(continued from previous page)

delivered her from demonic oppression, it broke not only the spiritual powers that dominated her, but the economic power of the syndicate that owned her.

Not surprisingly, the girl's bosses reacted to their loss and Paul paid for her liberation by going to jail. But despite the injustice, he and his team rejoiced with singing (v. 25) and were eventually vindicated (vv. 38–39).

Is there some whistle-blowing needed where you work or live? Are you willing to pay the price to bring equity or justice to others who are suffering?

THESSALONICA

YOU ARE THERE 17:1

* **Chief city of Macedonia and capital city of its district, second only to Corinth as the commercial center of Greece.**
* **Located on the Thermaic Gulf and the main seaport for the region.**
* **Founded by Cassander, king of Macedonia, in 316 B.C. to resettle war refugees from 26 towns that he had destroyed.**
* **Granted free-city status by Rome, allowing it to levy its own taxes, mint its own coins, and appoint local magistrates, known as politarchs. (Jason and other believers were dragged before these officials, Acts 17:5–9.)**
* **Located on the Egnatian Way, a Roman road extending across Macedonia from the Adriatic Sea to the Aegean Sea. The highway, along with a well-situated harbor, brought much commercial and military traffic through the city.**

FOR YOUR INFO 16:31–34

Families of the Early Church

Among the first people to join the Christian movement in the West were the Philippian jailer and his entire family (vv. 31–34). Families played an interesting role in the spread of the gospel during the early days of the church. Judging by Acts and the New Testament letters, acceptance of the faith seemed often to be a decision of an entire family or clan.

Consider the impact of family life, for better or worse, on the faith and commitment of several families and singles recorded in Acts and the New Testament letters.

Families of the Early Church

Family Name	Description
•Ananias •His wife Sapphira	These landowners in the early church observe the praise heaped on Barnabas for selling property and donating the proceeds to the movement. In like manner, they sell property and represent to Peter that they, too, are donating the funds. However, their collusion to keep back part of the money is uncovered and the Holy Spirit strikes them dead.
•Philip •His four daughters	This man is one of seven selected to manage distribution of food to widows. An evangelist, he crosses ethnic barriers by taking the gospel to Samaria. Later, he hosts Paul and his fellow travelers at his home in Caesarea, where his four daughters prophesy.
•Simon	Little is known about this tanner of Joppa except that he hosts Peter in his home during the apostle's momentous trip to Caesarea to take the gospel to Cornelius, a Gentile centurion.
•Mary •John Mark, her son •Rhoda, their maid	A woman of some means makes her home in Jerusalem available as a center of Christian activity. When Peter is released from prison, he goes to her house, where believers are in prayer. John Mark travels with cousin Barnabas, Mary's nephew, and later writes the first surviving narrative of Jesus' life and teachings.
•Barnabas	This landowner, donor, and leader in the early church helps bring Saul into the fellowship of believers, mentors him in the faith, and later works with him in the spread of the movement. He also mentors and defends cousin John Mark. At Antioch, he helps stabilize a new church that crosses many ethnic barriers.

Continued

FAMILIES OF THE EARLY CHURCH

Family Name	Description
Continued	
•Eunice •Her mother Lois •Eunice's son Timothy •His unnamed father, a Gentile	A Jewish mother and grandmother instill faith in Timothy, the product of a mixed marriage. Chosen and mentored by Paul, he becomes a pastor and fellow worker in the spread of Christianity.
•Lydia •Her household	This upscale garment dealer of Philippi and her family become the first believers in Europe. Probably a Gentile, she hosts Paul and his fellow travelers in her home, risking social and economic rejection but helping to found a church.
•A jailer of Philippi •His household	Shaken by an earthquake and the apparent escape of his prisoners, this man, probably a retired Roman soldier, is about to take his own life when Paul and Silas offer him the gospel. His entire family believes and he welcomes the apostles into his home.
•Priscilla •Aquila, her husband	This couple, possibly a mixed marriage between a Roman woman and a Jewish man, become partners in the tent manufacturing business with Paul. Together they mentor a teacher named Apollos. They also help to lead congregations in Corinth, Rome, and Ephesus, at least some of which are in their home.
•Saul, later called Paul •His sister •Her son	A young Jewish man with Roman citizenship starts out as a well-trained Pharisee determined to stamp out the Christian movement. But a dramatic encounter with the risen Christ causes him to make a complete turnabout, and he ends up as the faith's most ardent and widely traveled spokesperson. Apparently his nephew and perhaps his sister join him in the faith.
•Felix •Drusilla, his third wife	This Roman procurator, or governor, of Judea marries the Jewish Drusilla, youngest daughter of Herod Agrippa I, linking him to the notorious Herod family (Acts 12:1–2). Like the Herods, he considers himself above the law because of his influence with the courts. When Paul is brought before him, he hopes to collect a bribe. Later, their son, Agrippa, dies at the eruption of Mount Vesuvius in A.D. 79.
•Herod Agrippa II •Bernice, his sister and lover	The son of Herod Agrippa I becomes Roman governor over part of Palestine. His sister Bernice first marries a man named Marcus, then her uncle Herod, king of Chalcis. After his death she marries Polemo, king of Cilicia, but deserts him shortly after the wedding. Making her way to Jerusalem, she becomes the lover of her brother, by whom she has two sons. During this time Paul is brought before the couple to make a defense. Later, during the Jewish revolt, Agrippa flees Palestine for Rome, where he rules in absentia. Meanwhile, Bernice becomes mistress of the victorious Roman general and emperor, Vespasian, then of his son Titus.
•Publius •His father	The leading citizen of Malta welcomes shipwrecked Paul and his fellow travelers to his estate, hosting the group for three days. Paul heals his father of feverish dysentery, thereby attracting many others with illnesses.
•Philemon •Apphia, possibly his wife •Onesimus, their runaway slave	Probably a businessman of Colosse, this man's family hosts church in their home. When Paul sends back his runaway slave, Onesimus, he is challenged to break with the normal discipline and regard him as a brother in the faith rather than a rebellious slave. According to tradition, Onesimus becomes the first bishop of Ephesus.
•Onesiphorus •His household	A relative unknown of Scripture, this man receives high praise from Paul for his diligence in seeking out the imprisoned apostle in Rome and bringing him refreshment and help there and in Ephesus.

◆

The Gospels also portray many different families. They faced issues not unlike the ones families face today. See "Families of the Gospels," Luke 20:34.

3 explaining and demonstrating that the Christ had to suffer
and rise again from the dead, and *saying,* "This Jesus whom
17:4 I preach to you is the Christ." 4 And some
of them were persuaded; and a great
multitude of the devout Greeks, and not a few of the leading women, joined Paul and Silas.

5 But the Jews who were not persuaded, becoming envious,[a] took some of the evil men from the marketplace, and
gathering a mob, set all the city in an uproar and attacked
the house of Jason, and sought to bring them out to the
people. 6 But when they did not find them, they dragged Jason and some brethren to the rulers of the city, crying out,
"These who have turned the world upside down have come
here too. 7 Jason has harbored them, and these are all acting
contrary to the decrees of Caesar, saying there is another
king—Jesus." 8 And they troubled the crowd and the rulers
of the city when they heard these things. 9 So when they had
taken security from Jason and the rest, they let them go.

More Conflict in Berea

17:10 see pg. 488 10 Then the brethren immediately sent
Paul and Silas away by night to Berea.
When they arrived, they went into the synagogue of the
Jews. 11 These were more fair-minded than those in Thessalonica, in that they received the word with all readiness,
and searched the Scriptures daily *to find out* whether these
things were so. 12 Therefore many of them believed, and also
not a few of the Greeks, prominent women as well as men.
13 But when the Jews from Thessalonica learned that the
word of God was preached by Paul at Berea, they came
there also and stirred up the crowds. 14 Then immediately
the brethren sent Paul away, to go to the sea; but both Silas
17:15 see pg. 489 and Timothy remained there. 15 So those
who conducted Paul brought him to
Athens; and receiving a command for Silas and Timothy to
come to him with all speed, they departed.

Distress and Debate at Athens

17:15–34 see pg. 488 16 Now while Paul waited for them at
Athens, his spirit was provoked within
him when he saw that the city was given over to idols.
17:17 17 Therefore he reasoned in the synagogue
with the Jews and with the *Gentile* worshipers, and in the marketplace daily with those who happened to be there. 18 Then[a] certain Epicurean and Stoic

17:5 [a]NU-Text omits *who were not persuaded;* M-Text omits *becoming envious.*
17:18 [a]NU-Text and M-Text add *also.*

The Leading Women

CONSIDER THIS 17:4 *Thessalonica gave women more opportunities than most cities of the first-century world. Women there were known for their business contributions, their support of public projects, and their leadership in city government. When the gospel arrived, many of the "leading women" responded (v. 4), unlike their counterparts in Antioch of Pisidia (13:50). The difference is hard to explain, but it shows that success doesn't necessarily keep people from responding to the message of Christ.*

Thessalonica was named in honor of a woman, the wife of Cassander, sister of Alexander the Great, and daughter of Philip II of Macedonia.

philosophers encountered him. And some said, "What does
this babbler want to say?"

Others said, "He seems to be a proclaimer of foreign
gods," because he preached to them Jesus and the resurrection.

19And they took him and brought him to the Areopagus,
saying, "May we know what this new doctrine *is* of which
you speak? 20For you are bringing some strange things to
our ears. Therefore we want to know what these things
mean." 21For all the Athenians and the foreigners who were
there spent their time in nothing else but either to tell or to
hear some new thing.

22Then Paul stood in the midst of the Areopagus and said,
"Men of Athens, I perceive that in all things you are very religious; 23for as I was passing through and considering the
objects of your worship, I even found an altar with this inscription:

TO THE UNKNOWN GOD.

Therefore, the One whom you worship without knowing,
Him I proclaim to you: 24God, who made the world and
everything in it, since He is Lord of heaven and earth, does
not dwell in temples made with hands. 25Nor is He worshiped with men's hands, as though He needed anything,
since He gives to all life, breath, and all things. 26And He
has made from one blood[a] every nation of men to dwell on
all the face of the earth, and has determined their pre-
appointed times and the boundaries of their dwellings, 27so
that they should seek the Lord, in the hope that they might
grope for Him and find Him, though He is not far from
each one of us; 28for in Him we live and move and have our
being, as also some of your own poets have said, 'For we are
also His offspring.' 29Therefore, since we are the offspring of
God, we ought not to think that the Divine Nature is like
gold or silver or stone, something shaped by art and man's
devising. 30Truly, these times of ignorance God overlooked,
but now commands all men everywhere to repent, 31be-
cause He has appointed a day on which He will judge the
world in righteousness by the Man whom He has ordained.
He has given assurance of this to all by raising Him from
the dead."

32And when they heard of the resurrection of the dead,
some mocked, while others said, "We will hear you again
on this *matter*." 33So Paul departed from among them.
17:34 see pg. 490
34However, some men joined him and
believed, among them Dionysius the Are-
opagite, a woman named Damaris, and others with them.

(Bible text continued on page 490)

17:26 [a]NU-Text omits *blood.*

Adapt Your Witness!

CONSIDER THIS 17:17 *At Athens Paul addressed the Greeks in three very different settings—the synagogue, the Areopagus (the supreme tribunal), and the agora, or marketplace. This required three different approaches and points to Paul's great ability in the rhetorical arts.*

It's particularly interesting that Paul spoke out in the marketplace. As there apparently were few if any believers in Athens, he had to work "from the outside in" to present the gospel to Athenian workers. By contrast, believers today work in all levels of industry and commerce.

Paul's example raises a challenging question: Are you willing—and prepared—to represent Christ and His message and values where you work? Your faith cannot be a purely personal affair. God has appointed you to your workplace to carry the message of Christ to your coworkers and customers, just as he appointed Paul to go to the agora of Athens.

BEREA

YOU ARE THERE 17:10

- A city in southwest Macedonia located along the major east-west trade route, 45 miles west of Thessalonica.
- Capital city of the Macedonian region.
- Large and prosperous at the time of Paul, it prospered even more later under Byzantine rule; by the time of the Ottoman Turks (sixteenth century A.D.) it had become Europe's chief trade center for the Middle East.
- Sopater, Paul's companion from Berea (Acts 20:4), may have been converted when the fair-minded Bereans searched the Scriptures daily (17:11).

PAUL'S SECOND JOURNEY, PART THREE

CONSIDER THIS 17:15–34

PAUL, APOSTLE TO THE INTELLECTUALS

At Athens the gospel collided with a centuries-old culture rooted in intellectualism and discourse. Certainly Paul had encountered Greek philosophy elsewhere; indeed, he had grown up with it in Tarsus. But his visit to Athens brought him into direct contact with the inheritors of the city's celebrated intellectual tradition (Acts 17:18).

Was Paul intimidated by the arrogance and cynicism of the leisurely Epicureans and Stoics (vv. 18–21)? Some believe that he was (based on passages like 1 Cor. 2:1–5). Yet even though he might have felt more apprehension addressing them than any other audience, Acts gives no hint that he felt inferior. On the contrary, he addressed them at their own forum, the Areopagus, building on common ground by discussing their altar "to the unknown god" and citing one of their poets (Acts 17:28).

Was Paul's strategy effective? If judged by the number of converts, no. Only a handful believed. The rest dismissed him immediately or else postponed judgment pending later discussion—which apparently never came, as Paul departed.

On that basis, some believe that the apostle was wrong for ever going to Athens. In fact, some contend that Paul was so disillusioned by the experience that for a

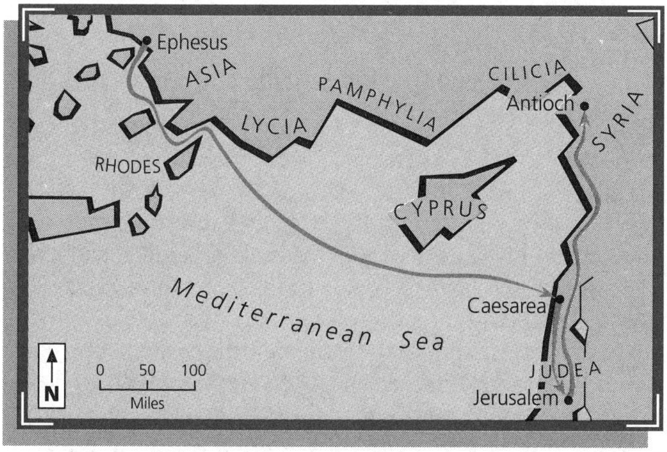

PAUL'S SECOND JOURNEY, PART FOUR

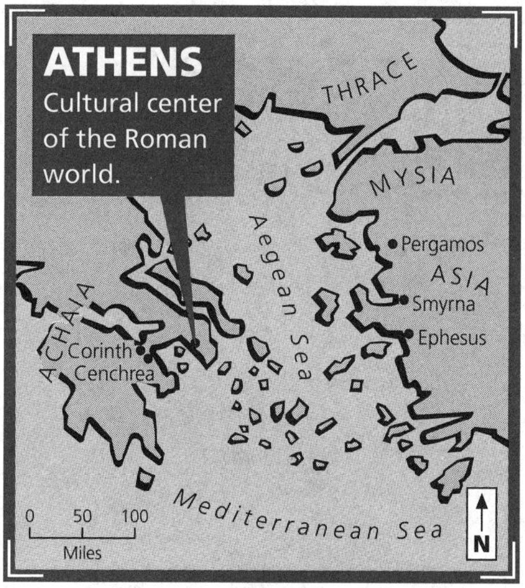

ATHENS

YOU ARE THERE 17:15

- Principal city of ancient Greece and capital of the district of Attica.
- Name derived from the Greek goddess Athena.
- Renowned in the ancient world for its philosophers, schools, and academies.
- As a free city, governed itself independently and paid no taxes to Rome.
- Though Paul won several converts to the gospel there, it may have been years later before a church began.

time he left the ministry to make tents at Corinth (18:1–3). Supposedly, his words in 1 Cor. 1:18—2:5 denouncing philosophy as so much "foolosophy" reflect that view. As a result, some conclude that it is a waste of time to offer the gospel to intellectuals.

Luke doesn't tell us exactly why Paul left Athens, but nothing suggests disillusionment. He never "left" the ministry, just as he had never abandoned his trade, tentmaking (see "Paul's 'Real' Job," Acts 18:1–3). While working with Aquila and Priscilla at Corinth, Paul continued to preach in the synagogue and in the house of Justus (18:4, 7), a ministry that lasted more than 18 months (18:11). Later in Ephesus he followed the same pattern for two years (19:8–10).

Paul's approach to the Athenian intellectuals should encourage believers today to actively participate in universities and other centers of learning. Those that God calls to work within the academic disciplines have an outstanding model to follow—Paul, God's apostle to the intellectuals. ◆

Moses is another example that demonstrates "The Value of Learning," Acts 7:22.

CHAPTER 18

Partnership with Priscilla and Aquila

18:1–3

18:2

1After these things Paul departed from
Athens and went to Corinth. 2And he
found a certain Jew named Aquila, born
in Pontus, who had recently come from
Italy with his wife Priscilla (because Claudius had commanded all the Jews to depart from Rome); and he came to
them. 3So, because he was of the same trade, he stayed with
them and worked; for by occupation they were tentmakers.
4And he reasoned in the synagogue every Sabbath, and persuaded both Jews and Greeks.

A Strategic Partnership

A CLOSER LOOK 18:2

In teaming up with Priscilla and Aquila, Paul not only made a smart business move, he also cultivated lifelong friends. Find out more about this outstanding first-century couple by reading "Priscilla and Aquila," Rom. 16:3–5.

Dionysius and Damaris

CONSIDER THIS 17:34

Apparently none of the Epicurean or Stoic philosophers of Athens responded to Paul's message about Christ, but Luke does name a council member and a woman as the nucleus of a group that believed (v. 34).

Dionysius was a member of the court and likely a person of some standing. Later writers name him as the first bishop of the church in Athens.

As for Damaris, it is remarkable that a woman should be among the first believers. Greek women of the day rarely took part in philosophical discourses. They generally stayed at home in seclusion while their husbands, freed by slaves from the menial tasks of life, pursued leisurely activities such as gymnastics, politics, and philosophy.

There are several possibilities to explain how Damaris managed to hear Paul and decide to follow Christ. One is that she was among a class of women known as hetairai, *specially trained companions to wealthy men who were educated in subjects usually reserved for men, such as rhetoric and philosophy. Their purpose was to entertain their partners. The role of* hetairai *was not as respected as that of wives, but they en-*

(continued on next page)

Paul's "Real" Job

CONSIDER THIS 18:1–3

Though the ministry today is viewed as a full-time profession, some of the first gospel workers earned all or part of their living through other occupations. Paul was a tentmaker (v. 3), a trade he may have learned as a boy in Tarsus (see 11:25 and "Saul," 13:1).

That kind of "bivocationalism" is worth considering in today's world. Many minority pastors in urban settings work at second and third jobs, since their churches cannot support them financially. And in developing countries, "secular" skills are desperately needed in supplying food, shelter, and economic development.

Jesus also could have made His living through a "secular" job, as did most rabbis of His day. See "Jesus the Carpenter," Mark 6:3, and "Scribes," Luke 20:39.

If Paul supported himself through an occupation other than his ministry, shouldn't Christian workers today at least consider that as an option? See "Paying Vocational Christian Workers," 1 Cor. 9:1–23.

A Synagogue Ruler Believes

5When Silas and Timothy had come from Macedonia, Paul was compelled by the Spirit, and testified to the Jews *that* Jesus *is* the Christ. 6But when they opposed him and blasphemed, he shook *his* garments and said to them, "Your blood *be* upon your *own* heads; I *am* clean. From now on I will go to the Gentiles." 7And he departed from there and entered the house of a certain *man* named Justus,[a] *one* who worshiped God, whose house was next door to the synagogue. 8Then Crispus, the ruler of the synagogue, believed on the Lord with all his household. And many of the Corinthians, hearing, believed and were baptized.

18:7–8

18:9–10 see pg. 492

9Now the Lord spoke to Paul in the night by a vision, "Do not be afraid, but speak, and do not keep silent; 10for I am with you, and no one will attack you to hurt you; for I have many people in this city." 11And he continued *there* a year and six months, teaching the word of God among them.

Jewish Leaders Oppose the Gospel

12When Gallio was proconsul of Achaia, the Jews with one accord rose up against Paul and brought him to the

18:7 [a]NU-Text reads *Titius Justus.*

"Not Many Mighty" . . . But a Few

CONSIDER THIS 18:7–8

A majority of converts to early Christianity, at least those in Corinth, were from the lower classes; there were "not many mighty," as Paul put it (1 Cor. 1:26–28).

But even if there were not many mighty, at least there were some. Several prominent citizens were attracted to the new religion, including Justus who lived next door to the synagogue (probably in a house of some size), Crispus, the ruler of the synagogue (Acts 18:7–8), and Erastus, the city treasurer (Rom. 16:23). Once again the gospel showed its incredible power to break down social barriers, creating a new people of God.

(continued from previous page)

joyed far more freedom and opportunity—including the opportunity to attend the philosophical discussions held daily in the marketplace and the Areopagus (vv. 17, 19).

Of course, there is no way to know for certain whether Damaris was a hetaira. *But no matter what her role in the society was, she courageously went against the prevailing culture by siding with Paul, Dionysius, and the message about the resurrected Jesus.*

judgment seat, [13]saying, "This *fellow* persuades men to worship God contrary to the law."
[14]And when Paul was about to open *his* mouth, Gallio
said to the Jews, "If it were a matter of wrongdoing
or wicked crimes, O Jews, there would be reason why I
should bear with you. [15]But if it is a question of words
and names and your own law, look *to it* yourselves; for
I do not want to be a judge of such *matters*." [16]And he
18:17 drove them from the judgment seat.
[17]Then all the Greeks[a] took Sosthenes,
the ruler of the synagogue, and beat *him* before
the judgment seat. But Gallio took no notice of these
things.

Paul Returns to Antioch

18:18 [18]So Paul still remained a good while.
Then he took leave of the brethren and

18:17 [a]NU-Text reads *they all.*

Afraid in the City?

CONSIDER THIS 18:9–10 *The Lord's words to Paul (vv. 9–10) offer hope for believers who live and work in cities. While there are many evils in the city—as well as in the country—the city itself is not an evil. Nor does evil prefer urban over rural settings. In his nighttime vision, Paul derived comfort from the affirmation that God was at work in the city. It was not a strange place for him, nor a place of alienation and fear. He felt at home there.*

Today, cities continue to be strategic for the work of the church in an increasingly urbanized world. Believers might as well get used to living and working in them as God's people. After all, they will spend eternity in a heavenly city (Rev. 21:1–27)!

Paul intentionally went to the cities. The gospel he proclaimed had implications for an urban setting. *See "Paul's Urban Strategy," Acts 16:4.*

Sosthenes the Attorney

CONSIDER THIS 18:17 *Sosthenes (v. 17) could have been the prosecuting lawyer who brought the case against Paul—and lost. The unfortunate synagogue ruler was beaten in a moment of mob psychology.*

There is perhaps a happy ending to the story, however. A man named Sosthenes was with Paul a few years later in Ephesus, as the apostle was writing to the Corinthians. In his letter, Paul brings greetings from "Sosthenes our brother" (1 Cor. 1:1).

We cannot know whether they were one and the same Sosthenes, but the possibility that we are witnessing Paul's treatment of a former enemy brings us to ask: What is the role of the church today with regard to the oppressed and victimized? How does it handle targets of persecution—people who have been "beaten up" by the unfair and capricious systems of the world?

sailed for Syria, and Priscilla and Aquila *were* with him. He
had *his* hair cut off at Cenchrea, for he had taken a vow.
19And he came to Ephesus, and left them there; but he himself entered the synagogue and reasoned with the Jews.
20When they asked *him* to stay a longer time with them, he
did not consent, 21but took leave of them, saying, "I must
by all means keep this coming feast in Jerusalem;[a] but I will
return again to you, God willing." And he sailed from Ephesus.
22And when he had landed at Caesarea, and gone up and
greeted the church, he went down to Antioch. 23After he
had spent some time *there,* he departed and went over the
region of Galatia and Phrygia in order, strengthening all the
disciples.

Apollos Is Mentored in the Faith

18:24 see pg. 494
24Now a certain Jew named Apollos,
born at Alexandria, an eloquent man *and*

18:21 [a]NU-Text omits *I must* through *Jerusalem.*

Personality Profile: Apollos

FOR YOUR INFO 18:24–28

Name means: "Destroyer."

Home: Alexandria, Egypt.

Occupation: Itinerant teacher in the things of the Lord (though his doctrinal knowledge only went as far as John the Baptist); later became an evangelist at Corinth.

Known to be: Eloquent and extremely popular. The Corinthians set up a faction around him, and perhaps to avoid causing any further controversy or fuel any party spirit, he did not return to Corinth, despite Paul's request (1 Cor. 16:12).

Best known today for: Being taught "the way of God more accurately" by Priscilla and Aquila (Acts 18:26; see Rom. 16:3–5), after which he became even more "mighty in the Scriptures."

Cenchrea

YOU ARE THERE 18:18

- **Corinth's eastern seaport on the Saronic Gulf, used as a jumping-off point for trade with Asia. Sailors hauled small ships and their cargo across the Isthmus of Corinth on a man-made "ship road" rather than sailing 200 miles around the dangerous peninsula.**
- **Several temples to a variety of pagan deities have been excavated in the Cenchrean harbor.**
- **Shared Corinth's ethnic diversity, free-thinking spirit, and money-making entrepreneurship; also the site of the biennial Isthmian games, on which there was heavy betting.**
- **Home of Phoebe, who distinguished herself as courier of Paul's letter to Rome (Rom. 16:1–2).**
- **Site of modern Kichries, Greece.**

18:24–26
mighty in the Scriptures, came to Ephesus. 25This man had been instructed in
the way of the Lord; and being fervent in spirit, he spoke
and taught accurately the things of the Lord, though he
knew only the baptism of John. 26So he began to speak
boldly in the synagogue. When Aquila and Priscilla heard
him, they took him aside and explained to him the way of
God more accurately. 27And when he desired to cross to
Achaia, the brethren wrote, exhorting the disciples to receive him; and when he arrived, he greatly helped those
18:24–28 see pg. 493
who had believed through grace; 28for he
vigorously refuted the Jews publicly,
showing from the Scriptures that Jesus is the Christ.

Marketplace Mentors: Priscilla and Aquila

A CLOSER LOOK 18:24–26

Priscilla and Aquila served as spiritual mentors to Apollos (vv. 24–28), updating his theology and increasing his effectiveness in the spread of the gospel. For more on the importance of the mentoring process, see "Discipleship—Or Mentoring?" Acts 9:26–30. To learn about the couple with whom Paul partnered in business, see "Priscilla and Aquila," Rom. 16:3–5.

YOU ARE THERE 18:24

The Septuagint: Alexandria's Gift to Christianity

Scripture mentions Alexandria only four times (all in Acts: 6:9; 18:24; 27:6; 28:11). However, the city's influence on the New Testament and the church was far greater than these few references might lead one to believe, for Alexandria was the birthplace of the Greek Old Testament translation known as the Septuagint.

Scattered among the cities of the Alexandrian, Greek, and Roman Empires were millions of Hebrews. By the first century, more than one million lived in Egypt. In Alexandria they had separate districts from their Gentile neighbors, but nevertheless isolation from Jerusalem took its toll. Each successive generation moved further away from Judaism, adopting the Hellenistic ways of Alexandrian society.

The Septuagint was a response to this cultural assimilation. Tradition holds that Jewish leaders in Alexandria invited some 70 Greek-speaking elders from Israel to translate the Hebrew Scriptures into koinē*, the Greek commonly spoken as a trade language throughout the ancient world.*

Several legends attach the miraculous to their work, completed in the second century B.C. One holds that the

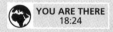

CHAPTER 19

Paul Arrives at Ephesus

1And it happened, while Apollos was at Corinth, that
Paul, having passed through the upper regions, came to
Ephesus. And finding some disciples 2he said to them, "Did
you receive the Holy Spirit when you believed?"
So they said to him, "We have not so much as heard
whether there is a Holy Spirit."
3And he said to them, "Into what then were you baptized?"
So they said, "Into John's baptism."
4Then Paul said, "John indeed baptized with a baptism
of repentance, saying to the people that they should believe
on Him who would come after him, that is, on Christ
Jesus."
5When they heard *this,* they were baptized in the name of
the Lord Jesus. 6And when Paul had laid hands on them,
the Holy Spirit came upon them, and they spoke with
tongues and prophesied. 7Now the men were about twelve
in all.

(Bible text continued on page 498)

translators were inspired by the Holy Spirit. Another claims that the 70 worked independently, but when finished their versions matched in every detail. At any rate, the translation, known as the Septuagint (Latin, septuaginta, *or LXX for 70), was a scholarly feat of astounding importance.*

This "Alexandrian Greek Urban Bible" became the Bible of the early church. It was the Bible Peter quoted at Pentecost, and the Bible that Apollos had grown up with. Conceived in a world-class, pluralistic city, it was the first Bible translated into the language of the people, and encouraged the use of koinē *for the New Testament. Even today the Septuagint is the authorized Bible of the Greek Orthodox Church.*

In short, the Alexandrian translation made Scripture intelligible and readable to common people, both Jew and Gentile. As a result, it became an indispensable tool in the spread of the gospel throughout the Roman world. ◆

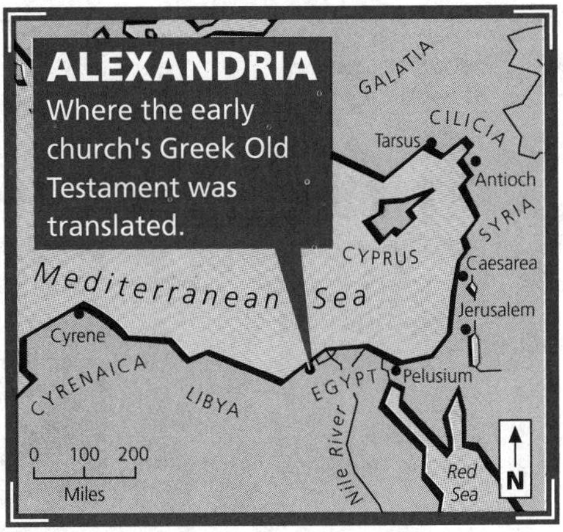

ALEXANDRIA

- **One of 21 cities founded by Alexander the Great named Alexandria or Alexander.**
- **Major port on the Nile delta, with a canal accessing the Mediterranean Sea.**
- **Perhaps the second-largest city of the Roman Empire, with a population of 300,000, perhaps 500,000 with slaves; Jews migrated there in large numbers.**
- **Renowned for shipbuilding (Acts 27:6; 28:11).**
- **Boasted the greatest "emporium," or trade center, of the ancient world. Exported papyrus, books, ivory, wood, glasswork, precious metals, bronze, perfumes, cosmetics, and domestic animals. Imported horses, wine and olive oil from Greece, timber from Cyprus, silk from Africa and the East, and precious stones.**
- **Site of a library housing 700,000 volumes, one of the "Seven Wonders of the Ancient World," making it the intellectual center of the Roman Empire.**
- **Birthplace of Apollos (18:24).**
- **John Mark, author of the second Gospel, may have founded a church there in A.D. 67. Later it became a major center of Christian philosophers and theologians.**

CONSIDER THIS
19:8–41

THE EPHESUS APPROACH:
HOW THE GOSPEL PENETRATED A CITY

Evangelism in Ephesus was explosive and unpredictable. People from vastly different backgrounds formed a diverse coalition of believers who had a far-reaching impact on the city's culture and economy (v. 10).

Laypeople Laid a Foundation

Start-up began with **Priscilla and Aquila**, the entrepreneurial couple that Paul met in Corinth (Acts 18:1–3). Joining Paul's team, they sailed with him to Ephesus, a major city of 350,000. While he traveled to Palestine and Galatia, they remained and set up key contacts, working in the **tent manufacturing industry** (18:18–23).

One beneficiary of their efforts was **Apollos**, a powerful orator from Alexandria who stirred things up in Paul's absence. Eloquent in delivery but incomplete in his theology, he learned from them about Jesus. After mentoring him in the faith, they sent him to Greece where he strengthened the believers, including their old friends at Corinth (18:24–28; 1 Cor. 3:6).

The Message Took Hold

Returning to Ephesus, Paul encountered a new breed of **religious zealots**. Like Apollos, they were unaware of Jesus, knowing

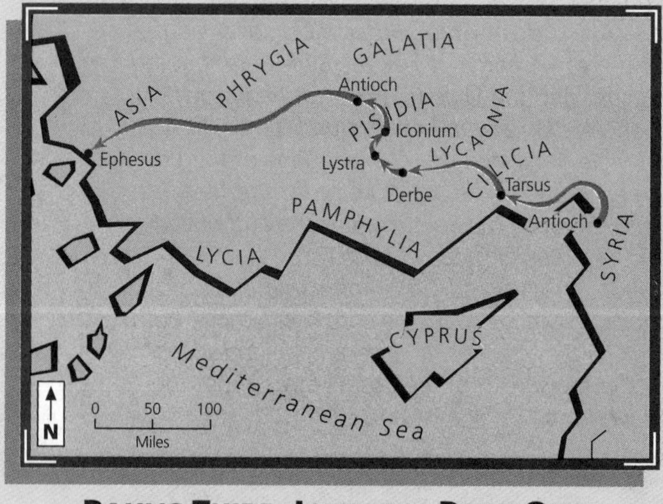

PAUL'S THIRD JOURNEY, PART ONE

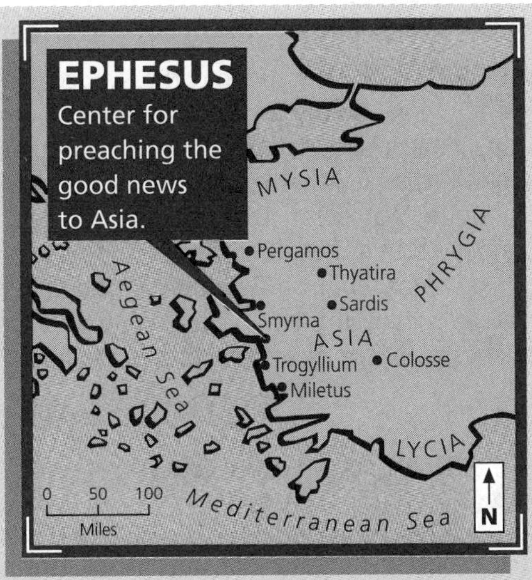

only of John the Baptist. But they became ecstatic as Paul related the fulfillment of John's ministry in Christ. Twelve of their number received the Holy Spirit, arousing the **religious establishment** (Acts 19:1–7).

Paul exploited the interest by initiating a three-month campaign in the local synagogue. However, his arguments met with opposition from obstinate **synagogue Jews** who maligned the movement publicly. In response, Paul relocated to the **school of Tyrannus** where for two years he engaged the Ephesians in a dialogue on Christianity during their midday, off-work hours (19:8–10).

Rapid Growth

Concentrated focus brought extraordinary results. The Christian message proved contagious among both **open-minded Jews and intellectually curious Gentiles**, impacting the city's **educational system**. **Residents and merchants** of Ephesus and from throughout Asia Minor were exposed. As word spread among **workers in regional commerce, the arts, and the transportation system**, "all . . . in Asia heard the word of the Lord" (19:10). Philemon's house church in Laodicea and probably other Asian churches were started by those attending Paul's "university lectureship."

Meanwhile, God validated Paul's message with dramatic miracles among the **sick and diseased**. This drew the notice of **health professionals**, including esoteric healing artists who become jealous. One group, the seven sons of Sceva, attempted to imitate the apostle through an occult ritual but were routed by the very powers over which they claimed to have mastery. The incident produced even more converts to Christianity, driving **occult practitioners and publishers** out of business (though not all; see 2 Tim. 3:8). The growing community of believers lit a bonfire that consumed magic books valued at no less than 400,000 hours of wages (Acts 19:11–20).

Economic Impact

At this point the civic leaders started receiving complaints from **artisans and craftsmen**, particularly **metalworkers**, about the economic impact of the message. Paul's meddlesome habit of attacking idolatry threatened the city's thriving **tourist trade**, centered around the internationally acclaimed temple to Diana, one of the "Seven Wonders of the Ancient World." The metalworkers, led by Demetrius, mobilized the entire city to save a key industry. Recruiting their associates in **other trade guilds**, they fomented a riot and rushed to the amphitheater.

THE THEATER AT EPHESUS

This brought **City Hall** into the act. At great

(continued on next page)

(continued from previous page)

pains to keep law and order—as well as his job—a Rome-appointed civil servant finally silenced the crowd and urged them to use the **court system** for redress of their grievances. His tactic forestalled violence, bought time, and saved the economy. It also spared Paul and his companions (19:23–41).

An Established Community

The riot brought Paul's lecture series to an end, but not the impact of the gospel. Departing the city, he left behind a growing, dynamic church, pastored by his young protégé, **Timothy** (16:1–3; 1 Tim. 1:3). Not only did these believers continue to penetrate their own community with the message of Christ, they also reached out to the many **travelers** to and from their strategically placed import-export city—**tourists and religious pilgrims, shipping merchants, sailors and other transportation workers, military personnel, political refugees**. Dozens of churches sprang up throughout Asia Minor, thanks to the Holy Spirit's coordinated use of three tentmakers (Priscilla, Aquila, and Paul), a fiery evangelist (Apollos), and countless unnamed laity. ◆

With its magnificent temple to Diana, Ephesus was a popular tourist spot in the ancient world. For more on Ephesus, see the Introduction to Ephesians.

The Ephesian outreach spawned numerous churches in Asia Minor. See "The Church at the End of the First Century A.D.," Rev. 1:20.

Lectures in the Synagogue and the School of Tyrannus

19:8–41 see pg. 496

[8]And he went into the synagogue and
spoke boldly for three months, reasoning
and persuading concerning the things of the kingdom of
God. [9]But when some were hardened and did not believe,
but spoke evil of the Way before the multitude, he departed
from them and withdrew the disciples, reasoning daily in
the school of Tyrannus. [10]And this continued for two years, so that all who
dwelt in Asia heard the word of the Lord Jesus, both Jews
and Greeks.

19:10

Occultists Are Converted

[11]Now God worked unusual miracles by the hands of
Paul, [12]so that even handkerchiefs or aprons were brought
from his body to the sick, and the diseases left them and the
evil spirits went out of them. [13]Then some of the itinerant
Jewish exorcists took it upon themselves to call the name of
the Lord Jesus over those who had evil spirits, saying, "We[a]
exorcise you by the Jesus whom Paul preaches." [14]Also
there were seven sons of Sceva, a Jewish chief priest, who
did so.
[15]And the evil spirit answered and said, "Jesus I know,
and Paul I know; but who are you?"
[16]Then the man in whom the evil spirit was leaped on
them, overpowered[a] them, and prevailed against them,[b] so
that they fled out of that house naked and wounded. [17]This
became known both to all Jews and Greeks dwelling in
Ephesus; and fear fell on them all, and the name of the Lord
Jesus was magnified. [18]And many who had believed came
confessing and telling their deeds. [19]Also, many of those
who had practiced magic brought their books together
and burned *them* in the sight of all. And they counted up
the value of them, and *it* totaled fifty thousand *pieces* of
silver. [20]So the word of the Lord grew mightily and prevailed.

The Gospel Challenges the Economy

19:21 see pg. 500

[21]When these things were accomplished, Paul purposed in the Spirit,
when he had passed through Macedonia and Achaia, to go
to Jerusalem, saying, "After I have been there, I must also
see Rome." [22]So he sent into Macedonia two of those who
ministered to him, Timothy and Erastus, but he himself
stayed in Asia for a time.

19:13 [a]NU-Text reads *I.* *19:16* [a]M-Text reads *and they overpowered.* [b]NU-Text reads *both of them.*

19:23–27

19:24

[23]And about that time there arose a
great commotion about the Way. [24]For a
certain man named Demetrius, a silversmith, who made silver shrines of Diana,[a]
brought no small profit to the craftsmen. [25]He called them
together with the workers of similar occupation, and said:
"Men, you know that we have our prosperity by this trade.
[26]Moreover you see and hear that not only at Ephesus, but
throughout almost all Asia, this Paul has persuaded and
turned away many people, saying that they are not gods
which are made with hands. [27]So not only is this trade of
ours in danger of falling into disrepute, but also the temple
of the great goddess Diana may be despised and her magnificence destroyed,[a] whom all Asia and the world worship."
[28]Now when they heard *this,* they were full of wrath and
cried out, saying, "Great *is* Diana of the Ephesians!" [29]So the
whole city was filled with confusion, and rushed into the
theater with one accord, having seized Gaius and
Aristarchus, Macedonians, Paul's travel companions. [30]And
when Paul wanted to go in to the people, the disciples
would not allow him. [31]Then some of the officials of Asia,
who were his friends, sent to him pleading that he would

19:24 [a]Greek *Artemis* *19:27* [a]NU-Text reads *she be deposed from her magnificence.*

Gospel and Property Conflicts

A CLOSER LOOK 19:23–27

Scripture has no argument with making a profit except when it compromises people or the truth. See "People, Property, and Profitability," Acts 16:19.

Personality Profile: Demetrius the Silversmith

FOR YOUR INFO 19:24

Home: Ephesus, a major tourist center renowned for its temple to Diana, one of the "Seven Wonders of the Ancient World" (see Introduction to Ephesians).

Profession: Silversmith and union leader of the local craft guild, specializing in silver statues of the goddess Diana.

Best known today for: Instigating a riot in Ephesus to get rid of Paul.

Ghetto Blaster

CONSIDER THIS 19:10

Anyone who lives or works in a large urban center today is no doubt familiar with the ghetto blaster, an oversized stereo box popular among urban youth for the same reason that many adults find it obnoxious—it shatters all peace and quiet with rap and rhythm.

When it comes to the gospel, a city itself can act like a ghetto blaster, amplifying the message to a level that cannot be ignored. As it reproduces the gospel's distinctive "sounds," city life exposes more and more people to the Good News.

That's what happened in Ephesus. The message reverberated out from that city such that "all who dwelt in Asia heard the word of the Lord" (v. 10). This is not to say that *every Asian* heard the gospel, but that the gospel was heard *all over Asia.* By penetrating the city, the gospel penetrated the region.

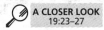

not venture into the theater. 32Some therefore cried one
thing and some another, for the assembly was confused,
and most of them did not know why they had come together. 33And they drew Alexander out of
the multitude, the Jews putting him for-
ward. And Alexander motioned with his hand, and wanted
to make his defense to the people. 34But when they found
out that he was a Jew, all with one voice cried out for about
two hours, "Great *is* Diana of the Ephesians!"

19:33

Alexander

A CLOSER LOOK
19:33

Paul later charged "Alexander the coppersmith," possibly this man, with doing him great harm. See "Alexander—A Confirmed Enemy," 2 Tim. 4:14–15.

CONSIDER THIS
19:21

ROME OR BUST

When Paul declared, "I must also see Rome" (v. 21), he wasn't talking about a tourist excursion; he was stating his bold intention to penetrate the capital of his world with the gospel. To him, Rome was a symbol of the center of power, the system that was driving the world. Jerusalem may have been important as a starting point, but the goal was Rome.

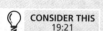

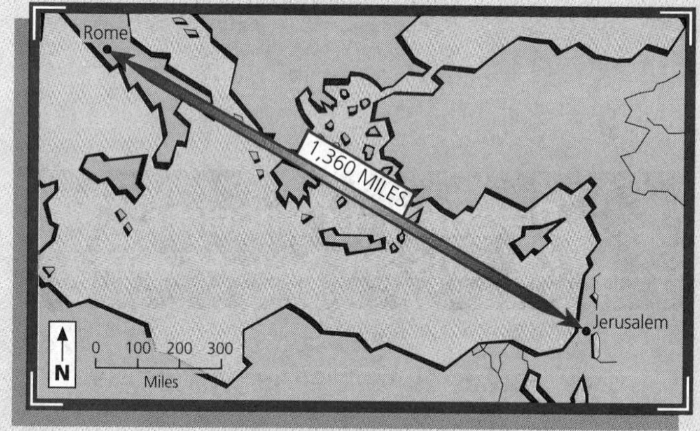

JERUSALEM TO ROME

In the center of Rome was a tall, marble obelisk indicating the distance from that point to every town in the empire—a graphic reminder of just how important Rome viewed itself. But Paul seemed to have a reverse model of that. Wherever he was, an internal marker seemed to remind him how far he was from Rome and how intent he

[35]And when the city clerk had quieted the crowd, he said:
"Men of Ephesus, what man is there who does not know
that the city of the Ephesians is temple guardian of the great
goddess Diana, and of the *image* which fell down from
Zeus? [36]Therefore, since these things cannot be denied, you
ought to be quiet and do nothing rashly. [37]For you have
brought these men here who are neither robbers of temples
nor blasphemers of your[a] goddess. [38]Therefore, if Demetrius
and his fellow craftsmen have a case against anyone, the
courts are open and there are proconsuls. Let them bring
charges against one another. [39]But if you have any other inquiry to make, it shall be determined in the lawful assem-

19:37 [a]NU-Text reads *our*.

was on getting there. The cities that he visited—including Jerusalem—became mileposts on his way to Rome.

The audacity of his plan is rather shocking: A tiny group living on the periphery of the Roman Empire aimed to conquer the cities and even the capital of the mightiest empire in world history with its new and strange beliefs. Incredibly, the movement prevailed!

That stunning achievement compels believers today to ask: What is our Rome? What are the forces shaping our world today? What is our strategy for gospel penetration? If Paul were alive today, where would he be headed as the strategic center of influence? Perhaps to the megacities of our world, like Mexico City with its 24 million people, half under the age of 15. Perhaps to Tokyo, the second largest city in the world and a major influence on the world's economy.

The point is that modern Christians walk in a tradition of people who declared, "We must get to Rome!" In the same way, we must not stay in our Jerusalems, our homes, our cultures. We are here for influence. We are here to spread the gospel. ◆

Paul's global vision came from Jesus, who sent His followers into "all the world." But spreading Christ's message involves more than just broadcasting a statement or set of facts. How does faith impact the world? See Mark 16:15.

Learn more about the imperial city at Acts 28:16.

AN INTERNATIONAL WORK GROUP

CONSIDER THIS 20:4

The rapidly growing Christian movement recruited members from a wide variety of places. That created significant cultural diversity, as the traveling team mentioned in v. 4 shows. Note the rich differences of background:

Macedonians

- **Sopater of Berea (perhaps the same as Sosipater in Rom. 16:21)**
- **Aristarchus (Acts 27:2) and Secundus of Thessalonica**

Galatians

- **Gaius of Derbe**
- **Timothy of Lystra, the product of a mixed marriage (Acts 16:1; see Introduction to 2 Timothy)**

Asians

- **Tychicus, possibly from Ephesus (Eph. 6:21–22; Col. 4:7–8)**
- **Trophimus of Ephesus (Acts 21:29)**

Others

- **Luke the physician from Antioch in Syria, who possibly was writing the Acts account while on the trip (see Introduction to Luke)**
- **Paul of Tarsus, Jerusalem, and Antioch in Syria (see Acts 13:1)**

This varied coalition shows how the people of God have a foundation for unity beyond all other causes. The common faith can bridge differences that even circumstances like a depression, war, or natural disaster cannot. It fulfills Jesus' prayer for His followers that they would demonstrate a oneness that demands the world's attention (John 17:20–23).

Develop Faith Whenever You Can

CONSIDER THIS 20:7–12 **The incidents at Troas (vv. 7–12) reflect a habit that believers do well to cultivate—gathering frequently in informal, small clusters to reflect on Scripture, pray, and support one another.**

The working people of that key Roman seaport gathered around the visitors to spend an evening together and learn more about the faith. They were following a pattern established at the beginning of the movement, of coming together around the apostles' teaching, fellowship, the breaking of bread, and prayer (2:42). In fact, their appetite for the experience was insatiable: even the shock of Eutychus' fall could not deter them (vv. 9–11)!

Home- or work-based groups of believers have frequently been the foundation of significant Christian movements throughout history. It's worth asking: Do you meet regularly with peers at work, home, or church to sort out your faith and its application to your world?

Troas was the site of a pivotal decision in Christianity. See "A Turning Point in Western Civilization," Acts 16:8.

bly. 40For we are in danger of being called in question for
today's uproar, there being no reason which we may give to
account for this disorderly gathering." 41And when he had
said these things, he dismissed the assembly.

CHAPTER 20

Macedonian Believers Are Revisited

1After the uproar had ceased, Paul called the disciples to
himself, embraced *them,* and departed to go to Macedonia.
2Now when he had gone over that region and encouraged
them with many words, he came to Greece 3and stayed
three months. And when the Jews plotted against him as he
was about to sail to Syria, he decided to return through
20:4 see pg. 501 Macedonia. 4And Sopater of Berea accompanied him to Asia—also Aristarchus
and Secundus of the Thessalonians, and Gaius of Derbe,
and Timothy, and Tychicus and Trophimus of Asia. 5These
men, going ahead, waited for us at Troas. 6But we sailed
away from Philippi after the Days of Unleavened Bread, and
in five days joined them at Troas, where we stayed seven
days.

Eutychus Falls to His Death and Is Raised

20:7–12 7Now on the first *day* of the week,
when the disciples came together to
break bread, Paul, ready to depart the next day, spoke to
them and continued his message until midnight. 8There
were many lamps in the upper room where they[a] were gathered together. 9And in a window sat a certain young man
named Eutychus, who was sinking into a deep sleep. He
was overcome by sleep; and as Paul continued speaking, he
fell down from the third story and was taken up dead. 10But
Paul went down, fell on him, and embracing *him* said, "Do
not trouble yourselves, for his life is in him." 11Now when
he had come up, had broken bread and eaten, and talked a
long while, even till daybreak, he departed. 12And they
brought the young man in alive, and they were not a little
comforted.

Farewell to the Ephesian Elders

20:13 13Then we went ahead to the ship and
sailed to Assos, there intending to take
Paul on board; for so he had given orders, intending himself
20:14 to go on foot. 14And when he met us at
Assos, we took him on board and came

20:8 [a]NU-Text and M-Text read *we.*

20:15
to Mitylene. 15We sailed from there, and
the next *day* came opposite Chios. The
following *day* we arrived at Samos and stayed at Trogyllium.
20:15–16 see pg. 505
The next *day* we came to Miletus. 16For
Paul had decided to sail past Ephesus, so
that he would not have to spend time in Asia; for he was
hurrying to be at Jerusalem, if possible, on the Day of Pentecost.
17From Miletus he sent to Ephesus and called for the elders of the church. 18And when they had come to him, he
said to them: "You know, from the first day that I came to
Asia, in what manner I always lived among you, 19serving
the Lord with all humility, with many tears and trials which
happened to me by the plotting of the Jews; 20how I kept
back nothing that was helpful, but proclaimed it to you,
and taught you publicly and from house to house, 21testify-
ing to Jews, and also to Greeks, repentance toward God and
faith toward our Lord Jesus Christ. 22And see, now I go
bound in the spirit to Jerusalem, not knowing the things
that will happen to me there, 23except that the Holy Spirit
testifies in every city, saying that chains and tribulations
await me. 24But none of these things move me; nor do I
count my life dear to myself,[a] so that I may finish my race
with joy, and the ministry which I received from the Lord
Jesus, to testify to the gospel of the grace of God.
25"And indeed, now I know that you all, among whom I
have gone preaching the kingdom of God, will see my face
no more. 26Therefore I testify to you this day that I *am* innocent of the blood of all *men.* 27For I have not shunned to declare to you the whole counsel of God. 28Therefore take
heed to yourselves and to all the flock, among which the
Holy Spirit has made you overseers, to shepherd the church
of God[a] which He purchased with His own blood. 29For I
know this, that after my departure savage wolves will come
in among you, not sparing the flock. 30Also from among
yourselves men will rise up, speaking perverse things, to
draw away the disciples after themselves. 31Therefore
watch, and remember that for three years I did not cease to
warn everyone night and day with tears.
32"So now, brethren, I commend you to God and to the
word of His grace, which is able to build you up and give
you an inheritance among all those who are sanctified. 33I
have coveted no one's silver or gold or apparel. 34Yes,[a] you
yourselves know that these hands have provided for my ne-
20:33–38 see pg. 506
cessities, and for those who were with
me. 35I have shown you in every way, by
laboring like this, that you must support the weak. And

20:24 [a]NU-Text reads *But I do not count my life of any value or dear to myself.*
20:28 [a]M-Text reads *of the Lord and God.* *20:34* [a]NU-Text and M-Text omit *Yes.*

Assos

YOU ARE THERE 20:13

- **Seaport located on a volcanic hill, 700 feet in altitude, overlooking the Gulf of Adramyttium on the Aegean Sea.**
- **Also known as Assus.**
- **Site of modern Behram Köi in Turkey.**
- **Impressively fortified with a thick wall two miles long and 65 feet high; also boasted a theater, public baths, and a rectangular *agora,* or marketplace.**
- **Competed with other Greek cities for the largest shrine by building a Doric temple to Athena. Emperor worship was also prevalent; like most Greek cities, Assos wanted Caesar to look upon it favorably.**
- **Home to the philosopher Aristotle for three years (348–345 B.C.).**

Mitylene

YOU ARE THERE 20:14

- **Chief city of the island of Lesbos off the coast of Asia Minor in the Aegean Sea.**
- **Name means "purity."**
- **Its sheltered, deep-water harbor faced the mainland, making it a logical overnight stay for anyone traveling along the coast.**
- **A favorite holiday resort for Roman soldiers.**

Chios

YOU ARE THERE 20:15

- **Small, mountainous island between Lesbos and Samos, just five miles off the coast of modern-day Turkey in the Aegean Sea.**
- **Modern Khios, meaning "open."**
- **Historically a "political football,"**

(continued on next page)

(continued from previous page)

wavering between conquest by empires, treaty alliances, and revolt for independence.
- **Renowned for its wine, wheat, citrus fruits, figs, and (today) the substance used in chewing gum.**
- **Claims to be the birthplace of Homer, the Greek poet to whom is ascribed *The Iliad* and *The Odyssey.* Tradition holds that he collected students at the foot of Chios' Mount Epos.**

SAMOS

- **Small, mountainous island in the Aegean Sea, separated from Asia Minor by the narrow Samos Strait.**
- **Important maritime island for Greece, later declared a free state by Rome.**
- **Known for producing fine wine, fruit, olives, and cotton.**

TROGYLLIUM

- **City 20 miles south of Ephesus, located on land that protrudes into the Aegean Sea within a mile of the island of Samos.**
- **Influenced by its neighbors to the north, the Lydians, who were the first to set up permanent retail shops and mint gold and silver coins to enhance economic activity.**
- **Some New Testament texts omit the single reference in Acts 20:15.**
- **A modern harbor in this region on the western tip of Trogyllium is designated St. Paul's Harbor.**

remember the words of the Lord Jesus, that He said, 'It is more blessed to give than to receive.' "
36And when he had said these things, he knelt down and
prayed with them all. 37Then they all wept freely, and fell on
Paul's neck and kissed him, 38sorrowing most of all for the
words which he spoke, that they would see his face no more. And they accompanied him to the ship.

CHAPTER 21

Paul Is Warned to Avoid Jerusalem

21:1 see pg. 508
1Now it came to pass, that when we had departed from them and set sail, running a straight course we came to Cos, the following *day* to
Rhodes, and from there to Patara. 2And finding a ship sail-
ing over to Phoenicia, we went aboard and set sail. 3When
we had sighted Cyprus, we passed it on the left, sailed to Syria, and landed at Tyre; for there the ship was to unload
her cargo. 4And finding disciples,[a] we stayed there seven days. They told Paul through the Spirit not to go up to
Jerusalem. 5When we had come to the end of those days, we departed and went on our way; and they all accompanied us, with wives and children, till *we were* out of the city.
And we knelt down on the shore and prayed. 6When we

21:4 [a]NU-Text reads *the disciples.*

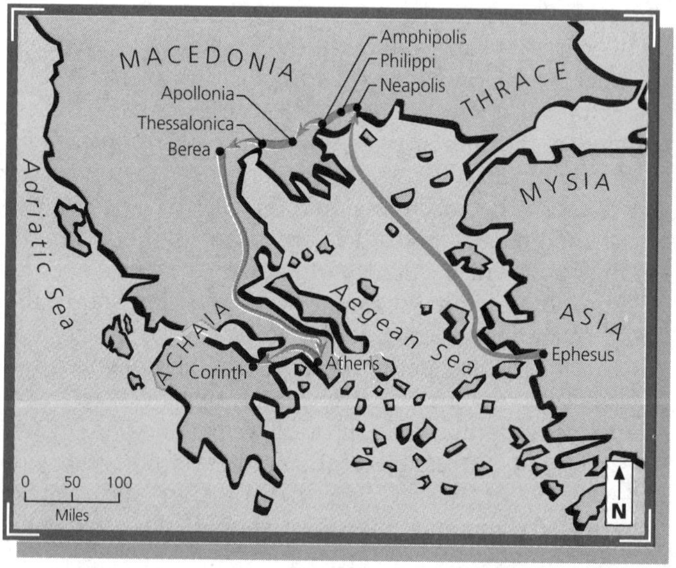

PAUL'S THIRD JOURNEY, PART TWO

had taken our leave of one another, we boarded the ship,
and they returned home.
21:7 see pg. 509
[7]And when we had finished *our* voyage
from Tyre, we came to Ptolemais, greeted
the brethren, and stayed with them one day. [8]On the next
day we who were Paul's companions[a] departed and came to
Caesarea, and entered the house of Philip the evangelist,
21:9 see pg. 506
who was *one* of the seven, and stayed
with him. [9]Now this man had four virgin
daughters who prophesied. [10]And as we stayed many days,
a certain prophet named Agabus came down from Judea.
[11]When he had come to us, he took Paul's belt, bound his
own hands and feet, and said, "Thus says the Holy Spirit,
'So shall the Jews at Jerusalem bind the man who owns this
belt, and deliver *him* into the hands of the Gentiles.' "
[12]Now when we heard these things, both we and those
from that place pleaded with him not to go up to Jerusalem.
[13]Then Paul answered, "What do you mean by weeping and
breaking my heart? For I am ready not only to be bound,
but also to die at Jerusalem for the name of the Lord Jesus."
[14]So when he would not be persuaded, we ceased, saying,
"The will of the Lord be done."
[15]And after those days we packed and went up to
Jerusalem. [16]Also some of the disciples from Caesarea went
with us and brought with them a certain Mnason of Cyprus,
an early disciple, with whom we were to lodge.

21:8 [a]NU-Text omits *who were Paul's companions.*

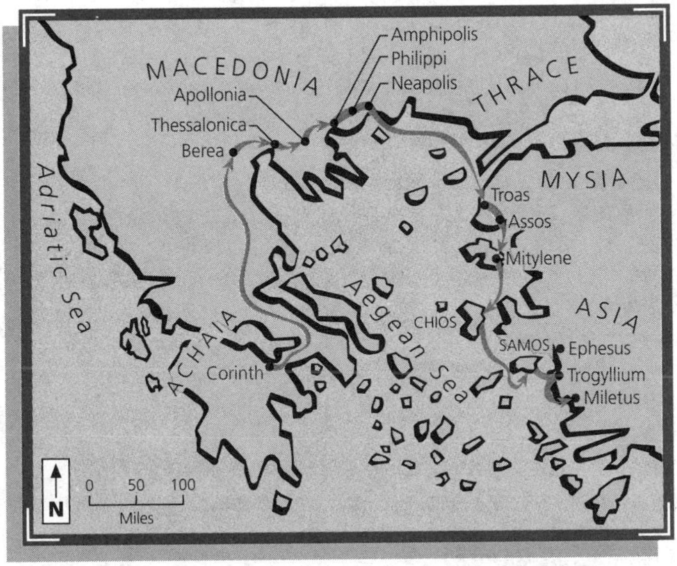

PAUL'S THIRD JOURNEY, PART THREE

MILETUS

YOU ARE THERE 20:15–16

- **Seaport on the west coast of Asia Minor and southernmost of the great cities of Greek culture.**
- **Located just south of present-day Söke, Turkey.**
- **Hippodamus of Miletus, an urban planner, rebuilt the city after it was destroyed during the Graeco-Persian Wars (c. 546–448 B.C.). Using a grid pattern of right angles with boulevards 30 feet wide, he created the "Hippodamian City," a model recreated throughout the Roman Empire.**
- **Leading merchants founded a marketing empire linking 70 to 90 smaller towns and cities further north, along the coast of the Black Sea.**
- **Exported its culture, Greek philosophy, and a trade language that became the common-speech Greek in which the New Testament was written.**
- **Noted for its civil strife between workers, who wanted a democracy, and the rich, who preferred dictatorship. At Miletus Paul warned the Ephesian elders against similar strife among believers (Acts 20:28–35).**
- **Already in decline commercially and strategically by the time of Paul's visit (c. A.D. 57), due to the silting up of its waterway.**

The Four Daughters of Philip

CONSIDER THIS
21:9

In his Pentecost sermon, Peter declared that the words of the Old Testament prophet Joel were coming to pass: "Your sons and your daughters shall prophesy" (Acts 2:17–18). The four virgin daughters of Philip were proof that it was so (21:9).

In the first century, prophets were recognized (not appointed) through the exercise of their God-given gifts, which they often dis-

(continued on next page)

Paul Arrives in Jerusalem

17And when we had come to Jerusalem, the brethren received us gladly. 18On the following *day* Paul went in with
us to James, and all the elders were present. 19When he had
greeted them, he told in detail those things which God had
done among the Gentiles through his ministry. 20And when
they heard *it*, they glorified the Lord. And they said to him,
"You see, brother, how many myriads of Jews there are who
have believed, and they are all zealous for the law; 21but
they have been informed about you that you teach all the
Jews who are among the Gentiles to forsake Moses, saying
that they ought not to circumcise *their* children nor to walk
according to the customs. 22What then? The assembly must
certainly meet, for they will[a] hear that you have come.
23Therefore do what we tell you: We have four men who
have taken a vow. 24Take them and be purified with them,
and pay their expenses so that they may shave *their* heads,
and that all may know that those things of which they were
informed concerning you are nothing, but *that* you yourself
also walk orderly and keep the law. 25But concerning the

21:22 [a]NU-Text reads *What then is to be done? They will certainly.*

CONSIDER THIS
20:33–38

"I Have Not Coveted"

Paul's emotional farewell to the Ephesian elders ended with a significant disclaimer: "I have [not] coveted" (v. 33). Paul seems to have been at pains to emphasize that he was not a deadbeat while among them, sponging off their generosity. Rather, he worked as a tentmaker, first in order to provide for himself and his companions, and second, to "support [help] the weak" (v. 34–35; see "Paul's 'Real' Job," 18:1–3).

These words merit our attention. First, they reveal a biblical work ethic that forsakes greed in favor of hard, honest labor and a trust in God to provide for basic needs. Then, as God blesses, a worker's abundance should overflow into generosity toward others in need. This pattern recurs throughout the New Testament (for example, Matt. 6:24–34; Luke 16:9–13; Eph. 4:28; 2 Thess. 3:6–15; 1 Tim. 6:6–10, 17–19).

However, Paul's statement also bears upon the reputation of churches and ministries today. A growing number of people regard Christian work and workers with skepticism, as little more than fundraising vehicles for a greedy clergy. Apparently Paul faced similar attitudes, and therefore chose to support himself during his stay in Ephesus. Is

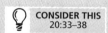

Gentiles who believe, we have written *and* decided that they
should observe no such thing,[a] except that they should
keep themselves from *things* offered to idols, from blood,
from things strangled, and from sexual immorality."
26Then Paul took the men, and the next day, having been
purified with them, entered the temple to announce the ex-
piration of the days of purification, at which time an offering should be made for each one of them.

A Mob Seeks to Kill Paul

27Now when the seven days were almost ended, the Jews
from Asia, seeing him in the temple, stirred up the whole
crowd and laid hands on him, 28crying out, "Men of Israel,
help! This is the man who teaches all *men* everywhere
against the people, the law, and this place; and furthermore
he also brought Greeks into the temple and has defiled this
holy place." 29(For they had previously[a] seen Trophimus the
Ephesian with him in the city, whom they supposed that
Paul had brought into the temple.)

21:25 [a]NU-Text omits *that they should observe no such thing, except.* *21:29* [a]M-Text omits *previously.*

(continued from previous page)

played during worship, bringing a word from the Lord. (The New Testament had not yet been written.) The role was highly esteemed by Paul (Eph. 4:11).

Philip's daughters broke the cultural norm of being wives and mothers, perhaps choosing to remain single in order to carry out their prophetic work.

there any reason why modern Christian leaders shouldn't at least consider that as an option today?

But Paul's words also present a stiff challenge to "laypeople." What about our attitudes toward work, income, and material things? How would we rate on a scale measuring greed versus generosity?

Paul goes beyond saying that generosity is just a nice virtue. "You must support the weak," he urges (v. 35, emphasis added), because it is the very thing that Christ taught. What must that have sounded like to people from the extraordinarily affluent city of Ephesus? It certainly is a powerful exhortation to us today. But it is backed up by two powerful examples—Paul (a tentmaker) and Christ (a carpenter). ◆

Like Paul, Jesus gave a direct, unequivocal command to guard against covetousness—longing for something we don't have. See "Watch Out for Greed!" Luke 12:15.

Paul knew firsthand the wealth and privileges of prominence in the Jewish community and of Roman citizenship. But he also suffered extraordinary hardships in the ministry. He survived both extremes. What was his secret? Find out at Phil. 4:10–13.

THE JERUSALEM RIOTS

CONSIDER THIS 21:30

By the time Paul was seized (v. 30), many years had passed since the euphoric Pentecost and its aftermath recorded in Acts 2–4. Whatever had happened to the Jerusalem church with its aggressive outreach and bold confidence? Where was it when these events took place? Its silence—or absence—at that point is a reminder that to preach in a city is one thing; to occupy and transform it is quite another. Urbanscapes everywhere, ancient and modern, are marked by steeples over buildings where the city church used to be.

Cos

YOU ARE THERE 21:1

- A massive, mountainous Greek island just off the west coast of Asia Minor.
- Settled by the Greeks, but known to rebel against Greece and side with Rome, which returned the loyalty: Rome's client Herod the Great was the island's benefactor, and Emperor Claudius proclaimed it exempt from paying Roman taxes.
- Known for its healthy climate and hot springs; gained prominence as a health resort; traditional site for Greece's first school of medicine and home of the famous physician, Hippocrates; a shrine to Asclepius, god of healing, was built there.
- Excavations have located a stadium, a wall, and Roman baths dating to the time of Paul's journey.
- Known to modern Greeks as Kos, to Italians as Koo, and to Turks as Istanköy.

Rhodes

- Largest and easternmost island in the Aegean Sea, opposite the southwest coast of Asia Minor.
- Name may derive from *Rhodē* ("rose"), daughter of the Greek god Poseidon. But some believe it comes from *erod,* the Phoenician word for "snake"; one species of poisonous snakes still survives there.
- Important center of commerce, cultural works, and year-round tourism.
- Site of the Colossus of Rhodes, which had a symbolic role similar to that of the Statue of Liberty.
- Paul only stopped briefly at the island as he hastened to Jerusalem for Pentecost (Acts 21:1).

(continued on next page)

21:30 see pg. 507

30And all the city was disturbed; and
the people ran together, seized Paul, and
dragged him out of the temple; and immediately the doors
were shut. 31Now as they were seeking to kill him, news
came to the commander of the garrison that all Jerusalem
was in an uproar. 32He immediately took soldiers and centurions, and ran down to them. And when they saw the
commander and the soldiers, they stopped beating Paul.
33Then the commander came near and took him, and commanded *him* to be bound with two chains; and he asked
who he was and what he had done. 34And some among the
multitude cried one thing and some another.
So when he could not ascertain the truth because of the
tumult, he commanded him to be taken into the barracks.
35When he reached the stairs, he had to be carried by the
soldiers because of the violence of the mob. 36For the multitude of the people followed after, crying out, "Away with
him!"
37Then as Paul was about to be led into the barracks, he
said to the commander, "May I speak to you?"
He replied, "Can you speak Greek? 38Are you not the
Egyptian who some time ago stirred up a rebellion and led
the four thousand assassins out into the wilderness?"
39But Paul said, "I am a Jew from Tarsus, in Cilicia, a citizen of no mean city; and I implore you, permit me to speak
to the people."

Paul Is Allowed to Address the People

40So when he had given him permission, Paul stood on
the stairs and motioned with his hand to the people. And

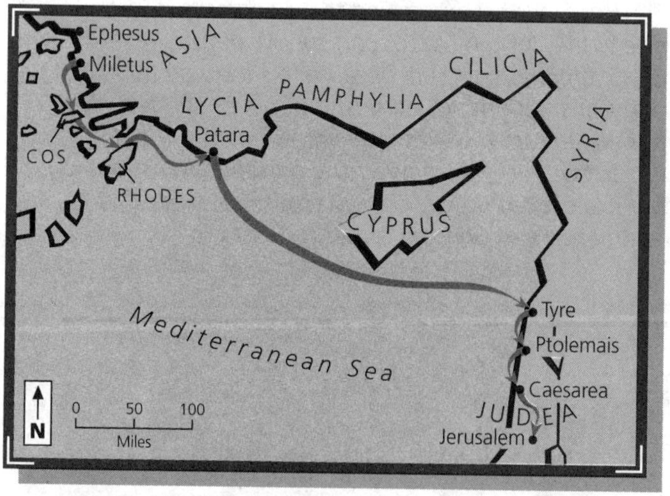

PAUL'S THIRD JOURNEY, PART FOUR

when there was a great silence, he spoke to *them* in the Hebrew language, saying,

CHAPTER 22

1“Brethren and fathers, hear my defense before you now.”
2And when they heard that he spoke to them in the Hebrew
language, they kept all the more silent.
Then he said: 3“I am indeed a Jew, born in Tarsus of Cilicia, but brought up in this city at the feet of Gamaliel,
taught according to the strictness of our fathers’ law, and
was zealous toward God as you all are today. 4I persecuted
this Way to the death, binding and delivering into prisons
both men and women, 5as also the high priest bears me witness, and all the council of the elders, from whom I also received letters to the brethren, and went to Damascus to
bring in chains even those who were there to Jerusalem to
be punished.
6“Now it happened, as I journeyed and came near Damascus at about noon, suddenly a great light from heaven
shone around me. 7And I fell to the ground and heard a
voice saying to me, ‘Saul, Saul, why are you persecuting
Me?’ 8So I answered, ‘Who are You, Lord?’ And He said to
me, ‘I am Jesus of Nazareth, whom you are persecuting.’
9“And those who were with me indeed saw the light and
were afraid,[a] but they did not hear the voice of Him who
spoke to me. 10So I said, ‘What shall I do, Lord?’ And the
Lord said to me, ‘Arise and go into Damascus, and there
you will be told all things which are appointed for you to
do.’ 11And since I could not see for the glory of that light,
being led by the hand of those who were with me, I came
into Damascus.
12“Then a certain Ananias, a devout man according to the
law, having a good testimony with all the Jews who dwelt
there, 13came to me; and he stood and said to me, ‘Brother
Saul, receive your sight.’ And at that same hour I looked up
at him. 14Then he said, ‘The God of our fathers has chosen
you that you should know His will, and see the Just One,
and hear the voice of His mouth. 15For you will be His witness to all men of what you have seen and heard. 16And
now why are you waiting? Arise and be baptized, and wash
away your sins, calling on the name of the Lord.’
17“Now it happened, when I returned to Jerusalem and
was praying in the temple, that I was in a trance 18and saw
Him saying to me, ‘Make haste and get out of Jerusalem
quickly, for they will not receive your testimony concerning
Me.’ 19So I said, ‘Lord, they know that in every synagogue I
imprisoned and beat those who believe on You. 20And when

22:9 [a]NU-Text omits *and were afraid.*

(continued from previous page)

PATARA

- **One of the largest and most prosperous cities of Lycia, a rugged coastal area of southwest Asia Minor shut off from the interior by 10,000-foot mountains.**
- **Freed by the Greeks from Persia in 546 B.C., the Lycians adopted Greek ways and language.**
- **With its excellent harbor, Patara enjoyed commercial success as an overhaul and crossover point, with favorable trade winds for ships venturing across the Mediterranean. It became one of the largest cities in the Lycian League, organized for mutual defense.**
- **Boasted a magnificent temple to Apollo, a prominent theater, an archway, and public baths.**

PTOLEMAIS

YOU ARE THERE 21:7

- **Seaport located in northern Palestine, 12 miles south of modern-day Lebanon and just across the bay from the port of Haifa.**
- **Originally Accho, but renamed Ptolemais by Ptolemy I, ruler of Egypt (323-285 B.C.) and descendant of one of Alexander’s generals.**
- **The only natural harbor on the eastern Mediterranean coast south of Phoenicia in ancient times.**
- **Likely one of the 20 cities given by King Solomon to Hiram of Tyre in exchange for building materials for the temple (1 Kin. 9:11–14).**
- **A retirement town for veterans under Emperor Claudius’ administration, who declared Ptolemais a colony of Rome.**

FAITH AND RIGHTS

CONSIDER THIS 22:25–29 **"Human rights" is not a new concept. Nearly every social structure has at least some rules to protect its members.**

As a Roman commander arrested Paul and ordered that he be beaten, Paul used his Roman citizenship to protect his rights (vv. 25–29). He had done the same thing at Philippi after being illegally jailed (16:36–40). In Jerusalem, he insisted on due process rather than endure unjust mob retaliation. He set the record straight so that the authorities could intervene appropriately.

Rumor, anger, or distortion regarding the faith need to be met forthrightly, as Paul's example shows. There's no need to allow discrimination to hinder one's practice of Christianity in society, particularly in one's workplace. As believers we need a clear understanding of the laws and rules and their application, and ensure that they are applied fairly on behalf of everyone—including ourselves.

the blood of Your martyr Stephen was shed, I also was
standing by consenting to his death,[a] and guarding the
clothes of those who were killing him.' 21Then He said to
me, 'Depart, for I will send you far from here to the Gentiles.' "
22And they listened to him until this word, and *then* they
raised their voices and said, "Away with such a *fellow* from
the earth, for he is not fit to live!" 23Then, as they cried out
and tore off *their* clothes and threw dust into the air, 24the
commander ordered him to be brought into the barracks,
and said that he should be examined under scourging, so
that he might know why they shouted so against him.
22:25–29 25And as they bound him with thongs,
Paul said to the centurion who stood by,
"Is it lawful for you to scourge a man who is a Roman, and
uncondemned?"
26When the centurion heard *that,* he went and told the
commander, saying, "Take care what you do, for this man is
a Roman."
27Then the commander came and said to him, "Tell me,
are you a Roman?"
He said, "Yes."
28The commander answered, "With a large sum I obtained this citizenship."
And Paul said, "But I was born *a citizen.*"
29Then immediately those who were about to examine
him withdrew from him; and the commander was also
afraid after he found out that he was a Roman, and because
he had bound him.

Paul Brought before the Jewish Leaders

30The next day, because he wanted to know for certain
why he was accused by the Jews, he released him from *his*
bonds, and commanded the chief priests and all their council to appear, and brought Paul down and set him before
them.

CHAPTER 23

23:1 1Then Paul, looking earnestly at the
council, said, "Men *and* brethren, I have
lived in all good conscience before God until this day."
23:2 2And the high priest Ananias commanded those who stood by him to strike
him on the mouth. 3Then Paul said to him, "God will strike
you, *you* whitewashed wall! For you sit to judge me according to the law, and do you command me to be struck contrary to the law?"

22:20 [a]NU-Text omits *to his death.*

4And those who stood by said, "Do you revile God's high
priest?"

23:5
see pg. 512

5Then Paul said, "I did not know,
brethren, that he was the high priest; for
it is written, 'You shall not speak evil of a ruler of your people.' "[a]
6But when Paul perceived that one part were Sadducees
and the other Pharisees, he cried out in the council, "Men
and brethren, I am a Pharisee, the son of a Pharisee; concerning the hope and resurrection of the dead I am being
judged!"
7And when he had said this, a dissension arose between
the Pharisees and the Sadducees; and the assembly was divided. 8For Sadducees say that there is no resurrection—
and no angel or spirit; but the Pharisees confess both.
9Then there arose a loud outcry. And the scribes of the
Pharisees' party arose and protested, saying, "We find no

23:5 [a]Exodus 22:28

Personality Profile: Ananias the High Priest

FOR YOUR INFO
23:2

Not to be confused with: Ananias, the liar (Acts 5:1); Ananias, the disciple who befriended Saul (9:10–19).

Home: Jerusalem.

Occupation: High priest and head of the Jewish council, making him the most powerful Hebrew official in Palestine.

Known to be: Greedy, open to bribes and extortion, and a collaborator with Rome. He was assassinated by a Jewish mob in A.D. 66 for his pro-Roman activities.

Best known today as: The high priest before whom Paul appeared following his arrest after returning to Jerusalem in about A.D. 58.

As the ranking member of the Jewish council, Ananias enjoyed many powers. See "Stephen's Trial and Murder," Acts 6:12.

Free to Be Bold

CONSIDER THIS
23:1

The foundation of a believer's witness must be honesty. If we can be open with God about our own sinfulness (Ps. 51) and our continuing struggle with sin (Rom. 7:14—8:1), we won't be prone to mislead others about sin and faith. God knows we aren't sinless and He calls us to be honest (1 John 1:8).

As Paul stood before the hostile Jewish council, he could honestly declare that he had a clear conscience (Acts 23:1). He said the same thing later when he and his accusers appeared before Governor Felix (24:16). That gave him tremendous freedom and boldness, even though his powerful opponents were hostile and wrong.

Honesty and a clear conscience are not the same as perfection. Paul was by no means perfect, just honest about his failures. He apologized, for example, after lashing out in anger (23:5). But he was real. He didn't cover up in an attempt to look good as a Christian witness.

Jesus does not ask us to project an impossibly perfect image. That would be a lie. Instead, He challenges us to admit our failures. He also delights in forgiving us when we do (Mark 11:25). If we can be honest about ourselves with others, it can give them hope for their own failings and turn them toward our gracious God.

evil in this man; but if a spirit or an angel has spoken to him, let us not fight against God."[a]

10Now when there arose a great dissension, the commander, fearing lest Paul might be pulled to pieces by them, commanded the soldiers to go down and take him by force from among them, and bring *him* into the barracks.

11But the following night the Lord stood by him and said, "Be of good cheer, Paul; for as you have testified for Me in Jerusalem, so you must also bear witness at Rome."

A Murder Plot Is Uncovered

12And when it was day, some of the Jews banded together
and bound themselves under an oath, saying that they
would neither eat nor drink till they had killed Paul. 13Now
there were more than forty who had formed this conspiracy.
14They came to the chief priests and elders, and said, "We
have bound ourselves under a great oath that we will eat
nothing until we have killed Paul. 15Now you, therefore, together with the council, suggest to the commander that he be brought down to you tomorrow,[a] as though you were going to make further inquiries concerning him; but we are ready to kill him before he comes near."

16So when Paul's sister's son heard of their ambush, he
went and entered the barracks and told Paul. 17Then Paul
called one of the centurions to *him* and said, "Take this young man to the commander, for he has something to tell
him." 18So he took him and brought *him* to the commander and said, "Paul the prisoner called me to *him* and asked *me* to bring this young man to you. He has something to say to you."

19Then the commander took him by the hand, went aside, and asked privately, "What is it that you have to tell me?"

20And he said, "The Jews have agreed to ask that you
bring Paul down to the council tomorrow, as though they
were going to inquire more fully about him. 21But do not
yield to them, for more than forty of them lie in wait for him, men who have bound themselves by an oath that they will neither eat nor drink till they have killed him; and now they are ready, waiting for the promise from you."

22So the commander let the young man depart, and commanded *him*, "Tell no one that you have revealed these things to me."

23And he called for two centurions, saying, "Prepare two hundred soldiers, seventy horsemen, and two hundred spearmen to go to Caesarea at the third hour of the night;

Paul Apologized for Losing His Cool

CONSIDER THIS 23:5 *Attacked in a humiliating and unjust way, Paul lashed out in anger (vv. 1–4). But when told that he had unknowingly insulted the high priest, he apologized (v. 5).*

Paul's example forces us to ask: Would you be willing to apologize for losing your cool, even if your opponent were attacking you and your values?

23:9 [a]NU-Text omits last clause and reads *what if a spirit or an angel has spoken to him?*
23:15 [a]NU-Text omits *tomorrow.*

✓ **23:24** ²⁴and provide mounts to set Paul on, and bring *him* safely to Felix the governor." ²⁵He wrote a letter in the following manner:

²⁶ Claudius Lysias,

To the most excellent governor Felix:

Greetings.

²⁷ This man was seized by the Jews and was about to be killed by them. Coming with the troops I rescued him, having learned that he was a Roman. ²⁸And when I wanted to know the reason they accused him, I brought him before their council. ²⁹I found out that he was accused concerning questions of their law, but had nothing charged against him deserving of death or chains. ³⁰And when it was told me that the Jews lay in wait for

◆ ◆ ◆ ◆ ◆ ◆ ◆ ◆ ◆ ◆ ◆ ◆ ◆ ◆ ◆ ◆ ◆

PERSONALITY PROFILE: FELIX

✓ **FOR YOUR INFO 23:24** **Name means:** "Happy."

Home: Caesarea, administrative center of Roman rule in Palestine.

Family: Married Drusilla, his third wife, youngest daughter of Herod Agrippa I (see "The Herods," 12:1–2).

Background: A Greek; a favorite of Emperor Claudius, who made him a freedman, and also of Emperor Nero.

Occupation: Procurator (governor) of Judea (A.D. 52–59).

Known for: Ruling with impunity because of his influence over the courts, until he was recalled by Nero; when Paul was brought before him, he tried to collect a bribe; others described him as heavy-handed, a procrastinator, and given to reveling in cruelty and lust, exercising "the powers of a king with the outlook of a slave."

Best known today for: Giving Paul a fair trial and keeping him in protective custody with liberal visitation rights, thereby foiling a Jewish plot to kill him.

ANTIPATRIS

 YOU ARE THERE 23:31 • Border town between Judea and Samaria, 25 miles south of Caesarea along a military road from Jerusalem.

• Former Canaanite city of Aphek (meaning "fortress"), rebuilt and renamed in the decade before Christ by Herod the Great, king of Judea, as a military outpost in honor of his father Antipater.

• Modern Ras el-`Ain, near present-day Petah Tiqwa, Israel. The tell (mound) of the former city is now one of the largest archaeological sites in the country.

This city was connected to the infamous Herod family. See Acts 12:1–2.

the man,[a] I sent him immediately to you, and also commanded his accusers to state before you the charges against him.

Farewell.

23:31 see pg. 513

31Then the soldiers, as they were commanded, took Paul and brought *him* by
night to Antipatris. 32The next day they left the horsemen to
go on with him, and returned to the barracks. 33When they
came to Caesarea and had delivered the letter to the governor, they also presented Paul to him. 34And when the governor had read *it,* he asked what province he was from. And
when he understood that *he was* from Cilicia, 35he said, "I
will hear you when your accusers also have come." And he
commanded him to be kept in Herod's Praetorium.

CHAPTER 24

Paul Faces Felix the Governor

24:1–26

1Now after five days Ananias the high priest came down with the elders and a certain orator *named* Tertullus. These gave evidence to the governor against Paul.
2And when he was called upon, Tertullus began his accu-

23:30 [a]NU-Text reads *there would be a plot against the man.*

CONSIDER THIS
24:1–26

Truth Can Trigger Opposition

Caring for others, speaking the truth, and living with integrity are not always rewarded in this broken world. God's grace often exposes the sin and guilt of people, sometimes triggering hostility. Believers can become a convenient target of anger.

Paul experienced that from the Jewish leaders in Jerusalem (vv. 1–26). Notice the varied forms of opposition they mobilized against him before Felix:

(1) They enlisted a skilled orator, Tertullus, who flattered the governor as he represented them in their case against Paul (vv. 1–3).

(2) They trumped up a variety of accusations that amounted to little more than name-calling (vv. 5–6). On a previous occasion, Jason of Thessalonica had experienced similar treatment for merely entertaining Paul and his team (17:5–9).

(3) They arrested Paul, and though they accused commander Lysias of violence, it was they who had been on the verge of a riot (23:7–10; 24:6–7).

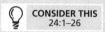

sation, saying: "Seeing that through you we enjoy great
peace, and prosperity is being brought to this nation by
your foresight, [3]we accept *it* always and in all places, most
noble Felix, with all thankfulness. [4]Nevertheless, not to be
tedious to you any further, I beg you to hear, by your cour-
tesy, a few words from us. [5]For we have found this man a
plague, a creator of dissension among all the Jews throughout the world, and a ringleader of the sect of the Nazarenes.
[6]He even tried to profane the temple, and we seized him,[a]
and wanted to judge him according to our law. [7]But the
commander Lysias came by and with great violence took
him out of our hands, [8]commanding his accusers to come to
you. By examining him yourself you may ascertain all these
things of which we accuse him." [9]And the Jews also as-
sented,[a] maintaining that these things were so.
[10]Then Paul, after the governor had nodded to him to
speak, answered: "Inasmuch as I know that you have been
for many years a judge of this nation, I do the more cheer-
fully answer for myself, [11]because you may ascertain that it
is no more than twelve days since I went up to Jerusalem to
worship. [12]And they neither found me in the temple disputing with anyone nor inciting the crowd, either in the synagogues or in the city. [13]Nor can they prove the things of

24:6 [a]NU-Text ends the sentence here and omits the rest of verse 6, all of verse 7, and the first clause of verse 8. *24:9* [a]NU-Text and M-Text read *joined the attack.*

(4) They engineered the testimony of others against him (v. 9).

(5) They demeaned the entire Christian movement, describing it in loaded terms like "plague" and "sect" (vv. 5, 14), not unlike some today who use sweeping negative generalizations and caricatures to dismiss religious activity.

(6) They apparently played politics with Felix, who was obviously used to settling disputes through bribes and other deals (v. 26; 25:9).

Recognizing this pattern can help us to avoid the mistake of personalizing all attacks on our faith. These are more often rooted in our opponents' sense of guilt or fear of judgment than in any justified assessment of our character or conduct. ◆

QUOTE UNQUOTE

CONSIDER THIS 24:22 *Felix had a "more accurate knowledge of the Way" (v. 22). Yet his knowledge did not lead to faith. So it is with many people:*

My non-Christian friends and acquaintances are zealous in what they "know" about Christianity, and which bears little or no relationship to anything I believe.

A friend of mine . . . writes about taking her brain-damaged child to a Jewish doctor. He said, "You people think of us as the people who killed your Christ." Spontaneously she replied, "Oh, no. We think of you as the people who gave him to us."

Madeleine L'Engle, *Walking On Water,* pp. 47–48

which they now accuse me. 14 But this I confess to you, that
according to the Way which they call a sect, so I worship
the God of my fathers, believing all things which are written
in the Law and in the Prophets. 15 I have hope in God,
which they themselves also accept, that there will be a resurrection of *the* dead,[a] both of *the* just and *the* unjust. 16 This
being so, I myself always strive to have a conscience without
offense toward God and men.

17 "Now after many years I came to bring alms and offerings to my nation, 18 in the midst of which some Jews from
Asia found me purified in the temple, neither with a mob
nor with tumult. 19 They ought to have been here before you
to object if they had anything against me. 20 Or else let those
who are *here* themselves say if they found any wrongdoing[a]
in me while I stood before the council, 21 unless *it is* for this
one statement which I cried out, standing among them,
'Concerning the resurrection of the dead I am being judged
by you this day.' "

24:22 see pg. 515

22 But when Felix heard these things,
having more accurate knowledge of *the*
Way, he adjourned the proceedings and said, "When Lysias
the commander comes down, I will make a decision on
your case." 23 So he commanded the centurion to keep Paul
and to let *him* have liberty, and told him not to forbid any of
his friends to provide for or visit him.

24 And after some days, when Felix came with his wife
Drusilla, who was Jewish, he sent for Paul and heard him

24:25–26

concerning the faith in Christ. 25 Now as
he reasoned about righteousness, self-
control, and the judgment to come, Felix was afraid and answered, "Go away for now; when I have a convenient time I
will call for you." 26 Meanwhile he also hoped that money
would be given him by Paul, that he might release him.[a]
Therefore he sent for him more often and conversed with
him.

Paul Faces Festus the Governor

27 But after two years Porcius Festus succeeded Felix; and
Felix, wanting to do the Jews a favor, left Paul bound.

CHAPTER 25

25:1

1 Now when Festus had come to the
province, after three days he went up

Paul and the Structures of Power

CONSIDER THIS
24:25–26

Chapters 23–25 make it plain that Paul was competent in and comfortable with the Roman judicial system and its procedures. He knew how to address Roman officials, respecting their position. At this point he obviously respected the political system. The state had not yet become the beast that John described in Revelation 13.

The problems Paul did encounter were not with the system but with its leaders. He faced two politicians, one dealing in bribes (Acts 24:25–26), the other in political favors (25:9). Seeking justice, Paul got caught in the middle.

24:15 [a]NU-Text omits *of the dead.* *24:20* [a]NU-Text and M-Text read *say what wrongdoing they found.* *24:26* [a]NU-Text omits *that he might release him.*

25:2

from Caesarea to Jerusalem. 2Then the
high priest[a] and the chief men of the Jews
informed him against Paul; and they petitioned him, 3ask-
ing a favor against him, that he would summon him to
Jerusalem—while *they* lay in ambush along the road to kill
him. 4But Festus answered that Paul should be kept at Caesarea, and that he himself was going *there* shortly. 5"Therefore," he said, "let those who have authority among you go
down with *me* and accuse this man, to see if there is any
fault in him."

6And when he had remained among them more than ten
days, he went down to Caesarea. And the next day, sitting
on the judgment seat, he commanded Paul to be brought.
7When he had come, the Jews who had come down from
Jerusalem stood about and laid many serious complaints
against Paul, which they could not prove, 8while he answered for himself, "Neither against the law of the Jews, nor
against the temple, nor against Caesar have I offended in
anything at all."

9But Festus, wanting to do the Jews a favor, answered
Paul and said, "Are you willing to go up to Jerusalem and
there be judged before me concerning these things?"

10So Paul said, "I stand at Caesar's judgment seat, where I
ought to be judged. To the Jews I have done no wrong, as
you very well know. 11For if I am an offender, or have committed anything deserving of death, I do not object to dying; but if there is nothing in these things of which these
men accuse me, no one can deliver me to them. I appeal to
Caesar."

25:12 see pg. 518

12Then Festus, when he had conferred
with the council, answered, "You have
appealed to Caesar? To Caesar you shall go!"

25:2 [a]NU-Text reads *chief priests.*

Personality Profile: Festus

FOR YOUR INFO 25:1

Home: Caesarea.

Occupation: Successor to Felix as governor of Judea (A.D. 59–61; see Acts 24:27).

Best known today for: Insisting that Jewish leaders meet with Paul in Caesarea, where the apostle was protected, thereby foiling a plot to kill him. Later, though, Festus suggested a retrial in Jerusalem as a favor to the Jews.

Caught Between a Novice and the Establishment

CONSIDER THIS 25:2

Paul found himself caught between Festus (v. 1), a brand new local governor appointed by the Romans (24:27), and the well-established Jewish council, the supreme court of the Hebrews (25:2; see "Stephen's Trial and Murder," Acts 6:12). The council could easily have outwitted the new official—at Paul's expense and to their own gain—if the case had been moved to their home turf in Jerusalem (25:9). So Paul appealed to a higher court, Caesar, to regain a balance of power (v. 11).

In doing so, Paul exercised his rights as a Roman citizen (see "Faith and Rights," 22:25–29). At the time of Acts 25, the reigning Caesar was Nero. He had not yet begun to persecute the Christians, as he did later in A.D. 64 (see 25:12).

In light of Paul's example here, it's worth asking: Do you know the proper routes of appeal in your workplace and community?

King Agrippa and Bernice Arrive

25:13

25:13–22

13And after some days King Agrippa
and Bernice came to Caesarea to greet
Festus. 14When they had been there
many days, Festus laid Paul's case before

Agrippa

A CLOSER LOOK 25:13 *King Agrippa came from a long and infamous line of royalty. See "The Herods," Acts 12:1–2.*

A Timely Diplomatic Visit

FOR YOUR INFO 25:13–22 *The visit of King Agrippa and Bernice to Caesarea proved timely (v. 13). As a new, relatively inexperienced Roman governor of Judea, Festus faced a delicate religious conflict between the Jews, led by their council, and the growing Christian movement, represented by Paul. Just as Festus began to rule on the case, Agrippa and Bernice arrived. Festus, the Jews, and Paul all benefited from the couple's expertise in Jewish history and affairs (v. 23; 26:3). The brother and sister had watched their father govern Judea and its population for several years before Agrippa inherited the office himself (see "The Herods," Acts 12:1–2, and "Families of the Early Church," Acts 16:31–34).*

Personality Profile: Nero

FOR YOUR INFO 25:12

Home: Rome.

Family: Son of an insanely controlling mother, Agrippina, who became Emperor Claudius' fourth wife; great-great-grandson of Augustus; raised and tortured by his menacing, mentally deranged uncle, Caligula. The family history bristled with incest, physical abuse, and political conspiracy.

Profession: Emperor of Rome (A.D. 54–68). Though noble in his youth, he made himself out to be a new god. He was the Caesar to whom Paul appealed for justice (Acts 25:9–11).

Reputation: Ascetic and maniacal in his devotion to music and the gods, especially during a 15-month arts tour in Greece; capricious as a ruler: he signed countless death warrants, yet once banned capital punishment; he laughed at revolts brewing in the empire; early Christians regarded him as the Antichrist; he died by suicide.

Best known today for: Supposedly fiddling while Rome burned (he was 35 miles away from Rome at his villa at Antium) and for persecuting Christians.

Find out about the other major political leaders of the Roman Empire and Palestine in the first century at "New Testament Political Rulers," Luke 3:1.

the king, saying: "There is a certain man left a prisoner by
Felix, 15about whom the chief priests and the elders of the
Jews informed *me,* when I was in Jerusalem, asking for a
judgment against him. 16To them I answered, 'It is not the
custom of the Romans to deliver any man to destruction[a]
before the accused meets the accusers face to face, and has
opportunity to answer for himself concerning the charge
against him.' 17Therefore when they had come together,
without any delay, the next day I sat on the judgment seat
and commanded the man to be brought in. 18When the accusers stood up, they brought no accusation against him of
such things as I supposed, 19but had some questions against
him about their own religion and about a certain Jesus, who
had died, whom Paul affirmed to be alive. 20And because I
was uncertain of such questions, I asked whether he was
willing to go to Jerusalem and there be judged concerning
these matters. 21But when Paul appealed to be reserved for
the decision of Augustus, I commanded him to be kept till I
could send him to Caesar."

22Then Agrippa said to Festus, "I also would like to hear
the man myself."

"Tomorrow," he said, "you shall hear him."

23So the next day, when Agrippa and Bernice had come
with great pomp, and had entered the auditorium with the
commanders and the prominent men of the city, at Festus'
command Paul was brought in. 24And Festus said: "King
Agrippa and all the men who are here present with us, you
see this man about whom the whole assembly of the Jews
petitioned me, both at Jerusalem and here, crying out that
he was not fit to live any longer. 25But when I found that he
had committed nothing deserving of death, and that he
himself had appealed to Augustus, I decided to send him.
26I have nothing certain to write to my lord concerning
him. Therefore I have brought him out before you, and especially before you, King Agrippa, so that after the examination has taken place I may have something to write. 27For it
seems to me unreasonable to send a prisoner and not to
specify the charges against him."

CHAPTER 26

26:1–32
see pg. 520

1Then Agrippa said to Paul, "You are
permitted to speak for yourself."

So Paul stretched out his hand and answered for himself:
2"I think myself happy, King Agrippa, because today I shall
answer for myself before you concerning all the things of
which I am accused by the Jews, 3especially because you are

(Bible text continued on page 521)

"TODAY I SHALL ANSWER FOR MYSELF BEFORE YOU. . . ." —Acts 26:2

25:16 [a]NU-Text omits *to destruction,* although it is implied.

CONSIDER THIS
26:1–32

AUDIENCE-SHAPED MESSAGES

As a Christian, do you know how to communicate the message of Christ to the different audiences you encounter? Or do you use the same old formula time after time, no matter who is listening? For that matter, do you remain silent when you have the opportunity to speak up for Christ, because you simply don't know what to say?

Paul had no prepackaged gospel message. He varied his approach with the situation. He was as aware of the differences between his audiences as he was of the content of his faith. Acts records numerous encounters, among them:

(1) Jews in the synagogue at Antioch of Pisidia (Acts 13:14–43).

- Paul reviewed the history of the Jewish faith, summarizing it from the Old Testament (vv. 17–22).
- He told how that history led to Jesus (vv. 23–37).
- He pointed out his audience's need to accept Jesus as their Messiah (vv. 38–41).
- He responded to their resistance by clearly explaining the alternative (vv. 46–48).

Result:

- Many chose to follow the way of Christ (v. 43).
- Others reacted negatively and opposed Paul (v. 45).
- Troublemakers incited city leaders to persecute Paul and his companions (v. 50).

(2) Intellectuals at Athens (17:16–33).

- Paul prepared by observing and reflecting on their culture (v. 16).
- He addressed them on their own turf, the Areopagus (vv. 19, 22).
- He established common ground, beginning with what was familiar and meaningful to them (vv. 22–23a, 28).
- He bridged to a description of God as the Creator and sustainer of life, distinguishing Him from the pagan idols that the Athenians worshiped (vv. 23b-29).
- He challenged them to repentance and appealed to the resurrection of Christ as proof that what he was telling them was true (vv. 30–31).

Result:

- Some mocked (v. 32).
- Some wanted to hear more (v. 32).
- Some believed (v. 34–35).

(3) An angry mob in Jerusalem (21:27—22:21).

- Paul built a bridge by reminding them of his own Jewish heritage (21:30).
- He reminded them that he, too, had once detested Jesus' followers; in fact, he had persecuted them (22:4–5).
- He explained the process by which he had changed his mind and joined a movement that he once opposed (vv. 6–17).

Result:

- Already at fever pitch (21:27–30), the crowd erupted violently, demanding Paul's death (22:22–23).

(4) High officials in a Roman court (26:1–32).

- Paul described his religious heritage (vv. 4–5).
- He related his view of his opponents' charges against him (vv. 6–8).
- He recalled his previous opposition to Jesus' followers (vv. 9–11).
- He recounted his own life-changing encounter with Christ (vv. 12–19).

(continued on next page)

expert in all customs and questions which have to do with the Jews. Therefore I beg you to hear me patiently.
4"My manner of life from my youth, which was spent from the beginning among my own nation at Jerusalem, all the Jews know.
5They knew me from the first, if they were willing to testify, that according to the strictest sect of our religion I lived a Pharisee.
6And now I stand and am judged for the hope of the promise made by God to our fathers.
7To this *promise* our twelve tribes, earnestly serving *God* night and day, hope to attain. For this hope's sake, King Agrippa, I am accused by the Jews.
8Why should it be thought incredible by you that God raises the dead?
9"Indeed, I myself thought I must do many things contrary to the name of Jesus of Nazareth.
10This I also did in Jerusalem, and many of the saints I shut up in prison, having received authority from the chief priests; and when they were put to death, I cast my vote against *them*.
11And I punished them often in every synagogue and compelled *them* to blaspheme; and being exceedingly enraged against them, I persecuted *them* even to foreign cities.
12"While thus occupied, as I journeyed to Damascus with authority and commission from the chief priests,
13at midday, O king, along the road I saw a light from heaven, brighter than the sun, shining around me and those who journeyed with me.
14And when we all had fallen to the ground, I heard a voice speaking to me and saying in the Hebrew language, 'Saul, Saul, why are you persecuting Me? *It is* hard for you to kick against the goads.'
15So I said, 'Who are You, Lord?' And He said, 'I am Jesus, whom you are persecuting.
16But rise and stand on your feet; for I have appeared to you for this purpose, to make you a minister and a witness both of the things which you have seen and of the things which I will yet reveal to you.
17I will deliver you from the *Jewish* people, as well as *from* the Gentiles, to whom I now[a] send you,
18to open their eyes, *in order* to turn *them* from darkness to light, and *from* the power of Satan to God, that they may receive forgiveness of sins and an inheritance among those who are sanctified by faith in Me.'
19"Therefore, King Agrippa, I was not disobedient to the heavenly vision,
20but declared first to those in Damascus and in Jerusalem, and throughout all the region of Judea, and *then* to the Gentiles, that they should repent, turn to God, and do works befitting repentance.
21For these reasons the Jews seized me in the temple and tried to kill *me*.
22Therefore, having obtained help from God, to this day I stand, witnessing both to small and great, saying no other things than those which the prophets and Moses said would

26:17 [a]NU-Text and M-Text omit *now*.

(continued from previous page)

- He explained the fundamentals of Jesus' message and the implications for his non-Jewish listeners (vv. 20–23).

Result:

- The rulers listened carefully (vv. 24, 31–32).
- They challenged his application of the gospel to them (vv. 24, 28).
- They passed him on in the Roman judicial process, thereby foiling a Jewish plot against him (vv. 31–32).

The gospel itself is forever the same, but as Christ's followers we are called to shape our message to fit our various audiences. How do your coworkers and friends differ from each other? What effect should that have on your life and message for them? What aspects of the good news would they most likely respond to? Do you know how they view faith? Why not ask them—before you speak? ◆

We can learn a lot about how to communicate the message of Christ by studying carefully how Jesus Himself interacted with people. The four Gospels record more than 40 meetings between Him and various individuals. See "Witnessing—Jesus' Style," Luke 24:48.

come— 23that the Christ would suffer, that He would be the
first to rise from the dead, and would proclaim light to the
Jewish people and to the Gentiles."
24Now as he thus made his defense, Festus said with a
loud voice, "Paul, you are beside yourself! Much learning is
driving you mad!"
25But he said, "I am not mad, most noble Festus, but
speak the words of truth and reason. 26For the king, before
whom I also speak freely, knows these things; for I am convinced that none of these things escapes his attention, since
this thing was not done in a corner. 27King Agrippa, do you
believe the prophets? I know that you do believe."
28Then Agrippa said to Paul, "You almost persuade me to
become a Christian."
29And Paul said, "I would to God that not only you, but
also all who hear me today, might become both almost and
altogether such as I am, except for these chains."
30When he had said these things, the king stood up, as
well as the governor and Bernice and those who sat with
them; 31and when they had gone aside, they talked among
themselves, saying, "This man is doing nothing deserving of
death or chains."
32Then Agrippa said to Festus, "This man might have
been set free if he had not appealed to Caesar."

CHAPTER 27

Shipwreck on the Way to Rome

1And when it was decided that we should sail to Italy,
they delivered Paul and some other prisoners to *one* named

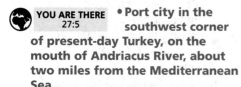

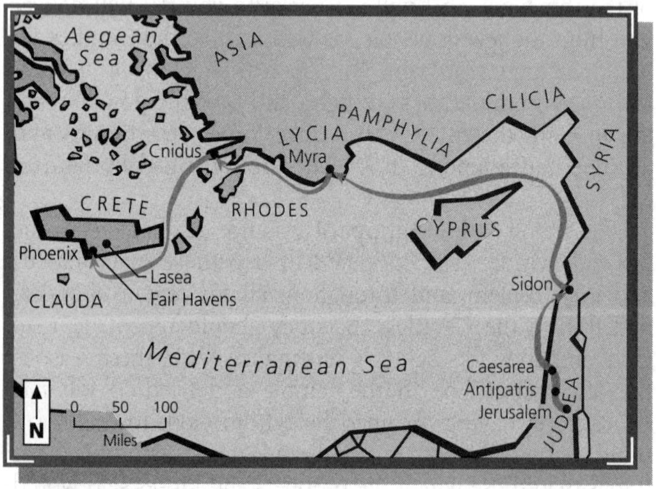

PAUL'S JOURNEY TO ROME, PART ONE

MYRA

YOU ARE THERE 27:5

- **Port city in the southwest corner of present-day Turkey, on the mouth of Andriacus River, about two miles from the Mediterranean Sea.**
- **Capital of Lycia and a leading city in the Lycean confederation.**
- **Now called Demre by the Turks.**
- **The Alexandrian vessel for which Paul and the party waited (Acts 27:6) was the largest type of ship available in that day, renowned for its seaworthiness.**
- **St. Nicholas—from whom we get the name Santa Claus—was born in nearby Patara and was the city's bishop under Constantine (fourth century A.D.). Legendary miracles have Nicholas appearing to save children and sailors from tragedy; devotion spread rapidly and widely, and he became the patron saint of Greece and Russia, of numerous fraternities and workers' guilds, and of Christmas.**

FAIR HAVENS AND LASEA

YOU ARE THERE 27:8

- **Fair Havens was a small bay on the south coast of Crete; Lasea was five miles inland.**
- **One of the more important harbors in the ancient world, according to first-century historian Pliny the Elder. But since the port was separated by five miles from the town, it was unsuitable for wintering.**

Julius, a centurion of the Augustan Regiment. 2So, entering
a ship of Adramyttium, we put to sea, meaning to sail along
the coasts of Asia. Aristarchus, a Macedonian of Thessalonica, was with us. 3And the next *day* we landed at Sidon.
And Julius treated Paul kindly and gave *him* liberty to go to
his friends and receive care. 4When we had put to sea from
there, we sailed under *the shelter of* Cyprus, because the
27:5 winds were contrary. 5And when we had
sailed over the sea which is off Cilicia and
Pamphylia, we came to Myra, *a city* of Lycia. 6There the centurion found an Alexandrian ship sailing to Italy, and he put
us on board.

7When we had sailed slowly many days, and arrived with
difficulty off Cnidus, the wind not permitting us to proceed,
27:8 we sailed under *the shelter of* Crete off
Salmone. 8Passing it with difficulty, we
came to a place called Fair Havens, near the city *of* Lasea.
27:9–11 9Now when much time had been
spent, and sailing was now dangerous be-
cause the Fast was already over, Paul advised them, 10say-
ing, "Men, I perceive that this voyage will end with disaster
and much loss, not only of the cargo and ship, but also our
lives." 11Nevertheless the centurion was more persuaded by
the helmsman and the owner of the ship than by the things
spoken by Paul. 12And because the harbor was not suitable
to winter in, the majority advised to set sail from there also,
if by any means they could reach Phoenix, a harbor of Crete
opening toward the southwest and northwest, *and* winter
there.

13When the south wind blew softly, supposing that they
had obtained *their* desire, putting out to sea, they sailed
close by Crete. 14But not long after, a tempestuous head
wind arose, called Euroclydon.[a] 15So when the ship was
caught, and could not head into the wind, we let *her* drive.
16And running under *the shelter of* an island called Clauda,[a]
we secured the skiff with difficulty. 17When they had taken
it on board, they used cables to undergird the ship; and
fearing lest they should run aground on the Syrtis[a] *Sands,*
they struck sail and so were driven. 18And because we were
exceedingly tempest-tossed, the next *day* they lightened the
ship. 19On the third *day* we threw the ship's tackle overboard with our own hands. 20Now when neither sun nor
stars appeared for many days, and no small tempest beat on
us, all hope that we would be saved was finally given up.

21But after long abstinence from food, then Paul stood in
the midst of them and said, "Men, you should have listened
to me, and not have sailed from Crete and incurred this dis-

27:14 [a]NU-Text reads *Euraquilon.* *27:16* [a]NU-Text reads *Cauda.* *27:17* [a]M-Text reads *Syrtes.*

"It Serves Them Right!"

CONSIDER THIS 27:9–11 **Paul's willingness to speak up (v. 10) is remarkable in that he was on his way to prison and had no need to warn anybody of anything. Nor did he have any control over the situation. Of course, he knew that God could preserve him from any and all dangers. Yet he reached out beyond his own interests and safety and spoke up for the safety of others.**

Is that your perspective, especially when things don't go your way? Or do you keep your mouth shut with the attitude . . .

- **"It serves them right!"**
- **"They won't pay attention anyway."**
- **"Let them stew in their own juices."**
- **"Why should I say anything? My boss doesn't listen anyway. It won't make any difference."**
- **"If they want to play that sort of game, I can, too."**
- **"I'll be out of here in a few weeks anyway."**
- **"She doesn't care about me. Why should I care about what happens to her?"**
- **"He made his bed, now let him lie in it."**

aster and loss. 22And now I urge you to take heart, for there
will be no loss of life among you, but only of the ship. 23For
there stood by me this night an angel of the God to whom I
belong and whom I serve, 24saying, 'Do not be afraid, Paul;
you must be brought before Caesar; and indeed God has
granted you all those who sail with you.' 25Therefore take
heart, men, for I believe God that it will be just as it was
told me. 26However, we must run aground on a certain island."

27Now when the fourteenth night had come, as we were
driven up and down in the Adriatic *Sea,* about midnight the
sailors sensed that they were drawing near some land.
28And they took soundings and found *it* to be twenty fathoms; and when they had gone a little farther, they took
soundings again and found *it* to be fifteen fathoms. 29Then,
fearing lest we should run aground on the rocks, they
dropped four anchors from the stern, and prayed for day to
come. 30And as the sailors were seeking to escape from the
ship, when they had let down the skiff into the sea, under
pretense of putting out anchors from the prow, 31Paul said
to the centurion and the soldiers, "Unless these men stay in
the ship, you cannot be saved." 32Then the soldiers cut
away the ropes of the skiff and let it fall off.

33And as day was about to dawn, Paul implored *them* all
to take food, saying, "Today is the fourteenth day you have
waited and continued without food, and eaten nothing.
34Therefore I urge you to take nourishment, for this is for
your survival, since not a hair will fall from the head of any
of you." 35And when he had said these things, he took
bread and gave thanks to God in the presence of them all;
and when he had broken *it* he began to eat. 36Then they
were all encouraged, and also took food themselves. 37And
in all we were two hundred and seventy-six persons on the
ship. 38So when they had eaten enough, they lightened the
ship and threw out the wheat into the sea.

39When it was day, they did not recognize the land; but
they observed a bay with a beach, onto which they planned
to run the ship if possible. 40And they let go the anchors
and left *them* in the sea, meanwhile loosing the rudder
ropes; and they hoisted the mainsail to the wind and made
for shore. 41But striking a place where two seas met, they
ran the ship aground; and the prow stuck fast and remained
immovable, but the stern was being broken up by the violence of the waves.

42And the soldiers' plan was to kill the prisoners, lest any
of them should swim away and escape. 43But the centurion,
wanting to save Paul, kept them from *their* purpose, and
commanded that those who could swim should jump *overboard* first and get to land, 44and the rest, some on boards

PAUL AND PUBLIUS

CONSIDER THIS
28:7–10

Paul's encounter with Publius (vv. 7–10) is reminiscent of Peter's meeting with Cornelius (Acts 10). It's interesting that Publius not only responded to the gospel, but also showed the castaways hospitality—something Christians have always valued. This is not uncommon: missionaries often receive from host cultures as much as they give. There is much to be learned from this passage about cross-cultural ministry.

and some on *parts* of the ship. And so it was that they all escaped safely to land.

CHAPTER 28

A Friendly Exchange at Malta

28:1

1Now when they had escaped, they then found out that the island was called Malta. 2And the natives showed us unusual kindness; for they kindled a fire and made us all welcome, because of the rain that was falling and because of the cold. 3But when Paul had gathered a bundle of sticks and laid *them* on the fire, a viper came out because of the heat, and fastened on his hand. 4So when the natives saw the creature hanging from his hand, they said to one another, "No doubt this man is a murderer, whom, though he has escaped the sea, yet justice does not allow to live." 5But he shook off the creature into the fire and suffered no harm. 6However, they were expecting that he would swell up or suddenly fall down dead. But after they had looked for a long time and saw no harm come to him, they changed their minds and said that he was a god.

28:7–10

7In that region there was an estate of the leading citizen of the island, whose name was Publius, who received us and entertained us courteously for three days. 8And it happened that the father of Publius lay sick of a fever and dysentery. Paul went in to him and prayed, and he laid his hands on him and healed him. 9So when this was done, the rest of those on the island who had diseases also came and were healed. 10They also honored us in many ways; and when we departed, they provided such things as were necessary.

Paul Arrives at Rome

28:11–13 see pg. 529
28:12 see pg. 526
28:13 see pg. 526

11After three months we sailed in an Alexandrian ship whose figurehead was the Twin Brothers, which had wintered at the island. 12And landing at Syracuse, we stayed three days. 13From there we circled round and reached Rhegium. And after one day the south wind blew; and the next day we came to Puteoli, 14where we found brethren, and were invited to stay with them seven days. And so we went toward Rome. 15And from there, when the brethren heard about us, they came to meet us as far as Appii Forum and Three Inns. When Paul saw them, he thanked God and took courage.

28:14–15
28:15 see pg. 526

(Bible text continued on page 528)

JOY ON THE WAY TO JAIL

CONSIDER THIS
28:14–15

Jail seldom produces joy. The condemnation of society and the grim realities of incarceration bring many reactions, but rarely happy ones. However, when the cause is just (28:25–28), the conscience clear (23:1; 24:16; 26:19), and friends loyal (28:15), imprisonment can take on a new dimension.

As Paul neared the end of his journey to face trial, believers from Rome and its environs welcomed him along the Appian highway from Puteoli to Rome (28:13–15). He had written them three years before, describing his deep longing for them (Rom. 1:9–15; 15:22–29). Even his chains and the prospect of prison could not cloud the joy of connecting with those fellow-believers.

Can Christians today surprise their culture by offering to become true friends to those in jail?

MALTA

YOU ARE THERE
28:1

- **A tiny island grouping in the Mediterranean Sea about 60 miles south of Sicily.**
- **Name means "refuge."**
- **Its strategic location has placed Malta between several ancient and modern powers vying for control of the Mediterranean region.**

Syracuse

YOU ARE THERE 28:12

- City with a good harbor on the straits of Messina, between Sicily and Italy.
- Initially a Greek colony, the city overthrew its Athenian tyrants during the Peloponnesian War (415–413 B.C.). Syracuse and Carthage (in modern-day Tunisia) shared centuries of prominence as the key cities west of Greece.
- Captured by Rome in 212 B.C.; made into a Roman colony by Caesar Augustus.
- Described by Cicero as the "largest and loveliest of all Greek cities"; boasted impressive public buildings: a temple to Athena, a Greek theater, a large amphitheater, a marketplace flanked by a forum, town hall, senate house, and a temple to Jupiter. Christian catacombs have also been found dating to the third and fourth centuries A.D.
- Noted for shipbuilding and fishing; once boasted the world's best navy.

Rhegium

YOU ARE THERE 28:13

- Name means "breach."
- Port city near the Strait of Messina, a treacherous body of water off Sicily. With its shoals, shallows, and narrow width, the strait spelled shipwreck for centuries of sea captains, and was to be passed only under the most favorable of conditions. Ships frequently harbored at Rhegium until the weather or winds changed, contributing to the city's maritime prominence.
- Messina was reputed to be the site of the mythical Scylla, a sea monster dominating shoreline rocks, and Charybdis, a whirlpool large enough to devour entire ships.
- Modern Reggio, Italy.

Puteoli

- The best harbor in Italy, located on the Bay of Naples in southern Italy; a stopover for seagoing vehicles and cargo heading to and from Rome.
- The largest ships—including Alexandrian ships such as the one Paul embarked on (Acts 28:11)—could dock there.
- When Paul arrived, a sizable Christian community was already functioning.
- Modern Pozzuoli, Italy.

Appii Forum and Three Inns

YOU ARE THERE 28:15

- Appii Forum, or the marketplace of Appius, was a town 43 miles southeast of Rome on the Appian Way, an ancient road to the Adriatic Sea built by Appius Claudius.
- Three Inns was located at a junction of the Appian Way and a road connecting Antium and Norba, 33 miles south of Rome.
- Travelers tended to frequent Three Inns more than Appii Forum, as the latter was inhospitable, with marshes, gnats, and intolerable drinking water, along with innkeepers and merchants notorious for taking advantage of weary travelers.

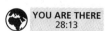

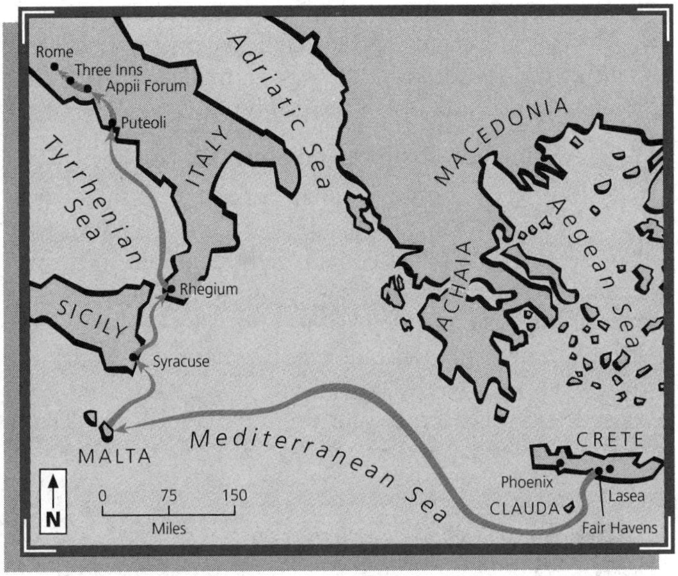

PAUL'S JOURNEY TO ROME, PART TWO

ALL ROADS LEAD TO ROME—AND BEYOND

CONSIDER THIS 28:28–31

Paul felt driven to get to Rome (Acts 19:21; Rom. 1:15), no doubt because it was the capital city. But he also intended to stop there on his way to Spain (Rom. 15:28).

Why was Spain significant? It's impossible to say exactly what Paul had in mind. But the Old Testament prophet Isaiah predicted that in the end times Gentiles would join Jews at Jerusalem to worship God, inaugurating a marvelous new era (Is. 66:19–24). Isaiah's text refers to "Tarshish," thought to mean Spain. Is it possible that Paul believed that getting the gospel to Rome meant being one step closer to the fulfillment of Isaiah's glorious vision (Acts 26:23; 28:28)?

We don't know whether Paul ever made it to Spain. He remained under house arrest in Rome until his trial before the emperor (Acts 28:16, 30–31). He may have been released, but tradition holds that he was eventually condemned and executed under Nero.

ROME

YOU ARE THERE 28:16

- **Political capital of the Roman Empire, which extended by the first century A.D. from the Atlantic Ocean to the Persian Gulf, and north Africa to Britain and northern Europe.**
- **Located on the Tiber river on seven hills, about 15 miles inland from the Tyrrhenian Sea.**
- **One of the two largest cities in the world in the first century (the other being Xian, China), with a population estimated at 1 million people, but declining to 50,000 by the sixth century due to numerous plagues, economic disasters, and a declining birth rate.**
- **A walled city of less than 25 square miles, it boasted the royal palace, ornate fountains, elaborate baths (some of which housed libraries and social clubs), the Circus Maximus, used for chariot racing and other games, and the 50,000-seat Coliseum. The Forum, where citizens engaged in political, religious, and commercial enterprises, was where Paul likely defended himself and the Christian movement.**
- **Some 82 temples were built or remodeled in the first half of the first century.**
- **Eventually became the center of the church in the West.**

When Paul arrived in Rome, he found a community of Christian believers already thriving there. See the Introduction to Romans.

28:16
see pg. 527
16Now when we came to Rome, the
centurion delivered the prisoners to the
captain of the guard; but Paul was permitted to dwell by
himself with the soldier who guarded him.

Some Jews Believe and Some Do Not

28:17–19
17And it came to pass after three days
that Paul called the leaders of the Jews together. So when they had come together, he said to them:
"Men *and* brethren, though I have done nothing against our
people or the customs of our fathers, yet I was delivered as
a prisoner from Jerusalem into the hands of the Romans,
18who, when they had examined me, wanted to let *me* go,
because there was no cause for putting me to death. 19But

CONSIDER THIS
28:17–19

A Response to Rejection

As believers called to proclaim the message of Christ, our role is not to change people; that's a job for the Holy Spirit (John 16:8). Instead, we need to give a full and careful disclosure of what God has done for us, realizing that it might result in rejection.

Paul knew very well that following Christ would lead to hostility and rejection (Acts 28:19). But in responding to criticism and defending himself legally, he made sure that his judges had the benefit of a full explanation, even though it took a special meeting that lasted all day (v. 23). Yet even that careful effort did not completely set the record straight or convince all of his hearers (vv. 24, 29).

Scripture records a long tradition of God-sent messengers whose words fell on deaf ears. For example:

- *Isaiah, who was told ahead of time that he was being sent to people who would not listen to him (Is. 6:9–12).*
- *the Lord Jesus, who also came to those who would not receive Him (John 1:11; 12:37–43).*
- *Barnabas and Paul, who turned to the Gentiles at Pisidian Antioch after Jews rejected their message (Acts 13:44–46).*
- *Paul, who turned to the Gentiles at Corinth after Jews rejected his message (Acts 18:5–6).*
- *Paul, who grieved over his countrymen's rejection of the gospel (Rom. 11:7–10).*

How should we respond to rejection? The key issue is to make sure that we give our hearers a chance to consider Christ. We must offer them as faithful and convincing a presentation as possible. But it may mean hostility and personal cost. Yet should we expect to suffer any less than Christ did (Phil. 1:29–30)? ◆

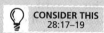

when the Jews[a] spoke against *it,* I was compelled to appeal
to Caesar, not that I had anything of which to accuse my
nation. 20For this reason therefore I have called for you, to
see *you* and speak with *you,* because for the hope of Israel I
am bound with this chain."
21Then they said to him, "We neither received letters from
Judea concerning you, nor have any of the brethren who
came reported or spoken any evil of you. 22But we desire to
hear from you what you think; for concerning this sect, we
know that it is spoken against everywhere."
23So when they had appointed him a day, many came to
him at *his* lodging, to whom he explained and solemnly testified of the kingdom of God, persuading them concerning
Jesus from both the Law of Moses and the Prophets, from
morning till evening. 24And some were persuaded by the
things which were spoken, and some disbelieved. 25So

28:19 [a]That is, the ruling authorities

PAUL'S RENTED HOUSE

CONSIDER THIS 28:30–31 *Paul rented a house at his own expense (v. 30), possibly in south Rome. Technically under house arrest, he spent his time in outreach to both Jews and Gentiles, but especially to Gentiles (vv. 28–29).*

The restrictions under which Paul lived should have held back his efforts to proclaim the gospel, but they "actually turned out for the furtherance of the gospel" (Phil. 1:12). Confined to his lodgings and handcuffed to one of the soldiers who guarded him in four-hour shifts, he was free to receive visitors and talk with them about the gospel. The guards and the official in charge of presenting his case were left in no doubt about the reason for his being in Rome. The message of Christ actually became a topic of discussion among them (1:13). This encouraged Christians in Rome to become more bold in their witness to the faith than ever before.

Paul's house in Rome was probably where a runaway slave named Onesimus came to faith. See the Introduction to Philemon.

HITTING THE COMMERCIAL HIGH SPOTS

CONSIDER THIS 28:11–13 **Springtime on the Mediterranean meant the return of cargo-laden ships from Alexandria, Egypt. They used westerly winds to deliver their goods to the empire's key ports.**

Paul was transported from Malta to Rome on one such vessel, a voyage that covered 180 nautical miles in less than two days at sea (v. 11). On the journey he was able to visit three important cities and continue his movement-building work: Syracuse; the dominant city of Sicily; Rhegium, a key harbor town on the Italian side of the Strait of Messina; and Puteoli, gateway to southern Italy, just 33 miles from Rome.

Throughout Christian history, the gospel has invariably traveled the routes of commerce. For example, many have been introduced to the good news through the witness of:

- **merchants doing business in foreign countries;**
- **employees of multinational corporations stationed overseas;**
- **consultants advising governments and businesses worldwide;**
- **medical personnel serving in developing nations;**
- **faculty and students studying and teaching around the world; and**
- **soldiers in foreign lands during war or occupation.**

Are you taking advantage of strategic opportunities to influence others with the message of Christ through your networks?

when they did not agree among themselves, they departed after Paul had said one word: "The Holy Spirit spoke rightly through Isaiah the prophet to our[a] fathers, 26saying,

'Go to this people and say:
"Hearing you will hear, and shall not understand;
And seeing you will see, and not perceive;
27 For the hearts of this people have grown dull.
Their ears are hard of hearing,
And their eyes they have closed,
Lest they should see with *their* eyes and hear with *their* ears,
Lest they should understand with *their* hearts and turn,
So that I should heal them." '[a]

28:28–31 see pg. 527

28"Therefore let it be known to you that the salvation of God has been sent to the Gentiles, and they will hear it!" 29And when he had said these words, the Jews departed and had a great dispute among themselves.[a]

"THE SALVATION OF GOD HAS BEEN SENT TO THE GENTILES. . . ." —Acts 28:28

Paul Preaches and Teaches

28:30–31 see pg. 529

30Then Paul dwelt two whole years in his own rented house, and received all who came to him, 31preaching the kingdom of God and teaching the things which concern the Lord Jesus Christ with all confidence, no one forbidding him.

28:25 [a]NU-Text reads *your.* *28:27* [a]Isaiah 6:9, 10 *28:29* [a]NU-Text omits this verse.

The Gospel Explained

What does it mean to be a Christian? Do you know? Many people today who call themselves Christians would be hard pressed to explain the term. Some would talk in generalities about "doing good." Others would say that Christianity means love. Others would say it means "following Jesus," though they have only the vaguest idea of what they are talking about.

Every Christian ought to read the book of Romans. It was written to explain the faith. While the first five books of the New Testament tell the story of Jesus, Romans examines the *message* of Jesus. It shows that His gospel is far more than just nice feelings or high moral sentiments. It is truth. It has intellectual content. It makes a difference in the way people think, and therefore in what they believe.

Romans

The gospel is more than high moral sentiments. It is truth.

C O N T E N T S

Have You Ever Wondered . . .

. . . Whether at the core all religions aren't really the same?
Read 1:18–23.

. . . Where the Bible addresses homosexuality?
Read 1:24–32.

. . . Why we have to know Jesus to be saved?
Read 3:5–26.

. . . Why doing good isn't good enough to get into heaven?
Read 3:27—4:25.

. . . Why, if you're saved, you can't just go ahead and sin freely since God forgives and you'll get into heaven anyway?
Read 6:1–23.

. . . Why you can't help but keep on sinning sometimes, even after you've given your life to God?
Read 7:1–25.

. . . Why there's so much pain and evil, even though God created the world?
Read 8:18–25.

. . . Whether God has given up on the Jews?
Read 9:1—11:36.

. . . Whether Christians are free from having to obey the government, since we serve a higher authority, God?
Read 13:1–7.

. . . Why Christians even bother with what others think?
Read 14:1—15:13.

A R T I C L E S

A Change of Plans (1:13)
God used Paul, a great visionary, to spread the gospel. Even so, Paul's plans did not always work out.

The Power of the Gospel (1:16)
Are you ever embarrassed to be identified as a follower of Christ?

The Law (2:12)
The Law was given specifically to Israel, but it rests on eternal moral principles that are consistent with God's character. Thus Gentiles will not be judged by the Law, but they will be judged by the same righteous standard that underlies the Law.

Abraham (4:1)
As father of the Hebrews, Abraham features prominently in the New Testament. His faith makes him important to the message of the gospel.

Promises (4:16–25)
Can God be depended on to honor His promises? Do we fulfill our commitments?

Real Freedom (6:15–22)
People throughout the world hunger for freedom. But ultimately, no one is totally "free."

Is Work a Curse? (8:20)
A stubborn myth persists that work is a punishment. Does Scripture support that idea?

Are We One People? (11:13–24)
What are the current challenges to the ethnic, racial, and cultural attitudes of believers?

Do You Suffer from "Comparisonitis"? (12:3)
You won't find this illness listed in medical textbooks, but it's a scourge as widespread and destructive as any physical or emotional malady known today.

Do Not Avenge Yourself (12:19–21)
Romans says vengeance belongs to God. What, then, can you do to those who hurt you?

The High Calling of Government Service (13:6)
If you work in government, you'll want to pay special attention to this article.

Are Sundays Special? (14:5–13)
Should Sunday be treated as a special day in light of God's instructions regarding a Sabbath?

Paul's Female Coworkers (16:1)
Not a few of Paul's most valued associates were women, several of whom are listed in Romans 16.

Who Was Paul's Mother (16:13)
Meet a woman who played such an important role in Paul's life that he never forgot her.

Why Did Jesus Die?

In Romans we find a carefully constructed argument that answers a crucial question: *Why did Jesus die?* The author, Paul, used his training as a Pharisee in writing this letter. As a rabbi, a teacher of the Law, he knew how to dissect theological issues and philosophical questions. In Romans he works his way through a sophisticated argument, not unlike a modern-day lawyer writing a brief. He asks and answers question after question until he has finished constructing a body of material that hangs together logically and theologically.

Romans shows that the gospel is big enough to deal with the weighty issues of the world—earth's ecology, ethical tensions arising from technology, world wars, humanity's capacity for self-destruction, human dignity, justice. Not everyone needs to look at Christianity on such a scale, but the great thinkers do. Romans does not disappoint: it offers the *big* picture of God's salvation.

This book may not be the easiest reading, but it is profoundly rewarding. Among the peaks of Scripture it looms like the Himalayas; its climax, chapter 8, towers up like Mount Everest. Scaling these vistas will give anyone's mental faculties a real workout—but the view is incomparable! Those who read and study Romans gain a grand perspective on what it means to be a Christian. They no longer have to guess at what the gospel is all about—they *know.* ◆

The Super-Powerful Gospel

We know almost nothing about the people to whom Romans was sent. Although Paul mentions the church at Rome (1:7), he wrote a general letter to a general readership, as if addressing it "to whom it may concern." Paul didn't start the church at Rome, nor had he ever visited there before writing this letter (1:13–15). In fact, He even intended to push beyond Rome to Spain (15:22–24).

But even if we know little about Paul's Roman readers, we know much about first-century Rome (see Acts 28:16). Rome was the greatest superpower of its day. Its influence extended from Britain to Africa and from Spain to Persia. This vast empire was governed very effectively by provincial heads, petty kings, and vassals of Rome. A pax Romana *(Roman peace) and a superior road system facilitated transportation and commerce and enabled the rapid spread of Christianity.*

Overall, Rome's government, economy, infrastructure, and defense were formidable enough to last for a thousand years. The Romans were a people in love with power. Perhaps that's why Paul described the gospel to the believers there in terms of power—God's power to save (Rom. 1:16). It's a gospel powerful enough to handle the empire, big enough to address issues on a global scale.

The salvation described in this book extends to . . .

- all aspects of life. *The gospel is not just personal or private, but public and universal as well. It deals with nations, with public policy, with science and technology, with race relations, with good and evil, with the cosmos, with the architecture of the world system.*
- all times and places. *Romans describes the grand sweep of history, from creation to Christ to the culmination of the world. At every point, God is carrying out His strategy for saving His creation from sin.*
- all kinds of people. *Jews and Gentiles, men and women, powerful and powerless, good and bad—all have a place in God's salvation story.*

Rome treated its Caesars like gods and gave them dominion over numerous territories and peoples. But the book of Romans affirms Christ as supreme Lord over all creation: over the past (chapters 3–5), over the present (chapters 6–8), over nations (chapters 9–11), and over daily living in a complex society (chapters 12–16). Christ is even Lord over the environment (chapter 8). Corrupted as it is and languishing under the crushing domination of Adam's sin, the world yearns for redemption. Fortunately, Adam's power to corrupt is exceeded by Christ's power to restore.

Overall, Romans presents a message for public people to embrace. The gospel is about God's power for anyone who lives and works in public systems and institutions. Is your faith big enough for the issues and tasks you face in your work and your world? If you're a marketplace Christian, Romans is a "must-read." ◆

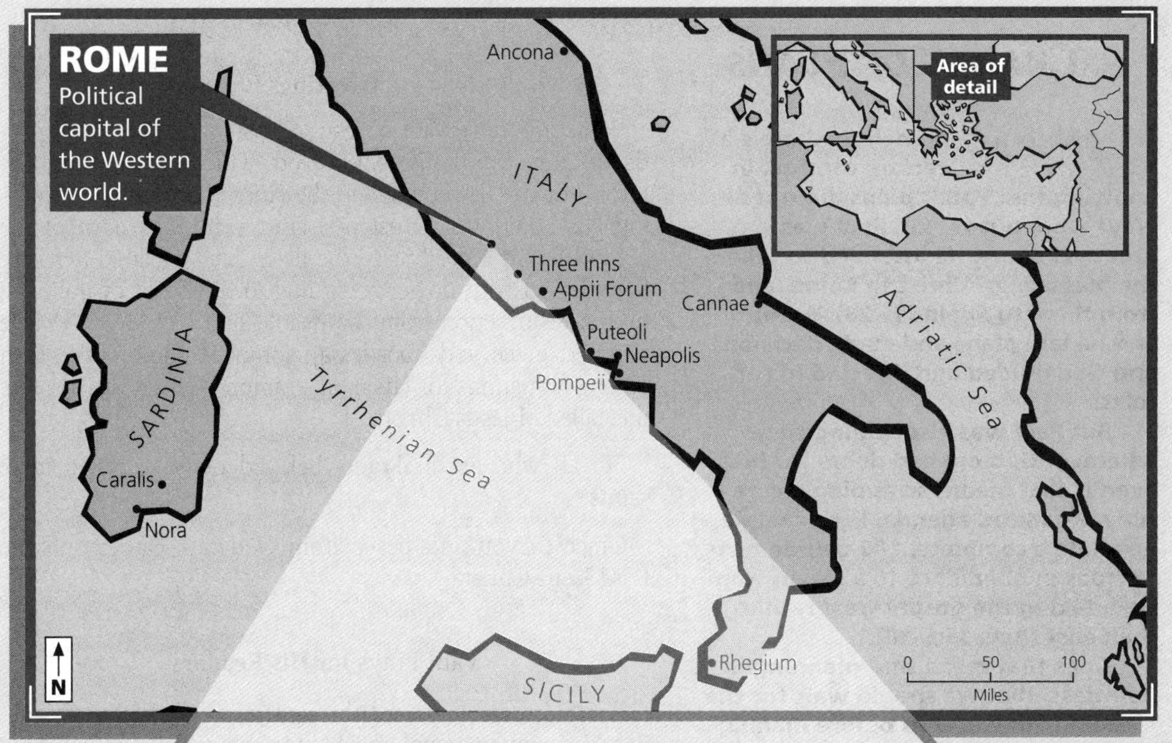
ROME
Political capital of the Western world.
Area of detail
Ancona
ITALY
Three Inns
Appii Forum
Cannae
Adriatic Sea
Puteoli
Neapolis
Pompeii
SARDINIA
Tyrrhenian Sea
Caralis
Nora
Rhegium
SICILY
0 50 100
Miles
N

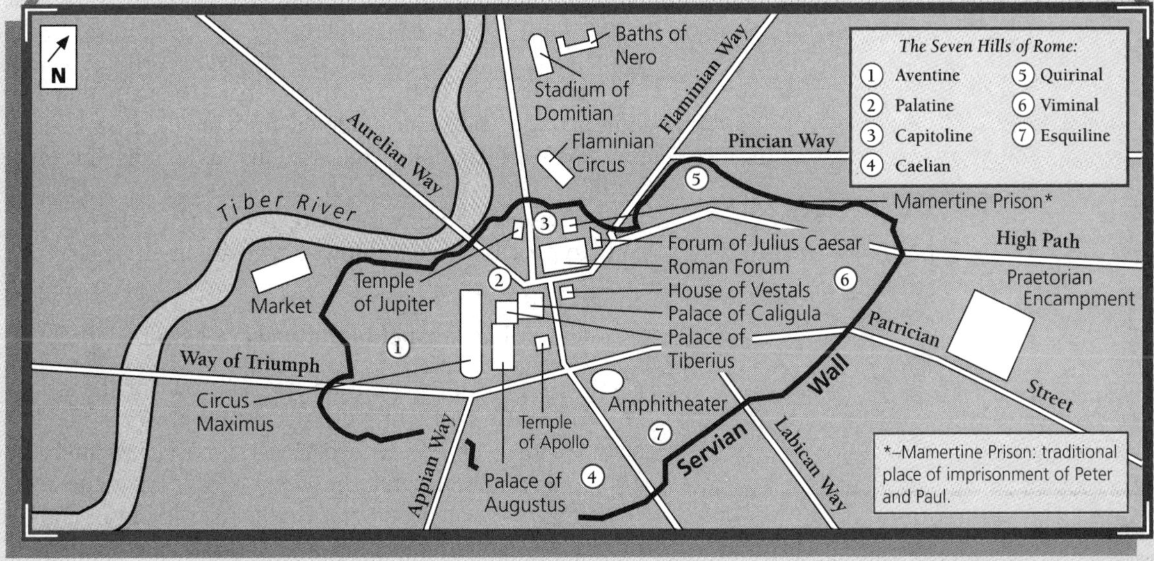
N
Baths of Nero
Stadium of Domitian
Flaminian Way
Flaminian Circus
Pincian Way
Aurelian Way
Tiber River
Mamertine Prison*
Forum of Julius Caesar
High Path
Roman Forum
Praetorian Encampment
Temple of Jupiter
House of Vestals
Market
Palace of Caligula
Patrician Street
Palace of Tiberius
Way of Triumph
Servian Wall
Circus Maximus
Amphitheater
Labican Way
Temple of Apollo
Appian Way
Palace of Augustus
The Seven Hills of Rome:
1 Aventine
2 Palatine
3 Capitoline
4 Caelian
5 Quirinal
6 Viminal
7 Esquiline
*–Mamertine Prison: traditional place of imprisonment of Peter and Paul.

A Change of Plans

CONSIDER THIS 1:13 **Somehow there's a certain comfort in knowing that Paul's plans did not always work out (v. 13). Paul was a great visionary. He intended to take the message of Christ to Rome, and from there to Spain (15:28). To that end he laid plans and made decisions, and God guided and directed his efforts.**

But Paul was also willing to go wherever God opened doors for him, even if that meant scrapping a carefully organized agenda. For example, he made a complete, 180-degree turn at Troas in obedience to a vision from God, taking the gospel west rather than east (Acts 16:6–10).

Does that mean that planning is pointless, that we should wait for the "leading" of the Lord before making any moves? Not if we judge by Paul's example. He understood that it's better to adapt and change one's plans than to have no plans at all.

Paul felt driven to get to Rome, but Spain was just as significant. See "All Roads Lead to Rome—and Beyond," Acts 28:28–31.

CHAPTER 1

Greetings

1 Paul, a bondservant of Jesus Christ, called *to be* an apostle, separated to the gospel of God 2 which He promised before through His prophets in the Holy Scriptures, 3 concerning His Son Jesus Christ our Lord, who was born of the
seed of David according to the flesh, 4 *and* declared *to be* the
Son of God with power according to the Spirit of holiness,
by the resurrection from the dead. 5 Through Him we have
received grace and apostleship for obedience to the faith
among all nations for His name, 6 among whom you also are
the called of Jesus Christ;

7 To all who are in Rome, beloved of God, called *to be*
saints:

Grace to you and peace from God our Father and the Lord Jesus Christ.

Paul Prays for His Readers

8 First, I thank my God through Jesus Christ for you all,
that your faith is spoken of throughout the whole world.
9 For God is my witness, whom I serve with my spirit in the
gospel of His Son, that without ceasing I make mention of
you always in my prayers, 10 making request if, by some
means, now at last I may find a way in the will of God to
come to you. 11 For I long to see you, that I may impart to
you some spiritual gift, so that you may be established—
12 that is, that I may be encouraged together with you by the
mutual faith both of you and me.

1:13 13 Now I do not want you to be unaware, brethren, that I often planned to
come to you (but was hindered until now), that I might
have some fruit among you also, just as among the other
Gentiles. 14 I am a debtor both to Greeks and to barbarians,
both to wise and to unwise. 15 So, as much as is in me, *I am*
ready to preach the gospel to you who are in Rome also.

The Gospel Is the Power of God

1:16 16 For I am not ashamed of the gospel
of Christ,[a] for it is the power of God to
salvation for everyone who believes, for the Jew first and
1:17 see pg. 538 also for the Greek. 17 For in it the righteousness of God is revealed from faith to
faith; as it is written, "The just shall live by faith."[a]

1:16 [a]NU-Text omits *of Christ.* *1:17* [a]Habakkuk 2:4

God Will Judge Sin

18For the wrath of God is revealed from heaven against all
ungodliness and unrighteousness of men, who suppress the
truth in unrighteousness, 19because what may be known of
God is manifest in them, for God has shown *it* to them.
20For since the creation of the world His invisible *attributes*
are clearly seen, being understood by the things that are
made, *even* His eternal power and Godhead, so that they are
without excuse, 21because, although they knew God, they
did not glorify *Him* as God, nor were thankful, but became
futile in their thoughts, and their foolish hearts were darkened. 22Professing to be wise, they became fools, 23and
changed the glory of the incorruptible God into an image
made like corruptible man—and birds and four-footed animals and creeping things.

24Therefore God also gave them up to uncleanness, in the
lusts of their hearts, to dishonor their bodies among themselves, 25who exchanged the truth of God for the lie, and
worshiped and served the creature rather than the Creator,
who is blessed forever. Amen.

26For this reason God gave them up to vile passions. For
even their women exchanged the natural use for what is
against nature. 27Likewise also the men, leaving the natural
use of the woman, burned in their lust for one another,
men with men committing what is shameful, and receiving
in themselves the penalty of their error which was due.

28And even as they did not like to retain God in *their*
knowledge, God gave them over to a debased mind, to do
those things which are not fitting; 29being filled with all unrighteousness, sexual immorality,[a] wickedness, covetousness, maliciousness; full of envy, murder, strife, deceit, evil-
mindedness; *they are* whisperers, 30backbiters, haters of
God, violent, proud, boasters, inventors of evil things, disobedient to parents, 31undiscerning, untrustworthy, unlov-
ing, unforgiving,[a] unmerciful; 32who, knowing the righteous
judgment of God, that those who practice such things are
deserving of death, not only do the same but also approve
of those who practice them.

CHAPTER 2

All Are Guilty, Whether Jew or Gentile

1Therefore you are inexcusable, O man, whoever you are
who judge, for in whatever you judge another you condemn yourself; for you who judge practice the same things.
2But we know that the judgment of God is according to
truth against those who practice such things. 3And do you
think this, O man, you who judge those practicing such

1:29 [a]NU-Text omits *sexual immorality.* *1:31* [a]NU-Text omits *unforgiving.*

THE POWER OF THE GOSPEL

CONSIDER THIS 1:16 **Are you ever embarrassed to be identified as a follower of Christ? Would coworkers or other associates ever assume that you are ashamed of your faith by the way you avoid talking about it or revealing your true thoughts and feelings?**

Paul felt no shame in the message of Christ, for he saw it as *powerful*—powerful enough to transform lives (v. 16).

How powerful is the gospel you believe in? Are you a channel or a barrier for the power of Christ in your workplace?

The first followers of Jesus experienced the power of the gospel in such a profound way that they changed the entire Roman world. *See "Power," Acts 1:8.*

things, and doing the same, that you will escape the judgment of God? 4Or do you despise the riches of His goodness, forbearance, and longsuffering, not knowing that the
goodness of God leads you to repentance? 5But in accordance with your hardness and your impenitent heart you
are treasuring up for yourself wrath in the day of wrath and
revelation of the righteous judgment of God, 6who "will
render to each one according to his deeds":[a] 7eternal life to
those who by patient continuance in doing good seek for
glory, honor, and immortality; 8but to those who are self-
seeking and do not obey the truth, but obey unrighteousness—indignation and wrath, 9tribulation and anguish, on
every soul of man who does evil, of the Jew first and also of
the Greek; 10but glory, honor, and peace to everyone who
works what is good, to the Jew first and also to the Greek.
11For there is no partiality with God.

2:6 [a]Psalm 62:12; Proverbs 24:12

CONSIDER THIS
1:17

RIGHTEOUSNESS

One of the greatest challenges confronting believers today is to communicate the message of Christ in terms that everyday people can understand. Words like "righteousness" (v. 17) have become unrecognizable to many in our culture, and even to many in the church.

Yet it's hard to talk about the gospel—and virtually impossible to understand Romans—without coming to terms with the word "righteousness" (Greek, dikaiosune*). In fact, the New Testament uses the term in one form or another no less than 228 times, at least 40 in Romans. What, then, does "righteousness" mean and how does the gospel reveal "the righteousness of God" (v. 17)?*

The word "righteous" goes back to a base, reg, *meaning "move in a straight line." Thus, "righteous"* (rightwise) *means "in the straight (or right) way." Used with reference to morality, "righteous" means living or acting in the* right *way.*

But what is the "right" way? In our society, people commonly say that everyone must determine what is right for oneself. However, Scripture offers a different standard—indeed, the ultimate standard of rightness *or "righteousness," God Himself. God's character reveals what is absolutely* right*. He is the measure of moral right and wrong.*

He is also the source of right living. It's important to understand that righteousness involves more than just determining whether or not one has lived up to the perfect standard that God sets. The fact is, no one has except Je-

2:12
see pg. 540

12 For as many as have sinned without
law will also perish without law, and as
many as have sinned in the law will be judged by the law
13 (for not the hearers of the law *are* just in the sight of God,
but the doers of the law will be justified; 14 for when Gentiles, who do not have the law, by nature do the things in
the law, these, although not having the law, are a law to
themselves, 15 who show the work of the law written in their
hearts, their conscience also bearing witness, and between
themselves *their* thoughts accusing or else excusing *them*)
16 in the day when God will judge the secrets of men by Jesus Christ, according to my gospel.

Being Jewish Is Not Enough

17 Indeed[a] you are called a Jew, and rest on the law, and
make your boast in God, 18 and know *His* will, and approve

2:17 [a]NU-Text reads *But if.*

sus (Rom. 3:23; 5:18–21). Thus, in a legal sense, all of us stand guilty before God. We are all "unrighteous." We have all "sinned" (literally, "missed the mark").

But the message of Romans is that God has done and is doing everything that needs to be done to restore things to the way He originally intended—to the right *way. For example, He dealt with sin through Jesus' death on the cross (5:6–11), and He transfers the* righteousness *of Christ to those who trust in Him (5:1–2). As believers, we can enjoy a restored relationship with God.*

That means that we can begin to live with righteousness, *that is, in a way that pleases God and fulfills His purposes for us. We can do that because He gives us the ability to do it (8:1–17). Rather than trying to "prove" ourselves good enough for Him or live up to impossible moral standards, we can relate to Him in love, expecting Him to help us as we make choices about how to live.*

The gospel, then, is "good news" because it reveals God's right *way. It tells us that He is a good God who, in love and mercy, has done something about the* wrong *way that the world has taken. How have you responded to that good news of God's righteousness?* ◆

Another term that is often misunderstood today is gospel. *To learn more about what it means, see "What Is the Gospel?" Luke 7:22.*

GOD WILL JUDGE THE SECRETS OF MEN BY JESUS CHRIST. . . .
—Romans 2:16

the things that are excellent, being instructed out of the law,
19and are confident that you yourself are a guide to the
blind, a light to those who are in darkness, 20an instructor
of the foolish, a teacher of babes, having the form of knowledge and truth in the law. 21You, therefore, who teach another, do you not teach yourself? You who preach that a
man should not steal, do you steal? 22You who say, "Do not
commit adultery," do you commit adultery? You who abhor
idols, do you rob temples? 23You who make your boast in
the law, do you dishonor God through breaking the law?
24For "the name of God is blasphemed among the Gentiles
because of you,"[a] as it is written.
25For circumcision is indeed profitable if you keep the
law; but if you are a breaker of the law, your circumcision
has become uncircumcision. 26Therefore, if an uncircumcised man keeps the righteous requirements of the law, will
not his uncircumcision be counted as circumcision? 27And
will not the physically uncircumcised, if he fulfills the law,
judge you who, *even* with *your* written *code* and circumci-

2:24 [a]Isaiah 52:5; Ezekiel 36:22

CONSIDER THIS
2:12

THE LAW

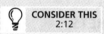

Paul's reference to "law" (v. 12) has to do not with laws in general, but with the specific code of rules and regulations that God gave to Moses on Mount Sinai. The Law was part of the covenant that set Israel apart as God's people. It governed their worship, their relationship to God, and their social relationships with one another. The Ten Commandments form a summary of that Law.

Israel was not the only nation to have a law code. Indeed, such collections were common in the ancient world. Most of them began by explaining that the gods gave the king power to reign, along with a pronouncement about how good and capable he was. Then came the king's laws grouped by subject. Finally, most of the codes closed with a series of curses and blessings.

What set the Mosaic Law apart from these other codes was, first of all, its origin. The Law was given by God Himself. It issued from His very nature; like Him it was holy, righteous, and good. Thus, all crimes in Israel were crimes against God (1 Sam. 12:9–10). He expected all of the people to love and serve Him (Amos 5:21–24). As their final judge, He disciplined those who violated the Law (Ex. 22:21–24; Deut. 10:18; 19:17), though He also held the nation responsible for insuring that justice was carried out (Deut. 13:6–10; 17:7; Num. 15:32–36).

Furthermore, God ruled over Israel, in effect, as the

sion, *are* a transgressor of the law? [28]For he is not a Jew who
is one outwardly, nor *is* circumcision that which *is* outward
in the flesh; [29]but *he is* a Jew who *is one* inwardly; and circumcision *is that* of the heart, in the Spirit, not in the letter;
whose praise *is* not from men but from God.

CHAPTER 3

Faith Alone Makes Heritage Valuable

[1]What advantage then has the Jew, or what *is* the profit of
circumcision? [2]Much in every way! Chiefly because to them
were committed the oracles of God. [3]For what if some did
not believe? Will their unbelief make the faithfulness of God
without effect? [4]Certainly not! Indeed, let God be true but
every man a liar. As it is written:

> "That You may be justified in Your words,
> And may overcome when You are judged."[a]

3:4 [a]Psalm 51:4

nation's King. Ancient kings often enacted laws to try to outdo their predecessors in image, economic power, and political influence. God, however, gave His law as an expression of love for His people, to advance their best interests (Ex. 19:5–6).

The Law can be divided into three categories—moral laws, ceremonial laws, and civil laws. The latter regulated in great detail matters having to do with leaders, the army, criminal cases, crimes against property, humane treatment, personal and family rights, property rights, and other social behavior.

The ceremonial laws contained specifications regarding public worship and ritual, giving high priority to the concept of holiness. Because God is holy (Lev. 21:8), Israel was to be holy in all its religious practices.

The Law was given specifically to Israel, but it rests on eternal moral principles that are consistent with God's character. Thus it is a summary of fundamental and universal moral standards. It expresses the essence of what God requires of people. That's why when God judges, He can be impartial. Gentiles will not be judged by the Law (Rom. 2:12), since it was not given to them, but they will still be judged by the same righteous standard that underlies the Law. ◆

**LET GOD BE TRUE BUT EVERY MAN A LIAR.
—Romans 3:4**

Nobody's Perfect

CONSIDER THIS 3:9–18 **It's common today for people to excuse their faults with the attitude, "Hey, nobody's perfect!" True enough. People can only be expected to be human—and that means fallible.**

Unfortunately, though, few people take that reality seriously enough. Indeed, when it comes to their standing before God, all too many take a different stance: they may not be perfect, but they're "good enough."

The question is, are they good enough for God? Romans 3 says they are not. That's what Paul means when he writes, "all are under sin" (v. 9) and then cites a number of Old Testament passages to back up his claim (vv. 10–18).

It's not that people are evil through and through, or that they never do any moral good. Quite the contrary. People are capable of impressive acts of courage, compassion, and justice. But in light of God's holy (morally perfect) character, which is the ultimate standard against which people's goodness is measured, people are indeed far from perfect. Their good behavior turns out to be the exception rather than the rule.

The good news that Paul writes about in Romans, however, is that God has reached out to humanity despite its imperfect ways. His attitude has not been one of rejection, as if to say, "They're not good enough for Me," but one of grace and compassion that says, in effect, "I will make them into good people—people as good as I AM—by means of Christ My Son."

Another popular notion today is that humankind is basically good, and that moral problems are simply the result of bad parenting, bad education, and the foibles of "society." Is that true? See "Are People Basically Good?" Rom. 7:21.

5But if our unrighteousness demonstrates the righteousness of God, what shall we say? *Is* God unjust who inflicts
wrath? (I speak as a man.) 6Certainly not! For then how will
God judge the world?
7For if the truth of God has increased through my lie to
His glory, why am I also still judged as a sinner? 8And *why*
not *say,* "Let us do evil that good may come"?—as we are
slanderously reported and as some affirm that we say. Their
condemnation is just.

All Stand Condemned before God

3:9–18 9What then? Are we better *than they?*
Not at all. For we have previously
charged both Jews and Greeks that they are all under sin.
10As it is written:

"There is none righteous, no, not one;
11 There is none who understands;
There is none who seeks after God.
12 They have all turned aside;
They have together become unprofitable;
There is none who does good, no, not one."[a]
13 "Their throat *is* an open tomb;
With their tongues they have practiced deceit";[a]
"The poison of asps *is* under their lips";[b]
14 "Whose mouth *is* full of cursing and bitterness."[a]
15 "Their feet *are* swift to shed blood;
16 Destruction and misery *are* in their ways;
17 And the way of peace they have not known."[a]
18 "There is no fear of God before their eyes."[a]

19Now we know that whatever the law says, it says to
those who are under the law, that every mouth may be
stopped, and all the world may become guilty before God.
20Therefore by the deeds of the law no flesh will be justified
in His sight, for by the law *is* the knowledge of sin.

The Way of Righteousness—By Faith

21But now the righteousness of God apart from the law is
revealed, being witnessed by the Law and the Prophets,
22even the righteousness of God, through faith in Jesus
Christ, to all and on all[a] who believe. For there is no difference; 23for all have sinned and fall short of the glory of God,
24being justified freely by His grace through the redemption
that is in Christ Jesus, 25whom God set forth *as* a propitiation by His blood, through faith, to demonstrate His righteousness, because in His forbearance God had passed over
the sins that were previously committed, 26to demonstrate

3:12 [a]Psalms 14:1–3; 53:1–3; Ecclesiastes 7:20 *3:13* [a]Psalm 5:9 [b]Psalm 140:3 *3:14* [a]Psalm 10:7 *3:17* [a]Isaiah 59:7, 8 *3:18* [a]Psalm 36:1 *3:22* [a]NU-Text omits *and on all.*

at the present time His righteousness, that He might be just
and the justifier of the one who has faith in Jesus.
27Where *is* boasting then? It is excluded. By what law? Of
works? No, but by the law of faith. 28Therefore we conclude
that a man is justified by faith apart from the deeds of the
law. 29Or *is He* the God of the Jews only? *Is He* not also the
God of the Gentiles? Yes, of the Gentiles also, 30since *there is*
one God who will justify the circumcised by faith and the
uncircumcised through faith. 31Do we then make void the
law through faith? Certainly not! On the contrary, we establish the law.

CHAPTER 4

Abraham Was Justified by Faith

4:1

1What then shall we say that Abraham
our father has found according to the
flesh?[a] 2For if Abraham was justified by works, he has *something* to boast about, but not before God. 3For what does the
Scripture say? "Abraham believed God, and it was accounted to him for righteousness."[a] 4Now to him who
works, the wages are not counted as grace but as debt.
5But to him who does not work but believes on Him who
justifies the ungodly, his faith is accounted for righteousness, 6just as David also describes the

4:6 see pg. 544

blessedness of the man to whom God imputes righteousness apart from works:

7 "Blessed *are those* whose lawless deeds are forgiven,
And whose sins are covered;
8 Blessed *is the* man to whom the LORD shall not impute
sin."[a]

9*Does* this blessedness then *come* upon the circumcised
only, or upon the uncircumcised also? For we say that faith
was accounted to Abraham for righteousness. 10How then
was it accounted? While he was circumcised, or uncircumcised? Not while circumcised, but while uncircumcised.
11And he received the sign of circumcision, a seal of the
righteousness of the faith which *he had while still* uncircumcised, that he might be the father of all those who believe,
though they are uncircumcised, that righteousness might be
imputed to them also, 12and the father of circumcision to
those who not only *are* of the circumcision, but who also
walk in the steps of the faith which our father Abraham *had
while still* uncircumcised.
13For the promise that he would be the heir of the world
was not to Abraham or to his seed through the law, but

4:1 [a]Or *Abraham our (fore)father according to the flesh has found?* *4:3* [a]Genesis 15:6
4:8 [a]Psalm 32:1, 2

ABRAHAM

CONSIDER THIS 4:1 **As father of the Hebrews, Abraham (v. 1) features prominently in the New Testament. Here in Romans 4, he is recalled as an individual. Elsewhere he represents the entire people of Israel, and especially those who have placed faith in God (for example, 9:7; 11:1; Gal. 3:6–9).**

Indeed, Abraham's faith is what makes him so important to the New Testament writers. God made important promises to him and his descendents, Isaac, Jacob, and Jacob's twelve sons—promises that God repeated throughout Israel's history. Abraham is remembered as the man who believed that God would do what He said He would do (Rom. 4:3)—a remarkable thing when we consider that at the time of the promises, Abraham had very little evidence that God would follow through, certainly far less than the New Testament writers or we who live today.

One of the most important promises was that God would send a Messiah, an "anointed one." Jesus claimed to be that Messiah. So the central question of the New Testament becomes, do we believe that? Do we take Jesus at His word? Do we accept His claim and its implications? Abraham believed God; do we?

Another important question raised by the coming of Jesus was, what happens to Israel? Even though many Jews believed Jesus' claims and followed Him, by and large the nation rejected Him. What did that mean for the promises of God? Paul deals with those issues in Romans 9–11 (see "Israel," Rom. 10:1).

DAVID

CONSIDER THIS 4:6 **If Abraham (v. 1) was honored as the patriarch of Israel, David (v. 6) was honored as the king of Israel. He was not the nation's first king, but He was God's choice for king (1 Sam. 16:1–13).**

If anyone might have a claim on being right with God and meriting His favor, then, it was David. After all, he was said to be a man after God's own heart (13:14; Acts 13:22). Furthermore, God established a covenant with him, promising that his heirs would have a right to the throne of Israel forever (2 Sam. 7:12; 22:51). He was even a direct ancestor of Jesus Christ (Matt. 1:6; Luke 3:31).

But David relied on none of these advantages (or "works," Rom. 4:5) when it came to his standing before God. Instead, he threw himself on God's mercy, trusting in His gracious character to forgive his sin and establish his "righteousness" (v. 6), or right standing in relation to God. Psalm 32, from which Romans 4:7–8 quotes, celebrates this delivery from sin that God brings about.

Do you rely on your own good works to establish your relationship with God? Romans 4 says you can never be good enough. That's why God offers an alternative—trusting in Jesus' righteousness to cover your sin and make it possible for you to know God.

It's virtually impossible to understand Romans without coming to terms with the word "righteousness." Learn more about what that word means at Rom. 1:17.

through the righteousness of faith. [14]For if those who are of
the law *are* heirs, faith is made void and the promise made
of no effect, [15]because the law brings about wrath; for
where there is no law *there is* no transgression.

God Rewarded Abraham's Faith

4:16–25

[16]Therefore *it is* of faith that *it might be*
according to grace, so that the promise
might be sure to all the seed, not only to those who are of
the law, but also to those who are of the faith of Abraham,
who is the father of us all [17](as it is written, "I have made
you a father of many nations"[a]) in the presence of Him
whom he believed—God, who gives life to the dead and
calls those things which do not exist as though they did;
[18]who, contrary to hope, in hope believed, so that he became the father of many nations, according to what was
spoken, "So shall your descendants be."[a] [19]And not being
weak in faith, he did not consider his own body, already
dead (since he was about a hundred years old), and the
deadness of Sarah's womb. [20]He did not waver at the
promise of God through unbelief, but was strengthened in
faith, giving glory to God, [21]and being fully convinced that
what He had promised He was also able to perform. [22]And
therefore "it was accounted to him for righteousness."[a]
[23]Now it was not written for his sake alone that it was imputed to him, [24]but also for us. It shall be imputed to us
who believe in Him who raised up Jesus our Lord from the
dead, [25]who was delivered up because of our offenses, and
was raised because of our justification.

CHAPTER 5

Through Faith We Have Peace with God

[1]Therefore, having been justified by faith, we have[a] peace
with God through our Lord Jesus Christ, [2]through whom
also we have access by faith into this grace in which we
stand, and rejoice in hope of the glory of God. [3]And not
only *that,* but we also glory in tribulations, knowing that
tribulation produces perseverance; [4]and perseverance, character; and character, hope. [5]Now hope does not disappoint,
because the love of God has been poured out in our hearts
by the Holy Spirit who was given to us.
[6]For when we were still without strength, in due time
Christ died for the ungodly. [7]For scarcely for a righteous
man will one die; yet perhaps for a good man someone
would even dare to die. [8]But God demonstrates His own
love toward us, in that while we were still sinners, Christ

4:17 [a]Genesis 17:5 *4:18* [a]Genesis 15:5 *4:22* [a]Genesis 15:6 *5:1* [a]Another ancient reading is, *let us have peace.*

died for us. [9]Much more then, having now been justified by
His blood, we shall be saved from wrath through Him.
[10]For if when we were enemies we were reconciled to God
through the death of His Son, much more, having been reconciled, we shall be saved by His life. [11]And not only *that,*
but we also rejoice in God through our Lord Jesus Christ,
through whom we have now received the reconciliation.

Through Faith Christ Makes Us Alive Again

[12]Therefore, just as through one man sin entered the
world, and death through sin, and thus death spread to all
men, because all sinned— [13](For until the law sin was in
the world, but sin is not imputed when there is no law.
5:14 [14]Nevertheless death reigned from Adam
to Moses, even over those who had not
sinned according to the likeness of the transgression of
Adam, who is a type of Him who was to come. [15]But the
free gift *is* not like the offense. For if by the one man's offense many died, much more the grace of God and the gift
by the grace of the one Man, Jesus Christ, abounded to
many. [16]And the gift *is* not like *that which came* through the
one who sinned. For the judgment *which came* from one *offense resulted* in condemnation, but the free gift *which came*
from many offenses *resulted* in justification. [17]For if by the
one man's offense death reigned through the one, much
more those who receive abundance of grace and of the gift
of righteousness will reign in life through the One, Jesus
Christ.)
[18]Therefore, as through one man's offense *judgment* came
to all men, resulting in condemnation, even so through one
Man's righteous act *the free gift came* to all men, resulting in
justification of life. [19]For as by one man's disobedience
many were made sinners, so also by one Man's obedience
many will be made righteous.
[20]Moreover the law entered that the offense might
abound. But where sin abounded, grace abounded much
more, [21]so that as sin reigned in death, even so grace might
reign through righteousness to eternal life through Jesus
Christ our Lord.

CHAPTER 6

Through Faith We Can Obey God

[1]What shall we say then? Shall we continue in sin that
grace may abound? [2]Certainly not! How shall we who died
to sin live any longer in it? [3]Or do you not know that as
many of us as were baptized into Christ Jesus were baptized

(Bible text continued on page 547)

PROMISES

CONSIDER THIS 4:16–25 **Do you believe that God can be depended on to honor His promises? Abraham did (vv. 20–21).**

All of us rely on the promises of others in our daily lives and work. Vendors promise to deliver products in specified quantities and qualities. Project groups promise to deliver results by certain dates. Companies promise to stand behind their products with "satisfaction guaranteed." If we can believe the promises of fallible human beings, how much more can we trust the promises of God, who never fails?

Of course, if we are one of God's people, we need to live and work with the same trustworthiness and reliability. When we give our word, we need to fulfill it. When we make a commitment, we need to honor it. When we enter into a contract, we need to abide by it. Otherwise, we bring discredit to God.

Trustworthiness is one of the traits of a godly "workstyle." See Titus 2:9–10.

ADAM

FOR YOUR INFO 5:14 **Adam (v. 14) was the first man, who, along with his wife, Eve, was created by God on the sixth day of creation and placed in the Garden of Eden (Gen. 1:26–28; 2:7–24). Thus they became the ancestors of all humanity.**

But Adam failed to keep God's command not to eat the fruit of a certain tree in the garden, resulting in a dramatic change—indeed, a tragic rupture—in the relationship between God and Adam and Eve and their descendants. His choice to disobey brought sin and death into the world (Rom. 5:12–19; 1 Cor. 15:22).

SLAVES

Paul uses a powerful image when he pictures one's relationship either to sin or to obedience as slavery (v. 16). The Roman Empire was heavily dependent on slaves to take care of its hard labor and menial tasks. In fact, many of Paul's Roman recipients may have been slaves, since perhaps half the population or more were under servitude by one historian's estimate.

Slaves were taken from the many nations that Rome conquered. Those assigned to the empire's widespread construction projects or to its mines had a hard lot. Fed a subsistence diet, they were worked to exhaustion. Injuries and disease were common, and once they were too sick to work, or in rare cases too old, they were abandoned.

Household slaves, however, enjoyed better conditions. Nearly every Roman home owned at least two or three servants, and some had hundreds. They assisted the women in maintaining their homes and raising their children. Slaves with occupational expertise proved particularly valuable in the workplace, and some businesses were entirely dependent on these imported, cheap laborers.

Slavery existed long before the Romans, of course. The Bible records several different forms of slavery in ancient times: domestic slavery, as illustrated by Hagar (Gen. 16:1); state slavery, as illustrated by the Israelites under Egypt (Ex. 5:6–19; 13:3); and temple slavery, as illustrated by the slaves of the Levites for temple service (Num. 31:25–47; Josh. 9:21–27).

Curiously, the Bible does not directly condemn slavery as an institution, though it contains warnings about the practice of slavery (Amos 1:6–9; Rev. 18:13). The Old Testament Law did regulate Israel's treatment of slaves (Ex. 21; Deut. 15). Repeatedly, the people were instructed not to rule over a fellow Israelite harshly (Lev. 25:39; Deut. 15:14). If a master beat a slave or harmed him, the law provided that the slave could go free (Ex. 21:26–27); and the killing of a slave called for a penalty (Ex. 21:20).

In the New Testament, slaves were advised to obey their masters (Eph. 6:5; Col. 3:22; Titus 2:9). Paul appealed to Philemon to receive back Onesimus, a runaway slave who became a Christian and therefore a brother (see the Introduction to Philemon). This was an illustration that in Christ, social distinctions such as slavery no longer apply (Gal. 3:28; Col. 3:11). Elsewhere Paul counseled believing slaves to seek freedom if they could (1 Cor. 7:21).

Under Jewish law, no Hebrew was to be the permanent slave of another Hebrew (Ex. 21:2; Lev. 25:37–43; Deut. 15:12). If a slave desired to continue with his master, he would have a mark made in the ear to signify that he had chosen to remain a slave (Ex. 21:5–6). A slave could also buy his freedom, or another person could buy his freedom for him (Lev. 25:47–49).

Among the Romans, an owner could free a slave outright, or the slave could purchase his freedom by paying his owner. Freedom could also be arranged if ownership was transferred to a god. The slave could then receive his freedom in return for contracting his services. He would continue with his master, but now as a free man.

Perhaps Paul had that sort of arrangement in mind when he described the moral choice of which master one would obey—sin or righteousness (Rom. 6:16). For as believers, we have been freed from sin, and in fact are now owned by God. We are now free to serve God. Yet we still have a choice to serve either sin or God. In light of the realities of slavery, it's worth considering: Which master are you serving? Which one is likely to treat you better? ◆

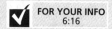

into His death? 4Therefore we were buried with Him
through baptism into death, that just as Christ was raised
from the dead by the glory of the Father, even so we also
should walk in newness of life.

5For if we have been united together in the likeness of His
death, certainly we also shall be *in the likeness* of *His* resurrection, 6knowing this, that our old man was crucified with
Him, that the body of sin might be done away with, that we
should no longer be slaves of sin. 7For he who has died has
been freed from sin. 8Now if we died with Christ, we believe that we shall also live with Him, 9knowing that Christ,
having been raised from the dead, dies no more. Death
no longer has dominion over Him. 10For *the death* that He
died, He died to sin once for all; but *the life* that He lives,
He lives to God. 11Likewise you also, reckon yourselves to
be dead indeed to sin, but alive to God in Christ Jesus our
Lord.

12Therefore do not let sin reign in your mortal body, that
you should obey it in its lusts. 13And do not present your
members *as* instruments of unrighteousness to sin, but present yourselves to God as being alive from the dead, and
your members *as* instruments of righteousness to God.
14For sin shall not have dominion over you, for you are not
under law but under grace.

We Are No Longer Enslaved to Sin

6:15–22

6:16

15What then? Shall we sin because we
are not under law but under grace? Certainly not! 16Do you not know that to
whom you present yourselves slaves to
obey, you are that one's slaves whom you obey, whether of
sin *leading* to death, or of obedience *leading* to righteousness? 17But God be thanked that *though* you were slaves of
sin, yet you obeyed from the heart that form of doctrine to
which you were delivered. 18And having been set free from
sin, you became slaves of righteousness. 19I speak in human
terms because of the weakness of your flesh. For just as you
presented your members *as* slaves of uncleanness, and of
lawlessness *leading* to *more* lawlessness, so now present your
members *as* slaves *of* righteousness for holiness.

20For when you were slaves of sin, you were free in regard
to righteousness. 21What fruit did you have then in the
things of which you are now ashamed? For the end of those
things *is* death. 22But now having been set free from sin,
and having become slaves of God, you have your fruit to
holiness, and the end, everlasting life. 23For the wages of sin
is death, but the gift of God *is* eternal life in Christ Jesus our
Lord.

Real Freedom

CONSIDER THIS 6:15–22 **One of the greatest motivating factors for people throughout the world today is the quest for freedom, for self-determination. Armies fight for it. Nations vote for it. Individuals work for it.**

But here in Romans 6, Scripture teaches that, ultimately, no one is ever totally "free." In the end, everyone serves either God or sin. In fact, Paul uses the word "slaves" to describe the relationship (vv. 16–20; see related article on "Slaves"). We are either slaves of righteousness or slaves of sin.

What does that imply for our understanding of the nature of freedom? Is complete autonomy possible? Is there such a thing as self-rule or political self-determination? Yes, in a limited sense. But here as elsewhere, Scripture describes real freedom as a change of masters: being set free from slavery to sin in order to become slaves to righteousness instead.

All of us are enslaved to sin from the moment of conception. Our only hope is Christ, who is able to emancipate us from that bondage (7:24–25). Then, having saved us, He enables us through His Holy Spirit to do what we could not do in and of ourselves—live in obedience to God's law (8:3–4). Therein lies true freedom.

CHAPTER 7

A New View of the Law

[1]Or do you not know, brethren (for I speak to those who
know the law), that the law has dominion over a man as
long as he lives? [2]For the woman who has a husband is
bound by the law to *her* husband as long as he lives. But if
the husband dies, she is released from the law of *her* husband. [3]So then if, while *her* husband lives, she marries another man, she will be called an adulteress; but if her husband dies, she is free from that law, so that she is no
adulteress, though she has married another man. [4]There-
fore, my brethren, you also have become dead to the law
through the body of Christ, that you may be married to another—to Him who was raised from the dead, that we
should bear fruit to God. [5]For when we were in the flesh,
the sinful passions which were aroused by the law were at
work in our members to bear fruit to death. [6]But now we
have been delivered from the law, having died to what we

CONSIDER THIS
7:7

SCYLLA AND CHARYBDIS

Ancient Greek mythology told of two dangers at sea known as Scylla and Charybdis. Scylla was a twelve-tentacled monster with six heads that grabbed at least six sailors from the decks of passing ships. Nearby lay Charybdis, an underwater terror able to suck down entire vessels in a giant whirlpool of seawater. These two dangers were arranged so that a ship could sail closer to one or the other, but could avoid neither.

The Christian life has two dangers not unlike Scylla and Charybdis. As believers travel along the journey of faith, they encounter two perils that cannot be avoided—law and lawlessness. Paul addresses both pitfalls in Romans 6–7.

In Romans, the Law (7:7; see 2:12) refers specifically to the Old Testament Law that God gave to Israel, but more generally to the moral expectations that God places on all humanity. Obviously such standards are not evil in themselves. Nevertheless, they become perilous because no one is humanly able to keep them all perfectly.

Paul illustrated that fact by citing the Tenth Commandment, "You shall not covet" (7:7; Ex. 20:17). That was a basic moral principle with which Paul was in total agreement. Yet when he examined his own life, he found "all manner of evil desire." In other words, the more Paul understood God's Law, the more aware he became of the sin in his life. Nor did knowing God's expectations make him

were held by, so that we should serve in the newness of the
Spirit and not *in* the oldness of the letter.

7:7

[7]What shall we say then? *Is* the law sin?
Certainly not! On the contrary, I would
not have known sin except through the law. For I would
not have known covetousness unless the law had said, "You
shall not covet."[a] [8]But sin, taking opportunity by the commandment, produced in me all *manner of* evil desire. For
apart from the law sin *was* dead. [9]I was alive once without
the law, but when the commandment came, sin revived and
I died. [10]And the commandment, which *was* to *bring* life, I
found to *bring* death. [11]For sin, taking occasion by the commandment, deceived me, and by it killed *me.* [12]Therefore
the law *is* holy, and the commandment holy and just and
good.

A Terrible Inner Conflict

[13]Has then what is good become death to me? Certainly
not! But sin, that it might appear sin, was producing death

7:7 [a]Exodus 20:17; Deuteronomy 5:21

capable of doing them. In fact, he found himself incapable of carrying them out (v. 19).

The end result was frustration and wretchedness (v. 24). How many Christians today feel similarly? They are keenly aware of the expectations of the Christian life, yet they are also aware of how poorly they carry out those expectations. As a result, they feel guilt and condemnation. So they become preoccupied with doing acts of morality rather than with the person of Christ. Such an attitude is called legalism.

However, if an overemphasis on law is perilous, its opposite, lawlessness, is just as perilous. Scripture says that all sin is lawlessness (6:19; 1 John 3:4), because to sin is to violate God's law, His moral expectations. But one sinful act has a way of spawning another, and yet another, until things snowball into a lifestyle of lawlessness. Some Christians end up in that condition—especially many who have previously suffered under legalism.

Scylla and Charybdis were myths of the Greeks, but the perils of law and lawlessness are no illusions. They are real dangers that Christians face every day. There is only one way to avoid either pitfall: Christ must produce in us the good that we cannot produce through our own human ability (8:1–4). If we want to fulfill the expectations of God, we must rely on the power of God to enable us to do so. Are you trusting Christ to reproduce His character in you? ◆

SERVE IN THE NEWNESS OF THE SPIRIT AND NOT IN THE OLDNESS OF THE LETTER.
—Romans 7:6

Are People Basically Good?

CONSIDER THIS 7:21 **Many of us want to believe that we are "basically good" people—or at least better than other people. In fact, it's popular today to subscribe to the view that humankind is basically good, and that moral problems are simply the result of bad parenting, bad education, and the foibles of "society."**

The Bible presents a different view, however. Scripture affirms the inherent dignity and value of every human being (Ps. 139:13–14; see "People At Work," Heb. 2:7). But it insists that each of us is born "in sin"—that is, apart from God, naturally tending toward wrong rather than right. That's what Paul addresses in Romans 7.

Original sin is a sobering concept, one that our pride would dearly love to do away with. But then, pride lies at the root of sin. Therefore, the first step toward rooting it out of our lives is to humbly admit our true condition—not to blame someone else, but rather to confess our sin to God and trust solely in His grace for forgiveness and acceptance (Luke 18:13).

This attitude of humility in light of our sin needs to become a way of life. Sin is so deeply entrenched within us that we can never safely say that we've mastered it (1 Cor. 4:4; 10:12). Instead, we live with limitation, admitting that we don't have all the answers to our own problems, let alone those that plague the world.

This perspective provides insight into the troubles that come our way. Sometimes they come as a result of our own sinful choices. Sometimes

(continued on next page)

in me through what is good, so that sin through the
commandment might become exceedingly sinful. 14For we
know that the law is spiritual, but I am carnal, sold under
sin. 15For what I am doing, I do not understand. For what I
will to do, that I do not practice; but what I hate, that I do.
16If, then, I do what I will not to do, I agree with the law
that *it is* good. 17But now, *it is* no longer I who do it, but sin
that dwells in me. 18For I know that in me (that is, in my
flesh) nothing good dwells; for to will is present with me,
but *how* to perform what is good I do not find. 19For the
good that I will *to do,* I do not do; but the evil I will not *to*
do, that I practice. 20Now if I do what I will not *to do,* it is
no longer I who do it, but sin that dwells in me.

7:21 21I find then a law, that evil is present
with me, the one who wills to do good.
22For I delight in the law of God according to the inward
man. 23But I see another law in my members, warring
against the law of my mind, and bringing me into captivity
to the law of sin which is in my members. 24O wretched
man that I am! Who will deliver me from this body of
death? 25I thank God—through Jesus Christ our Lord

So then, with the mind I myself serve the law of God, but
with the flesh the law of sin.

CHAPTER 8

In Christ There Is No More Condemnation

1*There is* therefore now no condemnation to those who
are in Christ Jesus,[a] who do not walk according to the flesh,
but according to the Spirit. 2For the law of the Spirit of life
in Christ Jesus has made me free from the law of sin and
death. 3For what the law could not do in that it was weak
through the flesh, God *did* by sending His own Son in the
likeness of sinful flesh, on account of sin: He condemned
sin in the flesh, 4that the righteous requirement of the law
might be fulfilled in us who do not walk according to the
flesh but according to the Spirit. 5For those who live according to the flesh set their minds on the things of the
flesh, but those *who live* according to the Spirit, the things
of the Spirit. 6For to be carnally minded *is* death, but to be
spiritually minded *is* life and peace. 7Because the carnal
mind *is* enmity against God; for it is not subject to the law
of God, nor indeed can be. 8So then, those who are in the
flesh cannot please God.

Believers Are People of the Spirit

9But you are not in the flesh but in the Spirit, if indeed
the Spirit of God dwells in you. Now if anyone does not

8:1 [a]NU-Text omits the rest of this verse.

have the Spirit of Christ, he is not His. 10And if Christ *is* in
you, the body *is* dead because of sin, but the Spirit *is* life because of righteousness. 11But if the Spirit of Him who raised
Jesus from the dead dwells in you, He who raised Christ
from the dead will also give life to your mortal bodies
through His Spirit who dwells in you.

12Therefore, brethren, we are debtors—not to the flesh, to
live according to the flesh. 13For if you live according to the
flesh you will die; but if by the Spirit you put to death the
deeds of the body, you will live. 14For as many as are led by
8:15–17
the Spirit of God, these are sons of God.
15For you did not receive the spirit of
bondage again to fear, but you received the Spirit of adoption by whom we cry out, "Abba, Father." 16The Spirit Himself bears witness with our spirit that we are children of
God, 17and if children, then heirs—heirs of God and joint
heirs with Christ, if indeed we suffer with *Him,* that we may
also be glorified together.

Believers Receive the Spirit's Help

18For I consider that the sufferings of this present time are
not worthy *to be compared* with the glory which shall be revealed in us. 19For the earnest expectation of the creation
8:20 see pg. 552
eagerly waits for the revealing of the sons
of God. 20For the creation was subjected
to futility, not willingly, but because of Him who subjected
8:21–22 see pg. 554
it in hope; 21because the creation itself
also will be delivered from the bondage
of corruption into the glorious liberty of the children of
God. 22For we know that the whole creation groans and
labors with birth pangs together until now. 23Not only *that,*
but we also who have the firstfruits of the Spirit, even we
ourselves groan within ourselves, eagerly waiting for the
adoption, the redemption of our body. 24For we were saved
in this hope, but hope that is seen is not hope; for why does
one still hope for what he sees? 25But if we hope for what
we do not see, we eagerly wait for *it* with perseverance.

26Likewise the Spirit also helps in our weaknesses. For we
do not know what we should pray for as we ought, but the
Spirit Himself makes intercession for us[a] with groanings
which cannot be uttered. 27Now He who searches the hearts

(Bible text continued on page 553)

8:26 [a]NU-Text omits *for us.*

An Inheritance?

A CLOSER LOOK 8:15–17

As God's adopted children, believers are promised an inheritance (vv. 15–17). What will that involve? See "What's In It for Me?" Eph. 1:11.

(continued from previous page)

God allows them as a way of building our character, especially our faith in Him (Ps. 119:67, 71–72; Heb. 12:7–11; James 1:2–4, 12–18).

Do you want true humility? It comes from seeing yourself in relation to God. See "Humility—The Scandalous Virtue," Phil. 2:3.

TO BE SPIRITUALLY MINDED IS LIFE AND PEACE.
—Romans 8:6

CONSIDER THIS
8:20

Is Work a Curse?

What was the curse that God put on creation (v. 20)? One of the most stubborn myths in Western culture is that God imposed work as a curse to punish Adam and Eve's sin (Gen. 3:1–19). As a result, some people view work as something evil. Scripture does not support that idea:

God Himself is a worker. The fact that God works shows that work is not evil, since by definition God cannot do evil. On the contrary, work is an activity that God carries out. See "God: The Original Worker," John 5:17.

God created people in His image to be His coworkers. He gives us ability and authority to manage His creation. See "People At Work," Heb. 2:7.

God established work before the fall. Genesis 1–2 record how God created the world. The account tells how He placed the first humans in a garden "to tend and keep it" (2:15). This work assignment was given before sin entered the world and God pronounced the curse (Gen. 3). Obviously, then, work cannot be a result of the fall since people were working before the fall.

God commends work even after the fall. If work were evil in and of itself, God would never encourage people to engage in it. But He does. For example, He told Noah and his family the same thing He told Adam and Eve—to have dominion over the earth (Gen. 9:1–7). In the New Testament, Christians are commanded to work (Col. 3:23; 1 Thess. 4:11).

Work itself was not cursed in the fall. A careful reading of Genesis 3:17–19 shows that God cursed the *ground* as a result of Adam's sin—but not work:

"Cursed is the ground for
  your sake;
In toil you shall eat of it
All the days of your life.
Both thorns and thistles it
  shall bring forth for you,
And you shall eat the herb of
  the field.
In the sweat of your face you
  shall eat bread
Till you return to the ground,
For out of it you were taken;
For dust you are,
And to dust you shall return."

Notice three ways that this curse affected work: (1) Work had been a joy, but now it would be "toil." People would feel burdened down by it, and even come to hate it. (2) "Thorns and thistles" would hamper people's efforts to exercise dominion. In other words, the earth would not be as cooperative as it had been. (3) People would have to "sweat" to accomplish their tasks. Work would require enormous effort and energy.

Most of us know all too well how burdensome work can be. Workplace stresses and pressures, occupational hazards, the daily grind, office politics, crushing boredom, endless routine, disappointments, setbacks, catastrophes, frustration, cutthroat competition, fraud, deception, injustice—there is no end of evils connected with work. But work itself is not evil. Far from naming it a curse, the Bible calls work and its fruit a gift from God (Eccl. 3:13; 5:18–19). ◆

Do you know that your job is actually an extension of Christ's rule over the world? See "People at Work," Heb. 2:7.

knows what the mind of the Spirit *is,* because He makes intercession for the saints according to *the will of* God.
8:28 28And we know that all things work together for good to those who love God,
to those who are the called according to *His* purpose. 29For
whom He foreknew, He also predestined *to be* conformed to
the image of His Son, that He might be the firstborn among
many brethren. 30Moreover whom He predestined, these He
also called; whom He called, these He also justified; and
whom He justified, these He also glorified.

Believers Are Loved by God

31What then shall we say to these things? If God *is* for us,
who *can be* against us? 32He who did not spare His own
Son, but delivered Him up for us all, how shall He not with
Him also freely give us all things? 33Who shall bring a
charge against God's elect? *It is* God who justifies. 34Who *is*
he who condemns? *It is* Christ who died, and furthermore is
also risen, who is even at the right hand of God, who also
makes intercession for us. 35Who shall separate us from the
love of Christ? *Shall* tribulation, or distress, or persecution,
or famine, or nakedness, or peril, or sword? 36As it is written:

"For Your sake we are killed all day long;
We are accounted as sheep for the slaughter."[a]

37Yet in all these things we are more than conquerors
through Him who loved us. 38For I am persuaded that neither death nor life, nor angels nor principalities nor powers,
nor things present nor things to come, 39nor height nor
depth, nor any other created thing, shall be able to separate
us from the love of God which is in Christ Jesus our Lord.

CHAPTER 9

The Implications of Faith for Israel

9:1 see pg. 556 1I tell the truth in Christ, I am not lying, my conscience also bearing me wit-
ness in the Holy Spirit, 2that I have great sorrow and continual grief in my heart. 3For I could wish that I myself were
accursed from Christ for my brethren, my countrymen[a] according to the flesh, 4who are Israelites, to whom *pertain*
the adoption, the glory, the covenants, the giving of the law,
the service *of God,* and the promises; 5of whom *are* the fathers and from whom, according to the flesh, Christ *came,*
who is over all, *the* eternally blessed God. Amen.

8:36 [a]Psalm 44:22 *9:3* [a]Or *relatives*

All **Things For Good?**

CONSIDER THIS 8:28 **Verse 28 is easy to quote to someone else. But what about when it's *your* turn to suffer? Is there comfort in this passage? Notice two important things as you consider Paul's words here:**

(1) All things work together *for* good but not all things *are* good. The loss of a job, a tyrannical boss, physical illness, or family troubles are not good *per se.* In fact, often they are the direct result of evil. That's important to observe. Believers are never promised immunity from the problems and pains of the world. Every day we must put up with much that is not good.

(2) Nevertheless, good can come out of bad! This verse promises that God uses all the circumstances of our lives—both the good and the bad—to shape outcomes that accomplish His purposes for us. And His purposes can only be good, because He is good by definition (James 1:17).

So how can you make this verse work for you as you face tough, troubling times?

- **Affirm your trust in God's presence.**
- **Align your goals with God's purposes.**
- **Accept the reliability of God's promises.**

6But it is not that the word of God has taken no effect.
For they *are* not all Israel who *are* of Israel, 7nor *are they* all
children because they are the seed of Abraham; but, "In
Isaac your seed shall be called."[a] 8That is, those who *are* the
children of the flesh, these *are* not the children of God; but
the children of the promise are counted as the seed. 9For
this *is* the word of promise: "At this time I will come and
Sarah shall have a son."[a]

10And not only *this,* but when Rebecca also had conceived
by one man, *even* by our father Isaac 11(for *the children* not
yet being born, nor having done any good or evil, that the
purpose of God according to election might stand, not of
works but of Him who calls), 12it was said to her, "The
older shall serve the younger."[a] 13As it is written, "Jacob I
have loved, but Esau I have hated."[a]

God Is Sovereign

14What shall we say then? *Is there* unrighteousness with
God? Certainly not! 15For He says to Moses, "I will have
mercy on whomever I will have mercy, and I will have com-

9:7 [a]Genesis 21:12 *9:9* [a]Genesis 18:10, 14 *9:12* [a]Genesis 25:23 *9:13* [a]Malachi 1:2, 3

CONSIDER THIS
8:21–22

THE LIBERATION OF CREATION

In Romans 8, Paul painted on a cosmic canvas a vast picture of the world, from its origin as God's beautiful creation to the impact of sin, and on to its ultimate restoration at the end of history. If you've ever wondered what's ultimately going to happen to the world, if you've ever worried about environmental disaster, if you've ever wished that evil could somehow be vanquished, this passage is "must reading."

Paul recognized that the world is both delightful and disastrous, orderly and chaotic. He offered a good news/bad news scenario. The bad news is that all of creation, including human beings and their environments, are corrupted by sin. Sin is so prevalent and so destructive that we need more than just a better earth—we need a new earth. Sin is not just personal, it's global. It's infused in the bloodstream of the whole world, where sinful people create systems and cultures that promote and protect evil, as well as good.

So much for the bad news. The good news is that God's salvation is equally universal in its availability and effects. His saving grace starts its work inside people, but eventually works its way out through their influence. God's power and purposes begin to penetrate their values,

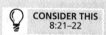

passion on whomever I will have compassion."[a] 16So then *it*
is not of him who wills, nor of him who runs, but of God
who shows mercy. 17For the Scripture says to the Pharaoh,
"For this very purpose I have raised you up, that I may
show My power in you, and that My name may be declared
in all the earth."[a] 18Therefore He has mercy on whom He
wills, and whom He wills He hardens.

19You will say to me then, "Why does He still find fault?
For who has resisted His will?" 20But indeed, O man, who
are you to reply against God? Will the thing formed say to
him who formed *it*, "Why have you made me like this?"
21Does not the potter have power over the clay, from the
same lump to make one vessel for honor and another for
dishonor?

22*What* if God, wanting to show *His* wrath and to make
His power known, endured with much longsuffering the
vessels of wrath prepared for destruction, 23and that He
might make known the riches of His glory on the vessels of
mercy, which He had prepared beforehand for glory, 24*even*
us whom He called, not of the Jews only, but also of the
Gentiles?

9:15 [a]Exodus 33:19 *9:17* [a]Exodus 9:16

worldview, relationships, career choices, and community involvements. As God's managers of the earth, they begin to reclaim the devil's territory, as it were, by redirecting social systems and cultural values so that people and places benefit instead of being exploited. What begins as personal conversion results in societal change as God's people slowly impact their families, coworkers, churches, communities, culture, and environment.

But this liberation of creation will be partial and imperfect until Christ returns to redeem it personally. In the meantime, the world groans like a woman in labor (v. 22), waiting for its delivery from sin. Christ calls His followers to participate in the world's systems, to promote His values and love as we have opportunity. As His people, we affirm both the salvation of persons and the transformation of places, participating with Him in the first skirmishes of the liberation of His creation. ◆

O MAN, WHO ARE YOU TO REPLY AGAINST GOD?
—Romans 9:20

25As He says also in Hosea:

"I will call them My people, who were not My people,
And her beloved, who was not beloved."[a]
26 "And it shall come to pass in the place where it was said to them,
'You *are* not My people,'
There they shall be called sons of the living God."[a]

27Isaiah also cries out concerning Israel:[a]

"Though the number of the children of Israel be as the sand of the sea,
The remnant will be saved.

9:25 [a]Hosea 2:23 *9:26* [a]Hosea 1:10 *9:27* [a]Isaiah 10:22, 23

FOR YOUR INFO
9:1

God's Heart for the Whole World

In Romans 9–11, Paul reminds us that God's heart reaches out to the whole world, both Jews and Gentiles:

Good News for the World in Romans 9–11

Passage	Teaching
9:24	•God in His mercy calls not only Jews but Gentiles as well.
9:25	•Gentiles, who were not God's people, have become children of the living God.
9:30	•Gentiles have received righteousness through their faith, just as Jews who have believed in Jesus.
10:3	•But Jews who seek God through the Law's requirements will never find righteousness because they do not seek it through faith. They seek to establish their own righteousness, not God's.
10:4	•Jesus is God's righteousness to everyone who believes.
9:33; 10:9,11	•Faith in Jesus is the key to salvation.
10:12–13	•When it comes to who can be saved, God makes no distinction between Jews and Gentiles.
10:20–21; 11:11	•The Gentiles, who were not looking for God, found Him. But the Jews, whom God continually reached out to, did not want Him.
11:1–2	•God has not given up on the Jews. Many have turned to God; Paul was one of them.
11:14	•The Gentiles found Christ through the witness of the Jews. Paul's great desire was for Jews to come to Christ through the witness of the Gentiles.
11:16–24	•Gentiles were grafted into God's tree of life as Jews rejected God and were broken off. But that leaves no room for pride or arrogance on the part of the Gentiles; rather, humility.
11:19–24	•Jews were "cut off" because they refused to believe. If they repent, God is able to graft them in again.
11:32	•God's desire is to have mercy on all.

By the time Paul wrote Romans, Gentiles had probably become a majority in the church. Paul saw the possibility of a church divided, and the tragedy that would result if that happened. See "Are We One People?" Rom. 11:13–24.

28 For He will finish the work and cut *it* short in
righteousness,
Because the LORD will make a short work upon
the earth."[a]

29And as Isaiah said before:

"Unless the LORD of Sabaoth[a] had left us a seed,
We would have become like Sodom,
And we would have been made like
Gomorrah."[b]

30What shall we say then? That Gentiles, who did
not pursue righteousness, have attained to righteousness, even the righteousness of faith; 31but Israel, pursuing the law of righteousness, has not attained to the law of righteousness.[a] 32Why? Because
they did not *seek it* by faith, but as it were, by the
works of the law.[a] For they stumbled at that stumbling stone. 33As it is written:

"Behold, I lay in Zion a stumbling stone and
rock of offense,
And whoever believes on Him will not be put
to shame."[a]

CHAPTER 10

Paul Longs for Israel's Salvation

10:1 see pg. 558

1Brethren, my heart's desire
and prayer to God for Israel[a] is
that they may be saved. 2For I bear them witness
that they have a zeal for God, but not according to
knowledge. 3For they being ignorant of God's righteousness, and seeking to establish their own righteousness, have not submitted to the righteousness
of God. 4For Christ *is* the end of the law for righteousness to everyone who believes.
5For Moses writes about the righteousness which
is of the law, "The man who does those things shall
live by them."[a] 6But the righteousness of faith
speaks in this way, "Do not say in your heart, 'Who
will ascend into heaven?' "[a] (that is, to bring Christ
down *from above*) 7or, " 'Who will descend into the
abyss?' "[a] (that is, to bring Christ up from the
dead). 8But what does it say? "The word is near
you, in your mouth and in your heart"[a] (that is, the
word of faith which we preach): 9that if you confess with your mouth the Lord Jesus and believe in
your heart that God has raised Him from the dead,
you will be saved. 10For with the heart one believes
unto righteousness, and with the mouth confession
is made unto salvation. 11For the Scripture says,
"Whoever believes on Him will not be put to
shame."[a] 12For there is no distinction between Jew
and Greek, for the same Lord over all is rich to all
who call upon Him. 13For "whoever calls on the
name of the LORD shall be saved."[a]

The Nation Needs to Hear the Gospel

14How then shall they call on Him in whom they
have not believed? And how shall they believe in
Him of whom they have not heard? And how shall
they hear without a preacher? 15And how shall they
preach unless they are sent? As it is written:

"How beautiful are the feet of those who preach
the gospel of peace,[a]
Who bring glad tidings of good things!"[b]

16But they have not all obeyed the gospel. For Isaiah says, "LORD, who has believed our report?"[a]
17So then faith *comes* by hearing, and hearing by
the word of God.
18But I say, have they not heard? Yes indeed:

"Their sound has gone out to all the earth,
And their words to the ends of the world."[a]

19But I say, did Israel not know? First Moses says:

"I will provoke you to jealousy by *those who are*
not a nation,
I will move you to anger by a foolish nation."[a]

20But Isaiah is very bold and says:

"I was found by those who did not seek Me;
I was made manifest to those who did not ask
for Me."[a]

21But to Israel he says:

"All day long I have stretched out My hands
To a disobedient and contrary people."[a]

(Bible text continued on page 559)

9:28 [a]NU-Text reads *For the LORD will finish the work and cut it short upon the earth.* *9:29* [a]Literally, in Hebrew, *Hosts* [b]Isaiah 1:9 *9:31* [a]NU-Text omits *of righteousness.* *9:32* [a]NU-Text reads *by works.* *9:33* [a]Isaiah 8:14; 28:16 *10:1* [a]NU-Text reads *them.* *10:5* [a]Leviticus 18:5 *10:6* [a]Deuteronomy 30:12 *10:7* [a]Deuteronomy 30:13 *10:8* [a]Deuteronomy 30:14 *10:11* [a]Isaiah 28:16 *10:13* [a]Joel 2:32 *10:15* [a]NU-Text omits *preach the gospel of peace, Who.* [b]Isaiah 52:7; Nahum 1:15 *10:16* [a]Isaiah 53:1 *10:18* [a]Psalm 19:4 *10:19* [a]Deuteronomy 32:21 *10:20* [a]Isaiah 65:1 *10:21* [a]Isaiah 65:2

FOR YOUR INFO
10:1

ISRAEL

Have you ever wondered what happened to the special relationship between God and the nation of Israel (v. 1)? Are the Jews still God's "chosen people"? Are the promises that God made to Abraham, Moses, David, and other Old Testament Hebrews still in effect? Or did God reject Israel when the nation rejected His Son, Jesus?

These are issues that Paul addresses in Romans 9–11. They are vitally important, because they relate to whether or not God is to be trusted.

Origins

God's relationship with Israel goes back thousands of years to the ancient Near East. The Bible presents Abraham (see Rom. 4:1) as the father of the nation. Abraham came from Ur, a city of ancient Sumer in Mesopotamia (Gen. 11:31), where he prospered before moving to the land of Canaan (Gen. 12:5).

There God entered into a covenant with Abraham, promising to bless his descendants and make them His special people (Gen. 12:1–3). Abraham was to remain faithful to God and to serve as a channel through which God's blessings could flow to the rest of the world.

Abraham's son Isaac had two sons, Esau and Jacob. God chose Jacob for the renewal of His promise to Abraham (Gen. 28:13–15). Jacob's name was changed to Israel after a dramatic struggle with God (Gen. 32:24–30; 35:9–15). The name Israel has been interpreted by different scholars as "prince with God," "he strives with God," "let God rule," or "God strives." The name was later applied to the descendants of Jacob through his twelve sons, the Hebrew people. These twelve tribes were called "Israelites," "children of Israel," and "house of Israel," identifying them clearly as the descendants of Israel.

God's Chosen People

God's covenant with Abraham was far more than a contract. A contract always has an end date, while a covenant, in the biblical sense, is a permanent arrangement. Furthermore, a contract generally involves only one part of a person, such as a skill, while a covenant covers a person's total being. Another striking feature is that God is holy, all-knowing, and all-powerful, yet He consented to enter into a covenant with Abraham and his descendants—weak, sinful, and imperfect as they were.

Thus, through Abraham, Israel became God's "chosen people." This covenant relationship was confirmed at Mount Sinai when the nation promised to perform "all the words which the Lord has said" (Ex. 24:3). When the people later broke their side of the agreement, they were called by their leaders to renew the covenant (2 Kin. 23:3).

God, of course, never breaks His promises, and throughout Israel's history, He has always lived up to His side of the covenant. That's why Paul can affirm that God has not "cast away" His people (Rom. 11:1). God's oath to raise up believing children to Abraham (Gen. 22:16–17) remains an "everlasting" covenant (Gen. 17:7).

This is good news for Jew and Gentile alike. For Jews it means that God has not abandoned His people. They still figure prominently in His plans and purposes. For Gentiles, it means that God is totally trustworthy. His word can be taken at face value. Are you basing your hope on the unalterable covenants of God? ◆

Because the Hebrews failed to honor their side of their covenant with God, He promised a new covenant through the prophet Jeremiah that would accomplish what the old covenant had failed to do. *See "The New Covenant," 1 Cor. 11:25.*

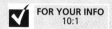

CHAPTER 11

God Has Not Given Up on His People

1 I say then, has God cast away His people? Certainly not! For I also am an Israelite, of the seed of
Abraham, *of* the tribe of Benjamin. 2 God has not
cast away His people whom He foreknew. Or do
you not know what the Scripture says of Elijah,
how he pleads with God against Israel, saying,
3 "LORD, they have killed Your prophets and torn
down Your altars, and I alone am left, and they
seek my life"? [a] 4 But what does the divine response
say to him? "I have reserved for Myself seven thousand men who have not bowed the knee to Baal."[a]
5 Even so then, at this present time there is a remnant according to the election of grace. 6 And if by
grace, then *it is* no longer of works; otherwise grace
is no longer grace.[a] But if *it is* of works, it is no
longer grace; otherwise work is no longer work.

7 What then? Israel has not obtained what it
seeks; but the elect have obtained it, and the rest
were blinded. 8 Just as it is written:

"God has given them a spirit of stupor,
Eyes that they should not see
And ears that they should not hear,
To this very day."[a]

9 And David says:

"Let their table become a snare and a trap,
A stumbling block and a recompense to them.
10 Let their eyes be darkened, so that they do not
see,
And bow down their back always."[a]

The Implications of Faith for Gentiles

11 I say then, have they stumbled that they should
fall? Certainly not! But through their fall, to provoke them to jealousy, salvation *has come* to the
Gentiles. 12 Now if their fall *is* riches for the world,
and their failure riches for the Gentiles, how much
more their fullness!

11:13–24
see pg. 560

13 For I speak to you Gentiles;
inasmuch as I am an apostle to
the Gentiles, I magnify my ministry, 14 if by any
means I may provoke to jealousy *those who are* my
flesh and save some of them. 15 For if their being
cast away *is* the reconciling of the world, what *will*
their acceptance *be* but life from the dead?

16 For if the firstfruit *is* holy, the lump *is* also *holy;*
and if the root *is* holy, so *are* the branches. 17 And if
some of the branches were broken off, and you, being a wild olive tree, were grafted in among them,
and with them became a partaker of the root and
fatness of the olive tree, 18 do not boast against the
branches. But if you do boast, *remember that* you
do not support the root, but the root supports you.

19 You will say then, "Branches were broken off
that I might be grafted in." 20 Well *said.* Because of
unbelief they were broken off, and you stand by
faith. Do not be haughty, but fear. 21 For if God did
not spare the natural branches, He may not spare
you either. 22 Therefore consider the goodness and
severity of God: on those who fell, severity; but toward you, goodness,[a] if you continue in *His* goodness. Otherwise you also will be cut off. 23 And they
also, if they do not continue in unbelief, will be
grafted in, for God is able to graft them in again.
24 For if you were cut out of the olive tree which is
wild by nature, and were grafted contrary to nature
into a cultivated olive tree, how much more will
these, who *are* natural *branches,* be grafted into
their own olive tree?

Israel Will Eventually Be Saved

25 For I do not desire, brethren, that you should
be ignorant of this mystery, lest you should be wise
in your own opinion, that blindness in part has
happened to Israel until the fullness of the Gentiles
has come in. 26 And so all Israel will be saved,[a] as it
is written:

"The Deliverer will come out of Zion,
And He will turn away ungodliness from
Jacob;
27 For this *is* My covenant with them,
When I take away their sins."[a]

28 Concerning the gospel *they are* enemies for
your sake, but concerning the election *they are*
beloved for the sake of the fathers. 29 For the gifts
and the calling of God *are* irrevocable. 30 For as you
were once disobedient to God, yet have now obtained mercy through their disobedience, 31 even so
these also have now been disobedient, that through
the mercy shown you they also may obtain mercy.

11:3 [a]1 Kings 19:10, 14 *11:4* [a]1 Kings 19:18 *11:6* [a]NU-Text omits the rest of this verse. *11:8* [a]Deuteronomy 29:4; Isaiah 29:10 *11:10* [a]Psalm 69:22, 23 *11:22* [a]NU-Text adds *of God.* *11:26* [a]Or *delivered* *11:27* [a]Isaiah 59:20, 21

[32]For God has committed them all to disobedience, that He might have mercy on all.

Paul's Prayer of Praise

[33]Oh, the depth of the riches both of the wisdom and knowledge of God! How unsearchable *are* His judgments and His ways past finding out!

34 "For who has known the mind of the LORD?
Or who has become His counselor?"[a]
35 "Or who has first given to Him
And it shall be repaid to him?"[a]

[36]For of Him and through Him and to Him *are* all things, to whom *be* glory forever. Amen.

CHAPTER 12

The Believer's Relationship to God

[1]I beseech you therefore, brethren, by the mercies of God, that you present your bodies a living sacrifice, holy, accept-

11:34 [a]Isaiah 40:13; Jeremiah 23:18 *11:35* [a]Job 41:11

CONSIDER THIS
11:13–24

ARE WE ONE PEOPLE?

By the time Paul wrote his letter to the Christians at Rome, Gentiles were probably becoming a majority of believers throughout the church. Jews had less and less influence theologically, culturally, or politically. Gradually—and tragically—the attitudes of pride and prejudice with which Jews had looked down on Gentiles were coming back to haunt them, as Gentile believers began to turn away from their Jewish brothers.

In Romans 9–11, Paul pleaded with his Gentile readers to remember that God has not forgotten Israel. God made promises to the nation that He cannot forsake (11:29). Furthermore, Gentiles have no room for arrogance: they were not originally included among God's people, but were allowed in, like branches grafted onto a tree (vv. 17–18).

Paul saw the possibility of a church divided, with Jewish and Gentile believers going their separate ways. If that happened, Gentiles would ignore the Jewish community altogether rather than show compassion and communicate the gospel so that Jews could be saved. That's why here, as elsewhere, Paul challenged believers to pursue unity in the body of Christ and charity among the peoples of the world.

able to God, *which is* your reasonable service. 2And do not
be conformed to this world, but be transformed by the renewing of your mind, that you may prove what *is* that good
and acceptable and perfect will of God.

The Believer's Position in the Body of Christ

12:3 see pg. 562

3For I say, through the grace given to
me, to everyone who is among you, not
to think *of himself* more highly than he ought to think, but
to think soberly, as God has dealt to each one a measure of
faith. 4For as we have many members in one body, but all
the members do not have the same function, 5so we, *being*
many, are one body in Christ, and individually members of
one another. 6Having then gifts differing according to the
grace that is given to us, *let us use them:* if prophecy, *let us*
prophesy in proportion to our faith; 7or ministry, *let us use it*
in *our* ministering; he who teaches, in

12:8

teaching; 8he who exhorts, in exhorta-
tion; he who gives, with liberality; he who leads, with diligence; he who shows mercy, with cheerfulness.
9*Let* love *be* without hypocrisy. Abhor what is evil. Cling
to what is good. 10*Be* kindly affectionate to one another with

QUOTE UNQUOTE

CONSIDER THIS 12:8 *If God has given you the capacity to give, give liberally (v. 8):*

We make a living by what we get.
We make a life by what we give.

Anonymous

Are we as believers today carrying out that exhortation? Unfortunately, the legacy that we've inherited is not encouraging. Had the church wholeheartedly embraced Paul's teaching, it would not have kept its tragic silence or participated in some of the great evils of the past 2,000 years. In fact, many of them probably could have been avoided, or at least resisted, had Christians paid careful attention to Romans 9–11.

We need to ask: What are the current challenges to the ethnic, racial, and cultural attitudes of believers? What tragic evils are currently operating that we need to be aware of and actively resisting? God's desire is clear—to have mercy on all (v. 32). Does that describe our heart? ◆

Paul was at pains to show that God's love and mercy extended to the whole world, both Jews and Gentiles. See how Paul accomplished that in Romans 9–11 by looking at the table, "God's Heart for the Whole World," Rom. 9:1.

brotherly love, in honor giving preference to one another;
11not lagging in diligence, fervent in spirit, serving the Lord;
12rejoicing in hope, patient in tribulation, continuing steadfastly in prayer; 13distributing to the needs of the saints,
given to hospitality.

The Believer's Service to the Community

14Bless those who persecute you; bless and do not curse.
15Rejoice with those who rejoice, and weep with those who
weep. 16Be of the same mind toward one another. Do not
set your mind on high things, but associate with the humble. Do not be wise in your own opinion.

17Repay no one evil for evil. Have regard for good things
in the sight of all men. 18If it is possible, as much as depends on you, live peaceably with all
men. 19Beloved, do not avenge your-
selves, but *rather* give place to wrath; for it is written,
"Vengeance *is* Mine, I will repay,"[a] says the Lord. 20Therefore

12:19–21

"If your enemy is hungry, feed him;
If he is thirsty, give him a drink;

12:19 [a]Deuteronomy 32:35

CONSIDER THIS
12:3

Do You Suffer from "Comparison-itis"?

One of the most debilitating diseases of the modern world is "comparisonitis"—the tendency to measure one's worth by comparing oneself to other people. You won't find this illness listed in any of the standard medical textbooks, nor will your company's disability or health insurance or worker's compensation program reimburse you for it. But make no mistake: comparisonitis is a scourge as widespread and destructive as any physical or emotional malady known today.

Do you suffer from it? Do you find ways to look down on others and think highly of yourself because you enjoy greater abilities, intelligence, status, or wealth than they? Or do you look down on yourself and envy others because you feel you are not as capable, smart, powerful, or rich as they?

Comparisonitis is an ancient disease. Certainly Paul was aware of how deadly it could be. That's why he offered an antidote for it—to see ourselves not as we stack up against others, nor as others evaluate us, but as God sees us *(v. 3). Ultimately, His estimation of our worth is what matters. And to Him we matter* a lot!

God does not define us according to culturally defined externals. Even our gender, ethnicity, family heritage, or

For in so doing you will heap coals of fire on his
head."[a]

21Do not be overcome by evil, but overcome evil with good.

CHAPTER 13

The Believer's Submission to the State

13:1–7 see pg. 564

1Let every soul be subject to the governing authorities. For there is no author-
ity except from God, and the authorities that exist are appointed by God. 2Therefore whoever
resists the authority resists the ordinance
of God, and those who resist will bring judgment on themselves. 3For rulers are not a terror to good works, but to
evil. Do you want to be unafraid of the authority? Do what
is good, and you will have praise from
the same. 4For he is God's minister to you
for good. But if you do evil, be afraid; for he does not bear
the sword in vain; for he is God's minister, an avenger to *execute* wrath on him who practices evil. 5Therefore *you* must

13:2 see pg. 565

13:4 see pg. 564

12:20 [a]Proverbs 25:21, 22

body type are not of primary importance to Him. No, He uses an altogether different set of criteria as the basis for how He deals with us, as several people in Scripture indicate:

- Paul *found that God's grace made him who he was (1 Cor. 15:10). He also discovered that despite his past, God had made him into a new person (2 Cor. 5:17).*
- Peter *learned that God's power gave him everything he needed to live his life and pursue godliness (2 Pet. 1:3).*
- Job *realized that all he had—family, friends, possessions, health—was ultimately from God (Job 1:21).*
- One of the psalmists *understood that God Himself had created him, "fearfully and wonderfully." Imagine what that did for his self-image! (Ps. 139:14).*

Do you suffer from comparisonitis? What needs to change in your self-assessment for you to see yourself as God sees you? ◆

Jesus told a parable that illustrates the deadly nature of comparisonitis. See "Comparisonitis Will Kill You," Luke 18:9–14.

Do Not Avenge Yourself

CONSIDER THIS 12:19–21 **Scripture is straightforward: no believer should avenge himself on others (v. 19). Why? Because God has reserved vengeance to Himself.**

What, then, can you do to those who hurt you? You must do them good, not evil (v. 21). If you do them evil, you will yourself be overcome by evil. You can't be too careful when it comes to vengeance. One of Satan's favorite tactics is to lure someone into doing evil by providing a "good" excuse for it. And retaliation feels so appealing.

But Scripture challenges you to overcome evil, both in yourself (the will to retaliate) and in those who harm you (by doing them good). Doing so will "heap coals of fire" on the heads of your enemies (v. 20). In other words, you may magnify their sense of guilt when they see that their evil against you is met by your good toward them. Indeed, their guilty conscience may drive them to repentance.

Does Paul mean that we can never defend ourselves or our property, or that criminals should go unpunished? See "An Eye for an Eye," Matt. 5:38–42; and "The Avengers," Rom. 13:4.

be subject, not only because of wrath but also for con-
13:6 see pg. 566
science' sake. 6For because of this you
also pay taxes, for they are God's minis-
ters attending continually to this very thing. 7Render therefore to all their due: taxes to whom taxes *are due,* customs
to whom customs, fear to whom fear, honor to whom
honor.

The Believer's Conduct

13:8 see pg. 567
8Owe no one anything except to love
one another, for he who loves another
has fulfilled the law. 9For the commandments, "You shall
not commit adultery," "You shall not murder," "You shall
not steal," "You shall not bear false witness,"[a] "You shall not
covet,"[b] and if *there is* any other commandment, are *all*
summed up in this saying, namely, "You shall love your
neighbor as yourself."[c] 10Love does no harm to a neighbor;
therefore love *is* the fulfillment of the law.
11And *do* this, knowing the time, that now *it is* high time
to awake out of sleep; for now our salvation *is* nearer than
when we *first* believed. 12The night is far spent, the day is at
hand. Therefore let us cast off the works of darkness, and
let us put on the armor of light. 13Let us walk properly, as in

13:9 [a]NU-Text omits *"You shall not bear false witness."* [b]Exodus 20:13–15, 17; Deuteronomy 5:17–19, 21 [c]Leviticus 19:18

THE AVENGERS

CONSIDER THIS 13:4

Governmental authorities are called by God to exact vengeance on those who do evil (v. 4). Is that inconsistent with Paul's command to believers not to avenge themselves (12:19–21)?

No, in Romans 12, Paul was addressing individuals in their private capacities. But in Romans 13, he was writing about representatives of governments in their official, public capacities. Private individuals are not to avenge themselves because God has reserved vengeance to Himself. But in doing so, God reserves the right to decide how He will bring about justice. Verse 4 indicates that one means He uses is government.

Jesus spoke along very similar lines. See "An Eye for an Eye," Matt. 5:38–42.

CONSIDER THIS 13:1–7

THE LIMITS OF POLITICAL AUTHORITY

When Paul wrote to the Roman believers about governing authorities (v. 1), there was no question as to what authorities he had in mind—the imperial government of Rome, probably led at the time by Nero. According to this passage, even Rome's harsh, corrupt system was established by God and deserved the respect and obedience of Christians.

However, Rome's authority—and all authority—was merely delegated authority. Ultimate authority belongs to God, as Paul pointed out. But that raises a tough question for believers, then as now: If governments are subordinate to God and accountable to Him for what they do, then aren't there limits on the extent to which believers must submit to them? Aren't there times when Christians need to obey God rather than human officials? If so, shouldn't the church pay attention to whether any particular civil government is usurping God's power and undermining His purposes rather than carrying out its intended function?

The early church had to wrestle with these issues.

the day, not in revelry and drunkenness, not in lewdness
and lust, not in strife and envy. [14]But put on the Lord Jesus
Christ, and make no provision for the flesh, to *fulfill its*
lusts.

CHAPTER 14

Controversial Practices

14:1–23 see pg. 568

[1]Receive one who is weak in the faith,
but not to disputes over doubtful things.
[2]For one believes he may eat all things, but he who is weak
eats *only* vegetables. [3]Let not him who eats despise him who
does not eat, and let not him who does not eat judge him
who eats; for God has received him. [4]Who are you to judge
another's servant? To his own master he stands or falls. Indeed, he will be made to stand, for God is able to make him
stand.

14:5 see pg. 566

14:5–13 see pg. 569

[5]One person esteems *one* day above another; another esteems every day *alike.*
Let each be fully convinced in his own
mind. [6]He who observes the day, ob-
serves *it* to the Lord;[a] and he who does not observe the day,
to the Lord he does not observe *it*. He who eats, eats to the

14:6 [a]NU-Text omits the rest of this sentence.

Rome's government was far more tolerant of Christians when Paul likely wrote Romans 13 than in the 90s, when John penned Revelation. Within that span of some 30 years, believers changed their view of Rome from God's "minister for good" (v. 4) to a usurper of power that deserved to fall. In fact, the book of Revelation is seen at one level as the story of Rome's fall.

Throughout church history, believers have struggled with whether to obey or resist evil governments. There are no easy answers. But one principle that Paul clearly affirms here is that government itself is intrinsically good, having been established by God. ◆

Governmental Authority

CONSIDER THIS 13:2 **Scripture challenges us as believers to subject ourselves to whatever governments we live under (vv. 1–7). Submission to authority is never easy. Human nature tends toward resistance and even rebellion, especially if government is imposed, incompetent, and/or corrupt. But as we struggle with how to respond to the systems in which we live, this passage offers some helpful perspectives:**

(1) God is the ultimate authority (v. 1). **Government as an institution has been established by God to serve His purposes. God raises up and does away with leaders.**

(2) Both followers and leaders are ultimately accountable to God (v. 2). **Submission to human authorities reflects our submission to God's authority.**

(3) God uses governments to carry out His good purposes on earth (v. 3). **Without question, some governments sometimes persecute those who do good. Paul had firsthand experience with that. But in the main, it's the lawbreaker, not the law-abiding citizen, who has something to fear from government.**

(4) Obedience is a matter of inner conviction as well as external law (v. 5). **Our motivation to obey must go beyond fear of punishment. As believers, we serve the highest of all authorities, God Himself.**

Our responses to authority tell others much about the sincerity of our commitment to Christ. See 1 Thess. 4:12; 1 Tim. 6:1; and Titus 2:9–10.

QUOTE UNQUOTE

CONSIDER THIS 14:5 *One modern-day believer who has become "fully convinced in his own mind" (v. 5) about Sundays has written:*

It is a gross error to suppose that the Christian cause goes forward solely or chiefly on weekends. What happens on the regular weekdays may be far more important, so far as the Christian faith is concerned, than what happens on Sundays.

Elton Trueblood, *Your Other Vocation,* p. 57

Lord, for he gives God thanks; and he who does not eat, to
the Lord he does not eat, and gives God thanks. 7For none
of us lives to himself, and no one dies to himself. 8For if we
live, we live to the Lord; and if we die, we die to the Lord.
Therefore, whether we live or die, we are the Lord's. 9For to
this end Christ died and rose[a] and lived again, that He
might be Lord of both the dead and the living. 10But why
do you judge your brother? Or why do you show contempt
for your brother? For we shall all stand before the judgment
seat of Christ.[a] 11For it is written:

"*As* I live, says the LORD,
Every knee shall bow to Me,
And every tongue shall confess to God."[a]

12So then each of us shall give account of himself to God.
13Therefore let us not judge one another anymore, but
rather resolve this, not to put a stumbling block or a cause
to fall in *our* brother's way.

Pursue Peace with Each Other

14I know and am convinced by the Lord Jesus that *there is*
nothing unclean of itself; but to him who considers any-

14:9 [a]NU-Text omits *and rose.* *14:10* [a]NU-Text reads *of God.* *14:11* [a]Isaiah 45:23

CONSIDER THIS 13:6

The High Calling of Government Service

The largest category of employment in many nations is government. That outrages some citizens, who see government as a massive, wasteful, scandal-plagued bureaucracy. But God takes a different view. If you work in government—as an elected or appointed official, a letter carrier, a police or military officer, a water-meter reader—you'll want to pay special attention to vv. 1–7.

Paul refers to governmental authorities as God's ministers *(vv. 4, 6), meaning "servants." It's the same word translated elsewhere as "deacons." The point is, if you work in government, you are ultimately God's worker. Your authority derives not just from the people, but from God Himself. (This is an amazing statement from Paul. He was not living under a democratically elected government, but under an imperial Roman system, probably headed by Nero!)*

Government, then, is established by God. That doesn't mean that He approves of everything governments or their representatives do. But good or bad, He chooses to allow them to exist and have authority. He actually works through them to accomplish His purposes.

As a government employee, you are a "minister for

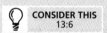

thing to be unclean, to him *it is* unclean. [15]Yet if your
brother is grieved because of *your* food, you are no longer
walking in love. Do not destroy with your food the one for
whom Christ died. [16]Therefore do not let your good be spoken of as evil; [17]for the kingdom of God is not eating and
drinking, but righteousness and peace and joy in the Holy
Spirit. [18]For he who serves Christ in these things[a] *is* acceptable to God and approved by men.
[19]Therefore let us pursue the things *which make* for peace
and the things by which one may edify another. [20]Do not
destroy the work of God for the sake of food. All things indeed *are* pure, but *it is* evil for the man who eats with offense. [21]*It is* good neither to eat meat nor drink wine nor *do*
anything by which your brother stumbles or is offended or
is made weak.[a] [22]Do you have faith?[a] Have *it* to yourself before God. Happy *is* he who does not condemn himself in
what he approves. [23]But he who doubts is condemned if he
eats, because *he does* not *eat* from faith; for whatever *is* not
from faith is sin.[a]

(Bible text continued on page 569)

14:18 [a]NU-Text reads *this.* *14:21* [a]NU-Text omits *or is offended or is made weak.* *14:22* [a]NU-Text reads *The faith which you have—have.* *14:23* [a]M-Text puts Romans 16:25–27 here.

◆ ◆ ◆ ◆ ◆ ◆ ◆ ◆ ◆ ◆ ◆ ◆ ◆ ◆ ◆

good." In what way? This passage describes one important category of governmental authority—policing citizens by motivating them to pursue good and punishing those who do evil. Of course, your work in the system may involve very different tasks. Still, God wants you to be a "minister for good" by helping society function, by meeting the needs of people, by protecting the rights of people, or by defending your country from attack.

With authority comes responsibility and accountability. As a "minister of God" you will answer to Him for your decisions and actions. If God promises to avenge the evil that citizens commit, how much more will He avenge the evil that those in authority commit? ◆

For a larger perspective on everyday work, see "People at Work," Heb. 2:7.

God gives government the right to revenge, but not private citizens. See "The Morality of Christ," Matt. 5:17–48.

DEBT-FREE LIVING

CONSIDER THIS 13:8 **Paul's admonition to owe nothing but love (v. 8) is a powerful reminder of God's distaste for all forms of unpaid debt.**

Usually we think of debt in terms of monetary loans. But in light of the context of this passage (13:1–7, 9–10), Paul seems to have a broader view of debt in mind (v. 7). He speaks to us of:

- ***Taxes,* levies placed on us by governing authorities, such as income and social security taxes.**
- ***Customs,* tolls and tariffs arising from trade and business, such as highway tolls, airport landing fees, and import fees.**
- ***Fear,* the respect we owe to those who enforce the law, such as police officers and military personnel.**
- ***Honor,* the praise we owe to those in high authority, such as judges and elected officials.**

All of us are debtors to God's grace. As He has shown us love, we need to extend love to those around us with whom we live and work—even those who tax and govern us.

CONSIDER THIS
14:1–23

MATTERS OF CONSCIENCE

One noticeable difference between Christianity and most other religions is that Christians are not bound by ritualistic rules. Paul discusses two examples here in Romans 14: special days of religious observance (vv. 5–13) and food (vv. 2–4, 14–23). However, the principles he sets forth apply to all matters of conscience, the "gray" areas of life for which Scripture prescribes no specific behavior one way or another.

Special observances and food were apparently trouble spots for the Roman believers. No doubt those from Jewish backgrounds brought their heritage of strict Sabbath-keeping and were shocked to find Gentile believers to whom Sabbath days were inconsequential. Likewise, some from pagan backgrounds may have encouraged the church to form its own counterparts to the festival days they had practiced in their former religions. Either way, the keeping of "holy days" created tension in the church.

So did the issue of eating meat. The pagan religions of the day offered meat as sacrifices to their idols. The meat was then sold to the general public. As it tended to be among the choicest cuts, it made for good eating. But many believers objected to eating such meat, or meat of any kind, lest they give tacit approval to the practice of idolatry. Others, however, saw no problem (v. 2). Again, Christians lined up on both sides of the issue. Predictably, people began to question each other's spirituality and dispute over whose position was "right" (v. 1).

Do these situations sound familiar? Perhaps meat sacrificed to idols is not an issue for believers today. But plenty of issues have managed to divide believers today. Does Paul offer any perspective on settling such disputes? Yes:

(1) No Christian should judge another regarding disputable things (vv. 3–4, 13). We may have opinions about what is right and wrong. But Christ is the Judge, for us and for others.

(2) Each person needs to come to his or her own convictions regarding matters of conscience (vv. 5, 22–23). God has given us a mind and the responsibility to think things through and decide what is best for ourselves in cases where the Scriptures are not clear. Unexamined morality is as irresponsible as no morality.

(3) We are not totally free to do as we please; we must answer to the Lord for our behavior (vv. 7–8, 12).

(4) We should avoid offending others by flaunting our liberty (v. 13). A "stumbling block" is an ancient metaphor for giving offense. It is easy to offend believers whose consciences are immature—that is, who lack the knowledge and confidence of their liberty in Christ (v. 2; 1 Cor. 8:9–12). This can happen in two ways: through trampling on their sensibilities by deliberately engaging in practices they find offensive; or through tempting them to engage in something they regard as sin. Even actions that are not inherently sinful can produce sin if they cause others to stumble.

(5) We should practice love, pursuing peace in the body and that which builds others up in the faith (vv. 15, 19). Christianity is just as concerned with community and healthy relationships as it is with morality. To be sure, there are matters that are worth fighting for. But where God is either silent or has left room for personal choice, believers need to practice tolerance and consider what is best for all. ◆

In a related text, Paul appeals to conscience for settling controversial issues. See "Gray Areas," 1 Cor. 8:1–13.

CHAPTER 15

Show Compassion to All

1We then who are strong ought to bear with the scruples
of the weak, and not to please ourselves. 2Let each of us
please *his* neighbor for *his* good, leading to edification. 3For
even Christ did not please Himself; but as it is written, "The
reproaches of those who reproached You fell on Me."[a] 4For
whatever things were written before were written for our
learning, that we through the patience and comfort of the
Scriptures might have hope. 5Now may the God of patience
and comfort grant you to be like-minded toward one another, according to Christ Jesus, 6that you may with one
mind *and* one mouth glorify the God and Father of our
Lord Jesus Christ.

15:7–12 see pg. 570

7Therefore receive one another, just as
Christ also received us,[a] to the glory of
God. 8Now I say that Jesus Christ has become a servant to
the circumcision for the truth of God, to confirm the
promises *made* to the fathers, 9and that the Gentiles might
glorify God for *His* mercy, as it is written:

"For this reason I will confess to You among the
Gentiles,
And sing to Your name."[a]

10And again he says:

"Rejoice, O Gentiles, with His people!"[a]

11And again:

"Praise the LORD, all you Gentiles!
Laud Him, all you peoples!"[a]

12And again, Isaiah says:

"There shall be a root of Jesse;
And He who shall rise to reign over the Gentiles,
In Him the Gentiles shall hope."[a]

13Now may the God of hope fill you with all joy and
peace in believing, that you may abound in hope by the
power of the Holy Spirit.

Paul's Confidence in His Readers

14Now I myself am confident concerning you, my
brethren, that you also are full of goodness, filled with all
knowledge, able also to admonish one another.[a] 15Neverthe-
less, brethren, I have written more boldly to you on *some*

15:3 [a]Psalm 69:9 *15:7* [a]NU-Text and M-Text read *you.* *15:9* [a]2 Samuel 22:50; Psalm 18:49 *15:10* [a]Deuteronomy 32:43 *15:11* [a]Psalm 117:1 *15:12* [a]Isaiah 11:10 *15:14* [a]M-Text reads *others.*

ARE SUNDAYS SPECIAL?

CONSIDER THIS 14:5–13 **In the Old Testament, God commanded the Hebrews to set aside one day a week as a "sabbath," a holy day of rest (Ex. 20:8–11; Is. 58:13–14; Jer. 17:19–27). Yet here in Romans, Paul seems to take a nondirective posture toward the Sabbath (14:5). Does that mean that there is no such thing as a "Lord's day," that God's people are no longer required to observe a Sabbath, whether it be Saturday or Sunday?**

Not exactly. For Paul, *every day* should be lived for the Lord because we are the Lord's possession (v. 8). If we act as if Sunday is the Lord's day but the other six days belong to us, then we've got a major misunderstanding. All seven days of the week belong to the Lord.

So the real question is, should one of those days be observed in a special way, in light of God's instructions regarding a sabbath? Paul says that neither pressure from other people nor tradition should bind our consciences. Instead, we are to seek guidance from the Spirit of God as to what we should do. Having inspired the Scriptures, God will help us determine what we should do as we study them.

For more on God's intentions regarding the Sabbath, see "The Sabbath," Heb. 4:1–13.

God's Rainbow

CONSIDER THIS 15:7–12 **Societies and their systems tend to encourage people to divide along racial, ethnic, and cultural lines, or else to abandon their distinctives by assimilating into the dominant power group. Paul called for a different approach. He didn't ask Jews to give up their Jewish heritage and become Gentiles, nor did he ask Gentiles to become Jews. Instead, he affirmed the rich ethnic backgrounds of both groups while challenging them to live together in unity (v. 7).**

That kind of unity is costly, and the attempt to practice it is always under attack. Yet that is the church that God calls us to—a diverse body of people who are unified around Christ. Our backgrounds—whether Japanese, Anglo-Saxon, African, Middle Eastern, Puerto Rican, Chinese, Italian, or whatever—are God's gifts to each of us and to the church. He has placed us in our families as He has seen fit. We can rejoice in the background He has given us and be enriched by the background He has given others.

points, as reminding you, because of the grace given to me
by God, 16that I might be a minister of Jesus Christ to the
Gentiles, ministering the gospel of God, that the offering of
the Gentiles might be acceptable, sanctified by the Holy
Spirit. 17Therefore I have reason to glory in Christ Jesus in
the things *which pertain* to God. 18For I will not dare to
speak of any of those things which Christ has not accomplished through me, in word and deed, to make the
Gentiles obedient— 19in mighty signs and wonders,
by the power of the Spirit of God, so that from Jerusalem and round about to Illyricum I have fully preached the
gospel of Christ. 20And so I have made it my aim to
preach the gospel, not where Christ was named, lest I
should build on another man's foundation, 21but as it is
written:

"To whom He was not announced, they shall see;
And those who have not heard shall understand."[a]

Paul Expects to Preach the Gospel at Rome

22For this reason I also have been much hindered from
coming to you. 23But now no longer having a place in these
parts, and having a great desire these many years to come to
15:24 you, 24whenever I journey to Spain, I
shall come to you.[a] For I hope to see you
on my journey, and to be helped on my way there by you,
if first I may enjoy your *company* for a while. 25But now I
am going to Jerusalem to minister to the saints. 26For it
pleased those from Macedonia and Achaia to make a certain
contribution for the poor among the saints who are in
Jerusalem. 27It pleased them indeed, and they are their
debtors. For if the Gentiles have been partakers of their
spiritual things, their duty is also to minister to them in
material things. 28Therefore, when I have performed this
and have sealed to them this fruit, I shall go by way of you
to Spain. 29But I know that when I come to you, I
shall come in the fullness of the blessing of the gospel[a] of
Christ.

30Now I beg you, brethren, through the Lord Jesus Christ,

15:21 [a]Isaiah 52:15 *15:24* [a]NU-Text omits *I shall come to you* (and joins *Spain* with the next sentence). *15:29* [a]NU-Text omits *of the gospel.*

Rest Stop in Rome

A CLOSER LOOK 15:24 *Many Bible readers assume that Paul's main goal in his work was to reach Rome, where he would preach the gospel to the leaders of the empire. But he intended to stop at Rome on his way to another strategic target, Spain (v. 24). He probably never made it that far. But why was Spain so important?* *See "All Roads Lead to Rome—and Beyond," Acts 28:28–31.*

and through the love of the Spirit, that you strive together
with me in prayers to God for me, 31that I may be delivered
from those in Judea who do not believe, and that my service
for Jerusalem may be acceptable to the saints, 32that I may
come to you with joy by the will of God, and may be refreshed together with you. 33Now the God of peace *be* with
you all. Amen.

CHAPTER 16

Personal Greetings

16:1

1I commend to you Phoebe our sister,
who is a servant of the church in
Cenchrea, 2that you may receive her in the Lord in a manner worthy of the saints, and assist her in whatever business

Personality Profile: Priscilla and Aquila

FOR YOUR INFO 16:3–5

Names mean: "Eagle" (Aquila); "ancient" (Priscilla, who was also called Prisca).

Background: Aquila was originally from Pontus in Asia Minor, bordering the Black Sea. They lived in Rome before Claudius forced all Jews to leave Rome. They then relocated to Corinth, and later to Ephesus. Eventually they returned to Rome.

Family: Priscilla might have grown up in a wealthy Roman family; Aquila might have been a Jewish freedman. Marrying across ethnic and socioeconomic lines was unusual in their day.

Occupation: Tentmaking—the manufacture of affordable mobile buildings for living, working, and traveling.

Best known today for: Taking Apollos the speaker aside and explaining to him the way of God more accurately (Acts 18:26); also helping to start at least three churches—at Rome, Corinth, and Ephesus.

Phoebe

CONSIDER THIS 16:1

Paul called Phoebe (v. 1) a *diakonos* (translated here as "servant," elsewhere as "deacon" or "minister") of the church at Cenchrea, the eastern port of Corinth. Does that means she held a formal position of responsibility? Possibly. Paul frequently referred to himself as a *diakonos* and used the same term in writing about male coworkers such as Apollos, Tychicus, Epaphras, and Timothy (1 Cor. 3:5; Eph. 6:21; Col. 1:7; 4:7; 1 Thess. 3:2).

Our understanding of exactly what it meant to be a *diakonos* in the early church is incomplete. Where the word appears in secular literature of the first century it refers to a helper of any sort who was not a slave. Whatever the role entailed, Paul commended Phoebe to the believers in Rome as a valued sister and one to be esteemed as one of his coworkers.

One important way that Phoebe may have assisted Paul was by taking his letter to Rome. The terms used to describe her suggest that she was a wealthy businesswoman of some influence. Perhaps she agreed to carry the document with her on business to the capital. Since couriers in the ancient world served as representatives of those who sent them, it is possible that Phoebe not only delivered the letter but also read it at different gatherings of Christians and discussed its contents with them.

Junia

CONSIDER THIS 16:7

Paul sends greetings to two fellow countrymen and fellow prisoners, Andronicus and Junia (v. 7). Was Junia a man or a woman? It is impossible to tell from the Greek text. The name could just as well be translated Ju-

(continued on next page)

(continued from previous page)

nias. However, in v. 3 Paul greets a couple, Priscilla and Aquila, then a man, Epaenetus (v. 4) and a woman, Mary (v. 5). Then he comes to Andronicus and Junia, whom he names together. Were they a couple, like Priscilla and Aquila? Again, it is impossible to say with certainty, but it is at least possible.

The interesting thing is that Paul describes these two as "of note among the apostles." That could mean either that they were actually apostles themselves or simply that the apostles held them in high esteem. If the former, and if Junia was a woman, that would mean that the early church had female apostles as well as male, and that it was not a movement led exclusively by men.

Right from the start the apostles were joined by women who had followed Christ. See "An Inclusive Prayer Meeting," Acts 1:14.

she has need of you; for indeed she has been a helper of
many and of myself also.

16:3–5 see pg. 571

3 Greet Priscilla and Aquila, my fellow
workers in Christ Jesus, 4 who risked their
own necks for my life, to whom not only I give thanks, but
also all the churches of the Gentiles. 5 Likewise *greet* the
church that is in their house.

Greet my beloved Epaenetus, who is the firstfruits of
Achaia[a] to Christ. 6 Greet Mary, who labored much for us.

16:7 see pg. 571

7 Greet Andronicus and Junia, my countrymen and my fellow prisoners, who are
of note among the apostles, who also were in Christ before
me.

8 Greet Amplias, my beloved in the Lord. 9 Greet Urbanus,
our fellow worker in Christ, and Stachys, my beloved.
10 Greet Apelles, approved in Christ. Greet those who are of
the *household* of Aristobulus. 11 Greet Herodion, my country-
man.[a] Greet those who are of the *household* of Narcissus
who are in the Lord.

16:12

12 Greet Tryphena and Tryphosa, who
have labored in the Lord. Greet the

16:13

beloved Persis, who labored much in the
Lord. 13 Greet Rufus, chosen in the Lord,

16:5 [a]NU-Text reads *Asia*. *16:11* [a]Or *relative*

FOR YOUR INFO
16:13

WHO WAS PAUL'S MOTHER?

In greeting Rufus and "his mother and mine*" (v. 13, italics added), Paul was probably not indicating his own actual mother, but rather a woman who played an important role in Paul's life.*

The apostle often used the image of a father or mother to describe his own unique relationship with certain Christians (1 Cor. 4:15; 1 Thess. 2:7), and some believers he called his children (1 Cor. 4:14; 1 Tim. 1:2; 2 Tim. 1:2; 2:1). He never explained exactly what he meant by those terms, but we can assume that those who received his letters knew what he meant. Apparently Paul had been instrumental in their lives in a way that a parent might be with a child.

In a similar way, the woman greeted in Romans 16:13 must have been especially important to Paul. Perhaps she had helped to nurture his faith, somewhat like Priscilla and Aquila with Apollos (see "Marketplace Mentors: Priscilla and Aquila," Acts 18:24–26; and "Apollos," Acts 18:24–28). Or perhaps she had helped to support Paul financially or in prayer. Whatever the case, he felt deeply enough toward her to refer to her as his mother.

Of Paul's actual mother, almost nothing is known. We

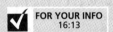

and his mother and mine. 14Greet Asyncritus, Phlegon, Her-
mas, Patrobas, Hermes, and the brethren who are with
them. 15Greet Philologus and Julia, Nereus and his sister,
and Olympas, and all the saints who are with them.
16Greet one another with a holy kiss. The[a] churches of
Christ greet you.

Warnings against False Teachers

17Now I urge you, brethren, note those who cause divisions and offenses, contrary to the doctrine which you
learned, and avoid them. 18For those who are such do not
serve our Lord Jesus[a] Christ, but their own belly, and by
smooth words and flattering speech deceive the hearts of
the simple. 19For your obedience has become known to all.
Therefore I am glad on your behalf; but I want you to be
wise in what is good, and simple concerning evil. 20And the
God of peace will crush Satan under your feet shortly.
The grace of our Lord Jesus Christ *be* with you. Amen.

Final Greetings and a Benediction

21Timothy, my fellow worker, and Lucius, Jason, and Sosipater, my countrymen, greet you.
22I, Tertius, who wrote *this* epistle, greet you in the Lord.

16:16 [a]NU-Text reads *All the churches.* *16:18* [a]NU-Text and M-Text omit *Jesus.*

can deduce that she must have been Jewish, because Paul was a Jew, and a Jewish heritage was determined through the mother. Paul said that he was born a Roman citizen (Acts 22:28), which meant his father must have been a Roman citizen before him. Apparently Paul was not their only child, for Luke mentions a sister (Acts 23:16).

However, we do have a clue as to the identity of the woman mentioned in Romans 16. The context implies that she was Rufus' actual mother. Rufus is probably the same man mentioned as one of the sons of Simon, the man who helped carry Jesus' cross (see Mark 15:21). If so, Rufus and his family were from Cyrene on the northern coast of Africa and were well known to the early church.

Whatever role Rufus' mother had in Paul's life, he certainly didn't forget her. Do you remember your mothers and fathers in the faith? ◆

Learn more about Paul's background through the two profiles, "Saul" and "Paul," Acts 13:2–3.

Paul's Female Coworkers

FOR YOUR INFO 16:12 **As Paul traveled throughout the Mediterranean, many believers labored with him to spread the message of Christ. Not a few of these valuable associates were women, several of whom are listed here in Romans 16.**

Paul literally owed his life to some of these coworkers. In several of his letters he lists their names and expresses his gratitude to them. Here are some of the women mentioned:

Women of the Early Church

- Apphia (Philem. 2)
- Euodia (Phil. 4:2–3)
- Junia (possibly a woman, Rom. 16:7)
- Lydia (Acts 16:13–40)
- Mary of Rome (Rom. 16:6)
- Nympha (Col. 4:15)
- Persis (Rom. 16:12)
- Phoebe (Rom. 16:1–2)
- Priscilla (Acts 18:1–28; Rom. 16:3; 1 Cor. 16:19; 2 Tim. 4:19)
- Syntyche (Phil. 4:2–3)
- Tryphena (Rom. 16:12)
- Tryphosa (Rom. 16:12)

Women also played a major part in Jesus' life and work, and helped take His message to the far reaches of the Roman world. See "The Women around Jesus," John 19:25; and the table, "Women and the Growth of Christianity," Phil. 4:3.

23Gaius, my host and *the host* of the whole
church, greets you. Erastus, the treasurer of the
city, greets you, and Quartus, a brother. 24The grace
of our Lord Jesus Christ *be* with you all. Amen.[a]
25Now to Him who is able to establish you according to my gospel and the preaching of Jesus
Christ, according to the revelation of the mystery
kept secret since the world began 26but now made
manifest, and by the prophetic Scriptures made
known to all nations, according to the commandment of the everlasting God, for obedience to the
faith— 27to God, alone wise, *be* glory through Jesus
Christ forever. Amen.[a]

16:24 [a]NU-Text omits this verse. *16:27* [a]M-Text puts Romans 16:25–27 after Romans 14:23.

A Collection of Sinners

Have you ever sighed, "I wish my church could be more like the church of the first century"? Perhaps you have in mind a small, closely knit community of believers who are radically committed to each other and, despite their number, are turning the community upside down with the gospel. What an exciting ideal! Unfortunately, the reality of the first churches probably wouldn't match it.

The church at Corinth is a good case in point. It had several excellent teachers and leaders, yet it struggled with the same problems many churches face today. The Corinthian church was an example of what churches look like, made up as they are of sinners saved by grace.

Depending on your expectations, the two Corinthian letters can make for encouraging reading. They point to the fact that there is no instant spirituality. Discipleship is a process. So if you and other believers around you sometimes seem less than Christlike, take heart! The Corinthians have walked this path before you. Despite their shortcomings, they held a special place in the heart of those who knew them best and helped them get started in the faith.

1 and 2 Corinthians

There is no instant spirituality.

Discipleship is a process.

CONTENTS

First-Century Christians, Twenty-first-Century Problems

The church at Corinth struggled with . . .

. . . Divisions over personalities and doctrine
(1 Cor. 1:10–17)

. . . Immaturity
(1 Cor. 3:1–9)

. . . Accountability
(1 Cor. 3:10–17; 5:1–2; 2 Cor. 1:12—2:4)

. . . Church discipline
(1 Cor. 5:3–13; 2 Cor. 2:5–11)

. . . Lawsuits
(1 Cor. 6:1–11)

. . . Immorality
(1 Cor. 6:18—7:1)

. . . Marriage and divorce
(1 Cor. 7:2–16)

. . . Insensitivity
(1 Cor. 8:1–13)

. . . Competing religions
(1 Cor. 10:1–14)

. . . Relating to unbelievers
(1 Cor. 10:27–30; 2 Cor. 6:11—7:1)

. . . Styles of worship
(1 Cor. 11:2–34)

. . . Prophecy and tongues
(1 Cor. 14:1–40)

. . . The nature of the gospel
(1 Cor. 15:1–11)

. . . Assistance for the poor
(1 Cor. 16:1–9; 2 Cor. 8:1—9:15)

. . . Money and generosity
(2 Cor. 9:6–15)

ARTICLES

Listening In on a Private Conversation

To read 1 & 2 Corinthians is to read someone else's mail. In contrast to Romans, these letters of Paul are very personal, and perhaps for that reason, very enlightening. What we have here are not fancy ideas dressed up in high-sounding words, but straight talk for a church working through everyday problems.

Actually, several letters passed between Paul and the Corinthians, including at least one between 1 & 2 Corinthians (2 Cor. 2:3). As in listening to one side of a telephone conversation, one has to infer what issues and questions made up the correspondence, based on the two letters that survive.

Paul had written a first, unpreserved letter from Ephesus (during his long stay mentioned in Acts 20:31) in which he warned the congregation about mixing with sexually immoral people (1 Cor. 5:9). That was an ever-present danger in Corinth. Most of the believers there had come from pagan backgrounds (12:2), and perhaps some had previously engaged in the idolatrous practices—including ritual prostitution—of the city's dozens of shrines and pagan temples. (The most prominent, the temple of Aphrodite, employed no less than 1,000 temple prostitutes.)

Paul's first letter must have failed to achieve its purpose, because certain problems persisted (1:11; 16:17). Apparently the Corinthians wrote a letter back to Paul, perhaps to justify their behavior, but also to ask him about other matters. He then wrote 1 Corinthians and minced no words in condemning the congregation's divisions and their continued tolerance of immorality. He also addressed their other concerns, as the repeated use of the words, "Now concerning," indicates (7:1, 25; 8:1; 12:1; 16:1).

But for all its stern language, 1 Corinthians also failed to correct the abuses. So Paul paid a visit to the church, but he was rebuffed (2 Cor. 2:1). Upon his return to Ephesus, he penned an extremely strident letter calculated to shock the stubborn Corinthians into obedience to Christ. (Most scholars believe that that letter has been lost. But some posit that it has been preserved in 2 Corinthians as chapters 10–13.)

Paul sent Titus to deliver the bombshell and then waited to hear the outcome. But Titus delayed in returning. As time passed, Paul felt increasingly alarmed that perhaps he had charged the epistle with a bit too much explosive. When he could contain his anxiety no longer, he set out for Corinth by way of Macedonia. But en route he encountered Titus, who, to his relief and joy, reported that the church had at last responded obediently. Heartened by this news, Paul wrote 2 Corinthians to bring healing to the relationship.

Christians today can profit by reading 1 and 2 Corinthians because they get behind the stereotyped images of what the church and the ministry are "supposed" to be. First Corinthians shows that churches are made up of real people living in the real world struggling with real problems. Likewise, 2 Corinthians shows that people in "full-time ministry" struggle with the same problems, doubts, and feelings as anyone else. As we read this correspondence, we need to ask, *If Paul came to my church and my community, what issues and problems would he see? And what would he say?*

Corinth

Beauty mingled with debauchery at Corinth. A "planned" city, it was less than 100 years old at the time of Paul. Stately gates at each city entrance opened onto well-maintained avenues with dozens of buildings and monuments built by the Roman emperors. City walls were lined with picturesque colonnades and countless residential shops. But Corinth was known less for its impressive architecture than its encouragement of gross immorality. *See "Corinth" at the Introduction to 2 Corinthians.*

The Power of Foolishness

CONSIDER THIS 1:18 **Paul recognized that the gospel appears foolish to most people (v. 18). Nowhere is that more apparent than in the workplace. In a tough, secular business environment, the message of Christ seems wholly out of place. Try to introduce it as relevant and you'll usually find stares of incredulity, if not outright protests.**

The irony is that the gospel is far more powerful than even the strongest players in the marketplace can imagine. But it remains impossible to receive except as the Holy Spirit opens a person's eyes.

This has a tremendous bearing on our witness as believers in the workplace. We need to keep communicating the message as persuasively and persistently as we can, all the while asking the Spirit to work His power, both in our own lives and in the lives of those around us.

One thing is certain about evangelism: both non-Christians and Christians feel uncomfortable with it. Fortunately, both have someone to help them in the process. See "Whose Job Is Evangelism?" John 16:8.

The message of the cross may be foolishness, but it was powerful enough to turn the Roman world upside down. See "Power," Acts 1:8.

CHAPTER 1

A Word of Greeting

1 Paul, called *to be* an apostle of Jesus Christ through the
will of God, and Sosthenes *our* brother,

2 To the church of God which is at Corinth, to those who
are sanctified in Christ Jesus, called *to be* saints, with all
who in every place call on the name of Jesus Christ our
Lord, both theirs and ours:

3 Grace to you and peace from God our Father and the
Lord Jesus Christ.

4 I thank my God always concerning you for the grace of
God which was given to you by Christ Jesus, 5 that you were
enriched in everything by Him in all utterance and all
knowledge, 6 even as the testimony of Christ was confirmed
in you, 7 so that you come short in no gift, eagerly waiting
for the revelation of our Lord Jesus Christ, 8 who will also
confirm you to the end, *that you may be* blameless in the
day of our Lord Jesus Christ. 9 God *is* faithful, by whom you
were called into the fellowship of His Son, Jesus Christ our
Lord.

The Corinthians Are Divided

10 Now I plead with you, brethren, by the name of our
Lord Jesus Christ, that you all speak the same thing, and
that there be no divisions among you, but *that* you be perfectly joined together in the same mind and in the same
judgment. 11 For it has been declared to me concerning you,
my brethren, by those of Chloe's *household,* that there are
1:12 contentions among you. 12 Now I say this,
that each of you says, "I am of Paul," or "I
am of Apollos," or "I am of Cephas," or "I am of Christ." 13 Is
Christ divided? Was Paul crucified for you? Or were you
baptized in the name of Paul?

14 I thank God that I baptized none of you except Crispus
and Gaius, 15 lest anyone should say that I had baptized in
my own name. 16 Yes, I also baptized the household of
Stephanas. Besides, I do not know whether I baptized any
other. 17 For Christ did not send me to baptize, but to
preach the gospel, not with wisdom of words, lest the cross
of Christ should be made of no effect.

Apollos

A CLOSER LOOK 1:12 *The name Apollos means "destroyer," but Apollos probably wouldn't have wanted the destructive factions that afflicted the church at Corinth. See "Apollos" at Acts 18:24–28.*

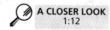

Wisdom Is Misunderstood

1:18

18For the message of the cross is foolishness to those who are perishing, but to us who are being saved it is the power of God. 19For it is written:

"I will destroy the wisdom of the wise,
And bring to nothing the understanding of the
prudent."[a]

20Where *is* the wise? Where *is* the scribe? Where *is* the disputer of this age? Has not God made foolish the wisdom of this world? 21For since, in the wisdom of God, the world through wisdom did not know God, it pleased God through the foolishness of the message preached to save those who believe. 22For Jews request a sign, and Greeks seek after wisdom; 23but we preach Christ crucified, to the Jews a stumbling block and to the Greeks[a] foolishness, 24but to those who are called, both Jews and Greeks, Christ the power of God and the wisdom of God. 25Because the foolishness of God is wiser than men, and the weakness of God is stronger than men.

1:23

1:26 see pg. 580

26For you see your calling, brethren, that not many wise according to the flesh, not many mighty, not many noble, *are called.* 27But God has chosen the foolish things of the world to put to shame the wise, and God has chosen the weak things of the world to put to shame the things which are mighty; 28and the base things of the world and the things which are despised God has chosen, and the things which are not, to bring to nothing the things that are, 29that no flesh should glory in His presence. 30But of Him you are in Christ Jesus, who became for us wisdom from God—and righteousness and sanctification and redemption— 31that, as it is written, "He who glories, let him glory in the LORD."[a]

CHAPTER 2

Paul's Initial Visit Was in Weakness

1And I, brethren, when I came to you, did not come with excellence of speech or of wisdom declaring to you the testimony[a] of God. 2For I determined not to know anything among you except Jesus Christ and Him crucified. 3I was with you in weakness, in fear, and in much trembling. 4And my speech and my preaching *were* not with persuasive words of human[a] wisdom, but in demonstration of the

(Bible text continued on page 581)

1:19 [a]Isaiah 29:14 *1:23* [a]NU-Text reads *Gentiles.* *1:31* [a]Jeremiah 9:24 *2:1* [a]NU-Text reads *mystery.* *2:4* [a]NU-Text omits *human.*

QUOTE UNQUOTE

CONSIDER THIS 1:23 *Paul's message was "Christ crucified" (v. 23). The gospel has not changed, and the same bold message is needed today:*

I simply argue that the cross be raised again at the center of the marketplace, as well as on the steeple of the church. I am recovering the claim that Jesus was not crucified between two candles, but on a cross between two thieves; on the town garbage heap; at a crossroad so cosmopolitan that they had to write his title in Latin and Greek . . . at the kind of place where cynics talk smut, and thieves curse, and soldiers gamble. Because that's where He died. And that is what He died about. And that is where churchmen ought to be and what churchmen should be about.

George MacLeod, Founder of the Scottish IONA Community, recipient of the Templeton Award for religious leadership

CONSIDER THIS
1:26

MYTH #5

10 MYTHS ABOUT CHRISTIANITY

MYTH: CHRISTIANITY IS JUST A CRUTCH FOR THE WEAK

Many people today accept a number of myths about Christianity, with the result that they never respond to Jesus as He really is. This is one of ten articles that speak to some of those misconceptions. For a list of all ten, see 1 Tim. 1:3–4.

The believers at Corinth tended to think more highly of themselves than they ought to have. The result was conflict and division in the church. So Paul pointed out that most of them had little of which to boast (v. 26; see also 6:9–11). On the whole they were weak, sinful people saved only by the grace of God.

Today, the grace of God still reaches out to the weak, the downcast, the broken, and the oppressed. Perhaps for that reason, people who pride themselves on their strength and self-sufficiency have little use for the gospel. Indeed, some despise a faith that resists the proud but promises hope to the humble.

Is Christianity just another crutch for people who can't make it on their own? In one sense, yes. "Those who are well have no need of a physician," Jesus said, "but those who are sick. I have not come to call the righteous, but sinners, to repentance" (Luke 5:31–32). Jesus bypasses those who pretend to be invincible, those who think they have it all together. Instead He reaches out to those who know that something is wrong, that their lives are "sick" with "illnesses" such as greed, lust, cruelty, and selfishness.

Jesus knows that no one is spiritually healthy. No one is righteous enough to stand before a holy God. That's why He came into this world, to restore people to God. The good news is that Christ gives us the power to overcome sin and the ways it pulls us down time after time.

What happens to the "weak" who avail themselves of this "crutch"? Consider Mother Teresa, who emerged from an insignificant nunnery to love the helpless and homeless of Calcutta and became a worldwide symbol of compassion. Or consider Alexander Solzhenitsyn, a forgotten political prisoner rotting away in the gulag system of Stalinist Russia. Surrendering himself to Jesus, he gained renewed strength to challenge a totalitarian regime on behalf of human dignity and freedom.

These are but two examples from the millions who have thrown away the self-styled crutches on which they used to limp along the road of life, opting instead for the seasoned wood of the cross of Christ which has transformed their weakness into strength.

In one sense, Christianity is a crutch for the weak. But those who dismiss it for that reason usually do so to deny their own inadequacies. They use that excuse as a way to evade the claims God has on their lives. They cannot accept that He takes wounded, fractured people and makes them whole. ◆

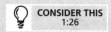

Spirit and of power, 5that your faith should not be in the
wisdom of men but in the power of God.

The Message Was God's Wisdom

6However, we speak wisdom among those who are mature, yet not the wisdom of this age, nor of the rulers of this
age, who are coming to nothing. 7But we speak the wisdom
of God in a mystery, the hidden *wisdom* which God ordained before the ages for our glory, 8which none of the
rulers of this age knew; for had they known, they would
not have crucified the Lord of glory.
9But as it is written:

> "Eye has not seen, nor ear heard,
> Nor have entered into the heart of man
> The things which God has prepared for those who love
> Him."[a]

10But God has revealed *them* to us through His Spirit. For
the Spirit searches all things, yes, the deep things of God.
11For what man knows the things of a man except the spirit
of the man which is in him? Even so no one knows the
things of God except the Spirit of God. 12Now we have received, not the spirit of the world, but the Spirit who is
from God, that we might know the things that have been
freely given to us by God.
13These things we also speak, not in words which man's
wisdom teaches but which the Holy[a] Spirit teaches, comparing spiritual things with spiritual. 14But the natural man
does not receive the things of the Spirit of God, for they are
foolishness to him; nor can he know *them*, because they are
2:15 spiritually discerned. 15But he who is
spiritual judges all things, yet he himself
is *rightly* judged by no one. 16For "who has known the mind
of the LORD that he may instruct Him?"[a] But we have the
mind of Christ.

CHAPTER 3

The Apostle's Role Misunderstood

1And I, brethren, could not speak to you as to spiritual
people but as to carnal, as to babes in Christ. 2I fed you with
milk and not with solid food; for until now you were not
able *to receive it*, and even now you are still not able; 3for
you are still carnal. For where *there are* envy, strife, and divisions among you, are you not carnal and behaving like *mere*
men? 4For when one says, "I am of Paul," and another, "I
am of Apollos," are you not carnal?

2:9 [a]Isaiah 64:4 *2:13* [a]NU-Text omits *Holy*. *2:16* [a]Isaiah 40:13

ARE WE TO JUDGE ALL THINGS?

CONSIDER THIS 2:15 **Paul's claim about judging all things (v. 15) sounds rather presumptuous. Is he urging believers to become moral policemen, passing judgment on everyone and everything around us?**

Yes and no. Paul was challenging the spiritually immature believers at Corinth to grow up by applying spiritual discernment to the world around them. In this passage he mentions three categories of people:

- ***natural*** **(v. 14), those without Christ, still living in the lost condition in which they were born;**
- ***spiritual*** **(v. 15), believers in Christ who have been born of the Spirit and in whom the Spirit of God lives and is producing growth; and**
- ***carnal*** **(3:1), believers who remain immature in the faith because they don't allow the Spirit to work in their lives.**

Spiritual people "judge" all things that come their way (v. 15) in the sense of scrutinizing, examining, and investigating spiritual value and implications. This is not something that we should do merely as individuals, but also corporately with other believers. For example, in the workplace Christians in various occupations need to band together to explore how the faith applies to particular vocations. By analyzing work situations in light of Scripture, we can discern what the issues are and how we might respond with Christlikeness.

"Judging all things" has nothing to do with damning others, but with recognizing and doing what God would want. Instead of pride, it calls for humility, since God will be the final Judge of everything we do (2 Cor. 5:10).

Who Gets the Credit?

CONSIDER THIS 3:5–8 **Paul pointed out that the work of planting the church at Corinth was a joint venture between himself, Apollos, and the Lord (vv. 5–8). Actually, many others were involved as well. But the point was that cooperation, not competition, is what God desires.**

Paul was speaking about the start-up of a church, but the principles apply in the workplace as well. An attitude of competition worries about who gets the credit for success, which is really a selfish concern. By contrast, cooperative efforts over time generally result in achievements far greater than what any individual could do in isolation. That's because the skill, insight, and energy in an organization's work force have enormous potential. But that potential will never be realized if everyone's chief objective is to take credit for results.

Who gets the credit where you work? Do you promote cooperation toward mutual goals rather than competition between individual agendas?

* * *

Apollos was a silver-tongued orator, but he learned much of his theology from a hard-working couple. See his profile, Acts 18:24–28.

The Ultimate Performance Review

CONSIDER THIS 3:13–15 **People often joke about standing before God and having their lives examined. But the picture Paul paints in vv. 9–15 is anything but funny. He is dead serious about a day of accountability for believers. Most of us are familiar with performance reviews on**

(continued on next page)

3:5–8
[5]Who then is Paul, and who *is* Apollos,
but ministers through whom you be-
lieved, as the Lord gave to each one? [6]I planted, Apollos watered, but God gave the increase. [7]So then neither he who
plants is anything, nor he who waters, but God who gives
the increase. [8]Now he who plants and he who waters are
one, and each one will receive his own reward according to
his own labor.

A New Building for God

3:9 see pg. 584
[9]For we are God's fellow workers; you
are God's field, *you are* God's building.
[10]According to the grace of God which was given to me, as
a wise master builder I have laid the foundation, and another builds on it. But let each one take heed how he builds
on it. [11]For no other foundation can anyone lay than that
which is laid, which is Jesus Christ. [12]Now if anyone builds
on this foundation *with* gold, silver, precious stones, wood,
3:13–15
hay, straw, [13]each one's work will become
clear; for the Day will declare it, because
it will be revealed by fire; and the fire will test each one's
work, of what sort it is. [14]If anyone's work which he has
built on *it* endures, he will receive a reward. [15]If anyone's
work is burned, he will suffer loss; but he himself will be
saved, yet so as through fire.
[16]Do you not know that you are the temple of God and
that the Spirit of God dwells in you? [17]If anyone defiles the
temple of God, God will destroy him. For the temple of
God is holy, which *temple* you are.
[18]Let no one deceive himself. If anyone among you seems
to be wise in this age, let him become a fool that he may become wise. [19]For the wisdom of this world is foolishness
with God. For it is written, "He catches the wise in their
own craftiness";[a] [20]and again, "The LORD knows the
thoughts of the wise, that they are futile."[a] [21]Therefore let
no one boast in men. For all things are yours: [22]whether
Paul or Apollos or Cephas, or the world or life or death, or
things present or things to come—all are yours. [23]And you
are Christ's, and Christ *is* God's.

CHAPTER 4

No Room for Boasting

[1]Let a man so consider us, as servants of Christ and stewards of the mysteries of God. [2]Moreover it is required in
4:3–5 see pg. 586
stewards that one be found faithful. [3]But
with me it is a very small thing that I

3:19 [a]Job 5:13 *3:20* [a]Psalm 94:11

should be judged by you or by a human court.[a] In fact, I do
not even judge myself. 4For I know of nothing against myself, yet I am not justified by this; but He who judges me is
the Lord. 5Therefore judge nothing before the time, until
the Lord comes, who will both bring to light the hidden
things of darkness and reveal the counsels of the hearts.
Then each one's praise will come from God.

6Now these things, brethren, I have figuratively transferred to myself and Apollos for your sakes, that you may
learn in us not to think beyond what is written, that none
of you may be puffed up on behalf of one against the other.
7For who makes you differ *from another?* And what do you
have that you did not receive? Now if you did indeed receive *it,* why do you boast as if you had not received *it?*

Fools for Christ

8You are already full! You are already rich! You have
reigned as kings without us—and indeed I could wish you
did reign, that we also might reign with you! 9For I think
that God has displayed us, the apostles, last, as men condemned to death; for we have been made a spectacle to the
world, both to angels and to men. 10We *are* fools for Christ's
sake, but you *are* wise in Christ! We *are* weak, but you *are*
strong! You *are* distinguished, but we *are* dishonored! 11To
the present hour we both hunger and thirst, and we are
poorly clothed, and beaten, and homeless. 12And we labor,
working with our own hands. Being reviled, we bless; being
persecuted, we endure; 13being defamed, we entreat. We
have been made as the filth of the world, the offscouring of
all things until now.

Paul's Care for the Corinthians

14I do not write these things to shame you, but as my
beloved children I warn *you.* 15For though you might have
ten thousand instructors in Christ, yet *you do* not *have* many
fathers; for in Christ Jesus I have begotten you through the
gospel. 16Therefore I urge you, imitate me. 17For this reason
I have sent Timothy to you, who is my beloved and faithful
son in the Lord, who will remind you of my ways in Christ,
as I teach everywhere in every church.

18Now some are puffed up, as though I were not coming
to you. 19But I will come to you shortly, if the Lord wills,
and I will know, not the word of those who are puffed up,
but the power. 20For the kingdom of God *is* not in word but
in power. 21What do you want? Shall I come to you with a
rod, or in love and a spirit of gentleness?

(Bible text continued on page 586)

4:3 [a]Literally *day*

(continued from previous page)

the job. Paul describes the ultimate performance review—the moment when we stand before God and He evaluates the worth of our lives on the earth, not for salvation but for reward or loss.

Paul uses the image of metal being purified in a refining fire (vv. 13–15). The fire burns away the worthless impurities, leaving only what is valuable. Based on the values set forth in many passages of Scripture, we can imagine the kinds of things that constitute "gold, silver, [and] precious stones": acts of charity and kindness; ethical decision-making; the pursuit of justice and fair play; keeping our word; courage and perseverance in the face of opposition and persecution; humility; communicating the message of Christ to coworkers; honoring our marriage vows; working diligently at the work God gives us; trusting God to keep His promises. Whatever is left when the fire burns down, Paul says, God will reward us for it (v. 14).

Conversely, we can envision what sorts of "wood, hay, [and] straw" will burn up: the lies we've told; ways we may have cheated customers; abuse heaped on family and relatives; manipulation of situations to our advantage; selfishness of all kinds; the squandering of income on trivial luxuries; turning a deaf ear to the poor; damage allowed to our environment; the systems created to lock ourselves into power and lock others out; the arrogance of self-sufficiency; lack of faith.

When the smoke clears, what will be left of your life?

CONSIDER THIS 3:9

WORKPLACE MYTHS

Paul called himself one of God's "fellow workers" (v. 9). In a similar way, every one of us is a coworker with God (see "People at Work," Heb. 2:7). Yet certain distorted views of work have taken on mythical proportions in Western culture. They've had devastating effect on both the people and the message of Christ. Here's a sampling of these pernicious myths, along with a few points of rebuttal:

Myth: Church work is the only work that has any real spiritual value.

In other words, everyday work in the "secular" world counts for nothing of lasting value. Only "sacred" work matters to God.

Fact: Christianity makes no distinction between the "sacred" and the "secular."

All of life is to be lived under Christ's lordship. So when it comes to work, all work has essential value to God, and workers will answer to Him for how they have carried out the work He has given to them (1 Cor. 3:13).

Myth: The heroes of the faith are ministers and missionaries. "Lay" workers remain second-class.

This follows from the previous idea. If "sacred" work is the only work with eternal value, then "sacred workers" (clergy) are the most valuable workers. The best that "laypeople" can do is to support the clergy and engage in "ministry" during their spare hours.

Fact: God has delegated His work to everybody, not just clergy.

Among the main characters of Scripture are ranchers, farmers, fishermen, vintners, ironworkers, carpenters, tentmakers, textile manufacturers, public officials, construction supervisors and workers, military personnel, financiers, physicians, judges, tax collectors, musicians, sculptors, dancers, poets, and writers, among others. Nowhere does God view these people or their work as "second class" or "secular." Rather, their work accomplishes God's work in the world. As we do our work each day, we reflect the very image of God, who is a working God (see "God: The Original Worker," John 5:17). He spent six days working on the creation (Gen. 1:31—2:3), so we merely follow God's example when we work five or six days out of the week.

Myth: Work is a part of the curse.

According to this belief, God punished Adam and Eve for their sin by laying the burden of work on them: "In the sweat of your face you shall eat bread till you return to the ground" (Gen. 3:19). That's why work is so often drudgery, and why the workplace is driven by greed and selfishness.

Fact: Work is a gift from God.

The Bible never calls work a curse, but rather a gift from God (Eccl. 3:13; 5:18–19). God gave Adam and Eve work to do long before they ever sinned (Gen. 2:15), and He commends and commands work long after the fall (Gen. 9:1–7; Col. 3:23; 1 Thess. 4:11; see "Is Work a Curse?" Rom. 8:20–22).

Myth: God is no longer involved in His creation.

For many, if not most, modern-day workers, God is irrelevant in the workplace. He may exist, but He has little to do with everyday matters of the work world. These people don't care much about what God does, and they assume He doesn't care much about what they do, either.

Fact: God remains intimately connected with both His world and its workers.

Scripture knows nothing of a detached Creator. He actively holds the creation together (Col. 1:16–17) and works toward its ultimate restoration from sin (John 5:17; Rom. 8:18–25). He uses the work of people to accomplish many of His purposes. Indeed, believers ultimately work for Christ as their Boss (see "Who's the Boss?" Col. 3:22–24). He takes an active interest in how they do their work (Titus 2:9–10).

Myth: You only go around once in life—so you better make the most of it!

This is the "heaven can wait" perspective. Here-and-now is what matters; it's where the excitement is. Heaven is just a make-believe world of gold-paved streets and never-ending choirs. Boring! Why not enjoy your reward right now? Go for it!

Fact: God is saving the greatest rewards for eternity—and work will be among them.

Scripture doesn't offer much detail about life after death, but it does promise a future society remade by God where work goes on—without the sweat, toil, pain, or futility of the curse (Is. 65:17–25; Rev. 22:2–5). And as for the question of rewards, God plans to hand out rewards for how believers have spent their lives—including their work (1 Cor. 3:9–15).

Myth: The most important day of the week is Friday.

"Thank God it's Friday!" the secular work ethic cries. Because work is drudgery, weekends are for escaping—and catching up. There's no idea of a Sabbath, just a couple of days of respite from the grinding routine.

Fact: God wants us to pursue cycles of meaningful work and restorative rest.

A biblical view of work places a high value on rest. God never intended us to work seven days a week. He still invites us to join Him in a day of rest, renewal, and celebration. That restores us to go back to our work with a sense of purpose and mission. "Thank God it's Monday!" we can begin to say. ◆

Avoiding Morbid Introspection

CONSIDER THIS 4:3–5 **Paul wisely recognized that even our most conscientious attempts to maintain pure motives fall far short (vv. 3–5). Indwelling sin taints everything we do. But Paul didn't allow that to discourage him from aiming at high motives. Neither did he despair of doing anything good. He was content to do his best in life and let God be his Judge.**

Are you free from the chronic worry that your motives are not always pristine? Are you living under the grace of God?

Paul knew that someday he would face the ultimate performance review, when God would evaluate both his motives and actions. See 1 Cor. 3:9–15.

Cover-ups Deceive Everybody

CONSIDER THIS 5:1–13 **Evil can never be remedied by ignoring or hiding it. In fact, covering it up is the worst that can happen, for like yeast, evil does its terrible work from within (vv. 6–8).**

The same is true of believers who live in consistent disobedience to God's expressed will. Their behavior will badly infect the larger groups of which they are a part. It can even lead to a distorted perception of sin in which the group tolerates or even approves of disobedience among its own members yet condemns outsiders for the very same activity (Rom. 1:32; 1 Cor. 5:9–10).

(continued on next page)

CHAPTER 5

Immorality Must Be Dealt With

5:1–13 1It is actually reported *that there is*
sexual immorality among you, and such
sexual immorality as is not even named[a] among the Gentiles—that a man has his father's wife! 2And you are puffed
up, and have not rather mourned, that he who has done
this deed might be taken away from among you. 3For I indeed, as absent in body but present in spirit, have already
judged (as though I were present) him who has so done this
deed. 4In the name of our Lord Jesus Christ, when you are
gathered together, along with my spirit, with the power of
our Lord Jesus Christ, 5deliver such a one to Satan for the
destruction of the flesh, that his spirit may be saved in the
day of the Lord Jesus.[a]
6Your glorying *is* not good. Do you not know that a little
leaven leavens the whole lump? 7Therefore purge out the
old leaven, that you may be a new lump, since you truly are
unleavened. For indeed Christ, our Passover, was sacrificed
for us.[a] 8Therefore let us keep the feast, not with old leaven,
nor with the leaven of malice and wickedness, but with the
unleavened *bread* of sincerity and truth.
9I wrote to you in my epistle not to keep company with
sexually immoral people. 10Yet *I* certainly *did* not *mean* with
the sexually immoral people of this world, or with the covetous, or extortioners, or idolaters, since then you would
need to go out of the world. 11But now I have written to
you not to keep company with anyone named a brother,
who is sexually immoral, or covetous, or an idolater, or a
reviler, or a drunkard, or an extortioner—not even to eat
with such a person.
12For what *have* I *to do* with judging those also who are
outside? Do you not judge those who are inside? 13But those
who are outside God judges. Therefore "put away from
yourselves the evil person."[a]

CHAPTER 6

Lawsuits before Unbelievers

6:1–11 1Dare any of you, having a matter
against another, go to law before the
unrighteous, and not before the saints? 2Do you not know
that the saints will judge the world? And if the world will be

5:1 [a]NU-Text omits *named.* *5:5* [a]NU-Text omits *Jesus.* *5:7* [a]NU-Text omits *for us.*
5:13 [a]Deuteronomy 17:7; 19:19; 22:21, 24; 24:7

judged by you, are you unworthy to judge the smallest
matters? 3Do you not know that we shall judge angels?
How much more, things that pertain to this life? 4If
then you have judgments concerning things pertaining
to this life, do you appoint those who are least esteemed
by the church to judge? 5I say this to your shame. Is
it so, that there is not a wise man among you, not even one,
who will be able to judge between his brethren? 6But
brother goes to law against brother, and that before unbelievers!
7Now therefore, it is already an utter failure for you that
you go to law against one another. Why do you not rather
accept wrong? Why do you not rather *let yourselves* be
cheated? 8No, you yourselves do wrong and cheat, and *you
do* these things *to your* brethren! 9Do you not know that the
unrighteous will not inherit the kingdom of God? Do not be
deceived. Neither fornicators, nor idolaters, nor adulterers,
nor homosexuals,[a] nor sodomites, 10nor thieves, nor covetous, nor drunkards, nor revilers, nor extortioners will inherit the kingdom of God. 11And such were some of you.
But you were washed, but you were sanctified, but you
were justified in the name of the Lord Jesus and by the
Spirit of our God.

Liberty Does Not Mean License

6:12 see pg. 589

12All things are lawful for me, but all
things are not helpful. All things are lawful for me, but I will not be brought under the power of
any. 13Foods for the stomach and the stomach for foods, but
God will destroy both it and them. Now the body *is* not for
sexual immorality but for the Lord, and the Lord for the
body. 14And God both raised up the Lord and will also raise
us up by His power.
15Do you not know that your bodies are members of
Christ? Shall I then take the members of Christ and make
them members of a harlot? Certainly not! 16Or do you not
know that he who is joined to a harlot is one body *with her?*
For "the two," He says, "shall become one flesh."[a] 17But he
who is joined to the Lord is one spirit *with Him.*
18Flee sexual immorality. Every sin that a man does is outside the body, but he who commits sexual immorality sins
against his own body. 19Or do you not know that your body
is the temple of the Holy Spirit *who is* in you, whom you
have from God, and you are not your own? 20For you were
bought at a price; therefore glorify God in your body[a] and
in your spirit, which are God's.

6:9 [a]That is, catamites *6:16* [a]Genesis 2:24 *6:20* [a]NU-Text ends the verse at *body.*

(continued from previous page)

Paul challenged the Corinthians to confront the subtle deterioration they had allowed within their congregation (1 Cor. 5:5). However, once the perpetrator had repented, they were then to seek his restoration. Even though corrective activity among believers may be severe, confrontation should always be to promote healing rather than to expel wrongdoers (compare Matt. 18:15–22; 2 Cor. 10:8). There are no throwaway people in the kingdom of God.

The Scandal of Litigating Christians

CONSIDER THIS 6:1–11

Scripture is explicit: for a Christian to take another Christian to court is "an utter failure" (v. 7). What, then, should we as believers do when we have disputes that normally call for litigation? Paul recommends that we take the matter before wise believers who can make a judgment (vv. 4–5). But suppose we can't arrange that? Then Paul says it would be better to "accept wrong" than to go before unbelievers for judgment.

Does that categorically rule out lawsuits between Christians today? Not necessarily. Modern Christians disagree over how to apply this passage. Our society is very different from the first-century Roman Empire. But we know that early churches took Paul's instructions literally. They forbade their members to resort to the pagan courts of the day. Instead, they appointed their own elders to judge civil disputes between members.

Those courts gained such a reputation for justice that they even attracted non-Christians, who found them preferable to the notoriously corrupt imperial courts. Eventually, church courts replaced secular courts

(continued on next page)

(continued from previous page)

and for some six centuries were the most important, if not the only, courts in Europe.

Some Christians today are trying to restore this judicial function of the church. In the United States, Christian attorneys are working with church leaders to arbitrate church members' disputes. The decisions can even be legally binding if the disputants agree to that in advance.

How do you settle legal problems when other believers are involved? Are you willing to try everything short of litigation *first,* before even considering going to court?

CHAPTER 7

Instructions to Married Believers

7:1
1Now concerning the things of which
you wrote to me:
It is good for a man not to touch a woman. 2Nevertheless,
because of sexual immorality, let each man have his own
7:3–6 see pg. 590
wife, and let each woman have her own
husband. 3Let the husband render to his
wife the affection due her, and likewise also the wife to her
husband. 4The wife does not have authority over her own
body, but the husband *does.* And likewise the husband does
not have authority over his own body, but the wife *does.*
5Do not deprive one another except with consent for a time,
that you may give yourselves to fasting and prayer; and
come together again so that Satan does not tempt you because of your lack of self-control. 6But I say this as a conces-

CONSIDER THIS
7:1

PRACTICAL LESSONS ON MARRIAGE

Have you ever listened in on half of a telephone conversation, trying to figure out what the whole conversation is about? That's what we have in 1 Corinthians 7—half of a very important conversation on marriage between Paul and the Corinthian believers. But we can glean many practical lessons from this passage, for marriage was undergoing profound changes then just as it is today.

Some of the believers in the early church had married before they became Christians. They wondered whether they should divorce their unbelieving spouses in order to remarry Christians and live more wholeheartedly for Christ.

An argument could be made for that. After all, if people's primary loyalty were now to Jesus, shouldn't that invalidate their pre-conversion marriage vows? (Of course, it would also provide them with a convenient excuse to escape bad marriages.)

But Paul didn't recommend that. He viewed the abandonment of one's family as a very serious matter (vv. 10–11), arguing that the believer should stay in the marriage as long as possible (vv. 12–13). However, God desires peace in relationships (v. 15), and that may not be possible in a family where Christian values are not shared. If the unbeliever wants to leave, he or she should be allowed to do so (v. 15).

Many churches in different cultures around the world today are faced with very similar circumstances. For example:

sion, not as a commandment. 7For I wish that all men were
even as I myself. But each one has his own gift from God,
one in this manner and another in that.

Instructions to Single Believers

8But I say to the unmarried and to the widows: It is good
for them if they remain even as I am; 9but if they cannot exercise self-control, let them marry. For it is better to marry
than to burn *with passion.*

Instructions to Those Married to Unbelievers

10Now to the married I command, *yet* not I but the Lord:
A wife is not to depart from *her* husband. 11But even if she
does depart, let her remain unmarried or be reconciled to
her husband. And a husband is not to divorce *his* wife.
12But to the rest I, not the Lord, say: If any brother has a
wife who does not believe, and she is willing to live with
him, let him not divorce her. 13And a woman who has a

- *the new believer who wonders what to do, since her husband isn't interested in church or religion.*
- *the inner-city congregation that has members who live in common-law marriages. What should the church tell them?*
- *the recent immigrant who tells his pastor that he has two families, one in each of two countries. "Should I get rid of one or both of those families?" he wonders.*
- *a tribal chief who wants to join the church—along with his five wives. What should he do with the wives? Divorce them all? Keep one? If so, which one?*

Paul offers no simple solutions for any of these situations, but he does share one piece of very good news: it is possible for one believer to "sanctify" a family, that is, to be an agent of God's love and grace, and perhaps to eventually bring other family members into the faith. No matter how unconventional the situation might be, Scripture doesn't counsel sudden changes. God may have work left to do in that family, and He may use the believer to do it—if he or she stays. ◆

WHAT CONTROLS YOU?

CONSIDER THIS 6:12 **As Christians we live under grace, not law. We enjoy a certain freedom of choice and commitment. But Paul reminds us that our choices and commitments, while freely made, do not always bring freedom (v. 12). Often they overpower us: we no longer possess our possessions—they possess us! We can be consumed by our jobs, our wealth, our houses, our hobbies, even our churches.**

Are there any ways to manage this problem? Here are a few suggestions:

(1) Determine your limits. What can you actually handle? What is realistic?

(2) Let time go by before making decisions and commitments. Sooner or later you need to decide, but very few choices are better made sooner than later.

(3) Pay attention to agreement or disagreement with your spouse and/or a close friend or associate. There is wisdom in mutual decision-making.

(4) To manage the commitment you are taking on, what are you willing to give up? Taking on new responsibilities means trading one set of problems for another. Are you prepared for that?

(5) Commit to giving away as well as taking on. That declares your freedom from the tyranny of things and responsibilities.

A New View of Sexuality

CONSIDER THIS 7:3–6

In an era when Greek women were often deprived both emotionally and sexually, Paul insisted that the Christian husband should recognize and fulfill the needs of his wife (vv. 3–6). He declared that marriage partners have authority over each other. That means that both husband and wife were forbidden from using sex as a means of control, but were to enjoy mutuality in that aspect of their marriage.

The gospel required a different understanding of sex and marriage than the surrounding culture's. Two thousand years later, it still does.

husband who does not believe, if he is willing to live with
her, let her not divorce him. 14For the unbelieving husband
is sanctified by the wife, and the unbelieving wife is sanctified by the husband; otherwise your children would be unclean, but now they are holy. 15But if the unbeliever departs,
let him depart; a brother or a sister is not under bondage in
such *cases.* But God has called us to peace. 16For how do
you know, O wife, whether you will save *your* husband? Or
how do you know, O husband, whether you will save *your*
wife?

Calling and Vocation

7:17

17But as God has distributed to each
one, as the Lord has called each one, so
let him walk. And so I ordain in all the churches. 18Was
anyone called while circumcised? Let him not become uncircumcised. Was anyone called while uncircumcised? Let
him not be circumcised. 19Circumcision is nothing and uncircumcision is nothing, but keeping the commandments of
God *is what matters.* 20Let each one remain in the same calling in which he was called. 21Were you called *while* a slave?
Do not be concerned about it; but if you can be made free,
rather use *it.* 22For he who is called in the Lord *while* a slave
is the Lord's freedman. Likewise he who is called *while* free
is Christ's slave. 23You were bought at a price; do not be-

CONSIDER THIS 7:17–24

Career Changes

Modern workers place a high value on mobility and freedom of choice. So how should Christians in our culture deal with Paul's admonition to remain in the situation where God has called us (vv. 17–24)? That sounds terribly antiquated in a society where the average person changes careers at least four times in life. In the ancient world, people normally worked for a lifetime at the same job.

Paul wrote that becoming a believer doesn't necessarily mean a career change. Wherever God has assigned us, that is our calling and we should pursue it to God's glory. On the other hand, there is nothing in the faith that locks a person into a work situation, any more than an unmarried woman must remain single all her life (7:8–9).

Paul's teaching about vocation parallels what he wrote about pre-conversion marriage (7:10–16). A believer is not compelled to leave his or her unbelieving spouse. On the other hand, the marriage may be dissolved if necessary to maintain peace. In the same way, believers should not use conversion as an excuse to leave their jobs.

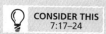

7:17–24

come slaves of men. 24Brethren, let each
one remain with God in that *state* in
which he was called.

Instructions Regarding Virgins

25Now concerning virgins: I have no commandment from
the Lord; yet I give judgment as one whom the Lord in His
mercy *has made* trustworthy. 26I suppose therefore that this
is good because of the present distress—that *it is* good for a
man to remain as he is: 27Are you bound to a wife? Do not
seek to be loosed. Are you loosed from a wife? Do not seek
a wife. 28But even if you do marry, you have not sinned; and
if a virgin marries, she has not sinned. Nevertheless such
will have trouble in the flesh, but I would spare you.
29But this I say, brethren, the time *is* short, so that from
now on even those who have wives should be as though
they had none, 30those who weep as though they did not
weep, those who rejoice as though they did not rejoice,
those who buy as though they did not possess, 31and those
who use this world as not misusing *it*. For the form of this
world is passing away.

7:32–35 see pg. 592

32But I want you to be without care. He
who is unmarried cares for the things of
the Lord—how he may please the Lord. 33But he who is
married cares about the things of the world—how he may

This is an important point because Christianity introduces new values into our lives that may make us anxious to escape our work environment. The atmosphere of language and jokes, competition and politics, quotas and numbers may begin to feel uncomfortable. Wouldn't it be easier to quit one's job and go to work for a Christian employer—or better yet, pursue a career in a church or ministry? But Paul didn't encourage that choice as the normal path. A job change may be a possibility, as Jesus' disciples found out. But it is not necessarily virtuous to leave our "nets," especially if our only reason is to escape the realities of the work world. ◆

It's actually an advantage for us to work alongside unbelievers so that we can communicate the message of Christ by how we do our jobs. See "Your Workstyle," Titus 2:9–10.

QUOTE UNQUOTE

CONSIDER THIS 7:17

Many believers today, like believers in Paul's day, struggle with how to bring their faith into their work. Should they quit their jobs and become vocational Christian workers? Paul did not encourage people to do that (v. 17). Here's a similar perspective from a twentieth-century believer:

Look: the question is not whether we should bring God into our work or not. We certainly should and must: as MacDonald says, "All that is not God is death." The question is whether we should simply (a) bring Him in in the dedication of our work to Him, in the integrity, diligence, and humility with which we do it, or also (b) make His professed and explicit service our job. The A vocation rests on all men whether they know it or not; the B vocation only on those who are specially called to it. Each vocation has its peculiar dangers and peculiar rewards.

C.S. Lewis, Letter to Sheldon Vanauken, Jan. 8, 1951

Gray Areas

CONSIDER THIS 8:1–13 **In first-century Corinth, meat sacrificed to idols (v. 1) proved to be an issue on which believers vehemently disagreed. It was a "gray" area of life, a matter for which there seemed to be no clear-cut instruction. How should Christians settle such disputes? Through a predetermined set of dos and don'ts? No, Paul offered a different perspective, one that appeals to conscience.**

Paul argued that food and drink

(continued on next page)

please *his* wife. 34There is[a] a difference between a wife and a
virgin. The unmarried woman cares about the things of the
Lord, that she may be holy both in body and in spirit. But
she who is married cares about the things of the world—
how she may please *her* husband. 35And this I say for your
own profit, not that I may put a leash on you, but for what
is proper, and that you may serve the Lord without distraction.

36But if any man thinks he is behaving improperly toward
his virgin, if she is past the flower of youth, and thus it
must be, let him do what he wishes. He does not sin; let
them marry. 37Nevertheless he who stands steadfast in his
heart, having no necessity, but has power over his own will,
and has so determined in his heart that he will keep his virgin,[a] does well. 38So then he who gives *her*[a] in marriage
does well, but he who does not give *her* in marriage does
better.

7:34 [a]M-Text adds *also.* *7:37* [a]Or *virgin daughter* *7:38* [a]NU-Text reads *his own virgin.*

YOU ARE THERE 7:32–35

Women and Work in the Ancient World

Paul's observation that a married woman must care about "the things of the world" (v. 34) hints at the busy lives that first century women lived, especially in the large cities of the Roman Empire.

The New Testament shows that women carried out a wide range of tasks: for example, drawing water, grinding grain, manufacturing tents, hosting guests, governing and influencing civic affairs, making clothes, teaching, prophesying and filling other spiritual functions, burying the dead, and doing the work of slaves, to name but a few. Additional evidence from the period reveals that women also served as wool workers, midwives, hairdressers, nurses, vendors, entertainers, political leaders, and even construction workers, among many other occupations.

If a woman was among the upper classes, she enjoyed relative economic security and social privileges. According to the Roman ideal, her role in society was to marry a citizen, produce legitimate heirs for him, and manage the household according to his orders. However, by the first century few families attained that ideal.

Wealthy women used slaves to perform such household tasks as cooking, making clothes, washing laundry, and caring for children (see "Children and Childcare," Matt. 19:14). Slaves also functioned as nurses, midwives, hairdressers, stenographers, and secretaries, and it was common for a high-ranking slave to be designated the household manager.

Instructions Regarding Remarriage

39 A wife is bound by law as long as her husband lives; but
if her husband dies, she is at liberty to be married to whom
she wishes, only in the Lord. 40 But she is happier if she remains as she is, according to my judgment—and I think I
also have the Spirit of God.

CHAPTER 8

The Controversy of Meat Offered to Idols

8:1–13

1 Now concerning things offered to
idols: We know that we all have knowl-
edge. Knowledge puffs up, but love edifies. 2 And if anyone
thinks that he knows anything, he knows nothing yet as he
ought to know. 3 But if anyone loves God, this one is known
by Him.
4 Therefore concerning the eating of things offered to

Female slaves were not only considered to be household property, but sexual property as well. The master of the house could legally force a slave to have sex with him, or with anyone he chose. Any children that she bore became his property. In this way a citizen could increase his number of slaves.

Women who were former slaves, or freeborn, lacked the economic security of either the citizen or the slave. Nevertheless, many women sought to buy their way out of slavery. Some of these working-class women earned their living as vendors, selling fish, grain, vegetables, clothing, or perfume. Others became wet nurses, and some chose to become entertainers or prostitutes, occupations that were considered beneath the dignity of respectable women. ◆

In Jewish homes, women were responsible not only for carrying out household tasks, but also for preparing the home for the Sabbath. See "Jewish Homemaking," Mark 1:29–31.

Not all first-century women centered their lives around domestic responsibilities totally. Lydia was a successful businesswoman in the purple trade (see profile at Acts 16:14) and Priscilla manufactured tents with her husband (see profile at Rom. 16:3–5).

(continued from previous page)

do not determine our relationship to God (v. 8). Meat offered to idols is inconsequential because, ultimately, there is no such thing as an idol (vv. 4–6). An idol is not God, so the mere fact that a priest blesses meat and offers it to an idol means nothing. From that point of view, Christians should be able to enjoy whatever food they want.

However, questionable practices may affect one's relationships with fellow believers or unbelievers (v. 9). As members of Christ's family we are obligated not to be a "stumbling block," but a loving neighbor. Our faith is not merely private, but has a corporate ethic and public responsibility as well.

So we live in a tension: God's grace frees us to choose as we please, but God's love requires us to ask questions of conscience about our choices. From what we eat, to whom we live and work with, to where we live, to what we do with our money and time—almost everything we do affects our neighbors (vv. 10–13). So we need to ask, are we treating them with love?

We need not allow others to manipulate us through legalistic criticism. But we do need discretion as to how our choices affect those around us. It's not enough to follow Christ just in our hearts; we also need to follow Him in our consciences.

Several other principles that apply to these issues can be found in "Matters of Conscience," Rom. 14:1–23.

idols, we know that an idol *is* nothing in the world, and
that *there is* no other God but one. 5For even if there are so-
called gods, whether in heaven or on earth (as there are
many gods and many lords), 6yet for us *there is* one God,
the Father, of whom *are* all things, and we for Him; and one
Lord Jesus Christ, through whom *are* all things, and
through whom we *live.*

7However, *there is* not in everyone that knowledge; for
some, with consciousness of the idol, until now eat *it* as a
thing offered to an idol; and their conscience, being weak,
is defiled. 8But food does not commend us to God; for neither if we eat are we the better, nor if we do not eat are we
the worse.

9But beware lest somehow this liberty of yours become a
stumbling block to those who are weak. 10For if anyone
sees you who have knowledge eating in an idol's temple,
will not the conscience of him who is weak be emboldened
to eat those things offered to idols? 11And because of your
knowledge shall the weak brother perish, for whom Christ

CONSIDER THIS
9:1–23

Paying Vocational Christian Workers

How much should pastors, missionaries, and others who work in churches and ministries be paid? Or should they be paid at all? Paul's example with the Corinthians offers some insight.

In Paul's day, philosophers traveled from city to city, teaching publicly for a fee. The more prestigious the teacher, the larger the fee. However, Paul charged the Corinthians *nothing when he came and delivered the gospel message. As a result, some were criticizing him, asserting that he must not be an authentic leader of the church if he was rendering his services for free.*

In reply, Paul explained himself (chapter 9). First, he insisted that those who labor spiritually should be supported materially by those with whom they work. He pointed to five familiar examples to support his position:

(1) Roman soldiers drew pay for their service (v. 7).
(2) Vintners enjoyed the fruits of their vineyards (v. 7).
(3) Shepherds received food from their flocks (v. 7).
(4) The Old Testament Law affirmed the right of laborers to receive fair compensation (vv. 8–10).
(5) The Law also allowed temple priests and attendants to live off of the sacrifices that the people brought (v. 13).

Paul also explained that the Lord Himself allowed those who preach the gospel to make their living from

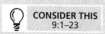

died? [12]But when you thus sin against the brethren, and
wound their weak conscience, you sin against Christ.
[13]Therefore, if food makes my brother stumble, I will never
again eat meat, lest I make my brother stumble.

CHAPTER 9

Paul's Own Example of Christian Liberty

9:1–23

[1]Am I not an apostle? Am I not free?
Have I not seen Jesus Christ our Lord?
Are you not my work in the Lord? [2]If I am not an apostle to
others, yet doubtless I am to you. For you are the seal of my
apostleship in the Lord.
[3]My defense to those who examine me is this: [4]Do we
have no right to eat and drink? [5]Do we have no right to take
along a believing wife, as *do* also the other apostles, the

9:6

brothers of the Lord, and Cephas? [6]Or *is*
it only Barnabas and I *who* have no right
to refrain from working? [7]Who ever goes to war at his own

that occupation (v. 14). Elsewhere the apostle wrote that church elders who rule well are worthy of "double honor" (1 Tim. 5:17–18). The context shows that Paul had payment in mind. In short, effective vocational Christian workers should be paid fairly for their labor.

Yet Paul refused payment in Corinth. Why? Because He felt that he owed it to God to communicate the gospel for free. When he considered his past and how God had saved him, the "chief of sinners" (1 Tim. 1:15), it was payment enough to be able to tell people about Jesus (1 Cor. 9:18).

Should workers in churches and ministries be paid? This passage insists that they have a right to a fair wage, and Christians today do well to pay attention to Paul's words here in light of the many workers who are leaving the ministry because of inadequate support. On the other hand, Paul's example opens the door to an alternative—the idea of carrying out ministry for free while supporting oneself through other means. That is also a model worth considering in a day when, for a variety of reasons, an increasing number of churches and ministries are strapped for funds. ◆

QUOTE UNQUOTE

CONSIDER THIS
9:6

Paul had a right to be paid for preaching the gospel (v. 6), but he did not use that right (vv. 12, 15–17). Instead, he made his living as a tentmaker. Perhaps his training as a Pharisee encouraged him in that direction:

Excellent is Torah study together with worldly business, for all Torah without work must ultimately fail and lead to sin.

Pirke Aboth ii:2

RACERS' STARTING BLOCKS

THE GAMES

YOU ARE THERE 9:24–27 **Paul's use of running, boxing, and other athletic feats (vv. 24–27) as metaphors for spiritual discipline was suited perfectly to the Corinthian culture. Corinth hosted numerous athletic events, including the prestigious Isthmian Games, one of four major athletic festivals of the Greeks.**

The Isthmian Games were held every other year and attracted athletes from all over Greece. The competitions were between individuals, not teams, who vied more for glory than for tangible prizes. At the Corinthian games, victors were crowned with pine needle garlands, the "perishable crown" to which Paul referred (v. 25).

However, when the heroes returned home, their cities might erect statues in their honor, have a parade, and write poems celebrating their feats. Sometimes a champion was even exempted from paying taxes, given free meals, and placed in the seat of honor at public events.

(continued on next page)

expense? Who plants a vineyard and does not eat of its
fruit? Or who tends a flock and does not drink of the milk
of the flock?
8Do I say these things as a *mere* man? Or does not the law
say the same also? 9For it is written in the law of Moses,
"You shall not muzzle an ox while it treads out the grain."[a]
Is it oxen God is concerned about? 10Or does He say *it* altogether for our sakes? For our sakes, no doubt, *this* is written, that he who plows should plow in hope, and he who
threshes in hope should be partaker of his hope. 11If we
have sown spiritual things for you, *is it* a great thing if we
reap your material things? 12If others are partakers of *this*
right over you, *are* we not even more?

A Servant to All

Nevertheless we have not used this right, but endure all
things lest we hinder the gospel of Christ. 13Do you not
know that those who minister the holy things eat *of the*
things of the temple, and those who serve at the altar partake of *the offerings of* the altar? 14Even so the Lord has commanded that those who preach the gospel should live from
the gospel.
15But I have used none of these things, nor have I written
these things that it should be done so to me; for it *would be*
better for me to die than that anyone should make my
boasting void. 16For if I preach the gospel, I have nothing to
boast of, for necessity is laid upon me; yes, woe is me if I do
not preach the gospel! 17For if I do this willingly, I have a
reward; but if against my will, I have been entrusted with a
stewardship. 18What is my reward then? That when I
preach the gospel, I may present the gospel of Christ[a] without charge, that I may not abuse my authority in the gospel.
19For though I am free from all *men,* I have made myself a
servant to all, that I might win the more; 20and to the Jews I
became as a Jew, that I might win Jews; to those *who are* under the law, as under the law,[a] that I might win those *who*
are under the law; 21to those *who are* without law, as without law (not being without law toward God,[a] but under law
toward Christ[b]), that I might win those *who are* without law;
22to the weak I became as[a] weak, that I might win the weak.
I have become all things to all *men,* that I might by all
means save some. 23Now this I do for the gospel's sake, that
I may be partaker of it with *you.*
9:24–27 24Do you not know that those who run
in a race all run, but one receives the

9:9 [a]Deuteronomy 25:4 *9:18* [a]NU-Text omits *of Christ.* *9:20* [a]NU-Text adds *though not being myself under the law.* *9:21* [a]NU-Text reads *God's law.* [b]NU-Text reads *Christ's law.* *9:22* [a]NU-Text omits *as.*

prize? Run in such a way that you may obtain *it.* 25And
everyone who competes *for the prize* is temperate in all
things. Now they *do it* to obtain a perishable crown, but we
for an imperishable *crown.* 26Therefore I run thus: not with
uncertainty. Thus I fight: not as *one who* beats the air. 27But I
discipline my body and bring *it* into subjection, lest, when I
have preached to others, I myself should become disqualified.

CHAPTER 10

The Example of Israel

1Moreover, brethren, I do not want you to be unaware
that all our fathers were under the cloud, all passed through
the sea, 2all were baptized into Moses in the cloud and in
the sea, 3all ate the same spiritual food, 4and all drank the
same spiritual drink. For they drank of that spiritual Rock
that followed them, and that Rock was Christ. 5But with
most of them God was not well pleased, for *their bodies*
were scattered in the wilderness.

6Now these things became our examples, to the intent
that we should not lust after evil things as they also lusted.
7And do not become idolaters as *were* some of them. As it is
written, "The people sat down to eat and drink, and rose up
to play."[a] 8Nor let us commit sexual immorality, as some of
them did, and in one day twenty-three thousand fell; 9nor
let us tempt Christ, as some of them also tempted, and were
destroyed by serpents; 10nor complain, as some of them also
complained, and were destroyed by the destroyer. 11Now
all[a] these things happened to them as examples, and they
were written for our admonition, upon whom the ends of
the ages have come.

10:12–13 see pg. 598

12Therefore let him who thinks he
stands take heed lest he fall. 13No temptation has overtaken you except such as is common to man;
but God *is* faithful, who will not allow you to be tempted
beyond what you are able, but with the temptation will also
make the way of escape, that you may be able to bear *it.*

Flee from Idolatry

14Therefore, my beloved, flee from idolatry. 15I speak as to
wise men; judge for yourselves what I say. 16The cup of
blessing which we bless, is it not the communion of the
blood of Christ? The bread which we break, is it not the
communion of the body of Christ? 17For we, *though* many,
are one bread *and* one body; for we all partake of that one
bread.

(Bible text continued on page 599)

10:7 [a]Exodus 32:6 *10:11* [a]NU-Text omits *all.*

(continued from previous page)

One of the important institutions associated with these athletic contests was the *gymnasium,* where young men were educated by the philosophers and trained in various physical routines. The name derived from the fact that the athletes trained and performed naked (*gumnos,* "naked"). That and the fact that gymnastic activities were closely tied to Greek culture made the institution repulsive to most Jewish people. But Paul's Corinthian readers were no doubt well acquainted with this prominent part of Greek life.

CONSIDER THIS
10:12–13

Pay Attention to Temptation!

Paul's warning to "take heed lest [you] fall" (v. 12) is as necessary today as it has ever been. For we, like all who have gone before us, are fallen, temptable, and subject to thinking and doing what is wrong. Few teachings of Scripture have more practical implications for day-to-day living.

Opportunities for temptation are almost endless. And since human nature is not getting any better, nor is any of us immune to the corrupted appetites of the flesh, we need to take Paul's warning seriously and watch out for temptation, or we will surely fall. Yet Scripture offers several alternatives for dealing with temptation as we find it:

(1) We should *avoid* temptation whenever possible. Proverbs 4:14–15 urges us, "Do not enter the path of the wicked, and do not walk in the way of evil. Avoid it, do not travel on it." Often we know beforehand whether a certain set of circumstances is likely to lead to sin. Therefore, the obvious way to avoid sin is to avoid those circumstances. Paul described a "way of escape" from temptation (1 Cor. 10:13). Often the escape is to stay away from the place or the people where temptation lurks.

As believers, we can help others in this regard. We can avoid setting up situations that encourage people to do wrong. Teachers, for example, can help students avoid cheating by making assignments, giving tests, and communicating expectations in ways that reduce the need or incentive to cheat. Likewise, business owners and managers can devise procedures that don't needlessly place employees in a position where they might be tempted to steal cash, inventory, or equipment. It's not that a teacher or employer can't trust students or employees, but that no one can trust human nature to be immune from temptation.

(2) We should *flee* from powerful temptations. Earlier in this letter, Paul warned the Corinthians to flee sexual immorality (6:18). Here he warned them to flee idolatry (v. 14). Elsewhere he warned Timothy to flee the lust for material possessions and wealth (1 Tim. 6:9–11), as well as youthful lusts (2 Tim. 2:22). The message is clear: don't toy with temptation. Flee from it!

(3) Chronic temptation is something we need to *confess* and offer to Christ and ask for His cleansing work. Some temptations are powerful inner struggles, with thoughts and attitudes that graphically remind us of how fallen we really are. What should we do with that kind of temptation? Rather than deny it or try to repress it, we should bring it to Christ. He alone is capable of cleaning up the insides of our minds.

(4) Finally, we must *resist* temptation until it leaves us. When Christ was tempted by the devil, He resisted until the devil went away (Matt. 4:1–11). James encouraged us to do the same (James 4:7). Resistance begins by bathing our minds with the Word of God and standing our ground. We have the promise, after all, that the temptations we experience will never go beyond the common experiences of others, or beyond our ability to deal with them (1 Cor. 10:13). That is great news! ◆

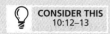

[18]Observe Israel after the flesh: Are not those who eat of
the sacrifices partakers of the altar? [19]What am I saying
then? That an idol is anything, or what is offered to idols is
anything? [20]Rather, that the things which the Gentiles sacrifice they sacrifice to demons and not to God, and I do not
want you to have fellowship with demons. [21]You cannot
drink the cup of the Lord and the cup of demons; you cannot partake of the Lord's table and of the table of demons.
[22]Or do we provoke the Lord to jealousy? Are we stronger
than He?

Do All to the Glory of God

[23]All things are lawful for me,[a] but not all things are helpful; all things are lawful for me,[b] but not all things edify.
[24]Let no one seek his own, but each one the other's *well-
being.*

10:25–26 see pg. 600

[25]Eat whatever is sold in the meat market, asking no questions for conscience'
sake; [26]for "the earth *is* the LORD's, and all its fullness."[a]
[27]If any of those who do not believe invites you *to dinner,*
and you desire to go, eat whatever is set before you, asking
no question for conscience' sake. [28]But if anyone says to
you, "This was offered to idols," do not eat it for the sake of
the one who told you, and for conscience' sake;[a] for "the
earth *is* the LORD's, and all its fullness."[b] [29]"Conscience," I
say, not your own, but that of the other. For why is my liberty judged by another *man's* conscience? [30]But if I partake
with thanks, why am I evil spoken of for *the food* over
which I give thanks?
[31]Therefore, whether you eat or drink, or whatever you
do, do all to the glory of God. [32]Give no offense, either to
the Jews or to the Greeks or to the church of God, [33]just as I
also please all *men* in all *things,* not seeking my own profit,
but the *profit* of many, that they may be saved.

CHAPTER 11

[1]Imitate me, just as I also *imitate* Christ.

Head Coverings for Women

11:2–16

11:3 see pg. 601

[2]Now I praise you, brethren, that you
remember me in all things and keep the
traditions just as I delivered *them* to you.
[3]But I want you to know that the head of
every man is Christ, the head of woman *is* man, and the
head of Christ *is* God. [4]Every man praying or prophesying,
having *his* head covered, dishonors his head. [5]But every

10:23 [a]NU-Text omits *for me.* [b]NU-Text omits *for me.* *10:26* [a]Psalm 24:1
10:28 [a]NU-Text omits the rest of this verse. [b]Psalm 24:1

HEAD COVERINGS

CONSIDER THIS 11:2–16 **Head coverings (vv. 4–6) were an important part of first-century wardrobes. Outdoors they provided both men and women protection from the intense sun and heat, as well as rain. In addition, a woman's head covering was a sign of modesty and commitment to her husband. Jewish and other women of the Near East wore veils in public, but Roman women never wore veils, and among the Greeks, some did and some did not. In some cultures, a woman without a veil was assumed to have loose morals.**

These cultural issues came to bear on the women believers at Corinth. Controversy arose over whether they were required to keep their heads covered during worship or not. Paul wrote that the churches had no universal policy on the matter (v. 16), indicating that the women had some freedom to choose how they would handle the issue.

Observing the custom to wear a

(continued on next page)

(continued from previous page)

covering may have been especially important in Corinth, where a favorite slogan was, "Everything is permissible" (compare 1 Cor. 6:12; 10:23). Paul was eager for Christians to maintain a good reputation and give no cause for offense so that people hearing the gospel would have no barriers to becoming followers of Christ.

woman who prays or prophesies with *her* head uncovered
dishonors her head, for that is one and the same as if her
head were shaved. 6For if a woman is not covered, let her
also be shorn. But if it is shameful for a woman to be shorn
or shaved, let her be covered. 7For a man indeed ought not
to cover *his* head, since he is the image and glory of God;
but woman is the glory of man. 8For man is not from
woman, but woman from man. 9Nor was man created for
the woman, but woman for the man. 10For this reason the
woman ought to have *a symbol of* authority on *her* head, because of the angels. 11Nevertheless, neither *is* man independent of woman, nor woman independent of man, in the
Lord. 12For as woman *came* from man, even so man also
comes through woman; but all things are from God.
13Judge among yourselves. Is it proper for a woman to

YOU ARE THERE
10:25–26

Food in the New Testament World

Meat sold in the Corinthian meat market (v. 25) was meat that had been offered to the Greek gods. Thus Paul had to address the moral question of whether a believer in Christ should buy and eat such food. His conclusion: don't worry about it; the earth and all its products belong to God (vv. 25–26).

Actually, ***beef*** *was something of luxury in ancient Greece and seldom eaten on a regular basis. A far more common source of meat was* ***fish****. Other items in a typical meal might be* ***cheese, leeks, olives, wine, oil, and vinegar****. Greece raised some* ***wheat,*** *but most of its* ***bread*** *was made from imported grain from Egypt or Asia Minor.*

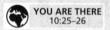

In Palestine, the land of "milk and honey" (Ex. 13:5), Hebrew farmers raised a variety of cereal grains such as ***wheat*** *and related products,* ***spelt, barley, and millet****. They also cultivated* ***cucumbers, squash, beans, lentils,***

pray to God with her head uncovered? [14]Does not even nature itself teach you that if a man has long hair, it is a dishonor to him? [15]But if a woman has long hair, it is a glory to
her; for *her* hair is given to her[a] for a covering. [16]But if anyone seems to be contentious, we have no such custom, nor
do the churches of God.

Impropriety in Worship

[17]Now in giving these instructions I do not praise *you,*
since you come together not for the better but for the
worse. [18]For first of all, when you come together as a
church, I hear that there are divisions among you, and in

11:15 [a]M-Text omits *to her.*

leeks, onions, and garlic. *Fruits and nuts included* ***melons, grapes and raisins, figs, apricots, oranges, almonds, and pistachios***.

Honey *was gathered from bees or made from* ***dates***. *Regional spices included* ***mint, anise, dill, and cummin***. *As in the rest of the Mediterranean,* ***olives*** *were plentiful. They were eaten green or ripe, or they might be pressed into* ***oil***, *which was used for cooking, seasoning, and as fuel for lamps.*

Beef and mutton *were a common part of the daily fare in Palestine, along with* ***milk, butter, and cheese***. *A noon meal for a workman might consist of two small loaves of* ***barley bread***—*one filled with cheese, the other with olives.*

Animals were divided into two classes by the Hebrews, clean and unclean (Lev. 11:1–47; Acts 10:9–15). Only ***clean animals***—*those that chewed the cud and had divided hooves—could be used for food (Lev. 11:3), except the fat (Lev. 3:16–17). Pigs and camels were ceremonially unclean and therefore unfit for food.* ***Camel's milk and cheese***, *however, were not forbidden.*

Many kinds of ***fish*** *could be eaten (Lev. 11:9–12), but not oysters or shrimp. Some twenty different species of* ***birds*** *were rejected (11:13–19). Insects that had legs and leaped, such as the* ***grasshopper***, *were fit for consumption.*

The major preservative for these foods was ***salt***. *An abundant supply was available from the Sea of Salt, or Dead Sea, in the south.* ◆

WHAT IS HEADSHIP?

CONSIDER THIS 11:3

What exactly did Paul mean when he used the word "head" (v. 3)? Some believe that the term by definition implies subordination of one person to another. Others disagree. For example, John Chrysostom, an early church leader, declared that only a heretic would understand "head" as chief or authority over. Rather, he understood the word as meaning absolute oneness, cause, or primal source.

Either way, it's important to note that while "the head of Christ is God" (v. 3), Christ is elsewhere shown to be equal with God (for example, John 1:1–3; 10:30; Col. 1:15). So the term "head" need not exclude the idea of equality. At the same time, even though Christ is the equal of God, He became obedient to the point of death (Phil. 2:5–8), demonstrating that equality need not rule out submission.

part I believe it. 19For there must also be factions among
you, that those who are approved may be recognized
among you. 20Therefore when you come together in one
place, it is not to eat the Lord's Supper. 21For in eating, each
one takes his own supper ahead of *others*; and one is hungry and another is drunk. 22What! Do you not have houses
to eat and drink in? Or do you despise the church of God
and shame those who have nothing? What shall I say to
you? Shall I praise you in this? I do not praise *you*.

The Proper Observance of the Lord's Supper

23For I received from the Lord that which I also delivered
to you: that the Lord Jesus on the *same* night in which He
was betrayed took bread; 24and when He had given thanks,
He broke *it* and said, "Take, eat;[a] this is My body which is
broken[b] for you; do this in remembrance
of Me." 25In the same manner *He* also

11:25

11:24 [a]NU-Text omits *Take, eat.* [b]NU-Text omits *broken.*

FOR YOUR INFO 11:25

THE NEW COVENANT

Even a casual reader of the Bible soon discovers that it is divided into two major sections, the Old Testament and the New Testament. But how many readers realize that "testament" is just another word for "covenant"? Thus, the New Testament describes the new covenant (v. 25), or agreement, that God has made with humanity, based on the death and resurrection of Jesus Christ.

In the Bible, a covenant involves much more than a contract or simple agreement. A contract has an end date, but a covenant is a permanent arrangement. Furthermore, a contract generally involves only one aspect of a person, such as a skill, while a covenant covers a person's total being.

God entered into numerous covenants with people in the Old Testament. For example: with Adam and Eve (Gen. 3:15); with Noah (Gen. 8:21–22; 2 Pet. 3:7, 15); with Abraham (Gen. 12:1–3); with Israel (Deut. 29:1—30:20); and with David (2 Sam. 7:12–16; 22:51).

The agreement with Israel was especially significant, because it established a special relationship between God and the Hebrews. They were made His "chosen people" through whom He would bring blessing and hope to the rest of the world. However, because the recipients of God's Law could not keep it perfectly, further provision was necessary for them as well as for the rest of humanity.

That's why God promised a new covenant through the prophet Jeremiah (Jer. 31:31). Under the new covenant,

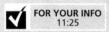

took the cup after supper, saying, "This cup is the new covenant in My blood. This do, as often as you drink *it,* in remembrance of Me."
[26]For as often as you eat this bread and drink this cup,
you proclaim the Lord's death till He comes.
[27]Therefore whoever eats this bread or drinks *this* cup of
the Lord in an unworthy manner will be guilty of the body
and blood[a] of the Lord. [28]But let a man examine himself,
and so let him eat of the bread and drink of the cup. [29]For
he who eats and drinks in an unworthy manner[a] eats and
drinks judgment to himself, not discerning the Lord's[b] body.
[30]For this reason many *are* weak and sick among you, and
many sleep. [31]For if we would judge ourselves, we would
not be judged. [32]But when we are judged, we are chastened
by the Lord, that we may not be condemned with the
world.

11:27 [a]NU-Text and M-Text read *the blood.* *11:29* [a]NU-Text omits *in an unworthy manner.* [b]NU-Text omits *Lord's.*

God would write His Law on human hearts. This suggested a new level of obedience and a new knowledge of the Lord.

The work of Jesus Christ brought the promised new covenant into being. When Jesus ate His final Passover meal with the Twelve, He spoke of the cup as "the new covenant in My blood" (Luke 22:20), the words that Paul quoted to the Corinthians to remind them of the need for purity and propriety in their worship (1 Cor. 11:25–34).

The new covenant in Jesus' blood rests directly on the sacrificial work of Christ on the cross (which was prefigured by Israel's system of sacrifices) and accomplishes the removal of sin and the cleansing of the conscience by faith in Him (Heb. 10:2, 22). So every time Christians celebrate the Lord's Supper, they remind themselves that God has fulfilled His promise: "I will be their God, and they shall be My people . . . I will be merciful to their unrighteousness, and their sins and their lawless deeds I will remember no more" (Heb. 8:10,12; compare Jer. 31:33–34). ◆

One of the striking features of God's covenant with Israel is that God is holy, all-knowing, and all-powerful, yet He consented to enter into a covenant with Abraham and his descendants—weak, sinful, and imperfect as they were. See "Israel," Rom. 10:1.

"TAKE, EAT; THIS IS MY BODY WHICH IS BROKEN FOR YOU."
—1 Corinthians 11:24

33 Therefore, my brethren, when you come together to eat,
wait for one another. 34 But if anyone is hungry, let him eat
at home, lest you come together for judgment. And the rest
I will set in order when I come.

CHAPTER 12

The Spirit Gives Gifts to Each Believer

1 Now concerning spiritual *gifts,* brethren, I do not want
you to be ignorant: 2 You know that[a] you were Gentiles,
carried away to these dumb idols, however you were led.
3 Therefore I make known to you that no one speaking by
the Spirit of God calls Jesus accursed, and no one can say
that Jesus is Lord except by the Holy Spirit.
4 There are diversities of gifts, but the same Spirit. 5 There
are differences of ministries, but the same Lord. 6 And there
are diversities of activities, but it is the same God who

12:2 [a]NU-Text and M-Text add *when.*

CONSIDER THIS
12:28–31

Are Some Jobs More Important Than Others?

Does a hierarchy of gifts (vv. 28–31) mean God values some jobs more than others? Judging by popular opinion, one might conclude that He does. In fact, for centuries Christians have subscribed to a subtle yet powerful hierarchy of vocations.

In our culture, that hierarchy tends to position clergy *(missionaries and evangelists, pastors and priests) at the top, members of the* "helping professions" *(doctors and nurses, teachers and educators, social workers) next, and* "secular" workers *(business executives, salespeople, factory laborers and farmers) at the bottom.*

So what determines the spiritual value of a job? How does God assign significance? The hierarchy assumes sacred and secular distinctions, and assigns priority to the sacred. But does God view vocations that way? No . . .

All legitimate work matters to God. *God Himself is a worker. In fact, human occupations find their origin in His work to create the world (Ps. 8:6–8). Work is a gift from Him to meet the needs of people and the creation.*

God creates people to carry out specific kinds of work. *God uniquely designs each of us, fitting us for certain kinds of tasks. He distributes skills, abilities, interests, and personalities among us so that we can carry out His work in the world. That work includes "spiritual" tasks, but also*

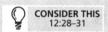

works all in all. [7]But the manifestation of the Spirit is given
to each one for the profit *of all:* [8]for to one is given the word
of wisdom through the Spirit, to another the word of
knowledge through the same Spirit, [9]to another faith by the
same Spirit, to another gifts of healings by the same[a] Spirit,
[10]to another the working of miracles, to another prophecy,
to another discerning of spirits, to another *different* kinds of
tongues, to another the interpretation of tongues. [11]But one
and the same Spirit works all these things, distributing to
each one individually as He wills.

[12]For as the body is one and has many members, but all
the members of that one body, being many, are one body, so
also *is* Christ. [13]For by one Spirit we were all baptized into
one body—whether Jews or Greeks, whether slaves or
free—and have all been made to drink into[a] one Spirit.
[14]For in fact the body is not one member but many.

12:9 [a]NU-Text reads *one.* *12:13* [a]NU-Text omits *into.*

extends to health, education, agriculture, business, law, communication, the arts, and so on.

God cares more about character and conduct than occupational status. *Paul's teaching in this passage is about gifts, not vocations. At the time Paul wrote it, there were few if any "professional" clergy in the church. Paul himself was a tentmaker by occupation, along with his friends, Aquila and Priscilla (1 Cor. 16:19; see Rom. 16:3–5). Other church leaders practiced a wide variety of professions and trades. God may assign rank among the spiritual gifts; but there's no indication that He looks at vocations that way.*

Furthermore, Scripture says there is something more important than gifts, "a more excellent way" (1 Cor. 12:31). Chapter 13 reveals it to be the way of Christlike love and character. Implication: If you want status in God's economy, excel at love, no matter what you do for work. Love has the greatest value to God (13:13; Matt. 22:35–40). ◆

Your work is like the work that God does, and it expresses something of who God is and what He wants done in the world. *See "People at Work," Heb. 2:7.*

Is it possible to hold a "secular" job and still seek the things of Christ? Or would it be better to quit and go into the ministry? *See "The Spirituality of Everyday Work," Col. 3:1–2.*

BY ONE SPIRIT WE WERE ALL BAPTIZED INTO ONE BODY. . . .
—1 Corinthians 12:13

Every Member Is Necessary

15If the foot should say, "Because I am not a
hand, I am not of the body," is it therefore not of
the body? 16And if the ear should say, "Because I
am not an eye, I am not of the body," is it therefore
not of the body? 17If the whole body *were* an eye,
where *would be* the hearing? If the whole *were* hearing, where *would be* the smelling? 18But now God
has set the members, each one of them, in the body
just as He pleased. 19And if they *were* all one member, where *would* the body *be?*

20But now indeed *there are* many members, yet
one body. 21And the eye cannot say to the hand, "I
have no need of you"; nor again the head to the
feet, "I have no need of you." 22No, much rather,
those members of the body which seem to be
weaker are necessary. 23And those *members* of the
body which we think to be less honorable, on these
we bestow greater honor; and our unpresentable
parts have greater modesty, 24but our presentable
parts have no need. But God composed the body,
having given greater honor to that *part* which lacks
it, 25that there should be no schism in the body,
but *that* the members should have the same care
for one another. 26And if one member suffers, all
the members suffer with *it;* or if one member is
honored, all the members rejoice with *it.*

27Now you are the body of Christ, and members
12:28–31 see pg. 604
individually. 28And God has appointed these in the church: first
apostles, second prophets, third teachers, after that
miracles, then gifts of healings, helps, administra-
tions, varieties of tongues. 29*Are* all apostles? *Are* all
prophets? *Are* all teachers? *Are* all workers of miracles? 30Do all have gifts of healings? Do all speak
with tongues? Do all interpret? 31But earnestly desire the best[a] gifts. And yet I show you a more excellent way.

CHAPTER 13

The Way of Love

13:1–13

1Though I speak with the
tongues of men and of angels,
but have not love, I have become sounding brass or
a clanging cymbal. 2And though I have *the gift of*
prophecy, and understand all mysteries and all
knowledge, and though I have all faith, so that I
could remove mountains, but have not love, I am
13:3
nothing. 3And though I bestow
all my goods to feed *the poor,* and
though I give my body to be burned,[a] but have not
love, it profits me nothing.

4Love suffers long *and* is kind; love does not
envy; love does not parade itself, is not puffed up;
5does not behave rudely, does not seek its own, is
not provoked, thinks no evil; 6does not rejoice in
iniquity, but rejoices in the truth; 7bears all things,
believes all things, hopes all things, endures all
things.

8Love never fails. But whether *there are* prophecies, they will fail; whether *there are* tongues,
they will cease; whether *there is* knowledge, it will
vanish away. 9For we know in part and we prophesy in part. 10But when that which is perfect
has come, then that which is in part will be done
away.

11When I was a child, I spoke as a child, I understood as a child, I thought as a child; but when I
13:12
became a man, I put away child-
ish things. 12For now we see in a
mirror, dimly, but then face to face. Now I know in
part, but then I shall know just as I also am
known.

13And now abide faith, hope, love, these three;
but the greatest of these *is* love.

12:31 [a]NU-Text reads *greater.* *13:3* [a]NU-Text reads *so I may boast.*

A Lifestyle of Love

A CLOSER LOOK 13:1–13 *In chapter 13, Paul described the lifestyle of love that Christ can produce in His followers. Elsewhere he painted a number of other pictures of what Christlikeness looks like. See "New Creatures with New Character," Gal. 5:22–23.*

Giving It All Away

A CLOSER LOOK 13:3 *Just as the Love Chapter suggests (v. 3), Christ told one man to sell all of his possessions and give the proceeds to the poor (Mark 10:17–27). Apparently He felt that doing so would bring eternal profit to the man. But the fellow could not bear to part with his goods. At least he was honest enough to turn away, even if in sadness, rather than fake love and end up with nothing. See "The Man Who Had It All—Almost," Mark 10:17–27.*

How should believers handle their money? See "Christians and Money," 1 Tim. 6:6–19.

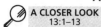

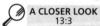

CHAPTER 14

The Value of Prophecy

1Pursue love, and desire spiritual *gifts,* but especially that
you may prophesy. 2For he who speaks in a tongue does not
speak to men but to God, for no one understands *him;* however, in the spirit he speaks mysteries. 3But he who prophesies speaks edification and exhortation and comfort to men.
4He who speaks in a tongue edifies himself, but he who
prophesies edifies the church. 5I wish you all spoke with
tongues, but even more that you prophesied; for[a] he who
prophesies *is* greater than he who speaks with tongues, unless indeed he interprets, that the church may receive edification.
6But now, brethren, if I come to you speaking with
tongues, what shall I profit you unless I speak to you either
by revelation, by knowledge, by prophesying, or by teaching? 7Even things without life, whether flute or harp, when
they make a sound, unless they make a distinction in the
sounds, how will it be known what is piped or played? 8For
if the trumpet makes an uncertain sound, who will prepare
for battle? 9So likewise you, unless you utter by the tongue
words easy to understand, how will it be known what is
spoken? For you will be speaking into the air. 10There are, it
may be, so many kinds of languages in the world, and none
of them *is* without significance. 11Therefore, if I do not know
the meaning of the language, I shall be a foreigner to him
who speaks, and he who speaks *will be* a foreigner to me.
12Even so you, since you are zealous for spiritual *gifts, let it
be* for the edification of the church *that* you seek to excel.

The Reason for Tongues

13Therefore let him who speaks in a tongue pray that he
may interpret. 14For if I pray in a tongue, my spirit prays,
but my understanding is unfruitful. 15What is *the conclusion*
then? I will pray with the spirit, and I will also pray with
the understanding. I will sing with the spirit, and I will also
sing with the understanding. 16Otherwise, if you bless with
the spirit, how will he who occupies the place of the uninformed say "Amen" at your giving of thanks, since he does
not understand what you say? 17For you indeed give thanks
well, but the other is not edified.
18I thank my God I speak with tongues more than you all;
19yet in the church I would rather speak five words with my
understanding, that I may teach others also, than ten thousand words in a tongue.
20Brethren, do not be children in understanding; however, in malice be babes, but in understanding be mature.

14:5 [a]NU-Text reads *and.*

QUOTE UNQUOTE

CONSIDER THIS 13:12 *One believer's reflections on seeing in a mirror dimly (v. 12):*

If we see dimly now with God as one image,
How well do we see with another sinner in the communication process here on earth?
No wonder human relations are so distorted.
But someday all hindrances will be removed!

Pete Hammond, *Marketplace Networks,* 1990

Not Permitted to Speak?

CONSIDER THIS 14:34 *When Paul writes that women should keep silent in the churches (v. 34), we are led to ask why in light of previous statements in the letter. He has already mentioned that women prayed and prophesied, presumably during worship services (11:5). Likewise, he has written that the Spirit gave gifts to everyone in the body (12:7, 11), and presumably some of the women received some of the speaking gifts. So why would he exhort the women to keep silent?*

One explanation is that the women in the congregation at Corinth probably had few opportunities for formal education and little exposure to large gatherings—except for the wild rites of their former religion. So when they came into the church, they may have assumed a similar approach to Christian worship. That would have been inappropriate, so Paul exhorted them to pursue a quieter, more orderly form of worship now that they were following the Lord.

21 In the law it is written:

"With *men of* other tongues and other lips
I will speak to this people;
And yet, for all that, they will not hear Me,"[a]

says the Lord.
22 Therefore tongues are for a sign, not to those who believe but to unbelievers; but prophesying is not for unbelievers but for those who believe. 23 Therefore if the whole
church comes together in one place, and all speak with
tongues, and there come in *those who are* uninformed or unbelievers, will they not say that you are out of your mind?
24 But if all prophesy, and an unbeliever or an uninformed
person comes in, he is convinced by all, he is convicted by
all. 25 And thus[a] the secrets of his heart are revealed; and so,
falling down on *his* face, he will worship God and report
that God is truly among you.

Order in Worship

26 How is it then, brethren? Whenever you come together,
each of you has a psalm, has a teaching, has a tongue, has a
revelation, has an interpretation. Let all things be done for
edification. 27 If anyone speaks in a tongue, *let there be* two
or at the most three, *each* in turn, and let one interpret.
28 But if there is no interpreter, let him keep silent in church,
and let him speak to himself and to God. 29 Let two or three
prophets speak, and let the others judge. 30 But if *anything* is
revealed to another who sits by, let the first keep silent.
31 For you can all prophesy one by one, that all may learn
and all may be encouraged. 32 And the spirits of the
prophets are subject to the prophets. 33 For God is not *the
author* of confusion but of peace, as in all the churches of
the saints.

14:34 34 Let your[a] women keep silent in the
churches, for they are not permitted to
speak; but *they are* to be submissive, as the law also says.
35 And if they want to learn something, let them ask their
own husbands at home; for it is shameful for women to
speak in church.

36 Or did the word of God come *originally* from you? Or
was it you only that it reached? 37 If anyone thinks himself to
be a prophet or spiritual, let him acknowledge that the
things which I write to you are the commandments of the
Lord. 38 But if anyone is ignorant, let him be ignorant.[a]

39 Therefore, brethren, desire earnestly to prophesy, and
do not forbid to speak with tongues. 40 Let all things be
done decently and in order.

14:21 [a]Isaiah 28:11, 12 *14:25* [a]NU-Text omits *And thus.* *14:34* [a]NU-Text omits *your.*
14:38 [a]NU-Text reads *if anyone does not recognize this, he is not recognized.*

CHAPTER 15

What the Gospel Is

[1]Moreover, brethren, I declare to you the gospel which I
preached to you, which also you received and in which you
stand, [2]by which also you are saved, if you hold fast that
word which I preached to you—unless you believed in
vain.
[3]For I delivered to you first of all that which I also received: that Christ died for our sins according to the Scriptures, [4]and that He was buried, and that He rose again the
third day according to the Scriptures, [5]and that He was seen
by Cephas, then by the twelve. [6]After that He was seen by
over five hundred brethren at once, of whom the greater
part remain to the present, but some have fallen asleep. [7]Af-
ter that He was seen by James, then by all the apostles.
[8]Then last of all He was seen by me also, as by one born out
of due time.

15:9–10
see pg. 610

[9]For I am the least of the apostles, who
am not worthy to be called an apostle,
because I persecuted the church of God. [10]But by the grace
of God I am what I am, and His grace toward me was not in
vain; but I labored more abundantly than they all, yet not I,
but the grace of God *which was* with me. [11]Therefore,
whether *it was* I or they, so we preach and so you believed.

Who Says There Is No Resurrection?

[12]Now if Christ is preached that He has been raised from
the dead, how do some among you say that there is no resurrection of the dead? [13]But if there is no resurrection of the
dead, then Christ is not risen. [14]And if Christ is not risen,
then our preaching *is* empty and your faith *is* also empty.
[15]Yes, and we are found false witnesses of God, because we
have testified of God that He raised up Christ, whom He
did not raise up—if in fact the dead do not rise. [16]For if *the*
dead do not rise, then Christ is not risen. [17]And if Christ is
not risen, your faith *is* futile; you are still in your sins!
[18]Then also those who have fallen asleep in Christ have perished. [19]If in this life only we have hope in Christ, we are of
all men the most pitiable.
[20]But now Christ is risen from the dead, *and* has become
the firstfruits of those who have fallen asleep. [21]For since by
man *came* death, by Man also *came* the resurrection of the
dead. [22]For as in Adam all die, even so in Christ all shall be
made alive. [23]But each one in his own order: Christ the
firstfruits, afterward those *who are* Christ's at His coming.

15:24

[24]Then *comes* the end, when He delivers
the kingdom to God the Father, when He

(Bible text continued on page 611)

The End of Authority

CONSIDER THIS 15:24 **Someday all authority, rule, and power will end—a sobering thought (v. 24). Peter mentioned a similar idea when he asked, in light of the end of the present time, what sort of people should we be (1 Pet. 3:10–13)? How should we live? No matter how hard we've worked to acquire and accrue power and position, it will eventually come to an end. That thought should challenge us to hold on lightly to the trappings of authority and use it wisely and responsibly for God's purposes.**

CONSIDER THIS
15:9–10

MYTH #6

10 MYTHS ABOUT CHRISTIANITY

MYTH: PEOPLE BECOME CHRISTIANS THROUGH SOCIAL CONDITIONING

Many people today accept a number of myths about Christianity, with the result that they never respond to Jesus as He really is. This is one of ten articles that speak to some of those misconceptions. For a list of all ten, see 1 Tim. 1:3–4.

Paul's statement that he persecuted the church prior to his conversion (vv. 9–10) is a strong piece of evidence against the commonly held notion that religious preference is mainly a result of upbringing.

Without question, cultural circumstances play a part in people's religious beliefs. A Hindu background would tend to predispose a person towards Hinduism, a Christian background toward Christianity, and so forth. But can social conditioning alone explain why people believe and behave as they do? After all, a Christian upbringing is no guarantee that a person won't someday abandon the faith. On the other hand, countless people who have had no exposure to Christianity in their youth nevertheless convert as adults.

The fact is, Christian conversion is much misunderstood. It is often regarded as sudden, irrational, selective, and even illusory. But what are its essential elements? Paul's experience is instructive. While certain aspects of his conversion were unique, four elements stand out that are present in every authentic conversion:

(1) *His conversion touched his conscience.* He recognized that he had been fighting God and that his vicious treatment of Christians was wrong (Acts 26:9–11; 1 Tim. 1:13).
(2) *His conversion touched his understanding.* He discovered that the Jesus he was persecuting was no less than the risen Messiah, the Son of God (Acts 9:22).
(3) *His conversion touched his will.* He gave in to Jesus and began following Him (Acts 26:19–20).
(4) *His conversion produced noticeable change in his life.* His ambitions, his character, his relationships, his outlook—everything changed as a result of his encounter with Christ (Phil. 3:7–11).

But suppose, as some have, that it all amounts to nothing but an illusion? Three tests can be applied to determine whether religious experience in general and Christianity in particular is illusory. First, there is the test of history. Christianity makes historical claims. Are those claims valid? Does history bear them out? Yes it does. There is nothing illusory about Jesus or His impact on the world. Nor are His claims illusory (see "Myth #1: Jesus Christ Was Only a Great Moral Teacher," Matt. 13:34–35). Likewise, His death and resurrection are well attested (see "Myth #2: There Is No Evidence That Jesus Rose From the Dead," Matt. 28:1–10). Nor is there any doubt about the reality of the church. In short, Christian faith is rooted in historical fact.

A second test is the test of character. When drunkards become sober and crooks become honest, when animists give up their mysticism and people enslaved by black magic are set free, when self-centered people become generous and unbelievers become giants of faith, it is very difficult to explain it away as illusion. Changed lives are not the only evidence of Christianity's authenticity, but they are certainly an impressive one.

(continued on next page)

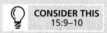

puts an end to all rule and all authority and power. 25For
He must reign till He has put all enemies under His feet.
26The last enemy *that* will be destroyed *is* death. 27For "He
has put all things under His feet."[a] But when He says "all
things are put under *Him,*" *it is* evident that He who put all
things under Him is excepted. 28Now when all things are
made subject to Him, then the Son Himself will also be subject to Him who put all things under Him, that God may be
all in all.

29Otherwise, what will they do who are baptized for the
dead, if the dead do not rise at all? Why then are they baptized for the dead? 30And why do we stand in jeopardy
every hour? 31I affirm, by the boasting in you which I have
in Christ Jesus our Lord, I die daily. 32If, in the manner of
men, I have fought with beasts at Ephesus, what advantage
is it to me? If *the* dead do not rise, "Let us eat and drink, for
tomorrow we die!"[a]

33Do not be deceived: "Evil company corrupts good habits." 34Awake to righteousness, and do not sin; for some do
not have the knowledge of God. I speak *this* to your shame.

A New Body

35But someone will say, "How are the dead raised up? And
with what body do they come?" 36Foolish one, what you
sow is not made alive unless it dies. 37And what you sow,
you do not sow that body that shall be, but mere grain—
perhaps wheat or some other *grain.* 38But God gives it a
body as He pleases, and to each seed its own body.

39All flesh *is* not the same flesh, but *there is* one *kind of*
flesh[a] of men, another flesh of animals, another of fish, *and*
another of birds.

40*There are* also celestial bodies and terrestrial bodies; but
the glory of the celestial *is* one, and the *glory* of the terrestrial *is* another. 41*There is* one glory of the sun, another glory
of the moon, and another glory of the stars; for *one* star differs from *another* star in glory.

15:42 see pg. 612

42So also *is* the resurrection of the
dead. *The body* is sown in corruption, it is
raised in incorruption. 43It is sown in dishonor, it is raised
in glory. It is sown in weakness, it is raised in power. 44It is
sown a natural body, it is raised a spiritual body. There is a
natural body, and there is a spiritual body. 45And so it is
written, "The first man Adam became a living being."[a] The
last Adam *became* a life-giving spirit.

46However, the spiritual is not first, but the natural, and
afterward the spiritual. 47The first man *was* of the earth,

(Bible text continued on page 613)

15:27 [a]Psalm 8:6 *15:32* [a]Isaiah 22:13 *15:39* [a]NU-Text and M-Text omit *of flesh.*
15:45 [a]Genesis 2:7

MYTH #6
10 MYTHS ABOUT CHRISTIANITY

(continued from previous page)

Finally there is the test of power. Delusions and neuroses tend to destroy people's character. They produce unbalanced behavior and keep people from achieving their goals. Christianity has precisely the opposite effect. It makes people whole. It even enables people to face death—a time when delusions are usually stripped away—with confidence and courage.

History, character, power: these cannot be attributed to social conditioning. Rather they strongly suggest that something far deeper lies behind Christianity, something good, powerful, and alive. ◆

Burial

Paul's doctrine of the resurrection (v. 42) flew in the face of prevailing ideas about the afterlife. To the Greek mind, death released a person's spirit from the prison of the body. The last thing a Greek would want was to be reunited with a corruptible body (v. 35).

Burial practices in Corinth and the other cities of the Roman Empire were largely a function of one's status in life. If the deceased was a member of the upper classes, the job of preparing the body was delegated to professional undertakers. They usually dressed the body in a toga adorned with badges and other tokens of the person's accomplishments and offices. Professional mourners and musicians then led a funeral procession to the burial site. Sometimes actors were recruited to follow the cortege, wearing masks that depicted the family's ancestors.

In Greek and Roman cultures, bodies were as likely to be cremated as buried. Either way, the rich tended to bury their dead in elaborate tombs. Some even formed cooperatives in which hundreds of urns were placed.

The poor, by contrast, laid their dead to rest in common, often unmarked graves. Or, if they lived in or near Rome, they might use the catacombs, a maze of underground tunnels outside the city. In the later years of the first century, Christians were not permitted to use regular cemeteries, so they resorted to the catacombs for their funerals. As persecution increased, some eventually fled there for survival.

Among the Hebrews, bodies were laid either in a shallow grave covered with stones or in a cave or tomb hewn out of stone and secured by a circular stone rolled and sealed over the entrance. Graves were often marked with a large, upright stone.

Due to the hot climate of Palestine, dead bodies decayed rapidly, so burial usually took place within a few hours after death. If someone died late in the day, burial took place the next day, but always within twenty-four hours after death.

The Hebrews did not follow the Greek custom of cremation, except in emergencies, nor did they generally use coffins. And even though they had historical ties to Egypt, they did not embalm their dead as the Egyptians did.

Mummification was invented by the Egyptians more than 3,000 years ago. They believed that the preservation of the body insured the continuation of the soul after death.

According to the Greek historian Herodotus, there were three different methods of embalming. The least expensive method involved emptying the intestines by flushing them with a cleaning

(continued on next page)

made of dust; the second Man *is* the Lord[a] from heaven.
48As *was* the *man* of dust, so also *are* those *who are* made of
dust; and as *is* the heavenly *Man*, so also *are* those *who are*
heavenly. 49And as we have borne the image of the *man* of
dust, we shall also bear[a] the image of the heavenly *Man*.
50Now this I say, brethren, that flesh and blood cannot inherit the kingdom of God; nor does corruption inherit incorruption. 51Behold, I tell you a mystery: We shall not all
sleep, but we shall all be changed— 52in a moment, in the
twinkling of an eye, at the last trumpet. For the trumpet
will sound, and the dead will be raised incorruptible, and
we shall be changed. 53For this corruptible must put on incorruption, and this mortal *must* put on immortality. 54So
when this corruptible has put on incorruption, and this
mortal has put on immortality, then shall be brought to pass
the saying that is written: "Death is swallowed up in victory."[a]

55 "O Death, where *is* your sting?[a]
O Hades, where *is* your victory?"[b]

56The sting of death *is* sin, and the strength of sin *is* the law.
57But thanks *be* to God, who gives us the victory through
our Lord Jesus Christ.
58Therefore, my beloved brethren, be steadfast, immovable, always abounding in the work of the Lord, knowing
that your labor is not in vain in the Lord.

CHAPTER 16

A Collection for Believers at Jerusalem

16:1–4 see pg. 615
1Now concerning the collection for the
saints, as I have given orders to the
churches of Galatia, so you must do also: 2On the first *day*
of the week let each one of you lay something aside, storing
up as he may prosper, that there be no collections when I
come. 3And when I come, whomever you approve by *your*
letters I will send to bear your gift to Jerusalem. 4But if it is
fitting that I go also, they will go with me.
5Now I will come to you when I pass through Macedonia
(for I am passing through Macedonia). 6And it may be that I
will remain, or even spend the winter with you, that you
may send me on my journey, wherever I go. 7For I do not
wish to see you now on the way; but I hope to stay a while
with you, if the Lord permits.

16:9–20 see pg. 614
8But I will tarry in Ephesus until Pentecost. 9For a great and effective door has
opened to me, and *there are* many adversaries.

15:47 [a]NU-Text omits *the Lord*. *15:49* [a]M-Text reads *let us also bear*. *15:54* [a]Isaiah 25:8
15:55 [a]Hosea 13:14 [b]NU-Text reads *O Death, where is your victory? O Death, where is your sting?*

(continued from previous page)

liquid, after which the body was soaked in natron. A second method called for placing the body in natron after the stomach and intestines had been dissolved by an injection of cedar oil.

The most elaborate method of embalming required the removal of the brain and all internal organs except the heart. The inner cavity of the body was then washed and filled with spices. The corpse was soaked in natron, then washed and wrapped in bandages of linen soaked with gum. Finally, the embalmed body was placed in a wooden coffin. These processes proved remarkably effective in preserving bodies from decay. ◆

Among Jews at the time of Christ, it was chiefly the women's task to prepare bodies for interment. See the article, "Funeral Preparations," John 12:1–8.

Greetings and Conclusion

16:10
[10]And if Timothy comes, see that he
may be with you without fear; for he
does the work of the Lord, as I also *do*. [11]Therefore let no
one despise him. But send him on his journey in peace, that
he may come to me; for I am waiting for him with the
brethren.
[12]Now concerning *our* brother Apollos, I strongly urged
him to come to you with the brethren, but he was quite unwilling to come at this time; however, he will come when he
has a convenient time.
[13]Watch, stand fast in the faith, be brave, be strong. [14]Let
all *that* you *do* be done with love.
[15]I urge you, brethren—you know the household of
Stephanas, that it is the firstfruits of Achaia, and *that* they
have devoted themselves to the ministry of the saints—

Timothy

A CLOSER LOOK 16:10

Timothy (v. 10) was one of Paul's most trusted and valued companions. To find out more about this promising young man, see his profile at the Introduction to 1 and 2 Timothy.

CONSIDER THIS 16:9–20

Enemies Become Family and Friends

Paul had once been a dangerous enemy to the followers of Christ. But his dramatic encounter with the Savior and subsequent change of heart brought him into the family of God (Acts 9:1–30). Courageous Christians such as Ananias (see 9:10) and Barnabas (see 4:36–37) began to nurture and aid the new believer. He had become a brother.

In the same way, Christ makes believers today into a new family. Having experienced the same gift from God—forgiveness and hope—we are now brothers and sisters in Christ.

Paul acknowledged several of his family of faith as he closed 1 Corinthians:

- *Young* Timothy *(1 Cor. 16:10–11), who needed acceptance and affirmation (see Timothy's profile at the Introduction to 1 and 2 Timothy).*
- *Gifted* Apollos *(v. 12), one of the Corinthians' former leaders (1:12) who was unable to go to them at that time (see "Apollos," Acts 18:24–28).*
- Stephanas *(vv. 15–16), baptized by Paul in the early days of the Corinthian church; the Corinthians needed to respect him.*

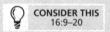

16that you also submit to such, and to everyone who works
and labors with *us*.
17I am glad about the coming of Stephanas, Fortunatus,
and Achaicus, for what was lacking on your part they supplied. 18For they refreshed my spirit and yours. Therefore
acknowledge such men.

16:19

19The churches of Asia greet you.
Aquila and Priscilla greet you heartily in
the Lord, with the church that is in their house. 20All the
brethren greet you.
Greet one another with a holy kiss.
21The salutation with my own hand—Paul's.
22If anyone does not love the Lord Jesus Christ, let him be
accursed.[a] O Lord, come![b]
23The grace of our Lord Jesus Christ *be* with you. 24My
love *be* with you all in Christ Jesus. Amen.

16:22 [a]Greek *anathema* [b]Aramaic *Maranatha*

Aquila and Priscilla

A CLOSER LOOK 16:19

Aquila and Priscilla (v. 19) were old friends of the Corinthians. In fact, they had been instrumental in starting the church at Corinth (Acts 18:1–11). To find out more about these valuable coworkers, business partners, and friends of Paul, see their profile at Rom. 16:3–5.

- Fortunatus and Achaicus *(vv. 17–18), encouragers of Paul who may have delivered to him the letter from the Corinthians that he was answering with 1 Corinthians; like Stephanas, they too needed recognition.*
- Priscilla and Aquila *(v. 19), co-founders of the Corinthian work and business partners with Paul (Acts 18:1–4); they now were leading a similar work at Ephesus and sent warm greetings to their brothers and sisters across the "wine dark" Aegean Sea (see "Priscilla and Aquila," Rom. 16:3–5).*

Once an enemy, Paul became a true friend, partner, and advocate of other believers. Just as others had once cared for him and his needs, he wrote to the Corinthians of the needs and concerns of his brothers and sisters in Christ.

Who are some of your friends in the faith? Who among them needs support or advocacy right now? To whom can you appeal on their behalf? ◆

MONEY: COMPASSION AND INTEGRITY

CONSIDER THIS 16:1–4

Money is powerful. It can bring out the best or the worst in a person. In our drive to gain lots of it or use it for personal comfort and convenience, we can become very cold and manipulative (1 Tim. 6:10). But that ought not to be the way for God's followers.

In 1 Corinthians 16, we see that Paul was coordinating a fund-raising drive to help some needy believers. He could have focused on the plight of the recipients. They were Christians in Jerusalem, perhaps suffering from persecution or famine. But instead he concentrated on how the Corinthians should initiate a regular pattern of giving to meet the need (1 Cor. 16:2). Their participation would be an act of loving worship as they met together on the first day of the week.

Paul also pointed out that the transfer of the funds would be carried out by responsible people chosen by the Corinthians themselves (v. 3). That guaranteed accountability and integrity. Apparently Paul was quite realistic about the human tendency toward manipulation and greed.

How are you using your money to alleviate suffering and meet the needs of others?

God is as interested in what Christians do with the money they keep as He is in the money they give away. See "Christians and Money," 1 Tim. 6:6–19.

2 Corinthians

CONTENTS

ARTICLES

Integrity In the Face of Competition (10:1)

When you face a competitive situation, are you tempted to do *whatever* it takes to win? Or can you keep the big picture, avoiding short-term gains in order to live with long-term, Christlike values?

When I Am Weak, Then I Am Strong (12:7–10)

It's hard to believe and it flies in the face of our culture's way of thinking, but weakness can make a person strong.

Spiritual Authority (13:10)

Anyone who exercises leadership among other believers will want to carefully study Paul's use of authority.

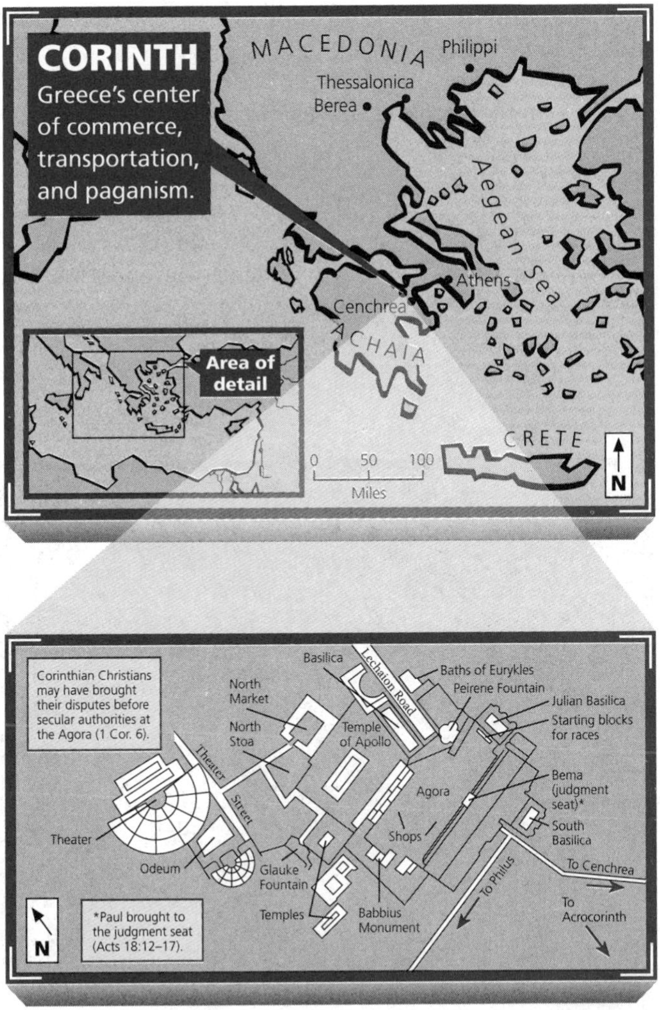

Corinth

- A major city of Greece situated on the Isthmus of Corinth between the Ionian Sea and the Aegean Sea.
- In New Testament times, perhaps the most celebrated city of the Roman Empire, second only to Rome.
- Less than 100 years old at the time of Paul.
- A "planned" city rebuilt from ashes by the Roman emperors.
- A transportation hub for both land and sea travel. Though not a seaport, its location on an isthmus linked two seaports and two bays. To save time and avoid potential disasters of sailing around Greece, shippers transported passengers and their goods across the isthmus and reloaded them onto ships on the other side.
- Greece's leading commercial center for trade, agriculture, and industry.
- Host city to numerous athletic events, gladiatorial contests, theater productions, and the Isthmian Games, one of four major athletic festivals of the Greeks.
- A major center for pagan religions. More than twelve temples have been excavated at Corinth, including the magnificent temple of Apollo, with its 38 Doric columns 24 feet high. The temple of Aphrodite, goddess of love, employed at least 1,000 temple prostitutes. The city had a widespread reputation for gross immorality.
- A city of diverse peoples and cultures, including Greeks, Roman colonists (mostly retired army veterans and freedmen), and Jews, some of whom migrated there during persecution under the emperor Claudius (Acts 18:1).

The Corinthians were first-century Christians but they struggled with a number of twenty-first-century problems. See the Introduction to 1 and 2 Corinthians.

CHAPTER 1

Comfort in the Midst of Trouble

1Paul, an apostle of Jesus Christ by the will of God, and
Timothy *our* brother,

To the church of God which is at Corinth, with all the
saints who are in all Achaia:

2Grace to you and peace from God our Father and the
Lord Jesus Christ.
3Blessed *be* the God and Father of our Lord Jesus Christ,
the Father of mercies and God of all comfort, 4who comforts us in all our tribulation, that we may be able to comfort those who are in any trouble, with the comfort with
which we ourselves are comforted by God. 5For as the sufferings of Christ abound in us, so our consolation also
abounds through Christ. 6Now if we are afflicted, *it is* for
your consolation and salvation, which is effective for enduring the same sufferings which we also suffer. Or if we are
comforted, *it is* for your consolation and salvation. 7And our
hope for you *is* steadfast, because we know that as you are
partakers of the sufferings, so also *you will partake* of the
consolation.

1:8 8For we do not want you to be ignorant, brethren, of our trouble which came
to us in Asia: that we were burdened beyond measure,
above strength, so that we despaired even of life. 9Yes, we
had the sentence of death in ourselves, that we should not
trust in ourselves but in God who raises the dead, 10who

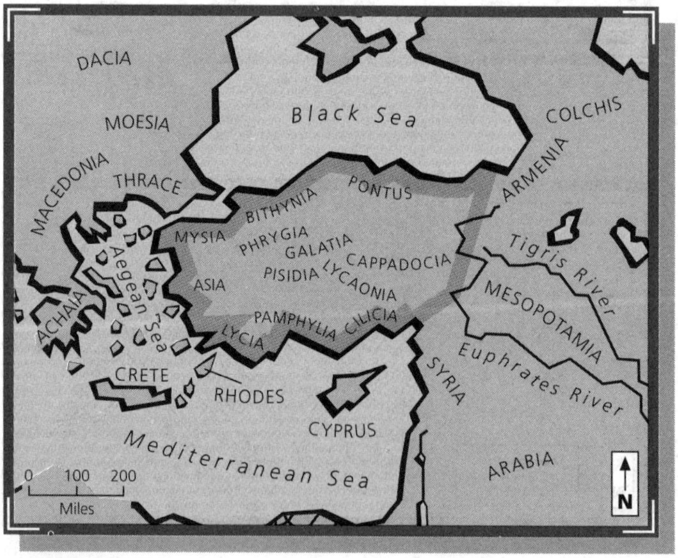

YOU OUGHT RATHER TO FORGIVE AND COMFORT. . . .
—2 Corinthians 2:7

ASIA MINOR

YOU ARE THERE 1:8

- **A peninsula, also called Anatolia, situated in the extreme western part of the continent of Asia.**
- **Bounded on the north by the Black Sea, the Sea of Marmara, and the Dardanelles; the Aegean Sea on the west; and Syria and the Mediterranean Sea on the south.**
- **Roughly identical with the modern nation of Turkey.**
- **A high plateau crossed by mountains, especially the Taurus Mountains near the southern coast.**
- **In the New Testament, the term "Asia" is ambiguous, sometimes referring to the peninsula of Asia Minor as a whole (Acts 19:26–27), but more often referring to proconsular Asia, situated in the western part of the peninsula (Acts 2:9; 6:9).**

The explosive impact of the gospel at Ephesus reverberated throughout Asia Minor, such that "all who dwelt in Asia heard the word of the Lord Jesus" (Acts 19:10). See "The Ephesus Approach," Acts 19:8–41.

delivered us from so great a death, and does[a] deliver us; in whom we trust that He will still deliver
us, 11you also helping together in prayer for us, that
thanks may be given by many persons on our[a] behalf for the gift *granted* to us through many.

Paul Defends His Integrity

12For our boasting is this: the testimony of our
conscience that we conducted ourselves in the
world in simplicity and godly sincerity, not with
fleshly wisdom but by the grace of God, and more
abundantly toward you. 13For we are not writing
any other things to you than what you read or understand. Now I trust you will understand, even to
the end 14(as also you have understood us in part),
that we are your boast as you also *are* ours, in the
day of the Lord Jesus.

Paul Explains His Plans

15And in this confidence I intended to come to
you before, that you might have a second benefit—
16to pass by way of you to Macedonia, to come
again from Macedonia to you, and be helped by
you on my way to Judea. 17Therefore, when I was
planning this, did I do it lightly? Or the things I
plan, do I plan according to the flesh, that with me
there should be Yes, Yes, and No, No? 18But *as* God
is faithful, our word to you was not Yes and No.
1:19–20
19For the Son of God, Jesus
Christ, who was preached
among you by us—by me, Silvanus, and Timothy
—was not Yes and No, but in Him was Yes. 20For
all the promises of God in Him *are* Yes, and in Him
Amen, to the glory of God through us. 21Now
He who establishes us with you in Christ and
has anointed us *is* God, 22who also has sealed us
and given us the Spirit in our hearts as a guarantee.
23Moreover I call God as witness against my soul,
that to spare you I came no more to Corinth. 24Not
that we have dominion over your faith, but are fellow workers for your joy; for by faith you stand.

CHAPTER 2

A Letter Instead of a Painful Visit

1But I determined this within myself, that I
would not come again to you in sorrow. 2For if I
make you sorrowful, then who is he who makes
me glad but the one who is made sorrowful by
me?
3And I wrote this very thing to you, lest, when I
came, I should have sorrow over those from whom
I ought to have joy, having confidence in you all
that my joy is *the joy* of you all. 4For out of much
affliction and anguish of heart I wrote to you, with
many tears, not that you should be grieved, but
that you might know the love which I have so
abundantly for you.

Forgiving a Repentant Brother

2:5–11 see pg. 620
5But if anyone has caused
grief, he has not grieved me, but
all of you to some extent—not to be too severe.
6This punishment which *was inflicted* by the majority *is* sufficient for such a man, 7so that, on the contrary, you *ought* rather to forgive and comfort *him,*
lest perhaps such a one be swallowed up with too
much sorrow. 8Therefore I urge you to reaffirm
your love to him. 9For to this end I also wrote, that
I might put you to the test, whether you are obedient in all things. 10Now whom you forgive anything, I also *forgive.* For if indeed I have forgiven
anything, I have forgiven that one[a] for your sakes
in the presence of Christ, 11lest Satan should take
advantage of us; for we are not ignorant of his devices.

Christ Leads in Triumph

12Furthermore, when I came to Troas to *preach*
Christ's gospel, and a door was opened to me by
the Lord, 13I had no rest in my spirit, because I did
not find Titus my brother; but taking my leave of
them, I departed for Macedonia.
14Now thanks *be* to God who always leads us in
triumph in Christ, and through us diffuses the fragrance of His knowledge in every place. 15For we

(Bible text continued on page 621)

1:10 [a]NU-Text reads *shall.* 1:11 [a]M-Text reads *your behalf.* 2:10 [a]NU-Text reads *For indeed, what I have forgiven, if I have forgiven anything, I did it.*

Affirmative Action

A CLOSER LOOK 1:19–20 *God doesn't equivocate in what He promises. Christ was His ultimate statement in the affirmative (vv. 19–20). Do you believe that God can be depended on to honor His word? See "Promises," Rom. 4:16–25.*

CONSIDER THIS
2:5–11

ACCOUNTABILITY

The discipline of a Corinthian believer (v. 6) points to one of the important functions of the body of Christ—to hold its members accountable for how they conduct their lives. In the case mentioned here, the censure of the church caused the offender to repent and change his ways, restoring his spiritual life and bringing joy to the church.

Accountability is easy to talk about but difficult to practice. No one likes to be judged by others. In modern society it's especially easy to feel that one's personal life is no one else's business. But a study of Scripture reveals a number of important principles about accountability:

(1) *As believers, we are accountable not only for our actions, but also for our attitudes.* In the performance-oriented work world, evaluations tend to measure results alone—higher sales, greater cost control, more clients served. Everything is quantitative. But God is interested in our innermost heart. He looks at the quality of our character. As God told Samuel, "The Lord does not see as man sees; for man looks at the outward appearance, but the Lord looks at the heart" (1 Sam. 16:7).

(2) *Accountability depends on trust.* To hold ourselves accountable to others is to to trust their judgment and to believe that they are committed to the same truths and values that we are. It also helps if we can sense that they have our best interests at heart. That's why Paul pleaded with the Corinthians to forsake their divisions and "be perfectly joined together in the same mind and in the same judgment" (1 Cor. 1:10). Without that unity, they would never submit to each other.

(3) *Accountability is directly related to the principle of submission.* Every person must struggle with the natural tendency toward rebellion against God. Accountability involves allowing others to enter into that struggle with us. But that means that sometimes we must defer to the judgment or counsel of another, especially when they challenge us with clear-cut Scriptural truth or the wisdom of personal experience. Paul told the Ephesians that part of living in the will of the Lord involves "submitting to one another in the fear of God" (Eph. 5:21).

It's not surprising that participation in the body of Christ would involve accountability, because all of us experience accountability in many other areas of life. For example, the government holds us accountable for obeying the law and paying taxes. Likewise, government officials are accountable to the public for their decisions. Employees are accountable to the boss for their work. Likewise, corporate officers are accountable to stockholders for quarterly financial results. In short, accountability touches us at home, at work, at church, and even at play.

But our attitudes toward accountability in general ultimately reflect our attitude toward accountability to God. If we are rebellious toward the One who created us and loves us most, how able will we be to submit to others? ◆

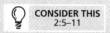

are to God the fragrance of Christ among those who are being saved and among those who are perishing. 16To the one
we are the aroma of death *leading* to death, and to the other
the aroma of life *leading* to life. And who *is* sufficient for
these things? 17For we are not, as so many,[a] peddling the
word of God; but as of sincerity, but as from God, we speak
in the sight of God in Christ.

CHAPTER 3

Paul's Best Defense: The Corinthians Themselves

1Do we begin again to commend ourselves? Or do we
need, as some *others,* epistles of commendation to you or
letters of commendation from you? 2You are our epistle
written in our hearts, known and read by all men; 3clearly
you are an epistle of Christ, ministered by us, written not
with ink but by the Spirit of the living God, not on tablets
of stone but on tablets of flesh, *that is,* of the heart.

4And we have such trust through Christ toward God.
5Not that we are sufficient of ourselves to think of anything
as *being* from ourselves, but our sufficiency *is* from God,
3:6 6who also made us sufficient as ministers
of the new covenant, not of the letter but
of the Spirit;[a] for the letter kills, but the Spirit gives life.

2:17 [a]M-Text reads *the rest.* 3:6 [a]Or *spirit*

The New Covenant

A CLOSER LOOK 3:6 *God promised a new covenant through the prophet Jeremiah in which He would write His Law on human hearts. This suggested a new level of obedience and a new knowledge of the Lord. See "The New Covenant," 1 Cor. 11:25.*

IMAGE-CONSCIOUS

CONSIDER THIS 3:7–18 When other people look at you, what do they see? What image do you project to coworkers, customers, friends, and neighbors? As Paul traveled through the cities of the Roman Empire, he always gave thought to how he would be perceived, but his biggest concern was whether observers would see Jesus in him.

To illustrate this principle, Paul recalled a phenomenon that occurred during the period in which Moses received the Law (vv. 7, 13). As Israel wandered through the wilderness, God revealed Himself to the people through what looked like a consuming fire (Ex. 24:17). But to Moses He spoke face to face (33:11). This encounter with the Living God had such an effect on Moses that his face would shine with an afterglow whenever he returned to the people. To dispel their fear, he put a veil over his face to hide the glory that resulted from his proximity to God.

Paul argues that we as believers have an even closer proximity to God than Moses did, for God Himself lives inside us (v. 8). Thus, when we meet others, they ought to see the glory of God shining out of us (vv. 9–11, 18). In other words, they ought to see Jesus.

Is that who people see when they look at us? Do they see Jesus' love, integrity, and power? Or do we "veil" the Light of the World (Matt. 5:14–16) under a mask of selfish ambition and worldly concerns?

The New Testament Ministry

3:7–18
see pg. 621

7But if the ministry of death, written
and engraved on stones, was glorious, so
that the children of Israel could not look steadily at the face
of Moses because of the glory of his countenance, which *glory*
was passing away, 8how will the ministry of the Spirit not be
more glorious? 9For if the ministry of condemnation *had*
glory, the ministry of righteousness exceeds much more in
glory. 10For even what was made glorious had no glory in this
respect, because of the glory that excels. 11For if what is passing away *was* glorious, what remains *is* much more glorious.
12Therefore, since we have such hope, we use great boldness of speech— 13unlike Moses, *who* put a veil over his
face so that the children of Israel could not look steadily at
the end of what was passing away. 14But their minds were
blinded. For until this day the same veil remains unlifted in
the reading of the Old Testament, because the *veil* is taken
away in Christ. 15But even to this day, when Moses is read, a

CONSIDER THIS
4:2

A Code of Ethics for Christian Witness

When believers present the message of Christ, we need to be like Paul, absolutely above board in our motives and manners (v. 2). We need to respect our hearers and refuse to do anything that would violate their integrity. Otherwise we become like a cult, peddling spiritual goods (2:17).

Here are some suggestions (from material distributed by Inter Varsity Christian Fellowship) to guide Christians in their witness:

Ethics for Witnessing
(1) We are Christians, called by God to honor Jesus Christ with our lives, abiding by biblically defined ethical standards in every area of life, public and private. This includes our efforts to persuade coworkers and others to believe the good news about Jesus Christ.
(2) Wherever we live and work, we seek to follow the mandate, motives, message, and model of Jesus, who still pursues and reclaims those lost in sin and rebelling against Him.
(3) We believe all people are created in God's image with the capacity to relate to their Creator and Redeemer. We disdain any effort to influence people which depersonalizes them or deprives them of their inherent value as persons.
(4) Since we respect the value of persons, we believe all are worthy of hearing about Jesus Christ. We also affirm the right of every person to survey other religious options. People are free to choose a different belief system than Christianity.

Continued

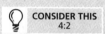

veil lies on their heart. [16]Nevertheless when one turns to the
Lord, the veil is taken away. [17]Now the Lord is the Spirit;
and where the Spirit of the Lord *is*, there *is* liberty. [18]But we
all, with unveiled face, beholding as in a mirror the glory of
the Lord, are being transformed into the same image from
glory to glory, just as by the Spirit of the Lord.

CHAPTER 4

Christ Is the Message

[1]Therefore, since we have this ministry, as we have re-
4:2 ceived mercy, we do not lose heart. [2]But
we have renounced the hidden things of
shame, not walking in craftiness nor handling the word of
God deceitfully, but by manifestation of the truth commending ourselves to every man's conscience in the sight of
God. [3]But even if our gospel is veiled, it is veiled to those
who are perishing, [4]whose minds the god of this age has

Continued

(5) We affirm the role and right of Christians to share the gospel of Christ in the marketplace of ideas. However, this does not justify any means to fulfill that end. We reject coercive techniques or manipulative appeals, especially those that play on emotions and discount or contradict reason or evidence. We will not bypass a person's critical faculties, prey upon psychological weaknesses, undermine a relationship with one's family or religious institution, or mask the true nature of Christian conversion. We will not intentionally mislead.

(6) We respect the individual integrity, intellectual honesty, and academic freedom of others, both believers and skeptics, and so we proclaim Christ without hidden agendas. We reveal our own identity, purpose, theological positions, and sources of information. We will use no false advertising and seek no material gain from presenting the gospel.

(7) We invite people of other religious persuasions to join us in true dialogue. We acknowledge our humanness—that we Christians are just as sinful, needy, and dependent on the grace of God as anyone else. We seek to listen sensitively in order to understand, and thus rid our witness of any stereotypes or fixed formulae which block honest communication.

(8) As our "brothers' keepers," we accept our responsibility to admonish any Christian brother or sister who presents the message of Christ in a way that violates these ethical guidelines.

JUST PLAIN JARS

CONSIDER THIS 4:7 **As humans, we are earthen vessels—plain old clay pots (v. 7). We may drape our human frame with fancy clothes, surround it with glittering possessions, transport it in rolling splendor, or rest it on a seat of power. But in the end, we are still just human beings. Certainly we have dignity and value in God's sight, but as believers we hold something of incomparably greater value—the treasure of Christ's grace and light!**

A child picks a fragrant bouquet of wildflowers for her mother and places them in an old mayonnaise jar for a vase. What does the mother pay attention to? What delights her heart? The flowers or the mayonnaise jar?

Our value as vessels lies in the incomparable beauty and splendor of what we hold, not in our shape or color.

blinded, who do not believe, lest the light of the gospel of
the glory of Christ, who is the image of God, should shine on
them. 5For we do not preach ourselves, but Christ Jesus the
Lord, and ourselves your bondservants for Jesus' sake. 6For
it is the God who commanded light to shine out of darkness, who has shone in our hearts to *give* the light of the
knowledge of the glory of God in the face of Jesus Christ.

Natural Messengers, Supernatural Power

4:7 see pg. 623

7But we have this treasure in earthen
vessels, that the excellence of the power
may be of God and not of us. 8*We are* hard-pressed on every
side, yet not crushed; *we are* perplexed, but not in despair;
9persecuted, but not forsaken; struck down, but not destroyed— 10always carrying about in the body the dying of
the Lord Jesus, that the life of Jesus also may be manifested
in our body. 11For we who live are always delivered to death
for Jesus' sake, that the life of Jesus also may be manifested
in our mortal flesh. 12So then death is working in us, but
life in you.

13And since we have the same spirit of faith, according to
what is written, "I believed and therefore I spoke,"[a] we also
believe and therefore speak, 14knowing that He who raised
up the Lord Jesus will also raise us up with Jesus, and will

4:13 [a]Psalm 116:10

CONSIDER THIS 5:10

The Judgment Seat

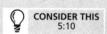

Have you ever felt wronged and had someone say, "Don't worry, you'll have your day in court"? All of us will eventually have our "day in court" before God when we stand before the judgment seat (bēma) *of Christ (v. 10).*

Paul's Corinthian readers must have been quite familiar with the bēma*. As in most cities of Greece, a large, richly decorated rostrum called the* bēma *stood in the middle of the marketplace at Corinth. It was used by the officials for purposes of public proclamations, commendations, and condemnations.*

Paul himself had been brought to the Corinthian bēma *by Jews who opposed his message. The case was heard by Gallio, the Roman proconsul (governor) of the region, who dismissed the complaint (Acts 18:12–17).*

But the bēma *was used for more than just tribunals. It was at the* bēma *that winners of Corinth's prestigious athletic contests were announced (see "The Games," 1 Cor. 9:24–27). Thus, Paul's statement that believers will appear*

present *us* with you. [15]For all things *are* for your sakes, that grace, having spread through the many, may cause thanksgiving to abound to the glory of God.

[16]Therefore we do not lose heart. Even though our outward man is perishing, yet the inward *man* is being renewed day by day. [17]For our light affliction, which is but for a moment, is working for us a far more exceeding *and* eternal weight of glory, [18]while we do not look at the things which are seen, but at the things which are not seen. For the things which are seen *are* temporary, but the things which are not seen *are* eternal.

CHAPTER 5

We Are Headed for Eternity with God

[1]For we know that if our earthly house, *this* tent, is destroyed, we have a building from God, a house not made with hands, eternal in the heavens. [2]For

5:2–5

in this we groan, earnestly desiring to be clothed with our habitation which is from heaven, [3]if indeed, having been clothed, we shall not be found naked. [4]For we who are in *this* tent groan, being burdened, not because we want to be unclothed, but further clothed, that mortality may be swallowed up by life. [5]Now He who has prepared us for this very thing *is* God, who also has given us the Spirit as a guarantee.

before the bēma *of Christ is as much a cause for joy and hope as it is for fear.*

One thing is certain: the judgment rendered at the bēma *will be fair, for Christ will be the Judge, and He Himself once stood before Pilate's* bēma *(Matt. 27:19; John 19:10). He knows what it feels like to have one's life weighed in the balance.*

However, the Lord will not be deciding the eternal fate of believers as He sits on His bēma*; that was settled at the moment of salvation (John 5:24). Instead, the* bēma *of Christ will be our chance as believers to look at our lives according to Christ's perfect assessment. It will be the ultimate opportunity to experience honest evaluation and true justice as we stand before Him.*

What will Christ say of you? Are you paying attention to your "deeds done in the body" in light of this moment of accountability? Are you striving to earn the Lord's praise in every area of life? ◆

WHAT DID YOU EXPECT?

CONSIDER THIS 5:2–5

In much of the world, evil abounds and Christians suffer. Yet many Western believers assume that health and wealth ought to be the norm. It's not just that they hope for these—they *expect* them, as if God somehow owes them prosperity in exchange for their faith or integrity or some other Christian virtue.

What a far cry from Paul's day, when "groaning" was the normal experience of people, believers and unbelievers alike (vv. 2, 4). Certainly Paul exulted in the "new creation" that God brings about (5:17). But having celebrated that marvelous reality, Paul went on to say that life in Christ involves troubles and pain (6:4–10). Only from our glorified bodies will God remove all suffering (5:1).

What does this say to modern Christians in the West? We may enjoy health, wealth, and success, but isn't that the exception rather than the rule, at least judging by the experience of believers throughout history and around the world today? How much do we really know about *normal* Christianity?

Paul directly attacked the idea that God rewards godliness with material blessing. See "The Dangers of Prosperity Theology," 1 Tim. 6:3–6.

[6]So *we are* always confident, knowing that while we are at
home in the body we are absent from the Lord. [7]For we
walk by faith, not by sight. [8]We are confident, yes, well
pleased rather to be absent from the body and to be present
with the Lord.

[9]Therefore we make it our aim, whether present or absent, to be well pleasing to Him. [10]For we
must all appear before the judgment seat
of Christ, that each one may receive the things *done* in the
body, according to what he has done, whether good or bad.
[11]Knowing, therefore, the terror of the Lord, we persuade
men; but we are well known to God, and I also trust are
well known in your consciences.

5:10 see pg. 624

A New Creation in Christ

[12]For we do not commend ourselves again to you, but
give you opportunity to boast on our behalf, that you may
have *an answer* for those who boast in appearance and not
in heart. [13]For if we are beside ourselves, *it is* for God; or if
we are of sound mind, *it is* for you. [14]For the love of Christ
compels us, because we judge thus: that if One died for all,

CONSIDER THIS
6:3–10

WELCOME TO STRESSFUL LIVING

For many people in the world today, tension, conflict, weariness, and suffering have become commonplace. Nevertheless, some offer the vain hope that life's troubles can be done away with, that we can somehow get to the point where things will always be great. They suggest that faith in Christ will deliver us into a state of serenity and ease and bring prosperity, health, and constant pleasure.

However, that was neither the experience nor the teaching of early Christians such as Paul, James, or Peter, and certainly not of their Lord Jesus. Paul described the life of a servant of God in terms of tribulation, distress, tumult, and sleeplessness (vv. 4–5). But he also linked these stress producers with rich treasures that money cannot buy: purity, kindness, sincere love, honor, good report, joy, and the possession of all things (vv. 6–10).

So as long as we live as God's people on this earth, we can expect a connection between trouble and hope. That connection is never pleasant, but our troubles can bring about lasting benefits:

> Jesus *told us that if we want to follow Him, we must deny ourselves and take up a cross. If we try to save our lives, we will only lose them. But if we lose our lives for His sake, we will find them (Matt. 16:24–25).*

then all died; 15and He died for all, that those who live
should live no longer for themselves, but for Him who died
for them and rose again.
16Therefore, from now on, we regard no one according to
the flesh. Even though we have known Christ according to
5:17 the flesh, yet now we know *Him thus* no
longer. 17Therefore, if anyone *is* in Christ,
he is a new creation; old things have passed away; behold,
all things have become new. 18Now all things *are* of God,
who has reconciled us to Himself through Jesus Christ, and
has given us the ministry of reconciliation, 19that is, that
God was in Christ reconciling the world to Himself, not imputing their trespasses to them, and has committed to us
the word of reconciliation.
20Now then, we are ambassadors for Christ, as though

A New Creation

A CLOSER LOOK 5:17 *In what sense do we become "a new creation" in Christ (v. 17)? Paul painted several pictures of what that looks like. See "New Creatures with New Character," Gal. 5:22–23.*

The writer to the Hebrews encouraged us that our troubles are often a sign that we are legitimate children of God, who lovingly disciplines us to train us in righteousness (Heb. 12:8–11).

James *encouraged us to rejoice in our various trials, because as they test our faith, they produce patience, which ultimately makes us mature in Christ (James 1:2–4).*

Peter *knew by personal experience the kind of pressure that can cause one's allegiance to Christ to waiver. He warned us that "fiery trials" are nothing strange, but that they actually allow us to experience something of Christ's sufferings so that we can ultimately experience something of His glory, too (1 Pet. 4:12–13).*

We can count on feeling stress if we're going to obey Christ. But we can take hope! That stress is preparing us for riches we will enjoy for eternity. ◆

OLD THINGS HAVE PASSED AWAY; BEHOLD, ALL THINGS HAVE BECOME NEW.
—2 Corinthians 5:17

God were pleading through us: we implore *you* on
Christ's behalf, be reconciled to God. 21For He
made Him who knew no sin *to be* sin for us, that
we might become the righteousness of God in
Him.

CHAPTER 6

Openness and Authenticity

1We then, *as* workers together *with Him* also
plead with *you* not to receive the grace of God in
vain. 2For He says:

> "In an acceptable time I have heard you,
> And in the day of salvation I have helped
> you."[a]

Behold, now *is* the accepted time; behold, now *is*
the day of salvation.

6:3–10
see pg. 626

3We give no offense in anything, that our ministry may not
be blamed. 4But in all *things* we commend ourselves as ministers of God: in much patience, in
tribulations, in needs, in distresses, 5in stripes, in
imprisonments, in tumults, in labors, in sleeplessness, in fastings; 6by purity, by knowledge, by longsuffering, by kindness, by the Holy Spirit, by sincere love, 7by the word of truth, by the power of
God, by the armor of righteousness on the right
hand and on the left, 8by honor and dishonor, by
evil report and good report; as deceivers, and *yet*
true; 9as unknown, and *yet* well known; as dying,
and behold we live; as chastened, and *yet* not
killed; 10as sorrowful, yet always rejoicing; as poor,
yet making many rich; as having nothing, and *yet*
possessing all things.
11O Corinthians! We have spoken openly to you,
our heart is wide open. 12You are not restricted by
us, but you are restricted by your *own* affections.
13Now in return for the same (I speak as to children), you also be open.

Avoid Immoral Partnerships

14Do not be unequally yoked together with unbelievers. For what fellowship has righteousness with
lawlessness? And what communion has light with
darkness? 15And what accord has Christ with Belial? Or what part has a believer with an unbeliever? 16And what agreement has the temple of
God with idols? For you[a] are the temple of the living God. As God has said:

> "I will dwell in them
> And walk among *them*.
> I will be their God,
> And they shall be My people."[b]

17Therefore

> "Come out from among them
> And be separate, says the Lord.
> Do not touch what is unclean,
> And I will receive you."[a]

18 "I will be a Father to you,
> And you shall be My sons and daughters,
> Says the LORD Almighty."[a]

CHAPTER 7

1Therefore, having these promises, beloved, let
us cleanse ourselves from all filthiness of the flesh
and spirit, perfecting holiness in the fear of God.

Be Open toward Each Other

2Open *your hearts* to us. We have wronged no
one, we have corrupted no one, we have cheated
no one. 3I do not say *this* to condemn; for I have
said before that you are in our hearts, to die together and to live together. 4Great *is* my boldness of
speech toward you, great *is* my boasting on your
behalf. I am filled with comfort. I am exceedingly
joyful in all our tribulation.
5For indeed, when we came to Macedonia, our
bodies had no rest, but we were troubled on every
side. Outside *were* conflicts, inside *were* fears.

7:6

6Nevertheless God, who comforts the downcast, comforted us
by the coming of Titus, 7and not only by his coming, but also by the consolation with which he was
comforted in you, when he told us of your earnest
desire, your mourning, your zeal for me, so that I
rejoiced even more.
8For even if I made you sorry with my letter, I do
not regret it; though I did regret it. For I perceive
that the same epistle made you sorry, though only
for a while. 9Now I rejoice, not that you were made
sorry, but that your sorrow led to repentance. For
you were made sorry in a godly manner, that you
might suffer loss from us in nothing. 10For godly

6:2 [a]Isaiah 49:8 *6:16* [a]NU-Text reads *we.* [b]Leviticus 26:12; Jeremiah 32:38; Ezekiel 37:27 *6:17* [a]Isaiah 52:11; Ezekiel 20:34, 41 *6:18* [a]2 Samuel 7:14

sorrow produces repentance *leading* to salvation, not to be
regretted; but the sorrow of the world produces death. 11For
observe this very thing, that you sorrowed in a godly manner: What diligence it produced in you, *what* clearing *of*
yourselves, what indignation, *what* fear, *what* vehement desire, *what* zeal, *what* vindication! In all *things* you proved
yourselves to be clear in this matter. 12Therefore, although I
wrote to you, *I did* not *do it* for the sake of him who had
done the wrong, nor for the sake of him who suffered
wrong, but that our care for you in the sight of God might
appear to you.
13Therefore we have been comforted in your comfort.
And we rejoiced exceedingly more for the joy of Titus, because his spirit has been refreshed by you all. 14For if in
anything I have boasted to him about you, I am not
ashamed. But as we spoke all things to you in truth, even so
our boasting to Titus was found true. 15And his affections
are greater for you as he remembers the obedience of you
all, how with fear and trembling you received him. 16There-
fore I rejoice that I have confidence in you in everything.

CHAPTER 8

The Example of the Macedonians

1Moreover, brethren, we make known to you the grace of
God bestowed on the churches of Macedonia: 2that in a

PERSONALITY PROFILE: TITUS

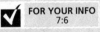

FOR YOUR INFO 7:6 **Not to be confused with:** The Roman general Titus who destroyed Jerusalem in A.D. 70 (see "Jerusalem Surrounded," Luke 21:20).

Background: Raised as a Greek-speaking Gentile.

Known for: Diplomacy, public relations, project management, and fund-raising. Paul praised him as dependable, reliable, and diligent.

Best known today for: His work with Paul as a traveling companion and coworker in establishing churches throughout the Roman world.

THE MAN OF THE HOUR

Titus was a man for tough tasks. According to Paul, he was dependable (2 Cor. 8:17), reliable (7:6), and diligent (8:17). He also had a great capacity for human affection (7:13–15). Tradition holds that he was the first bishop of Crete. Possessing both strength and tact, Titus calmed a desperate situation on more than one occasion. He serves as a good model for believers living under trying circumstances.

Titus' ethnic background proved to be important and useful to the early church. As an uncircumcised Gentile, he accompanied Paul and Barnabas to Jerusalem, where many of the Jewish Christians were debating whether non-Jews could be saved. Paul introduced him there as a living example of a great theological truth—that Gentiles need not be circumcised (that is, become Jews) in order to receive the grace of God (Gal. 2:1–3).

Does it really matter what you believe, as long as you do the right thing? Yes it does, thought Paul. That's why he wrote to Titus, his valued associate on Crete, urging him to teach "sound doctrine." He knew that correct living is a product of correct belief. To learn more about the situation, see the Introduction to Titus.

great trial of affliction the abundance of their joy and their
deep poverty abounded in the riches of their liberality. 3For
I bear witness that according to *their* ability, yes, and beyond *their* ability, *they were* freely willing, 4imploring us
with much urgency that we would receive[a] the gift and the
fellowship of the ministering to the saints. 5And not *only* as
we had hoped, but they first gave themselves to the Lord,
and *then* to us by the will of God. 6So we urged Titus, that
as he had begun, so he would also complete this grace in
you as well. 7But as you abound in everything—in faith, in
speech, in knowledge, in all diligence, and in your love for
us—*see* that you abound in this grace also.

The Example of Christ

8:8–9 8I speak not by commandment, but I
am testing the sincerity of your love by

8:4 [a]NU-Text and M-Text omit *that we would receive,* thus changing text to *urgency for the favor and fellowship . . . .*

CONSIDER THIS
8:8–9

CHRIST BECAME POOR

Almost anyone can "love" people in the abstract. But when it comes time to express that love—by lending a helping hand or writing a check—one can quickly determine the sincerity of a person's love for others. That was Paul's point in vv. 8–9. To illustrate it, he used the ultimate model of tangible love—Jesus Christ.

Christ became poor in order to make us rich. Consider what He gave up when He left heaven and took on a human body:

- *He left His Father, whose immediate presence He would not enjoy again for more than 30 years. How long would you be willing to be away from your closest companion and friend in order to help a group of people—especially if you knew that most of them would reject and despise you, and might even kill you?*
- *We can imagine that He left a joyful crowd that included Abraham, Isaac, Jacob, the angelic hosts, and all the redeemed saints who were worshiping Him, glorifying Him, and having fellowship with Him prior to His incarnation. He left those who loved Him to come and be misunderstood, rejected, scorned, hated, and scourged by most of those He came to help. Would you leave a position of honor and adoration to go help people who would by and large reject you?*
- *He left a heavenly home that far exceeded in splendor, majesty, and comfort the physical environment of His*

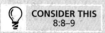

the diligence of others. 9For you know the grace of our Lord
Jesus Christ, that though He was rich, yet for your sakes He
became poor, that you through His poverty might become
rich.
10And in this I give advice: It is to your advantage not
only to be doing what you began and were desiring to do a
year ago; 11but now you also must complete the doing *of it;*
that as *there was* a readiness to desire *it,* so *there* also *may be*
a completion out of what *you* have. 12For if there is first a
willing mind, *it is* accepted according to what one has, *and*
not according to what he does not have.

8:13–15

13For *I do* not *mean* that others should
be eased and you burdened; 14but by an
equality, *that* now at this time your abundance *may supply*
their lack, that their abundance also may supply your
lack—that there may be equality. 15As it is written, "He who
gathered much had nothing left over, and he who *gathered*
little had no lack."[a]

8:15 [a]Exodus 16:18

earthly life. Would you give up the best accommodations this earth has to offer in order to help needy people in a bad neighborhood?

- *He left His pre-incarnate existence in the form of God, without limitations, to take on a physical body subject to fatigue, aches, and pains. Would you accept hunger, thirst, fatigue, pain, and limited physical abilities to help people who didn't even care whether you came or not?*

The statement that Christ became poor puts into perspective Jesus' command to the rich young ruler to sell what he had and give the proceeds to the poor (Mark 10:21), and His instruction to the disciples to sell what they had and give alms, providing themselves treasure in heaven (Luke 12:33). What Jesus asked them to do, He had already done—to such a degree, in fact, that their obedience could never equal His selflessness. ◆

Jesus worked as a carpenter and lived responsibly. But the fact remains, He was born poor and lived poor. In fact, He was homeless. *See Matt. 8:20.*

Christ may have been poor, but many of His followers today are not. How should wealthy believers handle their money? *See "Christians and Money," 1 Tim. 6:6–19.*

SOLIDARITY

CONSIDER THIS 8:13–15

Paul challenged the Corinthian Christians to participate in a fund-raising project to benefit believers at Jerusalem. But he seemed to be concerned with more than money. He wanted Gentile churches like Corinth to start practicing solidarity with their Jewish brothers and sisters (vv. 13–15, 24). It's almost as if the new churches owed something, in a sense, to the original church in Jerusalem.

REAPING THE BENEFITS

CONSIDER THIS 9:6–8 **Paul wanted the Corinthians to give generously toward a fund-raising project to help needy Christians. He linked generosity with spiritual benefits: the more one gives, the more one benefits (vv. 6–11).**

This principle goes beyond financial giving. At work, for example, you may donate toward the local United Way. But when a coworker asks for some of your time to talk about a problem, what is your response? Do you give your attention generously or grudgingly? When your boss gives you a special assignment, do you give the project just enough attention to get it over with, or do you jump in wholeheartedly with energy and creativity?

What about your time and emotional energy after hours? When your spouse or children need you, do you make yourself available generously or grudgingly? Do you give a fair contribution of yourself to assignments that you've volunteered for, or just a token effort?

We are constant recipients of God's generous grace. He promises that if we will give of ourselves, He'll enable us to have an abundance of resources for the work to which He has called us (v. 8).

Giving generously in order to gain spiritual benefits does not mean that God rewards godliness with material blessings. See "The Dangers of Prosperity Theology," 1 Tim. 6:3–6.

A Plan to Provide Material Help

16But thanks *be* to God who puts[a] the same earnest care
for you into the heart of Titus. 17For he not only accepted
the exhortation, but being more diligent, he went to you of
his own accord. 18And we have sent with him the brother
whose praise *is* in the gospel throughout all the churches,
19and not only *that,* but who was also chosen by the
churches to travel with us with this gift, which is administered by us to the glory of the Lord Himself and *to show*
your ready mind, 20avoiding this: that anyone should blame
us in this lavish gift which is administered by us— 21pro-
viding honorable things, not only in the sight of the Lord,
but also in the sight of men.
22And we have sent with them our brother whom we
have often proved diligent in many things, but now much
more diligent, because of the great confidence which *we
have* in you. 23If *anyone inquires* about Titus, *he is* my partner and fellow worker concerning you. Or if our brethren
are inquired about, they are messengers of the churches, the
glory of Christ. 24Therefore show to them, and[a] before the
churches the proof of your love and of our boasting on your
behalf.

CHAPTER 9

Implementing the Plan

1Now concerning the ministering to the saints, it is super-
fluous for me to write to you; 2for I know your willingness,
about which I boast of you to the Macedonians, that Achaia
was ready a year ago; and your zeal has stirred up the majority. 3Yet I have sent the brethren, lest our boasting of you
should be in vain in this respect, that, as I said, you may be
ready; 4lest if *some* Macedonians come with me and find
you unprepared, we (not to mention you!) should be
ashamed of this confident boasting.[a] 5Therefore I thought it
necessary to exhort the brethren to go to you ahead of time,
and prepare your generous gift beforehand, which *you had*
previously promised, that it may be ready as *a matter of* generosity and not as a grudging obligation.

The Blessings of Generosity

9:6–8 6But this *I say:* He who sows sparingly
will also reap sparingly, and he who sows
bountifully will also reap bountifully. 7*So let* each one *give* as
he purposes in his heart, not grudgingly or of necessity; for
God loves a cheerful giver. 8And God *is* able to make all
grace abound toward you, that you, always having all suffi-

8:16 [a]NU-Text reads *has put.* *8:24* [a]NU-Text and M-Text omit *and.* *9:4* [a]NU-Text reads *this confidence.*

ciency in all *things,* may have an abundance for every good
9:9–10 work. 9As it is written:

"He has dispersed abroad,
He has given to the poor;
His righteousness endures forever."[a]

10Now may[a] He who supplies seed to the sower, and
bread for food, supply and multiply the seed you have *sown*
and increase the fruits of your righteousness, 11while *you are*
enriched in everything for all liberality, which causes
thanksgiving through us to God. 12For the administration of
this service not only supplies the needs of the saints, but
also is abounding through many thanksgivings to God,
13while, through the proof of this ministry, they glorify God
for the obedience of your confession to the gospel of Christ,
and for *your* liberal sharing with them and all *men,* 14and by
their prayer for you, who long for you because of the exceeding grace of God in you. 15Thanks *be* to God for His indescribable gift!

CHAPTER 10

An Appeal for Obedience

10:1 see pg. 634
1Now I, Paul, myself am pleading with
you by the meekness and gentleness of
Christ—who in presence *am* lowly among you, but being
absent am bold toward you. 2But I beg *you* that when I am
present I may not be bold with that confidence by which I
intend to be bold against some, who think of us as if we
walked according to the flesh. 3For though we walk in the
flesh, we do not war according to the flesh. 4For the
weapons of our warfare *are* not carnal but mighty in God
for pulling down strongholds, 5casting down arguments and
every high thing that exalts itself against the knowledge of
God, bringing every thought into captivity to the obedience
of Christ, 6and being ready to punish all disobedience when
your obedience is fulfilled.

Paul Defends His Personal Integrity

7Do you look at things according to the outward appearance? If anyone is convinced in himself that he is Christ's,
let him again consider this in himself, that just as he *is*
Christ's, even so we *are* Christ's.[a] 8For even if I should boast
somewhat more about our authority, which the Lord gave
us[a] for edification and not for your destruction, I shall not
be ashamed— 9lest I seem to terrify you by letters. 10"For

9:9 [a]Psalm 112:9 *9:10* [a]NU-Text reads *Now He who supplies . . . will supply . . . .*
10:7 [a]NU-Text reads *even as we are.* *10:8* [a]NU-Text omits *us.*

WHO ARE THE POOR?

CONSIDER THIS 9:9–10 **By comparison to the many modern Christians who live in affluence, the Corinthian believers would appear poor. Yet Paul described the Christians of Macedonia as living in "deep poverty" (8:2), so they were much poorer even than the Corinthians. What does Scripture mean, then, when it says that God "has given to *the poor*" (9:9, italics added)? And what does that mean for believers today who are relatively affluent?**

The word for *poor* (v. 9) described someone who toiled for a living, what we would call a day laborer. Such persons were distinct from the truly destitute. The former may have had a difficult life, but at least they were in no danger of losing it. By contrast, the truly poor were in immediate danger of perishing if they didn't receive charitable aid.

Paul described God as dispersing to the *poor,* the day laborers, not food for survival but seed that they could sow to raise a crop (vv. 9–10). He indicated that God would aid the Corinthians so that they, in turn, could aid the completely destitute believers in Jerusalem.

So what does that mean for us as Christians today if we work at relatively stable, well-paid jobs, own our own homes, and manage to salt away at least some money for retirement? Paul would doubtless identify us as rich. We may work hard, but we have disposable income that most first-century Christians could have only imagined.

his letters," they say, "*are* weighty and powerful, but *his* bodily presence *is* weak, and *his* speech contemptible." 11 Let
such a person consider this, that what we are in word by
letters when we are absent, such *we will* also *be* in deed
when we are present.
12 For we dare not class ourselves or compare ourselves
with those who commend themselves. But they, measuring
themselves by themselves, and comparing themselves
among themselves, are not wise. 13 We, however, will not
boast beyond measure, but within the limits of the sphere
which God appointed us—a sphere which especially includes you. 14 For we are not overextending ourselves (as
though *our authority* did not extend to you), for it was to
you that we came with the gospel of Christ; 15 not boasting
of things beyond measure, *that is,* in other men's labors, but
having hope, *that* as your faith is increased, we shall be
greatly enlarged by you in our sphere, 16 to preach the
gospel in the *regions* beyond you, *and* not to boast in another man's sphere of accomplishment.
17 But "he who glories, let him glory in the LORD."[a] 18 For

10:17 [a]Jeremiah 9:24

CONSIDER THIS
10:1

INTEGRITY IN THE FACE OF COMPETITION

When you face a competitive situation, are you tempted to do whatever it takes to win? Paul faced severe competition at Corinth. In chapters 10–12, he described real danger to his work in Corinth:

- *Opposing leaders and teachers were making headway. Paul's people were tempted to cross over to them (10:15; 11:3–4, 12–15).*
- *Paul felt the pain of this loss very deeply (10:2–3; 11:2–3, 29).*
- *He felt threatened (10:8–11, 13–15; 11:5–6, 16–21).*
- *He loved the Corinthians and feared losing them so much that he became angry (11:11–15).*
- *He defended himself as a faithful servant who had suffered for the Corinthians and the gospel (10:13–18; 11:20–30; 12:11).*

As Paul wrestled with mixed feelings and sketchy information, he dealt in known principles of godliness and clear communication:

- *Paul was passionate about the problem. He wrote to the Corinthians extensively (see the Introduction to 1 and 2 Corinthians).*

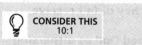

not he who commends himself is approved, but whom the
Lord commends.

CHAPTER 11

Paul Defends His Apostleship

[1]Oh, that you would bear with me in a little folly—and
indeed you do bear with me. [2]For I am jealous for you with
godly jealousy. For I have betrothed you to one husband,
that I may present *you as* a chaste virgin to Christ. [3]But I
fear, lest somehow, as the serpent deceived Eve by his craftiness, so your minds may be corrupted from the simplicity[a]
that is in Christ. [4]For if he who comes preaches another Jesus whom we have not preached, or *if* you receive a different spirit which you have not received, or a different gospel which you have not accepted—you may well put up
with it!

☑ 11:5

[5]For I consider that I am not at all inferior to the most eminent apostles. [6]Even
though *I am* untrained in speech, yet *I am* not in knowl-

11:3 [a]NU-Text adds *and purity.*

◆ ◆ ◆ ◆ ◆ ◆ ◆ ◆ ◆ ◆ ◆ ◆ ◆ ◆ ◆ ◆

- *He tried to visit Corinth to discuss matters openly (10:2, 11; 12:14; 13:1).*
- *He encouraged the Corinthians to test his prior works among them if they questioned his loyalty and integrity (10:13, 15; 11:22–27). It's interesting that he felt awkward in this self-defense (11:21, 23; 12:7–10).*
- *He gave a clear statement of the finances involved in his previous work in Corinth (11:7–9; 1 Cor. 16:1–4, 16).*
- *He appealed for negotiations in a way that would honor Christ and not duplicate the world's methods (2 Cor. 10:3–4; 13:8–10).*
- *He urged in-depth analysis of the situation (10:7; 13:1, 5, 8).*

Paul faced a real temptation to resort to any means not to lose his converts in Corinth. As readers we can feel the tension in these letters. But Paul waged spiritual warfare within himself first so that he could rise above vicious, underhanded solutions. He kept the big picture, avoiding short term gains in order to live with long-term, Christlike values. ◆

WHO WERE THE APOSTLES?

☑ FOR YOUR INFO 11:5

Paul was counted among a group of early church leaders known as "apostles" (v. 5). Each apostle was chosen by Jesus and given authority to carry out certain tasks, especially the task of making disciples of "all the nations" (Matt. 28:18).

The word *apostle* means "messenger." The term was first used of the twelve disciples whom Jesus sent out, two by two, into Galilee to expand His ministry of preaching and healing (Mark 3:14; 6:30). These same disciples, with the exception of Judas Iscariot, were recommissioned as apostles after Jesus' resurrection to be His witnesses throughout the world (Acts 1:8). After Jesus' ascension, the group brought their number to twelve again by choosing Matthias (1:23–26).

However, the term apostle came to apply to others besides the Twelve. It included people like Paul who had seen the risen Christ and were specially commissioned by Him (1 Cor. 15:10). James, the Lord's brother, was counted as an apostle (Gal. 1:19; see profile at the Introduction to James). And when Paul wrote that Jesus was seen not only by James but also by "all the apostles" (1 Cor. 15:7), he seemed to be describing a wider group than the Twelve to whom Jesus appeared earlier (1 Cor. 15:5).

The authority committed to the apostles by Christ was unique and foundational (1 Cor. 12:28; Eph. 4:11). The apostles could install elders or other leaders and teachers in the churches, and they could authorize believers to assume special responsibilities.

edge. But we have been thoroughly manifested[a]
among you in all things.
7Did I commit sin in humbling myself that you
might be exalted, because I preached the gospel of
God to you free of charge? 8I robbed other
churches, taking wages *from them* to minister to
you. 9And when I was present with you, and in
need, I was a burden to no one, for what I lacked
the brethren who came from Macedonia supplied.
And in everything I kept myself from being burdensome to you, and so I will keep *myself.* 10As the
truth of Christ is in me, no one shall stop me from
this boasting in the regions of Achaia. 11Why? Because I do not love you? God knows!
12But what I do, I will also continue to do, that I
may cut off the opportunity from those who desire
an opportunity to be regarded just as we are in the
things of which they boast. 13For such *are* false
apostles, deceitful workers, transforming themselves into apostles of Christ. 14And no wonder!
For Satan himself transforms himself into an angel
of light. 15Therefore *it is* no great thing if his ministers also transform themselves into ministers of
righteousness, whose end will be according to their
works.

Paul's Impeccable Credentials

16I say again, let no one think me a fool. If otherwise, at least receive me as a fool, that I also may
boast a little. 17What I speak, I speak not according
to the Lord, but as it were, foolishly, in this confidence of boasting. 18Seeing that many boast according to the flesh, I also will boast. 19For you put
up with fools gladly, since you *yourselves* are wise!
20For you put up with it if one brings you into
bondage, if one devours *you,* if one takes *from you,*
if one exalts himself, if one strikes you on the face.
21To *our* shame I say that we were too weak for
that! But in whatever anyone is bold—I speak foolishly—I am bold also.
22Are they Hebrews? So *am* I. Are they Israelites?
So *am* I. Are they the seed of Abraham? So *am* I.
23Are they ministers of Christ?—I speak as a fool—
I *am* more: in labors more abundant, in stripes
above measure, in prisons more frequently, in
deaths often. 24From the Jews five times I received
forty *stripes* minus one. 25Three times I was beaten
with rods; once I was stoned; three times I was
shipwrecked; a night and a day I have been in the
deep; 26*in* journeys often, *in* perils of waters, *in* perils of robbers, *in* perils of *my own* countrymen, *in*
perils of the Gentiles, *in* perils in the city, *in* perils
in the wilderness, *in* perils in the sea, *in* perils
among false brethren; 27in weariness and toil, in
sleeplessness often, in hunger and thirst, in fastings
often, in cold and nakedness— 28besides the other
things, what comes upon me daily: my deep concern for all the churches. 29Who is weak, and I am
not weak? Who is made to stumble, and I do not
burn *with indignation?*
30If I must boast, I will boast in the things which
concern my infirmity. 31The God and Father of our
Lord Jesus Christ, who is blessed forever, knows
that I am not lying. 32In Damascus the governor,
under Aretas the king, was guarding the city of the
Damascenes with a garrison, desiring to arrest me;
33but I was let down in a basket through a window
in the wall, and escaped from his hands.

CHAPTER 12

A Revelation from the Lord

1It is doubtless[a] not profitable for me to boast. I
will come to visions and revelations of the Lord: 2I
know a man in Christ who fourteen years ago—
whether in the body I do not know, or whether out
of the body I do not know, God knows—such a
one was caught up to the third heaven. 3And I
know such a man—whether in the body or out of
the body I do not know, God knows— 4how he
was caught up into Paradise and heard inexpressible words, which it is not lawful for a man to utter.
5Of such a one I will boast; yet of myself I will not
boast, except in my infirmities. 6For though I
might desire to boast, I will not be a fool; for I will
speak the truth. But I refrain, lest anyone should
think of me above what he sees me *to be* or hears
from me.

12:7–10

7And lest I should be exalted
above measure by the abundance
of the revelations, a thorn in the flesh was given to
me, a messenger of Satan to buffet me, lest I be exalted above measure. 8Concerning this thing I
pleaded with the Lord three times that it might depart from me. 9And He said to me, "My grace is
sufficient for you, for My strength is made perfect

11:6 [a]NU-Text omits *been.* *12:1* [a]NU-Text reads *necessary, though not profitable, to boast.*

in weakness." Therefore most gladly I will rather boast in
my infirmities, that the power of Christ may rest upon me.
10Therefore I take pleasure in infirmities, in reproaches, in
needs, in persecutions, in distresses, for Christ's sake. For
when I am weak, then I am strong.
11I have become a fool in boasting;[a] you have compelled
me. For I ought to have been commended by you; for in
nothing was I behind the most eminent apostles, though I
am nothing. 12Truly the signs of an apostle were accomplished among you with all perseverance, in signs and wonders and mighty deeds. 13For what is it in which you were
inferior to other churches, except that I myself was not burdensome to you? Forgive me this wrong!

Paul Says He Will Visit

14Now *for* the third time I am ready to come to you. And I
will not be burdensome to you; for I do not seek yours, but
you. For the children ought not to lay up for the parents,
but the parents for the children. 15And I will very gladly
spend and be spent for your souls; though the more abundantly I love you, the less I am loved.
16But be that *as it may,* I did not burden you. Nevertheless, being crafty, I caught you by cunning! 17Did I take advantage of you by any of those whom I sent to you? 18I
urged Titus, and sent our brother with *him.* Did Titus take
advantage of you? Did we not walk in the same spirit? Did
we not *walk* in the same steps?
19Again, do you think[a] that we excuse ourselves to you?
We speak before God in Christ. But *we do* all things,
beloved, for your edification. 20For I fear lest, when I come,
I shall not find you such as I wish, and *that* I shall be found
by you such as you do not wish; lest *there be* contentions,
jealousies, outbursts of wrath, selfish ambitions, back-
bitings, whisperings, conceits, tumults; 21lest, when I come
again, my God will humble me among you, and I shall
mourn for many who have sinned before and have not repented of the uncleanness, fornication, and lewdness which
they have practiced.

CHAPTER 13

Paul Challenges the Corinthians to Prepare

1This *will be* the third *time* I am coming to you. "By the
mouth of two or three witnesses every word shall be established."[a] 2I have told you before, and foretell as if I were
present the second time, and now being absent I write[a] to
those who have sinned before, and to all the rest, that if I

12:11 [a]NU-Text omits *in boasting.* *12:19* [a]NU-Text reads *You have been thinking for a long time. . . .* *13:1* [a]Deuteronomy 19:15 *13:2* [a]NU-Text omits *I write.*

When I Am Weak, Then I Am Strong

CONSIDER THIS 12:7–10 **Our world prizes strength—the physical strength of athletes, the financial strength of companies, the political strength of office-holders, and the military strength of armies. But Paul put a new twist on the notion of strength: weakness can make a person strong (vv. 7–10).**

Most of us would have no problem with God using our natural areas of strength, such as speaking, organizing, managing, or selling. But suppose He chose instead to use us in areas where we are weak? Moses claimed to be a poor speaker (Ex. 4:10), yet God used him as His spokesman on Israel's behalf. Peter tended to be impulsive and even hotheaded, yet God used him as one of the chief architects of the early church.

Weakness has a way of making us rely on God far more than our strengths do. What weakness in your life might God desire to use for His purposes?

SPIRITUAL AUTHORITY

CONSIDER THIS 13:10 **If you exercise leadership among other believers, you'll want to carefully study Paul's comment about his authority (v. 10). Like many of us, Paul liked to be in charge, and he felt frustrated when people failed to follow his lead, as the Corinthians had. As an apostle, he had spiritual authority over them, which at times led him to deal severely with them (1 Cor. 4:21; 5:5; compare Titus 1:13).**

But it's important to notice how Paul exercised his authority, especially as he grew older in the faith. He didn't lord it over others or try to use his authority to personal advantage. Nor did he abuse his power by using it to work out his own anger. Instead, he recognized that spiritual authority is given "for edification and not for destruction" (2 Cor. 10:8; 13:10), for building others up, not for tearing them down.

Is that how you use your position and authority? Do you exercise leadership in order to accomplish the best interests of those who follow you? As they carry out your directives, are they built up in Christ, or torn down?

Paul's method of leadership reflected a unique style of authority that Jesus encouraged. See "Servant-Leaders," Matt. 20:25–28.

come again I will not spare— 3since you seek a proof of
Christ speaking in me, who is not weak toward you, but
mighty in you. 4For though He was crucified in weakness,
yet He lives by the power of God. For we also are weak in
Him, but we shall live with Him by the power of God toward you.

5Examine yourselves *as to* whether you are in the faith.
Test yourselves. Do you not know yourselves, that Jesus
Christ is in you?—unless indeed you are disqualified. 6But I
trust that you will know that we are not disqualified.

7Now I[a] pray to God that you do no evil, not that we
should appear approved, but that you should do what is
honorable, though we may seem disqualified. 8For we can
do nothing against the truth, but for the truth. 9For we are
glad when we are weak and you are strong. And this also
13:10 we pray, that you may be made complete.
10Therefore I write these things being absent, lest being present I should use sharpness, according to the authority which the Lord has given me for edification and not for destruction.

Final Words

11Finally, brethren, farewell. Become complete. Be of good comfort, be of one mind, live in peace; and the God of love and peace will be with you.

12Greet one another with a holy kiss.

13All the saints greet you.

14The grace of the Lord Jesus Christ, and the love of God, and the communion of the Holy Spirit *be* with you all. Amen.

13:7 [a]NU-Text reads *we*.

Galatians

What happens when the gospel spreads from one culture to another? A collision often takes place, a clash of values and perceptions, too often with damage to the cause of Christ and the spiritual well-being of believers. Paul's letter to the Galatians shows that cultural conflicts began right from the start of the Christian movement.

Why should that be? Jesus told His followers to make disciples of "all the nations" (Matt. 28:19). The term "nations" (Greek, *ethnē*) literally means "peoples" or "people-groups," what we would call ethnic groups. In other words, Jesus specifically mandated that His followers cross ethnic, national, tribal, linguistic, and cultural lines to spread His message of salvation throughout the world.

In doing so, believers need to consider: What cultural "baggage" do we attach to our faith? Do we make certain assumptions about what Christianity should look like that are based less on biblical grounds than on cultural values and expectations? Is it possible that someone from a different background might serve the same Lord, but do so in a way that feels uncomfortable to us because of cultural differences?

Galatians offers insight into these questions. It is a brief letter, but it offers a powerful message for today, given our increasingly pluralistic society. As we are faced with diversity on every hand, the book reminds us to be clear about the essentials of the gospel, and not to confuse them with externals that really don't matter.

Be clear about the essentials of the gospel.

C O N T E N T S

A R T I C L E S

New Creatures with New Character (5:22–23)

If you are in Christ, you are a new creature. What does that look like? Scripture paints several pictures for us.

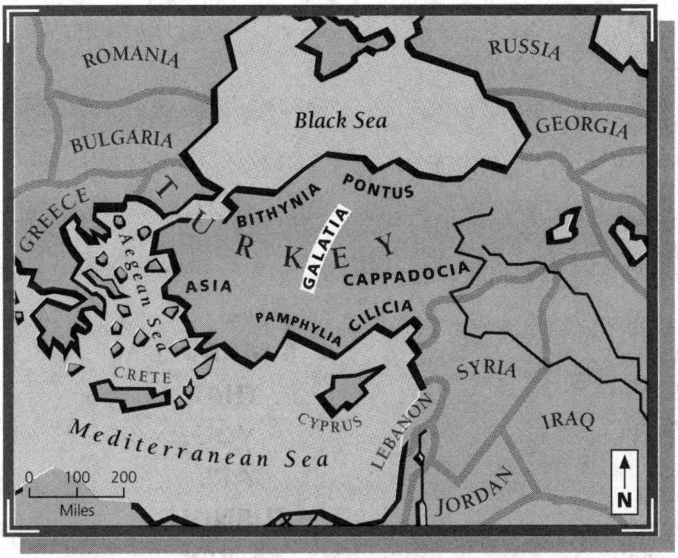

GALATIA AND SURROUNDING REGIONS

GALATIA

- **A loosely defined plateau region of central Asia Minor bounded on the east by Cappadocia, on the west by Asia, on the south by Pamphylia and Cilicia, and on the north by Bithynia and Pontus.**
- **Name derives from Celtic tribes driven out of Gaul (France) that settled the region in the third century B.C.**
- **Interconnected roads in Galatia provided easy access to roving tribes and marching armies. Cities had no walls and citizens cared little for defending themselves as they could always escape to nearby mountains.**
- **Conquered by Rome by 166 B.C. and given freedom on one condition—that the Celts would assist Rome in dividing and conquering the other groups around them. Thus, in Paul's day, Galatia was politically, economically, and militarily significant to Rome.**
- **North Galatia resisted Greek-Roman culture, keeping its own gods and Celtic language.**
- **South Galatia adopted the cult of emperor worship, and Judaism also persisted there for centuries after Christ.**
- **We know that Paul visited and established churches in the south (Acts 13:13—14:25), but we have no reliable record of any visits or churches to the north.**

ONLY CHRIST

Throughout Christian history, people have "added on" various requirements to the gospel message, almost always with an appeal to Scripture. Inevitably the result is a distortion of the faith that does great damage.

In first-century Galatia, the challenge came from Judaizers, teachers who insisted that belief in Jesus was not enough for salvation. One must also keep the Law of Moses, they said. In a way, one can understand their point of view. For centuries, Jews had held to the Law as the righteous path to favor with God (see Deut. 6:1–9; 30:15–20; compare Mark 12:28–34; Luke 10:25–28). The Judaizers perceived Jesus as perhaps building on the Law of Moses, but not replacing it.

However, their teaching greatly troubled the young believers in Galatia who had responded to Paul's message (Acts 13:13—14:26). If what the Judaizers said was true, Paul had been wrong and Christ alone did not really save a person.

Not surprisingly, Paul was outraged. He was furious with the deceptive claims of the Judaizers and zealous to defend the integrity of the gospel. So he composed the letter that we call Galatians, which may be his earliest surviving epistle, written perhaps in A.D. *48 or 49.*

If Galatians emphasizes anything, it is that Christ alone *is sufficient for salvation—nothing more and nothing less. Centuries later, after the church had again embraced add-ons to the faith, a young priest named Martin Luther claimed Galatians for his own, calling it the Magna Charta of Christian liberty. It helped usher in a reclamation of the faith in which salvation is based on Christ's grace, not on people's efforts.*

Still, every generation is marked by a tendency to classify believers according to their outward observances. Some are considered first-class, others second-class. In nearly every case, the resegregating of the church results from add-ons to the simple, pure gospel of Christ. But when believers hold to Christ alone, then their faith and the church will grow. That's the message of Galatians. ◆

I MARVEL THAT YOU ARE TURNING AWAY SO SOON . . . .
—Galatians 1:6

CHAPTER 1

To the Churches of Galatia

1Paul, an apostle (not from men nor through man, but
through Jesus Christ and God the Father who raised Him
from the dead), 2and all the brethren who are with me,

To the churches of Galatia:

3Grace to you and peace from God the Father and our
Lord Jesus Christ, 4who gave Himself for our sins, that He
might deliver us from this present evil age, according to the
will of our God and Father, 5to whom *be* glory forever and
ever. Amen.

Don't Turn Away from the True Gospel

6I marvel that you are turning away so soon from Him
who called you in the grace of Christ, to a different gospel,
7which is not another; but there are some who trouble you
and want to pervert the gospel of Christ. 8But even if we, or
an angel from heaven, preach any other gospel to you than
what we have preached to you, let him be accursed. 9As we
have said before, so now I say again, if anyone preaches any
other gospel to you than what you have received, let him be
accursed.

The Gospel Was Revealed by God

10For do I now persuade men, or God? Or do I seek to
please men? For if I still pleased men, I would not be a
bondservant of Christ.

1:11–24

11But I make known to you, brethren,
that the gospel which was preached by
me is not according to man. 12For I neither received it from
man, nor was I taught *it,* but *it came* through the revelation
of Jesus Christ.

1:13–17 see pg. 644

13For you have heard of my former
conduct in Judaism, how I persecuted
the church of God beyond measure and *tried to* destroy it.
14And I advanced in Judaism beyond many of my contem-
poraries in my own nation, being more exceedingly zealous
for the traditions of my fathers.

15But when it pleased God, who separated me from my
mother's womb and called *me* through His grace, 16to reveal
His Son in me, that I might preach Him among the Gentiles, I did not immediately confer with flesh and blood,
17nor did I go up to Jerusalem to those *who were* apostles
before me; but I went to Arabia, and returned again to
Damascus.

18Then after three years I went up to Jerusalem to see Peter,[a] and remained with him fifteen days. 19But I saw none

1:18 [a]NU-Text reads *Cephas.*

HOPE FOR YOU: WATCH PAUL GROW!

CONSIDER THIS 1:11–24 **The Bible offers many examples of people who struggled as they tried to live for God. Their stories are meant to encourage us. But sometimes comparing ourselves to the "heroes" of the faith only intimidates us. Paul, for instance, was a learned scholar, a fervent evangelist, a compassionate pastor, a competent businessman, and a diplomatic statesman. So when he tells us to follow his example as he follows Christ's example (1 Cor. 11:1), it sounds a bit unrealistic. How could we ever emulate a super-saint like Paul?**

But Paul didn't start out as a super-saint. Nor did he end up that way. In fact, he never saw himself that way. On the contrary, he grew in the faith with some difficulty. Notice how his view of himself changed over time (dates given are estimates):

c. A.D. 55: "I am the least of the apostles" (1 Cor. 15:9).

c. A.D. 57: "I know that in me... nothing good dwells" (Rom. 7:18).

c. A.D. 60: "[I am] less than the least of all the saints" (Eph. 3:8).

c. A.D. 63: "Jesus came...to save sinners, of whom I am chief" (1 Tim. 1:15).

(continued on next page)

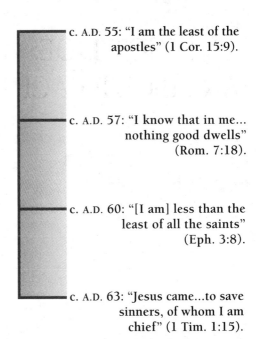

(continued from previous page)

Sounds as if Paul was perhaps more "average" than we often think. In fact, look carefully at some of the highlights (and lowlights) in his life (see Paul's profile, Acts 13:2–3). If one changes a few particulars and develops the whole-hearted commitment to God that Paul had, then his story could well be anyone's. That's because Paul was as human as any of us. His life challenges us to ask whether we are growing, struggling, and changing as he did. If so, then there's hope for us!

One of the keys to Paul's growth was the careful tutelage of a man named Barnabas. See "Barnabas—A Model for Mentoring," Acts 9:27.

It's interesting that sometimes when Paul compared Himself to other Christians of his day, he was all too aware of his own feet of clay. Apparently he suffered from the deadly disease of "comparisonitis." See Rom. 12:3.

of the other apostles except James, the Lord's brother.
20(Now *concerning* the things which I write to you, indeed,
before God, I do not lie.)
21Afterward I went into the regions of Syria and Cilicia.
22And I was unknown by face to the churches of Judea
which *were* in Christ. 23But they were hearing only, "He who
formerly persecuted us now preaches the faith which he
once *tried to* destroy." 24And they glorified God in me.

CHAPTER 2

The Apostles Approved Paul's Message

2:1–10

2:2

1Then after fourteen years I went up
again to Jerusalem with Barnabas, and
also took Titus with *me*. 2And I went up
by revelation, and communicated to
them that gospel which I preach among the Gentiles, but

Those Who Were of Reputation

A CLOSER LOOK 2:2

Who were the leaders described as being "of reputation" (v. 2)? See "The Twelve," Matt. 10:2, and "Who Were the Apostles?" 2 Cor. 11:5.

CONSIDER THIS 1:13–17

A Bigot Does an About-Face

In vv. 13–17, Paul recounts his dramatic confrontation with Christ on the Damascus road and his subsequent conversion (Acts 9:1–30). Imagine the emotional strain that placed on Saul (as he was called at the time): Jesus was alive! What members of the Way (the early Christians) had been saying about Him was all true! And Saul had killed many of them! What a shattering experience for one "advanced in Judaism" and "exceedingly zealous for the traditions" of his fathers (Gal. 1:14).

Perhaps that's why God made Saul blind for three days. He had a lot to sort out after meeting the risen Lord. It's not easy for someone to suddenly revise the entire theological basis on which he's been living, especially as a respected leader. No one wants to admit he's been wrong. No wonder Saul spent much of the time in prayer.

But God not only intended to change Saul's theology; He was determined to transform his bigoted view of the world. At the root of Saul's intense hatred of the Christian movement might well have been a belief that it would destroy Judaism by mixing it with foreign, Gentile elements (see "Stephen's Trial and Murder," Acts 6:12).

Imagine Saul's shock, then, when Ananias came to tell

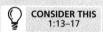

privately to those who were of reputation, lest by any
means I might run, or had run, in vain. 3Yet not even Titus
who *was* with me, being a Greek, was compelled to be circumcised. 4And *this occurred* because of false brethren secretly brought in (who came in by stealth to spy out our liberty which we have in Christ Jesus, that they might bring us
into bondage), 5to whom we did not yield submission even
for an hour, that the truth of the gospel might continue
with you.
6But from those who seemed to be something—whatever
they were, it makes no difference to me; God shows personal favoritism to no man—for those who seemed *to be
something* added nothing to me. 7But on the contrary, when
they saw that the gospel for the uncircumcised had been
committed to me, as *the gospel* for the circumcised *was* to
Peter 8(for He who worked effectively in Peter for the apostleship to the circumcised also worked effectively in me toward the Gentiles), 9and when James, Cephas, and John,
who seemed to be pillars, perceived the grace that had been
given to me, they gave me and Barnabas the right hand of
fellowship, that we *should go* to the Gentiles and they to the

(Bible text continued on page 647)

◆ ◆ ◆ ◆ ◆ ◆ ◆ ◆ ◆ ◆ ◆ ◆ ◆ ◆ ◆

him that God had chosen him to bear His name—to the Gentiles (Acts 9:15; 22:14–15; 26:16–18)! Unthinkable! Jews like Saul, who were utterly committed to holy living by all the laws and traditions of Judaism, had nothing to do with Gentiles (Acts 10:28). No wonder it took Saul years to re-evaluate his perspectives and bring them in line with the heart of God for the world (Acts 9:26–30; 22:17–21).

Paul's experience forces us to ask: What attitudes of prejudice keep you from recognizing God's heart for the whole world? What attitudes of bigotry operate where you live or work? Do you in any way challenge that thinking, or do you just keep silent—or worse, go along with it or even promote it? Would God be able to use you to bear His name to people from a different ethnic heritage? ◆

Believers often embrace cultural values whether they are biblical or not. We may reproduce and even defend sinful attitudes and actions that are normal for our surrounding culture. See "Society's Divisions Affect Believers," Acts 6:1.

Wise Believers Seek Counsel

CONSIDER THIS 2:1–10

If you've ever tried to resolve a deep-seated controversy, you may have found how easy it is to "agree to disagree" over a highly controversial issue, but how difficult it is to actually carry that out. It takes concerted effort. In his exchange with the apostles at Jerusalem (v. 1), Paul demonstrated how believers should honor one another by seeking each other's counsel, especially when strong convictions and difficult issues are at stake.

In this situation, Jewish followers of Christ were finding that their faith was influenced by deeply rooted ethnic and cultural bias against Gentiles. Paul had once been a champion of Judaism (1:13–14), but then became "the apostle to the Gentiles" (1:15; see Acts 13:2–3). Paul came to Jerusalem to meet with the leaders of the Jewish believers and discuss his activities.

Note several elements in the encounter between the two different positions:

(1) Paul voluntarily went to the leaders of the other side (vv. 1–2).
(2) He met privately to discuss a potentially volatile situation (v. 2).
(3) He sought the input of recognized leaders (vv. 2–9).

(continued on page 647)

FOR YOUR INFO
2:12

CIRCUMCISION

The fact that a certain group in the early church was referred to as "the circumcision" (v. 12) reflects how deeply controversial the ancient practice of circumcision had become. Originally mandated by God as a sign of His covenant relationship with Israel, circumcision became a mark of exclusivity, not only among the Jews, but among the early Jewish Christians.

Technically speaking, circumcision refers to the surgical removal of the male's foreskin. The procedure was widely practiced in the ancient world, including the Egyptian and Canaanite cultures. But they performed the rite at the beginning of puberty as an initiation into manhood. By contrast, the Hebrews circumcised infants as a sign of their responsibility to serve God as His special, holy people in the midst of a pagan world.

God instructed Abraham to circumcise every male child in his household, including servants (Gen. 17:11) as a visible, physical sign of the covenant between the Lord and His people. Any male not circumcised was to be "cut off from his people" (17:14) and regarded as a covenant breaker (Ex. 22:48). The custom was performed on the eighth day after birth (Gen. 17:12), at which time a name was given to the son (Luke 1:59; 2:21). In the early history of the Jews, the rite was performed by the father, but eventually was carried out by a specialist.

The Hebrew people came to take great pride in circumcision. In fact, it became a badge of their spiritual and national superiority. This attitude fostered a spirit of exclusivism instead of compassion to reach out to other nations as God intended. Gentiles came to be regarded as the "uncircumcision," a term of disrespect implying that non-Jewish peoples were outside the circle of God's love. The terms "circumcised" and "uncircumcised" became charged with emotion, as is plain from the discord the issue brought about in the early church.

A crisis erupted at Antioch when believers from Judea, known as Judaizers, taught the brethren, "Unless you are circumcised according to the custom of Moses, you cannot be saved" (Acts 15:1–2). In effect, the Judaizers insisted that a believer from a non-Jewish background must first become a Jew ceremonially by being circumcised before he could be admitted to the Christian brotherhood.

A council of apostles and elders was convened in Jerusalem to resolve the issue (Acts 15:6–29). Among those attending were Paul, Barnabas, Simon Peter, and James, leader of the Jerusalem church. To insist on circumcision for the Gentiles, Peter argued, would amount to a burdensome yoke (Acts 15:10). This was the decision handed down by the council.

Years later, reinforcing this decision, the apostle Paul wrote the believers at Rome that Abraham, "the father of circumcision" (Rom. 4:12), was saved by faith rather than by circumcision (Rom. 4:9–12). He declared circumcision to be of no value unless accompanied by an obedient spirit (Rom. 2:25–26).

Paul also spoke of the "circumcision of Christ" (Col. 2:11), a reference to His atoning death which "condemned sin in the flesh" (Rom. 8:3) and nailed "the handwriting of requirements" to the cross (Col. 2:14). In essence, Paul declared that the new covenant of Christ's shed blood has made forgiveness available to both Jew and Gentile and has made circumcision unnecessary. All that ultimately matters for both Jew and Gentile, Paul says, is a changed nature—a new creation that makes them one in Jesus Christ (Eph. 2:14–18). ◆

Among the Jews, circumcision was a sign of the covenant that God established with Israel, His chosen people. But in Christ, God established a new covenant, open to all people. See "The New Covenant," 1 Cor. 11:25.

2:10
circumcised. 10 *They desired* only that we
should remember the poor, the very
thing which I also was eager to do.

A Rebuke for Compromising the Gospel

11 Now when Peter[a] had come to Antioch, I withstood him
2:12
to his face, because he was to be blamed;
12 for before certain men came from
James, he would eat with the Gentiles; but when they came,
he withdrew and separated himself, fearing those who were
of the circumcision. 13 And the rest of the Jews also played
the hypocrite with him, so that even Barnabas was carried
away with their hypocrisy.

14 But when I saw that they were not straightforward
about the truth of the gospel, I said to Peter before *them* all,
"If you, being a Jew, live in the manner of Gentiles and not
as the Jews, why do you[a] compel Gentiles to live as Jews?[b]
15 We *who are* Jews by nature, and not sinners of the Gentiles, 16 knowing that a man is not justified by the works of
the law but by faith in Jesus Christ, even we have believed
in Christ Jesus, that we might be justified by faith in Christ
and not by the works of the law; for by the works of the law
no flesh shall be justified.

17 "But if, while we seek to be justified by Christ, we ourselves also are found sinners, *is* Christ therefore a minister
of sin? Certainly not! 18 For if I build again those things
which I destroyed, I make myself a transgressor. 19 For I
through the law died to the law that I might live to God. 20 I
have been crucified with Christ; it is no longer I who live,
but Christ lives in me; and the *life* which I now live in the
flesh I live by faith in the Son of God, who loved me and
gave Himself for me. 21 I do not set aside the grace of God;
for if righteousness *comes* through the law, then Christ died
in vain."

CHAPTER 3

Abraham Was Justified by Faith

3:1
see pg. 648
1 O foolish Galatians! Who has bewitched you that you should not obey
the truth,[a] before whose eyes Jesus Christ was clearly portrayed among you[b] as crucified? 2 This only I want to learn

2:11 [a]NU-Text reads *Cephas.* *2:14* [a]NU-Text reads *how can you.* [b]Some interpreters stop the quotation here. *3:1* [a]NU-Text omits *that you should not obey the truth.* [b]NU-Text omits *among you.*

Remember the Poor

A CLOSER LOOK 2:10

Recounting his meeting with the church leaders (v. 10), Paul reveals his attitude of generosity toward the poor. This was a constant theme throughout his life. In fact, elsewhere he says we must support the weak. See " 'I Have Not Coveted,' " Acts 20:33–38.

(continued from page 645)

(4) He evaluated his position and behavior in light of God's truth, in order to avoid working "in vain" (v. 2).

(5) He brought along an actual test case, uncircumcised Titus, which caused some to demand that Titus conform to the Jewish rite of circumcision (v. 3–5).

(6) Clarity was achieved, but in this case it did not require uniformity of practice (v. 9).

(7) The leaders reached agreement on another matter, serving the poor among both Jews and Gentiles (v. 10).

Commitment to Christ calls for believers to pay each other honor and respect. Even if they decide to "agree to disagree," they still need each other.

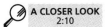

from you: Did you receive the Spirit by the works of the
law, or by the hearing of faith? 3Are you so foolish? Having
begun in the Spirit, are you now being made perfect by the
flesh? 4Have you suffered so many things in vain—if indeed
it was in vain?
5Therefore He who supplies the Spirit to you and works
miracles among you, *does He do it* by the works of the law,
3:6 or by the hearing of faith?— 6just as
Abraham "believed God, and it was ac-
counted to him for righteousness."[a] 7Therefore know that
only those who are of faith are sons of Abraham. 8And the
Scripture, foreseeing that God would justify the Gentiles by
faith, preached the gospel to Abraham beforehand, *saying,*
"In you all the nations shall be blessed."[a] 9So then those
who *are* of faith are blessed with believing Abraham.

3:6 [a]Genesis 15:6 *3:8* [a]Genesis 12:3; 18:18; 22:18; 26:4; 28:14

A CLOSER LOOK 3:6

Abraham

As the man who believed God, Abraham (v. 6) features prominently in the New Testament. See "Abraham," Rom. 4:1.

CONSIDER THIS 3:1

A Strong Rebuke

The book of Ecclesiastes speaks of "a time to love and a time to hate, a time of war and a time of peace" (Eccl. 3:8). When it came to a question of altering the gospel about Jesus, Paul realized that it was no time for peace, but for intense conflict. Here in Galatians and elsewhere, he issued a strong rebuke both to those who would pervert the message of Christ in order to preserve their traditions, and to those who followed them (Gal. 3:1).

Notice the strong feelings in some of Paul's statements on this subject (emphasis added):

- "I marvel *that you are turning away so soon from [Christ] . . . to a different gospel" (Gal. 1:6).*
- *"Even if we, or an angel from heaven, preach any other gospel to you than what we have preached to you,* let him be accursed*" (1:8).*
- *"As we have said before, so now I say again, if anyone preaches any other gospel to you than what you have received,* let him be accursed*" (1:9).*
- "O foolish Galatians! *Who has* bewitched *you . . . ?" (3:1).*
- "I am afraid for you, *lest I have labored for you in vain" (4:11).*

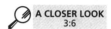

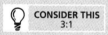

[10]For as many as are of the works of the law are under the
curse; for it is written, "Cursed *is* everyone who does not
continue in all things which are written in the book of the
law, to do them."[a] [11]But that no one is justified by the law in
the sight of God *is* evident, for "the just shall live by faith."[a]
[12]Yet the law is not of faith, but "the man who does them
shall live by them."[a]

[13]Christ has redeemed us from the curse of the law, having become a curse for us (for it is written, "Cursed *is* everyone who hangs on a tree"[a]), [14]that the blessing of Abraham
might come upon the Gentiles in Christ Jesus, that we
might receive the promise of the Spirit through faith.

[15]Brethren, I speak in the manner of men: Though *it is*
only a man's covenant, yet *if it is* confirmed, no one annuls
or adds to it. [16]Now to Abraham and his Seed were the
promises made. He does not say, "And to seeds," as of many,
but as of one, "And to your Seed,"[a] who is Christ. [17]And
this I say, *that* the law, which was four hundred and thirty
years later, cannot annul the covenant that was confirmed
before by God in Christ,[a] that it should make the promise

3:10 [a]Deuteronomy 27:26 *3:11* [a]Habakkuk 2:4 *3:12* [a]Leviticus 18:5 *3:13* [a]Deuteronomy 21:23 *3:16* [a]Genesis 12:7; 13:15; 24:7 *3:17* [a]NU-Text omits *in Christ.*

- *"I would like to be present with you now and to change my tone; for* I have doubts about you*"* *(4:20).*
- "I could wish that those who trouble you would even cut themselves off!" *(5:12).*
- "Beware of dogs, beware of evil workers, beware of the mutilation!" *(Phil. 3:2).*

Believers in Christ are called to be kind, humble, meek, and longsuffering; to bear with one another, to forgive each other, and above all to love one another as they seek the unity of the body (Col. 3:12–15). At the same time, they are called to "stand fast" in the faith (1 Cor. 16:13) and in their liberty in Christ (Gal. 5:1), and to "contend earnestly for the faith" (Jude 3). At times, that may mean anger and conflict when the very truth of the gospel is under attack.

The energy with which Paul defended the fundamentals of the faith should encourage us as believers today to ask: What challenges to the truth do we need to meet? Where are compromises being made to basic biblical principles? Is our commitment to the faith strong enough that we are willing to defend it against those who would pervert it to their own ends? ◆

ARE YOU NOW BEING MADE PERFECT BY THE FLESH?
—Galatians 3:3

We Are Family!

CONSIDER THIS 3:28 **In v. 28, Paul emphasizes that three major social distinctions no longer matter in Christ:**

- ***Ethnicity:* "neither Jew nor Greek."**
- ***Socioeconomic status:* "neither slave nor free."**
- ***Gender:* "neither male nor female."**

First-century culture was deeply divided along these lines. So was the church. But Paul stressed, "You are all *one* in Christ Jesus" (italics added).

Christians have become children of God through faith, which means we are all in the same family. We are no longer divided by ethnicity, social status, or gender, but have become brothers and sisters in God's family.

One powerful symbol of that new unity is baptism (v. 27). As part of the baptismal ceremony, a believer affirms the lordship of Christ and his or her commitment to a new way of life. Paul is possibly quoting from a first-century baptismal creed (v. 28) to remind us of our promise to "put on Christ," not in word but in deed.

In the early Christian communities that meant that both Gentiles and Jews could exercise their spiritual gifts. Both slaves and masters could pray or prophesy. Both women and men could enjoy full membership in the body. "Christ [was] all and in all" (Col. 3:11). The breaking down of traditional barriers wasn't just a future hope. The early church worked to make it a reality.

Which brings us to the question: What walls of ethnicity, status, or gender divide believers today? Are we willing to model reconciliation between different and even antagonistic groups? If not, then is our church truly a sign of God's kingdom, or merely a human institution?

of no effect. 18For if the inheritance *is* of the law, *it is* no
longer of promise; but God gave *it* to Abraham by promise.
19What purpose then *does* the law *serve?* It was added because of transgressions, till the Seed should come to whom
the promise was made; *and it was* appointed through angels
by the hand of a mediator. 20Now a mediator does not *medi-
ate* for one *only,* but God is one.
21*Is* the law then against the promises of God? Certainly
not! For if there had been a law given which could have
given life, truly righteousness would have been by the law.
22But the Scripture has confined all under sin, that the
promise by faith in Jesus Christ might be given to those
who believe. 23But before faith came, we were kept under
guard by the law, kept for the faith which would afterward
be revealed. 24Therefore the law was our tutor *to bring us* to
Christ, that we might be justified by faith. 25But after faith
has come, we are no longer under a tutor.

Believers Are Children of God by Faith

26For you are all sons of God through faith in Christ Jesus. 27For as many of you as were baptized into Christ have
3:28 put on Christ. 28There is neither Jew nor
Greek, there is neither slave nor free,
there is neither male nor female; for you are all one in
Christ Jesus. 29And if you *are* Christ's, then you are Abraham's seed, and heirs according to the promise.

CHAPTER 4

No Longer Slaves But Heirs

4:1–18 1Now I say *that* the heir, as long as he is
a child, does not differ at all from a slave,
though he is master of all, 2but is under guardians and
stewards until the time appointed by the father. 3Even so
we, when we were children, were in bondage under the elements of the world. 4But when the fullness of the time had
come, God sent forth His Son, born[a] of a woman, born under the law, 5to redeem those who were under the law, that
we might receive the adoption as sons.
6And because you are sons, God has sent forth the Spirit
of His Son into your hearts, crying out, "Abba, Father!"
4:7 7Therefore you are no longer a slave but a
son, and if a son, then an heir of[a] God
through Christ.

4:4 [a]Or *made* 4:7 [a]NU-Text reads *through God* and omits *through Christ.*

The Privileges of God's Children

A CLOSER LOOK 4:7 *Children enjoy privileges that slaves will never know (v. 7). See "What's In It for Me?" at Eph. 1:11, to learn more about the inheritance we will enjoy as God's children.*

[8]But then, indeed, when you did not know God, you
served those which by nature are not gods. [9]But now after
you have known God, or rather are known by God, how *is*
it that you turn again to the weak and beggarly elements, to
which you desire again to be in bondage? [10]You observe
days and months and seasons and years. [11]I am afraid for
you, lest I have labored for you in vain.

Whose Message Is to Be Believed?

[12]Brethren, I urge you to become like me, for I *became*
like you. You have not injured me at all. [13]You know that
because of physical infirmity I preached the gospel to you at
the first. [14]And my trial which was in my flesh you did not

CONSIDER THIS
4:1–18

RIGHTS

We live in a time when it seems that everyone is concerned about exercising their "rights." Indeed, society has become somewhat polarized as various groups form around their perceptions of rights that they feel they are being denied. The more intense the struggle to achieve those rights, the more social conflict seems to escalate.

Paul indicated to the Galatians that before God, no one has any rights; whatever rights humanity once had have been forfeited as a result of sin. To bring this situation home to his readers, Paul used the metaphor of a slave (vv. 1–3), an image that the Galatians probably knew well, as the Roman Empire depended heavily on slave labor (see Rom. 6:16).

The Galatians had become children of God, but before that they were in bondage to sin, to the "elements of the world" (v. 3; compare Col. 3:18–19). As slaves to sin, they had no rights before God. He owed them nothing. They belonged to sin, which they were forced to serve. Emancipation from that position had to come from a source other than their own power, ingenuity, or morality.

Such is the plight of all sinners before God—helpless and hopeless (Rom. 3:23, John 3:19–20). But just as God gave life, resources, and responsibility to humanity in the beginning (Gen. 1:26—2:4), so now He has given Christ His Son to rescue or "redeem" people from sin and grant them all the privileges of adoption into the family of God (vv. 4–7). No one deserves that, which is why receiving Christ's new life and the rights therein is truly a gift.

If as believers we have received these treasures from God, then we ought to let others know that the same opportunity is available to them. ◆

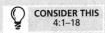

HAGAR

FOR YOUR INFO 4:24–25 **A helpless outcast serves as a metaphor for Paul's warning to the Galatians against turning to the Law for salvation. Hagar (vv. 24–25; Gen. 16:1–16) was an Egyptian slave of Sarah, the wife of the Old Testament patriarch Abraham (see 1 Pet. 3:6).**

God promised Abraham and Sarah that He would give them a son. But after ten years of waiting, Sarah presented Hagar to her husband so that he could father a child by her, according to the custom of the day. However, God viewed the substitution as a lack of faith.

When Hagar became pregnant, she mocked her mistress, who dealt with her harshly. Fleeing into the wilderness, Hagar encountered an angel of the Lord. The heavenly messenger revealed that the child she was to bear, Ishmael, would be the father of a great nation even though he was not the son that God had promised to Abraham and Sarah.

Hagar returned to Abraham's camp and bore Ishmael, who was accepted as Abraham's son. But when Ishmael was 14, Sarah gave birth to Isaac, the promised son. Later Ishmael mocked Isaac at the festival of Isaac's weaning. At Sarah's insistence, Hagar and her son were expelled from Abraham's family. However, God took care of them as they wandered in the wilderness.

The Lord also carried out His promise to make a great nation of Ishmael. He had twelve sons who had many descendents who lived as nomads in the deserts of northern Arabia. Tradition holds that all of the Arab peoples are descended from Hagar.

despise or reject, but you received me as an angel of God,
even as Christ Jesus. 15What[a] then was the blessing you *enjoyed?* For I bear you witness that, if possible, you would
have plucked out your own eyes and given them to me.
16Have I therefore become your enemy because I tell you
the truth?

17They zealously court you, *but* for no good; yes, they
want to exclude you, that you may be zealous for them.
18But it is good to be zealous in a good thing always, and
not only when I am present with you. 19My little children,
for whom I labor in birth again until Christ is formed in
you, 20I would like to be present with you now and to
change my tone; for I have doubts about you.

Two Alternatives—Freedom or Slavery

21Tell me, you who desire to be under the law, do you not
hear the law? 22For it is written that Abraham had two sons:
the one by a bondwoman, the other by a freewoman. 23But
he *who was* of the bondwoman was born according to the
4:24–25 flesh, and he of the freewoman through
promise, 24which things are symbolic.
For these are the[a] two covenants: the one from Mount Sinai
4:25–26 see pg. 655 which gives birth to bondage, which is
Hagar— 25for this Hagar is Mount Sinai
in Arabia, and corresponds to Jerusalem which now is, and is
in bondage with her children— 26but the Jerusalem above
is free, which is the mother of us all. 27For it is written:

"Rejoice, O barren,
You who do not bear!
Break forth and shout,
You who are not in labor!
For the desolate has many more children
Than she who has a husband."[a]

28Now we, brethren, as Isaac *was,* are children of promise.
29But, as he who was born according to the flesh then persecuted him *who was born* according to the Spirit, even so *it*
is now. 30Nevertheless what does the Scripture say? "Cast
out the bondwoman and her son, for the son of the bondwoman shall not be heir with the son of the freewoman."[a]
31So then, brethren, we are not children of the bondwoman
but of the free.

CHAPTER 5

Live in the Liberty of the Gospel

5:1–12 1Stand fast therefore in the liberty by
which Christ has made us free,[a] and do

(Bible text continued on page 654)

4:15 [a]NU-Text reads *Where.* *4:24* [a]NU-Text and M-Text omit *the.* *4:27* [a]Isaiah 54:1
4:30 [a]Genesis 21:10 *5:1* [a]NU-Text reads *For freedom Christ has made us free; stand fast therefore.*

CONSIDER THIS
5:1–12

MYTH #7

10 MYTHS ABOUT CHRISTIANITY

MYTH: CHRISTIANITY STIFLES PERSONAL FREEDOM

Many people today accept a number of myths about Christianity, with the result that they never respond to Jesus as He really is. This is one of ten articles that speak to some of those misconceptions. For a list of all ten, see 1 Tim. 1:3–4.

Freedom is the prevailing cry of the world today, the overwhelming preoccupation of individuals and nations. Yet even though Scripture speaks of a liberty that Christ offers (vv. 1–12), some people resist Christianity as itself an obstacle to freedom. Is this view of the faith justified?

On the face of it, it seems strange to identify Christianity as an enemy of freedom. After all, Christians have historically stood up for the poor, the oppressed, the captive, and the underprivileged. Likewise, liberation from ignorance, disease, and political oppression have invariably resulted wherever Christian faith and principles have been adopted. Why, then, would some view the faith as repressive?

Perhaps part of the answer lies in the problem of legalism. Whenever Christianity is made into a list of dos and don'ts, it becomes intolerant and restrictive. Instead of enjoying an intimate relationship with a loving God, the legalist is obsessed with rules and regulations, as if God were a celestial Policeman just waiting to catch us out of line.

To be sure, Christ does make demands on us that sometimes limit our autonomy. But true Christianity sees this as part of a relationship based on love and grace, not unlike a healthy marriage in which both partners sometimes sacrifice their own desires in order to serve the other.

But even if there were no legalists, many people would still resist Christianity because they resist any standards that would place absolute claims on them. To them, freedom means pure autonomy—the right to do whatever they want, with no accountability to anyone else.

But surely that leads to irresponsibility and license rather than freedom. Nor do people really live that way. Sooner or later they choose one course of action over another, based on some set of values. In other words, they surrender their will to standards, whether good or bad, and act accordingly. So it is not just the values of Christianity that "stifle" personal freedom, but values in general.

The real question, of course, is what kind of people are we? What is our character? Christians try to mold their character after the pattern of Jesus. He was the most liberated man who ever lived. His ultimate standard of behavior was, what does My Father want Me to do (John 8:29)? Did that code stifle His freedom? Hardly: He was utterly free of covetousness, hypocrisy, fear of others, and every other vice. At the same time He was free to be Himself, free to tell the truth, free to love people with warmth and purity, and free to surrender His life for others.

True Christian freedom is Christlike freedom. There is no hint of legalism about it. It accepts absolute moral standards that are well known and well proven, and it takes its inspiration from the most liberated human being who ever lived, Jesus of Nazareth. What is stifling about that? ◆

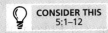

not be entangled again with a yoke of bondage. 2Indeed I,
Paul, say to you that if you become circumcised, Christ will
profit you nothing. 3And I testify again to every man who
becomes circumcised that he is a debtor to keep the whole
law. 4You have become estranged from Christ, you who *attempt to* be justified by law; you have fallen from grace. 5For
we through the Spirit eagerly wait for the hope of righteousness by faith. 6For in Christ Jesus neither circumcision

CONSIDER THIS
5:18

TEN COMMANDMENTS—TEN GREAT FREEDOMS

To live "under the law" (v. 18) is to live under the crushing expectation of fulfilling God's moral standards through one's own human ability. People who try to live that way are likely to end up in misery because sooner or later they are bound to fail (Rom. 7:7–24). Rather than experiencing the joy of a clean conscience, they feel enslaved to legalism and guilt.

The problem is not with God's moral standards but with the sinful nature of humanity. Fortunately, God provides the Holy Spirit to enable believers to carry out His holy standards, as summarized in the Ten Commandments. Thus, walking by the Spirit (v. 16) means that one is able to obey the spirit of the Ten Commandments ("the law") and experience powerful new freedoms to be the person God originally intended:

FREEDOMS FOR LIVING

	Original Commandment	New Freedoms
I	"You shall have no other gods before Me."	God is our Helper. If we hold onto Him we can find freedom from anxiety about our future, our relationships, our well-being, and our happiness.
II	"You shall not make for yourself a carved image."	God is our Teacher. If we hold onto Him we will learn what is true and avoid being talked into that which is false.
III	"You shall not take the name of the Lord your God in vain."	God is our Friend. If we hold onto Him, our prayers will not be futile; we need not try to force Him to help us. Nor should we invoke His name in pursuit of our own self-interest.
IV	"Remember the Sabbath day, to keep it holy."	God is our Master. If we hold onto Him, we will find fulfillment. We need not work ourselves to death.

Continued

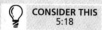

nor uncircumcision avails anything, but faith working through love.
7You ran well. Who hindered you from obeying the truth?
8This persuasion does not *come* from Him who calls you. 9A
little leaven leavens the whole lump. 10I have confidence in you, in the Lord, that you will have no other mind; but he who troubles you shall bear his judgment, whoever he is.
11And I, brethren, if I still preach circumcision, why do I

FREEDOMS FOR LIVING

	Original Commandment	New Freedoms
	Continued	
V	"Honor your father and your mother."	God is our Father in heaven. If we hold onto Him, we will experience His love. We need not be bound by the disappointments of our human relationships.
VI	"You shall not murder."	God is our Protector. If we hold onto Him, we can find freedom from competitiveness with our neighbor and instead act with love.
VII	"You shall not commit adultery."	God is the Author of true happiness. If we hold onto Him, we can find freedom to pursue true love rather than the caricatures of love promoted by our culture.
VIII	"You shall not steal."	God is our Provider. If we hold onto Him, we can learn to give instead of take. We can find freedom from worry about our material well-being and instead work honestly with the abilities He has given us.
IX	"You shall not bear false witness."	God is the Truth. If we hold onto Him, we can learn to speak truth and engender trust.
X	"You shall not covet."	God is the Giver of all good gifts. If we hold onto Him, we can find freedom from greed and instead live with generosity, compassion, and self-respect.

Just as the Ten Commandments provide powerful freedoms for living, they also serve as a guide for workplace behaviors and attitudes. See "Ten Commandments for Practical Living," James 2:8–13.

THE JERUSALEM ABOVE

CONSIDER THIS 4:25–26

Paul distinguished between a "Jerusalem which now is" (v. 25) and "the Jerusalem above" (v. 26). What was he talking about?

Paul was furious because teachers had come from Jerusalem to lay a Jewish agenda on the new believers in Galatia. It was a legalistic agenda. It claimed that one could not really be a Christian unless one first became a Jew. So when Paul mentioned the "Jerusalem which now is," he was referring to those teachers. They had enslaved Jerusalem itself with their teaching, and he resented their coming to Galatia to enslave Christians there.

By contrast, "the Jerusalem above" is free (v. 28)—free from legalism and free from sin. It is more than a city; it is a symbol of God's rule and kingdom.

Jerusalem is the place where God has fulfilled His promises in Christ, just as Isaac was delivered on the mountain there (v. 28).

still suffer persecution? Then the offense of the cross has
ceased. 12I could wish that those who trouble you would
even cut themselves off!

Liberty Means Living in Love

13For you, brethren, have been called to liberty; only do
not *use* liberty as an opportunity for the flesh, but through
love serve one another. 14For all the law is fulfilled in one
word, *even* in this: "You shall love your neighbor as yourself."[a] 15But if you bite and devour one another, beware lest
you be consumed by one another!

5:14 [a]Leviticus 19:18

FOR YOUR INFO
5:22–23

New Creatures with New Character

If you are in Christ, you are a new creature. The old habits and character traits that marked your life before Christ are passing away. He is making you entirely new (see 2 Cor. 5:17). What will that look like? Paul paints several pictures of new creatures with new character:

The Traits of New Creatures in Christ

1 Corinthians 13:3–8	Galatians 5:22–23	Philippians 4:8	Colossians 3:12–16
Love... •suffers long •is kind •does not envy •does not parade itself •is not puffed up •does not behave rudely •does not seek its own •is not provoked •thinks no evil •does not rejoice in iniquity •rejoices in the truth •bears all things •believes all things •hopes all things •endures all things	*The fruit of the Spirit is...* •love •joy •peace •longsuffering (patience) •kindness •goodness •faithfulness •gentleness •self-control	*Meditate on whatever things are...* •true •noble •just •pure •lovely •of good report •of any virtue •praiseworthy	*Put on these things...* •tender mercies •kindness •humility •meekness •longsuffering (patience) •Bear with one another. •Forgive one another. •Above all, put on love. •Let the peace of God rule in your hearts. •Be thankful. •Let the Word of Christ dwell in you richly. •Teach and admonish one another. •Sing with grace in your hearts.
"Now abide faith, hope, love, these three; but the greatest of these is love" (13:13).	"Against such there is no law... If we live in the Spirit, let us also walk in the Spirit" (5:23, 25).	"The things which you learned and received and heard and saw in me, these do, and the God of peace will be with you" (4:9).	"Whatever you do in word or deed, do all in the name of the Lord Jesus" (3:17).

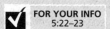

Liberty Means Living by the Spirit

[16]I say then: Walk in the Spirit, and you shall not
fulfill the lust of the flesh. [17]For the flesh lusts
against the Spirit, and the Spirit against the flesh;
and these are contrary to one another, so that you
5:18 see pg. 654
do not do the things that you
wish. [18]But if you are led by the
Spirit, you are not under the law.
[19]Now the works of the flesh are evident, which
are: adultery,[a] fornication, uncleanness, lewdness,
[20]idolatry, sorcery, hatred, contentions, jealousies,
outbursts of wrath, selfish ambitions, dissensions,
heresies, [21]envy, murders,[a] drunkenness, revelries,
and the like; of which I tell you beforehand, just as
I also told *you* in time past, that those who practice
such things will not inherit the kingdom of God.
5:22–23
[22]But the fruit of the Spirit is
love, joy, peace, longsuffering,
kindness, goodness, faithfulness, [23]gentleness, self-
control. Against such there is no law. [24]And those
who are Christ's have crucified the flesh with its
passions and desires. [25]If we live in the Spirit, let us
also walk in the Spirit. [26]Let us not become con-
ceited, provoking one another, envying one another.

CHAPTER 6

Liberty Means a Concern for Purity

6:1
[1]Brethren, if a man is overtaken in any trespass, you who
are spiritual restore such a one in a spirit of gentleness, considering yourself lest you also be tempted.
[2]Bear one another's burdens, and so fulfill the law
of Christ. [3]For if anyone thinks himself to be something, when he is nothing, he deceives himself.
[4]But let each one examine his own work, and then
he will have rejoicing in himself alone, and not in
another. [5]For each one shall bear his own load.

5:19 [a]NU-Text omits *adultery.* *5:21* [a]NU-Text omits *murders.* *6:14* [a]Or *by which* (the cross)

Liberty Means Caring about Other Believers

[6]Let him who is taught the word share in all
good things with him who teaches.
[7]Do not be deceived, God is not mocked; for
whatever a man sows, that he will also reap. [8]For
he who sows to his flesh will of the flesh reap corruption, but he who sows to the Spirit will of the
Spirit reap everlasting life. [9]And let us not grow
weary while doing good, for in due season we shall
reap if we do not lose heart. [10]Therefore, as we
have opportunity, let us do good to all, especially
to those who are of the household of faith.

A Handwritten Conclusion

[11]See with what large letters I have written to you
with my own hand! [12]As many as desire to make a
good showing in the flesh, these *would* compel you
to be circumcised, only that they may not suffer
persecution for the cross of Christ. [13]For not even
those who are circumcised keep the law, but they
desire to have you circumcised that they may boast
in your flesh. [14]But God forbid that I should boast
except in the cross of our Lord Jesus Christ, by
whom[a] the world has been crucified to me, and I to
the world. [15]For in Christ Jesus neither circumcision nor uncircumcision avails anything, but a new
creation.
[16]And as many as walk according to this rule,
peace and mercy *be* upon them, and upon the Israel of God.
[17]From now on let no one trouble me, for I bear
in my body the marks of the Lord Jesus.
[18]Brethren, the grace of our Lord Jesus Christ *be*
with your spirit. Amen.

Look to Yourselves!

A CLOSER LOOK 6:1

Paul warns us as believers that while we correct those who have fallen into sin, we should pay attention to our own vulnerability to temptation (v. 1). For more on this important topic, see "Pay Attention to Temptation!" 1 Cor. 10:12–13.

Ephesians

In some areas of the world today, Christianity is spreading so rapidly that experts predict that some countries and even some continents will be "Christianized" within a matter of years. However, encouraging as that may be, the roots of that new faith are often shallow and unstable, producing a Christianity that some have described as a mile wide and an inch deep.

Meanwhile, many Christians in the West tend to embrace what might be called a *subjective* gospel: what matters is not so much whether the message of Christ is true, but what it can do for *me*. Can it solve *my* problems, meet *my* needs, help *me* feel okay, improve *my* relationships? It's as if Jesus came primarily for *me*; what difference He makes for others in other times and places is of little consequence.

Paul's letter to the Ephesians was written for believers in both these kinds of circumstances. By unveiling some of what lies behind life in Christ, Ephesians brings depth to our day-to-day experience of the faith. For example, it explains how all three members of the Godhead brought about salvation through a carefully coordinated plan that began in eternity and continues in history. It also reveals the broad, diverse nature of the church. And it makes us aware of the vast forces of evil arrayed against God and His people, and what we must do to withstand the "spiritual hosts of wickedness in the heavenly places" (6:12).

In short, by paying careful attention to this letter, we as believers can develop depth and stability in our faith. We can discover a foundation that goes far beyond cultures and ideologies, and a purpose that transcends personal interests and preoccupations. As Paul says, we can "grow up in all things into Him who is the head—Christ" (4:15).

C O N T E N T S

A R T I C L E S

The Ultimate "New Testament Church"

Have you ever longed for your church to be more like the church of the New Testament? If so, carefully study the church at Ephesus. More material in the New Testament pertains historically to Ephesus than to any other community of believers, giving us the best picture we have of what a first-century congregation really looked like:

- *No less than 20 chapters, covering a period of more than 40 years, describe God's work and His people at Ephesus.*
- *More authors write about Ephesus than any other New Testament congregation:*
  Luke *described its founding in three chapters of Acts (18–20);*
  Paul *wrote Ephesians to the congregation there and sent two letters, 1 and 2 Timothy, to its young pastor;*
  John, *repeating a message from Christ, encouraged and warned the Ephesian believers in a letter preserved in the book of Revelation (2:1–7).*

The world of Ephesus feels remarkably like our own—tense with political intrigue and prejudices, divided between affluent, ambitious masters and a needy, dehumanized underclass, and strangely hopeful about its future. A reading of the entire New Testament record on the Ephesian church illustrates what it takes to live out the gospel in a challenging, world-class marketplace.

The start-up congregation in Ephesus proved remarkably fruitful. According to Luke, the message of Christ spread far inland from that major urban center until "all who dwelt in Asia heard the word of the Lord Jesus, both Jews and Greeks" (Acts 19:10). Judging from Revelation and the letters to Timothy, the Ephesian believers planted several daughter churches. In addition, some church historians believe that a fugitive slave, Onesimus, from Philemon's house church in Laodicea, may have been the same Bishop Onesimus who served at Ephesus around A.D. *110 (see the Introduction to Philemon).*

However, establishing such a thriving center of Christianity was not without cost. Paul probably devoted more time and energy to Ephesus than to any other city. He made at least three visits and spent three years there laying a foundation for the start-up effort. He was aided enormously by Priscilla and Aquila, his business partners (see Rom. 16:3–5). Later, young Timothy, Paul's protégé, carried on the work through tough times and apparently established faithful leadership to follow after him (see the Introduction to 2 Timothy and 2 Tim. 2:2).

Overall, the church at Ephesus serves as a case study in how to establish a community of faith in an increasingly urban world. The study begins with Luke's account of the church's beginnings (Acts 18–20). The letter that follows and 1 and 2 Timothy provide a window on what a growing church and its leaders need to keep in mind. Finally, the church receives an "audit," a warning to beware lest its spiritual life dissipate and its bright promise slip into decline (Rev. 2:1–7). ◆

EPHESUS

- **A major city of Greece between the Croessus mountain range and the Mediterranean Sea, seated at the mouth of the Cayster River in Paul's day. (Today the site of the ancient city is six miles inland, due to river silting.)**
- **First-century population estimated at 300,000, making Ephesus one of the larger cities of the Roman Empire.**
- **Extraordinarily prosperous as a commercial center, provincial capital, and port city in the eastern Roman Empire.**
- **Boasted numerous monuments, theaters, and temples, notably the temple of Diana (Acts 19:24–27). Ephesus was an international tourist center, so profitable that its leaders opened the first world bank.**
- **Renowned for religious pluralism, including emperor-worship, mystery cults, occult practices, Hellenized Judaism, and early Christianity.**
- **A frequent stop for Paul, who stayed almost three years and helped establish a church. He may have been jailed there, and probably wrote some of his letters there.**
- **Home to several Christian leaders, including Timothy, Erastus, and Onesiphorus.**
- **Timothy and the apostle John pastored there. The church experienced institutional development but was later denounced as having lost its first love (Rev. 2:4).**
- **Ephesian Christians held firm over four centuries. In A.D. 431 a church council was held there, condemning a false teaching called Nestorianism.**

Paul and the other believers at Ephesus penetrated the city and its systems so effectively that "all . . . in Asia heard the word of the Lord" (Acts 19:10). Find out more about their powerful strategy in "The Ephesus Approach," Acts 19:8–41.

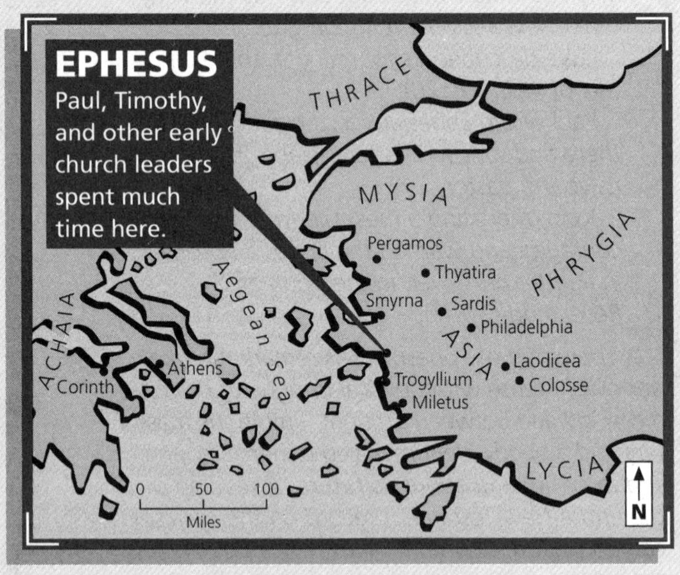

CHAPTER 1

Greeting

1 Paul, an apostle of Jesus Christ by the will of God,

To the saints who are in Ephesus, and faithful in Christ
Jesus:

2 Grace to you and peace from God our Father and the
Lord Jesus Christ.

Blessed Beyond Measure

1:3–14

3 Blessed *be* the God and Father of our
Lord Jesus Christ, who has blessed us
with every spiritual blessing in the heavenly *places* in
Christ, 4 just as He chose us in Him before the foundation of
the world, that we should be holy and without blame before Him in love, 5 having predestined us to adoption as
sons by Jesus Christ to Himself, according to the good pleasure of His will, 6 to the praise of the glory of His grace, by
which He made us accepted in the Beloved.
7 In Him we have redemption through His blood, the forgiveness of sins, according to the riches of His grace 8 which
He made to abound toward us in all wisdom and prudence,
9 having made known to us the mystery of His will, according to His good pleasure which He purposed in Himself,
10 that in the dispensation of the fullness of the times He
might gather together in one all things in Christ, both[a]
which are in heaven and which are on earth—in Him.

1:11 see pg. 664

11 In Him also we have obtained an inheritance, being predestined according to
the purpose of Him who works all things according to the
counsel of His will, 12 that we who first trusted in Christ
should be to the praise of His glory.
13 In Him you also *trusted*, after you heard the word of
truth, the gospel of your salvation; in whom also, having
believed, you were sealed with the Holy Spirit of promise,
14 who[a] is the guarantee of our inheritance until the redemption of the purchased possession, to the praise of His glory.

A Prayer for Eye Opening

15 Therefore I also, after I heard of your faith in the Lord
Jesus and your love for all the saints, 16 do not cease to give
thanks for you, making mention of you in my prayers:
17 that the God of our Lord Jesus Christ, the Father of glory,
may give to you the spirit of wisdom and revelation in the

1:18 see pg. 664

knowledge of Him, 18 the eyes of your understanding[a] being enlightened; that you

1:10 [a]NU-Text and M-Text omit *both.* *1:14* [a]NU-Text reads *which.* *1:18* [a]NU-Text and M-Text read *hearts.*

THE FOUNDATION

CONSIDER THIS 1:3–14

Many islands in the Pacific Ocean appear to be tiny points of land that rise only a few thousand feet above sea level. Yet the foundations of those peaks extend for miles underwater. In fact, if measured from their base, some would tower above the Himalayas.

In a similar way, the salvation that we enjoy today involves far more than our brief experience of it. It extends back through time and even beyond time into eternity, "before the foundation of the world" (v. 4). Indeed, salvation brings so many things into play that Paul wrote a 202-word run-on sentence (in the Greek) stretching across twelve verses (vv. 3–14) as he began to describe it. The exhausting, inspiring picture offers a breathtaking vista for the believer.

One thing it shows is that the salvation of every Christian involves all three persons of the Trinity. God the Father has selected us for His grace (vv. 4–5, 11). God the Son offered Himself as the sacrifice for sin, paying our penalty and extending forgiveness (v. 7). And God the Holy Spirit has "sealed" us in Christ, guaranteeing our relationship with God (vv. 13–14). This work of God began before the world was formed and has continued throughout history.

Thus the foundation of our faith is anchored in God Himself. In His wisdom He has superintended a massive chain of events of which our own lives are but the most recent links.

may know what is the hope of His calling, what are the
riches of the glory of His inheritance in the saints, [19]and
what *is* the exceeding greatness of His power toward us who
believe, according to the working of His mighty power
[20]which He worked in Christ when He raised Him from the
dead and seated *Him* at His right hand in the heavenly
places, [21]far above all principality and power and might and
dominion, and every name that is named, not only in this
age but also in that which is to come.
[22]And He put all *things* under His feet, and gave Him *to be*
head over all *things* to the church, [23]which is His body, the
fullness of Him who fills all in all.

What's In It for Me?

CONSIDER THIS 1:11 **Do you ever wonder what you're going to get out of following Christ? Peter and the other disciples wondered. "We have left all and followed You," Peter told Jesus. "Therefore what shall we have?" (Matt. 19:27). In other words, "What's the payoff? What's in this for me?"**

Paul describes some of the "payoff" for believers here in Ephesians 1:3–14. Because so much of it lies in the future, in another mode of existence, the language is strange and hard to understand. But in v. 11 he mentions an inheritance that is coming to us. What is it that we are going to receive "in Christ"?

Simply this: all that God has prepared for Christ in "the fullness of the times" is going to be ours as well (Rom. 8:15–17). This includes salvation from sin (Heb. 1:14), everlasting life (Matt. 19:29), and the kingdom of God (Matt. 25:34). In fact, we will inherit God Himself.

Is this just wishful thinking? No, God is already giving us glimpses of that inconceivable future. The Holy Spirit lives inside us as a guarantee of things to come (v. 14). He "seals" us, assuring that we remain in God's family and do not lose our inheritance. And while we move toward that day, He works within our lives to make us like Christ. Paul describes what that looks like in chapters 4–6.

Scripture also speaks of the inheritance of material goods that people receive from their parents. See "Will You Get What's Coming to You?" Luke 12:13–15.

All God's Children

CONSIDER THIS 1:18 *In the ancient world, conquering rulers often made a gift of conquered territories and other property to their children or to valued servants (Luke 19:12, 14, 17, 27). Such treasures formed an "inheritance" (Matt. 21:38). A similar idea appears in Ephesians 1:18, where Paul speaks of God's "inheritance in the saints."*

God is preparing an inheritance, a kingdom, for His Son, Jesus Christ. It will include people from throughout history, people the Bible calls "saints," or true believers. These are people that God has called and chosen to be His children. Paul wants the Ephesians—and us—to know that believers in Christ will be part of that joyful crowd.

God didn't have to do things that way. When sin entered the world He could have started all over again and created new and perfect creatures to present to His Son. But He chose to gather from the fallen, broken hordes of humanity a people for Himself. By telling us that we are going to be part of His inheritance, He's making a promise: the renovation that has started in our lives will continue until we are perfected and ready to be presented to Christ.

CHAPTER 2

Christ Has Overcome Sin

2:1 see pg. 666

1And you *He made alive,* who were
dead in trespasses and sins, 2in which
you once walked according to the course of this world, according to the prince of the power of the air, the spirit who
now works in the sons of disobedience, 3among whom also
we all once conducted ourselves in the lusts of our flesh,
fulfilling the desires of the flesh and of the mind, and were
by nature children of wrath, just as the others.
4But God, who is rich in mercy, because of His great love
with which He loved us, 5even when we were dead in trespasses, made us alive together with Christ (by grace you
have been saved), 6and raised *us* up together, and made *us*
sit together in the heavenly *places* in Christ Jesus, 7that in
the ages to come He might show the exceeding riches of His
grace in *His* kindness toward us in Christ Jesus. 8For by
grace you have been saved through faith, and that not of
yourselves; *it is* the gift of God, 9not of works, lest anyone
should boast. 10For we are His workmanship, created in
Christ Jesus for good works, which God prepared beforehand that we should walk in them.

Christ Has Abolished the Law's Enmity

11Therefore remember that you, once Gentiles in the
flesh—who are called Uncircumcision by what is called the
Circumcision made in the flesh by hands— 12that at that
time you were without Christ, being aliens from the
commonwealth of Israel and strangers from the covenants
of promise, having no hope and without God in the world.
13But now in Christ Jesus you who once were far off have
been brought near by the blood of Christ.

2:14–18

14For He Himself is our peace, who has
made both one, and has broken down
the middle wall of separation, 15having abolished in His
flesh the enmity, *that is,* the law of commandments *contained*
in ordinances, so as to create in Himself one new man *from*
the two, *thus* making peace, 16and that He might reconcile
them both to God in one body through the cross, thereby
putting to death the enmity. 17And He came and preached
peace to you who were afar off and to those who were near.

Breaking Down Walls

A CLOSER LOOK 2:14–18

Paul wrote about breaking down the walls that divide us (vv. 14–22). Antioch, the city from which Paul was sent out to take the gospel to Asia Minor, walled off the four dominant ethnic groups of its population—Greek, Syrian, African, and Jewish. For more, see "Antioch: A Model for the Modern Church?" Acts 13:1.

THIS BUILDING GETS LANDMARK STATUS

CONSIDER THIS 2:19–22

Many church buildings in the United States and Europe receive special protection from agencies such as the National Register of Historic Places. Historians do research on these landmark buildings, and visitors tour them to learn more about their architectural and cultural significance.

Paul regards the community of believers at Ephesus in a similar way (vv. 19–22). Apostles and prophets are the foundation of the building, and Christ is its cornerstone. Jews and Gentiles are chiseled into living bricks and mortar, until the whole group becomes the "dwelling place of God." Such mixed construction is so unique, so full of grace, that Paul gives the structure special recognition, "landmark status" as it were.

Suppose Paul were to visit your church—not the physical building, but the *people.* Would he find your group deserving of "landmark status"? What are you and your fellow believers doing to construct a holy dwelling place for God on the historic foundation blueprinted in Ephesians 2?

[18]For through Him we both have access by one Spirit to the Father.

2:19–22
see pg. 665

[19]Now, therefore, you are no longer
strangers and foreigners, but fellow citi-
zens with the saints and members of the household of God,
[20]having been built on the foundation of the apostles and
prophets, Jesus Christ Himself being the chief corner*stone,*
[21]in whom the whole building, being fitted together, grows
into a holy temple in the Lord, [22]in whom you also are being built together for a dwelling place of God in the Spirit.

CHAPTER 3

The Mystery of the Church

[1]For this reason I, Paul, the prisoner of Christ Jesus for
you Gentiles— [2]if indeed you have heard of the dispensation of the grace of God which was given to me for you,
[3]how that by revelation He made known to me the mystery
(as I have briefly written already, [4]by which, when you read,
you may understand my knowledge in the mystery of
Christ), [5]which in other ages was not made known to the

CONSIDER THIS
2:1

Alive Together

In the earliest days of Christianity, the few Gentiles in the church were often looked down on by Jewish believers who found it hard to accept that salvation had been offered to non-Jews. In Ephesus, however, Gentiles made up the majority of the church (see "The Ephesus Approach," Acts 19:8–41). Did they still regard themselves as second-class Christians? Or did they

New Life for Believers of All Kinds

Gentiles were...	God has...
•dead in trespasses and sins (2:1) •children of wrath (2:3) •dead in trespasses (2:5)	•made them alive (2:1) •loved them (2:4) •made them alive together with Christ (2:5) •raised them up (2:6) •seated them with Christ (2:6)
•without Christ (2:12) •aliens from the commonwealth of Israel (2:12) •strangers from the covenants of promise (2:12) •without hope and without God in the world (2:12)	•brought them near by the blood of Christ (2:13)
•far from God (2:17)	•provided access to Himself (2:18)
•strangers and foreigners (2:19)	•made them fellow citizens with the saints and members of the household of God (2:19) •built them into a holy temple or dwelling place of God (2:21–22)

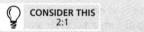

sons of men, as it has now been revealed by the Spirit to
His holy apostles and prophets: 6that the Gentiles should be
fellow heirs, of the same body, and partakers of His promise
in Christ through the gospel, 7of which I became a minister
according to the gift of the grace of God given to me by the
effective working of His power.
8To me, who am less than the least of all the saints, this
grace was given, that I should preach among the Gentiles
the unsearchable riches of Christ, 9and to make all see what
is the fellowship[a] of the mystery, which from the beginning
of the ages has been hidden in God who created all things
through Jesus Christ;[b] 10to the intent that now the manifold
wisdom of God might be made known by the church to the
principalities and powers in the heavenly *places,* 11according
to the eternal purpose which He accomplished in Christ Jesus our Lord, 12in whom we have boldness and access with
confidence through faith in Him. 13Therefore I ask that you
do not lose heart at my tribulations for you, which is your
glory.

3:9 [a]NU-Text and M-Text read *stewardship* (dispensation). [b]NU-Text omits *through Jesus Christ.*

perhaps reverse the discrimination and treat Jewish believers with prejudice?

Ephesians doesn't tell us, but it does describe in detail the new life that Christ has provided for Gentiles. Apparently they so dominated the Ephesian church that Paul could address them generally with the pronoun "you" as if to mean, "you Gentile believers" (Eph. 2:1, 11). Notice on the accompanying table what God has done for His Gentile children.

The interesting thing is that these privileges have not been provided for Gentiles separately from Jews, but together with them (2:5–6, 21–22; 4:16). In fact, God has torn down the "wall of separation" between the two groups in order to make from them one unified body (2:14–16).

These principles from the early church speak to divisions between Jew and Gentile, but they apply wherever believers face cultural diversity. The challenge of Ephesians is to see past differences to the common grace in which we stand, and "[bear] with one another in love, endeavoring to keep the unity of the Spirit in the bond of peace" (4:2–3). ◆

. . . WE HAVE BOLDNESS AND ACCESS WITH CONFIDENCE THROUGH FAITH IN HIM.
—Ephesians 3:12

A Prayer Can Restore Confidence

CONSIDER THIS 3:14–21 **Our troubles can easily cause us to lose the larger picture about life. Daily routines and pressures can create doubts about our significance. And because we are bound in a world of time, it's easy to assume that difficulties such as sickness, conflict, loneliness, insecurity, or fear will become a permanent state of affairs.**

The Ephesian believers lived with a lot of pressure. Their faith was born in a crucible of riots, courtroom conflict, and economic change (Acts 19:23–40). Later, when Paul wrote this letter to the Ephesians, he encouraged them to develop and maintain God's perspective on their lives and faith:

- ***Looking back* he rehearsed what God had done for them before they were even born (1:3–8).**
- ***Looking forward* he listed the future benefits that their faith would bring (1:9–14).**
- ***In the meantime* he prayed that they would be aware of and comprehend these realities, and experience God's power (1:15–23). He also prayed that their identity would be rooted in eternal truths and in God's present power in them (3:14–21).**

What doubts and stresses have caused you to lose perspective? Ephesians suggests that you relax—and join Paul in prayer. Take a look at the big picture of God's work on your behalf. It began long before you ar-

(continued on next page)

A Prayer to Experience Christ's Love

3:14–21
14For this reason I bow my knees to the
Father of our Lord Jesus Christ,[a] 15from
whom the whole family in heaven and earth is named,
16that He would grant you, according to the riches of His
glory, to be strengthened with might through His Spirit in
the inner man, 17that Christ may dwell in your hearts
through faith; that you, being rooted and grounded in love,
18may be able to comprehend with all the saints what *is* the
width and length and depth and height— 19to know the
love of Christ which passes knowledge; that you may be
filled with all the fullness of God.
20Now to Him who is able to do exceedingly abundantly
above all that we ask or think, according to the power that
works in us, 21to Him *be* glory in the church by Christ Jesus
to all generations, forever and ever. Amen.

CHAPTER 4

Walk Worthy of Your Calling

1I, therefore, the prisoner of the Lord, beseech you to
walk worthy of the calling with which you were called,
2with all lowliness and gentleness, with longsuffering, bearing with one another in love, 3endeavoring to keep the
unity of the Spirit in the bond of peace. 4*There is* one body
and one Spirit, just as you were called in one hope of your
calling; 5one Lord, one faith, one baptism; 6one God and
Father of all, who *is* above all, and through all, and in you[a]
all.
7But to each one of us grace was given according to the
measure of Christ's gift. 8Therefore He says:

"When He ascended on high,
He led captivity captive,
And gave gifts to men."[a]

9(Now this, "He ascended"—what does it mean but that He
also first[a] descended into the lower parts of the earth? 10He
who descended is also the One who ascended far above all
the heavens, that He might fill all things.)
11And He Himself gave some *to be* apostles, some
prophets, some evangelists, and some pastors and teachers,
4:12
12for the equipping of the saints for the
work of ministry, for the edifying of the
body of Christ, 13till we all come to the unity of the faith
and of the knowledge of the Son of God, to a perfect man,
to the measure of the stature of the fullness of Christ; 14that
we should no longer be children, tossed to and fro and car-

3:14 [a]NU-Text omits *of our Lord Jesus Christ.* *4:6* [a]NU-Text omits *you;* M-Text reads *us.*
4:8 [a]Psalm 68:18 *4:9* [a]NU-Text omits *first.*

ried about with every wind of doctrine, by the trickery of
men, in the cunning craftiness of deceitful plotting, [15]but,
speaking the truth in love, may grow up in all things into
Him who is the head—Christ— [16]from whom the whole
body, joined and knit together by what every joint supplies,
according to the effective working by which every part does
its share, causes growth of the body for the edifying of itself
in love.

Walk Differently than Unbelievers

[17]This I say, therefore, and testify in the Lord, that you
should no longer walk as the rest of[a] the Gentiles walk, in
the futility of their mind, [18]having their understanding
darkened, being alienated from the life of God, because of
the ignorance that is in them, because of the blindness of
their heart; [19]who, being past feeling, have given themselves
over to lewdness, to work all uncleanness with greediness.
[20]But you have not so learned Christ, [21]if indeed you have
heard Him and have been taught by Him, as the truth is in

4:22–24

Jesus: [22]that you put off, concerning your
former conduct, the old man which
grows corrupt according to the deceitful lusts, [23]and be renewed in the spirit of your mind, [24]and that you put on the
new man which was created according to God, in true righteousness and holiness.
[25]Therefore, putting away lying, "*Let* each one *of you*
speak truth with his neighbor,"[a] for we are members of one
another. [26]"Be angry, and do not sin":[a] do not let the sun go

4:28 see pg. 670

down on your wrath, [27]nor give place to
the devil. [28]Let him who stole steal no
longer, but rather let him labor, working with *his* hands
what is good, that he may have something to give him who
has need. [29]Let no corrupt word proceed out of your
mouth, but what is good for necessary edification, that it
may impart grace to the hearers. [30]And do not grieve the
Holy Spirit of God, by whom you were sealed for the day of
redemption. [31]Let all bitterness, wrath, anger, clamor, and
evil speaking be put away from you, with all malice. [32]And
be kind to one another, tenderhearted, forgiving one another, even as God in Christ forgave you.

4:17 [a]NU-Text omits *the rest of.* *4:25* [a]Zechariah 8:16 *4:26* [a]Psalm 4:4

Are You Fashion-conscious?

A CLOSER LOOK 4:22–24 *People who want to succeed in the business world know that they must pay careful attention to how they look. In vv. 22–24, Paul tells how to "dress for success," spiritually speaking: take off the old and put on the new. What do the fashions of faith look like? See "New Creatures with New Character," Gal. 5:22–23.*

(continued from previous page)

rived and long before your first steps in Christ. It will continue long after you pass from this life. Seeing things in this way can lend perspective to the harsh realities that may dominate your life right now.

QUOTE UNQUOTE

CONSIDER THIS 4:12 *Equipping the saints for the work of ministry (v. 12) is needed today more than ever:*

The First Reformation which came to its climax more than three centuries ago produced a great new power, by something analogous to a change of gears . . . . [T]he crucial step was that of making available the open Bible . . . .

Now, after more than three centuries, we can, if we will, change gears again. Our opportunity for a big step lies in opening the ministry to the ordinary Christian in much the same manner that our ancestors opened Bible reading to the ordinary Christian. To do this means, in one sense, the inauguration of a new Reformation while in another it means the logical completion of the earlier Reformation in which the implications of the position taken were neither fully understood nor loyally followed.

Elton Trueblood, *Your Other Vocation,* pp. 31–32

FROM DEADBEAT TO DONOR

CONSIDER THIS 4:28 **Does Christ affect people's work life? Yes, and Paul gives a concrete illustration of what "putting on the new man" means (vv. 24, 28). After Christ comes into his life, a person who has been a no-account thief stops stealing and takes an honest job. He becomes a contributing, productive member of society, doing good work. As a result, he is able to provide for his own needs and those of his family.**

But the transformation doesn't stop there. As God prospers him through his labor, he is able to give money away to help meet the needs of others. Christ changes a deadbeat into a donor!

How is Christ transforming your perspective on work and giving?

One reason that Christ has such a profound effect on people's work is that He gives it meaning and value. See "People at Work," Heb. 2:7.

The Bible has more to say about Christian character in the workplace. See "Who's the Boss?" Col. 3:22–24, and "Your 'Workstyle,'" Titus 2:9–10.

TIME FOR A CHECKUP

CONSIDER THIS 5:1–18 **How can we evaluate the quality of our faith? Are there any ways to assess spiritual progress and growth? Yes, Paul gives us a number of them here in Ephesians 5.**

Ephesians can be viewed as two halves of one big picture about giving

(continued on next page)

CHAPTER 5

Walk in Love

5:1–18
1Therefore be imitators of God as dear
children. 2And walk in love, as Christ
also has loved us and given Himself for us, an offering and a
sacrifice to God for a sweet-smelling aroma.
3But fornication and all uncleanness or covetousness, let
it not even be named among you, as is fitting for saints;
4neither filthiness, nor foolish talking, nor coarse jesting,
which are not fitting, but rather giving of thanks. 5For this
you know,[a] that no fornicator, unclean person, nor covetous
man, who is an idolater, has any inheritance in the kingdom
of Christ and God. 6Let no one deceive you with empty
words, for because of these things the wrath of God comes
upon the sons of disobedience. 7Therefore do not be partakers with them.

Walk as Children of Light

8For you were once darkness, but now *you are* light in the
Lord. Walk as children of light 9(for the fruit of the Spirit[a] is
in all goodness, righteousness, and truth), 10finding out
what is acceptable to the Lord. 11And have no fellowship
with the unfruitful works of darkness, but rather expose
them. 12For it is shameful even to speak of those things
which are done by them in secret. 13But all things that are
exposed are made manifest by the light, for whatever makes
manifest is light. 14Therefore He says:

"Awake, you who sleep,
Arise from the dead,
And Christ will give you light."

15See then that you walk circumspectly, not as fools but as
wise, 16redeeming the time, because the days are evil.
17Therefore do not be unwise, but understand what the
will of the Lord *is.* 18And do not be drunk with wine, in
which is dissipation; but be filled with the Spirit, 19speaking
to one another in psalms and hymns and spiritual songs,
singing and making melody in your heart to the Lord, 20giv-
ing thanks always for all things to God the Father in the
5:21
name of our Lord Jesus Christ, 21submit-
ting to one another in the fear of God.[a]

5:5 [a]NU-Text reads *For know this.* *5:9* [a]NU-Text reads *light.* *5:21* [a]NU-Text reads *Christ.*

A Lifestyle of Submission

A CLOSER LOOK 5:21 *Christ calls His people to a lifestyle of submission instead of selfish ambition (v. 21). The New Testament teaches that believers are to submit themselves to God, to their leaders, and to other believers. But what exactly does that mean? See "Submission," James 4:7.*

Instructions to Husbands and Wives

22Wives, submit to your own husbands, as to the Lord.
23For the husband is head of the wife, as also Christ is head
of the church; and He is the Savior of the body. 24Therefore,
just as the church is subject to Christ, so *let* the wives *be* to
their own husbands in everything.
25Husbands, love your wives, just as Christ also loved the
church and gave Himself for her, 26that He might sanctify
and cleanse her with the washing of water by the word,
27that He might present her to Himself a glorious church,
not having spot or wrinkle or any such thing, but that she
should be holy and without blemish. 28So husbands ought
to love their own wives as their own bodies; he who loves
his wife loves himself. 29For no one ever
hated his own flesh, but nourishes and
cherishes it, just as the Lord *does* the church. 30For we are

5:21–29

(Bible text continued on page 676)

A New Perspective on Marriage

CONSIDER THIS 5:21–29

In a great many pagan marriages of the first century, the husband was much older than his wife. He frequented other partners for sex, taking on a wife only to father legitimate children. Thus a girl of 13 or 14 entered an arranged marriage, frequently against her will and often with a man she had never previously met. There was little communication, cooperation, or affection—or expectation of these.

But new life in Christ called for new patterns in marriage (vv. 21–29). Paul instructed the husband to love his wife and seek her personal development—a radically new idea in that culture. The wife was to respond with commitment and loyalty. Her submission was not subordination but a wholehearted response to her husband's love.

New life in Christ also called for "A New View of Sexuality," 1 Cor. 7:3–6.

(continued from previous page)

and receiving faith. Chapters 1–3 describe what God has done for us in Christ. Chapters 4–6 describe what we are to do in response to what God has done for us.

We are called to live for God and to be imitators of God (5:1), just as children follow after the patterns seen in their parents. Here are some of the patterns that a godly lifestyle would include:

(1) Living in love, which means giving of ourselves sacrificially for the benefit of others, just as Christ has done for us (v. 2).
(2) Forsaking selfish pursuits such as self-seeking immorality and ruthless greed (vv. 3, 5).
(3) Replacing filthy talk, flippant chatter, and unkind jesting with communication rooted in thanksgiving to God and affirmation of others (vv. 4, 20).
(4) Exercising discernment about what we are told so as not to be susceptible to trickery from others (vv. 6–7, 15).
(5) Bowing out from situations where evil is the agenda (vv. 11–12).
(6) Managing our time well (v. 16).

Perhaps you'll want to develop your own list of Christlike patterns from this passage and others. Consider asking a close believing friend to assess your progress over several days or weeks. Allow these patterns of godliness to affect your own life before using them to evaluate others (Matt. 7:1–6).

The New Testament offers several portraits of what a godly lifestyle would look like. See "New Creatures with New Character," Gal. 5:22–23.

CONSIDER THIS
5:21—6:4

THE FAMILY: A CALL TO LONG-TERM WORK

"Family planning" is a controversial topic today that evokes strong feelings and images. But there is a place for "biblical family planning" in light of the reality of family life as a decades-long process to which God calls His people. Indeed, the family, along with work, is a focal point of life as God has designed it. That's why Paul devoted so much space in Ephesians to the issues of married couples (5:22–33), children (6:1–3), and fathers (6:4).

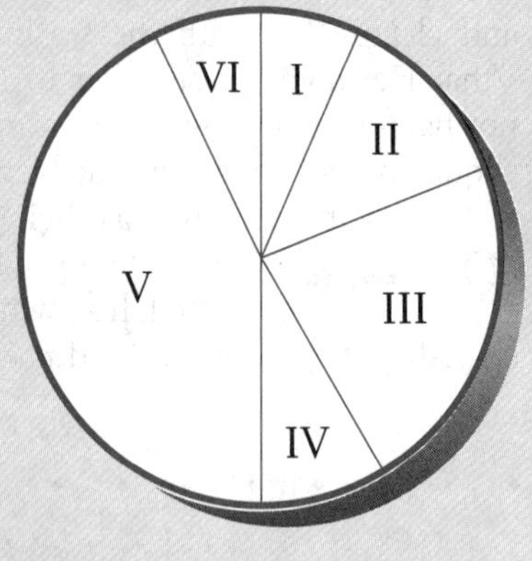

If a couple marry in their mid-20s and live into their mid-70s still married, they will spend 50 or more years of life together. That's a substantial commitment! One would never enter a business contract for that length of time without clarifying the work and costs involved. Yet do young people have any idea of the lifetime of work they are taking on when they repeat their marriage vows? Often not.

Perhaps it would help to know that there are roughly six phases of marriage. Each one requires husband and wife to work together as a team, combining their unique temperaments and strengths. As with any team activity, they must pull in the same direction if they expect to complete all six phases with their marriage intact.

Of course, not every couple or family follows the pattern outlined below. But what matters is not that a family adhere to a certain timetable, but that it recognize that there are seasons of family life, and that building relationships is a lifelong process. The following six periods are by no means distinct categories, but overlap quite a bit.

I. The Honeymoon Years

During this first period of marriage, two people from different family experiences and value systems begin to discover one another. Differences and similarities surface in areas such as finances, sexuality, faith, use of time, and personal habits. Each difference affords an opportunity for conflict and, hopefully, growth. Patterns that the couple establishes during this phase will tend to affect what happens during the next five phases.

The honeymoon typically ends with the birth or adoption of the first child. For some, it ends with the realization that there will be no children. In all too many cases, it ends with the dissolution of the marriage itself.

II. The Childbearing Years

The birth or adoption of the first child brings a rapid transition. New babies, though welcome, can feel like an "invasion," an abrupt intrusion into what up until then had been a relatively cozy twosome. Often the father particularly feels displaced as mother and infant bond through birth, nursing, and nurturing.

The childbearing years can be extraordinarily draining. Young parents often give out more than they take in from their children. They may be able to offset the deficit somewhat by revisiting some of the practices that they so valued during the "courtship" and "honeymoon" phases of their relationship. They'll need to "deposit" lots of emotional support into each other's "reserve bank accounts" if they hope to maintain a positive balance during the demanding child-focused years.

This period typically ends when the last child begins school.

III. The Child-rearing Years

As a couple's children pass through elementary and high school, new authority figures emerge, such as teachers, television personalities, scout masters, coaches, music teachers, youth pastors, and perhaps most influential of all, peers, both friends and bullies. Before, parents had the final word. Now others suggest or impose new values, decisions, and schedules.

That makes child rearing a great time for parents to help children think about themselves and the world. Discussion, prayer, and support can create an atmosphere of unity that is essential if young people are to face the many factors that compete with the family. If the parents are secure in their "bond of perfection," they can help their children tackle the tough issues—issues they themselves have been dealing with all along.

During the child-rearing years, which may stretch out over two decades or more, parents need to keep making deposits in their mate's bank of emotional support. One way to do that is to keep dating and to guard time alone with each other. Again, too many marriages never make it through the stresses and strains of the childbearing and child-rearing phases, and the families break apart.

IV. The Child-launching Years

With the onset of puberty, children begin to notice the opposite sex and discover "love" outside the home. This is the beginning of the "leaving" process, as children become adults in their own right and take steps toward independence, usually through work, college, and/or marriage.

In this phase, young adults tend to experience numerous "trial runs" of freedom, not all of which succeed. It helps for parents to remain available when their children have lost their way. Failure, whether in academic studies, financial matters, experiments in "freedom," or sexuality, offer important moments for learning, and sometimes for forgiveness. If young people never experience the freedom to fail, they may never learn to leave the nest and fly on their own.

V. The Empty-Nest Years

They're gone! Now it's just two again. Now the couple will find out whether they've grown together or apart over the years. Unfortunately, by this point many couples have developed a child- or career-centered marriage rather than a strong relationship between themselves. Though understandable, that can be tragic since the empty-nest phase typically outlasts the first four phases combined. No wonder so many marriages come apart as soon as the children have grown up and left. The couples have built their lives around their kids, and now they have nothing left in common.

By contrast, though, empty-nest couples who have built into each other can experience a joyous recovery of full attention to their marriage. They have more time to spend with each other, and often more money to spend. They may also have the bright privilege of welcoming grandchildren into the world.

VI. The Alone Years

The death of either spouse brings the survivor into the final phase of family life. For so many years, the person has lived in relation to his or her mate and children. Now, the sudden experience of being alone again exposes the level of individual growth experienced during marriage. Some couples never establish patterns that make for strong individuality. They become so intertwined and dependent on each other that the loss of the partner causes the surviving mate to crash or wither. But if the person has cultivated other relationships among friends and family and developed personal interests and hobbies, life can still be somewhat joyful, despite the painful loss of one's lifetime partner.

Where is your family among these six phases of family life? God calls couples to a lifetime of work. Are you practicing "biblical family planning" with a view toward the long haul? ◆

CONSIDER THIS
6:10–13

WHO IS THE ENEMY?

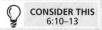

No matter who we are or what we do for a living, all of us are bound to face struggles in life. Financial pressures, job loss, personality conflicts, time demands, injury, illness, emotional pain, death—as Job's friend Eliphaz wryly noted, "Man is born to trouble, as the sparks fly upward" (Job 5:7).

When faced with setbacks like these, people often tend to blame God for their circumstances, or other people, or even themselves. However, Scripture urges us to consider another, more sinister source for troubles, what Paul called the "principalities" and "powers" in the heavenly places. Our struggle is not against God or other people but against "spiritual hosts of wickedness" (Eph. 6:11–12).

Certainly there's a place for human responsibility. But Paul is telling us that ultimately, people are not our enemy, sin and Satan are. If we intend to stand up to the onslaught of these powerful adversaries, we must fight them on their own turf—the spiritual—with weapons appropriate to the conflict (vv. 14–18).

Of course, it can be very difficult to persuade people of that in this day and age. Secular thinking dismisses all talk of the supernatural realm as so much superstition left over from the ancient world. At the same time, advocates of the occult have stimulated people's curiosity and have developed in many a fascination with evil rather than a determination to overcome it.

Nevertheless, the Bible is straightforward. It declares that evil forces exist in the spiritual realm that have a substantial influence on the world and human events. Paul called them "principalities." The word is often used in the New Testament, sometimes, as here, referring to fallen angels (Rom. 8:38; Col. 2:15), sometimes to human rulers (Titus 3:1; translated "authorities" in the NKJV), or sometimes to any type of ruler other than God Himself (Eph. 1:21; Col. 2:10).

Sometimes the presence of evil powers is evident, as in demon possession (see Luke 11:14). However, Satan and his hosts have numerous other ways to influence human activity and carry out their ultimate purpose, the capture of people away from God. For example, two means through which they can work are:

Belief systems. Philosophies and worldviews have a powerful effect on the way people live. By introducing lies into the very principles upon which entire societies are based, the evil one can wreak incredible havoc on the world.

Consider, for instance, the beliefs that fueled Nazism. Eventually they led to the most destructive war in history, which claimed tens of millions of lives. They brought about extermination camps in which millions of Jews and others were slaughtered. They disrupted entire nations and economies. Indeed, the aftermath of that dark era is still with us.

Again, none of this is to suggest that humans are excused from responsibility. But behind the visible, knowable element of human choice, one can detect or at least suspect the activity of forces with supernatural ability and evil intent, prompting people to accept and act on falsehoods.

That's why we cannot be too careful about the ideas we embrace, whether they come from religious teachers, educators, government leaders, or the media. Ideas have consequences, both in individual lives and entire nations. Our best protection against deception is a grounding in biblical truth (Eph. 6:14).

Human institutions and leaders. Human systems and people in authority make ideal targets of Satanic activity because of their influence on others. In the first century, one has only to consider the character and especially the spiritual choices of such groups as the Pharisees (Matt. 23:13–15, 31–36), the Jewish council (Acts 7:51–60), the Herods (see Acts 12:1–2), Caiaphas (see Matt. 26:3), Pilate (John 18:37–38; 19:10–11; 1 Cor. 2:8), and the Caesars, especially Nero (see Acts 25:12), to appreciate the counterattack that Satan must have launched after the coming of Christ and the founding of the church.

Scripture asserts that human authorities are established by God to carry out good purposes (Rom. 13:1–7). But because they are operated by humans, they are vulnerable to the influence of evil spiritual forces.

Paul knew that all too well. As he wrote the Ephesians, he sat chained to a Roman soldier for no other crime than the preaching of the gospel (Eph. 6:19–20). On another occasion, he instructed Timothy, the pastor at Ephesus, to have the people pray "for kings and all who are in authority, that we may lead a quiet and peaceable life in all godliness and reverence" because God "desires all men to be saved and to come to the knowledge of the truth" (1 Tim. 2:1–4).

There are many other ways in which the powers of darkness attempt to subvert the purposes of God. But it is pointless for us to try to determine at any moment whether something is being "caused" by a wicked spiritual power. A preoccupation with that leads only to foolish speculation.

Paul gives us a far more positive, constructive strategy for "standing firm" against our spiritual enemies: "put on the whole armor of God" (Eph. 6:11). That armor is made up entirely of spiritual weapons: truth, righteousness, the gospel of peace, faith, salvation, the word of God, and prayer (vv. 14–18). By learning to wear and to wield these powerful armaments, we can resist the carefully laid plans of the devil and, when the fight is over, still be standing. ◆

Work—A Platform for Evangelism?

CONSIDER THIS 6:5–9 **Our jobs put us in touch with people like no other activity. For 40 or more hours a week we toil, laugh, struggle, and interact with others to accomplish tasks. For that reason, many Christians view their workplace as a primary platform for spreading the gospel. Is that legitimate?**

It is certainly legitimate to treat our workplace as an opportunity for unbelievers to see Christianity by looking at us. Indeed, Paul challenges us to display a godly workstyle for that reason (Titus 2:9–10). However, we must never emphasize verbal witness to the detriment of our work, as if God sends us into the work world *only* to use it as a platform for evangelism.

Employers rightly look down on workers who are intruders, deceivers, or sluggards. In Ephesians 6:5–9, Paul challenges us to work with "sincerity of heart" and to pay close attention to the work itself, which he calls "doing the will of God." That's what impresses one's employer, as well as God.

What is God's intention for everyday work? See "People at Work," Heb. 2:7.

Some employers have become so disappointed with the work of believers that they no longer hire Christians. See 1 Tim. 6:1–2.

members of His body,[a] of His flesh and of His bones. [31]"For
this reason a man shall leave his father and mother and be
joined to his wife, and the two shall become one flesh."[a]
[32]This is a great mystery, but I speak concerning Christ and
the church. [33]Nevertheless let each one of you in particular
so love his own wife as himself, and let the wife *see* that she
respects *her* husband.

CHAPTER 6

Instructions to Children and Fathers

[1]Children, obey your parents in the Lord, for this is right.
[2]"Honor your father and mother," which is the first commandment with promise: [3]"that it may be well with you and
you may live long on the earth."[a]
5:21—6:4 see pg. 672 [4]And you, fathers, do not provoke your
children to wrath, but bring them up in
the training and admonition of the Lord.

Instructions to Servants and Masters

6:5 [5]Bondservants, be obedient to those
who are your masters according to the
flesh, with fear and trembling, in sincerity of heart, as to
Christ; [6]not with eyeservice, as men-pleasers, but as bondservants of Christ, doing the will of God from the heart,
[7]with goodwill doing service, as to the Lord, and not to
6:5–9 men, [8]knowing that whatever good anyone does, he will receive the same from
the Lord, whether *he is* a slave or free.
6:5–9 [9]And you, masters, do the same things
to them, giving up threatening, knowing
that your own Master also[a] is in heaven, and there is no
partiality with Him.

Spiritual Warfare

6:10–13 see pg. 674 [10]Finally, my brethren, be strong in the
Lord and in the power of His might.
[11]Put on the whole armor of God, that you may be able to
stand against the wiles of the devil. [12]For we do not wrestle
against flesh and blood, but against principalities, against
powers, against the rulers of the darkness of this age,[a]

5:30 [a]NU-Text omits the rest of this verse. *5:31* [a]Genesis 2:24 *6:3* [a]Deuteronomy 5:16 *6:9* [a]NU-Text reads *He who is both their Master and yours.* *6:12* [a]NU-Text reads *rulers of this darkness.*

A Promotion

A CLOSER LOOK 6:5–9 *What Paul wrote to "bondservants" (v. 5) redefined their occupational status. They were no longer just Roman slaves—they were employees of Jesus Christ! See "Who's the Boss?" Col. 3:22–24.*

against spiritual *hosts* of wickedness in the heavenly *places*.
13Therefore take up the whole armor of God, that you may
be able to withstand in the evil day, and having done all, to
stand.
14Stand therefore, having girded your waist with truth,
having put on the breastplate of righteousness, 15and having
shod your feet with the preparation of the gospel of peace;
16above all, taking the shield of faith with which you will be
able to quench all the fiery darts of the wicked one. 17And
take the helmet of salvation, and the sword of the Spirit,
which is the word of God; 18praying always with all prayer
and supplication in the Spirit, being watchful to this end
with all perseverance and supplication for all the saints—
19and for me, that utterance may be given to me, that I may
open my mouth boldly to make known the mystery of the
gospel, 20for which I am an ambassador in chains; that in it
I may speak boldly, as I ought to speak.

Concluding Matters

21But that you also may know my affairs *and* how I am
doing, Tychicus, a beloved brother and faithful minister in
the Lord, will make all things known to you; 22whom I have
sent to you for this very purpose, that you may know our
affairs, and *that* he may comfort your hearts.
23Peace to the brethren, and love with faith, from God the
Father and the Lord Jesus Christ. 24Grace *be* with all those
who love our Lord Jesus Christ in sincerity. Amen.

QUOTE UNQUOTE

CONSIDER THIS 6:5 *Sincerity of heart (v. 5) involves reaching out to coworkers in Christlike ways:*

The world is not a fun house hall of mirrors, everywhere reflecting distorted images of myself. The world is a wax museum of individuals needing to warm each other into full humanity through the touch of love.

Mark Quinn, Chicago public school teacher, "Five Guidelines to a Spirituality of Work"

Philippians

Some of the most powerful writings in history have been penned by leaders imprisoned for political reasons. Something about the confinement, uncertainty, and (often) mistreatment these prisoners have suffered seems to have helped them focus their minds on their fundamental convictions.

But whereas many imprisoned authors take a martyr's posture and rail against whatever system is oppressing them, Paul sounded a radically different note in his "prison epistle" to the Philippians: he focused on the Christ-centered life, the hallmark of which is joy—a remarkable theme considering that he may have been facing execution (Phil. 1:23), most likely in Rome (1:13; 4:22).

Can Paul's message have any relevance to believers today who live in a free society without threat of imprisonment or death for practicing their religion? Yes, by showing what ultimately matters. In the midst of freedom, affluence, and opportunity, it's easy to lose perspective, to pay more attention to peripheral things that, while attractive, really have little value, rather than substantial things that have great value.

The ultimate value is Christ. Whether elevated to heights of glory or, like Paul, reduced to prisoner status, we need to center our lives on Christ. Whatever happens, we need to hold onto Him. He alone must be our ultimate source of contentment, joy, and life.

The ultimate value is Christ.

CONTENTS

ARTICLES

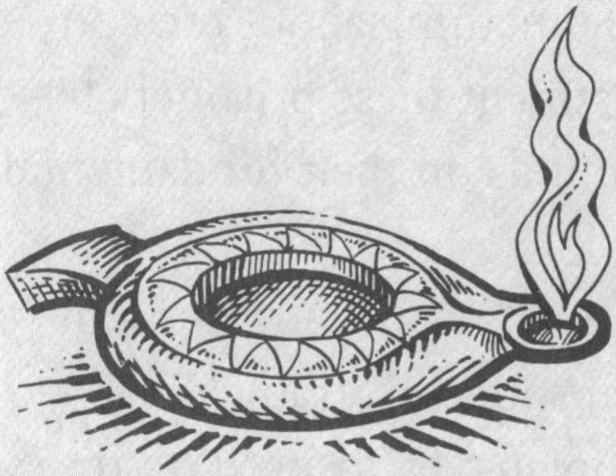

The Mind of Christ

The first church founded in the West was the church at Philippi (Acts 16:6–15). Living at a highly favored Roman military colony and a major crossroads on the Egnatian Way (one of the empire's "interstates"), the Philippians were proud and affluent. It's interesting that Paul's first convert was a businesswoman who sold purple, the most expensive of dyes, as valuable as gold and used for tribute and international trade (16:14).

Yet in writing to the believers in this prosperous community, Paul neither condemned the wealthy nor attacked profitable commerce. Rather, he emphasized Christ. Paul was well acquainted with position and power (Phil. 3:4–6). But he had surrendered everything to Christ and could say that "to me, to live is Christ" (1:21), that he was "a prisoner for Christ" (1:13), and that "I also count all things loss . . . that I may gain Christ" (3:8). Christ had laid hold of Paul (3:12) and Paul's sole passion was to bring glory to Him (3:8–9).

Paul longed for his friends in Philippi to have the same experience of Christ. He prayed that they would abound in Christ's love (1:9), that they would adopt Christ's mind (2:5–11), and that, like himself, they would follow in Christ's footsteps, experiencing His sufferings, death, and resurrection (3:10–11).

How could the Philippians translate their relationship with Christ into daily life? Paul told them that they would have to become "like-minded" with Christ and "set their minds on Christ." What would that look like? Paul painted a picture for them in 2:5–11. (Some scholars believe that this passage was an early hymn of the church. Could it have been among the songs Paul sang with Silas while in jail during his first visit to Philippi, Acts 16:25?)

For Christians in a prestigious city, Christ comes clothed in humility. Later, in Colossians, we see His power, glory, and lordship over creation emphasized. But here, Christ is shown to be human, vulnerable, and accessible. He lays down His rights and takes on a humble, virtually powerless posture of a servant.

Do you want honor and status, power and prestige? Our world offers them through selfish ambition and empty conceit (2:3). An alternative is the "lowliness of mind" that characterized Christ. In the short term, that may involve sacrifice and even suffering. But in the long run it means praise from God and joy in His pleasure. The path to glory is humility. The way to gain is loss. The way up is down. ◆

Philippi

Though "all roads led to Rome," much of the traffic to Rome from the east funneled through Philippi, which served as a gateway to Greece and Italy. To find out more about this strategic crossroads, *see "Philippi," Acts 16:12.*

CHAPTER 1

Grace and Peace

[1]Paul and Timothy, bondservants of Jesus Christ,

To all the saints in Christ Jesus who are in Philippi, with
the bishops[a] and deacons:

[2]Grace to you and peace from God our Father and the
Lord Jesus Christ.

Thanks for the Philippians' Gift

[3]I thank my God upon every remembrance of you, [4]al-
ways in every prayer of mine making request for you all
with joy, [5]for your fellowship in the gospel from the first
day until now, [6]being confident of this very thing, that He
who has begun a good work in you will complete *it* until
the day of Jesus Christ; [7]just as it is right for me to think
this of you all, because I have you in my heart, inasmuch as
both in my chains and in the defense and confirmation of
the gospel, you all are partakers with me of grace. [8]For God
is my witness, how greatly I long for you all with the affection of Jesus Christ.
[9]And this I pray, that your love may abound still more
and more in knowledge and all discernment, [10]that you
may approve the things that are excellent, that you may be
sincere and without offense till the day of Christ, [11]being
filled with the fruits of righteousness which *are* by Jesus
Christ, to the glory and praise of God.

In Prison for the Gospel

1:12–18 [12]But I want you to know, brethren,
that the things *which happened* to me have
actually turned out for the furtherance of the gospel, [13]so
that it has become evident to the whole palace guard, and
to all the rest, that my chains are in Christ; [14]and most of
the brethren in the Lord, having become confident by my
chains, are much more bold to speak the word without fear.
[15]Some indeed preach Christ even from envy and strife,
and some also from goodwill: [16]The former[a] preach Christ
from selfish ambition, not sincerely, supposing to add affliction to my chains; [17]but the latter out of love, knowing that
I am appointed for the defense of the gospel. [18]What then?
Only *that* in every way, whether in pretense or in truth,
Christ is preached; and in this I rejoice, yes, and will rejoice.
[19]For I know that this will turn out for my deliverance
through your prayer and the supply of the Spirit of Jesus

PAUL'S BROAD PERSPECTIVE

CONSIDER THIS 1:12–18 *Paul was deeply committed to the truth and integrity of the gospel. But in vv. 12–18 he generously credits others who were doing ministry, even though they had impure motives.*

This sets an important example for Christians today who feel strong loyalty to their particular tradition or institution. Like Paul, we need to accept and celebrate the fact that other believers with different perspectives and approaches may be helping people and accomplishing tasks that we never could.

1:1 [a]Literally *overseers* *1:16* [a]NU-Text reverses the contents of verses 16 and 17.

Christ, [20]according to my earnest expectation and hope that in nothing I shall be ashamed, but with all boldness, as always, so now also Christ will be magnified in my body,

1:21

whether by life or by death. [21]For to me, to live *is* Christ, and to die *is* gain. [22]But if *I* live on in the flesh, this *will mean* fruit from *my* labor; yet what I shall choose I cannot tell. [23]For[a] I am hard-pressed between the two, having a desire to depart and be with Christ, *which is* far better. [24]Nevertheless to remain in the flesh *is* more needful for you. [25]And being confident of this, I know that I shall remain and continue with you all for your progress and joy of faith, [26]that your rejoicing for me may be more abundant in Jesus Christ by my coming to you again.

A Call to Stand Firm

[27]Only let your conduct be worthy of the gospel of Christ, so that whether I come and see you or am absent, I may hear of your affairs, that you stand fast in one spirit, with one mind striving together for the faith of the gospel, [28]and not in any way terrified by your adversaries, which is to them a proof of perdition, but to you of salvation,[a] and that from God. [29]For to you it has been granted on behalf of Christ, not only to believe in Him, but also to suffer for His sake, [30]having the same conflict which you saw in me and now hear *is* in me.

CHAPTER 2

The Humble Example of Christ

[1]Therefore if *there is* any consolation in Christ, if any comfort of love, if any fellowship of the Spirit, if any affection and mercy, [2]fulfill my joy by being like-minded, having

2:3
see pg. 684

the same love, *being* of one accord, of one mind. [3]*Let* nothing *be done* through selfish ambition or conceit, but in lowliness of mind let each esteem others better than himself. [4]Let each of you look out not only for his own interests, but also for the interests of others.

2:5–8

[5]Let this mind be in you which was also in Christ Jesus, [6]who, being in the form of God, did not consider it robbery to be equal with God, [7]but made Himself of no reputation, taking the form of a bondservant, *and* coming in the likeness of men. [8]And being found in appearance as a man, He humbled Himself and became obedient to *the point of* death, even the death of the cross. [9]Therefore God also has highly exalted Him and given Him the name which is above every name, [10]that at

(Bible text continued on page 685)

1:23 [a]NU-Text and M-Text read *But.* *1:28* [a]NU-Text reads *of your salvation.*

To Live Is . . . ?

CONSIDER THIS 1:21 **Facing the prospect of his execution, Paul had to wrestle with what mattered most to him. It didn't take him long to come to a conclusion: Christ (v. 21). He felt that Christ not only made his life worth living, but death worth dying.**

What makes life worth living for you? Your family? Your work? The memory you hope to leave behind?

What makes death worth dying? Anything? Complete these thoughts:

- **"If I live for anything, it's . . . ."**
- **"Above all, I want to gain . . . ."**

Downward Mobility

CONSIDER THIS 2:5–8 *In contrast to the many people today who seek upward mobility, Jesus was, in a sense, downwardly mobile (vv. 5–8), moving from a position of ultimate power to utter powerlessness. In making this transition He set the best possible example of servant-leadership (see Matt. 20:25–28; John 13:2–17).*

However, in Colossians, Paul paints a different portrait of the Lord. See "Christ, the Lord of the World," Col. 1:15–18.

CONSIDER THIS
2:3

HUMILITY—THE SCANDALOUS VIRTUE

By recommending "lowliness of mind" (v. 3), Paul fired a broadside at the Philippian culture—and our own. Like us, the Greeks and Romans exalted the lifestyles of the rich and famous!

Lowliness of mind? Who would want that? A "lowly" (or humble) person meant a slave—a servile, groveling, wretched individual. And for Paul to associate the word "lowly" with "mind" was a laughable contradiction: everyone assumed that lowly people had no intelligence, and everyone honored higher thinking and self-conceit.

The idea of humility seemed especially out of place in Philippi. The town hosted a Roman military colony by the pretentious-sounding name of *Colonia Augusta Julia Pilippensis.* Unlike other conquered towns, it enjoyed the *jus Italicum* (law of Italy), which made it a sort of small, self-governing version of the empire. Pride and self-importance were part and parcel of Philippian life in Paul's day (see "Philippi," Acts 16:12).

Yet Paul insisted that Christians there cultivate humility—but not a grovelling, abject demeanor. No, biblical humility means not thinking of oneself more highly than is true (Rom. 12:3), but rather acknowledging what one is—with all of one's strengths and weaknesses, pluses and minuses, successes and failures.

Far from self-loathing, real humility makes people so truthful that they don't hesitate, when necessary, to tell about even their good qualities.

Do you want true humility? It comes from seeing yourself in relation to God. No wonder, then, that this virtue ran counter to the Roman worldview. Their concept of a god was grossly similar to their concept of humanity, and the mythological Roman gods were hardly noble.

By contrast, Jesus praised the humble, "the poor in spirit," (literally, "the destitute," Matt. 5:3). What would that attitude look like? David expresses it in Psalm 39:4–5:

> Lord, make me to know my end,
> And what is the measure of my days,
> That I may know how frail I am.
> Indeed, You have made my days as handbreadths,
> And my age is as nothing before You;
> Certainly every man at his best state is but vapor.
> Surely every man walks about like a shadow;
> Surely they busy themselves in vain;
> He heaps up riches,
> And does not know who will gather them.

Likewise, the prophet Micah warns that humility is one of three main virtues that ought to govern our lives (Mic. 6:8):

> He has shown you, O man, what is good;
> And what does the Lord require of you
> But to do justly,
> To love mercy,
> And to walk humbly with your God?

Humility is not an option for us as believers—it's an essential if we want to walk with God. Over and again, Scripture insists that we either walk humbly with Him, or not at all (Ps. 138:6; Is. 57:15; 1 Pet. 5:5–7). In short, a biblical lifestyle knows nothing of looking out chiefly for Number One. Just the opposite. With John the Baptist we need to say, "He must increase, but I must decrease" (John 3:30). ◆

Humility affects four crucial areas of everyday life:

(1) our view of ourselves. See "The Proper Measure of All Things," Heb. 2:6–8.
(2) our attitude toward controlling our circumstances. See "Who's in Charge Here?" James 4:13–16.
(3) how good or bad we think we are. See "Are People Basically Good?" Rom. 7:21.
(4) our perspective on status and power. See "Leadership Equals Humility?" Luke 22:24–27.

the name of Jesus every knee should bow, of those in
heaven, and of those on earth, and of those under the earth,
11and *that* every tongue should confess that Jesus Christ *is*
Lord, to the glory of God the Father.

Shine as Lights in the World

12Therefore, my beloved, as you have always obeyed, not
as in my presence only, but now much more in my absence,
work out your own salvation with fear and trembling; 13for
it is God who works in you both to will and to do for *His*
good pleasure.

2:15

14Do all things without complaining
and disputing, 15that you may become
blameless and harmless, children of God without fault in
the midst of a crooked and perverse generation, among
whom you shine as lights in the world, 16holding fast the
word of life, so that I may rejoice in the day of Christ that I
have not run in vain or labored in vain.

17Yes, and if I am being poured out *as a drink offering* on
the sacrifice and service of your faith, I am glad and rejoice
with you all. 18For the same reason you also be glad and rejoice with me.

Timothy and Paul Himself Hope to Come

19But I trust in the Lord Jesus to send Timothy to you
shortly, that I also may be encouraged when I know your
state. 20For I have no one like-minded, who will sincerely
care for your state. 21For all seek their own, not the things
which are of Christ Jesus. 22But you know his proven character, that as a son with *his* father he served with me in the
gospel. 23Therefore I hope to send him at once, as soon as I
see how it goes with me. 24But I trust in the Lord that I myself shall also come shortly.

Epaphroditus Is on His Way

2:25 see pg. 686

25Yet I considered it necessary to send
to you Epaphroditus, my brother, fellow
worker, and fellow soldier, but your messenger and the one
who ministered to my need; 26since he was longing for you
all, and was distressed because you had heard that he was
sick. 27For indeed he was sick almost unto death; but God
had mercy on him, and not only on him but on me also,
lest I should have sorrow upon sorrow. 28Therefore I sent
him the more eagerly, that when you see him again you may
rejoice, and I may be less sorrowful. 29Receive him therefore
in the Lord with all gladness, and hold such men in esteem;
30because for the work of Christ he came close to death, not
regarding his life, to supply what was lacking in your service toward me.

HONESTY AND ETHICAL STANDARDS

CONSIDER THIS 2:15 **Paul called his generation "crooked and perverse" (v. 15). But was his generation much different than ours? According to the Gallup Poll:**

By a large margin the U.S. public believes that ethics and standards of honesty are getting worse. This is a view held by all age groups and in each socio-economic level.

The public also does not give very high marks to people in most of the 24 occupations tested in a Gallup Poll in terms of honesty and ethical standards. Here is the full list, with the percentages who say the honesty and ethical standards are very high or high:

"ARE THEIR STANDARDS HIGH?"

Occupation	%
Clergymen	64
Druggists, pharmacists	61
Medical doctors	53
Dentists	51
College teachers	47
Engineers	46
Policemen	42
Bankers	38
TV reporters, commentators	33
Funeral directors	29
Newspaper reporters	26
Lawyers	24
Stockbrokers	19
Business executives	18
Senators	17
Building contractors	17
Local political officeholders	16
Congressmen	14
Realtors	13
State political officeholders	13
Insurance salesmen	13
Labor union leaders	12
Advertising practitioners	8
Car salesmen	6

(continued on next page)

(continued from previous page)

Given such a low opinion of the integrity of so many occupations, believers today have an outstanding opportunity to "shine as lights in the world" (v. 15).

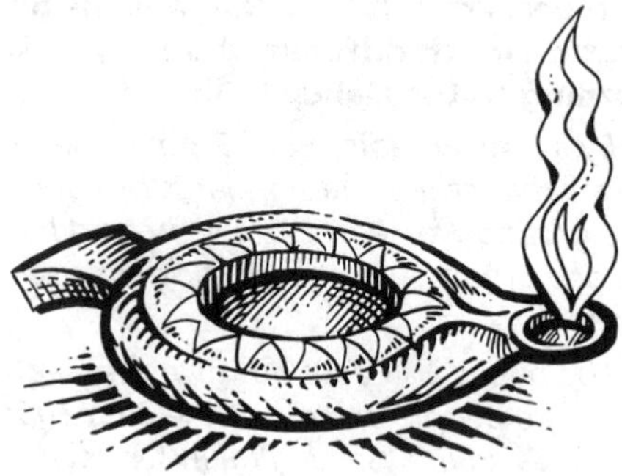

Paul wrote about the need for workplace Christians whose work and ethical integrity would be irresistibly attractive to coworkers. See "Your 'Workstyle,'" Titus 2:9–10.

CHAPTER 3

A Warning about Judaizers

1 Finally, my brethren, rejoice in the Lord. For me to write
the same things to you *is* not tedious, but for you *it is* safe.
2 Beware of dogs, beware of evil workers, beware of the
mutilation! 3 For we are the circumcision, who worship God
in the Spirit,[a] rejoice in Christ Jesus, and have no confi-

3:4–6

dence in the flesh, 4 though I also might
have confidence in the flesh. If anyone
else thinks he may have confidence in the flesh, I more so:
5 circumcised the eighth day, of the stock of Israel, *of* the
tribe of Benjamin, a Hebrew of the Hebrews; concerning the
law, a Pharisee; 6 concerning zeal, persecuting the church;
concerning the righteousness which is in the law, blameless.

What Really Matters

3:7–14

7 But what things were gain to me, these
I have counted loss for Christ. 8 Yet in-
deed I also count all things loss for the excellence of the
knowledge of Christ Jesus my Lord, for whom I have suffered the loss of all things, and count them as rubbish, that
I may gain Christ 9 and be found in Him, not having my
own righteousness, which *is* from the law, but that which *is*
through faith in Christ, the righteousness which is from
God by faith; 10 that I may know Him and the power of His

3:3 [a]NU-Text and M-Text read *who worship in the Spirit of God.*

PERSONALITY PROFILE: EPAPHRODITUS

FOR YOUR INFO 2:25

Name means: "Charming."

Not to be confused with: Epaphras, an associate of Paul's from Colosse (Col. 1:7; 4:12), whose name also means "charming."

Occupation: Unknown, but he may have been a coworker with Paul in the gospel ministry, for the apostle described him as a brother, fellow worker, and fellow soldier.

Best known today as: The messenger sent by the church at Philippi to take a gift to Paul, who was under house arrest in Rome, and also the bearer of Paul's letter back to the Philippian believers.

resurrection, and the fellowship of His sufferings, being
conformed to His death, 11if, by any means, I may attain to
the resurrection from the dead.
12Not that I have already attained, or am already perfected; but I press on, that I may lay hold of that for which
Christ Jesus has also laid hold of me. 13Brethren, I do not
count myself to have apprehended; but one thing *I do,* for-
getting those things which are behind and reaching forward
to those things which are ahead, 14I press toward the goal
for the prize of the upward call of God in Christ Jesus.

Paul Says to Follow His Example

15Therefore let us, as many as are mature, have this mind;
and if in anything you think otherwise, God will reveal
even this to you. 16Nevertheless, to *the degree* that we have
already attained, let us walk by the same rule,[a] let us be of
the same mind.

3:17

17Brethren, join in following my example, and note those who so walk, as you
have us for a pattern. 18For many walk, of whom I have told
you often, and now tell you even weeping, *that they are* the

3:16 [a]NU-Text omits *rule* and the rest of the verse.

PAUL'S DRIVENNESS

CONSIDER THIS 3:4–6

As we read Paul's description of his younger days (vv. 4–6), we discover a profound drivenness, as if he were out to prove something. Several clues suggest that he probably was. He was born outside of Palestine, in Tarsus, rather than in Judea. He devoted his life to intensive study of the Law. He attacked Christians with unusual vengeance. Perhaps it all added up to an intense desire to be accepted by the Jewish society in Jerusalem.

There are two major ways that minorities and other outsiders cope with rejection or discrimination by the larger society. One is to turn inward and refuse to participate in the dominant culture. The other is to remove or diminish differences and blend in with the majority. Perhaps one might be accepted, even if never treated as an equal. Paul seems possibly to have chosen the latter course.

TAKING STOCK

CONSIDER THIS 3:7–14

In Philippians 3, Paul takes stock of his life to determine what he has done that counts and what doesn't. His list of qualities and the conclusions he draws offer some important guideposts to help us assess our motives for and definitions of success:

(1) What does success look like to you? How have you arrived at that definition? What or who has influenced your vision of a successful life? What role, if any, have God's perspectives and purposes been given in your definition?

(2) What have you given up or sacrificed in order to pursue success?

(3) What have you determined to be worth your investment of time, energy, and/or money?

(4) How have your priorities and loyalties changed over time? Why?

(5) In what ways do you think God and His purposes are served by the life you are pursuing?

LEADING BY EXAMPLE

CONSIDER THIS 3:17

As Paul recognized (v. 17), leaders always lead by personal example, whether they are aware of it or not. And their example extends far beyond the nature of the task at hand. People pattern their motives and values after executives, supervisors, and other leaders.

Paul encouraged others to follow his example. What sort of example do you set for others? Are you aware of how you influence them? Are you close enough to the people around you, and in touch enough with your own tendencies, to have confidence in how others might follow you?

Euodia and Syntyche

CONSIDER THIS 4:2 *Paul described Euodia and Syntyche (v. 2) as having "labored" with him in the gospel (v. 3). His choice of words is significant. Elsewhere he affirmed other women who helped with the spread of the gospel (see "Paul's Female Co-workers," Rom. 16:12).*

Paul doesn't tell us about the exact nature of these two women's work, but he hints at the effectiveness of their ministry: he was eager to have them settle their dispute, probably because it crippled their work with others.

enemies of the cross of Christ: [19]whose end *is* destruction,
whose god *is their* belly, and *whose* glory *is* in their shame—
who set their mind on earthly things. [20]For our citizenship
is in heaven, from which we also eagerly wait for the Savior,
the Lord Jesus Christ, [21]who will transform our lowly body
that it may be conformed to His glorious body, according to
the working by which He is able even to subdue all things
to Himself.

CHAPTER 4

[1]Therefore, my beloved and longed-for brethren, my joy
and crown, so stand fast in the Lord, beloved.

A Word to Euodia and Syntyche

4:2 [2]I implore Euodia and I implore Syntyche to be of the same mind in the Lord.
4:3 [3]And[a] I urge you also, true companion,
help these women who labored with me
in the gospel, with Clement also, and the rest of my fellow
workers, whose names *are* in the Book of Life.

How to Have the Peace of God

[4]Rejoice in the Lord always. Again I will say, rejoice!
[5]Let your gentleness be known to all men. The Lord *is* at
hand.

4:3 [a]NU-Text and M-Text read *Yes.*

CONSIDER THIS 4:10–13

A Lifestyle of Contentment

Paul sounds so positive in vv. 10–13, so confident! It would be easy to assume that life was rosy when he wrote these words. But where was he? According to 1:12–14, in prison—quite possibly in Rome, facing a death sentence!

Given that sobering context, this passage speaks powerfully to the issue of contentment, not only with material possessions, but with circumstances as well.

Paul makes no idle boast here. He knew firsthand the wealth and privileges of prominence in the Jewish community and of Roman citizenship (3:4–6; Acts 22:3–5, 25–29; 26:4–5). On the other hand, he had suffered extraordinary hardships in his work—jailings, beatings, stonings, forcible ejection from several towns, shipwrecks—to say nothing of emotional and spiritual disappointments and setbacks (2 Cor. 11:23–33).

Either extreme would test a person's character. What was Paul's secret? "Christ who strengthens me." Rather than looking to the possessions he had or didn't have, or

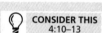

[6]Be anxious for nothing, but in everything by prayer and
supplication, with thanksgiving, let your requests be made
known to God; [7]and the peace of God, which surpasses all
understanding, will guard your hearts and minds through
Christ Jesus.

4:8

[8]Finally, brethren, whatever things are
true, whatever things *are* noble, whatever
things *are* just, whatever things *are* pure, whatever things
are lovely, whatever things *are* of good report, if *there* is any
virtue and if *there is* anything praiseworthy—meditate on
these things. [9]The things which you learned and received
and heard and saw in me, these do, and the God of peace
will be with you.

Praise for the Philippians' Gift

4:10–13

[10]But I rejoiced in the Lord greatly that
now at last your care for me has flour-
ished again; though you surely did care, but you lacked opportunity. [11]Not that I speak in regard to need, for I have

A New Way of Thinking

A CLOSER LOOK 4:8

The new way of thinking that Paul summarizes in v. 8 is only one of several pictures that Scripture paints of "New Creatures with New Character." See Gal. 5:22–23.

to his circumstances, good or bad, he looked to Christ to satisfy his needs. The result, he says, was contentment.

This passage poses a strong challenge to Christians living and working in today's society. Some of us live at the upper levels of material prosperity—"abounding," as Paul puts it. The temptation is to forget God (Luke 12:16–21). Likewise, much in our culture urges us to feel discontent with our lot—to long for more, for bigger, for better. Jesus warns against that attitude ("Watch Out for Greed!" Luke 12:15). On the other hand, failures and disappointments can also draw us away from trusting in the God who cares (see Luke 12:22–34). ◆

Where does contentment end and responsibility begin? What about setting goals and taking initiative? See "A Command to Work," 2 Thess. 3:6–12.

Women and the Growth of Christianity

FOR YOUR INFO 4:3

Euodia and Syntyche (v. 2) were only two of the many women who played a role in the spread of the gospel and the development of the early church.

What Women Did

Activity	Reference
Prayed	Acts 1:14
Received the Spirit	2:17
Were converted	2:41
Hosted the church in their homes	2:46–47; Col. 4:15
Received help	Acts 6:1–2
Were thrown in prison	8:3
Helped those in need	9:39
Were raised from the dead	9:40
Aided Paul and his companions	16:15
Were freed from evil spirits	16:18
Were often the first converts in a city	17:34
Traveled with Paul	18:18
Taught others	18:26
Served as couriers for Paul's letters	Rom. 16:1
Excelled in ministry and were described as "among the apostles"	Rom. 16:7, according to one possible translation
Worked alongside men in proclaiming the gospel	Phil. 4:3

Women also played a major part in Jesus' life and work. See "The Women around Jesus," John 19:25. For names of some of the women who worked alongside Paul, see the table, "Paul's Female Coworkers," Rom. 16:12.

learned in whatever state I am, to be content: [12]I
know how to be abased, and I know how to
abound. Everywhere and in all things I have
learned both to be full and to be hungry, both to
abound and to suffer need. [13]I can do all things
through Christ[a] who strengthens me.

[14]Nevertheless you have done well that you
shared in my distress. [15]Now you Philippians know
also that in the beginning of the gospel, when I departed from Macedonia, no church shared with me
concerning giving and receiving but you only. [16]For
even in Thessalonica you sent *aid* once and again
for my necessities. [17]Not that I seek the gift, but I
seek the fruit that abounds to your account. [18]In-
deed I have all and abound. I am full, having received from Epaphroditus the things *sent* from you,
a sweet-smelling aroma, an acceptable sacrifice,
well pleasing to God. [19]And my God shall supply
all your need according to His riches in glory by
Christ Jesus. [20]Now to our God and Father *be* glory
forever and ever. Amen.

Greetings for Everyone

[21]Greet every saint in Christ Jesus. The brethren
who are with me greet you. [22]All the saints greet
you, but especially those who are of Caesar's household.

[23]The grace of our Lord Jesus Christ be with you
all.[a] Amen.

4:13 [a]NU-Text reads *Him who.* *4:23* [a]NU-Text reads *your spirit.*

Colossians

Can Christianity compete in an age of "Star Wars," New Age thinking, and occult metaphysics? Absolutely! In fact, not only can the faith hold its own, it can be expected to prevail over competing worldviews and systems of thought. It happened before at Colosse.

Christians at Colosse, like many Christians today, were fond of mixing and matching the truths of Christ with ideas and practices from the surrounding non-Christian culture. The results were sometimes wild and always destructive. Some fell into extreme forms of legalism. Others took liberties with their "freedom" in Christ and succumbed to gross immorality. The doctrines of the faith were mingled with incompatible mysteries and the integrity of the gospel was compromised. As a result, Colossian Christianity was hard to distinguish from other religions of the day.

Sound familiar? If so, pay attention to Colossians. It speaks directly to the same kind of situation that exists today. Rather than conceding the idea of Christ as one god among many, Colossians establishes Him as God alone (capital "G")—*the* preeminent Lord of the universe, Creator of all things, the only One deserving of honor, worship, and obedience. If Philippians presents Christ in His humility (Phil. 2:5–11), Colossians presents Him in His exaltation.

In a day of moral and philosophical relativism, when many people hold to the idea that "what's true for you may not be true for me" and "all religions are basically the same," Colossians sounds a clarion call to a crucial absolute: Jesus is Lord! That made all the difference in the first century. It still does today.

C O N T E N T S

A R T I C L E S

The Dangers of Syncretism

First-century Colosse was an ideological swamp into which three main cultural streams drained. The first was Hellenism, the vestiges of Greek civilization that had dominated the world before the Romans. Hellenism brought a "dualistic" view of the world, the idea that things are either material or spiritual. A second stream was a form of Judaism that tended to be rigid and puritanical, leading to outright withdrawal from and condemnation of the world. A third influence was the local pagan culture. This included superstitious occultism and primitive, mystical rites.

These three streams blended together into a pseudo-philosophical swamp that mired the Colossian church in debates, divisions, and depravity. The problem was one of syncretism. *Syncretism involves the confusion of various ideas, beliefs, and practices.*

The syncretist has a mind like a blender. The person throws in notions from any number of systems of thought—even notions that contradict each other. Then they are ground into a single philosophical stew to generate a system that satisfies one's intellectual demands and preferences. Result: a custom-made worldview that invariably leads away from biblical truth.

Syncretism flourishes in times of rapid change and cultural upheaval. First-century Colosse experienced a lot of that. The region was dominated by a foreign superpower. The city was quickly being eclipsed by its neighbor, Laodicea. Frequent earthquakes made life precarious. In fact, one tremor in A.D. 61 devastated the town, forcing a relocation three miles to the south.

How the gospel reached Colosse is unknown, though Christians from Ephesus may have played a part (see "The Ephesus Approach," Acts 19:8–41). But once a church was established, it had to contend with the syncretism of its surrounding culture. Paul (who to our knowledge never visited Colosse) attempted to help by sending this letter, which he intended the believers to share with their brothers and sisters in Laodicea (Col. 4:16).

Paul's theme is straightforward: Christ is preeminent. He is Lord. He rules over the world as its Creator and Sustainer. Other religions may offer attractive claims and appealing rituals, but the gospel supersedes them all.

Such a claim has profound implications. It makes Christianity exclusive—not true along with all the other religions, but the *true religion. That may not be a popular position in today's world. Anyone who holds it can expect conflict and criticism. But were Paul here to speak to the issue, we can imagine that he would quickly turn to Colossians and affirm his words from the first century: "[Christ] is the image of the invisible God . . . All things were created through Him and for Him. And He is before all things, and in Him all things consist . . . This I say lest anyone should deceive you with persuasive words" (1:15–17; 2:4).*

The remarkable thing is that belief in Christ affects one's lifestyle in a positive way that syncretistic religion cannot. As Colossians clearly shows, Christ makes a profound difference in one's relationships, family life, work, and community involvements. Though He rules the world and governs the universe, He enters into the day-to-day lives of His followers. He comes to us where we are in order to bring us to where He is (3:3–4). ◆

COLOSSE

- A Roman city of Asia Minor located at the base of 8,000-foot-high Mount Cadmus in the Lycus River Valley east of Ephesus.
- Watered by a cascade descending through a gorge from Mount Cadmus.
- A prosperous industrial center especially famous for its textiles, but clearly in decline at the time of Christ, squeezed by its increasingly competitive neighbor, Laodicea.
- Survived a devastating earthquake in A.D. 61, but later its population moved three miles south to Chonai (modern Honaz).
- Judaism, Platonism, and mystery cults from the surrounding mountain peoples blended into strange, often contradictory religious practices. Cultic worship of angels persisted, with Michael as the favorite. He was credited with sparing the town in a time of disaster.
- Home of Archippus and Epaphras, associates of Paul who helped spread the gospel throughout Asia, up and down the Lycus Valley. The region was also home to Onesimus, a runaway slave who became a believer (see the Introduction to Philemon).

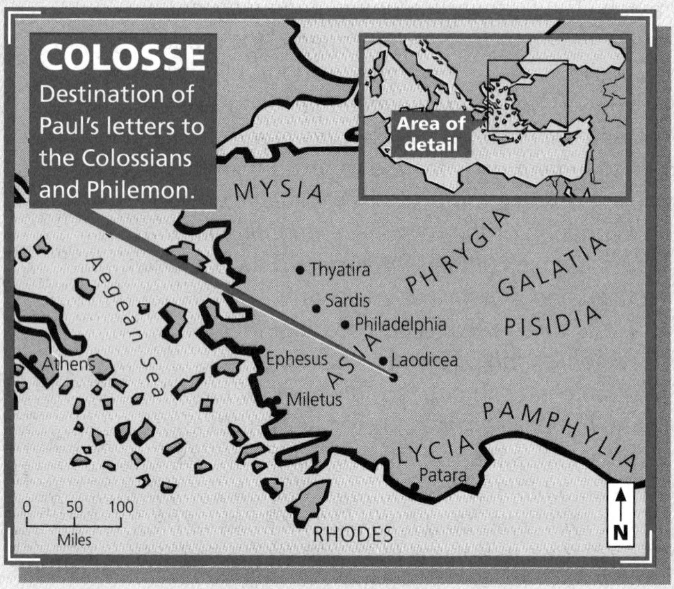

CHAPTER 1

Greeting

[1]Paul, an apostle of Jesus Christ by the will of God, and
Timothy our brother,

[2]To the saints and faithful brethren in Christ *who are* in
Colosse:

Grace to you and peace from God our Father and the
Lord Jesus Christ.[a]

Praise for Faith, Hope, and Love

[3]We give thanks to the God and Father of our Lord Jesus
Christ, praying always for you, [4]since we heard of your faith
in Christ Jesus and of your love for all the saints; [5]because
of the hope which is laid up for you in heaven, of which
you heard before in the word of the truth of the gospel,
[6]which has come to you, as *it has* also in all the world, and
is bringing forth fruit,[a] as *it is* also among you since the day
you heard and knew the grace of God in truth; [7]as you also
learned from Epaphras, our dear fellow servant, who is a
faithful minister of Christ on your behalf, [8]who also declared to us your love in the Spirit.
[9]For this reason we also, since the day we heard it, do not
cease to pray for you, and to ask that you may be filled with
the knowledge of His will in all wisdom and spiritual understanding; [10]that you may walk worthy of the Lord, fully
pleasing *Him,* being fruitful in every good work and increasing in the knowledge of God; [11]strengthened with all
might, according to His glorious power, for all patience and
longsuffering with joy; [12]giving thanks to the Father who
has qualified us to be partakers of the inheritance of the
saints in the light. [13]He has delivered us from the power of
darkness and conveyed *us* into the kingdom of the Son of
His love, [14]in whom we have redemption through His
blood,[a] the forgiveness of sins.

The Preeminence of Christ

1:15–18 [15]He is the image of the invisible God,
the firstborn over all creation. [16]For by
Him all things were created that are in heaven and that are
on earth, visible and invisible, whether thrones or domin-
ions or principalities or powers. All things were created

1:2 [a]NU-Text omits *and the Lord Jesus Christ.* *1:6* [a]NU-Text and M-Text add *and growing.*
1:14 [a]NU-Text and M-Text omit *through His blood.*

CHRIST, THE LORD OF THE WORLD

CONSIDER THIS 1:15–18 *In vv. 15–18, Paul presents Jesus as the cosmic Christ, Creator of the universe, Sustainer of earth and all of its ecological systems, and Ruler over the competing power networks of the world.*

This is quite a contrast from Jesus the Servant, as presented in Philippians 2:5–8. There He is Lord of the personal and the private, the One who speaks to someone's heart. Here in Colossians, Paul offers the Lord of the public who transcends individual needs to deal with global concerns.

These are not two different Christs, but the same Christ, Lord of all. And His rule over both domains—the public and the private—suggests the kinds of activities in which His followers need to engage. On the one hand, Christ lives in us to transform us personally. He wants to affect our individual jobs, our families, our local communities, and our personal relationships. On the other hand, Christ is at work globally, using people to transform societies and their systems, confront principalities and powers, and work for public justice and human rights.

Paul claimed that all things were created through and for Christ. How much of "all" is all? See "Life—The Big Picture," Mark 12:28–34.

1:17 through Him and for Him. [17]And He is
before all things, and in Him all things
consist. [18]And He is the head of the body, the church, who
is the beginning, the firstborn from the dead, that in all
things He may have the preeminence.
[19]For it pleased *the Father that* in Him all the fullness
should dwell, [20]and by Him to reconcile all things to Himself, by Him, whether things on earth or things in heaven,
having made peace through the blood of His cross.
[21]And you, who once were alienated and enemies in your
mind by wicked works, yet now He has reconciled [22]in the
body of His flesh through death, to present you holy, and
blameless, and above reproach in His sight— [23]if indeed
you continue in the faith, grounded and steadfast, and are
not moved away from the hope of the gospel which you
heard, which was preached to every creature under heaven,
of which I, Paul, became a minister.

Paul's Role in Preaching Christ

[24]I now rejoice in my sufferings for you, and fill up in my
flesh what is lacking in the afflictions of Christ, for the sake
of His body, which is the church, [25]of which I became a
minister according to the stewardship from God which was
given to me for you, to fulfill the word of God, [26]the mystery which has been hidden from ages and from generations, but now has been revealed to His saints. [27]To them
God willed to make known what are the riches of the glory
of this mystery among the Gentiles: which[a] is Christ in you,
the hope of glory. [28]Him we preach, warning every man and
teaching every man in all wisdom, that we may present
1:29 every man perfect in Christ Jesus. [29]To
this *end* I also labor, striving according to
His working which works in me mightily.

CHAPTER 2

Paul's Burden for the Colossians

[1]For I want you to know what a great conflict I have for
you and those in Laodicea, and *for* as many as have not seen
my face in the flesh, [2]that their hearts may be encouraged,
being knit together in love, and *attaining* to all riches of the
full assurance of understanding, to the knowledge of the
mystery of God, both of the Father and[a] of Christ, [3]in
whom are hidden all the treasures of wisdom and knowledge.

1:27 [a]M-Text reads *who*. *2:2* [a]NU-Text omits *both of the Father and*.

EVERY BREATH YOU TAKE

CONSIDER THIS 1:17 **People frequently use the term Mother Nature to describe the natural laws that bring order and predictability to the world. But Paul reminds us that Christ is ultimately the One who holds things together (v. 17), not some impersonal force or random chance. We depend on Him for every breath we draw. Since the first day of creation, He has been sustaining the world and providing for His creatures (Neh. 9:6; Ps. 36:6; Heb. 1:3).**

That lends tremendous dignity to human labor, especially since God has placed humanity over the creation as His managers. He values work that seeks to understand and oversee this world—for example, the work of the climatologist who studies the impact of humans on global ecology; the physicist who looks into the makeup of the atom and the application of that knowledge to human needs; and the publisher who helps distribute information and ideas to people. Jobs like these reflect God's work as Creator, and those who do them are actually partners with Christ in maintaining His creation.

God values everyday work because work is something that He Himself has done and continues to do. See "God: The Original Worker," John 5:17.

For more on how your job can help to accomplish God's purposes in the world, see "People at Work," Heb. 2:7.

4Now this I say lest anyone should deceive you with persuasive words. 5For though I am absent in the flesh, yet I
am with you in spirit, rejoicing to see your *good* order and
the steadfastness of your faith in Christ.

Continue in Christ

2:6 see pg. 698

6As you therefore have received Christ
Jesus the Lord, so walk in Him, 7rooted
and built up in Him and established in the faith, as you
have been taught, abounding in it[a] with thanksgiving.

Beware of False Teaching

8Beware lest anyone cheat you through philosophy and
empty deceit, according to the tradition of men, according
to the basic principles of the world, and not according to
Christ. 9For in Him dwells all the fullness of the Godhead
bodily; 10and you are complete in Him, who is the head of
all principality and power.
11In Him you were also circumcised with the circumcision made without hands, by putting off the body of the
sins[a] of the flesh, by the circumcision of Christ, 12buried
with Him in baptism, in which you also were raised with
Him through faith in the working of God, who raised Him
from the dead. 13And you, being dead in your trespasses
and the uncircumcision of your flesh, He has made alive together with Him, having forgiven you all trespasses, 14hav-
ing wiped out the handwriting of requirements that was
against us, which was contrary to us. And He has taken it
out of the way, having nailed it to the cross. 15Having dis-
armed principalities and powers, He made a public spectacle of them, triumphing over them in it.

2:16–17

16So let no one judge you in food or in
drink, or regarding a festival or a new
moon or sabbaths, 17which are a shadow of things to come,
but the substance is of Christ. 18Let no one cheat you of
your reward, taking delight in *false* humility and worship of
angels, intruding into those things which he has not[a] seen,

(Bible text continued on page 699)

2:7 [a]NU-Text omits *in it.* *2:11* [a]NU-Text omits *of the sins.* *2:18* [a]NU-Text omits *not.*

Stand Up for Your Convictions!

A CLOSER LOOK 2:16–17 *The community of believers at Colosse was plagued by opinionated people who tried to impose their preferences on others. Paul challenged his readers to stand up for their own convictions, and not to allow others to coerce them through intimidation or condemnation (vv. 16–17). His advice is similar to what he told the Christians at Rome about "Matters of Conscience" (Rom. 14:1–23).*

Jesus constantly faced judgment from religious leaders of His day over His treatment of the Sabbath. See "Jesus Confronts the Legalists," Luke 6:1–11.

QUOTE UNQUOTE

CONSIDER THIS 1:29 *Just as Paul strived to accomplish God's work, so many Christians today work hard to do the same:*

Using both the* [Wall Street] Journal *and the Bible, at the same time, sure makes our business lives complicated and difficult. But whoever said Christian faithfulness would be simple and easy?

John H. Rudy

CONSIDER THIS
2:6

Two Portraits of Jesus, Two Sides of Life

Paul urged the Colossians to follow the pattern of Christ (v. 6). But what does that pattern look like? In Philippians and Colossians, Paul paints two contrasting but complementary portraits of the Lord. Hanging side by side in the New Testament, they challenge believers to pay attention to two sides of life—the private and the public. Neither one is more important; both are crucial when it comes to living out the faith.

Notice how Jesus modeled two styles of living, and what that means for those of us who follow Christ today:

Two Ways Jesus Is Portrayed by Paul

Christ the Lord: Power over All	Christ the Servant: Lowest of the Lowly
As portrayed in Colossians, especially 1:15–20.	As portrayed in Philippians, especially 2:5–11.
Original audience: believers at Colosse, a dying town of Asia Minor.	*Original audience:* believers at Philippi, a proud, prosperous Roman colony in Macedonia.
Main features: Christ is... •the ruler of the universe. •the firstborn of creation. •the bodily expression of God. •the One who possesses all authority in heaven and on earth. •the "cosmic Christ" who confronts and exposes every opposing principality and power.	*Main features:* Christ is... •the model of humility, of "downward mobility." •the model of servant leadership. •the obedient Son who surrenders His power in order to accomplish His task among and on behalf of the powerless. •the One who dies in order to save.
Tends to produce a public faith that... is concerned with human rights, feeding the hungry, assisting the poor, and working on community development. Because Christ is Lord of the powers, He is Lord of governments, cities, systems, and economic structures. Christ's people pay attention to the social implications of the gospel.	*Tends to produce a private faith that...* is concerned with personal holiness, spiritual disciplines, individual growth, and one-on-one evangelism. Because Christ modeled servanthood, His people are called to put the interests of others ahead of their own. They especially pay attention to relationships and the personal, inner needs of people.
Examples today: •Running for public office. •Challenging businesses when they appear to have an adverse effect on people. •Serving meals to the homeless. •Advising public officials on matters of public policy. •Learning to initiate and manage institutional change. •Voting.	*Examples today:* •Bible study. •Friendship evangelism. •Missions. •Ministries that strengthen marriages and home life. •Support groups. •Counseling. •Prayer.

◆

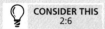

vainly puffed up by his fleshly mind, [19]and not holding fast
to the Head, from whom all the body, nourished and knit
together by joints and ligaments, grows with the increase
that is from God.
[20]Therefore,[a] if you died with Christ from the basic principles of the world, why, as *though* living in the world, do
you subject yourselves to regulations— [21]"Do not touch, do
not taste, do not handle," [22]which all concern things which
perish with the using—according to the commandments
and doctrines of men? [23]These things indeed have an appearance of wisdom in self-imposed religion, *false* humility,
and neglect of the body, *but are* of no value against the in-
dulgence of the flesh.

CHAPTER 3

Christ the Focus of Life

3:1–2 see pg. 702

[1]If then you were raised with Christ,
seek those things which are above, where
Christ is, sitting at the right hand of God. [2]Set your mind
on things above, not on things on the earth. [3]For you died,

3:1–4

and your life is hidden with Christ in
God. [4]When Christ *who is* our life appears, then you also will appear with Him in glory.

A Christlike Lifestyle

3:5 see pg. 700

[5]Therefore put to death your members
which are on the earth: fornication, uncleanness, passion, evil desire, and covetousness, which is
idolatry. [6]Because of these things the wrath of God is coming upon the sons of disobedience, [7]in which you yourselves once walked when you lived in them.
[8]But now you yourselves are to put off all these: anger,
wrath, malice, blasphemy, filthy language out of your
mouth. [9]Do not lie to one another, since you have put off
the old man with his deeds, [10]and have put on the new *man*
who is renewed in knowledge according to the image of

3:11 see pg. 701

Him who created him, [11]where there is
neither Greek nor Jew, circumcised nor
uncircumcised, barbarian, Scythian, slave *nor* free, but
Christ *is* all and in all.

3:12–17

[12]Therefore, as *the* elect of God, holy
and beloved, put on tender mercies,

2:20 [a]NU-Text and M-Text omit *Therefore.*

A New Wardrobe

A CLOSER LOOK 3:12–17 *In vv. 12–17, Paul challenges us as believers to "put on" a new wardrobe, one appropriate to our new life in Christ. For an expanded list of what that wardrobe includes, see "New Creatures with New Character," Gal. 5:22–23.*

Where's Your Head At?

CONSIDER THIS 3:1–4 *Paul urges us to focus on the "things above" rather than the "things on the earth" (vv. 1–4). The distinction between these two spheres has caused no end of misunderstanding. It has been said that heavenly things matter and earthly things don't. But that's not what Paul says. When he tells us to "set your mind on the things above," he's challenging us to make Christ the center of our lives, because Christ is what matters, certainly more than anything this world has to offer.*

And yet it is precisely because heavenly things matter that earthly things also matter a great deal—and why Paul immediately launches into a long exhortation about everyday issues such as character and conduct, relationships, and work (3:5—4:6). How we handle earthly affairs such as time, money, personal energy, emotions, our thought life, and our relationships reflects the focus of our mind. These "mundane" things show what matters to us.

kindness, humility, meekness, longsuffering; [13]bearing with
one another, and forgiving one another, if anyone has a
complaint against another; even as Christ forgave you,
so you also *must do.* [14]But above all these things put on
love, which is the bond of perfection. [15]And let the peace
of God rule in your hearts, to which also you were called
in one body; and be thankful. [16]Let the word of Christ
dwell in you richly in all wisdom, teaching and admonishing one another in psalms and hymns and spiritual
songs, singing with grace in your hearts to the Lord. [17]And
whatever you do in word or deed, *do* all in the name of
the Lord Jesus, giving thanks to God the Father through
Him.

Instructions for Families

[18]Wives, submit to your own husbands, as is fitting in the Lord.

[19]Husbands, love your wives and do not be bitter toward them.

[20]Children, obey your parents in all things, for this is well pleasing to the Lord.

CONSIDER THIS
3:5

Do-It-Yourself Idolatry

Most of us think of idolatry as a pagan bowing down to an image carved from stone or wood, reciting mysterious incantations, and carrying out peculiar rituals. But Paul says that idolatry is much more familiar to us than we realize. All it takes is simple greed (v. 5).

Does that mean it's wrong to want a bigger house, a newer car, a more prestigious job, a more dynamic personality, a more noticeable spirituality? No, none of these things is evil, in and of itself. The question is, what is the heart attitude that makes us want any of these things?

The difference between desire and greed is the difference between a small, blue circle of flame that cooks food on a gas range, and a raging inferno that threatens to burn down the house. Simple desire can be constructive; it motivates us to work and be productive. Proverbs 16:26 says that "a worker's appetite works for him." But greed is dangerous and destructive. It is desire out of control.

Control is the real issue. Will the thing we want serve

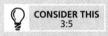

21Fathers, do not provoke your children, lest they become
discouraged.

Instructions to Servants and Masters

3:22 see pg. 705
22Bondservants, obey in all things your
masters according to the flesh, not with
eyeservice, as men-pleasers, but in sincerity of heart, fearing
3:22–24 see pg. 704
God. 23And whatever you do, do it
heartily, as to the Lord and not to men,
3:24
24knowing that from the Lord you will receive the reward of the inheritance; for[a]
you serve the Lord Christ. 25But he who does wrong will be
repaid for what he has done, and there is no partiality.

(Bible text continued on page 704)

3:24 [a]NU-Text omits *for.*

Your Reward

A CLOSER LOOK 3:24 *Do you ever wonder what you're going to get out of serving Christ? Paul promises "the reward of the inheritance" (v. 24). Find out more about it in the article, "What's In It for Me?" Eph. 1:11.*

our needs, or will our needs serve that thing? That's why Paul says that covetousness—or greed—is idolatry *(Eph. 5:5). To covet is to surrender our will to a thing—in effect, to make it our master, our god, the thing that we serve. But God insists: "You shall have no other gods before Me" (Ex. 20:3).*

Greed means that we want something other than God. He is not enough for us; we need something more to satisfy. It also means that we don't trust Him to follow through on His promises to supply what we need (Matt. 6:33; Rom. 8:32). Everyday greed, then, is nothing less than an attack on the very character of God. No wonder Paul warns so sternly against it! ◆

Jesus gives a direct, unequivocal command to guard against longing for something we don't have. See "Watch Out for Greed!" Luke 12:15.

The opposite of covetousness is contentment. What would that look like? See Phil. 4:10–13.

Bloodlines

CONSIDER THIS 3:11 **The city of Colosse included people from a wide variety of ethnic and cultural backgrounds (v. 11):**

- ***Greeks,* whose cultural heritage dominated the Roman world.**
- ***Jews,* who prided themselves as "God's chosen people."**
- ***Barbarians,* who spoke no Greek and therefore lacked social standing.**
- ***Scythians,* a crude, cruel warlike people from the north.**
- ***Slaves,* menial workers at the bottom of the society.**

Members from all these groups came to faith and joined the community of believers at Colosse. But their ethnic prejudices created problems, which Paul listed (vv. 8–9). He pulled no punches, calling them by their ugly names: anger, wrath, malice, blasphemy, filthy language, and lying. Paul challenged his culturally mixed group of readers to shed such behaviors like an old set of clothes and put on Christ instead, who "is all and in all." He was possibly reminding them of a first-century baptismal creed that reminded new converts that they were joining a new family in Christ (see "We Are Family!" Gal. 3:28).

God's family has no place for prejudice. Radically new ways of relating to others are called for (Col. 3:12–17). If believers today lived out these ideals, we would see God change our churches and begin to transform our culture.

CONSIDER THIS
3:1–2

THE SPIRITUALITY OF EVERYDAY WORK

What do vv. 1–2 imply about everyday work? Is it possible to hold a "secular" job and still "seek those things which are above" rather than "things on the earth"? Or would it be better to quit one's job and go into the ministry?

The issue here is *spirituality,* the capacity to know, experience, and respond to God. How is it possible to bring spirituality into "secular" work? Consider:

If Christ is Lord over all of life, then He must be Lord over work, too. Colossians 3 does not distinguish between the sacred and the secular, but between the life that Christ offers, (the "things above") and its alternative—spiritual death apart from Him (the "things on the earth"). This is clear from the preceding context (2:20) and the rest of chapter 3: "earthly" things include fornication, uncleanness, passion, etc. (vv. 5, 8); the "things above" include tender mercies, kindness, humility, etc. (vv. 12–15). Spirituality has to do with conduct and character, not just vocation.

It also has to do with the lordship of Christ. Christ is Lord over all of creation (1:15–18). Therefore, He is Lord over work. Whatever we do for work, we should do it "in the name of the Lord Jesus" (v. 17), that is, with a concern for His approval and in a manner that honors Him. In fact, Paul specifically addresses two categories of workers—slaves (v. 22–25) and masters (4:1)—in this manner.

The Spirit empowers us to live and work with Christlikeness. Spirituality has to do with character and conduct, regardless of where we work. Christ gives the Holy Spirit to help us live in a way that pleases Him. (Gal. 5:16–25.) That has enormous implications for how we do our jobs, our "workstyle" (Titus 2:9–10).

Furthermore, Scripture calls us "temples" of the Holy Spirit (1 Cor. 6:19). An intriguing image: In Exodus 31 and 35, the Spirit enabled Hebrew workers to use their skills in stonecutting, carpentry, lapidary arts, and so on to construct a beautiful, functional house of worship. In an even greater way, we can expect the Spirit to enable us to use our God-given skills and abilities to bring glory to God.

God values our work even when the product has no eternal value. A common measure of the significance of a job is its perceived value from the eternal perspective. Will the work "last"? Will it "really count" for eternity? The assumption is that God values work for eternity, but not work for the here and now.

By this measure, the work of ministers and missionaries has eternal value because it deals with the spiritual, eternal needs of people. By contrast, the work of the shoe salesman, bank teller, or typist has only limited value, because it meets only earthly needs. Implication: that kind of work doesn't really "count" to God.

But this way of thinking overlooks several important truths:

(1) God Himself has created a world which is time-bound and temporary (2 Pet. 3:10–11). Yet He values His work, declaring it to be "very good," good by its very nature (Gen. 1:31; Ps. 119:68; Acts 14:17).

(2) God promises rewards to people in everyday jobs, based on their attitude and conduct (Eph. 6:7–9; Col. 3:23—4:1).

(3) God cares about the everyday needs of people as well as their spiritual needs. He cares whether people have food, clothing, shelter, and so forth.

(4) God cares about people, who will enter eternity. To the extent that a job serves the needs of people, He values it because He values people. ◆

Because God cares about the everyday needs of people as well as their spiritual needs, He has given people the skills required to meet those everyday needs. See "People at Work," Heb. 2:7.

Are some jobs more important than others? See 1 Cor. 12:28–31.

The Gift of an Ethnic Heritage

CONSIDER THIS 4:10–11 **Culture provides people with a common set of experiences and values that bind them together over time. As Paul concludes his letter to the Colossians, he mentions three men who shared his Jewish heritage: Aristarchus, Mark the cousin of Barnabas, and Jesus who was called Justus (vv. 10–11). He says that they were the only Jews still working with him.**

Even though Paul was "the apostle to the Gentiles," he still cherished his Jewish roots. No Gentile could fully appreciate what it meant to grow up and live with the traditions of Judaism. But Aristarchus, Mark, and Justus could. No wonder Paul calls them "a comfort" to him.

God never asks us to reject our roots. We can affirm our ethnic heritage as a rich gift from Him, no matter how our surrounding culture regards it. To be sure, ethnicity ought not to create barriers with other people (Gal. 3:28; Col. 3:11). But we need not hide the cultural background from which God has called us. We need never deny who God has created us to be.

Workers for the Kingdom

CONSIDER THIS 4:11 **Do you ever wonder what your life contributes to the work of God in the world? If you are in a "secular" occupation, you may conclude that the only way to further the kingdom is to pray for and contribute financially to those who are in "full-time" Christian work. But are those your only options?**

Paul described Aristarchus, Mark, and Justus as "fellow workers for the kingdom" (v. 11), indicating that they may have been vocational Christian workers. However, there is no way to say whether they were employed in that work as a full-time occupation. In fact, if they followed Paul's example, they probably had other jobs through which they made their living (see "Paul's 'Real' Job," Acts 18:1–3).

The point is that drawing a paycheck for doing "ministry" is not the criterion by which to judge whether someone is a worker for God's kingdom. Kingdom work involves promoting the values, beliefs, and lifestyle of the kingdom. That may involve professional employment such as pastoring a church or serving on a mission field. But kingdom workers are also found among doctors, accountants, engineers, painters, salespeople, auto mechanics, and homemakers. Wherever believers are furthering the goals and objectives of Christ, they are working for His kingdom.

How does your life promote the purposes of God? Do you use your skills and abilities toward that end, whether or not pay is involved? Or have you given up and concluded that because you are not a vocational Christian worker, you aren't really serving the Lord with your life and career? If so, you'll want to reconsider what it means to be a worker for Christ's kingdom!

Is it really possible to hold a "secular" job and still please God with your life? Or would it be better to quit one's job and go into the ministry? See "The Spirituality of Everyday Work," Col. 3:1–2.

CHAPTER 4

3:22—4:1
see pg. 706
1Masters, give your bondservants what
is just and fair, knowing that you also
have a Master in heaven.

Instructions and Requests

4:2
see pg. 707
2Continue earnestly in prayer, being
vigilant in it with thanksgiving; 3mean-

CONSIDER THIS
3:22–24

Who's the Boss?

He had a menial, dead-end job. They assigned him tasks that no one else wanted—the "dumb-work," the dirty work, the dangerous work. They called him out at all hours of the day and night to satisfy the whims of his supervisors. He had little hope for advancement. In fact, he'd be lucky just to keep his job; plenty of others stood in line, ready to replace him. Whether he even lived or died mattered little. He was a first-century Roman slave.

Yet he mattered to God, and his work mattered, too. In writing to this lowly worker (vv. 22–24), Paul re-defined his occupational status: he was not just a Roman slave, he was an employee of Christ the Lord! That makes all the difference.

So it is for any Christian in the workplace. You may work for a giant multinational corporation or a mom-'n-pop pizza parlor. You may have 15 levels of bureaucracy over you, or be self-employed. It doesn't matter. Ultimately, Christ is your Boss. Consider what that means:

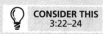

while praying also for us, that God would open to us a door
for the word, to speak the mystery of Christ, for which I am
also in chains, 4that I may make it manifest, as I ought to
speak.
5Walk in wisdom toward those *who are* outside, re-
deeming the time. 6*Let* your speech always *be* with grace,

(Bible text continued on page 707)

Christ gives you work to do. *Work is a gift from God. He has created you in His image to be a worker, giving you skills and abilities to accomplish His purposes. He has also sovereignly placed you in your occupation to do His work there. Even if your job is as lowly as a Roman slave's, it still has value and dignity to Christ.*

Christ is your Boss, but He uses human supervisors. *According to Colossians 3, people in authority over you are actually human representatives of Christ. They may not act very Christlike. But in working for them, you are ultimately working for Christ. Do you follow their instructions? Do you shirk your job when they're not around? Are you more interested in impressing them to gain approval and advancement than in getting the job done? How would your work ethic change if you saw Christ as your supervisor?*

Christ asks you to put your heart into your work. *If you serve Christ in your job, you have more reason than anyone else to work with integrity and enthusiasm. The job itself may be unchallenging or unpleasant. But Christ asks you to do it with dignity, to the best of your ability, as though working for Christ Himself.*

Christ will reward you for good, faithful work. *This passage says that Christ will review your work someday. You can expect praise and reward for working in a Christlike manner.* ◆

Many of the first Christians may have been slaves, since perhaps half the population or more of the Roman Empire were under servitude by one historian's estimate. Find out more about this important group in the article, "Slaves," Rom. 6:16.

One of the reasons that your work has dignity and value, even if you are a slave, is that you are a coworker with God. See "People at Work," Heb. 2:7.

Christ cares not only about what job you have, but how you go about doing it. See "Your 'Workstyle,'" Titus 2:9–10.

QUOTE UNQUOTE

CONSIDER THIS 3:22 *Paul's instructions to bondservants (v. 22) are as applicable to employees today as they were to slaves in the first century:*

When I hear someone say, "I couldn't work with a corporation with a profit motive or which demands more than forty hours a week," I say something like this: "Do you know that the Christian slaves to whom Paul wrote were working sixteen hours a day for masters that were fornicating with female slaves, making dirty business deals with traders from other parts of the Roman empire and going to baths and the gymnasium at night for orgies? To these slaves Paul says, 'Treat your masters as though they were Jesus. You are not working for them but for Jesus. And it is worship.'"

Paul Stevens, *Liberating the Laity,* p. 158

FOR YOUR INFO
3:22—4:1

WORK-WORLD CODES

Paul's letters have much to say to believers as we live out our faith in the work world. As he does here in 3:22—4:1, Paul usually speaks to both leaders and workers about the tough character and choices required to honor Christ in a difficult workplace environment. For example:

Guidelines for Managers and Others in Authority

Finance
- Workers deserve payment for their work (1 Cor. 9:7–14).
- You are accountable for fair employee compensation (Col. 4:1).
- Handle wealth very delicately (1Tim. 6:9–10, 17–18).

Work Relationships
- Bring your walk with Christ into each business relationship (2 Cor. 7:1).
- Value people highly (Gal. 5:14–15; Eph. 4:31–32).
- Treat and motivate employees with respect rather than threats (Eph. 6:5–9).
- Have a reasonable view of yourself (Rom. 12:3).

Communication
- Accusations must be verified (Matt. 18:15–35; 2 Cor. 13:1; 1 Tim. 5:19).
- Communication should always be gracious and truthful (Col. 4:6).

Responsibility
- Fulfill your commitments (Rom. 13:6–8).
- Remember your accountability (1 Cor. 3:9–15).
- Care for the poor and the weak (Rom. 12:13; Gal. 2:10).
- Learn how to handle times of bounty and leanness (Phil. 4:12).
- Remember, God's Son gets the ultimate credit (Col. 1:17–18).
- Be sure to care for your own family (1 Tim. 5:8).
- Discern needs and meet them (Titus 3:14).

Management
- View time not only in terms of time management, but also in light of the long-term implications of your decisions (2 Cor. 4:16–18; 2 Pet. 3:8–13).
- Help each employee discern the best thing to do (1 Thess. 5:14–15).
- Be willing to change your opinions (2 Cor. 5:16–17; Philem. 10–14).

Guidelines for Workers and Those under Authority

Tasks
- Don't try to get out of your current situation too quickly (1 Cor. 7:17–24).
- View stress and trouble in perspective (2 Cor. 4:7–18).

Supervisors
- Develop a respect for authority (Rom. 13:1–8).
- Do your work wholeheartedly and respectfully (Eph. 6:5–8; 1 Thess. 5:12–15).
- Give your employers obedient, hard work (Col. 3:22–25; 1 Thess. 4:11–12).
- Honor bosses, whether they are believers or not (1 Tim. 6:1–2).

Coworkers
- Develop a reasonable self-estimate (Rom. 12:3).
- Acknowledge differences and accept the contributions of others (1 Cor. 12:1–8).
- Help others, but do your job (Gal. 6:1–5).
- Learn to speak appropriately and sensitively (Col. 4:6).
- Understand others and treat them respectfully (1 Tim. 5:1–3).
- Develop a reputation for good relationships (Titus 3:1–2).

Responsibility
- Give your whole self to God (Rom. 12:1).
- Develop the art of discernment in order to live responsibly (Eph. 5:15–18).
- Do your work as if working for God—you are (1 Cor. 3:13; Col. 3:17).
- Don't let your responsibilities weigh you down with worry (Phil. 4:6).
- Take responsibility for yourself (1 Thess. 4:11–12; 2 Thess. 3:8–9).
- Develop a godly "workstyle" (Titus 2:9–10).

Finances
- Live frugally and do not steal—including pilfering (Eph. 4:28).
- Care for your family (1Tim. 5:8).

◆

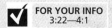

seasoned with salt, that you may know how you ought
to answer each one.

News, Greetings, and Final Words

7Tychicus, a beloved brother, faithful minister, and fellow
servant in the Lord, will tell you all the news about me. 8I
am sending him to you for this very purpose, that he[a] may
know your circumstances and comfort your hearts, 9with
Onesimus, a faithful and beloved brother,
who is *one* of you. They will make known
to you all things which *are happening*
here.
10Aristarchus my fellow prisoner greets
you, with Mark the cousin of Barnabas
(about whom you received instructions: if he comes to you,
welcome him), 11and Jesus who is called Justus. These *are*
my only fellow workers for the kingdom of God who are of
the circumcision; they have proved to be a comfort to me.
12Epaphras, who is *one* of you, a bondservant of Christ,
greets you, always laboring fervently for you in prayers, that
you may stand perfect and complete[a] in all the will of God.
13For I bear him witness that he has a great zeal[a] for you,
and those who are in Laodicea, and those in Hierapolis.
14Luke the beloved physician and Demas greet you. 15Greet
the brethren who are in Laodicea, and Nymphas and the
church that *is* in his[a] house.
16Now when this epistle is read among you, see that it is
read also in the church of the Laodiceans, and that you likewise read the epistle from Laodicea. 17And say to Archippus, "Take heed to the ministry which you have received in
the Lord, that you may fulfill it."
18This salutation by my own hand—Paul. Remember my
chains. Grace *be* with you. Amen.

4:10–11 see pg. 703

4:11 see pg. 703

4:8 [a]NU-Text reads *you may know our circumstances and he may.* *4:12* [a]NU-Text reads *fully assured.* *4:13* [a]NU-Text reads *concern.* *4:15* [a]NU-Text reads *Nympha . . . her house.*

QUOTE UNQUOTE

CONSIDER THIS 4:2 *Vigilance in prayer is a vital part of working with Christlikeness:*

Orare est laborare, laborare est orare.
(To pray is to work, to work is to pray.)

Motto of the Benedictine monks, C. A.D. 500

1 *and* 2 Thessalonians

What does a church look like when it functions the way it is supposed to? It may well resemble the church at Thessalonica. Of all the congregations mentioned in the New Testament, the Thessalonians were perhaps the model in carrying out the instructions of the apostles. Indeed, the story of their faith spread far and wide in the first century, impressing all who heard it (1:7–9).

Their example still proves instructive today. Many people in our culture are choosing to live increasingly isolated lives, putting distance between themselves and the needs of the world. By contrast, Christians are challenged to engage the world and penetrate it with the light of God's love. The Thessalonians did that in the first century; believers today can do the same. In a world that lacks hope, they can point toward the hope that is found in Christ.

The story of their faith spread far and wide.

C O N T E N T S

A R T I C L E S

WHEN HOPE FADES

Judging from his comments in the New Testament, the apostle Paul may have felt greater affection for the church at Thessalonica than for any other congregation (1 Thess. 2:7–8, 11). The believers there didn't just talk about the gospel, they *practiced* it.

In doing so they were emulating Paul, Silas, and Timothy, who had brought them the gospel. The threesome had taken great pains to live an exemplary life among them (2:9–10; 2 Thess. 3:7–9). The demonstration of a Christlike lifestyle lent credibility to the apostles' message, with the result that many Thessalonians were persuaded (Acts 17:1–4). Even those who were not recognized a power in the messengers, calling them men who had "turned the world upside down" (17:6).

For a time the gospel turned Thessalonica upside down. But after the apostles left and things quieted down, the new believers were left with an important reality of the faith—that lasting change occurs over time. That's why Paul's two letters call for responsible, long-term progress and the refusal to let hope fade. He reminds his readers of his example, how he worked among the Thessalonians (1 Thess. 2:9). They should work as well, he says, and keep on working rather than burning out in the midst of doing good (4:11; 5:12–14; 2 Thess. 3:6–13).

The work that Paul calls for is the everyday work of making a living and maintaining a home. And yet there is an inner work that takes place in and through that day-to-day toil. As the Thessalonians carried out their everyday responsibilities, God was building their character, so that Paul could speak of their "work of faith, labor of love, and patience of hope" (1 Thess. 1:3).

When hope fades, people lose heart and doubts begin to grow. Perhaps that was happening in Thessalonica. A major question that the two letters address is, what will happen in the end times (see 4:13—5:11; 2 Thess. 2:1–12)? And how should believers live as they await the return of the Lord? Again, Paul exhorts his readers to lifestyles of faithful service and steadfast hope. "The Lord is faithful," he declares (3:3). Therefore, His people should be faithful as well.

Two thousand years after the Thessalonians, believers still await the coming of the Lord. Has your hope faded? Have doubts crowded in so that you wonder whether God will keep His word? Has your lifestyle grown spiritually lax and undisciplined? The message of 1 and 2 Thessalonians remains: keep working, stay faithful, don't lose hope. God will honor His commitments. He challenges you to live in a way that points to that hope. ◆

. . . LET US NOT SLEEP, AS OTHERS DO, BUT LET US WATCH AND BE SOBER.

—1 Thessalonians 5:6

Thessalonica

Thessalonica was a thriving commercial and military center with a renowned history. Learn more about it at Acts 17:1.

WORK, LABOR, AND PATIENCE

CONSIDER THIS 1:3 *It's easy to see Paul's emphasis on faith, hope, and love, the trinity of Christian virtues (v. 3). But notice the words that precede these qualities:* work *of faith,* labor *of love, and* patience *of hope. These are marketplace terms. Christians in the workplace understand that useful results come only from hard work, diligent labor, and patience. The same is true in spiritual growth. (Heb. 6:9–12 mentions these same values.)*

QUOTE UNQUOTE

CONSIDER THIS 1:7 *The Thessalonians became examples of what the gospel can do (v. 7). Models of Christlikeness are still needed today:*

People are not particularly interested in our ideas; they are interested in our experiences. They are not searching for theories but for convictions. They want to penetrate our rhetoric in order to discover the reality of our lives.

Richard Halverson, Chaplain, United States Senate, and former pastor of Fourth Presbyterian Church, McLean, Virginia; from a church newsletter

CHAPTER 1

Greeting

1Paul, Silvanus, and Timothy,

To the church of the Thessalonians in God the Father and
the Lord Jesus Christ:

Grace to you and peace from God our Father and the
Lord Jesus Christ.[a]

The Thessalonians Act as Believers Should

2We give thanks to God always for you all, making men-
1:3 tion of you in our prayers, 3remembering
without ceasing your work of faith, labor
of love, and patience of hope in our Lord Jesus Christ in the
sight of our God and Father, 4knowing, beloved brethren,
your election by God. 5For our gospel did not come to you
in word only, but also in power, and in the Holy Spirit and
in much assurance, as you know what kind of men we were
among you for your sake.
6And you became followers of us and of the Lord, having
received the word in much affliction, with joy of the Holy
1:7 Spirit, 7so that you became examples to
all in Macedonia and Achaia who believe.
8For from you the word of the Lord has sounded forth, not
only in Macedonia and Achaia, but also in every place. Your
faith toward God has gone out, so that we do not need to
say anything. 9For they themselves declare concerning us
what manner of entry we had to you, and how you turned
to God from idols to serve the living and true God, 10and to
wait for His Son from heaven, whom He raised from the
dead, *even* Jesus who delivers us from the wrath to come.

CHAPTER 2

Fond Memories of Paul's First Visit

1For you yourselves know, brethren, that our coming to
you was not in vain. 2But even[a] after we had suffered before
and were spitefully treated at Philippi, as you know, we
were bold in our God to speak to you the gospel of God in
much conflict. 3For our exhortation *did* not *come* from error
or uncleanness, nor *was it* in deceit.
4But as we have been approved by God to be entrusted
with the gospel, even so we speak, not as pleasing men, but

1:1 [a]NU-Text omits *from God our Father and the Lord Jesus Christ.* *2:2* [a]NU-Text and M-Text omit *even.*

2:5

God who tests our hearts. 5For neither at
any time did we use flattering words, as
you know, nor a cloak for covetousness—God *is* witness.
6Nor did we seek glory from men, either from you or from
others, when we might have made demands as apostles of

2:7 see pg. 716

Christ. 7But we were gentle among you,
just as a nursing *mother* cherishes her
own children. 8So, affectionately longing for you, we were
well pleased to impart to you not only the gospel of God,
but also our own lives, because you had become dear to us.

2:9

9For you remember, brethren, our labor
and toil; for laboring night and day, that
we might not be a burden to any of you, we preached to
you the gospel of God.
10You *are* witnesses, and God *also*, how devoutly and
justly and blamelessly we behaved ourselves among you
who believe; 11as you know how we exhorted, and comforted, and charged[a] every one of you, as a father *does* his
own children, 12that you would walk worthy of God who
calls you into His own kingdom and glory.

A Model Church

2:13–14 see pg. 714

13For this reason we also thank God
without ceasing, because when you re-
ceived the word of God which you heard from us, you welcomed *it* not *as* the word of men, but as it is in truth, the
word of God, which also effectively works in you who believe. 14For you, brethren, became imitators of the churches
of God which are in Judea in Christ Jesus. For you also suffered the same things from your own countrymen, just as
they *did* from the Judeans, 15who killed both the Lord Jesus
and their own prophets, and have persecuted us; and they
do not please God and are contrary to all men, 16forbidding
us to speak to the Gentiles that they may be saved, so as always to fill up *the measure of* their sins; but wrath has come
upon them to the uttermost.

(Bible text continued on page 716)

2:11 [a]NU-Text and M-Text read *implored.*

The Value of Self-Support

A CLOSER LOOK 2:9

As an apostle, Paul had a right to be supported by others. However, he chose to forfeit that right so as not to be a burden on anyone and possibly cause them to reject the gospel (v. 9; compare 1 Cor. 9:7–12).

Paul's example is instructive to clergy and laity alike. For those who make their living in vocational Christian work, it opens the door to the idea of carrying out ministry while supporting oneself through other means. See "Paying Vocational Christian Workers," 1 Cor. 9:1–23. For all believers, it honors the principle of self-support to which every Christian is called. See "A Command to Work," 2 Thess. 3:6–12.

A Straightforward Approach

CONSIDER THIS 2:5

Many people in today's culture have grown cynical about religion. So as we believers think about presenting the gospel to others, we need to be careful to make our message credible and straightforward.

Paul mentions two dangers that he avoided so as not to compromise his credibility (v. 5): the use of "flattering words," which amounts to telling people what they want to hear, and "a cloak for covetousness," which involves hidden motives. To use either of these approaches is to deceive people. That's unacceptable for someone who presents himself as a representative of Christ.

The key to Paul's integrity was his realization that God Himself had entrusted him with the message (v. 4). The task of taking the gospel to the Gentiles was not something that Paul had thought up, but a calling from God (Gal. 1:11–17). Thus his aim was not to please people, but God.

Nor did he need to worry about his material well-being, even less to covet what others had. As a messenger of God, he could rely on God to provide for his needs and remain content in whatever circumstances came his way (Phil. 4:11–12). (This is not to suggest that Paul was irresponsible; he earned his living through his occupation as a tentmaker. See "Paul's 'Real' Job," Acts 18:1–3.)

As we consider ways in which to communicate Christ to people around us, what obstacles to our credibility might there be? Are there things about our methods or motives that conflict with the message with which we've been entrusted?

Some helpful suggestions for communicating the faith with integrity are contained in "A Code of Ethics for Christian Witness," 2 Cor. 4:2.

CONSIDER THIS
2:13–14

IS YOUR CHURCH UPSIDE-DOWN OR RIGHT SIDE UP?

The believers at Thessalonica became something of a model church in Paul's estimation by embracing the gospel with unreserved commitment and sincerity (v. 13; 1:8–9). What does a model church look like? We can gain some idea by looking at the New Testament's many glimpses of the early church worshiping the Lord, relating to one another, and effectively reaching out to its surrounding culture with the gospel.

It's interesting that the first believers apparently did not rely on hired staff to carry out most of the church's work, nor did they occupy many formal church buildings until the fourth century A.D. Nevertheless, they were enormously successful at carrying out the Lord's command to be His witnesses "to the end of the earth" (Acts 1:8). At Ephesus, for example, Christian outreach was so effective that "all of Asia [Minor] heard the word of the Lord" (19:10).

If we compare the pattern that seems to emerge from the New Testament with the way most churches in the West are structured today, we can see two models for describing church life.

The first model shows a chain-of-command, pyramid-like structure. At the top are the professional, "full-time" clergy who make up perhaps 1 percent of any local congregation.

A second level near the top are the "paraclergy," volunteers who are particularly active in congregational life. Their dedicated service within the programs and structures of the church is greatly appreciated by the clergy and is often used as a measure of their Christian commitment.

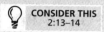

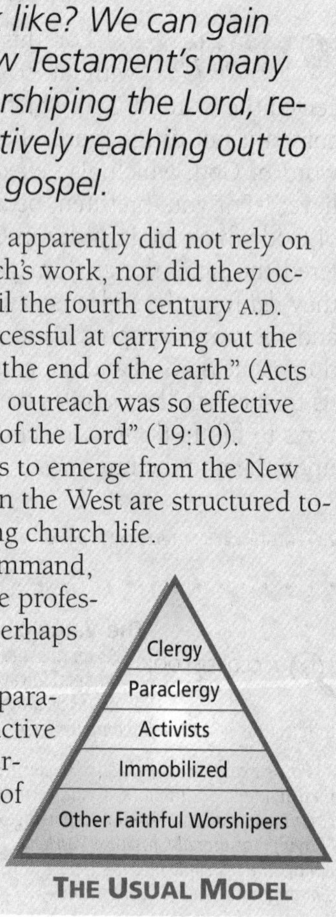

THE USUAL MODEL

Next are the "activists," some of whom may be among the paraclergy. These believers take a special interest in matters requiring action and the taking of a position. For example, they may advocate for a certain public policy, lead programs of social outreach, or lobby within the church to influence a particular decision. Sometimes activists stir up controversy and make others uncomfortable, but their zeal to apply the gospel is never in doubt.

Another important category to consider, especially in our own day, might be called "the immobilized." These are people in the midst of a crisis that dominates their experience, such as death, illness, divorce, or unemployment. Their situation makes it difficult for them to participate in ministry to others. Instead, they need the body to minister to them. Depending on the church, the immobilized and the other groups may comprise 20 to 30 percent or more of the congregation.

That leaves a majority of the church's faithful worshippers—perhaps 70 to 80 percent—available for ministries outside the church, out in the world among unbelievers. However, these potential "Monday ministers" are often overlooked by church leaders because their service is not directed toward the congregation itself. Yet because of their strategic location in the culture, they should be affirmed, equipped, and supported to impact the world for Christ (see "Faith Impacts the World," Mark 16:15–16).

When we examine the New Testament's description of the early church, we find all of the groups mentioned above. However, the way that these believers are organized and deployed for service is "upside-down" from the first model—or "right side up," depending on your point of view. The second model shows the difference.

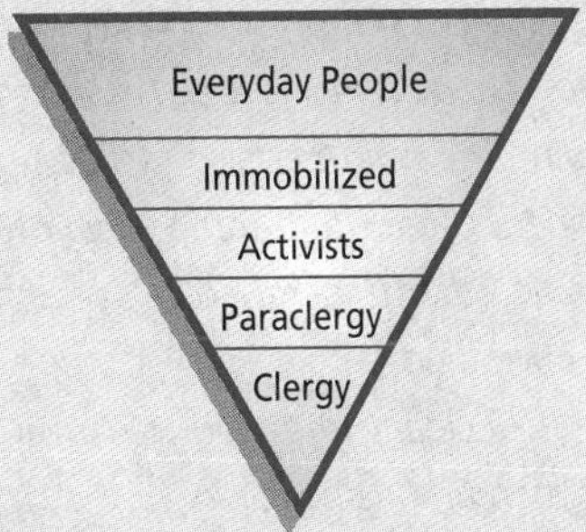

THE BIBLICAL MODEL

This is an outward-looking congregation in which the people of God view themselves as agents of Christ in the world. The pastors, teachers, and paraclergy function to "[equip] the saints for the work of ministry" (Eph. 4:12). They are, in effect, "internists" whose goal is to make Scripture "rise up and walk" in the minds and wills of everyday people.

As they do that, the larger congregation, the 70 to 80 percent majority above, become the "church scattered" as they live and work in the world, representing Christ.

Actually, both of the two diagrams shown are valid ways of understanding how a group of believers functions. As the first model suggests, the church needs to gather for worship, instruction, and the care of its members. In fact, the New Testament term for congregations of believers is *ekklēsia*, the "assembly." God's people are called out of the world and into the "church gathered," which functions as a home for safety, a hospital for restoration, a school for development, and an orchestra for worship.

This "gathered life," however, has its counterpart in the "scattered life" of God's people. As the second diagram suggests, the church looks outside itself to fulfill Christ's Great Commission (Matt. 28:18–20) in the world. Thus the "church scattered" becomes an army overcoming spiritual opposition, a social agency to meet the needs of wounded, hurting people, an agent of justice promoting righteousness in the community, and a communications company proclaiming the good news of salvation.

The church—gathered for equipping, scattered for service. Both dimensions are crucial. Where does your church place its emphasis? What ways can you think of to strengthen its internal growth and external outreach? ◆

The book of Acts shows a dynamic rhythm in the early church between gathering for the refinement of believers and the scattering of the church for encounter with the world. See "Reconnecting Sunday and Monday," Acts 2:46–47.

Paul Hindered from Visiting

[17]But we, brethren, having been taken away from you for
a short time in presence, not in heart, endeavored more eagerly to see your face with great desire. [18]Therefore we
wanted to come to you—even I, Paul, time and again—but
Satan hindered us. [19]For what *is* our hope, or joy, or crown
of rejoicing? *Is it* not even you in the presence of our Lord
Jesus Christ at His coming? [20]For you are our glory and joy.

CHAPTER 3

Timothy Sent to Thessalonica

3:1–10

[1]Therefore, when we could no longer
endure it, we thought it good to be left in
Athens alone, [2]and sent Timothy, our brother and minister
of God, and our fellow laborer in the gospel of Christ, to es-

THIS IS THE WILL OF GOD, YOUR SANCTIFICATION.
—1 Thessalonians 4:3

GENTLE AS A NURSING MOTHER

CONSIDER THIS 2:7 *Paul felt great love for the Thessalonian believers, and he drew upon a touching image to communicate his affection, that of a woman nursing an infant (v. 7).*

Most mothers in the first century world nursed their own infants. However, some wealthy women employed wet nurses. In that case, the child lived in the home of the wet nurse, who agreed to certain conditions such as not nursing other children and avoiding alcohol. The wet nurse took responsibility not only for feeding the child but also for raising it until it was weaned, often up to three years of age. Many contracts specified that the wet nurse's fee had to be returned if the child died.

Paul clearly intended to convey a sense of tender affection and responsible, loving care for his spiritual children, the Thessalonians. In doing so, he showed a side of spiritual leadership and nurture that Christian leaders do well to emulate today.

tablish you and encourage you concerning your faith, 3that
no one should be shaken by these afflictions; for you yourselves know that we are appointed to this. 4For, in fact, we
told you before when we were with you that we would suffer tribulation, just as it happened, and you know. 5For this
reason, when I could no longer endure it, I sent to know
your faith, lest by some means the tempter had tempted
you, and our labor might be in vain.

Timothy's Encouraging Report

6But now that Timothy has come to us from you, and
brought us good news of your faith and love, and that you
always have good remembrance of us, greatly desiring to
see us, as we also *to see* you— 7therefore, brethren, in all
our affliction and distress we were comforted concerning
you by your faith. 8For now we live, if you stand fast in the
Lord.

9For what thanks can we render to God for you, for all
the joy with which we rejoice for your sake before our God,
10night and day praying exceedingly that we may see your
face and perfect what is lacking in your faith?

Paul's Prayer for the Thessalonians

11Now may our God and Father Himself, and our Lord
Jesus Christ, direct our way to you. 12And may the Lord
make you increase and abound in love to one another and
to all, just as we *do* to you, 13so that He may establish
your hearts blameless in holiness before our God and Father at the coming of our Lord Jesus Christ with all His
saints.

CHAPTER 4

Maintain Sexual Purity

1Finally then, brethren, we urge and exhort in the Lord
Jesus that you should abound more and more, just as you
received from us how you ought to walk and to please God;
2for you know what commandments we gave you through
the Lord Jesus.

3For this is the will of God, your sanctification: that you
should abstain from sexual immorality; 4that each of you
should know how to possess his own vessel in sanctification
and honor, 5not in passion of lust, like the Gentiles who do
not know God; 6that no one should take advantage of and
defraud his brother in this matter, because the Lord *is* the
avenger of all such, as we also forewarned you and testified.
7For God did not call us to uncleanness, but in holiness.

ENCOURAGING THE BOSS

CONSIDER THIS 3:1–10 **Separation from close friends can bring feelings of loneliness and loss, especially when one is facing disappointment or failure. Paul felt that way in Athens. Despite his strident efforts to present and defend the gospel, he met with only lackluster response from the Athenians (Acts 17:16–34). Not surprisingly, his thoughts turned toward the Thessalonians with whom he felt an unusually deep bond (1 Thess. 2:8; 2:17—3:1).**

Anxious for news, Paul sent his valuable associate Timothy north for a visit (3:2). The young man's report buoyed Paul up. Even as one city was resisting Christ, another was responding to Him in powerful and encouraging ways (3:6–10).

Paul's emotional honesty here is refreshing and instructive. Rather than deny or spiritualize his pain, he acknowledged it and took action. He needed the warm affection of the Thessalonians and especially the capable companionship of Timothy. Rather than live as a "Lone Ranger Christian," Paul stayed connected to other believers and relied on them for insight, encouragement, and support. In this way he honored a basic principle of Christian community (Heb. 10:24–25).

Does your supervisor need encouragement, affirmation, or help in keeping the big picture? Often when people are under great stress or feeling a sense of failure, the only thing they hear is what's wrong. Can you encourage yours with a word about what is *right*?

QUOTE UNQUOTE

CONSIDER THIS 4:11–12 *Leading a disciplined life of honest work (vv. 11–12) can pay as many spiritual dividends as working in vocational ministry:*

I've always been glad myself that theology is not the thing that I earn my living by. On the whole, I'd advise you to get on with your tent-making. The performance of a duty will probably teach you quite as much about God as academic theology would do. Mind, I'm not certain: but that is the view I incline to.

C.S. Lewis, Letter to Sheldon Vanauken, Jan. 5, 1951

8Therefore he who rejects *this* does not reject man, but God,
who has also given[a] us His Holy Spirit.

Contribute to Society

9But concerning brotherly love you have no need that I
should write to you, for you yourselves are taught by God
to love one another; 10and indeed you do so toward all the
brethren who are in all Macedonia. But we urge you,
4:11 brethren, that you increase more and
more; 11that you also aspire to lead a
quiet life, to mind your own business, and to work with
4:11–12 your own hands, as we commanded you,
12that you may walk properly toward
those who are outside, and *that* you may lack nothing.

Concerning Believers Who Have Died

13But I do not want you to be ignorant, brethren, concerning those who have fallen asleep, lest you sorrow as
others who have no hope. 14For if we believe that Jesus died
and rose again, even so God will bring with Him those who
sleep in Jesus.[a]

(Bible text continued on page 720)

4:8 [a]NU-Text reads *who also gives.* *4:14* [a]Or *those who through Jesus sleep*

CONSIDER THIS 4:11

QUIET LIVING IN A HECTIC WORLD

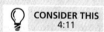

If any one word characterizes life in the modern world, it may be the word hectic. *The rat race. The grind. The fast lane. The laser lane. Things seem to move faster and faster, and anyone who can't keep up is in danger of being left behind.*

For that reason, Paul's exhortation to "lead a quiet life" (v. 11) seems out of step with contemporary culture. How can one lead a quiet life when technology accelerates change and increases complexity? When television and other media bring the world into our homes and broadcast private lives to the world? When a global economy makes everybody's business our business?

The challenge to lead a quiet life in a hectic world is considerable, but as believers we can take decisive steps that will benefit us personally and spiritually. Actually, Paul gives us an important first step in the exhortation to "work with [our] own hands." The focus is not on "hands" but on "your own": it was not manual labor that Paul insisted on, but self-support (see "A Command to Work," 2 Thess. 3:6–12).

As far as quiet living, Paul was probably not objecting

THE BLESSED HOPE

CONSIDER THIS 4:13–18 *Paul encouraged the believers at Thessalonica with the promise that the Lord will intervene (vv. 13–18). The resurrection is real! Fellowship with one another and with God is for real, whether it's here, there, or "in the air." This is the "blessed hope" that Paul offers by way of comfort (v. 18).*

The question this raises, however, is what is the interim hope for the church? Is it to flee the inner city and migrate to the suburbs, leaving behind city problems in search of healthier, wealthier prospects? Is that what Paul would recommend?

to noise and sound as such, but to needless distraction. One way that most people could bring a little more peace and quiet into their homes would be to cut their television viewing in half. Imagine the time left for family members and neighbors, personal reflection, and prayer!

However, the real thrust of this passage is not so much for believers to lower the noise level around them as to live peaceably with others, without disturbance or conflict (compare Rom. 12:18; Heb. 12:14). Minding our own business and working for ourselves are both means to that end, the end of "[walking] properly toward those who are outside [the faith]" (1 Thess. 4:12).

How can we live peaceably? By avoiding quarrels and complaints (Col. 3:13); by refusing to take offense when others hurt us (Matt. 5:7–12); by not getting entangled in the affairs of others (Prov. 6:1); and by humbly accepting the circumstances that God sends us for our good, rather than grumbling (Rom. 8:28; Phil. 4:11–12). ◆

QUOTE UNQUOTE

CONSIDER THIS 5:6 *Today there may be a reason why some believers "sleep, as others do" (v. 6):*

Many so-called believers have accepted a "decaffeinated" Christianity—it promises not to keep you awake at night.

Anglican Bishop Michael Marshall, as quoted in editor's column, *America Magazine*

Support the Weak

CONSIDER THIS 5:14 **Paul begins the concluding words of his letter with four sharp exhortations (v. 14). The "unruly"—the lazy, the undisciplined, those looking for a free ride—need a bit of a jolt. (Paul later gave them one in 2 Thess. 3:6–12.) Those who are losing heart need encouragement. And everyone needs patience.**

But Paul's third directive, "uphold the weak," has to do with one's responsibilities toward the poor. Wherever Scripture raises this issue, it challenges us to share at least some of our material wealth with people in desperate need. It is the only Christlike response there is.

Indeed, Christ serves as the ultimate model of compassion (see "Christ Became Poor," 2 Cor. 8:8–9). He even staked His credibility on His work among the the downtrodden and destitute when John the Baptist inquired as to whether He was the Christ (see "Some Surprising Evidence," Matt. 11:2–6).

Paul hardly needed to challenge the Thessalonian believers to be generous. He knew by experience that even though they lived in deep poverty, they were willing to give "beyond their ability" (2 Cor. 8:3) to help others in need.

If the Thessalonians, poor as they were, could give "beyond their ability," what should affluent believers today be giving?

Scripture has a great deal to say about our responsibilities to the poor and needy. See " 'I Have Not Coveted,' " Acts 20:33–38.

[15]For this we say to you by the word of the Lord, that we
who are alive *and* remain until the coming of the Lord will
by no means precede those who are asleep. [16]For the Lord
Himself will descend from heaven with a shout, with the
voice of an archangel, and with the trumpet of God. And
the dead in Christ will rise first. [17]Then we who are alive
and remain shall be caught up together with them in the
clouds to meet the Lord in the air. And thus we shall always
4:13–18 see pg. 719
be with the Lord. [18]Therefore comfort
one another with these words.

CHAPTER 5

Concerning the Times

[1]But concerning the times and the seasons, brethren, you
have no need that I should write to you. [2]For you yourselves know perfectly that the day of the Lord so comes as a
thief in the night. [3]For when they say, "Peace and safety!"
then sudden destruction comes upon them, as labor pains
upon a pregnant woman. And they shall not escape. [4]But
you, brethren, are not in darkness, so that this Day should
overtake you as a thief. [5]You are all sons of light and sons of
5:6 see pg. 719
the day. We are not of the night nor of
darkness. [6]Therefore let us not sleep, as
others *do,* but let us watch and be sober. [7]For those who
sleep, sleep at night, and those who get drunk are drunk at
night. [8]But let us who are of the day be sober, putting on
the breastplate of faith and love, and *as* a helmet the hope
of salvation. [9]For God did not appoint us to wrath, but to
obtain salvation through our Lord Jesus Christ, [10]who died
for us, that whether we wake or sleep, we should live together with Him.
[11]Therefore comfort each other and edify one another,
just as you also are doing.

The Community Life of Believers

[12]And we urge you, brethren, to recognize those who labor among you, and are over you in the Lord and admonish
you, [13]and to esteem them very highly in love for their
work's sake. Be at peace among yourselves.
5:14
[14]Now we exhort you, brethren, warn
those who are unruly, comfort the faint-
hearted, uphold the weak, be patient with all. [15]See that no
one renders evil for evil to anyone, but always pursue what
is good both for yourselves and for all.
[16]Rejoice always, [17]pray without ceasing, [18]in everything
give thanks; for this is the will of God in Christ Jesus for
you.
[19]Do not quench the Spirit. [20]Do not despise prophecies.

21Test all things; hold fast what is good. 22Abstain from
every form of evil.

Blessings and Greetings

23Now may the God of peace Himself sanctify you completely; and may your whole spirit, soul, and body be preserved blameless at the coming of our Lord Jesus Christ.
24He who calls you *is* faithful, who also will do *it*.

25Brethren, pray for us.

26Greet all the brethren with a holy kiss.

27I charge you by the Lord that this epistle be read to all
the holy[a] brethren.

28The grace of our Lord Jesus Christ *be* with you. Amen.

5:27 [a]NU-Text omits *holy*.

HE WHO CALLS YOU IS FAITHFUL.
—1 Thessalonians 5:24

2 Thessalonians

CONTENTS

ARTICLES

CHAPTER 1

Greetings

1Paul, Silvanus, and Timothy,

To the church of the Thessalonians in God our Father
and the Lord Jesus Christ:

2Grace to you and peace from God our Father and the
Lord Jesus Christ.

Praise for Withstanding Persecution

1:3–12

3We are bound to thank God always for
you, brethren, as it is fitting, because
your faith grows exceedingly, and the love of every one of
you all abounds toward each other, 4so that we ourselves
boast of you among the churches of God for your patience
and faith in all your persecutions and tribulations that you
endure, 5*which is* manifest evidence of the righteous judgment of God, that you may be counted worthy of the kingdom of God, for which you also suffer; 6since *it is* a righteous thing with God to repay with tribulation those who
trouble you, 7and to *give* you who are troubled rest with us
when the Lord Jesus is revealed from heaven with His
mighty angels, 8in flaming fire taking vengeance on those
who do not know God, and on those who do not obey the
gospel of our Lord Jesus Christ. 9These shall be punished
with everlasting destruction from the presence of the Lord
and from the glory of His power, 10when He comes, in that
Day, to be glorified in His saints and to be admired among
all those who believe,[a] because our testimony among you
was believed.
11Therefore we also pray always for you that our God
would count you worthy of *this* calling, and fulfill all the
good pleasure of *His* goodness and the work of faith with
power, 12that the name of our Lord Jesus Christ may be glorified in you, and you in Him, according to the grace of our
God and the Lord Jesus Christ.

CHAPTER 2

Discerning the Times

2:1–12
see pg. 724

1Now, brethren, concerning the coming
of our Lord Jesus Christ and our gather-
ing together to Him, we ask you, 2not to be soon shaken in
mind or troubled, either by spirit or by word or by letter, as
if from us, as though the day of Christ[a] had come. 3Let no
one deceive you by any means; for *that Day will not come*

(Bible text continued on page 725)

1:10 [a]NU-Text and M-Text read *have believed.* *2:2* [a]NU-Text reads *the Lord.*

FINISHING WELL

CONSIDER THIS 1:3–12 **What would be an appropriate epitaph on your tombstone? What statement would describe your life overall rather than whatever current circumstances you are temporarily facing right now?**

When Paul wrote to the believers in Thessalonica, they were in the midst of intense suffering (1:4–5). But Paul encouraged them to look beyond their immediate troubles to the return of Christ and the affirmation they would receive from Him at that time (vv. 6–7). Their enemies, who were really enemies of the Lord, would be judged and dealt with (vv. 8–9). By contrast, they would join with their Savior in joy and praise (v. 10). Paul went on in the next chapter to expand on this theme and its impact on the Thessalonians' current difficulties (2:1–12).

God calls us as His people to finish our lives well by holding on to the truths that last (2:15). He challenges us to maintain life-long faithfulness and not to be entirely caught up in the here and now, whether good or bad.

As you consider the long-term direction of your life, what memories are you creating in others about your values and reputation? What will people choose to remember about you?

The Dangers of Preoccupations

CONSIDER THIS 2:1–12 Are you anxious about the future of the world? Do dire predictions about coming disasters trouble you? Or do dramatic solutions to the world's many problems hold your curiosity?

Like many people today, the believers in Thessalonica were vulnerable to urgent warnings and announcements related to the future (vv. 1–2). In fact, certain false teachers of the day pandered to people's interest in such things, playing to their greatest hopes and worst fears about the return of Christ (v. 3; 1 Thess. 5:2–5). In response, Paul appealed for reason and critical thinking based on the clear instructions he had given (2 Thess. 2:3–12, 15).

As we read 2 Thessalonians today, we, like the letter's original readers, need to "stand fast and hold the traditions which [we] were taught," the truths of God's Word. We should avoid fanciful, fearful guesswork about events related to the Lord's return and instead be busy about our responsibilities at hand (3:6–13).

Father, Son, and Spirit for You!

CONSIDER THIS 2:13–17 One of the most important teachings of Christianity is the concept of the Trinity, the belief that God is one God, but exists in three Persons—Father, Son, and Holy Spirit. However, the Bible does not offer an explanation of this concept so much as a presentation of it. It assumes a Triune God but does not try to "prove" the Trinity.

In 2 Thessalonians, Paul seeks to enrich his readers' understanding of their new life in Christ by telling them about works done on their behalf by all three Persons of the Godhead. These same benefits are ours as believers today:

The Father *has selected us for salvation, loves us, and gives us consolation and hope (vv. 13, 16).*

The Son *shares His glory with us and provides comfort and stability in the faith (vv. 14, 16).*

The Spirit *purifies ("sanctifies") us and develops our faith (v. 13).*

As believers, we have a powerful, caring, active God working on our behalf. For the first-century Christians at Thessalonica, that was a distinct contrast to the many gods of the surrounding Greek and Roman cultures that were often passive, sometimes capricious, and terribly self-absorbed. Likewise in our own day, our God is infinitely more powerful and personal than the vague "higher power" to which many people allude.

The doctrine of the Trinity may be difficult to comprehend, but as always we see in a dim mirror when it comes to ultimate truth (1 Cor. 13:12). Nevertheless, we can obediently respond to what we know clearly and not dwell on things that are cloudy. One thing we know for sure: our God is for us in every way!

A Command to Work

CONSIDER THIS 3:6–12 God wants Christians to take responsibility to provide for their material needs and those of their families. In fact, v. 10 states this as a *command.*

God has created a world of resources for this purpose. He gives us authority, along with strength and skills, to use those resources to earn our living. Work is His gift to us, a means of supplying what we need.

Obviously, there are times when grown children must care for their parents or grand-

(continued on next page)

unless the falling away comes first, and the man of sin[a] is
revealed, the son of perdition, [4]who opposes and exalts
himself above all that is called God or that is worshiped, so
that he sits as God[a] in the temple of God, showing himself
that he is God.
[5]Do you not remember that when I was still with you I
told you these things? [6]And now you know what is restraining, that he may be revealed in his own time. [7]For the mystery of lawlessness is already at work; only He[a] who now restrains *will do so* until He[b] is taken out of the way. [8]And then
the lawless one will be revealed, whom the Lord will consume with the breath of His mouth and destroy with the
brightness of His coming. [9]The coming of the *lawless one* is
according to the working of Satan, with all power, signs,
and lying wonders, [10]and with all unrighteous deception
among those who perish, because they did not receive the
love of the truth, that they might be saved. [11]And for this
reason God will send them strong delusion, that they
should believe the lie, [12]that they all may be condemned
who did not believe the truth but had pleasure in unrighteousness.

Thanksgiving, Exhortation, and a Prayer

2:13–17

[13]But we are bound to give thanks to
God always for you, brethren beloved by
the Lord, because God from the beginning chose you for
salvation through sanctification by the Spirit and belief in
the truth, [14]to which He called you by our gospel, for the
obtaining of the glory of our Lord Jesus Christ. [15]Therefore,
brethren, stand fast and hold the traditions which you were
taught, whether by word or our epistle.
[16]Now may our Lord Jesus Christ Himself, and our God
and Father, who has loved us and given *us* everlasting consolation and good hope by grace, [17]comfort your hearts and
establish you in every good word and work.

CHAPTER 3

Paul Requests Prayer

[1]Finally, brethren, pray for us, that the word of the Lord
may run *swiftly* and be glorified, just as *it is* with you, [2]and
that we may be delivered from unreasonable and wicked
men; for not all have faith.
[3]But the Lord is faithful, who will establish you and guard
you from the evil one. [4]And we have confidence in the Lord
concerning you, both that you do and will do the things we
command you.

2:3 [a]NU-Text reads *lawlessness.* *2:4* [a]NU-Text omits *as God.* *2:7* [a]Or *he* [b]Or *he*

(continued from previous page)

parents (Mark 7:9–13; 1 Tim. 5:4). Likewise, the church community sometimes must assume responsibility for those in need. But responsibility always starts with the individual, as this passage makes plain.

Earlier, in 1 Thessalonians 4:12, Paul explains why: (1) Because of the testimony that Christians have among unbelievers. Believers who beg, borrow unnecessarily, or steal discredit Christ and the church. (2) Because God doesn't want His children to "lack" what they need. He doesn't call us to poverty, but to adequacy.

Our everyday work is something that God takes seriously. See "People at Work," Heb. 2:7.

God not only wants us to work, He wants us to work with a Christlike "workstyle." See Titus 2:9–10.

The idea that God rewards godliness with material blessing can lead people to be irresponsible about work. See "The Dangers of Prosperity Theology," 1 Tim. 6:3–6.

ARE YOU TIRED?

CONSIDER THIS 3:13

Do you grow weary of holding to high standards of integrity or performance? Do you resent a lack of recognition? Are you fed up as you see others around you maneuvering to get out of work, and do you seethe when they get away with it?

Paul's admonition in v. 13 is meant for believers who are "burned out" on doing good. Keep in mind that God never forgets you. You are the object of His attention and love. He sees the good that you do when no one else is around—and He'll never forget it!

NO WORK? NO EAT!

CONSIDER THIS 3:10 *Paul urged that those who would not work should not eat (v. 10). He may have been dealing with the laziness and idleness of those who thought there would be no tomorrow because they expected the immediate return of the Lord. Two thousand years later, we still anticipate the Second Coming. But it's interesting that nowadays people generally work as if there will be a tomorrow without a return.*

It's worth noting that these Macedonian believers, if they were the same ones that Paul referred to in 2 Corinthians 8:2, lived in abject poverty. It is common in poor communities—where jobs are few and many of those that do exist pay too little to support even the basics—for some to grow discouraged and give up all attempts at finding employment. That could also explain the "disorderly" behavior Paul rebuked (v. 6).

5Now may the Lord direct your hearts into the love of
God and into the patience of Christ.

Every Believer Has Work to Do

3:6–12 see pg. 724
6But we command you, brethren, in
the name of our Lord Jesus Christ, that
you withdraw from every brother who walks disorderly and
not according to the tradition which he[a] received from us.
3:7–9
7For you yourselves know how you
ought to follow us, for we were not disorderly among you; 8nor did we eat anyone's bread free of
charge, but worked with labor and toil night and day, that
we might not be a burden to any of you, 9not because we
do not have authority, but to make ourselves an example of
how you should follow us.
3:10
10For even when we were with you, we
commanded you this: If anyone will not
work, neither shall he eat. 11For we hear that there are some
who walk among you in a disorderly manner, not working
at all, but are busybodies. 12Now those who are such we
command and exhort through our Lord Jesus Christ that
they work in quietness and eat their own bread.
3:13 see pg. 725
13But *as for* you, brethren, do not grow
weary *in* doing good. 14And if anyone
does not obey our word in this epistle, note that person and
do not keep company with him, that he may be ashamed.
15Yet do not count *him* as an enemy, but admonish *him* as a
brother.

Peace and Grace from the Lord

16Now may the Lord of peace Himself give you peace always in every way. The Lord *be* with you all.
17The salutation of Paul with my own hand, which is a
sign in every epistle; so I write.
18The grace of our Lord Jesus Christ *be* with you all.
Amen.

3:6 [a]NU-Text and M-Text read *they*.

Paul's Example

A CLOSER LOOK 3:7–9 *Paul wrote that he had a right as an apostle to let others take care of him (v. 9). But he chose instead to earn his own living, setting an example of how believers should take responsibility to meet their own needs. Think of it: in effect, Paul was saying that if paid work was good enough for him, it's good enough for any of us.*

Paul's example also bears upon the reputation of churches and ministries today. Is there any reason why modern Christian leaders shouldn't at least consider doing as Paul did—earning a living outside the ministry to support their basic needs? See "I Have Not Coveted," Acts 20:33–38.

1 and 2 Timothy

One of the most difficult transitions for any organization to make is the transfer of power from the founders to a second generation of leadership. Countless entrepreneurs have brought disaster on their companies by refusing to relinquish control to others who are younger and, in their view, less competent. And even where visionaries gladly hand the reigns of authority over to qualified successors, there is no guarantee of continuity or success.

That's one reason why 1 and 2 Timothy make for such interesting reading. They are letters about the transfer of leadership to a new generation. In writing them, Paul was passing the torch to his son in the faith, Timothy, pastor of the church at Ephesus. Paul knew that his own time was drawing to a close, that his work would soon come to an end. Would the Ephesians continue in the faith? Would they hold to the truth of the gospel and practice Christlike love toward one another? Would young Timothy be adequate to the pastoral task? Would he teach his people sound doctrine, navigate through disputes and disappointments, and model a lifestyle of faith?

Whatever the condition of the local church where you worship—whatever its size, form of leadership, or spiritual condition—1 and 2 Timothy will prove instructive. They take us back to one of the very first cases of a church moving into its second generation. As a result, they reveal the essentials of church life and leadership, the key things to which everyone in the body needs to be paying attention.

C O N T E N T S

A R T I C L E S

Ten Myths About Christianity (1 Tim. 1:3–4)

Unfortunately, many people have accepted a number of myths about Christianity, with the result that they never respond to Jesus as He really is. Here's a list of ten myths about Christianity that are common in our culture.

Sorting Out the Truth (1:3–11)

When it comes to matters of the faith, it's wise to remain a bit skeptical—especially if someone claims to be God's special envoy.

The Prayer Breakfast Movement (2:1–7)

Prayer breakfasts are common today in many major cities. But city-wide prayer goes all the way back to Abraham's time, and Paul encouraged believers to petition God for those in authority.

Feel Like a Novice? (4:1–16)

Do you feel that proving yourself and gaining acceptance is an uphill battle? Are you tempted to declare, "I'll show 'em"? Paul offers some seasoned wisdom to people who are just starting out.

Widows (5:3)

Widows were common in the ancient world. Scripture gives clear instructions on their care, and there is no reason why those guidelines do not still apply to believers.

"I Won't Hire Christians!" (6:1–2)

"Imagine!" cries a business owner. "A former employee thought he could take advantage of me just because he knew I was a Christian!"

The Dangers of Prosperity Theology (6:3–6)

Does God reward godliness with material blessing? Not according to this passage.

Christians and Money (6:6–19)

Modern-day believers do well to carefully study Paul's discussion of money. He speaks to people who want to get rich, people who want to honor God, and those who are rich and want to honor God.

A Manual for Church Life

As we read Paul's instructions in 1 and 2 Timothy, we can feel his heart reaching out to the believers at Ephesus, where he had spent so much effort (Acts 19:1—20:1), and to his young protégé from Lystra. Paul wanted the congregation not merely to survive, but to thrive. So he wrote these two letters, which are among the earliest manuals we have for church organization. 1 Timothy emphasizes the life of the congregation, and 2 Timothy dwells on the life of the pastor.

Why were such instructions needed? Perhaps it was because of the gospel's unparalleled success at Ephesus. No longer was the Christian community there just a small body of new converts enjoying intimate fellowship on a first-name basis. The group had grown substantially over the years and was having an influence in cities throughout Asia Minor (see "The Ultimate 'New Testament Church' " at the Introduction to Ephesians). It was a diverse, multiethnic church struggling internally with issues of unity and doctrinal purity and externally with a pagan, sometimes hostile environment.

Ephesus was in many ways the church as it is supposed to be. But it had grown to the point where it needed organizational structure. For example:

- The church was attracting teachers who contradicted the gospel of Paul and Timothy, so it needed a clear statement of faith that would be regularly defended (1 Tim. 1:3–4, 18–20; 4:1–16).
- The gospel had impacted the commercial life of Ephesus, so church members needed to consider the public side of their faith (2:1–7).
- The worship service needed order (2:8–15).
- Standards were needed by which to appoint leaders (3:1–16) and hold them accountable (5:17–25).
- As its members advanced in years, the group had more and more widows to look after, so criteria were needed for determining who should receive help (5:3–16).
- Both masters and slaves, the rich and the poor, were joining the church, so it needed to develop a statement of policy regarding income and lifestyle (6:1–19).

From Paul's point of view, the key human actor in the work at Ephesus was Timothy. This man enjoyed an unusually close relationship with the apostle. Paul called him "my beloved and faithful son in the Lord" (1 Cor. 4:17) and his "true son in the faith" (1 Tim. 1:2). To the Philippians he boasted that no one else would have the same care for them as Timothy. Others were looking after their own affairs, Paul wrote, not the affairs of Christ. But not Timothy: "You know his proven character, that as a son with his father he served with me in the gospel" (Phil. 2:19–22).

So as he penned 2 Timothy, Paul was doing far more than writing a directive to a subordinate. He was opening his heart as a mentor to a man who would succeed him. He urged Timothy over and over to follow after him, to repeat the truths "which you have heard *from me*" (2 Tim. 1:13; 2:2, italics added), to "continue in the things which you have learned and been assured of, *knowing from whom you have learned them*" (3:14, italics added). These are more than encouragements to uphold standards or to pass along rituals. This is an older man reaching into the mind and heart and life of a younger man with the most powerful and enduring educational tool of all—his own personality. ◆

Timothy

Paul's young protégé Timothy traveled widely and worked among groups of believers in Greece, Macedonia, and Asia Minor. He also participated in the sending of six New Testament letters. See the profile on Timothy at the Introduction to 2 Timothy.

CHAPTER 1

A True Son in the Faith

[1]Paul, an apostle of Jesus Christ, by the commandment of
God our Savior and the Lord Jesus Christ, our hope,

[2]To Timothy, a true son in the faith:

Grace, mercy, *and* peace from God our Father and Jesus
Christ our Lord.

Counter False Teaching

1:3–4 see pg. 732

[3]As I urged you when I went into
Macedonia—remain in Ephesus that you
may charge some that they teach no other doctrine, [4]nor
give heed to fables and endless genealogies, which cause
disputes rather than godly edification which is in faith.
[5]Now the purpose of the commandment is love from a pure
heart, *from* a good conscience, and *from* sincere faith, [6]from
which some, having strayed, have turned aside to idle talk,
[7]desiring to be teachers of the law, understanding neither
what they say nor the things which they affirm.
[8]But we know that the law *is* good if one uses it lawfully,
[9]knowing this: that the law is not made for a righteous person, but for *the* lawless and insubordinate, for *the* ungodly
and for sinners, for *the* unholy and profane, for murderers
of fathers and murderers of mothers, for manslayers, [10]for
fornicators, for sodomites, for kidnappers, for liars, for per-
jurers, and if there is any other thing that is contrary to
sound doctrine, [11]according to the glori-
ous gospel of the blessed God which was
committed to my trust.

1:3–11

Paul's Testimony

[12]And I thank Christ Jesus our Lord who has enabled me,
because He counted me faithful, putting *me* into the ministry, [13]although I was formerly a blasphemer, a persecutor,
and an insolent man; but I obtained mercy because I did *it*
ignorantly in unbelief. [14]And the grace of our Lord was exceedingly abundant, with faith and love which are in Christ
Jesus. [15]This *is* a faithful saying and worthy of all acceptance, that Christ Jesus came into the world to save sinners,
of whom I am chief. [16]However, for this reason I obtained
mercy, that in me first Jesus Christ might show all longsuffering, as a pattern to those who are going to believe on
Him for everlasting life. [17]Now to the King eternal, immor-
tal, invisible, to God who alone is wise,[a] *be* honor and glory
forever and ever. Amen.

1:17 [a]NU-Text reads *to the only God.*

SORTING OUT THE TRUTH

CONSIDER THIS 1:3–11 **It seems as if everybody has one thing or another to sell. Even teachers try to persuade us to accept their ideas and claims about what is true. But when it comes to matters of faith, it's wise to remain slightly skeptical, especially if someone claims to be God's special envoy to you.**

Paul warned young project leader Timothy about exactly that sort of activity—false doctrines, myths, and endless genealogies (vv. 3–4). Here and in other passages, Paul gave guidelines for sorting out and testing what people say about faith issues and practices:

- **Do they call for the practice of love (v. 5)?**
- **Are they ambitious, striving for esteem and acclaim through their teaching (vv. 6–7)?**
- **Does their message promote internal moral standards that produce good behavior (vv. 8–10)?**
- **Is there evidence of a radical change for the better because of their walk with Christ (vv. 12–14)?**
- **Do they offer humble thanksgiving to God for what they have received (vv. 15–17)?**
- **Does their position build on the wisdom of predecessors (vv. 18–20)? (Paul contrasts those who called Timothy with two others whom he condemns.)**

When people make claims about spiritual things, weigh their words carefully against standards like these. Others around you may criticize any form of doubting, questioning, or evaluation. If so, they need to consider Paul's teaching in this passage. Scripture invites careful examination of statements about spiritual things so that we will distinguish what is from God and will last.

A Charge to Timothy

18This charge I commit to you, son Timothy, according to
the prophecies previously made concerning you, that by
them you may wage the good warfare, 19having faith and a
good conscience, which some having rejected, concerning
the faith have suffered shipwreck, 20of whom are Hymenaeus and Alexander, whom I delivered to Satan that
they may learn not to blaspheme.

CHAPTER 2

Instructions for Men and Women

2:1–7
1Therefore I exhort first of all that supplications, prayers, intercessions, *and* giving of thanks be made for all men, 2for kings and all who
are in authority, that we may lead a quiet and peaceable life
in all godliness and reverence. 3For this *is* good and acceptable in the sight of God our Savior, 4who desires all men to
be saved and to come to the knowledge of the truth. 5For
there is one God and one Mediator between God and men,
the Man Christ Jesus, 6who gave Himself a ransom for all, to
be testified in due time, 7for which I was appointed a
preacher and an apostle—I am speaking the truth in Christ[a]
and not lying—a teacher of the Gentiles in faith and truth.

2:8–15 see pg. 734
8I desire therefore that the men pray
everywhere, lifting up holy hands, with-
out wrath and doubting; 9in like manner also, that the
women adorn themselves in modest apparel, with propriety
and moderation, not with braided hair or gold or pearls or
costly clothing, 10but, which is proper for women professing godliness, with good works. 11Let a woman learn in silence with all submission. 12And I do not permit a woman
to teach or to have authority over a man, but to be in silence. 13For Adam was formed first, then Eve. 14And Adam
was not deceived, but the woman being deceived, fell into
transgression. 15Nevertheless she will be saved in childbearing if they continue in faith, love, and holiness, with
self-control.

CHAPTER 3

Standards for Leaders

3:1 see pg. 733
1This *is* a faithful saying: If a man desires the position of a bishop,[a] he desires a good work. 2A bishop then must be blameless, the

(Bible text continued on page 733)

2:7 [a]NU-Text omits *in Christ.* *3:1* [a]Literally *overseer*

The Prayer Breakfast Movement

CONSIDER THIS 2:1–7 **Paul urges prayer for "kings and all who are in authority" (vv. 1–2). In that spirit, Christians today pray for presidents, cabinet members, legislators, governors, mayors, and judges. In fact, a modern prayer breakfast movement has developed, with events held annually in many major cities.**

City-wide prayer for leaders recalls Abraham, who prayed for the doomed city of Sodom (Gen. 18:16–33). Abraham assumed that his prayers as a righteous man could preserve a city. In the same way, Paul affirms that believers ought to petition God for a "quiet and peaceable" community life (1 Tim. 2:2).

One interesting result of that peace—and a good reason for believers to serve in public office and/or to support in prayer those who do—is more effective evangelism (vv. 3–7).

CONSIDER THIS
1:3–4

SUMMARY

10 MYTHS ABOUT CHRISTIANITY

SUMMARY: THE TEN FAVORITE MYTHS PEOPLE BELIEVE ABOUT CHRISTIANITY

Truth and error have battled since the first days of the Christian faith. Paul urged Timothy to counter those who taught strange doctrines at Ephesus (vv. 3–4). Today, Christianity has become a major world religion with a well established set of beliefs. Nevertheless, believers still must contend with doctrinal error and misconceptions about the faith.

Unfortunately, many people have accepted a number of myths about Christianity, with the result that they never respond to Jesus as He really is. They reject the gospel on the basis of half-truths and lies rather than a clear understanding of Christ's message or its consequences. Below is a list of ten myths about Christianity that are common in our culture. Turn to the passages indicated for a discussion of these errors.

THE TEN FAVORITE MYTHS

#	Myth	See
1	Jesus Christ was only a great moral teacher.	Matt. 13:34–35
2	There is no evidence that Jesus rose from the dead.	Matt. 28:1–10
3	Science is in conflict with Christian faith.	John 4:48
4	It doesn't matter what you believe, all religions are basically the same.	Acts 4:12
5	Christianity is just a crutch for the weak.	1 Cor. 1:26
6	People become Christians through social conditioning.	1 Cor. 15:9–10
7	Christianity stifles personal freedom.	Gal. 5:1–12
8	Christianity is other-worldly and irrelevant to modern life.	Heb. 12:1–2
9	The Bible is unreliable and not to be trusted.	2 Pet. 1:16
10	All the evil and suffering in the world prove there is no God.	Rev. 20:1–10

Abandon the Myths—Go for the Truth!

Go for the truth about God. There are many things in the world that point to the truth about God—the kind of God that the Bible talks about, the God who made us, loves us, and communicates Himself to us.

Go for the truth about Jesus. Jesus claimed to be *the* truth (John 14:6). Everything in his life, teaching, death, and resurrection validates that astounding claim. So feel free to take a good, long look at Jesus. He won't disappoint you!

Go for the truth about yourself. Each of us is something of an enigma. At times we can be kind and thoughtful, generous and unselfish. Yet we can also be self-centered and vindictive, lustful and treacherous. What a contradiction! As the Roman poet Ovid put it, "I see the better way and I approve it—but I follow the worse." Or as Paul wrote, "The good that I will to do, I do not do; but the evil I will not to do, that I practice" (Rom. 7:19).

No wonder some people see only the good in human nature and dream of utopia, while others see little but moral squalor

(continued on next page)

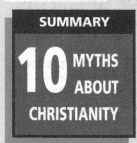

husband of one wife, temperate, sober-minded, of good be-
3:3 havior, hospitable, able to teach; [3]not
given to wine, not violent, not greedy for
money,[a] but gentle, not quarrelsome, not covetous; [4]one
who rules his own house well, having *his* children in submission with all reverence [5](for if a man does not know
how to rule his own house, how will he take care of the
church of God?); [6]not a novice, lest being puffed up with
pride he fall into the *same* condemnation as the devil.
[7]Moreover he must have a good testimony among those
who are outside, lest he fall into reproach and the snare of
the devil.
[8]Likewise deacons *must be* reverent, not double-tongued,
not given to much wine, not greedy for money, [9]holding the
mystery of the faith with a pure conscience. [10]But let these
also first be tested; then let them serve as deacons, being

3:3 [a]NU-Text omits *not greedy for money.*

A CLOSER LOOK 3:3

No Greedy Leaders!

Many church members today work in the marketplace where the mark of success is making and accumulating wealth. The same was true in Timothy's congregation at Ephesus. So Paul warns about those who are "greedy for money" (v. 3). He has much more to say about wealth in chapter 6. See "Christians and Money," 1 Tim. 6:6–19.

One Standard for All

CONSIDER THIS 3:1

In chapter 3, Paul outlines the criteria that qualify people for leadership in the church community. All of the items mentioned have to do with character. *God seems far more concerned with the personal integrity of leaders than with their education, eloquence, or charisma.*

Without question, the standards are high, but that doesn't imply a higher standard for church leaders than "ordinary" Christians. All *believers are called to these same high standards of Christlikeness. Paul is not creating a class of the spiritually elite here. He is simply indicating that the church should select its leadership from among people who are generally living up to the ideals of the gospel.*

SUMMARY 10 MYTHS ABOUT CHRISTIANITY

(continued from previous page)

and political chaos and fear cosmic destruction ahead. Christianity sees a bit of both: we are like semi-ruined temples that still bear the marks of their original splendor. Only the Architect who designed us can fully repair and restore us to our original purpose and beauty.

Go for the truth about growth. If we're going to be restored to God, change will be required. The first step is to turn our lives over to Him. Then He begins a process of growth that affects every aspect of life. The process takes time—a lifetime, in fact. Indeed, the process won't end until we meet Him after death.

For now, God helps us cultivate a close relationship with Himself. He develops our character so that we gradually become more like Christ. And He especially affects our relationships with other people so that we treat them as Jesus would. ◆

found blameless. 11Likewise, *their* wives *must be* reverent,
not slanderers, temperate, faithful in all things. 12Let deacons be the husbands of one wife, ruling *their* children
and their own houses well. 13For those who have served
well as deacons obtain for themselves a good standing and great boldness in the faith which is in Christ
Jesus.

Paul's Reason for Writing

14These things I write to you, though I hope to come to
you shortly; 15but if I am delayed, *I write* so that you may
know how you ought to conduct yourself in the house of
God, which is the church of the living God, the pillar and
ground of the truth. 16And without controversy great is the
mystery of godliness:

> God[a] was manifested in the flesh,
> Justified in the Spirit,
> Seen by angels,
> Preached among the Gentiles,
> Believed on in the world,
> Received up in glory.

3:16 [a]NU-Text reads *Who.*

CONSIDER THIS
2:8–15

A New Way to Worship

What is the proper way to worship God? For those who had grown up in the religious climate of Ephesus before the gospel, Christian worship called for altogether different behavior than they were used to practicing. So Paul offered guidelines for worship to the men and women in the Ephesian church (vv. 8–15).

Ephesus (see profile at the Introduction to Ephesians) was world-renowned for its magnificent temple of Artemis. Pagan cults flourished there, along with occult practices. In fact, books with magic recipes came to be known as "Ephesian books."

Nevertheless, the gospel bore great fruit there and the community of believers grew rapidly (see "The Ephesus Approach," Acts 19:8–41). Yet some of the new converts brought their old way of life into the church and began teaching other doctrines (1 Tim. 1:3–7). When it came to worship, many were used to wild rites and festivals. Ephesian women were particularly unacquainted with pub-

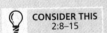

CHAPTER 4

Deception in Latter Times

4:1–16

[1]Now the Spirit expressly says that in
latter times some will depart from the
faith, giving heed to deceiving spirits and doctrines of
demons, [2]speaking lies in hypocrisy, having their own
conscience seared with a hot iron, [3]forbidding to marry,
and commanding to abstain from foods which God created
to be received with thanksgiving by those who believe
and know the truth. [4]For every creature of God *is* good,
and nothing is to be refused if it is received with thanksgiving; [5]for it is sanctified by the word of God and
prayer.

Live and Teach the Truth

[6]If you instruct the brethren in these things, you will be a
good minister of Jesus Christ, nourished in the words of
faith and of the good doctrine which you have carefully followed. [7]But reject profane and old wives' fables, and exercise yourself toward godliness. [8]For bodily exercise profits a
little, but godliness is profitable for all things, having
promise of the life that now is and of that which is to come.

◆ ◆ ◆ ◆ ◆ ◆ ◆ ◆ ◆ ◆ ◆ ◆ ◆ ◆ ◆

lic behavior, having been excluded for the most part from public gatherings, except pagan rituals.

So Paul described the correct way of worship. Men, who were apparently given to anger and doubts, needed to stop wrangling and start praying (v. 8). Likewise, women needed to focus on godliness and good works rather than clothing, jewelry, and hairstyles (vv. 9–10). And because some were apparently disruptive, they needed to practice restraint (v. 11)—not necessarily complete silence, but "quiet" (as the word is translated in 2 Thess. 3:12), since they likely participated in the prayers and other expressive parts of the worship gatherings (compare 1 Cor. 11:5; Eph. 5:19).

Today the message of Christ continues to attract people from a variety of backgrounds. Some, like the Ephesians, need to learn for the first time about worshiping God. Others bring cultural norms and expectations that are worth using in the worship experience, so long as they preserve biblical guidelines such as those that Paul gave to the Ephesians. ◆

FEEL LIKE A NOVICE?

CONSIDER THIS 4:1–6

Are you new at work or in your neighborhood? Has marriage recently brought you into a whole new family of relationships? Do you feel that proving yourself and gaining acceptance is an uphill battle? Are you tempted to declare, "I'll show 'em"?

Timothy was young in age and relatively untested as a trainee under Paul, his mentor. His pastorate in Ephesus was his first solo assignment. So Paul offered him some seasoned wisdom and perspective:

- **Tough times are to be expected in a broken world (vv. 1–3).**
- **We need to accept God's gifts with thanksgiving (vv. 4–5).**
- **Affirm the truth with others who share your faith (v. 6).**
- **Avoid getting caught up in the folklore that occurs in every environment (v. 7). It's not that stories are bad, but always search out the truth and make it your trademark (vv. 8–11).**
- **Overcome the skepticism of others with the basics like love, edifying conversation, and purity (v. 12).**
- **Work on your own skills and abilities with diligence (vv. 13–14).**

Over the long haul, perspectives like these will hold one in good stead, while the shortcuts of dirty politics, competition, and intrigue will fail.

WIDOWS

FOR YOUR INFO 5:3 **Widows (v. 3) were common in the ancient world due to a number of factors. First, women tended to marry earlier in life than men, usually in their early teens, because of societal expectations that they marry as virgins. The same did not apply to men, and most delayed marriage into their twenties and even thirties, as marriage incurred responsibility. That age disparity between husbands and wives, along with disease, wars, and other factors of mortality, created many widows.**

Among the Jews, widows were the responsibility of the community (Deut. 24:19–21). One feature of the system was for a brother of the deceased husband to take the widow as his wife and father an heir if no male heirs had been born (Deut. 25:5). Unremarried widows would be supported by family members or left to manage on their own as best they could. But in many cases widows were reduced to begging, prostitution, or slavery to survive.

Paul and the other leaders of the early church had no intention of tolerating that possibility in the Christian community. Here he gives clear instructions on the care of widows. Earlier, problems in the care of widows, along with ethnic tensions, had created conflict for the church at Jerusalem (Acts 6:1–7).

Today, the care of widows who lack either savings or adequate support from their families is often left to the state or nonprofit agencies. However, there is no reason why Paul's instructions regarding widows do not still apply to believers.

Widows who came in contact with Jesus found Him responsive to their needs. He offered them hope (Luke 7:11–15). He also used them frequently as object lessons of dependence on God and the need for justice (Mark 12:41–44; Luke 18:1–8; 21:1–4).

9This *is* a faithful saying and worthy of all acceptance. 10For
to this *end* we both labor and suffer reproach,[a] because we
trust in the living God, who is *the* Savior of all men, especially of those who believe. 11These things command and
teach.
12Let no one despise your youth, but be an example to
the believers in word, in conduct, in love, in spirit,[a] in faith,
in purity. 13Till I come, give attention to reading, to exhortation, to doctrine. 14Do not neglect the gift that is in you,
which was given to you by prophecy with the laying on of
the hands of the eldership. 15Meditate on these things; give
yourself entirely to them, that your progress may be evident
to all. 16Take heed to yourself and to the doctrine. Continue
in them, for in doing this you will save both yourself and
those who hear you.

CHAPTER 5

Treatment of Believers

1Do not rebuke an older man, but exhort *him* as a father,
younger men as brothers, 2older women as mothers,
younger women as sisters, with all purity.

Care for Widows

5:3 3Honor widows who are really widows.
4But if any widow has children or grand-
children, let them first learn to show piety at home and to
repay their parents; for this is good and[a] acceptable before
God. 5Now she who is really a widow, and left alone, trusts
in God and continues in supplications and prayers night
and day. 6But she who lives in pleasure is dead while she
lives. 7And these things command, that they may be blameless. 8But if anyone does not provide for his own, and especially for those of his household, he has denied the faith
and is worse than an unbeliever.
9Do not let a widow under sixty years old be taken into
the number, *and not unless* she has been the wife of one
man, 10well reported for good works: if she has brought up
children, if she has lodged strangers, if she has washed the
saints' feet, if she has relieved the afflicted, if she has diligently followed every good work.
11But refuse *the* younger widows; for when they have begun to grow wanton against Christ, they desire to marry,
12having condemnation because they have cast off their first
faith. 13And besides they learn *to be* idle, wandering about
from house to house, and not only idle but also gossips
and busybodies, saying things which they ought not.

(Bible text continued on page 738)

4:10 [a]NU-Text reads *we labor and strive.* *4:12* [a]NU-Text omits *in spirit.* *5:4* [a]NU-Text and M-Text omit *good and.*

CONSIDER THIS
5:3–16

EFFECTIVE CARE FOR THE NEEDY

Followers of Christ have the potential to be among the world's most effective agents for social service. They have the example of Christ to follow. They have the motivation of doing compassionate work in His name. They have the structure, community life, and pooled resources of their congregations. And they have the model of the early church, which provided standards for the systematic, ongoing care of widows (vv. 3–22).

We can learn a great deal about delivering services to the needy by carefully observing the principles that Paul set forth for Timothy and the believers at Ephesus. For example:

(1) The care described here was regular and ongoing for people who were "taken into the number" (v. 9), that is, put on a list of continuing recipients of the church's support. Presumably, the church was to give short-term support to people who needed help until they could get back on their feet; but not to able-bodied people who refused to work to support themselves (compare 2 Thess. 3:10).

(2) The care was for "widows who are really widows" (v. 3). The Old Testament described a widow as a woman who had no one to support her and therefore depended on the protection of the community (Ex. 22:22–24; Deut. 14:28–29; 24:17–22; 26:12–13). If a widow had able-bodied children or grandchildren, she needed to depend on them for provision, not the church (1 Tim. 5:4).

(3) A widow who was "taken into the number" incurred certain responsibilities in order to maintain her eligibility for the church's charity. For example, she needed to be frugal lest someone reproach her for living an extravagant lifestyle and the fellowship for supporting it (vv. 6–7). Likewise, she needed to meet certain criteria related to her earlier life and character (vv. 9–10). The point was not to keep a widow out of the program, but to ensure that she served her fellow believers in every way she could if she was going to receive support.

(4) Younger widows were expected to remarry and, as was common for that day, bear children (who presumably would care for their parents in old age). Again, the church needed to avoid offering long-term support to someone who had other options. To do so might contribute to wantonness, idleness, and gossip (vv. 11–14).

These instructions to Timothy mirror principles about systematic aid found elsewhere in Scripture. For example, Paul told the Corinthians that financial support should go only to the truly poor (see "Who Are the Poor?" 2 Cor. 9:9–10). Likewise, the aim of providing care is to give people enough food, clothing, and other aid for survival and health. It is not intended to give anyone a free ride, even less to underwrite an inflated standard of living (2 Cor. 8:13–15; 1 Tim. 6:6–10).

First Timothy 5 specifically addresses the care of widows, but its principles apply to a much broader range of human need. By using this and other biblical texts to develop social programs, believers can effectively render care in a way that honors the name of Christ and provides real help to needy people. ◆

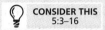

QUOTE UNQUOTE

CONSIDER THIS 6:7 *One of the world's wealthiest men concurred with Scripture's observation that we can carry nothing out of this world (v. 7) when he said:*

It is disgraceful to die a rich man.

Andrew Carnegie

[14]Therefore I desire that *the* younger *widows* marry, bear
children, manage the house, give no opportunity to the adversary to speak reproachfully. [15]For some have already
5:3–16 see pg. 737 turned aside after Satan. [16]If any believing man or[a] woman has widows, let them
relieve them, and do not let the church be burdened, that it
may relieve those who are really widows.

Dealing with Elders

[17]Let the elders who rule well be counted worthy of double honor, especially those who labor in the word and doctrine. [18]For the Scripture says, "You shall not muzzle an ox

5:16 [a]NU-Text omits *man or.*

CONSIDER THIS 6:1–2

"I Won't Hire Christians!"

He stood beside a window overlooking the shop floor below. A din of table saws, routers, and other equipment filtered up to the tiny cubicle. His desk was lost under mountains of papers, folders, catalogues, manuals, bills, and an ancient rotary phone.

Turning from the window he sighed and said, "I don't usually hire people who tell me they're Christians. I know that sounds mean. And I don't advertise it. I'm a Christian myself and I try to run this company the way I think God wants it run. But I won't hire Christians!"

"Why not?" he was asked.

"I've been burned once too often," he replied. "I've hired people just because they said they were Christians, and they turned out to be some of the worst employees I ever had.

"I remember one guy was always standing around preaching to the other guys instead of getting his work done. I couldn't afford him! Another guy kept coming in late, day after day. His supervisor warned him. Finally he fired him. Then the fellow came to me to try and get his job back. I told him the supervisor had made the right decision. Know what he said? 'I thought you were a Christian!' Imagine that! He thought he could take advantage of me just because he knew I was a Christian!

"After that I decided: no more Christians!" ◆

Every believer should understand why God has given us work. See "People at Work," Heb. 2:7.

When Christians enter the workplace, they need to exhibit a Christlike "workstyle." See Titus 2:9–10. They also need to remember "Who's the Boss?" Col. 3:22–24.

while it treads out the grain,"[a] and, "The laborer *is* worthy
of his wages."[b] [19]Do not receive an accusation against an elder except from two or three witnesses. [20]Those who are
sinning rebuke in the presence of all, that the rest also may
fear.

A Plea for Impartiality

[21]I charge *you* before God and the Lord Jesus Christ and
the elect angels that you observe these things without prejudice, doing nothing with partiality. [22]Do not lay hands on
anyone hastily, nor share in other people's sins; keep yourself pure.
[23]No longer drink only water, but use a little wine for
your stomach's sake and your frequent infirmities.
[24]Some men's sins are clearly evident, preceding *them* to
judgment, but those of some *men* follow later. [25]Likewise,
the good works *of some* are clearly evident, and those that
are otherwise cannot be hidden.

CHAPTER 6

Slaves Should Respect Masters

6:1–2

[1]Let as many bondservants as are under
the yoke count their own masters worthy
of all honor, so that the name of God and *His* doctrine may
not be blasphemed. [2]And those who have believing masters,
let them not despise *them* because they are brethren, but
rather serve *them* because those who are benefited are believers and beloved. Teach and exhort these things.

Godliness and Gain

6:3–6 see pg. 742

[3]If anyone teaches otherwise and does
not consent to wholesome words, *even*
the words of our Lord Jesus Christ, and to the doctrine
which accords with godliness, [4]he is proud, knowing nothing, but is obsessed with disputes and arguments over
words, from which come envy, strife, reviling, evil suspi-
cions, [5]useless wranglings[a] of men of corrupt minds and
destitute of the truth, who suppose that godliness is a *means
of* gain. From such withdraw yourself.[b]

6:6–19 see pg. 740

6:7

[6]Now godliness with contentment is
great gain. [7]For we brought nothing into
this world, *and it is* certain[a] we can carry
nothing out. [8]And having food and cloth-
ing, with these we shall be content. [9]But those who desire

(Bible text continued on page 743)

5:18 [a]Deuteronomy 25:4 [b]Luke 10:7 *6:5* [a]NU-Text and M-Text read *constant friction.* [b]NU-Text omits this sentence. *6:7* [a]NU-Text omits *and it is certain.*

QUOTE UNQUOTE

CONSIDER THIS 6:17–19 *Eighteenth-century hymn writer Charles Wesley's instructions regarding money repeat the themes that Paul gave to Timothy and the believers at Ephesus (vv. 17–19):*

Gain all you can by honest industry. Use all possible diligence in your calling. Lose no time. Gain all you can, by common sense, by using in your business all the understanding which God has given you. It is amazing to observe how few do this . . . . Having gained all you can by honest wisdom and unwearied diligence, the second rule of Christian prudence is, "Save all you can." Do not throw it away in idle expenses—to gratify pride, etc. If you desire to be a good and faithful steward . . . first provide things needful for yourself, food, raiment, etc. Second, provide these for your wife, your children, your servants, and others who pertain to your household. If then you have an overplus, do good to them that are of the household of faith. If there be still an overplus, do good to all men.

Charles Wesley, *The Use of Money.* (Wesley amassed some $250,000 from his writings, which made him a wealthy man according to the standards of his age.)

CONSIDER THIS
6:6–19

Christians and Money

Paul ridicules the idea that God is in the business of dispensing material gain in exchange for spiritual cooperation (v. 5). That launches him into a discussion of money that modern believers do well to study carefully, given the emphasis on money in our culture. He speaks to three categories of people: those who want to get rich (vv. 6–10), those who want to honor God (vv. 11–16), and those who are rich and want to honor God (vv. 17–19).

Contentment versus Covetousness (vv. 6–10)

Paul warns us strongly against "the love of money" (v. 10). But let's be sure we interpret his words correctly. He does not say that money itself is evil (nor does any other Scripture). Neither does he say that money is *the* fundamental root of evil, or that money lies at the root of *every* evil. Rather, the *love* of money (something inside people, not money itself) can be *a* root (but not the only root) of all *kinds* of evil (but not of all evil).

But don't let those qualifications soften the blow: people who love money are vulnerable to all kinds of evil, the worst of which, Paul points out, is straying from the faith (see "Do-It-Yourself Idolatry," Col. 3:5).

Given that danger, believers should by all means avoid greed. Jesus gave a direct, unequivocal command to that effect. He didn't tell us to guard against it in others, but in ourselves (see "Watch Out for Greed!" Luke 12:15).

Paul offers the alternative to greed, or covetousness, as contentment (vv. 6–8). However, his description of contentment—food and clothing—sounds incredibly spartan in our own culture that extols self-made millionaires and entertains itself by paying video visits to those who live in opulent, even decadent lifestyles. Are believers required to take vows of poverty like Franciscan monks (see "A Prayer of the Laity," Matt. 10:7–10)?

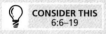

No, but Paul does remind us in this passage what poverty really is: lack of food, clothing, and shelter adequate for survival where one lives. If we have these, we ought to be content. If not, then we are truly destitute and dependent on the charity of others for survival. The biblical concept of poverty is not merely having less than the average income, or some percentage of it, in one's society, as contemporary sociologists and economists tend to define it (see "Who Are the Poor?" 2 Cor. 9:9–10).

Can Paul be serious? Is it really possible to be content, at least in our society, with merely the basics—food, clothing, and shelter? Paul should know. He experienced firsthand the wealth and privileges of prominence in the Jewish community and of Roman citizenship. Yet he also suffered extraordinary hardships in his work. Through it all he learned a secret that helped him maintain contentment. What was it? See "A Lifestyle of Contentment," Phil. 4:10–13.

A Charge to Timothy (vv. 11–16)

Paul's example was especially important to Timothy, his protégé in the faith (see the Introduction to 2 Timothy). He challenges the young pastor to pursue a lifestyle that values character over cash (1 Tim. 6:11). The words are addressed to Timothy, but they apply to anyone who wants to honor God in life. Timothy needed to watch out for greed just like any other believer (see "One Standard for All," 3:1; and "No Greedy Leaders!" 3:3).

Paul was especially on the lookout for greed. Interestingly, one of his main strategies for avoiding it was to earn his own living as a tentmaker, rather than live off the generosity of others (see "I Have Not Coveted!" Acts 20:33–38).

Commands for Rich Christians (vv. 17–19)

Apparently there were wealthy believers in Timothy's church at Ephesus. The city was extraordinarily prosperous. In fact, its tourist trade brought in so much revenue that the town leaders opened the first world bank. Paul had penetrated this vibrant economic life with the gospel, winning many converts (see "The Ephesus Approach," Acts 19:8–41). No doubt some of the rich Christians he addresses here brought their money with them into the faith—just like many in the modern church.

The question, then, especially in light of the teaching in 1 Tim. 6:6–10, is, what should people with money do if they want to honor God? Paul says they should start by examining their attitudes. Money has incredible power to create feelings of pride, superiority, and self-sufficiency (v. 17). So people of means have to learn to look beyond their money to God, the ultimate source of wealth.

But attitude is only half the battle. Sooner or later rich Christians need to take conscious, decisive action with their wealth. They need to put it into play serving God and others (v. 18).

What About You?

What is your deepest desire? Is it to be rich rather than righteous? If so, beware! Longing for wealth leads to many dangers—even to death. God wants you to grasp something far more permanent and satisfying—eternal life (vv. 12, 18). ◆

The ultimate model for how Christians, rich or poor, should handle wealth is Jesus. See Phil. 2:5–8.

SOME HAVE STRAYED FROM THE FAITH IN THEIR GREEDINESS.
—1 Timothy 6:10

CONSIDER THIS
6:3–6

THE DANGERS OF PROSPERITY THEOLOGY

Susan is a sales representative. She can make a big sale, but only if she mildly deceives the customer. She decides to tell the truth and she loses the sale. Should she expect God to honor her integrity by helping her make an even bigger sale in the future?

A contractor is deciding whether to award a job to Allen's firm or to another company. Allen really needs the business. So he prays at length that he will get the contract, and asks others to pray, too. Should he anticipate that God will somehow make the contractor award him the job? If not, should he expect God to arrange for other work to come along soon?

John and Joan are reviewing their finances. John has recently received a small bonus from his company, and they're wondering what to do with it. They finally decide to give ten percent of it to their church, and another ten percent to a mission. Can they expect God to bring them more money as a result?

Does God reward godliness with material blessing? Not according to v. 5. In fact, Paul describes those who teach that as being "destitute of the truth." They are guilty of fostering a "prosperity theology." That's a dangerous view:

It encourages perverted motives. God wants us to seek Him for His own sake, not for a "payoff" of physical well-being or financial gain. The reward of loving obedience is a closer relationship to God (John 14:15–18, 21–23). He also wants us to be content with what He provides us, not greedy for more (v. 6).

It misinterprets God's deepest concerns for us. If God wants us to have abundant material benefits, if He sees that they would be in our best interest, then we can trust Him to supply them. Otherwise, such "blessings" would be harmful. God loves us too much to destroy us with what we don't need or can't handle.

It misrepresents God's promises in Scripture. The Old Testament offers plenty of promises about material prosperity and blessing. But for the most part, those benefits were offered to the nation of Israel, not to individual believers.

Furthermore, God's promises are always offered to those who truly love Him, seek His will, and obey Him from a pure heart. The Lord Himself is always the end to be sought; material benefits are never an end in themselves.

A final note: God has established certain "moral laws" that benefit anyone who adheres to them. (The Proverbs are filled with prudent advice that rewards those who keep them.) For example, paying taxes avoids the trouble, fines, prison terms, and public censure associated with nonpayment. In this sense it "pays" to obey the law. But we shouldn't expect special blessing for doing what God wants us to do anyway (Luke 17:7–10). ◆

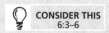

to be rich fall into temptation and a snare, and *into* many
foolish and harmful lusts which drown men in destruction
and perdition. 10For the love of money is a root of all *kinds*
of evil, for which some have strayed from the faith in their
greediness, and pierced themselves through with many sorrows.

Life's Focus Is Christ

11But you, O man of God, flee these things and pursue
righteousness, godliness, faith, love, patience, gentleness.
12Fight the good fight of faith, lay hold on eternal life, to
which you were also called and have confessed the good
confession in the presence of many witnesses. 13I urge you
in the sight of God who gives life to all things, and *before*
Christ Jesus who witnessed the good confession before Pontius Pilate, 14that you keep *this* commandment without spot,
blameless until our Lord Jesus Christ's appearing, 15which
He will manifest in His own time, *He who is* the blessed and
only Potentate, the King of kings and Lord of lords, 16who
alone has immortality, dwelling in unapproachable light,
whom no man has seen or can see, to whom *be* honor and
everlasting power. Amen.

A Word to the Wealthy

6:17–19 see pg. 739

17Command those who are rich in this
present age not to be haughty, nor to
trust in uncertain riches but in the living God, who gives us

6:18

richly all things to enjoy. 18*Let them* do
good, that they be rich in good works,
ready to give, willing to share, 19storing up for themselves a
good foundation for the time to come, that they may lay
hold on eternal life.

A Sacred Trust

20O Timothy! Guard what was committed to your trust,
avoiding the profane *and* idle babblings and contradictions
of what is falsely called knowledge— 21by professing it
some have strayed concerning the faith.
Grace *be* with you. Amen.

QUOTE UNQUOTE

CONSIDER THIS 6:18 *Are you rich in good works (v. 18)? A former communist party boss who became a vibrant believer pointed out the strategic importance of doing good with one's work life:*

The most important part of the Communist's day is, or should be, that which he spends at work. He sees his work as giving him wonderful opportunity to do a job for the cause. By way of contrast, the average [Christian] feels that his time for going into action on behalf of his beliefs begins after he has returned from his day's work, had a meal, changed and has just an hour or two left—when he is already tired—to give to his cause.

Douglas Hyde, *Dedication and Leadership,* p. 98

2 Timothy

C O N T E N T S

Personality Profile: Timothy

Name means: "Honored of God."

Home: Originally Lystra in Asia Minor. Later, as an associate of Paul, he traveled widely and worked among groups of believers in Macedonia, especially Thessalonica, and in Corinth and Ephesus.

Family: His father was Greek; his mother Eunice and his grandmother Lois were Jewish. His "spiritual father" was Paul.

Occupation: Traveling teacher and short-term pastor; tradition holds that he became bishop of Ephesus. He also helped in the sending of 2 Corinthians, Philippians, Colossians, 1 and 2 Thessalonians, and Philemon.

Best known today for: Joining Paul in his travels and being the recipient of two New Testament letters.

A R T I C L E S

CHAPTER 1

A Beloved Son

1Paul, an apostle of Jesus Christ[a] by the will of God, according to the promise of life which is in Christ Jesus,

2To Timothy, a beloved son:

Grace, mercy, *and* peace from God the Father and Christ
Jesus our Lord.

A Valuable Heritage

1:3

3I thank God, whom I serve with a
pure conscience, as *my* forefathers *did,* as
without ceasing I remember you in my prayers night and
day, 4greatly desiring to see you, being mindful of your

1:5 see pg. 746

tears, that I may be filled with joy, 5when
I call to remembrance the genuine faith
that is in you, which dwelt first in your grandmother Lois
and your mother Eunice, and I am persuaded is in you also.

1:6–7 see pg. 747

6Therefore I remind you to stir up the gift
of God which is in you through the lay-
ing on of my hands. 7For God has not given us a spirit of
fear, but of power and of love and of a sound mind.
8Therefore do not be ashamed of the testimony of our
Lord, nor of me His prisoner, but share with me in the sufferings for the gospel according to the power of God, 9who
has saved us and called *us* with a holy calling, not according
to our works, but according to His own purpose and grace
which was given to us in Christ Jesus before time began,
10but has now been revealed by the appearing of our Savior
Jesus Christ, *who* has abolished death and brought life and
immortality to light through the gospel, 11to which I was
appointed a preacher, an apostle, and a teacher of the Gentiles.[a] 12For this reason I also suffer these things; nevertheless I am not ashamed, for I know whom I have believed
and am persuaded that He is able to keep what I have committed to Him until that Day.

The Faithful and the Faithless

13Hold fast the pattern of sound words which you have
heard from me, in faith and love which are in Christ Jesus.
14That good thing which was committed to you, keep by
the Holy Spirit who dwells in us.
15This you know, that all those in Asia have turned away
from me, among whom are Phygellus and Hermogenes.
16The Lord grant mercy to the household of Onesiphorus,
for he often refreshed me, and was not ashamed of my

1:1 [a]NU-Text and M-Text read *Christ Jesus.* *1:11* [a]NU-Text omits *of the Gentiles.*

PAUL THE JEW—TEACHER OF THE GENTILES

CONSIDER THIS 1:3

What is your ethnic heritage? Are you proud to be who you are? Paul was. In v. 3 he openly identifies with his background as a Jew, affirming his connection to the "forefathers," people of faith such as Abraham, Isaac, Jacob, Joseph, Moses, and David.

But wait! Didn't he earlier call that same background a "loss" and "rubbish" as he considered his new life in Christ (Phil. 3:4–8)? Yes, at times he was highly critical of his culture, but only to the extent that it fostered self-righteous pride, exclusive attitudes, or a belief in salvation by the Law rather than by faith in Christ. In other words, Paul had perspective on his roots. He was able to value his heritage for the good things it gave him, yet reject its negative legacies.

Perhaps that was why Paul was so effective as a "teacher of the Gentiles" (v. 11)—a remarkable calling, given his training as a Pharisee and strict adherence to Hebrew traditions (see "A Bigot Does an About-Face," Gal. 1:13–17). God not only helped him reevaluate his ethnicity but in the process transformed his attitude toward non-Jews. He became a man who knew who he was, so he was no longer threatened by people from other cultures.

Consequently, Paul had much to offer Timothy, who came from a mixed background (Acts 16:1–3). Paul also serves as a model for believers today who need perspective on their roots in an increasingly diverse culture where ethnic and racial tensions run high.

God never asks us to reject our roots. We can affirm our ethnic heritage as a rich gift from Him, no matter how our surrounding culture regards it. See "The Gift of an Ethnic Heritage," Col. 4:10–11.

Eunice—A Mother's Legacy

FOR YOUR INFO 1:5 **Eunice (v. 5) was Jewish, but apparently her father was not very orthodox: he violated one of the clear commands of the Law in arranging a match for his daughter with a Gentile (Acts 16:1). Later, when Timothy was born, he wasn't circumcised (16:3). So it seems that neither Eunice's father nor husband were observant of Judaism.**

But Eunice was. Paul praised her for her "genuine faith," which she shared in common with Lois, her mother (2 Tim. 1:5). Eunice imparted that faith to her son, Timothy, and more than anyone else equipped him for a lifetime of usefulness for God.

Eunice is an encouragement for every woman faced with the daunting task of nurturing the spiritual life of her children, especially if she can't count on the help of a strong male. Eunice may have had no formal religious education and little encouragement from her family, except for Lois. But she had two crucial things going for her that offer hope for mothers today—the inherent power of being a mother and the dynamic power of a loving God.

How did the "genuine faith" that Timothy received from his mother work out in practical terms? See 1 Tim. 3:1–13 for a description.

chain; 17 but when he arrived in Rome, he sought me out
very zealously and found *me.* 18 The Lord grant to him that
he may find mercy from the Lord in that Day—and you
know very well how many ways he ministered *to me*[a] at
Ephesus.

CHAPTER 2

Pass On the Teaching

1 You therefore, my son, be strong in the grace that is in
2:2 see pg. 748
Christ Jesus. 2 And the things that you
have heard from me among many witnesses, commit these to faithful men who will be able to
teach others also. 3 You therefore must endure[a] hardship as a
good soldier of Jesus Christ. 4 No one engaged in warfare
entangles himself with the affairs of *this* life, that he may
please him who enlisted him as a soldier. 5 And also if anyone competes in athletics, he is not crowned unless he competes according to the rules. 6 The hardworking farmer must
be first to partake of the crops. 7 Consider what I say, and
may[a] the Lord give you understanding in all things.

A Sure Foundation

8 Remember that Jesus Christ, of the seed of David,
was raised from the dead according to my gospel, 9 for
which I suffer trouble as an evildoer, *even* to the point of
chains; but the word of God is not chained. 10 Therefore
I endure all things for the sake of the elect, that they
also may obtain the salvation which is in Christ Jesus with
eternal glory.
11 *This is* a faithful saying:

For if we died with *Him,*
We shall also live with *Him.*
12 If we endure,
We shall also reign with *Him.*
If we deny *Him,*
He also will deny us.
2:13
13 If we are faithless,
He remains faithful;
He cannot deny Himself.

14 Remind *them* of these things, charging *them* before the
Lord not to strive about words to no profit, to the ruin of
the hearers. 15 Be diligent to present yourself approved to

1:18 [a]*To me* is from the Vulgate and a few Greek manuscripts. *2:3* [a]NU-Text reads *You must share.* *2:7* [a]NU-Text reads *the Lord will give you.*

God, a worker who does not need to be ashamed, rightly
dividing the word of truth. [16]But shun profane *and* idle babblings, for they will increase to more ungodliness. [17]And
their message will spread like cancer. Hymenaeus and
Philetus are of this sort, [18]who have strayed concerning the
truth, saying that the resurrection is already past; and they
overthrow the faith of some. [19]Nevertheless the solid foundation of God stands, having this seal: "The Lord knows
those who are His," and, "Let everyone who names the
name of Christ[a] depart from iniquity."

Character and Conduct

[20]But in a great house there are not only vessels of gold
and silver, but also of wood and clay, some for honor and
some for dishonor. [21]Therefore if anyone cleanses himself
from the latter, he will be a vessel for honor, sanctified and
useful for the Master, prepared for every good work. [22]Flee
also youthful lusts; but pursue righteousness, faith, love,
peace with those who call on the Lord out of a pure heart.
[23]But avoid foolish and ignorant disputes, knowing that
they generate strife. [24]And a servant of the Lord must not
quarrel but be gentle to all, able to teach, patient, [25]in humility correcting those who are in opposition, if God perhaps will grant them repentance, so that they may know the
truth, [26]and *that* they may come to their senses *and escape*
the snare of the devil, having been taken captive by him to
do his will.

CHAPTER 3

Perilous Times Will Come

[1]But know this, that in the last days perilous times will
come: [2]For men will be lovers of themselves, lovers of
money, boasters, proud, blasphemers, disobedient to parents, unthankful, unholy, [3]unloving, unforgiving, slanderers, without self-control, brutal, despisers of good, [4]traitors,
headstrong, haughty, lovers of pleasure rather than lovers of
God, [5]having a form of godliness but denying its power.
And from such people turn away! [6]For of this sort are those
who creep into households and make captives of gullible
women loaded down with sins, led away by various lusts,
[7]always learning and never able to come to the knowledge
of the truth. [8]Now as Jannes and Jambres
resisted Moses, so do these also resist the
truth: men of corrupt minds, disapproved concerning the
faith; [9]but they will progress no further, for their folly will
be manifest to all, as theirs also was.

3:8–9 see pg. 751

(Bible text continued on page 749)

2:19 [a]NU-Text and M-Text read *the Lord.*

THE SPIRIT OF POWER

CONSIDER THIS 1:6–7 *Verses 6–7 offer both encouragement and exhortation. Paul links power—the ability to make things happen—with love and a sound mind. Conversely, power exercised without love and wisdom is inevitably destructive.*

A unique power accounted for the rapid spread of the message of Christ in the first century. See "Power," Acts 1:8.

HE REMAINS FAITHFUL

CONSIDER THIS 2:13 **Have you ever reneged on a business agreement? Or skipped out on an appointment? Or gone back on your word to a coworker? Or missed a crucial deadline on which everyone was counting? Have you ever broken promises to your spouse or children?**

Fortunately we can count on God to keep His commitments. Even though we as humans are frequently faithless, He remains faithful to His word (v. 13).

If we want to develop godly character, then one of our main objectives should be to honor our commitments. Psalm 15 describes a person who is moving closer to God as one who "swears to his own hurt and does not change." His word is his bond.

Faithfulness, trustworthiness, and reliability are key aspects of a godly "workstyle." See Titus 2:9–10.

CONSIDER THIS
2:2

Mentoring, Kingdom-Style

Paul describes the powerful process of mentoring in v. 2. Just as he had helped Timothy during a formative stage in his development, he challenged Timothy to mentor others, who in turn could become mentors and keep the reproductive cycle going. Christians today need to recover this pattern of older believers working with younger ones, which dates to the earliest days of the faith. Here are a few examples:

Jethro with Moses

A cattleman and father-in-law to Moses, Jethro took his overworked son-in-law through a performance review and taught him to delegate authority to associates (Ex. 18:1–27).

Boaz with Naomi and Ruth

A wealthy landowner and relative of Naomi, Boaz risked rejection from Jewish peers when he rescued the impoverished widow Naomi and her widowed immigrant daughter-in-law, Ruth. Ruth faced rejection among the Israelites but had respect and honor from Boaz (Ruth 1—4).

Deborah with Barak

A national leader and judge over Israel, Deborah guided Barak into battle and then accepted his call for her help, leading the campaign to victory over a Canaanite king. Together they celebrated in song, and the land enjoyed peace for 40 years (Judg. 4:4—-5:31).

Barnabas with Saul/Paul

A wealthy landowner from Cyprus, Barnabas stood up for Saul, the persecutor-turned-convert, introducing him to church leaders and vouching for his conversion. Coached by Barnabas (Acts 4:36–37; 9:26–30; 11:22–30), Paul became an outstanding leader in the burgeoning movement. (Barnabas' example serves as a textbook case in kingdom-style mentoring. See "Barnabas—A Model for Mentoring," Acts 9:27.)

Barnabas with John Mark

In a dramatic split with Paul, Barnabas took young John Mark home with him to Cyprus and rebuilt his confidence (Acts 15:36–39). Years later, Paul changed his opinion, describing John Mark as "useful to me for ministry" (2 Tim. 4:11).

Priscilla and Aquila with Apollos

Manufacturers of mobile living units (tents), Priscilla and Aquila drew alongside gifted but confused Apollos, tutoring him in the faith and then sponsoring his ministry (Acts 18:1–3, 24–28. Be sure to see the Priscilla and Aquila profile at Rom. 16:3–5).

Paul with Timothy

Pioneering leader Paul recruited young Timothy and built on the foundation laid by the young man's mother and grandmother (2 Tim. 1:5). Enlisting him as a fellow-traveler and tutoring him in the faith, Paul guided him in his first major assignment, the multiethnic start-up at Ephesus (Acts 16:1–3; Phil. 2:19–23; 2 Tim. 1–4).

Paul with Philemon

Paul helped Philemon, a wealthy leader in Colosse, deal with a runaway slave who had broken the law. He recommended full acceptance—even as a brother in the family—rather than insisting on the usual retribution (see the Introduction to Philemon). ◆

Consistency Needed in Hard Times

3:10–11

10But you have carefully followed my
doctrine, manner of life, purpose, faith,
longsuffering, love, perseverance, 11persecutions, afflictions,
which happened to me at Antioch, at Iconium, at Lystra—
what persecutions I endured. And out of *them* all the Lord
delivered me. 12Yes, and all who desire to live godly in
Christ Jesus will suffer persecution. 13But evil men and impostors will grow worse and worse, deceiving and being deceived. 14But you must continue in the things which you
have learned and been assured of, knowing from whom you
have learned *them,* 15and that from childhood you have
known the Holy Scriptures, which are able to make you
wise for salvation through faith which is in Christ Jesus.

3:16–17
see pg. 750

16All Scripture *is* given by inspiration of
God, and *is* profitable for doctrine, for re-
proof, for correction, for instruction in righteousness, 17that
the man of God may be complete, thoroughly equipped for
every good work.

CHAPTER 4

A Charge to Timothy

1I charge *you* therefore before God and the Lord Jesus
Christ, who will judge the living and the dead at[a] His appearing and His kingdom: 2Preach the word! Be ready in
season *and* out of season. Convince, rebuke, exhort, with all
longsuffering and teaching. 3For the time will come when
they will not endure sound doctrine, but according to their
own desires, *because* they have itching ears, they will heap
up for themselves teachers; 4and they will turn *their* ears
away from the truth, and be turned aside to fables. 5But you
be watchful in all things, endure afflictions, do the work of
an evangelist, fulfill your ministry.

Paul's Example and Reward

6For I am already being poured out as a drink offering,
and the time of my departure is at hand. 7I have fought the
good fight, I have finished the race, I have kept the faith.

(Bible text continued on page 752)

4:1 [a]NU-Text omits *therefore* and reads *and by* for *at*.

PREACH THE WORD! BE READY IN SEASON AND OUT OF SEASON.
—2 Timothy 4:2

Follow the Leader

A CLOSER LOOK
3:10–11

Paul felt confident in encouraging Timothy and others to follow his example (vv. 10–11). In light of his mentoring relationship to Timothy (2:2), it's clear that he realized that the values of Christ are as much caught as taught. See "Leading by Example," Phil. 3:17.

CONSIDER THIS
3:16–17

THE BIBLE: GETTING THE BIG PICTURE

As Paul indicates to Timothy (vv. 16–17) and many other passages affirm, the Bible is the ultimate authority for Christian faith and practice. It is crucial to interpret Scripture in light of its overall context.

The Bible as it has come down to us is laid out in two parts: the Old Testament, covering the period before Christ, and the New Testament, the period after Christ. The biblical record is a three-part story:

Part I: God's Original Creation (Gen. 1–2)

The eternal God created a perfect, beautiful world and put it under the management of Adam and Eve and their successors (Gen. 1–2). No one knows how long this part of the story lasted, but Scripture devotes only the first two of its 1,189 chapters to telling it.

Part II: The Human Dilemma and God's Response (Gen. 3—Rev. 20)

The second part of the story takes up all but the last two chapters of the Bible. Two story lines weave throughout the record. One reveals how the balance and beauty of creation is terribly damaged by sin and rebellion. The other unfolds God's response to rescue His creatures and the creation from this dilemma. His redemptive work is promised through Israel (as recorded in the Old Testament), provided through Christ (as recorded in the gospels), and then applied in and through the church (as told in Acts and the letters). The book of Revelation's first 20 chapters display events related to Christ's return to earth.

Part III: The Achievement of God's Original Design (Rev. 21–22)

The last two chapters of the Bible tell the final third of the story. They offer great hope to the reader by promising a new heaven and earth. God's original intentions for the creation will

(continued on next page)

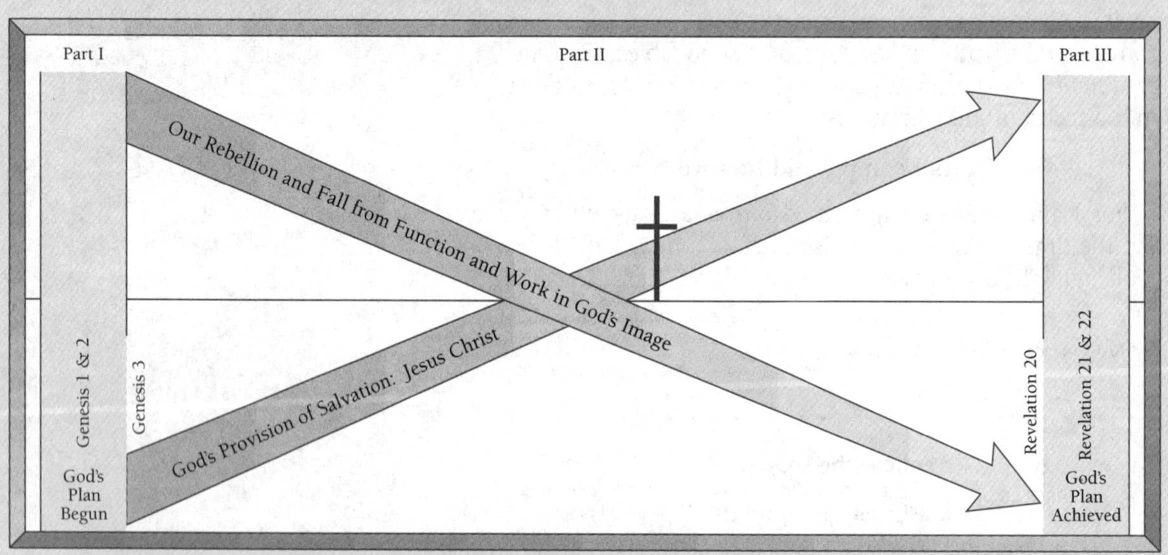

CREATION, REBELLION, AND RESTORATION

Counterfeit Christianity

CONSIDER THIS 3:8–9 **Wherever people accept the truth of God and begin practicing it, counterfeits soon surface. That's what Paul found at Ephesus, and what he warns Timothy about (vv. 8–9).**

He mentions two characters, Jannes and Jambres, whose names mean "he who seduces" and "he who is rebellious." Neither name is in the Old Testament, but Jewish legend held that these were the names of two Egyptian magicians who opposed Moses' demand of Pharaoh to free the Israelites. They tried to duplicate the miracles of Moses in an attempt to discredit him. But God showed that Moses' authority was more powerful (Ex. 7:11–12, 22).

Paul faced a similar experience at Ephesus. For two years he taught the message of Christ there, in a culture heavily steeped in pagan idolatry and occultism. God confirmed his teaching through powerful miracles and the release of many from evil spirits. But local exorcists attempted to duplicate the miracles. Their scheme backfired, however, to the benefit of the gospel (Acts 19:8–20).

Counterfeits to the truth of Christ abound today, as Paul predicted they would. If we effectively communicate the gospel to friends and coworkers, we can virtually count on the fact that competing systems and worldviews will soon appear. That's why we must "continue in the things which you have learned and been assured of," basing our lives and our witness on the firm foundation of Scripture (2 Tim. 3:14–17).

(continued from previous page)

finally and fully be achieved. This parallels and fulfills Genesis 1–2 and also reflects the values of Christ, who is the focus of the whole Bible.

Reading the Bible

Because the middle third of the account comprises 99 percent of the text, it grabs most of the attention of Bible readers. But to properly understand it, one must keep the first and third parts firmly in mind. Like two bookends, they frame and anchor the big picture of God's work throughout history. They provide the crucial context for the double story line of rebellion and restoration etched through the middle of the account.

That middle part often makes for rather painful reading. With forceful realism it shows the cruelty that sin unleashes on all of creation. Some readers would prefer to skip over or dismiss that aspect of the story. But God refuses to distort reality or put a positive "spin" on it. He includes the horrors of sin in His record as "examples to avoid" (1 Cor. 10:6). He lets nothing escape either exposure or resolution in Jesus Christ. ◆

How did the Bible come to be written? See 2 Pet. 1:21.

Alexander—A Confirmed Enemy

FOR YOUR INFO 4:14–15 **Wherever the gospel enjoys unusual success, believers will soon find someone determined to oppose it. In fact, it seems that the greater the impact that the message of Christ has, the more strident and determined will be the opposition.**

The man Alexander (v. 14) became a confirmed enemy of Paul and the church at Ephesus. Some identify him as a Jew who lived in the city during the riots instigated by Demetrius and the silversmiths to oppose Paul's preaching (Acts 19:21–41). The Jews tried to use Alexander to convince the Gentile Ephesians that they (the Jews) had nothing to do with Paul and the burgeoning Christian movement (v. 33).

Others, however, believe that Alexander was one of two heretical teachers at Ephesus mentioned by Paul (1 Tim. 1:19–20). With his associate Hymenaeus, Alexander was said to have "suffered shipwreck" concerning the faith, indicating that at one point he may have been counted among the believers. But Paul, apparently using his apostolic authority, "delivered [him] to Satan," which may have been some form of excommunication from the church.

Whoever Alexander was, Paul counted him as a confirmed enemy and warned Timothy to watch out for him (2 Tim. 4:15). However, rather than attack him, Paul left his fate in the Lord's hands, to repay him "according to his works."

Who are the confirmed enemies of the gospel where you live and work? Are you on guard against their attempts to discredit the cause of Christ?

No matter how mean-spirited people may become toward us or our witness to Christ, people are not really our enemies. We have far more powerful forces opposing us. See "Who Is the Enemy?" Eph. 6:10–13.

8Finally, there is laid up for me the crown of righteousness,
which the Lord, the righteous Judge, will give to me on that
Day, and not to me only but also to all who have loved His
appearing.

Personal News and Requests

9Be diligent to come to me quickly; 10for Demas has forsaken me, having loved this present world, and has departed for Thessalonica—Crescens for Galatia, Titus for
Dalmatia. 11Only Luke is with me. Get Mark and bring him
with you, for he is useful to me for ministry. 12And Tychicus
I have sent to Ephesus. 13Bring the cloak that I left with
Carpus at Troas when you come—and the books, especially
the parchments.

4:14–15 14Alexander the coppersmith did me
much harm. May the Lord repay him ac-
cording to his works. 15You also must beware of him, for he
has greatly resisted our words.

4:16–17 16At my first defense no one stood with
me, but all forsook me. May it not be
charged against them.

17But the Lord stood with me and strengthened me, so
that the message might be preached fully through me, and
that all the Gentiles might hear. Also I was delivered out of
the mouth of the lion. 18And the Lord will deliver me from
every evil work and preserve *me* for His heavenly kingdom.
To Him *be* glory forever and ever. Amen!

19Greet Prisca and Aquila, and the household of Onesiphorus. 20Erastus stayed in Corinth, but Trophimus I
have left in Miletus sick.

21Do your utmost to come before winter.

Eubulus greets you, as well as Pudens, Linus, Claudia,
and all the brethren.

22The Lord Jesus Christ[a] be with your spirit. Grace be
with you. Amen.

4:22 [a]NU-Text omits *Jesus Christ.*

"That All the Gentiles Might Hear"

A CLOSER LOOK 4:16–17 *As Paul wrote the last of this letter to Timothy, he knew that the end of his life was near. But right to the end, one goal was paramount—to preach the gospel to the Gentiles (v. 17). See "Paul the Jew—Teacher of the Gentiles," 1:3; and "A Bigot Does an About-Face," Gal. 1:13–17.*

Titus

Some people say that it doesn't really matter what you believe, as long as you do the right thing. However, Paul's letter to Titus contradicts that sort of thinking. He knew that people become what they think, and that everything they do is shaped by what they believe.

That's why he urged Titus, his valued associate who was pastoring a church on the island of Crete, to "speak the things which are proper for sound doctrine" (Titus 2:1). He knew that correct living is a product of correct belief. Error can never lead to godliness. Only truth produces genuine Christlikeness.

In our world today, many streams of thought lay claim to being "true." Yet they produce nothing that even approaches the character, integrity, and humility of Christ. That's why believers need to pay careful attention to the teaching they receive. Does it square with Scripture? Does it honor Christ? Does it acknowledge what Paul calls "the truth which accords with godliness" (1:1)?

Only truth produces genuine Christlikeness.

C O N T E N T S

A R T I C L E S

CRETE

- **An island in the Mediterranean Sea south of the Aegean Sea.**
- **Probably the same as the ancient Caphtor (Deut. 2:23; Amos 9:7) from which the Philistines (Caphtorim) originated.**
- **Associated with many legends, including those of King Minos and the Minotaur, a mythical half-bull, half-man monster.**
- **Captured by the Romans in 68–66 B.C. and made a Roman province.**
- **Inhabited by people known for their excesses. Paul quoted from the Greek poet Epimenides of Knossos (c. 600 B.C.) who wrote, "Cretans are always liars, evil beasts, lazy gluttons" (Titus 1:12).**

The Genuine Item

Just as 1 and 2 Timothy were meant to provide continuity for the church at Ephesus, Titus was meant to provide continuity for the church at Crete. What did believers there need? In a word, *authenticity.*

Crete had an ancient culture that was notorious for its corruption. In the face of this moral wasteland, believers needed to live counter-culturally. They needed to speak the truth and live the truth.

In the ancient world, people felt no need to emulate their gods (who were, after all, little better than humans, and in some cases much worse). But Christianity was just the opposite: believers needed to look like their God—and their God was not a liar. He was morally perfect or "holy," and His people needed to pursue holiness as well (2:14), no matter what the surrounding culture might sanction.

So Titus was to urge his people to "adorn the doctrine of God" (2:10), that is, to make the teaching about God attractive. Paul's words picture a fine gem that reflects light with beauty and radiance as it is placed in its appropriate setting. (Interestingly, Crete was a center for the jewelry trade.) So believers there were to stand out against the culture, reflecting the light of Christ attractively and deliberately.

As we read Titus we need to ask, what are the poets of our day saying about our culture? What is the moral reputation of our society? What is the spiritual climate? Like the Cretan believers, we need to speak the truth and live the truth. When people look at us, they need to see authentic Christianity, not a lukewarm, accommodating lifestyle that stands for nothing. We need to make the gospel attractive in such a way that unbelievers will be drawn to the matchless Light of the World. ◆

. . . ADORN THE DOCTRINE OF GOD OUR SAVIOR IN ALL THINGS.
—Titus 2:10

Titus

The man to whom Paul wrote this letter was someone the apostle could rely on in tense situations. Earlier he had represented Paul at Corinth. Now he was left on the island of Crete to bring order to the church there and establish leadership (1:5). Apparently Titus fulfilled his assignment rather well, for tradition holds that he was the first bishop of Crete. Learn more about Paul's "man of the hour" at "Titus," 2 Cor. 7:6.

CHAPTER 1

God Cannot Lie

[1]Paul, a bondservant of God and an apostle of Jesus
Christ, according to the faith of God's elect and the acknowledgment of the truth which accords with godliness,
1:2 [2]in hope of eternal life which God, who
cannot lie, promised before time began,
[3]but has in due time manifested His word through preaching, which was committed to me according to the commandment of God our Savior;

[4]To Titus, a true son in *our* common faith:

Grace, mercy, *and* peace from God the Father and the Lord Jesus Christ[a] our Savior.

Titus to Establish New Leaders

[5]For this reason I left you in Crete, that you should set in
order the things that are lacking, and appoint elders in
every city as I commanded you— [6]if a man is blameless, the

1:4 [a]NU-Text reads *and Christ Jesus.*

CONSIDER THIS
1:2

GOD CANNOT LIE

What understanding of God do your coworkers, friends, and family have? Is there a variety of opinion about spiritual issues among your peers? Do you face a mixture of hostility, detachment, distortion, or accusation that reflect badly on the faith?

Such was the case in Crete. New believers on that Mediterranean island heard no end of opinions about their new loyalty to Christ. The Greeks believed in many gods. Each one was to be served, honored, or placated. Jesus seemed to be just one more deity to add to the pantheon. To stabilize the situation, Paul sent his trainee Titus, instructing him to "set in order the things that are lacking, and appoint elders in every city" (v. 5).

As he wrote out Titus' job description, Paul emphasized that God does not lie (v. 2). Quite a contrast to the Cretans, who were known for their dishonesty. In fact, one of their own literary heroes, Epimenides, had remarked that "Cretans are always liars, evil beasts, and lazy gluttons." Paul added his affirmation to the assessment by writing, "This testimony is true" (vv. 12–13). He knew that he was dealing with a culture that thrived on trickery.

If the new believers were going to be faithful to a God who speaks truth, they would have to break that pattern.

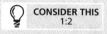

husband of one wife, having faithful children not accused of
dissipation or insubordination. 7For a bishop[a] must be
blameless, as a steward of God, not self-willed, not quick-
tempered, not given to wine, not violent, not greedy for
money, 8but hospitable, a lover of what is good, sober-
minded, just, holy, self-controlled, 9holding fast the faithful
word as he has been taught, that he may be able, by sound
doctrine, both to exhort and convict those who contradict.

Counter False Teachers

10For there are many insubordinate, both idle talkers and
deceivers, especially those of the circumcision, 11whose
mouths must be stopped, who subvert whole households,
teaching things which they ought not, for the sake of dishonest gain. 12One of them, a prophet of their own, said,
"Cretans *are* always liars, evil beasts, lazy gluttons." 13This
testimony is true. Therefore rebuke them sharply, that they
may be sound in the faith, 14not giving heed to Jewish fables and commandments of men who turn from the truth.

1:7 [a]Literally *overseer*

Therefore, Paul directed Titus to:

- *develop leaders who could be trusted (vv. 6–9).*
- *train all believers—young and old, male and female, slaves or free—to pursue changed lifestyles reflecting integrity, control, and purity (2:1–15).*
- *call all believers to lives characterized by action, not just words (1:16; 2:7, 14; 3:8–9, 14. See also James 1:19–27 and Matt. 7:21–23).*

Through these strategies, Titus and the Cretan believers would silence the critics of the faith (2:5, 8, 15).

God is not a liar. And followers of Christ are not just "wordsmiths" called to outdo the art of their culture in presenting a "new and improved" set of deceptions. No, Christians should be "new and improved" people known for their good deeds in contrast to a previous lifestyle of dishonesty, passion, and malice (3:1–3).

Are there distorted perceptions of the faith and of God in your sphere of influence? How can you live in a way that will speak to those and offer a clearer demonstration of true Christianity? How about gathering with other believers who live or work in similar environments, and together identifying the most strategic witness that could be offered? ◆

QUOTE UNQUOTE

CONSIDER THIS 1:15 *Another way of saying that "to the pure all things are pure" (v. 15) is:*

There is nothing so secular that it cannot be sacred, and that is one of the deepest messages of the Incarnation.

Madeleine L'Engle, *Walking On Water,* p. 50

1:15
see pg. 757

15To the pure all things are pure, but to
those who are defiled and unbelieving
nothing is pure; but even their mind and conscience are defiled. 16They profess to know God, but in works they deny
Him, being abominable, disobedient, and disqualified for
every good work.

CHAPTER 2

Develop Human Resources

1But as for you, speak the things which are proper for
sound doctrine: 2that the older men be sober, reverent, temperate, sound in faith, in love, in patience; 3the older
women likewise, that they be reverent in behavior, not slan-

CONSIDER THIS
2:9–10

YOUR "WORKSTYLE"

The term "lifestyle" describes the attitudes, behaviors, and expectations you have toward the life you lead. Similarly, the attitudes, behaviors, and expectations you have about your work could be termed your "workstyle." Paul highlights five key areas of a Christlike workstyle in vv. 9–10. How does yours compare? (See table opposite.)

According to verse 10, there's a purpose behind this godly workstyle: "that [workers] may adorn the doctrine of God our Savior in all things." Your attitudes and actions on the job can make the gospel of Christ attractive to coworkers and customers. What impression are you making? ◆

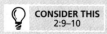

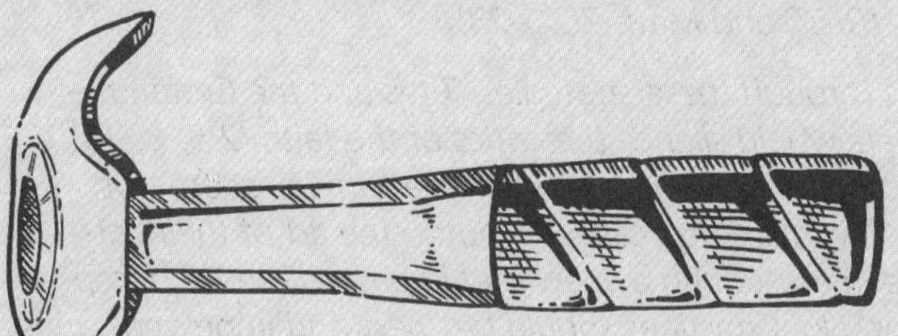

Did you know that in going to work every day, you bear the very image of God? See "People at Work," Heb. 2:7.

Christ never intended His followers to withdraw from the world to set up their own exclusive communities. Engagement, not isolation, is His desire. See "Called into the World," John 17:18.

No matter what position you hold at your job, no matter where you fit in the organization, you have a boss to answer to. See "Who's the Boss?" Col. 3:22–24.

derers, not given to much wine, teachers of good things—
4that they admonish the young women to love their husbands, to love their children, 5to be discreet, chaste, homemakers, good, obedient to their own husbands, that the
word of God may not be blasphemed.
2:7 6Likewise, exhort the young men to be
sober-minded, 7in all things showing

Moral Leadership

A CLOSER LOOK 2:7 *Do you exhibit moral leadership at work, at home, and in your community? Paul challenges Titus to show "a pattern of good works" (v. 7). He understood that the most effective leaders lead by example. See Phil. 3:17.*

SPEAK THE THINGS WHICH ARE PROPER FOR SOUND DOCTRINE.
—Titus 2:1

FIVE "WORKSTYLE" CATEGORIES

Description	Issue	Application
"obedient to their own masters"	Authority	Do you... •follow instructions? •comply with industry standards? •pay your fair share of taxes?
"well pleasing in all things"	Excellence	Do you... •take pride in your work? •use the right tools for the job, in the right way? •work just as hard even when the boss isn't around?
"not answering back"	Conflict	Do you... •seek to resolve conflicts in a healthy way? •respond with honesty and courtesy? •promote constructive cooperation instead of destructive competition?
"not pilfering"	Honesty & Integrity	Do you... •keep an honest accounting of your hours? •pay for personal expenses rather than charge them to company expense accounts? •avoid making personal long-distance calls on the company's phone?
"showing all good fidelity"	Loyalty & Dependability	Do you... •keep your word? •do what it takes to meet deadlines? •honor what your company stands for?

yourself *to be* a pattern of good works; in doctrine *showing*
integrity, reverence, incorruptibility,[a] 8sound speech that
cannot be condemned, that one who is an opponent may be
ashamed, having nothing evil to say of you.[a]

2:9–10 see pg. 758

2:9–10

9*Exhort* bondservants to be obedient to
their own masters, to be well pleasing in
all *things,* not answering back, 10not pilfering, but showing all good fidelity, that
they may adorn the doctrine of God our Savior in all things.

Build on What God Has Done

11For the grace of God that brings salvation has appeared
to all men, 12teaching us that, denying ungodliness and
worldly lusts, we should live soberly, righteously, and godly
in the present age, 13looking for the blessed hope and glorious appearing of our great God and Savior Jesus Christ,
14who gave Himself for us, that He might redeem us from

2:7 [a]NU-Text omits *incorruptibility.* *2:8* [a]NU-Text and M-Text read *us.*

Workplace Evangelism

A CLOSER LOOK 2:9–10

Paul implies that a believer's approach to work will influence the way coworkers see the gospel (v. 10). Today, many Christians view their job as a soapbox for spreading the gospel. Is that legitimate? See "Work—A Platform for Evangelism?" Eph. 6:5–9.

CONSIDER THIS 3:1–8

EVIDENCE BEFORE INFORMATION

What evidence can new believers offer to validate their new faith? How can their commitment to Christ be seen as more than just one more spiritual path among many? They need to put their best foot forward among non-believers, spiritually speaking, but how?

Believers on the island of Crete faced such a challenge, and it was enormous. The Cretan culture had many gods. Its people filled their time with much idle chatter, empty promises, and lies (Titus 1:10–13). So how could the Christians' loyalty to yet one more God be taken seriously, let alone make any difference in the society?

Paul acknowledged the dilemma that these early believers faced by opening his letter to Titus with the affirmation that God never lies (1:2). In the same way, God's people must be people of truth and unimpeachable integrity. How can that happen? Through fewer words and more deeds. That was the way to build consistent evidence of a new and credible lifestyle with lasting impact.

every lawless deed and purify for Himself *His* own special people, zealous for good works.

[15]Speak these things, exhort, and rebuke with all authority. Let no one despise you.

CHAPTER 3

Believers' Conduct in the Community

3:1

[1]Remind them to be subject to rulers
and authorities, to obey, to be ready for
every good work, [2]to speak evil of no one, to be peaceable,
gentle, showing all humility to all men. [3]For we ourselves
were also once foolish, disobedient, deceived, serving various lusts and pleasures, living in malice and envy, hateful
and hating one another. [4]But when the kindness and the
love of God our Savior toward man appeared, [5]not by
works of righteousness which we have done, but according
to His mercy He saved us, through the washing of regeneration and renewing of the Holy Spirit, [6]whom He poured out

Subject to Rulers

A CLOSER LOOK 3:1

Submission to human authorities (v. 1) reflects our submission to God's authority. See "Governmental Authority," Rom. 13:2.

The apostle called for that strategy among several sub-groups of the new believers: older men (2:2), older women (2:3), younger women (2:4–5), younger men (2:6), Titus himself (2:7–8), and slaves (2:9–10). Each of these groups was to carry out the deeds of faith listed in 3:1–8. In fact, Paul insisted that they all *"be careful to maintain good works" (v. 8). They were to avoid extended arguments as unprofitable and useless in their witness.*

Do your coworkers see the Christlike deeds of believers where you work? Or has their main exposure to the faith been little more than Christians filling the air with statements and ideas? Has your own walk with Christ produced any visible fruit in front of your associates, such as patience, staying power, compassion, loyalty, better management, hard work, or faithful service? That's the kind of evidence that shows whether faith in Christ has any power and impact. ◆

United for the Work

CONSIDER THIS 3:12–15

Working without phones, faxes, cars, or planes, a dedicated, diverse team of first-century believers spread the good news about Jesus throughout the Roman world. Paul mentioned several of these coworkers to Titus—Artemas, Tychicus, Zenas the lawyer, and Apollos (vv. 12–13)—but there were many others; for example, Barnabas (see Acts 4:36–37), Priscilla and Aquila (see Rom. 16:3–5), Silas (see Acts 15:34), and Junia (see Rom. 16:7).

The task of proclaiming the gospel in the face of sometimes fierce opposition knit these early believers together. They planned their travel not only around the tasks of ministry, but also around their relationships with each other. For example, Paul encouraged Titus to come to him at Nicopolis during a seasonal break (Titus 3:12). They also took care to provide necessities for each other (v. 13).

The principle emerges from this pattern that the cause of Christ goes forward even in the face of opposition when the workers are united for the work.

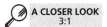

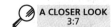

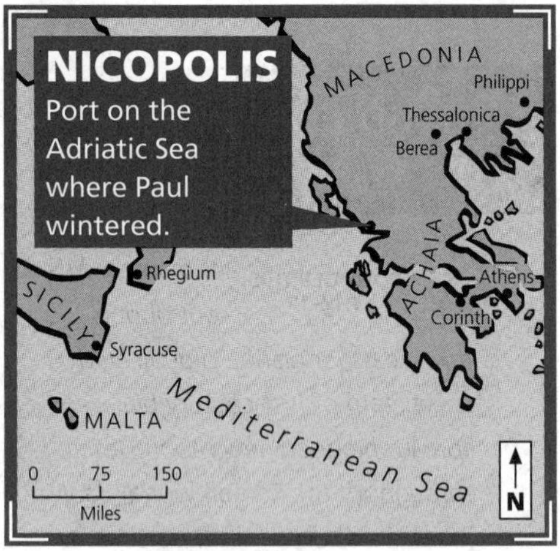

Nicopolis

YOU ARE THERE 3:12 **•The name of many cities in the first century, including the one at which Paul decided to spend a winter (Titus 3:12), probably in northwestern Greece on the Adriatic Sea.**
• Name means "city of victory."

3:7
on us abundantly through Jesus Christ
our Savior, 7that having been justified by
His grace we should become heirs according to the hope of
eternal life.

3:1–8 see pg. 760
8This is a faithful saying, and these
things I want you to affirm constantly,
that those who have believed in God should be careful to
maintain good works. These things are good and profitable
to men.

Unprofitable Disputes

9But avoid foolish disputes, genealogies, contentions, and
strivings about the law; for they are unprofitable and useless. 10Reject a divisive man after the first and second admonition, 11knowing that such a person is warped and sinning,
being self-condemned.

Plans and Greetings

3:12
12When I send Artemas to you, or Tychicus, be diligent to come to me at
Nicopolis, for I have decided to spend the winter there.
13Send Zenas the lawyer and Apollos on their journey with
haste, that they may lack nothing. 14And let our *people* also
learn to maintain good works, to *meet* urgent needs, that
they may not be unfruitful.

3:12–15 see pg. 761
15All who *are* with me greet you. Greet
those who love us in the faith.
Grace *be* with you all. Amen.

We Are Heirs

A CLOSER LOOK 3:7 *Is the idea of believers being "heirs" (v. 7) just wishful thinking? See "What's In It for Me?" Eph. 1:11.*

Philemon

Does Christ really make a difference in relationships? Does He really bring healing and the resolution of old grievances? Does He really surmount differences in social and economic status? The letter to Philemon offers powerful evidence that He does!

The Background of the Letter

Philemon provides a window on the story of Onesimus, a runaway slave, and Philemon, his master. The story begins with Paul's arrival in Ephesus. According to Acts 19:8–10, his work there for more than two years produced spectacular results: "all who dwelt in Asia [Minor] heard the word of the Lord Jesus, both Jews and Greeks."

Among those who responded to the gospel was Philemon, a wealthy man of Colosse, perhaps one of the many merchants doing business in the thriving economy of Ephesus. Philemon took his newfound faith back to Colosse and started or at least hosted a church in his home—perhaps the same group of believers to whom the letter to the Colossians was written (Col. 4:7–9).

Like most wealthy citizens of the Roman world, Philemon owned slaves. Scholars estimate that perhaps half the population of the empire may have been slaves. One of Philemon's slaves was Onesimus, possibly from Phrygia, the mountainous region in which Colosse sat. Whether Onesimus stole from his master, tired of his bondage, or thought he could take advantage of his master's new religion of love and grace, we don't know, but for some reason he ran away. ◆

The Prodigal Returns

Years later, Onesimus surfaced in Rome—where he ran into Paul! The apostle was living in rented quarters (Acts 28:30), perhaps in the Greek-speaking section in south Rome, where Onesimus would likely have gone. Like his former master, the fugitive turned to Christ and began growing in the faith. Paul came to regard him as "my son . . . whom I have begotten while in my chains" (Philem. 10), indicating a close relationship of mutual affection.

But Paul faced a dilemma. Should he hold onto him? The fellow proved useful and loyal. That's what Paul wanted to do (Philem. 13). But by law he was required to return the runaway slave to his master, or at least turn him over to the authorities. Yet what would happen to this new believer, his spiritual son and friend? Would he be punished or sold? Could Paul live with himself, knowing that in a sense, he had betrayed the man?

Paul's solution was to send Onesimus back to Philemon—but not without protection. He assigned an associate named Tychicus to escort the fugitive back, and to carry three letters—two general ones to the believers in Colosse and Laodicea (Col. 4:16), and a personal one to Philemon. As the latter makes clear, Paul was leaning heavily on his history with Philemon. He was also counting on the master to demonstrate spiritual maturity by forgiving the slave and accepting him as a brother in Christ. No doubt Philemon's standing among the community of believers would add further leverage, as people would be closely watching his response. ◆

The Rest of the Story

The letter to Philemon gives us only half of the conversation between Paul and Philemon. We don't know Philemon's response or what happened to Onesimus upon his return.

However, the name Onesimus appears among letters written by a bishop named Ignatius in about A.D. 110. Ignatius of Antioch was arrested and taken to Rome for trial. During the journey, he wrote a letter from Smyrna to the church at Ephesus in which he addressed the new bishop there, whose name was Onesimus. Many believe that this man was the same Onesimus who, as a slave, had run away from Philemon but later came to faith and returned.

Whatever the case, the Onesimus-Philemon story holds a number of significant lessons:

- It shows that in Christ, there is always room for reconciliation and a second chance for people.
- It illustrates how God works behind the scenes to bring people to faith and restore relationships.
- It shows the power of the gospel to work at a distance and effect change from city to city, coast to coast, and continent to continent.
- It shows the value of mentoring relationships, the way that older, seasoned believers can help younger followers of Christ work out problems and conflicts.
- It shows a measure of irony behind God's patience and providence: He had to send Onesimus thousands of miles away from his Christian master in order to bring him to faith!
- It shows that in Christ, people can change. Consider the many stages that Onesimus went through: from slave, to thief and runaway, to refugee, to convert, to penitent, to brother, and possibly to bishop. ◆

Personality Profile: Onesimus

Name means: "Useful" or "profitable."

Home: Originally from Phrygia, he worked in Colosse, lived for a while in Rome, but eventually returned to Colosse.

Occupation: Slave.

Best known today for: Running away from his master, Philemon, but returning to him after coming to faith.

Personality Profile: Philemon

Home: Colosse.

Family: His wife may have been Apphia (Philem. 2).

Occupation: Probably a businessman.

Special interests: He hosted a group of believers in his home.

Best known today for: Receiving a letter from Paul regarding the return of his runaway slave, Onesimus.

A General Greeting

[1]Paul, a prisoner of Christ Jesus, and Timothy *our* brother,

2 To Philemon our beloved *friend* and fellow laborer, [2]to the beloved[a] Apphia,
Archippus our fellow soldier, and to the church in your house:

[3]Grace to you and peace from God our Father and the Lord Jesus Christ.

God Praised for Philemon

[4]I thank my God, making mention of you always in my
prayers, [5]hearing of your love and faith which you have toward the Lord Jesus and toward all the saints, [6]that the
sharing of your faith may become effective by the acknowledgment of every good thing which is in you[a] in Christ Jesus. [7]For we have[a] great joy[b] and consolation in your love,

2 [a]NU-Text reads *to our sister Apphia.* 6 [a]NU-Text and M-Text read *us.*
7 [a]NU-Text reads *had.* [b]M-Text reads *thanksgiving.*

APPHIA

CONSIDER THIS 2

Apphia (v. 2) may have been the wife of Philemon and possibly the mother or sister of Archippus. In addition, some manuscripts give the phrase "to the beloved Apphia" as "to Apphia the [or our] sister." This as well as the placement of Apphia's name between two men, along with the terms used for each, suggest the possibility that Philemon, Apphia, and Archippus were leaders of the Christian community at Colosse.

Paul was addressing this letter not only to Philemon as the owner of Onesimus, but to all three of those named as well as to their church. Paul apparently did not intend that Philemon should act in isolation as he made his decision about what to do with Onesimus. By including Apphia and Archippus in his greeting, the apostle may have expected them to help Philemon make a wise, Christlike choice.

"PERHAPS . . ."

CONSIDER THIS 15–16

"I wonder why God allowed that to happen."

Countless people have uttered statements like that, either to themselves or out loud. In a world of many mysteries and uncertainties, they wonder *why?*

Is it worthwhile to ponder the reasons behind events or to question the ways of God? Some people think not. "God has His own reasons," they say. "Ours is not to know why. We ought not to question the purposes of God. Besides, there are some things we'll never know until we get to heaven, so why bother our heads with them now?"

But judging by Paul's words in vv. 15–16, thinking about what God may be up to in the events that come our way, what we might call "theological reflection," is both useful and encouraged. Paul had no scriptural text to turn to that would fully explain why Onesimus, of all people, had come to faith and was prepared to return to Philemon. So he offered Philemon his own reading of events.

Like Paul, we can and should reflect on the circumstances of our lives. We should think carefully about what God may be trying to show us or teach us. We should pay attention to the unusual or the unexpected, and even to the undesirable events that come our way. Such habits help us bring God and His Word into our understanding of life. We will never discover all the answers, but we may discover a bit more of God in our lives by wondering, "Perhaps . . ."

because the hearts of the saints have been refreshed by you,
brother.

Paul's Appeal for Onesimus

8 Therefore, though I might be very bold in Christ to command you what is fitting, 9 *yet* for love's sake I rather appeal
to you—being such a one as Paul, the aged, and now also a
prisoner of Jesus Christ— 10 I appeal to you for my son
Onesimus, whom I have begotten *while* in my chains, 11 who
once was unprofitable to you, but now is profitable to you
and to me.

12 I am sending him back.[a] You therefore receive him, that
is, my own heart, 13 whom I wished to keep with me, that
on your behalf he might minister to me in my chains for the
gospel. 14 But without your consent I wanted to do nothing,
that your good deed might not be by compulsion, as it
were, but voluntary.

15–16 see pg. 765

16

15 For perhaps he departed for a while
for this *purpose*, that you might receive
him forever, 16 no longer as a slave but
more than a slave—a beloved brother, especially to me but how much more to you, both in the flesh
and in the Lord.

12 [a]NU-Text reads *back to you in person, that is, my own heart.*

CONSIDER THIS
16

A Challenge to Slavery

Some people have criticized Paul and the early church, claiming that they did not call for an end to slavery. But Paul wrote the believers in Colosse, "There is neither . . . slave nor free, but Christ is all and in all" (Col. 3:11). Similarly, Galatians 3:28 reads, "There is neither slave nor free . . . you are all one in Christ Jesus."

In Christ, societal divisions and distinctions become immaterial, and practices that degrade and devalue people are condemned. It is true that first-century believers didn't actively campaign for an end to slavery, as far as we know. They never petitioned the government or urged slaves to rebel.

Yet here in Philemon we have a clear case of a believing slave owner being asked to put into practice the Christian ideals cited above. Philemon and Onesimus had an opportunity to demonstrate the gospel's power over slavery.

This was one of a number of cultural divisions that early believers broke down, such as:

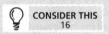

17–19

17–19

17If then you count me as a partner, receive him as *you would* me. 18But if he has
wronged you or owes anything, put that
on my account. 19I, Paul, am writing with
my own hand. I will repay—not to mention to you that you
owe me even your own self besides. 20Yes, brother, let me
have joy from you in the Lord; refresh my heart in the Lord.
21Having confidence in your obedience, I write to you,
knowing that you will do even more than I say. 22But,
meanwhile, also prepare a guest room for me, for I trust
that through your prayers I shall be granted to you.

Greetings and Farewell

23Epaphras, my fellow prisoner in Christ Jesus, greets
you, 24*as do* Mark, Aristarchus, Demas, Luke, my fellow laborers.
25The grace of our Lord Jesus Christ *be* with your spirit.
Amen.

Paul Mentors Philemon

A CLOSER LOOK 17–19

In this letter, Paul carries out a mentoring role for his friend, Philemon. He advises him on the difficult issue of dealing with a runaway slave who is also a brother in Christ. For more on mentoring relationships, see "Discipleship—Or Mentoring?" Acts 9:26–30.

- *Hellenists and Hebrews (Acts 6:1–7).*
- *Samaritans and Jews (Acts 8:5–8).*
- *Gentiles and Jews (Acts 8:26–40; 10:1–48).*
- *Women and men (Acts 16:14–15; 18:1–4, 24–28).*

Our society has formally done away with slavery. But there are systems still in place that abuse or oppress people. From the standpoint of the gospel, the issue is not whether they are legal, but whether they treat people as God would want them treated. If Paul were writing today, what would he challenge us as believers to do? What does "one in Christ" mean for the systems we participate in from day to day? ◆

Christians are all in the same family, no longer divided by ethnicity, social status, or gender. That has powerful implications for how we live. See "We Are Family!" Gal. 3:28.

LET ME PICK UP THE TAB

CONSIDER THIS 17–19

Paul tells Philemon that "if" Onesimus has stolen anything, he should send Paul a bill for it (vv. 18–19). But at this point he is writing somewhat tongue-in-cheek.

Paul knew that Onesimus really had "wronged" Philemon. Not only had he run away, apparently he had stolen property and owed Philemon restitution. Paul never questioned Philemon's right to have his slave returned or receive reimbursement for the theft. Conversion to Christ does not relieve anyone of obligations to others.

Nonetheless, Paul wanted Philemon to forgive Onesimus and receive him back as a brother (v. 16). But just in case the theft created a sticking point in the reconciliation, Paul volunteered to pay for the loss if Philemon was unwilling simply to forgive it. (Notice how Paul was imitating Christ in this regard.)

Of course, Paul anticipated that Philemon would be more than happy to bear the loss. After all, he owed Paul a large, intangible debt of gratitude for all that Paul had done for him (v. 19). So in effect, he would be returning Paul a favor by accepting Onesimus back unconditionally.

Is there a lesson here about favors and paybacks? Consider: often when we impose on others, asking them to do favors for us or for our friends, our main concern is for our own interests. But Paul's main concern was for Philemon—not for his financial loss, which was trifling, but for his spiritual gain, which was considerable.

The Roots of the Gospel

In 1976, Doubleday published Alex Haley's *Roots*, the story of Haley's descent from Africans brought to America as slaves. A subsequent television miniseries catapulted the work into best-seller status, fueling the burgeoning black pride movement and sparking a nationwide passion for tracing one's ancestry.

In many ways, the book of Hebrews is the *Roots* of the New Testament. It celebrates Christ as the fulfillment of Old Testament Judaism. Jewish Christians, who were quickly becoming a minority among first-century believers, were struggling with how their ancient heritage fit with the gospel. While warning them not to slip back into their old ways, the book showed that they need not disparage their background; there was still dignity and value to it, especially since so many of the seeds of Christianity had sprouted from it. Therefore, just as Gentiles did not need to become Jews to be accepted by God (the message of Galatians), so Jews did not need to become Gentiles.

If you've ever struggled to integrate your background, particularly your ethnic or cultural roots, with your faith in Christ, you'll do well to study Hebrews. God has used history—including the history of your own family—to accomplish His will and bring you to Himself.

Hebrews

Christ is the fulfillment of Judaism.

CONTENTS

ARTICLES

Creation: "Very Good," But Not Sacred! (11:3)

Is the universe itself divine? Is "Mother Nature" sacred?

Aiming to Please (11:6)

Sometimes we face conflicts because it's not always possible to please everybody. So when we have to make tough decisions about whom to please—and therefore whom to displease—how can we choose?

Christ Alone!

One of the most divisive issues in the early church was whether non-Jews could become Christians, and if so, to what extent they had to adopt Jewish practices. The church began, of course, among Jews. Since the earliest Christians shared much of the same religious, ethnic, and cultural background, there was little conflict over inclusiveness. But as the gospel spread to other groups, such as the Hellenists (Jews born outside of Palestine who spoke Greek), or the Jews' despised cousins the Samaritans, or Gentiles, tensions rose and conflicts broke out (for example, Acts 6:1; 11:1–2; 15:1–2).

In the case of Gentiles, some Jewish believers stridently opposed their inclusion. The only way that Gentiles could be acceptable to God, they argued, was by satisfying a precondition: they would have to be circumcised according to the Law of Moses. In effect, Gentiles would have to become Jews before they could become Christians.

This issue was first raised by Stephen, who in essence charged the Jewish council with using Judaism as an excuse for not believing in Jesus (Acts 7:2–53). Later, circumcision was hotly debated among church leaders in Jerusalem (11:1–18; 15:1–29; Gal. 2:1–10) and Antioch (Gal. 2:11–16). Eventually the Jerusalem church officially declared that Christ alone was necessary for salvation.

But that didn't stop false teachers from traveling many of the same paths as the apostles. Some arrived in Galatia and disturbed Gentiles there with a "different gospel" (Gal. 1:6–7). With holy indignation, Paul sent a strongly worded letter to the Galatians in which he insisted that salvation depends on Christ alone. Similar messages went to believers in Ephesus (Eph. 2:11–22), Philippi (Phil. 3:2–16), and Rome (Rom. 2:1—3:30; 11:11–32; 15:7–13).

The gospel of "Christ alone" prevailed. Before long, Gentiles outnumbered Jews in the church and the pendulum swung to the other extreme. "There is neither Jew nor Greek," the apostles said (Gal. 3:28; see also Eph. 2:14–18; Col. 3:11). So what value was left in Judaism if Christ alone was necessary for salvation? Why bother with an outdated system?

The Other Side of the Coin

Such issues troubled Jewish Christians. Although Jews throughout the empire were coming to faith, they were now a minority among believers. Would Christianity prove to be just one more episode in the inevitable loss of their Jewish heritage and assimilation into a Gentile world?

The letter to the Hebrews (along with Romans 9–11) spoke to those fears by showing the other side of the coin. Rather than dismiss the Jewish heritage, Hebrews affirmed it (Heb. 6:13–20).

- **It celebrated the richness of God's special relationship with Israel (1:1; 6:13–15).**
- **It showed God's work in Jewish history and the fulfillment of His plans for the nation in Christ (8:7–13; 10:15–17).**
- **It revealed significant parallels between details of the Old Testament heritage—such as smells, sounds, traditions, and names—and the new way of Christ (6:20—7:28; 9:1—10:14; 13:10–13).**

(continued on next page)

- **It recalled many of the heroes of Israel's history, such as Abraham (6:13—7:6; 11:8–19), Moses (2:2–6; 11:23–28), Aaron (4:14—5:10), Joshua (7:8–10), David (7:6–7), and others (11:4–40).**

What a treasure Jewish Christians could have in light of God's partnership with them! They need not be swallowed up by the Gentile cultures around them. Embracing Christ, they could still hold onto their roots and be themselves (6:13–19).

Hebrews was written to Jewish believers (1:1; 2:14–18; 3:1–6), but it encourages each of us to go back and re-examine, accept, and affirm our roots. That doesn't mean that everything in our past is honoring to God and worth preserving. Indeed, we may have to repudiate certain beliefs, traditions, or behaviors because they run counter to biblical truth.

Nevertheless, part of identifying ourselves with Christ involves a recognition of what God has made us to be from our backgrounds. By tracing the paths of history that He has used to prepare us for the gospel, we can discover delightful new insights into His wisdom, sovereignty, and grace. ◆

Who Wrote Hebrews?

Hebrews lacks a greeting or identification of its author, giving rise to numerous suggestions as to who wrote it. *See " 'I Have Written to You,' " Heb. 13:22.*

CHAPTER 1

God Has Spoken through Jesus

1:1 see pg. 774

1:2–3

[1]God, who at various times and in various ways spoke in time past to the fathers
by the prophets, [2]has in these last days
spoken to us by *His* Son, whom He has
appointed heir of all things, through whom also He made
the worlds; [3]who being the brightness of *His* glory and the
express image of His person, and upholding all things by
the word of His power, when He had by Himself[a] purged
our[b] sins, sat down at the right hand of the Majesty on high,
[4]having become so much better than the angels, as He has
by inheritance obtained a more excellent name than they.

Jesus Is Superior to the Angels

1:5–14 see pg. 776

[5]For to which of the angels did He ever
say:

"You are My Son,
Today I have begotten You"?[a]

And again:

"I will be to Him a Father,
And He shall be to Me a Son"?[b]

[6]But when He again brings the firstborn into the world,
He says:

"Let all the angels of God worship Him."[a]

[7]And of the angels He says:

"Who makes His angels spirits
And His ministers a flame of fire."[a]

[8]But to the Son *He says:*

"Your throne, O God, *is* forever and ever;
A scepter of righteousness *is* the scepter of Your
kingdom.
9 You have loved righteousness and hated lawlessness;
Therefore God, Your God, has anointed You
With the oil of gladness more than Your companions."[a]

1:3 [a]NU-Text omits *by Himself.* [b]NU-Text omits *our.* *1:5* [a]Psalm 2:7 [b]2 Samuel 7:14
1:6 [a]Deuteronomy 32:43 (Septuagint, Dead Sea Scrolls); Psalm 97:7 *1:7* [a]Psalm 104:4
1:9 [a]Psalm 45:6, 7

. . . **HIS SON, WHOM HE HAS APPOINTED HEIR OF ALL THINGS . . .**
—Hebrews 1:2

He's Got the Whole World In His Hands

A CLOSER LOOK 1:2–3 *We owe our day-to-day existence to God (vv. 2–3), not Mother Nature. See "Every Breath You Take," Col. 1:17.*

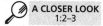

10And:

"You, LORD, in the beginning laid the foundation of the
earth,
And the heavens are the work of Your hands.
11 They will perish, but You remain;
And they will all grow old like a garment;
12 Like a cloak You will fold them up,
And they will be changed.
But You are the same,
And Your years will not fail."[a]

13But to which of the angels has He ever said:

1:12 [a]Psalm 102:25–27

FOR YOUR INFO
1:1

FATHERS AND PROPHETS

Who were the "fathers" and "prophets" privileged to hear God's voice "in time past" (v. 1)? The writer was referring to some of the Hebrews' most well-known ancestors and others to whom God made astonishing promises and through whom He communicated His Word, now known as the Old Testament. See if you can identify some of these important figures in Israelite history from the descriptions that follow (answers are given at the article, "Who Are These People?" Heb. 11:2):

OLD TESTAMENT FIGURES

1	The father of three sons in especially evil times, this man is warned of coming disaster and prepares for it despite his neighbors' ridicule. But when calamity strikes and destroys his opponents, he is vindicated by surviving. However, drunkenness leads him into sin with long-term consequences. Nevertheless, God makes an everlasting promise to him and his descendants.
2	A prisoner of war becomes a government trainee who resists cultural assimilation. Later, his coworkers hatch an evil plot which results in orders for his execution. However, by God's power he emerges unscathed and becomes the king's most trusted advisor. Through him God reveals great and awesome visions concerning history.
3	Born in poverty to a minority couple, this man is raised among the wealthy and powerful. But after committing murder, he flees to a remote land and adopts the life of a shepherd. Years later he stages a dramatic comeback, leading his people on the world's largest known expedition back to their homeland. Through him God reveals a moral code that still impacts civilization today.

Continued

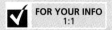

"Sit at My right hand,
Till I make Your enemies Your footstool"?[a]

1:14

14Are they not all ministering spirits sent forth to minister for those who will inherit salvation?

1:13 [a]Psalm 110:1

Inheriting Salvation

A CLOSER LOOK 1:14

Who are "those who will inherit salvation" (v. 14)? And what is it that they will inherit? See "What's In It For Me?" Eph. 1:11.

	Continued
4	One of the youngest sons of a family of shepherds develops musical ability and becomes a military prodigy. However, his prowess causes the existing leadership to view him as such a threat that he is marked for death. Nevertheless, he eventually becomes his nation's leader. Through him God causes to be composed a large portion of the Hebrews' songs of worship.
5	Himself the son of a king, he becomes the most powerful militarist, builder, and judge of his day, trading with foreign nations in military arms, construction materials, treasure cities, and wives. However, frustrations beset him and he writes of the hopelessness of life apart from God. Through him God reveals many practical nuggets of wisdom and the beauty of love.
6	Describing himself as nothing but "a herdsman and a tender of sycamore fruit," this man rises from obscurity and announces to a rebellious kingdom that God is sending invaders to punish it for its idol worship, corruption, and oppression of the poor. Through his message and its fulfillment, God shows that He can be counted on to keep His Word.
7	The answer to a barren woman's prayer, this man hears as a child the call of God to be His spokesman. Later he serves as a judge of his people and warns them against the perils of establishing a kingdom. Nevertheless, he presides over the anointing of two kings and records the early history of his nation's kingdom era.
8	A poet of deep emotional strength, this man is so outraged by his nation's sin that he cries out to God for judgment. Then when God reveals His plans, he challenges the justice of the proposal. A man of deep faith, he leaves behind a beautiful poem of praise in response to the mysterious ways of God.

For more Old Testament "guess-who's," see "Who Are These People?" Heb. 11:2.

"YOU ARE THE SAME, AND YOUR YEARS WILL NOT FAIL." —Hebrews 1:12

CHAPTER 2

A Warning

1Therefore we must give the more earnest heed to the
things we have heard, lest we drift away. 2For if the word
spoken through angels proved steadfast, and every transgression and disobedience received a just reward, 3how
shall we escape if we neglect so great a salvation, which at
the first began to be spoken by the Lord, and was confirmed to us by those who heard *Him,* 4God also bearing
witness both with signs and wonders, with various miracles, and gifts of the Holy Spirit, according to His own will?

Jesus—Lord over All the Earth

5For He has not put the world to come, of which we
2:6–8
speak, in subjection to angels. 6But one
testified in a certain place, saying:

"What is man that You are mindful of him,
Or the son of man that You take care of him?
2:7 see pg. 778
7You have made him a little lower than
the angels;
You have crowned him with glory and honor,[a]

2:7 [a]NU-Text and M-Text omit the rest of verse 7.

CONSIDER THIS 1:5–14

MANY ARE GREAT, BUT CHRIST IS THE GREATEST

The world has seen many great people in its history, but none equal to Jesus, the Son of God (v. 5). The writer shows that Christ is superior to:

- *The angels, Israel's divinely appointed guardians (1:4—2:18).*
- *Moses, Israel's great leader (3:1—4:7).*
- *Joshua, Israel's great general (4:8–13).*
- *Aaron, Israel's great high priest (4:14—7:28).*

Later, Hebrews lists a parade of people who showed great faith in their lives as they looked ahead to the coming of their spiritual brother, Christ (2:11–13; 11:1–40). They believed the promises of God to them, but they realized that the ultimate fulfillment of God's Word was yet to come through His Son.

Christ is the full disclosure of God and serves as the one fixed point amid all the chaotic periods of history—the "time past" of Old Testament history (1:1), the difficult times that the readers of Hebrews were enduring (12:4–13), and our own times in which we struggle

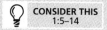

And set him over the works of Your hands.
8 You have put all things in subjection under his feet."[a]

For in that He put all in subjection under him, He left
nothing *that is* not put under him. But now we do not yet
see all things put under him. 9But we see Jesus, who was
made a little lower than the angels, for the suffering of
death crowned with glory and honor, that He, by the grace
of God, might taste death for everyone.
10For it was fitting for Him, for whom *are* all things and
by whom *are* all things, in bringing many sons to glory, to
make the captain of their salvation perfect through sufferings. 11For both He who sanctifies and those who are being
sanctified *are* all of one, for which reason He is not ashamed
to call them brethren, 12saying:

"I will declare Your name to My brethren;
In the midst of the assembly I will sing praise to You."[a]

13And again:

"I will put My trust in Him."[a]

And again:

"Here am I and the children whom God has given Me."[b]

2:8 [a]Psalm 8:4–6 *2:12* [a]Psalm 22:22 *2:13* [a]2 Samuel 22:3; Isaiah 8:17 [b]Isaiah 8:18

against spiritually hostile forces (see "Who Is the Enemy?" Eph. 6:10–13).

As we face the temptation to doubt God or forsake His ways, this letter assures us that our key resource is the incomparable Christ. He is:

- *God's communication to us (1:2).*
- *The heir of all things (1:2).*
- *The Creator of the worlds (1:3).*
- *A full reflection of God's glory (1:3).*
- *The Sustainer of all things (1:3).*
- *The One who has purged our sins (1:3).*
- *Our representative with God (1:3).*
- *Superior to the angels (1:4).*
- *The possessor of "a more excellent name" (1:4).*

The book of Hebrews invites us to get to know this incomparable Savior, our Lord and friend, Jesus! ◆

One reason we need to get to know Jesus is that He has faced the temptations we face—and conquered them! See "You Don't Understand," Matt. 4:3, and "Cocooning," Heb. 4:14–16.

The Proper Measure of All Things

CONSIDER THIS 2:6–8

"What is man?" David asked in Psalm 8:4–6. He found his answer not by looking at man in himself, but *man in relation to God.* Five hundred years later, the Greek philosopher Protagoras took a completely different approach by offering, "Man is the measure of all things." Today, our culture tends to side with Protagoras.

But the Bible shows that God is the true measure of all things. Adopting that perspective is the beginning of humility, the doorway to all the other virtues (see "The Way Up Is Down," Matt. 5:3).

Scripture constantly emphasizes the relative insignificance and transitoriness of humanity and the rest of creation in comparison to the greatness of eternal God. David asked, *What is man* in comparison to his Creator (Ps. 8:3–4)? *What is man* that he should merit God's attention and affection (Ps. 144:3–4)?

This lends perspective to so many of the idealistic, even utopian, plans to solve the problems of our world. There's nothing wrong with humans working cooperatively to solve problems. But it's a grave mistake to dismiss faith in God and rely instead on the omnipotence of a corporation, a state, or an international collective. To do so smacks of the same blind pride that brought judgment at the Tower of Babel (Gen. 11:1–9). It is cause for God to laugh (Ps. 2:1–4). If we as individuals are as fleeting as grass (Is. 40:6–7), then groups of us, no matter how large, are just as fleeting. We still need the wisdom and strength that only God can supply.

One of the benefits of seeing oneself in relation to God is that it cultivates "Humility—The Scandalous Virtue," Phil. 2:3.

14Inasmuch then as the children have partaken of flesh
and blood, He Himself likewise shared in the same, that
through death He might destroy him who had the power of
death, that is, the devil, 15and release those who through
fear of death were all their lifetime subject to bondage.
16For indeed He does not give aid to angels, but He does
give aid to the seed of Abraham. 17Therefore, in all things
He had to be made like *His* brethren, that He might be a
merciful and faithful High Priest in things *pertaining* to God,
to make propitiation for the sins of the people. 18For in that
He Himself has suffered, being tempted, He is able to aid
those who are tempted.

CHAPTER 3

Jesus Superior to Moses

3:1 see pg. 780

1Therefore, holy brethren, partakers of
the heavenly calling, consider the Apostle

CONSIDER THIS 2:7

PEOPLE AT WORK

Do you know that your job is an extension of Christ's rule over the world? Verse 7 cites Psalm 8:4–6 to support its point that Christ is Lord of the earth. But Psalm 8 also shows that God has given people authority over the world. It looks back to the Creation account (Gen. 1:26–30), where God created humanity in His image to be His coworkers in overseeing the creation. Consider what that means:

(1) You bear the very image of God. *Like Him, you are a person, which means you have dignity and value. You matter. Who you are and what you do are significant. God has created you for a reason, which gives your life ultimate meaning and purpose.*

(2) You are created to be a worker. *God is a worker, and since you are made in His image, your work expresses something of who He is and what He wants done in the world. Work (activity that advances your own well-being or that of someone else, or that manages the creation in a godly way) reflects the work that God does. That means your work has dignity and value. It matters to God.*

(3) You are God's coworker. *Genesis 1:26–30 makes it clear that God wants people to manage the world. He gives us authority to "subdue" the earth—to cultivate and develop it, bring it under our control, use it to meet our*

and High Priest of our confession, Christ Jesus, [2]who was
faithful to Him who appointed Him, as Moses also *was*
faithful in all His house. [3]For this One has been counted
worthy of more glory than Moses, inasmuch as He who
built the house has more honor than the house. [4]For every
house is built by someone, but He who built all things *is*
God. [5]And Moses indeed *was* faithful in all His house as a
servant, for a testimony of those things which would be
spoken *afterward,* [6]but Christ as a Son over His own house,
whose house we are if we hold fast the confidence and the
rejoicing of the hope firm to the end.[a]

Listen to Jesus

[7]Therefore, as the Holy Spirit says:

"Today, if you will hear His voice,
8 Do not harden your hearts as in the rebellion,
In the day of trial in the wilderness,

(Bible text continued on page 782)

3:6 [a]NU-Text omits *firm to the end.*

needs, explore its wonders, and learn to cooperate with its natural laws. He also gives us "dominion" over every plant and animal for similar purposes.

Your job can help accomplish that mandate, as you use your God-given skills and opportunities. He views your work as having not only dignity, but purpose and direction as well. He wants you to accomplish meaningful tasks as you labor with a Christlike work ethic. Ultimately, He wants you to bring Him glory as a faithful manager of the resources and responsibilities He has placed under your control. By approaching work from this perspective, you can find fulfillment and motivation as a partner with God Himself. ◆

Our work isn't exactly the same as God's work, is it? See "Creation: 'Very Good,' But Not Sacred!" Heb. 11:3.

Isn't work a part of the curse put on Adam and Eve? See Rom. 8:20–22.

Work has value in and of itself; it is something that God Himself does. See "God: The Original Worker," John 5:17.

As God's coworker, you have a responsibility to demonstrate Christlike character and conduct on the job. See "Your 'Workstyle,'" Titus 2:9–10.

IN ALL THINGS HE HAD TO BE MADE LIKE HIS BRETHREN . . .
—Hebrews 2:17

CONSIDER THIS 3:1

Who Is "Called," Anyway?

Nowadays people often speak of a "calling" to signify a career that one has made a lifelong passion, a vocation to which one feels deeply committed. In a similar way, many people use the term "calling" in connection with vocational Christian work. For instance, members of the clergy often describe their "call" to the ministry, a conviction that God has led them into that particular career to accomplish certain work for Him.

Hebrews tells us that all of us as believers partake of "the heavenly calling" (v. 1). What exactly does that mean? The Greek word translated "calling" comes from *kaleō*, meaning to call, invite, or summon. The word and its derivatives are used often in the New Testament. There is no single, definitive discussion of calling, but we can gain a fuller understanding by looking at some of the ways in which this subject is treated. For example, calling is used in connection with:

- An invitation to classes of people for salvation (Mark 2:17; 1 Cor. 1:9, 24; 2 Thess. 2:13–14).
- An invitation to individuals for salvation (Gal. 1:15–16; 2 Tim. 1:9).
- A summons to a Christlike lifestyle (Eph. 4:1; 1 Thess. 2:12).
- A designation of believers' position with God (1 Pet. 2:9; 1 John 3:1) or their identity with Christ, especially when it means suffering (1 Pet. 2:21; James 2:7).

A Summons to Faith and Obedience

It is the sense of identification with Christ and with other believers that Hebrews emphasizes when it calls us "holy brethren, partakers of the heavenly calling" (Heb. 3:1). Christ became human like us (2:14, 17) in order that we might become like Him—alive, free from sin, and holy.

One overriding theme for all of these treatments of calling is that the call of God is a summons to people to come to Him through faith in Christ and live as servants of His kingdom. Thus, salvation from sin and obedience to God are at the heart of what "calling" means in the New Testament.

A Higher Calling?

Why, then, did the idea of calling come to be connected with vocation? One reason is that Scripture records God calling individuals to particular tasks. Paul, for instance, said that he was "called" to be an apostle (Rom. 1:1; 1 Cor. 1:1). This has led some to propose the idea of a "general call" to all believers but a "special call" or "higher call" to certain believers for specific assignments, notably the "full-time" gospel ministry.

However, there is little evidence that Paul saw his calling chiefly as a "higher calling." Rather, he viewed himself in the main like any other believer, called by God to salvation and obedience. However, that calling had important implications for his vocation, because the Lord made clear from the start of Paul's walk with Christ what He wanted Paul to do: "He is a chosen vessel of Mine to bear My name before Gentiles, kings, and the children of Israel" (Acts 9:15). Henceforth, Paul regarded himself as "called to be an apostle." But the emphasis should be on the word *called* more than the word *apostle*.

Every Christian shares that same basic calling with Paul, as his opening words to the Romans demonstrate. He began the letter, as was his custom, with the greeting, "Paul, a bondservant of Jesus Christ, called to be an apostle, separated to the gospel of God" (Rom. 1:1). But the opening sentence (which is unbroken in the original Greek) goes on to say, "among whom you *also* are the called of Jesus Christ" (1:6, emphasis added). The word "also" indicates that the Roman believers' call was basically the same as Paul's. They were not all apostles, but they were all "called of Jesus Christ."

So it is for believers today. Like Paul and the rest of the New Testament Christians, we are all called with the same calling and thus stand as equals before God.

Calling and Careers

As with Paul, our calling has important implications for our jobs and careers. For one thing, it means a change of bosses: as God's children, we ultimately serve Christ (see "Who's the Boss?" Col. 3:22–24). It also means a change of conduct and character: as Christ's followers, we need to work with a Christlike "workstyle" (see Titus 2:9–10). And it means a new motivation when it comes to our paycheck: we work not only to meet our own needs, but to have money to meet the needs of others (see "From Deadbeat to Donor," Eph. 4:28, and "Christians and Money," 1 Tim. 6:6–19).

Does our calling affect our choice of career? It may, but not necessarily. It's interesting that Paul directed the Corinthians to remain in the calling in which they found themselves when they came to faith in Christ (1 Cor. 7:17–24). They did not need to change jobs just because they had become believers. Instead, they needed to be Christ's followers *wherever* they were. On the other hand, their relationship with Christ did not prevent them from changing occupational status if they could and if they wanted to.

The point is that no matter what we do for work—whether "full-time" vocational Christian work or "secular," everyday work—we are all called to serve Christ. In the end, what makes the issue of calling important is not us, but the One who calls us. ◆

Find out more about how God regards careers in the "secular" workplace. See "People at Work," Heb. 2:7.

9 Where your fathers tested Me, tried Me,
And saw My works forty years.
10 Therefore I was angry with that generation,
And said, 'They always go astray in *their* heart,
And they have not known My ways.'
11 So I swore in My wrath,
'They shall not enter My rest.' "[a]

12Beware, brethren, lest there be in any of you an evil
heart of unbelief in departing from the living God; 13but exhort one another daily, while it is called "Today," lest any of
you be hardened through the deceitfulness of sin. 14For we
have become partakers of Christ if we hold the beginning of
our confidence steadfast to the end, 15while it is said:

"Today, if you will hear His voice,
Do not harden your hearts as in the rebellion."[a]

16For who, having heard, rebelled? Indeed, *was it* not all
who came out of Egypt, *led* by Moses? 17Now with whom
was He angry forty years? *Was it* not with those who sinned,
whose corpses fell in the wilderness? 18And to whom did

3:11 [a]Psalm 95:7–11 *3:15* [a]Psalm 95:7, 8

CONSIDER THIS
4:1–13

The Sabbath

How would you explain the gospel to Jews living in the first century? How would you describe what it means to trust in Christ's work on the cross rather than working to merit it by strict observance of the Law? The writer of Hebrews found a useful comparison in the Sabbath (vv. 1–13).

When God completed His work of creation, He rested. *He stopped. It wasn't that He was tired and needed a break; He no longer needed to work because His work was finished. Creation was complete (v. 4; Gen. 2:1–2). In the same way, people don't need to work for salvation because in Christ salvation is finished. The way to God is open. We can rest from slavish adherence to the Law in an attempt to make ourselves acceptable to God. We need only trust in Christ's finished work on our behalf (Heb. 4:3; Rom. 10:4).*

The writer knew that nothing would dramatize what Christ accomplished like the Sabbath. Every seven days the Jews ceased from their work. They didn't just take a day off to catch up on chores or go to the lake, as many modern people do on Saturdays. They put an emphatic pause

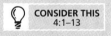

He swear that they would not enter His rest, but to those
who did not obey? 19So we see that they could not enter in
because of unbelief.

CHAPTER 4

A Promise of Rest

4:1–13

1Therefore, since a promise remains of
entering His rest, let us fear lest any of
you seem to have come short of it. 2For indeed the gospel
was preached to us as well as to them; but the word which
they heard did not profit them,[a] not being mixed with faith
in those who heard *it*. 3For we who have believed do enter
that rest, as He has said:

> "So I swore in My wrath,
> 'They shall not enter My rest,' "[a]

although the works were finished from the foundation of
the world. 4For He has spoken in a certain place of the seventh *day* in this way: "And God rested on the seventh day

4:2 [a]NU-Text and M-Text read *profit them, since they were not united by faith with those who heeded it.* *4:3* [a]Psalm 95:11

in life for an entire day. Society came to a screeching halt to remind everyone of what God had done (Ex. 20:8–11).

So when Hebrews equates rest in Christ with Sabbath rest, it draws on the heart of Jewish culture. Jesus is God's Sabbath rest when it comes to the work of salvation.

Every culture has powerful metaphors and symbols to describe its life. As you consider how to communicate Christ to people in your culture, what are some useful metaphors that you could use? How could you communicate the "old, old story" in "new, new" ways? ◆

Over the centuries Sabbath observance became so rigid that by the time of Christ it was "unlawful" even to do good on that day. See "Jesus Confronts the Legalists," Luke 6:1–11.

Do some of the activities that people engage in on Sundays bother you? Or maybe you wonder why Sundays seem like such a big deal to some Christians. See "Matters of Conscience," Rom. 14:1–23.

A PROMISE REMAINS OF ENTERING HIS REST. . . .
—Hebrews 4:1

QUOTE UNQUOTE

CONSIDER THIS 4:7 *Christ wants to start giving us life* today *(v. 7), right now, not at some distant point in the future:*

Many people spend their entire life indefinitely preparing to live.

Paul Tournier

from all His works";[a] 5and again in this *place:* "They shall
not enter My rest."[a]
6Since therefore it remains that some *must* enter it, and
those to whom it was first preached did not enter because
of disobedience, 7again He designates a
certain day, saying in David, "Today," after such a long time, as it has been said:

"Today, if you will hear His voice,
Do not harden your hearts."[a]

8For if Joshua had given them rest, then He would not afterward have spoken of another day. 9There remains therefore a rest for the people of God. 10For he who has entered
His rest has himself also ceased from his works as God *did*
from His.
11Let us therefore be diligent to enter that rest, lest anyone fall according to the same example of disobedience.
12For the word of God *is* living and powerful, and sharper than any two-edged
sword, piercing even to the division of soul and spirit, and
of joints and marrow, and is a discerner of the thoughts and

4:4 [a]Genesis 2:2 *4:5* [a]Psalm 95:11 *4:7* [a]Psalm 95:7, 8

CONSIDER THIS 4:14–16

COCOONING

One of the major developments in modern Western society is the phenomenon of "cocooning"—people pulling in, living private lifestyles in which they shut out the world and its concerns. Cocooners have interest only in what touches them, and they set up their environment so that they control what touches them.

Unfortunately, cocooning has subtly invaded the church, contributing to the "pulling in" of Christian faith. It shows up, for instance, in over-emphasis on the relationship of the individual to Christ and what He can do for each person, to the neglect of what Christ wants to do among communities of His people, including their corporate responsibilities to each other and the larger society.

The book of Hebrews speaks to the danger of cocooning as it describes Christ's work on our behalf (vv. 14–16):

(1) Christ chose to get involved. *He did not remain in His privileged position with the Father, but "passed through the heavens" (v. 14) to come to earth, becoming poor in order to make us spiritually rich. We can't imagine what that move cost Him (see "Christ Became Poor," 2 Cor. 8:8–9).*

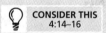

intents of the heart. [13]And there is no creature hidden from
His sight, but all things *are* naked and open to the eyes of
Him to whom we *must give* account.

Trials Are Shared by Christ

4:14–16

[14]Seeing then that we have a great High
Priest who has passed through the heav-
ens, Jesus the Son of God, let us hold fast *our* confession.
[15]For we do not have a High Priest who cannot sympathize
with our weaknesses, but was in all *points* tempted as *we
are, yet* without sin. [16]Let us therefore come boldly to the
throne of grace, that we may obtain mercy and find grace to
help in time of need.

CHAPTER 5

Jesus a Superior Priest

5:1–14
see pg. 786

[1]For every high priest taken from
among men is appointed for men in
things *pertaining* to God, that he may offer both gifts and
sacrifices for sins. [2]He can have compassion on those who
are ignorant and going astray, since he himself is also sub-

(2) Christ faced reality. *He is no stranger to real life. He never walled Himself off from what people go through every day (v. 15; see "You Don't Understand!" Matt. 4:3).*

(3) Christ empowers people. *He gives His people sufficient power to deal with life. One rationale for cocooning is the attitude, "When I'm done with work, I'm worn out. I can't be bothered with people's problems. I can hardly manage my own! If anything, I need to be a receiver of grace, not a dispenser of it." Result: the many take comfort, help, and peace from the few who give.*

But v. 16 challenges believers—individually and corporately—to "come boldly to the throne of grace." Why? In order to obtain mercy—a personal need of every individual—and "grace to help in time of need." Notice: grace to help. God's help relieves some of our cares and allows us the freedom and strength to "pass it on" by helping others. ◆

THE POWER OF GOD'S WORD

CONSIDER THIS
4:12

This publication that you are reading is based on the belief that Scripture really is the living and powerful Word of God (v. 12). As this verse shows, the Word speaks to heart matters—intentions and motives. Ultimately, people make choices and act on the basis of their underlying values and notions about what is true and right. God's Word is the authoritative standard by which all thoughts and actions are to be measured.

ject to weakness. [3]Because of this he is required as for the
people, so also for himself, to offer *sacrifices* for sins. [4]And
no man takes this honor to himself, but he who is called by
God, just as Aaron *was.*
[5]So also Christ did not glorify Himself to become High
Priest, *but it* was He who said to Him:

"You are My Son,
Today I have begotten You."[a]

[6]As *He* also *says* in another *place:*

"You *are* a priest forever
According to the order of Melchizedek";[a]

[7]who, in the days of His flesh, when He had offered up
prayers and supplications, with vehement cries and tears to
Him who was able to save Him from death, and was heard
because of His godly fear, [8]though He was a Son, *yet* He
learned obedience by the things which He suffered. [9]And
having been perfected, He became the author of eternal salvation to all who obey Him, [10]called by God as High Priest
"according to the order of Melchizedek," [11]of whom we
have much to say, and hard to explain, since you have become dull of hearing.

5:5 [a]Psalm 2:7 *5:6* [a]Psalm 110:4

CONSIDER THIS
5:1–14

Elementary Leadership Lessons

Leadership is often understood in terms of power, manipulation, assertiveness, and ambition. The literature of the work world is cluttered with "how to" books that profile the famous and successful who have fought and won by these cruel values. In the first century, the Roman Empire was dominated by very powerful and manipulative family dynasties riddled with competition, violence, greed, and dirty tricks.

But Jesus modeled a different way of leadership. Throughout the New Testament we are shown glimpses of His life and character. In them we discover a stark contrast to our world's soap opera of abuse and distortion.

Hebrews 5 is one such picture. It describes a true leader as a priest who is . . .

- *focused on people and how they connect with God (v. 1).*
- *compassionate with the weak and ignorant (v. 2).*
- *required to face sin head-on (v. 3).*

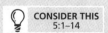

Press On to Maturity

[12]For though by this time you ought to be teachers, you
need *someone* to teach you again the first principles of the
oracles of God; and you have come to need milk and not
solid food. [13]For everyone who partakes *only* of milk *is* un-
skilled in the word of righteousness, for he is a babe. [14]But
solid food belongs to those who are of full age, *that is,* those
who by reason of use have their senses exercised to discern
both good and evil.

CHAPTER 6

Grow Beyond the Basics

6:1–20 see pg. 788

[1]Therefore, leaving the discussion of
the elementary *principles* of Christ, let us
go on to perfection, not laying again the foundation of repentance from dead works and of faith toward God, [2]of the
doctrine of baptisms, of laying on of hands, of resurrection
of the dead, and of eternal judgment. [3]And this we will[a] do
if God permits.
[4]For *it is* impossible for those who were once enlightened,
and have tasted the heavenly gift, and have become partakers of the Holy Spirit, [5]and have tasted the good word of

(Bible text continued on page 789)

6:3 [a]M-Text reads *let us do.*

- *not self-appointed, but rather called by God into his role (v. 4).*

Jesus was the perfect priest (vv. 5–10). The writer admits that this portrait is hard to grasp (vv. 11–14). However, those who seek to grow into Christlike maturity need to consider it carefully. Jesus provides for those who seek His help. All we need to do is ask (4:14–16).

Who are your heroes when it comes to leadership? Why? Do you aspire to a leadership style that lacks the character of Christ? Why not ask peers or friends what patterns they see in you? Use the evaluations of others to rewrite your agenda for growth. ◆

The families of first-century rulers were notorious for their villainy and intrigue. See "The Herods," Acts 12:1–2, and "Nero," Acts 25:12.

YOU NEED SOMEONE TO TEACH YOU AGAIN THE FIRST PRINCIPLES. . . .
—Hebrews 5:12

KNOWING *ABOUT* GOD IS NOT THE SAME AS *KNOWING* GOD

Many people have knowledge about religion, Christianity, and the Bible. But as the writer to the Hebrews warns, intellectual knowledge is not the same as vital faith. Knowing about God is not the same as having a personal relationship with Him.

This is clear from everyday relationships. Reading books on marriage is not the same as spending time with one's spouse. Knowing someone's phone number is a far cry from enjoying friendship with that person. Knowing who one's customers are is not the same as dealing with a specific customer.

In the same way, *knowing* God involves far more than knowing *about* Him. Information alone does not produce tangible faith. To be sure, right thinking is involved in faith, but faith is more than mere knowledge. For example, the recipients of Hebrews knew quite a bit about the faith, such as the the basic teachings about Christ, the need for repentance and for faith in God (6:1), and the meaning of baptism, ordination, the resurrection, and judgment (v. 2).

Nevertheless, without the constant work of cultivation (watering, weeding, fertilizing, pruning), spiritual weeds soon sprout and in time take over, producing thorns rather than good fruit or grain (vv. 7–8). In that case, the crop (faith) is worthless and destined for burning. To avoid that outcome, diligent tending and development are required (vv. 11–12). Perseverance is crucial: we must never "coast" on past experience or former tidbits of knowledge.

Hebrews 6 is a stern warning and a loving appeal for renewed commitment to Christ. Are you in need of spiritual renewal? What disciplines might help you get started on making your faith vital once again? Perhaps you might:

- Establish a small group with other believers in your workplace, industry, neighborhood, or family to meet regularly for prayer and discussion on how Christ enters into everyday situations.
- Volunteer for a program to serve the needy through your church or a community service agency.
- Speak out on workplace policies, decisions, or practices that you know to be unethical or harmful to others or the environment.
- Begin a regular habit of Bible reading and study in order to apply God's Word to your life.
- Get to know people in international missions work.
- Begin patterns of prayer such as: prayer for people with whom you live and work—even those you may not like; prayers of thanksgiving for the things God has done for you and for the responsibilities He has given to you; prayers of confession and repentance for sin or areas of neglect in your life; prayers that meditate on God and His Word; prayers that express your innermost feelings and thoughts to God.
- Keep a journal of developments and changes in your life.
- Take on a task that uses ability with which God has gifted you, especially if that ability is unused or underused elsewhere in your life.
- Consider whether you have ignored, offended, or hurt someone and need to repent of your error and apologize to that person.

The point is, faith works best when it is the central unifying factor in one's life. Christ must never be just one more thing to occasionally acknowledge;

(continued on next page)

God and the powers of the age to come, [6]if they fall away,[a]
to renew them again to repentance, since they crucify again
for themselves the Son of God, and put *Him* to an open
shame.
[7]For the earth which drinks in the rain that often comes
upon it, and bears herbs useful for those by whom it is cultivated, receives blessing from God; [8]but if it bears thorns
and briers, *it is* rejected and near to being cursed, whose
end *is* to be burned.

Great Expectations

6:9–12 [9]But, beloved, we are confident of better things concerning you, yes, things
that accompany salvation, though we speak in this manner.
[10]For God *is* not unjust to forget your work and labor of[a]
love which you have shown toward His name, *in that* you
have ministered to the saints, and do minister. [11]And we desire that each one of you show the same diligence to the full
6:12–15 assurance of hope until the end, [12]that
you do not become sluggish, but imitate
those who through faith and patience inherit the promises.
6:13 [13]For when God made a promise to
Abraham, because He could swear by no
one greater, He swore by Himself, [14]saying, "Surely blessing
I will bless you, and multiplying I will multiply you."[a]
[15]And so, after he had patiently endured, he obtained the
promise. [16]For men indeed swear by the greater, and an
oath for confirmation *is* for them an end of all dispute.
[17]Thus God, determining to show more abundantly to the
heirs of promise the immutability of His counsel, confirmed
it by an oath, [18]that by two immutable things, in which it *is*
impossible for God to lie, we might[a] have strong consolation, who have fled for refuge to lay hold of the hope set before *us*.
[19]This *hope* we have as an anchor of the soul, both sure

6:6 [a]Or *and have fallen away* *6:10* [a]NU-Text omits *labor of.* *6:14* [a]Genesis 22:17
6:18 [a]M-Text omits *might.*

Work, Labor, and Patience

A CLOSER LOOK 6:9–12 *Work, labor, and patience (vv. 10, 12)—these are marketplace terms that have important spiritual application. See "Work, Labor, and Patience," 1 Thess. 1:3.*

Promises to Abraham

A CLOSER LOOK 6:13 *God made important promises to Abraham (v. 13), who is remembered as the man who believed God—a remarkable thing in that Abraham had very little evidence that God would follow through. See "Abraham," Rom. 4:1.*

(continued from previous page)

rather, He must be the Lord of life and be brought into every area of life (see "Is Jesus Really Lord of All?" Luke 6:1–5). Hebrews 6 urges us to take our faith beyond only knowing to being and doing. ◆

Jesus made a connection between belief and practice by immediately following His Sermon on the Mount with "deeds in the valley." After warning His listeners against empty religious talk (Matt. 7:21–28), He demonstrated true spirituality by meeting needs. See "Being Like Jesus: To Be Like Jesus Means to Serve Others," Matt. 8:1—9:38.

"God Promised To . . ."

CONSIDER THIS 6:12–15 God has no problem committing Himself to people (v. 13). He has utter confidence that He can fulfill what He has promised. But His promises usually are not carried out for us immediately. God is not a vending machine dispensing treats at the press of a button. Nor should we expect to be able to call Him up and tell Him to send us what we need by overnight express. Like Abraham, we must receive His promises in faith, with great patience (vv. 12–13).

Actually, trusting in others and waiting for them to deliver is hardly foreign to us. Most of us face that every day in the workplace. We accept contracts for products and services weeks, months, or even years in advance of actual delivery.

Are you asking God to deliver on your time schedule? God wants to *grow* you rather than just *give* to you. He cultivates faith and perseverance by doing His work in our lives in His way and in His time.

and steadfast, and which enters the Presence *behind* the veil,
20where the forerunner has entered for us, *even* Jesus, having become High Priest forever according to the order of
Melchizedek.

CHAPTER 7

Melchizedek—An Illustration of Christ

7:1

1For this Melchizedek, king of Salem,
priest of the Most High God, who met
Abraham returning from the slaughter of the kings and
blessed him, 2to whom also Abraham gave a tenth part of
all, first being translated "king of righteousness," and then
also king of Salem, meaning "king of peace," 3without father, without mother, without genealogy, having neither beginning of days nor end of life, but made like the Son of
God, remains a priest continually.

4Now consider how great this man *was,* to whom even
the patriarch Abraham gave a tenth of the spoils. 5And indeed those who are of the sons of Levi, who receive the
priesthood, have a commandment to receive tithes from the
people according to the law, that is, from their brethren,
though they have come from the loins of Abraham; 6but he
whose genealogy is not derived from them received tithes
from Abraham and blessed him who had the promises.

FOR YOUR INFO 7:1

MELCHIZEDEK

One of the most mysterious figures in the Old Testament serves as an illustration for Christ. Melchizedek (v. 1) suddenly appears in the book of Genesis to bless Abraham after his defeat of Chedorlaomer, king of Elam, and his three allies (Gen. 14:18–20). Then, just as suddenly, Melchizedek disappears from the biblical record, until hundreds of years later David refers to him in Psalm 110.

Melchizedek ("king of righteousness") was a real man. Genesis reports that he was the king of Salem (Jerusalem) and a priest of God Most High. It was apparently in this priestly role that he first met Abraham returning from the rescue of his nephew Lot from Chedorlaomer. Melchizedek presented bread and wine, which was probably a demonstration of friendship and religious kinship. However, the parallel to Christ's Last Supper is unmistakable. Melchizedek also bestowed a blessing on Abraham, praising God for giving him victory in the battle.

In exchange, Abraham presented Melchizedek with a tithe (one-tenth) of the booty he had taken from the field

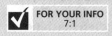

[7]Now beyond all contradiction the lesser is blessed by the
better. [8]Here mortal men receive tithes, but there he *receives*
them, of whom it is witnessed that he lives. [9]Even Levi, who
receives tithes, paid tithes through Abraham, so to speak,
[10]for he was still in the loins of his father when Melchizedek
met him.

[11]Therefore, if perfection were through the Levitical
priesthood (for under it the people received the law), what
further need *was there* that another priest should rise according to the order of Melchizedek, and not be called
according to the order of Aaron? [12]For the priesthood being
changed, of necessity there is also a change of the law. [13]For
He of whom these things are spoken belongs to another
tribe, from which no man has officiated at the altar.

Jesus Is Our High Priest

[14]For *it is* evident that our Lord arose from Judah, of
which tribe Moses spoke nothing concerning priesthood.[a]
[15]And it is yet far more evident if, in the likeness of
Melchizedek, there arises another priest [16]who has come,
not according to the law of a fleshly commandment, but according to the power of an endless life. [17]For He testifies:[a]

> "You *are* a priest forever
> According to the order of Melchizedek."[b]

7:14 [a]NU-Text reads *priests.* *7:17* [a]NU-Text reads *it is testified.* [b]Psalm 110:4

of battle. By this act, Abraham indicated that he recognized Melchizedek as a fellow-worshiper of the one true God as well as a priest who ranked higher spiritually than himself. Melchizedek's existence shows that there were people other than Abraham and his family who served the true God in ancient times.

In Psalm 110, a messianic psalm written by David, Melchizedek is seen as a type of Christ (v. 4). It's interesting that Jesus confounded His enemies by quoting from this Psalm (Matt. 22:43). They either failed to understand that Jesus was the Christ of whom David was speaking, or else they knew all too well but chose not to recognize Him as the Messiah.

The writer to the Hebrews recalls the incident between Abraham and Melchizedek and shows the parallels between Melchizedek and Christ. Both are kings of righteousness and peace. Both have a priesthood that is superior to the old Levitical order and the priesthood of Aaron (Heb. 7:1–10). ◆

IN THE LIKENESS OF MELCHIZEDEK, THERE ARISES ANOTHER PRIEST. . . .
—Hebrews 7:15

[18]For on the one hand there is an annulling of the former
commandment because of its weakness and unprofitable-

7:19–22

ness, [19]for the law made nothing perfect;
on the other hand, *there is the* bringing in
of a better hope, through which we draw near to God.
[20]And inasmuch as *He was* not *made priest* without an
oath [21](for they have become priests without an oath, but
He with an oath by Him who said to Him:

"The LORD has sworn
And will not relent,
'You *are* a priest forever[a]
According to the order of Melchizedek' "),[b]

[22]by so much more Jesus has become a surety of a better
covenant.
[23]Also there were many priests, because they were prevented by death from continuing. [24]But He, because He

7:21 [a]NU-Text ends the quotation here. [b]Psalm 110:4

FOR YOUR INFO
7:19–22

SOMETHING BETTER THAN LAW AND PRIESTS

Those who follow Christ enjoy the benefits of a "better hope" (v. 19) and a "better covenant" (v. 22) than the Mosaic Law and the sacrificial system described in the Old Testament (vv. 11–12).

The Mosaic Law:

- *Came from God.*
- *Prepared the way and pointed toward Christ (Matt. 5:17, Rom. 5:20, Gal. 3:19–25).*
- *Set the standard for holiness in every area of life, not just religious dimensions (1 John 3:4). (For example, Leviticus 17–26 and Exodus 21–23 are concentrated collections of what the entire Law teaches. They include laws regarding leaders, the army, criminal cases, property rights and crimes against property, humane treatment, personal and family rights, and social behavior.)*
- *Helped people know of their need for God because it exposed their bondage to sin (Rom. 7:7, 12, 14–25).*

The Levitical Priests:

- *Came from the tribe of Levi (Deut. 18:1).*
- *Functioned to: administer the Law to Israel (Mal. 2:6–7); represent the people before God by offering sacrifices (Lev. 4:20, 26, 31); judge matters in the land as a supreme court (Deut. 17:8–13).*
- *Preserved the Torah, copies of the Law (Deut. 31:24–26).*

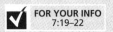

continues forever, has an unchangeable priesthood.
25Therefore He is also able to save to the uttermost those
who come to God through Him, since He always lives to
make intercession for them.
26For such a High Priest was fitting for us, *who is* holy,
harmless, undefiled, separate from sinners, and has become
higher than the heavens; 27who does not need daily, as
those high priests, to offer up sacrifices, first for His own
sins and then for the people's, for this He did once for all
when He offered up Himself. 28For the law appoints as high
priests men who have weakness, but the word of the oath,
which came after the law, *appoints* the Son who has been
perfected forever.

CHAPTER 8

A New Covenant

1Now *this is* the main point of the things we are saying:
We have such a High Priest, who is seated at the right hand

- *Cared for the temple after it was built.*
- *Foreshadowed the priesthood of Christ's followers (1 Pet. 2:9).*

The writer of Hebrews shows that Christ is superior to the Law and the Old Testament priests. He is God's provision to unite people directly with God.

Christ:

- *Offers a better hope than the Law (Heb. 7:18–20, 22).*
- *Is a permanent priest, no longer vulnerable to death (vv. 23–25).*
- *Always makes intercession for us (v. 25).*
- *Is holy, harmless, undefiled, separate from sinners, and has become higher than the heavens (v. 26).*
- *Has offered the one, final sacrifice for sins on our behalf—Himself (v. 27).*

No wonder we are called to submit to Christ and follow Him (10:19–22). He is our priest and our sacrifice, restoring us to God as beloved children. Have you declared your dependence on Christ and loyalty to Him? ◆

In what way does Jesus establish a "better covenant" than the old covenant? See "The New Covenant," 1 Cor. 11:25.

. . . HOLY, HARMLESS, UNDEFILED, SEPARATE FROM SINNERS . . . HIGHER THAN THE HEAVENS . . . .
—Hebrews 7:26

A New Contract That You'll Like

CONSIDER THIS 8:6–7 **Are you losing hope in your current situation? Do you long for a better arrangement? Perhaps you need a fresh start at work, in your family, your friendships, or your personal life. For too long you've felt trapped in old patterns.**

Hebrews addresses those kinds of circumstances. Thousands of years of Jewish history were built on God's covenant with Israel (see "Israel," Rom. 10:1). But Christ came to rewrite the script of history. He offers a superior covenant rooted in better promises and without fault (Heb. 8:6–7). As the prophet Jeremiah had foreseen, under the new arrangement wickedness will be forgiven, sins will be forgotten, and the old covenant will fade into the shadows before vanishing altogether (vv. 12–13; Jer. 31:31–34).

What an amazing message! We can have a fresh start. Bondage to old, seemingly unbreakable patterns can be broken and replaced. But first we must confess our condition and accept God's provision, which includes His agenda for change (1 John 1:8–10). Therein lies fresh start for our lives.

The same pattern of newness holds true for relationships. Owning our responsibility and admitting our faults opens the door to new ways (see Acts 19:18–20; James 5:16).

Have you learned the joy of confession, apology, and repentance? Do you need some breakthroughs among your peers, friends, or associates? Take the risk to speak the truth to them about your failings and seek a renewal in the relationship.

Many other passages of Scripture talk about the fresh start we can have in Christ, such as 2 Cor. 5:16–17; Col. 3:5–17; Titus 3:3–7; 1 Pet. 2:9–12.

of the throne of the Majesty in the heavens, 2a Minister of
the sanctuary and of the true tabernacle which the Lord
erected, and not man.
3For every high priest is appointed to offer both gifts and
sacrifices. Therefore *it is* necessary that this One also have
something to offer. 4For if He were on earth, He would not
be a priest, since there are priests who offer the gifts according to the law; 5who serve the copy and shadow of the
heavenly things, as Moses was divinely instructed when he
was about to make the tabernacle. For He said, "See *that*
you make all things according to the pattern shown you on
8:6–7 the mountain."[a] 6But now He has obtained a more excellent ministry, inas-
much as He is also Mediator of a better covenant, which
was established on better promises.

"They Shall Be My People"

7For if that first *covenant* had been faultless, then no place
would have been sought for a second. 8Because finding fault
with them, He says: "Behold, the days are coming, says the
LORD, when I will make a new covenant with the house of
Israel and with the house of Judah— 9not according to the
covenant that I made with their fathers in the day when I
took them by the hand to lead them out of the land of
Egypt; because they did not continue in My covenant, and I
disregarded them, says the LORD. 10For this *is* the covenant
that I will make with the house of Israel after those days,
says the LORD: I will put My laws in their mind and write
them on their hearts; and I will be their God, and they shall
be My people. 11None of them shall teach his neighbor, and
none his brother, saying, 'Know the LORD,' for all shall
know Me, from the least of them to the greatest of them.
12For I will be merciful to their unrighteousness, and their
sins and their lawless deeds[a] I will remember no more."[b]
13In that He says, "A new *covenant*," He has made the first
obsolete. Now what is becoming obsolete and growing old
is ready to vanish away.

CHAPTER 9

The Old Covenant

9:1–10 1Then indeed, even the first *covenant*
had ordinances of divine service and the
earthly sanctuary. 2For a tabernacle was prepared: the first
part, in which *was* the lampstand, the table, and the showbread, which is called the sanctuary; 3and behind the
second veil, the part of the tabernacle which is called the

8:5 [a]Exodus 25:40 8:12 [a]NU-Text omits *and their lawless deeds.* [b]Jeremiah 31:31–34

Holiest of All, 4which had the golden censer and the ark of
the covenant overlaid on all sides with gold, in which *were*
the golden pot that had the manna, Aaron's rod that bud-
ded, and the tablets of the covenant; 5and above it were the
cherubim of glory overshadowing the mercy seat. Of these
things we cannot now speak in detail.
6Now when these things had been thus prepared, the
priests always went into the first part of the tabernacle, performing *the services.* 7But into the second part the high
priest *went* alone once a year, not without blood, which he
offered for himself and *for* the people's sins *committed* in ignorance; 8the Holy Spirit indicating this, that the way into
the Holiest of All was not yet made manifest while the first
tabernacle was still standing. 9It *was* symbolic for the present time in which both gifts and sacrifices are offered which
cannot make him who performed the service perfect in regard to the conscience— 10*concerned* only with foods and
drinks, various washings, and fleshly ordinances imposed
until the time of reformation.

Eternal Redemption—Once for All

11But Christ came *as* High Priest of the good things to
come,[a] with the greater and more perfect tabernacle not
made with hands, that is, not of this creation. 12Not with
the blood of goats and calves, but with His own blood He
entered the Most Holy Place once for all, having obtained
eternal redemption. 13For if the blood of bulls and goats
and the ashes of a heifer, sprinkling the unclean, sanctifies
for the purifying of the flesh, 14how much more shall the
blood of Christ, who through the eternal Spirit offered
Himself without spot to God, cleanse your conscience from
dead works to serve the living God?
15And for this reason He is the Mediator
of the new covenant, by means of death, for the redemption
of the transgressions under the first covenant, that those
who are called may receive the promise of the eternal inheritance.
16For where there *is* a testament, there must also of necessity be the death of the testator. 17For a testament *is* in force
after men are dead, since it has no power at all while the
testator lives. 18Therefore not even the first *covenant* was

9:15

9:11 [a]NU-Text reads *that have come.*

An Eternal Inheritance?

A CLOSER LOOK 9:15 *Because so much of what God has in store for believers is on the other side of death, it is hard to explain. For instance, v. 15 talks about an "eternal inheritance." What is that? See "What's In It for Me?" Eph. 1:11.*

The Freedom of the New Covenant

FOR YOUR INFO 9:1–10 **Have you ever noticed how terms like "binding," "enforceable," and "limits" tend to make their way into negotiations of contracts and agreements? Words like that suggest that contracts rarely free people, but rather hedge them in with terms and commitments.**

The Bible presents two contracts, called *covenants,* between God and people: the old covenant (v. 1) described in the Old Testament ("testament" means covenant), which was based on God's law, and the new covenant described in the New Testament, which is based on God's grace.

Two Covenants Compared

THE OLD COVENANT: (Heb. 9:1–10)	THE NEW COVENANT: (Heb. 9:11–28)
Obsolete now that Christ has come (Heb. 8:13).	A better covenant brought about by Christ (Heb. 7:19; 8:6–7).
Originated at Mount Sinai (Gal. 4:24–25).	Originated from the Jerusalem above (Gal. 4:26–27).
Brought death and condemnation (2 Cor. 3:7–9).	Brings life (Eph. 2:1–13).
Impossible to obey perfectly because of human weakness and sin (Rom. 8:3).	Fulfilled perfectly by Christ (Luke 22:20; 1 Cor. 11:25).
Required annual atonement for sins (Heb. 9:7–8; 10:1–4).	Removes sin once for all and cleanses the conscience (Heb. 9:12; 10:2, 22).
Restricted access to God (Heb. 9:7–8).	Opened access to God for all (Heb. 9:15–16).

Actually, God's new covenant differs from a contract in that it is one-sided in initiative, not unlike a conqueror declaring the terms of victory.

(continued on next page)

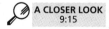

(continued from previous page)

However, God's covenant is vastly different from a victor's terms in that God's driving motivation is love, grace, and the desire to restore people into His family.

Based on His new covenant, God offers the forgiveness of sins and eternal life to all who respond and place faith in Jesus. Have you responded? Is there someone you need to tell about God's offer?

God entered into numerous covenants with people in the Old Testament. See "The New Covenant," 1 Cor. 11:25.

dedicated without blood. 19For when Moses had spoken
every precept to all the people according to the law, he took
the blood of calves and goats, with water, scarlet wool, and
hyssop, and sprinkled both the book itself and all the people, 20saying, "This *is* the blood of the covenant which God
has commanded you."[a] 21Then likewise he sprinkled with
blood both the tabernacle and all the vessels of the ministry.
22And according to the law almost all things are purified
with blood, and without shedding of blood there is no remission.

23Therefore *it was* necessary that the copies of the things
in the heavens should be purified with these, but the heavenly things themselves with better sacrifices than these.
24For Christ has not entered the holy places made with
hands, *which are* copies of the true, but into heaven itself,
now to appear in the presence of God for us; 25not that He
should offer Himself often, as the high priest enters the
Most Holy Place every year with blood of another— 26He
then would have had to suffer often since the foundation of
the world; but now, once at the end of the ages, He has appeared to put away sin by the sacrifice of Himself. 27And as
it is appointed for men to die once, but after this the judgment, 28so Christ was offered once to bear the sins of many.
To those who eagerly wait for Him He will appear a second
time, apart from sin, for salvation.

CHAPTER 10

The New Covenant Works

1For the law, having a shadow of the good things to come,
and not the very image of the things, can never with these
same sacrifices, which they offer continually year by year,
make those who approach perfect. 2For then would they
not have ceased to be offered? For the worshipers, once
purified, would have had no more consciousness of sins.
3But in those *sacrifices there is* a reminder of sins every year.
4For *it is* not possible that the blood of bulls and goats
could take away sins.

5Therefore, when He came into the world, He said:

"Sacrifice and offering You did not desire,
But a body You have prepared for Me.
6 In burnt offerings and *sacrifices* for sin
You had no pleasure.
7 Then I said, 'Behold, I have come—
In the volume of the book it is written of Me—
To do Your will, O God.' "[a]

9:20 [a]Exodus 24:8 *10:7* [a]Psalm 40:6–8

[8]Previously saying, "Sacrifice and offering, burnt offerings,
and *offerings* for sin You did not desire, nor had pleasure *in
them*" (which are offered according to the law), [9]then He
said, "Behold, I have come to do Your will, O God."[a] He
takes away the first that He may establish the second. [10]By
that will we have been sanctified through the offering of the
body of Jesus Christ once *for all.*

[11]And every priest stands ministering daily and offering
repeatedly the same sacrifices, which can never take away
sins. [12]But this Man, after He had offered one sacrifice for
sins forever, sat down at the right hand of God, [13]from that
time waiting till His enemies are made His footstool. [14]For
by one offering He has perfected forever those who are being sanctified.

[15]But the Holy Spirit also witnesses to us; for after He had said before,

[16]"This *is* the covenant that I will make with them after
those days, says the LORD: I will put My laws into their
hearts, and in their minds I will write them,"[a] [17]*then He
adds,* "Their sins and their lawless deeds I will remember no
more."[a] [18]Now where there is remission of these, *there is* no
longer an offering for sin.

Hold Onto Christ

10:19–25 see pg. 798

[19]Therefore, brethren, having boldness
to enter the Holiest by the blood of Jesus,
[20]by a new and living way which He consecrated for us,

10:19–39 see pg. 800

through the veil, that is, His flesh, [21]and
having a High Priest over the house of
God, [22]let us draw near with a true heart in full assurance of
faith, having our hearts sprinkled from an evil conscience

10:23

and our bodies washed with pure water.
[23]Let us hold fast the confession of *our*
hope without wavering, for He who promised *is* faithful.
[24]And let us consider one another in order to stir up love and
good works, [25]not forsaking the assembling of ourselves together, as *is* the manner of some, but exhorting *one another,*
and so much the more as you see the Day approaching.

Endurance Is Needed

[26]For if we sin willfully after we have received the knowledge of the truth, there no longer remains a sacrifice for

(Bible text continued on page 799)

10:9 [a]NU-Text and M-Text omit *O God.* *10:16* [a]Jeremiah 31:33 *10:17* [a]Jeremiah 31:34

"I WILL PUT MY LAWS INTO THEIR HEARTS, AND IN THEIR MINDS I WILL WRITE THEM."
—Hebrews 10:16

He Is Faithful

A CLOSER LOOK 10:23 *Do you believe that God is* faithful *(v. 23), that He can be depended on to honor His promises? See "Promises," Rom. 4:16–25.*

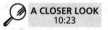

CONSIDER THIS
10:19–25

Coventry

The writer to the Hebrews draws a strong connection between prayer and the ability of believers to encourage each other toward "love and good works" (vv. 19–25). One church that has a long history of linking prayer for its people with the work they carry out is Coventry Cathedral in England.

Since 1043, when a Benedictine monastery was established there, parishioners at Coventry have applied the Lord's Prayer to their own work for God in the marketplace. In the fourteenth century, the merchant guild of St. Mary built a cathedral in the town to support the laity in their work, and the prayers continued.

Twice during World War II, German air raids demolished the town center, including Coventry Cathedral. The building lay in ruins until the mid-fifties, when work on a new cathedral was started. Finished in 1962, the new structure incorporates prayer panels that were preserved through the war. The panels, representing various industries in the town, bring together worship and work in a powerful way. They read:

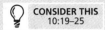

Hallowed be Thy Name in Industry:
God be in my hands and in my making.
[REFRAIN:]
Holy, Holy, Holy; Lord God of Hosts;
Heaven and earth are full of thy glory.

Hallowed be Thy Name in the Arts:
God be in my senses and in my creating.
[REFRAIN]

Hallowed be Thy Name in the Home:
God be in my heart and in my loving.
[REFRAIN]

Hallowed be Thy Name in Commerce:
God be at my desk and in my trading.
[REFRAIN]

Hallowed be Thy Name in Suffering:
God be in my pain and in my enduring.
[REFRAIN]

Hallowed be Thy Name in Government:
God be in my plans and in my deciding.
[REFRAIN]

Hallowed be Thy Name in Education:
God be in my mind and in my growing.
[REFRAIN]

Hallowed be Thy Name in Recreation:
God be in my limbs and in my leisure.
[REFRAIN]

Coventry's fame as a center of commerce and industry dates to the eleventh-century monastery. By 1400, the town had become the center of the Midlands' cloth industry, renowned for its excellent dyeing processes. It also boasted a theater. In 1545, the government chartered the first public school there. In the seventeenth century, industry shifted to watch- and clock-making for the next 200 years. By the late nineteenth century, the manufacture of bicycles and automobiles rose to prominence,

(continued on next page)

sins, [27]but a certain fearful expectation of judgment, and
fiery indignation which will devour the adversaries. [28]Any-
one who has rejected Moses' law dies without mercy on the
testimony of two or three witnesses. [29]Of how much worse
punishment, do you suppose, will he be thought worthy
who has trampled the Son of God underfoot, counted the
blood of the covenant by which he was sanctified a common thing, and insulted the Spirit of grace? [30]For we know
Him who said, "Vengeance is Mine, I will repay,"[a] says the
Lord.[b] And again, "The LORD will judge His people."[c] [31]It is
a fearful thing to fall into the hands of the living God.

[32]But recall the former days in which, after you were illuminated, you endured a great struggle with sufferings:
[33]partly while you were made a spectacle both by reproaches and tribulations, and partly while you became
companions of those who were so treated; [34]for you had
compassion on me[a] in my chains, and joyfully accepted the
plundering of your goods, knowing that you have a better
and an enduring possession for yourselves in heaven.[b]
[35]Therefore do not cast away your confidence, which has
great reward. [36]For you have need of endurance, so that after you have done the
will of God, you may receive the promise:

10:36

37 "For yet a little while,
And He[a] who is coming will come and will not tarry.
38 Now the[a] just shall live by faith;
But if *anyone* draws back,
My soul has no pleasure in him."[b]

[39]But we are not of those who draw back to perdition, but
of those who believe to the saving of the soul.

CHAPTER 11

The Hall of Faithfulness

11:1–40

11:2 see pg. 802

11:3 see pg. 800

[1]Now faith is the substance of things
hoped for, the evidence of things not
seen. [2]For by it the elders obtained a *good*
testimony.
[3]By faith we understand that the
worlds were framed by the word of God,

10:30 [a]Deuteronomy 32:35 [b]NU-Text omits *says the Lord.* [c]Deuteronomy 32:36
10:34 [a]NU-Text reads *the prisoners* instead of *me in my chains.* [b]NU-Text omits *in heaven.* *10:37* [a]*Or that which* *10:38* [a]NU-Text reads *My just one.* [b]Habakkuk 2:3, 4

Hang In There!

A CLOSER LOOK 10:36

God can be counted on to keep His promises, but can He count on us to wait until He delivers? See "God Promised To . . . ," Heb. 6:12–15.

(continued from previous page)

followed later by the rayon industry, telephone manufacturing, and electrical equipment. In 1958, England's first civic-funded theater was built there.

This vibrant economic life is certainly reflected in the prayer services at Coventry Cathedral and its support for the various guilds. Believers there have found an important way to "stir up love and good works." ◆

THE HALL OF FAITHFULNESS

CONSIDER THIS 11:1–40

Hebrews 11 takes us through a museum of Hebrew heroes—what we might call the Hall of Faithfulness, since faith is the operative value here (vv. 1–2). This is a remarkable collection of social winners and losers, all of whom are now with God because of their faith.

We look back on the lives of these "greats," but they in turn fill a stadium to watch us run the race of life (11:39—12:1). However, that race is not a solo event or one lonely individual against the world. It's more like a relay race, in which we have received a handoff from those who have preceded us. Now it's our turn to run, in full public view.

so that the things which are seen were not made of things
which are visible.
[4]By faith Abel offered to God a more excellent sacrifice
than Cain, through which he obtained witness that he was
righteous, God testifying of his gifts; and through it he being dead still speaks.
[5]By faith Enoch was taken away so that he did not see
death, "and was not found, because God had taken him";[a]
for before he was taken he had this testimony, that he
11:6
pleased God. [6]But without faith *it is* impossible to please *Him,* for he who comes
to God must believe that He is, and *that* He is a rewarder of
those who diligently seek Him.
[7]By faith Noah, being divinely warned of things not yet
seen, moved with godly fear, prepared an ark for the saving
of his household, by which he condemned the world and
became heir of the righteousness which is according to
faith.
[8]By faith Abraham obeyed when he was called to go out
to the place which he would receive as an inheritance. And
he went out, not knowing where he was going. [9]By faith he
dwelt in the land of promise as *in* a foreign country,

11:5 [a]Genesis 5:24

Creation: "Very Good," But Not Sacred!

CONSIDER THIS 11:3 **When God made the world, He declared it to be "very good" (Gen. 1:31). But is the universe itself divine? Is Mother Nature sacred? No, because God made the world and its natural systems out of nothing (Heb. 11:3). Nor is the creation self-sustaining; it depends on God for its continued existence (Col. 1:17; Heb. 1:3).**

This means that:

(1) People can work only within the framework of pre-existing physical realities. Humans are not God, and cannot call things into existence from what was nonexistent.

(2) The universe is not God. Some philosophies and religions teach

(continued on next page)

CONSIDER THIS 10:19–39

Toughening Timid Faith

For some followers of Christ, faith is not merely a private matter but a timid one as well. It's as if faith is such a delicate thing that unless one carefully protects it, the world will surely destroy it.

However, Hebrews challenges believers to a different way of living. Faith that is alive and growing need not be treated like a pet bunny rabbit that is periodically brought out of its cage to be adored and fed on special occasions, but then quickly returned to its haven of safety. To be sure, we live in a world of roaring lions (1 Pet. 5:8) and therefore must be on guard. Yet the safest way to live in a world of spiritual dangers is to build up our strength, not to hide our faith in secrecy. Hebrews offers some suggestions:

- *We can* take confidence *by freely entering into God's presence through Christ (vv. 19, 22).*
- *Our faith can* rest in full assurance *that because of Christs' work on our behalf, our sins have been forgiven (vv. 21–22).*
- *We can* keep a firm grip *on the basics of our faith, which rest on the integrity of Christ (v. 23).*

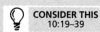

dwelling in tents with Isaac and Jacob, the heirs with him of
the same promise; 10for he waited for the city which has
foundations, whose builder and maker *is* God.

11:11 see pg. 804

11By faith Sarah herself also received
strength to conceive seed, and she bore a
child[a] when she was past the age, because she judged Him
faithful who had promised. 12Therefore from one man, and
him as good as dead, were born *as many* as the stars of the
sky in multitude—innumerable as the sand which is by the
seashore.

13These all died in faith, not having received the
promises, but having seen them afar off were assured of
them,[a] embraced *them* and confessed that they were
strangers and pilgrims on the earth. 14For those who say
such things declare plainly that they seek a homeland.
15And truly if they had called to mind that *country* from
which they had come out, they would have had opportunity to return. 16But now they desire a better, that is, a heavenly *country*. Therefore God is not ashamed to be called
their God, for He has prepared a city for them.

(Bible text continued on page 803)

11:11 [a]NU-Text omits *she bore a child.* *11:13* [a]NU-Text and M-Text omit *were assured of them.*

◆ ◆ ◆ ◆ ◆ ◆ ◆ ◆ ◆ ◆ ◆ ◆ ◆ ◆ ◆

- *As believers we can* stir each other up *to loving, active faith (v. 24).*
- *We can* meet with other believers *regularly for encouragement, accountability, worship, and prayer (v. 25).*
- *We can* leave judgment and repayment up to God, *who is the ultimate Judge of people (vv. 29–31).*
- *We can* keep a loose grip *on privilege, comfort, and possessions and instead show compassion toward those in need, such as prisoners (vv. 32–33).*
- *We can* condition ourselves for the long haul *so as to finish well (vv. 35–39).*

Spiritual strength and health means integrating our faith with every area of life. Faith is not just one more thing on a list of a hundred things, but rather the foundation of who we are. If our walk with Christ is real, it should become evident to others (James 2:14, 26; 3:13). Faith that is alive and growing is faith unleashed! ◆

(continued from previous page)

that the material universe and all it contains are a form of God, and/or that every human, animal, plant, and object contain a piece of God. But God is distinct from His creation.

(3) The earth is not sacred. Some conservationists ascribe a false value to creation by treating the earth and its flora and fauna as sacred. God wants humanity to manage the earth carefully, but not because the earth is sacred.

(4) The earth is a resource that God has given humans to manage. God has called His creation "very good" and has placed it under our rule for His glory and our benefit (Gen. 1:26–30). We are to tend it, cultivate it, conserve it, reshape it, mine it, and consume it with the certainty that each of us will give a full accounting to God for what we do with and to His world (Rom. 14:11–12; 1 Cor. 4:5).

◆ ◆

The fact that God's work was "very good" has enormous implications for work itself. See "God: The Original Worker," John 5:17.

AIMING TO PLEASE

CONSIDER THIS 11:6

Success is pleasing, and we often obtain success by pleasing others—our bosses, customers, shareholders, and so forth. But who do you most seek to please? Yourself? Other people? Or God? There is no inevitable conflict. Sometimes you can, with integrity, please all of these. But sometimes there is a dilemma because it's not always possible to please everybody. Preferences and standards may contradict each other. So when you have to make the tough decision about whom to please and therefore whom to displease, perhaps a better question is how much does pleasing God really matter to you?

FOR YOUR INFO
11:2

WHO ARE THESE PEOPLE?

Hebrews 11 is the Bible's "Hall of Faith," its review of Old Testament believers, called "the elders," who "obtained a good testimony" by exhibiting trust in God's promises (vv. 2, 39). Their faith is worth our praise and their example is worth following.

See if you can identify some of the "spiritual giants" mentioned in this chapter from the descriptions that follow (answers are given at the end of Hebrews):

EXAMPLES OF FAITH

(1) After deceiving his elderly father in order to trick his brother out of an inheritance, this man gets caught in the vicious intrigue of his wife's family. Struggling to break free and eager to build his own wealth, he resorts to lying. Later he loses most of what he has during a severe famine and dies as a refugee in a foreign land.

(2) The beautiful wife of a wealthy rancher, this woman joins her husband in a lie out of fear that his trading partner will kill him in order to marry her. Later, she resorts to using a surrogate to provide her husband with an heir. The union causes great trouble in the family and among its descendants. However, long after the time when she would be expected to conceive, she bears a son who becomes a sign of God's commitment to honoring His promises.

(3) While doing farm chores one day, this man is called by God to lead an uprising against his people's enemies. Unsure about the veracity of the message, he requests a sign from heaven, not once but twice. Later, after paring his "army" down to a small band of men, he uses stealth, surprise, and good timing to thoroughly rout the opposition.

(4) This wealthy man leaves a prosperous city for a land that he has never visited. Once there, however, his wealth multiplies beyond all expectation, and he and his nephew negotiate a major subdivision of the real estate. God gives him a new name.

(5) Raised in the family herding business, this man has jealous brothers who sell him to foreign slave traders. Eventually he winds up as a top-level manager, only to be imprisoned on false charges of sexual harassment. But a fortunate opportunity distinguishes him before the king and he ends up in a highly responsible position from which he manages large-scale grain storage and distribution.

(6) A handsome body builder with a penchant for charming women, this man is called by God to lead his people but proves unreliable because of weak character. Nevertheless, he wreaks havoc among the nation's enemies. After his foreign-born wife betrays him, he is made into an object of curiosity and scorn before a final prayer leads to a burst of God's power and vengeance on his enemies.

(7) The younger son of displaced parents, this man continues their legacy of working the land. He also takes a special interest in matters of faith and holiness. However, a disagreement with his jealous brother leads to his murder and the anguished grief of his mother.

(8) A manufacturer of dyed linen, this woman escapes the destruction of an invading army by housing two of its soldiers in stalks of flax. Later, she bears a son and through him becomes an ancestor of some of history's most important leaders.

◆

Answers to quiz at "Fathers and Prophets" (Heb. 1:1)

(1) Noah (Gen. 6–9)

(2) Daniel (Dan. 1–12)

(3) Moses (Exodus, Leviticus, Numbers, Deuteronomy)

(4) David (1 Sam. 16–31, Psalms)

(5) Solomon (2 Sam. 12, 1 Kin. 1–12, Proverbs, Ecclesiastes, Song of Solomon)

(6) Amos (Amos)

(7) Samuel (1 and 2 Samuel)

(8) Habbakuk (Habbakuk)

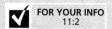

The Patriarchs

17By faith Abraham, when he was tested, offered up Isaac,
and he who had received the promises offered up his only
begotten *son,* 18of whom it was said, "In Isaac your seed
shall be called,"[a] 19concluding that God *was* able to raise
him up, even from the dead, from which he also received
him in a figurative sense.
20By faith Isaac blessed Jacob and Esau concerning things
to come.
21By faith Jacob, when he was dying, blessed each of the
sons of Joseph, and worshiped, *leaning* on the top of his
staff.
22By faith Joseph, when he was dying, made mention of
the departure of the children of Israel, and gave instructions
concerning his bones.

Moses and Israel

23By faith Moses, when he was born, was hidden three
months by his parents, because they saw *he was* a beautiful
child; and they were not afraid of the king's command.
24By faith Moses, when he became of age, refused to be
called the son of Pharaoh's daughter, 25choosing rather to
suffer affliction with the people of God than to enjoy the
passing pleasures of sin, 26esteeming the reproach of Christ
greater riches than the treasures in[a] Egypt; for he looked to
the reward.
27By faith he forsook Egypt, not fearing the wrath of the
king; for he endured as seeing Him who is invisible. 28By
faith he kept the Passover and the sprinkling of blood, lest
he who destroyed the firstborn should touch them.
29By faith they passed through the Red Sea as by dry *land,*
whereas the Egyptians, attempting *to do* so, were drowned.
30By faith the walls of Jericho fell down after they were
encircled for seven days. 31By faith the
harlot Rahab did not perish with those
who did not believe, when she had received the spies with
peace.

11:31

More People of Faith

32And what more shall I say? For the time would fail me
to tell of Gideon and Barak and Samson and Jephthah, also
of David and Samuel and the prophets: 33who through faith
subdued kingdoms, worked righteousness, obtained
promises, stopped the mouths of lions, 34quenched the violence of fire, escaped the edge of the sword, out of weakness were made strong, became valiant in battle, turned to

11:18 [a]Genesis 21:12 *11:26* [a]NU-Text and M-Text read *of.*

RAHAB

CONSIDER THIS 11:31 *Rahab the harlot was an example to the early church of a Gentile whose faith was accepted by God (v. 31). As a Canaanite woman of Jericho, she probably worshiped many gods according to elaborate pagan rituals. Yet somehow she recognized the uniqueness of the God of Israel (Josh. 2:11).*

How could she demonstrate her response to that God? One way was by her treatment of Israel's spies (2:1–24). By offering them a haven of safety, she was choosing to be at peace with their God. Through that simple but brave act, she modeled the concept of drawing near to God in faith, believing that He rewards those who seek Him (Heb. 11:6).

Her act of faith was a risky thing. Had she been caught hiding the spies, she would almost certainly have been executed. Thus her faith wasn't just a special feeling, but a conscious choice and a commitment to be for God, even if it meant standing against the entire city of Jericho.

11:35 flight the armies of the aliens. 35Women
received their dead raised to life again.
Others were tortured, not accepting deliverance, that
they might obtain a better resurrection. 36Still others had
trial of mockings and scourgings, yes, and of chains and imprisonment. 37They were stoned, they were sawn in two,
were tempted,[a] were slain with the sword. They wandered
about in sheepskins and goatskins, being destitute, afflicted,
tormented— 38of whom the world was not worthy. They
wandered in deserts and mountains, *in* dens and caves of
the earth.
39And all these, having obtained a good testimony
through faith, did not receive the promise, 40God having

11:37 [a]**NU-Text omits *were tempted.***

Women Received Their Dead Raised

A CLOSER LOOK 11:35

To be reminded of women who "received their dead raised to life again" (v. 35) was to be reminded of God's deliverance where it was least expected. Two strikingly similar Old Testament incidents were the prophet Elijah raising the son of a widow of Zarephath (1 Kin. 17:8–24) and his successor Elisha raising the son of a Shunammite woman (2 Kin. 4:8–37).

A New Testament example of the same miraculous response to faith was Jesus' raising of Lazarus, the brother of Mary and Martha. See John 11:1–45.

CONSIDER THIS 11:11

Why Believe Anyone?

Often many of us confront feelings of disappointment or frustration because people don't do what they promise. If we experience enough pain from enough broken commitments, we tend to become skeptical and unwilling to trust others. That mistrust can even spill over into our relationship with God.

Sarah (v. 11) must have often felt disappointment and confusion during the 75 years that she lived without bearing a child. God had promised her husband Abraham that his descendants would be more numerous than the dust of the earth or the stars in the sky (Gen. 13:16; 15:5). Yet month after month, Sarah remained barren. Was God telling the truth? Could He be trusted?

When Abraham was 99 and Sarah 90, the Lord again told them that they would have a child (17:1–22; 18:1–15). Both of them laughed at the idea of an aged couple conceiving a child. Abraham actually fell on the ground in laughter (17:17), while Sarah laughed to herself (18:12). Could God be serious? Could He be trusted?

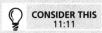

provided something better for us, that they should not be made perfect apart from us.

CHAPTER 12

Let Us Run the Race

12:1–2 see pg. 806

1Therefore we also, since we are surrounded by so great a cloud of witnesses,
let us lay aside every weight, and the sin which so easily en-
snares *us*, and let us run with endurance the race that is set
before us, 2looking unto Jesus, the author and finisher of
our faith, who for the joy that was set before Him endured
the cross, despising the shame, and has sat down at the
right hand of the throne of God.

God's Loving Discipline

12:3–13 see pg. 808

3For consider Him who endured such
hostility from sinners against Himself,
lest you become weary and discouraged in your souls. 4You
have not yet resisted to bloodshed, striving against sin.
5And you have forgotten the exhortation which speaks to
you as to sons:

"My son, do not despise the chastening of the LORD,
Nor be discouraged when you are rebuked by Him;

(Bible text continued on page 807)

However, Sarah's inclusion in Hebrews' "Hall of Faithfulness" suggests that in the end, hers was not the laugh of a skeptic but of a woman who realized that physically, what had been promised was impossible—but that the One who made the promise could and would keep it. She knew that God meant what He said, and that He was willing and able to do as He promised. Sarah's faith was not based on her lack of ability to conceive, but on her knowledge of God's power and truthfulness.

Faith is not a matter of stirring up feelings or convincing ourselves of what we know to be false. Faith involves getting to know God and learning to trust His character. Then as we consider His promises, we can take confidence, with Sarah, that He will make them come true. ◆

In Hebrews, Sarah serves as a model of faith. In 1 Peter, she serves as a model for Christian women to develop Christlike inner character. See "Sarah," 1 Pet. 3:6.

LET US RUN WITH ENDURANCE THE RACE THAT IS SET BEFORE US. . . .
—Hebrews 12:1

CONSIDER THIS
12:1–2

MYTH #8

10 MYTHS ABOUT CHRISTIANITY

MYTH: CHRISTIANITY IS OTHERWORLDLY AND IRRELEVANT TO MODERN LIFE

Many people today accept a number of myths about Christianity, with the result that they never respond to Jesus as He really is. This is one of ten articles that speak to some of those misconceptions. For a list of all ten, see 1 Tim. 1:3–4.

The writer of Hebrews encourages us to live with an eye toward the "cloud of witnesses" who watch us from heaven (v. 1) and to look to Jesus who sits at God's right hand (v. 2). Perhaps it is images such as these that cause some people to see Christianity as detached from the world. They prefer a worldview that seems more relevant to everyday life.

But the Christian worldview is very relevant. To be sure, Christians look to realities that lie beyond our natural universe. But we do so in order to gain perspective on life, to find a star by which to steer. Belief in the living God changes our outlook dramatically. We can see His hand in history. We can gain insight into His purposes for the world. As a result, we can find tremendous meaning and motivation for our lives and our day-to-day work.

Perhaps the greatest benefit of being absorbed with the person of Christ is that we no longer insulate ourselves from people for whom He cares. Human beings really matter. We take people seriously. As a result, we get involved with them for their welfare.

That means that we have a definite mandate for Christian social involvement. Wherever the tide of faith sweeps in, it brings a corresponding rise in social concern and service to the community. In England in the eighteenth and nineteenth centuries, a dedicated Christian named William Wilberforce led a lifelong struggle to abolish slavery, a fight he eventually won. Nearly all of the later social reforms of that era were brought about, not by the agnostic followers of John Stuart Mill, but by people who responded to the great Christian revivals of the day. The Great Reform Bill was passed largely through the influence of Christian parliamentarians. The Mines Act, forbidding the forced labor of women and children in the mines, and the Factories Act, limiting hours of work, were masterminded by the Earl of Shaftesbury. A believer named Dr. Barnardo founded homes for orphans. A Christian woman named Elizabeth Fry brought about prison reform. Another believer, Josephine Butler, lobbied Parliament to protect women and outlaw child prostitution.

There may be some Christians who are, as they say, "so heavenly minded that they are no earthly good." But believers who cultivate a Christlike mind and heart cannot help but get involved with the world around them. Just as Christ came into the world to do the will of His Father, so His servants go into the world to accomplish the Father's work. ◆

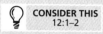

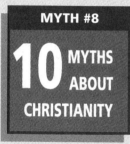

6 For whom the LORD loves He chastens,
And scourges every son whom He receives."[a]

[7]If[a] you endure chastening, God deals with you as with
sons; for what son is there whom a father does not chasten?
[8]But if you are without chastening, of which all have become partakers, then you are illegitimate and not sons.
[9]Furthermore, we have had human fathers who corrected
us, and we paid *them* respect. Shall we not much more readily be in subjection to the Father of spirits and live? [10]For
they indeed for a few days chastened *us* as seemed *best* to
them, but He for *our* profit, that *we* may be partakers of His
holiness. [11]Now no chastening seems to be joyful for the
present, but painful; nevertheless, afterward it yields the
peaceable fruit of righteousness to those who have been
trained by it.
[12]Therefore strengthen the hands which hang down, and
the feeble knees, [13]and make straight paths for your feet, so
that what is lame may not be *dislocated*, but rather be
healed.

New Life Means New Relationships

12:14–29
see pg. 810

[14]Pursue peace with all *people*, and holiness, without which no one will see the
Lord: [15]looking carefully lest anyone fall short of the grace
of God; lest any root of bitterness springing up cause trouble, and by this many become defiled; [16]lest there *be* any
fornicator or profane person like Esau, who for one morsel
of food sold his birthright. [17]For you know that afterward,
when he wanted to inherit the blessing, he was rejected, for
he found no place for repentance, though he sought it diligently with tears.
[18]For you have not come to the mountain that[a] may be
touched and that burned with fire, and to blackness and
darkness[b] and tempest, [19]and the sound of a trumpet and
the voice of words, so that those who heard *it* begged that
the word should not be spoken to them anymore. [20](For
they could not endure what was commanded: "And if so
much as a beast touches the mountain, it shall be stoned[a] or
shot with an arrow."[b] [21]And so terrifying was the sight *that*
Moses said, "I am exceedingly afraid and trembling."[a])
[22]But you have come to Mount Zion and to the city of the
living God, the heavenly Jerusalem, to an innumerable
company of angels, [23]to the general assembly and church of
the firstborn *who are* registered in heaven, to God the Judge
of all, to the spirits of just men made perfect, [24]to Jesus the

YOU HAVE COME TO MOUNT ZION AND TO THE CITY OF THE LIVING GOD. . . .
—Hebrews 12:22

12:6 [a]Proverbs 3:11, 12 *12:7* [a]NU-Text and M-Text read *It is for discipline that you endure; God. . . .* *12:18* [a]NU-Text reads *to that which.* [b]NU-Text reads *gloom.* *12:20* [a]NU-Text and M-Text omit the rest of this verse. [b]Exodus 19:12, 13 *12:21* [a]Deuteronomy 9:19

Mediator of the new covenant, and to the blood of sprinkling that speaks better things than *that of* Abel.
25See that you do not refuse Him who speaks. For if they
did not escape who refused Him who spoke on earth, much
more *shall we not escape* if we turn away from Him who
speaks from heaven, 26whose voice then shook the earth;
but now He has promised, saying, "Yet once more I shake[a]
not only the earth, but also heaven."[b] 27Now this, "Yet once
more," indicates the removal of those things that are being
shaken, as of things that are made, that the things which
cannot be shaken may remain.

12:26 [a]NU-Text reads *will shake.* [b]Haggai 2:6

FOR YOUR INFO
12:3–13

FAMILY HELPS IN THE NEW TESTAMENT LETTERS

Many of the first generation of believers were in difficult marriages and relationships when they entered the faith. Patterns from their backgrounds needed to be examined in light of their new commitment to Christ. The New Testament letters address these various family issues and talk about relationships based on Biblical values.

BIBLICAL GUIDANCE FOR FAMILIES

Texts	Issue	Summary
Rom. 9:6—11:36	Ethnic attitudes	Paul reviews some of the Jewish attitudes that had existed since the time of the patriarchs and appeals for humility and acceptance.
Rom. 14:1—15:6	Differences in spiritual maturity and convictions	Believers must practice grace and tolerance toward one another.
1 Cor. 5:1–13; 2 Cor. 2:1–11	Sexual immorality within families	Paul deals with a case of continuing incest within a believer's family.
1 Cor. 6:15–20; 1 Thess. 4:1–12	Temptation to sexual immorality	The body is God's temple; believers are to flee from sexual sins.
1 Cor. 7:1–7	Sexuality within marriage	Intimacy is crucial to the marriage relationship.
1 Cor. 7:8–20, 25–38	Singles and marriage	Paul expresses his own preference for singleness over marriage.
1 Cor. 7:39–40	Remarriage of widows	Remarriage to a believer is completely permissible.
Eph. 5:21–33; Col. 3:18–19; 1 Pet. 3:1–7	Spousal relationships	Paul and Peter challenge husbands and wives to mutual love and support.
Eph. 6:1–4; Col. 3:20–21	Child–parent relationships	The home should be characterized by obedient children and nurturing parents.
1 Tim. 3:1–13; Titus 1:5–16	Character	One of the major areas in which spiritual leaders should be evaluated is the home.
1 Tim. 5:3–16; James 1:27	Widows	Paul offers guidelines for the care of widows; James exhorts believers to meet the needs of widows and orphans.

[28]Therefore, since we are receiving a kingdom which can-
not be shaken, let us have grace, by which we may[a] serve
God acceptably with reverence and godly fear. [29]For our
God *is* a consuming fire.

CHAPTER 13

A Lifestyle of Love

13:1–6 see pg. 810

[1]Let brotherly love continue. [2]Do not
forget to entertain strangers, for by so

(Bible text continued on page 813)

12:28 [a]M-Text omits *may.*

For example, the writer to the Hebrews describes the fatherly discipline through which God develops His children (vv. 3–13). Readers can learn a great deal about parenting by examining the principles presented and following God's example.

The table opposite shows other passages that have at least some bearing on a variety of family-related issues. Believers today face the issues shown along with many others. Obviously, other biblical passages and principles could be mentioned. But by reading and discussing the texts and their implications with members of your family or with others, you can gain tremendous help from the New Testament's teaching on family matters. ◆

One of the most important things to understand about family life is that it goes through seasons in which the nature of the relationships change. In fact, building healthy family relationships is a lifelong process. See "The Family: A Call to Long-Term Work," Eph. 5:21—6:4.

. . . WE ARE RECEIVING A KINGDOM WHICH CANNOT BE SHAKEN . . . .
—Hebrews 12:28

CONSIDER THIS
12:14–29

TIME FOR A CHECKUP

A timeworn adage that makes a lot of sense in the world of business and industry is, "If it ain't broke, don't fix it!" However, that definitely does not apply when it comes to people's health. In fact, health experts report that preventive care can not only lead to better health and reduced risk from disease, but vastly reduce medical costs. People are unwise to neglect their physical condition.

This truth has its parallel in the spiritual realm, as the writer to the Hebrews shows. Twice the book warns its readers to pay attention to their spiritual condition (Heb. 6:1–20; 12:14–29). Notice the strong language used in chapter 12 to describe what can happen to us if we neglect our walk with Christ:

- *We can fall short of the grace of God (v. 15).*
- *Bitterness can take root and sprout up, causing trouble (v. 15).*
- *Many people can become defiled (v. 15).*
- *We may make a foolish or even catastrophic mistake like Esau did (vv. 16–17; Gen. 25:27–34; 27:1–45).*
- *We may refuse to listen when God speaks to us (v. 25).*
- *God's judgment may consume us (v. 29).*

CONSIDER THIS
13:1–6

LOVE NEVER FAILS

Are you ever in doubt about what you should do in a given situation? One rule of thumb that always applies is, Do unto others as you would have them do unto you (Matt. 7:12).

This "golden rule" is universally recognized. It summarizes the principle of love as an ethical cornerstone for life. In fact, Jesus taught that the greatest commandment was to love God with all of one's heart, soul, and mind, and the second greatest was to love one's neighbor as oneself (22:37–39). Likewise, James called love the "royal law" (James 2:8), and Paul wrote that of faith, hope, and love, love was the greatest; it never fails (1 Cor. 13:8, 13).

We also see this in Hebrews. Having summarized the vast changes brought about by the coming of Christ, the book's final chapter begins with a clear statement about one thing that has not changed, love. Love among believers must continue (Heb. 13:1). The writer goes on to list several ways in which that can happen:

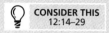

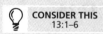

Those are dire consequences! Fortunately, the writer offers some ways to check our spirituality and make corrections where we detect trouble:

- *Are we pursuing peace with others (v. 14)? For example: how do we respond to conflicts at home, work or school?*
- *Are we pursuing holiness (v. 14)? For example: is our thought life focused on that which purifies (see Phil. 2:1–13; 4:8–9; 1 Thess. 4:1–8)?*
- *Are we listening carefully to God (v. 25)? For example: do we regularly wrestle with Scripture, allowing it to challenge us and keep us accountable?*
- *Do we live in grace, serving God in an acceptable way with reverence and respect (v. 28)? For example: are we growing in our appreciation for God and His salvation, and for other believers? Do we express that clearly and regularly? Would others describe us as "thankful" (see 1 Tim. 4:4; Col. 3:17)?*

How is your spiritual condition? Are there any symptoms to be concerned about? Any functions that seem weak or absent? What changes do you need to make to build yourself up into spiritual health and strength? ◆

◆ ◆ ◆ ◆ ◆ ◆ ◆ ◆ ◆ ◆ ◆ ◆ ◆ ◆ ◆

- *Hospitality toward strangers; in our day these might include immigrants, the homeless, and people of a different race than we are (v. 2).*
- *Remembrance of prisoners; it would be just as easy to forget them, but the principle of love says we ought to treat them as if chained with them (v. 3).*
- *Faithfulness to our marriage; this goes beyond sexual fidelity to active enrichment and development of our partner (v. 4).*
- *Contentment regarding money and possessions; this is a severe challenge in modern culture (vv. 5–6; see "Watch Out for Greed!" Luke 12:15, and "A Lifestyle of Contentment," Phil. 4:10–13).*

Christlike love is very practical. It seeks expression toward a wide variety of people. Is that love "continuing" in your life? ◆

TEMPORARY CITIES

CONSIDER THIS
13:14

Our world is increasingly urban, far more so than the first century, which boasted many impressive cities. Verse 14 provides a measure of realism and hope for Christians in the city. It says that our urban environments—and therefore our citizenship in earthly urban structures—are temporary. They are not "continuing"; they will eventually pass from the scene. Furthermore, if believers truly live for Christ in the city, we may well be driven out of the city, just as Christ was when He was dragged outside of Jerusalem and crucified (vv. 12–13). However, we also have the hope of a new Jerusalem which is to come—the everlasting city of God that will be our permanent, continuing home.

CONSIDER THIS
13:24

RESEARCHING YOUR OWN RELIGIOUS ROOTS

The book of Hebrews shows that God uses history to bring people to Himself. In the case of the Jews, God used generations of people and centuries of political events and religious symbolism to prepare the way for Christ. If you are Jewish, you have much to celebrate as you ponder God's sovereignty and grace in using your ancestors the Hebrews to bless "all the families of the earth" (Gen. 12:3; 22:18; Acts 3:25–26; Gal. 3:8).

However, God's participation in history extends far beyond the Jews. In fact, every believer is indebted to God's grace for superintending the circumstances that brought the gospel to him or her.

Have you ever traced the path between Jesus' proclamation of the gospel in the first century and your reception of it today? Do you know the religious roots of your own family and ancestors? Why not examine that heritage, either on your own or with a small group of believers? Doing so will help to personalize the gospel to your own life and experience. Here are some suggestions for getting started:

Gathering the Data

Begin by collecting as much information as you can about your genealogy. Widespread interest in genealogical studies in recent years has made this process easier. Many books, articles, libraries, data bases, organizations, seminars, and other resources exist to help you. In addition, you'll want to talk with your parents, grandparents, or other relatives who might have information about your family and its heritage. As you carry out your search, consider such questions as:

- When and where did your ancestors live?
- What was their culture like?
- What historical or political events or technological developments occurred during their times? How might those have affected people?
- What was the religious climate in which your ancestors lived? For example, what was the view of God, the nature of evil, the origins of the world, and the afterlife? Was one religion dominant, or were there many alternatives? How did religion affect people's day-to-day lives?
- When was the gospel first introduced to the society in which your ancestors lived? What was the reception? What has been the legacy since?
- Are there any notable religious figures in your ancestry or connected with people in your history?
- Overall, what has been your family's posture toward the message of Christ?
- What has been the role of religion in your family of origin? Where did its religious sentiments come from? Are there any surviving symbols of religion that might hold clues for investigation (family Bibles or other books, letters, documents, pictures, clothing, etc.)?
- When did you personally first hear the gospel?

Evaluating Your Religious Roots

As your knowledge about your ancestry grows, you can begin to piece together some idea of your religious heritage. Be careful not to jump to conclusions or make too much of sketchy details. You probably won't be able to come up with any definitive answers, but you can at least gain an appreciation for how God has worked in your past and what it took for Him to bring you to faith.

Of course, you may discover

(continued on next page)

doing some have unwittingly entertained angels. 3Remember
the prisoners as if chained with them—those who are mis-
treated—since you yourselves are in the body also.
4Marriage *is* honorable among all, and the bed undefiled;
but fornicators and adulterers God will judge.
5*Let your* conduct *be* without covetousness; *be* content
with such things as you have. For He Himself has said, "I
will never leave you nor forsake you."[a] 6So we may boldly
say:

"The LORD *is* my helper;
I will not fear.
What can man do to me?"[a]

Obey Leaders

7Remember those who rule over you, who have spoken
the word of God to you, whose faith follow, considering the
outcome of *their* conduct. 8Jesus Christ *is* the same yesterday, today, and forever. 9Do not be carried about[a] with various and strange doctrines. For *it is* good that the heart be
established by grace, not with foods which have not profited those who have been occupied with them.
10We have an altar from which those who serve the tabernacle have no right to eat. 11For the bodies of those animals,
whose blood is brought into the sanctuary by the high
priest for sin, are burned outside the camp. 12Therefore
Jesus also, that He might sanctify the people with His own
blood, suffered outside the gate. 13Therefore let us go forth
to Him, outside the camp, bearing His re-
proach. 14For here we have no continuing
city, but we seek the one to come.
15Therefore by Him let us continually of-
fer the sacrifice of praise to God, that is, the fruit of *our* lips,
giving thanks to His name. 16But do not forget to do good
and to share, for with such sacrifices God is well pleased.
17Obey those who rule over you, and be submissive, for
they watch out for your souls, as those who must give account. Let them do so with joy and not with grief, for that
would be unprofitable for you.

13:14 see pg. 811

13:15 see pg. 814

Greetings and Blessings

18Pray for us; for we are confident that we have a good
conscience, in all things desiring to live honorably. 19But I
especially urge *you* to do this, that I may be restored to you
the sooner.
20Now may the God of peace who brought up our Lord
Jesus from the dead, that great Shepherd of the sheep,

(Bible text continued on page 815)

13:5 [a]Deuteronomy 31:6, 8; Joshua 1:5 *13:6* [a]Psalm 118:6 *13:9* [a]NU-Text and M-Text read *away*.

(continued from previous page)

elements of your family's religious history that run counter to the gospel. But that, too, is important to know. You need not agree with what others believed or did in the past, but it's worth understanding the bolt of cloth from which you've been cut.

As you evaluate your data, consider such questions as:

- Is the gospel recent in your family's history, or has there been a long legacy of participation in the faith?
- If Christianity has been a part of your cultural or religious roots, what distinguishes your family's expression of Christianity from other traditions within the faith? Why? Where did that tradition come from and how and why did your family identify with it?
- What beliefs and practices among your religious roots would you disagree with or even denounce? Why?
- What has been the reception of your family to your personal faith in Christ? Why? How might the past contribute to their response?
- How might your understanding of the past affect the way in which you present the gospel to any unbelievers among your relatives?
- What is the story of how the gospel traveled from the apostles in the first century to your life today? What response can you make to God for superintending this process? ◆

QUOTE UNQUOTE

CONSIDER THIS 13:15 *Hebrews challenges us to speak up about our faith and give evidence of our relationship with God through the "fruit of our lips" (v. 15):*

A spiritual enemy in our time is privatization of personal faith. For too many so-called "committed Christians" their relationship with Jesus is like an extra-marital affair. It's a secret relationship. The love affair is real but hidden from the public eye. Some Christians become so skilled at concealing their personal faith in Christ that it takes the talent of an undercover agent to reveal their clandestine activity. The tragedy for those individuals is that undisclosed personal faith eventually produces an inner sense of psychological illegitimacy. The tragedy for the Kingdom is that God is silenced in the open forum so that people who ought to know Him do not even see Him as an option.

Donald C. Posterski, *Reinventing Evangelism*

"I HAVE WRITTEN TO YOU"

FOR YOUR INFO 13:22 **The author of Hebrews writes as if the original readers of the letter already knew who it was (v. 22). If only modern readers did! It would perhaps help us to better understand the epistle.**

Hebrews is one of only two letters in the New Testament that lacks a greeting or identification of its author (the other is 1 John). The King James Version calls the letter "The Epistle of Paul the Apostle to the Hebrews." But there is no such indication in the earliest manuscripts. And many people doubt whether Paul wrote the book. Among their reasons:

- **The language, vocabulary, and style differ from Paul's letters.**
- **Certain expressions that Paul often uses—"Christ Jesus," "in Christ," "the resurrection"—are all but absent.**
- **Hebrews approaches certain subjects, such as the law and faith, very differently from Paul's known writings.**
- **Early church sources mention other possible authors.**

Others challenge these points, however. Yet no one has conclusively demonstrated that Paul was the author. But if not, then who was? There has been no shortage of suggestions: Luke, Priscilla, Aquila, Clement of Rome, Silvanus, Philip the evangelist, Apollos, and Barnabas.

In the end, we do not know who wrote this letter. However, the anonymity of the author in no way diminishes the work's integrity, nor has it caused anyone to question its important place among the Scriptures.

through the blood of the everlasting covenant, [21]make you
complete in every good work to do His will, working in
you[a] what is well pleasing in His sight, through Jesus
Christ, to whom *be* glory forever and ever. Amen.

13:22

[22]And I appeal to you, brethren, bear
with the word of exhortation, for I have
written to you in few words. [23]Know that *our* brother Timothy has been set free, with whom I shall see you if he comes
shortly.

13:24
see pg. 812

[24]Greet all those who rule over you,
and all the saints. Those from Italy greet
you.

13:25

[25]Grace *be* with you all. Amen.

13:21 [a]NU-Text and M-Text read *us.*

FOR YOUR INFO
13:25

Answers to quiz at "Who Are These People?" (Heb. 11:2)
(1) Jacob (Heb. 11:21; Gen. 25–35, 43–50)
(2) Sarah (Heb. 11:11; Gen. 13–17, 20–22)
(3) Gideon (Heb. 11:32; Judg. 6–8)
(4) Abraham (Heb. 11:8; Gen. 11–26)
(5) Joseph (Heb. 11:22; Gen. 37–48)
(6) Samson (Heb. 11:32; Judg. 13–17)
(7) Abel (Heb. 11:4; Gen. 4)
(8) Rahab (Heb. 11:31; Josh. 2, 6)

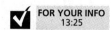

Faith and Life

You're a success. Your faith in Christ is helping you live responsibly, and now you're enjoying the fruits of that lifestyle. Your income is up. Your family life is stable. Your church is doing well. You have lots of friends. So what more do you need? What more can the gospel contribute to your life in the here and now than it already has?

To find out, read the letter of James. It was written to people who were prospering as a result of their faith, not unlike many Christians today. The gospel had brought a "social lift" to their lives, bettering their material circumstances. But what about those left behind, people still struggling to "make it"? What about trials and tribulations? Does success change the way one looks at trouble? What about sermons—is it really necessary to take them so seriously when things are going so well?

Perhaps you're finding it easy to be comfortable in the faith. But are you fruitful? James was written to help you consider whether Christ is affecting more than your income and lifestyle.

James

What more can the gospel contribute to your life?

C O N T E N T S

A R T I C L E S

Personality Profile: James

Not to be confused with: James the son of Zebedee and James the son of Alphaeus, two of the Twelve (see Matt. 10:2); James the Less, the son of Mary and brother of Joses (Mark 15:40); James the father of Judas (that is, of Thaddaeus; Matt. 10:3; Mark 3:18; Luke 6:16; Acts 1:13).

Home: Probably Nazareth.

Family: His father was probably Joseph; his mother was Mary; his older brother was Jesus; younger brothers were Joses, Judas, and Simon; he had sisters whom Scripture does not name.

Occupation: Unknown, but since his father and Jesus were carpenters, he may have been a carpenter, too.

Best known today for: Leading the church at Jerusalem and writing the book of James.

James—From Skeptic to True Believer

The James whose name appears as the author of James (1:1) was probably the oldest of Jesus' four younger brothers (Mark 6:3). Apparently he was at first skeptical about his brother's claims and ministry (Matt. 12:46–50; Mark 3:31–35; Luke 8:19–21; John 7:5). But after meeting the resurrected Lord (1 Cor. 15:7), he became a strong believer and was numbered among the apostles. He oversaw the church at Jerusalem, and helped resolve the dispute over Gentiles having to keep the Law (Acts 15:13–21).

Sermons to Successful Believers

James is a compact, hard-hitting letter about *practicing* the faith. It reads like a collection of sermons. In fact, except for a brief introduction, it bears none of the traits of an ancient letter. Each of its five chapters is packed with pointed illustrations and reminders designed to motivate the wills and hearts of relatively prosperous believers. James wanted them to grasp a truth taught by Jesus: "A tree is known by its fruit" (Matt. 12:33; compare James 1:9–11, 18; 3:12–18; 5:7–8, 17–18).

For James, religion is not about church membership, financial contributions, or even teaching in the Sunday school. The acid test of true religion is *doing the truth,* not just hearing it or speaking it. Action is the hallmark of authentic faith. In this respect, James mirrors Jesus' Sermon on the Mount. He forcefully condemns counterfeit religion that substitutes theory for practice. ◆

HUMAN RESOURCE DEVELOPMENT

CONSIDER THIS 1:2–5 **God has a three-stage "human resource development" program for believers (vv. 2–5). Stage one involves *trials*—as many as we need, as hard as they need to be. That leads to stage two, *patience*—waiting for God with trust and perseverance. The final result is stage three, *wisdom,* which is God's goal of growth for personnel in His kingdom.**

Do you want wisdom? Be careful when you ask for it! You could get a healthy dose of trials that demand patience. Eventually the process leads to wisdom—*if* you let it work.

CHAPTER 1

A Greeting to Scattered Believers

1James, a bondservant of God and of the Lord Jesus
Christ,

To the twelve tribes which are scattered abroad:

Greetings.

Trials and Temptations

1:2–5

2My brethren, count it all joy when you
fall into various trials, 3knowing that the
testing of your faith produces patience. 4But let patience
have *its* perfect work, that you may be perfect and
complete, lacking nothing. 5If any of you lacks wisdom,
let him ask of God, who gives to all liberally and without
reproach, and it will be given to him. 6But let him ask in
faith, with no doubting, for he who doubts is like a wave
of the sea driven and tossed by the wind. 7For let not
that man suppose that he will receive anything from
the Lord; 8*he is* a double-minded man, unstable in all his
ways.

1:9–11

9Let the lowly brother glory in his exaltation, 10but the rich in his humiliation,
because as a flower of the field he will pass away. 11For no
sooner has the sun risen with a burning heat than it withers
the grass; its flower falls, and its beautiful appearance
perishes. So the rich man also will fade away in his pursuits.

12Blessed *is* the man who endures temptation; for when
he has been approved, he will receive the crown of life
which the Lord has promised to those
who love Him. 13Let no one say when he
is tempted, "I am tempted by God"; for God cannot be
tempted by evil, nor does He Himself tempt anyone. 14But
each one is tempted when he is drawn away by his own desires and enticed. 15Then, when desire has conceived, it
gives birth to sin; and sin, when it is full-grown, brings
forth death.

1:13–18 see pg. 822

16Do not be deceived, my beloved brethren. 17Every good
gift and every perfect gift is from above, and comes down
from the Father of lights, with whom there is no variation
or shadow of turning. 18Of His own will He brought us
forth by the word of truth, that we might be a kind of firstfruits of His creatures.

True Faith Involves Practical Obedience

19 So then,[a] my beloved brethren, let every man be swift to
hear, slow to speak, slow to wrath; 20 for the wrath of man
does not produce the righteousness of God.
21 Therefore lay aside all filthiness and overflow of wickedness, and receive with meekness the implanted word, which
is able to save your souls.
22 But be doers of the word, and not hearers only, deceiving yourselves. 23 For if anyone is a hearer of the word and
not a doer, he is like a man observing his natural face in a
mirror; 24 for he observes himself, goes away, and immediately forgets what kind of man he was. 25 But he who looks
into the perfect law of liberty and continues *in it,* and is not
a forgetful hearer but a doer of the work, this one will be
blessed in what he does.
26 If anyone among you[a] thinks he is religious, and does
not bridle his tongue but deceives his own heart, this one's
religion *is* useless. 27 Pure and undefiled religion before God
and the Father is this: to visit orphans and widows in their
trouble, *and* to keep oneself unspotted from the world.

CHAPTER 2

True Faith Does Not Play Favorites

2:1–13 see pg. 823

1 My brethren, do not hold the faith of
our Lord Jesus Christ, *the Lord* of glory,
with partiality. 2 For if there should come into your assembly
a man with gold rings, in fine apparel, and there should
also come in a poor man in filthy clothes, 3 and you pay attention to the one wearing the fine clothes and say to him,
"You sit here in a good place," and say to the poor man,
"You stand there," or, "Sit here at my footstool," 4 have you
not shown partiality among yourselves, and become judges
with evil thoughts?

2:5–6 see pg. 823

5 Listen, my beloved brethren: Has God
not chosen the poor of this world *to be*
rich in faith and heirs of the kingdom which He promised
to those who love Him? 6 But you have dishonored the poor
man. Do not the rich oppress you and drag you into the
courts? 7 Do they not blaspheme that noble name by which
you are called?

The Royal Law

2:1–9 see pg. 822

8 If you really fulfill *the* royal law according to the Scripture, "You shall love
your neighbor as yourself,"[a] you do well; 9 but if you show

1:19 [a]NU-Text reads *Know this* or *This you know.* *1:26* [a]NU-Text omits *among you.*
2:8 [a]Leviticus 19:18

WHY THE RUSH?

CONSIDER THIS 1:9–11 **We live in a day of the "fast track," the "sound bite," and the "hurried child." But what is so attractive about the rush to achieve quick results? Is that the way life was intended to be?**

A study of James 1 shows that God wants people to *be someone* more than to *get somewhere.* Rather than measuring our worth through achievements and acquisitions, He evaluates our character, looking for such virtues as peace, truth, serenity, and strength of character. He values us for who we are and who we are becoming. He wants us to be:

- **People who can endure testing and trial (v. 4).**
- **People who trust God to provide for their needs and feel free to ask for His help (vv. 5–9).**
- **People who can discern between good and bad choices and make wise decisions (vv. 12–16).**
- **People who give generously to others, just as God has given generously to us (vv. 17–18).**
- **People who listen well and respond thoughtfully (vv. 19–21).**
- **People who act instead of just talking and whose actions benefit others (vv. 22–25).**
- **People who value and show compassion toward others who are in need, especially those forgotten by society (vv. 26–27).**

It takes time to develop character like that. But God is interested in long-term growth, not just a quick fix. We may need to slow down and take a long, hard look at the direction of our lives. If we're driven to gain as much as we can as fast as we can, we're headed down a road toward destruction.

Paul suggests some practical steps that we can take to slow down and become Christlike people. See "Quiet Living in a Hectic World," 1 Thess. 4:11.

THE ROOTS OF SIN

CONSIDER THIS 1:13–18 **Excuses for sin are many: "The devil made me do it"; "I couldn't help myself"; "It's not really my fault"; "I'm only human."**

James mentions another excuse that people give for sin: they blame God (v. 13). "If only He understood how hard it is to overcome temptation," they say. "He put me in a situation that was more than I could handle."

But the problem with that way of thinking is that sin is never rooted outside of us; it always comes from our own heart, often from our desire for what God has not given us (vv. 14–15; compare 1 Cor. 10:6).

In this sense, the roots of sin lie in covetousness or discontentment. We feel that we are worthy of more than what we have. But that means that sin is tied closely to pride—and God resists the proud (James 4:6).

But He gives grace to the humble. Therefore, the surest path to overcoming the temptation is to develop humility, which leads to contentment with the good gifts of God (1:17–18; see "Humility—The Scandalous Virtue," Phil. 2:3).

PLAYING FAVORITES

CONSIDER THIS 2:1–9 **Countless laws and legal battles have been and continue to be fought over civil rights and the effort to end discrimination. James calls on the ultimate law, the "royal law" (v. 8), to speak out against discrimination in the one place it ought least to exist—the church. He specifically condemns favoritism toward the rich and discrimination against the poor. When believers discriminate on the basis of**

(continued on next page)

partiality, you commit sin, and are convicted by the law as
transgressors. 10For whoever shall keep the whole law, and
yet stumble in one *point*, he is guilty of all. 11For He who
said, "Do not commit adultery,"[a] also said, "Do not
murder."[b] Now if you do not commit adultery, but you do
murder, you have become a transgressor of the law. 12So
speak and so do as those who will be judged by the law of
liberty. 13For judgment is without mercy
to the one who has shown no mercy.
Mercy triumphs over judgment.

2:8–13 see pg. 824

Faith without Works Is Dead

14What *does it* profit, my brethren, if someone says he has
faith but does not have works? Can faith save him? 15If a
brother or sister is naked and destitute of daily food, 16and
one of you says to them, "Depart in peace, be warmed and
filled," but you do not give them the things which are
needed for the body, what *does it* profit? 17Thus also faith by
itself, if it does not have works, is dead.

18But someone will say, "You have faith, and I have
works." Show me your faith without your[a] works, and I will
show you my faith by my[b] works. 19You believe that there is
one God. You do well. Even the demons believe—and tremble!
20But do you want to know, O foolish man, that faith
without works is dead?[a] 21Was not Abraham our father justified
by works when he offered Isaac his son on the altar?
22Do you see that faith was working together with his
works, and by works faith was made perfect? 23And the
Scripture was fulfilled which says, "Abraham believed God,
and it was accounted to him for righteousness."[a] And he
was called the friend of God. 24You see then that a man is
justified by works, and not by faith only.

2:25

25Likewise, was not Rahab the harlot
also justified by works when she received
the messengers and sent *them* out another way?

26For as the body without the spirit is dead, so faith without
works is dead also.

2:11 [a]Exodus 20:14; Deuteronomy 5:18 [b]Exodus 20:13; Deuteronomy 5:17
2:18 [a]NU-Text omits *your.* [b]NU-Text omits *my.* *2:20* [a]NU-Text reads *useless.*
2:23 [a]Genesis 15:6

Rahab

A CLOSER LOOK 2:25 *By offering the Israelite spies a safe haven in Jericho, Rahab the harlot (v. 25) demonstrated a commitment to the God of Israel. Through her simple but brave act, she was drawing near to Him, giving tangible evidence of her belief that He rewards those who seek Him. Find out more about this remarkable woman at Heb. 11:31.*

CHAPTER 3

The Test of Self-Control

1 My brethren, let not many of you become teachers,
knowing that we shall receive a stricter judgment. 2 For we
all stumble in many things. If anyone does not stumble in
word, he *is* a perfect man, able also to bridle the whole
body. 3 Indeed,[a] we put bits in horses' mouths that they may
obey us, and we turn their whole body. 4 Look also at ships:
although they are so large and are driven by fierce winds,
they are turned by a very small rudder wherever the pilot
desires. 5 Even so the tongue is a little member and boasts
great things.

See how great a forest a little fire kindles! 6 And the
tongue *is* a fire, a world of iniquity. The tongue is so set
among our members that it defiles the whole body, and sets
on fire the course of nature; and it is set on fire by hell. 7 For
every kind of beast and bird, of reptile and creature of the
sea, is tamed and has been tamed by mankind. 8 But no man
can tame the tongue. *It is* an unruly evil, full of deadly poison. 9 With it we bless our God and Father, and with it we
curse men, who have been made in the similitude of God.
10 Out of the same mouth proceed blessing and cursing. My
brethren, these things ought not to be so. 11 Does a spring
send forth fresh *water* and bitter from the same opening?
12 Can a fig tree, my brethren, bear olives, or a grapevine
bear figs? Thus no spring yields both salt water and fresh.[a]

(Bible text continued on page 825)

3:3 [a]NU-Text reads *Now if.* *3:12* [a]NU-Text reads *Neither can a salty spring produce fresh water.*

USHERS ON TRIAL

CONSIDER THIS 2:1–13 *To discriminate is to sin. Here in James 2, a congregation is on trial for discrimination, particularly the ushers. Their behavior is an example of how "faith without works" operates: without cause it excludes people on the basis of social standing rather than welcoming them into the household of God.*

Paul saw a similar case when he affirmed that, in Christ, "we are all one" (Gal. 3:28).

(continued from previous page)

socioeconomic status, they violate the core of God's law.

Yet it happens all the time, doesn't it? How about where you work, or in your church or community? Are only the wealthy considered likely candidates for church leadership? How do you respond to customers at work, visitors at church, or shoppers at a grocery store who look "down-and-out"?

On the other hand, does James' stern warning against favoring the rich and dishonoring the poor imply that we should favor the poor and dishonor the rich? Do you ever practice "reverse discrimination"? Does your church condemn wealthy people for their wealth? Do you assume that someone who has riches gained them by dishonesty or oppression, rather than by honest work and service?

James says that favoritism is as much a transgression of the law as adultery or murder (vv. 10–11). Apparently God takes economic discrimination seriously!

RICH IN . . . FAITH?

CONSIDER THIS 2:5–6 **James notes the tension between wealth and faith (vv. 5–6). None of us is exempt from the distracting and distorting effect of growing affluence. God does not condemn wealth, but He clearly warns us that we can't pursue wealth or trust in it and also pursue God and trust in His faithfulness (Matt. 6:24–34).**

Those of us who have wealth might consider several tough questions:

(1) What plans do we have for giving money away? Are we giving away more in the name of God now than we did last year or the year before?

(continued on next page)

(continued from previous page)

(2) What is our intention—to move to an even higher level of luxury, or to hold steady where we are, or even simplify our lifestyle and give away the excess?

(3) Can we name any ways in which our increased wealth has brought us closer to God?

Paul offers a discussion of wealth that modern believers do well to study carefully, given the emphasis on money in our culture. See "Christians and Money," 1 Tim. 6:6–19.

QUOTE UNQUOTE

CONSIDER THIS 3:13–18 *Do you want to be considered a wise person and a leader in the Christian community? James describes the nature of true wisdom and leadership (vv. 13–18). A modern-day writer expands on this theme:*

The purpose of Christian leadership training is not just to help ambitious men to the top, or to make little men who have done leadership courses feel bigger than they really are. Still less is it to produce fuehrers, either large or small.

It has much more to do with the making of integrated people. Ones who understand what they believe, are deeply dedicated to it, and who try unceasingly to relate their beliefs to every facet of their own lives and to the society in which they live.

Douglas Hyde, *Dedication and Leadership,* p. 157

TEN COMMANDMENTS FOR PRACTICAL LIVING

CONSIDER THIS 2:8–13 **Are the Ten Commandments that James refers to (vv. 8–11; Ex. 20:1–17) still realistic in today's culture? Absolutely. Jesus insisted that His followers honor them (see "The Morality of Christ," Matt. 5:17–48). But what might it look like to fulfill those ancient commandments in today's workplace? Here are some suggestions:**

GOD'S LAW IN PRACTICE

	Original Commandment	Modern Application
I	"You shall have no other gods before Me."	Show proper respect for authority.
II	"You shall not make for yourself a carved image."	Have a singleness of purpose.
III	"You shall not take the name of the Lord your God in vain."	Use effective communication in word and deed.
IV	"Remember the Sabbath day, to keep it holy."	Provide proper rest, recreation, and reflection.
V	"Honor your father and your mother."	Show respect for elders.
VI	"You shall not murder."	Show respect for human life, dignity, and rights.
VII	"You shall not commit adultery."	Maintain a stability of the sexes and family.
VIII	"You shall not steal."	Demonstrate the proper allocation of resources.
IX	"You shall not bear false witness."	Demonstate honesty and integrity.
X	"You shall not covet."	Maintain the right of ownership of property.

Adapted from *Ten Commandments for Practical Living,* ©1973 McNair Associates, used by permission.

True Wisdom

3:13–18

13Who *is* wise and understanding
among you? Let him show by good con-
duct *that* his works *are done* in the meekness of wisdom.
14But if you have bitter envy and self-seeking in your hearts,
do not boast and lie against the truth. 15This wisdom does
not descend from above, but *is* earthly, sensual, demonic.
16For where envy and self-seeking *exist,* confusion and
every evil thing *are* there. 17But the wisdom that is from
above is first pure, then peaceable, gentle, willing to yield,
full of mercy and good fruits, without partiality and without
hypocrisy. 18Now the fruit of righteousness is sown in peace
by those who make peace.

CHAPTER 4

Conflict, or Humility before God?

1Where do wars and fights *come* from among you? Do
they not *come* from your *desires for* pleasure that war in your
members? 2You lust and do not have. You murder and covet
and cannot obtain. You fight and war. Yet[a] you do not have
because you do not ask. 3You ask and do not receive, because you ask amiss, that you may spend *it* on your pleasures. 4Adulterers and[a] adulteresses! Do you not know that
friendship with the world is enmity with God? Whoever
therefore wants to be a friend of the world makes himself
an enemy of God. 5Or do you think that the Scripture says
in vain, "The Spirit who dwells in us yearns jealously"?
6But He gives more grace. Therefore He says:

"God resists the proud,
But gives grace to the humble."[a]

4:7 see pg. 826

7Therefore submit to God. Resist the
devil and he will flee from you. 8Draw
near to God and He will draw near to you. Cleanse *your*
hands, *you* sinners; and purify *your* hearts, *you* double-
minded. 9Lament and mourn and weep! Let your laughter
be turned to mourning and *your* joy to gloom. 10Humble
yourselves in the sight of the Lord, and He will lift you up.

Watch Out for Judgmental Attitudes

11Do not speak evil of one another, brethren. He who
speaks evil of a brother and judges his brother, speaks evil
of the law and judges the law. But if you judge the law, you

(Bible text continued on page 829)

4:2 [a]NU-Text and M-Text omit *Yet.* *4:4* [a]NU-Text omits *Adulterers and.*
4:6 [a]Proverbs 3:34

WHO'S IN CHARGE HERE?

CONSIDER THIS 4:13–16

All of us have hopes, dreams, and plans, and the Bible never discourages us from looking to the future with bright expectation. However, passages like vv. 13–16 enforce a crucial qualification. As we make our plans, whether in business, in relationships, in our personal lives, we must do so with a perspective on who is ultimately in charge—God! In other words, we need to plan with an attitude of humility.

Our tendency as humans is to seek control over our circumstances. Certainly the Bible encourages us to take responsibility for our lives (1 Thess. 4:11; 1 Pet. 2:12). But even so, we must ultimately submit to the sovereignty of God. The Old Testament prophet Isaiah likens us to clay in the hands of a potter; the divine Craftsman can do with us as He wishes (Is. 64:8; 1 Cor. 12:15–18).

As a result, we need to submit every intention to God—even our business proposals and plans. He may allow us to proceed according to our desires; or He may decide to alter our plans according to His own purposes. In either case, we need to accept what He decides to bring into our lives, without arguing and complaining (Rom. 9:20–21; Phil. 2:13–14).

The result: tremendous peace! We can feel confident that an infinitely wise, powerful, and good God ultimately controls our lives and our world. Of course, that doesn't mean that life will always go the way we want. Sometimes, from our human perspective, it will seem unfair, maybe even absurd. Nevertheless, God rules the world. Humility demands that we acknowledge and accept what He allows to happen in it.

Submitting to God involves "Humility—The Scandalous Virtue," Phil. 2:3.

FOR YOUR INFO
4:7

SUBMISSION

A popular slogan in recent years has been "peace through strength." But James might change that to "peace through humility." After all, the source of wars and fights are internal "desires for pleasure" (v. 1). Our cravings lead to friendship with the world and enmity toward God (vv. 2–4). Thus, peace in the world depends on peace with God, and that requires humility (v. 6).

The way to show humility before God is to submit to Him (v. 7). In fact, the New Testament calls believers to a lifestyle of submission, as the following table shows:

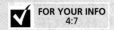

SUBMISSION BY BELIEVERS

Who Submits?	To Whom?	Text
Everyone (believers)	Governing authorities	Rom. 13:1, 5; Titus 3:1; 1 Pet. 2:13
Women	The church	1 Cor. 14:34
Corinthian believers	Paul's coworkers	1 Cor. 16:16
Believers	One another	Eph. 5:21
Wives	Their husbands	Eph. 5:22, 24; Col. 3:18; Titus 2:5; 1 Pet. 3:1, 5
The church	Christ	Eph. 5:24
Slaves	Their masters	Titus 2:9; 1 Pet. 2:18
Believers	God	Heb. 12:9; James 4:7
Young people	Those who are older	1 Pet. 5:5

Based on use of the Greek word *hupotassō* ("to place or arrange under," "to subject," "to submit")

In addition to these, the New Testament shows other relationships of submission as well:

FURTHER EXAMPLES OF SUBMISSION

Who/What Submits?	To Whom?	Text
Jesus	His parents	Luke 2:51
Demons	The 70 disciples	Luke 10:17, 20
Creation	God	Rom. 8:20
Everything	Christ	1 Cor. 15:27–28; Phil. 3:21
Christ	God the Father	1 Cor. 15:28
The world to come	Christ and His church	Heb. 2:5–8
Angels, authorities, powers	Christ	1 Pet. 3:22

Notice two instances of a lack of submission:

FAILURE TO SUBMIT

Who Did/Does Not Submit?	To Whom?	Text
The sinful mind	God and His law	Rom. 8:7
Israel	God's righteousness	Rom. 10:3

The fact that Christ submits to His Father shows that submission need not carry a sense of inferiority. In fact, it shows that submission in the ways that Scripture indicates is a Christlike behavior, and worthy of honor (Phil. 2:1–11).

It's worth mentioning that submission is only half the equation in the relationships shown above. For example, the church is called to submit to Christ, but Christ also has responsibilities toward the church: to love her, to give Himself up for her, to make her pure, to nourish and cherish her, to love her as He loves Himself (Eph. 5:25–33). ◆

Biblical humility does not involve a grovelling, abject demeanor, but rather acknowledging the reality about oneself—all of one's strengths and weaknesses, pluses and minuses, successes and failures. See "Humility—The Scandalous Virtue," Phil. 2:3.

CONSIDER THIS
5:13

LET'S CELEBRATE!

Does Christianity have to be morbid or cheerless? Should nonbelievers have all the fun? Does God disapprove of merrymaking? Is the only way to celebrate with wild wingdings and horrid hangovers?

No! Christians have ample reason to enjoy life, as James hints at when he urges us to sing songs of praise with those who are happy (v. 13). Likewise, Paul says (twice) to "rejoice in the Lord" (Phil. 3:1; 4:4). Even Jesus challenges a too-somber attitude. To be sure, He was "a Man of sorrows and acquainted with grief" (Is. 53:3). Yet His enemies called Him a "winebibber" (Matt. 11:19). He enlivened a wedding with a gift of fine wine (John 2:1–12) and attended a "great feast" with a converted tax collector and his friends (Luke 5:27–39).

We might also note that the Bible opens in celebration. God creates the world and then sets aside an entire day to commemorate what He has done (Gen. 2:1–3). In fact, He tells His people to follow that pattern weekly and annually (Ex. 20:8–11; Lev. 23:1–44). At the other end of Scripture, we find a wedding-like celebration in heaven as God removes all pain and suffering (Rev. 19:1–10). Hallelujah!

How, then, can we cultivate celebration and joy on earth, here and now? Scripture encourages us to be the joyous people of God who have hope:

Weddings

Weddings are a cause for celebration because the "one flesh" union of a man and a woman reflects God's image on earth. The Song of Solomon is an entire love poem that celebrates this theme.

Concerts and Artfests

Major events or accomplishments call for celebration in song, dance, poetry, and other arts. Scripture memorializes the victory or work of God among His people in numerous songs, such as those of Deborah (Judg. 5), Moses and Miriam (Ex. 15:1–21), Hannah (1 Sam. 2:1–10), David (Ps. 18), and Mary (Luke l:46–55). We do not have the words to the songs of Jephthah's daughter (Judg. 11:34), David's followers (1 Sam. 18:6–7), or Paul and Silas (Acts 16:25–26), but their songs of deliverance set a joyous pattern for us to follow.

Harvest Celebrations

Israel's agricultural economy revolved around harvest time, which it celebrated by honoring God in songs of joy and parading samples of produce (Ps. 126:5–6; Is. 9:3). Other festivals included the week-long feasts of unleavened bread, weeks, and tabernacles (Ex. 23:16; Lev. 23; Num. 28–29; Deut. 16:9–17). The Sabbath year festival, held every seven years (Lev. 25:1–7), and the year of jubilee celebrations, held every fiftieth year (Lev. 25:8–55), linked the nation's worship and celebration with social legislation.

Sabbath

Having finished His work, God established one day each week to remind His people that all of creation belongs to Him, that work is not endless, and that His people must depend on Him (Gen. 2:1–3; Ex. 20:8–11). Early Christians moved their weekly observance to the first day of the week to commemorate "Resurrection Day" or the "Lord's Day" (see Rev. 1:10), the day on which Jesus proved that He was "Lord of the Sabbath" (Matt. 12:1–14) by rising from the dead.

As was the Sabbath, the Lord's Day is a time for worship, celebration, rest, and renewal. Unfortunately, both in Jesus' day and our own, the joy of the day has too often been lost under layers of legalistic rules and restrictions, making it more of a burden than a delight. But Jesus declared that "the Sabbath was made for man, and not man for the Sabbath" (Mark 2:27).

(continued on next page)

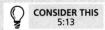

are not a doer of the law but a judge. 12There is one Law-
giver,[a] who is able to save and to destroy. Who[b] are you to
judge another?[c]

Trust God for the Future

4:13–16 see pg. 825

13Come now, you who say, "Today or
tomorrow we will[a] go to such and such a
city, spend a year there, buy and sell, and make a profit";
14whereas you do not know what *will happen* tomorrow. For
what *is* your life? It is even a vapor that appears for a little
time and then vanishes away. 15Instead you *ought* to say, "If
the Lord wills, we shall live and do this or that." 16But now
you boast in your arrogance. All such boasting is evil.
17Therefore, to him who knows to do good and does not
do *it,* to him it is sin.

CHAPTER 5

True Faith Reacts to Injustice

5:1–6

1Come now, *you* rich, weep and howl
for your miseries that are coming upon
you! 2Your riches are corrupted, and your garments are
moth-eaten. 3Your gold and silver are corroded, and their
corrosion will be a witness against you and will eat your
flesh like fire. You have heaped up treasure in the last days.
4Indeed the wages of the laborers who mowed your fields,
which you kept back by fraud, cry out; and the cries of the
reapers have reached the ears of the Lord of Sabaoth.[a] 5You
have lived on the earth in pleasure and luxury; you have
fattened your hearts as[a] in a day of slaughter. 6You have
condemned, you have murdered the just; he does not resist
you.

Patience and Perseverance

7Therefore be patient, brethren, until the coming of the
Lord. See *how* the farmer waits for the precious fruit of the
earth, waiting patiently for it until it receives the early and
latter rain. 8You also be patient. Establish your hearts, for
the coming of the Lord is at hand.
9Do not grumble against one another, brethren, lest you
be condemned.[a] Behold, the Judge is standing at the door!
10My brethren, take the prophets, who spoke in the name of
the Lord, as an example of suffering and patience. 11Indeed
we count them blessed who endure. You have heard of the
perseverance of Job and seen the end *intended by* the Lord—
that the Lord is very compassionate and merciful.

4:12 [a]NU-Text adds *and Judge.* [b]NU-Text and M-Text read *But who.* [c]NU-Text reads *a neighbor.* *4:13* [a]M-Text reads *let us.* *5:4* [a]Literally, in Hebrew, *Hosts* *5:5* [a]NU-Text omits *as.* *5:9* [a]NU-Text and M-Text read *judged.*

(continued from previous page)

Special Occasions

Scripture records a variety of occasions that called for special, spontaneous celebrations, such as escape from captivity (Ps. 126:1–3), conversion from sin (Acts 2:40–47; 16:25–34), and miraculous deliverance (Ex. 14:30—15:21). On occasions like these we need to pause to enjoy God's good gift, and to give thanks for what He has done in our lives. ◆

The Sabbath celebrated God's "rest" from His work of creation. Every seven days the Jews ceased from their work. They didn't just take a day off to catch up on chores or go to the lake, as many modern people do on Saturdays. They put an emphatic pause in life for an entire day. See "The Sabbath," Heb. 4:1–13.

GETTING YOURS

CONSIDER THIS 5:1–6

When James blasts the rich (vv. 1–6), is he condemning the possession of wealth? Is wealth inherently evil? No, but he is clearly warning those who get their wealth unjustly (v. 4) and live lavishly while ignoring their neighbors (vv. 5–6). Wealthy people of that kind are storing up judgment for themselves (v. 1).

God will call us to account for how we earn and spend our money. What will He say of you?

James' warning fits with other Scripture that discusses the use and abuse of wealth. See "Christians and Money," 1 Tim. 6:6–19.

ELIJAH

CONSIDER THIS 5:17–18 **What sort of person does it take to pray effectively? James offers Elijah as a model (vv. 17–18).**

In a way, Elijah seems an unlikely choice to be a model for ordinary people. After all, he was one of Israel's greatest prophets. He took on the evil Ahab and Jezebel, brought a punishment of drought on the land, called down fire from heaven, and was translated to heaven in a whirlwind accompanied by fiery chariots (1 Kin. 17–22, 2 Kin. 1–2). How much do we have in common with such a man? How could our prayers possibly emulate his?

Yet James insists that "Elijah was a man with a nature like ours." So apparently he did not pray because he was a great man; perhaps he became a great man because he prayed.

James shows some reasons why Elijah's prayer life was so effective:

- **He prayed; one cannot be effective in prayer unless one prays in the first place.**
- **He prayed fervently; he was aware of what he was praying, and kept praying with diligence and discipline.**
- **He prayed an "effective" prayer (v. 16); that is, he expected results.**
- **He was a righteous man (v. 16); he did not allow sin to cloud his conversation with God.**
- **He prayed specifically, first for a drought, then for rain, in accordance with God's word (for example, Deut. 28:12, 24); he prayed according to Scripture.**

Elijah was a great prophet granted extraordinary results by God. Nevertheless, there is no reason why any believer today cannot pray using the same principles as he did. Imagine what God might do in our world if Christians began praying like Elijah!

12But above all, my brethren, do not swear, either by
heaven or by earth or with any other oath. But let your
"Yes" be "Yes," and *your* "No," "No," lest you fall into judgment.[a]

The Power of Prayer

5:13 see pg. 828

13Is anyone among you suffering? Let
him pray. Is anyone cheerful? Let him
sing psalms. 14Is anyone among you sick? Let him call for
the elders of the church, and let them pray over him,
anointing him with oil in the name of the Lord. 15And the
prayer of faith will save the sick, and the Lord will raise him
up. And if he has committed sins, he will be forgiven.
16Confess *your* trespasses[a] to one another, and pray for one
another, that you may be healed. The effective, fervent

5:17–18

prayer of a righteous man avails much.
17Elijah was a man with a nature like
ours, and he prayed earnestly that it would not rain; and it
did not rain on the land for three years and six months.
18And he prayed again, and the heaven gave rain, and the
earth produced its fruit.

19Brethren, if anyone among you wanders from the truth,
and someone turns him back, 20let him know that he who
turns a sinner from the error of his way will save a soul[a]
from death and cover a multitude of sins.

5:12 [a]M-Text reads *hypocrisy.* *5:16* [a]NU-Text reads *Therefore confess your sins.*
5:20 [a]NU-Text reads *his soul.*

1 and 2 Peter

For Christians in the crucible.

Are you feeling beat up by life these days? Perhaps you've lost a job, or your family is in turmoil, or your health is poor. Perhaps a friend has turned against you, or an investment has gone bad, or the system has let you down. Whatever the circumstances, if life has become such a struggle that your faith itself feels under siege, then pay attention to 1 and 2 Peter! They were written for Christians in the crucible.

First Peter offers unique hope to people "grieved by various trials" (1:6), a hope rooted in the power of Jesus' triumph over death (1:3, 21) and the certainty of His return (1:13). What practical difference does that hope make? It dramatically affects one's behavior. Instead of caving in under the stress and pressure of adversity, the person of hope responds with Christlike dignity and moral integrity.

Second Peter shifts the emphasis from a hope by which we can live to a hope on which we can count. We can rely on God to provide us with "all things that pertain to life and godliness" (1:3). We can trust the Scriptures to guide us in the way of truth (1:16–21) and help us avoid error (2:1—3:7). We can also count on Jesus to return just as He said He would (3:8–18).

One of the great comforts of these letters is that we are not alone when we encounter disappointment, pain, or persecution. Jesus suffered the same kind of "fiery trial" and stands with us in our troubles. Best of all, He gave us an example of how to face the fires of adversity. Now 1 and 2 Peter invite us to "follow His steps" (1 Pet. 2:21).

C O N T E N T S

A R T I C L E S

Christians Against the System

In our culture, Christians enjoy privileges and freedoms that first-century believers could have only imagined. To be sure, Christians today may disapprove of many things that our increasingly secular society permits or encourages, and here and there we find believers discriminated against for their faith. Nevertheless, the system remains open to us. In fact, believers occupy positions of influence at all levels of society.

Things were far different for followers of Christ in the first century. As the gospel spread throughout the Roman Empire, it ran into hostility at the local level and eventually from Rome itself. Christians were harassed, threatened, arrested, jailed, beaten, and even killed for their unwavering commitment to Christ. During Domitian's reign as emperor (A.D. 81–96), official persecution intensified, turning many believers into migrants and driving some in Rome to live underground in the catacombs.

First Peter speaks to believers enduring "fiery trials" (4:12), people who had been rejected by the system. Likewise 2 Peter speaks to Christians whose faith may have been wavering as they endured long years of struggle, waiting for the return of the Lord and a deliverance from their oppressors.

The letters highlight a number of themes for Christians living under these conditions:

(1) The need for clarity as to position. The early Christians were enemies of Rome because the system defined them as enemies, not the other way around. The writer urged believers to submit to authorities, to persevere in the face of injustice, and to love their enemies rather than retaliate (1 Pet. 2:13–20; 3:13–17; 4:12–16).

(2) The need to affirm identity and worth. Some in the first century regarded Christians as evildoers (1 Pet. 2:12; 3:16; 4:4). By contrast, Peter gave the believers names and titles that affirmed their value to God—a chosen generation, a royal priesthood, a holy nation, God's own special people (2:9).

(3) The value of community. People under trial need each other. That's why Peter urged suffering saints to hold onto each other, to take care of each other, and to identify with other believers who are facing tough times (3:8–9).

(4) The crucial importance of character. When squeezed by opposition to their beliefs and morality, many people find it easy to compromise their ethical standards. Peter challenged his readers not to use persecution as an excuse to fail to grow in grace, but to stand firm in their faith and let suffering establish Christlike virtues within them (1:13–16; 2:1–2, 11–12; 2 Pet. 1:5–9; 3:17–18).

(5) The centrality of sound doctrine. Second Peter in particular warns against false teaching (2:1–22; 3:17–18). The author recognized that people under pressure tend to be vulnerable to powerful opportunists who capitalize on suffering to advance their own false ideas. When that happens, the enemy is no longer outside the community of faith, but within it. The result is inevitably a compromise of the truth and accommodation to evil. God deals very harshly with such false teachers (2:4–10).

(6) The importance of perseverance. Sometimes the only thing one can do under persecution is to endure. Peter's letters show believers how to do that, how to cope when they have no control over their circumstances or the outcome of their trials. Coping may be their only alternative to caving in—coping to the glory of God by never losing hope, never trading away their dignity, never letting their spirit give in. Keep on keeping on! That's the message of these books. ◆

QUOTE UNQUOTE

CONSIDER THIS 1:1 *The "pilgrims" who were dispersed abroad (v. 1) were probably ordinary believers from Jerusalem who had a powerful impact on the cultures where they located:*

The pagan Celsus admitted in the second century that it was the "wool workers, cobblers, laundry workers, and the most illiterate and bucolic yokels" who carried the gospel forth, even more than the bishops, the apologists, and the theologians.

Paul Stevens, *Liberating the Laity,* p. 22

CHAPTER 1

Greetings to Pilgrim Believers

1:1

1Peter, an apostle of Jesus Christ,
To the pilgrims of the Dispersion in
Pontus, Galatia, Cappadocia, Asia, and Bithynia, 2elect according to the foreknowledge of God the Father, in sanctification of the Spirit, for obedience and sprinkling of the
blood of Jesus Christ:

Grace to you and peace be multiplied.

Put Your Hope in Christ

3Blessed *be* the God and Father of our Lord Jesus Christ,
who according to His abundant mercy has begotten us
again to a living hope through the resurrection of Jesus
Christ from the dead, 4to an inheritance incorruptible and
undefiled and that does not fade away, reserved in heaven
for you, 5who are kept by the power of God through faith
for salvation ready to be revealed in the last time.
6In this you greatly rejoice, though now for a little while,
if need be, you have been grieved by various trials, 7that the
genuineness of your faith, *being* much more precious than
gold that perishes, though it is tested by fire, may be found
to praise, honor, and glory at the revelation of Jesus Christ,
8whom having not seen[a] you love. Though now you do not
see *Him,* yet believing, you rejoice with joy inexpressible
and full of glory, 9receiving the end of your faith—the salvation of *your* souls.
10Of this salvation the prophets have inquired and
searched carefully, who prophesied of the grace *that would
come* to you, 11searching what, or what manner of time, the
Spirit of Christ who was in them was indicating when He
testified beforehand the sufferings of Christ and the glories
that would follow. 12To them it was revealed that, not to
themselves, but to us[a] they were ministering the things
which now have been reported to you through those who
have preached the gospel to you by the Holy Spirit sent
from heaven—things which angels desire to look into.

An Encouragement to Holiness and Love

13Therefore gird up the loins of your mind, be sober, and
rest *your* hope fully upon the grace that is to be brought to
you at the revelation of Jesus Christ; 14as obedient children,
not conforming yourselves to the former lusts, *as* in your ignorance; 15but as He who called you *is* holy, you also be

1:8 [a]M-Text reads *known.* *1:12* [a]NU-Text and M-Text read *you.*

holy in all *your* conduct, [16]because it is written, "Be holy, for
I am holy."[a]

[17]And if you call on the Father, who without partiality
judges according to each one's work, conduct yourselves
throughout the time of your stay *here* in fear; [18]knowing
that you were not redeemed with corruptible things, *like* silver or gold, from your aimless conduct *received* by tradition
from your fathers, [19]but with the precious blood of Christ,
as of a lamb without blemish and without spot. [20]He indeed
was foreordained before the foundation of the world, but
was manifest in these last times for you [21]who through Him
believe in God, who raised Him from the dead and gave
Him glory, so that your faith and hope are in God.

[22]Since you have purified your souls in obeying the truth
through the Spirit[a] in sincere love of the brethren, love one
another fervently with a pure heart, [23]having been born
again, not of corruptible seed but incorruptible, through the
word of God which lives and abides forever,[a] [24]because

"All flesh *is* as grass,
And all the glory of man[a] as the flower of the grass.
The grass withers,
And its flower falls away,
25 But the word of the LORD endures forever."[a]

Now this is the word which by the gospel was preached to
you.

CHAPTER 2

The Way to Spiritual Growth

[1]Therefore, laying aside all malice, all deceit, hypocrisy,
envy, and all evil speaking, [2]as newborn babes, desire the
pure milk of the word, that you may grow thereby,[a] [3]if indeed you have tasted that the Lord *is* gracious.

God's New People

[4]Coming to Him *as to* a living stone, rejected indeed by
men, but chosen by God *and* precious, [5]you also, as living
stones, are being built up a spiritual house, a holy priesthood, to offer up spiritual sacrifices acceptable to God
through Jesus Christ. [6]Therefore it is also contained in the
Scripture,

"Behold, I lay in Zion
A chief cornerstone, elect, precious,

1:16 [a]Leviticus 11:44, 45; 19:2; 20:7 *1:22* [a]NU-Text omits *through the Spirit.* *1:23* [a]NU-Text omits *forever.* *1:24* [a]NU-Text reads *all its glory.* *1:25* [a]Isaiah 40:6–8 *2:2* [a]NU-Text adds *up to salvation.*

QUOTE UNQUOTE

CONSIDER THIS 2:9 *Peter's reference to "a royal priesthood" (v. 9) supports a Christian teaching known as the priesthood of believers:*

Most Protestants pay lip service to the Reformation doctrine of the priesthood of every believer, but they do not thereby mean to say that every Christian is a minister. Many hasten to add that all they mean by the familiar doctrine is that nobody needs to confess to a priest, since each can confess directly to God. The notion that this doctrine erases the distinction between laymen and minister is seldom presented seriously, and would, to some, be shocking, but it does not take much study of the New Testament to realize that the early Christians actually operated on this revolutionary basis.

Elton Trueblood, *Your Other Vocation,* p. 30

God's Family Album

CONSIDER THIS 2:9–10 **The names that Peter calls believers (vv. 9–10) are important because they reveal our identity. We know *who* we are because we know *whose* we are: we belong to God. We have received His call, mercy, and claim on our lives. As a result, we can commit ourselves to others and work with them to achieve common goals.**

Peter draws on the Exodus account for his language here: "I brought you [out of Egypt] to Myself . . . You shall be to Me a kingdom of priests" (Ex. 19:4–6). God first identified with and redeemed the people of Israel, then He made covenant agreements with them (see "Israel," Rom. 10:1, and "The New Covenant," 1 Cor. 11:25). Likewise for us, first God's grace secures our identity, then our commitment to His service.

Our modern culture tears at that sense of identity and security. If we want to effect change and serve others, we need to know *whose* we are and why. Do you? Can you find yourself in God's family portrait framed in this passage?

And he who believes on Him will by no means be put
to shame."[a]

7Therefore, to you who believe, *He is* precious; but to
those who are disobedient,[a]

"The stone which the builders rejected
Has become the chief cornerstone,"[b]

8and

"A stone of stumbling
And a rock of offense."[a]

They stumble, being disobedient to the word, to which
they also were appointed.

2:9 see pg. 835
9But you *are* a chosen generation, a
royal priesthood, a holy nation, His own
special people, that you may proclaim the praises of Him
who called you out of darkness into His marvelous light;
2:9–10
10who once *were* not a people but *are*
now the people of God, who had not obtained mercy but now have obtained mercy.

Living in the Community

11Beloved, I beg *you* as sojourners and pilgrims, abstain
from fleshly lusts which war against the soul, 12having your
conduct honorable among the Gentiles, that when they
speak against you as evildoers, they may, by *your* good
works which they observe, glorify God in the day of visitation.
13Therefore submit yourselves to every ordinance of man
for the Lord's sake, whether to the king as supreme, 14or to
governors, as to those who are sent by him for the punishment of evildoers and *for the* praise of those who do good.
15For this is the will of God, that by doing good you may
put to silence the ignorance of foolish men— 16as free, yet
not using liberty as a cloak for vice, but as bondservants of
God. 17Honor all *people.* Love the brotherhood. Fear God.
Honor the king.

The Challenge of Work Relationships

2:18–21
18Servants, *be* submissive to *your* masters with all fear, not only to the good
and gentle, but also to the harsh. 19For this *is* commendable, if because of conscience toward God one endures
grief, suffering wrongfully. 20For what credit *is it* if, when
you are beaten for your faults, you take it patiently? But

2:6 [a]Isaiah 28:16 *2:7* [a]NU-Text reads *to those who disbelieve.* [b]Psalm 118:22
2:8 [a]Isaiah 8:14

when you do good and suffer, if you take it patiently, this *is*
commendable before God. 21For to this you were called, because Christ also suffered for us,[a] leaving us[b] an example,
that you should follow His steps:

22 " Who committed no sin,
Nor was deceit found in His mouth";[a]

23who, when He was reviled, did not revile in return; when
He suffered, He did not threaten, but committed *Himself* to
Him who judges righteously; 24who Himself bore our sins
in His own body on the tree, that we, having died to sins,
might live for righteousness—by whose stripes you were
healed. 25For you were like sheep going astray, but have
now returned to the Shepherd and Overseer[a] of your souls.

CHAPTER 3

Christlike Families

1Wives, likewise, *be* submissive to your own husbands,
that even if some do not obey the word, they, without a
word, may be won by the conduct of their wives, 2when
they observe your chaste conduct *accompanied* by fear. 3Do
not let your adornment be *merely* outward—arranging the
hair, wearing gold, or putting on *fine* apparel— 4rather *let it*
be the hidden person of the heart, with the incorruptible
beauty of a gentle and quiet spirit, which is very precious in
the sight of God. 5For in this manner, in former times, the
holy women who trusted in God also adorned themselves,
being submissive to their own husbands,
6as Sarah obeyed Abraham, calling him
lord, whose daughters you are if you do good and are not
afraid with any terror.

3:6 see pg. 838

7Husbands, likewise, dwell with *them* with understanding, giving honor to the wife, as to the weaker vessel, and as
being heirs together of the grace of life, that your prayers
may not be hindered.

Relating to Other Believers

8Finally, all *of you be* of one mind, having compassion for
one another; love as brothers, *be* tenderhearted, *be* courte-
ous;[a] 9not returning evil for evil or reviling for reviling, but
on the contrary blessing, knowing that you were called to
this, that you may inherit a blessing. 10For

"He who would love life
And see good days,

2:21 [a]NU-Text reads *you.* [b]NU-Text and M-Text read *you.* *2:22* [a]Isaiah 53:9
2:25 [a]Greek *Episkopos* *3:8* [a]NU-Text reads *humble.*

It's Not Fair!

CONSIDER THIS 2:18–21 **Are you suffering at the hands of an unjust superior? Are you paid unfairly, or have you been cheated out of a raise? Have you been loaded down with more than your fair share of work? How should Christians react to injustices in the workplace?**

Healthy confrontation may be called for. There's a time to claim one's own rights or stand up for the rights of others. Scripture provides many examples and guidelines. For instance, Jesus gave instructions on how to deal with a believer in sin (Matt. 18:15–17), and Paul appealed to Caesar when he realized that justice was being withheld from him (Acts 25:8–12).

On the other hand, there is also a time to quietly suffer injustice as a matter of testimony, as Peter indicates (1 Pet. 2:18–21). Jesus told His followers the same thing (Matt. 5:38–42), and Paul discouraged lawsuits among believers for the sake of their testimony (1 Cor. 6:7).

Either way, Christians should never just ignore injustice. We may decide to quit if our employer is grossly unjust. But we should do so not out of cowardice or an unwillingness to endure hardship, but to honor Christ or else to find a constructive, godly alternative elsewhere.

Working for a difficult boss is one of the most important situations where a believer needs to work with a Christlike "workstyle." See Titus 2:9–10.

Faced with injustice, it might seem easier for believers to withdraw from the world. But engagement, not isolation, is Christ's desire for us. See "Called into the World," John 17:18.

Sarah . . . and Her Daughters

Sarah was no doubt well known to the Jewish believers to whom Peter was writing. Just as Jewish men valued their connection with Abraham (compare Matt. 3:9; John 8:39; Acts 13:26), so women regarded themselves as daughters of Sarah. Peter affirmed that desire by describing what it would mean for Christian women facing severe persecution: doing good and not giving in to fear (1 Pet. 3:5–6).

The book of Genesis does not record Sarah calling her husband lord, but the term was commonly used by members of a clan to show esteem to the head of the clan. By using such a title of respect, Sarah was honoring Abraham and demonstrating her submission to God by following her husband's leadership (vv. 1, 5).

Sarah exerted some leadership of her own by arranging for her servant Hagar to bear Abraham a son (Gen. 16:2–4; see "Hagar," Gal. 4:24–25), and later by urging him to send Hagar and her son Ishmael away (21:10–14). It's interesting that God instructed Abraham to listen to (obey) Sarah, even though Abraham was displeased with her plan.

In holding up Sarah as a model, Peter emphasized her good works and courageous faith (compare Heb. 11:11). She followed Abraham into some risky situations where courage and righteous living were required (Gen. 12:15; 20:2). In a similar way, Peter's readers were undergoing "fiery trials" as a result of their faith in Christ (1 Pet. 4:12). The key to their survival was not to capitulate to cultural standards of worth, but to develop a Christlike inner character, which is both beautiful and enduring (3:3–4).

Let him refrain his tongue from evil,
And his lips from speaking deceit.
11 Let him turn away from evil and do good;
Let him seek peace and pursue it.
12 For the eyes of the LORD *are* on the righteous,
And His ears *are open* to their prayers;
But the face of the LORD *is* against those who do evil."[a]

If You Should Suffer

13And who *is* he who will harm you if you become followers of what is good? 14But even if you should suffer for
righteousness' sake, *you are* blessed. "And do not be afraid
3:15–17 of their threats, nor be troubled."[a] 15But
sanctify the Lord God[a] in your hearts,
and always *be* ready to *give* a defense to everyone who asks
you a reason for the hope that is in you, with meekness and
fear; 16having a good conscience, that when they defame
you as evildoers, those who revile your good conduct in
Christ may be ashamed. 17For *it is* better, if it is the will of
God, to suffer for doing good than for doing evil.

18For Christ also suffered once for sins, the just for the
unjust, that He might bring us[a] to God, being put to death
in the flesh but made alive by the Spirit, 19by whom also

3:12 [a]Psalm 34:12–16 *3:14* [a]Isaiah 8:12 *3:15* [a]NU-Text reads *Christ as Lord.*
3:18 [a]NU-Text and M-Text read *you.*

Personality Profile: Sarah

FOR YOUR INFO 3:6

Name means: "Princess."

Also known as: Sarai, until the Lord changed her name (Gen. 17:15).

Home: Originally Haran in Mesopotamia (in modern Iraq); later, Canaan.

Family: Half-sister to her husband, Abraham; they had the same father but different mothers; mother to Isaac.

Best known today for: Bearing a promised son, Isaac, after she was past childbearing years.

He went and preached to the spirits in prison, [20]who formerly were disobedient, when once the Divine longsuffering waited[a] in the days of Noah, while *the* ark was being
prepared, in which a few, that is, eight souls, were saved
through water. [21]There is also an antitype which now saves
us—baptism (not the removal of the filth of the flesh, but
the answer of a good conscience toward God), through the
resurrection of Jesus Christ, [22]who has gone into heaven
and is at the right hand of God, angels and authorities and
powers having been made subject to Him.

CHAPTER 4

A Radically Different Lifestyle

[1]Therefore, since Christ suffered for us[a] in the flesh, arm
yourselves also with the same mind, for he who has suffered
in the flesh has ceased from sin, [2]that he no longer should
live the rest of *his* time in the flesh for the lusts of men, but
for the will of God. [3]For we *have spent* enough of our past
lifetime[a] in doing the will of the Gentiles—when we walked
in lewdness, lusts, drunkenness, revelries, drinking parties,
and abominable idolatries. [4]In regard to these, they think it
strange that you do not run with *them* in the same flood of
dissipation, speaking evil of *you*. [5]They will give an account
to Him who is ready to judge the living and the dead. [6]For
this reason the gospel was preached also to those who are
dead, that they might be judged according to men in the
flesh, but live according to God in the spirit.

Commitment to Other Believers

[7]But the end of all things is at hand; therefore be serious
and watchful in your prayers. [8]And above all things have
fervent love for one another, for "love will cover a multitude
of sins."[a] [9]*Be* hospitable to one another without grumbling.
[10]As each one has received a gift, minister it to one another,
as good stewards of the manifold grace of God. [11]If anyone
speaks, *let him speak* as the oracles of God. If anyone ministers, *let him do it* as with the ability which God supplies,
that in all things God may be glorified through Jesus Christ,
to whom belong the glory and the dominion forever and
ever. Amen.

Rejoice in Suffering

4:12–19
see pg. 840

[12]Beloved, do not think it strange concerning the fiery trial which is to try you,

(Bible text continued on page 841)

3:20 [a]NU-Text and M-Text read *when the longsuffering of God waited patiently.*
4:1 [a]NU-Text omits *for us.* *4:3* [a]NU-Text reads *time.* *4:8* [a]Proverbs 10:12

QUOTE UNQUOTE

CONSIDER THIS
3:15–17

Christians must "always be ready to give a defense for the hope that is in [them]" (v. 15). This is especially true at work. But witness involves the work itself as well as words:

If you are going to be really effective in your place of work, you must set out to be the best man at your job . . . .

I knew a man who . . . arrived on the job and, contrary to expectations, he did not talk, he did not agitate. He just got on with the work. And, for a period of some months, that is all he did . . . . His workmates began to see him in a new light . . . .

Only when he had already, to the surprise of everyone, established himself as a craftsman amongst craftsmen did he go into action. By this time he had the respect of every worker in the factory and in the trade union branch . . . . Within two years . . . he had obtained one of the most influential positions in his union, where he could profoundly influence policies which concerned the working lives and conditions of hundreds of thousands of Britain's key war-workers.

Douglas Hyde, *Dedication and Leadership*, pp. 99–100

Suffering Outweighs Comfort

CONSIDER THIS 4:12–19 Comfort and ease were never intended for sinners. We can't handle them. As someone has well said, sin gives us the terrible ability to misuse any good thing. We are deluded if we think we can rise above this less-than-perfect condition without outside help.

Christ's intervention highlights the seriousness of our situation. It took suffering and death for Him to break the bondage that holds all of God's creation in its vicious grip. That made it possible for us to enter into new life. Now His work continues in us and with us throughout our lives, and He gives us an opportunity to co-operate in our re-creation.

As believers, we inevitably find ourselves at war with our old ways, so we should not be surprised at pain and suffering in the walk of faith (1 Pet. 4:1). It is all part of the gift of believing (Phil. 1:29). It is the path to strength and steadiness (1 Pet. 5:10). It is the process of being completed (James 1:2–3).

Do you desire to arrive at a place of peace, joy, and serenity? Someday you will. That is not a false hope. But it is a *hope*: we won't enjoy those until we reach full maturity in Christ in the world to come (Rev. 7:9–17; 21:1–5; 22:1–6).

Don't Fleece the Flock!

CONSIDER THIS 5:2 Several flagrant abuses by prominent ministers, involving hundreds of millions of dollars, were exposed during the 1980s. As a result, many people adopted a general distrust of Christian ministers and ministries, and giving declined. The situation makes Peter's words to overseers (v. 2) required reading for all vocational Christian workers and their supporters. Clergy need to maintain the utmost integrity when it comes to finances.

Peter speaks here of *dishonest gain,* literally "filthy" or "shameful" money. What brings shame is not the money but the greed, which is nothing less than idolatry (Col. 3:5). No wonder Paul strenuously warned church leaders to beware of using ministry as a pretext for gain (1 Tim. 3:3, 8; 6:3–5; Titus 1:7).

Of course, it is not inevitable that ministers should fall to greed. Peter refused Simon's offer of a bribe in exchange for the power of the Holy Spirit (Acts 8:18–20). Likewise, Paul frequently refused the financial support to which he had a right as an apostle (1 Cor. 9:7–15).

Do you make your living in the ministry? If so, are you doing so willingly and eagerly, as Peter indicates? If not, why are you in the ministry?

Paul bent over backward to avoid any hint of financial impropriety. See "I Have Not Coveted," Acts 20:33–38.

as though some strange thing happened to you; 13but rejoice to the extent that you partake of Christ's sufferings, that when His glory is revealed, you may also be glad with exceeding joy. 14If you are reproached for the name of Christ, blessed *are you,* for the Spirit of glory and of God rests upon you.[a] On their part He is blasphemed, but on your part He is glorified. 15But let none of you suffer as a murderer, a thief, an evildoer, or as a busybody in other people's matters. 16Yet if *anyone suffers* as a Christian, let him not be ashamed, but let him glorify God in this matter.[a]

17For the time *has come* for judgment to begin at the house of God; and if *it begins* with us first, what will *be* the end of those who do not obey the gospel of God? 18Now

"If the righteous one is scarcely saved,
Where will the ungodly and the sinner appear?"[a]

19Therefore let those who suffer according to the will of God commit their souls *to Him* in doing good, as to a faithful Creator.

CHAPTER 5

Leaders and Followers

1The elders who are among you I exhort, I who am a fellow elder and a witness of the sufferings of Christ, and also a partaker of the glory that will be revealed: 2Shepherd the flock of God which is among you, serving as overseers, not by compulsion but willingly,[a] not for dishonest gain but eagerly; 3nor as being lords over those entrusted to you, but being examples to the flock; 4and when the Chief Shepherd appears, you will receive the crown of glory that does not fade away.

5:2

5:2–4

5Likewise you younger people, submit yourselves to *your* elders. Yes, all of *you* be submissive to one another, and be clothed with humility, for

"God resists the proud,
But gives grace to the humble."[a]

6Therefore humble yourselves under the mighty hand of God, that He may exalt you in due time, 7casting all your care upon Him, for He cares for you.

4:14 [a]NU-Text omits the rest of this verse. *4:16* [a]NU-Text reads *name.* *4:18* [a]Proverbs 11:31 *5:2* [a]NU-Text adds *according to God.* *5:5* [a]Proverbs 3:34

The Business of the Church

CONSIDER THIS 5:2–4 **There are many reasons why people seek positions of authority in a church. Some do it because they have authority at their normal job and therefore feel they should have authority at church. Some do it for just the opposite reason: authority is denied them at work, so they seek it in the church.**

Peter reminds overseers (vv. 2–4) that the presence or absence of authority or success on the job is more or less irrelevant to positions of authority at church. That may shock church members and leaders who have uncritically adopted models of church management from the business world. It's not that churches can't benefit from many of the practices found in business. Certainly in administration and finances, churches have much to learn from the efficient and effective policies of the marketplace. But the church is not a business, and philosophies and practices from that sphere need to be carefully evaluated and sifted in light of Scripture before they are put into effect.

... YOUR ADVERSARY THE DEVIL WALKS ABOUT LIKE A ROARING LION. . . .
—1 Peter 5:8

Watch Out for the Enemy

5:8
[8]Be sober, be vigilant; because[a] your
adversary the devil walks about like a
roaring lion, seeking whom he may devour. [9]Resist him,
steadfast in the faith, knowing that the same sufferings are
experienced by your brotherhood in the world. [10]But may[a]
the God of all grace, who called us[b] to His eternal glory by
Christ Jesus, after you have suffered a while, perfect, establish, strengthen, and settle *you.* [11]To Him *be* the glory and
the dominion forever and ever. Amen.

Final Greetings

[12]By Silvanus, our faithful brother as I consider him, I have written to you briefly, exhorting and testifying that this is the true grace of God in which you stand.

5:13
[13]She who is in Babylon, elect together
with *you,* greets you; and *so does* Mark
my son. [14]Greet one another with a kiss of love.

Peace to you all who are in Christ Jesus. Amen.

5:8 [a]NU-Text and M-Text omit *because.* *5:10* [a]NU-Text reads *But the God of all grace . . . will perfect, establish, strengthen, and settle you.* [b]NU-Text and M-Text read *you.*

A Hungry Lion

A CLOSER LOOK 5:8

Satan, who stalks the world like a lion (v. 8), knows that spiritual overconfidence is one sure-fire way to catch Christians off-guard. See "Pay Attention to Temptation!" at 1 Cor. 10:12–13.

The Church in "Babylon"

A CLOSER LOOK 5:13

"She who is in Babylon" sent greetings to Peter's readers (v. 13). Describing her as "elect together with you," Peter may have been indicating a group of believers rather than one person. But what did he mean by referring to Babylon? See "A Symbol of Evil," Rev. 14:8.

2 Peter

CHAPTER 1

Called, Equipped, and Growing

1Simon Peter, a bondservant and apostle of Jesus Christ,

To those who have obtained like precious faith with us by the righteousness of our God and Savior Jesus Christ:

2Grace and peace be multiplied to you in the knowledge
1:3–4 of God and of Jesus our Lord, 3as His divine power has given to us all things that
pertain to life and godliness, through the knowledge of Him
who called us by glory and virtue, 4by which have been
given to us exceedingly great and precious promises, that through these you may be partakers of the divine nature, having escaped the corruption *that is* in the world through lust.

5But also for this very reason, giving all diligence, add to
your faith virtue, to virtue knowledge, 6to knowledge self-
control, to self-control perseverance, to perseverance godliness, 7to godliness brotherly kindness, and to brotherly
kindness love. 8For if these things are yours and abound,
you will be neither barren nor unfruitful in the knowledge of
our Lord Jesus Christ. 9For he who lacks these things is
shortsighted, even to blindness, and has forgotten that he was cleansed from his old sins.

10Therefore, brethren, be even more diligent to make your call and election sure, for if you do these things you will
never stumble; 11for so an entrance will be supplied to you abundantly into the everlasting kingdom of our Lord and Savior Jesus Christ.

Peter's Intent in Writing

12For this reason I will not be negligent to remind you always of these things, though you know and are established
in the present truth. 13Yes, I think it is right, as long as I am
in this tent, to stir you up by reminding *you*, 14knowing that
shortly I *must* put off my tent, just as our Lord Jesus Christ
showed me. 15Moreover I will be careful to ensure that you always have a reminder of these things after my decease.
1:16 see pg. 844
16For we did not follow cunningly de-
vised fables when we made known to you the power and coming of our Lord Jesus Christ, but
were eyewitnesses of His majesty. 17For He received from
God the Father honor and glory when such a voice came to

(Bible text continued on page 845)

Do You Have What It Takes?

CONSIDER THIS 1:3–4

Do you think you have what it takes to "make it" in life? According to v. 3 you do. Peter says that God's power gives us what we need to experience real life in a way that pleases Him. God wants to affect every area of our lives—work, marriage and family, relationships, church, and community.

How can you make God's power operational in your experience? Peter says that it comes "through the knowledge of Him who called us." In other words, we must grow closer to Christ. Real power comes from having an understanding of our place in God's purposes and relying on His provisions.

CONSIDER THIS
1:16

MYTH #9

10 MYTHS ABOUT CHRISTIANITY

MYTH: THE BIBLE IS UNRELIABLE AND NOT TO BE TRUSTED

Many people today accept a number of myths about Christianity, with the result that they never respond to Jesus as He really is. This is one of ten articles that speak to some of those misconceptions. For a list of all ten, see 1 Tim. 1:3–4.

Is the Bible a trustworthy document? Are the Scriptures true as written? Or are they full of myths that may have symbolic value but little if any basis in fact? People have been questioning the biblical record almost from its beginnings. Peter, for instance, encountered skepticism as he presented the gospel in the first century. His claims about Jesus were nothing but cleverly devised fables, some said—a charge he vehemently denied (v. 16).

Today the Bible's credibility and authority are still attacked. Yet how many of its critics have carefully studied its teaching? How many have even looked at the story of how it came to be written?

A careful reader will recognize that the Bible is not so much a single book as a library of sixty-six books. It contains a variety of literary genres: history, poetry, narrative, exposition, parable, and "apocalyptic" (see Rev. 10:1–10). Its many authors wrote during a period of some two thousand years using three languages—Hebrew, Greek, and Aramaic. Probably all but one were Jews.

Remarkably, the writers tell one unified story:

- They offer the same understanding of God throughout. He is one God, Creator, Savior, and Judge. He is all-powerful, all-knowing, and eternal. His character is holy, good, loving, and just.
- They offer the same understanding of human nature. People are made in God's image and are capable of great good. Yet they are also sinful and capable of great wickedness. The great need of humanity is to be reconciled to God and to each another.
- They offer a common understanding of Jesus Christ. He is both God and man. He became a real human being in order to show the world the God it could not otherwise perceive. Something deeply significant happened as a result of His death on the cross, making it possible for God and humanity to be reconciled.
- They offer the same hope. God will accomplish His purposes for His Creation.

Aside from the internal evidence that Scripture is what it claims to be—the very words of God—is a growing body of external evidence that supports its reliability as a document. For example, scholars have found many contemporary sources that parallel the Scriptural record. For instance, Jesus is mentioned by two Roman writers of the first century, Tacitus (*Annals* 15.44) and Pliny the Younger (*Letters* 19.96), as well as by some Jewish writings of that period, including Josephus (*Antiquities* 18.3.3) and the Mishnah, a collection of traditions under compilation in Jesus' day.

Another body of research that proves invaluable for biblical studies is archaeology. Countless discoveries have helped to verify the text of Scripture, most notably the Dead Sea Scrolls. Likewise, digs throughout the Mediterranean have supported biblical references to various places and people and the

(continued on next page)

Him from the Excellent Glory: "This is My beloved Son, in
whom I am well pleased." 18And we heard this voice which
came from heaven when we were with Him on the holy
mountain.
19And so we have the prophetic word confirmed,[a] which
you do well to heed as a light that shines in a dark place,
until the day dawns and the morning star rises in your
hearts; 20knowing this first, that no prophecy of Scripture
1:21 is of any private interpretation,[a] 21for
prophecy never came by the will of man,
but holy men of God[a] spoke *as they were* moved by the Holy
Spirit.

CHAPTER 2

Beware of False Teachers

1But there were also false prophets among the people,
even as there will be false teachers among you, who will secretly bring in destructive heresies, even denying the Lord
who bought them, *and* bring on themselves swift destruction. 2And many will follow their destructive ways, because
of whom the way of truth will be blasphemed. 3By covetousness they will exploit you with deceptive words; for a
long time their judgment has not been idle, and their destruction does[a] not slumber.

God Will Protect

4For if God did not spare the angels who sinned, but cast
them down to hell and delivered *them* into chains of darkness, to be reserved for judgment; 5and did not spare the
ancient world, but saved Noah, *one of* eight *people,* a
preacher of righteousness, bringing in the flood on the
2:6–9 see pg. 846 world of the ungodly; 6and turning the
cities of Sodom and Gomorrah into
ashes, condemned *them* to destruction, making *them* an example to those who afterward would live ungodly; 7and
delivered righteous Lot, *who was* oppressed by the filthy
conduct of the wicked 8(for that righteous man, dwelling
among them, tormented *his* righteous soul from day to day
2:9 by seeing and hearing *their* lawless
deeds)— 9*then* the Lord knows how to

1:19 [a]Or *We also have the more sure prophetic word.* *1:20* [a]Or *origin* *1:21* [a]NU-Text reads *but men spoke from God.* *2:3* [a]M-Text reads *will not.*

Deliver Us from Temptation

A CLOSER LOOK 2:9 *God has committed Himself to help His children avoid, flee, confess, and resist temptation (v. 9). See "Pay Attention to Temptation!" at 1 Cor. 10:12–13.*

MYTH #9 10 MYTHS ABOUT CHRISTIANITY

(continued from previous page)

events of which they were a part thousands of years ago.

The more one examines the evidence, the more one becomes convinced that the Bible is more than a cleverly devised tale. It has the ring of authenticity. But in that case, readers ought to pay attention to its message. That is the ultimate issue. As Mark Twain aptly put it, it is not the things in the Bible that people can't understand that prove troublesome, but the things they can understand. Even if people are convinced that the Bible is true from cover to cover, will they heed its message? ◆

How Did the Bible Come to Us?

FOR YOUR INFO 1:21 **Peter wants us to feel confident that the Scriptures are as valid and trustworthy today as they were when they were first written (v. 21). He also gives some information on the process God used to get His Word written down in a permanent form.**

The "older testament," which exists today in 39 books, was written mostly in Hebrew over a thousand-year period, hundreds of years before Christ. The 27 books of the "newer testament" were written in Greek during the first century after Christ's birth. As the various writings came into existence over the centuries, the people of God corporately studied and recognized them as being the Word of God.

(continued on next page)

(continued from previous page)

The two testaments together tell a completed story. *Testament* means "covenant" or "agreement" between God and humanity (see "The New Covenant," 1 Cor. 11:25). The Old Testament is "old" in the sense that it reveals a covenant made at Mount Sinai (Ex. 19:3–6; 24:3–8; see "Israel," Rom. 10:1). The *New* Testament or covenant was accomplished by Christ through His death on the cross (Luke 22:20; 1 Cor. 11:25).

As we read Scripture, we need to make sure that we keep in mind its full context. See "The Bible: Getting the Big Picture," 2 Tim. 3:16–17.

SECOND CHANCES

CONSIDER THIS 2:6–9 **Peter asks us to consider Sodom and Gomorrah, which God did not spare (v. 6; Gen. 19:24). This and fifty other biblical references to those twin cities make two things clear: they could have been saved in spite of their evil, and God wants future generations like ours to avoid their mistakes.**

deliver the godly out of temptations and to reserve the unjust under punishment for the day of judgment, [10]and especially those who walk according to the flesh in the lust of
uncleanness and despise authority. *They are* presumptuous,
self-willed. They are not afraid to speak evil of dignitaries,
[11]whereas angels, who are greater in power and might, do
not bring a reviling accusation against them before the
Lord.

Interpersonal Relations

[12]But these, like natural brute beasts made to be caught
and destroyed, speak evil of the things they do not un-
2:13 derstand, and will utterly perish in their
own corruption, [13]*and* will receive the
wages of unrighteousness, *as* those who count it
pleasure to carouse in the daytime. *They are* spots and
blemishes, carousing in their own deceptions while
they feast with you, [14]having eyes full of adultery and
that cannot cease from sin, enticing unstable souls. *They
have* a heart trained in covetous practices, *and are* accursed children. [15]They have forsaken the right way
and gone astray, following the way of Balaam the *son* of
Beor, who loved the wages of unrighteousness; [16]but
he was rebuked for his iniquity: a dumb donkey speaking with a man's voice restrained the madness of the
prophet.
[17]These are wells without water, clouds[a] carried by a tempest, for whom is reserved the blackness of darkness forever.[b]
[18]For when they speak great swelling *words* of empti-
ness, they allure through the lusts of the flesh, through
lewdness, the ones who have actually escaped[a] from those
who live in error. [19]While they promise them liberty,
they themselves are slaves of corruption; for by whom a
person is overcome, by him also he is brought into bondage. [20]For if, after they have escaped the pollutions of
the world through the knowledge of the Lord and
Savior Jesus Christ, they are again entangled in them
and overcome, the latter end is worse for them than
the beginning. [21]For it would have been better for them
not to have known the way of righteousness, than
having known *it*, to turn from the holy commandment
delivered to them. [22]But it has happened to them according to the true proverb: "A dog returns to his own
vomit,"[a] and, "a sow, having washed, to her wallowing in
the mire."

2:17 [a]NU-Text reads *and mists.* [b]NU-Text omits *forever.* *2:18* [a]NU-Text reads *are barely escaping.* *2:22* [a]Proverbs 26:11

CHAPTER 3

Scoffers Will Come

[1]Beloved, I now write to you this second epistle (in *both of*
which I stir up your pure minds by way of reminder), [2]that
you may be mindful of the words which were spoken before by the holy prophets, and of the commandment of us,[a]
the apostles of the Lord and Savior, [3]knowing this first: that
scoffers will come in the last days, walking according to
their own lusts, [4]and saying, "Where is the promise of His
coming? For since the fathers fell asleep, all things continue
as *they were* from the beginning of creation." [5]For this they
willfully forget: that by the word of God the heavens were
of old, and the earth standing out of water and in the water,
[6]by which the world *that* then existed perished, being
flooded with water. [7]But the heavens and the earth *which*
are now preserved by the same word, are reserved for fire
until the day of judgment and perdition of ungodly men.

A New View of Time

3:8
see pg. 848

[8]But, beloved, do not forget this one
thing, that with the Lord one day *is* as a
thousand years, and a thousand years as one day. [9]The Lord
is not slack concerning *His* promise, as some count slack-
ness, but is longsuffering toward us,[a] not willing that any
should perish but that all should come to repentance.

Pursue Holiness and Maturity

[10]But the day of the Lord will come as a thief in the night,
in which the heavens will pass away with a great noise, and
the elements will melt with fervent heat; both the earth and
the works that are in it will be burned up.[a] [11]Therefore,
since all these things will be dissolved, what manner *of persons* ought you to be in holy conduct and godliness, [12]look-
ing for and hastening the coming of the day of God, because of which the heavens will be dissolved, being on fire,
and the elements will melt with fervent heat? [13]Nevertheless
we, according to His promise, look for new heavens and a
new earth in which righteousness dwells.

[14]Therefore, beloved, looking forward to these things, be
diligent to be found by Him in peace, without spot and
blameless; [15]and consider *that* the longsuffering of our Lord
is salvation—as also our beloved brother Paul, according to
the wisdom given to him, has written to you, [16]as also in all
his epistles, speaking in them of these things, in which are

3:2 [a]NU-Text and M-Text read *commandment of the apostles of your Lord and Savior* or *commandment of your apostles of the Lord and Savior.* *3:9* [a]NU-Text reads *you.* *3:10* [a]NU-Text reads *laid bare* (literally *found).*

QUOTE UNQUOTE

CONSIDER THIS 2:13 *Many people who "carouse in the day-time" (v. 13) do so because they are bored:*

Boredom is really a spiritual problem . . . . One way we try to avoid boredom is by owning and using material goods. We also try to escape boredom by pleasure without conscience.

Fr. Jerry Foley, "We Work at Our Leisure," *Connecting Faith and Life,* p. 25

KEEPING THE BIG PICTURE

CONSIDER THIS 3:8 **Where were you ten years ago? Does it seem like a distant memory, or as if it were only yesterday? Does the here and now totally consume you, dominating your perspective? Where do you expect to be ten years from now?**

As Peter neared the end of his life, he wrote a letter in which he offers some insight into the nature of time and eternity. He beckons us to view time in both thousand-year units and as mere days (3:8), recalling the beginnings of creation (vv. 4–6). He also projects into the future, when judgment will be rendered and new heavens and earth will be home to those who fear God (vv. 10–13). Peter reminds us that God values a day as much as a thousand years, affirming the importance of the here and now (v. 8). But he also affirms God's activity long before we came on the scene (v. 9).

Peter's perspective challenges us to live with a view toward eternity and values that last—purity, holiness, and righteousness (vv. 11, 14). We need to avoid getting caught up in the here and now and losing sight of our eternal destiny. Neither the joys of today nor the problems of this week can quite compare with what God has prepared for us in eternity. Peter urges us to stick with the basics of the faith and resist the fleeting enticements offered in this present moment (vv. 17–18).

some things hard to understand, which untaught and unstable *people* twist to their own destruction, as *they do* also
the rest of the Scriptures.
17You therefore, beloved, since you know *this* beforehand,
beware lest you also fall from your own steadfastness, being
led away with the error of the wicked; 18but grow in the
grace and knowledge of our Lord and Savior Jesus Christ.
To Him *be* the glory both now and forever. Amen.

1, 2 and 3 John

Oxford scholar C.S. Lewis once asked, "If you examined a hundred people who had lost their faith in Christianity, I wonder how many of them would turn out to have been reasoned out of it by honest argument? Do not most people simply drift away?" (*Mere Christianity*, p. 124).

Toward the end of the first century, some Christians began "drifting away" from the truth about Christ. They were losing touch with those who had known Jesus in the flesh as the founders of the church began to die off. They were also being seduced by competing doctrines, especially early forms of *gnosticism* (see 1 John 5:20). As a result, second- and third-generation believers began to grow cold in their love for each other and lukewarm in their commitment to the truth. They had, as the Lord put it to the Ephesians, "left [their] first love" (Rev. 2:4).

One response to this trend was the writing of 1, 2, and 3 John. These letters call Christians back to the basics—the truth about Christ and the love of Christ. For that reason, they are crucial for Christians today.

Back to the basics

C O N T E N T S

A R T I C L E S

Tough Love

John is often described as the "apostle of love" and 1, 2, and 3 John as the "love letters" of the New Testament. But these writings are far from mere sentimentalism. They're about "tough love," love that shoots straight, even if it hurts, because it cares for others and wishes them the best.

The tone of these letters has the feeling of an older believer pleading with a younger. Nine times in 1 John the writer addresses his readers as his "little children" and nine times among the three letters as "beloved." Likewise, he refers to himself as "the elder" (2 John 1, 3 John 1). His writing style is reflective and loosely structured, and he uses some of the simplest Greek in the New Testament.

One of the most notable features of 1 John in particular is the way in which the writer presents his material in formulaic expressions (for example 2:12–14; 5:6–8). These may be the beginnings of creedal statements and catechisms that package truth in a memorable way so as to lock it into the reader's thinking.

Such a strategy would be important in order to counter false teachers who denied Jesus' physical reality. Claiming to have special knowledge, they taught that God could not have become flesh. No wonder John opens his first letter with the powerful declaration, "That . . . which we have heard, which we have seen with our eyes, which we have looked upon, and our hands have handled, concerning the Word of life . . . that which we have seen and heard we declare to you" (1:1, 3). Here was a man—perhaps the last man in the early church—who had actually walked and talked with Jesus.

How does one discern genuine Christianity? John claims that there is a core truth to believe—that Jesus has come in the flesh—and that the practice of love and righteousness is the test of whether one truly believes in (and follows) that Jesus. His message is similar to Paul's word to the Ephesians that true spirituality involves "speaking the truth in love" (Eph. 4:15).

Two Short Letters with a Powerful Message

Perhaps because they are so brief, 2 and 3 John are often overlooked by Bible readers. Yet their message is crucial. Second John encourages believers to test ideas and spiritual claims against the litmus test of Christology: what do they say about Jesus? Deceivers are coming, the author warns, and God's people need to be on guard against deception. As believers today confront an onslaught of religious systems in a pluralistic society, John's warning remains extremely relevant.

Third John confronts disloyalty in the church. The hospitable and faithful Gaius contrasts with domineering Diotrephes, "who loves to have . . . preeminence" (v. 9). Diotrephes apparently felt no need of the apostles or their doctrine. Instead, he had become self-sufficient and, in fact, opposed to the church's leaders. John responds to this problem in an interesting way. He sets descriptions of Gaius and Diotrephes side by side and then simply encourages the rest of his readers to "imitate . . . what is good" (v. 11). Apparently he felt confident that the group would know which man was worthy of imitation. ◆

HE WHO LOVES GOD MUST LOVE HIS BROTHER ALSO.
—1 John 4:21

BINARY FAITH

Modern-day computers are built on the principles of binary mathematics. A binary system breaks down choices into two and only two alternatives—on or off, plus or minus, yes or no. This simple convention has enabled technicians to develop powerful machines and programs to accomplish a variety of complex tasks.

John's writing is somewhat binary in that it treats matters of faith in either-or categories. In contrast to the moral relativism that characterizes much of modern life, John requires that we look at spiritual things in black and white categories. Notice some of the strong contrasts that he draws in 1 John:

THE CHOICES IN JOHN'S FIRST LETTER

Either...	Or...	Texts
Light	Darkness	1:5–7; 2:9–11
Truth	Deception	1:8–10
Keeping God's commandments	Not keeping God's commandments	2:3–6
A new commandment	The old commandment	2:7–8
We love God	We love the world	2:15–16
Christ	The Antichrist	2:18, 22
Truth	Error	2:20–21; 4:1–3
Child of God	Child of the devil	3:1–10
Righteousness	Lawlessness	3:4–9
Life	Death	3:13–15; 5:11–12
Love	Hate	3:15–17; 4:20–21
Spirits confessing Christ	Spirits not confessing Christ	4:1–3
We are of God	We are not of God	4:4–11
Love	Fear	4:18–19

CHAPTER 1

With Our Own Eyes

1:1–10

1That which was from the beginning,
which we have heard, which we have
seen with our eyes, which we have looked upon, and our
hands have handled, concerning the Word of life— 2the life
was manifested, and we have seen, and bear witness, and
declare to you that eternal life which was with the Father
and was manifested to us— 3that which we have seen and
heard we declare to you, that you also may have fellowship
with us; and truly our fellowship *is* with the Father and
with His Son Jesus Christ. 4And these things we write to
you that your[a] joy may be full.

God's Offer and Our Response

5This is the message which we have heard from Him and
declare to you, that God is light and in Him is no darkness
at all. 6If we say that we have fellowship with Him, and
walk in darkness, we lie and do not practice the truth. 7But
if we walk in the light as He is in the light, we have fellowship with one another, and the blood of Jesus Christ His
Son cleanses us from all sin.

8If we say that we have no sin, we deceive ourselves, and
the truth is not in us. 9If we confess our sins, He is faithful
and just to forgive us *our* sins and to cleanse us from all
unrighteousness. 10If we say that we have not sinned, we
make Him a liar, and His word is not in us.

CHAPTER 2

Dealing with Sin

2:1–2

1My little children, these things I write
to you, so that you may not sin. And if
anyone sins, we have an Advocate with the Father, Jesus
Christ the righteous. 2And He Himself is the propitiation for
our sins, and not for ours only but also for the whole world.

Loving God and One Another

2:3–6 see pg. 854

3Now by this we know that we know
Him, if we keep His commandments. 4He

1:4 [a]NU-Text and M-Text read *our*.

The Advocate

A CLOSER LOOK 2:1–2 *As Christians we have an Advocate in Christ (v. 1). Not only is He our go-between with the Father when we do sin, but He also helps us avoid sin in the first place. Does that mean we should expect never to sin? See "Sinless Perfection?" 1 John 3:6.*

SOME BASICS OF WITNESS

CONSIDER THIS 1:1–10 **What exactly does it mean to "witness"? Many people associate the term with street evangelism. But street preachers can sometimes alienate people, although the boldness of their faith is acknowledged by all. What else, then, is needed for someone to be an effective representative for Christ?**

John was one of Jesus' closest associates (see his profile at the Introduction to John). In this first chapter of his first letter, John notes several basic elements of what it means to communicate Christ to others:

- **Our message grows out of our knowledge and experience of Christ (vv. 1–4).**
- **We make clear to others what we have heard from Christ (v. 5).**
- **We live out our faith on a continuous basis, thereby avoiding lives that contradict our message (vv. 6–7). "Walk" is a metaphor for living used often in the New Testament (for example, John 8:12; Rom. 4:12; Col. 3:7).**
- **When we fall short (as we all will, v. 10), we own up to it, avoiding deception about our walk or Christ's work (vv. 8–10).**

Truthfulness, clarity, consistency, and honesty should be basic qualities of Christ's followers. They are things that last in the eyes of God, and they matter most to those evaluating the faith. We should offer nothing less.

Rules That Lead to Joy

CONSIDER THIS 2:3–6 **Most parents expect obedience from their children as a sign of loyalty and trust. In a similar way, God expects His children to follow His commandments (vv. 4–5). In fact, when we obey God and act like Him, we show ourselves to be His (v. 6).**

We can be thankful that God has established rules and standards. Without such boundaries, we would not experience freedom but chaos. After all, we no longer inhabit Eden, but a broken world of sinners. We need moral safeguards that protect people's rights, delay gratification, enforce commitments, define relationships, ensure privacy, and demonstrate a respect for life.

Furthermore, we can be thankful that God is the One who has defined moral absolutes. Sinners could not be trusted to define goodness or justice.

God's original desire was for humans to have authority over all creation (Gen. 1:26–31). But sin and rebellion made us incapable of carrying out that responsibility (Gen. 3:22–24; Rom. 1:18–32). However, Christ has opened the way for us to re-establish our relationship with God and assume once again the responsibilities for which He created us:

- **He has provided for the forgiveness for our sins (John 3:16–19).**
- **He has provided renewal for all of our life (2 Cor. 5:16–21).**
- **He empowers us to carry out His work (Acts 1:6–8).**
- **He has established guidelines for proper conduct (1 John 2:7–17).**

When we follow God's commandments we experience true liberty. As His obedient children we can be fulfilled, fruitful, and joyful as we look forward to the promise of eternal life (v. 17).

who says, "I know Him," and does not keep His commandments, is a liar, and the truth is not in him. 5But whoever
keeps His word, truly the love of God is perfected in him.
By this we know that we are in Him. 6He who says he
abides in Him ought himself also to walk just as He walked.

7Brethren,[a] I write no new commandment to you, but an
old commandment which you have had from the beginning. The old commandment is the word which you heard
from the beginning.[b] 8Again, a new commandment I write
to you, which thing is true in Him and in you, because the
darkness is passing away, and the true light is already shining.

9He who says he is in the light, and hates his brother, is in
darkness until now. 10He who loves his brother abides in
the light, and there is no cause for stumbling in him. 11But
he who hates his brother is in darkness and walks in darkness, and does not know where he is going, because the
darkness has blinded his eyes.

Three Stages of Faith

12 I write to you, little children,
Because your sins are forgiven you for His name's sake.
13 I write to you, fathers,
Because you have known Him *who is* from the beginning.
I write to you, young men,
Because you have overcome the wicked one.
I write to you, little children,
Because you have known the Father.
14 I have written to you, fathers,
Because you have known Him *who is* from the beginning.
I have written to you, young men,
Because you are strong, and the word of God abides in you,
And you have overcome the wicked one.

Do Not Love the World

15Do not love the world or the things in the world. If anyone loves the world, the love of the Father is not in him.
16For all that *is* in the world—the lust of the flesh, the lust
of the eyes, and the pride of life—is not of the Father but is
of the world. 17And the world is passing away, and the lust
of it; but he who does the will of God abides forever.

18Little children, it is the last hour; and as you have heard
that the[a] Antichrist is coming, even now many antichrists

2:7 [a]NU-Text reads *Beloved.* [b]NU-Text omits *from the beginning.* *2:18* [a]NU-Text omits *the.*

have come, by which we know that it is the last hour.
19They went out from us, but they were not of us; for if they
had been of us, they would have continued with us; but
they went out that they might be made manifest, that none of
them were of us.
20But you have an anointing from the Holy One, and you
know all things.[a] 21I have not written to you because you do
not know the truth, but because you know it, and that no
lie is of the truth.
22Who is a liar but he who denies that Jesus is the Christ?
He is antichrist who denies the Father and the Son. 23Who-
ever denies the Son does not have the Father either; he who
acknowledges the Son has the Father also.
24Therefore let that abide in you which you heard from
the beginning. If what you heard from the beginning abides
in you, you also will abide in the Son and in the Father.
2:25
25And this is the promise that He has
promised us—eternal life.
26These things I have written to you concerning those
who *try to* deceive you. 27But the anointing which you have
received from Him abides in you, and you do not need that
anyone teach you; but as the same anointing teaches you
concerning all things, and is true, and is not a lie, and just
as it has taught you, you will[a] abide in Him.
28And now, little children, abide in Him, that when[a] He
appears, we may have confidence and not be ashamed before Him at His coming. 29If you know that He is righteous,
you know that everyone who practices righteousness is
born of Him.

CHAPTER 3

The Children of God

1Behold what manner of love the Father has bestowed on
us, that we should be called children of God![a] Therefore the
world does not know us,[b] because it did not know Him.
2Beloved, now we are children of God; and it has not yet
been revealed what we shall be, but we know that when He
is revealed, we shall be like Him, for we shall see Him as He
is. 3And everyone who has this hope in Him purifies himself, just as He is pure.
4Whoever commits sin also commits lawlessness, and sin
is lawlessness. 5And you know that He was manifested to
take away our sins, and in Him there is
no sin. 6Whoever abides in Him does not
sin. Whoever sins has neither seen Him nor known Him.

3:6
see pg. 856

2:20 [a]NU-Text reads *you all know.* 2:27 [a]NU-Text reads *you abide.* 2:28 [a]NU-Text reads *if.* 3:1 [a]NU-Text adds *And we are.* [b]M-Text reads *you.*

ETERNAL LIFE

CONSIDER THIS 2:25 **From beauty creams to vitamins to aerobics, many people today are pursuing a "fountain of youth." They want to avoid growing old, perhaps because it leads to the final, ultimate reality, death. That reality is so painful to most people that they won't even consider it. They make little or no preparation for their death and its aftermath.**

John offers the one way that a person can actually do something about his or her death. He speaks of a revolutionary promise that God has made—we can live happily forever (vv. 24–25)! God makes that promise of eternal life for those who put their faith in Jesus Christ.

Have you chosen to act on God's promise? Are you trusting in Christ for your eternal life? If not, why not do so now? If you already have, then tell someone else about God's promise today.

[7]Little children, let no one deceive you. He who practices
righteousness is righteous, just as He is righteous. [8]He who
sins is of the devil, for the devil has sinned from the beginning. For this purpose the Son of God was manifested,
that He might destroy the works of the devil. [9]Whoever
has been born of God does not sin, for His seed remains
in him; and he cannot sin, because he has been born of
God.

[10]In this the children of God and the children of the devil
are manifest: Whoever does not practice righteousness is
not of God, nor *is* he who does not love
his brother. [11]For this is the message that
you heard from the beginning, that we should love one another, [12]not as Cain *who* was of the wicked one and murdered his brother. And why did he murder him? Because
his works were evil and his brother's righteous.

3:11–13

Love Cares for Others' Needs

[13]Do not marvel, my brethren, if the world hates you.
[14]We know that we have passed from death to life, because
we love the brethren. He who does not love *his* brother[a]
abides in death. [15]Whoever hates his brother is a murderer,
and you know that no murderer has eternal life abiding in
him.

3:14 [a]NU-Text omits *his brother.*

CONSIDER THIS
3:6

Sinless Perfection?

Most followers of Christ would agree that they should pursue the highest moral integrity that they can. But John's statements in v. 6 appear to raise that standard to the point of sinless perfection. In fact, if the person who sins "has neither seen [Christ] nor known Him," then what hope is there for believers who fail?

Here is a case where the English language fails us. In English the word "sins" appears absolute and final: one sin and you're cut off from God. However, the form of the Greek verb here (hamartanei) *conveys a sense of continuous action: "No one who abides in Christ makes a habit of continually sinning." The point is that true believers diminish their old patterns of sin as they grow in Christ, replacing them with new patterns of faith and love.*

The situation is similar to losing weight by changing one's eating habits. No one obtains instant health, but over time and by sticking to a disciplined diet, one can make great strides in that direction.

3:16–21
[16]By this we know love, because He
laid down His life for us. And we also
ought to lay down *our* lives for the brethren. [17]But whoever
has this world's goods, and sees his brother in need, and
shuts up his heart from him, how does the love of God
abide in him?
[18]My little children, let us not love in word or in tongue,
but in deed and in truth. [19]And by this we know[a] that we
are of the truth, and shall assure our hearts before Him.
[20]For if our heart condemns us, God is greater than our
heart, and knows all things. [21]Beloved, if our heart does not
condemn us, we have confidence toward God. [22]And whatever we ask we receive from Him, because we keep His
commandments and do those things that are pleasing in His
sight. [23]And this is His commandment: that we should believe on the name of His Son Jesus Christ and love one another, as He gave us[a] commandment.

3:19 [a]NU-Text reads *we shall know.* *3:23* [a]M-Text omits *us.*

Take a Cardiogram

A CLOSER LOOK 3:16–21 *John gives us a way to check the condition of our heart (v. 17). He indicates that one vital way to assess our spiritual health is by our reaction to the poor. Of course, anyone can "love" in the abstract. That's why John goes on to challenge us to express our love in practical terms. That's what Jesus did. See "Christ Became Poor," 2 Cor. 8:8–9.*

Of course, the fact that we won't obtain sinless perfection in this life does not mean that we should deal lightly with sin. To do so would be an offense to God, as well as destructive to ourselves. Yes, God forgives individual sins, but if we persist in sinful patterns, we keep the power of Christ from operating in our lives. We also risk grave spiritual consequences, such as losing the ability to repent (Heb. 6:1–12).

Do you keep falling into in a particular area of sin? John says that the way out of that frustrating predicament is to learn to continually "abide" in Christ. Confess your sins to Him and then concentrate not so much on avoiding sin as on maintaining your relationship with Him. After all, He has come to keep you from sin (1 John 2:1–2). But if you turn away from Him and capitulate to sin's mastery, then, as John has written, you can neither see Him working in your life nor know the joy of His presence. ◆

MURDER ON THE JOB

CONSIDER THIS 3:11–13 **Why do mediocre workers often resent excellent workers? Why do people who lie to and steal from their employers and customers resent honest coworkers? Why does the person who cuts corners on the job feel ill-at-ease with someone who gives an honest day's work? Because the unrighteous hate the righteous, as John shows (vv. 11–13). They can't stand someone who has integrity. That person's honest lifestyle exposes their evil and wrongdoing, like a light that penetrates moral darkness.**

The reference to Cain (v. 12) is sobering. Cain killed his brother, Abel, out of resentment (Gen. 4:3–8; Heb. 11:4). In the same way, a worker with a poor attitude and substandard work usually resents a coworker whose work ethic and performance are consistently higher. Like Cain, he may "murder" his nemesis in his mind and heart, simply by begrudging his conscientious efforts.

The warning is clear: Pay attention to feelings of resentment against coworkers who outperform you. Consider what happened to Cain!

[24]Now he who keeps His commandments abides in Him,
and He in him. And by this we know that He abides in us,
by the Spirit whom He has given us.

CHAPTER 4

Discernment

4:1

[1]Beloved, do not believe every spirit,
but test the spirits, whether they are of
God; because many false prophets have gone out into the
world. [2]By this you know the Spirit of God: Every spirit that
confesses that Jesus Christ has come in the flesh is of God,
[3]and every spirit that does not confess that[a] Jesus Christ has
come in the flesh is not of God. And this is the *spirit* of the
Antichrist, which you have heard was coming, and is now
already in the world.
[4]You are of God, little children, and have overcome them,
because He who is in you is greater than he who is in the
world. [5]They are of the world. Therefore they speak *as* of
the world, and the world hears them. [6]We are of God. He
who knows God hears us; he who is not of God does not

4:3 [a]NU-Text omits *that* and *Christ has come in the flesh.*

CONSIDER THIS
5:1–3

LOVE IS MORE THAN ENTHUSIASM

John has been called the apostle of love, and 1 John certainly offers plenty of evidence to show why. For example, he writes that one way to know that we are born of God is that we love Him and keep His commandments (v. 2).

But what does John mean by love? People say they "love" all kinds of things today. One minute they "love" peanut butter and in the next they "love" their spouse. Likewise, they "love" pets, food, sports, vacations, cars, children—whatever!

Thankfully, Scripture defines love for us by describing God's love, using both nouns and verbs. As we examine various passages, we find that God's love is:

- *Lasting (Ps. 136; Rom. 8:28–39; 1 Cor. 13:8).*
- *Sacrificial (John 15:12–13; Rom. 5:8; 2 Cor. 5:14–15; Gal. 2:20; 1 John 3:16–17).*
- *Reconciling and healing (Matt. 5:38–48; Luke 6:27–31; 2 Cor. 5:17–19).*
- *Mutual between Father, Son, and Holy Spirit (Matt. 11:27–30; John 14:31).*
- *Effective; it involves not just emotions or words, but deeds that benefit people (1 John 3:18–19; 4:21; 5:1–3).*

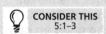

hear us. By this we know the spirit of truth and the spirit of
error.

Love Serves Others

7Beloved, let us love one another, for love is of God; and
everyone who loves is born of God and knows God. 8He
who does not love does not know God, for God is love. 9In
this the love of God was manifested toward us, that God
has sent His only begotten Son into the world, that we
might live through Him. 10In this is love, not that we loved
God, but that He loved us and sent His Son *to be* the propitiation for our sins. 11Beloved, if God so loved us, we also
ought to love one another.
12No one has seen God at any time. If we love one another, God abides in us, and His love has been perfected
in us. 13By this we know that we abide in Him, and He in
us, because He has given us of His Spirit. 14And we have
seen and testify that the Father has sent the Son *as* Savior of
the world. 15Whoever confesses that Jesus is the Son of
God, God abides in him, and he in God. 16And we have
known and believed the love that God has for us. God is
love, and he who abides in love abides in God, and God in
him.

◆ ◆ ◆ ◆ ◆ ◆ ◆ ◆ ◆ ◆ ◆ ◆ ◆ ◆ ◆

- *Fearless (Rom. 1:16; 1 John 4:18).*
- *Discerning (1 Tim. 1:3–7; 1 John 2:15–17; 4:1–7).*
- *Accepting, not condemning (Luke 15:11–32; 18:10–17; John 3:16–17; Rom. 8:1).*
- *Generous (Luke 10:25–37; Rom. 5:8, 15–17; 6:23; 1 Cor. 2:9; 1 Pet. 3:8–9).*

Perhaps the best summary of true, godly love is 1 Corinthians 13, "the love chapter," in which Paul describes the love of God as it needs to be among the believers at Corinth. Likewise, the ultimate expression of God's love is Christ, who offered Himself up for the sins of the world (John 3:16).

In what ways does your love need to develop? Have you grasped the dimensions of God's love for you? How can you cultivate Christlike love and make it more tangible in your life, work, and relationships? ◆

As noted, people use the word "love" to describe very different relationships today. But in the New Testament there are four distinct words for love, each with its own shade of meaning. Find out about them at "What Kind of Love Is This?" Matt. 22:34–40.

Tough-minded Believers

CONSIDER THIS 4:1

Christianity has rightly been characterized as a religion of love, but it's important not to take that emphasis to an unhealthy extreme. If, in the name of love, we uncritically accept every idea or value of others, we open ourselves up to error. God never asks us to put our brains in neutral when it comes to matters of faith.

John repeatedly appeals for love (1 John 2:10; 3:3, 10–24; 4:7–12, 16–21), but he also places a premium on truth—not the wishy-washy opinions that pass for "truth" in our society, but the absolute, eternal truths of God's Word. For example, John challenges us to "test the spirits" (4:1) and learn to discern between truth and error (v. 6). He calls for us to avoid sin, which requires that we discern what is sinful (2:1; 3:4–10). He tells us to distinguish between the things of the world and the will of God (2:15–17), and he appeals for us to identify deceivers and avoid them (2:18–29; 3:7).

Paul echoes this appeal to be tough-minded when it comes to our faith. To be spiritual, he writes, means to be able to "judge" (discern or test) all things (1 Cor. 2:15). Likewise, we are to have the mind of Christ: tough in discernment, loving toward all, and fearless in the face of judgment (Phil. 2:5–11, 17–18).

Are you discerning on issues of faith and spirituality? If not, consider starting your own study of the Scriptures to understand what they say and mean, or perhaps enroll in a Bible class where you can learn more about God's truth in a systematic way.

17Love has been perfected among us in this: that we may
have boldness in the day of judgment; because as He is, so
are we in this world. 18There is no fear in love; but perfect
love casts out fear, because fear involves torment. But he
who fears has not been made perfect in love. 19We love
Him[a] because He first loved us.

20If someone says, "I love God," and hates his brother, he
is a liar; for he who does not love his brother whom he has
seen, how can[a] he love God whom he has not seen? 21And
this commandment we have from Him: that he who loves
God *must* love his brother also.

4:19 [a]NU-Text omits *Him*. *4:20* [a]NU-Text reads *he cannot.*

FOR YOUR INFO
5:20

The Danger of Gnosticism

One reason John was so concerned that his readers exercise discernment (1 John 4:1; 2 John 1–2, 4; 3 John 3–4) was that a system of false teachings known as gnosticism *was then becoming popular.*

The name gnosticism comes from the Greek word for knowledge, gnōsis. *The gnostics believed that a special knowledge about the nature of the world was the way to salvation. For that reason, several writers of the New Testament condemned early manifestations of the philosophy as false. Paul, for example, emphasized a wisdom and knowledge that comes from God as opposed to idle speculations and fables (Col. 2:8–23; 1 Tim. 1:4; 2 Tim. 2:16–19; Titus 1:10–16). Likewise John, both in his Gospel and the epistles, countered heretical teaching which, in a broad sense, could be considered gnostic.*

Roots in Greek Dualism

The gnostic teachers accepted the Greek idea of a radical dualism between God (spirit) and the world (matter). According to their worldview, the created order was evil, inferior, and opposed to the good. They believed that the earth is surrounded by a number of cosmic spheres which separate humans from God. These spheres are ruled by archōns *(spiritual powers) who guard their spheres by barring the souls of those who are seeking to ascend from the realm of darkness and captivity which is below to the realm of light which is above.*

The gnostics also taught that humans are composed of body, soul, and spirit. Since the body and soul are part of people's earthly existence, they were held to be evil. Enclosed in the soul, they said, is the spirit, the divine sub-

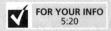

CHAPTER 5

If You Love God, Obey Him

5:1–3 see pg. 858

1Whoever believes that Jesus is the
Christ is born of God, and everyone who
loves Him who begot also loves him who is begotten of
Him. 2By this we know that we love the children of God,
when we love God and keep His commandments. 3For this
is the love of God, that we keep His commandments. And

5:4–5

His commandments are not burdensome.
4For whatever is born of God overcomes
the world. And this is the victory that has overcome the

stance of man. According to gnostic teaching, this spirit is asleep and ignorant, and needs to be awakened and liberated by knowledge. Thus the aim of salvation in gnosticism is to release the inner man from his earthly dungeon so that he can return to the realm of light where the soul is reunited with God.

These beliefs led to two extremes of ethical behavior. Some gnostics became ascetics, trying to separate themselves from matter in order to avoid contamination by evil. Paul may have been opposing such a view in 1 Timothy 4:1–5. Other gnostics felt that since they had received divine knowledge and were truly informed as to their divine nature, it didn't matter how they lived; they thought their "knowledge" gave them freedom to participate in all sorts of indulgences.

Impact on the Church

Gnostic teachings, when blended with Christian beliefs, created serious heresies. They also had a disruptive effect on fellowship within the church. Those who were "enlightened" thought of themselves as being superior to those who did not have such knowledge, and divisions arose. Again, the New Testament writers severely condemned this attitude of superiority. Christians are "one body," the apostles argued (1 Cor. 12) and should love one another (1 Cor. 13; 1 John 4). Whatever spiritual gifts God has given are for the entire Christian community, not just individual use. Moreover, they should promote humility rather than pride (1 Cor. 12–14; Eph. 4:11–16). ◆

QUOTE UNQUOTE

CONSIDER THIS 5:4–5 *Christians are not those who must leave the world in order to experience life, but those who "overcome the world" (vv. 4–5) through their relationship with Christ:*

When the gnostic escapes the world, it becomes very possible for him to be a christian [sic] ***on the side, even in his spare time. But the christian whose life has been transformed from aimless wandering to determined pilgrimage will find no respite. The christian and the cosmos are inextricably bound together until death do them part.***

Philip J. Lee, Jr., *Against the Protestant Gnostics*, pp. 25–26

world—our[a] faith. 5Who is he who overcomes the
world, but he who believes that Jesus is the Son of
God?

Certainty about Eternal Life

6This is He who came by water and blood—Jesus
Christ; not only by water, but by water and blood.
And it is the Spirit who bears witness, because the
Spirit is truth. 7For there are three that bear witness
in heaven: the Father, the Word, and the Holy
Spirit; and these three are one. 8And there are three
that bear witness on earth:[a] the Spirit, the water,
and the blood; and these three agree as one.

9If we receive the witness of men, the witness of
God is greater; for this is the witness of God which[a]
He has testified of His Son. 10He who believes in
the Son of God has the witness in himself; he who
does not believe God has made Him a liar, because
he has not believed the testimony that God has
given of His Son. 11And this is the testimony: that
God has given us eternal life, and this life is in His
Son. 12He who has the Son has life; he who does
not have the Son of God does not have life. 13These
things I have written to you who believe in the
name of the Son of God, that you may know that
you have eternal life,[a] and that you may *continue to*
believe in the name of the Son of God.

14Now this is the confidence that we have in
Him, that if we ask anything according to His will,
He hears us. 15And if we know that He hears us,
whatever we ask, we know that we have the peti-
tions that we have asked of Him.

Avoiding Sin

16If anyone sees his brother sinning a sin *which
does* not *lead* to death, he will ask, and He will give
him life for those who commit sin not *leading* to
death. There is sin *leading* to death. I do not say
that he should pray about that. 17All unrighteousness is sin, and there is sin not *leading* to
death.

18We know that whoever is born of God does not
sin; but he who has been born of God keeps himself,[a] and the wicked one does not touch him.

19We know that we are of God, and the whole
world lies *under the sway of* the wicked one.

5:20 see pg. 860

20And we know that the Son of
God has come and has given us
an understanding, that we may know Him who is
true; and we are in Him who is true, in His Son Jesus Christ. This is the true God and eternal life.

21Little children, keep yourselves from idols.
Amen.

5:4 [a]M-Text reads *your.* *5:8* [a]NU-Text and M-Text omit the words from *in heaven* (verse 7) through *on earth* (verse 8). Only four or five very late manuscripts contain these words in Greek. *5:9* [a]NU-Text reads *God, that.* *5:13* [a]NU-Text omits the rest of this verse. *5:18* [a]NU-Text reads *him.*

2 John

To the Elect Lady

1 [1]The Elder,

To the elect lady and her children, whom I love in truth, and not only I, but also all those who have known the truth, [2]because of the truth which abides in us and will be with us forever:

[3]Grace, mercy, *and* peace will be with you[a] from God the Father and from the Lord Jesus Christ, the Son of the Father, in truth and love.

3 [a]NU-Text and M-Text read *us*.

The Elect Lady

FOR YOUR INFO 1 *The identity of the "elect lady" (v. 1) is unknown. Some believe that she was an individual woman, and that John chose to use this title instead of her personal name in order to protect her from persecution. Others believe that the term is symbolic, referring to a group of believers, perhaps the church at Ephesus.*

If indeed John was writing to a particular woman, she must have been a wise and loving mother as John's praise for her children attests (vv. 4–6). He warned her not to welcome those who spread false teaching (vv. 9–10). His closing remarks also hint that the "elect lady" and John shared a close friendship (vv. 12–13). Though the name of this woman (if she was an individual woman) is lost to us today, this description of her reveals a person whose faith in Christ was influential in the lives of her family and others around her.

Although most first-century cultures isolated and even discriminated against women, Christ invited women to follow Him. See "The Women around Jesus," John 19:25. Women also played an important role in the development of early church. See the table, "Women and the Growth of Christianity," Phil. 4:3.

Hospitality and Discernment

CONSIDER THIS 7–11 **We live in a day in which any and everything is tolerated. No matter how outlandish or how strenuously we disagree with what others cherish or embrace, we accept their right to their opinion. There seems to be no basis for saying "no" anymore. Ours is an age of "I'm okay, you're okay."**

But that is just not true. It would be more honest to affirm, "I'm *not* okay and you're *not* okay. We both need help that we can count on."

The early church faced a similar predicament. After Jesus' death and resurrection, many claimed to know Him and His message, even though their versions of the story differed remarkably. For instance, Paul faced a conflicting gospel in Galatia and at Philippi and vehemently challenged his opponents' claims (Gal. 1:6–9; Phil. 3:1–4). Likewise, John warned against those who distort the truth (1 John 2:18–29; 4:1–6; 3 John 9–11).

The recipient of 2 John, possibly a woman (v. 1), was given to hospitality (v. 10)—a wonderfully Christlike virtue. But John was concerned to help her become more discerning and not lend the reputation of her household to those who would distort the truth about Christ (vv. 7, 11). He knew that not all who claim Christ are true followers. So believers must develop discernment if they are to remain loyal to truth.

Do you know the basics of what the Bible teaches? Can you detect error in the statements of others? When you do, do you know how to lovingly disagree on major issues of faith and truth?

Joy over Truth and Love

4I rejoiced greatly that I have found *some* of your
children walking in truth, as we received commandment from the Father. 5And now I plead with
you, lady, not as though I wrote a new commandment to you, but that which we have had from the
beginning: that we love one another. 6This is love,
that we walk according to His commandments.
This is the commandment, that as you have heard
from the beginning, you should walk in it.

Watch Out for False Teachers

7–11
see pg. 863
7For many deceivers have
gone out into the world who
do not confess Jesus Christ *as* coming in the
flesh. This is a deceiver and an antichrist. 8Look
to yourselves, that we[a] do not lose those things
we worked for, but *that* we[b] may receive a full reward.
9Whoever transgresses[a] and does not abide in the
doctrine of Christ does not have God. He who
abides in the doctrine of Christ has both the Father
and the Son. 10If anyone comes to you and does
not bring this doctrine, do not receive him into
your house nor greet him; 11for he who greets him
shares in his evil deeds.

John Plans to Visit in Person

12Having many things to write to you, I did not
wish *to do so* with paper and ink; but I hope to
come to you and speak face to face, that our joy
may be full.
13The children of your elect sister greet you.
Amen.

8 [a]NU-Text reads *you.* [b]NU-Text reads *you.* 9 [a]NU-Text reads *goes ahead.*

3 John

A Greeting

1The Elder,

To the beloved Gaius, whom I love in truth:

Encouragement for Gaius

2
2Beloved, I pray that you may prosper
in all things and be in health, just as your
soul prospers. 3For I rejoiced greatly when brethren came
and testified of the truth *that is* in you, just as you walk in
the truth. 4I have no greater joy than to hear that my children walk in truth.[a]
5Beloved, you do faithfully whatever you do for the
brethren and[a] for strangers, 6who have borne witness of
your love before the church. *If* you send them forward on
their journey in a manner worthy of God, you will do well,
7because they went forth for His name's sake, taking nothing from the Gentiles. 8We therefore ought to receive[a] such,
that we may become fellow workers for the truth.

Disappointing Diotrephes

9–11
see pg. 866
9I wrote to the church, but Diotrephes,
who loves to have the preeminence
among them, does not receive us. 10Therefore, if I come, I
will call to mind his deeds which he does, prating against
us with malicious words. And not content with that, he
himself does not receive the brethren, and forbids those
who wish to, putting *them* out of the church.
11Beloved, do not imitate what is evil, but what is good.
He who does good is of God, but[a] he who does evil has not
seen God.

The Testimony of Demetrius

12Demetrius has a *good* testimony from all, and from the
truth itself. And we also bear witness, and you know that
our testimony is true.

John Will Come in Person

13I had many things to write, but I do not wish to write to
you with pen and ink; 14but I hope to see you shortly, and
we shall speak face to face.
Peace to you. Our friends greet you. Greet the friends by
name.

4 [a]NU-Text reads *the truth.* *5* [a]NU-Text adds *especially.* *8* [a]NU-Text reads *support.*
11 [a]NU-Text and M-Text omit *but.*

Prosperity

CONSIDER THIS 2 **John's greeting (v. 2) raises an important issue. It is clear that he expects God to give physical and material well-being to Gaius. Is that what believers today should be asking God for? Should we expect God to prosper us physically and financially? Is this verse an indication that He will? Notice three important things:**

(1) John is praying for Gaius' prosperity, not Gaius praying for his own prosperity.

(2) This is part of a formal greeting or blessing. We say very similar things today like, "Good luck," or "Have a good day," or "Stay healthy, kid."

(3) The Greek word here for *prosper* means "to travel well on a journey." That fits with its use in a blessing. Furthermore, it is not something one should actively pursue, but rather a gift that one should look for, a sense of "wholeness" like the Old Testament concept of *shalom* that people enjoy when they follow God's precepts and live in His power.

(4) We don't know what Gaius' circumstances may have been, only that his soul was prospering. John may be saying, "You are doing so well in the faith; I wish you were doing as well in your health and the rest of your life."

(5) John's main concern is that Gaius would walk in the truth (vv. 3–4), not that he would have a big bank account or be in tip-top shape.

Overall, it would be foolish to construct a general principle of material blessing from this verse, especially when so many other passages warn against that very thing.

Paul describes those who teach that God rewards godliness with material blessing as being "destitute of the truth." See "The Dangers of Prosperity Theology," 1 Tim. 6:3–6.

CONSIDER THIS
9–11

A STUDY IN CONTRASTS OF FAITH

What traits does Christ desire in a faithful follower? How does godliness reveal itself? What are the differences between a good representative of the faith and a bad one?

In 3 John, John contrasts two men, Gaius and Diotrephes. Notice the patterns of each one:

A GOOD EXAMPLE AND A BAD ONE
Gaius (vv. 1–8)
•Attended to things that made for a godly inner spiritual life (v. 2).
•Was well regarded by other believers for his life and activities (v. 3).
•Made truth central to his communication (vv. 3–4).
•Showed hospitality to believers and others (vv. 5–6).
•Showed generosity to traveling gospel workers, freeing them from dependence on outside sources (v. 7).
•Did not aspire to fame or an exalted position in the fellowship, in contrast to others (v. 9).
Diotrephes (vv. 9–10)
•Loved prominence (v. 9).
•Did not welcome John's communication (v. 9).
•Demeaned John's reputation with malicious information (v. 10).
•Was not hospitable to other believers (v. 10).
•Hindered others in the congregation in their desire to be hospitable (v. 10).
•Expelled believers who resisted his activities (v. 10).

As always, the true test of the integrity of one's faith is whether one's actions are befitting to a follower of Christ. It's easy to talk about religious things, but words are of little value unless they translate into works that benefit others and bring glory to God (compare Matt. 7:21–29; Titus 1:16; 2:7–8; 3:8–11; James 1:19–27; 2:14–26).

Whom are you more like—Gaius or Diotrephes? What could people point to in your life that gives evidence of a faith that benefits others and honors Christ? ◆

Suppose you were on trial as Jesus was. What would be some of the best evidence against you, that you were "guilty" of following Christ? Would there be anything conclusive? Consider the checklist at "Is There Enough Evidence to Convict You?" Mark 14:53–64.

John's juxtaposition of Gaius and Diotrephes is another example of his use of strong contrasts to describe matters of faith. See the table, "Binary Faith," at the Introduction to 1 John.

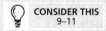

Jude

An exposé of false teachers.

One of the most popular forms of journalism today is the exposé, the report that unmasks pretenders and brings to light the carefully concealed misdeeds of individuals and institutions. The exposé appeals to people's desire for the truth to be told and for wrongdoers to be subjected to public scrutiny. Such stories carry an implicit warning to others: "You may decide to do wrong, but sooner or later you're going to be found out."

The book of Jude is the New Testament's exposé of false teachers in the body of Christ. Using graphic word pictures and recalling a rogue's gallery of deceivers from the Old Testament, Jude documents a history of subversive forces that threatened to destroy Israel and threatened to destroy the early church. Watch out, the letter warns, because "certain men have crept in unnoticed . . . ungodly men, who turn the grace of our God into lewdness and deny the only Lord God and our Lord Jesus Christ" (Jude 4). By blowing the whistle on such impostors, Jude makes sure that they will no longer be "unnoticed."

The author doesn't give us advice on how to do away with false teachers. He merely urges us to guard ourselves by building ourselves up in the faith (vv. 20–21). The best protection against deception is a mature grasp of God's revealed truth.

Contend Earnestly for the Faith

No one knows exactly when Jude was written, but it was apparently late enough in the first century for Jude to tell his readers, "remember the words which were spoken before by the apostles of our Lord Jesus Christ" (v. 17). By the time he wrote, faith had become *the* faith "once for all delivered to the saints" (v. 3), suggesting a formal and even codified body of belief and practice. That spiritual treasure was under attack, so Jude urged believers to "contend earnestly for the faith" (v. 3).

However, the battle was not with outsiders, such as the Jewish council, the Roman government, or the many esoteric philosophies and mystery religions of the day. Instead, the danger came from within. Curiously, Jude never named names, except from the Old Testament: sinful Israel (v. 5; Num. 14:22–23), rebellious angels (v. 6), Sodom and Gomorrah (v. 7; Gen. 19:24–25), Cain (v. 11; Gen. 4:3–8), Balaam (v. 11; Num. 22–24), and Korah (v. 11; Num. 16:19–35).

For Jude's readers, who were probably Jewish Christians, these references were virtual code names for subversion and rebellion against God. They were as well known a warning then as a skull and crossbones marking poison are today. Jude was warning his readers that like those who had caused so much evil for the ancient Hebrews, mockers and false teachers were now infiltrating the church, poisoning it with error. However, the author avoided naming names, perhaps because his readers might have faced reprisals if he did so.

At any rate, the oblique way in which Jude makes these references is an ironic return to Judas Iscariot. The danger is inside the camp, Jude warned, but you don't always know who it is. And just like the disciples at the last supper, the readers of Jude would be asking, "Which of us is it?" (Matt. 26:20–22; John 13:25).

Little has changed in the two thousand years since Jude was written. Believers still need to be on their guard against doctrinal error and persuasive teachers who lead people away from the truth about Jesus. In reading this letter, we are reminded that Christianity is no game. The Old Testament rebels mentioned in Jude came to very bad ends. So will today's false teachers and those who follow them. Jude is a very sobering book. It warns us in stark terms not to play with sin. ◆

The Faithful Judas

Jude is an English form of the name Judas—an infamous name among believers both then and now because of Judas Iscariot, whom the New Testament never mentions without reminding the reader that it was Judas Iscariot who betrayed Jesus to the Jewish leaders (for example, Matt. 10:4; Mark 3:19; John 12:4).

In contrast to Judas Iscariot, the author of Jude was a devoted defender of the Lord and the faith. We know little about the man, except that he called himself "a bondservant of Jesus Christ and the brother of James" (Jude 1). If that James was James the apostle, the half-brother of Jesus (Matt. 13:55; Gal. 1:19), then Jude must also have been a half-brother of Jesus.

Whoever this man was, he was very familiar with the Old Testament and with apocryphal books that dated from the intertestamental period. These books, written during a time of political turmoil in the history of the Jewish people, from about 200 B.C. to about A.D. 100, are of dubious origin and contain certain fabrications, and so were excluded from the Old Testament canon.

However, they were quite popular at the time of Christ, and Jesus and Jude probably read them in their youth. In fact, Jude may have used some of these writings in putting together his letter. For example, Jude 14 may be a reference to the apocryphal Book of Enoch 1:9. ◆

A Bondservant of Jesus

1Jude, a bondservant of Jesus Christ, and brother of
James,

To those who are called, sanctified[a] by God the Father,
and preserved in Jesus Christ:

2Mercy, peace, and love be multiplied to you.

Contend for the Faith

3Beloved, while I was very diligent to write to you concerning our common salvation, I found it necessary to write
to you exhorting you to contend earnestly for the faith
which was once for all delivered to the saints. 4For certain
men have crept in unnoticed, who long ago were marked
out for this condemnation, ungodly men, who turn the
grace of our God into lewdness and deny the only Lord
God[a] and our Lord Jesus Christ.

Examples from History

5But I want to remind you, though you once knew this,
that the Lord, having saved the people out of the land of
6–13
Egypt, afterward destroyed those who did
not believe. 6And the angels who did not
keep their proper domain, but left their own abode, He has
reserved in everlasting chains under darkness for the judgment of the great day; 7as Sodom and Gomorrah, and the
cities around them in a similar manner to these, having
given themselves over to sexual immorality and gone after
strange flesh, are set forth as an example, suffering the
vengeance of eternal fire.

False Teachers Described and Condemned

8–16
see pg. 870
8Likewise also these dreamers defile the
flesh, reject authority, and speak evil of
dignitaries. 9Yet Michael the archangel, in contending with
the devil, when he disputed about the body of Moses, dared
not bring against him a reviling accusation, but said, "The
Lord rebuke you!" 10But these speak evil of whatever they
do not know; and whatever they know naturally, like brute
beasts, in these things they corrupt themselves. 11Woe to
them! For they have gone in the way of Cain, have run
greedily in the error of Balaam for profit, and perished in
the rebellion of Korah.
12These are spots in your love feasts, while they feast with
you without fear, serving *only* themselves. *They are* clouds
without water, carried about[a] by the winds; late autumn

1 [a]NU-Text reads *beloved.* *4* [a]NU-Text omits *God.* *12* [a]NU-Text and M-Text read *along.*

The Power Behind Porn

CONSIDER THIS
6–13

Pornography exposes more than skin. Jude connects the illicit sex in Sodom and Gomorrah (v. 7) with demonic powers (v. 6; see "Who Is the Enemy?" Eph. 6:10–13). The real evil behind porn is not that it is so shameful or unfulfilling, though it is, like "clouds without water" (vv. 12–13). Nor is the evil that the peddling of raw sex and lustful pleasure makes someone else rich, though it does (v. 11). Jude hints at the real sources of power and profit behind the porn market: demonic evil that traffics in human sex.

trees without fruit, twice dead, pulled up by the roots;
13raging waves of the sea, foaming up their own shame;
wandering stars for whom is reserved the blackness of darkness forever.

14Now Enoch, the seventh from Adam, prophesied about
these men also, saying, "Behold, the Lord comes with ten
thousands of His saints, 15to execute judgment on all, to
convict all who are ungodly among them of all their ungodly deeds which they have committed in an ungodly way,
and of all the harsh things which ungodly sinners have spoken against Him."

Stay in the Love of God

16These are grumblers, complainers, walking according to
their own lusts; and they mouth great swelling *words,* flattering people to gain advantage. 17But you, beloved, remember the words which were spoken before by the apostles of our Lord Jesus Christ: 18how they told you that there
would be mockers in the last time who would walk according to their own ungodly lusts. 19These are sensual persons,
who cause divisions, not having the Spirit.

CONSIDER THIS
8–16

Sad Fallouts Are Inevitable

In today's age of acceptance and tolerance, it is not easy or popular to disagree with others. It seems that the one truth everyone must bow to is that everybody has the right to their own beliefs, and what's true for one may not be true for another. To suggest that someone else could be wrong, or worse, to claim that there is such a thing as ultimate, absolute truth, is highly offensive in our culture.

But how can everything be true? That seems to be a contradiction in logic, if we agree with Webster that truth can be defined as fact, the state of something being the case, or as actuality, the body of real things, events, or facts. Jesus claimed to be the truth, not just a truth (John 14:6). He regularly spoke of telling the truth to his listeners (for example, Matt. 5:18, 26; Mark 10:15, 29; Luke 21:3, 32; John 3:3–11; 16:7–23). So what God communicated through Christ is extraordinarily important and must not be compromised.

But as Jude demonstrates, not all who begin to follow God's truth finish well:

- *When Israel fled from Egypt, some disbelieved—and died (v. 5; Num. 14:26–45).*

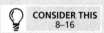

20But you, beloved, building yourselves up on your most
holy faith, praying in the Holy Spirit, 21keep yourselves in
the love of God, looking for the mercy of our Lord Jesus
Christ unto eternal life.
22And on some have compassion, making a distinction;[a]
23but others save with fear, pulling *them* out of the fire,[a]
hating even the garment defiled by the flesh.

A Doxology

24 Now to Him who is able to keep you[a] from stumbling,
And to present *you* faultless
Before the presence of His glory with exceeding joy,
25 To God our Savior,[a]
Who alone is wise,[b]
Be glory and majesty,
Dominion and power,[c]
Both now and forever.
Amen.

22 [a]NU-Text reads *who are doubting* (or *making distinctions*). *23* [a]NU-Text adds *and on some have mercy with fear* and omits *with fear* in first clause. *24* [a]M-Text reads *them.* *25* [a]NU-Text reads *To the only God our Savior.* [b]NU-Text adds *Through Jesus Christ our Lord.* [c]NU-Text adds *Before all time.*

- *Some angels turned away from God and were banished from their positions (v. 6; Matt. 25:41; 2 Pet. 2:4).*
- *Sodom and Gomorrah stand as evidence that sin can bring about destruction (v. 7; Gen. 13:10—19:28).*
- *Cain chose selfishness, greed, hatred and murder (v. 11; Gen. 4:3–8).*
- *Balaam gave in to error and lost his clarity regarding the truth of God (v. 11; Num. 22–24; 2 Pet. 2:15–16).*
- *Korah mistakenly opposed God's leaders and paid for it dearly (v. 11; Num. 16).*

God's people are not called to be bigots who flaunt their connection with the truth. But we are called to be loyal to the truth of Christ, and we should challenge people to avoid anything less than what God offers (Jude 17–23). We're not to be a "truth squad," inflated with our own importance. But neither are we to be Milquetoasts who will agree to anything for the sake of peace. No, we must proclaim God's truth with mercy (v. 22) to those who will perish without it (v. 23). ◆

THEY TOLD YOU THAT THERE WOULD BE MOCKERS IN THE LAST TIME. . . .
—Jude 18

Christ the Lord of History

At the end of the twentieth century, the nations of the world seem to be emerging from under the ominous threat of nuclear holocaust. Yet even as an era of safety seems to be at hand, many warn of new possibilities for global catastrophe through widespread destruction of the world's ecology. In both cases, disaster on a scale described as "apocalyptic" has been forecast—the end of the world as we know it.

How will history end? That is the theme of this last book in the New Testament. Originally known as the *Apocalypse,* which means the "unveiling" or "disclosure" of things known only to God, the book pulls the curtain back to reveal the end of the world. What we find is a dramatic tale told in highly symbolic language. Nevertheless, its ultimate point is easily grasped: Christ will emerge as the Lord of history. The world will change—indeed, it will be made new—but Jesus remains "the Alpha and the Omega, the Beginning and the End . . . who is and who was and who is to come, the Almighty" (Rev. 1:8).

Revelation

Jesus remains "the Alpha and the Omega . . . the Almighty."

C O N T E N T S

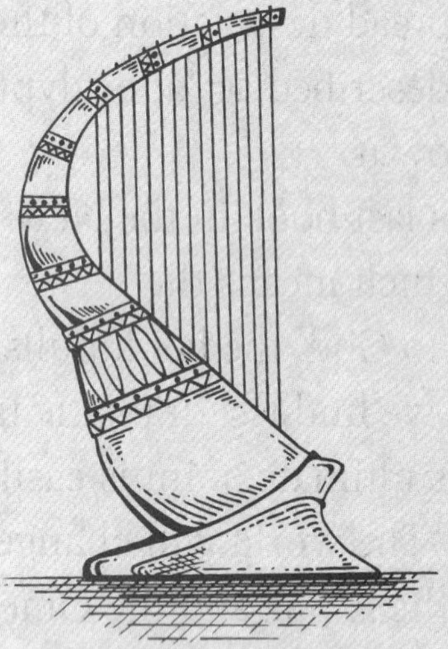

A R T I C L E S

Will Evil Ever Get Its Reward? (20:1–5)

Sometimes it seems like fairness never happens in matters of business, government, the law, and world affairs. But God will not turn His back on injustice. Scripture promises that He will deal with evil in absolute, final ways.

There's a Welcome Here (22:17)

Revelation closes with a powerful invitation from Jesus to join Him in an exciting journey that leads to eternal life!

THE AEGEAN SEA AND SURROUNDING REGIONS

JOHN'S VISION—MYSTERY, NOT MAGIC

Revelation has been perhaps the most debated book in the Bible. Throughout history people have offered various interpretations to try to explain its meaning. Some have seen it as allegorical. Others have taken it more literally and tried to link it to historical events.

An important consideration for anyone who reads the book is that it is written in a genre known as *apocalyptic*. Apocalyptic literature seeks to reveal divine mysteries that would otherwise remain hidden. Yet in conveying its message, it speaks in figurative rather than literal terms (see "The Genre of Apocalyptic Literature," Rev. 10:1–10). Revelation is the only New Testament example of apocalyptic writing, but examples can be found in the Old Testament at Dan. 7–12, Is. 24–27, Ezek. 37–41, and Zech. 9–12.

If Revelation and other apocalyptic texts are supposed to unveil hidden realities, how is it that they remain difficult to understand? Why do they couch their messages in symbolism rather than speak plainly? One reason may be that apocalyptic writings tend to appear during times of great danger. A writer may find it safer to hide his meaning in images that his readers will understand but his opponents will not.

Revelation, for example, may have been written during the reign of the Roman Emperor Domitian (A.D. 81–96). He was the first Roman emperor to demand that the entire empire honor him as "Lord and God." John, who had been exiled to the island of Patmos under Domitian (see Rev. 1:9), may have been warning first-century believers not to give in to the emperor's wishes (compare 22:8–9). The apostle's images of "Babylon the great, the mother of harlots" and of a seven-headed beast that lives on seven mountains (17:1–11) are commonly taken to be a veiled reference to Rome.

However, in addition to the danger of the times, another reason for the mystical nature of apocalyptic literature may have to do with its attempt to convey heavenly realities in earthly terms. In Revelation, John runs out of words in his efforts to describe the indescribable. Consequently, he resorts to metaphors, similes, and symbols to express what he has seen, heard, and experienced (for example, 1:13–16; 4:1, 3, 6–7). But these images are only approximations; the realities are beyond human words to express.

How, then, should we interpret this book? First, we need to accept it as real, not as fantasy. To be sure, Revelation is a vision that takes us beyond everyday experience, but that does not make it imaginary. We can trust that Jesus appeared to John, just as the writer says (1:1).

In addition, while we may wonder about the meaning of specific details, we cannot miss the book's overall outcome in which God triumphs over every adversary—Satan, sin, evil, and death. History comes to its fulfillment in Christ. His kingdom is victorious, His eternal reign is established, and His people enter a joyful eternity worshiping and working for Him. ◆

CHAPTER 1

Greetings to All

1The Revelation of Jesus Christ, which God gave Him to
show His servants—things which must shortly take place.
And He sent and signified *it* by His angel to His servant
John, 2who bore witness to the word of God, and to the testimony of Jesus Christ, to all things that he saw. 3Blessed *is*
he who reads and those who hear the words of this
prophecy, and keep those things which are written in it; for
the time *is* near.

4John, to the seven churches which are in Asia:

Grace to you and peace from Him who is and who was
and who is to come, and from the seven Spirits who are before His throne, 5and from Jesus Christ, the faithful witness,
the firstborn from the dead, and the ruler over the kings of
the earth.

To Him who loved us and washed[a] us from our sins in
His own blood, 6and has made us kings[a] and priests to His
God and Father, to Him *be* glory and dominion forever and
ever. Amen.

7Behold, He is coming with clouds, and every eye will see
Him, even they who pierced Him. And all the tribes of the
earth will mourn because of Him. Even so, Amen.

8"I am the Alpha and the Omega, *the* Beginning and *the*
End,"[a] says the Lord,[b] "who is and who was and who is to
come, the Almighty."

John Sees a Vision of Jesus

1:9
see pg. 880

9I, John, both[a] your brother and companion in the tribulation and kingdom
and patience of Jesus Christ, was on the island that is called
Patmos for the word of God and for the testimony of Jesus

1:10
see pg. 878

Christ. 10I was in the Spirit on the Lord's
Day, and I heard behind me a loud voice,
as of a trumpet, 11saying, "I am the Alpha and the Omega,
the First and the Last," and,[a] "What you see, write in a book
and send *it* to the seven churches which are in Asia:[b] to
Ephesus, to Smyrna, to Pergamos, to Thyatira, to Sardis, to
Philadelphia, and to Laodicea."

12Then I turned to see the voice that spoke with me. And
having turned I saw seven golden lampstands, 13and in the
midst of the seven lampstands *One* like the Son of Man,
clothed with a garment down to the feet and girded about

HE IS COMING WITH CLOUDS, AND EVERY EYE WILL SEE HIM. . . .
—Revelation 1:7

1:5 [a]NU-Text reads *loves us and freed;* M-Text reads *loves us and washed.* *1:6* [a]NU-Text and M-Text read *a kingdom.* *1:8* [a]NU-Text and M-Text omit *the Beginning and the End.* [b]NU-Text and M-Text add *God.* *1:9* [a]NU-Text and M-Text omit *both.* *1:11* [a]NU-Text and M-Text omit *I am* through third *and.* [b]NU-Text and M-Text omit *which are in Asia.*

the chest with a golden band. 14His head and hair *were*
white like wool, as white as snow, and His eyes like a flame
of fire; 15His feet *were* like fine brass, as if refined in a furnace, and His voice as the sound of many waters; 16He had
in His right hand seven stars, out of His mouth went a
sharp two-edged sword, and His countenance *was* like the
sun shining in its strength. 17And when I saw Him, I fell at
His feet as dead. But He laid His right hand on me, saying
to me,[a] "Do not be afraid; I am the First and the Last. 18I *am*
He who lives, and was dead, and behold, I am alive forever-
more. Amen. And I have the keys of Hades and of Death.
19Write[a] the things which you have seen, and the things
which are, and the things which will take place after this.
1:20 see pg. 880
20The mystery of the seven stars which
you saw in My right hand, and the seven
golden lampstands: The seven stars are the angels of the
seven churches, and the seven lampstands which you saw[a]
are the seven churches.

CHAPTER 2

Ephesus Has Left Her First Love

1"To the angel of the church of Ephesus write,
'These things says He who holds the seven stars in His

1:17 [a]NU-Text and M-Text omit *to me.* *1:19* [a]NU-Text and M-Text read *Therefore, write.*
1:20 [a]NU-Text and M-Text omit *which you saw.*

FOR YOUR INFO
1:10

THE LORD'S DAY

John's reference to the Lord's Day (v. 10), generally regarded as referring to Sunday, suggests that to first-century Christians the first day of the week was particularly significant. That raises the question of whether Sundays are special today.

We know that the early church gave special honor to Sunday, the first day of the week, as the day on which Jesus was raised from the dead. Every week on that day they celebrated His resurrection and met for worship and instruction (1 Cor. 16:2). This observance of a special day was both a parallel and a contrast to the Jewish Sabbath, or day of rest, at the end of the week. The Sabbath celebrated God's rest from creation (see "The Sabbath," Heb. 4:1–13).

Some Jewish Christians continued to observe the Sabbath, as well as the Jewish festival days. But many Gentiles in the church did not. Apparently this created tension, especially when the observance of Jewish practices began to be linked by some to salvation. A council of church leaders at Jerusalem did not include a demand for Sabbath obser-

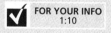

right hand, who walks in the midst of the seven golden
lampstands: 2"I know your works, your labor, your patience, and that you cannot bear those who are evil. And
you have tested those who say they are apostles and are not,
and have found them liars; 3and you have persevered and
have patience, and have labored for My name's sake and
have not become weary. 4Nevertheless I have *this* against
you, that you have left your first love. 5Remember therefore
from where you have fallen; repent and do the first works,
or else I will come to you quickly and remove your lampstand from its place—unless you repent. 6But this you have,
that you hate the deeds of the Nicolaitans, which I also
hate.

7"He who has an ear, let him hear what the Spirit says to
the churches. To him who overcomes I will give to eat from
the tree of life, which is in the midst of the Paradise of
God." '

Smyrna Is Suffering

8"And to the angel of the church in Smyrna write,

'These things says the First and the Last, who was dead,
and came to life: 9"I know your works, tribulation, and
poverty (but you are rich); and *I know* the blasphemy of
those who say they are Jews and are not, but *are* a synagogue of Satan. 10Do not fear any of those things which you

(Bible text continued on page 881)

vance in its decision regarding Gentile converts (Acts 15:20, 28–29).

Likewise, in writing to the Romans, Paul urged everyone to decide for themselves whether one day should be esteemed above another; but by all means, no one should judge another for his convictions (see "Matters of Conscience," Rom. 14:1–23; compare Gal. 4:10; Col. 2:16–17).

It's interesting that the phrase "the Lord's Day" occurs only this one time in Rev. 1:10. In Asia Minor, where the churches to which John was writing were located, people celebrated the first day of each month as the Emperor's Day. Some believe that a day of the week was also called by this name. Thus, by calling the first day of the week the Lord's Day, John may have been making a direct challenge to emperor worship, as he does elsewhere in the book. ◆

HEAR WHAT THE SPIRIT SAYS TO THE CHURCHES.
—Revelation 2:7

Patmos

YOU ARE THERE 1:9

- A small rocky island in the Aegean Sea off the southwest coast of Asia Minor.
- Site of John's exile under Emperor Domitian (A.D. 81–96) and the place where he wrote the book of Revelation. Because of its desolate and barren nature, Patmos was used by the Romans to banish criminals. Prisoners were forced to work at hard labor in the mines and quarries of the island.

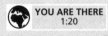

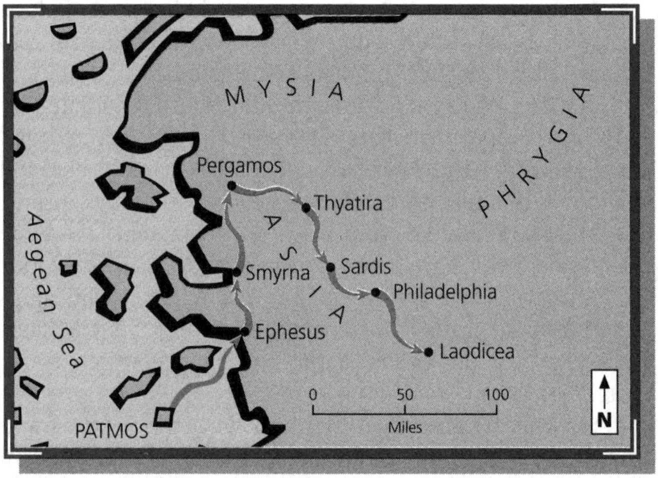

From Patmos to the Seven Churches

YOU ARE THERE 1:20

The Church at the End of the First Century

First-century believers faced stiff opposition from political authorities determined to stop the spread of their message. Nevertheless, despite increasingly harsh treatment, they were able to go a long way toward fulfilling the Lord's mandate to take the gospel "to the end of the earth" (Acts 1:8). In fact, within about three decades they had won converts throughout the Roman Empire, including the capital, Rome itself.

One reason for these spectacular results was a concentration on reaching cities (see "Paul's Urban Strategy," Acts 16:4). In Ephesus, for example, Christian leaders influenced strategic groups of workers who not only turned the city upside down with their new faith, but took the gospel inland so that "all who dwelt in Asia heard the word of the Lord" (Acts 19:10; see "The Ephesus Approach," Acts 19:8–41).

In Revelation, John writes letters from the Lord to some of the churches that were probably established through the Ephesus initiative (see the table, "Seven Churches to Study," Rev. 3:1). The seven mentioned were provincial capitals in what is now Turkey. A courier would have taken a circular route to deliver the epistles to the seven cities, which in turn would have served as distribution points to other churches in the region.

By the time John wrote to these churches, Christians were probably facing intense persecution under Emperor Domitian (A.D. 81–96). He extended the practice of emperor worship to demand that all citizens in the empire re-

are about to suffer. Indeed, the devil is about to throw *some*
of you into prison, that you may be tested, and you will
have tribulation ten days. Be faithful until death, and I will
give you the crown of life.
11 “He who has an ear, let him hear what the Spirit says to
the churches. He who overcomes shall not be hurt by the
second death.” ’

Pergamos Is Confused

12 “And to the angel of the church in Pergamos write,
‘These things says He who has the sharp two-edged
sword: 13 “I know your works, and where you dwell, where
Satan’s throne *is*. And you hold fast to My name, and did
not deny My faith even in the days in which Antipas *was*
My faithful martyr, who was killed among you, where Satan
dwells. 14 But I have a few things against you, because you
have there those who hold the doctrine of Balaam, who

◆ ◆ ◆ ◆ ◆ ◆ ◆ ◆ ◆ ◆ ◆ ◆ ◆ ◆ ◆

fer to him as “Lord and God.” He also used political, economic, and social measures to suppress what he perceived to be resistance, including the burgeoning Christian movement. It was probably during this period that believers in Rome began to seek refuge in the catacombs, deep underground tunnels intended as burial chambers for the dead.

Internally, many of the churches struggled with poverty, heresy, and dissension. In Revelation, heretical teachers are variously referred to as teachers of Balaam (2:14), Jezebel (2:20), the Nicolaitans (2:6, 15), and the Synagogue of Satan (2:9; 3:9). We don’t know exactly what the nature of these heresies was, though one possibility is gnosticism (see article at the end of 1 John). But we do know that problems of syncretism and worldliness were common (see the Introduction to Colossians).

John sends the Lord’s letters to seven groups of believers living at the end of the first century. But Revelation is an open letter to all Christians, including those of us who follow Christ today. In John’s day believers were faced with false teachers and the persecution that resulted from a resurgent cult of emperor worship. Revelation challenged them to loyalty to the truth and perseverance under suffering.

What challenges to their faith do Christians face today? What would Christ say to them? What words of warning might apply to today’s life and faith? ◆

THYATIRA

YOU ARE THERE 2:18

- **A city of the province of Lydia in western Asia Minor located on the road from Pergamos to Sardis.**
- **Situated on the southern bank of the Lycus River, a branch of the Hermus River.**
- **Although never a large city, a thriving manufacturing and commercial center during New Testament times. Archaeologists have uncovered evidence of many trade guilds and unions here. Membership in these guilds, necessary for financial and social success, often involved pagan customs and practices such as superstitious worship, feasts using food sacrificed to idols, and loose sexual morality.**
- **Original home of Lydia of Philippi (see Acts 16:14), the first person known to have responded to the gospel in Europe.**
- **Modern name of Thyatira, Akhisar, means “white castle.”**

taught Balak to put a stumbling block before the children of
Israel, to eat things sacrificed to idols, and to commit sexual
immorality.
15Thus you also have those who hold the doctrine of the Nicolaitans, which thing I hate.[a]
16Repent, or else I will come to you quickly and will fight against them
with the sword of My mouth.

2:15 [a]NU-Text and M-Text read *likewise* for *which thing I hate.*

FOR YOUR INFO 3:1

SEVEN CHURCHES TO STUDY

What is your church like? What would Jesus say if He sent a letter to it, as He did to the churches of Asia Minor (2:1—3:22)? Here is a comparison of the seven churches mentioned in Revelation. See if there are any parallels between these churches and the congregation with whom you worship today:

Church	Description	Praised for	Warned about
Ephesus (2:1–7)	The Loveless Church	•labor •patience •not bearing those who are evil •testing false apostles •perseverance •hating the deeds of the Nicolaitans	•leaving their first love
Smyrna (2:8–11)	The Persecuted Church	•tribulation •poverty	•faithfulness under persecution
Pergamos (2:12–17)	The Compromising Church	•holding fast to Christ's name •not denying the faith, even faced with martyrdom	•allowing false teaching having to do with immorality and idolatry •holding to the doctrine of the Nicolaitans
Thyatira (2:18–29)	The Corrupt Church	•love •service •faith •patience	•allowing Jezebel to teach and seduce to immorality and idolatry •holding fast and overcoming
Sardis (3:1–6)	The Dead Church	•a few faithful people	•deadness, even though they had a reputation for being alive
Philadelphia (3:7–13)	The Faithful Church	•a little strength •keeping Christ's word •not denying Christ's name •perseverance	•holding fast what they had and overcoming during coming tribulations
Laodicea (3:14–20)	The Lukewarm Church		•being lukewarm •pretending to be well off spiritually when they were impoverished •need for repentance and overcoming

As you study the seven churches to whom Christ dictated letters, with which group do you most identify? What words of warning might apply to your church? What changes might your church need to make?

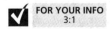

17“He who has an ear, let him hear what the Spirit says to
the churches. To him who overcomes I will give some of the
hidden manna to eat. And I will give him a white stone, and
on the stone a new name written which no one knows except him who receives *it*.” ’

Thyatira Is Too Tolerant

2:18 see pg. 881

18“And to the angel of the church in
Thyatira write,
‘These things says the Son of God, who has eyes like a
flame of fire, and His feet like fine brass: 19“I know your
works, love, service, faith,[a] and your patience; and *as* for

2:20–23

your works, the last *are* more than the
first. 20Nevertheless I have a few things
against you, because you allow[a] that woman[b] Jezebel, who
calls herself a prophetess, to teach and seduce[c] My servants
to commit sexual immorality and eat things sacrificed to
idols. 21And I gave her time to repent of her sexual immorality, and she did not repent.[a] 22Indeed I will cast her
into a sickbed, and those who commit adultery with her
into great tribulation, unless they repent of their[a] deeds. 23I
will kill her children with death, and all the churches shall
know that I am He who searches the minds and hearts. And
I will give to each one of you according to your works.
24“Now to you I say, and[a] to the rest in Thyatira, as many
as do not have this doctrine, who have not known the
depths of Satan, as they say, I will[b] put on you no other burden. 25But hold fast what you have till I come. 26And he
who overcomes, and keeps My works until the end, to him
I will give power over the nations—

27 ‘He shall rule them with a rod of iron;
They shall be dashed to pieces like the potter’s
vessels’[a]—

as I also have received from My Father; 28and I will give
him the morning star.
29“He who has an ear, let him hear what the Spirit says to
the churches.” ’

CHAPTER 3

Sardis Is Sleeping

3:1

1“And to the angel of the church in
Sardis write,
‘These things says He who has the seven Spirits of God
and the seven stars: “I know your works, that you have a

(Bible text continued on page 885)

2:19 [a]NU-Text and M-Text read *faith, service.* *2:20* [a]NU-Text and M-Text read *I have against you that you tolerate.* [b]M-Text reads *your wife Jezebel.* [c]NU-Text and M-Text read *and teaches and seduces.* *2:21* [a]NU-Text and M-Text read *time to repent, and she does not want to repent of her sexual immorality.* *2:22* [a]NU-Text and M-Text read *her.* *2:24* [a]NU-Text and M-Text omit *and.* [b]NU-Text and M-Text omit *will.* *2:27* [a]Psalm 2:9

JEZEBEL

FOR YOUR INFO
2:20–23

The name Jezebel (v. 20) instantly signified evil for John’s readers. King Ahab’s wife, Jezebel, left a bad taste in Israel (1 Kin. 16:31; 21:25; 2 Kin. 9:7–10, 22). After her passing, Jews avoided naming their daughters Jezebel.

Here in Revelation 2, a Jezebel is teaching people to worship false gods and encouraging immorality. The pagan religions of the day, including the emperor-worship of the Romans, usually involved idol worship and sometimes included sexual activity.

This Jezebel was no follower of Christ, but a false prophet leading people astray. Yet the believers at Thyatira stood by, watching and tolerating her teaching and promotion of sexual promiscuity in the name of religion.

FOR YOUR INFO
3:17–18

A History of Money

The words attributed to the Laodiceans, "I am rich, have become wealthy, and have need of nothing" (v. 17) are easy to understand since Laodicea became an extremely wealthy city under the Romans. When the city was destroyed by an earthquake in A.D. 61, the Laodiceans took a posture of self-sufficiency by refusing aid from Rome for rebuilding. In doing so, they continued a long tradition associated with money.

From Barter to Metals

In ancient times, people used a system of barter, or trading of property, to exchange value. Land became an important commodity, but produce, and especially livestock, was more convenient. Grain, oil, wine, and spices were also popular tools of trade.

Gradually metals began to replace goods and services as items of exchange. Copper or bronze was in demand for weapons, farming tools, and religious offerings. The early Egyptians and others shaped gold and silver into rings, bars, or rounded nodules for easier trading. Scripture records that Jacob's children used "bundles of money" (Gen. 42:35), which may have been metal rings tied together with strings.

Silver became especially important in real estate transactions. Omri, for example, purchased the village and hill of Samaria for two talents of silver (1 Kin. 16:24; compare Gen. 23:15–16; 2 Sam. 24:24). Eventually silver became so commonly used as money that the Hebrew word for "silver" came to mean "money" (Gen. 17:13).

Gold, the most valuable of metals, was also used for major transactions. King Hiram of Tyre paid 120 talents of gold to Solomon for several cities near his land (1 Kin. 9:13–14). Later, Hezekiah paid Sennacherib 300 talents of silver and 30 talents of gold to obtain peace (2 Kin. 18:14). Silver, gold, and copper (probably a copper-bronze alloy) were used to mint Israel's first coins.

Standardized Value

In their early use as money, metals were probably in their raw form or in varying stages of refinement. However, in that form it was difficult to transport them and to determine their true value. Thus metals began to be refined into wedges or bars of known weight and value (Josh. 7:21) or into various forms of jewelry. Gold and silver were also kept as ingots, vessels, dust, or small fragments that could be melted and used immediately. These small pieces of metal were often carried in leather pouches that could be easily hidden (Gen. 42:35).

The Bible frequently refers to "pieces" of silver or gold. The confusing term *shekel* did not denote any one value or weight at first, although it later became the name of a Jewish coin. Fractions of the shekel are mentioned in the Old Testament as well (for example, Ex. 38:26; Lev. 27:25; Neh. 10:32). These pieces were probably fragments of gold or silver bars rather than shaped coins.

The largest unit of silver was the talent, shaped in pellets or rings, with approximately the value of one ox.

Eventually pieces of metal were standardized, then stamped to designate their weight and value. Coins still had to be weighed, however, since their edges might have been trimmed or filed. Ancient coins often show other marks, indicating they may have been probed to assure their silver content.

The basic unit of Roman coinage was the silver denarius, probably equal to a laborer's daily wage, as in the parable of the vineyard workers (Matt. 20:9–10, 13). It was also used for paying tribute, or taxes, to the Roman emperor, whose image it carried. Jesus was shown a

(continued on next page)

name that you are alive, but you are dead. 2Be watchful,
and strengthen the things which remain, that are ready to
die, for I have not found your works perfect before God.[a]
3Remember therefore how you have received and heard;
hold fast and repent. Therefore if you will not watch, I will
come upon you as a thief, and you will not know what hour
I will come upon you. 4You[a] have a few names even in
Sardis who have not defiled their garments; and they shall
walk with Me in white, for they are worthy. 5He who overcomes shall be clothed in white garments, and I will not
blot out his name from the Book of Life; but I will confess
his name before My Father and before His angels.

6"He who has an ear, let him hear what the Spirit says to
the churches."'

Philadelphia Is Working

7"And to the angel of the church in Philadelphia write,

'These things says He who is holy, He who is true, "He
who has the key of David, He who opens and no one shuts,
and shuts and no one opens":[a] 8"I know your works. See, I
have set before you an open door, and no one can shut it;[a]
for you have a little strength, have kept My word, and have
not denied My name. 9Indeed I will make *those* of the synagogue of Satan, who say they are Jews and are not, but lie—
indeed I will make them come and worship before your
feet, and to know that I have loved you. 10Because you have
kept My command to persevere, I also will keep you from
the hour of trial which shall come upon the whole world, to
test those who dwell on the earth. 11Behold,[a] I am coming
quickly! Hold fast what you have, that no one may take
your crown. 12He who overcomes, I will make him a pillar
in the temple of My God, and he shall go out no more. I
will write on him the name of My God and the name of the
city of My God, the New Jerusalem, which comes down out
of heaven from My God. And *I will write on him* My new
name.

13"He who has an ear, let him hear what the Spirit says to
the churches."'

Laodicea Is Lukewarm

14"And to the angel of the church of the Laodiceans[a]
write,

'These things says the Amen, the Faithful and True Witness, the Beginning of the creation of God: 15"I know your
works, that you are neither cold nor hot. I could wish you
were cold or hot. 16So then, because you are lukewarm, and

3:2 [a]NU-Text and M-Text read *My God.* *3:4* [a]NU-Text and M-Text read *Nevertheless you have a few names in Sardis.* *3:7* [a]Isaiah 22:22 *3:8* [a]NU-Text and M-Text read *which no one can shut.* *3:11* [a]NU-Text and M-Text omit *Behold.* *3:14* [a]NU-Text and M-Text read *in Laodicea.*

(continued from previous page)

denarius by the Pharisees who wanted to trick him into opposing Roman taxation (Matt. 22:15–22).

Scripture warns believers against "the love of money," but it does not teach that money itself is evil (see "Christians and Money," 1 Tim. 6:6–19). Instead, it encourages Christ's followers to work at a steady job to earn a living in order to provide for one's own needs as well as to help others who have material needs (see "From Deadbeat to Donor," Eph. 4:28, and "A Command to Work," 2 Thess. 3:6–12). ◆

For more on the value of biblical units of coinage, see the table, "Money in the New Testament," Rev. 16:21.

neither cold nor hot,[a] I will vomit you out of My mouth.
3:17–18 see pg. 884
17Because you say, 'I am rich, have become wealthy, and have need of noth-
ing'—and do not know that you are wretched, miserable,
3:18
poor, blind, and naked—18I counsel you
to buy from Me gold refined in the fire,
that you may be rich; and white garments, that you may be
clothed, *that* the shame of your nakedness may not be revealed; and anoint your eyes with eye salve, that you may
see. 19As many as I love, I rebuke and chasten. Therefore be
zealous and repent. 20Behold, I stand at the door and
knock. If anyone hears My voice and opens the door, I will

3:16 [a]NU-Text and M-Text read *hot nor cold.*

YOU ARE THERE 3:18

CLOTHING

John records the promise of white garments (v. 18), probably a symbol for purity and health. But clothing of the more practical kind was as important to the first-century Laodiceans as it is to modern Westerners.

In the ancient world, wool and flax provided most of the raw material for creating fabric. The more rural the household, the more likely that spinning and weaving were done in the home. Urban households probably depended on merchants for material and even finished garments. Cleaning and dyeing eventually developed into distinct occupations.

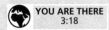

Among the Greeks, spinning, weaving, and decorating cloth were so much the responsibility of females that those skills became metaphors for "women's wiles." Women in Roman cities were likewise encouraged to occupy their time working with wool. The task was synonymous with being a virtuous wife and mother. In fact, Emperor Augustus (27 B.C.—A.D. 14) was so eager to re-establish traditional Roman values that he wore woolen clothes made by his wife to encourage women to return to their looms.

Among the Jews, some men but mostly women made fabric. Jews who intended to strictly observe the Law were careful not to mix wool and flax in the same garment, following the prohibitions of Deut. 22:11 and Lev. 19:19. They also sewed fringes with a blue thread on the corners onto their outer garments as a sign of remembrance of the commandments of God (Deut. 22:12, Num. 15:38–40).

come in to him and dine with him, and he with Me. 21To
him who overcomes I will grant to sit with Me on My
throne, as I also overcame and sat down with My Father on
His throne.
22"He who has an ear, let him hear what the Spirit says to
the churches." ' "

CHAPTER 4

Worship in Heaven

1After these things I looked, and behold, a door *standing*
open in heaven. And the first voice which I heard *was* like a
trumpet speaking with me, saying, "Come up here, and I
will show you things which must take place after this."

"I WILL SHOW YOU THINGS WHICH MUST TAKE PLACE AFTER THIS."
—Revelation 4:1

Mediterranean clothing typically consisted of a tunic made of two pieces of wool joined together at the top, with an opening to pass over the head. The garment was often red, yellow, black, or a combination of these colors, and might be decorated with two vertical stripes of a contrasting color. Another garment, the mantle, was a single piece of cloth, often yellow or brown with a pattern woven into it. ◆

2Immediately I was in the Spirit; and behold, a throne set
in heaven, and *One* sat on the throne. 3And He who sat
there was[a] like a jasper and a sardius stone in appearance;
and *there was* a rainbow around the throne, in appearance
like an emerald. 4Around the throne *were* twenty-four
thrones, and on the thrones I saw twenty-four elders sitting,
clothed in white robes; and they had crowns[a] of gold on
their heads. 5And from the throne proceeded lightnings,
thunderings, and voices.[a] Seven lamps of fire *were* burning
before the throne, which are the[b] seven Spirits of God.

6Before the throne *there was*[a] a sea of glass, like crystal.
And in the midst of the throne, and around the throne, *were*
four living creatures full of eyes in front and in back. 7The
first living creature *was* like a lion, the second living creature like a calf, the third living creature had a face like a
man, and the fourth living creature *was* like a flying eagle.
8*The* four living creatures, each having six wings, were full

4:3 [a]M-Text omits *And He who sat there was* (which makes the description in verse 3 modify the throne rather than God). *4:4* [a]NU-Text and M-Text read *robes, with crowns.* *4:5* [a]NU-Text and M-Text read *voices, and thunderings.* [b]M-Text omits *the.* *4:6* [a]NU-Text and M-Text add *something like.*

CONSIDER THIS
4:10–11

Two Great Works of God

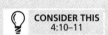

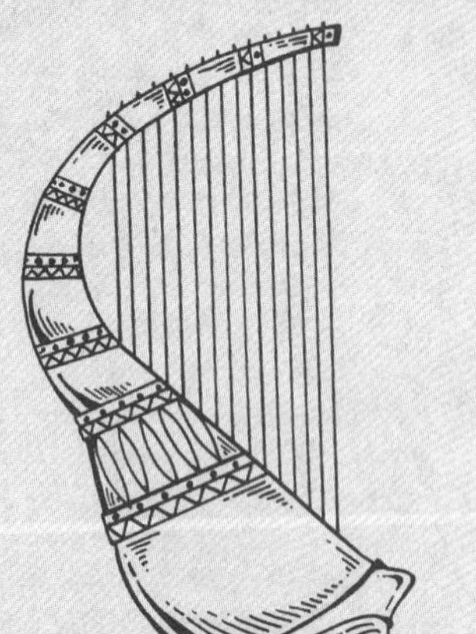

In calling believers to faithfulness, Revelation records several heavenly songs that focus on two great works of God—creation and redemption:

- A creation hymn (4:11). *God created the universe and sustains it for our benefit (Gen. 1:1–31). Four creatures sing, "You are worthy, O Lord."*
- A redemption hymn (5:9–12). *In Christ, God has offered up the necessary sacrifice to rescue us from sin. Four creatures, twenty-four elders, and myriads of the heavenly host sing, "You are worthy."*

Finally, these two great gifts of God, creation and redemption, cause every creature in heaven and earth to give praise by singing, "Blessing and honor and glory and power be to Him" (5:13).

Believers today need to give thanks to God for both of these mighty acts. We also need to respond to these acts through our lives and work. For example, through an emphasis on the creative activity of God, believers might participate in efforts on behalf of the environment or on projects to aid the needy who control few of the resources of creation. Likewise, through an emphasis on the re-

of eyes around and within. And they do not rest day or
night, saying:

"Holy, holy, holy,[a]
Lord God Almighty,
Who was and is and is to come!"

9Whenever the living creatures give glory and honor and
thanks to Him who sits on the throne, who lives forever
4:10–11 and ever, 10the twenty-four elders fall
down before Him who sits on the throne
and worship Him who lives forever and ever, and cast their
crowns before the throne, saying:

11 "You are worthy, O Lord,[a]
To receive glory and honor and power;
For You created all things,
And by Your will they exist[b] and were created."

4:8 [a]M-Text has *holy* nine times. 4:11 [a]NU-Text and M-Text read *our Lord and God.* [b]NU-Text and M-Text read *existed.*

demptive activity of God, believers will work hard to communicate the message of Christ's saving grace to all the people of the earth.

Ideally, followers of Christ will strike a balance between these two, rather than choose one emphasis over another. After all, we have been called by God to obey two mandates: (1) to be good stewards of God's creation by exercising dominion over the earth and its resources (Gen. 1:26–31); and (2) to carry out Christ's mandate to make disciples of all peoples (Matt. 28:18–20).

John reinforces these challenges through two additional passages:

- *"Do not harm the earth, the sea, or the trees" (7:3).*
- *"I looked and behold, a great multitude which no one could number, of all nations, tribes, peoples and tongues, standing before the throne" (7:9).*

Do you tend to emphasize one aspect of God's work—creation or redemption—to the neglect of the other? How can you and your church recover this dual calling from God? ◆

"YOU ARE WORTHY, O LORD, TO RECEIVE GLORY AND HONOR AND POWER."
—Revelation 4:11

FINALLY, FULL EQUALITY

CONSIDER THIS 5:9–10 **Will there ever be an end to discrimination, racism, elitism, and injustice? Will people ever regard each other as equals? John's vision of "every tribe and tongue and people and nation" standing before God and singing His praise (v. 9) gives us assurance that in the end, we will all experience full equality.**

Scripture begins with a creation that was "very good" (Gen. 1:31). Adam and Eve were given authority over creation and responsibility to tend the garden as full partners. However, the horrible entrance of sin ruins this original design. Is there any reason to hope that God's original intention will be recovered?

Yes, Revelation 5 offers images of the original reality one day coming true again:

- **One who is worthy to provide a renewed future arrives (vv. 1–5).**
- **The Spirits of God pervade the creation (v. 6).**
- **Believers from every tribe and nation are among the leadership (v. 9).**
- **All of them are empowered to be "kings and priests to our God" who will reign on the earth (v. 10).**
- **Unhindered praise and worship breaks forth, uniting representatives of all peoples before God (vv. 11–14).**

God's original design will ultimately become a reality. Meanwhile, believers today are called to be signposts of Christ's coming kingdom so that others may choose to welcome Him into their lives.

Is there evidence in your life, family, and work that this kingdom is beginning in you?

CHAPTER 5

A Sealed Book

1And I saw in the right *hand* of Him who sat on the
throne a scroll written inside and on the back, sealed with
seven seals. 2Then I saw a strong angel proclaiming with a
loud voice, "Who is worthy to open the scroll and to loose
its seals?" 3And no one in heaven or on the earth or under
the earth was able to open the scroll, or to look at it.

4So I wept much, because no one was found worthy to
open and read[a] the scroll, or to look at it. 5But one of the elders said to me, "Do not weep. Behold, the Lion of the tribe
of Judah, the Root of David, has prevailed to open the scroll
and to loose[a] its seven seals."

6And I looked, and behold,[a] in the midst of the throne
and of the four living creatures, and in the midst of the elders, stood a Lamb as though it had been slain, having
seven horns and seven eyes, which are the seven Spirits of
God sent out into all the earth. 7Then He came and took the
scroll out of the right hand of Him who sat on the throne.

8Now when He had taken the scroll, the four living creatures and the twenty-four elders fell down before the Lamb,
each having a harp, and golden bowls full of incense, which
5:9–10 are the prayers of the saints. 9And they
sang a new song, saying:

"You are worthy to take the scroll,
And to open its seals;
For You were slain,
And have redeemed us to God by Your blood
Out of every tribe and tongue and people and nation,
10 And have made us[a] kings[b] and priests to our God;
And we[c] shall reign on the earth."

11Then I looked, and I heard the voice of many angels
around the throne, the living creatures, and the elders; and
the number of them was ten thousand times ten thousand,
and thousands of thousands, 12saying with a loud voice:

"Worthy is the Lamb who was slain
To receive power and riches and wisdom,
And strength and honor and glory and blessing!"

13And every creature which is in heaven and on the earth
and under the earth and such as are in the sea, and all that
are in them, I heard saying:

5:4 [a]NU-Text and M-Text omit *and read.* *5:5* [a]NU-Text and M-Text omit *to loose.* *5:6* [a]NU-Text and M-Text read *I saw in the midst . . . a Lamb standing.* *5:10* [a]NU-Text and M-Text read *them.* [b]NU-Text reads *a kingdom.* [c]NU-Text and M-Text read *they.*

"Blessing and honor and glory and power
Be to Him who sits on the throne,
And to the Lamb, forever and ever!"[a]

14Then the four living creatures said, "Amen!" And the
twenty-four[a] elders fell down and worshiped Him who lives
forever and ever.[b]

CHAPTER 6

Seals of Wrath and Chaos

6:1–17 see pg. 892

1Now I saw when the Lamb opened
one of the seals;[a] and I heard one of the
four living creatures saying with a voice like thunder,
"Come and see." 2And I looked, and behold, a white horse.
He who sat on it had a bow; and a crown was given to him,
and he went out conquering and to conquer.
3When He opened the second seal, I heard the second living creature saying, "Come and see."[a] 4Another horse, fiery
red, went out. And it was granted to the one who sat on it
to take peace from the earth, and that *people* should kill one
another; and there was given to him a great sword.
5When He opened the third seal, I heard the third living
creature say, "Come and see." So I looked, and behold, a
black horse, and he who sat on it had a pair of scales in his
hand. 6And I heard a voice in the midst of the four living
creatures saying, "A quart[a] of wheat for a denarius,[b] and
three quarts of barley for a denarius; and do not harm the
oil and the wine."
7When He opened the fourth seal, I heard the voice of the
fourth living creature saying, "Come and see." 8So I looked,
and behold, a pale horse. And the name of him who sat on
it was Death, and Hades followed with him. And power was
given to them over a fourth of the earth, to kill with sword,
with hunger, with death, and by the beasts of the earth.
9When He opened the fifth seal, I saw under the altar the
souls of those who had been slain for the word of God and
for the testimony which they held. 10And they cried with a
loud voice, saying, "How long, O Lord, holy and true, until
You judge and avenge our blood on those who dwell on the
earth?" 11Then a white robe was given to each of them; and
it was said to them that they should rest a little while
longer, until both *the number of* their fellow servants and
their brethren, who would be killed as they *were,* was completed.

5:13 [a]M-Text adds *Amen.* *5:14* [a]NU-Text and M-Text omit *twenty-four.* [b]NU-Text and M-Text omit *Him who lives forever and ever.* *6:1* [a]NU-Text and M-Text read *seven seals.* *6:3* [a]NU-Text and M-Text omit *and see.* *6:6* [a]Greek *choinix;* that is, approximately one quart [b]This was approximately one day's wage for a worker.

ANGELS—SERVANTS OF GOD

FOR YOUR INFO 7:1 **The four angels that John saw standing at the four corners of the earth (v. 1) are among the countless ministering spirits that serve God and His people (Heb. 1:7, 14). Angels figure prominently in the book of Revelation (for example, 1:20; 5:2, 11; 7:2, 11; 8:2, 6; 12:7; 14:6; 15:1; 18:21; 20:1; 22:8). But they also played a part in many other**

(continued on next page)

12I looked when He opened the sixth seal, and behold,[a]
there was a great earthquake; and the sun became black as
sackcloth of hair, and the moon[b] became like blood. 13And
the stars of heaven fell to the earth, as a fig tree drops its
late figs when it is shaken by a mighty wind. 14Then the sky
receded as a scroll when it is rolled up, and every mountain
and island was moved out of its place. 15And the kings of
the earth, the great men, the rich men, the commanders,[a]
the mighty men, every slave and every free man, hid themselves in the caves and in the rocks of the mountains, 16and
said to the mountains and rocks, "Fall on us and hide us
from the face of Him who sits on the throne and from the
wrath of the Lamb! 17For the great day of His wrath has
come, and who is able to stand?"

CHAPTER 7

Representatives from Israel

7:1

1After these things I saw four angels
standing at the four corners of the earth,

6:12 [a]NU-Text and M-Text omit *behold.* [b]NU-Text and M-Text read *the whole moon.*
6:15 [a]NU-Text and M-Text read *the commanders, the rich men.*

CONSIDER THIS 6:1–17

WORSHIP OR WRATH?

For some people, Christ makes very little difference in how one looks at life. Faith doesn't really matter. But in Revelation 4–10, John provides us with a peek into the future and the prospect of life or death forever. Clearly, the time we spend on earth is but a brief preamble to something much larger.

CHRIST MAKES ALL THE DIFFERENCE

With Christ: Worship	Without Christ: Wrath
Splendor and beauty (4:2–8)	Peace gone from earth (6:4)
Praise and adoration (4:8–11)	Killing unleashed (6:5)
Access provided (5:1–8)	Death reigns (6:8)
Outbursts of worship (5:9)	Earth collapses (6:12–17)
Entitlement given (5:10)	Fires and earthquakes (8:5)
Affirmation (5:11–14)	Destruction surges (8:7–10)
Martyrs restored (6:9–11)	Many die (8:11)
Protection given (7:2–8)	Darkness pervades earth (8:12)
Suffering ceases (7:9–17)	Woes are announced (8:13)
God's mystery completed (10:7)	Plagues torment the lost (9:2–11)
Bitter becomes sweet (10:9)	Many die (9:18)
	Repentance is rejected (9:20–21)

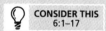

holding the four winds of the earth, that the wind should
not blow on the earth, on the sea, or on any tree. 2Then I
saw another angel ascending from the east, having the seal
of the living God. And he cried with a loud voice to the four
angels to whom it was granted to harm the earth and the
sea, 3saying, "Do not harm the earth, the sea, or the trees till
we have sealed the servants of our God on their foreheads."
4And I heard the number of those who were sealed. One
hundred *and* forty-four thousand of all the tribes of the
children of Israel *were* sealed:

5 of the tribe of Judah twelve thousand *were* sealed;[a]
of the tribe of Reuben twelve thousand *were* sealed;
of the tribe of Gad twelve thousand *were* sealed;
6 of the tribe of Asher twelve thousand *were* sealed;
of the tribe of Naphtali twelve thousand *were* sealed;
of the tribe of Manasseh twelve thousand *were* sealed;
7 of the tribe of Simeon twelve thousand *were* sealed;
of the tribe of Levi twelve thousand *were* sealed;

7:5 [a]In NU-Text and M-Text *were sealed* is stated only in verses 5a and 8c; the words are understood in the remainder of the passage.

◆ ◆ ◆ ◆ ◆ ◆ ◆ ◆ ◆ ◆ ◆ ◆ ◆ ◆ ◆

This section offers us a bird's-eye view of the coming apocalypse on earth and the promised joy of heaven (4:1). The contrasts are severe. Those who embrace Christ and His provision for sin can anticipate a celebration that exceeds their greatest expectations. Those without Christ have cause to tremble for their refusal to accept His offer of deliverance from the wrath to come.

The message is plain: only in Christ is there hope of escaping wrath. That way of escape is offered right now. Waiting to accept Christ's offer only increases the risk of experiencing adverse judgment. It also deprives one of new life today.

If you have not yet responded to Christ's offer of eternal life, why not do so right now? There is much more to life than the here and now. The choice you make has eternal consequences. ◆

(continued from previous page)

events of the New Testament, as the following table shows:

THE MINISTRY OF ANGELS
•Calmed Joseph's doubts about Mary's faithfulness (Matt. 1:20–25).
•Warned Joseph to flee from Herod's plan to kill Jesus (Matt. 2:13).
•Encouraged Joseph to return to Israel with his family (Matt. 2:19–20).
•Ministered to Jesus after His temptation in the wilderness (Matt. 4:11).
•Told the women at the empty tomb that Jesus was alive (Matt. 28:2–6).
•Foretold to Zacharias the birth of John the Baptist (Luke 1:11–20).
•Told Mary that she would bear the Christ (Luke 1:26–38).
•Announced Jesus' birth to shepherds near Bethlehem (Luke 2:8–15).
•Appeared to Jesus in the Garden of Gethsemane to give Him strength (Luke 22:43).
•Promised the crowd observing Jesus' ascension that He would return in like manner (Acts 1:10–11).
•Brought Peter and John out of prison (Acts 5:17–20).
•Told Philip to go into the desert where he met the Ethiopian treasurer (Acts 8:26).
•Told the centurion Cornelius to send for Peter (Acts 10:3–8).
•Released Peter from prison (Acts 12:7).
•Struck down Herod for not giving glory to God (Acts 12:23).
•Stood by Paul during a storm at sea to assure him that he would stand before Caesar (Acts 27:23–24).

Learn more about angels and the role they played in Jesus' birth, resurrection, and ascension at the article, "Spiritual Realities Beyond You," Matt. 8:29.

A Great Multitude of All Nations

CONSIDER THIS 7:9 **Jesus sent His followers to make disciples of all the nations (*ethnē*, "peoples"; see "To All the Nations," Matt. 28:19). As John takes us into the throne room of heaven, we see the fulfillment of Jesus' mandate. There, standing before the Lamb (Christ) is a crowd so large that it cannot be counted, made up of "all nations, tribes, peoples, and tongues" (Rev. 7:9).**

Actually, two groups are present—representatives from God's people, the Jews (vv. 3–8), and countless Gentile believers (vv. 9–10). Just as Jesus said it would, the gospel has spread out from Jerusalem to reach people from "the end of the earth" (Acts 1:8). Now Jews and Gentiles have come together to receive the salvation that God has promised. Now God dwells among His people. Jesus is their Shepherd, supplying all their needs (Rev. 7:14–17).

In response to this spectacular, worldwide, multiethnic salvation, the creatures of heaven and earth fall down before God in worship and song (vv. 11–12). What a breathtaking picture this is!

But of course this vision lies in the future. For now, we live in a world wracked by ethnic divisions and racial prejudice. Yet knowing that God intends to populate heaven with people from every ethnic background has important implications for those of us who claim to follow Christ. If God's heart reaches out to the whole world, then our hearts need to as well.

of the tribe of Issachar twelve thousand *were* sealed;
8 of the tribe of Zebulun twelve thousand *were* sealed;
of the tribe of Joseph twelve thousand *were* sealed;
of the tribe of Benjamin twelve thousand *were* sealed.

A Great Multitude from Every Nation

7:9 [9]After these things I looked, and behold, a great multitude which no one
could number, of all nations, tribes, peoples, and tongues,
standing before the throne and before the Lamb, clothed
with white robes, with palm branches in their hands, [10]and
crying out with a loud voice, saying, "Salvation *belongs* to
our God who sits on the throne, and to the Lamb!" [11]All the
angels stood around the throne and the elders and the four
living creatures, and fell on their faces before the throne and
worshiped God, [12]saying:

"Amen! Blessing and glory and wisdom,
Thanksgiving and honor and power and might,
Be to our God forever and ever.
Amen."

[13]Then one of the elders answered, saying to me, "Who
are these arrayed in white robes, and where did they come
from?"
[14]And I said to him, "Sir,[a] you know."
So he said to me, "These are the ones who come out of
the great tribulation, and washed their robes and made
them white in the blood of the Lamb. [15]Therefore they are
before the throne of God, and serve Him day and night in
His temple. And He who sits on the throne will dwell
among them. [16]They shall neither hunger anymore nor
thirst anymore; the sun shall not strike them, nor any heat;
[17]for the Lamb who is in the midst of the throne will shepherd them and lead them to living fountains of waters.[a] And
God will wipe away every tear from their eyes."

CHAPTER 8

One Last Seal

8:1 see pg. 896 [1]When He opened the seventh seal,
there was silence in heaven for about half
an hour. [2]And I saw the seven angels who stand before God,

7:14 [a]NU-Text and M-Text read *My lord.* *7:17* [a]NU-Text and M-Text read *to fountains of the waters of life.*

and to them were given seven trumpets. 3Then another
angel, having a golden censer, came and stood at the
altar. He was given much incense, that he should offer *it*
with the prayers of all the saints upon the golden altar
which was before the throne. 4And the smoke of the incense, with the prayers of the saints, ascended before God
from the angel's hand. 5Then the angel took the censer,
filled it with fire from the altar, and threw *it* to the earth.
And there were noises, thunderings, lightnings, and an
earthquake.

A Sound of Trumpets

6So the seven angels who had the seven trumpets prepared themselves to sound.
7The first angel sounded: And hail and fire followed, mingled with blood, and they were thrown to the earth.[a] And a
third of the trees were burned up, and all green grass was
burned up.
8Then the second angel sounded: And *something* like a
great mountain burning with fire was thrown into the sea,
and a third of the sea became blood. 9And a third of the living creatures in the sea died, and a third of the ships were
destroyed.
10Then the third angel sounded: And a great star fell from
heaven, burning like a torch, and it fell on a third of the
rivers and on the springs of water. 11The name of the star
is Wormwood. A third of the waters became wormwood,
and many men died from the water, because it was made
bitter.
12Then the fourth angel sounded: And a third of the sun
was struck, a third of the moon, and a third of the stars, so
that a third of them were darkened. A third of the day did
not shine, and likewise the night.
13And I looked, and I heard an angel[a] flying through the
midst of heaven, saying with a loud voice, "Woe, woe, woe
to the inhabitants of the earth, because of the remaining
blasts of the trumpet of the three angels who are about to
sound!"

CHAPTER 9

Two More Trumpets and Woe

1Then the fifth angel sounded: And I saw a star fallen
from heaven to the earth. To him was given the key to the

8:7 [a]NU-Text and M-Text add *And a third of the earth was burned up.* *8:13* [a]NU-Text and M-Text read *eagle.*

"AND HE WHO SITS ON THE THRONE WILL DWELL AMONG THEM."
—Revelation 7:15

bottomless pit. 2And he opened the bottomless pit, and
smoke arose out of the pit like the smoke of a great furnace.
So the sun and the air were darkened because of the smoke
of the pit. 3Then out of the smoke locusts came upon the
earth. And to them was given power, as the scorpions of the
earth have power. 4They were commanded not to harm the grass of the

9:4 see pg. 898

FOR YOUR INFO 8:1

The Structure of Revelation

A cascade of dramatic events pours from the book of Revelation as the book unfolds. John narrates his vision in a torrent of images such as the seventh seal (v. 1), many of which may seem confusing to some readers. However, close observation reveals that the action is not random. John's vision is told in a tightly woven structure that offers important clues to understanding the book.

One way to summarize the material in Revelation is based on the three time frames that Jesus told John to write about: "Write the things which you have seen, and the things which are, and the things which will take place after this" (1:19). This yields the following outline for the book:

- *I. "The things which you have seen" (1:1–20)*
  - *A. Greetings and praise (1:1–8)*
  - *B. A vision of the risen Christ (1:9–20)*
- *II. "The things which are" (2:1—3:22)*
  - *A. Letter to the church at Ephesus (2:1–7)*
  - *B. Letter to the church at Smyrna (2:8–11)*
  - *C. Letter to the church at Pergamos (2:12–17)*
  - *D. Letter to the church at Thyatira (2:18–29)*
  - *E. Letter to the church at Sardis (3:1–6)*
  - *F. Letter to the church at Philadelphia (3:7–13)*
  - *G. Letter to the church at Laodicea (3:14–22)*
- *III. "The things which will take place after this" (4:1—22:21)*
  - *A. Worship in heaven (4:1—5:14)*
  - *B. Seven seals (6:1—8:5)*
  - *C. Seven trumpets (8:6—11:19)*
  - *D. Seven signs (12:1—14:20)*
  - *E. Seven bowls (15:1—16:21)*
  - *F. The final judgment and the triumph of God (17:1—20:15)*
  - *G. A new heaven and new earth (21:1—22:5)*
  - *H. Conclusion (22:6–21)*

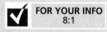

earth, or any green thing, or any tree, but only those men
who do not have the seal of God on their foreheads. 5And
they were not given *authority* to kill them, but to torment
them *for* five months. Their torment *was* like the torment of
a scorpion when it strikes a man. 6In those days men will
seek death and will not find it; they will desire to die, and
death will flee from them.

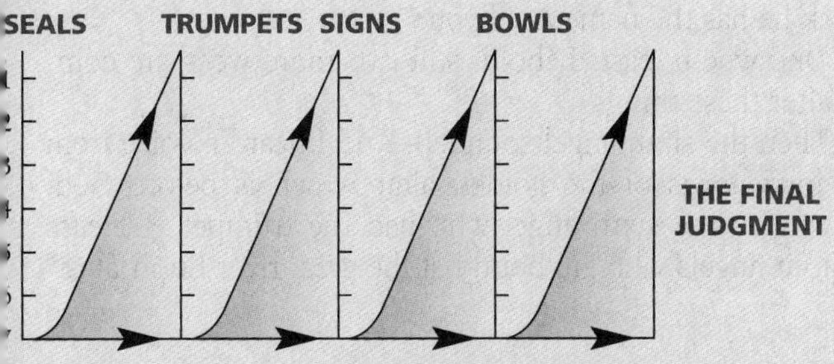

THE STRUCTURE OF REVELATION

In the portion of the book devoted to the seven seals, seven trumpets, seven signs, and seven bowls (6:1—16:21), a common pattern repeats. In each case, six of the seven items play out their action and then there is a break during which God's people are challenged to perseverance and faithfulness. Then the seventh item unfolds.

Some have suggested that the seventh item in each group holds or gives rise to the action that follows: the seventh seal contains the seven trumpets, the seventh trumpet contains the seven signs, the seventh sign contains the seven bowls, and the seventh bowl contains the final judgment. This suggests that the apocalyptic events increase in their intensity with each passing event, spiraling toward the final defeat of evil and the triumph of Christ.

Throughout these events, a message to believers remains clear: God is in control; ultimately His will will be done; therefore His people need to stand firm, trust in His power, and wait for deliverance from whatever trials befall them. ◆

In addition to the structure of Revelation, it's important to read the book as a kind of literature known as apocalyptic *in order to appreciate its meaning. See "The Genre of Apocalyptic Literature," Rev. 10:1–10.*

IN THOSE DAYS MEN WILL SEEK DEATH AND WILL NOT FIND IT.
—Revelation 9:6

7The shape of the locusts was like horses prepared for
battle. On their heads were crowns of something like gold,
and their faces *were* like the faces of men. 8They had hair
like women's hair, and their teeth were like lions' *teeth.* 9And
they had breastplates like breastplates of iron, and the
sound of their wings *was* like the sound of chariots with
many horses running into battle. 10They had tails like scorpions, and there were stings in their tails. Their power *was*
9:11 to hurt men five months. 11And they had
as king over them the angel of the bottomless pit, whose name in Hebrew *is* Abaddon, but in
Greek he has the name Apollyon.

12One woe is past. Behold, still two more woes are coming after these things.

13Then the sixth angel sounded: And I heard a voice from
the four horns of the golden altar which is before God,
14saying to the sixth angel who had the trumpet, "Release
the four angels who are bound at the great river Euphrates."

CONSIDER THIS
9:4

FAITH AND THE ENVIRONMENT

Global warming. Overpopulation. Acid rain. The destruction of rain forests. Is the Bible concerned with the earth's ecology? Or does it teach that the earth's resources exist purely for people's pleasure, to be used as they will, with little thought for long-term consequences?

"The earth is the Lord's, and all its fullness," declared the psalmist (Ps. 24:1). Again, "The earth is full of [God's] possessions" (Ps. 104:24). These and many other passages indicate that creation is not ours to plunder, but rather a resource which God has entrusted to our management, to be used in service to each other (Ps. 104:13, 23, 31). We will ultimately answer to God for its use.

In John's description of the end times, there is much destruction and violence. But not all is to be consumed. Nor does the earth exist only for people's pleasure and consumption. The command not to harm "the grass of the earth, or any green thing, or any tree" (v. 4) is a curious echo of Gen. 1:29–30: "every herb that yields seed which is on the face of all the earth, and every tree whose fruit yields seed . . . every beast of the earth, to every bird of the air, and to everything that creeps on the earth."

The same concern for earth's resources occurs when God sends one of His angels to cry with a loud voice to the

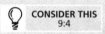

[15]So the four angels, who had been prepared for the hour
and day and month and year, were released to kill a third of
mankind. [16]Now the number of the army of the horsemen
was two hundred million; I heard the number of them.
[17]And thus I saw the horses in the vision: those who sat on
them had breastplates of fiery red, hyacinth blue, and sulfur
yellow; and the heads of the horses *were* like the heads of
lions; and out of their mouths came fire, smoke, and brimstone. [18]By these three *plagues* a third of mankind was
killed—by the fire and the smoke and the brimstone which
came out of their mouths. [19]For their power[a] is in their
mouth and in their tails; for their tails *are* like serpents,
having heads; and with them they do harm.
[20]But the rest of mankind, who were not killed by these
plagues, did not repent of the works of their hands, that

(Bible text continued on page 902)

9:19 [a]NU-Text and M-Text read *the power of the horses.*

◆ ◆ ◆ ◆ ◆ ◆ ◆ ◆ ◆ ◆ ◆ ◆ ◆ ◆ ◆

four angels "to whom it was granted to harm the earth and the sea . . . 'Do not harm the earth, the sea, or the trees' " (7:2–3). Likewise, the new heaven and earth include a "pure river of water of life, clear as crystal . . . the tree of life, which bore twelve fruits, each tree yielding its fruit every month. The leaves of the tree were for the healing of the nations" (22:1–2).

When God created the world's resources, He declared them to be "very good" (Gen. 1:31). He assigned people to care for them, develop them, and use them for good (1:26–31). This management role is part of our calling to live according to the image and likeness of God. He has made us to be more than mere consumers who gratify their own desires. He wants us to serve Him as we manage His creation. Our work is a gift from God to develop and deliver the benefits of that resource to other people (see "People at Work," Heb. 2:7).

Do you treat the world with respect as a resource for which God has given you responsibility? Does your work please God and serve other people? Can you think of ways to do a better job of managing the environment in a way that God would approve? ◆

NAMES FOR SATAN IN THE NEW TESTAMENT

FOR YOUR INFO 9:11 **Two names are given to the "angel of the bottomless pit" (v. 11), Abaddon ("destruction") and Apollyon ("destroyer"). There is no mistaking this reference to Satan, the archenemy of God (the name Satan means "adversary"). Other names used for him in the New Testament reveal his evil character:**

SATAN'S MANY ALIASES

- Beelzebub, the ruler of the demons (Matt. 12:24)
- The wicked one (Matt. 13:19, 38)
- The enemy (Matt. 13:39)
- Murderer (John 8:44)
- Liar (John 8:44)
- The ruler of this world (John 12:31; 14:30)
- The god of this age (2 Cor. 4:4)
- Belial (2 Cor. 6:15, according to some interpretations)
- The prince of the power of the air (Eph. 2:2)
- The tempter (1 Thess. 3:5)
- A roaring lion (1 Pet. 5:8)
- The adversary (1 Pet. 5:8)
- The dragon (Rev. 12:7)
- The accuser of our brethren (Rev. 12:10)
- The serpent of old (Rev. 20:2)
- The deceiver (Rev. 20:10)

Satan leads a vast army of fallen angels who are in open rebellion against God. See "Demons," Luke 11:14.

FOR YOUR INFO 10:1–10

The Genre of Apocalyptic Literature

An angel from heaven, straddling land and sea (vv. 1, 3). A voice from heaven (v. 4). The number seven (vv. 4, 7). Prophecies about "peoples, nations, tongues, and kings" (v. 11). These are features of the style of literature known as apocalyptic, *of which Revelation is the preeminent example. It's important to understand this genre if one wants to understand the book's meaning. Although Revelation is more than just a typical apocalyptic work, in that it is part of Scripture, it pays to study such literature as a category.*

The Greek word *apocalypse* means a "revelation," "unveiling," or "disclosure." Thus apocalyptic literature seeks to reveal certain mysteries about heaven and earth, humankind and God, angels and demons, the life of the world today, and the world to come. This type of writing arose among the Jews and Christians during the period from 200 B.C. to A.D. 200.

Characteristics

Apocalyptic literature employs a number of literary devices, styles, and motifs that set it apart from other literature, including:

- *visions* as a way of revealing secrets from heaven about the present and future. Often these visions are caused by some trauma or major event that creates a crisis in the writer's experience (for example, Rev. 1:10). Often one vision leads to others.
- *ethical conclusions* drawn on the basis of the writer's visionary experiences. For instance, John's seven letters to seven churches in Rev. 2–3 are written after the apostle sees a vision and is commissioned by God to write (1:19). The letters call the churches to specific ethical and moral decisions.
- *anonymous or attributed authorship.* Revelation is an exception among apocalyptic works in that it gives the name of its author (1:1, 9). Many non-canonical apocalyptic books attribute their origins to famous prophets of the past, such as Ezra, Enoch, Jeremiah, and Moses. This may be a way to add credibility to the work.

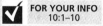

- *the use of powerful symbolism.* Apocalyptic books stretch the reader's imagination through highly dramatic images in which actions and outcomes occur in extremes. Numerology is especially important. Those for whom the books were originally intended presumably knew the meaning of the symbols used by the authors, connecting them to events of the time.
- *a stark contrast between good and evil.* Apocalyptic writing is dualistic in that it separates things into definite categories of good and evil, right and wrong. In Revelation, for example, one is either on the side of God, who is holy, righteous, and just, or on the side of Satan, who is surrounded by abominations, idolatries, and wickedness.
- *a concern with end times.* The future plays prominently in these writings. The authors look ahead to coming events, on the one hand offering hope to those who long for justice and delivery from evil, and on the other issuing warnings to those who are in rebellion against God's ways.

Messages

Through apocalyptic writing, authors communicate important messages to their readers. The following themes occur in all the apocalyptic writings:

- *The end is coming soon.* Apocalyptic writers frequently connect the arrival of the end times with the near future. This sense of immediacy lends urgency to the message.
- *The whole cosmos is involved.* The end of the world is not a solitary event for the earth alone; it extends to the whole universe. Apocalyptic writings emphasize worldwide events and cataclysmic judgments.
- *History is divided into fixed segments.* Along with a pessimistic view of history, apocalyptic literature takes the view that history has been determined by God before creation. World history has been divided into fixed time periods, and people simply live out a predetermined drama. Many of the writings divide history into two major periods—the present world, ruled by Satan and his legions, and the world to come, in which wickedness will be abolished and God will rule supreme.
- *Angels and demons.* Spirits are common figures in the apocalyptic genre who are actively involved in the drama of events. Pointing to Satan and his demons (fallen angels) explains the problem of evil. Likewise, angels who have not fallen are used by God to protect and serve His faithful people.
- *A new heaven and a new earth.* The end times as portrayed in apocalyptic writings bring a return to the beginning of creation. Out of heaven will come a new heaven and a new earth. The old will be destroyed, replaced by a new creation where God will rule.
- *A Messiah.* A Messiah or mediator between God and man appears in most of the apocalyptic writings as one who accomplishes the final salvation of the world. In Revelation, the Messiah is shown to be Christ, the "King of kings and Lord of lords" (19:16).

Because the book of Revelation forms a part of God's revealed Word, it is in a class by itself among the apocalyptic works of its period. Like the rest of the inspired Scriptures, it is reliable and authoritative, and possesses an integrity and a trustworthiness not found in uninspired writings that resemble it as to its genre. But studying apocalyptic literature helps us to identify Revelation's themes, and thereby to better understand God's message to us in it. ◆

they should not worship demons, and idols of gold, silver, brass, stone, and wood, which can neither see nor
hear nor walk. 21And they did not repent of their murders or their sorceries[a] or their sexual immorality or their
thefts.

CHAPTER 10

The Little Book

10:1–10 see pg. 900

1I saw still another mighty angel coming down from heaven, clothed with a
cloud. And a rainbow *was* on his head, his face *was*
like the sun, and his feet like pillars of fire. 2He had a
little book open in his hand. And he set his right foot on
the sea and *his* left *foot* on the land, 3and cried with a loud

9:21 [a]NU-Text and M-Text read *drugs.*

CONSIDER THIS 11:17

POWER

Business, government, nonprofit organizations, and churches all feel the impact of people pursuing and defending power. Here in John's vision of God triumphing over evil, God holds the ultimate power (v. 17).

What does the New Testament teach about power?

- *There is tremendous power in humility. It gives us strength that is a gift from God to be used for His purposes. See "The Power of Humility," Matt. 3:11.*
- *Forgiveness is powerful and liberating and is a power that Jesus has delegated to His followers. See "The Power of Forgiveness," Matt. 9:4–8.*
- *When others observe us and the way we use power and authority, they ought to see Jesus. See " 'You Remind Me of . . . ,' " Mark 6:14–16.*
- *Like fire, power can be used to accomplish good. But always lurking in its shadow is the temptation of abuse. See "Three Dangers of Power," Luke 3:14.*
- *Jesus described the power that He supplies as the right and ability to lay down one's life for others. See "The Power of Self-Sacrifice," John 10:17–18.*
- *All power ultimately comes from God, and we are ultimately accountable to Him for how we use power. See "Seeing Behind Power," John 19:10–11.*
- *Jesus gives His followers a unique kind of power to accomplish His tasks. See "Power," Acts 1:8.*
- *God's power has little or nothing to do with outward ap-*

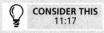

voice, as *when* a lion roars. When he cried out, seven
thunders uttered their voices. 4Now when the seven
thunders uttered their voices,[a] I was about to write; but I
heard a voice from heaven saying to me,[b] "Seal up the
things which the seven thunders uttered, and do not write
them."

5The angel whom I saw standing on the sea and on the
land raised up his hand[a] to heaven 6and swore by Him who
lives forever and ever, who created heaven and the things
that are in it, the earth and the things that are in it, and the
sea and the things that are in it, that there should be delay
no longer, 7but in the days of the sounding of the seventh
angel, when he is about to sound, the mystery of God
would be finished, as He declared to His servants the
prophets.

10:4 [a]NU-Text and M-Text read *sounded.* [b]NU-Text and M-Text omit *to me.*
10:5 [a]NU-Text and M-Text read *right hand.*

pearances or worldly acclaim. See " 'Give Me Power!' " Acts 8:18–19.

- *Paul was competent in and comfortable with the powerful Roman judicial system and its procedures, even when he faced officials who dealt in bribes and political favors. See "Paul and the Structures of Power," Acts 24:25–26.*
- *The message of Christ is powerful enough to transform lives. See "The Power of the Gospel," Rom. 1:16.*
- *The gospel appears foolish to many people. Yet the irony is that it is far more powerful than even the strongest players in our culture can imagine. See "The Power of Foolishness," 1 Cor. 1:18.*
- *Sometimes we give away the control of our lives to things like status and possessions. When we do, they overpower us: we no longer possess our possessions—they possess us! See "What Controls You?" 1 Cor. 6:12.*
- *Our world prizes strength and power, but Scripture puts a new twist on the notion of strength: weakness can make a person strong. See "When I Am Weak, Then I Am Strong," 2 Cor. 12:7–10.*
- *Do you have what it takes to "make it" in life? Scripture teaches that God's power gives us what we need to experience real life in a way that pleases Him. See "Do You Have What It Takes?" 2 Pet. 1:3–4.* ◆

WHEN HE CRIED OUT, SEVEN THUNDERS UTTERED THEIR VOICES.
—Revelation 10:3

8 Then the voice which I heard from heaven
spoke to me again and said, "Go, take the little
book which is open in the hand of the angel who
stands on the sea and on the earth."
9 So I went to the angel and said to him, "Give me
the little book."
And he said to me, "Take and eat it; and it will
make your stomach bitter, but it will be as sweet as
honey in your mouth."
10 Then I took the little book out of the angel's
hand and ate it, and it was as sweet as honey in my
mouth. But when I had eaten it, my stomach became bitter. 11 And he[a] said to me, "You must
prophesy again about many peoples, nations,
tongues, and kings."

CHAPTER 11

Two Witnesses and a Second Woe

1 Then I was given a reed like a measuring rod.
And the angel stood,[a] saying, "Rise and measure
the temple of God, the altar, and those who worship there. 2 But leave out the court which is outside the temple, and do not measure it, for it has
been given to the Gentiles. And they will tread the
holy city underfoot *for* forty-two months. 3 And I
will give *power* to my two witnesses, and they will
prophesy one thousand two hundred and sixty
days, clothed in sackcloth."
4 These are the two olive trees and the two lampstands standing before the God[a] of the earth. 5 And
if anyone wants to harm them, fire proceeds from
their mouth and devours their enemies. And if anyone wants to harm them, he must be killed in this
manner. 6 These have power to shut heaven, so that
no rain falls in the days of their prophecy; and they
have power over waters to turn them to blood, and
to strike the earth with all plagues, as often as they
desire.
7 When they finish their testimony, the beast
that ascends out of the bottomless pit will make
war against them, overcome them, and kill them.
8 And their dead bodies *will lie* in the street of
the great city which spiritually is called Sodom
and Egypt, where also our[a] Lord was crucified.
9 Then *those* from the peoples, tribes, tongues,
and nations will see their dead bodies three-and-
a-half days, and not allow[a] their dead bodies to
be put into graves. 10 And those who dwell on
the earth will rejoice over them, make merry,
and send gifts to one another, because these
two prophets tormented those who dwell on the
earth.
11 Now after the three-and-a-half days the breath
of life from God entered them, and they stood on
their feet, and great fear fell on those who saw
them. 12 And they[a] heard a loud voice from heaven
saying to them, "Come up here." And they ascended to heaven in a cloud, and their enemies
saw them. 13 In the same hour there was a great
earthquake, and a tenth of the city fell. In the
earthquake seven thousand people were killed, and
the rest were afraid and gave glory to the God of
heaven.
14 The second woe is past. Behold, the third woe
is coming quickly.

The Seventh Trumpet

15 Then the seventh angel sounded: And there
were loud voices in heaven, saying, "The
kingdoms[a] of this world have become *the kingdoms*
of our Lord and of His Christ, and He shall reign
forever and ever!" 16 And the twenty-four elders
who sat before God on their thrones fell on their

11:17
see pg. 902

faces and worshiped God, 17 saying:

"We give You thanks, O Lord God Almighty,
The One who is and who was and who is to
come,[a]
Because You have taken Your great power and
reigned.
18 The nations were angry, and Your wrath has
come,
And the time of the dead, that they should be
judged,
And that You should reward Your servants the
prophets and the saints,
And those who fear Your name, small and
great,
And should destroy those who destroy the
earth."

10:11 [a]NU-Text and M-Text read *they.* *11:1* [a]NU-Text and M-Text omit *And the angel stood.* *11:4* [a]NU-Text and M-Text read *Lord.* *11:8* [a]NU-Text and M-Text read *their.* *11:9* [a]NU-Text and M-Text read *nations see . . . and will not allow.* *11:12* [a]M-Text reads *I.* *11:15* [a]NU-Text and M-Text read *kingdom . . . has become.* *11:17* [a]NU-Text and M-Text omit *and who is to come.*

19Then the temple of God was opened in heaven, and the
ark of His covenant[a] was seen in His temple. And there
were lightnings, noises, thunderings, an earthquake, and
great hail.

CHAPTER 12

A Woman Gives Birth

12:1–2 see pg. 906

1Now a great sign appeared in heaven:
a woman clothed with the sun, with the
moon under her feet, and on her head a garland of twelve
stars. 2Then being with child, she cried out in labor and in
pain to give birth.
3And another sign appeared in heaven: behold, a great,
fiery red dragon having seven heads and ten horns, and
seven diadems on his heads. 4His tail drew a third of the
stars of heaven and threw them to the earth. And the
dragon stood before the woman who was ready to give
birth, to devour her Child as soon as it was born. 5She bore
a male Child who was to rule all nations with a rod of iron.
And her Child was caught up to God and His throne. 6Then
the woman fled into the wilderness, where she has a place
prepared by God, that they should feed her there one thousand two hundred and sixty days.

War in Heaven

7And war broke out in heaven: Michael and his angels
fought with the dragon; and the dragon and his angels
fought, 8but they did not prevail, nor was a place found for
them[a] in heaven any longer. 9So the great dragon was cast
out, that serpent of old, called the Devil and Satan, who
deceives the whole world; he was cast to the earth, and his
angels were cast out with him.
10Then I heard a loud voice saying in heaven, "Now salvation, and strength, and the kingdom of our God, and the
power of His Christ have come, for the accuser of our
brethren, who accused them before our God day and night,
has been cast down. 11And they overcame him by the blood
of the Lamb and by the word of their testimony, and they
did not love their lives to the death. 12Therefore rejoice, O
heavens, and you who dwell in them! Woe to the inhabitants of the earth and the sea! For the devil has come down
to you, having great wrath, because he knows that he has a
short time."

War on Earth

13Now when the dragon saw that he had been cast to the
earth, he persecuted the woman who gave birth to the male

11:19 [a]M-Text reads *the covenant of the Lord*. *12:8* [a]M-Text reads *him*.

WOMEN AGAINST EVIL

CONSIDER THIS 12:1–17 **Women have often been identified in folk wisdom as a peculiar source of evil. For example, confusion over the temptation in the Garden of Eden (Gen. 3:1–16) has sometimes resulted in holding women particularly responsible for sin.**

But in Revelation 12, John describes a woman who is the source of all life and the parent of the One who will rule the nations, Christ (vv. 2, 5). When she is pursued by a dragon that opposes God's work and seeks its destruction (vv. 3–4), God cares for her and prepares a place of refuge for her (v. 6).

This leads to a cosmic war between the angel Michael and the dragon (vv. 7–13). The evil dragon loses and the woman emerges safe and sound (vv. 13–16). Nevertheless, the dragon, which is mortally wounded, declares war on the woman's children (v. 17). This suggests that our bondage to sin and battles against evil are not ultimately the fault of a woman, but of powerful forces beyond our imagining (see "Spiritual Realities Beyond You," Matt. 8:29, and "Who Is the Enemy?" Eph. 6:10–13).

Child. 14But the woman was given two wings of a great
eagle, that she might fly into the wilderness to her place,
where she is nourished for a time and times and half a time,
from the presence of the serpent. 15So the serpent spewed
water out of his mouth like a flood after the woman, that he
might cause her to be carried away by the flood. 16But the
earth helped the woman, and the earth opened its mouth
and swallowed up the flood which the dragon had spewed
out of his mouth. 17And the dragon was
enraged with the woman, and he went
to make war with the rest of her offspring, who keep the
commandments of God and have the testimony of Jesus
Christ.[a]

12:1–17 see pg. 905

12:17 [a]NU-Text and M-Text omit *Christ.*

FOR YOUR INFO 12:1–2

WOMEN IN REVELATION

John's first-century readers no doubt understood more of Revelation than we do today. Nevertheless, even they may have struggled with some of the complex imagery and bizarre descriptions. One interesting group of characters in the narrative is women, such as the woman in labor (vv. 1–2).

The women in Revelation are described in extremes of moral character, either very good or very bad. These heavy contrasts are typical of apocalyptic literature, which tends to be dualistic (see 10:1–10). This, along with the unusual actions that these women take, suggest that we understand them as symbols rather than literal women.

Jezebel (2:20–23)

Christ rebukes the church at Thyatira for allowing "that woman Jezebel" to teach people to worship false gods and to encourage immorality. In the Old Testament, Jezebel was the wife of King Ahab. Together, they were perhaps the most wicked of the Jewish rulers (see "Jezebel," 2:20–23). Note that Christ says that He will judge not only Jezebel, but her children as well—people who follow her ways.

The Woman Giving Birth (12:1–6, 13–17)

This woman stands in marked contrast to Jezebel. Attacked by an evil dragon, she finds protection and refuge provided by God. Her identity has been variously interpreted. Because she bears the Child (capital C), some have seen her as Mary, the mother of Jesus, others as Israel, the collective "mother" that brought forth the Messiah. The

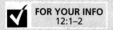

CHAPTER 13

The Great Beast from the Sea

13:1

1Then I[a] stood on the sand of the sea.
And I saw a beast rising up out of the sea,
having seven heads and ten horns,[b] and on his horns ten

13:1 [a]NU-Text reads *he.* [b]NU-Text and M-Text read *ten horns and seven heads.*

Beastly Rome

A CLOSER LOOK 13:1

The beast from the sea (v. 1) has long been understood to be a symbol for the Roman Empire. This image of a power that deserved to fall was a far cry from the one that Paul urged Christians to obey. See "The Limits of Political Authority," Rom. 13:1–7.

attempts of the dragon to destroy her, along with "the rest of her offspring" (v. 17), may be references to Satan's attempts to destroy Israel and disrupt the Messianic line.

Babylon, the Great Harlot (14:8; 17:1–6, 15–18; 18:1–24)

Old Testament prophets (for example, Hosea; Ezek. 16:8–58) often referred to adulterers and prostitutes to represent people who practiced idolatry. Just as an adulteress is unfaithful to her husband, so God's people are unfaithful to Him when they allow their hearts to be divided and they worship other gods (see "Understanding Prostitution," Matt 21:31–32).

The harlot in Revelation 17 is identified as Babylon, which first-century readers would probably have identified as Rome (see "A Symbol of Evil," 14:8). In contrast to the new Jerusalem that descends from heaven with glory and blessing (Rev. 21), Babylon is shattered and destroyed in judgment for persecuting God's people and corrupting the peoples of the earth with wickedness (Rev. 18).

The Wife (Bride) of the Lamb (19:7–8)

As the marriage feast of the Lamb approaches, a bride has made herself ready. The description of this woman clothing herself in righteous acts (19:8) suggests that she may represent the church. ◆

AND THE DRAGON WAS ENRAGED WITH THE WOMAN. . . .
—Revelation 12:17

crowns, and on his heads a blasphemous name. [2]Now the
beast which I saw was like a leopard, his feet were like *the
feet of* a bear, and his mouth like the mouth of a lion. The
dragon gave him his power, his throne, and great authority.
[3]And *I saw* one of his heads as if it had been mortally
wounded, and his deadly wound was healed. And all the
13:1–18 world marveled and followed the beast.
[4]So they worshiped the dragon who gave
authority to the beast; and they worshiped the beast, saying,
"Who *is* like the beast? Who is able to make war with him?"
[5]And he was given a mouth speaking great things and
blasphemies, and he was given authority to continue[a] for
forty-two months. [6]Then he opened his mouth in blasphemy against God, to blaspheme His name, His tabernacle, and those who dwell in heaven. [7]It was granted to him
to make war with the saints and to overcome them. And authority was given him over every tribe,[a] tongue, and nation.

13:5 [a]M-Text reads *make war.* *13:7* [a]NU-Text and M-Text add *and people.*

CONSIDER THIS
13:1–18

God Restrains Evil

The presence of pain, suffering, and evil in the world causes some people to wonder whether a good God exists, and if He does, why He doesn't put an end to it if He can. John's vision of a beast rising up out of the sea (v. 1) and causing great havoc in the world does not explain why there is evil, but it does sound an important note of encouragement: the evils of the world happen only by "permission" and those that do occur have precise limits imposed on them by God. Notice that the beast "was given authority to continue for forty-two months" *(v. 5, emphasis added).*

Clearly, God has placed restraints on evil. We have not and will not experience the full onslaught of pain and suffering that could be delivered. This restraining work of God can be seen in several incidents in the Old Testament:

- Adam and Eve (Gen. 3:22–24). *After Adam and Eve sinned, God sent them out of the garden and sealed it off. According to Genesis, this was not a matter of retaliation by God but a protection from the possibility of eating from the tree of life and being separated from Him forever.*
- The Flood (Gen. 6:5–8). *When evil had corrupted the entire world, God acted with "severe mercy" by sending the flood. This restricted evil and made possible a second start for the earth.*

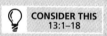

8All who dwell on the earth will worship him, whose names
have not been written in the Book of Life of the Lamb slain
from the foundation of the world.
9If anyone has an ear, let him hear. 10He who leads into
captivity shall go into captivity; he who kills with the sword
must be killed with the sword. Here is the patience and the
faith of the saints.
11Then I saw another beast coming up out of the earth,
and he had two horns like a lamb and spoke like a dragon.
12And he exercises all the authority of the first beast in his
presence, and causes the earth and those who dwell in it to
worship the first beast, whose deadly wound was healed.
13He performs great signs, so that he even makes fire come
down from heaven on the earth in the sight of men. 14And
he deceives those[a] who dwell on the earth by those signs
which he was granted to do in the sight of the beast, telling

(Bible text continued on page 911)

13:14 [a]M-Text reads *my own people.*

- The Tower of Babel (Gen. 11:1–9). *Again, widespread evil threatened to consume the creation. God intervened by confusing the languages of the peoples to limit their collusion in wickedness. This was a case of God preserving sinful humanity from itself.*
- Job (Job 1:6—2:10). *Satan wanted to prove to God that Job's faithfulness was merely the result of God blessing him. So God granted Satan limited permission to inflict suffering.*

John was writing to believers to help them maintain a realistic view of good and evil in the midst of intense persecution. Today, as we watch televised reports of death and disaster around the world and as we experience pain and suffering in our own families and among our neighbors and associates, we too need to maintain a godly perspective. God has placed limits on evil. The very fact that we have a distaste for it reflects that we do indeed bear God's image as His creatures. ◆

There can be no question that evil and pain are a massive problem to both belief and behavior. But the Bible does give us ground to stand on as we try to live in a world where suffering is real. See "Ten Myths about Christianity, Myth #10: Evil and Suffering in the World Prove There Is No God," Rev. 20:1–10.

HERE IS THE PATIENCE AND THE FAITH OF THE SAINTS.
—Revelation 13:10

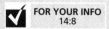

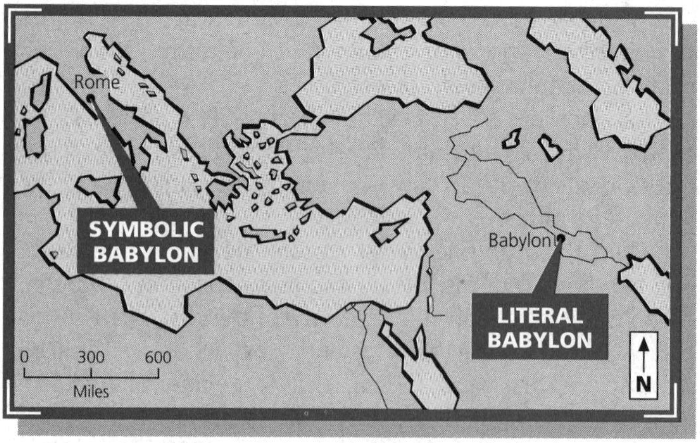

THE TWO BABYLONS

FOR YOUR INFO
14:8

A SYMBOL OF EVIL

In Revelation, Babylon (v. 8) probably represents, more than a city, an entire world system in rebellion against God. The Old Testament prophets often prophesied the fall of Babylon, the capital of an empire that destroyed Jerusalem and carried away God's people into captivity. So here Babylon becomes a fitting image for a society that persecutes believers but which God will ultimately destroy.

In the first century, Babylon may have been a code word for Rome, built as it was on seven hills (17:9). Under the Roman Emperor Domitian (A.D. 81–96), Christians were severely persecuted, especially for refusing to participate in the cult of emperor worship. Each mention of Babylon in Revelation shows that it is linked with evil and resistance to God:

BABYLON IN REVELATION

- Babylon is brought down for making "all the nations drink the wine of the wrath of her fornication" (14:8).
- Babylon is shattered by God, who remembers the city's ways and gives it "the cup of the wine of the fierceness of His wrath" (16:19).
- Babylon is given the title, "Mystery, Babylon the Great, the Mother of Harlots and of the Abominations of the Earth" (17:5).
- Babylon falls and becomes "a dwelling place of demons, a prison for every foul spirit, and a cage for every unclean and hated bird" (18:2).
- Babylon is mourned as it wallows in terrifying torment; those who watch cry out, "Alas, alas, that great city Babylon, that mighty city! For in one hour your judgment has come" (18:10).
- Babylon "shall be thrown down, and shall not be found anymore" (18:21).

those who dwell on the earth to make an image to the beast
who was wounded by the sword and lived. 15He was
granted *power* to give breath to the image of the beast, that
the image of the beast should both speak and cause as
many as would not worship the image of the beast to be
killed. 16He causes all, both small and great, rich and poor,
free and slave, to receive a mark on their right hand or on
their foreheads, 17and that no one may buy or sell except
one who has the mark or[a] the name of the beast, or the
number of his name.
18Here is wisdom. Let him who has understanding calculate the number of the beast, for it is the number of a man:
His number *is* 666.

13:17 [a]NU-Text and M-Text omit *or.*

Historically, Babylon oppressed and captured Judah. In the same way, John's figurative Babylon oppresses the people of God and holds them captive under its mighty grip. History is a war between two cities: "Babylon," the capital of idolatry and oppression, and "Jerusalem," the center of Christ's peace and justice.

John's buildup to the clash of these two titans is epic in scope and drama. The climax comes here in chapter 14, where judgment finally falls on Babylon, and the bowls, plagues, and intoxicating wine of God's wrath are poured out on her. A tremendous tidal wave of evil sloshes back and forth in the passage, like the last great battles of World War II. But the outcome is assured; Christ will prevail. ◆

HE CAUSES ALL . . . TO RECEIVE A MARK ON THEIR RIGHT HAND OR ON THEIR FOREHEADS. . . .
—Revelation 13:16

CHAPTER 14

The Lamb Calls His Own

1 Then I looked, and behold, a[a] Lamb standing on Mount
Zion, and with Him one hundred *and* forty-four thousand,
having[b] His Father's name written on their foreheads. 2 And I
heard a voice from heaven, like the voice of many waters,
and like the voice of loud thunder. And I heard the sound
of harpists playing their harps. 3 They sang as it were a new
song before the throne, before the four living creatures, and
the elders; and no one could learn that song except the
hundred *and* forty-four thousand who were redeemed from
the earth. 4 These are the ones who were not defiled with
women, for they are virgins. These are the ones who follow
the Lamb wherever He goes. These were redeemed[a] from
among men, *being* firstfruits to God and to the Lamb. 5 And
in their mouth was found no deceit,[a] for they are without
fault before the throne of God.[b]

"Blessed are the dead who die in the Lord from now on."
—Revelation 14:13

Angels with Announcements

6 Then I saw another angel flying in the midst of heaven,
having the everlasting gospel to preach to those who dwell
on the earth—to every nation, tribe, tongue, and people—
7 saying with a loud voice, "Fear God and give glory to Him,
for the hour of His judgment has come; and worship Him
who made heaven and earth, the sea and springs of water."

14:8 see pg. 910

8 And another angel followed, saying,
"Babylon[a] is fallen, is fallen, that great
city, because she has made all nations drink of the wine of
the wrath of her fornication."

9 Then a third angel followed them, saying with a loud
voice, "If anyone worships the beast and his image, and receives *his* mark on his forehead or on his hand, 10 he himself
shall also drink of the wine of the wrath of God, which is
poured out full strength into the cup of His indignation. He
shall be tormented with fire and brimstone in the presence
of the holy angels and in the presence of the Lamb. 11 And
the smoke of their torment ascends forever and ever; and
they have no rest day or night, who worship the beast and
his image, and whoever receives the mark of his name."

12 Here is the patience of the saints; here *are* those[a] who
keep the commandments of God and the faith of Jesus.

13 Then I heard a voice from heaven saying to me,[a] "Write:
'Blessed *are* the dead who die in the Lord from now on.' "

14:1 [a]NU-Text and M-Text read *the.* [b]NU-Text and M-Text add *His name and.*
14:4 [a]M-Text adds *by Jesus.* *14:5* [a]NU-Text and M-Text read *falsehood.* [b]NU-Text and M-Text omit *before the throne of God.* *14:8* [a]NU-Text reads *Babylon the great is fallen, is fallen, which has made;* M-Text reads *Babylon the great is fallen. She has made.*
14:12 [a]NU-Text and M-Text omit *here are those.* *14:13* [a]NU-Text and M-Text omit *to me.*

"Yes," says the Spirit, "that they may rest from their labors, and their works follow them."

Reaping the Earth's Harvest

14Then I looked, and behold, a white cloud, and on the
cloud sat *One* like the Son of Man, having on His head a
golden crown, and in His hand a sharp sickle. 15And another angel came out of the temple, crying with a loud
voice to Him who sat on the cloud, "Thrust in Your sickle
and reap, for the time has come for You[a] to reap, for the
harvest of the earth is ripe." 16So He who sat on the cloud
thrust in His sickle on the earth, and the earth was reaped.
17Then another angel came out of the temple which is in
heaven, he also having a sharp sickle.
18And another angel came out from the altar, who had
power over fire, and he cried with a loud cry to him who
had the sharp sickle, saying, "Thrust in your sharp sickle
and gather the clusters of the vine of the earth, for her
grapes are fully ripe." 19So the angel thrust his sickle into
the earth and gathered the vine of the earth, and threw *it*
into the great winepress of the wrath of God. 20And the
winepress was trampled outside the city, and blood came
out of the winepress, up to the horses' bridles, for one thousand six hundred furlongs.

CHAPTER 15

A Vision of Seven Plagues

15:1–8

1Then I saw another sign in heaven,
great and marvelous: seven angels having
the seven last plagues, for in them the wrath of God is complete.
2And I saw *something* like a sea of glass mingled with fire,
and those who have the victory over the beast, over his image and over his mark[a] *and* over the number of his name,
standing on the sea of glass, having harps of God. 3They
sing the song of Moses, the servant of God, and the song of
the Lamb, saying:

"Great and marvelous *are* Your works,
Lord God Almighty!
Just and true *are* Your ways,
O King of the saints![a]
4 Who shall not fear You, O Lord, and glorify Your name?
For *You* alone *are* holy.
For all nations shall come and worship before You,
For Your judgments have been manifested."

14:15 [a]NU-Text and M-Text omit *for You.* *15:2* [a]NU-Text and M-Text omit *over his mark.*
15:3 [a]NU-Text and M-Text read *nations.*

QUOTE UNQUOTE

CONSIDER THIS 15:1–8 *Although Revelation is not fiction, it nevertheless narrates a story that goes beyond ordinary experience. Compare John's description of the evil beasts (13:1–17) with his portrayal of the heavenly temple (15:1–8):*

In all but a few writers the "good" characters are the least successful, and every one who has ever tried to make even the humblest story ought to know why . . . . Heaven understands Hell and Hell does not understand Heaven, and all of us, in our measure, share the Satanic . . . blindness. To project ourselves into a wicked character, we have only to stop doing something, and something that we are already tired of doing; to project ourselves into a good one, we have to do what we cannot and become what we are not.

C. S. Lewis, *A Preface to Paradise Lost,* pp. 100–101

5After these things I looked, and behold,[a] the temple of
the tabernacle of the testimony in heaven was opened. 6And
out of the temple came the seven angels having the seven
plagues, clothed in pure bright linen, and having their
chests girded with golden bands. 7Then one of the four
living creatures gave to the seven angels seven golden
bowls full of the wrath of God who lives forever and ever.
8The temple was filled with smoke from the glory of God
and from His power, and no one was able to enter the temple till the seven plagues of the seven angels were completed.

15:5 [a]NU-Text and M-Text omit *behold.*

FOR YOUR INFO
16:21

MONEY IN THE NEW TESTAMENT

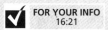

The hail that falls from heaven is described as weighing "the weight of a talent" (v. 21). A talent was a measure normally used as a monetary unit (for example, Matt. 25:15). The table below shows the various monetary systems used among New Testament peoples.

NEW TESTAMENT MONETARY UNITS

Unit	Equivalents	Translations
Jewish Weights		
Talent	3,000 shekels; 6,000 bekas	talent
Shekel	4 days' wages; 2 bekas; 20 gerahs	shekel
Beka	1/2 shekel; 10 gerahs	bekah
Gerah	1/20 shekel	gerah
Persian Coins		
Daric	2 days' wages; 1/2 Jewish silver shekel	drachma
Greek Coins		
Tetradrachma (Stater)	4 drachmas	piece of money
Didrachma	2 drachmas	tribute
Drachma	1 day's wage	piece of silver
Lepton	1/2 of a Roman kodrantes	mite
Roman Coins		
Aureus	25 denarii	
Denarius	1 day's wage	denarius
Assarius	1/16 of a denarius	copper coin
Kodrantes	1/4 of an assarius	penny, quadrans

Learn more about the origins and use of money among ancient peoples in the article, "A History of Money," Rev. 3:17–18.

CHAPTER 16

Seven Bowls Pour Out

1 Then I heard a loud voice from the temple saying to the
seven angels, "Go and pour out the bowls[a] of the wrath of
God on the earth."
2 So the first went and poured out his bowl upon the
earth, and a foul and loathsome sore came upon the men
who had the mark of the beast and those who worshiped
his image.
3 Then the second angel poured out his bowl on the sea,
and it became blood as of a dead *man;* and every living
creature in the sea died.
4 Then the third angel poured out his bowl on the rivers
and springs of water, and they became blood. 5 And I heard
the angel of the waters saying:

"You are righteous, O Lord,[a]
The One who is and who was and who is to be,[b]
Because You have judged these things.
6 For they have shed the blood of saints and prophets,
And You have given them blood to drink.
For[a] it is their just due."

7 And I heard another from[a] the altar saying, "Even so,
Lord God Almighty, true and righteous *are* Your judgments."
8 Then the fourth angel poured out his bowl on the sun,
and power was given to him to scorch men with fire. 9 And
men were scorched with great heat, and they blasphemed
the name of God who has power over these plagues; and
they did not repent and give Him glory.
10 Then the fifth angel poured out his bowl on the throne
of the beast, and his kingdom became full of darkness; and
they gnawed their tongues because of the pain. 11 They blasphemed the God of heaven because of their pains and their
sores, and did not repent of their deeds.
12 Then the sixth angel poured out his bowl on the great
river Euphrates, and its water was dried up, so that the way
of the kings from the east might be prepared. 13 And I saw
three unclean spirits like frogs *coming* out of the mouth of
the dragon, out of the mouth of the beast, and out of the
mouth of the false prophet. 14 For they are spirits of demons,
performing signs, *which* go out to the kings of the earth
and[a] of the whole world, to gather them to the battle of that
great day of God Almighty.

(Bible text continued on page 918)

"YOU ARE RIGHTEOUS, O LORD . . . BECAUSE YOU HAVE JUDGED THESE THINGS."
—Revelation 16:5

16:1 [a]NU-Text and M-Text read *seven bowls.* *16:5* [a]NU-Text and M-Text omit *O Lord.* [b]NU-Text and M-Text read *who was, the Holy One.* *16:6* [a]NU-Text and M-Text omit *For.* *16:7* [a]NU-Text and M-Text omit *another from.* *16:14* [a]NU-Text and M-Text omit *of the earth and.*

FOR YOUR INFO 17:4

COLORS IN THE BIBLE

The woman that John sees in the wilderness sits on a scarlet beast and wears purple and scarlet (vv. 3–4). In apocalyptic literature, color plays an important role in conveying symbolic meanings (see "The Genre of Apocalyptic Literature," Rev. 10:1–10). Here, the purple and scarlet suggest that the woman has become affluent, probably through evil means.

Individual colors mentioned in the Bible fall into two major types—natural colors and artificial colors.

ARTIFICIAL COLORS IN THE BIBLE	
PURPLE	The most precious of ancient dyes (see "The Trade in Purple," Acts 16:14) made from a shellfish found in the Mediterranean Sea. A total of 250,000 mollusks was required to make one ounce of the dye, which partly accounts for its great price. It was highly valued within the nation of Israel. Used in several features of the tabernacle (Ex. 26:1; 27:16) and the temple (2 Chr. 2:14); the color of royal robes (Judg. 8:26); the garments of the wealthy (Prov. 31:22; Luke 16:19); the vesture of a harlot (Rev. 17:4); and the robe placed on Jesus (Mark 15:17, 20). The color of royalty.
BLUE	Also derived from a species of shellfish; fabric dyed this color used in the tabernacle (Ex. 26:1) and the temple (2 Chr. 2:7); also used for royal trappings (Esth. 1:6; 8:15) and clothing for the rich (Jer. 10:9; Ezek. 23:6).
RED	Existed in several shades; dye extracted from the bodies of insects. Crimson linen used in the temple (2 Chr. 2:7, 14; 3:14); the color must have been indelible or permanent (Jer. 4:30), as crimson is used figuratively of sin (Is. 1:18). Scarlet cord tied around the wrist of Zerah (Gen. 38:28–30); used a great deal in the tabernacle (Ex. 25:4); the color of the cord hung form Rahab's window (Josh. 2:18); a mark of prosperity (2 Sam. 1:24; Prov. 31:21); the color of the robe placed on Jesus (Matt. 27:28), though scarlet and purple were not always distinguished (Mark 15:17); color of the beast ridden by the harlot Babylon (Rev. 17:3) along with some of her garments (Rev. 17:4) and those of her followers (Rev. 18:16). Vermilion used in decorating homes of the wealthy (Jer. 22:14) and in the painting of idols (Ezek. 23:14).

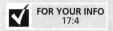

Artificial colors, such as paints and dyes, were used widely in the ancient world. The Israelites had an advanced textile industry. They were skilled not only in weaving but also in dyeing. Since dyes were made from vegetable sources or from shellfish, quality control was difficult. The completed colors were often impure and inexact. These problems were compounded by the fact that many dyes were closely guarded family recipes which were sometimes lost or changed.

NATURAL COLORS IN THE BIBLE	
BLUE	Used to describe the color of a wound, but may refer to the wound itself (Prov. 20:30). Sometimes describes the sky.
BROWN	A dark, blackish color referred only to sheep (Gen. 30:32–33, 35, 40).
BLACK	One of the more commonly used colors in Scripture; describes the color of the middle of the night (Prov. 7:9); diseased skin (Job 30:30); healthy hair (Song 5:11; Matt. 5:36); corpses' faces (Lam. 4:8); the sky (Jer. 4:28); the darkening of the sun and the moon (Joel 2:10); horses (Zech. 6:2, 6; Rev. 6:5); and marble (Esth. 1:6). The color of famine and death.
GRAY	Used only to describe the hair of the elderly (Gen. 42:38).
GREEN	Normally describes vegetation; used of pastures (Ps. 23:2); herbage (2 Kin. 19:26); trees in general (Deut. 12:2; Luke 23:31; Rev. 8:7); the marriage bed (in a figurative sense, Song 1:16); a hypocrite compared to a papyrus plant (Job 8:16); and grass (Mark 6:39). A word meaning "greenish" describes plague spots (Lev. 13:49; 14:37) as well as the color of gold.
RED	Describes natural objects such as Jacob's stew (Gen. 25:30); the sacrificial heifer (Num. 19:2); wine (Prov. 23:31); newborn Esau (Gen. 25:25); Judah's eyes (Gen. 49:12, KJV); the eyes of the drunkard (Prov. 23:29); and the dragon (Rev. 12:3). The color of blood, it often symbolizes life; it also suggests the carnage of war.
WHITE	The color of animals (Gen. 30:35); manna (Ex. 16:31); both hair and pustules located in plague sores (Lev. 13:3–39); garments (Eccl. 9:8; Dan. 7:9); the robes of the righteous (Rev. 19:8); horses (Zech. 1:8; Rev. 6:2; 19:11); forgiven sins (Ps. 51:7; Is. 1:18); a refined remnant (Dan. 11:35; 12:10); the beloved one (Song 5:10); the white of an egg (Job 6:6); the shining garments of angels (Rev. 15:6) and of the transfigured Christ (Matt. 17:2); hair (Matt. 5:36); gravestones (Matt. 23:27); and the great throne of judgment (Rev. 20:11). Portrays purity, righteousness, and joy, and a white horse symbolizes victory.
YELLOW	Indicates the greenish cast of gold (Ps. 68:13) and the light-colored hair in a leprous spot (Lev. 13:30, 32).

◆

The Delusions of Luxury

CONSIDER THIS 18:1–24 **Just as overeating can make a person sick and too much insulation in a home can trap toxic air inside, too much wealth can be dangerous to the moral and spiritual health of an individual, a city, or a nation. In fact, Jesus warned about the "deceitfulness of riches" (Matt. 13:22). Luxury can easily delude us into spiritual carelessness, greed, and ultimate ruin.**

Such is the case of Babylon in John's vision of her fall (Rev. 18:2–3, 7–8). Historically, Babylon achieved wealth, power, and dominance through constant warfare, oppression, and deception. It was known throughout the ancient world for plundering others for its own gain. Here in Revelation, Babylon is probably a symbol not only of Rome, but of a world system that operates in open rebellion against God (see "A Symbol of Evil," Rev. 14:8).

But there is a heavy price to pay for the self-indulgent lifestyle that Babylon's people live, and for the injustices they resort to in maintaining it. Cruelty and deception do not go unanswered:

- **The city becomes a dwelling place for demons (v. 2).**
- **Her patterns of luxury become addictive, similar to alcoholism, sexual excess, and a lifestyle of greed (v. 3).**
- **Insulated from pain, she lives in denial of her true condition (vv. 4–8).**
- **Her economic systems are taken away and her trading partnerships are dissolved (vv. 11–18; 22–23).**

(continued on next page)

15"Behold, I am coming as a thief. Blessed *is* he who
watches, and keeps his garments, lest he walk naked and
they see his shame."
16And they gathered them together to the place called in
Hebrew, Armageddon.[a]
17Then the seventh angel poured out his bowl into the air,
and a loud voice came out of the temple of heaven, from
the throne, saying, "It is done!" 18And there were noises and
thunderings and lightnings; and there was a great earthquake, such a mighty and great earthquake as had not occurred since men were on the earth. 19Now the great city
was divided into three parts, and the cities of the nations
fell. And great Babylon was remembered before God, to give
her the cup of the wine of the fierceness of His wrath.
20Then every island fled away, and the mountains were not
16:21 see pg. 914 found. 21And great hail from heaven fell
upon men, *each hailstone* about the
weight of a talent. Men blasphemed God because of the
plague of the hail, since that plague was exceedingly great.

CHAPTER 17

The Harlot Babylon

1Then one of the seven angels who had the seven bowls
came and talked with me, saying to me,[a] "Come, I will
show you the judgment of the great harlot who sits on
many waters, 2with whom the kings of the earth committed
fornication, and the inhabitants of the earth were made
drunk with the wine of her fornication."
3So he carried me away in the Spirit into the wilderness.
And I saw a woman sitting on a scarlet beast *which was* full
of names of blasphemy, having seven heads and ten horns.
17:4 see pg. 916 4The woman was arrayed in purple and
scarlet, and adorned with gold and pre-
cious stones and pearls, having in her hand a golden cup
full of abominations and the filthiness of her fornication.[a]
5And on her forehead a name *was* written:

MYSTERY,
BABYLON THE GREAT,
THE MOTHER OF HARLOTS AND OF THE
ABOMINATIONS OF THE EARTH.

6I saw the woman, drunk with the blood of the saints and
with the blood of the martyrs of Jesus. And when I saw her,
I marveled with great amazement.
7But the angel said to me, "Why did you marvel? I will
tell you the mystery of the woman and of the beast that car-

16:16 [a]M-Text reads *Megiddo.* *17:1* [a]NU-Text and M-Text omit *to me.* *17:4* [a]M-Text reads *the filthiness of the fornication of the earth.*

ries her, which has the seven heads and the ten horns. 8The
beast that you saw was, and is not, and will ascend out of
the bottomless pit and go to perdition. And those who
dwell on the earth will marvel, whose names are not written
in the Book of Life from the foundation of the world, when
they see the beast that was, and is not, and yet is.[a]
9"Here *is* the mind which has wisdom: The seven heads
are seven mountains on which the woman sits. 10There are
also seven kings. Five have fallen, one is, *and* the other has
not yet come. And when he comes, he must continue a
short time. 11The beast that was, and is not, is himself also
the eighth, and is of the seven, and is going to perdition.
12"The ten horns which you saw are ten kings who have
received no kingdom as yet, but they receive authority for
one hour as kings with the beast. 13These are of one mind,
and they will give their power and authority to the beast.
14These will make war with the Lamb, and the Lamb will
overcome them, for He is Lord of lords and King of kings;
and those *who are* with Him *are* called, chosen, and faithful."
15Then he said to me, "The waters which you saw, where
the harlot sits, are peoples, multitudes, nations, and
tongues. 16And the ten horns which you saw on[a] the beast,
these will hate the harlot, make her desolate and naked, eat
her flesh and burn her with fire. 17For God has put it into
their hearts to fulfill His purpose, to be of one mind, and to
give their kingdom to the beast, until the words of God are
fulfilled. 18And the woman whom you saw is that great city
which reigns over the kings of the earth."

CHAPTER 18

Babylon's Corruption

18:1–24

1After these things I saw another angel
coming down from heaven, having great
authority, and the earth was illuminated with his glory.
2And he cried mightily[a] with a loud voice, saying, "Babylon
the great is fallen, is fallen, and has become a dwelling place
of demons, a prison for every foul spirit, and a cage for
every unclean and hated bird! 3For all the nations have
drunk of the wine of the wrath of her fornication, the kings
of the earth have committed fornication with her, and the
merchants of the earth have become rich through the abundance of her luxury."
4And I heard another voice from heaven saying, "Come
out of her, my people, lest you share in her sins, and lest

17:8 [a]NU-Text and M-Text read *and shall be present.* *17:16* [a]NU-Text and M-Text read *saw, and the beast.* *18:2* [a]NU-Text and M-Text omit *mightily.*

(continued from previous page)

- **All of her possessions disappear and ultimately she is left desolate (v. 19).**

What happens to Babylon is instructive for those of us who follow Christ, especially as we live in a culture of affluence. Is there a note of warning in this text for us?

you receive of her plagues. 5For her sins have reached[a] to
heaven, and God has remembered her iniquities. 6Render to
her just as she rendered to you,[a] and repay her double according to her works; in the cup which she has mixed, mix
double for her. 7In the measure that she glorified herself
and lived luxuriously, in the same measure give her torment
and sorrow; for she says in her heart, 'I sit *as* queen, and am
no widow, and will not see sorrow.' 8Therefore her plagues
will come in one day—death and mourning and famine.
And she will be utterly burned with fire, for strong *is* the
Lord God who judges[a] her.
9"The kings of the earth who committed fornication and
lived luxuriously with her will weep and lament for her,
when they see the smoke of her burning, 10standing at a
distance for fear of her torment, saying, 'Alas, alas, that
great city Babylon, that mighty city! For in one hour your
judgment has come.'

18:5 [a]NU-Text and M-Text read *have been heaped up.* *18:6* [a]NU-Text and M-Text omit *to you.* *18:8* [a]NU-Text and M-Text read *has judged.*

CONSIDER THIS
19:6–10

THERE IS HOPE FOR THE FAMILY

The fact that John's vision ends in a marriage between Christ (the Lamb) and His bride the church (vv. 6–10) offers great hope to families. In this world, almost every family experiences some pain and suffering in its relationships. After all, families are made up of people who struggle under the burden of sin.

Of course, things were not intended to be that way. In the beginning, God instituted the family when He created Adam and Eve and joined them together as "one flesh" (Gen. 2:24). However, their sin and rebellion against God brought havoc into their relationship and into all subsequent families. In their own family they soon experienced violence as Cain murdered his brother Abel, causing an ongoing cycle of trouble (4:1–16).

Even in a fallen world, however, God desires His best for the family structure. Scripture holds out great hope for the restoration of marriage. For example:

- *It encourages parents to raise children in an environment of truth and integrity (Deut. 6:2–9).*
- *It offers a touching illustration of aid to a family devastated by death and the prospect of poverty (Ruth 1–4).*
- *It shows a family destroyed by senseless evil but restored twofold by a faithful God (Job 1:13–21; 2:9; 42:10–17).*

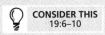

Collapse of the Global Economy

11"And the merchants of the earth will weep and mourn
over her, for no one buys their merchandise anymore:
12merchandise of gold and silver, precious stones and
pearls, fine linen and purple, silk and scarlet, every kind of
citron wood, every kind of object of ivory, every kind of object of most precious wood, bronze, iron, and marble; 13and
cinnamon and incense, fragrant oil and frankincense, wine
and oil, fine flour and wheat, cattle and sheep, horses and
chariots, and bodies and souls of men. 14The fruit that your
soul longed for has gone from you, and all the things which
are rich and splendid have gone from you,[a] and you shall
find them no more at all. 15The merchants of these things,
who became rich by her, will stand at a distance for fear of
her torment, weeping and wailing, 16and saying, 'Alas, alas,
that great city that was clothed in fine linen, purple, and
scarlet, and adorned with gold and precious stones and
pearls! 17For in one hour such great riches came to nothing.'

18:14 [a]NU-Text and M-Text read *been lost to you.*

- *It affirms the beauty of sexual love within marriage in terms of passion, fidelity, and integrity (Song of Solomon).*
- *It encourages the restoration of broken relationships, just as God will do with His people (Hos. 1:2—2:23).*
- *It offers guidelines for marriage in terms of mutual submission, loyalty, love, and discipline for children that does not alienate them—a way of relating that is similar to Christ's relationship to His bride the church (Eph. 5:21—6:4).*

God's original design for the family will not be destroyed. Right now you may be experiencing the struggle of human relationships or even the pain of a broken family. But you can take hope from the knowledge that God's healing and love will ultimately win out, and He will "wipe away every tear . . . there shall be no more death, nor sorrow, nor crying" (21:4). ◆

Scripture offers a great deal of help on a variety of family-related issues. See the table, "Family Helps in the New Testament Letters," Heb. 12:3–13.

"AND THE MERCHANTS OF THE EARTH WILL WEEP AND MOURN OVER HER. . . ."
—Revelation 18:11

MAGIC AND SORCERY

FOR YOUR INFO 18:23 **There is today a growing interest in occult beliefs and practices, such as fortune-telling, witchcraft, and astrology. But John reveals the true nature of the occult when he writes that the sorcery of Babylon has deceived all the nations (v. 23).**

Occult practices were common among the pagan nations of the ancient world. But attempts to contact or control evil spirits were expressly forbidden to the Hebrews, and the prohibition extends to believers today. Among the practices that Deuteronomy 18:10–12 calls "an abomination to the Lord" are:

- **child sacrifice (making one's son or daughter "pass through the fire").**
- **witchcraft.**
- **soothsaying, a form of divination which may have been similar to tea leaf reading or astrology.**
- **interpreting omens.**
- **sorcery.**
- **conjuring spells.**
- **consulting mediums.**
- **spiritism.**
- **calling up the dead.**

In the New Testament, the gospel exposed two sorcerers, Simon (Acts 8:9–25) and Elymas (Acts 13:6–8). They may have been something like the "itinerant Jewish exorcists," also mentioned in the book of Acts (Acts 19:13), who attempted to drive evil spirits out of people in the name of Jesus.

The New Testament word translated "sorcery" comes from the same Greek word as our English word, "pharmacy." Obviously this has to do with drugs; a more relevant and contemporary application could hardly be found. The denunciations of Revela-

(continued on next page)

Every shipmaster, all who travel by ship, sailors, and as
many as trade on the sea, stood at a distance 18and cried out
when they saw the smoke of her burning, saying, 'What *is*
like this great city?'
19"They threw dust on their heads and cried out, weeping
and wailing, and saying, 'Alas, alas, that great city, in which
all who had ships on the sea became rich by her wealth! For
in one hour she is made desolate.'
20"Rejoice over her, O heaven, and *you* holy apostles[a] and
prophets, for God has avenged you on her!"
21Then a mighty angel took up a stone like a great millstone and threw *it* into the sea, saying, "Thus with violence
the great city Babylon shall be thrown down, and shall not
be found anymore. 22The sound of harpists, musicians,
flutists, and trumpeters shall not be heard in you anymore.
No craftsman of any craft shall be found in you anymore,
and the sound of a millstone shall not be heard in you any-
18:23 more. 23The light of a lamp shall not
shine in you anymore, and the voice of
bridegroom and bride shall not be heard in you anymore.
For your merchants were the great men of the earth, for by
your sorcery all the nations were deceived. 24And in her was
found the blood of prophets and saints, and of all who were
slain on the earth."

CHAPTER 19

Rejoicing in Heaven

1After these things I heard[a] a loud voice of a great multitude in heaven, saying, "Alleluia! Salvation and glory and
honor and power *belong* to the Lord[b] our God! 2For true
and righteous *are* His judgments, because He has judged
the great harlot who corrupted the earth with her fornication; and He has avenged on her the blood of His servants
shed by her." 3Again they said, "Alleluia! Her smoke rises up
forever and ever!" 4And the twenty-four elders and the four
living creatures fell down and worshiped God who sat on
the throne, saying, "Amen! Alleluia!" 5Then a voice came
from the throne, saying, "Praise our God, all you His servants and those who fear Him, both[a] small and great!"
19:6–10 see pg. 920
6And I heard, as it were, the voice of a
great multitude, as the sound of many
waters and as the sound of mighty thunderings, saying, "Alleluia! For the[a] Lord God Omnipotent reigns! 7Let us be
glad and rejoice and give Him glory, for the marriage of the

18:20 [a]NU-Text and M-Text read *saints and apostles.* *19:1* [a]NU-Text and M-Text add *something like.* [b]NU-Text and M-Text omit *the Lord.* *19:5* [a]NU-Text and M-Text omit *both.* *19:6* [a]NU-Text and M-Text read *our.*

Lamb has come, and His wife has made herself ready." [8]And
to her it was granted to be arrayed in fine linen, clean and
bright, for the fine linen is the righteous acts of the saints.
[9]Then he said to me, "Write: 'Blessed *are* those who are
called to the marriage supper of the Lamb!' " And he said to
me, "These are the true sayings of God." [10]And I fell at his
feet to worship him. But he said to me, "See *that you do* not
do that! I am your fellow servant, and of your brethren who
have the testimony of Jesus. Worship God! For the testimony of Jesus is the spirit of prophecy."

The Rule of Christ Restored

[11]Now I saw heaven opened, and behold, a white horse.
And He who sat on him *was* called Faithful and True, and
in righteousness He judges and makes war. [12]His eyes *were*
like a flame of fire, and on His head *were* many crowns. He
had[a] a name written that no one knew except Himself. [13]He
was clothed with a robe dipped in blood, and His name is
called The Word of God. [14]And the armies in heaven,
clothed in fine linen, white and clean,[a] followed Him on
white horses. [15]Now out of His mouth goes a sharp[a] sword,
that with it He should strike the nations. And He Himself
will rule them with a rod of iron. He Himself treads the
winepress of the fierceness and wrath of Almighty God.
[16]And He has on *His* robe and on His thigh a name written:

KING OF KINGS
AND LORD OF LORDS.

[17]Then I saw an angel standing in the sun; and he cried
with a loud voice, saying to all the birds that fly in the
midst of heaven, "Come and gather together for the supper
of the great God,[a] [18]that you may eat the flesh of kings, the
flesh of captains, the flesh of mighty men, the flesh of
horses and of those who sit on them, and the flesh of all
people, free[a] and slave, both small and great."
[19]And I saw the beast, the kings of the earth, and their
armies, gathered together to make war against Him who sat
on the horse and against His army. [20]Then the beast was
captured, and with him the false prophet who worked signs in his presence, by which he deceived those who received the mark of the beast and those who worshiped his image. These two were cast alive into the lake of fire burning with
brimstone. [21]And the rest were killed with the sword which
proceeded from the mouth of Him who sat on the horse. And all the birds were filled with their flesh.

19:12 [a]M-Text adds *names written, and.* *19:14* [a]NU-Text and M-Text read *pure white linen.* *19:15* [a]M-Text adds *two-edged.* *19:17* [a]NU-Text and M-Text read *the great supper of God.* *19:18* [a]NU-Text and M-Text read *both free.*

(continued from previous page)

tion 9:21; 18:23; 21:8; and 22:15 apply to those who use drugs to bring on trances during which they claim to have supernatural knowledge or power.

WILL EVIL EVER GET ITS REWARD?

CONSIDER THIS 20:1–5 **Anyone who pays attention to today's headlines is likely to wonder, whatever happened to ethics and justice? Sometimes it seems like fairness never happens in matters of business, government, the law, and world affairs. But for those who long to see justice reign, the Bible offers powerful hope.**

God will not turn His back on injustice. His character demands that He give people what is coming to them. Moreover, Scripture promises that He will deal with evil in absolute, final ways. John's vision foresees that triumphant accomplishment:

- **God will bind evil and cast it into a bottomless pit (vv. 2–3).**
- **He will place a seal on the source of evil (v. 3).**
- **He will administer judgment and restore believers who have been killed unjustly (v. 4).**
- **He will deal finally with Satan after allowing him one last attempt to deceive (vv. 7–9); the devil's punishment will include eternal torment (vv. 10, 14).**
- **the dead will stand before God and be judged (vv. 11–15).**

This picture offers tremendous hope to anyone concerned about the injustices of our world today. As we seek to deliver God's righteousness into our communities, workplaces, and families, it's a relief to know that no human being—no matter how impartial and objective or biased and corrupt—is the final judge. Ultimate justice will someday be administered by One who can be thoroughly trusted—God, through Christ.

CHAPTER 20

Judgments on Satan

20:1–5

1Then I saw an angel coming down from heaven, having the key to the bottomless pit and a great chain in his hand. 2He laid hold of the dragon, that serpent of old, who is *the* Devil and Satan, and bound him for a thousand years; 3and he cast him into the bottomless pit, and shut him up, and set a seal on him, so that he should deceive the nations no more till the thousand years were finished. But after these things he must be released for a little while.

4And I saw thrones, and they sat on them, and judgment was committed to them. Then *I saw* the souls of those who had been beheaded for their witness to Jesus and for the word of God, who had not worshiped the beast or his image, and had not received *his* mark on their foreheads or on their hands. And they lived and reigned with Christ for a[a] thousand years. 5But the rest of the dead did not live again until the thousand years were finished. This *is* the first resurrection. 6Blessed and holy *is* he who has part in the first resurrection. Over such the second death has no power, but they shall be priests of God and of Christ, and shall reign with Him a thousand years.

7Now when the thousand years have expired, Satan will be released from his prison 8and will go out to deceive the nations which are in the four corners of the earth, Gog and Magog, to gather them together to battle, whose number *is* as the sand of the sea. 9They went up on the breadth of the earth and surrounded the camp of the saints and the beloved city. And fire came down from God out of heaven and devoured them. 10The devil, who deceived them, was cast into the lake of fire and brimstone where[a] the beast and the false prophet *are*. And they will be tormented day and night forever and ever.

20:1–10 see pg. 926

The Great White Throne Judgment

11Then I saw a great white throne and Him who sat on it, from whose face the earth and the heaven fled away. And there was found no place for them. 12And I saw the dead, small and great, standing before God,[a] and books were opened. And another book was opened, which is *the Book* of Life. And the dead were judged according to their works, by the things which were written in the books. 13The sea gave up the dead who were in it, and Death and Hades delivered up the dead who were in them. And they were judged, each one according to his works. 14Then Death and Hades were cast into the lake of fire. This is the second

20:4 [a]M-Text reads *the.* *20:10* [a]NU-Text and M-Text add *also.* *20:12* [a]NU-Text and M-Text read *the throne.*

death.[a] 15And anyone not found written in the Book of Life
was cast into the lake of fire.

CHAPTER 21

A New Heaven and a New Earth

21:1
see pg. 928

21:1–2

1Now I saw a new heaven and a new
earth, for the first heaven and the first
earth had passed away. Also there was no
more sea. 2Then I, John,[a] saw the holy
city, New Jerusalem, coming down out of heaven from God,
prepared as a bride adorned for her husband. 3And I heard
a loud voice from heaven saying, "Behold, the tabernacle of
God *is* with men, and He will dwell with them, and they
shall be His people. God Himself will be with them *and be*
their God. 4And God will wipe away every tear from their
eyes; there shall be no more death, nor sorrow, nor crying.
There shall be no more pain, for the former things have
passed away."
5Then He who sat on the throne said, "Behold, I make all
things new." And He said to me,[a] "Write, for these words are
true and faithful."
6And He said to me, "It is done![a] I am the Alpha and the
Omega, the Beginning and the End. I will give of the fountain of the water of life freely to him who thirsts. 7He who
overcomes shall inherit all things,[a] and I will be his God
and he shall be My son. 8But the cowardly, unbelieving,[a]
abominable, murderers, sexually immoral, sorcerers, idolaters, and all liars shall have their part in the lake which
burns with fire and brimstone, which is the second death."

The New Jerusalem

9Then one of the seven angels who had the seven bowls
filled with the seven last plagues came to me[a] and talked
with me, saying, "Come, I will show you the bride, the
Lamb's wife."[b] 10And he carried me away in the Spirit to a
great and high mountain, and showed me the great city, the
holy[a] Jerusalem, descending out of heaven from God, 11hav-
ing the glory of God. Her light *was* like a most precious
stone, like a jasper stone, clear as crystal. 12Also she had a
great and high wall with twelve gates, and twelve angels at
the gates, and names written on them, which are *the names*
of the twelve tribes of the children of Israel: 13three gates on
the east, three gates on the north, three gates on the south,
and three gates on the west.

(Bible text continued on page 927)

20:14 [a]NU-Text and M-Text add *the lake of fire.* *21:2* [a]NU-Text and M-Text omit *John.* *21:5* [a]NU-Text and M-Text omit *to me.* *21:6* [a]M-Text omits *It is done.* *21:7* [a]M-Text reads *overcomes, I shall give him these things.* *21:8* [a]M-Text adds *and sinners.* *21:9* [a]NU-Text and M-Text omit *to me.* [b]M-Text reads *I will show you the woman, the Lamb's bride.* *21:10* [a]NU-Text and M-Text omit *the great* and read *the holy city, Jerusalem.*

THE NEW JERUSALEM

CONSIDER THIS
21:1–2

As John draws Revelation to a close, he offers a glimpse of a new Jerusalem descending from heaven (v. 2). It is Jerusalem as it was intended to be—fulfilling its prophetic calling as a light to the nations, a place of justice and peace, and the capital city and dwelling place of God.

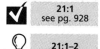

CONSIDER THIS
20:1–10

MYTH #10

10 MYTHS ABOUT CHRISTIANITY

MYTH: ALL THE EVIL AND SUFFERING IN THE WORLD PROVES THERE IS NO GOD

Many people today accept a number of myths about Christianity, with the result that they never respond to Jesus as He really is. This is one of ten articles that speak to some of those misconceptions. For a list of all ten, see 1 Tim. 1:3–4.

Few stories offer a more dramatic or thrilling climax than the closing chapters of Revelation. The scene of God finally and ultimately destroying Satan and his hosts (vv. 1–10) brings a bright, joyful conclusion not only to the Revelation of John, but to the entire Bible. Once and for all, evil will be banished, never again to trouble God's creation.

Yet while Christians look forward to that day with hope, many other people reject God and the gospel precisely because of evil in the world. Their reasoning goes something like this:

(1) A God who is good and loving would not allow evil and suffering in His world.
(2) Yet evil exists in the world.
(3) If God is all-powerful, He could remove evil if He wanted to.
(4) Yet evil remains. In fact, at times it seems to grow worse.
(5) Therefore, a good and powerful God must not exist.

This is a powerful argument, and there can be no question that evil and pain are a massive problem to both belief and behavior. Christianity offers no knock-down solution, but the Bible does give us ground to stand on as we try to live in a world where suffering is real.

(1) The Bible teaches that God did not create evil. The world He made was utterly good (Gen. 1:31). Where, then, did evil come from? The record finds people themselves turning against God, using His gift of free will to rebel against Him. With that moral rebellion, the perfection of God's world came tumbling down and people began to suffer.

The Bible also claims that behind human wickedness lies a great outside influence, Satan. This fallen angel hates God and everything to do with Him. He is out to destroy both humanity and the environment and does everything He can to attack God and His purposes. To that end he promotes much of the evil and suffering that we see. (See "Spiritual Realities Beyond You," Matt. 8:28–34.)

(2) The Bible teaches that even though God did not create evil, nor does He will it, He nevertheless uses it to accomplish His purposes. For instance, God sometimes uses pain in a profound way to draw people to Himself, especially when they otherwise would not respond to Him. Likewise, the struggle against evil has led many to strive for good. Like an irritating grain of sand in an oyster, it has produced pearls of character in countless people—courage, endurance, self-sacrifice, compassion.

(3) Why then, if God is all-powerful, does He not remove evil from the world? The question assumes, of course, that He has done nothing. But in fact, He has, is, and will. First, God Himself came into this world, with all its sorrow, pain, and wickedness, and lived as a man. Jesus was well acquainted with suffering. He knew poverty, thirst, hunger, injustice, physical abuse, heartbreak, and betrayal. He ended his life in excruciating

(continued on next page)

14Now the wall of the city had twelve foundations, and on
them were the names[a] of the twelve apostles of the Lamb.
15And he who talked with me had a gold reed to measure
the city, its gates, and its wall. 16The city is laid out as a
square; its length is as great as its breadth. And he measured
the city with the reed: twelve thousand furlongs. Its length,
breadth, and height are equal. 17Then he measured its wall:
one hundred *and* forty-four cubits, *according* to the measure
of a man, that is, of an angel. 18The construction of its wall
was *of* jasper; and the city *was* pure gold, like clear glass.
19The foundations of the wall of the city *were* adorned with
all kinds of precious stones: the first foundation *was* jasper,
the second sapphire, the third chalcedony, the fourth emerald, 20the fifth sardonyx, the sixth sardius, the seventh
chrysolite, the eighth beryl, the ninth topaz, the tenth
chrysoprase, the eleventh jacinth, and the twelfth amethyst.
21The twelve gates *were* twelve pearls: each individual gate
was of one pearl. And the street of the city *was* pure gold,
like transparent glass.
22But I saw no temple in it, for the Lord God Almighty
and the Lamb are its temple. 23The city had no need of the
sun or of the moon to shine in it,[a] for the glory[b] of God illuminated it. The Lamb *is* its light. 24And the nations of those
who are saved[a] shall walk in its light, and the kings of the
earth bring their glory and honor into it.[b] 25Its gates shall
not be shut at all by day (there shall be no night there).
26And they shall bring the glory and the honor of the nations into it.[a] 27But there shall by no means enter it anything that defiles, or causes[a] an abomination or a lie, but
only those who are written in the Lamb's Book of Life.

CHAPTER 22

Eden Is Restored

22:1–11 see pg. 929

22:2 see pg. 930

1And he showed me a pure[a] river of
water of life, clear as crystal, proceeding
from the throne of God and of the Lamb.
2In the middle of its street, and on either
side of the river, *was* the tree of life, which bore twelve
fruits, each *tree* yielding its fruit every month. The leaves of
the tree *were* for the healing of the nations. 3And there shall
be no more curse, but the throne of God and of the Lamb
shall be in it, and His servants shall serve Him. 4They shall
see His face, and His name *shall be* on their foreheads.
5There shall be no night there: They need no lamp nor light

21:14 [a]NU-Text and M-Text read *twelve names.* *21:23* [a]NU-Text and M-Text omit *in it.* [b]M-Text reads *the very glory.* *21:24* [a]NU-Text and M-Text omit *of those who are saved.* [b]M-Text reads *the glory and honor of the nations to Him.* *21:26* [a]M-Text adds *that they may enter in.* *21:27* [a]NU-Text and M-Text read *anything profane, nor one who causes.* *22:1* [a]NU-Text and M-Text omit *pure.*

MYTH #10
10 MYTHS ABOUT CHRISTIANITY

(continued from previous page)

pain. So God certainly understands our condition. He has personally experienced it.

In the process, God dealt with the problem of evil at its root. On the cross, Jesus took on Himself the wickedness of every man and woman who has ever lived in order to do away with it. We may never fully understand what happened in that incredible act of self-sacrifice. But we know that Christ broke the grip of evil that holds the world captive. Already we can see among God's people a glimpse of the new life that He has brought about (Rom. 8:4, 11).

(4) That brings us to God's final solution to evil, which John describes in Revelation 20. In the end, God will triumph by doing away with evil itself and those who promote it. He will restore His creation and His creatures to their original purpose, to the original relationship they enjoyed with Him. Suffering will be but a memory. Goodness, justice, and peace will characterize the moral climate of God's new heaven and earth. ◆

of the sun, for the Lord God gives them light. And they
shall reign forever and ever.

"I Am Coming Quickly!"

6Then he said to me, "These words *are* faithful and true."
And the Lord God of the holy[a] prophets sent His angel to
show His servants the things which must shortly take place.
7"Behold, I am coming quickly! Blessed *is* he who keeps
the words of the prophecy of this book."
8Now I, John, saw and heard[a] these things. And when I
heard and saw, I fell down to worship before the feet of the
angel who showed me these things.

(Bible text continued on page 930)

22:6 [a]NU-Text and M-Text read *spirits of the prophets.* *22:8* [a]NU-Text and M-Text read *am the one who heard and saw.*

FOR YOUR INFO 21:1

GENESIS AND REVELATION—THE FIRST AND LAST VOLUMES

The word "Bible" comes from the Greek word *biblos*, which means "book." The Bible is a complete book, unified in its theme and message. But it is also a collection of sixty-six books, a virtual library of God's Word to humanity. Genesis, the first book in the Bible, and Revelation, the last, help to define the collection, showing us the beginning and the end of history.

Here in Revelation 21, John reveals a new heaven and earth. In reading it, we can't help but look back to the beginnings of the world:

Genesis	Revelation
God creates the world.	God creates a new heaven and earth.
The devil introduces sin into the world.	The devil is defeated and destroyed; sin is done away with.
Humanity falls into sin.	God restores people to their original sinlessness.
The world is subjected to a curse.	The curse is removed.
People are separate from God.	People live with God forever.
People shed tears and know sorrow.	God wipes away every tear and removes sorrow.
People are barred from the tree of life.	People may eat freely from the tree of life.
Death enters the world.	Death is done away with and people live forever.
The languages of humanity are confused and the peoples scattered.	The peoples of the world are brought together before Christ and they sing His praises together.

One way to view the Bible is to see it as a magnificent three-part story. See "The Bible: Getting the Big Picture," 2 Tim. 3:16–17.

CONSIDER THIS
22:1–11

A Glance at Work in the Bible

As John's Revelation draws to a close, we see creation restored to its original intention (vv. 1–11). Since work plays such an important role in the world—whether Eden, today, or the end time—this is a good place to review Scripture's teaching on work, considered according to three different eras: work as it was originally intended, work in a fallen world, and work as it will be when Christ returns.

Main Point	Key Texts	Related Articles
Creation of Work: Work according to God's original design.		
God reveals Himself as the primary Worker and Creator.	Gen. 1:1–25; Ps. 19:1–6	"Our Daily Bread," Matt. 6:11; "The Divine Partnership," John 1:3; "He's Got the Whole World in His Hands," Heb. 1:2–3; "Creation: 'Very Good,' But Not Sacred!" Heb. 11:3
God creates us in His likeness and image as coworkers.	Gen. 1:26–31; 2:15–25; Ps. 8:1–9	"Every Breath You Take," Col. 1:17; "People at Work," Heb. 2:7
Distortion of Work: Work under the curse and influenced by the principalities and powers that oppose God.		
Sin introduces toil, sweat, and pain into work and family.	Gen. 3:16–24; 4:11–12; Rom. 8:20–22	"Is Work a Curse?" Rom. 8:20
Complications intensify in the workplace.	Gen. 39:1–23	"Workplace Myths," 1 Cor. 3:9; "Honesty and Ethical Standards," Phil. 2:15; "It's Not Fair!" 1 Pet. 2:18–21
The danger of exploitation in the workplace appears.	Ex. 1:8–22	"Work-World Codes," Col. 3:22—4:1
Work is not only for our own benefit but for others, including the poor and oppressed.	Ex. 23:10–11; Deut. 15:7–11; Eph. 4:28	"From Deadbeat to Donor," Eph. 4:28
God still equips people for work with His Word and the Spirit.	Ex. 31:2–11	"People at Work," Heb. 2:7
People lack fulfillment by idolizing work or making it an end in itself.	Eccl. 2:4–26; Luke 12:13–34	"Do-It-Yourself Idolatry," Col. 3:5
But God still rules and work can be a gift that fits God's design.	Eccl. 2:24—3:17	"A Command to Work," 2 Thess. 3:6–12
Work is a gift of God and will be blessed.	Ps. 104:1–35; 127:1–5; Eccl. 3:12–13; 5:18–20	"People at Work," Heb. 2:7
Jesus re-established and illustrated God's original design for work.	John 4:34–38; 5:1–18	"Jesus the Carpenter," Mark 6:3; "Paul's 'Real' Job," Acts 18:1–3
Our agony in this life continues as we seek release from sin and the renewal of creation.	Eccl. 1:2–3; Rom. 8:18–30	"Is Work a Curse?" Rom. 8:20
God's people are to illustrate their new citizenship in heaven through good work here and now.	Eph. 6:5–9; Col. 3:17–23; Titus 2:1—3:15; James 2:1–26	"A Promotion," Eph. 6:5–9; "Who's the Boss?" Col. 3:22–24; "'I Won't Hire Christians!'" 1 Tim. 6:1–2; "Your 'Workstyle,'" Titus 2:9–10
Restoration of Work: Work as it will be when Christ returns.		
God will someday restore His original design; His people will work without the burden of sin.	Is. 65:17–25; Rev. 15:1–4; 22:1–11	

Why not use this overview of the Bible's teaching on work as an outline of study for yourself, others at your church, or coworkers who want to know what God has to say on the subject?

To understand more about Scripture's teaching on the three different time periods shown—God's original design, life in a fallen world, and the period after Christ returns—see "The Bible: Getting the Big Picture," 2 Tim. 3:16–17.

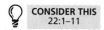

9Then he said to me, "See *that you do* not *do that.* For[a] I
am your fellow servant, and of your brethren the prophets,
and of those who keep the words of this book. Worship
God." 10And he said to me, "Do not seal the words of the
prophecy of this book, for the time is at hand. 11He who is
unjust, let him be unjust still; he who is filthy, let him be
filthy still; he who is righteous, let him be righteous[a] still;
he who is holy, let him be holy still."

12"And behold, I am coming quickly, and My reward *is*
with Me, to give to every one according to his work. 13I am
the Alpha and the Omega, *the* Beginning and *the* End, the
First and the Last."[a]

14Blessed *are* those who do His commandments,[a] that
they may have the right to the tree of life, and may enter
through the gates into the city. 15But[a] outside *are* dogs and
sorcerers and sexually immoral and murderers and idolaters, and whoever loves and practices a lie.

16"I, Jesus, have sent My angel to testify to you these
things in the churches. I am the Root and the Offspring of
David, the Bright and Morning Star."

22:9 [a]NU-Text and M-Text omit *For.* *22:11* [a]NU-Text and M-Text read *do right.*
22:13 [a]NU-Text and M-Text read *the First and the Last, the Beginning and the End.*
22:14 [a]NU-Text reads *wash their robes.* *22:15* [a]NU-Text and M-Text omit *But.*

CONSIDER THIS
22:2

Fresh Fruit Salad!

When you think of the new heavens and new earth that God will someday create, what images come to mind? John's vision includes a unique species of tree, the tree of life that bears twelve kinds of fruits—a different fruit every month (v. 2)!

Trees that productive will afford little rest for the workers who cultivate and harvest them. Yet surely those fruit pickers will be happy because the text also says, "there shall be no more curse*" (v. 3, italics added). Work will be free of the painful toil and drudgery that now characterizes it (see also Rev. 21:4).*

This view of the new creation, with delightful work and enjoyable results, is very similar to the description of God's future society in Isaiah 65:17–23. There the picture includes such attractive images as:

- *joy and rejoicing (v. 18).*
- *an end to weeping and crying (v. 19).*
- *building and living in one's own house (v. 21).*
- *owning, planting, and enjoying the fruit of one's vineyard (vv. 21–22).*

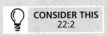

22:17

[17]And the Spirit and the bride say,
"Come!" And let him who hears say,
"Come!" And let him who thirsts come. Whoever desires,
let him take the water of life freely.

A Final Warning

[18]For[a] I testify to everyone who hears the words of the
prophecy of this book: If anyone adds to these things, God
will add[b] to him the plagues that are written in this book;
[19]and if anyone takes away from the words of the book of
this prophecy, God shall take away[a] his part from the Book[b]
of Life, from the holy city, and *from* the things which are
written in this book.
[20]He who testifies to these things says, "Surely I am coming quickly."
Amen. Even so, come, Lord Jesus!
[21]The grace of our Lord Jesus Christ *be* with you all.[a]
Amen.

22:18 [a]NU-Text and M-Text omit *For.* [b]M-Text reads *may God add.* *22:19* [a]M-Text reads *may God take away.* [b]NU-Text and M-Text read *tree of life.* *22:21* [a]NU-Text reads *with all;* M-Text reads *with all the saints.*

- *enjoying the work of one's hands (v. 22).*
- *an end to laboring in vain or bringing children into a world of trouble (v. 23).*

These statements from Revelation and Isaiah recall the original design that God had for His creation, a creation that was "very good" (Gen. 1:31). God created people to be His coworkers in managing the resources of His world for the benefit of all (see "People at Work," Heb. 2:7). God will restore that ideal. As Paul promised, the world will be freed from its sufferings, futility, and bondage to corruption and be made again to fulfill its original design (Rom. 8:18–25).

What a hope to look forward to—the reign of God over a joyful new world where trouble-free families work painlessly together and enjoy fresh fruit salad month after month! ◆

Most of us know all too well how burdensome work can be. Yet the Bible calls it a gift from God. See "Is Work a Curse?" Rom. 8:20–22.

There's a Welcome Here

CONSIDER THIS 22:17

Perhaps you or someone you know feels hesitant about spiritual things. Matters of faith may feel forbidding, even scary. Religion may seem like nothing but judgment and condemnation.

Yet Jesus came not to condemn, but to save. His primary purpose was to offer life to dying people, inviting them to experience forgiveness, healing, and hope. "Come!" He says to those who are thirsty, "Whoever desires, let him take the water of life freely" (v. 17; see also John 7:37–38).

Centuries prior to Jesus' coming, a prophet foretold this invitation (Is. 55:1, 3):

Ho! Everyone who thirsts,
Come to the waters;
And you who have no money,
Come, buy and eat.
Yes, come, buy wine and milk
Without money and without price . . .
Incline your ear, and come to Me.
Hear, and your soul shall live.

This is a powerful invitation because the same Jesus who makes it wields the power to withdraw it from those who refuse His call and continue to live in rebellion and sin (Rev. 22:14–15, 18–19). Just as He has authority to welcome us into eternal life, so He has the authority not to welcome us. Yet in His grace He chooses to offer life to sinful people.

You may be confused about many issues of religion, but hear God's gracious offer: Jesus wants to forgive your sins and welcome you into new life. If you haven't already accepted His invitation, why not do so now and begin the exciting journey that leads to eternal life!

Acknowledgments

Weights and Measures

Themes to Study in the New Testament

Index to Key New Testament Passages

The Four Gospels Side by Side

Jobs and Occupations Index

ACKNOWLEDGMENTS

Matthew 13:34–35: "Ten Myths About Christianity, Myth #1: Jesus Christ Was Only a Great Moral Teacher." Adapted by permission from *Ten Myths About Christianity* by Michael Green and Gordon Carkner, Lion Publishing, 1988. Quotation from C.S. Lewis, *Mere Christianity,* Macmillan, 1978, used by permission of HarperCollins Publishers.

Matthew 20:28: quotation from *Honest To God,* by John A.T. Robinson, SCM Press Ltd. 1963. Used by permission. © J.A.T. Robinson, 1963.

Matthew 23:1–30: excerpt from *A Severe Mercy* by Sheldon Vanauken. Copyright ©1977, 1980 by Sheldon Vanauken. Reprinted by permission of HarperCollins Publishers Inc.

Matthew 28:1–10: "Ten Myths About Christianity, Myth #2: There Is No Evidence That Jesus Rose from the Dead." Adapted by permission from *Ten Myths About Christianity* by Michael Green and Gordon Carkner, Lion Publishing, 1988.

Mark 2:17: quotation reprinted from *Walking on Water* by Madeleine L'Engle, ©1980 by Crosswicks. Used by permission of Harold Shaw Publishers, Wheaton, IL.

Mark 16:15: quotation from *National Catholic Reporter,* October 27, 1989.

John 4:48: "Ten Myths About Christianity, Myth #3: Science Is In Conflict with Christian Faith." Adapted by permission from *Ten Myths About Christianity* by Michael Green and Gordon Carkner, Lion Publishing, 1988.

John 5:17: "God—The Original Worker." Adapted by permission from Doug Sherman and William Hendricks, *Your Work Matters to God,* NavPress, 1987.

John 15:18–20: quotation from A. W. Tozer, *A Treasury of A.W. Tozer,* Baker Book House, 1980.

John 18:37–38: quotation reprinted from *Walking on Water* by Madeleine L'Engle, ©1980 by Crosswicks. Used by permission of Harold Shaw Publishers, Wheaton, IL.

Acts 4:12: "Ten Myths About Christianity, Myth #4: It Doesn't Matter What You Believe, All Religions Are Basically the Same." Adapted by permission from *Ten Myths About Christianity* by Michael Green and Gordon Carkner, Lion Publishing, 1988.

Acts 4:13: quotation from Elton Trueblood, *Your Other Vocation,* Harper & Brothers, 1952, used by permission of HarperCollins Publishers.

Acts 24:22: quotation reprinted from *Walking on Water* by Madeleine L'Engle, ©1980 by Crosswicks. Used by permission of Harold Shaw Publishers, Wheaton, IL.

Romans 8:20: "Is Work a Curse?" Adapted by permission from Doug Sherman and William Hendricks, *Your Work Matters to God,* NavPress, 1987.

Romans 14:5: quotation from Elton Trueblood, *Your Other Vocation,* Harper & Brothers, 1952, used by permission of HarperCollins Publishers.

1 Corinthians 1:26: "Ten Myths About Christianity, Myth #5: Christianity Is Just a Crutch for the Weak." Adapted by permission from *Ten Myths About Christianity* by Michael Green and Gordon Carkner, Lion Publishing, 1988.

1 Corinthians 7:17: excerpt from *A Severe Mercy* by Sheldon Vanauken. Copyright ©1977, 1980 by Sheldon Vanauken. Reprinted by permission of HarperCollins Publishers Inc.

1 Corinthians 13:12: quotation from Pete Hammond, *Marketplace Networks,* InterVarsity Christian Fellowship of the USA, 1990.

1 Corinthians 15:9–10: "Ten Myths About Christianity, Myth #6: People Become Christians Through Social Conditioning." Adapted by permission from *Ten Myths About Christianity* by Michael Green and Gordon Carkner, Lion Publishing, 1988.

2 Corinthians 4:2: "A Code of Ethics for Christian Witness." Used by permission of InterVarsity Christian Fellowship of the USA.

Galatians 5:1–12: "Ten Myths About Christianity, Myth #7: Christianity Stifles Personal Freedom." Adapted by permission from *Ten Myths About Christianity* by Michael Green and Gordon Carkner, Lion Publishing, 1988.

Galatians 5:18: "Ten Commandments—Ten Great Freedoms." Used by permission of InterVarsity Christian Fellowship of the USA.

Ephesians 4:12: quotation from Elton Trueblood, *Your Other Vocation,* Harper & Brothers, 1952, used by permission of HarperCollins Publishers.

Ephesians 6:5: quotation from Mark Quinn, "Five Guidelines to a Spirituality of Work," *Initiatives,* newsletter of the National Center for the Laity, 1989.

Philippians 2:15: "Honesty & Ethical Standards." From a speech given by George Gallup, Jr., December 2, 1987, as reported in *Emerging Trends,* Princeton Religion Research Center, 1988.

Colossians 3:22: reprinted from *Liberating the Laity* by R. Paul Stevens. ©1985 by InterVarsity Christian Fellowship of the USA. Used by permission of InterVarsity Press, P.O. Box 1400, Downers Grove, IL 60515.

1 Thessalonians 1:7: quotation from speech by Richard Halverson as reported in the newsletter of Fourth Presbyterian Church, McLean, VA.

1 Thessalonians 4:11–12: excerpt from *A Severe Mercy* by Sheldon Vanauken. Copyright ©1977, 1980 by Sheldon Vanauken. Reprinted by permission of HarperCollins Publishers Inc.

1 Thessalonians 5:6: remarks by Anglican Bishop Michael Marshall, as quoted in editor's column, *America Magazine,* 1990.

1 Timothy 1:3–4: "Ten Myths About Christianity." Adapted by permission from *Ten Myths About Christianity* by Michael Green and Gordon Carkner, Lion Publishing, 1988.

1 Timothy 6:18: quotation from *Dedication and Leadership* by Douglas Hyde. ©1966 by the University of Notre Dame Press. Reprinted by permission.

Acknowledgments

Titus 1:15: quotation reprinted from *Walking on Water* by Madeleine L'Engle, ©1980 by Crosswicks. Used by permission of Harold Shaw Publishers, Wheaton, IL.

Hebrews 2:7: "People at Work." Adapted by permission from Doug Sherman and William Hendricks, *Your Work Matters to God,* NavPress, 1987.

Hebrews 12:1–2: "Ten Myths About Christianity, Myth #8: Christianity Is Otherwordly and Irrelevant to Modern Life." Adapted by permission from *Ten Myths About Christianity* by Michael Green and Gordon Carkner, Lion Publishing, 1988.

Hebrews 13:15: reprinted from *Reinventing Evangelism* by Donald C. Posterski. ©1989 by Donald C. Posterski. Used by permission of InterVarsity Press, P.O. Box 1400, Downers Grove, IL 60515.

James 2:8–13: "Ten Commandments for Practical Living." Adapted from *Ten Commandments for Practical Living,* ©1973, McNair Associates, used by permission.

James 3:13–18: quotation from *Dedication and Leadership* by Douglas Hyde. ©1966 by the University of Notre Dame Press. Reprinted by permission.

1 Peter 1:1: reprinted from *Liberating the Laity* by R. Paul Stevens. ©1985 by InterVarsity Christian Fellowship of the USA. Used by permission of InterVarsity Press, P.O. Box 1400, Downers Grove, IL 60515.

1 Peter 2:9: quotation from Elton Trueblood, *Your Other Vocation,* Harper & Brothers, 1952, used by permission of HarperCollins Publishers.

1 Peter 3:15–17: quotation from *Dedication and Leadership* by Douglas Hyde. ©1966 by the University of Notre Dame Press. Reprinted by permission.

2 Peter 1:16: "Ten Myths About Christianity, Myth #9: The Bible Is Unreliable and Not to Be Trusted." Adapted by permission from *Ten Myths About Christianity* by Michael Green and Gordon Carkner, Lion Publishing, 1988.

2 Peter 2:13: quotation from Fr. Jerry Foley, "We Work At Our Leisure," from *Connecting Faith and Life,* Sheed and Ward, 1986.

1 John 5:4–5: quotation from Philip J. Lee, Jr., *Against the Protestant Gnostics,* Oxford University Press, 1989.

Revelation 15:1–8: quotation from C.S. Lewis, *A Preface to Paradise Lost,* Oxford University Press, 1942.

Revelation 20:1–10: "Ten Myths About Christianity, Myth #10: Evil and Suffering in the World Proves There Is No God." Adapted by permission from *Ten Myths About Christianity* by Michael Green and Gordon Carkner, Lion Publishing, 1988.

A diligent effort has been made to secure permission to reprint previously published material. Any oversight should be brought to the attention of the publisher for rectification in a subsequent printing.

WEIGHTS AND MEASURES

WEIGHTS

Unit	Weight	Equivalents	Translations
Jewish Weights			
Talent	c. 75 pounds for common talent, c. 150 pounds for royal talent	60 minas; 3,000 shekels	talent
Mina (Maneh)	1.25 pounds	50 shekels	mina
Shekel	c. .4 ounce (11.4 grams) for common shekel c. .8 ounce for royal shekel	2 bekas; 20 gerahs	shekel
Beka	c. .2 ounce (5.7 grams)	1/2 shekel; 10 gerahs	half a shekel
Gerah	c. .02 ounce (.57 grams)	1/20 shekel	gerah
Roman Weight			
Litra	12 ounces		pound

MEASURES OF LENGTH

Unit	Length	Equivalents	Translations
Day's journey	c. 20 miles		day's journey
Roman mile	4,854 feet	8 stadia	mile
Sabbath day's journey	3,637 feet	6 stadia	Sabbath day's journey
Stadion	606 feet	1/8 Roman mile	furlong
Rod	9 feet (10.5 feet in Ezekiel)	3 paces; 6 cubits	measuring reed, reed
Fathom	6 feet	4 cubits	fathom
Pace	3 feet	1/3 rod; 2 cubits	pace
Cubit	18 inches	1/2 pace; 2 spans	cubit
Span	9 inches	1/2 cubit; 3 handbreadths	span
Handbreadth	3 inches	1/3 span; 4 fingers	handbreadth
Finger	.75 inchs	1/4 handbreadth	finger

LIQUID MEASURES			
Unit	**Measure**	**Equivalents**	**Translations**
Kor	60 gallons	10 baths	kor
Metretes	10.2 gallons		gallons
Bath	6 gallons	6 hins	measure, bath
Hin	1 gallon	2 kabs	hin
Kab	2 quarts	4 logs	kab
Log	1 pint	1/4 kab	log

DRY MEASURES			
Unit	**Measure**	**Equivalents**	**Translations**
Homer	6.52 bushels	10 ephahs	homer
Kor	6.52 bushels	1 homer; 10 ephahs	kor, measure
Lethech	3.26 bushels	1/2 kor	half homer
Ephah	.65 bushel, 20.8 quarts	1/10 homer	ephah
Modius	7.68 quarts		basket
Seah	7 quarts	1/3 ephah	measure
Omer	2.08 quarts	1/10 ephah; 1 4/5 kag	omer
Kab	1.16 quarts	4 logs	kab
Choenix	1 quart		measure
Xestes	1 1/6 pints		pot
Log	.58 pint	1/4 kab	log

For a table of monetary units see Rev. 16:21.

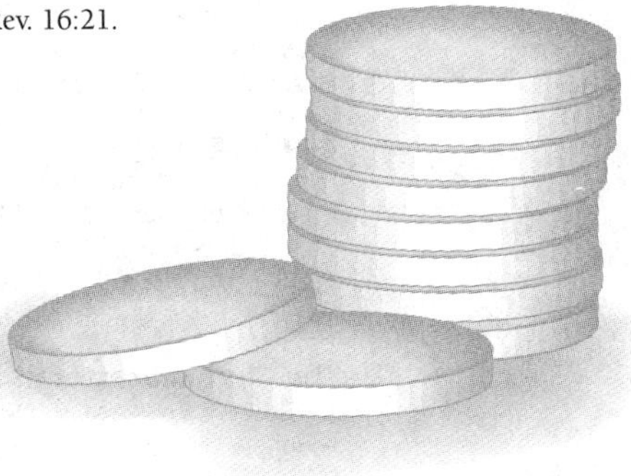

Themes to Study in the New Testament

The New Testament speaks to numerous practical themes, as shown below. Studying the texts associated with a given issue will help you apply God's Word to your experience. To study a theme, refer to the articles listed for that theme. Within the articles you'll find references to additional helps, Bible texts, and related themes.

The Church

What is the church? A building? An institution? A community of believers? Is there such a thing as an "ideal" or "model" church? What can we learn about the church as we study its infancy recorded in the New Testament? What implications are there for the church today? The articles below and their related texts will help you get started as you think about the church and your place in it:

The Nature of the Church

The King Declares His Kingdom (Matt. 4:17)
Significance for Little People (Mark 2:3–17)
Is Jesus Really Lord of All? (Luke 6:1–5)
Sorting Out Membership (Luke 13:22–23)
With Us (John 14:16–18)
The Network (John 15:1–10)
A New Reality Gets a New Name (Acts 11:26)
Ten Myths about Christianity, Myth #5: Christianity Is Just a Crutch for the Weak (1 Cor. 1:26)
This Building Gets Landmark Status (Eph. 2:19–22)
Is Your Church Upside-down or Right Side Up? (1 Thess. 2:13–14)
God's Family Album (1 Pet. 2:9–10)
Worship or Wrath? (Rev. 6:1–17)

The Character of the Church

To Be Like Jesus Means to Commit to Other Believers (Matt. 3:1–17)
To Be Like Jesus Means to Serve Others (Matt. 8:1—9:38)
To Be Like Jesus Means to Affirm Other Leaders (Matt. 10:1–42)
Are You Confused about Greatness, Too? (Mark 9:33–37)
The Hallmark of Love (John 13:31–35)
Society's Divisions Affect Believers (Acts 6:1)
The Scandal of Litigating Christians (1 Cor. 6:1–11)
Support the Weak (1 Thess. 5:14)
One Standard for All (1 Tim. 3:1)
Ushers on Trial (James 2:1–13)
Playing Favorites (James 2:1–9)
Rules That Lead to Joy (1 John 2:3–6)
Sad Fallouts Are Inevitable (Jude 8–16)

The Early Church

The Women Who Followed Jesus (Luke 8:1–3)
Jesus—A Rabbi for Women, Too (Luke 23:49)
Families of the Early Church (Acts 16:31–34)
"Not Many Mighty"...But a Few (Acts 18:7–8)
The Church at the End of the First Century (Rev. 1:20)
Seven Churches to Study (Rev. 3:1)

"Making Disciples of All the Nations"

Pluralism at Pentecost (Acts 2:5)
Come One, Come All! (Acts 10:34)
Ethnic Walls Break Down (Acts 10:44–45)
Antioch: A Model for the Modern Church? (Acts 13:1)
A Church That Defies Market Research (Acts 15:22–35)
Are We One People? (Rom. 11:13–24)
Enemies Become Family and Friends (1 Cor. 16:9–20)
A Strong Rebuke (Gal. 3:1)
We Are Family! (Gal. 3:28)
Breaking Down Walls (Eph. 2:14–18)

The Church Gathered for Refinement

To Be Like Jesus Means to Serve Others (Matt. 8:1—9:38)
The Synagogue (Mark 1:21)
The Network (John 15:1–10)
Reconnecting Sunday and Monday (Acts 2:46–47)
Sharing Things in Common (Acts 4:32–35)
Society's Divisions Affect Believers (Acts 6:1)
Barnabas—A Model for Mentoring (Acts 9:27)
A Church That Defies Market Research (Acts 15:22–35)
Not Permitted to Speak? (1 Cor. 14:34)
Work, Labor, and Patience (1 Thess. 1:3)
Is Your Church Upside-down or Right Side Up? (1 Thess. 2:13–14)
A New Way to Worship (1 Tim. 2:8–15)
Widows (1 Tim. 5:3)
Effective Care for the Needy (1 Tim. 5:3–16)
Mentoring, Kingdom-Style (2 Tim. 2:2)
Coventry (Heb. 10:19–25)
Let's Celebrate! (James 5:13)
Tough-minded Believers (1 John 4:1)
Hospitality and Discernment (2 John 7–11)

Sundays

Does God Work on Sundays? (John 5:16–17)
Reconnecting Sunday and Monday (Acts 2:46–47)
Are Sundays Special? (Rom. 14:5–13)
The Sabbath (Heb. 4:1–13)
The Lord's Day (Rev. 1:10)

The Church Scattered for Impact

To All the Nations (Matt. 28:19)
People Priorities in the City (Mark 5:21–43)
Life—The Big Picture (Mark 12:28–34)
Faith Impacts the World (Mark 16:15–16)
Jesus' First Sermon Included Surprises (Luke 4:16–27)
The Spirit of the Lord Is upon...You! (Luke 4:18)
The Underclass (Luke 7:20–23)
Can Laity Get the Job Done? (Luke 9:1–62)
Sorting Out Membership (Luke 13:22–23)
You Alone Can't Bring Them to Jesus (John 6:44)
Whose Job Is Evangelism? (John 16:8)
Called into the World (John 17:18)
Reconnecting Sunday and Monday (Acts 2:46–47)

Where Has God Placed You? (Acts 8:26–39)
The Ephesus Approach (Acts 19:8–41)
The Power of the Gospel (Rom. 1:16)
A Straightforward Approach (1 Thess. 2:5)
Is Your Church Upside-down or Right Side Up? (1 Thess. 2:13–14)

Leaders
To Be Like Jesus Means to Serve Others (Matt. 8:1—9:38)
To Be Like Jesus Means to Affirm Other Leaders (Matt. 10:1–42)
The Twelve (Matt. 10:2)
Would You Choose These for Leaders? (Matt. 26:35–74)
Can Laity Get the Job Done? (Luke 9:1–62)
Leadership Equals Humility? (Luke 22:24–27)
The Order of the Towel (John 13:1–20)
An International Work Group (Acts 20:4)
"I Have Not Coveted" (Acts 20:33–38)
Paying Vocational Christian Workers (1 Cor. 9:1–23)
Who Were the Apostles? (2 Cor. 11:5)
A Straightforward Approach (1 Thess. 2:5)
Is Your Church Upside-down or Right Side Up? (1 Thess. 2:13–14)
One Standard for All (1 Tim. 3:1)
No Greedy Leaders! (1 Tim. 3:3)
Mentoring, Kingdom-Style (2 Tim. 2:2)
United for the Work (Titus 3:12–15)
Don't Fleece the Flock (1 Pet. 5:2)
The Business of the Church (1 Pet. 5:2–4)

The Church in the World
"The Gates of Hell" (Matt. 16:18)
Faith Impacts the World (Mark 16:15–16)
Is Jesus Really Lord of All? (Luke 6:1–5)
Whose Job Is Evangelism? (John 16:8)
Called into the World (John 17:18)
Reconnecting Sunday and Monday (Acts 2:46–47)
A Confusing Reputation (Acts 5:12–16)
Where Has God Placed You? (Acts 8:26–39)
Confusing Responses (Acts 14:11–19)
Paul's Urban Strategy (Acts 16:4)
The Ephesus Approach (Acts 19:8–41)
Truth Can Trigger Opposition (Acts 24:1–26)
Audience-shaped Messages (Acts 26:1–32)
The Power of the Gospel (Rom. 1:16)
God's Heart for the Whole World (Rom. 9:1)
A Straightforward Approach (1 Thess. 2:5)
Quiet Living in a Hectic World (1 Thess. 4:11)

Ethics and Character
God calls His people to integrity and compassion. But because all of us are sinners who have rebelled against God and come into bondage to our own self-interests, following God's calling does not come naturally. Instead we find in ourselves agendas and patterns of behavior that fall far short of Christ's example of goodness and humane treatment of others.

How can we change? How can born sinners develop into ethical people? To find out, start by studying the categories, articles, and passages below:

Accountability
Do You Suffer From "Comparisonitis"? (Rom. 12:3)
The Ultimate Performance Review (1 Cor. 3:13–15)
Taking Stock (Phil. 3:7–14)

Behavior on the Job
See "Work"

Christlike Character
Being Like Jesus (series; Matt. 10:25)
The Spirit of the Lord Is Upon...You! (Luke 4:18)
The Cost of Following Jesus (Luke 14:25–32)
Sinless Perfection? (1 John 3:6)

Decision Making
Judge Not! (Matt. 7:1–5)
Trick Questions Foiled (Matt. 22:23–33)
A Reckless Choice (Mark 6:23)
Convenience Makes for Odd Choices (Luke 23:1–25)
A Double Standard? (John 8:2–3)
The Blessing of a Clean Conscience (John 18:1–11)
Matters of Conscience (Rom. 14:1–23)
Are We to Judge All Things? (1 Cor. 2:15)
Gray Areas (1 Cor. 8:1–13)
Welcome to Stressful Living (2 Cor. 6:3–10)

Humility
The Power of Humility (Matt. 3:11)
The Way Up Is Down (Matt. 5:3)
Are You a Friend of Someone in Need? (Luke 5:17–26)
Competition versus Compassion (Luke 9:46–48)
The Right Kind of Fear (Luke 12:4–7)
Compassion and Anger in One Person? (Luke 19:41–46)
Leadership Equals Humility? (Luke 22:24–27)
The Quest for Greatness (Luke 22:24–30)
The Power of Self Sacrifice (John 10:17–18)
The Order of the Towel (John 13:1–20)
Paul Apologized for Losing His Cool (Acts 23:5)
Humility—The Scandalous Virtue (Phil. 2:3)

Integrity
Is Evasion Ethical? (Matt. 21:24–27)
Trick Questions Foiled (Matt. 22:23–33)
Can You Be Trusted? (Luke 1:18–19)
Convenience Makes for Odd Choices (Luke 23:1–25)
The Blessing of a Clean Conscience (John 18:1–11)
Real Estate Deal Deadly (Acts 5:2–10)
Promises (Rom. 4:16–25)
Matters of Conscience (Rom. 14:1–23)
Cover-ups Deceive Everybody (1 Cor. 5:1–13)
Integrity in the Face of Competition (2 Cor. 10:1)
New Creatures with New Character (Gal. 5:22–23)
Honesty and Ethical Standards (Phil. 2:15)
Work-World Codes (Col. 3:22—4:1)
Finishing Well (2 Thess. 1:3–12)
One Standard for All (1 Tim. 3:1)
"I Won't Hire Christians!" (1 Tim. 6:1–2)

Justice
An Eye for an Eye (Matt. 5:38–42)
Judge Not! (Matt. 7:1–5)
No Forgiveness! (Matt. 12:31–32)
Seventy Times Seven—Still Not Enough! (Matt. 18:21–35)
Jesus and Unjust Pay (Matt. 20:1–16)
The Final Exam (Matt. 25:31–46)
Jesus' First Sermon Included Surprises (Luke 4:16–27)
Running to Extremes (Luke 6:29)
The Underclass (Luke 7:20–23)
Are You the Older Brother? (Luke 15:25–30)
Doing Your Duty (Luke 17:5–10)
A Double Standard? (John 8:2–3)
Discrimination on the Basis of Wealth (John 19:1–6)

Forgiveness Abounds (John 21:15–23)
Faith and Rights (Acts 22:25–29)
Do Not Avenge Yourself (Rom. 12:19–21)
The Avengers (Rom. 13:4)
Rights (Gal. 4:1–18)
God Restrains Evil (Rev. 13:1–18)
Will Evil Ever Get Its Reward? (Rev. 20:1–15)

Love

What Kind of Love Is This? (Matt. 22:34–40)
Love My Enemies? (Luke 6:27–31)
Love Your Neighbor (Luke 10:27–28)
The Good Neighbor (Luke 10:30–37)
The Hallmark of Love (John 13:31–35)
New Creatures with New Character (Gal. 5:22–23)
Love Is More than Enthusiasm (1 John 5:1–3)

Money and Wealth

Living Within Your Limits (Matt. 16:22–23)
Jesus and Unjust Pay (Matt. 20:1–16)
Tainted Money (Matt. 27:3–10)
It's All Relative (Mark 12:43–44)
Running to Extremes (Luke 6:29)
The Underclass (Luke 7:20–23)
The Real Bottom Line (Luke 9:25)
Watch Out for Greed! (Luke 12:15)
Confused Value? (Luke 15:1–31)
Holding Wealth or Serving Others? (Luke 18:18–30)
A Remedy for Tax Fraud (Luke 19:1–10)
Discrimination on the Basis of Wealth (John 19:1–6)
Wealth: Hold It Lightly (Acts 4:37—5:11)
Gospel and Property Conflicts (Acts 19:23–27)
Debt-Free Living (Rom. 13:8)
What Controls You? (1 Cor. 6:12)
Money: Compassion and Integrity (1 Cor. 16:1–4)
Who Are the Poor? (2 Cor. 9:9–10)
A Lifestyle of Contentment (Phil. 4:10–13)
Support the Weak (1 Thess. 5:14)
No Greedy Leaders! (1 Tim. 3:3)
The Dangers of Prosperity Theology (1 Tim. 6:3–6)
Christians and Money (1 Tim. 6:6–19)
Don't Fleece the Flock (1 Pet. 5:2)
The Delusions of Luxury (Rev. 18:1–24)

Morality

The Morality of Christ (Matt. 5:17–48)
What About Old Testament Law? (Matt. 5:19)
An Eye for an Eye (Matt. 5:38–42)
Always the Poor (Mark 14:7)
Jesus Confronts the Legalists (Luke 6:1–11)
The Letter and the Spirit (Luke 14:1–6)
A Double Standard? (John 8:2–3)
The Blessing of a Clean Conscience (John 18:1–11)
The Law (Rom. 2:12)
Are People Basically Good? (Rom. 7:21)
Matters of Conscience (Rom. 14:1–23)
Gray Areas (1 Cor. 8:1–13)
New Creatures with New Character (Gal. 5:22–23)
One Standard for All (1 Tim. 3:1)
Ten Commandments for Practical Living (James 2:8–13)
Rules That Lead to Joy (1 John 2:3–6)

Power and Authority

To Be Like Jesus Means to Serve Others (Matt. 8:1—9:38)
Under Authority (Matt. 8:5–13)
The Power of Forgiveness (Matt. 9:4–8)
Servant-Leaders (Matt. 20:25–28)
A New Style of Fame (Matt. 21:8–11)
Would You Choose These for Leaders? (Matt. 26:35–74)
Significance for Little People (Mark 2:3–17)
Are You Confused about Greatness, Too? (Mark 9:33–37)
Three Dangers of Power (Luke 3:14)
Authority and Responsibility (Luke 12:35–48)
A Shrewd Manager (Luke 16:1–13)
Leadership Equals Humility? (Luke 22:24–27)
The Quest for Greatness (Luke 22:24–30)
Wait for Power (Luke 24:49)
The Power of Self-Sacrifice (John 10:17–18)
Under Authority (John 12:49)
The Order of the Towel (John 13:1–20)
A Model of Servant Leadership (John 13:2–17)
Leaders Start as Servants (Acts 6:5–6)
"It Serves Them Right" (Acts 27:9–11)
Who Gets the Credit? (1 Cor. 3:5–8)
One Standard for All (1 Tim. 3:1)
No Greedy Leaders! (1 Tim. 3:3)
Mentoring, Kingdom-Style (2 Tim. 2:2)
Elementary Leadership Lessons (Heb. 5:1–14)
Don't Fleece the Flock (1 Pet. 5:2)

Public Ethics

Sulfa Drugs and Street Lights (Matt. 5:13–16)
The Public Side of Faith (Matt. 14:13–14)
Jesus and Taxation (Matt. 17:24–27)
Taxes (Mark 12:14)
Faith Impacts the World (Mark 16:15–16)
Jesus' First Sermon Included Surprises (Luke 4:16–27)
What Does Leprosy Have to Do with AIDS? (Luke 5:12–15)
The Underclass (Luke 7:20–23)
God and the Environment (Luke 12:6–7)
A Remedy for Tax Fraud (Luke 19:1–10)
Be Willing to Pay the Price (Acts 16:16–24)
Free to Be Bold (Acts 23:1)
The Limits of Political Authority (Rom. 13:1–7)
The Avengers (Rom. 13:4)
The Scandal of Litigating Christians (1 Cor. 6:1–11)
A Code of Ethics for Christian Witness (2 Cor. 4:2)
Rights (Gal. 4:1–18)
Honesty and Ethical Standards (Phil. 2:15)
Support the Weak (1 Thess. 5:14)
A Command to Work (2 Thess. 3:6–12)
A Challenge to Slavery (Philem. 16)

Right and Wrong

The Morality of Christ (Matt. 5:17–48)
Jesus Confronts the Legalists (Luke 6:1–11)
The Letter and the Spirit (Luke 14:1–6)
The Blessing of a Clean Conscience (John 18:1–11)
Righteousness (Rom. 1:17)
Are People Basically Good? (Rom. 7:21)

Success

True Success Means Faithfulness (Matt. 25:14–30)
A Kingdom Perspective on Significance (Mark 13:33)
The Real Bottom Line (Luke 9:25)
Competition versus Compassion (Luke 9:46–48)
Success (John 3:30)
Who Gets the Credit? (1 Cor. 3:5–8)

Temptation

Wealth's Temptation (Matt. 4:8–10)
"All Will Be Yours" (Luke 4:5–8)

Watch Out for Greed (Luke 12:15)
Real Estate Deal Deadly (Acts 5:2–10)
Are People Basically Good? (Rom. 7:21)
Pay Attention to Temptation! (1 Cor. 10:12–13)
The Delusions of Luxury (Rev. 18:1–24)

Miscellaneous

City Kids Die over Adult Matters (Matt. 2:16–18)
Does Change Threaten You? (Luke 5:36–39)
Who Is Blessed? (Luke 11:27–28)
The Value of a Disabled Woman (Luke 13:10–17)
Holy Interruptions (Luke 18:35–43)
The Road Less Traveled (John 4:4–42)
Resistance—Unpopular Obedience (Acts 7:57–60)
Conflict Resolution (Acts 11:2–18)
Confusing Responses (Acts 14:11–19)
When I Am Weak, Then I Am Strong (2 Cor. 12:7–10)
Hope For You: Watch Paul Grow! (Gal. 1:11–24)
Feel Like a Novice? (1 Tim. 4:1–16)
Let Me Pick Up the Tab (Philem. 17–19)
Knowing *About* God Is Not the Same as *Knowing* God (Heb. 6:1–20)

The Family

There is great confusion in society today about the family. On the one hand, expectations are often high and unmet. On the other hand, many people's expectations are so low as to render the concept of the family meaningless. Tension, conflict, pain, and loss often dominate family relationships so that positive qualities such as love, commitment, pleasure, and security are all but impossible.

Scripture has much to say about the nature of the family. The articles listed below will help you study this theme in order to apply biblical truth to your own family relationships:

Jesus' Family

Jesus' Roots (Matt. 1:1–16)
The Women in Jesus' Genealogy (Matt. 1:3–6)
Asian-born Jesus Becomes a Refugee in Africa (Matt. 2:13–15)
Jesus—A Homeless Man? (Matt. 8:20)
Is Jesus For or Against Family? (Mark 3:31–35)
Jesus the Carpenter (Mark 6:3)
Mary, the Mother of Jesus (Luke 1:26–56)
A Poor Family's Sacrifice (Luke 2:22–24)
Jesus, the Son of...(Luke 3:23–28)
Jesus' Family Experienced Pain, Too (Luke 3:36–38)
James (Introduction to James)
Jude (Introduction to Jude)

Families of the New Testament

A Poor Family Comes into Wealth (Matt. 2:11)
A Surprise in Peter's Household (Matt. 8:14–15)
Hateful Herodias (Matt. 14:3)
A Pushy Mother (Matt. 20:20–23)
Families of the Gospels (Luke 20:34)
Ananias and Sapphira (Acts 5:1)
The Herods (Acts 12:1–2)
Families of the Early Church (Acts 16:31–34)
The Four Daughters of Philip (Acts 21:9)

See also the personality profiles of individual family members listed elsewhere.

Family Backgrounds

Jesus' Roots (Matt. 1:1–16)
To Be Like Jesus Means to Accept Our Roots (Matt. 1:1–17)
The Women in Jesus' Genealogy (Matt. 1:3–6)
Jesus, the Son of...(Luke 3:23–28)
Jesus' Family Experienced Pain, Too (Luke 3:36–38)
Researching Your Own Religious Roots (Heb. 13:24)

Family Life Issues

Family Loyalty (Matt. 12:46–50)
Children and Childcare (Matt. 19:14)
Jewish Homemaking (Mark 1:29–31)
Honor Your Parents (Mark 7:9–13)
Divorce (Mark 10:2–12)
A Poor Family's Sacrifice (Luke 2:22–24)
How Poor Was the Widow? (Luke 21:1–4)
Practical Lessons on Marriage (1 Cor. 7:1)
A New View of Sexuality (1 Cor. 7:3–6)
What Is Headship? (1 Cor. 11:3)
The Family: A Call to Long-Term Work (Eph. 5:21—6:4)
A New Form of Marriage (Eph. 5:21–29)
The Value of Self-Support (1 Thess. 2:9)
Widows (1 Tim. 5:3)
Effective Care for the Needy (1 Tim. 5:3–16)
Family Helps in the New Testament Letters (Heb. 12:14–29)
Love Is More than Enthusiasm (1 John 5:1–3)

Other

A Poor Family Comes into Wealth (Matt. 2:11)
City Kids Die over Adult Matters (Matt. 2:16–18)
Jesus Weeps for the Children (Matt. 23:37–39)
Jewish Homemaking (Mark 1:29–31)
The Friend of Children (Mark 10:13–16)
Betrothal (Luke 1:27)
Please Bless Our Children (Luke 18:15–17)
A Woman in Labor (John 16:21–22)
Enemies Become Family and Friends (1 Cor. 16:9–20)
We Are Family! (Gal. 3:28)
All God's Children (Eph. 1:18)
God's Family Album (1 Pet. 2:9–10)
There Is Hope for the Family (Rev. 19:6–10)

Getting to Know Jesus

Jesus Christ is the center around which Christianity and all of Scripture revolve. He invites everyone to know Him, and the New Testament helps us do that by recording His life, work, teaching, death, and resurrection. To know Jesus is to know God. It is also the way to know what God intended us to be like, before sin began its terrible work on us. The articles listed below will help you get started in learning about the Son of God:

Being Like Jesus

A good place to begin your study would be to read the series of articles in Matthew under the heading, "Being Like Jesus." The lead article can be found at Matt. 10:25.

The Life and Work of Jesus

Jesus' Roots (Matt. 1:1–16)
Asian-born Jesus Becomes a Refugee in Africa (Matt. 2:13)
Jesus' Galilean Ministry (map, Matt. 4:25)
Jesus—A City Preacher (Matt. 9:35)
Jesus the Carpenter (Mark 6:3)
The Miracles of Jesus (Mark 8:11–12)
Jesus the Student (Luke 2:46–47)
Jesus, the Son of... (Luke 3:23–28)
Jesus' Family Experienced Pain, Too (Luke 3:36–38)
Jesus' First Sermon Included Surprises (Luke 4:16–27)

Herod Finally Meets Jesus (Luke 23:8)
Jesus—A Rabbi for Women, Too (Luke 23:49)

Jesus' Nature and Character
Ten Myths about Christianity, Myth #1: Jesus Christ Was Only a Great Moral Teacher (Matt. 13:34–35)
The Names of Jesus (Matt. 17:5)
For or Against Family? (Mark 3:31–35)
You Are the Christ (Mark 8:27–33)
Is Jesus Really Lord of All? (Luke 6:1–5)
Compassion and Anger in One Person? (Luke 19:41–46)
Many Men Would Be Gods, But Only One God Would Be Man (John 8:52–59)
A Model of Servant Leadership (John 13:2–17)
Christ, the Lord of the World (Col. 1:15–18)
Many Are Great, But Christ Is the Greatest (Heb. 1:5–14)

Jesus and People
Jesus' Roots (Matt. 1:1–16)
Jesus' Global Connections (Matt. 8:10)
Jews, Gentiles and Jesus (Matt. 15:24)
The Great Physician (Mark 1:32–34)
Jesus and Ethnicity (Mark 7:24–30)
The Miracles of Jesus (Mark 8:11–12)
Compassion and Anger in One Person? (Luke 19:41–46)
Herod Finally Meets Jesus (Luke 23:8)
Jesus—The Name You Can Trust (Acts 3:1)
Alive Together (Eph. 2:1)

Jesus Our Example
Jesus—A Homeless Man? (Matt. 8:20)
Jesus—A City Preacher (Matt. 9:35)
Jesus and Taxation (Matt. 17:24–27)
Jesus and Unjust Pay (Matt. 20:1–16)
Trick Questions Foiled (Matt. 22:23–33)
Jesus Weeps for the Children (Matt. 23:37–39)
Jesus the Carpenter (Mark 6:3)
Jesus Died Poor (Mark 15:24)
Jesus Is for Gentiles, Too (Luke 1:1–4)
An International Savior (Luke 2:29–32)
Jesus the Student (Luke 2:46–47)
Jesus' Family Experienced Pain, Too (Luke 3:36–38)
Jesus' First Sermon Included Surprises (Luke 4:16–27)
Good Men Cry (Luke 13:34)
Compassion and Anger in One Person? (Luke 19:41–46)
His Last Words (Luke 24:45–49)
Witnessing—Jesus' Style (Luke 24:48)
A Model of Servant Leadership (John 13:2–17)
Christ Became Poor (2 Cor. 8:8–9)
Humility—The Scandalous Virtue (Phil. 2:3)
Downward Mobility (Phil. 2:5–8)
Two Portraits of Jesus, Two Sides of Life for Christians (Col. 2:6)

Jesus' Parables
Another way to learn about Christ is to study His teaching through His stories, called parables. For a listing see "The Parables of Jesus," Luke 8:4.

Four Gospels
The New Testament offers four accounts of Jesus' life, known as the four Gospels—Matthew, Mark, Luke, and John. Each one offers a different perspective. If you are unfamiliar with the life and teaching of Jesus, consider reading an entire Gospel at one sitting. The shortest of the four is Mark.

GOVERNMENT
What should be the Christian's relationship to governmental authorities? How did Jesus deal with the political authorities of His day? How did the early church not only survive but thrive in an increasingly hostile political climate? To find out the answers to these and related questions, study the articles below and the passages to which they relate:

The Nature and Value of Government
Under Authority (John 12:49)
The Limits of Political Authority (Rom. 13:1–7)
Governmental Authority (Rom. 13:2)
The Avengers (Rom. 13:4)
The High Calling of Government Service (Rom. 13:6)
The Church at the End of the First Century (Rev. 1:20)
A Symbol of Evil (Rev. 14:8)

The Church and Government
Faith Impacts the World (Mark 16:15–16)
"We Ought to Obey God Rather than Men" (Acts 5:22–32)
Stephen's Trial and Murder (Acts 6:12)
Where Has God Placed You? (Acts 8:26–39)
"Not Many Mighty"...But a Few (Acts 18:7–8)
The Ephesus Approach (Acts 19:8–41)
Faith and Rights (Acts 22:25–29)
Paul and the Structures of Power (Acts 24:25–26)
Caught Between a Novice and the Establishment (Acts 25:2)

New Testament Government Officials
Party Politics of Jesus' Day (Matt. 16:1)
Caiaphas (Matt. 26:3)
Augustus (Luke 2:1)
New Testament Political Rulers (Luke 3:1)
Roman Politics in the First Century A.D. (Luke 22:25)
The Treasurer of Ethiopia (Acts 8:27–39)
Cornelius (Acts 10:1)
Claudius (Acts 11:28)
The Herods (Acts 12:1–2)
Sosthenes the Attorney (Acts 18:17)
Felix (Acts 23:24)
Festus (Acts 25:1)
Nero (Acts 25:12)

LAITY IN THE NEW TESTAMENT
When we examine the New Testament's description of the early church, we find that pastors, teachers, and other leaders functioned "for the equipping of the saints for the work of ministry" (Eph. 4:12). In other words, ministry belonged to the saints or "laity" (from *laos,* "people"), Christians who live and work in the everyday world. Study the articles below to find out what the New Testament has to say about the value, calling, and work of laypeople:

Laypeople and the Church
A Prayer of the Laity (Matt. 10:7–10)
Reconnecting Sunday and Monday (Acts 2:46–47)
Discipleship—Or Mentoring? (Acts 9:26–30)
Who Were the Apostles? (2 Cor. 11:5)
Spiritual Authority (2 Cor. 13:10)
Is Your Church Upside-down or Right Side Up? (1 Thess. 2:13–14)
Who Is "Called," Anyway? (Heb. 3:1)
Coventry (Heb. 10:19–25)

Laypeople and the Community
Faith Impacts the World (Mark 16:15–16)
Called into the World (John 17:18)
The Ephesus Approach (Acts 19:8–41)
Quiet Living in a Hectic World (1 Thess. 4:11)
The Prayer Breakfast Movement (1 Tim. 2:1–7)

Laypeople and Work
Work-World Stories Describe the Kingdom (Matt. 13:1)
Is Work a Curse? (Rom. 8:20–22)
Workplace Myths (1 Cor. 3:9)
Career Changes (1 Cor. 7:17–24)
Are Some Jobs More Important than Others? (1 Cor. 12:28–31)
Work—A Platform for Evangelism? (Eph. 6:5–9)
The Spirituality of Everyday Work (Col. 3:1–2)
Workers for the Kingdom (Col. 4:11)
A Command to Work (2 Thess. 3:6–12)
People at Work (Heb. 2:7)
Ten Commandments for Practical Living (James 2:8–13)

Other
The Twelve (Matt. 10:2)
Being Like Jesus (series; Matt. 10:25)
Would You Choose These for Leaders? (Matt. 26:35–74)
Wealthy People in the New Testament (Matt. 27:57)
Significance for Little People (Mark 2:3–17)
A Kingdom Perspective on Significance (Mark 13:33)
Can Laity Get the Job Done? (Luke 9:1–62)
Delegation and Affirmation (Luke 10:1)
Barnabas—A Model for Mentoring (Acts 9:27)
Just Plain Jars (2 Cor. 4:7)
Hope for You—Watch Paul Grow! (Gal. 1:11–24)
Mentoring, Kingdom-Style (2 Tim. 2:2)
The Hall of Faithfulness (Heb. 11:1–40)
God's Family Album (1 Pet. 2:9–10)

Also study the lives of individual laypeople through the list of personality profiles presented elsewhere in this section.

Men
What does it mean to be a man? How can men live with Christlike character? By studying the men of the New Testament and the passages that speak to masculine concerns, you can begin to learn what God intends for a man, and how men can grow and serve Christ in every area of life:

The Man Jesus
Jesus' Roots (Matt. 1:1–16)
Jesus: A Homeless Man? (Matt. 8:20)
Jesus the Carpenter (Mark 6:3)
Jesus and Ethnicity (Mark 7:24–30)
The Friend of Children (Mark 10:13–16)
Is Jesus Really Lord of All? (Luke 6:5)
Compassion and Anger in One Person? (Luke 19:41–46)
Jesus—A Rabbi for Women, Too (Luke 23:49)
Witnessing, Jesus' Style (Luke 24:48)
Jesus Speaks to a Woman (John 4:27)
Many Men Would Be Gods, But Only One God Would Be Man (John 8:52–59)
A Model of Servant-Leadership (John 13:2–17)
The Proper Measure of All Things (Heb. 2:6–8)

Men in the New Testament
Matthew, the Social Outcast (Introduction to Matthew)
A Rich Man Enters the Kingdom (Matt. 9:9–13)
The Twelve (Matt. 10:2)
Caiaphas, the Religious Power Broker (Matt. 26:3)
Judas Iscariot, the Betrayer (Matt. 26:14)
John the Baptist, a Voice Crying in the Wilderness (Mark 1:6)
Peter, the First Disciple (Mark 1:16)
Significance for Little People (Mark 2:3–17)
A Respected Leader Takes a Risk (Mark 5:22–23)
Jesus the Carpenter (Mark 6:3)
The Man Who Had It All—Almost (Mark 10:17–27)
Barabbas (Mark 15:7)
Luke, the Gentile Author (Introduction to Luke)
Zacharias (Luke 1:5–25)
Augustus (Luke 2:1)
Simeon (Luke 2:25–35)
Isaiah (Luke 4:17)
Who Was the Neighbor? (Luke 10:37)
Are You the Older Brother? (Luke 15:25–30)
Families of the Gospels (Luke 20:34)
John—The Apostle of Love (Introduction to John)
Andrew the Networker (John 1:40)
Lazarus (John 11:1–45)
Skeptics Welcome (John 20:24–31)
Barnabas—"Joe Encouragement" (Acts 4:36–37; 9:27)
Ananias and Sapphira (Acts 5:1)
Stephen's Trial and Murder (Acts 6:12)
Philip the Evangelist (Acts 8:5–13)
Simon the Magician (Acts 8:9)
The Treasurer of Ethiopia (Acts 8:27–29)
Ananias the Disciple (Acts 9:10)
Cornelius (Acts 10:1)
Claudius (Acts 11:28)
Saul/Paul (Acts 13:2–3)
Why Did John Mark Go Home? (Acts 13:13)
Silas (Acts 15:34)
John Mark (Acts 15:37)
Families of the Early Church (Acts 16:31–34)
Apollos (Acts 18:24–28)
Demetrius the Silversmith (Acts 19:24)
An International Work Group (Acts 20:4)
Ananias the High Priest (Acts 23:2)
Felix (Acts 23:24)
Festus (Acts 25:1)
Nero (Acts 25:12)
Abraham (Rom. 4:1)
David (Rom. 4:6)
Priscilla and Aquila (Rom. 16:3–5)
Enemies Become Family and Friends (1 Cor. 16:9–20)
Titus, The Man of the Hour (2 Cor. 7:6)
Hope for You—Watch Paul Grow! (Gal. 1:11–24)
A Bigot Does an About-Face (Gal. 1:13–17)
Epaphroditus (Phil. 2:25)
The Gift of an Ethnic Heritage (Col. 4:10–11)
Timothy (Introduction to 2 Timothy)
Philemon (Introduction to Philemon)
Onesimus (Introduction to Philemon)
Fathers and Prophets (Heb. 1:1)
The Hall of Faithfulness (Heb. 11:1–40)
Who Are These People? (Heb. 11:2)
James (Introduction to James)
Elijah (James 5:17–18)
A Study in Contrasts of Faith (3 John 9–11)

A Man's Character
See "Ethics and Character"

Other
A New Respect for Women (Matt. 5:32)

Those Women Again! (Luke 24:11)
Gentle as a Nursing Mother (1 Thess. 2:7)

People to Know in the New Testament

Scripture provides many things to many people, such as doctrine, comfort, guidance, and principles for day-to-day life. Another treasure in God's Word is a host of people who lived and worked in public and private places. Their stories are told so we can learn from their examples (whether good or bad) as we see how they struggled with issues of faith and life:

Matthew, the Social Outcast (Introduction to Matthew)
The Women in Jesus' Genealogy (Matt. 1:3–6)
A Rich Man Enters the Kingdom (Matt. 9:9–13)
The Hemorrhaging Woman (Matt. 9:20–22)
The Twelve (Matt. 10:2)
A Pushy Mother (Matt. 20:20–23)
Judas Iscariot, the Betrayer (Matt. 26:14)
Would You Choose These for Leaders? (Matt. 26:35–74)
Wealthy People in the New Testament (Matt. 27:57)
John the Baptist, a Voice Crying in the Wilderness (Mark 1:6)
Peter, the First Disciple (Mark 1:16)
Significance for Little People (Mark 2:3–17)
A Respected Leader Takes a Risk (Mark 5:22–23)
The Man Who Had It All—Almost (Mark 10:17–27)
Barabbas (Mark 15:7)
Why So Many Marys? (Mark 15:40)
Luke, the Gentile Author (Introduction to Luke)
Zacharias (Luke 1:5–25)
Elizabeth (Luke 1:24)
Mary, the Mother of Jesus (Luke 1:26–56)
Simeon (Luke 2:25–35)
Anna (Luke 2:36–38)
Isaiah (Luke 4:17)
The Women Who Followed Jesus (Luke 8:1–3)
Mary of Magdala (Luke 8:2)
Who Was the Neighbor? (Luke 10:37)
Martha of Bethany (Luke 10:38–42)
Who Was the Queen of Sheba? (Luke 11:31)
The Value of a Disabled Woman (Luke 13:10–17)
Are You the Older Brother? (Luke 15:25–30)
Families of the Gospels (Luke 20:34)
The Servant Girl (Luke 22:56–57)
Jesus—A Rabbi for Women, Too (Luke 23:49)
Those Women Again! (Luke 24:11)
John—The Apostle of Love (Introduction to John)
Andrew the Networker (John 1:40)
Lazarus (John 11:1–45)
Mary of Bethany (John 11:1–2)
The Women Around Jesus (John 19:25)
Skeptics Welcome (John 20:24–31)
Barnabas—"Joe Encouragement" (Acts 4:36–37; 9:27)
Ananias and Sapphira (Acts 5:1)
Stephen's Trial and Murder (Acts 6:12)
The Conversion of Samaritans to the Gospel—and of Peter and John to Samaritans (Acts 8:4–25)
Philip the Evangelist (Acts 8:5–13)
Simon the Magician (Acts 8:9)
The Treasurer of Ethiopia (Acts 8:27–29)
Ananias the Disciple (Acts 9:10)
Tabitha (Acts 9:36)
Cornelius (Acts 10:1)
Saul/Paul (Acts 13:2–3)
Why Did John Mark Go Home? (Acts 13:13)
Silas (Acts 15:34)
John Mark (Acts 15:37)
Lydia (Acts 16:14)
Families of the Early Church (Acts 16:31–34)
Apollos (Acts 18:24–28)
An International Work Group (Acts 20:4)
The Four Daughters of Philip (Acts 21:9)
Abraham (Rom. 4:1)
David (Rom. 4:6)
Phoebe (Rom. 16:1–2)
Priscilla and Aquila (Rom. 16:3–5)
Junia (Rom. 16:7)
Paul's Female Coworkers (Rom. 16:12)
Who Was Paul's Mother? (Rom. 16:13)
Enemies Become Family and Friends (1 Cor. 16:9–20)
Titus, the Man of the Hour (2 Cor. 7:6)
Hope for You—Watch Paul Grow! (Gal. 1:11–24)
A Bigot Does an About-Face (Gal. 1:13–17)
Epaphroditus (Phil. 2:25)
The Gift of an Ethnic Heritage (Col. 4:10–11)
Timothy (Introduction to 2 Timothy)
Eunice—A Mother's Legacy (2 Tim. 1:5)
Mentoring, Kingdom-Style (2 Tim. 2:2)
Philemon (Introduction to Philemon)
Onesimus (Introduction to Philemon)
Apphia (Philem. 2)
Fathers and Prophets (Heb. 1:1)
The Hall of Faithfulness (Heb. 11:1–40)
Who Are These People? (Heb. 11:2)
Rahab (Heb. 11:31)
Women Received Their Dead Raised (Heb. 11:35)
James (Introduction to James)
Elijah (James 5:17–18)
Sarah (1 Pet. 3:6)
The Elect Lady (2 John 1)
A Study in Contrasts of Faith (3 John 9–11)

Power

Our society places a great deal of emphasis on power. What does the New Testament teach on this issue? See the following articles and their related texts:

Exercising of Power

The Power of Humility (Matt. 3:11)
The Power of Forgiveness (Matt. 9:4–8)
Three Dangers of Power (Luke 3:14)
The Power of Self Sacrifice (John 10:17–18)
Seeing Behind Power (John 19:10–11)
The Power of Foolishness (1 Cor. 1:18)
Are We to Judge All Things? (1 Cor. 2:15)
Who Gets the Credit? (1 Cor. 3:5–8)
Power (Rev. 11:17)

Leadership

To Be Like Jesus Means to Serve Others (Matt. 8:1—9:38)
Under Authority (Matt. 8:5–13)
Servant-Leaders (Matt. 20:25–28)
A New Style of Fame (Matt. 21:8–11)
Significance for Little People (Mark 2:3–17)
Are You Confused about Greatness, Too? (Mark 9:33–37)
Authority and Responsibility (Luke 12:35–48)
A Shrewd Manager (Luke 16:1–13)
Leadership Equals Humility? (Luke 22:24–27)
The Quest for Greatness (Luke 22:24–30)
Under Authority (John 12:49)

The Order of the Towel (John 13:1–20)
A Model of Servant-Leadership (John 13:2–17)
Empowering Leadership (John 14:13)
One Standard for All (1 Tim. 3:1)
No Greedy Leaders! (1 Tim. 3:3)
Don't Fleece the Flock! (1 Pet. 5:2)
Do You Have What It Takes? (2 Pet. 1:3–4)

Spiritual Power

Spiritual Realities Beyond You (Matt. 8:29)
Power (Acts 1:8)
"Give Me Power!" (Acts 8:18–19)
The Power of the Gospel (Rom. 1:16)
Who Is the Enemy? (Eph. 6:10–13)
The Spirit of Power (2 Tim. 1:6–7)
The Power of God's Word (Heb. 4:12)

Other

"You Remind Me of..." (Mark 6:14–16)
Paul and the Structures of Power (Acts 24:25–26)
"It Serves Them Right" (Acts 27:9–11)
What Controls You (1 Cor. 6:12)
Just Plain Jars (2 Cor. 4:7)
When I Am Weak, Then I Am Strong (2 Cor. 12:7–10)
The Power Behind Porn (Jude 6–13)

Race and Ethnicity

We all have roots. No matter who we are, the history of our family has had a profound impact on us. Yet these powerful influences are often unrecognized, and they frequently cause people to misunderstand others from different backgrounds. Nevertheless, God values all the people of the world and seeks to bring them into His eternal family. To that end, Scripture calls Christ's followers to overcome barriers of race, ethnicity, language, and culture. While our ultimate allegiance must be to Christ, we need not deny our own roots or those of others. We can celebrate the riches of diversity. Find out more of what the New Testament has to say about this crucial issue through the following articles and their related texts:

Jesus and Ethnicity

Jesus' Roots (Matt. 1:1–16)
Asian-born Jesus Becomes a Refugee in Africa (Matt. 2:13–15)
Jesus' Global Connections (Matt. 8:10)
Jews, Gentiles, and Jesus (Matt. 15:24)
Jesus the Galilean (Mark 1:14)
Jesus and Ethnicity (Mark 7:24–30)
Jesus Is for Gentiles, Too (Luke 1:1–4)
An International Savior (Luke 2:29–32)
Jesus, the Son of... (Luke 3:23–28)
Ethnic Games with Religious Roots (John 4:19–23)
Jesus Is Called a Samaritan Demoniac (John 8:48)
Jesus Excludes Only the Faithless (John 12:20–36)

The Early Church Confronts Ethnic Barriers

Opportunities Look like Barriers (Acts 1:4)
Jerusalem—Merely the Beginning (Acts 1:12–26)
Off to a Good Start (Acts 2:1)
Pluralism at Pentecost (Acts 2:5)
A Surprising First Fulfillment of Acts 1:8 (Acts 2:8–11)
Society's Divisions Affect Believers (Acts 6:1)
A Growing Movement Confronts Ethnic Prejudice (Acts 6:2–6)
Stephen's New View of History (Acts 7:1–53)
The Message Leaves Jerusalem (Acts 8:1)
The Conversion of the Samaritans to the Gospel—And of Peter and John to Samaritans (Acts 8:4–25)
Come One, Come All! (Acts 10:34)
Ethnic Walls Break Down (Acts 10:44–45)
The Movement Expands Beyond Palestine (Acts 11:19–26)
A New Reality Gets a New Name (Acts 11:26)
"Sure You're Saved...Sort Of" (Acts 15:1–21)
A Church That Defies Market Research (Acts 15:22–25)
The Ephesus Approach (Acts 19:8–41)
Rome or Bust (Acts 19:21)
An International Work Group (Acts 20:4)
All Roads Lead to Rome—And Beyond (Acts 28:28–31)

The Inclusiveness of the Gospel

To Be Like Jesus Means to Accept Our Roots (Matt. 1:1–17)
The Twelve (Matt. 10:2)
To All the Nations (Matt. 28:19)
Luke, the Gentile Author (Introduction to Luke)
A Soldier's Surprising Faith (Luke 7:1–10)
The Gospel in a Pluralistic Society (John 3:21)
Samaria (John 4:4)
Called Into the World (John 17:18)
The Treasurer of Ethiopia (Acts 8:27–39)
Saul/Paul (Acts 13:2–3)
Lydia (Acts 16:14)
God's Heart for the Whole World (Rom. 9:1)
God's Rainbow (Rom. 15:7–12)
Circumcision (Gal. 2:12)
We Are Family! (Gal. 3:28)
Breaking Down Walls (Eph. 2:14–18)
Bloodlines (Col. 3:11)
God's Family Album (1 Pet. 2:9–10)
Finally, Full Equality (Rev. 5:9–10)
A Great Multitude of All Nations (Rev. 7:9)

Rebukes against Prejudice

No Better than Gentiles (Mark 10:32–45)
Condemnation or Compassion? (Luke 9:51–56)
Who Was the Neighbor? (Luke 10:37)
Where Are the Others? (Luke 17:11–19)
Are We One People? (Rom. 11:13–24)
A Bigot Does an About-Face (Gal. 1:13–17)
A Strong Rebuke (Gal. 3:1)
Paul's Drivenness (Phil. 3:4–6)
A Challenge to Slavery (Philem. 15–16)
Ushers on Trial (James 2:1–13)

The Value of Diversity

The Gift of an Ethnic Heritage (Col. 4:10–11)
Paul the Jew—Teacher of the Gentiles (2 Tim. 1:3, 11)
Fathers and Prophets (Heb. 1:1)
Who Are These People? (Heb. 11:2)
Researching Your Own Religious Roots (Heb. 13:24)

The Roman World Transformed

The Roman Empire was one of the greatest superpowers the world has ever seen. Nevertheless, much of its greatness was fueled by the normal human drives of power and pleasure. One has only to look at the legacy of the emperors, such as Nero (Acts 25:12), or the rulers that Rome installed or tolerated, such as the Herods (12:1–2) and Pontius Pilate, to realize that much of the empire's foundation ultimately rested on the self-interest of its leaders.

But an upstart movement with a radically different approach to leadership and change challenged and eventually overcame that pattern. Quietly at first, but with determination and mounting effectiveness, Jesus and His followers transformed their world, as the New Testament and other writings of that period show. Here is an overview of some of the revolutionary changes brought on by the burgeoning movement that came to be known as Christianity:

The Significance of People Changed

Little people took center stage in importance and focus. See...

- The Twelve (Matt. 10:2)
- Significance for Little People (Mark 2:3–17)
- Personality Profile: Mary of Magdala (Luke 8:2)
- Personality Profile: Mary of Bethany (John 11:1–2)
- The Hall of Faithfulness (Heb. 11:1–40)

Rich and poor connected in new ways. See...

- A Rich Man Enters the Kingdom (Matt. 9:9–13)
- A Burial Fit for a King (Mark 15:42—16:1)
- The Women Who Followed Jesus (Luke 8:1–3)
- Barnabas—"Joe Encouragement" (Acts 4:36–37; 9:27)
- "Not Many Mighty"...But a Few (Acts 18:7–8)

Women were affirmed in a culture that devalued them. See...

- Jesus—A Rabbi for Women, Too (Luke 23:49)
- An Inclusive Prayer Meeting (Acts 1:14)
- Personality Profile: Tabitha (Acts 9:36)
- Personality Profile: Lydia (Acts 16:14)
- Personality Profile: Priscilla and Aquila (Rom. 16:3–5)
- Paul's Female Coworkers (Rom. 16:12)
- Widows (1 Tim. 5:3)

Children were valued in a world that devalued them. See...

- Children and Childcare (Matt. 19:14)
- Jesus Weeps for the Children (Matt. 23:37–39)
- The Friend of Children (Mark 10:13–16)
- The Family: A Call to Long-term Work (Eph. 5:21—6:4)
- There Is Hope for the Family (Rev. 19:6–10)

Entire Systems Changed

Submissiveness and humility were urged in place of oppression and injustice. See...

- The Way Up Is Down (Matt. 5:3)
- Leaders Start as Servants (Acts 6:5–6)
- Do Not Avenge Yourself (Rom. 12:19–21)
- Humility—The Scandalous Virtue (Phil. 2:3)
- Work World Codes (Col. 3:22—4:1)
- Submission (James 4:7)

Opponents, criminals, and ne'er-do-wells were rehabilitated and became leaders. See...

- Matthew, the Social Outcast (Introduction to Matthew)
- Simon the Magician (Acts 8:9)
- Profiles of Saul/Paul (Acts 13:2–3)
- From Deadbeat to Donor (Eph. 4:28)
- Personality Profile: Onesimus (Introduction to Philemon)

People from different races and ethnic backgrounds were reconnected. See...

- A Growing Movement Confronts Ethnic Prejudice (Acts 6:2–6)
- Personality Profile: the Treasurer of Ethiopia (Acts 8:27–39)
- Ethnic Walls Break Down (Acts 10:44–45)
- A Church That Defies Market Research (Acts 15:22–35)
- A Bigot Does an About-Face (Gal. 1:13–17)

Slavery was quietly but effectively challenged at its roots. See...

- Slaves (Rom. 6:16)
- Work World Codes (Col. 3:22—4:1)
- Personality Profile: Philemon (Introduction to Philemon)
- Personality Profile: Onesimus (Introduction to Philemon)
- A Challenge to Slavery (Philem. 16)

Competing religions and worldviews were challenged and displaced. See..

- Paul, Apostle to the Intellectuals (Acts 17:15–34)
- The Ephesus Approach (Acts 19:8–41)
- God Cannot Lie (Titus 1:2)
- The Dangers of Syncretism (Introduction to Colossians)
- Gnosticism (1 John 5:20)

Government was called to be more honorable. See...

- Paul and the Structures of Power (Acts 24:25–26)
- Governmental Authority (Rom. 13:2)
- The High Calling of Government Service (Rom. 13:6)

Rights were restructured. See...

- The Power of Self-Sacrifice (John 10:17–18)
- Do Not Avenge Yourself (Rom. 12:19–21)
- Rights (Gal. 4:1–18)
- A Challenge to Slavery (Philem. 16)

Values Changed

Wealth was re-evaluated. See...

- The Man Who Had It All—Almost (Mark 10:17–27)
- Wealth: Hold It Lightly (Acts 4:37—5:11)
- Downward Mobility (Phil. 2:5–8)
- Christians and Money (1 Tim. 6:6–19)
- Prosperity (3 John 2)

Possessions were seen as a call to stewardship. See...

- Gospel and Property Conflicts (Acts 19:23–27)
- Giving It All Away (1 Cor. 13:3)
- Money: Compassion and Integrity (1 Cor. 16:1–4)
- A Lifestyle of Contentment (Phil. 4:10–13)

People were given new worth. See...

- The Underclass (Luke 7:20–23)
- People, Property, and Profitability (Acts 16:19)
- Mentoring, Kingdom-Style (2 Tim. 2:2)
- Let Me Pick Up the Tab (Philem. 17–19)

Morality was redefined. See...

- New Creatures with New Character (Gal. 5:22–23)
- Honesty and Ethical Standards (Phil. 2:15)
- Your "Workstyle" (Titus 2:9–10)
- Ten Commandments for Practical Living (James 2:8–13)

Are you a part of a group of believers in which the faith is producing some of these changes? Do you know of congregations or home fellowships that accomplish these kinds of "faith works"? Can you take initiative to begin something along these lines among your own Christian associates?

Urban Life

For the first time in history, more of the world's people soon will live in cities than in rural areas. Modern technology will further "urbanize" the world by delivering the values and attitudes of city dwellers to even the most remote villages.

How does faith function in this "modern" era? To find out, consider some of what the New Testament has to say about the impact of society on people of faith, and vice versa:

The City

City Kids Die over Adult Matters (Matt. 2:16–18)
Can a Noisy, Dirty, Smelly City Also Be Holy? (Matt. 4:5)
The Holy City (Matt. 23:37)
The Underclass (Luke 7:20–23)
The Septuagint: Alexandria's Gift to Christianity (Acts 18:24)
The Jerusalem Above (Gal. 4:25–26)
Temporary Cities (Heb. 13:14)
Beastly Rome (Rev. 13:1)
A Symbol of Evil (Rev. 14:8)
The New Jerusalem (Rev. 21:1–2)

Jesus and the City

To Be Like Jesus Means to Engage the World's Pain (Matt. 1:18—2:23)
The King Declares His Kingdom (Matt. 4:17)
Jesus' Global Connections (Matt. 8:10)
Jesus—A Homeless Man? (Matt. 8:20)
A Public Statement (Luke 1:46–55)
An International Savior (Luke 2:29–32)
Jesus' First Sermon Included Surprises (Luke 4:16–27)
He Healed Them All (Luke 4:40)
Jesus Confronts the Legalists (Luke 6:1–11)
The Value of a Disabled Woman (Luke 13:10–17)
Good Men Cry (Luke 13:34)
Confused Value? (Luke 15:1–31)
Called into the World (John 17:18)

The Church and the City

Sulfa Drugs and Street Lights (Matt. 5:13–16)
People Priorities in the City (Mark 5:21–43)
What Does Leprosy Have to Do with AIDS? (Luke 5:12–15)
The Gospel in a Pluralistic Society (John 3:21)
Churches—Keys to the Cities (Acts 11:22)
Antioch: A Model for the Modern Church? (Acts 13:1)
A Church That Defies Market Research (Acts 15:22–35)
Paul's Urban Strategy (Acts 16:4)
Afraid in the City? (Acts 18:9–10)
The Ephesus Approach (Acts 19:8–41)
Ghetto Blaster (Acts 19:10)
Rome or Bust (Acts 19:21)
The Jerusalem Riots (Acts 21:30)
Solidarity (2 Cor. 8:13–15)
This Building Gets Landmark Status (Eph. 2:19–22)
Quiet Living in a Hectic World (1 Thess. 4:11)
The Prayer Breakfast Movement (1 Tim. 2:1–7)
The Church at the End of the First Century (Rev. 1:20)
Seven Churches to Study (Rev. 3:1)

The Environment

God and the Environment (Luke 12:6–7)
The Liberation of Creation (Rom. 8:21)
Faith and the Environment (Rev. 9:4)

Faith in the Public Arena

The Public Side of Our Faith (Matt. 14:13–14)
The Final Exam (Matt. 25:31–46)
Faith Impacts the World (Mark 16:15–16)
Sacred Space (John 1:51)
Be Willing to Pay the Price (Acts 16:16–24)
Free to Be Bold (Acts 23:1)
Matters of Conscience (Rom. 14:1–23)
Gray Areas (1 Cor. 8:1–13)
A Code of Ethics for Christian Witness (2 Cor. 4:2)
Honesty and Ethical Standards (Phil. 2:15)

Pluralism and Diversity

The Twelve: Similar or Diverse? (Luke 6:12–16)
Pluralism at Pentecost (Acts 2:5)
A Growing Movement Confronts Ethnic Prejudice (Acts 6:2–6)
Ethnic Walls Break Down (Acts 10:44–45)
Issues of Faith and Culture (Acts 15:6)
Rights (Gal. 4:1–18)
Who Is the Enemy? (Eph 6:10–13)
Christ, the Lord of the World (Col. 1:15–18)
Support the Weak (1 Thess. 5:14)
(Introduction to Philemon)
A Great Multitude of All Nations (Rev. 7:9)

The Poor

Always the Poor (Mark 14:7)
The Underclass (Luke 7:20–23)
The Good Neighbor (Luke 10:30–37)
Holding Wealth or Serving Others? (Luke 18:18–30)
Sharing Things in Common (Acts 4:32–35)

Urban Systems and Structures

Party Politics of Jesus' Day (Matt. 16:1)
Jesus and Taxation (Matt. 17:24–27)
Centurions (Mark 15:39)
The Census (Luke 2:1–3)
New Testament Political Rulers (Luke 3:1)
A Remedy for Tax Fraud (Luke 19:1–10)
Banking (Luke 19:23)
Owners or Tenants? (Luke 20:9–19)
Roman Politics in the First Century A.D. (Luke 22:25)
Paul and the Structures of Power (Acts 24:25–26)
The Limits of Political Authority (Rom. 13:1–7)
The Scandal of Litigating Christians (1 Cor. 6:1–11)
Who Is the Enemy? (Eph. 6:10–13)
The Power Behind Porn (Jude 6–13)

See also the separate listing of city profiles in the New Testament.

Wealth and Poverty

If you can afford to own this Bible it probably means that you are "rich" in that you have choices in life. By contrast, poverty means not having options such as what to eat, where to live, or to whom to relate. Wealth and poverty are major topics in Scripture. For example, the Gospels preserve more of what Jesus spoke about money than about heaven. So serving and following Christ involves acting responsibly in regard to money, whether we consider ourselves rich or poor. Consider discussing the following articles and their related passages with other believers, especially among your coworkers:

Wealthy People in the New Testament

A Rich Man Enters the Kingdom (Matt. 9:9–13)
Who Were Those Tax Collectors? (Matt. 9:10)
Wealthy People in the New Testament (Matt. 27:57)

The Man Who Had It All—Almost (Mark 10:17–27)
A Burial Fit for a King (Mark 15:42—16:1)
Set for Life—But What about Eternity? (Luke 16:19–31)
"Not Many Mighty"...But a Few (Acts 18:7–8)
Demetrius the Silversmith (Acts 19:24)

Words to the Wealthy
Growing Fat at the Poor's Expense (Matt. 23:14)
True Success Means Faithfulness (Matt. 25:14–30)
The Real Bottom Line (Luke 9:25)
Watch Out for Greed (Luke 12:15)
Confused Value? (Luke 15:1–31)
A Shrewd Manager (Luke 16:1–13)
Holding Wealth or Serving Others? (Luke 18:18–30)
Success (John 3:30)
Discrimination on the Basis of Wealth (John 19:1–6)
Wealth—Hold It Lightly (Acts 4:37—5:11)
Downward Mobility (Phil. 2:5–8)
The Dangers of Prosperity Theology (1 Tim. 6:3–6)
Christians and Money (1 Tim. 6:6–19)
Cocooning (Heb. 4:14–16)
Rich in...Faith? (James 2:5–6)
Prosperity (3 John 2)
The Delusions of Luxury (Rev. 18:1–24)

Poor People in the New Testament
A Poor Family Comes into Wealth (Matt. 2:11)
Jesus—A Homeless Man? (Matt. 8:20)
A Poor Family's Sacrifice (Luke 2:22–24)
The Underclass (Luke 7:20–23)
How Poor Was the Widow? (Luke 21:1–4)
Slaves (Rom. 6:16)
Christ Became Poor (2 Cor. 8:8–9)
Who Are the Poor? (2 Cor. 9:9–10)

Words Concerning the Poor
Growing Fat at the Poor's Expense (Matt. 23:14)
Always the Poor (Mark 14:7)
Discrimination on the Basis of Wealth (John 19:1–6)
Little Is Much with God (Acts 7:3–44)
The Value of Self-Support (1 Thess. 2:9)
Support the Weak (1 Thess. 5:14)
No Work? No Eat! (2 Thess. 3:10)
Effective Care for the Needy (1 Tim. 5:3–16)

The Challenge of Wealth
Wealth's Temptation (Matt. 4:8–10)
Living Within Your Limits (Matt. 16:22–23)
Tainted Money (Matt. 27:3–10)
It's All Relative (Mark 12:43–44)
Running to Extremes (Luke 6:29)
The Real Bottom Line (Luke 9:25)
Watch Out for Greed (Luke 12:15)
Confused Value? (Luke 15:1–31)
Holding Wealth or Serving Others? (Luke 18:18–30)
Owners or Tenants? (Luke 20:9–19)
New Life Means New Lifestyles (Acts 2:42–47)
Sharing Things in Common (Acts 4:32–35)
People, Property, and Profitability (Acts 16:19)
"I Have Not Coveted" (Acts 20:33–38)
Giving It All Away (1 Cor. 13:3)
Money: Compassion and Integrity (1 Cor. 16:1–4)
To Live Is...? (Phil. 1:21)
A Lifestyle of Contentment (Phil. 4:10–13)
The Dangers of Prosperity Theology (1 Tim. 6:3–6)
Christians and Money (1 Tim. 6:6–19)
Cocooning (Heb. 4:14–16)
Rich in...Faith? (James 2:5–6)
Prosperity (3 John 2)
The Delusions of Luxury (Rev. 18:1–24)

Charitable Contributions
Anonymous Donors (Matt. 6:1–4)
Tithing (Matt. 23:23–24)
A Parting Gift (Mark 14:3–9)
From Deadbeat to Donor (Eph. 4:28)
The Value of Self-Support (1 Thess. 2:9)
No Work? No Eat! (2 Thess. 3:10)
Effective Care for the Needy (1 Tim. 5:3–16)
Let Me Pick Up the Tab (Philem. 17–19)

Inheritance
Will You Get What's Coming to You? (Luke 12:13–15)
What's In It for Me? (Eph. 1:11)
Getting Yours (James 5:1–6)

Money
Banking (Luke 19:23)
Trade in Ancient Israel (End of John)
A History of Money (Rev. 3:17–19)
Money in the New Testament (Rev. 16:21)

Taxes
Jesus and Taxation (Matt. 17:24–27)
Taxes (Mark 12:14)
A Remedy for Tax Fraud (Luke 19:1–10)

Other
Some Surprising Evidence (Matt. 11:2–6)
Jesus and Unjust Pay (Matt. 20:1–16)
Jesus' First Sermon Included Surprises (Luke 4:16–27)
A Job to Do (Luke 19:11–27)
Debt-Free Living (Rom. 13:8)
The Scandal of Litigating Christians (1 Cor. 6:1–11)
Paying Vocational Christian Workers (1 Cor. 9:1–23)
All God's Children (Eph. 1:18)
Taking Stock (Phil. 3:7–14)
No Greedy Leaders! (1 Tim. 3:3)
Aiming to Please (Heb. 11:6)
Ushers on Trial (James 2:1–13)
Don't Fleece the Flock! (1 Pet. 5:2)
Clothing (Rev. 3:18)
A Symbol of Evil (Rev. 14:8)

Witness and Evangelism
What does it mean to "be a witness" for Christ? What is evangelism all about? How can believers influence others to consider and accept the message about Jesus?

The topics of witness, evangelism, the gospel, and missions are vitally important to the story of the New Testament and to the church today. Study the following articles and their related passages to learn more about the Scriptures' teaching in these areas:

The Gospel Message
Evidence for the Resurrection—Jesus' Appearances (Mark 16:1–8)
What is the Gospel? (Luke 7:22)
Many Men Would Be Gods, But Only One God Would Be Man (John 8:52–59)
The Power of the Gospel (Rom. 1:16)

Righteousness (Rom. 1:17)
Nobody's Perfect (Rom. 3:9–18)
Are People Basically Good? (Rom. 7:21)
Ten Myths about Christianity (series; 1 Tim. 1:3–4)
Knowing *About* God Is Not the Same as *Knowing* God (Heb. 6:13)
Worship or Wrath? (Rev. 6:1–17)
There's a Welcome Here (Rev. 22:17)

The Example of Jesus
Being Like Jesus (series, Matt. 10:25)
Jews, Gentiles, and Jesus (Matt. 15:24)
The Miracles of Jesus (Mark 8:11–12)
Jesus Is for Gentiles, Too (Luke 1:1–4)
Jesus' First Sermon Included Surprises (Luke 4:16–27)
The Spirit of the Lord Is upon...You! (Luke 4:18)
Jesus Excludes Only the Faithless (John 12:20–36)

The Church's Mandate
The Public Side of Our Faith (Matt. 14:13–14)
To All the Nations (Matt. 28:19)
Faith Impacts the World (Mark 16:15–16)
Can Laity Get the Job Done? (Luke 9:1–62)
The Gospel in a Pluralistic Society (John 3:21)
Whose Job Is Evangelism? (John 16:8)
Power (Acts 1:8)
The Ephesus Approach (Acts 19:8–41)
The Spirit of Power (2 Tim. 1:6–7)

Communicating the Message by What We Say
Is Your Witness Falling on Deaf Ears? (Mark 4:3–20)
Witnessing—Jesus' Style (Luke 24:48)
Carrots, Not Sticks (Acts 2:37–38)
Adapt Your Witness! (Acts 17:17)
Free to Be Bold (Acts 23:1)
Truth Can Trigger Opposition (Acts 24:1–26)
Audience-shaped Messages (Acts 26:1–32)
Some Basics of Witness (1 John 1:1–10)

Communicating the Message by What We Do
Being Like Jesus (series, Matt. 10:25)
Is There Enough Evidence to Convict You? (Mark 14:53–64)
Are You a Friend of Someone in Need? (Luke 5:17–26)
Does Anyone Believe You? (John 7:5)
A Confusing Reputation (Acts 5:12–16)
New Creatures with New Character (Gal. 5:22–23)
"I Won't Hire Christians!" (1 Tim. 6:1–2)
Your "Workstyle" (Titus 2:9–10)
Evidence before Information (Titus 3:1–8)

Strategic Evangelism
Opportunities Look like Barriers (Acts 1:4)
Where Has God Placed You? (Acts 8:26–39)
A Church That Defies Market Research (Acts 15:22–35)
A Code of Ethics for Christian Witness (2 Cor. 4:2)
Work—A Platform for Evangelism? (Eph. 6:5–9)

Other
Faith Unfolds Slowly (Mark 4:33–34)
Set for Life—But What about Eternity? (Luke 16:19–31)
You Alone Can't Bring Them to Jesus (John 6:44)
A Radically Changed Perspective (Acts 9:15)
Come One, Come All (Acts 10:34)
A New Reality Gets a New Name (Acts 11:26)
Be Willing to Pay the Price (Acts 16:16–24)
God's Heart for the Whole World (Rom. 9:1)
Paul the Jew—Teacher of the Gentiles (2 Tim. 1:3)
God Cannot Lie (Titus 1:2)
A Great Multitude of All Nations (Rev. 7:9–17)

Women

The New Testament was written in an age when women faced very different roles and expectations than they experience today. Nevertheless, Jesus took women seriously. He enjoyed important friendships with a number of women and affirmed their value and significance. Here are some articles to study as you consider what Scripture has to say about women and subjects that pertain to them:

Jesus and Women
The Women in Jesus' Genealogy (Matt. 1:3–6)
A New Respect for Women (Matt. 5:32)
Family Loyalty (Matt. 12:46–50)
Persistence Pays Off (Matt. 15:21–28)
Significance for Little People (Mark 2:3–17)
People Priorities in the City (Mark 5:21–43)
The Women Who Followed Jesus (Luke 8:1–3)
The Value of a Disabled Woman (Luke 13:10–17)
Jesus—A Rabbi for Women, Too (Luke 23:49)
Those Women Again! (Luke 24:11)
The Road Less Traveled (John 4:4–42)
A Double Standard (John 8:2–3)
The Women around Jesus (John 19:25)
The Proper Measure of All Things (Heb. 2:6–8)

Women in the New Testament
The Women in Jesus' Genealogy (Matt. 1:3–6)
The Hemorrhaging Woman (Matt. 9:20–22)
Hateful Herodias (Matt. 14:3)
Persistence Pays Off (Matt. 15:21–28)
Children and Childcare (Matt. 19:14)
A Pushy Mother (Matt. 20:20–23)
"Harlots Enter the Kingdom" (Matt. 21:31–32)
Jewish Homemaking (Mark 1:29–31)
Significance for Little People (Mark 2:3–17)
Why So Many Marys? (Mark 15:40)
Elizabeth (Luke 1:24)
Mary, the Mother of Jesus (Luke 1:26–56)
Anna (Luke 2:36–38)
The Women Who Followed Jesus (Luke 8:1–3)
Mary of Magdala (Luke 8:2)
Martha of Bethany (Luke 10:38–42)
Who Was the Queen of Sheba? (Luke 11:31)
The Value of a Disabled Woman (Luke 13:10–17)
Families of the Gospels (Luke 20:34)
The Servant Girl (Luke 22:56–57)
Jesus—A Rabbi for Women, Too (Luke 23:49)
Those Women Again! (Luke 24:11)
Mary of Bethany (John 11:1–2)
Funeral Preparations (John 12:1–8)
A Woman in Labor (John 16:21–22)
The Women around Jesus (John 19:25)
An Inclusive Prayer Meeting (Acts 1:14)
Ananias and Sapphira (Acts 5:1)
Tabitha (Acts 9:36)
Lydia (Acts 16:14)
Families of the Early Church (Acts 16:31–34)
The Four Daughters of Philip (Acts 21:9)
Phoebe (Rom. 16:1)
Priscilla and Aquila (Rom. 16:3–5)
Junia (Rom. 16:7)
Paul's Female Coworkers (Rom. 16:12)

Who Was Paul's Mother? (Rom. 16:13)
Women and Work in the Ancient World (1 Cor. 7:32–35)
Euodia and Syntyche (Phil. 4:2)
Widows (1 Tim. 5:3)
Eunice—A Mother's Legacy (2 Tim. 1:5)
Apphia (Philem. 2)
The Hall of Faithfulness (Heb. 11:1–40)
Who Are These People? (Heb. 11:2)
Rahab (Heb. 11:31)
Women Received Their Dead Raised (Heb. 11:35)
Sarah (1 Pet. 3:6)
The Elect Lady (2 John 1)
Jezebel (Rev. 2:20–23)
Women against Evil (Rev. 12:1–17)

A Woman's Character

See "Ethics and Character"

Other

The Way Up Is Down (Matt. 5:3)
A New Respect for Women (Matt. 5:32)
Children and Childcare (Matt. 19:14)
A New View of Sexuality (1 Cor. 7:3–6)
Head Coverings (1 Cor. 11:2–16)
What Is Headship? (1 Cor. 11:3)
Not Permitted to Speak? (1 Cor. 14:34)
We Are Family! (Gal. 3:28)
Gentle as a Nursing Mother (1 Thess. 2:7)
A New Way to Worship (1 Tim. 2:8–15)
Submission (James 4:7)
Finally, Full Equality (Rev. 5:9–10)

Work

In today's world some people see their work as a long, dark tunnel between leisurely weekends, others as a passion bordering on addiction; some as a curse from God, others as a divine calling. What does the New Testament say about this crucial area that so dominates day-to-day life? Find out by studying the articles listed below and their related passages:

The Nature and Value of Work

Our Daily Bread (Matt. 6:11)
Life—The Big Picture (Mark 12:28–34)
Is Jesus Really Lord of All? (Luke 6:1–5)
A Job to Do (Luke 19:11–27)
God—The Original Worker (John 5:17)
Reconnecting Sunday and Monday (Acts 2:46–47)
Is Work a Curse? (Rom. 8:20)
Workplace Myths (1 Cor. 3:9)
Are Some Jobs More Important than Others? (1 Cor. 12:28–31)
Every Breath You Take (Col. 1:17)
The Spirituality of Everyday Work (Col. 3:1–2)
A Command to Work (2 Thess. 3:6–12)
No Work? No Eat! (2 Thess. 3:10)
People at Work (Heb. 2:7)
Who Is "Called," Anyway? (Heb. 3:1)
A Glance at Work in the Bible (Rev. 22:1–11)
Fresh Fruit Salad (Rev. 22:2)

The Believer's "Workstyle"

Conflict Resolution (Acts 11:2–18)
The Ultimate Performance Review (1 Cor. 3:13–15)
New Creatures with New Character (Gal. 5:22–23)
Honesty and Ethical Standards (Phil. 2:15)
Work World Codes (Col. 3:22—4:1)
Work, Labor, and Patience (1 Thess. 1:3)
One Standard for All (1 Tim. 3:1)
"I Won't Hire Christians!" (1 Tim. 6:1–2)
Your "Workstyle" (Titus 2:9–10)
Ten Commandments for Practical Living (James 2:8–13)

Career Changes and Planning

Levi's Feast—A Career Transition Party (Luke 5:28–29)
Career Changes (1 Cor. 7:17–24)
From Deadbeat to Donor (Eph. 4:28)

Communicating the Gospel in the Workplace

Sulfa Drugs and Street Lights (Matt. 5:13–16)
The Public Side of Our Faith (Matt. 14:13–14)
Faith Impacts the World (Mark 16:15–16)
Called into the World (John 17:18)
Where Has God Placed You? (Acts 8:26–39)
A Code of Ethics for Christian Witness (2 Cor. 4:2)
Work: A Platform for Evangelism? (Eph. 6:5–9)
"I Won't Hire Christians!" (1 Tim. 6:1–2)
Your "Workstyle" (Titus 2:9–10)

Competition and Conflict

Competition versus Compassion (Luke 9:46–48)
Compassion and Anger in One Person? (Luke 19:41–46)
Paul Apologized for Losing His Cool (Acts 23:5)
"It Serves Them Right" (Acts 27:9–11)
Integrity in the Face of Competition (2 Cor. 10:1)
Murder on the Job (1 John 3:11–13)

Honesty and Integrity

Doing Your Duty (Luke 17:5–10)
The Blessing of a Clean Conscience (John 18:1–11)
Real Estate Deal Deadly (Acts 5:2–10)
Welcome to Stressful Living (2 Cor. 6:3–10)

Money and Profits

Jesus and Unjust Pay (Matt. 20:1–16)
Growing Fat at the Poor's Expense (Matt. 23:14)
People, Property, and Profitability (Acts 16:19)
Debt-Free Living (Rom. 13:8)
From Deadbeat to Donor (Eph. 4:28)
Downward Mobility (Phil. 2:5–8)
Prosperity (3 John 2)

Success and Significance

True Success Means Faithfulness (Matt. 25:14–30)
A Kingdom Perspective on Significance (Mark 13:33)
The Real Bottom Line (Luke 9:25)
Success (John 3:30)
To Live Is...? (Phil 1:21)
Taking Stock (Phil. 3:7–14)
Aiming to Please (Heb. 11:6)

Supervisors and Subordinates

The Dangers of Power (Luke 3:14)
Delegation and Affirmation (Luke 10:1)
A Shrewd Manager (Luke 16:1–13)
The Quest for Greatness (Luke 22:24–30)
Under Authority (John 12:49)
A Model of Servant-Leadership (John 13:2–17)
Barnabas—A Model for Mentoring (Acts 9:27)
People, Property, and Profitability (Acts 16:19)
Who Gets the Credit? (1 Cor. 3:5–8)
The Ultimate Performance Review (1 Cor. 3:13–15)
Who's the Boss? (Col. 3:22–24)
Encouraging the Boss (1 Thess. 3:1–10)
Submission (James 4:7)
Who's in Charge Here? (James 4:13–16)
Power (Rev. 11:17)

See also the Jobs and Occupations Index, and the list of articles under "Ethics" in this section.

Index to Large Articles

See also the introduction to each book in the New Testament.

Index to Maps

A number of maps help you put the events of the New Testament into geographical perspective:

Locator Maps

A locator map shows where a certain place is with reference to the surrounding area:

Index to City and Regional Profiles

The world of the Bible was far more urban than many modern readers realize. Jesus, Paul, and others in the first century grew up and carried out most of their work among the cities of the Roman Empire, which were connected by an extensive network of relatively safe, well-maintained roads. Many of the profiles below tell about these important urban centers.

City and Regional Profiles By Reference

Index to Personality Profiles

In writing to the Corinthian believers, Paul pointed out that the things that happened to Old Testament people "happened to them as examples, and they were written for our admonition" (1 Cor. 10:11). In a similar way, the New Testament provides believers today with many illustrations of people responding to God in one way or another. By studying the personality profiles below and reading the related biblical texts, you can learn much about these individuals, whose lives the Holy Spirit chose to record in Scripture for our benefit.

Index to Tables, Lists, and Diagrams

Index to Tables, Lists, and Diagrams

Index to Key New Testament Passages

The following index provides access to selected passages of the New Testament that speak most directly to practical concerns in today's world. Use this index along with the other helps and annotations to see quickly what the New Testament says about each subject.

(Passages are listed alphabetically by brief content summaries. The words 'a' and 'the' are ignored in the alphabetizing.)

Passages referred to in a Gospel might also be found in one or more other Gospels, in slightly different form. See "The Four Gospels Side by Side" for a listing of such parallel passages.)

Duty

Education

Enmity

Environment

Envy

Ethnicity

Evangelism

Evil

Faith

Family

Fellowship

Friendship

Government

The Four Gospels Side by Side

(The publishers gratefully acknowledge the use of *Gospel Parallels,* edited by Burton H. Throckmorton, Jr., in preparing this chart.)

	Matthew	Mark	Luke	John
I. Before Jesus' Public Ministry				
1. Introductions	—	—	1:1–4	1:1–18
2. The promise of John the Baptist's birth	—	—	1:5–25	—
3. An angel greets Mary; Mary visits Elizabeth	—	—	1:26–56	—
4. John the Baptist born	—	—	1:57–80	—
5. Jesus born; the shepherds see Him	1:18–25	—	2:1–20	—
6. The wise men visit	2:1–12	—	—	—
7. Jesus circumcised and presented in the temple	—	—	2:21–40	—
8. Escape to Egypt; Herod kills children; return from Egypt	2:13–23	—	—	—
9. Jesus at age twelve	—	—	2:41–52	—
II. Preparation for Jesus' Public Ministry				
10. The preaching of John the Baptist	3:1–12	1:1–8	3:1–18	1:19–34
11. John put in prison	—	—	3:19–20	—
12. The baptism of Jesus	3:13–17	1:9–11	3:21–22	—
13. The ancestors of Jesus	1:1–17	—	3:23–38	—
14. The devil tests Jesus	4:1–11	1:12–13	4:1–13	—
III. Jesus' Public Ministry in Galilee				
15. Jesus makes wine from water; visits Capernaum	—	—	—	2:1–12
16. Jesus clears out the temple during Passover	—	—	—	2:13–15
17. Nicodemus visits Jesus at night	—	—	—	3:1–21
18. Jesus baptizes (through His followers) in Judea; John the Baptist again tells of Jesus	—	—	—	3:22—4:3
19. Jesus speaks with a woman of Samaria	—	—	—	4:4–42
20. Jesus arrives in Galilee; His first preaching there	4:12–17	1:14–15	4:14–15	4:43–45
21. Jesus first rejected in Nazareth	—	—	4:16–30	—
22. Many fish caught; the first disciples called	4:18–22	1:16–20	5:1–11	1:35–41
23. Jesus in Capernaum; a man with an evil spirit healed	7:28–29	1:21–28	4:31–37	7:46
24. Peter's mother-in-law and others healed	8:14–17	1:29–34	4:38–41	—
25. Jesus leaves Capernaum	—	1:35–38	4:42–43	—
26. Jesus travels and preaches in Galilee	4:23–25	1:39	4:44	—
A. The Sermon on the Mount (or the Plain)				
27. Introduction	5:1–2	—	6:20	—
28. Blessings promised	5:3–12	—	6:20–23	—
29. Warnings of troubles	—	—	6:24–26	—
30. Stories about salt and about light	5:13–16	9:50	11:33–36; 14:34–35	—
31. About the law	5:17–20	—	16:16–17	—

	Matthew	Mark	Luke	John
A. The Sermon on the Mount (or the Plain) *(continued)*				
32. About murder	5:21–26	—	12:57–59	—
33. About being faithful in marriage	5:27–30	—	—	—
34. About divorce	5:31–32	—	16:18	—
35. About promises and revenge	5:33–42	—	6:29–30	—
36. About love for enemies	5:43–48	—	6:27–28, 32–36	—
37. About giving and prayer	6:1–8	—	—	—
38. The Lord's Prayer	6:9–15	—	11:1–4	—
39. About going without eating; about treasures	6:16–21	—	12:33–34	—
40. About eyes and light	6:22–23	—	11:34–36	—
41. Serving two masters	6:24	—	16:13	—
42. About worry	6:25–34	—	12:22–31	—
43. About judging others	7:1–5	—	6:37–42	—
44. What belongs to God	7:6	—	—	—
45. God's answer to prayer	7:7–11	—	11:9–13	—
46. The Golden Rule	7:12	—	6:31	—
47. The narrow gate	7:13–14	—	13:23–24	—
48. A tree and its fruit	7:15–20	—	6:43–45	—
49. A warning to obey God	7:21–23	—	6:46; 13:26–27	—
50. Two builders	7:24–27	—	6:47–49	—
51. The end of the Sermon	7:28–29	—	—	7:26
B. Continuing Jesus' Public Ministry in Galilee				
52. A man healed of leprosy	8:1–4	1:40–45	5:12–16	—
53. An army officer's servant healed	8:5–13	—	7:1–10	4:46–54
54. A widow's son healed at Nain	—	—	7:11–17	—
55. What it means to follow Jesus	8:18–22	—	9:57–62	—
56. A crippled man healed at Capernaum	9:1–8	2:1–12	5:17–26	5:8–9
57. Jesus chooses Matthew	9:9–13	2:13–17	5:27–32	—
58. People ask about going without eating	9:14–17	2:18–22	5:33–39	—
59. A man healed at a pool; witnesses about Jesus	—	—	—	5:1–47
60. Two blind men healed	9:27–31	—	—	—
61. Jesus heals a man who could not talk	9:32–34	3:22–27	11:14–23	—
62. The twelve apostles sent out	9:35—10:16	—	10:1–16	1:42; 4:35
63. The disciples warned about trouble	10:17–25	13:9–13	21:12–17	13:16; 14:26; 15:20
64. Don't be afraid of people	10:26–33	—	12:2–12	14:26
65. Division in families	10:34–36	—	12:49–56	—
66. The cost of following Jesus	10:37–39	—	14:25–33	12:25
67. End of Jesus' talk with His disciples	10:40—11:1	—	10:16	5:23; 12:44–45
68. John the Baptist's question to Jesus	11:2–6	—	7:18–23	—
69. Jesus talks about John the Baptist	11:7–19	—	7:24–35	—
70. Jesus predicts trouble for unbelieving towns	11:20–24	—	10:13–15	—
71. Jesus gives thanks to the Father	11:25–27	—	10:21–22	3:35; 7:29; 10:14–15; 17:2

	MATTHEW	MARK	LUKE	JOHN
B. Continuing Jesus' Public Ministry in Galilee *(continued)*				
72. Comfort for the tired	11:28–30	—	—	—
73. Picking grains of wheat on the Sabbath	12:1–8	2:23–28	6:1–5	5:10
74. Jesus heals a man with a crippled hand	12:9–14	3:1–6	6:6–11	—
75. Jesus heals many people	12:15–21	3:7–12	6:17–19	—
76. Twelve apostles chosen	10:1–4	3:13–19	6:12–16	1:42
77. A woman pours perfume on Jesus	26:6–13	14:3–9	7:36–50	12:1–8
78. Women who helped Jesus	—	—	8:1–3	—
79. Jesus accused; lesson about when people fight	12:22–37	3:20–30	11:14–23	7:20; 8:48, 52
80. Looking for signs from heaven	12:38–42	8:11–12	11:29–32	—
81. The return of an evil spirit	12:43–45	—	11:24–26	—
82. Jesus' mother and brothers	12:46–50	3:31–35	8:19–21	15:14
83. Jesus teaches with stories: a farmer, weeds, seed growing, a mustard seed, leaven, hidden treasure, a pearl, a fish net, new and old treasures	13:1–52	4:1–34	8:4–18; 10:23–24; 13:18–21	12:40
84. Jesus calms a storm	8:23–27	4:35–41	8:22–25	—
85. The man near Gadara with evil spirits	8:28–34	5:1–20	8:26–39	—
86. A dying girl and a sick woman's faith	9:18–26	5:21–43	8:40–56	—
87. The people of Nazareth reject Jesus again	13:53–58	6:1–6	—	4:44; 6:42; 7:5, 15
88. The twelve apostles sent out	9:35; 10:1–14	6:6–13	9:1–6	—
89. Herod thinks Jesus is John the Baptist back from death	14:1–2	6:14–16	9:7–9	—
90. The death of John the Baptist	14:3–12	6:17–29	—	—
91. The twelve apostles return; five thousand people fed	14:13–21	6:30–44	9:10–17	6:1–14
92. Jesus walks on water	14:22–33	6:45–52	—	6:15–21
93. Jesus speaks of the bread of life	—	—	—	6:22–71
94. Healings at Gennesaret	14:34–36	6:53–56	—	—
95. What really makes people unclean	15:1–20	7:1–23	—	—
96. A Canaanite woman's daughter healed	15:21–28	7:24–30	—	—
97. Many healed, including a man who was deaf and mute	15:29–31	7:31–37	—	—
98. Four thousand people fed	15:32–39	8:1–10	—	—
99. Pharisees want a sign from heaven	16:1–4	8:11–13	11:29–32; 12:54–56	6:30
100. A teaching about leaven	16:5–12	8:14–21	12:1	—
101. A blind man at Bethsaida healed	—	8:22–26	—	9:1–7
102. Who Jesus is; He predicts His suffering and death	16:13–23	8:27–33	9:18–22	6:68–69; 20:21–23
103. What it means to follow Jesus	16:24–28	8:34—9:1	9:23–27	12:25
104. The glory of Jesus	17:1–8	9:2–8	9:28–36	1:14
105. The coming of Elijah	17:9–13	9:9–13	—	—
106. A boy with epilepsy healed	17:14–21	9:14–29	9:37–43a	14:9
107. Jesus predicts His suffering and death a second time	17:22–23	9:30–32	9:43b–45	7:1
108. Paying the temple tax	17:24–27	—	—	—
109. A discussion about greatness	18:1–5	9:33–37	9:46–48	3:3, 5; 12:44–45; 13:20

	Matthew	Mark	Luke	John
B. Continuing Jesus' Public Ministry in Galilee *(continued)*				
110. For or against Jesus	—	9:38–41	9:49–50	—
111. Temptations to sin	18:6–9	9:42–48	17:1–2	—
112. About salt	5:13	9:49–50	14:34–35	—
113. About a lost sheep	18:10–14	—	15:1–10	—
114. When someone sins	18:15–20	—	17:3	20:23
115. Forgiving many times	18:21–22	—	17:3–4	—
116. An official who refused to forgive	18:23–35	—	—	—
117. Jesus teaches in Jerusalem at the Feast of Tabernacles	—	—	—	7:1–53
118. A woman caught in sin	—	—	—	8:1–11
119. Jesus is the light of the world; some people try to stone Him	—	—	—	8:12–59
120. Jesus heals a man born blind	—	—	—	9:1–41
121. The good shepherd	—	—	—	10:1–20
C. Luke's Special Section				
122. Samaritan villagers refuse to welcome Jesus	—	—	9:51–56	—
123. What it means to be a follower of Jesus	8:18:22	—	9:57–62	—
124. Seventy followers sent out	9:35—10:16	—	10:1–16	4:35; 5:23
125. The seventy followers return	—	—	10:17–20	12:31
126. Jesus thanks His Father	11:25–27	—	10:21–22	10:15; 17:2
127. The disciples are blessed	13:16–17	—	10:23–24	—
128. An expert in the Law questions Jesus	22:34–40	12:28–31	10:25–28	—
129. The good Samaritan	—	—	10:29–37	—
130. Martha and Mary	—	—	10:38–42	11:1–3
131. The friend at midnight	—	—	11:5–8	—
132. Answer to prayer	7:7–11	—	11:9–13	—
133. Jesus and the ruler of demons	9:32–34; 12:22–30	—	11:14–23	—
134. Being really blessed	—	—	11:27–28	—
135. A sign from God for the people	12:38–42; 16:1–4	8:11–12	11:29–32	—
136. About light	5:14–16; 6:22–23	—	11:33–36	—
137. Jesus condemns the Pharisees	23:1–36	12:37–40	11:37—12:1	—
138. Telling others about Jesus without fear	10:19–20, 26–33; 12:32	4:22; 8:38	12:2–12	14:26
139. About a rich fool	—	—	12:13–21	—
140. Worries about earthly things	6:16–21; 25–34	—	12:22–34	—
141. Watchfulness and faithfulness	24:43–51	13:32–33	12:35–46	13:4–5
142. What a master expects	—	—	12:47–48	—
143. Knowing what to do	10:34–36; 16:1–4	—	12:49–56	12:27
144. Settling with an accuser	5:25–26	—	12:57–59	—
145. Turn back to God; a tree without figs	—	—	13:1–9	—
146. Jesus heals a woman on the Sabbath	—	—	13:10–17	—
147. About a mustard seed; about yeast	13:31–33	4:30–32	13:18–21	—

	Matthew	Mark	Luke	John
C. Luke's Special Section *(continued)*				
148. Being kept out of God's kingdom	7:13–14; 25:10–12; 7:22–23	—	13:22–30	—
149. Leaving Galilee	—	—	13:31–33	—
150. Jesus loves Jerusalem	23:37–39	—	13:34–35	—
151. A man with dropsy (swollen legs) healed	—	—	14:1–6	—
152. Being a humble guest	—	—	14:7–14	—
153. The great banquet	22:1–14	—	14:15–24	—
154. The cost of being a disciple	10:26–33, 37–39	—	14:25–35	—
155. A lost sheep; a lost coin	18:12–14	—	15:1–10	—
156. A lost son comes home	—	—	15:11–32	—
157. A dishonest manager	6:24	—	16:1–13	—
158. God sees the heart	—	—	16:14–15	—
159. About the law and about divorce	5:17–20, 31–32; 11:12–13	—	16:16–18	—
160. A rich man and Lazarus	—	—	16:19–31	—
161. About causing sin	18:6–9	9:42–48	17:1–2	—
162. About forgiving	18:15, 21–22	—	17:3–4	—
163. About faith	17:20	—	17:5–6	—
164. A servant's duty	—	—	17:7–10	—
165. Jesus heals ten men with leprosy	—	—	17:11–19	—
166. About God's kingdom	24:23–25	13:21–23	17:20–21	—
167. The day of the Son of Man	24:26–28, 37–41	—	17:22–37	—
168. About a widow and a crooked judge	—	—	18:1–8	—
169. About a Pharisee and a tax collector	—	—	18:9–14	—
IV. The Judean Ministry				
A. The Journey to Jerusalem				
170. About divorce	19:1–12	10:1–12	—	—
171. Jesus blesses children	19:13–15	10:13–16	18:15–17	3:3, 5
172. A rich young man	19:16–30	10:17–31	18:18–30	—
173. Workers in a vineyard	20:1–16	—	—	—
174. Jesus again tells about His death	20:17–19	10:32–34	18:31–34	—
175. James and John want to be first	20:20–28	10:35–45	22:24–27	—
176. Jesus heals the blind	20:29–34	10:46–52	18:35–43	—
177. Zacchaeus meets Jesus	—	—	19:1–10	—
178. A man who left his servants with money	25:14–30	—	19:11–27	—
B. The Days in Jerusalem				
179. Entry into Jerusalem; Jesus in the temple	21:1–17	11:1–11	19:28–46	12:12–50; 2:13–15
180. Jesus at the Feast of Dedication in Jerusalem	—	—	—	10:22–39
181. Jesus brings Lazarus to life at Bethany	—	—	—	10:40—11:44
182. The plot to kill Jesus	—	—	—	11:45–53
183. Jesus at Ephraim; the coming of the Passover	—	—	—	11:54–57

	MATTHEW	MARK	LUKE	JOHN
B. The Days in Jerusalem *(continued)*				
184. Jesus puts a curse on a fig tree	21:18–19	11:12–14	—	—
185. Jesus clears out the temple	21:12–13	11:15–19	19:45–48	2:13–17
186. The meaning of the dried-up fig tree	21:20–22	11:20–26	—	14:13–14
187. A question about Jesus' authority	21:23–27	11:27–33	20:1–8	2:18
188. About two sons	21:28–32	—	—	—
189. About the renters of a vineyard	21:33–46	12:1–12	20:9–19	—
190. The great banquet	22:1–14	—	14:16–24	—
191. Paying taxes to Caesar	22:15–22	12:13–17	20:20–26	3:2
192. Life in the future world	22:23–33	12:18–27	20:27–40	—
193. The most important commandment	22:34–40	12:28–34	10:25–28	—
194. About David's son	22:41–46	12:35–37	20:41–44	—
195. Pharisees and teachers of the Law condemned	23:1–36	12:38–40	20:45–47; 11:37–52	—
196. Jesus loves Jerusalem	23:37–39	—	13:34–35	—
197. A widow's offering	—	12:41–44	21:1–4	—
198. The temple to be destroyed	24:1–3	13:1–4	21:5–7	—
199. Signs of Christ's coming	24:4–8	13:5–8	21:8–11	—
200. Warning about trouble	24:9–14	13:9–13	21:12–19	14:26; 15:21; 16:2
201. The abomination of desolation	24:15–22	13:14–20	21:20–24	—
202. False messiahs to come	24:23–25	13:21–23	17:20–23	—
203. The coming of the Son of Man	24:26–28	—	17:23–24, 37	—
204. When the Son of Man appears	24:29–31	13:24–27	21:25–28	—
205. A lesson from a fig tree	24:32–33	13:28–29	21:29–31	—
206. The time of Christ's appearing unknown	24:34–36	13:30–32	21:32–33	—
207. Be on guard	—	13:33–37	—	—
208. A warning to watch out	—	—	21:34–36	—
209. The Son of Man's appearing to be sudden	24:37–41	—	7:26–27, 34–35	—
210. Watchfulness and faithfulness	24:42–51	—	12:39–46	—
211. About ten virgins	25:1–13	—	—	—
212. About three servants	25:14–30	—	19:12–27	—
213. The final judgment	25:31–46	—	—	5:28–29
214. Jesus teaches in the temple each day	—	—	21:37–38	—
C. Jesus Is Arrested and Crucified				
215. The plot to kill Jesus	26:1–5	14:1–2	22:1–2	11:47–53
216. Perfume poured on Jesus at Bethany	26:6–13	14:3–9	7:36–50	12:1–11
217. Judas betrays Jesus	26:14–16	14:10–11	22:3–6	18:2–5
218. Preparing for the Passover meal	26:17–19	14:12–16	22:7–13	—
219. Jesus washes the feet of His disciples	—	—	—	13:1–20
220. The one who will betray Jesus	26:20–25	14:17–21	22:14, 21–23	13:21–30
221. The Lord's Supper	26:26–29	14:22–25	22:15–20	—
222. Betrayal predicted; greatness in the kingdom; two swords	19:28; 20:25–28	10:42–45	22:21–38	13:4–5, 12–14, 36–38
223. Jesus the true vine; he teaches and prays for His followers	—	—	—	13:31—17:26
224. They go to the Mount of Olives; Peter promises to be loyal	26:30–35	14:26–31	22:39; 22:31–34	13:36–38; 16:32; 18:1

	MATTHEW	MARK	LUKE	JOHN
C. Jesus Is Arrested and Crucified *(continued)*				
225. Jesus prays in Gethsemane	26:36–46	14:32–42	22:40–46	18:1; 12:27; 14:31; 18:11
226. Jesus is arrested	26:47–56	14:43–52	22:47–53	18:2–12, 20
227. The council questions Jesus; Peter says he doesn't know Him	26:57–75	14:53–72	22:54–71	18:13–27
228. Jesus taken to Pilate	27:1–2	15:1	23:1	18:28–32
229. The death of Judas	27:3–10	—	—	—
230. Pilate questions Jesus	27:11–14	15:2–5	23:2–5	18:33–37; 19:6, 9–10
231. Jesus brought to Herod	—	—	23:6–16	—
232. Jesus sentenced to death	27:15–26	15:6–15	23:17–25	18:38–40; 19:4–16
233. Soldiers mock Jesus	27:27–31	15:16–20	—	19:1–3
234. Jesus nailed to a cross at Golgotha	27:32–44	15:21–32	23:26–43	19:17–24
235. Jesus dies and is buried	27:45–61	15:33–47	23:44–56	19:25–42
236. The guards at the tomb	27:62–66	—	—	—
V. The Resurrection				
237. The empty tomb	28:1–10	16:1–11	24:1–12	20:1–18
238. The Roman soldiers bribed	28:11–15	—	—	—
239. Jesus appears to two disciples on the road to Emmaus	—	16:12–13	24:13–35	—
240. Jesus appears in Jerusalem	—	—	24:36–39	—
241. Jesus appears to the disciples twice	—	—	—	20:19–29
242. Jesus appears at Lake Tiberias	—	—	—	21:1–24
243. Jesus appears on a mountain in Galilee	28:16–20	16:14–16	—	—
244. Believers to do wondrous things	—	16:17–18	—	—
245. Jesus ascends to heaven	—	16:19	24:50–53	—
246. The disciples go and preach everywhere	—	16:20	—	—
247. The end of John's gospel	—	—	—	20:30–31; 21:25

JOBS AND OCCUPATIONS INDEX

The ancient Near East has often been called the "cradle of civilization." Highly developed cultures flourished in the region long before Abraham (about 2100 B.C.). Many skills that eventually developed into occupations and trades originated there. The following are mentioned or inferred in the Bible. Where Old Testament references are given, we suggest that you consult a copy of the complete Bible.

This listing is based on the New King James Version (NKJV), but mentions translations of words from the King James Version (KJV), the New Revised Standard Version (NRSV), the New International Version (NIV), and the New American Standard Bible (NASB).

(Related terms that are treated separately in this index are indicated by bold type. Other terms are expressed in italics.)

A

◆ACCOUNTANT

Even though the word *accountant* does not appear in the Bible, the principles and methods of accounting do. Wherever a census or an inventory of financial assets or offerings is recorded (Ex. 30:11–15; 2 Sam. 24; 2 Chron. 13–28; Ezra 2; Neh. 7:6–72; Luke 2:2; see "The Census," Luke 2:1–3), accountants were probably involved. In the New Testament, the language of accounting (adding, reasoning, computing) is used with regard to rational conclusions and moral inventory rather than fiscal reckoning. Paul, for example, "added up" his works of the flesh and counted them as a net "loss" compared to the unsurpassable worth of knowing Christ (Phil. 3:4–8).

◆ACTOR, ACTRESS

The Bible does not refer specifically to professional actors and actresses, perhaps because the acting profession was forbidden to the Jews because of its pagan associations. However, when Jesus called the Pharisees "hypocrites" (Matt. 23:13–30), he was using a word that had come to mean "play-actors." The deceptive religious leaders feigned biblical virtues in order to win people's praise. For example, they "disfigured" their faces with a sad countenance while fasting, essentially putting on a mask, in order to look contrite (Matt. 6:16).

In the first century, actors traveled a circuit of Greek and Roman cities to perform before large audiences in the culture's many theaters, some with a seating capacity of 20,000 or more. The riot at Ephesus began at such a forum (see Acts 19:29).

◆ADVOCATE

One who "pleads another's case" or is "called alongside to give advice" or counsel was known as an advocate, not unlike a modern-day **lawyer**. The word is used primarily in the New Testament, mostly of Jesus or the Holy Spirit. Jesus acts as a righteous Advocate, pleading our case as lost sinners before a righteous God (1 John 2:1). When the term is applied to the Holy Spirit (John 14:16; 15:26; 16:7), it is variously translated as *Advocate* (NRSV), *Helper* (NKJV, NASB), *Comforter* (KJV), or **Counselor** (NIV). (See **Counselor**; **Lawyer**.)

◆AMBASSADOR

In ancient times, kings and rulers spoke to other nations through official representatives, or *envoys.* These ambassadors offered congratulations (1 Kin. 5:1; Is. 39:2), sought favors (Num. 20:14), made treaties (Josh. 9:4–6), and registered protests (Judg. 11:12). The treatment that an ambassador received represented the host nation's response to the ambassador's ruler. Insults could lead to war (2 Sam. 10:4–6). In the New Testament, Paul describes himself as "Christ's ambassador" (Eph. 6:20), as are all Christians (2 Cor. 5:20, according to one interpretation).

◆ANNOUNCER

Modern-day television hosts and radio disc jockeys may have had forerunners in biblical **heralds** who were responsible for bearing a message, often in preparation for the appearance of a king or other royal figure (Dan. 3:4). The Aramaic word for herald is sometimes translated "to preach" (Matt. 3:1; 4:17); consequently, New Testament preachers are heralds of the King, Jesus (1 Tim. 2:7; 2 Tim. 1:11). (See **Messenger**.)

◆APOTHECARY

Some translations use this word or *confectioner* for the *pharmacist* who prepared or sold drugs, medicines, and perfumes. (See **Perfumer**; **Physician**.)

◆ARCHER

Archers were trained from childhood to serve in ancient armies. These warriors were the first to engage the enemy from a distance. To draw an ancient war bow required an estimated 100-pound pull. Arrows could pierce almost any armor. A number of Old Testament nations had men who were famous archers (1 Sam. 31:3; 1 Chr. 8:40; Is. 22:6). Abraham's son Ishmael (Gen. 21:20) and Isaac's son Esau (Gen. 27:3) grew up to be archers, though probably not in an army. (See **Hunter**; **Soldier**.)

◆ARCHITECT

Biblical references to the tabernacle, temple, palaces, fortifications, and the like, attest to the need for architects. Walled cities in biblical times required architects (see, for example, the book of Nehemiah). The New Testament speaks of God as the preeminent Architect, calling Him the "builder" and "maker" (architect) of the heavenly city, the New Jerusalem (Heb. 11:10). (See **Builder**.)

◆ARMORBEARER

An armorbearer carried weapons for a military commander or champion. They were also responsible for finishing the job of killing enemies brought down by their masters, using clubs or swords. The Old Testament leaders Abimilech (Judg. 9:54), Jonathan (1 Sam. 14:6–17), and Joab (2 Sam. 18:15) had armorbearers. David acted as Saul's armorbearer for a time (1 Sam. 16:21). However, after David became king, commanders fought from chariots, and armorbearers are no longer mentioned in the Bible.

◆ARMORER

This person was a smith skilled in making armor or a leather worker who made shields. In the days of Saul, armorers were primarily Philistines. Armorers are not mentioned directly in the Bible, but their presence is inferred from the Hebrew soldiers' use of shields, helmets, breastplates of scale-like plates, and leg armor. Paul

◆ARMORER *(continued)*

speaks of God in a figurative sense as the great armorer of spiritual soldiers (Eph. 6:14–17).

◆ARTIFICER

(See **Metalworker**.)

◆ARTISAN

(See **Metalworker**.)

◆ARTIST

The Bible makes no direct mention of artists, but the fact that they existed in Hebrew culture is evident from the many paintings and etchings found on clay tablets, bas-reliefs, and engraved images in ivory and stone. Jews construed the Second Commandment (Ex. 20:4) as prohibiting the artistic portrayal of humans.

◆ASTROLOGER

(See **Astronomer**.)

◆ASTRONOMER

Although the model of the universe adopted by ancient peoples was inaccurate, their attempts to explain how the universe works can be traced back thousands of years. In ancient times, the positions of the planets in relation to each other was thought to have an impact on the course of history. This accounts for astronomy's origins in *astrology,* the study of the heavenly bodies and their movements in an attempt to predict the future.

Isaiah taunted the Babylonians to go to their powerless "astrologers, the stargazers, and the monthly prognosticators" for their salvation (Is. 47:13). The word for astrologer appears eight times in Daniel, in association with **magicians**, *sorcerers, Chaldeans, wise men,* and **soothsayers** (Dan. 1:20; 2:2, 10, 27; 4:7; 5:7, 11, 15). Some Bible scholars believe the wise men or Magi who saw the star of the infant Jesus (Matt. 2:1–12) were astrologers from Mesopotamia.

In the Bible, astronomical references are often poetic (Amos 5:8). Their main purpose is to show God's glory rather than provide scientific details about the universe. The important truth for the Hebrews as they observed the stars was that "the heavens declare the glory of God; and the firmament shows His handiwork" (Ps. 19:1).

◆ATHLETE

Of all the biblical writers, Paul used the most metaphors from the world of sports to describe spiritual realities. The Greeks of Paul's day celebrated four major athletic festivals, including the original Olympic games (see "The Games," 1 Cor. 9:24–27). The apostle likened the Christian life to that of a track and field **runner** (Acts 20:24; Rom. 9:16; Gal. 2:2; 5:7; Phil. 2:16; 2 Tim. 4:7; compare Heb. 12:1–2), a *wrestler* (Eph. 6:12), and a *boxer* (1 Cor. 9:26; 2 Tim. 4:7). He noted that athletes were obliged to compete according to rules (2 Tim. 2:5), and that they competed for a prize (1 Cor. 9:24–27; Phil. 3:12–14; 1 Thess. 2:19; 2 Tim. 4:8).

Among the Romans, sporting events evolved beyond vigorous competition into life-and-death struggles. In Nero's day, for example, Christians were sometimes sent into an amphitheater to fight for their lives (1 Cor. 4:9; 15:32; Heb. 10:32–33).

Jewish culture apparently did not develop the same appreciation for athletic

◆ATHLETE *(continued)*

contests or train athletes professionally, partly because of the nudity that was often involved. Yet Jews did esteem the ancient sport of running. (See **Runner**.)

◆ATTENDANT

Some translations use this word for one who rendered household services. (See **Servant**.)

◆AUTHOR

The books collected in the Bible were written by about forty writers from various walks of life. Yet even though the Bible is itself a written work, the usual sense of the word author is not mentioned as a profession. In a broader sense, Jesus is called the Author of eternal salvation and of our faith (Heb. 5:9; 12:2). (See **Writer**; **Editor**.)

B

◆BAKER

Bread was a major food in the ancient world (Gen. 3:19; Judg. 7:13; John 6:13). Most baking was done by women in the home (Gen. 18:6; Lev. 26:26; 1 Sam. 8:13; see "Jewish Homemaking," Mark 1:29–31, and "Grinding the Grain," Luke 17:35). However, the Pharaoh of Egypt employed a chief baker (Gen. 40:2, 16), and a street in old Jerusalem was renowned for its bakers and their shops (Jer. 37:21). Bakers prepared dough from cereal grains, mostly wheat and barley, but sometimes beans, lentils, millet, and spelt (Ezek. 4:9). They baked it on an open fire of wood or coals (Is. 44:19) or in a clay, bell-shaped oven (Lev. 7:9; Hos. 7:4; Matt. 6:30), using iron grids or pans (1 Chr. 9:31; 23:29; Ezek. 4:3).

◆BANKER

Bankers and banking were not part of the Jewish culture until the Babylonian captivity. Money as such did not exist at that time. Lending to other Jews for profit was forbidden (Deut. 23:19–20), though loans to foreigners were permitted. Even so, the Law recognized that there would inevitably be some people in debt to others, and it made provision to keep debtors from falling hopelessly behind (Deut. 15:1–6). National wealth was safeguarded in the temple or at the king's palace, while common people hid their treasures and valuables. When Nebuchadnezzar's troops ransacked the temple (2 Kin. 25:13–17), they were in effect robbing a bank.

In the New Testament, Jesus urged His followers to go beyond the letter of the Law, which said to lend without interest, to the spirit of the Law, by giving without expecting a return of even the principal (Luke 6:35). By Roman times, bankers were becoming common among the Jews (Matt. 25:27; see "Banking," Luke 19:23). Under Roman law, bankers could put a debtor in prison. But echoing the Law, Jesus challenged His followers to cancel others' debts, just as God has cancelled our debts (Matt. 6:25–26; 18:25, 30). (See "A History of Money," Rev. 3:17, and "Money in the New Testament," Rev. 16:21.)

◆BARBER

Both men and women in Old Testament times normally wore their hair long, eliminating the need for barbering as a profession. In fact, Israelite men were forbidden to cut the forelocks of their hair (Lev. 19:27), and a shaved or bald head was a sign of disgrace (2 Kin. 2:23–24; Is. 3:24; 15:2; Jer. 48:37). Both men and women prized beautifully styled hair (Song 4:1; 5:11). Long hair contributed to Samson's strength, but also to his capture (Judg. 16:13–19). Likewise, Absalom's locks gave

◆BARBER *(continued)*

him a handsome appeal (2 Sam. 14:25–26), but also brought about his death (2 Sam. 18:9–15).

There were some circumstances that called for barbering. Men who took a Nazarite vow shaved their heads (Num. 6:18). And God ordered Ezekiel's barber to shave the prophet's head as a sign of judgment (Ezek. 5:1).

By New Testament times, men apparently wore their hair shorter than women's, especially in the Roman cities such as Corinth (1 Cor. 11:14–15), so barbers were more in demand. Even so, barbers tended to work for the rich and for royalty. Christian women were urged to style their hair simply, not expensively (1 Tim. 2:9; 1 Pet. 3:3).

◆BASKETMAKER

Ancient Near Eastern societies required lightweight containers to transport goods by hand or donkey. Thus women wove baskets from natural fibers such as palm fronds, straw, reeds, rushes, sedges, and grasses. Baskets came in all sizes and shapes, but a shape resembling earthenware pots was common. Scripture mentions baskets large enough to hold a person (Acts 9:25) or a human head (2 Kin. 10:7), and small enough to house birds (Jer. 5:27) and carry bread (Ex. 29:3).

◆BEEKEEPER

From the many biblical references to honey (for example, Ex. 3:8, 17; 16:31; Prov. 24:13; Matt. 3:4), it is possible to infer that beekeepers were common in Palestine. But honey could also have been obtained wild (Judg. 14:8–9), and the word might have been used of a syrup made from grapes and dates.

◆BEGGAR

Scripture describes people reduced to begging because of divine judgment or wickedness (1 Sam. 2:7–8; Ps. 109:10; Luke 16:3), physical handicaps (Mark 10:46; Luke 18:35; John 9:8), or laziness (Prov. 20:4). Nearly every society and every city in biblical times had a large "underclass," people scraping by on the margins of society. Few cultures provided for these desperate, destitute wanderers, though God did command Israel to care for the poor (Deut. 15:1–11; see "The Underclass," Luke 7:20–23).

◆BLACKSMITH

Some translations use this word for the craftsman who worked with metals, especially in making swords and spears (1 Sam. 13:19). (See **Armorer**; **Metalworker**.)

◆BLEACHER

(See **Fuller**.)

◆BODYGUARD

Many bodyguards mentioned in Scripture may also have been **soldiers**, **armor-bearers**, *prison guards*, **runners**, **slaves**, or *servants*. Examples include bodyguards for the Pharaoh of Egypt (Gen. 37:36; 39:1), Joseph (Gen. 40:3), David (2 Sam. 23:22), certain Israelite kings (2 Kin. 11:19), and Paul (Acts 28:16).

◆BOTANIST

The presence of botanists in Bible times is easily inferred from the thriving agricultural economies of the ancient Near East (see "Trade in the Ancient World" at the end of John). Apparently Solomon was rather knowledgeable in this area, as vari-

◆BOTANIST *(continued)*

ous gardens and orchards are listed among his great accomplishments (1 Kin. 4:33; Eccl. 2:5–6). In the New Testament, Paul alluded to the techniques of botany when he spoke of the Gentiles as a wild olive tree being "grafted" into God's tree of salvation (Rom. 11:17–21). (See **Gardener**.)

◆BREWER

"Strong" or intoxicating drink is mentioned some twenty times in the Bible, and wine more than 240 times. Ancient brewers are known to have produced beers from various cereals beginning more than 8,000 years ago, and beer was known in Egypt and Mesopotamia. The process involved burying barley in pots to force germination, then mixing it with water to ferment naturally. Sometime between the tenth and seventh centuries B.C., hops were added to the process (see "Winemaking," John 2:3). (See **Winemaker**.)

◆BRICKLAYER

The biblical record of brickmaking goes back to the construction of a tower at Babel (Gen. 11:3). Excavations and wall paintings in Egypt show Hebrews making clay bricks (compare Ex. 1:14) and that the Egyptians used bricks that were sun-dried and large by today's standards (10 by 20 by 4 inches). Clay bricks were made with straw which decomposed to release chemicals that made the bricks stronger (compare Ex. 5:6–19). It's interesting that after the Hebrews had been slaves in Egypt, they later made brickworkers of their prisoners of war (2 Sam. 12:31).

◆BUILDER

The first building project mentioned in Scripture is the walled dwelling that Cain constructed to protect himself (Gen. 4:17). Later, descendants of Noah built a tower at Babel to go up to heaven, to make a name for themselves (Gen. 11:4). Hebrew slaves built storage cities for the Pharaoh of Egypt (Ex. 1:11). Later in Palestine, their descendants built walled cities and unwalled towns, houses, palaces, the temple, and many other structures. After the Babylonian exile, Nehemiah served as a *general contractor* to rebuild the walls of Jerusalem.

In the New Testament era, the Herods were especially active in sponsoring construction projects (see profile at Acts 12:1–2). One of the major ones was the city of Sepphoris in Galilee, which Herod Antipas rebuilt as a provincial capital during the time of Jesus' youth. It is easy to imagine that Jesus and His father, Joseph, who were both **carpenters**, worked on projects in the city, given its proximity to Nazareth. In a similar way, the Roman emperors built Corinth as a "planned" city, favoring it with numerous imperial building projects (see Introduction to 2 Corinthians). (See **Architect**; **Carpenter**.)

◆BUTCHER

The work of the many wild game hunters and livestock ranchers in the ancient world gave rise to the occupation of butcher. In the Old Testament, the Law prescribed that some animals be considered "clean" and others "unclean" (Lev. 11), perhaps partially for reasons of health and survival. In the New Testament, an issue related to meat surfaced in Corinth and other Gentile cities, where meat offered to idols was for sale. Paul affirmed that it was all right, in good conscience, for believers to eat whatever the butchers prepared and sold at the Gentile meat markets (1 Cor. 10:25). (See **Cook**.)

◆BUTLER

The only mention of a butler in Scripture is the chief butler whom Joseph met in prison (Gen. 40). However, the occupation was closely related to that of *cupbearer.* Ancient rulers had to be very cautious about what they ate or drank, as the prospect of poisoning was ever present, either from attempts on their lives or from spoiled food. The butler or cupbearer tasted the ruler's food first in order to test its safety.

Solomon employed cupbearers and waiters (1 Kin. 10:5; 2 Chr. 9:4), and Pharaoh's butler mentioned above probably oversaw a staff of such officials. Nehemiah was a cupbearer to King Artaxerxes (Neh. 1:11), which made him a very powerful official with an expense account and direct access to the king. This enabled him to arrange for the rebuilding of the wall at Jerusalem.

◆BUYER

While the word *buyer* occurs just three times in Scripture (Prov. 20:14; Is. 24:2; Ezek. 7:12), the concept of buying and selling occurs often. A wide range of commodities were sold in and exported from Palestine, including oil, wine, wheat, barley, nuts, honey, fruits, fish, salt, and spices. A list of some of the many commodities being imported into Palestine in Solomon's time is recorded in Ezekiel 27 (see "Trade in Ancient Israel" at the end of John). (See **Merchant**.)

C

◆CAMEL DRIVER

The camel driver was one who herded and rode camels. Camels were used to cross the desert between Mesopotamia and Palestine about 1800 B.C. The Old Testament mentions the Midianites, who were desert nomads and camel drivers whose thousands of camels were used to wage war (Judg. 6:1–6) and peace (Is. 60:6). David named a camel driver, Obil the Ishmaelite, to his state government to head up the camel division (1 Chr. 27:30). The Queen of Sheba probably brought many camel drivers with her on her visit to Jerusalem to see Solomon's riches (1 Kin. 10:2).

◆CANDYMAKER

The Hebrews enjoyed making and giving royal "dainties," sweet "delicacies," and "rich and splendid" foodstuffs (Gen. 49:20; Ps. 141:4; Prov. 23:3; Rev. 18:14). This implies that candymaking has a long history. Women were the principal candymakers, using dates, honey, nuts, and gum extract.

◆CAPTAIN

In the Bible, the term captain can mean **prince**, *officer, chief, ruler, leader,* **author**, *initiator,* or **commander**—in a military, civilian, or spiritual sense. In the New Testament period, military captains commanded as many as 1,000 Roman soldiers constituting a military cohort, tribune, or garrison (Mark 6:21; Acts 21:31–37; Rev. 6:15; 19:18). Civilian captains in government were called **magistrates** (Acts 16:20–38). The chief officer on duty in the temple precinct was a *temple captain* (Luke 22:4, 52; Acts 4:1; 5:24, 26). In a spiritual sense, the Captain of our salvation is Jesus Christ (Heb. 2:10; 12:2; see Josh. 5:14–15; 2 Chr. 13:12). (See **Government Official**.)

◆CAPTAIN (SHIP)

(See **Sailor**.)

◆CARPENTER

Carpenters worked with wood, metal, and stone to produce furniture and farm implements, and to construct houses and public buildings. During the reigns of David and Solomon, Israel relied almost exclusively on foreign carpenters, especially those from Tyre (2 Sam. 5:11; 1 Kin. 5:18; 1 Chr. 14:1). Later, however, Jewish carpenters were used to repair the temple (2 Kin. 22:5–6; 2 Chr. 24:12).

Scripture makes reference to handtools such as the axe and hatchet (Deut. 19:5; Ps. 74:6; Jer. 10:3), the hammer (Judg. 4:21), the saw (Is. 10:15), the plumb line, the ruler, the plane, and the compass (Is. 44:13–14; Zech. 2:1).

Two of the best known carpenters in the Bible are Noah (Gen. 6) and Jesus (see "Jesus the Carpenter," Mark 6:3). (See **Builder**.)

◆CARVER

Artisans known as carvers were skilled at whittling, cutting, or chipping wood, stone, ivory, clay, bronze, gold, silver, or glass. Bezalel and Aholiab received special mention in Moses' day for their work on the tabernacle (Ex. 31:1–6). Skilled carvers were sought after (2 Chr. 2:7), and carved panels, windows, and woodwork were signs of great wealth. Some carvers specialized in making idols (Jer. 10:4; Rev. 18:12), thus bringing judgment from God. (See **Metalworker**.)

◆CATTLEMAN

Scripture presents Jabal as "the father of those who dwell in tents and have livestock" (Gen. 4:20). A similar description applied to Abraham (Gen. 13:2). To own many cattle was a sign of God's blessing (Ps. 107:38). God provides for cattle (2 Kin. 3:17; Ps. 104:14); indeed, He owns "the cattle on a thousand hills" (Ps. 50:10). Some translations classify livestock of all kinds—cows, sheep, goats, donkeys—as "cattle," and the word can also be translated "beasts" or "animals." (See **Shepherd**.)

◆CAULKER

Some carpenters were skilled at applying tar to the hulls of boats to make them watertight (Ezek. 27:9, 27). In the Old Testament, the best caulkers were the "wise men" of Phoenicia, a nation renowned in the ancient world for its shipbuilding. (See **Shipbuilder**.)

◆CENSUS TAKER

The job of the census taker was associated with military conscription and tax collection. Consequently, it was unpopular in Bible times. Several censuses are mentioned in the Bible: Moses' censuses during the Exodus (Ex. 30:11–16; Num. 1), David's numbering of the people (2 Sam. 24), a census under Solomon (2 Chr. 2:17), and the Roman census that brought Joseph and Mary to Bethlehem where Jesus was born (Luke 2:1–5). (See **Accountant, Tax Collector**.)

◆CENTURION

The centurion was the backbone of the relatively small but well-organized citizen army of Rome (see "Centurions," Mark 15:39). A centurion was a non-commissioned officer commanding at least 100 men. Six centuries of men made up a cohort or regiment. Ten cohorts, about 6,000 men, made up a legion.

It's interesting that all of the individual centurions mentioned in the New Testament are reported to have been of good repute, and even exceptional faith. Jesus commended a centurion who cared for his dying servant (Luke 7:1–10). The Gospel writers report that the centurion who oversaw Jesus' crucifixion confessed

◆CENTURION *(continued)*

faith in Christ (Matt. 27:54; Mark 15:39; Luke 23:47). In Acts, the centurion Cornelius embraced the gospel, opening the door to Gentiles in the early church (Acts 10). A centurion named Julius saved Paul's life (Acts 27:1–11). (See **Soldier**.)

◆CHAMBERLAIN

(See **Eunuch**.)

◆CHANCELLOR

Some translations use this word for a bureaucratic chief or **magistrate**. (See **Government Official**.)

◆CHARIOTEER

A charioteer was a soldier who fought from a chariot. Chariots were introduced in Mesopotamia about 2800 B.C. These machines served as mobile firing platforms. They came in many different forms. They could be two-wheeled or four-wheeled, drawn by two to four horses. As the technology developed, chariots were made to hold a driver, a bowman, and a shield-bearer to protect both the warrior and the driver.

In Bible times, Solomon employed the most charioteers outside of Egypt. At one point, he deployed 1,400 chariots throughout the land in fortified "chariot cities" (1 Kin. 10:26), and later built 4,000 stalls for his horses and chariots (2 Chr. 9:25). (See **Soldier**.)

◆CHEESEMAKER

Cheesemaking has a long history, dating at least to Job's day (Job 10:10). David and his brothers enjoyed cheese or "curds" (1 Sam. 17:18; 2 Sam. 17:29). A cheese made from sweet milk was probably like our cottage cheese (Deut. 32:14) or goat cheese (Prov. 27:27). A valley outside Jerusalem was named The Valley of the Cheesemakers due to the cottage industry carried on there. (See **Dairyman**.)

◆CHOIRMASTER

More than one-third of the Psalms are by or dedicated to a choirmaster or chief musician. Several choirmasters were named by David to the task of leading corporate worship—Asaph, Heman, Ethan, Jeduthun, Chenaniah, and their descendants (1 Chr. 15:16–24; 25:1–7). These choir directors no doubt helped to organize and instruct the 288 men said to be skilled as temple musicians (1 Chr. 25:7). (See **Musician**; **Singer**.)

◆CITY CLERK

City clerks were important officials in the Greek city-states. They were responsible for record-keeping, recording minutes of official assemblies, caring for the city archives, handling official communications such as public readings, and annually distributing money to the poor. They also served on a number of boards and handled countless administrative details. The city clerk of Ephesus (Acts 19:35) was also president of the assembly. His importance and prominence are shown by the fact that his name frequently appeared on coins of the period.

◆COMMANDER

This word can imply either civilian governance or military service, similar to the word **captain**. (See **Captain**; **Government Official**.)

◆COMPTROLLER

(See **Government Official**.)

◆CONFECTIONER

(See **Apothecary**; **Perfumer**.)

◆CONTROLLER

(See **Government Official**.)

◆COOK

The Hebrew word usually translated cook literally means "slaughterer," one who kills and dresses animals. Thus the king's cooks apparently killed animals to be prepared for the royal table. Cooks may have been either women servants (1 Sam. 8:13) or male professionals (Luke 17:8). In most Hebrew households, cooking was the woman's job (Gen. 18:6; 27:9; see "Jewish Homemaking," Mark 1:29–31), while men did the butchering (Gen. 18:7). Gideon is named as a cook and a baker (Judg. 6:19). (See **Butcher**.)

◆COPPERSMITH

Scripture makes many references to copper and coppersmiths (Ex. 38:8; Deut. 8:9; Ezra 8:27; Job 28:2; Ezek. 22:18). Archaeological excavations of copper tools, vases, polished mirrors, and the like show that coppersmithing was a common occupation in ancient times. Copper mines in Tyre and Cyprus supplied the artisans of Palestine. In time they learned to make bronze, an alloy of copper and tin which could take a finer polish and was harder than pure copper. The first coppersmith mentioned in the Bible is Tubal-Cain, a descendant of Cain who instructed others in working with "bronze and iron" (Gen. 4:22). In the New Testament, Paul mentions Alexander the coppersmith as having done him and the gospel much harm (2 Tim. 4:14). (See **Metalworker**.)

◆COPYIST

(See **Scribe**.)

◆COSMETOLOGIST

Cosmetology as a profession is not mentioned in Scripture, but archaeologists have found ancient toilet kits, ointment pots, small make-up instruments, and even a cosmetics factory from 2,500 years ago. The practice of beautifying the skin and eyes with cosmetics, salves, alabaster ointments, and the like is very old (Ex. 30:25; Neh. 3:8; Ezek. 23:40). However, early Christian women were admonished to distinguish themselves by focusing more on the beauty of their souls than that of their bodies (1 Tim. 2:9; 1 Pet. 3:3–4). (See **Perfumer**.)

◆COUNSELOR

Ancient kings had trusted officials who served as counselors (1 Chr. 27:32; Ezra 4:5), though not all counselors were professionals (2 Chr. 22:3). In the New Testament, Joseph of Arimathea is called a counselor, reflecting his membership in the Jewish council, or Sanhedrin (Mark 15:43; Luke 23:50, KJV). Israel anticipated that the coming Messiah would be a Counselor (Is. 9:6). (See **Advocate**.)

◆COURT REPORTER

(See **Government Official**.)

◆CRAFTSMAN

(See **Designer, Metalworker**.)

◆CREDITOR

(See **Banker**.)

◆CRIMINAL

The first criminal mentioned in Scripture, in the sense of one human sinning against another, was Cain, who murdered his brother (Gen. 4:8). Apparently a criminal mentality and rebellion against God's law characterized Cain's descendants (Gen. 4:23–24). In Hebrew society, the Law punished various criminals by mutilation, scourging, paying monetary damages and fines, enslavement, and death (Gen. 9:6; Ex. 21–22). One means of capital punishment was stoning (see John 10:31). Among the Romans and other Gentile empires, crucifixion was practiced (see Luke 23:33).

Paul described the transformation that can occur when a criminal turns to Christ and follows Him (see "From Deadbeat to Donor," Eph. 4:28).

◆CUPBEARER

(See **Butler**.)

◆CUSTODIAN

(See **Keeper**; **Watchman**.)

◆CUSTOMS OFFICER

This occupation was similar to that of the **tax collector**, as taxes and customs were often collected by the same person. In the first century, both taxes and customs were owed to Rome (Rom. 13:7). The KJV has Matthew, the tax collector, sitting at "the receipt of custom" when called by Jesus to follow Him (Matt. 9:9). (See **Census Taker**; **Tax Collector**.)

D

◆DAIRYMAN

Along with bread, dairy products were staples of the Hebrew diet (Prov. 30:33; 1 Sam. 17:18). Milkers of cows, goats, sheep, and camels had to make use of the milk right away, as there was no way to keep fresh milk from spoiling. However, one way to give it a longer "shelf life" was to culture it into butter (Ps. 55:21), curds (Is. 7:22), or cheese (Job 10:10). Dairymen sold these products in the marketplaces of towns and cities, probably transporting them there on donkeys. (See **Cheesemaker**.)

◆DANCER

Apparently the Hebrews did not have professional dancers as did Egypt, Babylon, and other pagan nations. However, Scripture indicates that children danced in play (Job 21:11; Luke 7:32) and adults danced in joy, notably Miriam (Ex. 15:20) and David (2 Sam. 6:14; Ps. 30:11). God's people were encouraged to dance before Him as a joyous act of congregational worship (Ps. 149:3; 150:4). And other occasions called for dance—festivals (Judg. 21:23), the celebration of war heroes (1 Sam. 18:6–7), and family reunions (Luke 15:25). The Hebrew words associated with dancing reveal that it involved skipping, whirling about, and leaping.

◆DEALER

(See **Merchant**.)

◆DEPUTY

(See **Government Official**.)

◆DESIGNER

The skills of designers were used in commissioned public works of art for the tabernacle, the temple, and other building projects. Designers often worked in concert with *engravers,* **weavers**, **metalworkers**, **carpenters**, and other craftsmen (Ex. 35:35; 38:23). Bezalel and Aholiab were two designers called by God to oversee the construction of the tabernacle. They were filled with the Spirit and knowledgeable in several crafts (Ex. 31:1–11). (See **Metalworker**.)

◆DIVINER

The Old Testament Law condemned the practitioner of magic, sorcery, and divination as a "false prophet." Diviners used a variety of occult practices to contact or control evil spirits or foretell the future: trances, dreams, mediums, enchantments, clairvoyance, the stars, even examining the livers of animals. (see "Magic and Sorcery," Rev. 18:23).

Divination was widespread in the ancient Near East from earliest times: in Egypt (Ex. 7:11), Canaan (Lev. 18:3, 21; 19:26, 31), Arabia (Is. 2:6), Babylon (Ezek. 21:21; Dan. 5:11), Samaria (Acts 8:9), Macedonia (Acts 16:16), and Asia (Acts 19:13, 19). Even the Israelites lapsed at times into the use of divination (2 Kin. 17:17; 21:6).

Because of their idolatry and deception, diviners and similar practitioners are strongly condemned in Scripture, for example by the Law (Deut. 18:9–14), the prophets (Is. 2:6; 8:19; 47:9, 12; Jer. 14:14; 29:8) and Paul (Acts 13:6–12).

◆DOCTOR

The KJV calls the "learned" men in Scripture "doctors of the law" (Luke 2:46; 5:17; Acts 5:34), meaning teachers and experts of the Mosaic Law. In some other translations the term doctor is used to refer to members of the medical profession. (See **Lawyer**, **Physician**.)

◆DOORKEEPER

(See **Eunuch**; **Porter**.)

◆DRESSMAKER

(See **Tailor**.)

◆DRIVER

(See **Camel Driver**, **Charioteer**, **Overseer**.)

◆DYER

Dyeing was an ancient art among families working in linen (1 Chr. 4:21). Dyers often developed specialized formulas for their craft which they passed on to successive generations. One of the most important dyes of the Mediterranean world was purple, made from the shell of the murex, a species of clam. Purple cloth and dye were extremely valuable. The first known Christian in Europe, Lydia, was a "seller of purple" (see profile and "The Trade in Purple," Acts 16:14).

In the Old Testament, the patriarch Jacob made a "tunic of many colors" for his favored son Joseph (Gen. 37:3), which probably involved the use of various dyes. Later, the Israelite tabernacle made use of purple dye that was probably imported from Phoenicia.

◆DYER *(continued)*

The dyer of wool was usually the **fuller** of wool, as well, so that he or she cleansed and dressed the wool before coloring it. (See **Fuller**.)

E

◆EMBALMER

Egyptian embalmers prepared the dead for burial by treating the body to prevent decay. Modern-day discoveries by archaeologists show that they developed this skill to near perfection. Joseph, who became a ruler in Egypt and the adopted son of a Pharaoh, had his father Jacob embalmed (Gen. 50:2–3) and was himself embalmed (Gen. 50:26). However, this was probably done to preserve the bodies for an anticipated trip back to Palestine (Gen. 50:13–14; Josh. 24:32). Otherwise the Hebrews did not embalm the dead, nor did they cremate bodies as the Greeks and Romans often did. Rather they washed and scented the body before dressing it in the person's own clothes or else wrapping it in specially prepared sheets (see "Funeral Preparations," John 12:1–8, and "Burial," 1 Cor. 15:42). These funeral preparations were frequently carried out by women. (See **Undertaker**.)

◆EMBROIDERER

Decorative needlework, or "painting with a needle," was the work of an embroiderer. Ancient embroiderers decorated clothes with colorful, highly stylized geometric designs, particularly for the rich (Judg. 5:30; Ps. 45:14; Luke 20:46). In Israel, embroiderers decorated priestly garments and the appointments of the tabernacle (Ex. 26:1, 36; 27:16; 28:4, 15). Embroidering, **weaving**, and **tapestry making** were separate occupations, but some translations use the terms interchangeably. (See **Tailor**, **Tapestry Maker**, **Weaver**.)

◆ENCHANTER

(See **Diviner**.)

◆ENGRAVER

(See **Metalworker**.)

◆ENVOY

(See **Ambassador**.)

◆EUNUCH

The eunuch or chamberlain was responsible for guarding the king's bedroom and harem (Esth. 1:10–15). These men were castrated so as to remove all possibility of unfaithfulness (Is. 56:3). They were highly trusted and influential officials. The Ethiopian eunuch under Queen Candace apparently also was in charge of her royal treasury (Acts 8:27). (See **Porter**.)

◆EXECUTIONER

The Old Testament distinguishes between murder (illegally taking another's life, Ex. 20:13) and execution. Under the Law, many crimes were punishable by death (Gen. 9:6; Deut. 13:10; 21:22). It was the executioner's task to carry out that punishment, though some crimes called for stoning by the men of the community (see "Stoning," John 10:31). Personal vengeance was prohibited (Deut. 24:16). The New Testament records several executions that were legal under Roman law (Matt. 14:10; Acts 12:1–2). The most infamous was the crucifixion of Jesus (see "Crucifixion," Luke 23:3).

◆EXORCIST

Peoples of the ancient world generally believed in spirit powers and that a person could be taken over by an evil power. Many methods were used to cast out these demons, including potions, spells, and chanting. Acts even records an attempt by one group of exorcists to use Jesus' name as a magic spell.

New Testament teaching affirms the existence of evil spirits, but it also emphasizes Christ's total victory over them (see "Demons," Luke 11:14, and "Who Is the Enemy?" Eph. 6:10–13). Jesus expelled demons quickly and easily (see "Whatever Became of 'Demon Possession'?" Luke 9:38–42). He did not practice the mysterious and often complicated rituals of the exorcist (Matt. 12:24–28).

F

◆FANNER

Some translations use this word for the one who sifts wheat from the chaff using a forked fanning instrument. (See **Winnower**.)

◆FARMER

Terms in the Bible that refer to farmer include *plowman* (Is. 28:24), **husbandman** (2 Chr. 26:10, KJV), **vinedresser** (Is. 61:5; John 15:1–8), **gardener** (John 20:15), and *tiller* (Gen. 4:2). This was one of the major occupations of the ancient Hebrews, along with **shepherding**. Cain was the first farmer (Gen. 4:2). Olive and fig trees were the principal crops among fruit farmers in ancient Palestine. Other crops included almonds, apples, dates, grapes, mulberries, pomegranates (Joel 1:11–12). Farmers of ancient times were responsible for all aspects of farming. The plowing, planting, tending, and harvesting were done by farmers and their own families. Very prosperous farmers could hire helpers (see **Laborer**). In the New Testament, a farmer is one who owns the land or rents it and raises crops (Matt. 21:33).

◆FISHERMAN

Fishing was one of the most important and common occupations held in Bible times. Fishermen used various kinds of spears, nets, hooks, and lines (Job 41:7; Is. 19:8; Matt. 13:47–48; Mark 1:16; Luke 5:2; see "The World of the Fishermen," Luke 5:1–11). Several of Jesus' disciples were professional fishermen (Matt. 4:18–22).

◆FOOTMAN

Heralds who ran before a king's chariot to announce his coming were sometimes called footmen (Jer. 12:5). Most biblical references are to "foot soldiers" or infantrymen (for example, 1 Sam. 4:10, 15:4; 22:17, KJV). (See **Announcer**; **Messenger**; **Soldier**.)

◆FOREMAN

(See **Overseer**.)

◆FORESTER

The Bible makes frequent reference to forests. Yet the forests of Palestine were depleted during a brief 13–year period to enable the construction of Solomon's aptly named House of the Forest of Lebanon (1 Kin. 7:2). Nevertheless, loggers were said to be conservationists who practiced reforestation (Is. 44:14). A man named Asaph was "the keeper of the king's forest" in Nehemiah's time (Neh. 2:8). He was a regional governor responsible for land use and for developing and restricting the

◆FORESTER *(continued)*

lumber industry. Nehemiah secured a logging permit from Asaph to fell timber for use in reconstructing the walls of Jerusalem. (See **Builder**; **Carpenter**; **Woodworker**.)

◆FOUNDRY WORKER, FOUNDER, FORGER

The foundry worker melted, refined, and cast ore into precious or other useful metals (Jer. 6:29). Once cast, the metal could be pounded flat or engraved (Jer. 10:9). It was hot, dirty work involving stoking and cleaning furnaces, making castings, and pouring molten metal into clay molds. Huram of Tyre was brought to Jerusalem by Solomon to cast two bronze pillars, topped with capitals and laced with a pomegranate design, for the temple (1 Kin. 7:13–22). (See **Refiner**; **Metalworker**.)

◆FOWLER

The Egyptians had a particular taste for fowl and so became innovative as "fowlers." Ancient fowlers used a variety of devices to seek, catch, and kill wild fowl, such as decoys, traps (Amos 3:5), nets (Prov. 1:17), bait, bows and arrows, slings, lures, dogs, and bird lime smeared on branches. The Mosaic Law forbade taking a mother bird and her young together; only the young were to be taken (Deut. 22:6–7). Used figuratively, the fowler depicts the wicked, scheming enemies of the righteous (Ps. 91:3; 124:7; Hos. 9:8). (See **Hunter**.)

◆FULLER (BLEACHER)

The fuller's job was to clean, shrink, thicken, and sometimes dye newly cut wool or cloth. The Hebrew term means "to trample" or "to tread," suggesting at least one means by which the fuller carried out the craft.

Fullers removed oily and gummy substances from the material so that it would be fit for use. They used "fuller's soap," probably containing alkaline as found in white clay, putrid urine, or niter; the kind of soap known today did not exist then. The alkaline was washed out by treading on the material repeatedly in clean, running water. The material was then dried and bleached in the sun.

The fulling process created an unpleasant odor, and therefore fullers usually worked outside the city gates. A location outside of Jerusalem was known as the Fuller's Field (2 Kin. 18:17; Is. 7:3).

The day of God's judgment is compared to "fullers' soap" (Mal. 3:2, KJV; "launderers'," NKJV). Likewise, Jesus' garments at the transfiguration are described as having been whiter than any human fuller could make them (Mark 9:3, KJV; launderer, NKJV). (See **Dyer**.)

G

◆GARDENER

Scripture references to gardens, plants and orchards are as abundant as the varieties (for example, 1 Kin. 4:33; Eccl. 2:5; Amos 9:14). With more than 300 botanical terms and incidental reference to gardens, we can conclude that gardening was an important skill in Bible times. Adam was the first gardener (Gen. 2:15). Yet the one gardener directly mentioned in Scripture, the person that Mary Magdalene supposed the resurrected Jesus to be (John 20:15), was probably not one who did actual gardening, but functioned as a watchman. (See **Botanist**; **Farmer**; **Watchman**.)

◆GATEKEEPER

(See **Porter**.)

◆GLASSWORKER

Glass was known as early as 2600 B.C. Around 1400 B.C., the Egyptians were able to make glass similar to pottery by winding hot glass rods around a sand core and then joining the layers by reheating them. While glassworkers are not mentioned specifically in the Bible, several New Testament references to transparent glass suggest the existence of the occupation by that time.

◆GLEANER

Fruit and grain farmers were instructed to leave certain gleanings in the field, unharvested, for poor laborers or gleaners (Lev. 19:9–10; Ruth 2). (See **Laborer**.)

◆GOATHERDER

(See **Shepherd**.)

◆GOLDSMITH

Goldsmiths refined, purified, and worked with gold (Is. 41:7). Israelite goldsmiths fashioned gold-plated vessels and interior furnishings for the tabernacle (Ex. 25:11, 24; 26:29, 32; 30:3), along with solid gold pieces (Ex. 25:18, 29, 31). They also made fine gold wire, thread, and bells for embroidering the priests' garments (Ex. 28). However, some molded and hammered out idols (Ex. 32; Ps. 115:4; Is. 2:7). The New Testament describes God as like a goldsmith, molding Christian character like "gold refined by fire" (1 Cor. 3:12–13; 1 Pet. 1:7; Rev. 3:18). (See **Metalworker**; **Refiner**.)

◆GOVERNOR

The English word governor, meaning "to lead" or "to rule," is used to translate eleven different Hebrew words and four different Greek words. As applied to Joseph, the term indicates that he was second in command in Egypt as a *chief deputy*, **prince**, or *viceroy* in Pharaoh's court (Gen. 41:40; 42:6; 45:26; Acts 7:10). In the New Testament, the term is used of several Roman officials including Pilate (Matt. 27:2), Quirinius (Luke 2:2), Felix (Acts 23:26), and Festus (Acts 26:30), where governor also implied a sort of *chief financial officer* (see "New Testament Political Rulers," Luke 3:1, and "Roman Politics in the First Century A.D.," Luke 22:25). These political appointees were responsible to Rome for the military, judicial, and financial administration of their districts. In one place the KJV uses the word "governor" to mean a *custodian* or *manager* of property or people (Gal. 4:2). (See **Steward**.)

◆GOVERNMENT OFFICIAL

Many different officials are mentioned in Scripture. Depending on the translation, one finds **chancellors**, *commissioners, comptrollers, controllers, courtiers, deputies,* **magistrates**, *officers, presidents, procurers, quartermasters,* **recorders**, **secretaries**, **treasurers**, *trustees,* and *viceroys,* to name several. These officials may have been *government administrators* (Gen. 41:34), religious or military **overseers** (1 Kin. 4:5), **secretaries** (Ex. 5:6–8), **commanders** (Num. 11:16), or *assistants* to the king (Esth. 1:8). However, little is known about most of these positions. For an extended account of one government official, read the life of Joseph (Gen. 39–50).

◆GUARD

(See **Keeper**; **Jailer**; **Soldier**; **Watchman**.)

H

◆HARLOT
(See **Prostitute**.)

◆HARVESTER
(See **Laborer**.)

◆HEALER
(See **Nurse**; **Physician**.)

◆HELMSMAN
(See **Sailor**.)

◆HERALD
(See **Announcer**.)

◆HERDSMAN
(See **Cattleman**; **Shepherd**.)

◆HEWER
(See **Woodworker**.)

◆HEWER OF STONE
(See **Mason**.)

◆HISTORIAN
The fact that the Scriptures exist points to the important role of the historian, *chronicler,* or **recorder**. The Bible names several historians, such as Jehoshaphat (2 Sam. 8:16; 20:24) and Joah (2 Kin. 18:18; Is. 36:22). These chroniclers recorded significant events and stories from their nation's history. Often the events were compiled in chronological order and presented in a way intended to explain the cause of events. Biblical histories also served a spiritual purpose, as we see in Luke's writings especially. (See **Recorder**; **Scribe**.)

◆HORSEMAN
Horses are mentioned often in the Bible but were of little importance to the average Hebrew, who found it more practical to keep a donkey to ride or an ox to pull a plow. Sometimes horsemen were used as mail carriers (Esth. 8:10), but for the most part, horses were thought of in terms of war.

God warned the Israelites not to place their faith in the strength and speed of horses (Ps. 20:7) or to "multiply" horses (Deut. 17:16). Nevertheless, David and Solomon built up large mounted forces, even importing horses from other countries. Solomon had a sizeable cavalry as well as horses to draw war chariots. (See **Charioteer**; **Soldier**.)

◆HOUSEHOLDER
Householders were what we would call heads of households, persons with authority over what went on in a given home. Jesus also called them *landowners* or *masters of the house.* He frequently included such figures in His teaching (see "Treasures New and Old," Matt. 13:52; 20:1; 21:33).

◆HUNTER

Hunting was a common means of food and fur provision in ancient times, but there are few references to hunters as such in the Bible. Only two are mentioned by name: Nimrod, the "mighty hunter before the LORD" (Gen. 10:9; 1 Chr. 1:10), and Esau, the skillful hunter and brother of Jacob (Gen. 25:27; 27:3, 30).

A variety of wild game are mentioned in Scripture: roe deer, gazelles, harts, antelope, mountain sheep, and wild goats, among others (Deut. 12:15, 22; 14:5; Lev. 17:13). Methods of hunting included bows and arrows (Gen. 21:20), digging pits, and nets, snares and traps (Is. 24:17; Ezek. 19:4–8; Amos 3:5). Hunting for sport was popular among ancient kings. Landowners also became hunters at times to protect their crops. (See **Archer**; **Fowler**.)

◆HUSBANDMAN

Some translations use this older word for one who plows and cultivates land. (See **Farmer**.)

I

◆INNKEEPER

In Old Testament times, most travelers stayed in private dwellings or slept in the open. But by New Testament times, some people managed inns (Luke 10:34–35). However, these facilities were often neither comfortable nor safe and provided no food and few amenities. According to tradition, innkeepers were infamous for their dishonesty, which may be one reason why Christians were encouraged to open their homes in hospitality to strangers. The inn at which Mary and Joseph stopped but found full could have been a large private dwelling, as it was customary for such homeowners to rent out dwelling quarters during festival times (Luke 2:7). (See "Travel," Acts 13:3–4.)

◆INSTRUCTOR

Instructors of all kinds—priestly catechists, pastor-evangelists, and godly parents—were charged with teaching, mentoring, and discipling successive generations. Luke was an instructor in the faith for Theophilus (Luke 1:1–4). Paul chided the Corinthians that though they might have "ten thousand instructors in Christ," he was their spiritual father (1 Cor. 4:15). Many of the Proverbs praise parents who take on the role of instructor (Prov. 1:8; 4:1). God frequently used angels to instruct people when a difficult message needed fuller explanation (Luke 1–2; Acts 10:22).

◆INTERPRETER

The job of an interpreter sometimes resembles that of an instructor in that the term implies one who can "explain fully or give the understanding of something in different words." In the Bible, interpreters were used to translate languages (Gen. 42:23), explain dreams (Gen. 40:8; 41:8), or reveal the meaning of tongues or prophecies (1 Cor. 12:10, 30; 14:26–28). Ambassadors often served kings as interpreters (2 Chr. 32:31; Ezra 4:7), along with magicians, astrologers, and sorcerers (Dan 2:2–4; 4:6). Daniel and his friends were recruited for this purpose (Dan. 1:3–5; 2:14–49; 4:19–27; 5:13–29). Angels also served as interpreters of God's message (Luke 1–2; Acts 10:22). (See **Ambassador**; **Astrologer**; **Instructor**; **Magician**.)

◆IRONWORKER

(See **Metalworker**.)

J

◆JAILER

Jailers and *keepers of prisons* were usually soldiers in Bible times. Prisons were damp, dark, and rigorous places of detention (Ps. 107:10). Numerous biblical persons spent time in jail: Joseph, who was given responsibility over other prisoners (Gen. 39:20–23; 40:3–4); Samson (Judg. 16:21, 25); the prophet Jeremiah, who was imprisoned in four different places of detention (Jer. 37–38); John the Baptist (Mark 6:17, 27); and Peter and John (Acts 4:3; 5:18; 12:3–5). Before his conversion, Paul arrested Christians and had them put into prison (Acts 8:3). Later, he was himself frequently imprisoned on behalf of the gospel (Acts 16:23; 28:30). However, he used the opportunity to bring his jailers to faith (Acts 16:23–37; Phil. 1:12–14). (See **Keeper**.)

◆JEWELER

Ancient peoples were fond of jewelry. The Old Testament mentions jewelry as a sign of wealth and blessing (Ezek. 23:26; Is. 61:10). It was given to brides as a present (Gen. 24:22, 30, 53), or as part of a dowry. The priestly garments, especially the breastplate, were adorned with beautiful gem stones, rings, and chains crafted by a skilled jeweler (Ex. 28:15–28). In the New Testament, Jesus told a story about a woman who lost a coin that may have been part of a set of ten silver coins worn as jewelry, as was common in that day (see "The Woman Who Searched as God Searches," Luke 15:8–10). (See **Metalworker**.)

◆JUDGE

Judges in the Bible dispensed justice, governed, and provided legal protection. It's interesting that the first and last judge mentioned in Scripture is God Himself (Gen. 18:25; Rev. 19:11; 20:1–13). To some extent following this divine model, the Old Testament patriarchs acted as judges in matters of their households (Gen. 21; 22; 27). Moses was judge over all Israel and he appointed elders to be subsidiary judges under him (Ex. 18:13–27; Deut. 1:12–17). After Israel entered the Promised Land, the nation was ruled by a cycle of judges or deliverers such as Othniel, Ehud, Deborah, Gideon, Jephthah, and Samson. Under the monarchy, justice ultimately resided with the king (1 Kin. 3:16–28). All along, however, God was viewed Israel's final Judge, Deliverer, and King (Judg. 8:23; 11:27; Is. 33:22).

By the time of the New Testament, the high court of Israel had become the Sanhedrin, although there were also judges in every town (Luke 18:2; see "Stephen's Trial and Murder," Acts 6:12). In the early church, members were forbidden to use the pagan courts. Instead, believers appointed their own elders to judge civil disputes between Christians (see "The Scandal of Litigating Christians," 1 Cor. 6:1–11). Christ is the ultimate Judge over His people (see "The Judgment Seat," 2 Cor. 5:10).

K

◆KEEPER

This generic job description applied to many occupations in the Bible: *trustees* or **treasurers** of the city treasury (Rom. 16:23); keepers of prisons, also known as *guards* or **jailers** (Gen. 39:20–23; 40:3–4); night **watchmen** (2 Kin. 11:5); **foresters** (Neh. 2:8); keepers of the vineyard, or **vinedressers** (Is. 5:1–30; Matt. 21:33–44); and keepers of the wardrobe (2 Kin. 22:14), the doors (2 Kin. 23:4), and the gates, also known as *gatekeepers, doorkeepers,* or **porters** (1 Chr. 9:19). Keepers of a harem (Esth. 2:3, 14) were called **eunuchs** or *chamberlains.* Keepers of animals included **shepherds** (Gen. 4:2; 1 Sam. 17:20) and *herdsmen* or **cattlemen** (Gen. 4:20).

◆KING, QUEEN

The majority of the large ancient civilizations were controlled by kings and queens who usually inherited their position and power and ruled for life. Much has been written about the dynasties of the Pharaohs in Egypt, as well as the bright but brief monarchy in Israel. Unlike the rulers of the Gentiles, the Hebrew kings were not viewed as gods, though their right to rule was given by God.

In the New Testament, several kings are mentioned, including Herod (Matt. 2:1) and his grandson Agrippa (Acts 25:24). However, they were not really kings but **governors** over Roman territories (see "The Herods," Acts 12:1–2). Interestingly, even though Herod was called the "king of the Jews," it was Jesus who was born into that position and later crucified by Pilate under that title (Matt. 27:37). Elsewhere, Scripture affirms that Jesus is the King of kings and Lord of lords (1 Tim. 6:15; Rev. 17:14; 19:16).

L

◆LABORER (WORKER)

The term *laborer* indicates either a field hand (Matt. 9:37–38; 20:1, 2, 8; James 5:4; see **Farmer**; **Harvester**; **Gleaner**; **Reaper**) or a worker in a general sense (Matt. 10:10, some translations; 1 Tim. 5:18). A laborer's job might entail more manual work, less pay, and less skill (but no less value) than a skilled occupation, but not necessarily: for example, Luke calls the fellow craftsmen of the silversmiths at Ephesus "workers of similar occupation" (Acts 19:25, emphasis added). While laborers are often poor and oppressed, their heritage in life is good, joyful and worthwhile, even a "gift of God" (Eccl. 5:18–20). Jesus called for more "laborers" to harvest fields of souls (Matt. 9:37–38).

◆LAUNDERER

(See **Fuller**.)

◆LAWYER

The term *lawyer* is found only in the New Testament and means something entirely different from the profession of lawyers today. By the first century, the Law (the first five books of the Old Testament) had been expounded upon by generations of Jewish teachers. Their intent was to interpret and apply the Law to every situation of life. This ongoing work created a vast body of commentary which its custodians claimed was just as binding as the actual commandments of Moses. These experts in the Law, known as lawyers, **scribes**, or **doctors** of the law (Luke 2:46; 5:17; Acts 5:34, KJV), were employed in studying, interpreting, and expounding the Law. They also acted as court **judges**. In the New Testament they are found opposing John the Baptist (Luke 7:30) and Jesus (Matt. 22:34–40; Luke 14:3). (See **Advocate**; **Doctor**; **Judges**; **Scribe**.)

◆LEATHERWORKER

(See **Tanner**.)

◆LENDER

The practice of moneylending was under strict regulation in the Old Testament (Deut. 15:1–11; 23:19–20; 24:10–11; 28:12, 44). The Law prohibited interest-bearing loans to the poor, especially to fellow Hebrews. The people were urged instead to give generously and without taking anything in pledge. Nonetheless, Israel repeatedly broke these regulations and had to take corrective measures. Even Nehemiah was guilty of lending at interest and had to make amends (Neh. 5). Jesus brought the concept of canceling debts into sharper focus by applying it to forgiveness (Matt. 18:23–35).

◆LIBRARIAN

Scrolls and parchments were readily available to visiting speakers in a synagogue (Luke 4:17). The Book of the Law (possibly Deuteronomy) was found "in the house of the Lord" by Hilkiah (2 Kin. 22:8; see Ezra 6:1). This finding implies temple archives or perhaps a temple library, and thus a librarian.

◆LINEN WORKER

(See **Dyer**.)

◆LOBBYIST

Moses and Aaron were perhaps the prototype of lobbyists who attempt to persuade those in power to adopt a particular course of action. With God's help, the two leaders ultimately were able to convince Pharaoh to allow the Israelites to leave Egypt (Ex. 7–12). Another effective lobbyist was Nehemiah, who persuaded King Artaxerxes to rebuild Jerusalem, and in fact to underwrite the project. It's interesting to observe some of the methods that Nehemiah used to lobby his cause: prayer, pouting, bold speech, carefully written letters, first-hand inspections, and progress reports. In a similar way, the Old Testament prophets often went to great lengths to convince others to accept God's ways. Ezekiel staged a hunger strike and shaved off all of his hair (Ezek. 4–5). Jeremiah used props to illustrate his message—a ruined, useless belt (Jer 13:1–11), a broken clay pot (Jer. 19:1–12), and yoked straps and crossbars (Jer. 27). In the New Testament, Paul lobbied the authorities in Rome and Jerusalem to accept the gospel, or at least permit its advance (see "Faith and Rights," Acts 22:25–29, and "Paul and the Structures of Power," Acts 24:25–26). (See **Orator**; **Prophet**.)

◆LOGGER

(See **Forester**.)

M

◆MAGICIAN

Occult practices, such as fortune-telling and witchcraft, were common among the pagan nations of the ancient world. But attempts to contact or control evil spirits were expressly forbidden to the Hebrews, and the prohibition extends to believers today (see "Magic and Sorcery," Rev. 18:23).

◆MAGISTRATE

This term has many meanings, depending on its context. Sometimes a magistrate was like a **judge** (Ezra 7:25; Luke 12:58; Acts 16:20), with ruling, even priestly, authority (Judg. 18:7; Acts 23:5). Among the Jews in Jesus' day, some magistrates were "rulers of synagogues" (Matt. 9:18, 23; Luke 8:41; 12:11), subject to a larger ruling body known as the Sanhedrin (see "The Synagogue," Mark 1:21, and "Stephen's Trial and Murder," Acts 6:12).

◆MAID, MAIDSERVANT

Two Hebrew words are variously translated *bond-, hand-,* or *maidservant, maiden, bondwoman,* or *female servant,* or **slave**. In general, these girls or women served the wives and daughters of rich or important men (Gen. 16:1–3). They were treated more like property than their male counterparts; some were even sold into slavery by their fathers (Ex. 21:7). They performed menial tasks, such as grinding flour (Ex. 11:5; see "Slaves," Rom. 6:16, and "Women and Work in the Ancient World," 1 Cor. 7:32–35). Some functioned as surrogate mothers (1 Sam. 1:11) and as con-

◆MAID, MAIDSERVANT *(continued)*

cubines (Judg. 19:9). Sarah's maidservant Hagar was given to Abraham so that he could father a child by her, according to the custom of the day (see Gal. 4:24–25). (See **Servant**; **Slave**.)

◆MANAGER

(See **Overseer**.)

◆MARINER

(See **Sailor**.)

◆MASON

Masons were employed in cutting stone to make hedges, walls, buildings, memorials, and other functional or ornamental objects. Stoneworkers also hewed out wine vats, cisterns, tombs, and water tunnels. Judging from the many examples of stone works in Scripture (2 Sam. 5:11; 2 Kin. 22:6; 1 Chr. 22:2; 2 Chr. 24:12), this was an important occupation. The Jews may have learned the craft from their sojourn in Egypt (Ex. 1:11, 14) or from the master builders at Phoenicia (2 Sam. 5:11; 1 Chr. 14:1).

In quarrying out rock, masons drove wooden wedges into stone and soaked them until they expanded, causing the rock to crack. After separating a block of rough stone, they trimmed it with a saw, axe, or pick. Some masons were known for their ability to "square" or "quarry" stone so it joined neatly with other stones to create a smooth face (1 Kin. 5:17–18; 6:7).

The Old Testament likened the Word of God to the quarry worker's hammer (Jer. 23:29).

Other names for stonemasons include *stonecutters* and *hewers of stone*. (See **Builder**.)

◆MEDIATOR

(See **Messenger**; **Priest**.)

◆MERCHANT

Merchants are referred to by various Bible translations as *traders, dealers,* and *merchandisers.* Merchants sold their merchandise in open bazaars or marketplaces in the cities of the Mediterranean (Neh. 3:32; 13:16; Ezek. 27:24; Matt. 11:16; Mark 7:4). Scripture warned them against being unscrupulous by using false weights and measures (Deut. 25:13–16; Hos. 12:7; Amos 8:5), and the book of Revelation depicts how they could take their trade to scandalous excess (Rev. 18:3–23). By contrast, the virtuous woman of Proverbs 31 is praised for her honest merchandising skills.

◆MESSENGER

The job of messenger in Scripture is related to several other occupations: **ambassador** (Prov. 13:17), *mediator* (Job. 33:23), and *military courier* (1 Sam. 4:17; 23:27; 2 Sam. 2:19; 11:22–25). The messenger is also associated with the **footman** or **runner** (2 Kin. 6:32–33; Jer. 51:31) and with the **horseman** and **watchman** (2 Kin. 9:18). The word is also used of the **prophets** (Hag 1:13), the Lord's servant (Is. 42:19), and John the Baptist (Mal. 3:1; Mark 1:2). (See **Announcer**.)

◆METALWORKER

This category includes those who dug ore out of the ground, refined the ore into metal, and worked the metal into useful objects. Refining metal is an ancient skill that was well developed by the time of Abraham, when smiths were using bellows to increase the heat of their furnaces in order to melt iron ore for extraction. Even before then, copper was mixed with tin to form bronze, or mixed with zinc to form brass. Metalworkers produced high quality items such as vessels, jewelry, and coins.

Smiths were commonly named for the metals they worked. The first metalworker mentioned in the Bible is Tubal-Cain, a descendant of Cain who instructed others in working with "bronze and iron" (Gen. 4:22). Two metalworkers named in the New Testament are Demetrius, a silversmith at Ephesus (Acts 19:24–28), and Alexander the coppersmith (2 Tim. 4:14).

Various translations use different terms to describe metalworkers: *artificer, artisan,* **blacksmith**, *bronze worker, craftsman, engraver,* **forger**, **founder**, *metalsmith,* **refiner**, and *smelter.* (See **Foundry Worker**.)

◆MIDWIFE

Midwives helped other women give birth to their babies (Gen. 35:17; see "A Woman in Labor," John 16:21–22). The task involved coaching the mother through the delivery, cutting the umbilical cord, bathing the baby, and rubbing it with salt in the belief that it promoted good health (Ezek. 16:4). Newborns were "swaddled" or wrapped snugly in cloth in a way that bound the baby's arms to its body. If twins were born, the midwife marked the firstborn (Gen. 38:28). Midwives were sometimes relatives or friends of the mother, but often professionals such as the Hebrew midwives who refused to obey the Egyptian Pharaoh's orders to kill all the boy babies at birth (Ex. 1:15–22). (See **Nurse**.)

◆MILITARY RECRUITER

(See **Census Taker**.)

◆MILLER

Grinding the grain was the work of a miller, often a maidservant (Ex. 11:5). In the division of labor, men were usually in the fields gathering grain, while women did the grinding of grain (Matt. 24:40–41) using a household hand-mill (see "Grinding the Grain," Luke 17:35). Thus the millstone became an invaluable asset, never to be used as a pledge and thus put at risk of being lost (Deut. 24:6). The saying, "to have a large millstone hung around one's neck" (Matt. 18:6; Mark 9:42; Luke 17:2; compare Judg. 9:53) indicated humiliating and unbearable punishment, similar to Samson's being forced to push a heavy grinder that would normally have been turned by donkeys or oxen (Judg. 16:21).

◆MINER

(See **Foundry Worker**.)

◆MONEY CHANGER

Money changers set up open-air stalls outside the temple to change ceremonially unclean foreign currency into local money for offerings. These cashiers often cheated their customers, a practice especially irksome since their service was indispensable. Jesus turned over the tables of corrupt money changers, charging that they had made His father's house a den of thieves and a house of merchandise (Mark 11:15–17; John 2:13–20). (See **Banker**.)

◆MOURNER

Many ancient Near Eastern cultures employed professional mourners, usually women, for public expressions of grief at funerals (Eccl. 12:5; Jer. 9:17–18; Amos 5:16; see "The Mourners," Matt. 9:23). Even the poor hired pipers, flute players, and at least one wailer to make the proper lamentations. Men sometimes joined women as singers and wailers at funerals (2 Chr. 35:24–25). An entourage of women mourned Jesus' death (Luke 23:27–28).

◆MUSICIAN

Scripture provides ample evidence that music was a major part of Israel's worship, suggesting that musicians were vital to the culture. While temple music was mostly a voluntary service, paid musicians were called upon for special occasions (Matt. 9:23; Mark 5:38). The study and practice of musical instruments goes back to Cain's family and Jubal, who apparently invented the harp and the flute (Gen. 4:21). David's early fame as a harp player came to the attention of Saul, who employed David as a "music therapist" for his sin-sick soul (1 Sam. 16:14–23). Other stringed instruments noted in Scripture include the lyre, the psaltery, and the sackbut. Wind instruments include the flute, the ram's horn, and the trumpet. The silver or brass cymbal was a main feature of the temple orchestra. (English translations vary in their rendering of instruments' names.) (See **Singer**; **Mourner**.)

N

◆NOBLEMAN

(See **Prince**.)

◆NURSE

One term for nurse in Hebrew applied in some of its usages to males as well as females and meant "to foster." The more common term meant "to give milk." One well-known biblical nurse was the Hebrew woman fetched by the Pharaoh's daughter to raise Moses (Ex. 2:7–9)—a case in which the biological mother became a paid professional nurse to her own child. Moses later came to see himself as a "nursing [foster] father" (KJV) in relation to the Hebrews (Num. 11:12). Likewise, Paul was like a nurse to his spiritual children (1 Thess. 2:7). The word meaning "to foster" is applied to Mordecai, the man who raised Esther (Esth. 2:7). Both words are used, respectively, with reference to the kings and queens in Isaiah's prophecy who will serve and wait upon God's chosen people (Is. 49:23).

The tasks of a female nurse included suckling the children of Hebrew women and carrying infants on their shoulders or hips (Is. 49:22; see "Children and Childcare," Matt. 19:14.). Some family nurses were honored and shared between the generations (Gen. 24:59; 35:8; Ruth 4:16). Some heroic nurses took endangered children into protective custody to raise on their own (2 Kin. 11:2; 2 Chr. 22:11; 2 Sam. 4:4). (See **Midwife**; **Physician**.)

O

◆OARSMAN

(See **Sailor**.)

◆OFFICER

(See **Government Official**.)

◆ORATOR

Perhaps because communication in ancient societies tended to be oral rather than visual, rhetoricians and their teachers, coaches, and speech writers were in great demand. For example, the Jews who opposed Paul in Jerusalem employed Tertullus, a professional orator, to make their case before the Gentile governor Felix (Acts 24:1–9). Roman courts operated according to rules of etiquette and oratory. One could lose one's case simply by crudeness of speech. Paul was a highly trained speaker who was able to defend himself in such settings (Acts 24:10–21; 25:9–12; 26:1–28). A study of Paul's speech at the Areopagus (Acts 17:22–31) demonstrates the range of his abilities, even though the power of his preaching did not depend on such skill (1 Cor. 2:4; see "Paul, Apostle to the Intellectuals," Acts 17:15, and "Adapt Your Witness," Acts 17:17).

◆ORNITHOLOGIST

Bird lovers, watchers, and cultivators were many in Scripture, which refers to birds more than 300 times and mentions about 50 species. (Modern-day ornithologists have catalogued almost 400 kinds of birds in the Palestine area.) Adam and Noah included birds in their work as "zoologist" and "zookeeper" (Gen. 2:19–21; 6:19—7:3). The food list in Leviticus 11:2–23 includes a great number of birds, but 44 other books of the Bible name at least one. Among those mentioned: the bittern, chicken, cormorant, crane, cuckoo, dove, eagle, falcon, hawk, heron, osprey, ostrich, owl, partridge, peacock, pelican, pigeon, quail, raven, sparrow, stork, swallow, turtledove, and vulture (translations vary). Migratory patterns, food, songs, nesting, and the habitats of birds are also noted.

◆OVERSEER

An overseer controlled or managed groups of people or projects. In the Old Testament, a captain in Pharaoh's guard bought Joseph from slave traders and made him the "overseer" of his house (Gen. 39:4–5). This was a position of great authority (38:8–9). Elsewhere, overseers were responsible for getting tasks done (2 Chr. 2:8) and sometimes helped to rule others (Neh. 11:9). Overseers responsible for slaves were sometimes called *taskmasters* (see "Slaves," Rom. 6:16, and "Philemon" at the Introduction to Philemon). Those who oversaw the Israelite slaves in Egypt were remembered as particularly cruel (Ex. 1:11–14). Overseers also were known as *drivers, foremen,* and *slavemasters.* In the New Testament, certain leaders in the churches are referred to as overseers, sometimes translated as "bishops" (Acts 20:28; Phil. 1:1; 1 Tim. 3:2; Titus 1:7).

P

◆PERFUMER

Perfume making is an ancient art, as perfumes were used to mask unpleasant body odors in a world where bathing tended to be infrequent. Perfumers and cooks are frequently associated in ancient literature, since their skills were related. Egyptian tomb paintings of the fifteenth century B.C. depict the process of making perfume from flowers. In the Old Testament, tabernacle and temple worship required professional perfumers to make scents for the priest and incense for burning (Ex. 30:25, 35; 1 Chr. 9:30). These perfumers formed professional guilds (Neh. 3:8). In the KJV, perfumers are sometimes called *apothecaries* or *confectioners.* (See **Cosmetologist**.)

◆PHARMACIST

(See **Apothecary**.)

◆PHILOSOPHER

A philosopher is literally a "lover of wisdom." The only philosophers directly mentioned in Scripture are the Epicureans and Stoics whom Paul encountered at Athens (Acts 17:18). However, their presence in the account reflects the fact that philosophers heavily influenced the thinking of the Greek and Roman cultures.

Elsewhere Scripture offers what could be called philosophical reflection and discussion. The book of Job, for example, records the thinking of Job and his three friends as they struggled to make sense of the evils that befell Job. Ecclesiastes presents the conclusions of a person looking back on life to determine what is of value and significance. Many of Paul's letters, while not philosophical treatises, offer a starting point for philosophical inquiry.

It has sometimes been said that philosophy by its very nature is opposed to faith. However, while philosophers have often started from assumptions and come to conclusions that go against Scripture, there is no indication that God discourages intellectual inquiry (see "The Value of Learning," Acts 7:22, and "Paul: Apostle to the Intellectuals," Acts 13:2–3). At the same time, Scripture reminds us that ultimately Christ is the "wisdom of God," a concept that may appear to be foolishness to some (1 Cor 1:24).

◆PHYSICIAN

The Bible alludes frequently to sickness and health issues. The practice of medicine began in ancient times and gradually developed in knowledge and technique. Simple but relatively effective medicines were made from mineral, animal, and plant substances. Eventually specialists began to experiment with surgery and other invasive medical procedures. For example, archaeologists have found skulls from the sixth century B.C. which show evidence of *trepanning,* an attempt to surgically relieve pressure on the brain.

The only type of surgery mentioned directly in the Bible is circumcision, the ceremonial removal of the Hebrew male's foreskin eight days after birth (Gen. 17:10–14; see "Circumcision," Gal. 2:12).

The only physician mentioned by name in Scripture is Luke (Col. 4:14; see profile at the Introduction to Luke). However, Jesus and His followers performed miraculous healings of numerous people as a sign that He is indeed the Messiah.

◆PILOT

(See **Sailor**.)

◆PLASTERER

Plastering the walls of a home to form a smooth surface (Lev. 14:42–43) is an ancient and widespread craft, known to have been done sometimes by homeowners themselves. Higher quality plaster was made with heated broken limestone and gypsum; lower quality, used only in very dry climates, was made with clay and straw. Plaster, sometimes called "whitewash" (Deut. 27:2–4), was applied to the altar in the tabernacle and engraved while still wet. Years later in Babylon, a hand suddenly appeared and inscribed a message from God on a plastered wall in King Belshazzar's palace (Dan. 5:5). (See **Bricklayer**.)

◆PLOWMAN

(See **Farmer**.)

◆POET

Poetry was important throughout the ancient world, and nearly every culture had skilled lyricists to capture the essential experiences and emotions of the society.

◆POET *(continued)*

The Hebrew poets were especially prolific; in fact, an entire section of the Old Testament is made up of poetry composed under the inspiration of the Holy Spirit (Job, Psalms, Proverbs, Ecclesiastes, and Song of Solomon), and verse can also be found in other books. Poetry is seen as well in the structure of several New Testament passages (such as Luke 1:46–55, 68–79).

◆POLICEMAN

(See **Keeper**; **Sergeant**.)

◆PORTER

Porters and gatekeepers were essentially security guards who stood at the entrance to public buildings, the temple (1 Chr. 9:23; 26:12; 2 Chr. 23:19), and the homes of public officials (John 18:17) and the wealthy (Mark 13:34). Jesus also referred to a doorkeeper at the entrance to a sheepfold (John 10:3). The job required watchful attention and the ability to handle sudden developments. Nevertheless, it must have been a relatively lowly position as implied by the Psalmist's statement that he would "rather be a doorkeeper in the house of my God than dwell in the tents of wickedness" (Ps. 84:10). (See "'The Gates of Hell,'" Matt. 16:18.)

◆POTTER

The pottery wheel is known to have been in use for thousands of years. Israel employed professional potters who sat at the edge of a small pit, turning the pottery wheel with their feet. Before working with the clay, however, the potter would tread it by foot, kneading it into the right consistency. Otherwise, weak spots could develop when he threw the piece on his wheel, leading to cracks when the piece was baked or put to use. Jeremiah enacted the role of a potter to make a powerful point that people are like unformed, pliable clay in the hands of God (Jer. 18–19).

◆PREACHER

The words associated with preachers and preaching are found primarily in the New Testament. Preaching was not seen as it is today in terms of an occupation, but more generally as a task or function involving the duties of a herald. For example, Peter described Noah as a "preacher of righteousness" (2 Pet. 2:5). Paul referred to himself as a "preacher of the gospel" (1 Tim. 2:7; 2 Tim. 1:11). To the Romans he pointed out the importance of a "preacher" in the spread of the gospel, meaning one who has been sent to communicate the message of Christ to unbelievers (Rom. 10:14–15). (See **Announcer**.)

◆PRIEST

In Israel, priests were official ministers and worship leaders who represented the people before God and conducted various rituals to atone for their sins. Originally this function was carried out by the father of a family (Job 1:5). But with the appointment of Aaron by God as the first *high priest* over Israel, the priesthood was formally established (Num. 8:9–18).

By the time of the New Testament, the position of priests had changed considerably. The temple functions were taken over by the *chief priests*. Rank-and-file priests were overshadowed by the **scribes** and Pharisees, two groups that arose to interpret the Law for the people.

The office of priest was ultimately fulfilled in Jesus Christ. The Son of God became a man in order to offer Himself as a sacrifice "once to bear the sins of many" (Heb. 2:9–14; 9:28). As a result, there is no longer a need for human priests to

◆PRIEST *(continued)*

offer a sacrifice to atone for people's sins. Christ made Himself a permanent sacrifice through His death on the cross (see "Something Better Than Law and Priests," Heb. 7:19–22).

◆PRINCE, PRINCESS

This term applied not only to royalty, but to persons in positions of authority and responsibility (Gen. 12:15; 17:20; Ex. 2:14). (See **King**; **Queen**.)

◆PROCURER

(See **Buyer**.)

◆PROGNOSTICATOR

(See **Astronomer**.)

◆PROPHET

Prophets were people who spoke for God and communicated His message, often at great risk to themselves. The Old Testament prophets received a call directly from God, sometimes even before birth (Jer. 1:5; compare Luke 1:13–16). Otherwise, they had no special qualifications and came from all walks of life. Some were called for a lifetime, others were given only a brief ministry. But one trait characterized them all: a faithful proclamation of God's word and not their own (Jer. 23:16; Ezek. 13:2).

Sometimes prophets made their points by dramatic means. For example, Isaiah went barefoot and unclothed for three years (Is. 20:2–3). Ezekiel lay on his left side for 390 days and on his right side for 40 more (Ezek. 4:1–8). Zechariah broke two staffs (Zech. 11:7–14). A prophet's activities aroused curiosity and caused people to think, but sometimes they also invited scorn (Jer. 11:21).

In the early church, some believers were given the gift of prophecy, such as Agabus and the four daughters of Philip (Acts 21:8–11). These people, who spoke by the Holy Spirit, gave direction to the church in the period before the New Testament had been fully written.

◆PROSTITUTE

Prostitution is known to have been a part of pagan religious rites since at least 3000 B.C. Intercourse with a temple prostitute was believed to induce fertility. In Israel, ritual prostitution was forbidden (Deut. 23:17). However, commercial prostitutes practiced their trade and made themselves easily recognizable (Prov. 5:3–20; 6:24–29; 7:6–27), accepting payment in money, grain, wine, or livestock (see "'Harlots Enter the Kingdom,'" Matt. 21:31–32).

In contrast to the religious elite of His day, Jesus became known as a friend of sinners who welcomed those in need of forgiveness, including prostitutes (Matt. 11:19; Luke 7:36–50).

The harlot Rahab was praised in the New Testament as an example of a Gentile whose faith was accepted by God (see Heb. 11:31; compare Josh. 2:1–24; 6:22–25; James 2:25).

◆PUBLICAN

The derivation of the word "publican" from the Latin, *publicanus,* suggests a "provincial general." The publican is not to be confused with the **customs officer** or **tax collector**. Publicans were wealthy men, usually Gentiles, who contracted with the Roman government to be responsible for the taxes of a particular district.

◆PUBLICAN *(continued)*

Each province was assessed a certain amount of taxes by Rome, and the publican employed tax collectors to bring in that amount. Anything he could gather over and above the assessed amount was his to keep as a commission or "collection fee."

The shrewd publican, often backed by military force, collected import-export surcharges, road and bridge user fees, and as many other levies as he could (see "Taxes," Mark 12:14). This led to unscrupulous practices, and to hatred by the Jews toward these Gentile "sinners" who were in league with Rome (Matt. 9:9–11). (See **Tax Collector**.)

◆PUBLISHER

One can find no evidence of publishing as an industry in Scripture, as technologies such as the printing press and papermaking were undeveloped in Bible times. Furthermore, ancient cultures tended to concentrate information in the hands of a few powerful leaders rather than disperse it throughout the societies. Nevertheless, a form of publishing can be seen in Esther, when laws from the king were distributed to the people, apparently in some written form (Esth. 3:14; 8:13). In a similar manner, the king of Nineveh "published" a decree mandating acts of repentance after Jonah's warning of impending judgment (Jon. 3:6–9). (See **Author**; **Scribe**; **Writer**.)

Q

◆QUARRY WORKER

(See **Mason**.)

R

◆RABBI

This title, meaning "my teacher," showed honor and respect to a teacher of the Jewish Law. In Jesus' day, the term did not signify an ordained person, as it does today, but was simply a term of dignity given by the Jews to a distinguished teacher. (See **Instructor**; **Scribe**.)

◆REAPER

(See **Laborer**.)

◆RECORDS CLERK (RECORDER)

This government worker was a functionary with some official standing, ranked with scribes and priests (2 Sam. 20:24; 1 Kin. 4:3). The job was mostly concerned with calling to remembrance the history of a particular sovereign's reign. In that sense, the records clerk was like a *registrar* or *court reporter*. Apparently, he mostly registered deeds of property and genealogies of people. Genealogical records were important, for example, to certify eligibility for the priesthood (Neh. 7:63). When foreign dignitaries visited, the recorder played a prominent ceremonial role (2 Kin. 18:18; Is. 36:3, 22). (See **Government Official**; **Scribe**; **Historian**.)

◆REFINER

Allusions to this profession are made in the Bible wherever God examines or purifies His people as if refining ore in a furnace (Ps. 66:10; Is. 48:10; Ezek. 22:17–22; Zech. 13:9; Mal. 3:2–3). In the New Testament, the refiner's fire is symbolic of the fire of God's testing (Matt. 3:10–12; 1 Cor. 3:13–15; 1 Pet. 1:6–7). (See **Foundry Worker**.)

◆REGISTRAR

(See **Government Official**; **Records Clerk**; **Scribe**; **Historian**.)

◆ROADMAKER

While the Bible does not mention roadmakers as such, it refers to "paths" (Prov. 8:2) and to "highways and hedges" (Luke 14:23). Palestine was crossed by the Way of the Sea (Is. 9:1), also called "the way of the land of the Philistines" (Ex. 13:17) and, under the Romans, the Via Maris, the most important international highway throughout the biblical period. A second major highway in the region was the King's Highway (Num. 20:17; 21:22; Judg. 21:19), which provided a secondary road to Egypt and access to the spice routes of Arabia. In addition, an internal system of secondary roads provided links between the many cities of the area (see "Travel," Acts 13:3–4).

The call to prepare for the Messiah by "mak[ing] straight in the desert a highway for our God" (Is. 40:1–5; Matt. 3:3–5) evokes the imagery of roadmaking. In a way, that call was literally carried out: The relative peace established by Rome in the years before Christ enabled an extensive system of ancient roads in the Mediterranean world to be refurbished—just in time to aid the spread of the gospel.

◆ROBBER

(See **Criminal**.)

◆ROPEMAKER

Scripture refers frequently to rope and, by inference, ropemakers. Thus these artisans had a hand in helping the Philistines capture Samson (Judg. 15:13; 16:7) and in helping the spies escape from Jericho (Josh. 2:15). Ropemakers also contributed the cords that held the tabernacle together (Ex. 35:18), as well as the rope by which Judas hung himself (Matt. 27:5). In the shipbuilding trade, ropemakers produced the tackle and sheets that helped trim sails and steer rudders on ships (Is. 32:23; Acts 27:40). They also made heavy-duty bowstrings, animal traps, pulley systems, and plumb lines.

◆RUNNER

Runners were employed as royal messengers for kings. They sometimes competed with chariots and horsemen (1 Sam. 8:11; 2 Sam. 15:1; 1 Kin. 1:5), where "the race is not to the swift" (Eccl. 9:11). In this sense, they were **athletes**, but were more akin to mail carriers. (See **Announcer**; **Messenger**.)

S

◆SAGE

(See **Astrologer**.)

◆SAILOR

Despite their proximity to the Mediterranean, the Hebrews had little affinity for the sea and apparently had no navy. Nevertheless, the Bible makes frequent reference to sailing and shipping (Ps. 104:26; 107:23; Acts 27). Solomon built a merchant fleet, but many of the crews were Phoenician (1 Kin. 9:27). When Jonah ran away from God's call to Nineveh, he traveled on a Phoenician ship (Jon. 1:3). Later, dur-

◆SAILOR *(continued)*

ing the New Testament era, the headquarters of shipping shifted to Alexandria, which was renowned for its cargo ships (see Acts 18:24, and "Travel," Acts 13:3–4; compare Acts 27:6; 28:11).

The ship's **captain** (Jon. 1:6) is sometimes called the *pilot* (Ezek. 27:27–29), the *helmsman* (Acts 27:11), or the *shipmaster* (Rev. 18:17). He was responsible for the safety of the vessel, its crew, and its cargo. (See **Shipbuilder**.)

◆SCRIBE

The title of "scribe" can be confusing. Sometimes the term is used interchangeably with **lawyer**, meaning a *teacher* of the law. During some periods of Jewish history, particularly the reigns of David and Solomon, the scribe was a significant administrator similar to a secretary of state or **chancellor** (2 Sam. 8:17; 20:25; 1 Kin. 4:3). In other times, scribes were more like **recorders**, *chroniclers,* or **historians**, recording history as it happened and keeping the official archives. The two books of Chronicles, for example, are believed to have been compiled from historical archives by an authoritative scribe, perhaps Ezra. He was particularly noted for his commitment to studying and promoting the Law (Ezra 7:6; Neh. 8:1–9).

In Jesus day, scribes had become a learned class in Israel who studied the Scriptures and served as *copyists, editors,* and *teachers* (see "Scribes," Luke 20:39). To become a scribe required a lifetime of study, often beginning at age 14 and continuing to the age of 40. Once qualified, scribes could act as **judges**, be called **rabbis**, and occupy positions in law, government, and education. They joined the *chief* **priests** and aristocratic families who made up the Jewish council. They were held in great esteem by the people.

One category of scribes were the *copyists* who copied by hand the various Hebrew and Greek Scriptures onto rolls of parchment or sheets of papyrus. This time-consuming work was done by a team of scribes gathered at a *scriptorium,* in some ways the precursor to the modern publishing house. At first the documents were reproduced on scrolls. But eventually the bound book was invented, enabling the copyist to write on both sides of a page. These *codices,* as the documents were subsequently called, were a major advance in publishing technology. (See **Author**; **Lawyer**; **Writer**.)

◆SCULPTOR

(See **Stoneworker**.)

◆SEAMSTER, SEAMSTRESS

(See **Tailor**.)

◆SECRETARY

In Hebrew society, the job of writing and corresponding for others was done by a **scribe** or **recorder** (Jer. 36:26, 32). However, scribes typically had many more administrative and teaching duties to fulfill (see "Scribes," Luke 20:39). Like many secretaries today, secretaries in the ancient world took dictation, usually in shorthand, and also composed letters for a communicator. Paul may have dictated some of his letters to such a person, called by some an *amanuensis* or *stenographer* (Rom. 16:22; Gal. 6:11; 2 Thess. 3:17). (See **Scribe**.)

◆SECURITY GUARD

(See **Watchman**.)

◆SENTRY

(See **Watchman**.)

◆SERVANT

(See **Slave**.)

◆SHEEPBREEDER

(See **Shepherd**.)

◆SHEEPSHEARER

(See **Shepherd**.)

◆SHEPHERD (SHEEPHERDER)

The first shepherd mentioned in Scripture is Abel (Gen. 4:2). Later, Abraham, Isaac, and Jacob owned vast herds of livestock, including sheep (Gen. 13:7; 26:20; 30:36). However, when Jacob relocated his family to Egypt, his son Joseph counseled him to tell Pharaoh that his family's occupation was raising livestock, resulting in their isolation in Goshen, "for every shepherd is an abomination to the Egyptians" (Gen. 46:31–34). Among the other prominent biblical people who spent at least part of their lives as shepherds were Rachel, Moses, David, and Amos.

Sheep and goat herding were major occupations of Palestine throughout its history. Sheep and goats were sometimes herded together, sometimes separately. Other occupations grew up around sheep herding, including breeders and shearers who cut the sheep's wool.

Shepherds were expected to be faithful and diligent, so much so that their occupation was often used as a metaphor for spiritual direction and leadership, either positively or negatively (Jer. 23:1–4; John 10:1–5). Sheep came to know their shepherd's voice so well that they would follow only him. Shepherds provided water and food for their flocks (Ps. 23:2; Jer. 31:10), and when an animal was lost, they were expected to go out and find it (Ezek. 34:12; Luke 15:4–5). Small lambs, unable to keep up with the flock, were often carried by the shepherd (Is. 40:11). Shepherds also protected their flocks, risking their lives if necessary (1 Sam. 17:34–37; Amos 3:12; John 10:11).

In the Old Testament, God is often called a Shepherd (Ps. 23; Is. 40:11). He protects and seeks out His flock, Israel (Jer. 31:10; Ezek. 34:12). Likewise, in the New Testament Jesus refers to Himself as the Good Shepherd who cares for, protects, and redeems His people (John 10:2–16). He even suffers for the sheep (Matt. 26:31) and separates them from the goats at the day of judgment (Matt. 25:32). As the Great Shepherd of the sheep (Heb. 13:20), Jesus calls spiritual leaders to be under-shepherds (Acts 20:28–30; 1 Pet. 5:2).

◆SHIPBUILDER

Shipbuilding stems from the days of Noah (Gen. 6:13–22). However, the Hebrews were not much of a seafaring people, and they mainly relied on others to build and sail their ships, especially the Phoenicians. Hebrew poetry extols the Phoenician shipbuilders for their perfect ships, tall masts, inlaid decks, strong oars, and embroidered sails (Ezek. 27:3–7). In the New Testament, the cargo ships of Alexandria (see Acts 18:24) were prized by sailors and merchants of the Mediterranean (See "Travel in the Ancient World" Acts 13:3–4). Paul sailed on such a vessel on the last leg of his trip to Rome (Acts 28:11). (See **Caulker**; **Ropemaker**; **Sailor**.)

◆SHIPMASTER

(See **Sailor**.)

◆SILVERSMITH

The silversmith refined and molded silver into bowls, cups, trumpets, basins, jewelry, candlesticks, coins (Gen. 23:16; Matt. 22:19–20), and the like. Scripture contains more than 200 references to silver and those who worked it. During Solomon's era, however, the silversmith was virtually out of work as gold was apparently so plenteous that silver "was accounted as nothing" (1 Kin. 10:21). In the New Testament, Demetrius, a silversmith of Ephesus, led a guild of related craftsmen in a protest against the gospel, which was destroying their extremely profitable trade in shrines to the goddess Diana (Acts 19:24–28). (See **Metalworker**.)

◆SINGER

More than fifty singers are named and their songs recorded in Scripture, in addition to the 150 compositions collected in Psalms. Singers were professional vocalists, usually trained. David's royal court enjoyed the singing of both male and female vocalists (2 Sam. 19:35), and he also organized 4,000 Levites and "skilled men" as temple musicians (1 Chr. 25). Many of these were choir members "instructed in the songs of the Lord" (25:7). Temple singers were originally all men, aged 30 to 50, and may have belonged to a performing artists' guild. They were employed in the work "night and day" (1 Chr. 9:33). They lodged together, took separate purification vows, and were supported by others to do their work (Neh. 12:29,45–47). After the Babylonian exile, women also participated in the choirs (Ezra 2:65). Women also sang as professional **mourners** (see "The Mourners," Matt. 9:23, and "Burial," 1 Cor. 15:42). (See **Mourner**; **Musician**.)

◆SLAVE

Virtually every major ancient civilization depended heavily on the service of slaves, conquered peoples set to a variety of tasks by their masters. Scripture states that the Hebrews became slaves of the Egyptians, under whom they carried out forced labor "in mortar, in brick, and in all manner of service in the field" (Ex. 1:8–14). In the Roman Empire of Paul's day, half the population or more may have been slaves, according to one historian's estimate.

Slave labor varied widely, depending on the interests of the ruling masters and the abilities of individual slaves. Joseph was sold as a slave to the Egyptian Potiphar, who made him an **overseer** of his household with a high level of responsibility (Gen. 39:1–9). Likewise Daniel and other young Hebrew males were brought in captivity to Babylon, where they were trained for high levels of government service (Dan. 1:1–7, 18–21). Later the Romans preferred Greek slaves as **tutors** or **instructors** to their young.

However, the majority of slaves in the ancient world were little more than property to be bought and sold as needed. Male slaves were often assigned to construction projects or the mines, where they were worked to exhaustion (see "Slaves," Rom. 6:16). Female slaves or **maidservants** were sold to men for service to their wives and daughters, and in many cultures for the sexual pleasure of the men as well (see "Women and Work in the Ancient World," 1 Cor. 7:32–35).

Not all slavery was between nations, however. According to the Old Testament, the Israelites had both Jewish and Gentile slaves. Jews who were too poor to pay their debts or who were convicted of theft sometimes sold themselves into slavery. In contrast to other cultures of the day, Jewish Law protected slaves and even granted them certain rights (Ex. 21:2–11; Lev. 25:39–55; Deut. 21:10–14).

Often Scripture refers to **servants**, or those who were "under the authority of

◆SLAVE *(continued)*

another." Some were like *day laborers* or *hired hands* who were paid for their work and free to leave when the job was finished (Ex. 21:1–11; compare Matt. 20:1–15). Jacob was such a servant for a time to Laban (Gen. 29). Jesus spoke of a household servant plowing, tending sheep, and preparing a meal (Luke 17:7–10).

Curiously, the Bible does not directly condemn slavery as an institution, though it contains oblique warnings about the practice of slavery (Amos 1:6–9; Rev. 18:13). The New Testament teaches that in Christ, the hierarchy of master over slave is done away (Gal. 3:28; Col. 3:11). Paul appealed to Philemon to put that ideal into practice by receiving back Onesimus, a runaway slave who became a Christian, as a brother (see the Introduction to Philemon and "A Challenge to Slavery," Philem. 15–16). Even so, Scripture exhorts slaves to obey their masters (Eph. 6:5; Col. 3:22; Titus 2:9). (See **Maid**; **Maidservant**; **Steward**.)

◆SLAVEMASTER

(See **Overseer**.)

◆SMELTER

(See **Foundry Worker**.)

◆SMITH

Some translations use this generic word for one who worked with metals. (See **Metalworker**.)

◆SOLDIER

Even though Israel conquered the Promised Land by waging war, it did not have a standing army until Solomon's time (1 Kin. 10:26). However, all 20-year-old males were liable for emergency military duty (Num. 1:3), with a few exceptions (Deut. 20:5–8). Saul maintained a body of chosen capable fighters (1 Sam. 13:15), and David recruited a force of "mighty men" (1 Sam. 22:2; 1 Chr. 11:10–47). Under David, each tribe had a well-delineated chain of command and trained its adult males to use military weapons (1 Chr. 12).

The Bible mentions several specific kinds of soldiers, including the *guard,* **bodyguard**, or *escort* assigned to protect a particular person or place, such as *prison guards* (Gen. 40:3–4) and *palace guards* (2 Kin. 11:4–11); and the **charioteer** who was often a skilled **horseman** and commanded by a captain of the chariots (1 Kin. 22:33–34). (See **Archer**; **Armorbearer**; **Armorer**; **Captain**; **Centurion**; **Horseman**.)

◆SOOTHSAYER

Soothsaying is rarely mentioned in the Bible, but it appears to describe some form of divination (Deut. 18:10). Because the Hebrew word for "soothsaying" sounds like the word for cloud, some scholars believe it refers to cloud reading. It may have been similar to tea leaf reading or astrology, which is a reading of the stars. In any case, God forbids this occult practice (Deut. 18:10, 14; Lev. 19:26). Wicked King Manasseh was guilty of soothsaying (2 Kin. 21:6; 2 Chr. 33:6), and the Old Testament prophets strongly condemned it (Is. 2:6; 57:3; Jer. 27:9; Mic. 5:12). (See **Astrologer**; **Diviner**; **Magician**.)

◆SORCERER, SORCERESS

(See **Diviner**; **Magician**; **Witch**; **Wizard**.)

◆SPY

Moses sent twelve spies to scout out the Promised Land. Ten returned with discouraging reports, while two, Joshua and Caleb, encouraged the people to go forward (Num. 13). Later, Joshua sent spies into Jericho, who escaped capture only through the help of Rahab (Josh. 2). Another group of five spies for the tribe of Dan compromised in their mission by adopting the idolatry of Micah of Ephraim (Judg. 18).

In the New Testament, the chief priests and scribes had Jesus followed and sent spies to catch Him saying something treasonous (Luke 20:20). Later, Paul accused the Judaizers of sending spies among the leaders of the church (Gal. 2:4). However, on one occasion Paul benefitted from the intelligence brought by a "spy," his sister's son, who reported on a plot to kill the apostle (Acts 23:16–21). (See **Watchman**.)

◆STARGAZER

(See **Astrologer**.)

◆STENOGRAPHER

(See **Secretary**.)

◆STEWARD

Stewards, like **overseers**, were entrusted with responsibility for their superiors' goods (Gen. 43:19). In the New Testament, a steward is sometimes referred to as a *guardian* or *curator* (Matt. 20:8; Gal. 4:2), or as a manager or household superintendent (Luke 8:2–3; 1 Cor. 4:1–2). Paul called himself a "steward" of Christ's household, responsible to Christ for carrying out his task of preaching the gospel to the Gentiles (1 Cor. 4:1). All Christians have been given resources and responsibilities by God and are accountable to Him for their stewardship over those gifts (1 Pet. 4:10). (See **Overseer**.)

◆STONECUTTER

(See **Mason**.)

T

◆TAILOR.

The work of tailoring is implied rather than specifically mentioned in Scripture. In Israel, most of a family's clothing was made by the women (see "Jewish Homemaking," Mark 1:29–31). For instance, Hannah made a "little robe" for her son Samuel (1 Sam. 2:19). Likewise, the "virtuous woman of Proverbs" is praised for her skill in making clothing for her family (Prov. 31:13–24).

This work began by spinning thread or yarn and weaving cloth. Everyday clothing tended to be loose fitting and thus did not require much shaping. However, the rich and royalty demanded more ornate design in their garments. Intricate weaving and embroidery were required for the beautiful, stone-studded priestly garments prescribed by Moses (Ex. 28). In the New Testament, Lydia became a successful businesswoman by trading in *purple,* the name for both an expensive dye and the clothing dyed that color (see profile at Acts 16:14). (See **Weaver**.)

◆TANNER

Tanners converted animal skins into leather and fashioned useful or ornamental items from it. Tanning was widespread in the ancient world. Originally, Israelite

◆TANNER *(continued)*

families did their own tanning, but with the growth of cities, leather craftsmen arose. Peter stayed with one such tanner named Simon (Acts 10:6).

Tanning skins was an involved process, requiring much skill. The hides were soaked until the fat, blood, and hair were removed. After the leather was tanned, it was used for many purposes, including tents (Ex. 26:14), sandals (Ezek. 16:10), hats, skirts, and aprons.

◆TAPESTRY MAKER

Sometimes called *carpetmakers* or *rugmakers,* the more inclusive term is tapestry maker. Rugs in Bible times were braided with strips of cotton, wool, or other fibers. Because these braided strands varied in color and length, they were coiled and sewn together to obtain the desired pattern and size. The virtuous woman of Proverbs is praised for making her own tapestries (Prov. 31:22). By contrast, the seductive prostitute of Proverbs 7 has her bedroom chamber adorned with rugs and blankets or wall-hangings from a tapestry maker (7:16). (See **Weaver**.)

◆TASKMASTER

(See **Overseer**.)

◆TAX COLLECTOR

Tax collectors were contract workers who collected taxes for the government during Bible times. Some translations call them "publicans," but publicans were actually the ones who employed tax collectors to do the actual collecting of monies. Between Rome, the temple system, and other taxing authorities, Jews in Jesus' time were probably paying between 30 and 40 percent of their income in taxes and religious dues. Not surprisingly, tax collectors were despised by their fellow citizens who viewed them as mercenaries working for the Romans (see "Who Were Those Tax Collectors?" Matt. 9:10, and "Taxes," Mark 12:14). (See **Publicans**.)

◆TEACHER

(See **Instructor**; **Lawyer**.)

◆TENTMAKER

This ancient craft had to do with the manufacture of affordable, mobile shelters for living, working, and traveling. Construction involved cutting and sewing together cloth, often made of goat's hair, and attaching ropes and loops. Paul's native province of Cilicia exported cilicium cloth made from goat's hair, and his hometown of Tarsus was known for its tentmaking industry (see Acts 11:25). Thus Paul may have picked up the trade as a boy (see "Paul's 'Real' Job," Acts 18:1–3). Later he partnered with Priscilla and Aquila (see profile at Rom. 16:3–5) and earned his living in that manner while preaching the gospel.

◆TETRARCH

The term tetrarch is a title meaning "ruler of a fourth part." Sometimes it is translated "king." Four members of the Herod family named in the New Testament were Roman tetrarchs (see "The Herods," Acts 12:1–2): Herod the Great (Matt. 2), who was tetrarch before he was king (according to the historian Josephus); his son Herod Antipas, called "Herod the Tetrarch" (Matt. 14:1; Acts 13:1); Herod Philip, the brother of Antipas (Mark 6:17); and Lysanias, tetrarch of Abilene (Luke 3:1). A tetrarch's privileges and power were royal, but inferior to those of a real king or emperor. (See **Government Official**.)

◆THIEF
(See **Criminal**.)

◆TILLER
(See **Farmer**.)

◆TOWN CLERK
(See **City Clerk**.)

◆TRADER
(See **Merchant**.)

◆TRAPPER
(See **Hunter**.)

◆TREASURER
The Bible mentions several treasurers, powerful government officials who could sometimes even be heir to a throne (2 Chr. 26:21). They advised and reported to ancient monarchs on financial matters. Ezra was given authority by King Artaxerxes over the treasurers in the districts near Jerusalem (Ezra 7:21).

Nehemiah appointed several treasurers to work in concert with one another in distributing resources (Neh. 13:13). The New Testament highlights an Ethiopian treasurer who became a believer (Acts 8:26–40). (See **Government Official**.)

◆TRUSTEE
(See **Government Official**.)

◆TUTOR
Tutors are hardly mentioned in Scripture, but they were quite common in the ancient world, especially among the Greeks and Romans. Usually the trusted slave of a wealthy family, a tutor supervised the activities of the family's children, especially its sons, acting as a guide and guardian. When boys reached the age of 16, they were considered adults and no longer in need of a tutor. Paul wrote that the Law was a "tutor" to bring us to Christ (Gal. 3:24–25). In the Old Testament, a man named Jehiel functioned as a tutor to the sons of King David (1 Chr. 27:32). (See **Instructor**.)

U

◆UNDERTAKER
Most undertakers in Israel were not professionals but family of the deceased (Luke 9:59), or in Jesus' case, friends (Mark 16:1; John 19:38–40; see "A Burial Fit for a King," Mark 15:42). The early church possibly appointed a certain group of people to undertake this responsibility and attend to the dead person's property (Acts 5:6; 8:2).

Haste characterized the burial customs of the ancient Near East due to the hot climate of Palestine, where dead bodies decayed rapidly (see "Funeral Preparations," John 12:1–8, and "Burial," 1 Cor. 15:42). Among the Hebrews, preparation for burial involved washing the body, scenting it with oils and spices, and wrapping it in sheets (John 19:38–40) or the person's own clothes. Bodies were buried in a shallow grave covered with stones or placed in a cave or tomb hewn out of stone. The Jews did not embalm bodies as the Egyptians did, or cremate them as the Greeks and Romans did. (See **Embalmer**.)

V

◆VICEROY

(See **Government Official**.)

◆VINEDRESSER

Scripture highlights the vocation of the vinedresser in many ways. Isaiah warns Israel of judgment in the woeful song of the vineyard (Is. 5:1–30). Jesus warns the Pharisees of similar judgment in His parable of the wicked vinedressers (Matt. 21:33–44). Jesus also called Himself the true vine and His Father the vinedresser (John 15:1–8). Grape vines required constant digging, weeding, and pruning to bring growth to the fruit and not to the shoots, lest the vines be overcome by thorns and weeds (Prov. 24:30–31; Luke 13:7). During the captivity of Judah in Babylon, God raised up the poor, even the foreigners, to dress the vines (2 Kin. 25:12; Is. 61:5; Jer. 52:16), not unlike today's migrant farm workers. (See **Farmer**; **Laborer**.)

W

◆WAITER, WAITRESS

(See **Butler**.)

◆WARRIOR

(See **Soldier**.)

◆WATCHMAN

The duty of a watchman was to stand guard over or "watch" over something valuable, perhaps a treasure, a person, or a city. From the height and protection of a watch tower, a guard watched over cities and fields, looking for thieves or ravaging animals (Ps. 80:13; Song 2:15). Nehemiah appointed watchmen to guard the walls of Jerusalem during their rebuilding (Neh. 4:9; 7:3). Some watchmen also worked as *guardians* or *policemen,* patrolling a city (Ps. 127:1; Song 5:7).

The Jews divided the night into three military watches, which the watchman was required to call out (2 Sam. 18:24–27; Is. 21:11–12; see "Telling Time," Matt. 14:25). Under the Romans they adopted the Roman method of dividing the night into four watches (Mark 13:35). A 24–hour, round-the-clock watch was posted at Jesus' tomb (Matt. 27:64–66; 28:11).

In a metaphorical or spiritual sense, prophets and teachers were God's appointed watchmen to keep His people morally alert (Ezek. 33:2–7; 2 Tim. 4:5).

◆WATER CARRIER

Going to the well or spring to bring back a household's daily water supply was lowly work. Wells and springs were generally situated outside city gates (John 4:5–8). Sometimes the task was assigned to young men (Ruth 2:9), but usually to women (Gen. 24:3; 1 Sam. 9:11) or servants (John 2:5–9). Water was carried home in water pots and goatskin bags, sometimes borne by a donkey. Some translations refer to this occupation as *drawer of water.*

◆WEAVER

Weaving was known in the ancient world from about 2000 B.C. Almost every household had a loom, and in Israel women spent much time at this task (Prov. 31:13–24). Women also made their own yarn or thread from animal hair or plant

◆WEAVER *(continued)*

fibers. Among other peoples, however, such as the Egyptians and Assyrians, weaving was a man's job. Professional weavers in urban areas created professional weaver guilds. (See **Embroiderer**.)

◆WELL DIGGER

Well diggers were relatively skilled workers in ancient Palestine, where little rain fell during most of the year. Wells and cisterns were crucial to the region's economy. Wars were sometimes fought over wells and water rights (Gen. 21:25–30; 26:20–22). In David's time, Jerusalem was provided with an elaborate underground system of shafts and tunnels that led to a water source (2 Sam. 5:8). Some wells bore specific names and survive to this day; for example, Jacob's Well (John 4:6).

◆WINE MAKER

Wine was a valuable trade commodity for ancient peoples, including the Israelites (2 Chr. 2:10, 15–16; Ezra 6:9; 7:22). Wine was an important part of the everyday diet and a popular beverage for special occasions (Ps. 104:15). Apparently shouts of joy typified the occasion of treading grapes in the wine presses (Is. 16:10; Jer. 48:33; see "Winemaking," John 2:3). Even ordinary people owned wine presses and gave the firstfruits of them in worship (Num. 18:27, 30; Deut. 14:15). Times of reformation and renewal called for bringing "new wine" into the storehouses (2 Chr. 31:5; Neh. 13:5). Jesus made use of this image by saying that the "wine" of the good news called for new wineskins to hold it (Luke 5:36–38).

It's interesting that of the more than 240 references to wine in the Bible, only about a tenth have to do with "strong" drink or drunkenness. Most use wine to refer to abundance, sustenance, and the blessing of God (for example, Gen. 27:28; Neh. 5:18; Esth. 1:7; Hos. 2:8). Jesus blessed a wedding party at Cana with gallons of new wine (see "Water Into Wine," John 2:3–12), and initiated His new covenant with wine (Luke 22:17–20).

Winepressing is also used as a symbol of God's wrath in judgment (Lam. 1:15; Joel 3:13; Rev. 14:18–20; 19:15). (See **Brewer**; **Vinedresser**.)

◆WINNOWER

Those who winnowed or separated grain from the chaff are sometimes called **fanners** (Jer. 51:2, KJV). The grain was beaten to loosen the kernels. The kernels were then trampled underfoot to loosen the chaff covering the grain. After each stage, the fanner would pitch the grain into the air with a winnowing fork, or fan, an implement still used by Syrian farmers. The wind blew the useless chaff away to be burned (Ruth 3:2; Job 21:18; Ps. 1:4; Matt. 3:12) while the valuable grain fell to the ground. The winnower used a five- or six-pronged pitchfork in the first stage and a shovel for the second stage (Is. 30:24). Most references in the Bible to winnowing or fanning are metaphorical. Just as a winnower separates wheat and chaff, so God separates true believers from unbelievers and hypocrites at the Last Day (Jer. 23:28–29; Luke 3:17).

◆WITCH, WIZARD

Witchcraft involved divination or sorcery that attempted to avoid or alter God's revealed will. In the Old Testament, God condemned pagan nations for practicing witchcraft (Deut. 18:9–14; Jer. 27:8–11; 29:8–9; Nah. 3:1–4). Saul was punished for visiting the witch of Endor (1 Sam. 28; 1 Chr. 10:13). (See **Diviner**; **Magician**.)

◆WOODWORKER

This general term covers a variety of trades involved in making wood into usable items. Archaeology has confirmed Scripture's testimony that ancient Palestine had forests. Even so, wood was scarce and rather expensive. Thus, good woodworkers also practiced conservation and reforestation (Is. 44:14). Their projects involved many people working in concert. *Lumberjacks* and *woodcutters* felled trees (1 Kin. 5:6). *Hewers* trimmed and readied the lumber for transportation. **Laborers** transported it (1 Kin. 5:13–14). **Carpenters** fashioned it into houses, furniture, tools, and other useful items (2 Kin. 22:6). Those who specialized as **carvers** carved wood into bas-relief and statues (Is. 40:20; Jer. 10:3–4). (See **Builder**; **Carpenter**; **Forester**.)

◆WRESTLER

(See **Athlete**.)

◆WRITER

More than 400 terms for writing can be found in the Bible. The origins of this craft can be traced to crude inscriptions on clay tablets made in prehistoric times. Writing and writing instruments were well developed by the time of Moses, enabling him to write down the Law (Ex. 17:4; 24:4). Note, however, that the two stone tablets of the Law were said to be written with "the finger of God" (Ex. 31:18). Another form of writing mentioned in Scripture is the "inward [or spiritual] writing" in which a message is written on the "tablet of your heart" (Prov. 3:3; 7:3; Jer. 17:1; 2 Cor. 3:3).

Materials on which ancient peoples wrote included clay, wax, stone, bricks, metal, and the inner side of papyrus bark. The latter was called *biblos,* from which we derive the word *bible.* Papyrus manuscripts were perishable, and some penmen were kept busy full-time transcribing records onto new papyrus. Needless to say, were it not for faithful copywriters, we would have no Bible today. (See **Author**; **Scribe**.)

Z

◆ZOOLOGIST

God brought "every beast of the field and every bird of the air" to Adam for him to name and classify according to its kind (Gen. 2:19–20), making Adam the first "zoologist." Likewise, Noah also classified animals and birds according to their kind (Gen. 6:19—7:3). Scripture reports that he took aboard the ark complete sets (seven) of all the "clean" animals and birds, plus two of the "unclean" variety, plus a 40–day supply of food for all, making Noah a "zookeeper" as well as a "zoologist." (See **Ornithologist**.)

Jobs and Occupations Index—By Category

To read about job classifications in a certain category, see the alphabetical listings in the main Jobs and Occupations Index, as indicated under each category name.

Health and Education

Hospitality and Household Services

Legal and Social Services

Manufacturing

Military and Defense

Mining and Metals

Real Estate and Construction

Retailing, Wholesale, and Marketing

Science, Industry, and Technology

Transportation and Travel

Miscellaneous

Notes

Notes

Notes

Notes

Notes

Notes

Notes

Notes

Notes